Accounting Trends & Techniques

Today's Financial Reporting Practices

D1160104

10819-341

AICPA®

SIXTY-FIFTH EDITION

1 2 3 4 5 6 7 8 9 0 AAP 1 9 8 7 6 5 4 3 2 1

ISSN 1531-4340   01-26-12

ISBN 978-0-87051-981-9

Notice to readers: This book does not represent an official position of the American Institute of Certified Public
Accountants, and it is distributed with the understanding that the authors and publisher are not rendering legal,
accounting, or other professional services via this publication.

Publisher: Amy M. Plent
Director, Accounting & Auditing Publications: Amy Eubanks
Senior Technical Manager: Doug Bowman
Technical Manager: Keira Kraft
Developmental Editor: David Cohen
Project Manager: M. Donovan Scott

The 2011 edition of *Accounting Trends & Techniques* was developed by

Raymond J. Petrino, CPA
Content Matter Expert

David J. Cohen
Developmental Editor
AICPA Publications Product Development

Keira A. Kraft, CPA
Technical Manager
AICPA Accounting and Auditing Publications

Kristy L. Illuzzi, CPA
Senior Technical Manager
AICPA Accounting and Auditing Publications

Anjali V. Patel, CPA
Technical Manager
AICPA Accounting and Auditing Publications

Special acknowledgment and sincere thanks are due to the following individuals for their efforts, without whom this book would not be possible:

Mark Bond
Sandy Carlin
Jennifer Hogge
Lisa Hopson
Stephanie Jordan

Kathleen V. Karatas
Kathy Keough
Gene P. Leporiere
Thomas Moore
Karen Venturini

About This Edition of *Accounting Trends & Techniques*

Accounting Trends & Techniques (*Trends*) compiles annual reporting and disclosure data and examples from a survey of the annual reports of publicly-traded entities. *Trends* provides accounting professionals with an invaluable resource for incorporating new and existing accounting and reporting guidance into financial statements using presentation techniques adopted by some of the most recognized entities headquartered in the United States.

Organization and Content

This 2011 edition of *Trends* surveyed annual reports of 500 carefully selected non-regulated entities with fiscal periods ending between January and December 2010. The industry classifications of survey entities (as shown in Table 1-1) were obtained from Morningstar, Inc.

To provide you with the most useful and comprehensive look at current financial reporting techniques and methods, *Trends* is topically organized and offers the following:

- Descriptive guidance that includes current reporting requirements under U.S. generally accepted accounting principles (GAAP). U.S. GAAP is generally considered to be the requirements of the Financial Accounting Standards Board (FASB) *Accounting Standards Codification*™ (ASC). Select Securities and Exchange Commission (SEC) guidance is also included.
- Statistical tables that track reporting trends.
- Illustrative examples from the surveyed annual reports showing reporting techniques.
- Detailed indexes.

Guidance

Trends offers discerning, plain English guidance covering the significant U.S. GAAP accounting and financial statement reporting requirements in narrative form. These narratives use common headings (recognition and measurement, presentation, and disclosure) to achieve a consistent presentation throughout all the sections. Although not a substitute for the authoritative accounting and reporting standards, *Trends'* reporting guidance boils down the complex requirements with a focus on your clear understanding of the content. The related authoritative sources for each requirement are cited within the narratives (for example, FASB ASC 310, *Receivables*, or Regulation S-K).

SEC rules and interpretative releases may expand, modify, or decrease accounting and disclosure requirements for foreign private issuers, regardless of whether they file their annual financial statements with the SEC in Forms 10-K, 20-F, or 40-F (Canadian issuers). Therefore, it is critical to consider SEC requirements, as well as those of FASB ASC, when reviewing the financial statements of SEC registrants. A general reference to FASB ASC in this publication does not include the SEC materials. When requirements are taken from an SEC rule or regulation, that rule or regulation will be cited directly.

Reporting Trends

Statistical tables throughout Trends present reporting trends across the available choices in recognition, measurement, presentation, and disclosure in such diverse reporting matters as financial statement format and terminology and the treatment of transactions and events reflected in the financial statements. To distinguish them from content excerpted from a survey entity's financial statements, these tables are presented with a shaded background.

Illustrative Reporting Examples

Trends presents carefully selected excerpts from the annual reports of the survey entities to illustrate current reporting techniques and various presentation practices already subjected to the audit requirements mandated by the Public Company Accounting Oversight Board (PCAOB). Every edition of *Trends* includes all new annual report excerpts that were chosen to be particularly relevant and useful to financial statement preparers in illustrating current reporting practices.

Because survey entities may present disclosures on specific topics within different footnotes in their annual filings, including those ostensibly about a separate accounting topic, the excerpts presented in *Trends* to illustrate a given topic may have been taken from footnotes about other topics.

Indexes

Indexes in this edition include the "Appendix of 500 Entities," which alphabetically lists each of the 500 survey entities included in the current edition and notes where in the text excerpts from their annual reports can be found; the "Index of Authoritative Accounting & Auditing Guidance," which provides for easy cross-referencing of pronouncements to the applicable descriptive narratives; and a detailed "Subject Index," which is fully cross-referenced to all significant topics included throughout the narratives.

FASB ASC

Because FASB ASC is the source of authoritative U.S. GAAP for nongovernmental entities, in addition to guidance issued by the SEC, the guidance within *Trends* refers only to the appropriate FASB ASC reference for all standards.

Note that the effective dates of recently released guidance affect the timing of its inclusion in the financial statements of the survey entities, thereby affecting the availability of illustrative excerpts for potential inclusion in each edition of *Trends*. This 2011 edition of *Trends* includes survey entities having fiscal years ending within calendar year 2010. Technical guidance for which this edition supplies illustrative annual report excerpts includes the following, among other recently issued guidance:

- Accounting Standards Update (ASU) No. 2010-28, *Intangibles-Goodwill and Other (Topic 350): When to Perform Step 2 of the Goodwill Impairment Test for Reporting Units with Zero or Negative Carrying Amounts (a consensus of the FASB Emerging Issues Task Force)*
- ASU No. 2010-06, *Fair Value Measurements and Disclosures (Topic 820): Improving Disclosures about Fair Value Measurements*
- ASU No. 2009-17, *Consolidations (Topic 810): Improvements to Financial Reporting by Enterprises Involved with Variable Interest Entities*
- ASU No. 2009-16, *Transfers and Servicing (Topic 860): Accounting for Transfers of Financial Assets*
- ASU No. 2009-15, *Accounting for Own-Share Lending Arrangements in Contemplation of Convertible Debt Issuance or Other Financing—a consensus of the FASB Emerging Issues Task Force*

Convergence of U.S. GAAP and IFRSs

Converging the standards of FASB and the International Accounting Standards Board (IASB) has been the primary focus of both organizations' boards throughout 2011. The commitment for global convergence gained momentum in 2002, when FASB and the IASB signed what is known as the Norwalk Agreement. At that meeting, FASB and IASB pledged to use their best efforts to (a) make their existing financial reporting standards fully compatible as soon as is practicable, and (b) coordinate their future work programs to ensure that, once achieved, compatibility is maintained. That agreement was reaffirmed in a February 2006 Memorandum of Understanding (MoU), which was based on the following three principles:

- Convergence of accounting standards can best be achieved through the development of high quality, common standards over time.
- Trying to eliminate differences between two standards that are in need of significant improvement is not the best use of FASB's and IASB's resources—instead, a new common standard should be developed that improves the financial information reported to investors.

- Serving the needs of investors means that FASB and IASB should seek convergence by replacing standards in need of improvement with jointly developed new standards.

At a joint meeting in April 2008, FASB and the IASB again affirmed their commitment to developing common, high quality standards, and agreed on a path to completing the MoU projects, including projected completion dates. In September 2008, and again in April 2011, the two boards jointly published an update of their 2006 MoU to report the progress they had made since. During 2011, the boards regularly updated project completion dates as difficulties in completing projects arose. Some projects (for example, Income Taxes) were removed from the convergence schedules when the boards agreed that convergence was unlikely to be achieved in the short time available, whereas other projects have reached the exposure draft milestone. Each board believes that these standards, when completed, would improve the quality, consistency, and comparability of financial information for investors and capital markets around the world.

Lastly, in May 2011, the SEC produced a work plan to outline how convergence efforts may be carried out. Many of the panelists favored the "condorsement" approach, whereby FASB would endorse new IFRSs one at a time as part of the convergence process, instead of following a "Big Bang" approach of converging several IFRSs at one time. Both IASB and FASB provide extensive information about convergence projects and other projects on their respective web sites, often with links to the relevant page on the opposite partner's site.

Private Company Financial Reporting

In October 2011, the Financial Accounting Federation (FAF) board of trustees announced a plan to establish a new Private Company Standards Improvement Council (PCSIC) that would identify, propose, deliberate, and formally vote on specific exceptions or modifications to U.S. GAAP for private companies. The PCSIC, jointly with FASB, would develop a set of specific criteria to determine whether and when exceptions or modifications to U.S. GAAP are warranted for private companies. Based on those criteria, the PCSIC would identify aspects of existing U.S. GAAP that its members believe require exceptions or modifications and then vote on specific changes. Any proposed changes to existing U.S. GAAP would be subject to ratification by FASB and undergo thorough due process, including public comment. The PCSIC would be overseen by the FAF board of trustees. The trustees seek public comment on the plan to establish a PCSIC until January 2012; a final decision will be made on the plan following the end of the comment period.

Related Products

Trends presents and analyzes financial reporting information for public, nonregulated entities across many sectors. To see a similar presentation and analysis for IFRSs, employee benefit plans, not-for-profit entities, and state and local governments, please see the related publications in the AICPA's *Trends & Techniques* series:

- *IFRS Accounting Trends & Techniques*
- *Employee Benefit Plans Accounting Trends & Techniques*
- *Not-for-Profit Entities Accounting Trends & Techniques*
- *State and Local Governments Accounting Trends & Techniques*

AICPA also recently launched *eXacct: Financial Reporting Tools & Techniques*, a powerful new Web-based tool that builds on the *Trends* framework to holistically address accounting, financial reporting, and enhanced business reporting. *eXacct* provides all the content you've come to expect from *Trends*—the guidance, reporting trends, and illustrative reporting examples—in an interactive, online format. *eXacct* augments the print edition of *Trends* by providing complete annual reports—in multiple formats—for all of the 500 *Trends* survey companies, as well as all available XBRL filings from the survey companies and full XBRL tag information. *eXacct*'s XBRL functionality makes XBRL tags and content fully searchable, highlighting company extensions with the click of a button, giving you the analytical tools to inform your own XBRL reporting. A subscription to this robust online tool allows you to search, browse, filter, download, and use *Trends*, annual report, and XBRL data exactly as you need them and is available at www.cpa2biz.com.

Notice

Trends is a nonauthoritative practice aid and is not designed to provide a comprehensive understanding of all the requirements contained in U.S. GAAP. The guidance provided herein may not discuss all relevant accounting guidance on a given topic and should not be relied upon for its completeness. Users are encouraged to consult FASB ASC for complete, authoritative discussion of U.S. GAAP. Users are also encouraged to consult the complete body of SEC rules and regulations for regulatory requirements. In addition, *Trends* does not include reporting requirements relating to other matters such as internal control or agreed-upon procedures.

Authoritative guidance on accounting treatments in accordance with U.S. GAAP can be made only by reference to the FASB ASC, which is copyright of the FAF and can be acquired directly from FASB.

Trends has not been reviewed, approved, disapproved, or otherwise acted on by any senior technical committee of the AICPA and does not represent official positions or pronouncements of the AICPA. The financial statement excerpts selected for inclusion in *Trends* are provided herein only as a reference. In as much as these excerpts originate from various sources beyond the control of the AICPA, neither the authors nor the publisher endorse them and AICPA specifically disclaims any liability with regard to their use. All such information is provided without warranty of any kind.

The use of this publication requires the exercise of individual professional judgment. It is not a substitute for the original authoritative accounting and auditing guidance. Users are urged to refer directly to applicable authoritative pronouncements, when appropriate. As an additional resource, users may call the AICPA Technical Hotline at 1.877.242.7212.

Feedback

We hope that you find this year's edition of *Trends* to be informative and useful. Please let us know! What features do you like? What do you think can be improved or added? We encourage you to give us your comments and questions about all aspects of *Trends*. Please direct your feedback to Keira Kraft, using the following contact information. All feedback is greatly appreciated and kept strictly confidential.

Keira Kraft—Professional Publications
AMERICAN INSTITUTE OF CERTIFIED PUBLIC ACCOUNTANTS
220 Leigh Farm Road
Durham, NC 27707-8110
Telephone: 919.402.4819
E-mail: kkraft@aicpa.org

You can also contact the Accounting and Auditing Publications team of the AICPA directly via e-mail at

A&Apublications@aicpa.org

TABLE OF CONTENTS

Section   **Paragraph**

Section   **Paragraph**

LIST OF TABLES

Table   **Paragraph**

Section 1: General Topics

SURVEY ENTITIES

1.01 In years prior to fiscal year 2008, 600 entities were used in the survey. All tables of significant accounting trends will be based on a survey of 500 entities for the 2008–10 fiscal years and 600 entities for the years prior to fiscal year 2008.

1.02 All 500 entities included in the survey are registered with the Securities and Exchange Commission (SEC). Many of the survey entities have securities traded on one of the major stock exchanges: 80 percent on the New York Stock Exchange and 19 percent on NASDAQ. The remaining entities were traded on the American Stock Exchange or "over-the-counter" exchanges.

1.03 Each year, entities are selected from the latest Fortune 1000 listing to replace those entities that were deleted from the survey (see the "Appendix of 500 Entities" for a comprehensive listing of the 500 entities, as well as those that were added and removed in this edition). Generally, entities are deleted from the survey when they are acquired; become privately held and, therefore, are no longer registered with the SEC; fail to timely issue a report; or cease operations.

1.04

TABLE 1-1: INDUSTRY CLASSIFICATIONS OF SURVEY ENTITIES

	2010
Basic Materials/Agricultural Inputs	3
Basic Materials/Aluminum	1
Basic Materials/Building Materials	10
Basic Materials/Chemicals	9
Basic Materials/Coal	2
Basic Materials/Copper	1
Basic Materials/Gold	1
Basic Materials/Industrial Metals & Minerals	2
Basic Materials/Lumber & Wood Production	2
Basic Materials/Paper & Paper Products	7
Basic Materials/Specialty Chemicals	7
Basic Materials/Steel	8
Communication Services/Pay TV	3
Communication Services/Telecom Services	7
Consumer Cyclical /Rubber & Plastics	1
Consumer Cyclical/Advertising Agencies	2
Consumer Cyclical/Apparel Manufacturing	9
Consumer Cyclical/Apparel Stores	4
Consumer Cyclical/Auto & Truck Dealerships	2
Consumer Cyclical/Auto Manufacturers	1
Consumer Cyclical/Auto Parts	8
Consumer Cyclical/Broadcasting—TV	1
Consumer Cyclical/Department Stores	6
Consumer Cyclical/Footwear & Accessories	7
Consumer Cyclical/Home Furnishings & Fixtures	10

1.04

TABLE 1-1: INDUSTRY CLASSIFICATIONS OF SURVEY ENTITIES—*(continued)*

Consumer Cyclical/Home Improvement Stores	2
Consumer Cyclical/Leisure	7
Consumer Cyclical/Lodging	3
Consumer Cyclical/Luxury Goods	2
Consumer Cyclical/Marketing Services	1
Consumer Cyclical/Media—Diversified	6
Consumer Cyclical/Packaging & Containers	9
Consumer Cyclical/Personal Services	3
Consumer Cyclical/Publishing	8
Consumer Cyclical/Recreational Vehicles	4
Consumer Cyclical/Residential Construction	10
Consumer Cyclical/Resorts & Casinos	3
Consumer Cyclical/Restaurants	10
Consumer Cyclical/Rubber & Plastics	3
Consumer Cyclical/Specialty Retail	12
Consumer Cyclical/Textile Manufacturing	1
Consumer Defensive/Beverages—Brewers	1
Consumer Defensive/Beverages—Soft Drinks	3
Consumer Defensive/Beverages—Wineries & Distilleries	2
Consumer Defensive/Confectioners	1
Consumer Defensive/Department Stores	1
Consumer Defensive/Discount Stores	5
Consumer Defensive/Education & Training Services	2
Consumer Defensive/Farm Products	6
Consumer Defensive/Food Distribution	2
Consumer Defensive/Grocery Stores	9
Consumer Defensive/Household & Personal Products	11
Consumer Defensive/Packaged Foods	14
Consumer Defensive/Pharmaceutical Retailers	3
Consumer Defensive/Tobacco	4
Energy/Oil & Gas Drilling	1
Energy/Oil & Gas E&P	5
Energy/Oil & Gas Equipment & Services	4
Energy/Oil & Gas Integrated	6
Energy/Oil & Gas Refining & Marketing	4
Healthcare/Biotechnology	1
Healthcare/Diagnostics & Research	1
Healthcare/Drug Manufacturers—Major	7
Healthcare/Health Care Plans	3
Healthcare/Medical Care	2
Healthcare/Medical Devices	5
Healthcare/Medical Distribution	2
Healthcare/Medical Instruments & Supplies	10
Industrials/Aerospace & Defense	12
Industrials/Business Equipment	7
Industrials/Business Services	13
Industrials/Conglomerates	4
Industrials/Diversified Industrials	33

(continued)

1.04

TABLE 1-1: INDUSTRY CLASSIFICATIONS OF SURVEY ENTITIES—*(continued)*

Industrials/Engineering & Construction	6
Industrials/Farm & Construction Equipment	7
Industrials/Industrial Distribution	3
Industrials/Integrated Shipping & Logistics	2
Industrials/Metal Fabrication	4
Industrials/Railroads	1
Industrials/Rental & Leasing Services	2
Industrials/Security & Protection Services	1
Industrials/Staffing & Outsourcing Services	6
Industrials/Tools & Accessories	5
Industrials/Truck Manufacturing	2
Industrials/Trucking	3
Industrials/Waste Management	2
Real Estate/REIT—Industrial	3
Technology/Communications Equipment	7
Technology/Computer Distribution	2
Technology/Computer Systems	5
Technology/Consumer Electronics	2
Technology/Contract Manufacturers	2
Technology/Data Storage	4
Technology/Electronic Components	8
Technology/Electronic Gaming & Multimedia	1
Technology/Electronics Distribution	2
Technology/Information Technology Services	4
Technology/Internet Content & Information	3
Technology/Scientific & Technical Instruments	3
Technology/Semiconductor Equipment & Materials	3
Technology/Semiconductor Memory	2
Technology/Semiconductors	10
Technology/Software—Application	8
Technology/Software—Infrastructure	4
Technology/Solar	1
Total Entities	**500**

Note: Because the industry classifications used in Accounting Trends & Techniques changed in 2010, no prior year data are available.

1.05

TABLE 1-2: SIZE OF SURVEY ENTITIES BY AMOUNT OF REVENUE

Table 1-2 indicates the relative size of the survey entities as measured by dollar amount of revenue.

	2010	2009	2008
Less than $100,000,000	3	3	3
Between $100,000,000 and $500,000,000	9	13	10
Between $500,000,000 and $1,000,000,000	18	19	8
Between $1,000,000,000 and $2,000,000,000	72	75	53
Between $2,000,000,000 and $3,000,000,000	63	67	65
Between $3,000,000,000 and $4,000,000,000	52	44	53
Between $4,000,000,000 and $5,000,000,000	42	42	37
Between $5,000,000,000 and $10,000,000,000	96	93	105
More than $10,000,000,000	145	144	166
Total Entities	**500**	**500**	**500**

GENERAL FINANCIAL STATEMENT CONSIDERATIONS

RECOGNITION AND MEASUREMENT

1.06 Financial Accounting Standards Board (FASB) *Accounting Standards Codification* (ASC) 105-10-05-2 explains that if the necessary guidance for a transaction or event is not specified within a source of authoritative U.S. generally accepted accounting principles (GAAP), an entity should first consider accounting principles for similar transactions or events within a source of authoritative U.S. GAAP for that entity and then consider nonauthoritative guidance from other sources. When those accounting principles either prohibit the application of the accounting treatment to the particular transaction or event or indicate that the accounting treatment should not be applied by analogy, an entity should not follow those accounting principles.

1.07 FASB ASC 105-10-05-3 explains that accounting and financial reporting practices not included in FASB ASC are nonauthoritative. FASB Concept Statements are not considered authoritative sources of U.S. GAAP, and no preference is given to the FASB Concept Statements over other nonauthoritative sources. FASB ASC does not state that consistency with the FASB Concept Statements in connection with an entity's application of an accounting treatment is necessary. Sources of nonauthoritative accounting guidance include the following:
- Practices that are widely recognized and prevalent, either generally or in the industry
- FASB Concept Statements
- AICPA Issues Papers
- International Financial Reporting Standards of the International Accounting Standards Board
- Pronouncements of professional associations or regulatory agencies

- Technical Questions and Answers included in AICPA *Technical Practice Aids*
- Accounting textbooks, handbooks, and articles

The appropriateness of other sources of accounting guidance depends on its relevance to particular circumstances, the specificity of the guidance, the general recognition of the issuer or author as an authority, and the extent of its use in practice.

1.08 As discussed in FASB ASC 105-10-05-1, U.S. GAAP, as codified in FASB ASC, includes the rules and interpretive releases of the SEC as sources of authoritative GAAP as a convenience to SEC registrants. In addition to SEC rules and interpretive releases, the SEC staff issues Staff Accounting Bulletins that represent practices that the staff follows when administering SEC disclosure requirements. SEC staff announcements and observer comments made at meetings of the Emerging Issues Task Force publicly announce the staff's views on certain accounting issues for SEC registrants.

1.09 In June 2009, FASB issued the last FASB statement referenced in that form: FASB Statement No. 168, *The FASB Accounting Standards Codification™ and the Hierarchy of Generally Accepted Accounting Principles—a replacement of FASB Statement No. 162.* This standard established FASB ASC as the source of authoritative U.S. accounting and reporting standards for nongovernmental companies, in addition to guidance issued by the SEC, and was effective for financial statements issued for interim and annual periods ending after September 15, 2009.

1.10 In FASB ASC's Notice to Constituents (NTC), FASB suggests the use of plain English references to describe broad FASB ASC topics going forward in financial statements and related footnote disclosures. FASB provides the following example of plain English references in the NTC when referring to the requirements of FASB ASC 815, *Derivatives and Hedging*: "as required by the Derivatives and Hedging Topic of the FASB Accounting Standards Codification."

1.11 A natural business year is the period of 12 consecutive months that end when the business activities of an entity have reached the lowest point in their annual cycle. In many instances, the natural business year of an entity ends December 31.

1.12

TABLE 1-3: FASB ASC REFERENCING

Table 1-3 indicates the method in which the survey entities referenced FASB ASC.

	Number of Entities	
	2010	2009
Plain English references throughout..............	350	236
Specific FASB ASC references throughout......................................	78	98
Dual Referencing (use of both plain English and specific references is the same paragraph, typically by using a parenthetical)...................................	34	35
Mix of both plain English and FASB ASC references..................................	38	—
Legacy referencing to old standard names only (for example, SFAS No. 157)..............	—	2
Pre-codification financial statements.............	—	129
Total Entities.................................	**500**	**500**

PRESENTATION

1.13 Rule 14a-3 of the Securities Exchange Act of 1934 states that annual reports furnished to stockholders in connection with the annual meetings of stockholders should include audited financial statements: balance sheets as of the end of the two most recent fiscal years and statements of income and cash flows for each of the three most recent fiscal years. Rule 14a-3 also states that the following information, as specified in SEC Regulation S-K should be included in the annual report to stockholders:

- Selected quarterly financial data
- Changes in, and disagreements with, accountants on accounting and financial disclosure
- Summary of selected financial data for the last five years
- Description of business activities
- Segment information
- Listing of company directors and executive officers
- Market price of, and dividends on, the company's common stock for each quarterly period within the two most recent fiscal years
- Management's discussion and analysis (MD&A) of financial condition and results of operations
- Quantitative and qualitative disclosures about market risk

1.14 FASB ASC 205-10-45-2 states only that it is ordinarily desirable for an entity to present the statement of financial position; the income statement; and the statement of changes in equity for one or more preceding years, in addition to those of the current year.

1.15 Paragraphs 3–4 of FASB ASC 205-10-45 require these statements to be comparable, and any exceptions to comparability should be described as required by FASB ASC 250, *Accounting Changes and Error Corrections.* An entity is required to repeat, or at least refer to, any notes to financial statements,

other explanations, or accountants' reports that contain quali-
fications for prior years that appeared in the comparative statements when originally issued, to the extent this information
remains significant. Multiple rules set forth in SEC Regulation
S-X provide guidance to SEC registrants on the form and ordering of financial statements, the presentation of amounts, the
omission of certain items, and requirements for supplemental
schedules. Rule 14a-3 requires that annual reports to stockholders should include comparative balance sheets and statements
of income and cash flows for each of the three most recent fiscal
years. All the survey entities are SEC registrants and conformed
to the aforementioned requirements of Rule 14a-3.

1.16 FASB ASC permits an entity to offset a liability with an
asset only when the following certain conditions discussed in
FASB ASC 210-20-45-1 are met:
- Each of two parties owes the other determinable amounts.
- The reporting party has the right to set off the amount
  owed with the amount owed by the other party.
- The reporting party intends to set off.
- The right of setoff is enforceable by law.

DISCLOSURE

1.17 SEC Regulations S-X and S-K and AU section 431,
Adequacy of Disclosure in Financial Statements (AICPA, *Professional Standards*), state the need for adequate disclosure in financial statements. Normally, the financial statements alone cannot
present all information necessary for adequate disclosure without considering appended notes that disclose information. All
surveyed entities provided footnote disclosures to their financial
statements.

1.18 FASB ASC 235, *Notes to Financial Statements*, sets forth
guidelines about the content and format of disclosures of accounting policies. FASB ASC 235-10-50-1 requires that the
significant accounting policies of an entity be presented as an
integral part of the financial statements of the entity. FASB
ASC 235-10-50-6 states that the preferable format is to present
a summary of significant accounting policies preceding notes
to financial statements or as the initial note under the same or
a similar title.

1.19 FASB ASC 205-10-50-1 requires an entity to provide
information explaining changes due to reclassifications or other
reasons that affect the manner of, or basis for, presenting corresponding items for two or more periods. FASB ASC 250-10
does not require an entity to present an opening balance sheet
of the earliest period presented when an entity retrospectively
applies a change in accounting policy or restates to correct an
error.

1.20 FASB ASC 275, *Risks and Uncertainties*, requires reporting entities to disclose information about the risks and uncertainties resulting from the nature of their operations, the use
of estimates in preparing financial statements, and significant
concentrations in certain aspects of the entity's operations.

1.21

TABLE 1-4: DISCLOSURE OF ACCOUNTING POLICIES

Table 1-4 shows the nature of information frequently disclosed in summaries
of accounting policies and the number of survey entities disclosing such
information.

	Number of Entities		
	2010	2009	2008
Revenue recognition	491	485	486
Consolidation policy	473	477	481
Use of estimates	476	476	469
Property	484	475	453
Cash equivalents	485	474	475
Depreciation methods	488	456	469
Amortization of intangibles	395	456	451
Interperiod tax allocation	314	449	438
Impairment	457	436	415
Financial instruments	433	435	440
Inventory pricing	430	429	416
Stock-based compensation	425	414	408
Translation of foreign currency	389	383	376
Nature of operations	403	365	363
Earnings per share calculation	327	297	300
Accounts receivable	351	349	333
Advertising costs	258	244	250
Employee benefits	263	229	195
Research and development costs	202	185	172
Credit risk concentrations	220	181	190
Fiscal years	171	150	145
Environmental costs	150	129	131
Capitalization of interest	114	98	86

PRESENTATION AND DISCLOSURE EXCERPTS

Plain English References

1.22

SCHNITZER STEEL INDUSTRIES, INC. (AUG)

NOTES TO CONSOLIDATED FINANCIAL STATEMENTS

Note 3—Recent Accounting Pronouncements (in part)

Recently Adopted Accounting Standards

In September 2006, the Financial Accounting Standards
Board ("FASB") issued guidance that defines fair value, establishes a framework for measuring fair value, and expands
fair value measurement disclosure. This guidance, as it relates to non-financial assets and liabilities that are recognized or disclosed at fair value in the financial statements on
a non-recurring basis, was effective for the Company for the
fiscal year ended August 31, 2010. Assets acquired through
business combinations completed during the year ended
August 31, 2010 were valued in accordance with this guidance. Non-recurring, non-financial asset fair value measurements also include those used in the Company's test of

recoverability of goodwill and indefinite-lived intangible assets, in which the Company determines whether fair values of its applicable reporting segments exceed their carrying values.

In December 2007, the FASB issued amended guidance regarding business combinations, establishing principles and requirements for how an acquirer recognizes and measures identifiable assets acquired, liabilities assumed, any resulting goodwill and any noncontrolling interest in an acquiree in its financial statements, as well as requiring that all transaction costs be expensed as incurred. This guidance also provides for disclosures to enable users of the financial statements to evaluate the nature and financial effects of a business combination. This amended guidance became effective for the Company beginning September 1, 2009 and has been applied prospectively to all business combinations completed in fiscal 2010. Transaction costs of $1 million related to acquisitions that had not been completed at the time of adoption were expensed and all subsequent transaction costs have been expensed as incurred.

In December 2007, the FASB issued new guidance regarding the accounting and reporting for noncontrolling interests in subsidiaries. This guidance clarifies that noncontrolling interests in subsidiaries should be accounted for as a component of equity separate from the parent's equity. Additionally, the guidance requires that income from noncontrolling interests be presented below net income to derive a net income figure attributable to the parent entity. This guidance became effective for the Company beginning September 1, 2009 and the applicable classification and presentation provisions were applied retrospectively.

In December 2008, the FASB issued guidance relating to an employer's disclosures about the plan assets of a defined benefit pension or post retirement plan. The guidance requires additional disclosure regarding investment policies and strategies, fair value of each major asset category based on risks of the assets, inputs and valuation techniques used to estimate fair value, fair value measurement hierarchy for each asset category and significant concentrations of risk information. This guidance was effective for the Company for the fiscal year ended August 31, 2010 and the disclosures have been incorporated accordingly. See Note 15—Employee Benefits.

In June 2009, the FASB established the FASB Accounting Standards Codification (the "Codification") as the single source of authoritative US GAAP for all non-governmental entities. The Codification changes the referencing and organization of accounting guidance and became effective for us beginning September 1, 2009. There were no changes to US GAAP as a result of the issuance of the FASB Codification.

In January 2010, an accounting standards update was issued by the FASB to improve disclosure requirements related to fair value measurement. This update requires additional disclosures relating to significant transfers in and out of Levels 1 and 2 fair value measurements, along with the reason for the transfer and separate presentation of purchases, sales, issuances and settlements in the reconciliation of Level 3 fair value measurements. The update was effective for the Company in the third quarter of the fiscal year ended August 31, 2010, except for disclosures relating to Level 3 activity, which will be effective for the fiscal year ending August 31, 2012 and will be applied prospectively and thus will not have any impact on previously issued financial information. See Note 14—Derivative Financial Instruments and Fair Value Measurements.

In February 2010, the FASB issued amended guidance on subsequent events. Under this amended guidance, SEC filers are no longer required to disclose the date through which subsequent events have been evaluated in originally issued and revised financial statements. This guidance was effective immediately and the Company adopted these new requirements in the second quarter of fiscal 2010. In preparing the accompanying audited financial statements the Company has reviewed events that occurred after August 31, 2010, the balance sheet date, noting no material subsequent events.

1.23

APPLIED MATERIALS, INC. (OCT)

NOTES TO CONSOLIDATED FINANCIAL STATEMENTS

Note 1. Summary of Significant Accounting Policies (in part)

Recent Accounting Pronouncements

In March 2010, the FASB issued updated authoritative guidance that amends the requirements for evaluating whether a decision maker or service provider has a variable interest entity and clarified that a quantitative approach should not be the sole consideration in assessing the criteria for variable interest entity determination. The guidance also clarifies that related parties should be considered in applying all of the decision maker and service provider criteria. This is in addition to the authoritative guidance the FASB issued in June 2009 that applies to determining whether an entity is a variable interest entity and requiring an enterprise to perform an analysis to determine whether the enterprise's variable interest or interests give it a controlling financial interest in a variable interest entity. Under this guidance, an enterprise has a controlling financial interest when it has (1) the power to direct the activities of a variable interest entity that most significantly impact the entity's economic performance and (2) the obligation to absorb losses of the entity or the right to receive benefits from the entity that could potentially be significant to the variable interest entity. The guidance also requires an enterprise to assess whether it has an implicit financial responsibility to ensure that a variable interest entity operates as designed when determining whether it has power to direct the activities of the variable interest entity that most significantly impact the entity's economic performance. The guidance also requires ongoing assessments of whether an enterprise is the primary beneficiary of a variable interest entity, requires enhanced disclosures, and eliminates the scope exclusion for qualifying special-purpose entities. This guidance is effective for Applied beginning in the first quarter of fiscal 2011. The implementation of this authoritative guidance is not expected to have a material impact on Applied's financial position or results of operations.

In January 2010, the FASB issued authoritative guidance for fair value measurements, which requires additional disclosures and clarifications to existing disclosures. This authoritative guidance requires a reporting entity to disclose separately the amounts of significant transfers in and out of Level 1 and Level 2 fair value measurements and also to describe the reasons for these transfers. This authoritative guidance also requires enhanced disclosure of activity in

Level 3 fair value measurements. The new disclosures and clarifications of existing disclosures for Level 1 and Level 2 fair value measurements became effective for Applied in the second quarter of fiscal 2010. Disclosures regarding activity within Level 3 fair value measurements become effective the first interim reporting period after December 15, 2010 and will be effective for Applied in the second quarter of fiscal 2011. Applied is evaluating the potential impact of the implementation of this authoritative guidance on its consolidated financial statements. See Note 4 for information and related disclosures regarding Applied's fair value measurements.

In June 2009, the FASB issued authoritative guidance on variable interest entities, which requires revised evaluations of whether entities represent variable interest entities, ongoing assessments of control over such entities, and additional disclosures for variable interests. In December 2009, the FASB issued authoritative guidance on the financial reporting by entities involved with variable interest entities which amends previously issued guidance on variable interest entities. The amendments in this authoritative guidance replace the quantitative-based risks and rewards calculation for determining which reporting entity, if any, has a controlling financial interest in a variable interest entity with an approach focused on identifying which reporting entity has the power to direct the activities of a variable interest entity that most significantly impact the entity's economic performance and (1) the obligation to absorb losses of the entity or (2) the right to receive benefits from the entity. This authoritative guidance becomes effective for Applied in fiscal 2011. The implementation of this authoritative guidance is not expected to have a material impact on Applied's financial position or results of operations.

Specific FASB ASC References

1.24

AUTODESK, INC. (JAN)

NOTES TO CONSOLIDATED FINANCIAL STATEMENTS

Note 1. Business and Summary of Significant Accounting Policies (in part)

Accounting Standards Adopted in Fiscal 2010

With the exception of those discussed below, there have been no recent accounting pronouncements or changes in accounting pronouncements during the fiscal year ended January 31, 2010 that are of significance, or potential significance to the Company.

In June 2009, the Financial Accounting Standards Board ("FASB") issued The FASB Accounting Standards Codification and the Hierarchy of Generally Accepted Accounting Principles. This statement, which became effective on July 1, 2009, established the Accounting Standards Codification ("ASC") as the source of authoritative GAAP recognized by the FASB to be applied by nongovernmental entities, and is codified in ASC Topic 105, "Generally Accepted Accounting Principles." The ASC did not change GAAP, but instead reorganizes the U.S. GAAP pronouncements into accounting Topics. As the ASC did not change GAAP, the adoption of ASC Topic 105 did not have a material effect on Autodesk's

consolidated financial position, results of operations or cash flows.

In February 2010, the FASB issued Accounting Standards Update ("ASU") 2010-09 regarding ASC Topic 855 "Subsequent Events." This ASU removes the requirement for SEC filers to disclose the date through which management evaluated subsequent events in the financial statements, and was effective upon its issuance. Autodesk adopted the ASU upon issuance. The adoption did not have an impact on Autodesk's consolidated financial position, results of operations or cash flows.

In August 2009, the FASB issued ASU 2009-05 regarding ASC Topic 820, "Fair Value Measurements and Disclosures." This ASU provides guidance on how to measure liabilities at fair value within the scope of ASC Topic 820. This Update provides clarification that in circumstances in which a quoted price in an active market for the identical liability is not available, a reporting entity is required to measure fair value using one or more of the following techniques: 1) A valuation technique that uses: a. The quoted price of the identical liability when traded as an asset, or b. Quoted prices for similar liabilities or similar liabilities when traded as assets, or 2) Another valuation technique that is consistent with the principles of ASC Topic 820. Two examples would be an income approach or a market approach. Autodesk adopted the changes represented by this ASU during Autodesk's fiscal quarter ended October 31, 2009. The adoption of ASU 2009-05 did not have a material impact on Autodesk's consolidated financial position, results of operations or cash flows.

In April 2009, the FASB issued three related FASB Staff Positions ("FSP"): (i) FSP 157-4, "Determining Fair Value When the Volume and Level of Activity for the Asset or Liability have Significantly Decreased and Identifying Transactions That Are Not Orderly" ("FSP 157-4"), (ii) FSP Statement of Financial Accounting Standard ("SFAS") 115-2 and SFAS 124-2, "Recognition and Presentation of Other-Than-Temporary Impairments" ("FSP SFAS 115-2" and "SFAS 124-2"), and (iii) FSP SFAS 107-1 and Accounting Principles Board ("APB") 28-1, "Interim Disclosures about Fair Value of Financial Instruments" ("FSP SFAS 107" and "APB 28-1"). FSP 157-4 provides guidance on how to determine the fair value of assets and liabilities under SFAS 157, "Fair Value Measurements" ("SFAS 157") in the current economic environment and reemphasizes that the objective of a fair value measurement remains the determination of an exit price. If Autodesk were to conclude that there has been a significant decrease in the volume and level of activity of the asset or liability in relation to normal market activities, quoted market values may not be representative of fair value and the Company may conclude that a change in valuation technique or the use of multiple valuation techniques may be appropriate. FSP SFAS 115-2 and SFAS 124-2 modify the requirements for recognizing other-than-temporarily impaired debt securities and revise the existing impairment model for such securities by modifying the current intent and ability indicator in determining whether a debt security is other-than-temporarily impaired. FSP SFAS 107 and APB 28-1 enhance the disclosure of instruments under the scope of SFAS 157 for both interim and annual periods. Autodesk adopted these FSPs during the quarter ended July 31, 2009. The adoption did not have a material effect on the Company's consolidated financial position, results of operations or cash flows.

In April 2009, the FASB issued FSP 141R-1, "Accounting for Assets Acquired and Liabilities Assumed in a Business Combination That Arise from Contingencies" ("FSP 141R-1").

FSP 141R-1 amends the provisions in Statement of Financial Accounting Standards No. 141 (revised 2007) "Business Combinations" ("SFAS 141R") for the initial recognition and measurement, subsequent measurement and accounting, and disclosures for assets and liabilities arising from contingencies in business combinations. FSP 141R-1 eliminates the distinction between contractual and non-contractual contingencies, including the initial recognition and measurement criteria in SFAS 141R and instead carries forward most of the provisions in SFAS 141 for acquired contingencies. FSP 141R-1 was effective for Autodesk for contingent assets and contingent liabilities acquired in business combinations for which the acquisition date was on or after February 1, 2009. The adoption of FSP 141R-1 did not have a material effect on the Company's consolidated financial position, results of operations or cash flows.

Recently Issued Accounting Standards

In January 2010, the FASB issued ASU 2010-06 regarding ASC Topic 820 "Fair Value Measurements and Disclosures." This ASU requires additional disclosure regarding significant transfers in and out of Levels 1 and 2 fair value measurements and the reasons for the transfers. In addition, this ASU requires the Company to present separately information about purchases, sales, issuances, and settlements, (on a gross basis rather than as one net number), in the reconciliation for fair value measurements using significant unobservable inputs (Level 3). ASU 2010-06 clarifies existing disclosures regarding fair value measurement for each class of assets and liabilities and the valuation techniques and inputs used to measure fair value for recurring and nonrecurring fair value measurements that fall in either Level 2 or Level 3. This update also includes conforming amendments to the guidance on employers' disclosures about postretirement benefit plan asset (Subtopic 715-20). The changes under ASU 2010-06 will be effective for Autodesk's fiscal year beginning February 1, 2010, except for the disclosures about purchases, sales, issuances and settlements in the roll forward of activity in Level 3 fair value measurements, which are effective for Autodesk's fiscal year beginning February 1, 2011. Autodesk believes that the adoption of these new accounting pronouncements will not have a material impact on its consolidated financial position, results of operations or cash flows.

In October 2009, the FASB issued ASU 2009-13 regarding ASC Subtopic 605-25 "Revenue Recognition—Multiple-element Arrangements." This ASU addresses criteria for separating the consideration in multiple-element arrangements. ASU 2009-13 will require companies to allocate the overall consideration to each deliverable by using a best estimate of the selling price of individual deliverables in the arrangement in the absence of vendor-specific objective evidence or other third-party evidence of the selling price. In October 2009, the FASB also issued ASU 2009-14 regarding ASC Topic 985 "Software: Certain Revenue Arrangements That Include Software Elements." This ASU modifies the scope of ASC Subtopic 965-605, "Software Revenue Recognition," to exclude (a) non-software components of tangible products and (b) software components of tangible products that are sold, licensed, or leased with tangible products when the software components and non-software components of the tangible product function together to deliver the tangible product's essential functionality. The changes under ASU 2009-13 and 2009-14 will be effective prospectively for revenue arrangements entered into or materially modified in fiscal years beginning on or after June 15, 2010, and early adoption is permitted. Autodesk currently plans to adopt the changes under ASU 2009-13 and 2009-14 effective February 1, 2011. Autodesk is currently assessing the impact that the adoption of these new accounting pronouncements will have on its consolidated financial position, results of operations or cash flows.

In June 2009, the FASB issued SFAS 166, "Accounting for Transfers of Financial Assets-an amendment of FASB Statement No. 140" and SFAS 167, "Amendments to FASB Interpretation No. 46(R)," which update accounting for securitizations and special-purpose entities. SFAS 166 eliminates the concept of a "qualifying special-purpose entity," changes the requirements for derecognizing financial assets and requires additional disclosures. SFAS 167 amends the evaluation criteria to identify the primary beneficiary of a variable interest entity provided by FASB Interpretation No. 46(R), "Consolidation of Variable Interest Entities—An Interpretation of ARB No. 51." This statement also amends the consolidation guidance applicable to variable interest entities. Additionally, SFAS 167 requires ongoing reassessments of whether an enterprise is the primary beneficiary of the variable interest entity. These statements will be effective for Autodesk's fiscal year beginning February 1, 2010. Autodesk believes that the adoption of SFAS 166 or 167 will not have a material effect on its consolidated financial position, results of operations and cash flows.

1.25

THOR INDUSTRIES, INC. (JUL)

NOTES TO CONSOLIDATED FINANCIAL STATEMENTS

A. Summary of Significant Accounting Policies (in part)

Accounting Pronouncements

In June 2009, the FASB issued SFAS No. 167, "Amendments to FASB Interpretation No. 46(R)" (SFAS 167). SFAS No. 167 amends ASC 810-10 (formerly FASB Interpretation No. 46(R)) by adding previously considered qualifying special purpose entities (the concept of these entities was eliminated by SFAS No. 166). In addition, companies must perform an analysis to determine whether the Company's variable interest or interests give it a controlling financial interest in a variable interest entity. Companies must also reassess on an ongoing basis whether the Company is the primary beneficiary of a variable interest entity. SFAS 167 is effective for fiscal years beginning after November 15, 2009. The Company does not expect the adoption of SFAS 167 to have a material impact on the Company's financial statements.

In January 2010, the FASB issued Accounting Standards Update ("ASC") 2010-06 (Financial Reporting Considerations Related to Fair Value Measurement Disclosures), which amends ASC 820 (formerly Statement 157). The ASU was issued in response to requests from financial statement users for additional information about fair value measurements. Under the ASU:

- A reporting entity is now required to disclose separately the amounts of, and reasons for, significant transfers (1)

between Level 1 and Level 2 of the fair value hierarchy and (2) into and out of Level 3 of the fair value hierarchy for the reconciliation of Level 3 measurements.
- A reporting entity is no longer permitted to adopt a policy recognizing transfers into Level 3 as of the beginning of the reporting period and transfers out of Level 3 as of the end of the reporting period. Rather, an entity must disclose and follow a consistent policy for determining when transfers between levels are recognized.

The Company adopted this ASU effective April 30, 2010. The adoption of the ASU did not have a material impact on the financial statements.

B. Investments and Fair Value Measurements (in part)

ASC 820-10, Fair Value Measurements and Disclosures, defines fair value, establishes a framework for measuring fair value under generally accepted accounting principles and enhances disclosures about fair value measurements. Fair value is defined as the exchange price that would be received for an asset or paid to transfer a liability (i.e., an exit price) in the principal or most advantageous market for the asset or liability in an orderly transaction between market participants on the measurement date. Valuation techniques used to measure fair value must maximize the use of observable inputs and minimize the use of unobservable inputs. The stan-dard describes a fair value hierarchy based on three levels of inputs, of which the first two are considered observable and the last unobservable, that may be used to measure fair value which are the following:

Level 1—Quoted prices in active markets for identical assets or liabilities.

Level 2—Inputs other than Level 1 that are observable, either directly or indirectly, such as quoted prices for similar assets or liabilities; quoted prices in markets that are not active; or other inputs that are observable or can be corroborated by observable market data for substantially the full term of the assets or liabilities.

Level 3—Unobservable inputs that are supported by little or no market activity and that are significant to the fair value of the assets or liabilities.

Quarterly Financial Data

1.26

YAHOO! INC. (DEC)

NOTES TO CONSOLIDATED FINANCIAL STATEMENTS

Selected Quarterly Financial Data (Unaudited)

(In thousands, except per share amounts)	March 31, 2009[1]	June 30, 2009[2]	Sept. 30, 2009[3]	Dec. 31, 2009[4]	March 31, 2010[5]	June 30, 2010[6]	Sept. 30, 2010[7]	Dec. 31, 2010[8]
Revenue	$1,580,042	$1,572,897	$1,575,399	$1,731,977	$1,596,960	$1,601,379	$1,601,203	$1,525,109
Gross profit	$ 879,305	$ 860,444	$ 866,501	$ 982,319	$ 890,577	$ 918,657	$ 920,449	$ 967,423
Net income attributable to Yahoo! Inc.	$ 117,558	$ 141,387	$ 186,093	$ 152,954	$ 310,191	$ 213,321	$ 396,131	$ 312,020
Net income attributable to Yahoo! Inc. common stockholders per share—basic	$ 0.08	$ 0.10	$ 0.13	$ 0.11	$ 0.22	$ 0.15	$ 0.30	$ 0.24
Net income attributable to Yahoo! Inc. common stockholders per share—diluted	$ 0.08	$ 0.10	$ 0.13	$ 0.11	$ 0.22	$ 0.15	$ 0.29	$ 0.24
Shares used in per share calculation—basic	1,391,526	1,394,783	1,401,961	1,402,339	1,398,308	1,378,374	1,333,753	1,306,036
Shares used in per share calculation—diluted	1,406,510	1,414,295	1,424,854	1,416,974	1,413,432	1,390,240	1,343,094	1,311,682

[1] Net income attributable to Yahoo! Inc. for the quarter ended March 31, 2009 includes net restructuring charges of $5 million.

[2] Net income attributable to Yahoo! Inc. for the quarter ended June 30, 2009 includes a pre-tax gain of $67 million in connection with the Company's sale of its Gmarket shares and net restructuring charges of $65 million.

[3] Net income attributable to Yahoo! Inc. for the quarter ended September 30, 2009 includes Yahoo!'s gain on sale of the Company's direct investment in Alibaba.com of $98 million and net restructuring charges of $17 million.

[4] Net income attributable to Yahoo! Inc. for the quarter ended December 31, 2009 includes net restructuring charges of $40 million.

[5] Net income attributable to Yahoo! Inc. for the quarter ended March 31, 2010 includes a pre-tax gain of $66 million in connection with the sale of Zimbra, Inc. and net restructuring charges of $4 million. During the quarter ended March 31, 2010, Yahoo! recorded $43 million for the reimbursement of transition costs incurred in 2009.

[6] Net income attributable to Yahoo! Inc. for the quarter ended June 30, 2010 includes net restructuring charges of $10 million.

[7] Net income attributable to Yahoo! Inc. for the quarter ended September 30, 2010 includes a pre-tax gain of $186 million in connection with the sale of HotJobs and net restructuring charges of $6 million.

[8] Net income attributable to Yahoo! Inc. for the quarter ended December 31, 2010 includes net restructuring charges of $38 million. Beginning in the fourth quarter of 2010 when Yahoo! completed the transition of algorithmic and paid search services to the Microsoft platform in the U.S. and Canada, revenue was impacted by the required change in revenue presentation and the revenue share with Microsoft associated with the transition pursuant to the Search Agreement. For transitioned markets, Yahoo! now reports an 88 percent revenue share for search advertising services provided by Microsoft. Yahoo!'s income tax provision was also reduced by the effect of certain tax benefits as discussed in Note 9—"Income Taxes" in the Notes to the consolidated financial statements.

1.27

HARLEY-DAVIDSON, INC. (DEC)

NOTES TO CONSOLIDATED FINANCIAL STATEMENTS

Supplementary Data

Quarterly Financial Data (Unaudited)

(In millions, except per share data)	1st Quarter Mar. 28, 2010	1st Quarter Mar. 29, 2009	2nd Quarter June 27, 2010	2nd Quarter June 28, 2009	3rd Quarter Sep. 26, 2010	3rd Quarter Sep. 27, 2009	4th Quarter Dec. 31, 2010	4th Quarter Dec. 31, 2009
Motorcycles:								
Revenue	$1,037.3	$1,278.4	$1,135.1	$1,135.7	$1,087.1	$1,108.5	$917.1	$ 764.5
Operating income (loss)[(a)(b)]	$ 126.1	$ 231.0	$ 157.9	$ 174.2	$ 101.5	$ 130.7	$ (6.8)	$(221.8)
Financial Services:								
Revenue	$ 169.8	$ 104.7	$ 173.7	$ 124.0	$ 172.8	$ 137.0	$166.3	$ 129.2
Operating income (loss)[(c)(d)]	$ 26.7	$ 11.2	$ 60.8	$ (90.5)	$ 50.9	$ (31.5)	$ 43.5	$ (7.1)
Consolidated:								
Income (loss) before taxes[(e)]	$ 130.2	$ 234.4	$ 196.7	$ 83.2	$ 130.5	$ 99.2	$ (67.0)	$(238.1)
Income (loss) from continuing operations	$ 68.7	$ 128.1	$ 139.3	$ 33.4	$ 93.7	$ 56.4	$ (42.1)	$(147.2)
Loss from discontinued operations[(f)]	$ (35.4)	$ (10.7)	$ (68.1)	$ (13.6)	$ (4.9)	$ (29.9)	$ (4.7)	$ (71.5)
Net income (loss)	$ 33.3	$ 117.4	$ 71.2	$ 19.8	$ 88.8	$ 26.5	$(46.8)	$(218.7)
Earnings (loss) per common share from continuing operations:								
Basic	$ 0.30	$ 0.55	$ 0.60	$ 0.14	$ 0.40	$ 0.24	$(0.18)	$ (0.63)
Diluted	$ 0.29	$ 0.55	$ 0.59	$ 0.14	$ 0.40	$ 0.24	$(0.18)	$ (0.63)
Loss per common share from discontinued operations:								
Basic	$ (0.15)	$ (0.05)	$ (0.29)	$ (0.06)	$ (0.02)	$ (0.13)	$(0.02)	$ (0.31)
Diluted	$ (0.15)	$ (0.05)	$ (0.29)	$ (0.06)	$ (0.02)	$ (0.13)	$(0.02)	$ (0.31)
Earnings (loss) per common share:								
Basic	$ 0.14	$ 0.51	$ 0.30	$ 0.08	$ 0.38	$ 0.11	$(0.20)	$ (0.94)
Diluted	$ 0.14	$ 0.50	$ 0.30	$ 0.08	$ 0.38	$ 0.11	$(0.20)	$ (0.94)

[(a)] Operating income (loss) for the Motorcycles segment includes restructuring expense and other impairments as discussed in Note 4 for the following periods (in millions):

	1st Quarter Mar. 28, 2010	1st Quarter Mar. 29, 2009	2nd Quarter June 27, 2010	2nd Quarter June 28, 2009	3rd Quarter Sep. 26, 2010	3rd Quarter Sep. 27, 2009	4th Quarter Dec. 31, 2010	4th Quarter Dec. 31, 2009
Motorcycles:								
Restructuring expense	$ 49.3	$ 30.4	$ 30.1	$ 15.1	$ 39.3	$ 36.6	$ 17.7	$ 83.1
Asset impairment	—	—	—	—	—	14.2	—	3.8
Pension and postretirement healthcare plan curtailment	(1.0)	4.5	—	—	28.2	—	—	33.3
Total restructuring expense and other impairments	$ 48.3	$ 34.9	$ 30.1	$ 15.1	$ 67.5	$ 50.8	$ 17.7	$ 120.2

[(b)] Operating income (loss) for the Motorcycles segment includes approximately $19 million of costs associated with the Company's efforts to expand its presence in Brazil as discussed in Item 7, "Management's Discussion and Analysis of Financial Condition and Results of Operations."

[(c)] Operating income (loss) for the Financial Services segment includes restructuring expense as discussed in Note 4 for the quarters ended September 27, 2009 and December 31, 2009 of $1.2 million and $2.1 million, respectively.

[(d)] Operating income (loss) for the Financial Services segment includes a goodwill impairment charge as discussed in Note 5 for the quarter ended June 28, 2009 of $28.4 million.

[(e)] Income (loss) before taxes includes a loss on debt extinguishment as discussed in Note 13 for the quarter ended December 31, 2010 of $85.2 million.

[(f)] Loss from discontinued operations includes pre-tax impairment charges as discussed in Note 3 for the following periods (in millions):

	1st Quarter Mar. 28, 2010	1st Quarter Mar. 29, 2009	2nd Quarter June 27, 2010	2nd Quarter June 28, 2009	3rd Quarter Sep. 26, 2010	3rd Quarter Sep. 27, 2009	4th Quarter Dec. 31, 2010	4th Quarter Dec. 31, 2009
Loss from discontinued operations:								
Impairment charges (pre-tax)	$ 35.0	$ —	$ 76.8	$ —	$ —	$ 18.9	$ —	$ 96.5

Selected Information for Five Years

1.28

CATERPILLAR INC. (DEC)

FIVE-YEAR FINANCIAL SUMMARY

	Years ended December 31				
(Dollars in millions except per share data)	**2010**	**2009**	**2008**	**2007**	**2006**
Sales and revenues	$42,588	$32,396	$51,324	$44,958	$41,517
Sales	$39,867	$29,540	$48,044	$41,962	$38,869
Percent inside the United States	32%	31%	33%	37%	46%
Percent outside the United States	68%	69%	67%	63%	54%
Revenues	$ 2,721	$ 2,856	$ 3,280	$ 2,996	$ 2,648
Profit[4][6]	$ 2,700	$ 895	$ 3,557	$ 3,541	$ 3,537
Profit per common share[1][6]	$ 4.28	$ 1.45	$ 5.83	$ 5.55	$ 5.37
Profit per common share—diluted[2][6]	$ 4.15	$ 1.43	$ 5.66	$ 5.37	$ 5.17
Dividends declared per share of common stock	$ 1.740	$ 1.680	$ 1.620	$ 1.380	$ 1.150
Return on average common stockholders' equity[3][5][6]	27.4%	11.9%	46.8%	44.4%	45.9%
Capital expenditures:					
Property, plant and equipment	$ 1,575	$ 1,504	$ 2,320	$ 1,682	$ 1,531
Equipment leased to others	$ 1,011	$ 968	$ 1,566	$ 1,340	$ 1,082
Depreciation and amortization	$ 2,296	$ 2,336	$ 1,980	$ 1,797	$ 1,602
Research and development expenses	$ 1,905	$ 1,421	$ 1,728	$ 1,404	$ 1,347
As a percent of sales and revenues	4.5%	4.4%	3.4%	3.1%	3.2%
Wages, salaries and employee benefits	$ 9,187	$ 7,416	$ 9,076	$ 8,331	$ 7,512
Average number of employees	98,504	99,359	106,518	97,444	90,160
December 31					
Total assets[6]	$64,020	$60,038	$67,782	$56,132	$51,449
Long-term debt due after one year:					
Consolidated	$20,437	$21,847	$22,834	$17,829	$17,680
Machinery and Engines	$ 4,505	$ 5,652	$ 5,736	$ 3,639	$ 3,694
Financial Products	$15,932	$16,195	$17,098	$14,190	$13,986
Total debt:					
Consolidated	$28,418	$31,631	$35,535	$28,429	$27,296
Machinery and Engines	$ 5,204	$ 6,387	$ 7,824	$ 4,006	$ 4,277
Financial Products	$23,214	$25,244	$27,711	$24,423	$23,019

[1] Computed on weighted-average number of shares outstanding.

[2] Computed on weighted-average number of shares outstanding diluted by assumed exercise of stock-based compensation awards, using the treasury stock method.

[3] Represents profit divided by average stockholders' equity (beginning of year stockholders' equity plus end of year stockholders' equity divided by two).

[4] Profit attributable to common stockholders.

[5] Effective January 1, 2009, we changed the manner in which we accounted for noncontrolling interests. Prior periods have been revised, as applicable.

[6] In 2007 we changed the manner in which we accounted for uncertain tax positions.

1.29

THE MCGRAW-HILL COMPANIES, INC. (DEC)

FIVE-YEAR FINANCIAL REVIEW

(In millions, except per share data and number of employees)	2010	2009	2008	2007	2006
Income statement data:					
Revenue	$ 6,168.3	$ 5,951.8	$ 6,355.1	$ 6,772.3	$ 6,255.1
Segment operating profit	1,601.1	1,382.8	1,483.8	1,836.7	1,589.9
Income before taxes on income	1,339.4[1]	1,178.9[2]	1,299.1[3]	1,636.3[4]	1,413.5[5]
Provision for taxes on income	487.5	429.1	479.7	609.0	522.6
Net income attributable to The McGraw-Hill Companies, Inc.	828.1	730.5	799.5	1,013.6	882.2
Earnings per common share:					
Basic	2.68	2.34	2.53	3.01	2.47
Diluted	2.65	2.33	2.51	2.94	2.40
Dividends per share	0.94	0.90	0.88	0.82	0.73
Operating statistics:					
Return on average equity	40.4%	45.7%	54.1%	46.6%	30.3%
Income before taxes on income as a percent of revenue	21.7%	19.8%	20.4%	24.2%	22.6%
Net income as a percent of revenue	13.4%	12.6%	12.9%	15.2%	14.2%
Balance sheet data:					
Working capital	$ 613.7	$ 484.4	$ (228.0)	$ (314.6)	$ (210.1)
Total assets	7,046.6	6,475.3	6,080.1	6,391.4	6,042.9
Total debt	1,198.3	1,197.8	1,267.6	1,197.4	2.7
Equity	2,291.4	1,929.2	1,352.9	1,677.8	2,730.0
Number of employees	20,755	21,077	21,649	21,171	20,214

[1] Includes the impact of the following items: a $15.6 million pre-tax charge for subleasing excess space in our New York facilities, a $10.6 million pre-tax restructuring charge, a $7.3 million pre-tax gain on the sale of certain equity interests at our Standard & Poor's segment and a $3.8 million pre-tax gain on the sale of McGraw-Hill Education's Australian secondary education business.

[2] Includes the impact of the following items: a $15.2 million net pre-tax restructuring charge, a $13.8 million pre-tax loss on the sale of Vista Research, Inc. and a $10.5 million pre-tax gain on the sale of *BusinessWeek*.

[3] Includes a $73.4 million pre-tax restructuring charge.

[4] Includes the impact of the following items: a $43.7 million pre-tax restructuring charge and a $17.3 million pre-tax gain on sale of the mutual fund data business.

[5] Includes the impact of the following items: a $31.5 million pre-tax restructuring charge, a $21.1 million pre-tax reduction in operating profit related to the transformation of Sweets from a primarily print catalogue to bundled print and online services, and stock-based compensation expense of $136.2 million incurred as a result of a new accounting standard for share-based payments (included in this expense is a one-time charge for the elimination of our restoration stock option program of $23.8 million).

Management's Discussion and Analysis of Financial Condition and Results of Operations

1.30

APPLE INC. (SEP)

MANAGEMENT'S DISCUSSION AND ANALYSIS OF FINANCIAL CONDITION AND RESULTS OF OPERATIONS

Item 7

This section and other parts of this Form 10-K contain forward-looking statements that involve risks and uncertainties. Forward-looking statements can also be identified by words such as "anticipates," "expects," "believes," "plans," "predicts," and similar terms. Forward-looking statements are not guarantees of future performance and the Company's actual results may differ significantly from the results discussed in the forward-looking statements. Factors that might cause such differences include, but are not limited to, those discussed in the subsection entitled "Risk Factors" above, which are incorporated herein by reference. The following discussion should be read in conjunction with the consolidated financial statements and notes thereto included in Item 8 of this Form 10-K. All information presented herein is based on the Company's fiscal calendar. Unless otherwise stated, references in this report to particular years or quarters refer to the Company's fiscal years ended in September and the associated quarters of those fiscal years. The Company assumes no obligation to revise or update any forward-looking statements for any reason, except as required by law.

Executive Overview

The Company designs, manufactures, and markets a range of personal computers, mobile communication and media devices, and portable digital music players, and sells a variety of related software, services, peripherals, networking solutions, and third-party digital content and applications. The Company's products and services include Mac computers, iPhone, iPad, iPod, Apple TV, Xserve, a portfolio of consumer and professional software applications, the Mac OS X and iOS operating systems, third-party digital content and applications through the iTunes Store, and a variety of accessory, service and support offerings. The Company sells its products worldwide through its retail stores, online stores, and direct sales force, and third-party cellular network carriers, wholesalers, retailers, and value-added resellers. In addition, the Company sells a variety of third-party Mac, iPhone, iPad and iPod compatible products, including application software, printers, storage devices, speakers, headphones, and various other accessories and peripherals through its online and retail stores. The Company sells to SMB, education, enterprise, government, and creative markets.

The Company is committed to bringing the best user experience to its customers through its innovative hardware, software, peripherals, services, and Internet offerings. The Company's business strategy leverages its unique ability to design and develop its own operating systems, hardware, application software, and services to provide its customers new products and solutions with superior ease-of-use, seamless integration, and innovative industrial design. The Company believes continual investment in research and development is critical to the development and enhancement of innovative products and technologies. In conjunction with its strategy, the Company continues to build and host a robust platform for the discovery and delivery of third-party digital content and applications through the iTunes Store. Within the iTunes Store, the Company has expanded its offerings through the App Store and iBookstore, which allow customers to browse, search for, and purchase third-party applications and books through either a Mac or Windows-based computer or by wirelessly downloading directly to an iPhone, iPad or iPod touch. The Company also works to support a community for the development of third-party software and hardware products and digital content that complement the Company's offerings. Additionally, the Company's strategy includes expanding its distribution network to effectively reach more customers and provide them with a high-quality sales and post-sales support experience. The Company is therefore uniquely positioned to offer superior and well-integrated digital lifestyle and productivity solutions.

The Company participates in several highly competitive markets, including personal computers with its Mac computers; mobile communications and media devices with its iPhone, iPad and iPod product families; and distribution of third-party digital content and applications with its online iTunes Store. While the Company is widely recognized as a leading innovator in the markets where it competes, these markets are highly competitive and subject to aggressive pricing. To remain competitive, the Company believes that increased investment in research and development and marketing and advertising is necessary to maintain or expand its position in the markets where it competes. The Company's research and development spending is focused on further developing its existing Mac line of personal computers; the Mac OS X and iOS operating systems; application software for the Mac; iPhone, iPad and iPod and related software; development of new digital lifestyle consumer and professional software applications; and investing in new product areas and technologies. The Company also believes increased investment in marketing and advertising programs is critical to increasing product and brand awareness.

The Company utilizes a variety of direct and indirect distribution channels, including its retail stores, online stores, and direct sales force, and third-party cellular network carriers, wholesalers, retailers, and value-added resellers. The Company believes that sales of its innovative and differentiated products are enhanced by knowledgeable salespersons who can convey the value of the hardware, software, and peripheral integration, demonstrate the unique digital lifestyle solutions that are available on its products, and demonstrate the compatibility of the Mac with the Windows platform and networks. The Company further believes providing direct contact with its targeted customers is an effective way to demonstrate the advantages of its products over those of its competitors and providing a high-quality sales and after-sales support experience is critical to attracting new and retaining existing customers. To ensure a high-quality buying experience for its products in which service and education are emphasized, the Company continues to expand and improve its distribution capabilities by expanding the number of its own retail stores worldwide. Additionally, the Company has invested in programs to enhance reseller sales by placing high quality Apple fixtures, merchandising materials and other resources within selected third-party reseller locations. Through the Apple Premium Reseller Program, certain third-party resellers focus on the Apple platform by providing a high level of integration and support services, and product expertise.

Critical Accounting Policies and Estimates

The preparation of financial statements and related disclosures in conformity with U.S. generally accepted accounting principles ("GAAP") and the Company's discussion and analysis of its financial condition and operating results require the Company's management to make judgments, assumptions and estimates that affect the amounts reported in its consolidated financial statements and accompanying notes. Note 1, "Summary of Significant Accounting Policies" of Notes to Consolidated Financial Statements in this Form 10-K describes the significant accounting policies and methods used in the preparation of the Company's consolidated financial statements. Management bases its estimates on historical experience and on various other assumptions it believes to be reasonable under the circumstances, the results of which form the basis for making judgments about the carrying values of assets and liabilities. Actual results may differ from these estimates and such differences may be material.

Management believes the Company's critical accounting policies and estimates are those related to revenue recognition, valuation and impairment of marketable securities, inventory valuation and inventory purchase commitments, warranty costs, income taxes, and legal and other contingencies. Management considers these policies critical because they are both important to the portrayal of the Company's financial condition and operating results, and they require management to make judgments and estimates about inherently uncertain matters. The Company's senior management has reviewed these critical accounting policies and related disclosures with the Audit and Finance Committee of the Company's Board of Directors.

Revenue Recognition

Net sales consist primarily of revenue from the sale of hardware, software, digital content and applications, peripherals, and service and support contracts. The Company recognizes revenue when persuasive evidence of an arrangement exists, delivery has occurred, the sales price is fixed or determinable, and collection is probable. Product is considered delivered to the customer once it has been shipped and title and risk of loss have been transferred. For most of the Company's product sales, these criteria are met at the time the product is shipped. For online sales to individuals, for some sales to education customers in the U.S., and for certain other sales, the Company defers recognition of revenue until the customer receives the product because the Company retains a portion of the risk of loss on these sales during transit. The Company recognizes revenue from the sale of hardware products (e.g., Macs, iPhones, iPads, iPods and peripherals), software bundled with hardware that is essential to the functionality of the hardware, and third-party digital content sold on the iTunes Store in accordance with general revenue recognition accounting guidance. The Company recognizes revenue in accordance with industry specific software accounting guidance for the following types of sales transactions: (i) standalone sales of software products, (ii) sales of software upgrades and (iii) sales of software bundled with hardware not essential to the functionality of the hardware.

For multi-element arrangements that include tangible products containing software essential to the tangible product's functionality and undelivered software elements relating to the tangible product's essential software, the Company allocates revenue to all deliverables based on their relative selling prices. In such circumstances, the Company uses a hierarchy to determine the selling price to be used for allocating revenue to deliverables: (i) vendor-specific objective evidence of fair value ("VSOE"), (ii) third-party evidence of selling price ("TPE") and (iii) best estimate of the selling price ("ESP"). VSOE generally exists only when the Company sells the deliverable separately and is the price actually charged by the Company for that deliverable. ESPs reflect the Company's best estimates of what the selling prices of elements would be if they were sold regularly on a stand-alone basis.

For all past and current sales of iPhone, iPad, Apple TV and for sales of iPod touch beginning in June 2010, the Company indicated it might from time-to-time provide future unspecified software upgrades and features free of charge to customers. The Company has identified two deliverables in arrangements involving the sale of these devices. The first deliverable is the hardware and software essential to the functionality of the hardware device delivered at the time of sale. The second deliverable is the embedded right included with the purchase of iPhone, iPad, iPod touch and Apple TV to receive on a when-and-if-available basis, future unspecified software upgrades and features relating to the product's essential software. The Company has allocated revenue between these two deliverables using the relative selling price method. Because the Company has neither VSOE nor TPE for the two deliverables, the allocation of revenue has been based on the Company's ESPs. Amounts allocated to the delivered hardware and the related essential software are recognized at the time of sale provided the other conditions for revenue recognition have been met. Amounts allocated to the embedded unspecified software upgrade right are deferred and recognized on a straight-line basis over the 24-month estimated life of each of these devices. All product cost of sales, including estimated warranty costs, are recognized at the time of sale. Costs for engineering and sales and marketing are expensed as incurred. If the estimated life of the hardware product should change, the future rate of amortization of the revenue allocated to the software upgrade right will also change.

The Company's process for determining its ESP for deliverables without VSOE or TPE involves management's judgment. The Company's process considers multiple factors that may vary depending upon the unique facts and circumstances related to each deliverable. The Company believes its customers, particularly consumers, would be reluctant to buy unspecified software upgrade rights related to iPhone, iPad, iPod touch and Apple TV. This view is primarily based on the fact that unspecified upgrade rights do not obligate the Company to provide upgrades at a particular time or at all, and do not specify to customers which upgrades or features will be delivered. Therefore, the Company has concluded if it were to sell upgrade rights on a standalone basis, including those rights associated with iPhone, iPad, iPod touch and Apple TV, the selling price would be relatively low. Key factors considered by the Company in developing the ESPs for these upgrade rights include prices charged by the Company for similar offerings, the Company's historical pricing practices, the nature of the upgrade rights (e.g., unspecified and when-and-if-available), and the relative ESP of the upgrade rights as compared to the total selling price of the product. The Company may also consider, when appropriate, the impact of other products and services, including advertising services, on selling price assumptions when developing and reviewing its ESPs for software upgrade rights and related deliverables. The Company may also consider additional factors as appropriate, including the pricing of competitive alternatives if they exist, and product-specific business objectives. If the facts and circumstances underlying the factors considered change or should future facts and circumstances lead the Company to consider additional factors, the Company's ESP for software upgrades related to future sales for these devices could change.

Beginning in the third quarter of 2010 in conjunction with the announcement of iOS 4, the Company's ESPs for the embedded software upgrade rights included with iPhone, iPad and iPod touch reflect the positive financial impact expected by the Company as a result of its introduction of a mobile advertising platform for these devices and the expectation of customers regarding software that includes or supports an advertising component. iOS 4 supports iAd, the Company's new mobile advertising platform, which enables applications on iPhone, iPad and iPod touch to feature media-rich advertisements within applications.

The Company records reductions to revenue for estimated commitments related to price protection and for customer incentive programs, including reseller and end-user rebates, and other sales programs and volume-based incentives. For transactions involving price protection, the Company recognizes revenue net of the estimated amount to be refunded, provided the refund amount can be reasonably and reliably estimated and the other conditions for revenue recognition have been met. The Company's policy requires that, if refunds cannot be reliably estimated, revenue is not recognized until reliable estimates can be made or the price protection lapses. For customer incentive programs, the estimated cost of these programs is recognized at the later of the date at which the Company has sold the product or the date at which the program is offered. The Company also records reductions to revenue for expected future product returns based on the Company's historical experience. Future market conditions and product transitions may require the Company to increase customer incentive programs and incur incremental price protection obligations that could result in additional reductions to revenue at the time such programs are offered. Additionally, certain customer incentive programs require management to estimate the number of customers who will actually redeem the incentive. Management's estimates are based on historical experience and the specific terms and conditions of particular incentive programs. If a greater than estimated proportion of customers redeem such incentives, the Company would be required to record additional reductions to revenue, which would have a negative impact on the Company's results of operations.

Valuation and Impairment of Marketable Securities

The Company's investments in available-for-sale securities are reported at fair value. Unrealized gains and losses related to changes in the fair value of investments are included in accumulated other comprehensive income, net of tax, as reported in the Company's Condensed Consolidated Balance Sheets. Changes in the fair value of investments impact the Company's net income only when such investments are sold or an other-than-temporary impairment is recognized. Realized gains and losses on the sale of securities are determined by specific identification of each security's cost basis. The Company regularly reviews its investment portfolio to determine if any investment is other-than-temporarily impaired due to changes in credit risk or other potential valuation concerns, which would require the Company to record an impairment charge in the period any such determination is made. In making this judgment, the Company evaluates, among other things, the duration and extent to which the fair value of an investment is less than its cost, the financial condition of the issuer and any changes thereto, and the Company's intent to sell, or whether it is more likely than not it will be required to sell, the investment before recovery of the investment's amortized cost basis. The Company's assessment on whether an investment is other-than-temporarily impaired or not, could change in the future due to new developments or changes in assumptions related to any particular investment.

Inventory Valuation and Inventory Purchase Commitments

The Company must order components for its products and build inventory in advance of product shipments. The Company records a write-down for inventories of components and products, including third-party products held for resale, which have become obsolete or are in excess of anticipated demand or net realizable value. The Company performs a detailed review of inventory each fiscal quarter that considers multiple factors including demand forecasts, product life cycle status, product development plans, current sales levels, and component cost trends. The industries in which the Company competes are subject to a rapid and unpredictable pace of product and component obsolescence and demand changes. If future demand or market conditions for the Company's products are less favorable than forecasted or if unforeseen technological changes negatively impact the utility of component inventory, the Company may be required to record additional write-downs, which would negatively affect its results of operations in the period when the write-downs were recorded.

The Company records accruals for estimated cancellation fees related to component orders that have been cancelled or are expected to be cancelled. Consistent with industry practice, the Company acquires components through a combination of purchase orders, supplier contracts, and open orders based on projected demand information. These commitments typically cover the Company's requirements for periods ranging from 30 to 150 days. If there is an abrupt and substantial decline in demand for one or more of the Company's products or an unanticipated change in technological requirements for any of the Company's products, the Company may be required to record additional accruals for cancellation fees that would negatively affect its results of operations in the period when the cancellation fees are identified and recorded.

Warranty Costs

The Company provides for the estimated cost of hardware and software warranties at the time the related revenue is recognized based on historical and projected warranty claim rates, historical and projected cost-per-claim, and knowledge of specific product failures that are outside of the Company's typical experience. Each quarter, the Company reevaluates its estimates to assess the adequacy of its recorded warranty liabilities considering the size of the installed base of products subject to warranty protection and adjusts the amounts as necessary. If actual product failure rates or repair costs differ from estimates, revisions to the estimated warranty liability would be required and could materially affect the Company's results of operations.

The Company periodically provides updates to its applications and operating system software to maintain the software's compliance with specifications. The estimated cost to develop such updates is accounted for as warranty cost that is recognized at the time related software revenue is recognized. Factors considered in determining appropriate accruals related to such updates include the number of units delivered, the number of updates expected to occur, and the historical cost and estimated future cost of the resources necessary to develop these updates.

Income Taxes

The Company records a tax provision for the anticipated tax consequences of the reported results of operations. In accordance with GAAP, the provision for income taxes is computed using the asset and liability method, under which deferred tax assets and liabilities are recognized for the expected future tax consequences of temporary differences between the financial reporting and tax bases of assets and liabilities, and for operating losses and tax credit carryforwards. Deferred tax assets and liabilities are measured using the currently enacted tax rates that apply to taxable income in effect for the years in which those tax assets are expected to be realized or settled. The Company records a valuation allowance to reduce deferred tax assets to the amount that is believed more likely than not to be realized.

The Company only recognizes the tax benefit from an uncertain tax position if it is more likely than not that the tax position will be sustained on examination by the taxing authorities, based on the technical merits of the position. The tax benefits recognized in the financial statements from such positions are then measured based on the largest benefit that has a greater than 50% likelihood of being realized upon ultimate settlement.

Management believes it is more likely than not that forecasted income, including income that may be generated as a result of certain tax planning strategies, together with future reversals of existing taxable temporary differences, will be sufficient to fully recover the deferred tax assets. In the event that the Company determines all or part of the net deferred tax assets are not realizable in the future, the Company will make an adjustment to the valuation allowance that would be charged to earnings in the period such determination is made. In addition, the calculation of tax liabilities involves significant judgment in estimating the impact of uncertainties in the application of GAAP and complex tax laws. Resolution of these uncertainties in a manner inconsistent with management's expectations could have a material impact on the Company's financial condition and operating results.

Legal and Other Contingencies

As discussed in Part I, Item 3 of this Form 10-K under the heading "Legal Proceedings" and in Note 8 "Commitments and Contingencies" in Notes to Consolidated Financial Statements, the Company is subject to various legal proceedings and claims that arise in the ordinary course of business. In accordance with GAAP, the Company records a liability when it is probable that a loss has been incurred and the amount is reasonably estimable. There is significant judgment required in both the probability determination and as to whether an exposure can be reasonably estimated. In management's opinion, the Company does not have a potential liability related to any current legal proceedings and claims that would individually or in the aggregate materially adversely affect its financial condition or operating results. However, the outcomes of legal proceedings and claims brought against the Company are subject to significant uncertainty. Should the Company fail to prevail in any of these legal matters or should several of these legal matters be resolved against the Company in the same reporting period, the operating results of a particular reporting period could be materially adversely affected.

Net Sales

Fiscal years 2010, 2009 and 2008 each spanned 52 weeks. An additional week is included in the first fiscal quarter approximately every six years to realign fiscal quarters with calendar quarters.

The following table summarizes net sales and Mac unit sales by operating segment and net sales and unit sales by product during the three years ended September 25, 2010 (in millions, except unit sales in thousands and per unit amounts):

	2010	Change	2009	Change	2008
Net Sales by Operating Segment:					
Americas net sales	$24,498	29%	$18,981	15%	$16,552
Europe net sales	18,692	58%	11,810	28%	9,233
Japan net sales	3,981	75%	2,279	32%	1,728
Asia-Pacific net sales	8,256	160%	3,179	18%	2,686
Retail net sales	9,798	47%	6,656	(9)%	7,292
Total net sales	$65,225	52%	$42,905	14%	$37,491
Mac Unit Sales by Operating Segment:					
Americas Mac unit sales	4,976	21%	4,120	4%	3,980
Europe Mac unit sales	3,859	36%	2,840	13%	2,519
Japan Mac unit sales	481	22%	395	2%	389
Asia-Pacific Mac unit sales	1,500	62%	926	17%	793
Retail Mac unit sales	2,846	35%	2,115	4%	2,034
Total Mac unit sales	13,662	31%	10,396	7%	9,715
Net Sales by Product:					
Desktops[a]	$ 6,201	43%	$ 4,324	(23)%	$ 5,622
Portables[b]	11,278	18%	9,535	9%	8,732
Total Mac net sales	17,479	26%	13,859	(3)%	14,354
iPod	8,274	2%	8,091	(12)%	9,153
Other music related products and services[c]	4,948	23%	4,036	21%	3,340
iPhone and related products and services[d]	25,179	93%	13,033	93%	6,742
iPad and related products and services[e]	4,958	NM	0	NM	0
Peripherals and other hardware[f]	1,814	23%	1,475	(13)%	1,694
Software, service and other sales[g]	2,573	7%	2,411	9%	2,208
Total net sales	$65,225	52%	$42,905	14%	$37,491

(continued)

	2010	Change	2009	Change	2008
Unit Sales by Product:					
Desktops [a]	4,627	45%	3,182	(14)%	3,712
Portables [b]	9,035	25%	7,214	20%	6,003
Total Mac unit sales	13,662	31%	10,396	7%	9,715
Net sales per Mac unit sold [h]	$ 1,279	(4)%	$ 1,333	(10)%	$ 1,478
iPod unit sales	50,312	(7)%	54,132	(1)%	54,828
Net sales per iPod unit sold [h]	$ 164	10%	$ 149	(11)%	$ 167
iPhone units sold	39,989	93%	20,731	78%	11,627
iPad units sold	7,458	NM	0	NM	0

[a] Includes iMac, Mac mini, Mac Pro and Xserve product lines.
[b] Includes MacBook, MacBook Air and MacBook Pro product lines.
[c] Includes iTunes Store sales, iPod services, and Apple-branded and third-party iPod accessories.
[d] Includes revenue recognized from iPhone sales, carrier agreements, services, and Apple-branded and third-party iPhone accessories.
[e] Includes revenue recognized from iPad sales, services and Apple-branded and third-party iPad accessories.
[f] Includes sales of displays, wireless connectivity and networking solutions, and other hardware accessories.
[g] Includes sales of Apple-branded operating system and application software, third-party software, Mac and Internet services.
[h] Derived by dividing total product-related net sales by total product-related unit sales.
NM = Not Meaningful

Fiscal Year 2010 Versus 2009

Net sales during 2010 increased $22.3 billion or 52% compared to 2009. Several factors contributed positively to these increases, including the following:

- Net sales of iPhone and related products and services were $25.2 billion in 2010 representing an increase of $12.1 billion or 93% compared to 2009. Net sales of iPhone and related products and services accounted for 39% of the Company's total net sales for the year. iPhone unit sales totaled 40 million in 2010, which represents an increase of 19.3 million or 93% compared to 2009. iPhone year-over-year growth was attributable primarily to continued growth from existing carriers, expanded distribution with new international carriers and resellers, and strong demand for iPhone 4, which was released in the U.S. in June 2010 and in many other countries over the remainder of 2010. As of September 25, 2010, the Company distributed iPhone in 89 countries through 166 carriers.
- Net sales of iPad and related products and services were $5.0 billion and unit sales of iPad were 7.5 million during 2010. iPad was released in the U.S. in April 2010 and in various other countries over the remainder of 2010. As of September 25, 2010, the Company distributed iPad in 26 countries. The Company distributes iPad through its direct channels, certain cellular network carriers' distribution channels and certain third-party resellers. Net sales of iPad and related products and services accounted for 8% of the Company's total net sales for 2010, reflecting the strong demand for iPad during the five months following its release.
- Mac net sales increased by $3.6 billion or 26% in 2010 compared to 2009, and Mac unit sales increased by 3.3 million or 31% in 2010 compared to 2009. Net sales per Mac unit sold decreased by 4% in 2010 compared to 2009 due primarily to lower average selling prices of Mac portable systems. Net sales of the Company's Macs accounted for 27% of the Company's total net sales in 2010 compared to 32% in 2009. During 2010, net sales and unit sales of the Company's Mac

portable systems increased by 18% and 25%, respectively, primarily attributable to strong demand for MacBook Pro, which was updated in April 2010. Net sales and unit sales of the Company's Mac desktop systems increased by 43% and 45%, respectively, as a result of higher sales of iMac, which was updated in July 2010.
- Net sales of other music related products and services increased $912 million or 23% during 2010 compared to 2009. This increase was due primarily to growth of the iTunes Store which generated total net sales of $4.1 billion for 2010. The results of the iTunes Store reflect growth of the iTunes App Store, continued growth in the installed base of iPhone, iPad, and iPod customers, and the expansion of third-party audio and video content available for sale and rent via the iTunes Store. The Company continues to expand its iTunes content and applications offerings around the world. Net sales of other music related products and services accounted for 8% of the Company's total net sales for 2010.
- Net sales of iPods increased $183 million or 2% during 2010, while iPod unit sales declined by 7% during 2010 compared to 2009. Net sales per iPod unit sold increased by 10% to $164 in 2010 compared to 2009, due to a shift in product mix toward iPod touch. iPod touch had strong growth in each of the Company's reportable operating segments. Net sales of iPods accounted for 13% of the Company's total net sales for the year compared to 19% in 2009.

Fiscal Year 2009 Versus 2008

Net sales during 2009 increased $5.4 billion or 14% compared to 2008. Several factors contributed positively to these increases, including the following:

- iPhone revenue and net sales of related products and services amounted to $13.0 billion in 2009, an increase of $6.3 billion or 93% compared to 2008. The year-over-year iPhone revenue growth is largely attributable to the year-over-year increase in iPhone handset unit sales. iPhone handset unit sales totaled 20.7 million during 2009, which represents an increase of 9.1 million or 78% during 2009 compared to 2008. This growth is attributed primarily to expanded distribution and strong overall demand for iPhones. iPhone 3GS was released in the U.S. on June 19, 2009 and in many other countries over the remainder of 2009.

- Net sales of other music-related products and services increased $696 million or 21% during 2009 compared to 2008. The increase was due predominantly to increased net sales of third-party digital content and applications from the iTunes Store, which experienced double-digit growth in each of the Company's geographic segments during 2009 compared to the same period in 2008. The Company believes this is attributable primarily to continued interest in and growth of the iTunes App Store, continued growth in the Company's base of iPhone, iPad, and iPod customers, and the expansion of third-party audio and video content available for sale and rent via the iTunes Store.

Partially offsetting the favorable factors discussed above, net sales during 2009 were negatively impacted by certain factors, including the following:

- Net sales of iPods decreased $1.1 billion or 12% during 2009 compared to 2008. iPod unit sales decreased by 1% during 2009 compared to 2008. Net sales per iPod unit sold decreased 11% to $149 in 2009 compared to 2008, resulting from lower average selling prices across all of the iPod product lines, due primarily to price reductions taken with the introduction of new iPods in September 2009 and September 2008 and a stronger U.S. dollar, offset partially by a higher mix of iPod touch sales.
- Mac net sales declined 3% during 2009 compared to 2008, while Mac unit sales increased by 7% over the same period. Net sales per Mac unit sold decreased by 10% during 2009 compared to 2008, due primarily to lower average selling prices across all Mac portable and desktop systems and a stronger U.S. dollar. Net sales of Macs accounted for 32% of the Company's total net sales for 2009. During 2009, Mac portable systems net sales and unit sales increased by 9% and 20%, respectively, compared to 2008. This growth was driven by strong demand for MacBook Pro, which was updated in June 2009 and October 2008, and which experienced double-digit net sales and unit growth in each of the Company's reportable operating segments compared to the same period in 2008. The Company also had a higher mix of Mac portable systems sales, which is consistent with overall personal computer market trends. Net sales and unit sales of the Company's Mac desktop systems decreased by 23% and 14%, respectively, during 2009 compared to 2008. The decrease in net sales of Mac desktop systems was due mainly to a shift in product mix towards lower-priced desktops, lower average selling prices across all Mac desktop systems and a stronger U.S. dollar.

Segment Operating Performance

The Company manages its business primarily on a geographic basis. The Company's reportable operating and reporting segments consist of the Americas, Europe, Japan, Asia-Pacific and Retail operations. The Americas, Europe, Japan and Asia-Pacific reportable segment results do not include the results of the Retail segment. The Americas segment includes both North and South America. The Europe segment includes European countries as well as the Middle East and Africa. The Asia-Pacific segment includes Australia and Asia, but does not include Japan. The Retail segment operates Apple retail stores in 11 countries, including the U.S. Each reportable operating segment provides similar hardware and software products and similar services. Further information regarding the Company's operating segments may be found in Note 9, "Segment Information and Geographic Data" in Notes to Consolidated Financial Statements of this Form 10-K.

Americas

During 2010, net sales in the Americas segment increased $5.5 billion or 29% compared to 2009. This increase in net sales was driven by increased iPhone revenue, strong demand for iPad, continued demand for Mac desktop and portable systems, and higher sales of third-party digital content and applications from the iTunes Store. Americas Mac net sales and unit sales increased 18% and 21%, respectively, during 2010 compared to 2009, largely due to strong demand for MacBook Pro. The Americas segment represented 37% and 44% of the Company's total net sales in 2010 and 2009, respectively.

During 2009, net sales in the Americas segment increased $2.4 billion or 15% compared to 2008. The increase in net sales during 2009 was attributable to the significant year-over-year increase in iPhone revenue, higher sales of third-party digital content and applications from the iTunes Store, and increased sales of Mac portable systems, partially offset by a decrease in sales of Mac desktop systems and iPods. Americas Mac net sales decreased 6% due primarily to lower average selling prices, while Mac unit sales increased by 4% on a year-over-year basis. The increase in Mac unit sales was due primarily to strong demand for the MacBook Pro. The Americas segment represented approximately 44% of the Company's total net sales in both 2009 and 2008.

Europe

During 2010, net sales in Europe increased $6.9 billion or 58% compared to 2009. The growth in net sales was due mainly to a significant increase in iPhone revenue attributable to continued growth from existing carriers and country and carrier expansion, increased sales of Mac desktop and portable systems and strong demand for iPad, partially offset by a stronger U.S. dollar. Europe Mac net sales and unit sales increased 32% and 36%, respectively, during the year due to strong demand for MacBook Pro and iMac. The Europe segment represented 29% and 28% of the Company's total net sales in 2010 and 2009, respectively.

During 2009, net sales in Europe increased $2.6 billion or 28% compared to 2008. The increase in net sales was due mainly to increased iPhone revenue and strong sales of Mac portable systems, offset partially by lower net sales of Mac desktop systems, iPods, and a stronger U.S. dollar. Mac unit sales increased 13% in 2009 compared to 2008, which was driven primarily by increased sales of Mac portable systems, particularly MacBook Pro, while total Mac net sales declined as a result of lower average selling prices across all Mac products. iPod net sales decreased year-over-year as a result of lower average selling prices, partially offset by increased unit sales of the higher priced iPod touch. The Europe segment represented 28% and 25% of total net sales in 2009 and 2008, respectively.

Japan

During 2010, Japan's net sales increased $1.7 billion or 75% compared to 2009. The primary contributors to this growth were significant year-over-year increases in iPhone revenue, strong demand for iPad, and to a lesser extent strength in the Japanese Yen. Mac net sales increased by 8% driven by a 22% increase in unit sales due primarily to strong demand for MacBook Pro and iMac, partially offset by lower average selling prices in Japan on a year-over-year basis. The Japan segment represented 6% and 5% of the Company's total net sales for 2010 and 2009, respectively.

Japan's net sales increased $551 million or 32% in 2009 compared to 2008. The primary contributors to this growth were increased iPhone revenue, stronger demand for certain Mac portable systems and iPods, and strength in the Japanese Yen, partially offset by decreased sales of Mac desktop systems. Net sales and unit sales of Mac portable systems increased during 2009 compared to 2008, driven primarily by stronger demand for MacBook Pro. Net sales and unit sales of iPods increased during 2009 compared to 2008, driven by strong demand for iPod touch and iPod nano. The Japan segment represented approximately 5% of the Company's total net sales in both 2009 and 2008.

Asia-Pacific

Net sales in Asia-Pacific increased $5.1 billion or 160% during 2010 compared to 2009. The significant growth in Asia-Pacific net sales was due mainly to increased iPhone revenue, which was primarily attributable to country and carrier expansion and continued growth from existing carriers. Asia-Pacific net sales were also favorably affected by strong demand for Mac portable and desktop systems and for iPad. Particularly strong year-over-year growth was experienced in China, Korea and Australia. The Asia-Pacific segment represented 13% and 7% of the Company's total net sales for 2010 and 2009, respectively.

Net sales in Asia-Pacific increased $493 million or 18% during 2009 compared to 2008 reflecting strong growth in sales of iPhone and Mac portable systems, offset partially by a decline in sales of iPods and Mac desktop systems, as well as a strengthening of the U.S. dollar against the Australian dollar and other Asian currencies. Mac net sales and unit sales grew in the Asia-Pacific region by 4% and 17%, respectively, due to increased sales of the MacBook Pro. The Asia-Pacific segment represented approximately 7% of the Company's total net sales in both 2009 and 2008.

Retail

Retail net sales increased $3.1 billion or 47% during 2010 compared to 2009. The increase in net sales was driven primarily by strong demand for iPad, increased sales of Mac desktop and portable systems and a significant year-over-year increase in iPhone revenue. Mac net sales and unit sales grew in the Retail segment by 25% and 35%, respectively, during 2010. The Company opened 44 new retail stores during the year, 28 of which were international stores, ending the year with 317 stores open compared to 273 stores at the end of 2009. With an average of 288 stores and 254 stores opened during 2010 and 2009, respectively, average revenue per store increased to $34.1 million in 2010, compared to $26.2 million in 2009. The Retail segment represented 15% and 16% of the Company's total net sales in 2010 and 2009, respectively.

Retail net sales decreased $636 million or 9% during 2009 compared to 2008. The decline in net sales was driven largely by a decrease in net sales of iPhones, iPods and Mac desktop systems, offset partially by strong demand for Mac portable systems. The year-over-year decline in Retail net sales was attributable to continued third-party channel expansion, particularly in the U.S. where most of the Company's stores are located, and also reflects the challenging consumer-spending environment in 2009. The Company opened 26 new retail stores during 2009, including 14 international stores, ending the year with 273 stores open. This compares to 247 stores open as of September 27, 2008. With an average of 254 stores and 211 stores opened during 2009 and 2008, respectively, average revenue per store decreased to $26.2 million for 2009 from $34.6 million in 2008.

The Retail segment reported operating income of $2.4 billion during 2010 and $1.7 billion during both 2009 and 2008. The increase in Retail operating income during 2010 compared to 2009 was attributable to higher overall net sales. Despite the decline in Retail net sales during 2009 compared to 2008, the Retail segment's operating income was flat at $1.7 billion in 2009 compared to 2008 due primarily to a higher gross margin percentage in 2009 consistent with that experienced by the overall company.

Expansion of the Retail segment has required and will continue to require a substantial investment in fixed assets and related infrastructure, operating lease commitments, personnel, and other operating expenses. Capital asset purchases associated with the Retail segment since its inception totaled $2.2 billion through the end of 2010. As of September 25, 2010, the Retail segment had approximately 26,500 full-time equivalent employees and had outstanding lease commitments associated with retail space and related facilities of $1.7 billion. The Company would incur substantial costs if it were to close multiple retail stores and such costs could adversely affect the Company's financial condition and operating results.

Gross Margin

Gross margin for the three years ended September 25, 2010, are as follows (in millions, except gross margin percentages):

	2010	2009	2008
Net sales	$65,225	$42,905	$37,491
Cost of sales	39,541	25,683	24,294
Gross margin	$25,684	$17,222	$13,197
Gross margin percentage	39.4%	40.1%	35.2%

The gross margin percentage in 2010 was 39.4% compared to 40.1% in 2009. This decline in gross margin is primarily attributable to new products that have higher cost structures, including iPad, partially offset by a more favorable sales mix of iPhone, which has a higher gross margin than the Company average.

The gross margin percentage in 2009 was 40.1% compared to 35.2% in 2008. The primary contributors to the increase in 2009 as compared to 2008 were a favorable sales mix toward products with higher gross margins and lower commodity and other product costs, which were partially offset by product price reductions.

The Company expects its gross margin percentage to decrease in future periods compared to levels achieved during

2010 and anticipates gross margin levels of about 36% in the first quarter of 2011. This expected decline is largely due to a higher mix of new and innovative products that have higher cost structures and deliver greater value to customers, and expected and potential future component cost and other cost increases.

The foregoing statements regarding the Company's expected gross margin percentage are forward-looking and could differ from anticipated levels because of several factors, including but not limited to certain of those set forth below in Part I, Item 1A, "Risk Factors" under the subheading *"Future operating results depend upon the Company's ability to obtain key components including but not limited to microprocessors, NAND flash memory, DRAM and LCDs at favorable prices and in sufficient quantities,"* which is incorporated herein by reference. There can be no assurance that targeted gross margin percentage levels will be achieved. In general, gross margins and margins on individual products will remain under downward pressure due to a variety of factors, including continued industry wide global product pricing pressures, increased competition, compressed product life cycles, product transitions and expected and potential increases in the cost of key components including but not limited to microprocessors, NAND flash memory, DRAM and LCDs, as well as potential increases in the costs of outside manufacturing services and a potential shift in the Company's sales mix towards products with lower gross margins. In response to these competitive pressures, the Company expects it will continue to take product pricing actions, which would adversely affect gross margins. Gross margins could also be affected by the Company's ability to manage product quality and warranty costs effectively and to stimulate demand for certain of its products. Due to the Company's significant international operations, financial results can be significantly affected in the short-term by fluctuations in exchange rates.

Operating Expenses

Operating expenses for the three years ended September 25, 2010, are as follows (in millions, except for percentages):

	2010	2009	2008
Research and development	$1,782	$1,333	$1,109
Percentage of net sales	2.7%	3.1%	3.0%
Selling, general and administrative	$5,517	$4,149	$3,761
Percentage of net sales	8.5%	9.7%	10.0%

Research and Development Expense ("R&D")

R&D expense increased 34% or $449 million to $1.8 billion in 2010 compared to 2009. This increase was due primarily to an increase in headcount and related expenses in the current year to support expanded R&D activities. Also contributing to this increase in R&D expense in 2010 was the capitalization in 2009 of software development costs of $71 million related to Mac OS X Snow Leopard. Although total R&D expense increased 34% during 2010, it declined as a percentage of net sales given the 52% year-over-year increase in net sales in 2010. The Company continues to believe that focused investments in R&D are critical to its future growth and competitive position in the marketplace and are directly related to timely development of new and enhanced products that are central to the Company's core business strategy. As such, the Com-

pany expects to make further investments in R&D to remain competitive.

R&D expense increased 20% or $224 million to $1.3 billion in 2009 compared to 2008. This increase was due primarily to an increase in headcount in 2009 to support expanded R&D activities and higher stock-based compensation expenses. Additionally, $71 million of software development costs were capitalized related to Mac OS X Snow Leopard and excluded from R&D expense during 2009, compared to $11 million of software development costs capitalized during 2008. Although total R&D expense increased 20% during 2009, it remained relatively flat as a percentage of net sales given the 14% increase in revenue in 2009.

Selling, General and Administrative Expense ("SG&A")

SG&A expense increased $1.4 billion or 33% to $5.5 billion in 2010 compared to 2009. This increase was due primarily to the Company's continued expansion of its Retail segment, higher spending on marketing and advertising programs, increased stock-based compensation expenses and variable costs associated with the overall growth of the Company's net sales.

SG&A expenses increased $388 million or 10% to $4.1 billion in 2009 compared to 2008. This increase was due primarily to the Company's continued expansion of its Retail segment in both domestic and international markets, higher stock-based compensation expense and higher spending on marketing and advertising.

Other Income and Expense

Other income and expense for the three years ended September 25, 2010, are as follows (in millions):

	2010	2009	2008
Interest income	$ 311	$407	$653
Other income (expense), net	(156)	(81)	(33)
Total other income and expense	$ 155	$326	$620

Total other income and expense decreased $171 million or 52% to $155 million during 2010 compared to $326 million and $620 million in 2009 and 2008, respectively. The overall decrease in other income and expense is attributable to the significant declines in interest rates on a year-over-year basis, partially offset by the Company's higher cash, cash equivalents and marketable securities balances. The weighted average interest rate earned by the Company on its cash, cash equivalents and marketable securities was 0.75%, 1.43% and 3.44% during 2010, 2009 and 2008, respectively. Additionally the Company incurred higher premium expenses on its foreign exchange option contracts, which further reduced the total other income and expense. During 2010, 2009 and 2008, the Company had no debt outstanding and accordingly did not incur any related interest expense.

Provision for Income Taxes

The Company's effective tax rates were 24%, 32% and 32% for 2010, 2009 and 2008, respectively. The Company's effective rates for these periods differ from the statutory federal income tax rate of 35% due primarily to certain undistributed foreign earnings for which no U.S. taxes are provided because such earnings are intended to be indefinitely reinvested outside the U.S. The lower effective tax rate in 2010 as compared to 2009 is due primarily to an increase in foreign earnings on which U.S. income taxes have not been provided as such earnings are intended to be indefinitely reinvested outside the U.S.

As of September 25, 2010, the Company had deferred tax assets arising from deductible temporary differences, tax losses, and tax credits of $2.4 billion, and deferred tax liabilities of $5.0 billion. Management believes it is more likely than not that forecasted income, including income that may be generated as a result of certain tax planning strategies, together with future reversals of existing taxable temporary differences, will be sufficient to fully recover the deferred tax assets. The Company will continue to evaluate the realizability of deferred tax assets quarterly by assessing the need for and amount of a valuation allowance.

The Internal Revenue Service (the "IRS") has completed its field audit of the Company's federal income tax returns for the years 2004 through 2006 and proposed certain adjustments. The Company has contested certain of these adjustments through the IRS Appeals Office. The IRS is currently examining the years 2007 through 2009. All IRS audit issues for years prior to 2004 have been resolved. During the third quarter of 2010, the Company reached a tax settlement with the IRS for the years 2002 through 2003. In addition, the Company is subject to audits by state, local, and foreign tax authorities. Management believes that adequate provision has been made for any adjustments that may result from tax examinations. However, the outcome of tax audits cannot be predicted with certainty. If any issues addressed in the Company's tax audits are resolved in a manner not consistent with management's expectations, the Company could be required to adjust its provision for income taxes in the period such resolution occurs.

Liquidity and Capital Resources

The following table presents selected financial information and statistics as of and for the three years ended September 25, 2010 (in millions):

	2010	2009	2008
Cash, cash equivalents and marketable securities	$51,011	$33,992	$24,490
Accounts receivable, net	$ 5,510	$ 3,361	$ 2,422
Inventories	$ 1,051	$ 455	$ 509
Working capital	$20,956	$20,049	$18,645
Annual operating cash flow	$18,595	$10,159	$ 9,596

As of September 25, 2010, the Company had $51 billion in cash, cash equivalents and marketable securities, an increase of $17 billion from September 26, 2009. The principal component of this net increase was the cash generated by operating activities of $18.6 billion, which was partially offset by payments for acquisition of property, plant and equipment of $2 billion and payments made in connection with business acquisitions, net of cash acquired, of $638 million.

The Company's marketable securities investment portfolio is invested primarily in highly rated securities, generally with a minimum rating of single-A or equivalent. As of September 25, 2010 and September 26, 2009, $30.8 billion and $17.4 billion, respectively, of the Company's cash, cash equivalents and marketable securities were held by foreign subsidiaries and are generally based in U.S. dollar-denominated holdings. The Company believes its existing balances of cash, cash equivalents and marketable securities will be sufficient to satisfy its working capital needs, capital asset purchases, outstanding commitments and other liquidity requirements associated with its existing operations over the next 12 months.

Capital Assets

The Company's capital expenditures were $2.6 billion during 2010, consisting of approximately $404 million for retail store facilities and $2.2 billion for other capital expenditures, including product tooling and manufacturing process equipment and corporate facilities and infrastructure. The Company's actual cash payments for capital expenditures during 2010 were $2 billion.

The Company anticipates utilizing approximately $4.0 billion for capital expenditures during 2011, including approximately $600 million for retail store facilities and approximately $3.4 billion for product tooling and manufacturing process equipment, and corporate facilities and infrastructure, including information systems hardware, software and enhancements.

Historically the Company has opened between 25 and 50 new retail stores per year. During 2011, the Company expects to open 40 to 50 new stores, over half of which are expected to be located outside of the U.S.

Off-Balance Sheet Arrangements and Contractual Obligations

The Company has not entered into any transactions with unconsolidated entities whereby the Company has financial guarantees, subordinated retained interests, derivative instruments, or other contingent arrangements that expose the Company to material continuing risks, contingent liabilities, or any other obligation under a variable interest in an unconsolidated entity that provides financing, liquidity, market risk, or credit risk support to the Company.

The following table presents certain payments due by the Company under contractual obligations with minimum firm commitments as of September 25, 2010 and excludes amounts already recorded on the Consolidated Balance Sheet (in millions):

	Total	Payments Due in Less Than 1 Year	Payments Due in 1–3 Years	Payments Due in 4–5 Years	Payments Due in More Than 5 Years
Operating leases	$ 2,089	$ 266	$ 527	$ 470	$ 826
Purchase obligations	8,700	8,700	0	0	0
Other obligations	1,096	912	176	6	2
Total	$11,885	$9,878	$ 703	$ 476	$ 828

Lease Commitments

As of September 25, 2010, the Company had total outstanding commitments on noncancelable operating leases of $2.1 billion, $1.7 billion of which related to the lease of retail space and related facilities. The Company's major facility leases are typically for terms not exceeding 10 years and generally provide renewal options for terms not exceeding five additional years. Leases for retail space are for terms ranging from five to 20 years, the majority of which are for ten years, and often contain multi-year renewal options.

Purchase Commitments with Contract Manufacturers and Component Suppliers

The Company utilizes several contract manufacturers to manufacture sub-assemblies for the Company's products and to perform final assembly and test of finished products. These contract manufacturers acquire components and build product based on demand information supplied by the Company, which typically covers periods ranging from 30 to 150 days. The Company also obtains individual components for its products from a wide variety of individual suppliers. Consistent with industry practice, the Company acquires components through a combination of purchase orders, supplier contracts, and open orders based on projected demand information.

Such purchase commitments typically cover the Company's forecasted component and manufacturing requirements for periods ranging from 30 to 150 days. As of September 25, 2010, the Company had outstanding off-balance sheet third-party manufacturing commitments and component purchase commitments of $8.2 billion.

The Company has entered into prepaid long-term supply agreements to secure the supply of certain inventory components, which generally expire between 2011 and 2015. In August 2010, the Company entered into a long-term supply agreement under which it has committed to prepay $500 million in 2011. These prepayments will be applied to certain inventory component purchases made over the life of each respective agreement.

Other Obligations

Other outstanding obligations were $1.1 billion as of September 25, 2010, which related to advertising, research and development, product tooling and manufacturing process equipment, Internet and telecommunications services and other obligations.

The Company's other non-current liabilities in the Consolidated Balance Sheets consist primarily of deferred tax liabilities, gross unrecognized tax benefits and the related gross interest and penalties. As of September 25, 2010, the Company had non-current deferred tax liabilities of $4.3 billion. Additionally, as of September 25, 2010, the Company had gross unrecognized tax benefits of $943 million and an additional $247 million for gross interest and penalties classified as non-current liabilities. At this time, the Company is unable to make a reasonably reliable estimate of the timing of payments in connection with these tax liabilities; therefore, such amounts are not included in the above contractual obligation table.

Indemnifications

The Company generally does not indemnify end-users of its operating system and application software against legal claims that the software infringes third-party intellectual property rights. Other agreements entered into by the Company sometimes include indemnification provisions under which the Company could be subject to costs and/or damages in the event of an infringement claim against the Company or an indemnified third-party. However, the Company has not been required to make any significant payments resulting from such an infringement claim asserted against it or an indemnified third-party and, in the opinion of management, does not have a liability related to unresolved infringement claims subject to indemnification that would materially adversely affect its financial condition or operating results. Therefore, the Company did not record a liability for infringement costs as of either September 25, 2010 or September 26, 2009.

The Company has entered into indemnification agreements with its directors and executive officers. Under these agreements, the Company has agreed to indemnify such individuals to the fullest extent permitted by law against liabilities that arise by reason of their status as directors or officers and to advance expenses incurred by such individuals in connection with related legal proceedings. It is not possible to determine the maximum potential amount of payments the Company could be required to make under these agreements due to the limited history of prior indemnification claims and the unique facts and circumstances involved in each claim. However, the Company maintains directors and officers liability insurance coverage to reduce its exposure to such obligations, and payments made under these agreements historically have not materially adversely affected the Company's financial condition or operating results.

Forward-Looking Information

1.31

VISTEON CORPORATION (DEC)

FORWARD-LOOKING STATEMENTS

Certain statements contained or incorporated in this Annual Report on Form 10-K which are not statements of historical fact constitute "Forward-Looking Statements" within the meaning of the Private Securities Litigation Reform Act of 1995 (the "Reform Act"). Forward-looking statements give current expectations or forecasts of future events. Words such as "anticipate," "expect," "intend," "plan," "believe," "seek," "estimate" and other words and terms of similar meaning in connection with discussions of future operating or financial performance signify forward-looking statements. These statements reflect the Company's current views with respect to future events and are based on assumptions and estimates, which are subject to risks and uncertainties including those discussed in Item 1A under the heading "Risk Factors" and elsewhere in this report. Accordingly, undue reliance should not be placed on these forward-looking statements. Also, these forward-looking statements represent the

Company's estimates and assumptions only as of the date of this report. The Company does not intend to update any of these forward-looking statements to reflect circumstances or events that occur after the statement is made and qualifies all of its forward-looking statements by these cautionary statements.

You should understand that various factors, in addition to those discussed elsewhere in this document, could affect the Company's future results and could cause results to differ materially from those expressed in such forward-looking statements, including:

- Visteon's ability to satisfy its future capital and liquidity requirements; Visteon's ability to access the credit and capital markets at the times and in the amounts needed and on terms acceptable to Visteon; Visteon's ability to comply with covenants applicable to it; and the continuation of acceptable supplier payment terms.
- Visteon's ability to satisfy its pension and other postretirement employee benefit obligations, and to retire outstanding debt and satisfy other contractual commitments, all at the levels and times planned by management.
- Visteon's ability to access funds generated by its foreign subsidiaries and joint ventures on a timely and cost effective basis.
- Changes in the operations (including products, product planning and part sourcing), financial condition, results of operations or market share of Visteon's customers.
- Changes in vehicle production volume of Visteon's customers in the markets where it operates, and in particular changes in Ford's and Hyundai Kia's vehicle production volumes and platform mix.
- Increases in commodity costs or disruptions in the supply of commodities, including steel, resins, aluminum, copper, fuel and natural gas.
- Visteon's ability to generate cost savings to offset or exceed agreed upon price reductions or price reductions to win additional business and, in general, improve its operating performance; to achieve the benefits of its restructuring actions; and to recover engineering and tooling costs and capital investments.
- Visteon's ability to compete favorably with automotive parts suppliers with lower cost structures and greater ability to rationalize operations; and to exit non-performing businesses on satisfactory terms, particularly due to limited flexibility under existing labor agreements.
- Restrictions in labor contracts with unions that restrict Visteon's ability to close plants, divest unprofitable, noncompetitive businesses, change local work rules and practices at a number of facilities and implement cost-saving measures.
- The costs and timing of facility closures or dispositions, business or product realignments, or similar restructuring actions, including potential asset impairment or other charges related to the implementation of these actions or other adverse industry conditions and contingent liabilities.
- Significant changes in the competitive environment in the major markets where Visteon procures materials, components or supplies or where its products are manufactured, distributed or sold.
- Legal and administrative proceedings, investigations and claims, including shareholder class actions, in-

quiries by regulatory agencies, product liability, warranty, employee-related, environmental and safety claims and any recalls of products manufactured or sold by Visteon.
- Changes in economic conditions, currency exchange rates, changes in foreign laws, regulations or trade policies or political stability in foreign countries where Visteon procures materials, components or supplies or where its products are manufactured, distributed or sold.
- Shortages of materials or interruptions in transportation systems, labor strikes, work stoppages or other interruptions to or difficulties in the employment of labor in the major markets where Visteon purchases materials, components or supplies to manufacture its products or where its products are manufactured, distributed or sold.
- Changes in laws, regulations, policies or other activities of governments, agencies and similar organizations, domestic and foreign, that may tax or otherwise increase the cost of, or otherwise affect, the manufacture, licensing, distribution, sale, ownership or use of Visteon's products or assets.
- Possible terrorist attacks or acts of war, which could exacerbate other risks such as slowed vehicle production, interruptions in the transportation system or fuel prices and supply.
- The cyclical and seasonal nature of the automotive industry.
- Visteon's ability to comply with environmental, safety and other regulations applicable to it and any increase in the requirements, responsibilities and associated expenses and expenditures of these regulations.
- Visteon's ability to protect its intellectual property rights, and to respond to changes in technology and technological risks and to claims by others that Visteon infringes their intellectual property rights.
- Visteon's ability to quickly and adequately remediate control deficiencies in its internal control over financial reporting.
- Other factors, risks and uncertainties detailed from time to time in Visteon's Securities and Exchange Commission filings.

Liquidity and Capital Resources

1.32

PULTEGROUP, INC. (DEC)

LIQUIDITY AND CAPITAL RESOURCES

We finance our land acquisitions, development, and construction activities by using internally-generated funds and existing credit arrangements. We routinely monitor current and expected operational requirements and financial market conditions to evaluate the use of available financing sources, including securities offerings. Based on our current financial condition and credit relationships, we believe that our operations and borrowing resources are sufficient to provide for our current and foreseeable capital requirements. However, we continue to evaluate the impact of market conditions on our liquidity and may determine that modifications are appropriate if the current difficult market conditions extend beyond our expectations or if we incur additional land-related charges.

At December 31, 2010, we had cash and equivalents of $1.5 billion and no borrowings outstanding under our unsecured revolving credit facility (the "Credit Facility"). We also had $3.4 billion of senior notes outstanding. Other financing included limited recourse land-collateralized financing totaling $0.6 million. Sources of our working capital include our cash and equivalents, our Credit Facility, and our unsecured letter of credit facility (the "LOC Agreement"). An additional source of liquidity during 2010 was the receipt of federal tax refunds aggregating $934.7 million. Such refunds resulted primarily from the carryback of taxable losses provided by the Worker, Homeownership, and Business Assistance Act of 2009.

We follow a diversified investment approach for our cash and equivalents by maintaining such funds with a diversified portfolio of banks within our group of relationship banks in high quality, highly liquid, short-term investments, generally money market funds and federal government or agency securities. We monitor our investments with each bank on a daily basis and do not believe our cash and equivalents are exposed to any material risk of loss. However, given the volatility in the global financial markets, there can be no assurances that losses of principal balance on our cash and equivalents will not occur.

Our ratio of debt to total capitalization, excluding our land-collateralized debt, was 61.4% at December 31, 2010, and 47.4% net of cash and equivalents.

In June 2009, we entered into the LOC Agreement, a five-year, unsecured letter of credit facility that permits the issuance of up to $200.0 million of letters of credit. The LOC Agreement supplements our existing letter of credit capacity included in our Credit Facility (described below). At December 31, 2010, $167.2 million of letters of credit were outstanding under the LOC Agreement.

Given the difficult conditions in the homebuilding industry in recent years, we have reduced the borrowing capacity under the Credit Facility as the result of a combination of reduced working capital needs and challenges in meeting the Credit Facility's financial covenants. On December 23, 2010, we entered into the Fifth Amendment to Third Amended and Restated Credit Agreement (the "Fifth Amendment"), which decreased the borrowing capacity under the Credit Facility from $750.0 million to $250.0 million and also reduced the required level of cash and equivalents to be maintained in certain liquidity reserve accounts. Previously, on December 11, 2009, we entered into the Fourth Amendment and Waiver to Third Amended and Restated Credit Agreement, which reduced the borrowing capacity under the Credit Facility from $1.2 billion to $750.0 million, replaced the maximum debt to capitalization ratio with a maximum debt to tangible capital limit, reduced the tangible net worth minimum, and waived any default under the previous Credit Facility resulting from failure to comply with the tangible net worth financial covenant.

Under the terms of the Credit Facility, we have the capacity to issue letters of credit totaling up to $250.0 million. Borrowing availability is reduced by the amount of letters of credit outstanding. The Credit Facility includes a borrowing

base limitation when we do not have an investment grade senior unsecured debt rating from at least two of Fitch Ratings, Moody's Investor Service, and Standard and Poor's Corporation (the "Rating Agencies"). We currently do not have investment grade ratings from any of the Rating Agencies and are therefore subject to the borrowing base limitation. Given the uncertainty of current market conditions, we anticipate operating under the borrowing base limitation for the remainder of the Credit Facility's term. Under the borrowing base limitation, the sum of our senior debt and the amount drawn on the Credit Facility may not exceed an amount based on certain percentages of various categories of our unencumbered inventory and other assets. At December 31, 2010, we had no borrowings outstanding and full availability of the remaining $28.4 million under the Credit Facility after consideration of $221.6 million of outstanding letters of credit. As a result, the borrowing base limitation did not restrict our borrowing availability at December 31, 2010.

We are also required to maintain certain liquidity reserve accounts in the event we fail to satisfy an interest coverage test. Specifically, if the interest coverage ratio (as defined in the Credit Facility) is less than 2.0 to 1.0, we are required to maintain cash and equivalents in designated accounts with certain banks. While our access to and utilization of cash and equivalents maintained in liquidity reserve accounts is not restricted, failure to maintain sufficient balances within the liquidity reserve accounts restricts our ability to utilize the Credit Facility. We maintained the required cash and equivalents of $250.0 million within the liquidity reserve accounts at December 31, 2010, calculated under the Credit Facility as two times the amount by which the interest incurred over the last four quarters exceeds interest income over the last four quarters, excluding Financial Services, with a maximum amount of $250.0 million to be maintained in the liquidity reserve accounts effective with the Fifth Amendment. Additionally, failure to satisfy the interest coverage test can also result in an increase to LIBOR margin and letter of credit pricing. Our interest coverage ratio for the quarter ended December 31, 2010 was negative 0.66. For the period ending March 31, 2011, we will be required to maintain cash and equivalents of $250.0 million within the liquidity reserve accounts.

The Credit Facility contains certain financial covenants. We are required to not exceed a debt to tangible capital ratio as well as to meet a tangible net worth covenant each quarter. At December 31, 2010, our debt to tangible capital ratio (as defined in the Credit Facility) was 57.5% (compared with the requirement not to exceed 60.0%) while our tangible net worth (as defined in the Credit Facility) cushion was $436.2 million. Accordingly, we were in compliance with all of the covenants under the Credit Facility as of December 31, 2010. However, the required debt to tangible capital ratio adjusts to 57.5% as of both March 31 and June 30, 2011 and 55.0% as of the end of each quarter thereafter. In the event we are not able to reduce our debt to tangible capital ratio below our current level, our compliance with the required covenant levels may be adversely impacted. Violations of the financial covenants in the Credit Facility, if not waived by the lenders or cured, could result in an optional maturity date acceleration by the lenders, which might require repayment of any borrowings and replacement or cash collateralization of any letters of credit outstanding under the Credit Facility. In the event these violations were not waived by the lenders or cured, the violations could also result in a default under our

$3.4 billion of senior notes. Based on current market conditions, we believe that we may need to take action in order to avoid violating the debt to tangible capital ratio, potentially as early as March 31, 2011. Possible actions could include: negotiating changes to the Credit Facility's financial covenants with our group of lenders or arranging a new credit facility; terminating the Credit Facility, which would release the funds currently maintained in the liquidity reserve accounts ($250.0 million) and using our available cash to collateralize required letters of credit ($221.6 million at December 31, 2010); or replacing the Credit Facility with a separate letter of credit facility, similar to our existing LOC Agreement. While there can be no assurances that we could complete any of these actions given the uncertainties in the homebuilding industry and the financial markets, we believe that the combination of these potential actions will allow us to avoid any violations of covenants under either the Credit Facility or senior notes for the near term.

Pulte Mortgage provides mortgage financing for many of our home sales and uses its own funds and borrowings made available pursuant to certain third party and intercompany borrowings. Pulte Mortgage uses these resources to finance its lending activities until the mortgage loans are sold to third party investors, generally within 30 days. At December 31, 2009, Pulte Mortgage had a combination of repurchase lending agreements in place with various banks that provided borrowing capacity totaling $175.0 million. Given our strong liquidity and the cost of third party financing relative to existing mortgage rates, Pulte Mortgage allowed each of its third party borrowing arrangements to expire during 2010 and began funding its operations using internal Company resources. At December 31, 2010, we elected to fund $74.5 million of Pulte Mortgage's financing needs via a repurchase agreement with the Company. In order to satisfy regulatory requirements in certain states, Pulte Mortgage also maintains a $2.5 million repurchase lending agreement with a bank that expires in October 2011. There were no borrowings outstanding under this facility as of December 31, 2010.

Pursuant to the two $100 million stock repurchase programs authorized by our Board of Directors in October 2002 and 2005, and the $200 million stock repurchase authorization in February 2006 (for a total stock repurchase authorization of $400 million), we have repurchased a total of 9,688,900 shares for a total of $297.7 million. There have been no repurchases under these programs since 2006. We had remaining authorization to purchase common stock aggregating $102.3 million at December 31, 2010.

For the last three years, we have generated significant positive cash flow primarily through the liquidation of land inventory without a corresponding level of reinvestment combined with refunds of income taxes paid in prior years. We have used this positive cash flow to, among other things, increase our cash reserves as well as retire outstanding debt. Over the last three years, we have retired $3.1 billion of debt, including debt assumed with the Centex merger (see Note 8 to the Consolidated Financial Statements for additional details regarding these retirements). The majority of this debt was retired prior to its stated maturity. In the fourth quarter of 2010, we retired $898.5 million of senior notes. Additionally, we voluntarily used $111.2 million to repurchase at a discount prior to their maturity certain community development district obligations with an aggregate principal balance of $124.1 million in order to improve the future financial performance of the related communities (see Note 16 to the

Consolidated Financial Statements) and also voluntarily used $74.5 million of Company funds to finance Pulte Mortgage's lending operations rather than continue to use third party financing arrangements. However, we do not anticipate that we will be able to continue to generate positive cash flow at these same levels in the near future. Additionally, should growth conditions return to the homebuilding industry, we will need to invest significant capital into our operations to support such growth.

Our net cash provided by operating activities amounted to $580.3 million in 2010, $738.9 million in 2009 and $1.2 billion in 2008. During 2010, we received federal income tax refunds of $934.7 million compared with $362.0 million and $212.1 million in 2009 and 2008, respectively. After adjusting for these tax refunds, operating cash flow was negative for 2010. Generally, the primary drivers of cash flow from operations are inventory levels and profitability. For the years ended 2008 through 2010, our net losses were largely attributable to noncash asset impairments, including land-related charges and goodwill impairments. Cash flows from operations in 2010 were negatively impacted by the voluntary repurchase of certain community development district obligations for $111.2 million (see above) and using $74.5 million to internally finance Pulte Mortgage's lending operations. During 2010, inventory levels and residential mortgage loans available-for-sale decreased slightly while operating cash flows in 2009 and 2008 benefited from a significant net decrease in inventory and residential mortgage loans available-for-sale.

Net cash used by investing activities was $19.5 million at December 31, 2010, compared to net cash provided by investing activities of $1.7 billion in 2009 and net cash used in investing activities of $55.9 million in 2008. The net cash used in 2010 was primarily the result of investments in unconsolidated entities and capital expenditures, partially offset by distributions from unconsolidated entities and a reduction in residential mortgage loans held for investment. Our contributions to unconsolidated entities and investments in capital expenditures have declined in recent years as the result of the reduction in our overall land investments. Substantially all of the cash provided by investing activities in 2009 was the result of cash acquired through the Centex merger. For 2008, the majority of the cash used by investing activities related to contributions to our unconsolidated entities.

Net cash used in financing activities totaled $948.4 million, $2.2 billion, and $567.7 million in 2010, 2009, and 2008, respectively. Net cash used in 2010 was primarily the result of the repurchase of senior notes as mentioned above as well as repayments made under Financial Services credit arrangements. The large increase in net cash used in financing activities in 2009 was largely attributable to $2.0 billion used to retire outstanding debt combined with reductions in amounts outstanding under our Financial Services credit arrangements. Net cash used in 2008 was largely attributable to the repurchase of outstanding senior notes combined with reductions in amounts outstanding under our Financial Services credit arrangements.

On November 24, 2008, our Board of Directors discontinued the regular quarterly dividend on our common stock effective in the first quarter of 2009.

Inflation

We, and the homebuilding industry in general, may be adversely affected during periods of high inflation because of higher land and construction costs. Inflation may also increase our financing, labor, and material costs. In addition, higher mortgage interest rates significantly affect the affordability of permanent mortgage financing to prospective homebuyers. While we attempt to pass to our customers increases in our costs through increased sales prices, the current industry conditions have resulted in lower sales prices in substantially all of our markets. If we are unable to raise sales prices enough to compensate for higher costs, or if mortgage interest rates increase significantly, affecting our prospective homebuyers' willingness or ability to adequately finance home purchases, our revenues, gross margins, and net income would be adversely affected.

Seasonality

We experience variability in our quarterly results from operations due to the seasonal nature of the homebuilding industry. Historically, we have experienced significant increases in revenues and cash flow from operations during the fourth quarter based on the timing of home settlements. However, the challenging market conditions experienced since early 2006 have lessened the seasonal variations of our results. Given the current significant uncertainty in the homebuilding industry, we can make no assurances as to when and whether our historical seasonality will recur.

New Accounting Standards

1.33

URS CORPORATION (DEC)

ADOPTED AND OTHER RECENTLY ISSUED ACCOUNTING STANDARDS

A new accounting standard on transfers of financial assets became effective for us at the beginning of our 2010 fiscal year. This standard eliminates the concept of a qualifying special-purpose entity, limits the circumstances under which a financial asset is derecognized and requires additional disclosures concerning a transferor's continuing involvement with transferred financial assets. The adoption of this standard did not have a material impact on our consolidated financial statements.

A new accounting standard on consolidation of VIEs became effective for us at the beginning of our 2010 fiscal year. This standard amends the accounting and disclosure requirements for the consolidation of a VIE. It requires additional disclosures about the significant judgments and assumptions used in determining whether to consolidate a VIE, the restrictions on a consolidated VIE's assets and on the settlement of a VIE's liabilities, the risk associated with involvement in a VIE, and the financial impact on a company due to its involvement with a VIE. As the standard requires ongoing quarterly evaluation of the application of the new requirements, changes in circumstances could result in the identification of additional VIEs to be consolidated or existing VIEs to be deconsolidated in any reporting period. We adopted this standard prospectively and based on the carrying values of the entities at the date of adoption. The adoption of this standard did not have

a material impact on our consolidated financial statements. For additional disclosures, see Note 5, "Joint Ventures," to our "Consolidated Financial Statements and Supplementary Data" included under Item 8 of this report.

An accounting standard update related to recurring and nonrecurring fair value measurements was issued. This update requires new disclosures on significant transfers of assets and liabilities between Level 1 and Level 2 of the fair value hierarchy (including the reasons for these transfers) and the reasons for any transfers in or out of Level 3. It also requires a reconciliation of recurring Level 3 measurements including purchases, sales, issuances and settlements on a gross basis. The accounting update clarifies certain existing disclosure requirements and requires fair value measurement disclosures for each class of assets and liabilities as opposed to each major category of assets and liabilities. It also clarifies that entities are required to disclose information about both the valuation techniques and inputs used in estimating Level 2 and Level 3 fair value measurements. Except for the disclosures on the reconciliation of recurring Level 3 measurements, the other new disclosures and clarifications of existing disclosures were effective for us beginning with the first quarter of our 2010 fiscal year. The adoption of this standard did not have a material impact on our consolidated financial statements. See Note 10, "Fair Values of Debt Instruments, Investments and Derivative Instruments," to our "Consolidated Financial Statements and Supplementary Data" included under Item 8 of this report for our fair value measurement disclosure. The information about the activity in Level 3 fair value measurements on a gross basis will be effective for us beginning with the first quarter of our 2011 fiscal year. We currently do not expect that the adoption of this portion of the standard will have a material impact on our consolidated financial statements.

An accounting standard update related to disclosures about the credit quality of financing receivables and the allowance for credit losses was issued. This update is intended to provide additional disclosures on a disaggregated basis about the nature of credit risk inherent in the company's portfolio of financing receivables, how the risk is analyzed and assessed in arriving at the allowance for credit losses, and the changes and reasons for those changes in the allowance for credit losses. We adopted the additional disclosures required by this accounting standard update at the end of our 2010 fiscal year. See Note 1, "Business, Basis of Presentation, and Accounting Policies" to our "Consolidated Financial Statements and Supplementary Data" included under Item 8 of this report for the additional disclosures. The adoption of this standard did not have a material impact on our consolidated financial statements. The additional disclosures related to the activity during the reporting period will be effective for us beginning with the first quarter of our 2011 fiscal year. We do not expect that the adoption of this portion of the standard will have a material impact on our consolidated financial statements.

An accounting standard update related to the way companies test for impairment of goodwill was issued. Pursuant to this accounting update, goodwill of the reporting unit is not impaired if the carrying amount of a reporting unit is greater than zero and its fair value exceeds its carrying amount. Hence, the second step of the impairment test is not required. However, if the carrying amount of a reporting unit is zero or negative, the second step of the impairment test is required to be performed to measure the amount of impairment loss, if any, when it is more likely than not that goodwill impairment exists. In considering whether it is more likely than not that a goodwill impairment exists, a company must evaluate whether there are adverse qualitative factors. Consistent with before, this test must be performed annually or in the interim if an event occurs or circumstances exist that indicate that it is more likely than not that goodwill impairment exists. This standard is effective for us beginning in the first quarter of our 2011 fiscal year. We currently do not expect that the adoption of this standard will have a material impact on our consolidated financial statements.

Market Risk Information

1.34

TRW AUTOMOTIVE HOLDINGS CORP. (DEC)

QUANTITATIVE AND QUALITATIVE DISCLOSURES ABOUT MARKET RISKS

Item 7A

Our primary market risk arises from fluctuations in foreign currency exchange rates, interest rates and commodity prices. We manage foreign currency exchange rate risk, interest rate risk and, to a lesser extent, commodity price risk by utilizing various derivative instruments. We limit the use of such instruments to hedging activities; we do not use such instruments for speculative or trading purposes. If we did not use derivative instruments, our exposure to such risks would be higher. We are exposed to credit loss in the event of nonperformance by the counterparty to the derivative financial instruments. We attempt to manage this exposure by entering into agreements directly with a number of major financial institutions that meet our credit standards and that are expected to fully satisfy their obligations under the contracts. However, given historical disruptions in the financial markets,

including the bankruptcy, insolvency or restructuring of certain financial institutions, there is no guarantee that the financial institutions with whom we contract will be able to fully satisfy their contractual obligations.

Foreign Currency Exchange Rate Risk. We utilize derivative financial instruments to manage foreign currency exchange rate risks. We enter into forward contracts and, to a lesser extent, options to hedge portions of our foreign currency denominated forecasted revenues, purchases and the subsequent cash flow from adverse movements in exchange rates. Foreign currency exposures are reviewed monthly and any natural offsets are considered prior to entering into a derivative financial instrument.

During 2010, we repaid approximately $520 million of our U.S. dollar-denominated debt resulting in an increase in the percentage of debt denominated in foreign currencies compared to total debt. As of December 31, 2010, approximately 24% of our total debt was in foreign currencies, as compared to 19% as of December 31, 2009.

Interest Rate Risk. We are subject to interest rate risk in connection with variable- and fixed-rate debt. In order to manage interest costs, we may occasionally utilize interest rate swap agreements to exchange fixed- and variable-rate interest payment obligations over the life of the agreements. As of December 31, 2010, approximately 1% of our total debt was at variable interest rates, as compared to 18% (or 5% when considering the effect of interest rate swaps) as of December 31, 2009.

Commodity Price Risk. From time to time, we may utilize derivative financial instruments to manage select commodity price risks. Forward purchase agreements generally meet the criteria to be accounted for as normal purchases. Forward purchase agreements which do not or no longer meet these criteria are classified and accounted for as derivatives.

Sensitivity Analysis. We utilize a sensitivity analysis model to calculate the fair value, cash flows or statement of operations impact that a hypothetical 10% change in market rates would have on our debt and derivative instruments. For derivative instruments, we utilized applicable forward rates in effect as of December 31, 2010 to calculate the fair value or cash flow impact resulting from this hypothetical change in market rates. The analyses also do not factor in a potential change in the level of variable rate borrowings or derivative instruments outstanding that could take place if these hypothetical conditions prevailed. The results of the sensitivity model calculations follow:

(Dollars in millions)	Assuming a 10% U.S.$ Strengthening	Assuming a 10% U.S.$ Weakening	Favorable (Unfavorable) Change in
Market Risk			
Foreign Currency Rate Sensitivity:			
— Forward sales contracts of U.S.$ and net purchased U.S.$ put options	$(53)	$ 55	Fair value
— Forward purchase contracts of U.S.$ and net purchased U.S.$ call options	$ 21	$(21)	Fair value
— Foreign currency denominated debt	$ 43	$(43)	Fair value

(Dollars in millions)	Assuming a 10% Decrease in Rates	Assuming a 10% Increase in Rates	Favorable (Unfavorable) Change in
Interest Rate Sensitivity:			
Debt			
— Fixed rate	$38	$(39)	Fair value
— Variable rate	$—	$ —	Cash flow

Critical Accounting Policies

1.35

TIME WARNER INC. (DEC)

NOTES TO CONSOLIDATED FINANCIAL STATEMENTS

1. Description of Business, Basis of Presentation and Summary of Significant Accounting Policies (in part)

Summary of Critical and Significant Accounting Policies

The following is a discussion of each of the Company's critical accounting policies, including information and analysis of estimates and assumptions involved in their application, and other significant accounting policies.

The Securities and Exchange Commission ("SEC") considers an accounting policy to be critical if it is important to the Company's financial condition and results of operations and if it requires significant judgment and estimates on the part of management in its application. The development and selection of these critical accounting policies have been determined by Time Warner's management and the related disclosures have been reviewed with the Audit and Finance Committee of the Board of Directors of the Company. Due to the significant judgment involved in selecting certain of the assumptions used in these areas, it is possible that different parties could choose different assumptions and reach different conclusions. The Company considers the policies relating to the following matters to be critical accounting policies:

- Impairment of Goodwill and Intangible Assets (see pages 82 to 83);
- Multiple-Element Transactions (see page 88);
- Income Taxes (see pages 89 to 90);
- Film Cost Recognition, Participations and Residuals and Impairments (see page 87);
- Gross versus Net Revenue Recognition (see pages 88 to 89); and
- Sales Returns, Pricing Rebates and Uncollectible Accounts (see pages 79 to 80).

Disclosure of Accounting Policies

1.36

JOY GLOBAL INC. (OCT)

NOTES TO CONSOLIDATED FINANCIAL STATEMENTS

2. Significant Accounting Policies

Our significant accounting policies are as follows:

Basis of Presentation and Principles of Consolidation— The Consolidated Financial Statements are presented in accordance with accounting principles generally accepted in the United States ("GAAP"). The Consolidated Financial Statements include the accounts of Joy Global Inc. and our subsidiaries, all of which are wholly owned. All significant intercompany balances and transactions have been eliminated.

Use of Estimates—The preparation of financial statements in conformity with GAAP requires us to make estimates and assumptions that affect the reported amounts of assets and liabilities at the date of the financial statements, and the reported amounts of revenues and expenses during the reporting period. Ultimate realization of assets and settlement of liabilities in the future could differ from those estimates.

Cash Equivalents—All highly liquid investments with original maturities of three months or less when issued are considered cash equivalents. These primarily consist of money market funds and to a lesser extent, certificates of deposit and commercial paper. Cash equivalents were $517.7 million and $201.7 million at October 29, 2010 and October 30, 2009, respectively.

Inventories—Our inventories are carried at the lower of cost or net realizable value using the first-in, first-out ("FIFO") method for all inventories. We evaluate the need to record adjustments for inventory on a regular basis. Our policy is to evaluate all inventories including raw material, work-in-process, finished goods, and spare parts. Inventory in excess of our estimated usage requirements is written down to its estimated net realizable value. Inherent in the estimates of net realizable value are estimates related to our future manufacturing schedules, customer demand, possible alternative uses and ultimate realization of potentially excess inventory.

Property, Plant and Equipment—Property, plant and equipment are stated at historical cost. Expenditures for major renewals and improvements are capitalized, while maintenance and repair costs that do not significantly improve the related asset or extend its useful life are charged to expense as incurred. For financial reporting purposes, plant and equipment are depreciated primarily by the straight-line method over the estimated useful lives of the assets which generally range from 5 to 45 years for improvements, from 10 to 45 years for buildings, from 3 to 12 years for machinery and equipment and 3 to 5 years for software. Depreciation expense was $51.5 million, $49.3 million and $48.8 million for 2010, 2009, and 2008, respectively. Depreciation claimed for income tax purposes is computed by accelerated methods.

Impairment of Long-Lived Assets—We assess the realizability of our held and used long-lived assets to evaluate such assets for impairment whenever events or circumstances indicate that the carrying amount of such assets (or group of assets) may not be recoverable. Impairment is determined to exist if the estimated future undiscounted cash flows related to such assets are less than the carrying value. If impairment is determined to exist, any related impairment loss is calculated based on the fair value of the asset compared to its carrying value.

Goodwill and Intangible Assets—Intangible assets include drawings, patents, trademarks, technology, customer relationships and other specifically identifiable assets. Indefinite-lived intangible assets are not being amortized. Assets not subject to amortization are evaluated for impairment annually or more frequently if events or changes occur that suggest impairment in carrying value. Finite-lived intangible assets are amortized to reflect the pattern of economic benefits consumed, which is primarily the straight-line method. Intangible assets that are subject to amortization are evaluated for potential impairment whenever events or circumstances indicate that the carrying amount may not be recoverable.

Goodwill represents the excess of the purchase price over the fair value of identifiable net assets acquired in a business combination. Goodwill is tested for impairment using the two-step approach, in accordance with Accounting Standards Codification ("ASC") No. 350, "Goodwill and Other." Goodwill is assigned to specific reporting units, which we have identified as our operating segments, and tested for impairment at least annually, during the fourth quarter of our fiscal year, or more frequently upon the occurrence of an event or when circumstances indicate that a reporting unit's carrying amount is greater than its fair value. We recognize an impairment charge if the carrying amount of a reporting unit exceeds its fair value and the carrying amount of the reporting unit's goodwill exceeds the implied fair value of that goodwill. The fair value of goodwill is established using the discounted cash flow method and market approach. We performed our goodwill impairment testing in the fourth quarter of fiscal 2010 and no impairment was identified.

Risks and Uncertainties—As of October 29, 2010, we employed 11,900 employees worldwide, with 5,600 employed in the United States. Collective bargaining agreements or similar type arrangements cover 37% of our U.S. workforce and 30% of our international employees. In 2011, union agreements are to expire for 3% of our employees with the largest covering the AMICUS union at our facilities in the United Kingdom and the Teamster Union at our facility in Meadowlands, Pennsylvania.

Foreign Currency Translation—Exchange gains or losses incurred on transactions conducted by one of our operations in a currency other than the operation's functional currency are normally reflected in cost of sales in our Consolidated Statement of Income. An exception is made where the transaction is a long-term intercompany loan that is not expected to be repaid in the foreseeable future, in which case the transaction gain or loss is included in shareholders' equity as an element of accumulated other comprehensive income (loss). Assets and liabilities of international operations that have a functional currency that is not the U.S. dollar are translated into U.S. dollars at year-end exchange rates and revenue and expense items are translated using weighted average exchange rates. Any adjustments arising on translations are included in shareholders' equity as an element of accumulated other comprehensive income (loss). Assets and liabilities of operations which have the U.S. dollar as their functional currency (but which maintain their accounting records in local currency) have their values remeasured into U.S. dollars at year-end exchange rates, except for non-monetary items for which historical rates are used. Exchange gains or losses arising on remeasurement of the values into U.S. dollars are recognized in cost of sales. Pre-tax foreign exchange gains included in operating income were $5.7 million, $0.4 million, and $3.3 million in 2010, 2009, and 2008, respectively.

Foreign Currency Hedging and Derivative Financial Instruments—We enter into derivative contracts, primarily foreign currency forward contracts, to protect against fluctuations in exchange rates. These contracts are for committed transactions, and receivables and payables denominated in foreign currencies and not for speculative purposes. ASC No. 815, "Derivatives and Hedging," requires companies to record derivatives on the balance sheet as assets or liabilities, measured at fair value, if certain designation and documentation requirements are established at hedge inception. Any changes in fair value of these instruments are recorded in the income statement as cost of sales or in the balance sheet as other comprehensive income (loss).

Revenue Recognition—We recognize revenue on aftermarket products and services when the following criteria are satisfied: persuasive evidence of an arrangement exists, product delivery and title transfer has occurred or the services have been rendered, the price is fixed and determinable, and collectability is reasonably assured. We recognize revenue on long-term contracts, such as for the manufacture of mining shovels, drills, draglines, roof support systems and conveyor systems, using the percentage-of-completion method. We generally recognize revenue using the percentage-of-completion method for original equipment. When using the percentage-of-completion method, sales and gross profit are recognized as work is performed based on the relationship between actual costs incurred and total estimated costs at completion. Sales and gross profit are adjusted prospectively for revisions in estimated total contract costs and contract values. Estimated losses are recognized in full when identified.

We have life cycle management contracts with customers to supply parts and service for terms of 1 to 13 years. These contracts are established based on the conditions the equipment will be operating in, the time horizon that the program will cover, and the expected operating cycle that will be required for the equipment. Based on this information, a model is created representing the projected costs and revenues of servicing the respective machines over the specified contract terms. Accounting for these contracts requires us to make various estimates, including estimates of the relevant machine's long-term maintenance requirements. Under these contracts, customers are generally billed monthly based on hours of operation or units of production achieved by the equipment, with the respective deferred revenues recorded when billed. Revenue is recognized in the period in which parts are supplied or services provided. These contracts are reviewed quarterly by comparison of actual results to original estimates or most recent analysis, with revenue recognition adjusted appropriately for future estimated costs. If a loss is expected at any time, the full amount of the loss is recognized immediately.

We have customer agreements that are multiple element arrangements as defined by ASC No. 605-25 "Multiple-Element Arrangements." The agreements are assessed for multiple elements based on the following criteria: the delivered item has value to the customer on a standalone basis, there is objective and reliable evidence of the fair value of the undelivered item and the arrangement includes a general right of return relative to the delivered item and delivery or performance of the undelivered item is considered probable and substantially in the control of the vendor. Revenue is then allocated to each identified unit of accounting based on our estimate of their relative fair values.

Revenue recognition involves judgments, including assessments of expected returns, the likelihood of nonpayment, and estimates of expected costs and profits on long-term contracts. We analyze various factors, including a review of specific transactions, historical experience, creditworthiness of customers, and current market and economic conditions, in determining when to recognize revenue. Changes in judgments on these factors could impact the timing and amount of revenue recognized with a resulting impact on the timing and amount of associated income.

Comprehensive Income (Loss)—ASC No. 220, "Comprehensive Income," requires the reporting of comprehensive income in addition to net income. Comprehensive income is a more inclusive financial reporting method that includes disclosure of financial information that historically has not been recognized in the calculation of net income. We have chosen to report Comprehensive Income (Loss) and Accumulated Other Comprehensive Income (Loss) which encompasses net income, foreign currency translation, unrecognized pension obligations, and unrealized gain (loss) on derivatives in the Consolidated Statement of Shareholders' Equity. Accumulated other comprehensive loss consists of the following:

(In millions)	October 29, 2010	October 30, 2009	October 31, 2008
Unrecognized pension and other postretirement obligations	$(436.1)	$(500.6)	$(278.0)
Unrealized gain (loss) on derivatives	2.7	(0.6)	(19.9)
Foreign currency translation	53.8	29.0	(48.0)
Accumulated other comprehensive loss	$(379.6)	$(472.2)	$(345.9)

The unrecognized pension and other postretirement obligation is net of a $103.5 million, $125.6 and $47.3 million income tax benefit as of October 29, 2010, October 30, 2009 and October 31, 2008, respectively. Unrealized (loss) gain on derivatives is net of $1.4 million, $(0.3) million, and $(11.9) million of income tax effects at October 29, 2010, October 30, 2009 and October 31, 2008, respectively.

Sales Incentives—In accordance with ASC No. 605-50, "Customer Payments and Incentives," we account for cash consideration (such as sales incentives and cash discounts) given to our customers or resellers as a reduction of net sales.

Allowance for Doubtful Accounts—We establish an allowance for doubtful accounts on a specific account identification basis through a review of several factors, including the aging status of our customers accounts', financial condition of our customers, and historical collection experience.

Shipping and Handling Fees and Costs—We account for shipping and handling fees and costs in accordance with ASC No. 605-45, "Principal Agent Considerations." Under ASC No. 605-45, amounts billed to a customer in a sale transaction related to shipping costs are reported as net sales and the related costs incurred for shipping are reported as cost of sales.

Income Taxes—Deferred income taxes are recognized for the tax consequences of temporary differences by applying enacted statutory tax rates applicable to future years to differences between the financial statement carrying amounts and the tax bases of existing assets and liabilities, and for tax loss carryforwards. Valuation allowances are provided for deferred tax assets where it is considered more likely than not that we will not realize the benefit of such assets. Certain tax benefits existed as of our emergence from protection under Chapter 11 of the U.S. Bankruptcy Code in 2001 but were offset by valuation allowances. Realization of net operating loss, tax credits, and other deferred tax benefits from pre-emergence attributes will be credited to additional paid in capital.

Research and Development Expenses—Research and development costs are expensed as incurred. Such costs incurred in the development of new products or significant improvements to existing products amounted to $29.8 million, $22.3 million and $16.4 million for fiscal 2010, 2009, and 2008, respectively.

Earnings Per Share—Basic earnings per share is computed by dividing net earnings by the weighted average number of common shares outstanding during the reporting period. Diluted earnings per share is computed similar to basic earnings per share except that the weighted average number of shares outstanding is increased to include additional shares from the assumed exercise of stock options, performance shares, and restricted stock units if dilutive. See Note 9—Earnings Per Share for further information.

Accounting For Share-Based Compensation—We account for awards of stock in accordance with ASC No. 718, "Compensation—Stock Compensation." ASC No. 718 requires measurement of the cost of employee services received in exchange for an award of equity instruments based on the grant date fair value of the award. Compensation expense is recognized using the straight-line method over the vesting period of the award.

Reclassifications—Certain prior year amounts have been reclassified to conform to the current year presentation. The reclassifications did not impact net income or earnings per share.

New Accounting Pronouncements—In December 2009, the Financial Accounting Standards Board ("FASB") issued

Accounting Standards Update ("ASU") No. 2009-17, "Consolidations (Topic 810): Improvements to Financial Reporting by Enterprises Involved with Variable Interest Entities." ASU No. 2009-17 clarifies how a company determines when an entity that is insufficiently capitalized or is not controlled through voting should be consolidated. This statement is effective for us beginning in the first quarter of fiscal 2011 (which commenced on October 30, 2010). We do not expect a material impact from the adoption of ASU No. 2009-17 on our consolidated financial statements.

In October 2009, FASB issued ASU No. 2009-13, "Revenue Recognition (Topic 605): Multiple-Deliverable Revenue Arrangements—a consensus of the FASB Emerging Issues Task Force." ASU No. 2009-13 establishes the accounting and reporting guidance for arrangements under which a vendor will perform multiple revenue-generating activities. Specifically, this ASU addresses how to separate deliverables and how to measure and allocate arrangement consideration to one or more units of accounting. This statement is effective for us beginning in the first quarter of fiscal 2011 (which commenced on October 30, 2010) and, when adopted, will change our accounting treatment for multiple-element revenue arrangements on a prospective basis. We do not expect a material impact from the adoption of ASU No. 2009-13 on our consolidated financial statements.

In June 2009, FASB issued SFAS No. 167, "Amendments to FASB Interpretation No. 46(R)." SFAS No. 167 changes how a company determines when an entity that is insufficiently capitalized or is not controlled through voting should be consolidated. The determination of whether a company is required to consolidate an entity is based on, among other things, an entity's purpose and design and a company's ability to direct the activities of the entity that most significantly impact the entity's economic performance. This statement is effective for us in fiscal 2011. We do not expect a material impact from the adoption of SFAS No. 167 on our consolidated financial statements.

In December 2007, FASB issued ASC No. 805, "Business Combinations." ASC No. 805 requires the measurement at fair value of assets acquired, the liabilities assumed, and any non-controlling interest in the acquiree as of the acquisition date. ASC No. 805 also requires that acquisition related costs and costs to restructure the acquiree be expensed as incurred. ASC No. 805 became effective for us beginning in fiscal 2010. The adoption of ASC No. 805 did not have a significant effect on our consolidated financial statements and related disclosures.

In December 2007, FASB issued ASC No. 810, "Consolidation." The objective of ASC No. 810 is to improve the transparency and comparability of financial information that is provided as it relates to a parent and non-controlling interests. ASC No. 810 requires clear identification of ownership interests in subsidiaries held by other parties and the amount of consolidated net income attributable to the parent and other parties. The codification also requires changes in parent ownership interests to be accounted for consistently, while the parent retains its controlling interest in the subsidiary. ASC No. 810 became effective for us beginning in fiscal 2010. The adoption of ASC No. 810 did not have a significant effect on our consolidated financial statements and related disclosures.

Nature of Operations

1.37

COLGATE-PALMOLIVE COMPANY (DEC)

NOTES TO CONSOLIDATED FINANCIAL STATEMENTS

1. Nature of Operations

The Company manufactures and markets a wide variety of products in the U.S. and around the world in two distinct business segments: Oral, Personal and Home Care; and Pet Nutrition. Oral, Personal and Home Care products include toothpaste, toothbrushes and mouth rinses, bar and liquid hand soaps, shower gels, shampoos, conditioners, deodorants and antiperspirants, laundry and dishwashing detergents, fabric conditioners, household cleaners, bleaches and other similar items. These products are sold primarily to wholesale and retail distributors worldwide. Pet Nutrition products include specialty pet nutrition products manufactured and marketed by Hill's Pet Nutrition. The principal customers for Pet Nutrition products are veterinarians and specialty pet retailers. Principal global and regional trademarks include Colgate, Palmolive, Mennen, Speed Stick, Lady Speed Stick, Softsoap, Irish Spring, Protex, Sorriso, Kolynos, Elmex, Tom's of Maine, Ajax, Axion, Fabuloso, Soupline, Suavitel, Hill's Science Diet and Hill's Prescription Diet.

The Company's principal classes of products accounted for the following percentages of worldwide sales for the past three years:

	2010	2009	2008
Oral Care	43%	41%	41%
Home Care	22%	23%	23%
Personal Care	22%	22%	22%
Pet Nutrition	13%	14%	14%
Total	100%	100%	100%

1.38

MERCK & CO., INC. (DEC)

NOTES TO CONSOLIDATED FINANCIAL STATEMENTS

1. Nature of Operations

The Company is a global health care company that delivers innovative health solutions through its prescription medicines, vaccines, biologic therapies, animal health, and consumer care products, which it markets directly and through its joint ventures. The Company's operations are principally managed on a products basis and are comprised of four operating segments, which are the Pharmaceutical, Animal Health, Consumer Care and Alliances segments, and one reportable segment, which is the Pharmaceutical segment. The Pharmaceutical segment includes human health pharmaceutical and vaccine products marketed either directly by the Company or through joint ventures. Human health pharmaceutical products consist of therapeutic and preventive agents, sold by prescription, for the treatment of human disorders. The Company sells these human health pharmaceutical products primarily to drug wholesalers and retailers, hospitals, government agencies and managed health care providers such as health maintenance organizations, pharmacy benefit managers and other institutions. Vaccine products consist of preventive pediatric, adolescent and adult vaccines, primarily administered at physician offices. The Company sells these human health vaccines primarily to physicians, wholesalers, physician distributors and government entities. The Company also has animal health operations that discover, develop, manufacture and market animal health products, including vaccines, which the Company sells to veterinarians, distributors and animal producers. Additionally, the Company has consumer care operations that develop, manufacture and market over-the-counter, foot care and sun care products, which are sold through wholesale and retail drug, food chain and mass merchandiser outlets in the United States and Canada.

On November 3, 2009, Merck & Co., Inc. ("Old Merck") and Schering-Plough Corporation ("Schering-Plough") merged (the "Merger"). In the Merger, Schering-Plough acquired all of the shares of Old Merck, which became a wholly-owned subsidiary of Schering-Plough and was renamed Merck Sharp & Dohme Corp. Schering-Plough continued as the surviving public company and was renamed Merck & Co., Inc. ("New Merck" or the "Company"). However, for accounting purposes only, the Merger was treated as an acquisition with Old Merck considered the accounting acquirer. Accordingly, the accompanying financial statements reflect Old Merck's stand-alone operations as they existed prior to the completion of the Merger. The results of Schering-Plough's business have been included in New Merck's financial statements only for periods subsequent to the completion of the Merger. Therefore, New Merck's financial results for 2009 do not reflect a full year of legacy Schering-Plough operations. References in these financial statements to "Merck" for periods prior to the Merger refer to Old Merck and for periods after the completion of the Merger to New Merck.

Description of Business

1.39

YUM! BRANDS, INC. (DEC)

NOTES TO CONSOLIDATED FINANCIAL STATEMENTS

Note 1—Description of Business

YUM! Brands, Inc. and Subsidiaries (collectively referred to as "YUM" or the "Company") comprises the worldwide operations of KFC, Pizza Hut, Taco Bell, Long John Silver's ("LJS") and A&W All-American Food Restaurants ("A&W") (collectively the "Concepts"). YUM is the world's largest quick service restaurant company based on the number of system units, with more than 37,000 units of which approximately 48% are located outside the U.S. in more than 110 countries and territories. YUM was created as an independent, publicly-owned company on October 6, 1997 (the "Spin-off Date") via a tax-free distribution by our former parent, PepsiCo, Inc., of our Common Stock to its shareholders.

References to YUM throughout these Consolidated Financial Statements are made using the first person notations of "we," "us" or "our."

Through our widely-recognized Concepts, we develop, operate, franchise and license a system of both traditional and non-traditional quick service restaurants. Each Concept has proprietary menu items and emphasizes the preparation of food with high quality ingredients as well as unique recipes and special seasonings to provide appealing, tasty and attractive food at competitive prices. Our traditional restaurants feature dine-in, carryout and, in some instances, drive-thru or delivery service. Non-traditional units, which are principally licensed outlets, include express units and kiosks which have a more limited menu and operate in non-traditional locations like malls, airports, gasoline service stations, convenience stores, stadiums, amusement parks and colleges, where a full-scale traditional outlet would not be practical or efficient. We also operate multibrand units, where two or more of our Concepts are operated in a single unit. In addition, we continue to pursue the combination of Pizza Hut and WingStreet, a flavored chicken wings concept we have developed.

YUM consists of six operating segments: KFC-U.S., Pizza Hut-U.S., Taco Bell-U.S., LJS/A&W-U.S., YUM Restaurants International ("YRI" or "International Division") and YUM Restaurants China ("China Division"). For financial reporting purposes, management considers the four U.S. operating segments to be similar and, therefore, has aggregated them into a single reportable operating segment ("U.S."). The China Division includes mainland China ("China"), and the International Division includes the remainder of our international operations.

At the beginning of 2010 we began reporting information for our Thailand and KFC Taiwan businesses within our International Division as a result of changes to our management reporting structure. These businesses now report to the President of YRI, whereas previously they reported to the President of the China Division. While this reporting change did not impact our consolidated results, segment information for previous periods has been restated to be consistent with the current period presentation throughout the Financial Statements and Notes thereto. For the years ended December 26, 2009 and December 27, 2008 this restatement resulted in decreases in Company sales of $270 million and $282 million, respectively, and decreases in Operating profit of $6 million and $9 million, respectively, for the China Division. Any impact of the restatement on the China Division reported figures was offset by the impact to the International Division reported figures.

Use of Estimates

1.40

VIAD CORP (DEC)

NOTES TO CONSOLIDATED FINANCIAL STATEMENTS

Note 1. Summary of Significant Accounting Policies (in part)

Significant Accounting Policies

Use of Estimates. The preparation of financial statements in conformity with GAAP requires management to make estimates and assumptions that affect the amounts reported in the consolidated financial statements and accompanying notes. These estimates and assumptions include, but are not limited to:

- Estimated fair value of Viad's reporting units used to perform annual impairment testing of recorded goodwill;
- Estimated fair value of intangible assets with indefinite lives, for purposes of impairment testing;
- Estimated allowances for uncollectible accounts receivable;
- Estimated provisions for income taxes, including uncertain tax positions;
- Estimated valuation allowances related to deferred tax assets;
- Estimated liabilities for losses related to self-insured liability claims;
- Estimated liabilities for losses related to environmental remediation obligations;
- Estimated sublease income associated with restructuring liabilities;
- Assumptions used to measure pension and postretirement benefit costs and obligations;
- Assumptions used to determine share-based compensation costs under the fair value method; and
- Allocation of purchase price of acquired businesses.

Actual results could differ from these and other estimates.

1.41

XEROX CORPORATION (DEC)

NOTES TO CONSOLIDATED FINANCIAL STATEMENTS

Note 1—Summary of Significant Accounting Policies (in part)

Use of Estimates

The preparation of our Consolidated Financial Statements, in accordance with accounting principles generally accepted in the United States of America, requires that we make estimates and assumptions that affect the reported amounts of assets and liabilities, as well as the disclosure of contingent assets and liabilities at the date of the financial statements, and the reported amounts of revenues and expenses during the reporting period. Significant estimates and assumptions are used for, but not limited to: (i) allocation of revenues and fair values in leases and other multiple element arrangements; (ii) accounting for residual values; (iii) economic lives of leased assets; (iv) revenue recognition for services under the percentage-of-completion method; (v) allowance for doubtful accounts; (vi) inventory valuation; (vii) restructuring and related charges; (viii) asset impairments; (ix) depreciable lives of assets; (x) useful lives of intangible assets; (xi) amortization period for customer contract costs (xii) pension and post-retirement benefit plans; (xiii) income tax reserves and valuation allowances; and (xiv) contingency and litigation reserves. Future events and their effects cannot be predicted with certainty; accordingly, our accounting estimates require the exercise of judgment. The accounting estimates used in the preparation of our Consolidated Financial Statements will change as new events occur, as more experience is acquired, as additional information is obtained and as our operating environment changes. Actual results could differ from those estimates.

The following table summarizes certain significant charges that require management estimates for the three years ended December 31, 2010:

	Years Ended December 31		
(In millions)	2010	2009	2008
Expense/(Income)			
Restructuring provisions and asset impairments	$483	$ (8)	$429
Provisions for receivables[1]	180	289	199
Provisions for litigation and regulatory matters	(4)	9	781
Provisions for obsolete and excess inventory	31	52	115
Depreciation and obsolescence of equipment on operating leases	313	329	298
Depreciation of buildings and equipment	379	247	257
Amortization of internal use software	70	53	56
Amortization of product software	7	5	—
Amortization of acquired intangible assets[2]	316	64	58
Amortization of customer contract costs	12	—	—
Defined pension benefits—net periodic benefit cost	304	232	174
Other post-retirement benefits—net periodic benefit cost	32	26	77
Deferred tax asset valuation allowance provisions	22	(11)	17

[1] Includes net receivable adjustments of $(8), $(2) and $11 for 2010, 2009 and 2008, respectively.

[2] Includes amortization of $4 for patents, which is included in cost of sales for each period presented.

1.42

W. R. GRACE & CO. (DEC)

NOTES TO CONSOLIDATED FINANCIAL STATEMENTS

1. Basis of Presentation and Summary of Significant Accounting and Financial Reporting Policies (in part)

Use of Estimates—The preparation of financial statements in conformity with U.S. generally accepted accounting principles (U.S. GAAP) requires management to make estimates and assumptions that affect the reported amount of assets and liabilities and disclosure of contingent assets and liabilities at the date of the Consolidated Financial Statements, and the reported amounts of revenues and expenses for the periods presented. Actual amounts could differ from those estimates, and the differences could be material. Changes in estimates are recorded in the period identified. Grace's accounting measurements that are most affected by management's estimates of future events are:

- Contingent liabilities, which depend on an assessment of the probability of loss and an estimate of ultimate resolution cost, such as asbestos-related matters (see Notes 2 and 3), income taxes (see Note 10), environmental remediation (see Note 13), and litigation (see Note 13);
- Pension and postretirement liabilities that depend on assumptions regarding participant life spans, future inflation, discount rates and total returns on invested funds (see Note 11);
- Realization values of net deferred tax assets and insurance receivables, which depend on projections of future income and cash flows and assessments of insurance coverage and insurer solvency; and
- Recoverability of goodwill, which depends on assumptions used to value reporting units, such as observable market inputs, projections of future cash flows and weighted average cost of capital.

The accuracy of management's estimates may be materially affected by the uncertainties arising under Grace's Chapter 11 proceeding.

Significant Accounting Policies and Estimates

1.43

THE PROCTER & GAMBLE COMPANY (JUN)

SIGNIFICANT ACCOUNTING POLICIES AND ESTIMATES (in part)

In preparing our financial statements in accordance with U.S. GAAP, there are certain accounting policies that may require a choice between acceptable accounting methods or may require substantial judgment or estimation in their application. These include income taxes, certain employee benefits and acquisitions, goodwill and intangible assets. We believe these accounting policies, and others set forth in Note 1 to the Consolidated Financial Statements, should be reviewed as they are integral to understanding the results of operations and financial condition of the Company.

The Company has discussed the selection of significant accounting policies and the effect of estimates with the Audit Committee of the Company's Board of Directors.

Income Taxes

Our annual tax rate is determined based on our income, statutory tax rates and the tax impacts of items treated differently for tax purposes than for financial reporting purposes. Tax law requires certain items to be included in the tax return at different times than the items are reflected in the financial statements. Some of these differences are permanent, such as expenses that are not deductible in our tax return, and some differences are temporary, reversing over time, such as depreciation expense. These temporary differences create deferred tax assets and liabilities.

Deferred tax assets generally represent the tax effect of items that can be used as a tax deduction or credit in future years for which we have already recorded the tax benefit in our income statement. Deferred tax liabilities generally represent tax expense recognized in our financial statements for which payment has been deferred, the tax effect of expenditures for which a deduction has already been taken in our tax return but has not yet been recognized in our financial statements or assets recorded at fair value in business combinations for which there was no corresponding tax basis adjustment.

Inherent in determining our annual tax rate are judgments regarding business plans, planning opportunities and expectations about future outcomes. Realization of certain deferred tax assets is dependent upon generating sufficient taxable income in the appropriate jurisdiction prior to the expiration of the carry-forward periods. Although realization is not assured, management believes it is more likely than not that our deferred tax assets, net of valuation allowances, will be realized.

We operate in multiple jurisdictions with complex tax policy and regulatory environments. In certain of these jurisdictions, we may take tax positions that management believes are supportable, but are potentially subject to successful challenge by the applicable taxing authority. These interpretational differences with the respective governmental taxing authorities can be impacted by the local economic and fiscal environment. We evaluate our tax positions and establish liabilities in accordance with the applicable accounting guidance on uncertainty in income taxes. We review these tax uncertainties in light of changing facts and circumstances, such as the progress of tax audits, and adjust them accordingly. We have a number of audits in process in various jurisdictions. Although the resolution of these tax positions is uncertain, based on currently available information, we believe that the ultimate outcomes will not have a material adverse effect on our financial position, results of operations or cash flows.

Because there are a number of estimates and assumptions inherent in calculating the various components of our tax provision, certain changes or future events such as changes in tax legislation, geographic mix of earnings, completion of tax audits or earnings repatriation plans could have an impact on those estimates and our effective tax rate.

Employee Benefits

We sponsor various post-employment benefits throughout the world. These include pension plans, both defined contribution plans and defined benefit plans, and other post-employment benefit (OPEB) plans, consisting primarily of health care and life insurance for retirees. For accounting purposes, the defined benefit pension and OPEB plans require assumptions to estimate the projected and accumulated benefit obligations, including the following variables: discount rate; expected salary increases; certain employee-related factors, such as turnover, retirement age and mortality; expected return on assets and health care cost trend rates. These and other assumptions affect the annual expense and obligations recognized for the underlying plans. Our assumptions reflect our historical experiences and management's best judgment regarding future expectations. In accordance with U.S. GAAP, the net amount by which actual results differ from our assumptions is deferred. If this net deferred amount exceeds 10% of the greater of plan assets or liabilities, a portion of the deferred amount is included in expense for the following year. The cost or benefit of plan changes, such as increasing or decreasing benefits for prior employee service (prior service cost), is deferred and included in expense on a straight-line basis over the average remaining service period of the employees expected to receive benefits.

The expected return on plan assets assumption is important, since many of our defined benefit pension plans and our primary OPEB plan are funded. The process for setting the expected rates of return is described in Note 8 to the Consolidated Financial Statements. For 2010, the average return on assets assumptions for pension plan assets and OPEB assets were 7.1% and 9.1%, respectively. A change in the rate of return of 0.5% for both pension and OPEB assets would impact annual after-tax benefit expense by less than $45 million.

Since pension and OPEB liabilities are measured on a discounted basis, the discount rate is a significant assumption. Discount rates used for our U.S. defined benefit pension and OPEB plans are based on a yield curve constructed from a portfolio of high quality bonds for which the timing and amount of cash outflows approximate the estimated payouts of the plan. For our international plans, the discount rates are set by benchmarking against investment grade corporate bonds rated AA or better. The average discount rate on the defined benefit pension plans of 5.0% represents a weighted average of local rates in countries where such plans exist. A 0.5% change in the discount rate would impact annual after-tax defined benefit pension expense by less than $65 million. The average discount rate on the OPEB plan of 5.4% reflects the higher interest rates generally applicable in the U.S., which is where a majority of the plan participants receive benefits. A 0.5% change in the discount rate would impact annual after-tax OPEB expense by less than $30 million.

Certain defined contribution pension and OPEB benefits in the U.S. are funded by the Employee Stock Ownership Plan (ESOP), as discussed in Note 8 to the Consolidated Financial Statements.

Acquisitions, Goodwill and Intangible Assets

We account for acquired businesses using the purchase method of accounting. Under the purchase method, our Consolidated Financial Statements reflect the operations of an acquired business starting from the completion of the acquisition. In addition, the assets acquired and liabilities assumed must be recorded at the date of acquisition at their respective estimated fair values, with any excess of the purchase price over the estimated fair values of the net assets acquired recorded as goodwill.

Significant judgment is required in estimating the fair value of intangible assets and in assigning their respective useful lives. Accordingly, we typically obtain the assistance of third-party valuation specialists for significant items. The fair value estimates are based on available historical information and on future expectations and assumptions deemed reasonable by management, but are inherently uncertain.

We typically use an income method to estimate the fair value of intangible assets, which is based on forecasts of the expected future cash flows attributable to the respective assets. Significant estimates and assumptions inherent in the valuations reflect a consideration of other marketplace participants, and include the amount and timing of future cash flows (including expected growth rates and profitability), the underlying product or technology life cycles, economic barriers to entry, a brand's relative market position and the discount rate applied to the cash flows. Unanticipated market or macroeconomic events and circumstances may occur, which could affect the accuracy or validity of the estimates and assumptions.

Determining the useful life of an intangible asset also requires judgment. Certain brand intangibles are expected to have indefinite lives based on their history and our plans to continue to support and build the acquired brands. Other acquired intangible assets (e.g., certain trademarks or brands, customer relationships, patents and technologies) are expected to have determinable useful lives. Our assessment as to brands that have an indefinite life and those that have a determinable life is based on a number of factors including competitive environment, market share, brand history, underlying product life cycles, operating plans and the macroeconomic environment of the countries in which the brands are sold. Our estimates of the useful lives of determinable-lived intangibles are primarily based on these same factors. All of our acquired technology and customer-related intangibles are expected to have determinable useful lives.

The costs of determinable-lived intangibles are amortized to expense over their estimated life. The value of indefinite-lived intangible assets and residual goodwill is not amortized, but is tested at least annually for impairment. Our impairment testing for goodwill is performed separately from our impairment testing of indefinite-lived intangibles. We test goodwill for impairment by reviewing the book value compared to the fair value at the reportable unit level. We test individual indefinite-lived intangibles by reviewing the individual book values compared to the fair value. We determine the fair value of our reporting units and indefinite-lived intangible assets based on the income approach. Under the income approach, we calculate the fair value of our reporting units based on the present value of estimated future cash flows. Considerable management judgment is necessary to evaluate the impact of operating and macroeconomic changes and to estimate future cash flows to measure fair value. Assumptions used in our impairment evaluations, such as forecasted growth rates and cost of capital, are consistent with internal projections and operating plans. We believe such assumptions and estimates are also comparable to those that would be used by other marketplace participants. When certain events or changes in operating conditions occur, indefinite-lived intangible assets may be reclassified to a determinable life asset and an additional impairment assessment may be performed. We did not recognize any material impairment charges for goodwill or intangible assets during the years presented.

Our annual impairment testing for both goodwill and indefinite-lived intangible assets indicated that all reporting unit and intangible asset fair values exceeded their respective recorded values. However, future changes in the judgments, assumptions and estimates that are used in our impairment testing for goodwill and indefinite-lived intangible assets, including discount and tax rates or future cash flow projections, could result in significantly different estimates of the fair values. A significant reduction in the estimated fair values could result in impairment charges that could materially affect the financial statements in any given year. The recorded value of goodwill and intangible assets from recently acquired businesses are derived from more recent business operating plans and macroeconomic environmental conditions and therefore are more susceptible to an adverse change that could require an impairment charge.

For example, because the Gillette intangible and goodwill amounts represent values as of a relatively more recent acquisition date, such amounts are more susceptible to an impairment risk if business operating results or macroeconomic conditions deteriorate. Gillette indefinite-lived intangible assets represent approximately 89% of the $26.5 billion of indefinite-lived intangible assets at June 30, 2010. Goodwill allocated to stand-alone reporting units consisting primarily of businesses purchased as part of the Gillette acquisition represents 42% of the $54.0 billion of goodwill at June 30, 2010. This includes the Male Grooming and Appliance businesses, which are components of the Grooming segment, and the Batteries business, which is part of the Fabric Care and Home Care segment.

With the exception of our Appliances and Salon Professional businesses, all of our other reporting units have fair values that significantly exceed recorded values. As noted above, the Appliances business was acquired as part of the Gillette acquisition and is a stand-alone goodwill reporting unit. The Salon Professional business consists primarily of operations acquired in the Wella acquisition and is part of the Beauty segment. As a result of the organization changes to the structure of the Beauty GBU effected on July 1, 2009 (see the Recent Business Developments section and Note 11 to our Consolidated Financial Statements), the Salon Professional business recently became a new stand-alone goodwill reporting unit. These businesses represent some of our more discretionary consumer spending categories. The Appliances business has goodwill of $1.5 billion, while the Salon Professional business has a goodwill balance of $809 million. The estimated fair values of our Appliances and Salon Professional businesses exceed their carrying values by 18% and 20%, respectively. Because these businesses are more discretionary in nature, their operations and underlying fair values were disproportionately impacted by the economic downturn that began in fiscal 2009, which led to a reduction in home and personal grooming appliance purchases and in visits to hair salons. Our valuation of the Appliances and Salon Professional businesses has them returning to sales and earnings growth rates consistent with our long-term business plans. Failure to achieve these business plans or a further deterioration of the macroeconomic conditions could result in a valuation that would trigger an impairment of the goodwill and intangible assets of these businesses.

Vulnerability Due to Certain Concentrations

1.44

VISHAY INTERTECHNOLOGY, INC. (DEC)

NOTES TO CONSOLIDATED FINANCIAL STATEMENTS

Note 14—Current Vulnerability Due to Certain Concentrations

Market Concentrations

While no single customer comprises greater than 10% of net revenues, a material portion of the Company's revenues are derived from the worldwide communications and computer markets. These markets have historically experienced wide variations in demand for end products. If demand for these end products should decrease, the producers thereof could reduce their purchases of the Company's products, which could have a material adverse effect on the Company's results of operations and financial position.

Credit Risk Concentrations

Financial instruments with potential credit risk consist principally of cash and cash equivalents, accounts receivable, and notes receivable. The Company maintains cash and cash equivalents with various major financial institutions. Concentrations of credit risk with respect to receivables are generally limited due to the Company's large number of customers and their dispersion across many countries and industries. At December 31, 2010 and 2009, the Company had no significant concentrations of credit risk.

Sources of Supplies

Many of the Company's products require the use of raw materials that are produced in only a limited number of regions around the world or are available from only a limited number of suppliers. The Company's consolidated results of operations may be materially and adversely affected if the Company has difficulty obtaining these raw materials, the quality of available raw materials deteriorates, or there are significant price increases for these raw materials. For periods in which the prices of these raw materials are rising, the Company may be unable to pass on the increased cost to the Company's customers, which would result in decreased margins for the products in which they are used. For periods in which the prices are declining, the Company may be required to write down its inventory carrying cost of these raw materials which, depending on the extent of the difference between market price and its carrying cost, could have a material adverse effect on the Company's net earnings.

From time to time, there have been short-term market shortages of raw materials utilized by the Company. While these shortages have not historically adversely affected the Company's ability to increase production of products containing these raw materials, they have historically resulted in higher raw material costs for the Company. The Company cannot assure that any of these market shortages in the future would not adversely affect the Company's ability to increase production, particularly during periods of growing demand for the Company's products.

Tantalum

Vishay is a major consumer of the world's annual production of tantalum. Tantalum, a metal purchased in powder or wire form, is the principal material used in the manufacture of tantalum capacitors. There are few suppliers that process tantalum ore into capacitor grade tantalum powder.

The Company was obligated under two contracts entered into in 2000 with Cabot Corporation to make purchases of tantalum through 2006. The Company's purchase commitments were entered into at a time when market demand for tantalum capacitors was high and tantalum powder was in short supply. Since that time, the price of tantalum has decreased significantly, and accordingly, the Company wrote down the carrying value of its tantalum inventory on-hand and recognized losses on purchase commitments. As of December 31, 2006, the Company has fulfilled all obligations under the Cabot contracts and is no longer required to purchase tantalum from Cabot at prices fixed by the contracts.

Our minimum tantalum purchase commitments under the contracts with Cabot exceeded our production requirements for tantalum capacitors over the term of the contract. Tantalum powder and wire have an indefinite shelf life; therefore, we believe that we will eventually use all of the material in our inventory. At December 31, 2010 and 2009, the Company had tantalum with a book value of $0 and $13,032,000, respectively, classified as other assets, representing the value of quantities which were not expected to be used within one year.

Geographic Concentration

We have operations outside the United States, and, excluding VPG, approximately 77% of our revenues during 2010 were derived from sales to customers outside the United States. Some of our products are produced in countries which are subject to risks of political, economic, and military instability. This instability could result in wars, riots, nationalization of industry, currency fluctuations, and labor unrest. These conditions could have an adverse impact on our ability to operate in these regions and, depending on the extent and severity of these conditions, could materially and adversely affect our overall financial condition and operating results.

Our business has been in operation in Israel for 40 years. We have never experienced any material interruption in our operations attributable to these factors, in spite of several Middle East crises, including wars. However, we might be adversely affected if events were to occur in the Middle East that interfered with our operations in Israel.

1.45

AK STEEL HOLDING CORPORATION (DEC)

NOTES TO CONSOLIDATED FINANCIAL STATEMENTS

Note 1—Summary of Significant Accounting Policies (in part)

Concentrations of Credit Risk: The Company operates in a single business segment and is primarily a producer of carbon, stainless and electrical steels and steel products, which are sold to a number of markets, including automotive, in-

dustrial machinery and equipment, construction, power distribution and appliances. The following presents net sales by product line:

(In millions)	2010	2009	2008
Stainless and electrical	$2,136.9	$1,736.2	$3,234.5
Carbon	3,620.1	2,207.6	4,188.4
Tubular	210.7	131.7	221.4
Other, primarily conversion services	0.6	1.3	—
Total	$5,968.3	$4,076.8	$7,644.3

The following sets forth the percentage of the Company's net sales attributable to various markets:

	Year Ended December 31		
	2010	2009	2008
Automotive	36%	36%	32%
Infrastructure and Manufacturing	25%	31%	29%
Distributors and Converters	39%	33%	39%

No customer accounted for more than 10% of net sales of the Company during 2010, 2009 or 2008. The Company sells domestically to customers primarily in the Midwestern and Eastern United States and to foreign customers, primarily in Canada, Mexico and Western Europe. Net sales to customers located outside the United States totaled $823.3 million, $767.0 million and $1,267.9 million for 2010, 2009 and 2008, respectively. Approximately 28% and 29% of trade receivables outstanding at December 31, 2010 and 2009, respectively, are due from businesses associated with the U.S. automotive industry. Except in a few situations where the risk warrants it, collateral is not required on trade receivables. While the Company believes its recorded trade receivables will be collected, in the event of default the Company would follow normal collection procedures.

1.46

ARDEN GROUP, INC. (DEC)

NOTES TO CONSOLIDATED FINANCIAL STATEMENTS

5. Significant Supplier

During 2010, the Company procured approximately 15% of its product through Unified Grocers, Inc. (Unified), a grocery wholesale cooperative. As a member-patron, the Company is required to provide Unified with certain minimum deposits in order to purchase product from the cooperative. As of January 1, 2011, the Company had approximately $1,628,000 on deposit with Unified in addition to approximately $694,000 related to ownership of equity shares in Unified. There is no established public trading market for Unified's shares. The deposit and equity ownership are recorded under other assets on the Consolidated Balance Sheets.

Unified pays dividends annually in December of each year. Dividends are paid in arrears and are based on a percentage of the Company's qualifying purchases from Unified, which percentage is typically established by Unified at or after the end of each year. The Company accrues patronage dividend income as a reduction of cost of sales ratably throughout the year based on a review of prior dividend history, projected purchase volume and an estimate of Unified's current year patronage earnings. The accrual is adjusted each year, as needed, based on the actual amount received from Unified in December.

1.47

THE BOEING COMPANY (DEC)

NOTES TO CONSOLIDATED FINANCIAL STATEMENTS

Note 18—Significant Group Concentrations of Risk

Credit Risk (in millions)

Financial instruments involving potential credit risk are predominantly with commercial aircraft customers and the U.S. government. Of the $10,496 in gross accounts receivable and gross customer financing included in the Consolidated Statements of Financial Position as of December 31, 2010, $4,996 related to commercial aircraft customers ($570 of accounts receivable and $4,426 of customer financing) and $2,969 related to the U.S. government. Of the $5,033 in gross customer financing, $4,310 related to customers we believe have less than investment-grade credit. AirTran Airways, American Airlines, Continental Airlines and Hawaiian Airlines were associated with 27%, 16%, 9% and 8%, respectively, of our financing portfolio. Financing for aircraft is collateralized by security in the related asset. As of December 31, 2010, there was $9,865 of financing commitments related to aircraft on order including options and proposed as part of sales campaigns described in Note 11, of which $8,490 related to customers we believe have less than investment-grade credit.

BDS Fixed-Price Development Contracts

Fixed-price development work is inherently uncertain and subject to significant variability in estimates of the cost and time required to complete the work. Significant BDS fixed-price development contracts include AEW&C, P-8I, KC-767 International Tanker and commercial and military satellites. The operational and technical complexities of these contracts create financial risk, which could trigger termination provisions, order cancellations or other financially significant exposure. Changes to cost and revenue estimates could also result in lower margins or a material charge for reach-forward losses in 2011.

Commercial Airplane Development Programs

Significant risks are inherent throughout the development of new commercial airplanes and new commercial airplane derivatives. Currently both the 787-8 and 747-8 freighter are in the demanding flight test and certification stages of program development. The 787-9 and 747-8 Intercontinental airplanes are also in development. These programs require substantial investments and research and development as well as investments in working capital and infrastructure. They also entail significant commitments to customers and suppliers and require substantial internal resources. Performance issues on these programs could have a material adverse impact on our consolidated results and financial position in 2011.

Other Risk

As of December 31, 2010, approximately 36% of our total workforce was represented by collective bargaining agreements and approximately 1% of our total workforce was represented by agreements expiring during 2011.

SEGMENT REPORTING

PRESENTATION

1.48 FASB ASC 280, *Segment Reporting*, requires that a public business enterprise report a measure of segment profit or loss, certain specific revenue and expense items, and segment assets. FASB ASC 280-10-05-1 requires that all public business enterprises report information about the revenues derived from the enterprise's products or services or groups of similar products and services; about the countries in which the enterprise earns revenues and holds assets; and about major customers, regardless of whether that information is used in making operating decisions. Even if a public company has only one operating segment, FASB ASC 280 requires that it report information about geographic areas and major customers. However, FASB ASC does not require an enterprise to report information that is impracticable to present because the necessary information is not available, and the cost to develop it would be excessive.

1.49 According to FASB ASC 280-10-50-1, an operating segment of a public entity has all of the following characteristics:
- It engages in business activities from which it may earn revenues and incur expenses, including revenues and expenses relating to transactions with other components of the same public entity.
- Its operating results are regularly reviewed by the public entity's chief operating decision maker to make decisions about resources to be allocated to the segment and assess its performance.
- Its discrete financial information is available.

1.50 FASB ASC 280-10-50-30 requires reconciliations of total segment revenues, total segment profit or loss, total segment assets, and other amounts disclosed for segments to corresponding amounts in the enterprise's general-purpose financial statements. FASB ASC 350-20-50-1 states that entities that report segment information should provide information about the changes in the carrying amount of goodwill during the period for each reportable segment.

1.51

TABLE 1-5: SEGMENT INFORMATION

Table 1-5 shows the type of segment information most frequently presented as an integral part of the financial statements of the survey entities.

	Number of Entities		
	2010	2009	2008
Industry Segments			
Revenue	408	386	412
Operating income or loss	362	291	305
Identifiable assets	306	312	313
Depreciation expense	331	339	344
Capital expenditures	305	311	316
Goodwill	230	235	232
Other, described	135	N/C*	N/C*
Geographic Area			
Revenue	346	256	253
Operating income or loss	61	35	27
Identifiable assets	282	52	54
Depreciation expense	45	24	21
Capital expenditures	45	24	22
Goodwill	20	9	10
Other, described	47	N/C*	N/C*
Entity does not report by segment	35	N/C*	N/C*

* N/C = Not compiled. Line item was not included in the table for the year shown.

PRESENTATION AND DISCLOSURE EXCERPTS

Segment Information

1.52

PALL CORPORATION (JUL)

NOTES TO CONSOLIDATED FINANCIAL STATEMENTS

NOTE 18—Segment Information and Geographies
(in thousands)

The Company serves customers through two global vertically integrated businesses: Life Sciences and Industrial.

Refer to Note 1, Accounting Policies and Related Matters, regarding the Company reorganization of its operating segments during the fourth quarter of fiscal year 2010. Based on this reorganization, segment information for prior periods has been restated to reflect these changes. All discussions and amounts reported in this report are based on the reorganized segment structure.

The Life Sciences business group is focused on developing, manufacturing and selling products to customers in the Medical, BioPharmaceuticals and Food & Beverage markets. The Industrial business group is focused on developing, manufacturing and selling products to customers in the Aeropower, Microelectronics and Energy & Water markets. The chief executive officer manages the Company and makes key decisions about the allocation of Company resources based on the two businesses. The Company's reportable segments, which are also its operating segments, consist of its two vertically integrated businesses, Life Sciences and Industrial.

The Company's subsidiaries sell both Life Sciences and Industrial products. As such, certain overhead costs of these subsidiaries are shared by the businesses. Additionally these business groups are supported by shared and corporate services groups that facilitate the Company's corporate governance and business activities globally.

Cash and cash equivalents, short-term investments, investments and retirement benefit assets and income taxes all of which are managed at the Corporate level, are included in Corporate/Shared Services assets. Furthermore assets not specifically identified to a business group are also included in Corporate/Shared Services assets. Accounts receivable and inventory are in all cases specifically identified to a business group.

Expenses associated with the corporate operations, interest expense, net, the provision for income taxes, as well as restructuring and other charges are currently excluded from the measurement and evaluation of the profitability of the Company's reportable segments.

(In thousands, except per share data)	2010	2009	2008
Segment Information:			
Sales:			
Life Sciences	$1,237,835	$1,166,275	$1,227,736
Industrial	1,164,097	1,162,883	1,343,909
Total	$2,401,932	$2,329,158	$2,571,645
Operating Profit:			
Life Sciences	280,089	234,055	237,292
Industrial	164,544	152,068	206,337
Total operating profit	444,633	386,123	443,629
General corporate expenses	53,411	56,478	53,960
Earnings before ROTC, interest expense, net, loss on extinguishment of debt and income taxes	391,222	329,645	389,669
ROTC	17,664	30,723	31,538
Interest expense, net	14,324	28,136	32,576
Loss on extinguishment of debt	31,513	—	—
Earnings before income taxes	$ 327,721	$ 270,786	$ 325,555
Depreciation and Amortization:			
Life Sciences	$ 54,882	$ 51,838	$ 53,426
Industrial	36,922	36,170	38,381
Subtotal	91,804	88,008	91,807
Corporate	1,824	1,431	1,398
Total	$ 93,628	$ 89,439	$ 93,205
Capital Expenditures:			
Life Sciences	$ 59,882	$ 73,915	$ 71,704
Industrial	32,175	42,033	33,631
Subtotal	92,057	115,948	105,335
Corporate/Shared Services	44,256	17,101	18,519
Total	$ 136,313	$ 133,049	$ 123,854
Identifiable Assets:			
Life Sciences	$1,068,697	$1,020,194	
Industrial	903,740	924,948	
Subtotal	1,972,437	1,945,142	
Corporate/Shared Services	1,026,775	895,670	
Total	$2,999,212	$2,840,812	
Geographic Information:			
Sales:			
Western Hemisphere	$ 789,361	$ 769,702	$ 810,659
Europe	945,952	960,307	1,106,983
Asia	666,619	599,149	654,003
Total	$2,401,932	$2,329,158	$2,571,645
Identifiable Assets:			
Western Hemisphere	$1,098,019	$1,074,641	
Europe	621,959	643,184	
Asia	304,671	271,212	
Eliminations	(52,212)	(43,895)	
Subtotal	1,972,437	1,945,142	
Corporate/Shared Services	1,026,775	895,670	
Total	$2,999,212	$2,840,812	

Sales by the Company's U.S. operations to unaffiliated customers totaled approximately $733,000, $715,000 and $754,000 in fiscal years 2010, 2009 and 2008, respectively. Included therein are export sales of approximately $43,300, $86,000 and $66,000 in fiscal years 2010, 2009 and 2008, respectively. Sales by the Company's subsidiaries in Germany amounted to approximately $225,000, $234,000 and $278,000 in fiscal years 2010, 2009 and 2008, respectively.

Sales by the Company's subsidiary in Japan amounted to approximately $230,000, $214,000 and $235,000 in fiscal years 2010, 2009 and 2008, respectively. The Company considers its foreign operations to be of major importance to its future growth prospects. The risks related to the Company's foreign operations include the local political and regulatory developments as well as the regional economic climate.

1.53

SYSCO CORPORATION (JUN)

NOTES TO CONSOLIDATED FINANCIAL STATEMENTS

19. Business Segment Information

The company has aggregated its operating companies into a number of segments, of which only Broadline and SYGMA are reportable segments as defined in the accounting literature related to disclosures about segments of an enterprise. The Broadline reportable segment is an aggregation of the company's United States, Canadian and European Broadline segments. Broadline operating companies distribute a full line of food products and a wide variety of non-food products to its customers. SYGMA operating companies distribute a full line of food products and a wide variety of non-food products to certain chain restaurant customer locations. "Other" financial information is attributable to the company's other operating segments, including the company's specialty produce, custom-cut meat and lodging industry segments and a company that distributes to international customers.

The accounting policies for the segments are the same as those disclosed by Sysco. Intersegment sales represent specialty produce and meat company products distributed by the Broadline and SYGMA operating companies. The segment results include certain centrally incurred costs for shared services that are charged to our segments. These centrally incurred costs are charged based upon the relative level of service used by each operating company consistent with how Sysco's management views the performance of its operating segments. Management evaluates the performance of each of our operating segments based on its respective operating income results, which include the allocation of certain centrally incurred costs.

Included in corporate expenses, among other items, are:
- Gains and losses recognized to adjust corporate-owned life insurance policies to their cash surrender values;
- Share-based compensation expense;
- Expenses related to the company's Business Transformation Project; and
- Corporate-level depreciation and amortization expense.

The following table sets forth the financial information for Sysco's business segments:

(In thousands)	Fiscal Year		
	2010 (53 Weeks)	2009	2008
Sales:			
Broadline	$29,737,718	$29,234,199	$29,824,553
SYGMA	4,891,279	4,839,036	4,574,880
Other	3,158,855	3,242,115	3,590,738
Intersegment sales	(544,357)	(462,020)	(468,060)
Total	$37,243,495	$36,853,330	$37,522,111
Operating income:			
Broadline	$ 2,075,647	$ 1,959,963	$ 1,931,881
SYGMA	47,311	30,193	8,261
Other	122,483	101,355	136,533
Total segments	2,245,441	2,091,511	2,076,675
Corporate expenses	(269,573)	(219,300)	(196,726)
Total operating income	1,975,868	1,872,211	1,879,949
Interest expense	125,477	116,322	111,541
Other expense (income), net	802	(14,945)	(22,930)
Earnings before income taxes	$ 1,849,589	$ 1,770,834	$ 1,791,338
Depreciation and amortization:			
Broadline	$ 275,639	$ 265,526	$ 258,171
SYGMA	23,822	26,753	30,467
Other	34,389	37,629	36,692
Total segments	333,850	329,908	325,330
Corporate	56,126	52,431	47,199
Total	$ 389,976	$ 382,339	$ 372,529
Capital expenditures:			
Broadline	$ 393,824	$ 342,550	$ 393,067
SYGMA	25,436	5,053	4,977
Other	25,259	40,857	36,565
Total segments	444,519	388,460	434,609
Corporate	150,085	76,101	81,354
Total	$ 594,604	$ 464,561	$ 515,963
Assets:			
Broadline	$ 6,218,985	$ 5,637,998	$ 5,809,060
SYGMA	392,883	366,539	414,044
Other	937,605	914,764	1,005,740
Total segments	7,549,473	6,919,301	7,228,844
Corporate	2,764,228	3,228,885	2,781,771
Total	$10,313,701	$10,148,186	$10,010,615

The sales mix for the principal product categories for each
fiscal year is as follows:

(In thousands)	2010 (53 Weeks)	2009	2008
Canned and dry products	$ 7,152,628	$ 7,091,420	$ 6,820,363
Fresh and frozen meats	6,405,820	6,394,447	6,606,347
Frozen fruits, vegetables, bakery and other	5,220,307	5,122,415	5,105,353
Poultry	3,862,486	3,709,553	3,808,844
Dairy products	3,709,410	3,750,684	4,000,780
Fresh produce	3,179,947	3,017,018	3,183,540
Paper and disposables	2,906,426	2,911,029	2,964,006
Seafood	1,739,949	1,740,292	1,878,830
Beverage products	1,408,376	1,322,300	1,297,543
Janitorial products	907,189	940,097	988,781
Equipment and smallwares	599,267	661,309	704,050
Medical supplies	151,690	192,766	163,674
Total	$37,243,495	$36,853,330	$37,522,111

Information concerning geographic areas is as follows:

(In thousands)	Fiscal Year		
	2010 (53 Weeks)	2009	2008
Sales:[1]			
United States	$33,268,481	$33,378,485	$33,842,824
Canada	3,550,605	3,134,989	3,380,159
Other	424,409	339,856	299,128
Total	$37,243,495	$36,853,330	$37,522,111
Long-lived assets:[2]			
United States	$ 2,884,728	$ 2,725,200	$ 2,655,714
Canada	291,514	223,320	233,879
Other	27,581	30,680	197
Total	$ 3,203,823	$ 2,979,200	$ 2,889,790

[1] Represents sales to external customers from businesses operating in these countries.
[2] Long-lived assets represents net property, plant and equipment reported in the country in which they are held.

1.54

WASTE MANAGEMENT, INC. (DEC)

NOTES TO CONSOLIDATED FINANCIAL STATEMENTS

21. Segment and Related Information

We currently manage and evaluate our operations primarily through our Eastern, Midwest, Southern, Western and Wheelabrator Groups. These five Groups are presented below as our reportable segments. Our four geographic operating Groups provide collection, transfer, disposal (in both solid waste and hazardous waste landfills) and recycling services. Our fifth Group is the Wheelabrator Group, which provides waste-to-energy services and manages waste-to-energy facilities and independent power production plants. We serve residential, commercial, industrial, and municipal customers throughout North America. The operations not managed through our five operating Groups are presented herein as "Other."

Summarized financial information concerning our reportable segments for the respective years ended December 31 is shown in the following table (in millions):

	Gross Operating Revenues	Intercompany Operating Revenues[c]	Net Operating Revenues	Income From Operations[d],[e]	Depreciation and Amortization	Capital Expenditures[f]	Total Assets[g],[h]
2010							
Eastern	$ 2,943	$ (508)	$ 2,435	$ 516	$ 270	$ 201	$ 4,272
Midwest	3,048	(453)	2,595	533	275	203	4,929
Southern	3,461	(403)	3,058	844	269	230	3,256
Western	3,173	(438)	2,735	569	210	223	3,715
Wheelabrator	889	(125)	764	214	64	38	2,574
Other[a]	963	(35)	928	(135)	50	182	1,744
	14,477	(1,962)	12,515	2,541	1,138	1,077	20,490
Corporate and Other[b]	—	—	—	(425)	56	90	1,679
Total	$14,477	$(1,962)	$12,515	$2,116	$1,194	$1,167	$22,169
2009							
Eastern	$ 2,960	$ (533)	$ 2,427	$ 483	$ 276	$ 216	$ 4,326
Midwest	2,855	(426)	2,429	450	261	218	4,899
Southern	3,328	(431)	2,897	768	274	242	3,250
Western	3,125	(412)	2,713	521	226	195	3,667
Wheelabrator	841	(123)	718	235	57	11	2,266
Other[a]	628	(21)	607	(136)	29	128	1,112
	13,737	(1,946)	11,791	2,321	1,123	1,010	19,520
Corporate and Other[b]	—	—	—	(434)	43	66	2,281
Total	$13,737	$(1,946)	$11,791	$1,887	$1,166	$1,076	$21,801

(continued)

	Gross Operating Revenues	Intercompany Operating Revenues[c]	Net Operating Revenues	Income From Operations[d],[e]	Depreciation and Amortization	Capital Expenditures[f]	Total Assets[g],[h]
2008							
Eastern	$ 3,319	$ (599)	$ 2,720	$ 523	$ 284	$ 318	$ 4,372
Midwest	3,267	(475)	2,792	475	287	296	4,626
Southern	3,740	(493)	3,247	872	294	303	3,218
Western	3,387	(428)	2,959	612	238	295	3,686
Wheelabrator	912	(92)	820	323	56	24	2,359
Other[a]	897	(47)	850	(60)	32	81	873
	15,522	(2,134)	13,388	2,745	1,191	1,317	19,134
Corporate and Other[b]	—	—	—	(511)	47	45	1,676
Total	$15,522	$(2,134)	$13,388	$2,234	$1,238	$1,362	$20,810

[a] Our "Other" net operating revenues and "Other" income from operations include (i) the effects of those elements of our in-plant services, landfill gas-to-energy operations, and third-party subcontract and administration revenues managed by our Upstream ®, Renewable Energy and Strategic Accounts organizations, respectively, that are not included with the operations of our reportable segments; (ii) our recycling brokerage and electronic recycling services; and (iii) the impacts of investments that we are making in expanded service offerings such as portable self-storage and fluorescent lamp recycling. In addition, our "Other" income from operations reflects the impacts of (i) non-operating entities that provide financial assurance and self-insurance support for the Groups or financing for our Canadian operations; and (ii) certain year-end adjustments recorded in consolidation related to the reportable segments that were not included in the measure of segment profit or loss used to assess their performance for the periods disclosed.

[b] Corporate operating results reflect the costs incurred for various support services that are not allocated to our five Groups. These support services include, among other things, treasury, legal, information technology, tax, insurance, centralized service center processes, other administrative functions and the maintenance of our closed landfills. Income from operations for "Corporate and other" also includes costs associated with our long-term incentive program and any administrative expenses or revisions to our estimated obligations associated with divested operations.

[c] Intercompany operating revenues reflect each segment's total intercompany sales, including intercompany sales within a segment and between segments. Transactions within and between segments are generally made on a basis intended to reflect the market value of the service.

[d] For those items included in the determination of income from operations, the accounting policies of the segments are the same as those described in Note 3.

[e] The income from operations provided by our four geographic Groups is generally indicative of the margins provided by our collection, landfill, transfer and recycling businesses. The operating margins provided by our Wheelabrator Group (waste-to-energy facilities and independent power production plants) have historically been higher than the margins provided by our base business generally due to the combined impact of long-term disposal and energy contracts and the disposal demands of the regions in which our facilities are concentrated. However, the revenues and operating results of our Wheelabrator Group have been unfavorably affected by a significant decrease in the rates charged for electricity under our power purchase contracts, which correlate with natural gas prices in the markets where we operate. Exposure to market fluctuations in electricity prices increased for the Wheelabrator Group in 2009 due in large part to the expiration of several long-term energy contracts. Additionally, the Company's current focus on the expansion of our waste-to-energy business both internationally and domestically has increased Wheelabrator's costs and expenses, which has negatively affected the comparability of their operating results for the periods presented. From time to time the operating results of our reportable segments are significantly affected by certain transactions or events that management believes are not indicative or representative of our results. Refer to Note 12 and Note 13 for an explanation of transactions and events affecting the operating results of our reportable segments.

[f] Includes non-cash items. Capital expenditures are reported in our reportable segments at the time they are recorded within the segments' property, plant and equipment balances and, therefore, may include amounts that have been accrued but not yet paid.

[g] The reconciliation of total assets reported above to "Total assets" in the Consolidated Balance Sheets is as follows (in millions):

	December 31		
	2010	**2009**	**2008**
Total assets, as reported above	$22,169	$21,801	$20,810
Elimination of intercompany investments and advances	(693)	(647)	(583)
Total assets, per Consolidated Balance Sheets	$21,476	$21,154	$20,227

[h] Goodwill is included within each Group's total assets. As discussed above, for segment reporting purposes, our material recovery facilities and secondary processing facilities are included as a component of their respective geographic Group and our recycling brokerage business and electronics recycling services are included as part of our "Other" operations. The following table shows changes in goodwill during 2009 and 2010 by reportable segment (in millions):

	Eastern	**Midwest**	**Southern**	**Western**	**Wheelabrator**	**Other**	**Total**
Balance, December 31, 2008	$1,488	$1,300	$643	$1,208	$788	$35	$5,462
Acquired goodwill	10	45	36	7	—	27	125
Divested goodwill, net of assets held-for-sale	2	—	—	—	—	—	2
Translation adjustments	—	37	—	6	—	—	43
Balance, December 31, 2009	1,500	1,382	679	1,221	788	62	5,632
Acquired goodwill	4	17	4	20	—	32	77
Divested goodwill, net of assets held-for-sale	—	—	—	—	—	—	—
Translation and other adjustments	—	15	—	2	—	—	17
Balance, December 31, 2010	$1,504	$1,414	$683	$1,243	$788	$94	$5,726

The table below shows the total revenues by principal line of business (in millions):

	Years Ended December 31		
	2010	2009	2008
Collection	$ 8,247	$ 7,980	$ 8,679
Landfill	2,540	2,547	2,955
Transfer	1,318	1,383	1,589
Wheelabrator	889	841	912
Recycling	1,169	741	1,180
Other[a]	314	245	207
Intercompany[b]	(1,962)	(1,946)	(2,134)
Operating revenues	$12,515	$11,791	$13,388

[a] The "Other" line-of-business includes landfill gas-to-energy operations, Port-O-Let ® services, portable self-storage and fluorescent lamp recycling.

[b] Intercompany revenues between lines of business are eliminated within the Consolidated Financial Statements included herein.

Net operating revenues relating to operations in the United States and Puerto Rico, as well as Canada are as follows (in millions):

	Years Ended December 31		
	2010	2009	2008
United States and Puerto Rico	$11,784	$11,137	$12,621
Canada	731	654	767
Total	$12,515	$11,791	$13,388

Property and equipment (net) relating to operations in the United States and Puerto Rico, as well as Canada are as follows (in millions):

	December 31		
	2010	2009	2008
United States and Puerto Rico	$10,558	$10,251	$10,355
Canada	1,310	1,290	1,047
Total	$11,868	$11,541	$11,402

1.55

ORACLE CORPORATION (MAY)

NOTES TO CONSOLIDATED FINANCIAL STATEMENTS

16. Segment Information

ASC 280, *Segment Reporting*, establishes standards for reporting information about operating segments. Operating segments are defined as components of an enterprise about which separate financial information is available that is evaluated regularly by the chief operating decision maker, or decision making group, in deciding how to allocate resources and in assessing performance. Our chief operating decision maker is our Chief Executive Officer. We are organized geographically and by line of business. While our Chief Executive Officer evaluates results in a number of different ways, the line of business management structure is the primary basis for which the allocation of resources and financial results are assessed. As a result of our acquisition of Sun, we entered into a new hardware systems business with two operating segments as described further below. We have three businesses—software, hardware systems and services—which are further divided into seven operating segments. Our software business is comprised of two operating segments: (1) new software licenses and (2) software license updates and product support. Our hardware systems business is comprised of two operating segments: (1) hardware systems products and (2) hardware systems support. Our services business is comprised of three operating segments: (1) consulting, (2) On Demand and (3) education.

The new software licenses line of business is engaged in the licensing of database and middleware software as well as our applications software. Database and middleware software includes database management software, application server software, business intelligence software, identification and access management software, content management software, portal and user interaction software, Service-Oriented Architecture and business process management software, data integration software and development tools. As a result of our acquisition of Sun, we acquired certain software technologies that expanded and enhanced our existing database and middleware software product offerings, including Java, which is a global software development platform used in a wide range of computers, networks and devices. Applications software provides enterprise information that enables companies to manage their business cycles and provide intelligence in functional areas such as customer relationship management, financials, human resources, maintenance management, manufacturing, marketing, order fulfillment, product lifecycle management, enterprise project portfolio management, enterprise performance management, procurement, sales, services, enterprise resource planning and supply chain planning.

The software license updates and product support line of business provides customers with rights to unspecified software product upgrades and maintenance releases, internet access to technical content, as well as internet and telephone access to technical support personnel during the support period.

The hardware systems products line of business consists primarily of computer server and storage product offerings. Most of our computer servers are based on our SPARC family of microprocessors and on Intel Xeon microprocessors. Our servers range from high performance computing servers to cost efficient, entry-level servers, and run with our Solaris Operating System, Linux and certain other operating systems environments. Our storage products are designed to securely manage, protect, archive and restore customers' data assets and consist of tape, disk and networking solutions for open systems and mainframe server environments. Customers that purchase our hardware systems products may also elect to purchase our hardware systems support offerings. Our hardware systems support offerings provide customers with software updates for the software components that are essential to the functionality of our hardware systems and storage products and can include product repairs, maintenance services, and technical support services.

The consulting line of business primarily provides services to customers in business strategy and analysis, business process simplification, solutions integration and the implementation, enhancement and upgrade of our database, middleware and applications software. On Demand includes Oracle On Demand and Advanced Customer Services. Oracle On Demand provides multi-featured software and hardware management and maintenance services for customers that are delivered at our data center facilities, select partner data centers or customer facilities. Advanced Customer Services consists of solution lifecycle management services, industry-specific solution support centers, hardware systems expert services, packaged offerings that support the installation and optimization of our hardware products and remote and on-site expert services. The education line of business provides instructor-led, media-based and internet-based training in the use of our software and hardware products.

We do not track our assets by operating segments. Consequently, it is not practical to show assets by operating segments results.

The following table presents a summary of our businesses' and operating segments' results:

(In millions)	Year Ended May 31		
	2010	2009	2008
New software licenses:			
Revenues[1]	$ 7,525	$ 7,112	$ 7,501
Sales and distribution expenses	3,980	4,006	4,040
Margin[2]	$ 3,545	$ 3,106	$ 3,461
Software license updates and product support:			
Revenues[1]	$13,175	$11,997	$10,507
Software license update and product support expenses	958	1,012	933
Margin[2]	$12,217	$10,985	$ 9,574
Total software business:			
Revenues[1]	$20,700	$19,109	$18,008
Expenses	4,938	5,018	4,973
Margin[2]	$15,762	$14,091	$13,035
Hardware systems products:			
Revenues	$ 1,493	$ —	$ —
Hardware systems products expenses	850	—	—
Sales and distribution expenses	307	—	—
Margin[2]	$ 336	$ —	$ —
Hardware systems support:			
Revenues[1]	$ 912	$ —	$ —
Hardware systems support expenses	408	—	—
Margin[2]	$ 504	$ —	$ —
Total hardware systems business:			
Revenues[1]	$ 2,405	$ —	$ —
Expenses	1,565	—	—
Margin[2]	$ 840	$ —	$ —
Consulting:			
Revenues[1]	$ 2,705	$ 3,221	$ 3,454
Services expenses	2,319	2,686	2,914
Margin[2]	$ 386	$ 535	$ 540
On Demand:			
Revenues[1]	$ 887	$ 780	$ 695
Services expenses	679	566	569
Margin[2]	$ 208	$ 214	$ 126
Education:			
Revenues[1]	$ 337	$ 385	$ 452
Services expenses	247	282	314
Margin[2]	$ 90	$ 103	$ 138
Total services business:			
Revenues[1]	$ 3,929	$ 4,386	$ 4,601
Services expenses	3,245	3,534	3,797
Margin[2]	$ 684	$ 852	$ 804
Totals:			
Revenues[1]	$27,034	$23,495	$22,609
Expenses	9,748	8,552	8,770
Margin[2]	$17,286	$14,943	$13,839

[1] Operating segment revenues differ from the external reporting classifications due to certain software license products that are classified as service revenues for management reporting purposes. Software license updates and product support revenues for management reporting included $86 million, $243 million and $179 million of revenues that we did not recognize in the accompanying consolidated statements of operations in fiscal 2010, 2009 and 2008, respectively. In addition, we did not recognize hardware systems support revenues related to hardware systems support contracts that would have otherwise been recorded by Sun as an independent entity, in the amount of $128 million in fiscal 2010. See Note 10 for an explanation of these adjustments and the following table for a reconciliation of operating segment revenues to total revenues.

[2] The margins reported reflect only the direct controllable costs of each line of business and do not include allocations of product development, information technology, marketing and partner programs, and corporate and general and administrative expenses incurred in support of the lines of business. Additionally, the margins do not reflect the amortization of intangible assets, acquisition related and other expenses, restructuring costs, or stock-based compensation.

The following table reconciles operating segment revenues to total revenues as well as operating segment margin to income before provision for income taxes:

(In millions)	Year Ended May 31		
	2010	2009	2008
Total revenues for reportable segments	$27,034	$23,495	$22,609
Software license updates and product support revenues[1]	(86)	(243)	(179)
Hardware systems support revenues[1]	(128)	—	—
Total revenues	$26,820	$23,252	$22,430
Total margin for reportable segments	$17,286	$14,943	$13,839
Software license updates and product support revenues[1]	(86)	(243)	(179)
Hardware systems support revenues[1]	(128)	—	—
Hardware systems products expenses[2]	(29)	—	—
Product development and information technology expenses	(3,479)	(2,984)	(3,012)
Marketing and partner program expenses	(503)	(439)	(460)
Corporate and general and administrative expenses	(755)	(634)	(677)
Amortization of intangible assets	(1,973)	(1,713)	(1,212)
Acquisition related and other	(154)	(117)	(124)
Restructuring	(622)	(117)	(41)
Stock-based compensation	(421)	(340)	(257)
Interest expense	(754)	(630)	(394)
Non-operating income (expense), net	(139)	108	351
Income before provision for income taxes	$ 8,243	$ 7,834	$ 7,834

[1] Software license updates and product support revenues for management reporting include $86 million, $243 million and $179 million of revenues that we did not recognize in the accompanying condensed consolidated statements of operations for fiscal 2010, 2009 and 2008, respectively. In addition, we did not recognize hardware systems support revenues related to hardware systems support contracts that would have otherwise been recorded by Sun as an independent entity, in the amount of $128 million for fiscal 2010. See Note 10 for an explanation of these adjustments and this table for a reconciliation of operating segment revenues to total revenues.

[2] Represents the effects of fair value adjustments to our inventories acquired from Sun that were sold to customers in the periods presented. Business combination accounting rules require us to account for inventories assumed from our acquisitions at their fair values. The amount included in hardware systems products expenses above is intended to adjust these expenses to the hardware systems products expenses that would have been otherwise recorded by Sun as a standalone entity upon the sale of these inventories. If we assume inventories in future acquisitions, we will be required to assess their fair values, which may result in fair value adjustments to those inventories.

Geographic Information

Disclosed in the table below is geographic information for each country that comprised greater than three percent of our total revenues for fiscal 2010, 2009 or 2008.

(In millions)	As of and for the Year Ended May 31					
	2010		2009		2008	
	Revenues	Long Lived Assets[1]	Revenues	Long Lived Assets[1]	Revenues	Long Lived Assets[1]
United States	$11,472	$2,141	$10,190	$1,466	$ 9,650	$1,465
United Kingdom	1,685	136	1,587	89	1,655	110
Japan	1,349	505	1,189	485	1,068	207
Germany	1,112	20	956	5	983	9
France	965	24	856	8	858	21
Canada	888	10	737	13	737	15
Other countries	9,349	660	7,737	462	7,479	532
Total	$26,820	$3,496	$23,252	$2,528	$22,430	$2,359

[1] Long-lived assets exclude goodwill, intangible assets, equity investments and deferred taxes, which are not allocated to specific geographic locations as it is impracticable to do so.

ACCOUNTING CHANGES AND ERROR CORRECTIONS

PRESENTATION

1.56 FASB ASC 250 defines various types of accounting changes, including a change in accounting principle, and provides guidance on the manner of reporting each type of change.

1.57 Paragraphs 1–2 of FASB ASC 250-10-45 include the presumption that, once adopted, an entity should not change an accounting principle (policy) to account for events and transactions of a similar type. FASB ASC 250-10-45-2 permits an entity to change an accounting principle in certain circumstances, such as when required to do so by new authoritative accounting guidance that mandates the use of a new accounting principle, interprets an existing principle, expresses a preference for an accounting principle, or rejects a specific principle. This paragraph also permits an entity to change an accounting principle if it can justify the use of an allowable alternative accounting principle on the basis that it is preferable.

1.58 FASB ASC 250-10-45-1 does not consider the following to be changes in accounting principle:
- Initial adoption of an accounting principle for new events or transactions
- Initial adoption of an accounting principle for new events or transactions that previously were immaterial in their effect
- Adoption or modification of an accounting principle for substantively different transactions or events from those occurring previously

1.59 FASB ASC 250-10-45-5 requires an entity to apply a change in accounting principle retrospectively to all prior periods, unless it is impracticable to do so. Retrospective application requires cumulative adjustments to the carrying amounts of assets and liabilities at the beginning of the earliest period presented; an adjustment, if any, to the opening balance of retained earnings or other relevant equity account; and adjusted financial statements for each individual prior period presented to reflect the period-specific effects of applying the new accounting principle. FASB ASC 250-10-45-7 provides an impracticability exception for period-specific effects or all periods. However, FASB ASC 250-10-45-8 permits only direct effects of the change, including any related income tax effects, to be included in the retrospective adjustment and prohibits an entity from including indirect effects that would have been recognized if the newly adopted accounting principle had been followed in prior periods. If indirect effects are actually incurred and recognized, an entity should only report for those indirect effects in the period in which the accounting change is made.

1.60 FASB ASC 250-10-45-17 requires an entity to account for a change in accounting estimate prospectively in the period of change if the change affects that period only or in the period of change and future periods if the change affects both.

1.61 Paragraphs 18–19 of FASB ASC 250-10-45 recognize that it may be difficult to distinguish between a change in an accounting principle and a change in an accounting estimate. Additional guidance is provided for those circumstances when an entity's change in estimate is affected by a change in accounting principle, recognizing that the effect of a change in accounting principle or the method of applying it may be inseparable from the effect of the change in accounting estimate. An example of such change is a change in the method of depreciation, amortization, or depletion for long-lived nonfinancial assets. Although an entity is permitted to apply this change prospectively as a change in accounting estimate, an entity should only make a change in accounting estimate affected by a change in accounting principle if the entity can justify the new accounting principle on the basis that it is preferable.

1.62 Paragraphs 23–24 of FASB ASC 250-10-45 require an entity to correct any error in the financial statements of a prior period discovered after the financial statements are issued or available to be issued by restating the prior-period financial statements. Such errors are required to be reported as an error correction by restating the prior-period financial statements retrospectively with adjustments to the financial statements.

DISCLOSURE

1.63 As discussed in FASB ASC 250-10-50, among the required disclosures for a change in accounting principle, the reason should be disclosed, including an explanation about why the new method is preferable. Specific disclosures are also required for a change in accounting estimate, a change in reporting entity, correction of an error in previously-issued financial statements, and error corrections related to prior interim periods of the current fiscal year. As indicated in Table 1-6, most of the accounting changes disclosed by the survey entities were changes made to conform to requirements stated in newly Accounting Standards Updates.

1.64

TABLE 1-6: ACCOUNTING CHANGES AND ERROR CORRECTIONS*

Table 1-6 lists the accounting changes and error corrections disclosed by the survey entities.

	Number of Entities 2010
Change in Accounting Principle	
Depreciation method	2
Stock-based compensation	2
Defined benefit pension and other postretirement	14
Business combinations	43
Fair value measurements	30
Derivatives and hedging activities	1
Noncontrolling interests	35
Financial instruments with debt and equity characteristics	16
Earnings per share	6
Other, described	53
Change in Accounting Estimate	
Impairment or disposal of long-lived assets	1
Depreciable lives	3
Income tax (uncertainties)	5
Fair value measurements	3
Derivatives and hedging activities	—
Other, described	6
Correction of an Error	
Prior-period financial statement misstatements	6
Other, described	5

* NOTE: Due to the implementation of greater detail for accounting changes in this edition, no prior year data are available.

PRESENTATION AND DISCLOSURE EXCERPTS

Change in Accounting Principle: Share-Based Compensation

1.65

THE CLOROX COMPANY (JUN)

NOTES TO CONSOLIDATED FINANCIAL STATEMENTS

Note 1. Summary of Significant Accounting Policies (in part)

New Accounting Pronouncements (in part)
On July 1, 2009, the Company adopted a new accounting standard that provides that unvested share-based payment awards that contain nonforfeitable rights to dividends or dividend equivalents, whether paid or unpaid, are participating securities that must be included in the computation of earnings per share pursuant to the two-class method. These payment awards were previously not considered participating securities. Accordingly, the Company's unvested perfor-

mance units, restricted stock awards and restricted stock units that provide such nonforfeitable rights are now considered participating securities in the calculation of net earnings per share (EPS). The Company's share-based payment awards granted in fiscal year 2010 are not participating securities. The new standard requires the retrospective adjustment of the Company's earnings per share data. The impact of the retrospective adoption of the new accounting standard on the fiscal year 2009 and 2008 reported EPS data was as follows:

	Basic		Diluted	
	As Previously Reported	As Restated	As Previously reported	As Restated
Year ended June 30, 2009	$3.86	$3.82	$3.81	$3.79
Year ended June 30, 2008	3.30	3.27	3.24	3.23

The calculation of EPS under the new accounting standard is disclosed in Note 15.

Note 15. Earnings Per Share (in part)

The Company computes EPS using the two-class method (See Note 1), which is an earnings allocation formula that determines EPS for common stock and participating securities.

EPS for common stock is computed by dividing net earnings applicable to common stock by the weighted average number of common shares outstanding each period on an unrounded basis. Net earnings applicable to common stock includes dividends paid to common shareholders during the period plus a proportionate share of undistributed net earnings which is based on the weighted average number of shares of common stock and participating securities outstanding during the period.

Diluted EPS for common stock reflects the earnings dilution that could occur from common shares that may be issued through stock options, restricted stock awards, performance units and restricted stock units that are not participating securities. Excluded from this calculation are amounts allocated to participating securities.

The following are reconciliations of net earnings to net earnings (in millions) applicable to common stock, and the number of common shares outstanding (in thousands) used to calculate basic EPS to those used to calculate diluted EPS for fiscal years ended June 30:

	2010	2009	2008
Net earnings	$603	$537	$461
Less: Earnings allocated to participating securities	3	5	5
Net earnings applicable to common stock	$600	$532	$456

	Weighted Average Number of Shares Outstanding		
	2010	2009	2008
Basic	140,272	139,015	139,633
Dilutive effect of stock options and other (excludes participating securities)	1,262	1,154	1,564
Diluted	141,534	140,169	141,197

Change in Accounting Principle: Pension and Other Postretirement Benefits

1.66

AT&T INC. (DEC)

NOTES TO CONSOLIDATED FINANCIAL STATEMENTS

Note 1. Summary of Significant Accounting Policies (in part)

Pension and Other Postretirement Benefits (In millions). In January 2011, we announced a change in our method of recognizing actuarial gains and losses for pension and other postretirement benefits for all benefit plans. Historically, we have recognized the actuarial gains and losses as a component of the Stockholders' Equity on our consolidated balance sheets on an annual basis and have amortized them into our operating results over the average future service period of the active employees of these plans, to the extent such gains and losses were outside of a corridor. We have elected to immediately recognize actuarial gains and losses in our operat-

ing results, noting that it is generally preferable to accelerate the recognition of deferred gains and losses into income rather than to delay such recognition. This change will improve transparency in our operating results by more quickly recognizing the effects of economic and interest rate conditions on plan obligations, investments and assumptions. These gains and losses are generally only measured annually as of December 31 and accordingly will be recorded during the fourth quarter. Additionally, for purposes of calculating the expected return on plan assets, we will no longer use a permitted averaging technique for the market-related value of plan assets but instead will use actual fair value of plan assets. We have applied these changes retrospectively, adjusting all prior periods. The cumulative effect of the change on retained earnings as of January 1, 2008, was a reduction of $1,533, with an offset to accumulated other comprehensive income (OCI). The annual recognition of actuarial gains and losses, which is reported as "Actuarial loss on pension and postretirement benefit plans" on our consolidated statement of cash flows total $2,521 in 2010, $215 in 2009 and $25,150 in 2008. This change did not have a material impact on cash provided by or used in operations for any period presented.

The following table presents our results under our historical method and as adjusted to reflect the accounting change:

(In millions)	Historical Accounting Method	As Adjusted	Effect of Change
At December 31, 2010 or for the year ended			
Cost of services and sales (exclusive of depreciation and amortization shown separately below)	$ 51,379	$ 52,263	$ 884
Selling, general and administrative	31,221	33,065	1,844
Depreciation and amortization[1,2]	19,456	19,379	(77)
Income tax (benefit) expense[2]	(155)	(1,162)	(1,007)
Income from continuing operations	21,045	19,400	(1,645)
Net income attributable to AT&T[2]	21,508	19,864	(1,644)
Basic earnings per share attributable to AT&T	$ 3.64	$ 3.36	$ (0.28)
Diluted earnings per share attributable to AT&T	3.62	3.35	(0.27)
Property, plant and equipment—net[1]	$103,564	$103,196	$ (368)
Deferred income taxes	22,210	22,070	(140)
Retained earnings	50,859	31,792	(19,067)
Accumulated other comprehensive income	(16,128)	2,712	18,840
At December 31, 2009 or for the year ended			
Cost of services and sales (exclusive of depreciation and amortization shown separately below)	$ 50,517	$ 50,571	$ 54
Selling, general and administrative	30,943	31,427	484
Depreciation and amortization[1,2]	19,602	19,515	(87)
Income tax (benefit) expense[2]	6,146	6,091	(55)
Income from continuing operations	12,824	12,427	(397)
Net income attributable to AT&T[2]	12,535	12,138	(397)
Basic earnings per share attributable to AT&T	$ 2.12	$ 2.06	$ (0.06)
Diluted earnings per share attributable to AT&T	2.12	2.05	(0.07)
Property, plant and equipment—net[1]	$100,052	$ 99,519	$ (533)
Deferred income taxes	23,781	23,579	(202)
Retained earnings	39,366	21,944	(17,422)
Accumulated other comprehensive income	(14,412)	2,678	17,090
At December 31, 2008 or for the year ended			
Cost of services and sales (exclusive of depreciation and amortization shown separately below)	$ 49,878	$ 56,688	$ 6,810
Selling, general and administrative	30,752	48,772	18,020
Depreciation and amortization[1,2]	19,766	19,673	(93)
Income tax (benefit) expense[2]	7,034	(2,210)	(9,244)
Income (loss) from continuing operations	13,130	(2,362)	(15,492)
Net income (loss) attributable to AT&T[2]	12,867	(2,625)	(15,492)
Basic earnings (loss) per share attributable to AT&T	$ 2.17	$ (0.44)	$ (2.61)
Diluted earnings (loss) per share attributable to AT&T	2.16	(0.44)	(2.60)
Property, plant and equipment—net[1]	$ 99,037	$ 98,415	$ (622)
Deferred income taxes	19,171	18,935	(236)
Retained earnings	36,591	19,566	(17,025)
Accumulated other comprehensive income	(17,057)	(418)	16,639

[1] A portion of pension and postretirement costs are capitalized as a part of construction labor.
[2] The effect of the accounting change is also reflected in our consolidatd statements of cash flows, included in "Net income (loss)" and relevant adjustments to reconcile net income (loss) to net cash provided by operating activities.

Change in Accounting Principle: Business Combinations

1.67

ORACLE CORPORATION (MAY)

NOTES TO CONSOLIDATED FINANCIAL STATEMENTS

1. Organization and Significant Accounting Policies (in part)

Business Combinations

In fiscal 2010, we adopted ASC 805, Business Combinations, which revised the accounting guidance that we were required to apply for our acquisitions in comparison to prior fiscal years. The underlying principles are similar to the previous guidance and require that we recognize separately from goodwill the assets acquired and the liabilities assumed, generally at their acquisition date fair values. Goodwill as of the acquisition date is measured as the excess of consideration transferred and the net of the acquisition date fair values of the assets acquired and the liabilities assumed. While we use our best estimates and assumptions as a part of the purchase price allocation process to accurately value assets acquired and liabilities assumed at the acquisition date, our estimates are inherently uncertain and subject to refinement. As a result, during the measurement period, which may be up to one year from the acquisition date, we record adjustments to the assets acquired and liabilities assumed, with the corresponding offset to goodwill. Upon the conclusion of the measurement period or final determination of the values of assets acquired or liabilities assumed, whichever comes first, any subsequent adjustments are recorded to our consolidated statements of operations.

As a result of adopting the revised accounting guidance provided for by ASC 805 as of the beginning of fiscal 2010, certain of our policies differ when accounting for acquisitions in fiscal 2010 and prospective periods in comparison to the accounting for acquisitions in fiscal 2009 and prior periods, including:

- The fair value of in-process research and development is recorded as an indefinite-lived intangible asset until the underlying project is completed, at which time the intangible asset is amortized over its estimated useful life, or abandoned, at which time the intangible asset is expensed (prior to fiscal 2010, in-process research and development was expensed at the acquisition date);
- The direct transaction costs associated with the business combination are expensed as incurred (prior to fiscal 2010, direct transaction costs were included as a part of the purchase price);
- The costs to exit or restructure certain activities of an acquired company are accounted for separately from the business combination (prior to fiscal 2010, these restructuring and exist costs were included as a part of the assumed obligations in deriving the purchase price allocation); and

- Any changes in estimates associated with income tax valuation allowances or uncertain tax positions after the measurement period are generally recognized as income tax expense with application of this policy also applied prospectively to all of our business combinations regardless of the acquisition date (prior to fiscal 2010, any such changes were generally included as a part of the purchase price allocation indefinitely).

Costs to exit or restructure certain activities of an acquired company or our internal operations are accounted for as one-time termination and exit costs pursuant to ASC 420, *Exit or Disposal Cost Obligations*, and, as noted above, are accounted for separately from the business combination. A liability for a cost associated with an exit or disposal activity is recognized and measured at its fair value in our consolidated statement of operations in the period in which the liability is incurred. When estimating the fair value of facility restructuring activities, assumptions are applied regarding estimated sub-lease payments to be received, which can differ materially from actual results. This may require us to revise our initial estimates which may materially affect our results of operations and financial position in the period the revision is made.

For a given acquisition, we generally identify certain pre-acquisition contingencies as of the acquisition date and may extend our review and evaluation of these pre-acquisition contingencies throughout the measurement period (up to one year from the acquisition date) in order to obtain sufficient information to assess whether we include these contingencies as a part of the purchase price allocation and, if so, to determine the estimated amounts.

If we determine that a pre-acquisition contingency (non-income tax related) is probable in nature and estimable as of the acquisition date, we record our best estimate for such a contingency as a part of the preliminary purchase price allocation. We often continue to gather information for and evaluate our pre-acquisition contingencies throughout the measurement period and if we make changes to the amounts recorded or if we identify additional pre-acquisition contingencies during the measurement period, such amounts will be included in the purchase price allocation during the measurement period and, subsequently, in our results of operations.

In addition, uncertain tax positions and tax related valuation allowances assumed in connection with a business combination are initially estimated as of the acquisition date and we reevaluate these items quarterly with any adjustments to our preliminary estimates being recorded to goodwill provided that we are within the measurement period and we continue to collect information in order to determine their estimated values. Subsequent to the measurement period or our final determination of the tax allowance's or contingency's estimated value, changes to these uncertain tax positions and tax related valuation allowances will affect our provision for income taxes in our consolidated statement of operations and could have a material impact on our results of operations and financial position.

Change in Accounting Principle: Noncontrolling Interests

1.68

COLLECTIVE BRANDS, INC. (JAN)

NOTES TO CONSOLIDATED FINANCIAL STATEMENTS

Note 21—Impact of Recently Issued Accounting Standards (in part)

In December 2007, the FASB issued new guidance for the accounting for noncontrolling interests. The new guidance, which is now a part of ASC 810, "Consolidation," estab-lishes accounting and reporting standards for the noncontrolling interest in a subsidiary and for the deconsolidation of a subsidiary. The new guidance requires consolidated net earnings to be reported at amounts that include the amounts attributable to both the parent and the noncontrolling interest. It also requires disclosure, on the face of the Condensed Consolidated Statement of Earnings, of the amounts of consolidated net earnings attributable to the parent and to the noncontrolling interest. In addition, this new guidance establishes a single method of accounting for changes in a parent's ownership interest in a subsidiary that do not result in deconsolidation and requires that a parent recognize a gain or loss in net income when a subsidiary is deconsolidated. The Company adopted this new guidance on February 1, 2009, the impact of which was retrospectively applied and resulted in the noncontrolling interest being separately presented as a component of equity on the Consolidated Balance Sheets and Consolidated Statements of Equity and Comprehensive Income.

CONSOLIDATED STATEMENTS OF SHAREOWNERS' EQUITY AND COMPREHENSIVE INCOME (LOSS) (in part)

(Dollars in millions, shares in thousands)	Collective Brands, Inc. Shareowners'					Non-Controlling Interests	Total Equity	Comprehensive Income (Loss)
	Outstanding Common Stock		Additional Paid-In Capital	Retained Earnings	Accumulated Other Comprehensive Income (Loss)			
	Shares	Dollars						
Balance at February 3, 2007	64,996	$0.7	$ 0.7	$698.1	$ 0.6	$12.7	$712.8	
Net earnings	—	—	—	42.7	—	7.7	50.4	$ 50.4
Translation adjustments	—	—	—	—	14.3	0.1	14.4	14.4
Net change in fair value of derivative, net of taxes of $9.2 (Note 8)	—	—	—	—	(14.3)	—	(14.3)	(14.3)
Changes in unrecognized amounts of pension benefits, net of taxes of $4.5 (Note 10)	—	—	—	—	(6.5)	—	(6.5)	(6.5)
Issuances of common stock under stock plans	1,291	—	8.7	—	—	—	8.7	
Purchases of common stock	(2,438)	—	(26.9)	(21.5)	—	—	(48.4)	
Amortization of unearned nonvested shares	—	—	4.9	—	—	—	4.9	
Income tax benefit of stock option exercise	—	—	2.6	—	—	—	2.6	
Stock option expense	—	—	10.0	—	—	—	10.0	
Restricted stock cancellation	(96)	—	—	—	—	—	—	
Adoption of uncertain tax positions accounting guidance (Note 13)	—	—	—	(11.2)	—	(0.9)	(12.1)	
Distributions to noncontrolling interests	—	—	—	—	—	(2.4)	(2.4)	
Comprehensive income								44.0
Comprehensive income attributable to noncontrolling interests								(7.8)
Comprehensive income attributable to Collective Brands, Inc.								36.2
Balance at February 2, 2008	63,753	0.7	—	708.1	(5.9)	17.2	720.1	
Net (loss) earnings	—	—	—	(68.7)	—	8.7	(60.0)	(60.0)
Translation adjustments	—	—	—	—	(18.9)	(0.7)	(19.6)	(19.6)
Net change in fair value of derivative, net of taxes of $0.8 (Note 8)	—	—	—	—	1.2	—	1.2	1.2
Changes in unrecognized amounts of pension benefits, net of taxes of $7.1 (Note 10)	—	—	—	—	(12.0)	—	(12.0)	(12.0)
Issuances of common stock under stock plans	433	—	1.2	—	—	—	1.2	
Purchases of common stock	(153)	—	(1.9)	—	—	—	(1.9)	
Amortization of unearned nonvested shares	—	—	11.1	—	—	—	11.1	
Stock option expense	—	—	9.5	—	—	—	9.5	
Restricted stock cancellation	(308)	—	(2.1)	—	—	—	(2.1)	
Contributions from noncontrolling interests	—	—	—	—	—	4.6	4.6	
Distributions to noncontrolling interests	—	—	—	—	—	(6.1)	(6.1)	
Comprehensive loss								(90.4)
Comprehensive income attributable to noncontrolling interests								(8.0)
Comprehensive loss attributable to Collective Brands, Inc.								(98.4)
Balance at January 31, 2009	63,725	0.7	17.8	639.4	(35.6)	23.7	646.0	

(continued)

(Dollars in millions, shares in thousands)	Outstanding Common Stock		Additional Paid-In Capital	Retained Earnings	Accumulated Other Comprehensive Income (Loss)	Non-Controlling Interests	Total Equity	Comprehensive Income (Loss)
	Shares	Dollars						
Balance at January 31, 2009	63,725	$0.7	$17.8	$639.4	$(35.6)	$23.7	$646.0	
Net earnings	—	—	—	82.7	—	5.6	88.3	$88.3
Translation adjustments	—	—	—	—	8.0	0.1	8.1	8.1
Net change in fair value of derivatives, net of taxes of $2.2 (Note 8)	—	—	—	—	3.9	—	3.9	3.9
Changes in unrecognized amounts of pension benefits, net of taxes of $0.3 (Note 10)	—	—	—	—	1.4	—	1.4	1.4
Issuances of common stock under stock plans	882	—	8.2	—	—	—	8.2	
Purchases of common stock	(389)	—	(7.6)	—	—	—	(7.6)	
Amortization of unearned nonvested shares	—	—	5.4	—	—	—	5.4	
Stock option expense	—	—	10.9	—	—	—	10.9	
Restricted stock cancellation	(62)	—	—	—	—	—	—	
Contributions from noncontrolling interests	—	—	—	—	—	5.5	5.5	
Distributions to noncontrolling interests	—	—	—	—	—	(6.2)	(6.2)	
Comprehensive income								101.7
Comprehensive income attributable to noncontrolling interests								(5.7)
Comprehensive income attributable to Collective Brands, Inc.								$96.0
Balance at January 30, 2010	64,156	$0.7	$34.7	$722.1	$(22.3)	$28.7	$763.9	

Collective Brands, Inc. Shareowners'

Change in Accounting Principle: Convertible Debt

1.69

XILINX, INC. (MAR)

NOTES TO CONSOLIDATED FINANCIAL STATEMENTS

Note 2. Summary of Significant Accounting Policies and Concentrations of Risk (in part)

Adoption of New Accounting Standard for Convertible Debentures

Beginning in fiscal 2010, the Company retrospectively adopted the authoritative guidance for convertible debentures issued by the Financial Accounting Standards Board (FASB), which affected the Company's 3.125% junior subordinated convertible debentures (debentures). The guidance specifies that issuers of convertible debt instruments should separately account for the liability (debt) and equity (conversion option) components of such instruments in a manner that reflects the borrowing rate for a similar non-convertible debt. The liability component is recognized at fair value, based on the fair value of a similar instrument that does not have a conversion feature at issuance. The equity component is based on the excess of the principal amount of the debentures over the fair value of the liability component, after adjusting for an allocation of debt issuance costs and the deferred tax impact. Such excess represents the estimated fair value of the conversion feature and is recorded as additional paid-in capital. The Company's debentures were issued at a coupon rate of 3.125%, which was below the rate of a similar instrument that did not have a conversion feature at that time (7.20%). Therefore, the valuation of the debt component resulted in a discounted carrying value of the debentures compared to the principal. This debt discount is amortized as additional non-cash interest expense over the expected life of the debt, which is also the stated life of the debt. The consolidated financial statements have been retrospectively adjusted for all periods presented in accordance with the authoritative guidance for convertible debentures.

The effect of the retrospective adoption on individual line items on the Company's consolidated balance sheet was as follows:

(In thousands)	March 28, 2009		
	As Previously Reported	Adjustments[1]	As Adjusted
Other assets	$216,905	$ (13,614)[2]	$ 203,291
Convertible debentures	690,125	(338,015)	352,110
Deferred tax liabilities	82,648	113,541	196,189
Additional paid-in capital	856,232	229,513	1,085,745
Retained earnings	$897,771	$ (18,653)	$ 879,118

[1] The amounts represent the net effect of the adoption of the accounting standard for convertible debentures in the first quarter of fiscal 2010 and the repurchase of a portion of the debentures.

[2] Other assets as of March 28, 2009 decreased by $13.6 million due to a decrease to long-term deferred tax assets of $7.0 million and a retroactive adjustment of debt issuance costs from other assets to additional paid-in capital of $6.6 million upon the adoption of the accounting standard for convertible debentures. The reclassification resulted in a cumulative decrease in amortization of debt issuance costs of $488 thousand as of March 28, 2009.

The effect of the retrospective adoption on individual line items on the Company's consolidated statements of income for the periods indicated was as follows:

	Year Ended March 28, 2009			Year Ended March 29, 2008		
(In thousands, except per share amounts)	As Previously Reported	Adjustments	As Adjusted	As Previously Reported	Adjustments	As Adjusted
Gain on early extinguishment of convertible debentures	$110,606	$(35,571)[1]	$ 75,035	$ —	$ —	$ —
Interest and other income, net	12,189	(4,587)[2]	7,602	52,750	(4,605)[2]	48,145
Provision for income taxes	122,544	(26,237)	96,307	100,047	127	100,174
Net income	375,640	(13,921)	361,719	374,047	(4,732)	369,315
Net income per common share—basic	$ 1.36	$ (0.05)	$ 1.31	$ 1.27	$ (0.02)	$ 1.25
Net income per common share—diluted	$ 1.36	$ (0.05)	$ 1.31	$ 1.25	$ (0.01)	$ 1.24

[1] Gain on early extinguishment of convertible debentures decreased due to the allocation of the original gain to additional paid-in capital.

[2] Interest and other income (expense), net decreased due to additional interest expense recorded retroactively, partially offset by a reduction of amortization of debt issuance costs.

For fiscal 2010, the retrospective adoption increased interest expense by $3.7 million and decreased provision for income taxes by $1.4 million, and thereby reducing net income by $2.3 million (or $0.01 of net income per basic and diluted common share).

The retrospective adoption does not change the Company's net cash provided by (used in) operating, investing or financing activities for any periods.

Note 14. Convertible Debentures and Revolving Credit Facility (in part)

3.125% Junior Subordinated Convertible Debentures

In March 2007, the Company issued $1.00 billion principal amount of 3.125% junior convertible debentures due March 15, 2037, to an initial purchaser in a private offering. The debentures are subordinated in right of payment to the Company's existing and future senior debt and to the other liabilities of the Company's subsidiaries. The debentures were initially convertible, subject to certain conditions, into shares of Xilinx common stock at a conversion rate of 32.0760 shares of common stock per $1 thousand principal amount of debentures, representing an initial effective conversion price of approximately $31.18 per share of common stock. The conversion rate is subject to adjustment for certain events as outlined in the indenture governing the debentures but will not be adjusted for accrued interest. Due to the accumulation of cash dividend distributions to common stockholders, the conversion rate for the debentures was adjusted to 32.8092 shares of common stock per $1 thousand principal amount of debentures, representing an adjusted conversion price of $30.48 per share at the end of fiscal 2010.

The Company received net proceeds from issuance of the debentures of $980.0 million after deduction of issuance costs of $20.0 million. During fiscal 2009, the Company paid $193.2 million in cash to repurchase $310.4 million (principal amount) of its debentures, resulting in approximately $689.6 million of principal amount of debt outstanding as of April 3, 2010. The debt issuance costs, as adjusted for the retrospective adoption of the authoritative guidance for convertible debentures issued by the FASB, are recorded in long-term other assets and are being amortized to interest expense over 30 years. Cash interest of 3.125% (per annum) is payable semiannually in arrears on March 15 and September 15, beginning on September 15, 2007. However,

the Company recognizes an effective interest rate of 7.20% on the carrying value of the debentures. The effective rate is based on the interest rate for a similar instrument that does not have a conversion feature. The debentures also have a contingent interest component that may require the Company to pay interest based on certain thresholds beginning with the semi-annual interest period commencing on March 15, 2014 (the maximum amount of contingent interest that will accrue is 0.50% per year) and upon the occurrence of certain events, as outlined in the indenture governing the debentures.

Beginning in fiscal 2010, the Company retrospectively adopted the authoritative guidance for convertible debentures issued by the FASB. The authoritative guidance specifies that issuers of convertible debt instruments should separately account for the liability (debt) and equity (conversion option) components of such instruments in a manner that reflects the borrowing rate for a similar non-convertible debt. See "Adoption of New Accounting Standard for Convertible Debentures" included in "Note 1. Basis of Presentation" for further information relating to the adoption.

The carrying values of the liability and equity components of the debentures, after the retrospective adoption, are reflected in the Company's consolidated balance sheets as follows:

(In thousands)	April 3, 2010	Mar. 28, 2009
Liability component:		
Principal amount of convertible debentures	$ 689,635	$ 689,635
Unamortized discount of liability component	(334,123)	(338,015)
Unamortized discount of embedded derivative from date of issuance	(1,562)	(1,620)
Carrying value of liability component	353,950	350,000
Carrying value of embedded derivative component	848	2,110
Convertible debentures—net carrying value	$ 354,798	$ 352,110
Equity component—net carrying value	$ 229,513	$ 229,513

The remaining debt discount is being amortized as additional non-cash interest expense over the expected remaining life of the debentures using the effective interest rate of 7.20%. As of April 3, 2010, the remaining term of the debentures is 27 years. Interest expense related to the debentures was included in interest and other income (expense), net on the consolidated statements of income and was recognized as follows:

(In thousands)	2010	2009*	2008*
Contractual coupon interest	$21,816	$28,293	$31,250
Amortization of debt issuance costs	223	379	383
Amortization of embedded derivative	58	73	84
Amortization of debt discount	3,892	4,789	4,889
Total interest expense related to the debentures	$25,989	$33,534	$36,606

* As adjusted for the retrospective adoption of the accounting standard for convertible debentures in the first quarter of fiscal 2010 (see Note 2).

1.70

ARCHER DANIELS MIDLAND COMPANY (JUN)

NOTES TO CONSOLIDATED FINANCIAL STATEMENTS

Note 1. Summary of Significant Accounting Policies (in part)

New Accounting Standards (in part)

On July 1, 2009, the Company adopted the amended guidance in ASC Topic 470-20, *Debt with Conversion and Other Options*, which specifies that issuers of convertible debt instruments that may settle in cash upon conversion must bifurcate the proceeds from the debt issuance between the debt and equity components in a manner that reflects the entity's nonconvertible debt borrowing rate when interest cost is recognized in subsequent periods. The equity component reflects the fair value of the conversion feature of the notes at adoption. The amended guidance was retrospectively applied to the Company's $1.15 billion, 0.875% Convertible Series Notes for all periods presented as further described in Note 8.

Note 8. Debt and Financing Arrangements (in part)

In February 2007, the Company issued $1.15 billion principal amount of convertible senior notes due in 2014 (the Notes) in a private placement. The Notes were issued at par and bear interest at a rate of 0.875% per year, payable semi-annually. The Notes are convertible based on a conversion rate of 22.8423 shares per $1,000 principal amount of Notes (which is equal to a conversion price of approximately $43.78 per share). The Notes may be converted, subject to adjustment, only under the following circumstances: 1) during any calendar quarter beginning after March 31, 2007, if the closing price of the Company's common stock for at least 20 trading days in the 30 consecutive trading days ending on the last trading day of the immediately preceding quarter is more than 140% of the applicable conversion price per share, which is $1,000 divided by the then applicable conversion

rate, 2) during the five consecutive business day period immediately after any five consecutive trading day period (the note measurement period) in which the average of the trading price per $1,000 principal amount of Notes was equal to or less than 98% of the average of the product of the closing price of the Company's common stock and the conversion rate at each date during the note measurement period, 3) if the Company makes specified distributions to its common stockholders or specified corporate transactions occur, or 4) at any time on or after January 15, 2014, through the business day preceding the maturity date. Upon conversion, a holder would receive an amount in cash equal to the lesser of 1) $1,000 and 2) the conversion value, as defined. If the conversion value exceeds $1,000, the Company will deliver, at the Company's election, cash or common stock or a combination of cash and common stock for the conversion value in excess of $1,000. If the Notes are converted in connection with a change in control, as defined, the Company may be required to provide a make-whole premium in the form of an increase in the conversion rate, subject to a stated maximum amount. In addition, in the event of a change in control, the holders may require the Company to purchase all or a portion of their Notes at a purchase price equal to 100% of the principal amount of the Notes, plus accrued and unpaid interest, if any. In accordance with ASC Topic 470-20, the Company recognized the Notes proceeds received in 2007 as long-term debt of $853 million and equity of $297 million. The discount is being amortized over the life of the Notes using the effective interest method. Discount amortization expense of $40 million, $39 million, and $37 million for 2010, 2009, and 2008, respectively, were included in interest expense related to the Notes.

1.71

GRIFFON CORPORATION (SEP)

NOTES TO CONSOLIDATED FINANCIAL STATEMENTS

Note 3—Adoption of New Accounting Pronouncements (in part)

Retrospective Adjustment for Adoption of Convertible Debt Guidance (in part; in thousands)

In May 2008, the FASB issued new guidance to clarify that the liability and equity components of convertible debt instruments that may be settled in cash upon conversion (including partial cash settlement) must be separately accounted for in a manner that will reflect the entity's nonconvertible debt borrowing rate when interest cost is recognized. This guidance, which is applicable to Griffon's 4% convertible subordinated notes due 2023 issued in 2003 (the "2023 Notes") and 4% convertible subordinated notes due 2017 issued in December 2009 (the "2017 Notes"), became effective for Griffon as of October 1, 2009 and is implemented retrospectively, as required, for the 2023 Notes.

At September 30, 2010, the 2023 Notes had an outstanding balance of $532, with no unamortized discount or capital in excess of par value component balance as substantially all of these notes were put to Griffon in July 2010. At September 30, 2009, the 2023 Notes had an outstanding balance of $79,380, an unamortized discount balance of $2,820, a net carrying value of $76,560 and a capital in excess of par value component balance, net of tax, of $18,094. The stock price was below the conversion price for all periods presented. Griffon used 8.5% as the nonconvertible debt borrowing rate to discount the 2023 Notes. For more information, see the Long-Term Debt footnote.

For the 2023 Notes, the effective interest rate and interest expense was as follows:

(In thousands)	Years Ended September 30		
	2010	2009	2008
Effective interest rate	9.4%	9.0%	8.9%
Interest expense related to the coupon	$1,998	$3,472	$ 5,200
Amortization of the discount	2,105	3,576	4,720
Amortization of deferred issuance costs	217	530	601
Total interest expense on the 2023 Notes	$4,320	$7,578	$10,521

The cumulative effect of the adjustments prior to September 30, 2009 was recognized in the September 30, 2009 balance sheet as follows:

(in thousands)	As of September 30, 2009	
	Reported	As Adjusted
Other Assets	$ 30,648	$ 29,132
All other assets	1,114,759	1,114,759
Total Assets	$1,145,407	$1,143,891
Notes payable & current portion of LT debt	$ 81,410	$ 78,590
Long-term debt	98,394	98,394
All other liabilities	278,700	278,700
Total liabilities	458,504	455,684
Capital in excess of par value	420,749	438,843
Retained earnings	438,782	421,992
All other shareholders' equity	(172,628)	(172,628)
Total Shareholders' Equity	686,903	688,207
Total Liabilities and shareholders' equity	$1,145,407	$1,143,891

The prior year statements of operations have been adjusted as follows:

(In thousands)	September 30, 2009		September 30, 2008	
	Reported	As Adjusted	Reported	As Adjusted
Income from operations	$25,147	$25,147	$ 12,044	$ 12,044
Other income (expense)				
Interest expense	(9,562)	(13,091)	(12,345)	(16,909)
Interest income	1,539	1,539	1,970	1,970
Gain from debt extinguishment, net	7,360	4,488	—	—
Other, net	1,522	1,522	2,713	2,713
Total other income (expense)	859	(5,542)	(7,662)	(12,226)
Income (loss) before taxes and discontinued operations	26,006	19,605	4,382	(182)
Provision for income taxes	4,005	1,687	4,294	2,651
Income (loss) from continuing operations	22,001	17,918	88	(2,833)
Income (loss) from discontinued operations	790	790	(40,591)	(40,591)
Net income (loss)	$22,791	$18,708	$(40,503)	$(43,424)
Basic earnings (loss) per common share:				
Income (loss) from continuing operations	$ 0.37	$ 0.31	$ 0.00	$ (0.09)
Income (loss) from discontinued operations	0.01	0.01	(1.24)	(1.24)
Net income (loss)	0.39	0.32	(1.24)	(1.33)
Weighted average shares outstanding	58,699	58,699	32,667	32,667
Diluted earnings (loss) per common share:				
Income (loss) from continuing operations	$ 0.37	$ 0.30	$ 0.00	$ (0.09)
Income (loss) from discontinued operations	0.01	0.01	(1.24)	(1.24)
Net income (loss)	0.39	0.32	(1.24)	(1.32)
Weighted average shares outstanding	59,002	59,002	32,836	32,836

Change in Accounting Principle: Earnings Per Share

1.72

BROWN SHOE COMPANY, INC. (JAN)

NOTES TO CONSOLIDATED FINANCIAL STATEMENTS

1. Summary of Significant Accounting Policies (in part)

Earnings (Loss) Per Common Share Attributable to Brown Shoe Company, Inc. Shareholders

At the beginning of 2009, the Company was required to begin using the two-class method to calculate basic and diluted earnings (loss) per common share attributable to Brown Shoe Company, Inc. shareholders as unvested restricted stock awards are considered participating units because they entitle holders to non-forfeitable rights to dividends or dividend equivalents during the vesting term. Under the two-class method, basic earnings (loss) per common share attributable to Brown Shoe Company, Inc. shareholders is computed by dividing the net earnings (loss) attributable to Brown Shoe Company, Inc. after allocation of earnings to participating securities by the weighted-average number of common shares outstanding during the year. Diluted earnings (loss) per common share attributable to Brown Shoe Company, Inc. shareholders is computed by dividing the net earnings (loss) attributable to Brown Shoe Company, Inc. after allocation of earnings to participating securities by the weighted-average number of common shares and potential dilutive securities outstanding during the year. Potential dilutive securities consist of outstanding stock options. See Note 2 to the consoli-

dated financial statements for additional information related to the calculation of earnings (loss) per common share attributable to Brown Shoe Company, Inc. shareholders.

Impact of New Accounting Pronouncements (in part)

In June 2008, the FASB issued guidance which addresses whether instruments granted in share-based payment awards are participating securities prior to vesting and, therefore, must be included in the earnings allocation in calculating earnings per share under the two-class method. Under this pronouncement, unvested share-based payment awards that contain non-forfeitable rights to dividends or dividend equivalents should be treated as participating securities in computing earnings per share. However, in periods of net loss, no effect is given to the Company's participating securities since they do not contractually participate in the losses of the Company. The guidance is effective for fiscal years beginning after December 15, 2008, and for interim periods within those years, and shall be applied retrospectively to all prior periods. Accordingly, due to the adoption of the standard at the beginning of 2009, restricted stock awards are now considered participating units in the calculation of basic and diluted earnings (loss) per common share attributable to Brown Shoe Company, Inc. shareholders. See Note 2 to the consolidated financial statements for the calculation of basic and diluted earnings (loss) per common share attributable to Brown Shoe Company, Inc. shareholders.

2. Earnings (Loss) Per Share

As discussed in Note 1, the Company began using the two-class method to compute basic and diluted earnings (loss) per common share attributable to Brown Shoe Company, Inc. shareholders at the beginning of 2009. In periods of net loss, no effect is given to the Company's participating securities since they do not contractually participate in the losses of the Company. The following table sets forth the computation of basic and diluted earnings (loss) per common share attributable to Brown Shoe Company, Inc. shareholders:

(In thousands, except per share amounts)	2009	2008	2007
Numerator			
Net earnings (loss) attributable to Brown Shoe Company, Inc. before allocation of earnings to participating securities	$ 9,500	$(133,238)	$60,427
Less: Earnings allocated to participating securities	(361)	—	(670)
Net earnings (loss) attributable to Brown Shoe Company, Inc. after allocation of earnings to participating securities	$ 9,139	$(133,238)	$59,757
Denominator			
Denominator for basic earnings (loss) per common share attributable to Brown Shoe Company, Inc. shareholders	41,585	41,525	43,223
Dilutive effect of share-based awards	64	—	693
Denominator for diluted earnings (loss) per common share attributable to Brown Shoe Company, Inc. shareholders	41,649	41,525	43,916
Basic earnings (loss) per common share attributable to Brown Shoe Company, Inc. shareholders	$ 0.22	$ (3.21)	$ 1.38
Diluted earnings (loss) per common share attributable to Brown Shoe Company, Inc. shareholders	$ 0.22	$ (3.21)	$ 1.36

Options to purchase 1,679,335 and 194,243 shares of common stock in 2009 and 2007, respectively, were not included in the denominator for diluted earnings per common share attributable to Brown Shoe Company, Inc. shareholders because the effect would be antidilutive. Due to the Company's net loss attributable to Brown Shoe Company, Inc. in 2008, the denominator for diluted loss per common share attributable to Brown Shoe Company, Inc. shareholders is the same as the denominator for basic loss per common share attributable to Brown Shoe Company, Inc. shareholders.

Change in Accounting Principle: Inventory

1.73

SNYDER'S-LANCE, INC. (DEC)

NOTES TO CONSOLIDATED FINANCIAL STATEMENTS

Note 2. Change in Accounting Method

Prior to December 6, 2010, inventories were valued using both the LIFO and the FIFO methods. Effective December 6, 2010, we changed our method of accounting for the finished goods, work-in-progress and raw material inventories previously on the LIFO method to the FIFO method. We believe the change is preferable as the FIFO method better reflects the current value of inventory on the Consolidated Balance Sheets and provides better matching of manufacturing costs and revenues. The change also conforms all of our raw materials, work-in-process and finished goods to a single costing method (FIFO).

We applied this change in method of inventory costing by retrospectively adjusting the prior years' financial statements.

The effect of the change on the Consolidated Statements of Income for the years ended December 26, 2009 and December 27, 2008, was as follows:

	Increase/(Decrease)	
(In thousands, except share data)	2009	2008
Cost of sales	$ 1,128	$(1,715)
Income before interest and income taxes	(1,128)	1,715
Income tax expense	(362)	593
Net income	(766)	1,122
Basic earnings per share	(0.02)	0.03
Diluted earnings per share	(0.02)	0.03

The effect on the Consolidated Balance Sheet at December 26, 2009, was as follows:

(In thousands)	Increase/(Decrease)
Inventories	$ 5,836
Deferred income tax asset	(2,013)
Retained earnings	3,823

Had we not changed our policy for accounting for inventory, pre-tax income for both the fourth quarter and the year ended January 1, 2011 would have been $0.2 million lower ($0.1 million reduction after-tax, with no effect on earnings per basic

or diluted share). As a result of the accounting change, retained earnings as of December 29, 2007, increased from $163.4 million using the LIFO method to $166.8 million using the FIFO method. There was no impact to net cash provided by operating activities as a result of this change in accounting policy.

Note 6. Inventories

Both the LIFO and FIFO methods were previously used to value inventory. Effective December 6, 2010, we changed the accounting policy for those inventories previously valued using LIFO, to FIFO. Refer to Note 2 for more information.

Inventories at January 1, 2011 and December 26, 2009 consisted of the following:

(In thousands)	2010	2009[*]
Finished goods	$55,658	$33,060
Raw materials	17,015	11,732
Supplies, etc.	24,263	19,081
Total inventories	$96,936	$63,873

[*] 2009 amounts have been reclassified to reflect the change in accounting for inventory, see Note 2.

The increase in inventory during 2010 was primarily due to the Merger.

Change in Accounting Principle: Revenue Recognition

1.74

LOCKHEED MARTIN CORPORATION (DEC)

NOTES TO CONSOLIDATED FINANCIAL STATEMENTS

Note 1—Significant Accounting Policies (in part)

Sales and earnings—We record net sales and estimated profits on a percentage-of-completion (POC) basis for cost-reimbursable and fixed-price design, development, and production (DD&P) contracts. Revenue is recorded on time-and-materials contracts as the work is performed based on agreed-upon hourly rates and allowable costs. The POC method for DD&P contracts depends on the nature of the products provided under the contract. For example, for contracts that require us to perform a significant level of development effort in comparison to the total value of the contract and/or to deliver less than substantial quantities of similar items, sales are recorded using the cost-to-cost method to measure progress toward completion. Under the cost-to-cost method of accounting, we recognize sales and an estimated profit as costs are incurred based on the proportion that the incurred costs bear to total estimated costs. For contracts that require us to provide a substantial number of similar items without a significant level of development effort, we record sales and profit on a percentage-of-completion basis using units-of-delivery as the basis to measure progress toward completing the contract.

When adjustments in estimated contract revenues or estimated costs at completion are required on DD&P contracts, any changes from prior estimates are recognized in the current period for the inception-to-date effect of the changes. When estimates of total costs to be incurred on a contract exceed total estimates of revenue to be earned, a provision for the entire loss on the contract is recorded in the period in which the loss is determined.

Award fees and incentives, as well as penalties related to contract performance, are considered in estimating sales and profit rates on DD&P contracts. We consider estimates of award fees in estimating sales and profit rates based on past experience and anticipated performance. We record incentives or penalties when there is sufficient information to assess anticipated contract performance. We do not recognize incentive provisions that increase or decrease earnings based solely on a single significant event until the event occurs. We only include amounts representing contract change orders, claims, or other items in contract value when they can be reliably estimated and realization is probable.

For cost-reimbursable contracts for services that provide for award and incentive fees, we record net sales as services are performed, except for the award and incentive fees. Award and incentive fees are recorded when they are fixed or determinable, generally at the date the amount is communicated to us by the customer. This approach results in the recognition of such fees at contractual intervals (typically every six months) throughout the contract and is dependent on the customer's processes for notification of awards and issuance of formal notifications. Under a fixed-price service contract, we get paid a predetermined fixed amount for a specified scope of work and generally have full responsibility for the costs associated with the contract and the resulting profit or loss. We record net sales under fixed-price service contracts on a straight-line basis over the period of contract performance, unless evidence suggests that net sales are earned or the obligations are fulfilled in a different pattern. Costs for all service contracts are expensed as incurred.

Change in Accounting Principle—Effective January 1, 2011, we changed our methodology for recognizing net sales for service contracts with the U.S. Government. We will recognize sales on those contracts using the POC method similar to our DD&P contracts as described above. As such, we expect that approximately 95% of our consolidated net sales will be recognized using the POC method. We believe the POC method is preferable, as consistent revenue recognition application across all contracts with the U.S. Government better reflects the underlying economics of those contracts and aligns our financial reporting with others in our industry. Beginning with our first quarter 2011 financial statements, all prior periods presented will be retrospectively adjusted to apply the new method of accounting. The effect of this change is expected to be less than one percent of net sales and segment operating profit in 2011, and was not material to prior periods.

1.75

CISCO SYSTEMS, INC. (JUL)

NOTES TO CONSOLIDATED FINANCIAL STATEMENTS

2. Summary of Significant Accounting Policies (in part)

(n) Revenue Recognition—The Company recognizes revenue when persuasive evidence of an arrangement exists, delivery has occurred, the fee is fixed or determinable, and collectibility is reasonably assured. In instances where final acceptance of the product, system, or solution is specified by the customer, revenue is deferred until all acceptance criteria have been met. For hosting arrangements, the Company recognizes revenue based on customer utilization. Technical support services revenue is deferred and recognized ratably over the period during which the services are to be performed, which is typically from one to three years. Advanced services revenue is recognized upon delivery or completion of performance.

The Company uses distributors that stock inventory and typically sell to systems integrators, service providers, and other resellers. In addition, certain products are sold through retail partners. The Company refers to this as its two-tier system of sales to the end customer. Revenue from distributors and retail partners generally is recognized based on a sell-through method using information provided by them. Distributors and retail partners participate in various cooperative marketing and other programs, and the Company maintains estimated accruals and allowances for these programs. The Company accrues for warranty costs, sales returns, and other allowances based on its historical experience. Shipping and handling fees billed to customers are included in net sales, with the associated costs included in cost of sales.

In October 2009, the FASB amended the accounting standards for revenue recognition to remove from the scope of industry-specific software revenue recognition guidance tangible products containing software components and nonsoftware components that function together to deliver the product's essential functionality. In October 2009, the FASB also amended the accounting standards for multiple-deliverable revenue arrangements to:

(i) Provide updated guidance on whether multiple deliverables exist, how the deliverables in an arrangement should be separated, and how consideration should be allocated;

(ii) Require an entity to allocate revenue in an arrangement using estimated selling prices (ESP) of deliverables if a vendor does not have vendor-specific objective evidence of selling price (VSOE) or third-party evidence of selling price (TPE); and

(iii) Eliminate the use of the residual method and require an entity to allocate revenue using the relative selling price method.

The Company elected to early adopt this accounting guidance at the beginning of its first quarter of fiscal 2010 on a prospective basis for applicable transactions originating or materially modified after July 25, 2009. This guidance does not generally change the units of accounting for the Company's revenue transactions. Most products and services qualify as separate units of accounting and the revenue is recognized when the applicable revenue recognition criteria are met. The Company's arrangements generally do not include any provisions for cancellation, termination, or refunds that would significantly impact recognized revenue.

Many of the Company's products have both software and nonsoftware components that function together to deliver the products' essential functionality. The Company's product offerings fall into the following categories: routing, switching, advanced technologies, and other products, the last of which includes emerging technologies items. The Company also provides technical support and advanced services. The Company has a broad customer base that encompasses virtually all types of public and private entities, including enterprise businesses, service providers, commercial customers, and consumers. The Company and its salesforce are not organized by product divisions and the Company's products and services can be sold standalone or together in various combinations across the Company's geographic segments or customer markets. For example, service provider arrangements are typically larger in scale with longer deployment schedules and involve the delivery of a variety of product technologies, including high-end routing, video and network management software, among others, along with technical support and advanced services. The Company's enterprise and commercial arrangements are typically unique for each customer and smaller in scale and may include network infrastructure products such as routers and switches or collaboration technologies such as unified communications and Cisco TelePresence systems products along with technical support services. Consumer products, including Linksys wireless routers and Pure Digital video recorders, are sold in standalone arrangements directly to distributors and retailers without support, as customers generally only require repair or replacement of defective products or parts under warranty.

The Company enters into revenue arrangements that may consist of multiple deliverables of its product and service offerings due to the needs of its customers. For example, a customer may purchase routing products along with a contract for technical support services. This arrangement would consist of multiple elements, with the products delivered in one reporting period and the technical support services delivered across multiple reporting periods. Another customer may purchase networking products along with advanced service offerings, in which all the elements are delivered within the same reporting period. In addition, distributors and retail partners purchase products or technical support services on a standalone basis for resale to an end user or for purposes of stocking certain products, and these transactions would not result in a multiple element arrangement. For transactions entered into prior to the first quarter of fiscal 2010, the Company primarily recognized revenue based on software revenue recognition guidance. For the vast majority of the Company's arrangements involving multiple deliverables, such as sales of products with services, the entire fee from the arrangement was allocated to each respective element based on its relative selling price, using VSOE. In the limited circumstances when the Company was not able to determine VSOE for all of the deliverables of the arrangement, but was able to obtain VSOE for any undelivered elements, revenue was allocated using the residual method. Under the residual method, the amount of revenue allocated to delivered elements equaled the total arrangement consideration less the aggregate selling price of any undelivered elements, and no revenue was recognized until all elements without VSOE had been delivered. If VSOE of any undelivered items did not exist, revenue from the entire arrangement was initially deferred and recognized at the earlier of (i) delivery of those elements for which VSOE did not exist or (ii) when VSOE could be established. However, in limited cases where technical support services were the only undelivered element without VSOE, the entire arrangement fee was recognized ratably as a single unit of accounting over the technical services contractual period. The residual and ratable revenue recognition methods were generally used in a limited number of arrangements containing advanced and emerging technologies, such as Cisco TelePresence systems products. Several of these technologies are sold as solution offerings, whereas products or services are not sold on a standalone basis.

In many instances, products are sold separately in standalone arrangements as customers may support the products themselves or purchase support on a time-and-materials basis. Advanced services are sometimes sold in standalone engagements such as general consulting, network management, or security advisory projects and technical support services are sold separately through renewals of annual contracts. As a result, for substantially all of the arrangements with multiple deliverables pertaining to routing and switching products and related services, as well as most arrangements containing advanced and emerging technologies, the Company has used and intends to continue using VSOE to allocate the selling price to each deliverable. Consistent with its methodology under previous accounting guidance, the Company determines VSOE based on its normal pricing and discounting practices for the specific product or service when sold separately. In determining VSOE, the Company requires that a substantial majority of the selling prices for a product or service fall within a reasonably narrow pricing range, generally evidenced by approximately 80% of such historical standalone transactions falling within plus or minus 15% of the median rates. In addition, the Company considers the geographies in which the products or services are sold, major product and service groups and customer classifications, and other environmental or marketing variables in determining VSOE.

In certain limited instances, the Company is not able to establish VSOE for all deliverables in an arrangement with multiple elements. This may be due to the Company infrequently selling each element separately, not pricing products within a narrow range, or only having a limited sales history, such as in the case of certain advanced and emerging technologies. When VSOE cannot be established, the Company attempts to establish selling price of each element based on TPE. TPE is determined based on competitor prices for similar deliverables when sold separately. Generally, the Company's go-to-market strategy typically differs from that of its peers and its offerings contain a significant level of customization and differentiation such that the comparable pricing of products with similar functionality cannot be obtained. Furthermore, the Company is unable to reliably determine what similar competitor products' selling prices are on a standalone basis. Therefore, the Company is typically not able to determine TPE.

When the Company is unable to establish selling price using VSOE or TPE, the Company uses ESP in its allocation of arrangement consideration. The objective of ESP is to determine the price at which the Company would transact a sale if the product or service were sold on a standalone basis. ESP is generally used for new or highly customized offerings and solutions or offerings not priced within a narrow range, and it applies to a small proportion of the Company's arrangements with multiple deliverables.

The Company determines ESP for a product or service by considering multiple factors, including, but not limited to, geographies, market conditions, competitive landscape, internal costs, gross margin objectives, and pricing practices. The determination of ESP is made through consultation with and formal approval by the Company's management, taking into consideration the go-to-market strategy.

The Company regularly reviews VSOE, TPE, and ESP and maintains internal controls over the establishment and updates of these estimates. There were no material impacts during the fiscal year nor does the Company currently expect a material impact in the near term from changes in VSOE, TPE, or ESP.

Net sales as reported for the fiscal year ended July 31, 2010, and the Company's estimate of the pro forma net sales that would have been reported if the transaction entered into or materially modified during fiscal 2010 were subject to previous accounting guidance, are shown in the following table (in millions):

| | Fiscal Year Ended July 31, 2010 | |
	As Reported	Pro Forma Basis as if the Previous Accounting Guidance Were in Effect
Net sales	$40,040	$39,802

The estimated impact to net sales of the accounting standard was primarily to net product sales.

The new accounting standards for revenue recognition if applied in the same manner to the year ended July 25, 2009 would not have had a material impact on net sales for that fiscal year. In terms of the timing and pattern of revenue recognition, the new accounting guidance for revenue recognition is not expected to have a significant effect on net sales in periods after the initial adoption when applied to multiple-element arrangements based on current go-to-market strategies due to the existence of VSOE across most of the Company's product and service offerings. However, the Company expects that this new accounting guidance will facilitate the Company's efforts to optimize its offerings due to better alignment between the economics of an arrangement and the accounting. This may lead to the Company engaging in new go-to-market practices in the future. In particular, the Company expects that the new accounting standards will enable it to better integrate products and services without VSOE into existing offerings and solutions. As these go-to-market strategies evolve, the Company may modify its pricing practices in the future, which could result in changes in selling prices, including both VSOE and ESP. As a result, the Company's future revenue recognition for multiple-element arrangements could differ materially from the results in the current period. The Company is currently unable to determine the impact that the newly adopted accounting guidance could have on its revenue as these go-to-market strategies evolve.

The Company's arrangements with multiple deliverables may have a standalone software deliverable that is subject to the existing software revenue recognition guidance. The revenue for these multiple-element arrangements is allocated to the software deliverable and the nonsoftware deliverables based on the relative selling prices of all of the deliverables in the arrangement using the hierarchy in the new revenue accounting guidance. In the limited circumstances where the Company cannot determine VSOE or TPE of the selling price

for all of the deliverables in the arrangement, including the software deliverable, ESP is used for the purposes of performing this allocation.

Change in Accounting Principle: Transfers of Financial Assets and Variable Interest Entities

1.76

TIME WARNER INC. (DEC)

NOTES TO CONSOLIDATED FINANCIAL STATEMENTS

1. Description of Business, Basis of Presentation and Summary of Significant Accounting Policies (in part)

Accounting Guidance Adopted in 2010

Amendments to Accounting for Transfers of Financial Assets and VIEs

On January 1, 2010, the Company adopted guidance on a retrospective basis that (i) eliminated the concept of a qualifying special-purpose entity ("SPE"), (ii) eliminated the exception from applying existing accounting guidance related to variable interest entities ("VIEs") that were previously considered qualifying SPEs, (iii) changed the approach for determining the primary beneficiary of a VIE from a quantitative risk and reward model to a qualitative model based on control and (iv) requires the Company to assess each reporting period whether any of the Company's variable interests give it a controlling financial interest in the applicable VIE.

The Company's investments in entities determined to be VIEs principally consist of certain investments at its Networks segment, primarily HBO Asia, HBO South Asia and certain entities that comprise HBO Latin America Group ("HBO LAG"), which operate multi-channel pay and basic cable television services. As of December 31, 2010, the Company held an 80% economic interest in HBO Asia, a 75% economic interest in HBO South Asia and an approximate 80% economic interest in HBO LAG. The Company previously consolidated these entities; however, as a result of adopting this guidance, because voting control is shared with the other partners in each of the three entities, the Company determined that it is no longer the primary beneficiary of these entities and, effective January 1, 2010, accounts for these investments using the equity method. As of December 31, 2010 and December 31, 2009, the Company's aggregate investment in these three entities was $597 million and $362 million, respectively, and was recorded in investments, including available-for-sale securities, in the consolidated balance sheet.

These investments are intended to enable the Company to more broadly leverage its programming and digital strategy in the territories served and to capitalize on the growing multi-channel television market in such territories. The Company provides programming as well as certain services, including distribution, licensing, technological and administrative support, to HBO Asia, HBO South Asia and HBO LAG. These entities are financed through cash flows from their operations, and the Company is not obligated to provide them with any additional financial support. In addition, the assets of these entities are not available to settle the Company's obligations.

The adoption of this guidance with respect to these entities resulted in an increase (decrease) to revenues, operating income and net income attributable to Time Warner Inc. shareholders of $(397) million, $(75) million and $9 million, respectively, for the year ended December 31, 2009 and an increase (decrease) of $(82) million, $(16) million and $4 million, respectively, for the year ended December 31, 2008. The impact on the consolidated balance sheet as of December 31, 2009 and consolidated statement of cash flows for the years ended December 31, 2009 and 2008 was not material.

The Company also held variable interests in two wholly owned SPEs through which the activities of its accounts receivable securitization facilities were conducted. The Company determined it was the primary beneficiary of these entities because of its ability to direct the key activities of the SPEs that most significantly impact their economic performance. Accordingly, as a result of adopting this guidance, the Company consolidated these SPEs, which resulted in an increase to securitized receivables and non-recourse debt of $805 million as of December 31, 2009. In addition, for the year ended December 31, 2008, cash provided by operations increased by $231 million, with an offsetting decrease to cash used by financing activities. There was no change to cash provided by operations for the year ended December 31, 2009. The impact on the consolidated statement of operations for the years ended December 31, 2009 and 2008 was not material. During the first quarter of 2010, the Company repaid the $805 million that was outstanding under these facilities and terminated the two facilities on March 19, 2010 and March 24, 2010, respectively.

Change in Accounting Estimates

1.77

FURNITURE BRANDS INTERNATIONAL, INC. (DEC)

NOTES TO CONSOLIDATED FINANCIAL STATEMENTS

20. Change in Estimates (In Thousands)

During 2010 we recorded changes in estimates related to certain international tax and trade compliance matters. As a result of favorable settlements and actions taken by the Company as well as other conditions during 2010, our potential exposure and our estimate of the probable cost to resolve the matters decreased and we recognized a corresponding reduction in selling, general, and administrative expenses of $5,937.

During 2009 we recorded changes in estimates related to changes in inventory valuation allowances and changes in the accrual for lease termination costs. The inventory valuation allowances were increased by $32,981 due to our decision to accelerate the disposal of slow moving inventory and the accrual for closed store lease liabilities was increased by $7,537 due to deteriorating market conditions for commercial leases. During 2008 we recorded changes in estimates related to changes in inventory valuation allowances, changes in the allowances for doubtful accounts, and changes in the accrual for lease termination costs. The inventory valuation allowances were increased by $39,800, the allowance for doubtful accounts was increased by $35,241, and the accrual

for closed store lease liabilities was increased by $23,158. The increases in estimates were required due to deteriorating economic conditions and our decision to accelerate the disposal of slow moving inventory.

1.78

KIMBALL INTERNATIONAL, INC. (JUN)

NOTES TO CONSOLIDATED FINANCIAL STATEMENTS

Note 1. Summary of Significant Accounting Policies (in part)

Change in Estimates: The Company periodically performs assessments of the useful lives of assets. In evaluating useful lives, the Company considers how long assets will remain functionally efficient and effective, given levels of technology, competitive factors, and the economic environment. If the assessment indicates that the assets will continue to be used for a longer period than previously anticipated, the useful life of the assets is revised, resulting in a change in estimate. Changes in estimates are accounted for on a prospective basis by depreciating the assets' current carrying values over their revised remaining useful lives.

Effective July 1, 2009, the Company revised the useful lives of Surface Mount Technology production equipment from 5 years to 7 years. Additionally, effective October 1, 2008, the Company revised the useful lives of Enterprise Resource Planning software from 7 years to 10 years. The effect of these changes in estimates, compared to the original depreciation and amortization, for fiscal year 2010 was a pre-tax reduction in depreciation and amortization expense of, in thousands, ($2,148). The pre-tax reduction in amortization expense for fiscal year 2009 was, in thousands, ($1,402). The pre-tax (decrease) increase to depreciation and amortization expense in future periods is expected to be, in thousands, ($1,010), $141, $1,052, $1,272, and $1,225 in the five years ending June 30, 2015, and $531 thereafter.

Correction of Errors

1.79

THE TIMKEN COMPANY (DEC)

NOTES TO CONSOLIDATED FINANCIAL STATEMENTS

Note 17—Prior-Period Adjustments

During the third quarter of 2010, the Company recorded an adjustment related to its 2009 Consolidated Financial Statements. (Loss) income from discontinued operations, net of income taxes, decreased $1.3 million (after-tax) due to a correction of an error related to a foreign currency translation adjustment for the Company's Canadian operations that were sold as part of the NRB divestiture. The Company realized during the third quarter of 2010 that this adjustment should have been written-off in the fourth quarter of 2009 and recognized as part of the loss on the sale of the NRB operations.

Management of the Company concluded the effect of the third quarter adjustment was immaterial to the Company's 2009 and third-quarter 2010 financial statements, as well as to the full-year 2010 financial statements.

During the first quarter of 2010, the Company recorded a $14.1 million adjustment to other comprehensive income for deferred taxes on postretirement prescription drug benefits, specifically the employer subsidy provided by the U.S. government under the Medicare Part D program (the Medicare subsidy). The Company determined it had provided deferred taxes on postretirement benefit plan accruals recorded through other comprehensive income net of the Medicare subsidy, rather than on a gross basis. The cumulative impact of this error resulted in a cumulative understatement of deferred tax assets totaling $14.1 million and a corresponding overstatement of accumulated other comprehensive loss. Management concluded the effect of the adjustment was not material to the Company's prior three fiscal years and the first quarter of 2010 financial statements, as well as the estimated full-year 2010 financial statements.

During the first quarter of 2009, the Company recorded two adjustments related to its 2008 Consolidated Financial Statements. Net income (loss) attributable to noncontrolling interest increased by $6.1 million (after-tax) due to a correction of an error related to the $18.4 million goodwill impairment loss the Company recorded in the fourth quarter of 2008 for the Mobile Industries segment. In recording this goodwill impairment loss, the Company did not recognize that a portion of the loss related to two separate subsidiaries in India and South Africa of which the Company holds less than 100% ownership. In addition, income (loss) from continuing operations before income taxes decreased by $3.4 million, or $0.04 per share, ($2.0 million after-tax or $0.02 per share) due to a correction of an error related to $3.4 million of in-process research and development costs that were recorded in other current assets with the anticipation of being paid for by a third-party. However, the Company subsequently realized that the balance could not be substantiated through a contract with a third party. The net effect of these errors understated 2008 net income attributable to The Timken Company of $267.7 million by $4.1 million. Furthermore, the net effect of these errors overstated the Company's first quarter 2009 net income attributable to The Timken Company of $0.9 million by $4.1 million. Had these adjustments been

recorded in the fourth quarter of 2008, rather than the first quarter of 2009, the results for the first quarter of 2009 would have been a net loss attributable to The Timken Company of $3.2 million. Management of the Company concluded the effect of the first quarter adjustments was immaterial to the Company's 2008 and first-quarter 2009 financial statements, as well as to the full-year 2009 financial statements.

1.80

LA-Z-BOY INCORPORATED (APR)

NOTES TO CONSOLIDATED FINANCIAL STATEMENTS

Note 1. Accounting Policies (in part)

Principles of Consolidation (in part)

During the third quarter of fiscal 2010, we corrected our historical financial statements related to one of our VIEs. This VIE previously amortized leasehold improvements over a period that exceeded the appropriate useful life in accordance with our accounting policy. The cumulative effect was a $3.3 million reduction to fixed assets and retained earnings as of April 25, 2009, to record the previously unrecognized amortization. The correction resulted in an increase in our net loss for the fiscal years ended April 29, 2006, April 26, 2008, and April 25, 2009, of $0.2 million, $0.4 million and $1.3 million, respectively, as well as a decrease in our net income for the fiscal year ended April 28, 2007, of $0.3 million. We determined that the cumulative impact of this correction was material to our fiscal 2010 year. However, we determined that the corrections were not material, either individually or in the aggregate, to any of our historical fiscal years or interim periods. Consequently, we revised our historical financial statements for the prior periods. Because our analysis concluded that these corrections were immaterial to any prior period, we did not amend our previous filings with the Securities and Exchange Commission.

The following tables set forth the impact of the immaterial corrections to our consolidated statements of operations for the fiscal years ended April 25, 2009, and April 26, 2008, and our consolidated balance sheet as of April 25, 2009:

| | Year Ended 4/25/2009 | | |
| | 4/25/2009 | | 4/25/2009 |
(Amounts in thousands, except per share data)	(As Previously Reported)	Adjustments	(As Adjusted)
Net loss attributable to La-Z-Boy Incorporated	$(121,347)	$(1,325)	$(122,672)
Diluted net loss attributable to La-Z-Boy Incorporated per share	$ (2.36)	$ (0.03)	$ (2.39)

| | Year Ended 4/26/2008 | | |
| | 4/26/2008 | | 4/26/2008 |
(Amounts in thousands, except per share data)	(As Previously Reported)	Adjustments	(As Adjusted)
Net loss attributable to La-Z-Boy Incorporated	$(13,537)	$ (389)	$(13,926)
Diluted net loss attributable to La-Z-Boy Incorporated per share	$ (0.27)	$(0.00)	$ (0.27)

| | As of 4/25/2009 | | |
| | 4/25/2009 | | 4/25/2009 |
(Amounts in thousands)	(As Previously Reported)	Adjustments	(As Adjusted)
Property, plant and equipment, net	$150,234	$(3,338)	$146,896
Retained earnings	$ 70,769	$(3,338)	$ 67,431

1.81

HUBBELL INCORPORATED (DEC)

NOTES TO CONSOLIDATED FINANCIAL STATEMENTS

Note 1—Significant Accounting Policies (in part)

Revision to Financial Statement Presentation

During the third quarter of 2010, we determined that the December 31, 2009 deferred tax assets and deferred tax liabilities related to the Burndy acquisition were misclassified, primarily as a result of improperly applying the jurisdictional netting rules of the income taxes accounting guidance. The Company has assessed the materiality of this correction in accordance with the SEC Staff Accounting Bulletin ("SAB") No. 99 "Materiality" and has concluded that the previously issued financial statements are not materially misstated. In accordance with the SEC's SAB No. 108 "Considering the Effects of Prior Year Misstatements when Quantifying Misstatements in Current Year Financial Statements," the Company has corrected the immaterial misstatement by revising the prior period balance sheet by decreasing current deferred tax assets (reflected in Deferred taxes and other) by $17.1 million, decreasing non-current deferred tax assets (reflected in Intangible assets and other) by $44.6 million and by decreasing its non-current deferred tax liability (reflected in Other Non-current liabilities) by $61.7 million. This revision did not impact the statement of income or the statement of cash flows for any period.

Note 12—Income Taxes (in part)

Deferred tax assets and liabilities result from differences in the basis of assets and liabilities for tax and financial statement purposes. The components of the deferred tax assets/(liabilities) at December 31, were as follows (in millions):

	2010	2009
Deferred Tax Assets:		
Inventory	$ 8.0	$ 6.4
Income tax credits	18.8	16.6
Accrued liabilities	13.8	17.4
Pension	35.7	34.4
Postretirement and post employment benefits	18.8	11.2
Stock-based compensation	11.3	10.2
Net operating loss carryforwards	75.9	86.6
Miscellaneous other	1.4	0.8
Gross deferred tax assets	183.7	183.6
Valuation allowance	(2.6)	(2.2)
Total net deferred tax assets	$181.1	$181.4
Deferred Tax Liabilities:		
Acquisition basis difference	115.7	107.4
Property, plant, and equipment	27.7	29.5
Total deferred tax liabilities	$143.4	$136.9
Total net deferred tax asset	$ 37.7	$ 44.5
Deferred Taxes are Reflected in the Consolidated Balance Sheet as Follows:		
Current tax assets (included in deferred taxes and other)	$ 24.7	$ 46.7
Non-current tax assets (included in intangible assets and other)	34.2	19.3
Non-current tax liabilities (included in other non-current liabilities)	(21.2)	(21.5)
Total net deferred tax asset	$ 37.7	$ 44.5

During 2010, the Company determined that the December 31, 2009 deferred tax assets and deferred tax liabilities related to the Burndy acquisition were misclassified, primarily as a result of improperly applying the jurisdictional netting rule of the income taxes accounting guidance. As a result, the Company revised the December 31, 2009 balance sheet by decreasing current deferred tax assets by $17.1 million, decreasing non-current deferred tax assets by $44.6 million and by decreasing its non-current deferred tax liability by $61.7 million. In 2010, the Company also finalized the tax attributes associated with the Burndy acquisition and as a result recorded an additional $19.5 million of deferred tax assets. Both of these revisions have been reflected in the December 31, 2009 data presented in the table above.

CONSOLIDATION

RECOGNITION AND MEASUREMENT

1.82 FASB ASC 810-10-10 states that the purpose of consolidated financial statements is to present, primarily for the benefit of the owners and creditors of the parent, the results of operations and the financial position of a parent and all its subsidiaries as if the consolidated group were a single economic entity. It is presumed that consolidated financial statements are more meaningful than separate financial statements and are usually necessary for a fair presentation when one of the entities in the consolidated group directly or indirectly has a controlling financial interest in the other entities.

1.83 As explained by FASB ASC 810-10-05-8, the "General" subsections of FASB ASC 810, *Consolidation*, apply to certain legal entities in which equity investors do not have sufficient equity at risk for the legal entity to finance its activities without additional subordinated financial support, or as a group, the holders of the equity investment at risk lack any of the following three characteristics:

- The power, through voting or similar rights, to direct the activities of a legal entity that most significantly affect the entity's economic performance
- The obligation to absorb the expected losses of the legal entity
- The right to receive the expected residual returns of the legal entity

Consolidated financial statements are usually necessary for a fair presentation if one of the entities in the consolidated group directly or indirectly has a controlling financial interest, typically a majority voting interest. Application of the majority voting interest requirement to certain types of entities may not identify the party with a controlling financial interest because that interest may be achieved through other arrangements. FASB ASC 810-10-25-38A explains that a reporting entity with a variable interest in a variable interest entity (VIE) should assess whether the reporting entity has a controlling financial interest in the VIE and, thus, is the VIE's primary beneficiary. The reporting enterprise with a variable interest(s) that provides the reporting entity with a controlling financial interest in a VIE will have both the following characteristics: (*a*) the power to direct the activities of a VIE that most significantly affect the VIE's performance and (*b*) the obligation to absorb losses of the VIE that could potentially be significant to the VIE or the right to receive benefits from the VIE that could potentially be significant to the VIE. Only one reporting entity, if any, is expected to be identified as the primary beneficiary of a VIE. Although more than one reporting entity could have the obligation to absorb losses previously mentioned, only one reporting entity (if any) will have the power to direct the activities of a VIE that most significantly affect the VIE's economic performance. Further, the concept of a qualifying special-purpose entity no longer exists in FASB ASC.

1.84　　FASB ASC 810 also establishes accounting and reporting standards for the noncontrolling interest in a subsidiary and the deconsolidation of a subsidiary. A *noncontrolling interest* is the portion of equity (net assets) in a subsidiary not directly or indirectly attributable to a parent. A noncontrolling interest is sometimes called a minority interest.

PRESENTATION

1.85　　FASB ASC 810-10-45-23 requires that a change in a parent's ownership interest while the parent retains its controlling financial interest in its subsidiary should be accounted for as equity transactions (investments by owners and distributions to owners acting in their capacity as owners). Therefore, no gain or loss shall be recognized in consolidated net income or comprehensive income. The carrying amount of the noncontrolling interest should be adjusted to reflect the change in its ownership interest in the subsidiary. Any difference between the fair value of the consideration received or paid and the amount by which the noncontrolling interest is adjusted should be recognized in equity attributable to the parent.

1.86　　Paragraphs 4–5 of FASB ASC 810-10-40 state that a parent should deconsolidate a subsidiary or derecognize a group of assets specified in FASB ASC 810-10-40-3A as of the date the parent ceases to have a controlling financial interest in that subsidiary or group of assets. If a parent deconsolidates a subsidiary or derecognizes a group of assets through a nonreciprocal transfer to owners, such as a spinoff, the applicable guidance is in FASB ASC 845-10. Otherwise, a parent should account for the deconsolidation of a subsidiary or derecognition of a group of assets by recognizing a gain or loss in net income attributable to the parent. This gain or loss is measured as the difference between (*a*) the aggregate of the fair value of any consideration received; the fair value of any retained noncontrolling interest in the former subsidiary of the group of assets at the date the subsidiary is deconsolidated or the group of assets is derecognized, and the carrying amount of any noncontrolling interest in the former subsidiary, including any accumulated other comprehensive income attributable to the noncontrolling interest, at the date the subsidiary is deconsolidated and (*b*) the carrying amount of the former subsidiary's assets and liabilities or the carrying amount of the group of assets.

DISCLOSURE

1.87　　FASB ASC 810-10-50 states in part that consolidated financial statements should disclose the consolidation policy that is being followed. In most cases, this can be made apparent by the headings or other information in the financial statements, but in other cases, a footnote is required.

1.88　　FASB ASC 810-10-50-1A also requires disclosure on the face of the consolidated financial statements of the amounts of consolidated net income and consolidated comprehensive income attributable to the parent and noncontrolling interest. Disclosures in the consolidated financial statements should clearly identify and distinguish between the interests of the parent's owners and the interests of the noncontrolling owners of a subsidiary. Those disclosures include a reconciliation of the beginning and ending balances of the equity attributable to the parent and noncontrolling owners and a schedule showing the effects of changes in a parent's ownership interest in a subsidiary on the equity attributable to the parent.

PRESENTATION AND DISCLOSURE EXCERPTS

Consolidation

1.89

HARLEY-DAVIDSON, INC. (DEC)

NOTES TO CONSOLIDATED FINANCIAL STATEMENTS

1. Summary of Significant Accounting Policies (in part)

Principles of Consolidation and Basis of Presentation—The consolidated financial statements include the accounts of Harley-Davidson, Inc. and its wholly-owned subsidiaries (the Company), including the accounts of the groups of companies doing business as Harley-Davidson Motor Company (HDMC), Harley-Davidson Financial Services (HDFS) and Buell Motorcycle Company (Buell). In addition, certain variable interest entities (VIEs) related to secured financing are consolidated as the Company is the primary beneficiary. All intercompany accounts and transactions are eliminated.

All of the Company's subsidiaries are wholly owned and are included in the consolidated financial statements. Substantially all of the Company's international subsidiaries use their respective local currency as their functional currency. Assets and liabilities of international subsidiaries have been translated at period-end exchange rates, and income and expenses have been translated using average exchange rates for the period.

The Company operates in two principal business segments: Motorcycles & Related Products (Motorcycles) and Financial Services (Financial Services).

During 2008, the Company acquired Italian motorcycle manufacturer MV Agusta (MV). On October 15, 2009, the Company announced its intent to divest MV and completed the sale of MV on August 6, 2010. MV is presented as a discontinued operation for all periods.

New Accounting Standards (in part)

Consolidation of Off-Balance Sheet Special Purpose Entities

In June 2009, the Financial Accounting Standards Board (FASB) issued Statement of Financial Accounting Standards (SFAS) No. 166, "Accounting for Transfers of Financial

Assets, an amendment of FASB Statement No. 140." SFAS No. 166 amended the guidance within Accounting Standards Codification (ASC) Topic 860, "Transfers and Servicing," primarily by removing the concept of a qualifying special purpose entity as well as removing the exception from applying FASB Interpretation No. 46(R), "Consolidation of Variable Interest Entities." Upon the effective adoption date, former QSPEs as defined under prior U.S. GAAP had to be evaluated for consolidation within an entity's financial statements. Additionally, the guidance within ASC Topic 860 requires enhanced disclosures about the transfer of financial assets as well as an entity's continuing involvement, if any, in transferred financial assets. In connection with term asset-backed securitization transactions prior to 2009, HDFS utilized QSPEs as defined under prior U.S. GAAP which were not subject to consolidation in the Company's financial statements.

In June 2009, the FASB issued SFAS No. 167, "Amendments to FASB Interpretation No. 46(R)." SFAS No. 167 amended the guidance within ASC Topic 810, "Consolidations," by adding formerly off-balance sheet QSPEs to its scope (the concept of these entities was eliminated by SFAS No. 166). In addition, companies must perform an analysis to determine whether the company's variable interest or interests give it a controlling financial interest in a variable interest entity (VIE). Companies must also reassess on an ongoing basis whether they are the primary beneficiary of a VIE.

Effects of Adoption on January 1, 2010

The Company was required to adopt the new guidance within ASC Topic 810 and ASC Topic 860 as of January 1, 2010. The Company determined that the formerly unconsolidated QSPEs that HDFS utilized were VIEs, of which the Company was the primary beneficiary, and consolidated them into the Company's financial statements beginning January 1, 2010. In accordance with ASC Topic 810, the Company measured the initial carrying values of the assets and liabilities of the VIEs by determining what those values would have been on January 1, 2010 as if the new guidance had been in effect when the Company first met the conditions as the primary beneficiary. The Company's VIEs are discussed in further detail in Note 7.

The initial adoption of the new accounting guidance within ASC Topic 810 and ASC Topic 860 did not impact the Company's statement of operations. The following table summarizes the effects on the Company's balance sheet of adopting the new guidance within ASC Topic 810 and ASC Topic 860 on January 1, 2010 (in thousands):

	As of December 31, 2009	Effect of Consolidation	As of January 1, 2010
Finance receivables held for investment[1]	$ 4,961,894	$ 1,922,833	$ 6,884,727
Allowance for finance credit losses[1]	$ (150,082)	$ (49,424)	$ (199,506)
Investment in retained securitization interests[1]	$ 245,350	$ (245,350)	$ —
Restricted cash held by variable interest entities[2]	$ —	$ 198,874	$ 198,874
Other current assets[2]	$ 462,106	$ 40,224	$ 502,330
Accrued liabilities	$ (514,084)	$ (11,952)	$ (526,036)
Long-term debt	$(5,446,130)	$(1,892,313)	$(7,338,443)
Retained earnings	$(6,324,268)	$ 40,591	$(6,283,677)
Accumulated other comprehensive loss	$ 417,898	$ (3,483)	$ 414,415

[1] These three lines items were reported together as finance receivables held for investment, net prior to January 1, 2010.

[2] At December 31, 2009, the Company had $167.7 million of restricted cash related to its 2009 on-balance sheet term-asset backed securitization transactions and its asset-backed commercial paper conduit facility. These amounts were reported within Other current assets as of December 31, 2009.

Financial Statement Comparability to Prior Periods

The new accounting guidance within ASC Topic 810 and ASC Topic 860 is adopted on a prospective basis. Prior periods have not been restated and therefore will not be comparable to the current period as discussed below.

Under the new accounting guidance, the Company's securitization transactions are considered secured borrowings rather than asset sales. Beginning in 2010, the Company recognizes interest income and credit losses on the previously unconsolidated securitized receivables and interest expense on the related debt. The Company's statement of operations no longer includes income from securitizations which consisted of an initial gain or loss on new securitization transactions, income on the investment in retained securitization interests and servicer fees. In addition, the Company no longer incurs charges related to other-than-temporary impairments on its investment in retained securitization interests as that asset has been derecognized.

Finance receivables consolidated as part of the adoption of the new accounting guidance, as well as finance receivables securitized as part of the Company's 2009 on-balance sheet securitization transactions and finance receivables restricted as collateral under the Company's asset-backed commercial paper conduit facility, are reported on the Company's balance sheet as restricted finance receivables held for investment by VIEs. Prior to the adoption of the new accounting guidance, finance receivables held by VIEs were included in finance receivables held for investment. In addition, finance receivable securitization debt is now reported as debt held by VIEs.

Historically, U.S. retail motorcycle finance receivables intended for securitization through off-balance sheet securitization transactions were initially classified as finance receivables held for sale. Accordingly, all of the related cash flows were classified as operating cash flows in the statement of cash flows. After the adoption of the new guidance within ASC Topic 810 and ASC Topic 860, all retail finance receivables are considered held for investment, as the Company has the intent and ability to hold the finance receivables for the foreseeable future, or until maturity. The adoption guidance within ASC Topic 810 and ASC Topic 860 requires the Company to apply the standards on a prospective basis as if they had always been in effect. Therefore, the Company has classified post-January 1, 2010 cash flows related to all of its retail motorcycle finance receivables as investing cash flows in the statement of cash flows.

1.90

TRINITY INDUSTRIES, INC. (DEC)

NOTES TO CONSOLIDATED FINANCIAL STATEMENTS

Note 1. Summary of Significant Accounting Policies (in part)

Principles of Consolidation (in part)

The financial statements of Trinity Industries, Inc. and its consolidated subsidiaries ("Trinity," "Company," "we" or "our") include the accounts of all majority owned subsidiaries. The equity method of accounting is used for companies in which the Company has significant influence and 50% or less ownership. All significant intercompany accounts and transactions have been eliminated.

On January 1, 2010, the Company adopted the provisions of a new accounting standard, Accounting Standards Codification ("ASC") 810-10, requiring the inclusion of the consolidated financial statements of TRIP Holdings and subsidiary in the consolidated financial statements of the Company as of January 1, 2010. Prior to January 1, 2010, the Company's investment in TRIP Holdings was accounted for using the equity method. Accordingly, the consolidated balance sheet of the Company as of December 31, 2010 and the consolidated statements of operations, cash flows, and stockholders' equity for the year ended December 31, 2010 include the accounts of all subsidiaries including TRIP Holdings. As a result of adopting this pronouncement, we determined the effects on Trinity's consolidated financial statements as if TRIP Holdings had been included in the Company's consolidated financial statements from TRIP Holdings' inception and recorded a charge to retained earnings of $105.4 million, net of $57.7 million of tax benefit, and a noncontrolling interest of $129.9 million as of January 1, 2010. Prior periods were not restated. All significant intercompany accounts and transactions have been eliminated. Profits have been deferred on sales of railcars from the Rail or Leasing Group to TRIP Holdings and will be amortized over the life of the related equipment. Additionally, any future profits on the sale of railcars to TRIP Holdings will be deferred and amortized over the life of the related equipment. The noncontrolling interest represents the non-Trinity equity interest in TRIP Holdings. In September 2010, Trinity increased its ownership interest in TRIP Holdings to 57.1%. The effect of adopting this accounting standard was an increase to net income from continuing operations and net income attributable to Trinity Industries, Inc. of $5.3 million or $0.07 per basic diluted share. The effect of adopting this accounting standard was an increase to income from continuing operations and net income attributable to Trinity Industries, Inc. of $5.3 million or $0.07 per share.

1.91

BALL CORPORATION (DEC)

NOTES TO CONSOLIDATED FINANCIAL STATEMENTS

1. Critical and Significant Accounting Policies (in part)

The preparation of the company's consolidated financial statements in conformity with accounting principles generally accepted in the United States of America (U.S. GAAP) requires Ball's management to make estimates and assumptions that affect the reported amounts in our consolidated financial statements and the accompanying notes including various claims and contingencies related to lawsuits, taxes, environmental and other matters arising during the normal course of business. These estimates are based on management's best judgment, knowledge of existing facts and circumstances and actions that may be undertaken in the future. Ball's management evaluates the estimates on an ongoing basis using the company's historical experience, as well as other factors believed to be appropriate under the circumstances, such as current economic conditions, and adjusts or revises the estimates as circumstances change. As future events and their effects cannot be determined with precision, actual results may differ from these estimates. The financial statements reflect all adjustments necessary, in the opinion of management, for the fair presentation of results.

Significant Accounting Policies (in part)

Principles of Consolidation and Basis of Presentation (in part)

The consolidated financial statements include the accounts of Ball Corporation, its subsidiaries and variable interest entities in which Ball Corporation is considered to be the primary beneficiary (collectively, Ball, the company, we or our). Equity investments in which the company exercises significant influence but does not control and is not the primary beneficiary are accounted for using the equity method of accounting. Investments in which the company does not exercise significant influence over the investee are accounted for using the cost method of accounting. Intercompany transactions are eliminated.

5. Business Consolidation and Other Activities

Following is a summary of business consolidation (charges)/gains included in the consolidated statements of earnings for the years ended December 31:

($ in millions)	2010	2009	2008
Metal beverage packaging, Americas & Asia	$ —	$ (6.8)	$(40.6)
Metal beverage packaging, Europe	(3.2)	—	—
Metal food & household products packaging, Americas	18.3	(2.6)	1.6
Corporate other costs	(4.1)	(12.0)	(4.8)
	$11.0	$(21.4)	$(43.8)

2010

Metal Beverage Packaging, Europe

During the fourth quarter of 2010, the company recorded a charge of $2.6 million to write off capitalized installation costs associated with the decision not to complete a plant in Lublin, Poland. Also included in the fourth quarter were charges totaling $0.6 million for transaction costs incurred for the January 2011 acquisition of Aerocan S.A.S. (See Note 23.)

Metal Food and Household Products Packaging, Americas

In September 2010, Ball announced the closure of its metal food container manufacturing plant in Richmond, British Columbia. The plant, which produces steel cans for the Alaskan and Canadian salmon industry, will cease production in the first quarter of 2011, and its production capacity will be consolidated into other Ball facilities. In connection with the closure, the company recorded a charge of $4.6 million primarily for severance and other employee benefits. In the fourth quarter of 2010, the company completed the sale and subsequent leaseback of its Richmond, British Columbia, facility resulting in a $5.1 million gain on the sale net of estimated lease exit costs and other individually insignificant items.

During the third quarter of 2010, the company identified an accrual of a pension liability related to a Canadian plant closure that occurred in 2006. The amount of the accrual was $17.8 million ($14.5 million after tax) and was the result of recognizing the final settlement of the pension plan prior to the actual settlement of the pension obligation as defined in the pension accounting guidance. A third quarter 2010 out-of-period adjustment eliminated the excess pension liability balance related to the final settlement. The accrual for the pension settlement liability, as determined at that time, will be charged to earnings from accumulated other comprehensive earnings (loss) upon final settlement of the related pension obligation when the criteria in the accounting guidance are deemed to have been met and all regulatory clearances have been given. Management has assessed the impact of this adjustment and does not believe these amounts were quantitatively or qualitatively material, individually or in the aggregate, to any previously issued financial statements, including the results of operations for 2006, or to the 2010 results of operations.

Corporate and Other Costs

In the third and fourth quarter of 2010, charges totaling $1.0 million were recorded primarily for transaction costs related to the acquisition of Neuman (discussed in Note 3). In the second quarter of 2010, charges of $3.1 million were recorded primarily to establish a reserve associated with an environmental matter at a previously owned facility.

2009

Metal Beverage Packaging, Americas and Asia

During the fourth quarter, income of $4.2 million was recorded to reflect the reversal of previously recorded employee benefit charges taken primarily related to the closures of the Puerto Rico and Kansas City plants, which were announced in the fourth quarter of 2008. The reversal was due to the original estimates of group insurance and other employee-related costs being higher than actual experience rates. These gains were partially offset by other charges recognized in the fourth quarter totaling $1.0 million primarily for fixed asset disposals where original adjustments to net realizable value were insufficient.

A charge of $0.7 million was also recorded in the fourth quarter for acquisition costs required to be expensed related to the acquisition in the PRC of the remaining outstanding shares of Jianlibao. (See Note 3.) During the third quarter, a charge of $1 million was recorded, primarily for additional costs of winding down the Puerto Rico and Kansas City plants, the closures of which were announced in the fourth quarter of 2008. In the second quarter of 2009, a charge of $3.3 million was taken for severance and other employee benefits related to a reduction of personnel in the plants and headquarters of the Americas portion of this segment. Most of the costs were paid by the end of 2009. In the first quarter of 2009, a charge of $5 million was taken related to accelerated depreciation for operations that ceased at the Kansas City plant.

Metal Food & Household Products Packaging, Americas

In the fourth quarter, Ball recorded a charge of $2.6 million primarily for higher than originally estimated employee benefit and lease termination costs related to previously announced plant closures.

Corporate Other Costs

Charges of $12.0 million were recorded in 2009 primarily for transaction costs required to be expensed for the acquisition of three metal beverage can plants and one beverage can end plant from AB InBev. (See Note 3.)

2008

Metal Beverage Packaging, Americas & Asia

On October 30, 2008, the company announced the closure of two North American metal beverage can plants. A plant in Kansas City, Missouri, which primarily manufactured specialty beverage cans, was closed by the end of the first quarter of 2009 with manufacturing volumes absorbed by other North American beverage can plants. A plant in Puerto Rico, which manufactured 12-ounce beverage cans, was closed at the end of 2008. A pretax charge of $40.7 million was recorded in the fourth quarter of 2008. The charge included $17 million for employee severance, pension and other employment benefit costs; and $9 million of accelerated depreciation and $14 million for the write down to net realizable value of certain fixed assets and related spare parts. The carrying value of fixed assets remaining for sale in connection with the plant closures was $4.9 million at December 31, 2010.

On April 23, 2008, the company announced plans to close a U.S. metal beverage packaging plant in Kent, Washington. A charge of $11.2 million was recorded during the second and third quarters and included $9.2 million for employee severance, pension and other employee benefit costs and $2 million primarily related to accelerated depreciation and the write down to net realizable value of certain fixed assets, related spare parts and tooling inventory. The plant was shut down during the third quarter, and the land and building was sold in the fourth quarter for a gain of $4.1 million. All remaining costs, excluding pension costs of $5.2 million, were paid during 2009.

A gain of $7.2 million was recorded in the second quarter for the recovery of previously expensed costs in a prior metal beverage business consolidation charge. This reflects a decision made in the second quarter to continue to operate existing end-making equipment and not install a new beverage can end module that would have been part of a multi-year project. The remaining reserves were utilized in 2010.

During 2007, the company settled a dispute with a U.S. customer, which was primarily related to the pricing of the aluminum component of the containers it supplied. The customer received $85.6 million on settlement of the dispute, and Ball retained all of the customer's beverage can and end supply through 2015. The customer received a one-time payment of approximately $70.3 million in January 2008 with the remainder of the settlement to be recovered over the life of the contract through 2015.

Metal Food & Household Products Packaging, Americas

During 2008 the company recorded a net pretax gain of $1.6 million for business consolidation activities. In addition to costs recorded in the fourth quarter of 2007, during the third quarter of 2008, a charge of $4.5 million was recorded for lease cancellation costs on final shutdown of the Commerce, California, facility. In the fourth quarter, a $6.1 million gain was recorded primarily related to management's decision in the fourth quarter to remain in the custom and decorative tinplate can business based on market conditions. All remaining reserves related to Commerce and Tallapoosa, Georgia (see 2007 discussion below), excluding lease cancellation costs, were utilized during 2009.

Corporate Other Costs

During 2008 pretax charges of $4.8 million were recorded for estimated environmental costs related to previously closed and sold facilities.

Summary

Following is a summary of reserve activity by segment related to business consolidation activities for the year ended December 31, 2010. The reserve balances are included in other current liabilities on the consolidated balance sheets.

($ in millions)	Metal Beverage Packaging, Americas & Asia	Metal Beverage Packaging, Europe	Metal Food & Household Products Packaging, Americas	Corporate and Other Costs	Total
Balance at December 31, 2008	$ 28.2	$ —	$ 11.1	$ 7.7	$ 47.0
Charges (gains) in continuing operations	6.8	—	2.6	11.3	20.7
Charges (gains) in discontinued operations	—	—	—	23.8	23.8
Cash payments and other activity	(24.6)	—	(6.4)	(32.6)	(63.6)
Balance at December 31, 2009	10.4	—	7.3	10.2	27.9
Charges (gains) in continuing operations	—	3.2	(18.3)	4.1	(11.0)
Charges (gains) in discontinued operations	—	—	—	10.4	10.4
Cash payments and other activity	(2.9)	(3.2)	20.5	(13.7)	0.7
Balance at December 31, 2010	$ 7.5	$ —	$ 9.5	$ 11.0	$ 28.0

BUSINESS COMBINATIONS

RECOGNITION AND MEASUREMENT

1.92 FASB ASC 805, *Business Combinations*, requires that the acquisition method be used for all business combinations. An acquirer is required to recognize the identifiable acquired assets, the liabilities assumed, and any noncontrolling interest in the acquiree at the acquisition date, measured at their fair values as of that date. Additionally, FASB ASC 805 requires costs incurred to affect the acquisition to be recognized as expenses as incurred, rather than included in the cost allocated to the acquired assets and assumed liabilities. However, the costs to issue debt or equity securities should be recognized in accordance with other applicable GAAP. In a business combination achieved in stages, FASB ASC 805 also requires the acquirer to remeasure its previously-held equity interest in the acquiree at its acquisition date fair value and recognize the resulting gain or loss, if any, in earnings. For all business combinations, the guidance requires the acquirer to recognize goodwill as of the acquisition date, measured as the excess of (a) over (b):

   a. The aggregate of the following:
      i. The transferred consideration measured in accordance with FASB ASC 805-30, which generally requires acquisition-date fair value
      ii. The fair value of any noncontrolling interest in the acquiree
      iii. In a business combination achieved in stages, the acquisition-date fair value of the acquirer's previously-held equity interest in the acquiree
   b. The net of the acquisition-date amounts of the identifiable acquired assets and the assumed liabilities, measured in accordance with FASB ASC 805

If the amounts in (b) are in excess of those in (a), a bargain purchase has occurred. Before recognizing a gain on a bargain purchase, the acquirer shall reassess whether it has correctly identified all the acquired assets and assumed liabilities and should recognize any additional assets or liabilities identified in that review. If an excess still remains, the acquirer should recognize the resulting gain in earnings on the acquisition date.

DISCLOSURE

1.93   FASB ASC 805-10-50 requires the acquirer to disclose information that enables financial statement users to evaluate the nature and financial statement effect of a business combination that occurs during the current reporting period or after the reporting date but before the financial statements are issued or available to be issued. To meet this objective, the following items should be disclosed:

- The name and a description of the acquiree
- The acquisition date
- The percentage of voting equity interests acquired
- The primary reasons for the business combination and a description of how control was obtained
- For public business entities
  - The amounts of revenue and earnings of the acquiree since the acquisition date included in the consolidated income statement for the reporting period
  - The revenue and earnings of the combined entity for the current reporting period as though the acquisition date for all business combinations that occurred during the year had been as of the annual reporting period (supplemental pro forma information)
  - If comparative financial statements are presented, the revenue and earnings of the combined entity for the comparable prior reporting period as though the acquisition date for all business combinations that occurred during the current year had occurred as of the beginning of the comparable prior annual reporting period (supplemental pro forma information)

If any of the preceding disclosures for public business entities are impracticable, the acquirer should disclose that fact and explain why. Additional disclosures are required for transactions that are recognized separately from the acquisition of assets and assumptions of liabilities in the business combination and for business combinations achieved in stages.

Author's Note

In December 2010, FASB Accounting Standards Update (ASU) No. 2010-29, *Business Combinations (Topic 805): Disclosure of Supplementary Pro Forma Information for Business Combinations (a consensus of the FASB Emerging Issues Task Force)*, was issued. This ASU clarifies that if comparative financial statements are presented, the pro forma revenue and earnings of the combined entity for the comparable prior reporting period should be reported as though the acquisition date for all business combinations that occurred during the current year had been as of the beginning of the comparable prior annual reporting period. Further, a public business entity will also be required to disclose the nature and amount of any material, nonrecurring pro forma adjustments directly attributable to the business combination(s) included in the reported pro forma revenue and earnings. The amendments in this ASU are effective prospectively for business combinations for which the acquisition date is on or after the beginning of the first annual reporting period beginning on or after December 15, 2010. Early adoption is permitted.

1.94

TABLE 1-7: BUSINESS COMBINATION DISCLOSURES

The nature of information commonly disclosed for business combinations is listed in Table 1-7.

	2010	2009	2008
Method of Payment			
Cash only	171	147	194
Cash and stock	20	13	20
Stock only	2	8	5
Other, described	9	5	10
Intangible assets not subject to amortization	72	156	202
Intangible assets subject to amortization	151	114	176
Preliminary allocation of acquisition cost	96	81	118
Contingent payments	30	26	42
Purchased research and development costs	16	25	25
Fair value of noncontrolling interest	9	4	N/C*
Bargain purchase gain (negative goodwill)	3	2	N/C*
Other, described	19	N/C*	N/C*

* N/C = Not compiled. Line item was not included in the table for the year shown.

PRESENTATION AND DISCLOSURE EXCERPTS

Business Combinations

1.95

CATERPILLAR INC. (DEC)

NOTES TO CONSOLIDATED FINANCIAL STATEMENTS

23. Business Combinations and Alliances

Electro-Motive Diesel, Inc.

In August 2010, we acquired 100 percent of the equity in privately held Electro-Motive Diesel, Inc. (EMD) for approximately $901 million, consisting of $928 million paid at closing less a final net working capital adjustment of $27 million received in the fourth quarter of 2010. Headquartered in LaGrange, Illinois with additional manufacturing facilities in Canada and Mexico, EMD designs, manufactures and sells diesel-electric locomotives for commercial railroad applications and sells its products to customers throughout the world. EMD has a significant field population in North America and throughout the world supported by an aftermarket business offering customers replacement parts, maintenance solutions, and a range of value-added services. EMD is also a global provider of diesel engines for marine propulsion, offshore and land-based oil well drilling rigs, and stationary power generation. The acquisition supports our strategic plan to grow our presence in the global rail industry. The EMD acquisition will enable us to provide rail and transit customers a range of locomotive, engine and emissions solutions, as well as aftermarket product and parts support and a full line of rail-related services and solutions.

The transaction was financed with available cash. Tangible assets acquired of $890 million, recorded at their fair values, primarily were receivables of $186 million, inventories of $549 million and property, plant and equipment of $131 million. Finite-lived intangible assets acquired of $329 million were primarily related to customer relationships and also included intellectual property and trade names. The finite-lived intangible assets are being amortized on a straight-line basis over a weighted-average amortization period of approximately 15 years. An additional intangible asset acquired of $18 million, related to in-process research and development, is considered indefinite-lived until the completion or abandonment of the development activities. Liabilities assumed of $518 million, recorded at their fair values, primarily included accounts payable of $124 million and accrued expenses of $161 million. Additionally, net deferred tax liabilities were $104 million. Goodwill of $286 million, substantially all of which is non-deductible for income tax purposes, represents the excess of cost over the fair value of the net tangible and intangible assets acquired. Factors that contributed to a purchase price resulting in the recognition of goodwill include EMD's strategic fit into our product and services portfolio, aftermarket support opportunities and the acquired assembled workforce. The results of the acquired business for the period from the acquisition date are included in the accompanying consolidated financial statements and are reported in the "All Other" category in Note 22. Assuming this transaction had been made at the beginning of any period presented, the consolidated pro forma results would not be materially different from reported results.

FCM Rail Ltd.

In May 2010, we acquired 100 percent of the equity in privately held FCM Rail Ltd. (FCM) for approximately $97 million, including the assumption of $59 million in debt. We paid $32 million at closing and an additional $1 million post-closing adjustment paid in October 2010. There is also an additional $5 million to be paid by May 2012. FCM is one of the largest lessors of maintenance-of-way (MOW) equipment in the United States, and is located in Fenton, Michigan. This acquisition strengthens Progress Rail's position in the MOW industry by expanding its service offerings.

The transaction was financed with available cash. Tangible assets acquired of $93 million, primarily consisting of property, plant and equipment, were recorded at their fair values. Finite-lived intangible assets acquired of $10 million related to customer relationships are being amortized on a straight-line basis over 15 years. Liabilities assumed of $82 million, including $59 million of assumed debt, were recorded at their fair values. Goodwill of $17 million, non-deductible for income tax purposes, represents the excess of cost over the fair value of net tangible and finite-lived intangible assets acquired. The results of the acquired business for the period from the acquisition date are included in the accompanying consolidated financial statements and reported in the "All Other" category in Note 22. Assuming this transaction had been made at the beginning of any period presented, the consolidated pro forma results would not be materially different from reported results.

GE Transportation's Inspection Products Business

In March 2010, we acquired the Inspection Products business from GE Transportation's Intelligent Control Systems division for approximately $46 million, which includes $1 million paid for post-closing adjustments. The acquired business has operations located primarily in the United States, Germany and Italy that design, manufacture and sell hot wheel and hot box detectors, data acquisition systems, draggers and other related inspection products for the global freight and passenger rail industries. The acquisition supports our strategic initiative to expand the scope and product range of our rail signaling business and will provide a foundation for further global expansion of this business.

The transaction was financed with available cash. Tangible assets acquired of $12 million and liabilities assumed of $9 million were recorded at their fair values. Finite-lived intangible assets acquired of $28 million related to customer relationships and intellectual property are being amortized on a straight-line basis over a weighted-average amortization period of approximately 13 years. Goodwill of $15 million, approximately $8 million of which is deductible for income tax purposes, represents the excess of cost over the fair value of the net tangible and finite-lived intangible assets acquired. The results of the acquired business for the period from the acquisition date are included in the accompanying consolidated financial statements and are reported in the "All Other" category in Note 22. Assuming this transaction had been made at the beginning of any period presented, the consolidated pro forma results would not be materially different from reported results.

JCS Company, Ltd.

In March 2010, we acquired 100 percent of the equity in privately held JCS Company Ltd. (JCS) for approximately $34 million, consisting of $32 million paid at closing and an additional $2 million post-closing adjustment paid in June 2010. Based in Pyongtaek, South Korea, JCS is a leading manufacturer of centrifugally cast metal face seals used in many of the idlers and rollers contained in our undercarriage components. JCS is also a large supplier of seals to external customers in Asia and presents the opportunity to expand our customer base. The purchase of this business provides Caterpillar access to proprietary technology and expertise, which we will be able to replicate across our own seal production processes.

The transaction was financed with available cash. Tangible assets acquired of $22 million and liabilities assumed of $8 million were recorded at their fair values. Finite-lived intangible assets acquired of $12 million related to intellectual property and customer relationships are being amortized on a straight-line basis over a weighted-average amortization period of approximately 9 years. Goodwill of $8 million, non-deductible for income tax purposes, represents the excess of cost over the fair value of net tangible and finite-lived intangible assets acquired. The results of the acquired business for the period from the acquisition date are included in the accompanying consolidated financial statements and reported in the "Core Components" segment in Note 22. Assuming this transaction had been made at the beginning of any period presented, the consolidated pro forma results would not be materially different from reported results.

NC² Joint Venture

In September 2009, we entered into a joint venture with Navistar International Corporation (Navistar), resulting in a new company, NC² Global LLC (NC²). NC² will develop, manufacture, market, distribute and provide product support for heavy and medium duty trucks outside of North America, the Indian subcontinent, Myanmar (Burma) and Malaysia. Initially, NC² will focus its activities in Australia, Brazil, and South Africa. NC²'s product line will feature both conventional and cab-over truck designs and will be sold under both the Caterpillar and International brands.

Under the joint venture operating agreement, Caterpillar and Navistar each contributed $19 million during 2009 and $80 million during 2010. Our investment in NC², accounted for by the equity method, is included in Investments in unconsolidated affiliated companies in Statement 2.

Lovat Inc.

In April 2008, we acquired 100 percent of the equity in privately held Lovat Inc. (Lovat) for approximately $49 million. Based in Toronto, Canada, Lovat is a leading manufacturer of tunnel boring machines used globally in the construction of subway, railway, road, sewer, water main, mine access and high voltage cable and telecommunications tunnels. Expansion into the tunnel boring business is a strong fit with our strategic direction and the customers we serve around the world.

The transaction was financed with available cash and commercial paper borrowings. Net tangible assets acquired and liabilities assumed of $10 million were recorded at their fair values. Finite-lived intangible assets acquired of $17 million related to customer relationships, intellectual property and trade names are being amortized on a straight-line basis over a weighted-average amortization period of approximately 6 years. Goodwill of $22 million, non-deductible for income tax purposes, represents the excess of cost over the fair value of net tangible and finite-lived intangible assets acquired. The results of the acquired business for the period from the acquisition date are included in the accompanying consolidated financial statements and reported in the "Mining" segment in Note 22. Assuming this transaction had been made at the beginning of any period presented, the consolidated pro forma results would not be materially different from reported results.

Gremada Industries Inc.

In July 2008, we acquired certain assets and assumed certain liabilities of Gremada Industries, Inc. (Gremada), a supplier to our remanufacturing business. The cost of the acquisition was $62 million, consisting of $60 million paid at closing and an additional $2 million post-closing adjustment paid in August 2008. Gremada is a remanufacturer of transmissions, torque converters, final drives and related components. This acquisition increases our product and service offerings for our existing customers, while providing a platform for further growth opportunities.

This transaction was financed with available cash and commercial paper borrowings. Net tangible assets acquired and liabilities assumed of $21 million were recorded at their fair values. Goodwill of $41 million, deductible for income tax purposes, represents the excess of cost over the fair value of net tangible assets acquired. The results of the acquired business for the period from the acquisition date are included in the accompanying consolidated financial statements and are reported in the "All Other" category in Note 22. Assuming this transaction had been made at the beginning of any period presented, the consolidated pro forma results would not be materially different from reported results.

Shin Caterpillar Mitsubishi Ltd. (SCM)

On August 1, 2008, SCM completed the first phase of a share redemption plan whereby SCM redeemed half of MHI's shares in SCM for $464 million. This resulted in Caterpillar owning 67 percent of the outstanding shares of SCM and MHI owning the remaining 33 percent. As part of the share redemption, SCM was renamed Caterpillar Japan Ltd. (Cat Japan). Both Cat Japan and MHI have options, exercisable beginning August 1, 2013, to require the redemption of the remaining shares owned by MHI, which if exercised, would make Caterpillar the sole owner of Cat Japan. The share redemption plan is part of our comprehensive business strategy for expansion in the emerging markets of Asia and the Commonwealth of Independent States and will allow Cat Japan's manufacturing, design and process expertise to be fully leveraged across the global Caterpillar enterprise.

The change in Caterpillar's ownership interest from 50 percent to 67 percent was accounted for as a business combination. The $464 million redemption price was assigned to 17 percent of Cat Japan's assets and liabilities based upon their respective fair values as of the transaction date. The revaluation resulted in an increase in property, plant and equipment of $78 million and an increase in inventory of $8 million over the book value of these assets. Finite-lived intangible assets of $54 million were recognized and related primarily to customer relationships, intellectual property and trade names. These intangibles are being amortized on a straight-line basis over a weighted-average amortization period of approximately 9 years. Deferred tax liabilities of $57 million were also recognized as part of the business combination. Goodwill of $206 million, non-deductible for income tax purposes, represents the excess of the redemption price over the 17 percent of Cat Japan's net tangible and finite-lived intangible assets that were reported at their fair values.

Because Cat Japan is accounted for on a lag, we consolidated Cat Japan's August 1, 2008 financial position on September 30, 2008. We began consolidating Cat Japan's results of operations in the fourth quarter of 2008. Including the amounts assigned as part of the business combination, the initial consolidation of Cat Japan's financial position resulted in a net increase in assets of $2,396 million (primarily property, plant and equipment of $1,279 million, inventory of $640 million, receivables of $612 million, and goodwill and intangibles of $260 million partially offset by a $528 million reduction in investment in unconsolidated affiliates) and a net increase in liabilities of $2,045 million (including $1,388 million in debt). Cat Japan's functional currency is the Japanese yen.

The remaining 33 percent of Cat Japan owned by MHI has been reported as redeemable noncontrolling interest and classified as mezzanine equity (temporary equity) in Statement 2. On September 30, 2008, the redeemable noncontrolling interest was reported at its estimated future redemption value of $464 million with the difference between the $351 million book value of the 33 percent interest and the redemption value reported as a $113 million reduction of Profit employed in the business. See Note 24 for information on the subsequent reporting of the redeemable noncontrolling interest.

Cat Japan is included in the "Cat Japan" segment in Note 22. Assuming this transaction had been made at the beginning of any period presented, the consolidated pro forma results would not be materially different from reported results.

1.96

FRONTIER COMMUNICATIONS CORPORATION (DEC)

NOTES TO CONSOLIDATED FINANCIAL STATEMENTS

(2) Recent Accounting Literature and Changes in Accounting Principles

Business Combinations

Business combinations are accounted for utilizing the guidance of Accounting Standards Codification (ASC) Topic 805, formerly Statement of Financial Accounting Standards (SFAS) No. 141R, as amended by FSP SFAS No. 141(R)-1 which became effective on January 1, 2009. ASC Topic 805 requires an acquiring entity in a transaction to recognize all of the assets acquired and liabilities assumed at fair value at the acquisition date, to recognize and measure preacquisition contingencies, including contingent consideration, at fair value (if possible), to remeasure liabilities related to contingent consideration at fair value in each subsequent reporting period and to expense all acquisition related costs. We are accounting for our July 1, 2010 acquisition of approximately 4.0 million access lines from Verizon Communications Inc. (Verizon) (the Transaction or the Merger) using the guidance included in ASC Topic 805. We incurred approximately $137.1 million and $28.3 million of acquisition and integration related costs in connection with the Transaction during 2010 and 2009, respectively. Such costs are required to be expensed as incurred and are reflected in "Acquisition and integration costs" in our consolidated statements of operations.

(3) Acquisitions

The Transaction

On July 1, 2010, Frontier acquired the defined assets and liabilities of the local exchange business and related landline activities of Verizon in Arizona, Idaho, Illinois, Indiana, Michigan, Nevada, North Carolina, Ohio, Oregon, South Carolina, Washington, West Virginia and Wisconsin and in portions of California bordering Arizona, Nevada and Oregon (collectively, the Territories), including Internet access and long distance services and broadband video provided to designated customers in the Territories (the Acquired Business). Frontier is considered the accounting acquirer of the Acquired Business.

Our consolidated statement of operations for the year ended December 31, 2010 includes $1,748.1 million of revenue and $231.5 million of operating income related to the results of operations of the Acquired Business from the date of its acquisition on July 1, 2010.

The allocation of the purchase price of the Acquired Business is based on the fair value of assets acquired and liabilities assumed as of July 1, 2010, the effective date of the Merger. Our assessment of fair value is preliminary, and will be adjusted for information that is currently not available to us, primarily related to the tax basis of assets acquired, certain accruals and contingencies, pension assets and liabilities, and other assumed postretirement benefit obligations.

The fair value amounts recorded for the allocation of the purchase price as of July 1, 2010 are preliminary and certain items are subject to change. The most significant items include: legal and tax accruals, including sales and utility tax liabilities for the states of Washington and Indiana, pending the finalization of examinations and valuations of various cases; other accrued liabilities pending receipt of supporting documentation; deferred income tax assets and liabilities, pending Verizon providing us with tax values for the assets and liabilities of the Acquired Business; and pension and other postretirement liabilities, pending completion of actuarial studies and the related transfer of pension assets.

The preliminary allocation of the purchase price presented below represents the effect of recording the preliminary estimates of the fair value of assets acquired, liabilities assumed and related deferred income taxes as of the date of the Merger, based on the total transaction consideration of $5.4 billion. The following allocation of purchase price includes minor revisions to the initial preliminary allocation that was reported as of September 30, 2010. These preliminary estimates will be revised in future periods and the revisions may materially affect the presentation of our consolidated financial results. Any changes to the initial estimates of the fair value of the assets and liabilities will be recorded as adjustments to those assets and liabilities and residual amounts will be allocated to goodwill.

($ In thousands)	
Total transaction consideration:	$5,411,705
Current assets	$ 479,993
Property, plant & equipment	4,417,567
Goodwill	3,649,871
Other intangibles—primarily customer list	2,537,100
Other assets	75,092
Current liabilities	(509,234)
Deferred income taxes	(1,303,626)
Long-term debt	(3,456,782)
Other liabilities	(478,276)
Total net assets acquired	$5,411,705

The Transaction provides for a post-closing adjustment for working capital, pension liabilities transferred and pension assets. Frontier and Verizon have not finalized the results of these calculations. If an adjustment is made for the working capital "true-up," the purchase price allocation will be revised.

The fair value of the total consideration issued to acquire the Acquired Business amounted to $5.4 billion and included $5.2 billion for the issuance of Frontier common shares and cash payments of $105.0 million. As a result of the Merger, Verizon stockholders received 678,530,386 shares of Frontier common stock. Immediately after the closing of the Merger, Verizon stockholders owned approximately 68.4% of the combined company's outstanding equity, and existing

Frontier stockholders owned approximately 31.6% of the combined company's outstanding equity.

The following unaudited pro forma financial information presents the combined results of operations of Frontier and the Acquired Business as if the acquisition had occurred as of January 1, 2009. The pro forma information is not necessarily indicative of what the financial position or results of operations actually would have been had the acquisition been completed as of January 1, 2009. In addition, the unaudited pro forma financial information is not indicative of, nor does it purport to project, the future financial position or operating results of Frontier. The unaudited pro forma financial information excludes acquisition and integration costs and does not give effect to any estimated and potential cost savings or other operating efficiencies that could result from the Merger.

UNAUDITED PRO FORMA CONDENSED COMBINED STATEMENTS OF OPERATIONS INFORMATION

($ in millions, except per share amounts)	For the Year Ended December 31	
	2010	2009
Revenue	$5,652	$6,071
Operating income	$1,192	$1,373
Net income attributable to common shareholders of Frontier	$ 324	$ 433
Basic and diluted net income per common share attributable to common shareholders of Frontier	$ 0.33	$ 0.44

1.97

BOSTON SCIENTIFIC CORPORATION (DEC)

NOTES TO CONSOLIDATED FINANCIAL STATEMENTS

Note B—Acquisitions

During 2010, we paid approximately $200 million in cash to acquire Asthmatx, Inc. and certain other strategic assets. We did not consummate any material acquisitions during 2009. During 2008, we paid approximately $40 million in cash to acquire CryoCor, Inc. and Labcoat, Ltd. Each of these acquisitions is described in further detail below. The purchase price allocations presented for our 2010 acquisitions are preliminary, pending finalization of the valuation surrounding deferred tax assets and liabilities, and will be finalized in 2011.

Our consolidated financial statements include the operating results for each acquired entity from its respective date of acquisition. We do not present pro forma information for these acquisitions given the immateriality of their results to our consolidated financial statements.

2010 Acquisitions

Asthmatx, Inc.

On October 26, 2010, we completed the acquisition of 100 percent of the fully diluted equity of Asthmatx, Inc. Asthmatx designs, manufactures and markets a less-invasive, catheter-based bronchial thermoplasty procedure for the treatment of severe persistent asthma. The acquisition was intended to broaden and diversify our product portfolio by expanding into the area of endoscopic pulmonary intervention. We are integrating the operations of the Asthmatx business into our Endoscopy division. We paid approximately $194 million at the closing of the transaction using cash on hand, and may be required to pay future consideration up to $250 million that is contingent upon the achievement of certain revenue-based milestones.

As of the acquisition date, we recorded a contingent liability of $54 million, representing the estimated fair value of the contingent consideration we currently expect to pay to the former shareholders of Asthmatx upon the achievement of certain revenue-based milestones. The acquisition agreement provides for payments on product sales using technology acquired from Asthmatx of up to $200 million through December 2016 and, in addition, we may be obligated to pay a one-time revenue-based milestone payment of $50 million, no later than 2019, for a total of $250 million in maximum future consideration.

The fair value of the contingent consideration liability associated with the $200 million of potential payments was estimated by discounting, to present value, the contingent payments expected to be made based on our estimates of the revenues expected to result from the acquisition. We used a risk-adjusted discount rate of 20 percent to reflect the market risks of commercializing this technology, which we believe is appropriate and representative of market participant assumptions. For the $50 million milestone payment, we used a probability-weighted scenario approach to determine the fair value of this obligation using internal revenue projections and external market factors. We applied a rate of probability to each scenario, as well as a risk-adjusted discount factor, to derive the estimated fair value of the contingent consideration as of the acquisition date. This fair value measurement is based on significant unobservable inputs, including management estimates and assumptions and, accordingly, is classified as Level 3 within the fair value hierarchy prescribed by ASC Topic 820, *Fair Value Measurements and Disclosures* (formerly FASB Statement No. 157, *Fair Value Measurements*). In accordance with ASC Topic 805, *Business Combinations* (formerly FASB Statement No. 141(R), *Business Combinations*), we will re-measure this liability each reporting period and record changes in the fair value through a separate line item within our consolidated statements of operations. Increases or decreases in the fair value of the contingent consideration liability can result from changes in discount periods and rates, as well as changes in the timing and amount of revenue estimates. During the fourth quarter of 2010, we recorded expense of $2 million in the accompanying statements of operations representing the increase in fair value of this obligation between the acquisition date and December 31, 2010.

The components of the preliminary purchase price as of the acquisition date for our 2010 acquisitions are as follows:

(In millions)	Asthmatx	All Other	Total
Cash	$194	$ 5	$199
Fair value of contingent consideration	54	15	69
	$248	$20	$268

We accounted for these acquisitions as business combinations and, in accordance with Topic 805, we have recorded the assets acquired and liabilities assumed at their respective fair values as of the acquisition date. The following summarizes the preliminary purchase price allocations:

(In millions)	Asthmatx	All Other	Total
Goodwill	$ 68	$ 5	$ 73
Amortizable intangible assets	176	3	179
Indefinite-lived intangible assets	45	12	57
Other net assets	2		2
Deferred income taxes	(43)		(43)
	$248	$20	$268

Transaction costs associated with these acquisitions were expensed as incurred through selling, general and administrative costs in the statement of operations and were not material in 2010.

We allocated the preliminary purchase price to specific intangible asset categories as follows:

	Amount Assigned (In Millions)			Weighted Average Amortization Period (In Years)	Range of Risk-Adjusted Discount Rates used in Purchase Price Allocation
	Asthmatx	All Other	Total		
Amortizable Intangible Assets					
Technology—core	$168		$168	12.0	28.0%
Technology—developed	8	$ 3	11	5.5	27.0%–35.5%
	176	3	179	11.6	
Indefinite-Lived Intangible Assets					
Purchased research and development	45	12	57		29.0%–36.0%
	$221	$15	$236		

Core technology consists of technical processes, intellectual property, and institutional understanding with respect to products and processes that we will leverage in future products or processes and will carry forward from one product generation to the next. Developed technology represents the value associated with marketed products that have received regulatory approval, primarily the Alair ® Bronchial Thermoplasty System acquired from Asthmatx, which is approved for distribution in CE Mark countries and received FDA approval in April 2010. The amortizable intangible assets are being amortized on a straight-line basis over their assigned useful lives.

Purchased research and development represents the estimated fair value of acquired in-process research and development projects, including the second generation of the Alair ® product, which have not yet reached technological feasibility. The indefinite-lived intangible assets will be tested for impairment on an annual basis, or more frequently if impairment indicators are present, in accordance with our accounting policies described in Note A—Significant Accounting Policies, and amortization of the purchased research and development will begin upon completion of the project. As of the acquisition date, we estimate that the total cost to complete the in-process research and development programs acquired from Asthmatx is between $10 million and $15 million. We currently expect to launch the second generation of the Alair ® product in the U.S. in 2014, in our Europe/Middle East/Africa (EMEA) region and certain Inter-Continental countries in 2016, and Japan in 2017, subject to regulatory approvals. We expect material net cash inflows from such products to commence in 2014, following the launch of this technology in the U.S.

We believe that the estimated intangible asset values so determined represent the fair value at the date of each acquisition and do not exceed the amount a third party would pay for the assets. We used the income approach, specifically the discounted cash flow method, to derive the fair value of the amortizable intangible assets and purchased research and development. These fair value measurements are based on significant unobservable inputs, including management estimates and assumptions and, accordingly, are classified as Level 3 within the fair value hierarchy prescribed by Topic 820.

We recorded the excess of the purchase price over the estimated fair values of the identifiable assets as goodwill, which is non-deductible for tax purposes. Goodwill was established due primarily to revenue and cash flow projections associated with future technology, as well as synergies expected to be gained from the integration of these businesses into our existing operations, and has been allocated to our reportable segments as follows based on the relative expected benefit from the business combinations, as follows:

(In millions)	Asthmatx	All Other	Total
U.S.	$17	$5	$22
EMEA	44		44
Inter-Continental	4		4
Japan	3		3
	$68	$5	$73

2009 Acquisitions

Our policy is to expense certain costs associated with strategic investments outside of business combinations as purchased research and development as of the acquisition date. Our adoption of Statement No. 141(R) (Topic 805) did not change this policy with respect to asset purchases. In accordance with this policy, we recorded purchased research and development charges of $21 million in 2009, associated with entering certain licensing and development arrangements. Since the technology purchases did not involve the transfer of processes or outputs as defined by Statement No. 141(R) (Topic 805), the transactions did not qualify as business combinations.

2008 Acquisitions

Labcoat, Ltd.

In December 2008, we completed the acquisition of the assets of Labcoat, Ltd., a development-stage drug-coating company, for a purchase price of $17 million, net of cash acquired.

CryoCor, Inc.

In May 2008, we completed our acquisition of 100 percent of the fully diluted equity of CryoCor, Inc., and paid a cash purchase price of $21 million, net of cash acquired. CryoCor was developing products using cryogenic technology for use in treating atrial fibrillation.

In 2008, in accordance with accounting guidance applicable at the time, we consummated the acquisitions of Labcoat and CryoCor and recorded $43 million of purchased research and development charges, including $17 million associated with Labcoat and $8 million attributable to CryoCor, as well as $18 million associated with entering certain licensing and development arrangements. During 2010, we suspended the Labcoat and CryoCor in-process research and development projects.

Payments Related to Prior Period Acquisitions

Certain of our acquisitions involve contingent consideration arrangements. Payment of additional consideration is generally contingent on the acquired company reaching certain performance milestones, including attaining specified revenue levels, achieving product development targets or obtaining regulatory approvals. In August 2007, we entered an agreement to amend our 2004 merger agreement with the principal former shareholders of Advanced Bionics Corporation. Previously, we were obligated to pay future consideration contingent primarily on the achievement of future performance milestones. The amended agreement provided a new schedule of consolidated, fixed payments, consisting of

$650 million that was paid in 2008, and a final $500 million payment, paid in 2009. We received cash proceeds of $150 million in 2008 related to our sale of a controlling interest in the Auditory business acquired with Advanced Bionics, and received additional proceeds of $40 million in 2009 related to the sale of our remaining interest in this business. Refer to *Note C—Divestitures and Assets Held for Sale* for a discussion of this transaction. During 2010, we made total payments of $12 million related to prior period acquisitions. During 2009, including the $500 million payment to the former shareholders of Advanced Bionics, we made total payments of $523 million related to prior period acquisitions. During 2008, we paid $675 million related to prior period acquisitions, consisting primarily of the $650 million payment made to the principal former shareholders of Advanced Bionics.

As of December 31, 2010, the estimated maximum potential amount of future contingent consideration (undiscounted) that we could be required to make associated with acquisitions consummated prior to 2010 is approximately $260 million. In accordance with accounting guidance applicable at the time we consummated these acquisitions, we do not recognize a liability until the contingency is resolved and consideration is issued or becomes issuable. Topic 805 now requires the recognition of a liability equal to the expected fair value of future contingent payments at the acquisition date for all acquisitions consummated after January 1, 2009. In connection with our 2010 business combinations, we recorded liabilities of $69 million representing the estimated fair value of contingent payments expected to be made, including $54 million associated with Asthmatx and $15 million attributable to other acquisitions. The maximum amount of future contingent consideration (undiscounted) that we could be required to make associated with our 2010 acquisitions is approximately $275 million. Included in the accompanying consolidated balance sheets is accrued contingent consideration of $71 million as of December 31, 2010 and $6 million as of December 31, 2009.

1.98

BARNES & NOBLE, INC. (JAN)

NOTES TO CONSOLIDATED FINANCIAL STATEMENTS

4. Acquisition of B&N College (In Thousands)

On September 30, 2009, the Company completed the acquisition of B&N College from Leonard Riggio and Louise Riggio (Sellers) pursuant to a Stock Purchase Agreement dated as of August 7, 2009 among the Company and the Sellers. Mr. Riggio is the Chairman of the Company's Board of Directors and a significant stockholder. As part of the transaction, the Company acquired the Barnes & Noble trade name that had been owned by B&N College and licensed to the Company.

As a result of the Acquisition, the Company expects to capitalize on the revenue stream derived from the sale of textbooks and course-related materials, emblematic apparel and gifts, trade books, school and dorm supplies, and convenience and café items. Combining both businesses under a unified brand will enable the Company to benefit from the growing online college textbook and eBook markets.

On September 30, 2009, in connection with the closing of the Acquisition described above, the Company issued the Sellers (i) a senior subordinated note in the principal amount of $100,000, payable in full on December 15, 2010, with interest of 8% per annum payable on the unpaid principal amount (the Senior Seller Note), and (ii) a junior subordinated note in the principal amount of $150,000, payable in full on the fifth anniversary of the closing of the Acquisition, with interest of 10% per annum payable on the unpaid principal amount (the Junior Seller Note; and together with the Senior Seller Note, the Seller Notes). On December 22, 2009, the Company consented to the pledge and assignment of the Senior Seller Note by the Sellers as collateral security.

The purchase price paid to the Sellers was $596,000, consisting of $346,000 in cash and $250,000 in Seller Notes. However, the cash paid to the Sellers was reduced by $82,352 in cash bonuses paid by B&N College to 192 members of its management team and employees, not including Leonard Riggio. The Company financed the Acquisition through $250,000 of seller financing, $150,000 from the Credit Facility and the remainder from both the Company's and B&N College's cash on hand.

The Acquisition was accounted for as a business purchase pursuant to Accounting Standards Codification (ASC) 805, *Business Combinations* (ASC 805). Acquisition-related expenses totaled $10,400 and have been recorded as selling and administrative expenses in the Company's consolidated statement of operations for the 52 weeks ended May 1, 2010. As required by ASC 805-20, the Company allocated the purchase price to assets and liabilities based on their estimated fair value at the Acquisition date. The following table represents the allocation of the purchase price to the acquired net assets and resulting adjustment to goodwill (in thousands):

Cash Paid	$ 263,648
Seller Notes	$ 250,000
Fair value of total consideration	$ 513,648
Allocation of purchase price:	
Current assets	$ 609,786
Non-current assets	114,683
Trade name	245,000
Customer relationships	255,000
Goodwill	274,070
Total assets acquired	$1,498,539
Deferred taxes	234,631
Liabilities assumed	750,260
	$ 513,648

Acquired intangible assets consisted primarily of the trade name and customer relationships.

Trade Name

The Company previously licensed the "Barnes & Noble" trade name from B&N College under certain agreements. The Acquisition gave the Company exclusive ownership of its trade name. The estimated fair value ascribed to the trade name of $245,000 represents solely the estimated incremental value acquired as part of the Acquisition, which is not representative of the value of the "Barnes & Noble" trade name taken as a whole. The trade name has been classified as an indefinite life intangible asset.

Customer Relationships

The estimated fair value of customer relationships of B&N College is $255,000. Customers are comprised of existing college and university contractual relationships at the date of the Acquisition.

Amortization of Fair Value Ascribed to Customer Relationships

Historical customer attrition rates imply a life of 50 years; however, the useful life was shortened to 25 years since the majority of the value of discounted cash flows are captured in this period. The $255,000 will be amortized evenly over the 25-year period. The Company recorded $5,950 in amortization during the 52 weeks ended May 1, 2010, related to these intangibles.

The Company also recorded a short-term deferred tax liability of $26,810 and a long-term deferred tax liability of $207,821 related to the difference between the book basis and the tax basis of the net assets acquired. In addition, the Company stepped up the value of other assets and liabilities, resulting in goodwill of $272,879, which is not deductible for income tax purposes.

The following audited condensed financial information of B&N College since the date of the Acquisition on September 30, 2009 was included in the Company's consolidated results of operations for the 52 weeks ended May 1, 2010:

(In thousands)	52 Weeks Ended May 1, 2010
Sales	$836,458
Net loss	$ 3,344

The following unaudited pro forma condensed financial information assumes that the Acquisition was accounted for using the acquisition method of accounting for business combinations in accordance with ASC 805 and represents a pro forma presentation based upon available information of the combining companies giving effect to the Acquisition as if it had occurred on May 4, 2008, the first date of B&N College's prior fiscal year, with adjustments for amortization expense of intangible assets, depreciation expense for the fair value of property and equipment above its book value, termination or changes in certain compensation arrangements, termination of textbook royalties, non-operating expenses not acquired in the Acquisition, interest expense and income tax expense:

(In thousands)	52 Weeks Ended May 1, 2010	13 Weeks Ended May 2, 2009	52 Weeks Ended January 31, 2009
Sales	$6,786,661	$1,302,769	$6,907,179
Net income (loss) from continuing operations attributable to Barnes & Noble, Inc.	$ 53,514	$ (27,730)	$ 96,554
Income (loss) from continuing operations attributable to Barnes & Noble, Inc. per common share			
Basic	$ 0.93	$ (0.52)	$ 1.52
Diluted	$ 0.92	$ (0.52)	$ 1.48

The unaudited pro forma condensed financial information is based on the assumptions and adjustments which give effect to events that are: (i) directly attributable to the Acquisition; (ii) expected to have a continuing impact; and (iii) factually supportable. The unaudited pro forma condensed financial information is presented for informational purposes only and is not necessarily indicative of the operating results that would have been achieved had the Acquisition been consummated as of the dates indicated or of the results that may be obtained in the future.

In accordance with ASC 280, *Disclosures about Segments of an Enterprise and Related Information*, the Company performed an evaluation on the effect of the Acquisition on the identification of operating segments, considering the way the business is managed (focusing on the financial information distributed) and the manner in which the chief operating decision maker interacts with other members of management. As a result of this assessment, the Company has determined that it now has two operating segments: B&N Retail and B&N College. See Note 20 for more detail on segment information.

COMMITMENTS

DISCLOSURE

1.99 FASB ASC 440, *Commitments*, requires the disclosure of commitments such as those for unused letters of credit; long-term leases; assets pledged as security for loans; pension plans; cumulative preferred stock dividends in arrears; plant acquisition, obligations to reduce debts, maintain working capital, and restrict dividends; and unconditional purchase obligations.

1.100

TABLE 1-8: COMMITMENTS

Table 1-8 lists the various commitments disclosed in the annual reports of the survey entities.

	Number of Entities		
	2010	2009	2008
Restriction on amount of retained earnings available for dividends	62	N/C*	N/C*
Restriction on amount of treasury stock that a company can acquire	28	N/C*	N/C*
Requirement that a certain level of working capital or net worth be maintained	25	N/C*	N/C*
Acquisition of additional assets (mergers)	79	N/C*	N/C*
Level of net worth	37	N/C*	N/C*
Minimum level of cash flow/EBITDA	46	N/C*	N/C*
Lease covenants or other related lease restrictions	94	N/C*	N/C*
Restriction on amounts of additional debt that a company can incur (leverage/coverage ratio)	216	N/C*	N/C*
Construction of property/acquisition of PP&E, other capital expenditure restrictions	52	72	77
Financing/support agreements	42	47	45
Sales/marketing agreements	30	41	40
Additional payments in association with a business acquisition	19	38	46
Existence of employment contracts, separation agreements	19	35	35
Royalty/licensing agreements	23	26	34
Other—described	139	44	27

* N/C = Not compiled. Line item was not included in the table for the year shown.

PRESENTATION AND DISCLOSURE EXCERPTS

Restrictive Covenants

1.101

LEAR CORPORATION (DEC)

NOTES TO CONSOLIDATED FINANCIAL STATEMENTS

(8) Long-Term Debt (in part)

The indenture governing the Notes contains restrictive covenants that, among other things, limit the ability of the Company and its subsidiaries to: (i) incur additional debt, (ii) pay dividends and make other restricted payments, (iii) create or permit certain liens, (iv) issue or sell capital stock of the Company's restricted subsidiaries, (v) use the proceeds from sales of assets and subsidiary stock, (vi) create or permit restrictions on the ability of the Company's restricted subsidiaries to pay dividends or make other distributions to the Company, (vii) enter into transactions with affiliates, (viii) enter into sale and leaseback transactions and (ix) consolidate or merge or sell all or substantially all of the Company's assets. The foregoing limitations are subject to exceptions as set forth in the Notes. In addition, if in the future the Notes have an investment grade credit rating from both Moody's Investors Service and Standard & Poor's Ratings Services and no default has occurred and is continuing, certain of these covenants will, thereafter, no longer apply to the Notes for so long as the Notes have an investment grade credit rating by both rating agencies.

The indenture governing the Notes contains customary events of default that include, among other things (subject in certain cases to customary grace and cure periods): (i) non-payment of principal or interest, (ii) breach of certain covenants contained in the indenture governing the Notes, (iii) failure to pay certain other indebtedness or the acceleration of certain other indebtedness prior to maturity if the total amount of such indebtedness unpaid or accelerated exceeds $100 million or its foreign currency equivalent, (iv) the rendering of a final and nonappealable judgment for the payment of money in excess of $100 million or its foreign currency equivalent that is not timely paid or its enforcement stayed, (v) the failure of the guarantees by the subsidiary guarantors to be in full force and effect in all material respects and (vi) certain events of bankruptcy or insolvency. Generally, if an event of default occurs (subject to certain exceptions), the trustee or the holders of at least 25% in aggregate principal amount of the then outstanding Notes of any series may declare all of the Notes of such series to be due and payable immediately.

As of December 31, 2010, the Company was in compliance with all covenants under the indenture governing the Notes.

1.102

L-3 COMMUNICATIONS HOLDINGS, INC. (DEC)

NOTES TO CONSOLIDATED FINANCIAL STATEMENTS

10. Debt (in part)

Covenants (in part)

Financial and other restrictive covenants. The Revolving Credit Facility and Senior Subordinated Notes indentures contain financial and other restrictive covenants that limit, among other things, the ability of the subsidiaries of L-3 Communications to borrow additional funds, and the ability of L-3 Communications and its subsidiaries to incur liens, make investments, merge or consolidate, dispose of assets, pay dividends or repurchase its common stock. The Company's Revolving Credit Facility contains covenants that require that (1) the Company's consolidated leverage ratio be less than or equal to 4.0 to 1.0; (2) the Company's consolidated interest coverage ratio be greater than or equal to 3.0 to 1.0; and (3) the Company's consolidated senior leverage ratio be less than or equal to 3.5 to 1.0, in each case, as of the end of any fiscal quarter. Calculations of the financial covenants are to exclude, among other things, certain items such as impairment losses on goodwill or other intangible assets, non-cash gains or losses from discontinued operations, gains or losses in connection with asset dispositions, and gains or losses with respect to judgments or settlements in connection with litigation matters. As of December 31, 2010, the Company was in compliance with its financial and other restrictive covenants.

The Senior Indenture contains covenants customary for investment grade notes, including covenants that restrict the ability of L-3 Communications and its wholly-owned domestic subsidiaries to create, incur, assume or permit to exist any lien, except permitted liens (as defined in the Senior Indenture) and restrict the ability of L-3 Communications and its subsidiaries to enter into certain sale and leaseback transactions (as defined in the Senior Indenture).

The Senior Subordinated Notes indentures contain covenants that restrict the ability of L-3 Communications to incur indebtedness and issue capital stock that matures or is redeemable 91 days or less after the maturity date of such series of notes, and the ability of its restricted subsidiaries to incur indebtedness or issue preferred stock, unless the Company's fixed charge coverage ratio would have been at least 2.0 to 1.0 on a pro forma basis. The covenants are subject to several material exceptions, including an exception for indebtedness under the Company's credit facilities up to a specified amount.

Restricted Payments. L-3 Holdings relies on dividends paid by L-3 Communications to generate the funds necessary to pay dividends on and repurchase its common stock. The Revolving Credit Facility contains provisions that limit the ability of L-3 Communications to pay dividends, repurchase L-3 Holdings' common stock or other distributions with respect to any capital stock and make investments in L-3 Holdings. However, the Revolving Credit Facility permits L-3 Communications to:

- Fund payments of interest on indebtedness of L-3 Holdings and to fund payments of dividends on disqualified preferred stock issued by L-3 Holdings, so long as (1) any such indebtedness or disqualified preferred stock is guaranteed by L-3 Communications and (2) the proceeds received by L-3 Holdings from the issuance of such indebtedness or disqualified preferred stock have been invested by L-3 Holdings in L-3 Communications;

- Fund payments and prepayments of principal of indebtedness of L-3 Holdings and to fund optional and mandatory redemptions of disqualified preferred stock issued by L-3 Holdings, so long as (1) any such indebtedness or disqualified preferred stock is guaranteed by L-3 Communications and (2) the amount of such fundings does not exceed the sum of (a) the aggregate amount of investments made by L-3 Holdings in L-3 Communications with the proceeds from any issuance of indebtedness or disqualified preferred stock by L-3 Holdings that is guaranteed by L-3 Communications and (b) the amount of any premium, penalty, or accreted value payable in connection with such payment, prepayment or redemption;

- Pay other dividends on and make other redemptions of its equity interests (including for the benefit of L-3 Holdings) and make other investments in L-3 Holdings, so long as no default or event of default has occurred and is continuing, up to an aggregate amount of $2.0 billion, increased (or decreased) on a cumulative basis at the end of each quarter, commencing with the quarter ended December 31, 2009 by an amount equal to 50% of the consolidated net income (or deficit) of L-3 Communications for the quarter, plus (1) 100% of the proceeds from any issuance of capital stock (other than disqualified preferred stock) by L-3 Holdings after October 23, 2009, provided those proceeds were invested in L-3 Communications, plus (2) 100% of the proceeds from any issuance of indebtedness or disqualified preferred stock by L-3 Holdings after October 23, 2009 provided those proceeds were invested in L-3 Communications and the indebtedness or disqualified preferred stock is not guaranteed by L-3 Communications, plus (3) 100% of the proceeds from any issuance of capital stock (other than disqualified preferred stock) by L-3 Communications after October 23, 2009.

Disqualified preferred stock discussed above is stock, other than common stock, that is not classified as a component of shareholders' equity on the balance sheet. At December 31, 2010, L-3 Holdings and L-3 Communications did not have any disqualified preferred stock.

The Senior Subordinated Notes indentures contain provisions that limit the ability of L-3 Communications to pay dividends to L-3 Holdings and make investments in L-3 Holdings, subject to exceptions. Subject to certain limitations, the indentures permit L-3 Communications to make such restricted payments so long as it would be able to incur at least one dollar of additional indebtedness under the fixed charge coverage ratio test described above and meet other conditions.

1.103

SEABOARD CORPORATION (DEC)

NOTES TO CONSOLIDATED FINANCIAL STATEMENTS

Note 8—Notes Payable and Long-term Debt (in part)

Of the 2010 foreign subsidiary obligations, $16,352,000 was payable in U.S. dollars, $221,000 was payable in Argentine pesos. Of the 2009 foreign subsidiary obligations, $688,000 was denominated in CFA francs, $232,000 was payable in Argentine pesos.

The terms of the note agreements pursuant to which the senior notes, IDRBs, bank debt and credit lines were issued require, among other terms, the maintenance of certain ratios and minimum net worth, the most restrictive of which requires consolidated funded debt not to exceed 50% of consolidated total capitalization; an adjusted leverage ratio of less than 3.5 to 1.0; requires the maintenance of consolidated tangible net worth, as defined, of not less than $1,150,000,000 plus 25% of cumulative consolidated net income beginning March 29, 2008; limits aggregate dividend payments to $10,000,000 plus 50% of consolidated net income less 100% of consolidated net losses beginning January 1, 2002 plus the aggregate amount of Net Proceeds of Capital Stock for such period ($645,864,000 as of December 31, 2010) or $15,000,000 per year under certain circumstances; limits the sum of subsidiary indebtedness and priority indebtedness to 10% of consolidated tangible net worth; and limits Seaboard's ability to acquire investments and sell assets under certain circumstances. Seaboard is in compliance with all restrictive debt covenants relating to these agreements as of December 31, 2010.

1.104

SMITHFIELD FOODS, INC. (APR)

NOTES TO CONSOLIDATED FINANCIAL STATEMENTS

Note 10. Debt (in part)

Debt Covenants

Our various debt agreements contain covenants that limit additional borrowings, acquisitions, dispositions, leasing of assets and payments of dividends to shareholders, among other restrictions.

Our senior unsecured and secured notes limit our ability to incur additional indebtedness, subject to certain exceptions, when our interest coverage ratio is, or after incurring additional indebtedness would be, less than 2.0 to 1.0 (the Incurrence Test). As of May 2, 2010, we did not meet the Incurrence Test. Due to the trailing twelve month nature of the Incurrence Test, we do not expect to meet the Incurrence Test again until the second quarter of fiscal 2011 at the earliest. The Incurrence Test is not a maintenance covenant and our failure to meet the Incurrence Test is not a default. In addition to limiting our ability to incur additional indebtedness, our failure to meet the Incurrence Test restricts us from engaging in certain other activities, including paying cash dividends, repurchasing our common stock and making certain investments. However, our failure to meet the Incurrence Test does not preclude us from borrowing on the ABL Credit Facility or from refinancing existing indebtedness. Therefore we do not expect the limitations resulting from our inability to satisfy the Incurrence Test to have a material adverse effect on our business or liquidity.

Our ABL Credit Facility contains a covenant requiring us to maintain a fixed charges coverage ratio of at least 1.1 to 1.0 when the amounts available for borrowing under the ABL Credit Facility are less than the greater of $120 million or 15% of the total commitments under the facility (currently $1.0 billion). We currently are not subject to this restriction and we do not anticipate that our borrowing availability will decline below those thresholds during fiscal 2010, although there can be no assurance that this will not occur because our borrowing availability depends upon our borrowing base calculated for purposes of that facility.

During the first quarter of fiscal 2010, we determined that we previously and unintentionally breached a non-financial covenant under our senior unsecured notes relating to certain foreign subsidiaries' indebtedness. We promptly cured this minor breach by amending certain debt agreements of the subsidiaries and extinguishing other indebtedness of the subsidiaries, and, as a result, no event of default occurred under our senior unsecured notes or any other facilities.

Leasing Commitments

1.105

NETAPP, INC. (APR)

NOTES TO CONSOLIDATED FINANCIAL STATEMENTS

18. Commitments and Contingencies (in part)

Operating Leases—We lease office space in several U.S. locations. Outside the United States, larger leased sites include sites in The Netherlands, Australia, Belgium, France, Germany, India, Japan, and the United Kingdom. We also lease equipment and vehicles.

As of April 30, 2010, we have four leasing arrangements (Leasing Arrangements 1, 2, 3 and 4) for facilities in Sunnyvale, California with BNPPLC which require us to lease certain of our land to BNPPLC for a period of 99 years, and to lease approximately 0.6 million square feet of office space for our headquarters in Sunnyvale costing up to $149.6 million. Under these leasing arrangements, we pay BNPPLC minimum lease payments, which vary based on LIBOR plus a spread or a fixed rate on the costs of the facilities on the respective lease commencement dates. We make payments for each of the leases for a term of five years. We have the option to renew each of the leases for two consecutive five-year periods upon approval by BNPPLC. Upon expiration (or upon any earlier termination) of the lease terms, we must elect one of the following options: (i) purchase the buildings from BNPPLC at cost; (ii) if certain conditions are met, arrange for the sale of the buildings by BNPPLC to a third party for an amount equal to at least 85% of the costs (residual guarantee), and be liable for any deficiency between the net proceeds received from the third party and such amounts; or (iii) pay BNPPLC supplemental payments for an amount equal to at least 85% of the costs (residual guarantee), in which event we may recoup some or all of such payments by arranging for a sale of each or all buildings by BNPPLC during the ensuing two-year period. The following table summarizes the costs, the residual guarantee, the applicable LIBOR plus spread or fixed rate at April 30, 2010, and the date we began to make payments for each of our leasing arrangements (in millions):

Leasing Arrangements	Cost	Residual Guarantee	LIBOR Plus Spread or Fixed Rate	Lease Commencement Date	Term
1	$48.5	$41.2	3.99%	January 2008	5 years
2	$80.0	$68.0	1.08%	December 2007	5 years
3	$10.5	$ 8.9	3.97%	December 2007	5 years
4	$10.6	$ 9.0	3.99%	December 2007	5 years

These leases require us to maintain specified financial covenants with which we were in compliance as of April 30, 2010. Such financial covenants include a maximum ratio of Total Debt to Earnings before Interest, Taxes, Depreciation and Amortization and a minimum amount of Unencumbered Cash and Short-Term Investments.

Future annual minimum lease payments under all non-cancelable operating leases with an initial term in excess of one year as of April 30, 2010 are as follows (in millions):

	2011	2012	2013	2014	2015	Thereafter	Total
Office operating lease payments	$26.7	$22.3	$ 17.8	$15.1	$13.0	$20.4	$115.3
Real estate lease payments	3.6	3.6	129.5	—	—	—	136.7
Equipment operating lease payments	24.3	10.7	4.6	0.4	—	—	40.0
Less: Sublease income	(5.8)	(0.8)	(0.6)	(0.4)	(0.2)	—	(7.8)
Total lease commitments	$48.8	$35.8	$151.3	$15.1	$12.8	$20.4	$284.2

Included in real estate lease payments pursuant to four financing arrangements with BNP Paribas Leasing Corporation (BNPPLC) are (i) lease commitments of $3.6 million in each of the fiscal years 2011 and 2012; $2.4 million in fiscal 2013, which are based on the LIBOR rate at April 30, 2010 plus a spread or a fixed rate, for terms of five years; and (ii) at the expiration or termination of the lease, a supplemental payment obligation equal to our minimum guarantee of $127.1 million in the event that we elect not to purchase or arrange for sale of the buildings.

In fiscal 2010, we determined that it was probable that the fair value of the properties under synthetic lease would be below the guaranteed residual at the end of the initial lease terms. Our current estimate of this shortfall is $36.9 million. We are accruing for this deficiency over the remaining initial terms of the respective leases of thirty-two months.

Capital Expenditures

1.106

FRONTIER COMMUNICATIONS CORPORATION (DEC)

NOTES TO CONSOLIDATED FINANCIAL STATEMENTS

(20) Commitments and Contingencies (in part)

We anticipate total capital expenditures of approximately $750 million to $780 million for 2011 related to our Frontier legacy properties and the Acquired Business. Although we from time to time make short-term purchasing commitments to vendors with respect to these expenditures, we generally do not enter into firm, written contracts for such activities.

In connection with the Transaction, the Company undertook activities to plan and implement systems conversions and other initiatives necessary to effectuate the closing (Phase 1). The Company incurred operating expenses, including deal costs, of approximately $135.6 million and capital expenditures of approximately $90.6 million in 2010 related to these integration initiatives in Phase 1. The Company continues to engage in activities to enable the Company to implement its "go to market" strategy in its new markets and to complete the conversions of all the remaining systems into one platform (Phase 2). The Company also incurred $1.5 million of integration costs and $6.4 million in capital expenditures related to the commencement of these Phase 2 activities during 2010. The Company currently expects to incur operating expenses and capital expenditures of approximately $90 million and $60 million, respectively, in 2011 related to these Phase 2 initiatives.

In addition, the Federal Communications Commission (FCC) and certain state regulatory commissions, in connection with granting their approvals of the Transaction, specified certain capital expenditure and operating requirements for the acquired Territories for specified periods of time postclosing. These requirements focus primarily on certain capital investment commitments to expand broadband availability and speeds to at least 85% of the households throughout the acquired Territories with minimum speeds of 3 megabits per second (Mbps) by the end of 2013 and 4 Mbps by the end of 2015. To satisfy all or part of certain capital investment commitments to three state regulatory commissions, we placed an aggregate amount of $115.0 million in cash into escrow accounts and obtained the letter of credit for $190.0 million in the third quarter of 2010. Another $72.4 million of cash in an escrow account, with an associated liability (reflected in Other liabilities), was acquired in connection with the Merger to be used for service quality initiatives in the state of West Virginia. As of December 31, 2010, the Company had a restricted cash balance in these escrow accounts in the aggregate amount of $187.5 million. The aggregate amount of these escrow accounts and the letter of credit will decrease over time as Frontier makes the required capital expenditures in the respective states.

Financing Commitments

1.107

THE BOEING COMPANY (DEC)

NOTES TO CONSOLIDATED FINANCIAL STATEMENTS

Note 11—Liabilities, Commitments and Contingencies (in part)

Financing Commitments (In millions)

Financing commitments totaled $9,865 and $10,409 as of December 31, 2010 and 2009. We anticipate that a significant portion of these commitments will not be exercised by the customers as we continue to work with third party financiers to provide alternative financing to customers. However, there can be no assurances that we will not be required to fund greater amounts than historically required.

We have entered into standby letters of credit agreements and surety bonds with financial institutions primarily relating to the guarantee of future performance on certain contracts. Contingent liabilities on outstanding letters of credit agreements and surety bonds aggregated approximately $7,599 and $7,052 as of December 31, 2010 and 2009.

In connection with the formation of ULA, we and Lockheed Martin Corporation (Lockheed) each committed to provide up to $200 to support its working capital requirements through December 1, 2011. ULA did not request any funds under the commitment as of December 31, 2010. We and Lockheed have also each committed to provide ULA with up to $232 of additional capital contributions in the event ULA does not have sufficient funds to make a required payment to us under an inventory supply agreement.

Royalty and Advertising Obligations

1.108

WOLVERINE WORLD WIDE, INC. (DEC)

NOTES TO CONSOLIDATED FINANCIAL STATEMENTS

8. Litigation and Contingencies (in part; in thousands)

The Company has future minimum royalty and advertising obligations due under the terms of certain licenses held by the Company. These minimum future obligations are as follows:

(In thousands)	2011	2012	2013	2014	2015
Minimum royalties	1,693	880	898	916	934
Minimum advertising	1,941	1,999	2,059	2,121	2,184

Minimum royalties are based on both fixed obligations and assumptions regarding the consumer price index. Royalty obligations in excess of minimum requirements are based upon future sales levels. In accordance with these agreements, the Company incurred royalty expense of $3,028, $2,861 and $3,198 for 2010, 2009 and 2008, respectively.

The terms of certain license agreements also require the Company to make advertising expenditures based on the level of sales. In accordance with these agreements, the Company incurred advertising expense of $2,998, $2,682 and $3,018 for 2010, 2009 and 2008, respectively.

Purchase Agreements

1.109

TIFFANY & CO. (JAN)

NOTES TO CONSOLIDATED FINANCIAL STATEMENTS

L. Commitments and Contingencies (in part)

Diamond Sourcing Activities

The Company will, from time to time, secure supplies of diamonds by agreeing to purchase a defined portion of a mine's output. Under such arrangements, management anticipates that it will purchase approximately $75,000,000 of rough diamonds in 2010. Purchases beyond 2010 that are contingent upon mine production cannot be reasonably estimated.

Contractual Cash Obligations and Contingent Funding Commitments

At January 31, 2010, the Company's contractual cash obligations and contingent funding commitments were: inventory purchases of $291,322,000 (which includes the $75,000,000 obligation discussed in Diamond Sourcing Activities above); non-inventory purchases of $4,552,000; construction-in-progress of $17,857,000 and other contractual obligations of $29,649,000.

CONTINGENCIES

RECOGNITION AND MEASUREMENT

1.110 The FASB ASC glossary defines a *contingency* as an existing condition, situation, or set of circumstances involving uncertainty about possible gain (gain contingency) or loss (loss contingency) to an entity that will ultimately be resolved when one or more future events occur or fail to occur. FASB ASC 450-20 sets forth guidance for the recognition and disclosure of loss contingencies. An estimated loss from a loss contingency should be accrued by a charge to income if both of the following conditions are met:

- Information available before the financial statements are issued or available to be issued indicates that it is probable that an asset had been impaired or a liability had been incurred at the date of the financial statements. It is implicit in this condition that it must be probable that one or more future events will occur confirming the fact of the loss.
- The amount of loss can be reasonably estimated.

1.111 Disclosure is preferable to accrual when a reasonable estimate of loss cannot be made. Even losses that are reasonably estimable should not be accrued if it is not probable that an asset has been impaired or a liability has been incurred at the date of the entity's financial statements because those losses relate to a future period, rather than the current period. If some amount within a range of loss appears at the time to be a better estimate than any other amount within the range, that amount should be accrued. When no amount within the range is a better estimate than any other amount, however, the minimum amount in that range should be accrued. Select loss contingency disclosures do not apply to loss contingencies arising from an entity's recurring estimation of its allowance for credit losses. FASB ASC 450-30 states the guidance for the recognition and disclosure for gain contingencies and explains that a contingency that might result in a gain usually should not be reflected in the financial statements because to do so might be to recognize revenue before its realization. When contingency disclosures exist, public companies generally present a balance sheet caption for contingencies, in accordance with Rule 5-02 of Regulation S-X.

1.112

TABLE 1-9: CONTINGENCIES

Table 1-9 lists the loss and gain contingencies disclosed in the annual reports of the survey entities.

	Number of Entities		
	2010	2009	2008
Loss Contingencies			
Litigation	344	379	404
Environmental	193	203	225
Possible tax assessments	133	145	166
Insurance	101	132	160
Government investigations	107	95	122
Warranties	25	N/C*	N/C*
Other, described	33	63	66
Gain Contingencies			
Operating loss carryforward	262	429	423
Tax credits and other tax credit carryforwards	212	273	255
Capital loss carryforward	60	69	65
Alternative minimum tax carryforward	22	44	40
Plaintiff litigation	13	42	55
Asset sale receivable	—	8	8
Investment credit carryforward	3	7	11
Potential tax refund	7	7	4
Charitable contribution carryforward	3	4	5
Other, described	6	6	3

* N/C = Not compiled. Line item was not included in the table for the year shown.

PRESENTATION AND DISCLOSURE EXCERPTS

Legal Matters

1.113

BOSTON SCIENTIFIC CORPORATION (DEC)

NOTES TO CONSOLIDATED FINANCIAL STATEMENTS

Note L—Commitments and Contingencies (in part)

The medical device market in which we primarily participate is largely technology driven. Physician customers, particularly in interventional cardiology, have historically moved quickly to new products and new technologies. As a result, intellectual property rights, particularly patents and trade secrets, play a significant role in product development and differentiation. However, intellectual property litigation is inherently complex and unpredictable. Furthermore, appellate courts can overturn lower court patent decisions.

In addition, competing parties frequently file multiple suits to leverage patent portfolios across product lines, technologies and geographies and to balance risk and exposure between the parties. In some cases, several competitors are parties in the same proceeding, or in a series of related proceedings, or litigate multiple features of a single class of de-

vices. These forces frequently drive settlement not only for individual cases, but also for a series of pending and potentially related and unrelated cases. In addition, although monetary and injunctive relief is typically sought, remedies and restitution are generally not determined until the conclusion of the trial court proceedings and can be modified on appeal. Accordingly, the outcomes of individual cases are difficult to time, predict or quantify and are often dependent upon the outcomes of other cases in other geographies. Several third parties have asserted that certain of our current and former product offerings infringe patents owned or licensed by them. We have similarly asserted that other products sold by our competitors infringe patents owned or licensed by us. Adverse outcomes in one or more of the proceedings against us could limit our ability to sell certain products in certain jurisdictions, or reduce our operating margin on the sale of these products and could have a material adverse effect on our financial position, results of operations or liquidity.

In particular, although we have resolved multiple litigation matters with Johnson & Johnson, described herein, we continue to be involved in patent litigation with them, particularly relating to drug-eluting stent systems. Adverse outcomes in one or more of these matters could have a material adverse effect on our ability to sell certain products and on our operating margins, financial position, results of operation or liquidity.

In the normal course of business, product liability, securities and commercial claims are asserted against us. Similar claims may be asserted against us in the future related to events not known to management at the present time. We are substantially self-insured with respect to product liability claims and intellectual property infringement, and maintain an insurance policy providing limited coverage against securities claims. The absence of significant third-party insurance coverage increases our potential exposure to unanticipated claims or adverse decisions. Product liability claims, securities and commercial litigation, and other legal proceedings in the future, regardless of their outcome, could have a material adverse effect on our financial position, results of operations and liquidity. In addition, the medical device industry is the subject of numerous governmental investigations often involving regulatory, marketing and other business practices. These investigations could result in the commencement of civil and criminal proceedings, substantial fines, penalties and administrative remedies, divert the attention of our management and have an adverse effect on our financial position, results of operations and liquidity.

We generally record losses for claims in excess of the limits of purchased insurance in earnings at the time and to the extent they are probable and estimable. In accordance with ASC Topic 450, *Contingencies* (formerly FASB Statement No. 5, *Accounting for Contingencies*), we accrue anticipated costs of settlement, damages, losses for general product liability claims and, under certain conditions, costs of defense, based on historical experience or to the extent specific losses are probable and estimable. Otherwise, we expense these costs as incurred. If the estimate of a probable loss is a range and no amount within the range is more likely, we accrue the minimum amount of the range.

Our accrual for legal matters that are probable and estimable was $588 million as of December 31, 2010 and $2.316 billion as of December 31, 2009, and includes estimated costs of settlement, damages and defense. The decrease in our accrual is due primarily to the payment of $1.725 billion to Johnson & Johnson in connection with the patent litigation settlement discussed below. We continue to assess certain litigation and claims to determine the amounts, if any, that management believes will be paid as a result of such claims and litigation and, therefore, additional losses may be accrued and paid in the future, which could materially adversely impact our operating results, cash flows and our ability to comply with our debt covenants.

In management's opinion, we are not currently involved in any legal proceedings other than those specifically identified below, which, individually or in the aggregate, could have a material effect on our financial condition, operations and/or cash flows. Unless included in our legal accrual or otherwise indicated below, a range of loss associated with any individual material legal proceeding cannot be estimated.

Patent Litigation (in part)

Litigation with Johnson & Johnson (including its subsidiary, Cordis Corporation)

On April 13, 1998, Cordis Corporation filed suit against Boston Scientific Scimed, Inc. and us in the U.S. District Court for the District of Delaware, alleging that our former NIR ® stent infringed three claims of two patents (the Fischell patents) owned by Cordis and seeking damages and injunctive relief. On May 2, 2005, the District Court entered judgment that none of the three asserted claims was infringed, although two of the claims were not invalid. The District Court also found the two patents unenforceable for inequitable conduct. Cordis appealed the non-infringement finding of one claim in one patent and the unenforceability of that patent. We cross appealed the finding that one of the two claims was not invalid. Cordis did not appeal as to the second patent. On June 29, 2006, the Court of Appeals upheld the finding that the claim was not invalid, remanded the case to the District Court for additional factual findings related to inequitable conduct, and did not address the finding that the claim was not infringed. On August 10, 2009, the District Court reversed its finding that the two patents were unenforceable for inequitable conduct. On August 24, 2009, we asked the District Court to reconsider and on March 31, 2010, the District Court denied our request for reconsideration. On April 2, 2010, Cordis filed an appeal and on April 9, 2010, we filed a cross appeal.

On each of May 25, June 1, June 22 and November 27, 2007, Boston Scientific Scimed, Inc. and we filed a declaratory judgment action against Johnson & Johnson and Cordis Corporation in the U.S. District Court for the District of Delaware seeking a declaratory judgment of invalidity of four U.S. patents (the Wright and Falotico patents) owned by them and of non-infringement of the patents by the PROMUS® coronary stent system, supplied to us by Abbott Laboratories. On February 21, 2008, Johnson & Johnson and Cordis filed counterclaims for infringement seeking an injunction and a declaratory judgment of validity. On June 25, 2009, we amended our complaints to allege that the four patents owned by Johnson & Johnson and Cordis are unenforceable. On January 20, 2010, the District Court found the four patents owned by Johnson & Johnson and Cordis invalid. On February 17, 2010, Johnson & Johnson and Cordis appealed the District Court's decision. The oral argument on appeal occurred on January 11, 2011.

On February 1, 2008, Wyeth Corporation and Cordis Corporation filed an amended complaint against Abbott Laboratories, adding us and Boston Scientific Scimed, Inc. as additional defendants to the complaint. The suit alleges that the PROMUS® coronary stent system, supplied to us by Abbott, infringes three U.S. patents (the Morris patents) owned by Wyeth and licensed to Cordis. The suit was filed in the U.S. District Court for the District of New Jersey seeking monetary and injunctive relief. A Markman hearing was held on July 15, 2010. On November 3, 2010, the District Court granted a motion to bifurcate damages from liability in the case. A liability trial is scheduled to begin September 12, 2011. On January 7, 2011, Wyeth and Cordis withdrew their infringement claim as to one of the patents.

On September 22, 2009, Cordis Corporation, Cordis LLC and Wyeth Corporation filed a complaint for patent infringement against Abbott Laboratories, Abbott Cardiovascular Systems, Inc., Boston Scientific Scimed, Inc. and us alleging that the PROMUS® coronary stent system, supplied to us by Abbott, infringes a patent (the Llanos patent) owned by Cordis and Wyeth that issued on September 22, 2009. The suit was filed in the U.S. District Court for the District of New Jersey seeking monetary and injunctive relief. On September 22, 2009, we filed a declaratory judgment action in the U.S. District Court for the District of Minnesota against Cordis and Wyeth seeking a declaration that the patent is invalid and not infringed by the PROMUS® coronary stent system, supplied to us by Abbott. On January 19, 2010, the Minnesota District Court transferred our suit to the U.S. District Court for the District of New Jersey and on February 17, 2010, the Minnesota case was dismissed. On July 13, 2010, Cordis filed a motion to amend the complaint to add an additional patent, which the New Jersey District Court granted on August 2, 2010. Cordis filed an amended complaint on August 9, 2010. On September 3, 2010 we filed an answer to the amended complaint along with counterclaims of invalidity and non-infringement.

On December 4, 2009, Boston Scientific Corporation and Boston Scientific Scimed, Inc. filed a complaint for patent infringement against Cordis Corporation alleging that its Cypher Mini™ stent product infringes a U.S. patent (the Jang patent) owned by us. The suit was filed in the U.S. District Court for the District of Minnesota seeking monetary and injunctive relief. On January 19, 2010, Cordis filed its answer as well as a motion to transfer the suit to the U.S. District Court for the District of Delaware. On April 16, 2010, the Minnesota District Court granted Cordis' motion to transfer the case to Delaware. A trial has been scheduled to begin on May 5, 2011.

On January 15, 2010, Cordis Corporation filed a complaint against us and Boston Scientific Scimed, Inc. alleging that the PROMUS® coronary stent system, supplied to us by Abbott, infringes three patents (the Fischell patents) owned by Cordis. The suit was filed in the U.S. District Court for the District of Delaware and seeks monetary and injunctive relief. A trial is scheduled to begin on April 9, 2012.

1.114

AK STEEL HOLDING CORPORATION (DEC)

NOTES TO CONSOLIDATED FINANCIAL STATEMENTS

Note 9—Environmental and Legal Contingencies (in part; in millions)

Butler Works Retiree Healthcare Benefits Litigation

As previously reported, on June 18, 2009, three former hourly members of the Butler Armco Independent Union filed a purported class action against AK Steel in the United States District Court for the Southern District of Ohio, Case No. 1-09CV00423 (the "2009 Retiree Action"), alleging that AK Steel did not have a right to make changes to their healthcare benefits. On June 29, 2009, the plaintiffs filed an amended complaint. The named plaintiffs in the 2009 Retiree Action sought, among other things, injunctive relief for themselves and the other members of a proposed class, including an order retroactively rescinding certain changes to retiree healthcare benefits negotiated by AK Steel with its union. The proposed class the plaintiffs sought to represent consisted originally of all union-represented retirees of AK Steel other than those retirees who were included in the class covered by the Middletown Works Retiree Healthcare Benefits Litigation described below. On August 21, 2009, AK Steel filed an answer to the amended complaint and filed a motion for summary judgment. On September 14, 2009, plaintiffs filed a motion for partial summary judgment and responded to defendant's motion. On October 14, 2009, plaintiffs filed a motion for preliminary injunction, seeking to prevent certain scheduled January 2010 changes to retiree healthcare from taking effect. On November 25, 2009, AK Steel filed its opposition to the motion for a preliminary injunction, opposition to plaintiffs' motion for partial summary judgment, and reply in support of its motion for summary judgment. A hearing on the then-pending motions was held on December 8, 2009. During the course of the hearing, plaintiffs' counsel notified the court that the pending motion for a preliminary injunction was limited to retirees from the Company's Butler Works in Butler, Pennsylvania. On January 29, 2010, the trial court issued an opinion and order granting plaintiffs' motion for a preliminary injunction and barring the Company from effecting any further benefit reductions or new healthcare charges for Butler Works hourly retirees until final judgment in the case.

On February 2, 2010, AK Steel filed a notice of appeal to the United States Court of Appeals for the Sixth Circuit seeking a reversal of the decision to grant the preliminary injunction. Absent a reversal of the decision to impose the preliminary injunction, the negotiated changes to retiree healthcare for the Company's Butler Works retirees would be rescinded and the Company's other postretirement benefit ("OPEB") obligations would increase by approximately $145.0 based upon then-current valuation assumptions. This amount reflects the value of the estimated additional healthcare and welfare benefits the Company would pay out with respect to the Butler hourly retirees.

In the third quarter of 2010, the Company reached a tentative settlement agreement (the "Hourly Class Settlement") with the Butler Works hourly retirees who initiated the litigation. The appeal pending in the Sixth Circuit Court of Appeals was stayed pending finalization of the Hourly Class Settlement. The participants in the Hourly Class Settlement consist generally of all retirees and their surviving spouses who worked for AK Steel at Butler Works and retired from AK Steel on or before December 31, 2006 (the "Hourly Class Members"). Pursuant to the Hourly Class Settlement, AK Steel agreed to continue to provide company-paid health and life insurance to Hourly Class Members through December 31, 2014, and to make combined lump sum payments totaling $86.0 to a Voluntary Employees Beneficiary Association trust (the "VEBA Trust") and to plaintiffs' counsel. More specifically, AK Steel will make three cash contributions to the VEBA Trust as follows: $21.4 on August 1, 2011; $30.0 on July 31, 2012; and $26.0 on July 31, 2013. The balance of the $86.0 in lump sum payments will be paid to plaintiffs' attorneys on August 1, 2011, to cover plaintiffs' obligations with respect to attorneys' fees. Effective January 1, 2015, AK Steel will transfer to the VEBA Trust all OPEB obligations owed to the Hourly Class Members under the Company's applicable health and welfare plans and will have no further liability for any claims incurred by the Hourly Class Members after December, 31, 2014, relating to their OPEB obligations. The VEBA Trust will be utilized to fund all such future OPEB obligations to the Hourly Class Members. Trustees of the VEBA will determine the scope of the benefits to be provided to the Hourly Class Members.

After reaching the Hourly Class Settlement, the Company was notified that a separate group of retirees from the Butler Works who were previously salaried employees and who had been members of the Butler Armco Independent Salaried Union also were asserting similar claims and desired to settle those claims on a basis similar to the settlement with the hourly employees. The participants in this group consist generally of all retirees and their surviving spouses who worked for AK Steel at Butler Works and retired from AK Steel between January 1, 1985, and on or before September 30, 2006 (the "Salaried Class Members"). If the Salaried Class Members were to prevail on their claims, the Company's other postretirement benefit obligation would have increased by approximately $8.5 based upon then-current valuation assumptions. This amount reflects the value of the estimated additional healthcare and welfare benefits the Company would pay out with respect to the Salaried Class Members. After negotiation with counsel representing the Salaried Class Members, the Company also reached a tentative settlement agreement with the Salaried Class Members (the "Salaried Class Settlement"). The stay referenced above of the appeal pending in the Sixth Circuit Court of Appeals pending finalization of the Hourly Class Settlement also applies to the Salaried Class Settlement.

Pursuant to the Salaried Class Settlement, AK Steel agreed to continue to provide company-paid health and life insurance to Salaried Class Members through December 31, 2014, and to make combined lump sum payments totaling $5.0 to a VEBA Trust and to plaintiffs' counsel. AK Steel will make three cash contributions to the VEBA Trust as follows: approximately $1.2 on August 1, 2011; approximately $1.7 on July 31, 2012; and approximately $1.6 on July 31, 2013. The balance of the $5.0 in lump sum payments will be paid to plaintiffs' attorneys on August 1, 2011, to cover plaintiffs' obligations with respect to attorneys' fees. Effective January 1, 2015, AK Steel will transfer to the VEBA Trust all OPEB obligations owed to the Salaried Class Members under the Company's applicable health and welfare plans and will have no further liability for any claims incurred by the Salaried Class Members after December 31, 2014, relating to their OPEB obligations. The VEBA Trust will be utilized to fund all such future OPEB obligations to the Salaried Class Members. Trustees of the VEBA will determine the scope of the benefits to be provided to the Salaried Class Members.

The tentative settlements (hereinafter collectively referred to as the "Butler Retiree Settlement") with both the Hourly Class Members and the Salaried Class Members (hereinafter collectively referred to as the "Class Members") were subject to approval by the Court. On September 17, 2010, the plaintiffs filed an Unopposed Motion to File a Second Amended Complaint and an Unopposed Amended Motion for an Order Conditionally Certifying Classes, and the parties jointly filed a Joint Motion for Preliminary Approval of Class Action Settlement Agreements and Proposed Class Notice. On September 24, 2010, the Court held a hearing on these motions and issued orders granting the joint motion for preliminary approval of the Butler Retiree Settlement, conditionally certifying the two classes, and allowing the filing of a second amended complaint. The second amended complaint was deemed filed as of September, 24, 2010 and defined the class represented by the Plaintiffs to consist of the Class Members. Notice of the settlement was sent to all Class Members on October 1, 2010. The Class Members were given the opportunity to object to the Butler Retiree Settlement in writing and at a hearing conducted by the Court to determine whether to approve that Settlement. The deadline for filing objections was November 15, 2010 and only one objection was filed prior to that date. That objection subsequently was withdrawn. On December 20, 2010, the parties filed their motions for approval of the Butler Retiree Settlement. Plaintiffs further filed a motion for approval of attorney fees and expenses. A Fairness Hearing with respect to the settlement occurred on January 10, 2011. There were no objections to the Butler Retiree Settlement or to the proposed attorney fee award expressed during the Fairness Hearing. On January 10, 2011, the Court issued written orders granting final approval to the Butler Retiree Settlement, as well as the proposed attorney fee award. The final judgment (the "Judgment") formally approving the Butler Retiree Settlement and the attorney fee award also was entered on January 10, 2011. The Butler Retiree Settlement became effective on that date. No appeal from that Judgment has been taken and the time for filing such an appeal has expired.

As of December 31, 2010, the Company's total OPEB liability for all of its retirees was approximately $795.4. Following entry of the Judgment approving the Butler Retiree Settlement, the Company's total OPEB liability (prior to any funding of the VEBA Trust) will increase by approximately $30.0 in 2011. A one-time, pre-tax charge of approximately $14.2, based upon then-current valuation assumptions, will be recorded in the first quarter of 2011 to reverse previous amortization of the prior plan amendment. In addition, the Company recorded a one-time charge of $9.1 in the fourth quarter of 2010 related to the Butler Retiree Settlement. The remaining portion of the plan amendment will be amortized over approximately five years. The Company's only remaining liability with respect to the OPEB obligations to the Class Members will be to provide existing company-paid health and life insurance to Class Members through December 31, 2014, and to contribute the payments due to the VEBA Trust under the settlements. The Company's OPEB liability will be reduced after each of the annual contributions to the VEBA Trust under the terms of the settlements. In addition, its OPEB liability will be reduced by the amounts of the continued payments of uncapped benefits through December 31, 2014. After December 31, 2014, the Company will have no liabil-

ity or responsibility with respect to OPEB obligations to the Class Members.

For accounting purposes, a settlement of the Company's OPEB obligations related to the Class Members will be deemed to have occurred when AK Steel makes the last payment called for under the Settlement.

Middletown Works Retiree Healthcare Benefits Litigation

As previously reported, on June 1, 2006, AK Steel notified approximately 4,600 of its current retirees (or their surviving spouses) who formerly were hourly and salaried members of the Armco Employees Independent Federation ("AEIF") that AK Steel was terminating their existing healthcare insurance benefits plan and implementing a new plan more consistent with current steel industry practices that would require the retirees to contribute to the cost of their healthcare benefits, effective October 1, 2006. On July 18, 2006, a group of nine former hourly and salaried members of the AEIF filed a class action (the "Middletown Retiree Action") in the United States District Court for the Southern District of Ohio (the "Court"), Case No. 1-06CV0468, alleging that AK Steel did not have a right to make changes to their healthcare benefits. The named plaintiffs in the Middletown Retiree Action sought, among other things, injunctive relief (including an order retroactively rescinding the changes) for themselves and the other members of the class. On August 4, 2006, the plaintiffs in the Middletown Retiree Action filed a motion for a preliminary injunction seeking to prevent AK Steel from implementing the previously announced changes to healthcare benefits with respect to the AEIF-represented hourly employees. AK Steel opposed that motion, but on September 22, 2006, the trial court issued an order granting the motion. On October 8, 2007, the Company announced that it had reached a tentative settlement (the "Middletown Retiree Settlement") of the claims of the retirees in the Middletown Retiree Action. The Middletown Retiree Settlement was opposed by certain objecting class members, but their objections were rejected by the trial court and on appeal. After the appeal of the objecting participants was dismissed, the Middletown Retiree Settlement became final on July 6, 2009.

Under terms of the Middletown Retiree Settlement, AK Steel has transferred to a Voluntary Employees Beneficiary Association trust (the "VEBA Trust") all OPEB obligations owed to the covered retirees under the Company's applicable health and welfare plans and will have no further liability for any claims incurred by those retirees after the effective date of the Middletown Retiree Settlement relating to their OPEB obligations. The VEBA Trust will be utilized to fund the future OPEB obligations to the covered retirees. Under the terms of the Middletown Retiree Settlement, AK Steel was obligated to initially fund the VEBA Trust with a contribution of $468.0 in cash within two business days of the effective date of that Settlement. AK Steel made this contribution on March 4, 2008. AK Steel further committed under the Middletown Retiree Settlement to make three subsequent annual cash contributions of $65.0 each, for a total contribution of $663.0. AK Steel has timely made the first two of these three annual cash contributions of $65.0, leaving AK Steel obligated to make one more cash contribution in March of 2011.

Prior to the Middletown Retiree Settlement, the Company's total OPEB liability for all of its retirees was approximately $2.0 billion. Of that amount, approximately $1.0 billion was attributable to the retirees covered by the Middletown Retiree Settlement. Immediately following the judgment approving that Settlement, the Company's total OPEB liability was reduced by approximately $339.1. This reduction in the Company's OPEB liability is being treated as a negative plan amendment and amortized as a reduction to net periodic benefit cost over approximately eleven years. This negative plan amendment will result in an annual net periodic benefit cost reduction of approximately $30.0 in addition to the lower interest costs associated with the lower OPEB liability. Upon payment on March 4, 2008, of the initial $468.0 contribution by AK Steel to the VEBA Trust in accordance with the terms of the Middletown Retiree Settlement, the Company's total OPEB liability was reduced further to approximately $1.1 billion. The Company's total OPEB liability was further reduced by the two $65.0 payments referred to above. The Company's total OPEB liability will be reduced further after the remaining $65.0 payment due in March 2011 is made. In total, it is expected that the $663.0 Middletown Retiree Settlement ultimately will reduce the Company's total OPEB liability by approximately $1.0 billion.

For accounting purposes, a settlement of the Company's OPEB obligations related to the Class Members will be deemed to have occurred when AK Steel makes the last $65.0 payment called for under the Middletown Retiree Settlement. In the first quarter of 2011, the Company will recognize the settlement accounting at the date of the final payment, which will result in a non-cash adjustment to the income statement for a portion of the accumulated gains and losses measured at that date. The amount recognized will be prorated based on the portion settled of the total liability as of March 2008.

Tax Contingencies

1.115

PRAXAIR, INC. (DEC)

NOTES TO CONSOLIDATED FINANCIAL STATEMENTS

Note 17. Commitments and Contingencies (in part)

The company accrues non income-tax liabilities for contingencies when management believes that a loss is probable and the amounts can be reasonably estimated, while contingent gains are recognized only when realized. In the event any losses are sustained in excess of accruals, they will be charged against income at that time. Commitments represent obligations, such as those for future purchases of goods or services, that are not yet recorded on the company's balance sheet as liabilities. The company records liabilities for commitments when incurred (i.e., when the goods or services are received).

Praxair is subject to various lawsuits and government investigations that arise from time to time in the ordinary course of business. These actions are based upon alleged environmental, tax, antitrust and personal injury claims, among others. Praxair has strong defenses in these cases and intends to defend itself vigorously. However, it is possible that the company may incur losses in connection with some of these actions in excess of accrued liabilities. Management does not anticipate that in the aggregate such losses would have a material adverse effect on the company's consolidated financial position or liquidity; however, it is possible that the final outcomes could have a significant impact on the company's reported results of operations in any given period.

Among such matters are:

- Claims by the Brazilian taxing authorities against several of the company's Brazilian subsidiaries relating to non-income and income tax matters. During May 2009, the Brazilian government published Law 11941/2009 instituting a new voluntary amnesty program ("Refis Program") which allowed Brazilian companies to settle certain federal tax disputes at reduced amounts. During the 2009 third quarter, Praxair decided that it was economically beneficial to settle many of its outstanding federal tax disputes and these disputes were enrolled in the Refis Program and settled (see Note 2). During January 2010, the Brazilian state of Rio de Janeiro ("Rio") published Law 5647/2010 instituting a new state amnesty program ("Rio Amnesty Program") which allows Brazilian companies to settle certain disputes with the state of Rio at reduced amounts. During the 2010 first quarter, Praxair decided that it was economically beneficial to settle several of its outstanding disputes with the state of Rio and these disputes were enrolled in the Program and settled. The final settlements related to both the Refis and Rio Amnesty Programs are subject to final calculation and review by the Brazilian federal and Rio state governments, respectively, and the company currently anticipates these reviews will conclude during the next year. Any differences from amounts recorded will be adjusted to income at that time.

  After enrollment in the amnesty programs, at December 31, 2010 the most significant remaining claims relate to a state VAT tax matter associated with a procedural issue and a federal income tax matter where the taxing authorities are challenging the tax rate that should be applied to income generated by a subsidiary company. The total estimated exposure relating to such claims, including interest and penalties, as appropriate, is approximately $173 million. Praxair has not recorded any liabilities related to such claims based on management judgments, after considering judgments and opinions of outside counsel. Because litigation in Brazil historically takes many years to resolve, it is very difficult to estimate the timing of resolution of these matters; however, it is possible that certain of these matters may be resolved within the near term. The company is vigorously defending against the proceedings.

1.116

INGRAM MICRO INC. (DEC)

NOTES TO CONSOLIDATED FINANCIAL STATEMENTS

Note 10—Commitments and Contingencies (in part; in thousands)

Our Brazilian subsidiary has been assessed for commercial taxes on its purchases of imported software for the period January to September 2002. The principal amount of the tax assessed for this period was 12,700 Brazilian reais. Although we believe we have valid defenses to the payment of the assessed taxes, as well as any amounts due for the unassessed period from October 2002 to December 2005, after consultation with counsel and consideration of legislation enacted in February 2007, it is our opinion that it is probable that we may be required to pay all or some of these taxes. Accordingly, we recorded a net charge to cost of sales of $30,134 in 2007 to establish a liability for these taxes assessable through December 2005. The legislation enacted in February 2007 provides that such taxes are not assessable on software imports after January 1, 2006. In the fourth quarters of 2010, 2009 and 2008, we released a portion of this commercial tax reserve amounting to $9,112, $9,758 and $8,224 respectively, (15,500, 17,100 and 19,600 Brazilian reais at a December 2010 exchange rate of 1.666, December 2009 exchange rate of 1.741 and December 2008 exchange rate of 2.330 Brazilian reais to the U.S. dollar, respectively). These partial reserve releases were related to the unassessed periods from January through December 2005, January through December 2004 and January through December 2003, respectively, for which it is our opinion, after consultation with counsel, that the statute of limitations for an assessment from Brazilian tax authorities has expired. The remaining amount of liability at January 1, 2011 and January 2, 2010 was 12,700 Brazilian reais and 28,200 Brazilian reais, respectively, (approximately $7,600 and $16,200 at January 1, 2011 and January 2, 2010, respectively, based on the exchange rate prevailing on those dates of 1.666 and 1.741 Brazilian reais, respectively, to the U.S. dollar).

While the tax authorities may seek to impose interest and penalties in addition to the tax as discussed above, which potentially aggregate to approximately $15,000 as of January 1, 2011 based on the exchange rate prevailing on that date of 1.666 Brazilian reais to the U.S. dollar, we continue to believe that we have valid defenses to the assessment of interest and penalties and that payment is not probable. We will continue to vigorously pursue administrative and judicial action to challenge the current, and any subsequent assessments. However, we can make no assurances that we will ultimately be successful in defending any such assessments, if made.

Environmental Matters

1.117

ANADARKO PETROLEUM CORPORATION (DEC)

NOTES TO CONSOLIDATED FINANCIAL STATEMENTS

2. Deepwater Horizon Events (in part)

Background In April 2010, the Macondo well in the Gulf of Mexico, in which Anadarko holds a 25% non-operating leasehold interest, discovered hydrocarbon accumulations. During suspension operations, the well blew out, an explosion occurred on the *Deepwater Horizon* drilling rig, and the drilling rig sank, resulting in the release of hydrocarbons into the Gulf of Mexico. Eleven people lost their lives in the explosion and subsequent fire, and others sustained personal injuries. Response and cleanup efforts are being conducted by BP Exploration & Production Inc. (BP), the operator and 65% owner of the Macondo lease, and by other parties, all

under the direction of the Unified Command of the United States Coast Guard (USCG).

On July 15, 2010, after several attempts to contain the oil spill, BP successfully installed a capping stack that shut in the well and prevented the further release of hydrocarbons. Installation of the capping stack was a temporary solution that was followed by a successful "static kill" cementing operation completed on August 5, 2010. The Macondo well was permanently plugged on September 19, 2010, when BP completed a "bottom kill" cementing operation in connection with the successful interception of the well by a relief well. Investigations by the federal government and other parties into the cause of the well blowout, explosion, and resulting oil spill, as well as other matters arising from or relating to these events, are ongoing.

Based on information provided by BP to the Company, BP has incurred costs of approximately $16.5 billion (including costs associated with USCG invoices totaling $606 million) through December 31, 2010, related to spill response and containment, relief-well drilling, grants to certain Gulf Coast states for cleanup costs, local tourism promotion, monetary damage claims and federal costs. In addition, BP has incurred more than $1.4 billion of costs since December 31, 2010.

BP has sought reimbursement from Anadarko for amounts BP has paid or committed to pay for spill-response efforts, grants, damage claims and costs incurred by the federal government through provisions of the operating agreement (OA), which is the contract governing the relationship between BP and the non-operating OA parties to the Mississippi Canyon Block 252 lease in which the Macondo well is located (Lease). BP has invoiced the Company an aggregate $4.0 billion for what BP considers to be Anadarko's 25% proportionate share of actual costs through December 31, 2010. In addition, BP has invoiced Anadarko for anticipated near-term future costs related to the Deepwater Horizon events. Anadarko has withheld reimbursement to BP for Deepwater Horizon event-related invoices pending the completion of various ongoing investigations into the cause of the well blowout, explosion, and subsequent release of hydrocarbons. Final determination of the root causes of the Deepwater Horizon events could materially impact the Company's potential obligations under the OA.

BP, Anadarko and other parties, including parties that do not own an interest in the Lease, such as the drilling contractor, have received correspondence from the USCG referencing their identification as a "responsible party or guarantor" (RP) under the Oil Pollution Act of 1990 (OPA), and the United States Department of Justice (DOJ) has also filed a civil lawsuit against such parties seeking to, among other things, confirm each party's identified RP status. Under OPA, RPs may be held jointly and severally liable for costs of well control, spill response, and containment and removal of hydrocarbons, as well as other costs and damage claims directly related to the spill and spill cleanup. The USCG has directly invoiced the identified RPs for reimbursement of spill-related response costs incurred by the USCG and other federal and state agencies. The identified RPs each received identical invoices for total costs, without specification or stipulation of any allocation of costs between or among the identified RPs. To date, as operator, BP has paid all USCG invoices, thereby satisfying the joint and several obligation of the identified RPs to the USCG for these costs. BP has also made repeated public statements regarding its intention to continue to pay

100% of costs associated with cleanup efforts, claims and reimbursements related to the Deepwater Horizon events.

The following analysis applies relevant accounting guidance to the Deepwater Horizon events to determine the Company's liability accrual as of December 31, 2010. The process for quantifying the Company's Deepwater Horizon event-related liability accrual involves the identification of all potential costs and the grouping of these costs in a manner that enables the Company to apply relevant accounting guidance to each cost based upon the qualitative characteristics of such costs. This is appropriate because satisfaction of liability-recognition criteria may vary depending upon the type of costs being analyzed. For example and as discussed more fully below, contingent contractual liabilities (such as those arising under the OA) and contingent environmental liabilities (such as those arising under OPA) are subject to substantially similar liability-recognition criteria; however, circumstances under which such criteria are considered satisfied are different.

As discussed and analyzed below, after applying the relevant accounting guidance to the Company's Deepwater Horizon event-related contingent liabilities, the Company's aggregate liability accrual for these amounts is zero as of December 31, 2010. The zero liability accrual is not intended to represent an opinion of the Company that it will not incur any future liability related to the Deepwater Horizon events. Rather, the zero liability accrual is based on currently available facts and the application of accounting rules to this set of facts where the relevant accounting rules do not allow for loss recognition where a potential loss is not considered "probable" or cannot be reasonably estimated.

In quantifying its potential Deepwater Horizon event-related liabilities, the Company has made certain assumptions regarding facts that are the subject of continuing investigations, the duration and extent of ongoing cleanup activities, and current and potential future damage claims. Thus, the Company's zero liability accrual for the Deepwater Horizon events is subject to change in the future, perhaps materially. Below is a discussion of the Company's current analysis, under applicable accounting guidance, of its potential liability for (i) amounts invoiced by BP under the OA, (ii) OPA-related environmental costs, and (iii) other contingent liabilities.

OA Contingent Liabilities—OA contingent liabilities relate to Anadarko's potential responsibility for a 25% share of costs incurred by BP through December 31, 2010, for which BP has sought reimbursement from Anadarko under the OA. Accounting standards require the Company to accrue contingent liabilities arising under the terms of the OA if it is both "probable" that a liability has been incurred and the amount of the liability can be reasonably estimated.

With respect to the operator's duties and liabilities, the OA provides the following:

- BP, as operator, owes duties to the non-operating parties (including Anadarko) to perform the drilling of the well in a good and workmanlike manner and to comply with all applicable laws and regulations;
- BP, as operator, is not liable to non-operating parties for losses sustained or liabilities incurred, except for losses resulting from the operator's gross negligence or willful misconduct; and
- Liability for losses, damages, costs, expenses, or claims involving activities or operations shall be borne by each party in proportion to its participating interest, except that when liability results from the gross negligence or willful misconduct of a party, that party shall

be solely responsible for liability resulting from its gross negligence or willful misconduct.

The Company believes publicly available evidence indicates that the blowout of the well, the explosion on the *Deepwater Horizon* drilling rig, and the subsequent release of hydrocarbons were preventable and the direct result of BP's decisions, omissions and actions, and likely constitute gross negligence or willful misconduct by BP. BP has issued public statements indicating that it disagrees with this assessment. Under the OA, liabilities arising as a result of gross negligence or willful misconduct by BP are the sole responsibility of BP and are not chargeable to other OA parties, including Anadarko. In light of the foregoing, Anadarko does not consider OA contingent liabilities for Deepwater Horizon event-related costs invoiced by BP to the Company to satisfy the standard of "probable" required for loss recognition. Accordingly, as of December 31, 2010, pursuant to applicable accounting guidance, the Company has not recognized a liability in its Consolidated Balance Sheets for Deepwater Horizon event-related costs that have been invoiced by BP to Anadarko under the OA.

In the future, the Company may recognize a liability for Deepwater Horizon event-related costs invoiced by BP under the OA if new information arising from the legal discovery or adjudication process, hearings, other investigations, expert analysis, or testing alters the Company's current assessment as to the likelihood of the Company incurring a liability for its existing OA contingent obligations. In addition, BP, as the operator, may have enforceable indemnity obligations to certain of its contractors, for which BP may be able to obtain reimbursement from the Company under the OA for the Company's share of any such costs incurred by BP, notwithstanding BP's own gross negligence. The Company currently is not positioned to assess the validity of BP's ostensible indemnity obligations to its contractors, nor is the Company knowledgeable as to whether BP has incurred actual costs as a result of these indemnity provisions. As a result, the Company currently does not consider any losses attributable to potential indemnity obligations to be "probable," and is furthermore unable to reasonably estimate the amount of any such potential loss.

OPA-Related Environmental Costs—Under OPA, Anadarko may be held jointly and severally liable with all RPs for OPA-related environmental costs associated with the Deepwater Horizon events. Anadarko's treatment by the USCG as an identified RP arises as a result of Anadarko's status as a co-lessee in the Lease.

Applicable accounting guidance requires the Company to accrue an environmental liability if it is both "probable" that a liability has been incurred and the amount of the liability can be reasonably estimated. Under accounting guidance applicable to environmental liabilities, a liability is presumed "probable" if the entity is both identified as an RP and associated with the environmental event. The Company's co-lessee status in the Lease and the subsequent identification and treatment of the Company as an RP satisfies these standards and therefore establishes the presumption that the Company's potential environmental liabilities related to the Deepwater Horizon events are "probable." Given that such liabilities are probable, applicable accounting guidance requires the Company to (i) estimate, on a gross basis, a range of total potential OPA-related environmental costs for the Deepwater Horizon events, and (ii) separately assess and estimate the Company's allocable share of the gross estimated costs.

OPA-related environmental costs that have been paid by BP and subsequently invoiced to Anadarko under the OA are accounted for as OA contingent liabilities (discussed above) rather than OPA-related environmental costs (discussed herein). Payment of OPA-related environmental costs by BP satisfies these liabilities for all identified RPs, including Anadarko, and has resulted in BP seeking reimbursement from Anadarko for these costs through the OA, thereby creating an OA contingent liability. The Company assumes that all OPA-related environmental costs incurred by BP and reported to the Company have been paid by BP, thereby satisfying those joint and several OPA-related environmental costs for all identified RPs.

Gross OPA-Related Environmental Cost Estimate—The Company estimates the range of gross OPA-related environmental costs for all identified RPs to be $4.0 billion to $5.0 billion, excluding (i) $16.5 billion of costs incurred by BP as of December 31, 2010, which are considered and analyzed as OA contingent liabilities, and (ii) amounts the Company currently cannot reasonably estimate, which include OPA damage claims that may be filed subsequent to the first quarter of 2011, potential costs associated with penalties and fines, the costs associated with natural resource damage (NRD) assessments and NRD claims, and civil litigation damages. The costs that the Company currently cannot reasonably estimate may be significant.

Anadarko's gross OPA-related environmental cost estimate is comprised of spill-response costs and OPA damage claims. This cost estimate is based on cost information received from BP, certain assumptions discussed below, and publicly available information from the Gulf Coast Claims Facility (GCCF). The GCCF is an independent claims facility that was established in June 2010, as part of an agreement between the federal government and BP, to assist claimants in the submission and resolution of claims for costs and damages incurred as a result of the Deepwater Horizon events. As a non-operator, the Company is limited to formulating its estimates of spill-response costs and OPA damages based upon information provided by BP, publicly available information, and management's assumptions regarding a number of variables associated with the Deepwater Horizon events that remain uncertain or unknown. Although the Macondo well has been permanently plugged, the scope and extent of damages and cleanup activities continue to evolve, resulting in significant uncertainty as to the spill's ultimate impacts and associated costs. Accordingly, the Company believes that actual gross OPA-related environmental costs may vary, perhaps materially, from the Company's estimate.

Spill-Response Costs and Assumptions—Estimated spill-response costs are based on cost information received from BP, which was used to estimate activity-based cost run-rates for spill-response activities, which, in turn, were projected forward according to the Company's estimates of the potential duration and extent of the spill response and cleanup.

The Company's current cost estimate is based on the following assumptions:

- Costs to operate, demobilize and decontaminate off-shore well-site equipment and resources will continue through the first quarter of 2011; and
- At a minimum, costs will continue through the end of the first quarter of 2011, and end prior to the beginning of the third quarter of 2011, for the following activities:
  —Shallow-water marine cleanup;
  —Demobilization and decontamination of vessels deployed in open-water cleanup;

—Shoreline cleanup; and
—Federal, state and local spill mitigation and co-ordination.

The above costs may continue for periods longer than those assumed by the Company for purposes of formulating its cost estimate. However, the scope and extent of the above costs continue to evolve over time, which adversely impacts the Company's ability to reasonably estimate certain costs that may continue beyond the above-stated periods. The Company will continue to monitor and estimate costs as the scope and extent of required activities becomes more certain.

OPA Damage Claims—OPA damages (other than NRD, discussed below) include costs associated with increased public-service expenses, damages to real or personal property, damages to subsistence users of natural resources, lost revenues, and lost profits and earning capacity. These damages are assessed pursuant to OPA and are limited, in general, to $75 million. However, the $75 million limit has not been applied for purposes of formulating the Company's cost-range estimate and may not be applicable where there is a finding of gross negligence, willful misconduct, or a violation of an applicable federal safety, construction, or operating regulation by an RP, an agent or employee of an RP, or a person acting pursuant to a contractual relationship with an RP.

The Company's cost estimate includes potential OPA damage claims and costs to administer those claims based on data received from BP and publicly available information from the GCCF. This claims information has been used to formulate estimates of the number of claims to be paid, the average expected per-claim payout, and costs to administer claims and operate claims offices projected for claims filed through the end of the first quarter of 2011.

The Company believes that new claims will continue to be filed beyond the end of the first quarter of 2011; however, the Company is currently unable to reasonably estimate the number, magnitude and administrative cost of claims that will be filed subsequent to the first quarter of 2011. The Company lacks visibility into, among other things, the processes associated with OPA damage claim approvals and claims administration, which significantly hinders the Company's ability to formulate a long-term estimate of potential OPA damage claims. Accordingly, the Company's cost estimate does not include amounts attributable to OPA damage claims that could be made subsequent to the end of the first quarter of 2011.

Allocable Share of Gross OPA-Related Environmental Costs—As discussed above, under applicable accounting guidance, the Company is required to estimate its allocable share of gross OPA-related environmental costs based on the Company's estimate of the allocation method and percentage that may ultimately apply. No agreed-upon or stipulated allocation of gross OPA-related environmental costs currently exists. As a result, the Company considered the following factors for purposes of estimating a range of its allocable share of these costs:

- *BP's payment to date of Deepwater Horizon event-related costs*—To date, BP has paid all Deepwater Horizon event-related costs and has repeatedly stated publicly and in congressional testimony that it will continue to pay all of these costs. The liability of all RPs for amounts payable under OPA is satisfied as BP funds these amounts. Accordingly, Anadarko's minimum allocable share of gross OPA-related environmental costs is zero where BP continues to fund 100% of OPA-related environmental costs. Furthermore, the Company believes that in order for BP to obtain reimbursement from Anadarko under the OA for OPA-related environmental costs paid by BP, BP must establish that it is entitled to reimbursement under the terms of the OA. As discussed above, the Company does not consider BP to be entitled to cost reimbursement under the OA.

- *Anadarko's OA sharing percentage*—If BP ceases paying any portion of the Deepwater Horizon event-related costs, the federal government could seek payment from all potential RPs under the joint and several liability provisions of OPA. Under this scenario, the Company estimates its maximum allocation of gross OPA-related environmental costs could be 25%, which is equivalent to Anadarko's OA sharing percentage. The Company does not consider an allocable percentage in excess of 25% to be reasonable based on BP's public statements that it intends to continue to honor its commitments in the Gulf of Mexico, the Company's assessment of BP's ability to continue funding all OPA-related environmental costs and the Company's assessment of the other OA party's ability to fund its share of potential costs. This estimate of a maximum allocation percentage assumes no allocation of gross OPA-related environmental costs to RPs that are not a party to the OA (non-OA RPs).
- *Allocation to non-OA RPs*—In addition to the parties to the OA, identified as RPs (including the Company), two non-OA RPs have been identified by the federal government. The allocation of costs to all potential RPs, including non-OA RPs, would likely reduce Anadarko's potential allocable share of gross OPA-related environmental costs to an amount less than Anadarko's 25% OA sharing percentage.

Based on the above, the Company has concluded that a range of 0-25% is appropriate as an estimate of its potential allocable share of gross OPA-related environmental costs. In prior periods, the Company concluded that no single allocation percentage within the 0-25% range was more likely than another, resulting in the Company accruing a liability of zero for its potential share of gross OPA-related environmental costs as required by applicable accounting guidance. At December 31, 2010, the Company considers zero to be the most likely allocable percentage within the original 0-25% range for allocation of gross OPA-related environmental costs and, under the applicable accounting guidance, continues to have a liability accrual of zero. The Company's assessment as to the most likely allocation percentage changed as a result of BP's continued funding of 100% of OPA-related environmental costs and BP's repeated public commentary regarding its ability and intent to continue to honor its Deepwater Horizon-related commitments. BP's funding and public commentary has continued subsequent to the release of BP's own investigation report as well as the National Commission on the BP Deepwater Horizon Oil Spill and Offshore Drilling's final report, which the Company considers significant in concluding that zero is the most likely allocation percentage within the 0-25% range.

1.118

LOCKHEED MARTIN CORPORATION (DEC)

NOTES TO CONSOLIDATED FINANCIAL STATEMENTS

Note 14—Legal Proceedings, Commitments, and Contingencies (in part)

Environmental Matters

We are involved in environmental proceedings and potential proceedings relating to soil and groundwater contamination, disposal of hazardous waste, and other environmental matters at several of our current or former facilities, or at third-party sites where we have been designated as a potentially responsible party (PRP). At December 31, 2010 and 2009, the aggregate amount of liabilities recorded relative to environmental matters was $935 million and $877 million. Approximately $807 million and $748 million are recorded in other liabilities on the Balance Sheets, with the remainder recorded in other current liabilities. A portion of environmental costs is eligible for future recovery in the pricing of our products and services on U.S. Government contracts. We have recorded assets totaling $810 million and $740 million at December 31, 2010 and 2009 for the estimated future recovery of these costs, as we consider the recovery probable based on government contracting regulations and our history of receiving reimbursement for such costs. Approximately $699 million and $630 million are recorded in other assets on the Balance Sheets, with the remainder recorded in other current assets.

Environmental cleanup activities usually span several years, which make estimating liabilities a matter of judgment because of such factors as changing remediation technologies, assessments of the extent of contamination, and continually evolving regulatory environmental standards. We consider these and other factors in estimates of the timing and amount of any future costs that may be required for remediation actions, which results in the calculation of a range of estimates for a particular environmental site.

We perform quarterly reviews of the status of our environmental sites and the related liabilities and assets. We record a liability when it is probable that a liability has been incurred and the amount can be reasonably estimated. The amount of liability recorded is based on our best estimate of the costs to be incurred for remediation at a particular site within a range of estimates for that site or, in cases where no amount within the range is better than another, we record an amount at the low end of the range. We do not discount the recorded liabilities, as the amount and timing of future cash payments are not fixed or cannot be reliably determined.

We cannot reasonably determine the extent of our financial exposure in all cases at this time. There are a number of former operating facilities that we are monitoring or investigating for potential future remediation. In some cases, although a loss may be probable, it is not possible at this time to reasonably estimate the amount of any obligation for remediation activities because of uncertainties with respect to assessing the extent of the contamination or the applicable regulatory standard. We also are pursuing claims for contribution to site cleanup costs against other PRPs, including the U.S. Government.

In January 2011, both the U.S. Environmental Protection Agency and the California Office of Environmental Health Hazard Assessment announced plans to regulate two chemicals, perchlorate and hexavalent chromium, to a level that is expected to be substantially lower than the existing standard established in California. The rulemaking process is a lengthy one and may take one or more years to complete. If a substantially lower standard is adopted, we would expect a material increase in our estimates for remediation at several existing sites.

We are conducting remediation activities, including under various consent decrees and orders relating to soil or groundwater contamination at certain sites of former or current operations. Under an agreement related to our Burbank and Glendale, California sites, the U.S. Government reimburses us an amount equal to approximately 50% of expenditures for certain remediation activities in its capacity as a PRP under the Comprehensive Environmental Response, Compensation and Liability Act (CERCLA).

Self-Insurance

1.119

THE MCCLATCHY COMPANY (DEC)

NOTES TO CONSOLIDATED FINANCIAL STATEMENTS

Note 9. Commitments and Contingencies (in part)

Self-Insurance—The Company retains the risk for workers' compensation resulting from uninsured deductibles per accident or occurrence that are subject to annual aggregate limits. Losses up to the deductible amounts are accrued based upon known claims incurred and an estimate of claims incurred but not reported. For the year ended December 26, 2010, the Company compiled its historical data pertaining to the self-insurance experiences and actuarially developed the ultimate loss associated with its self-insurance programs for workers' compensation liability. Management believes that the actuarial valuation provides the best estimate of the ultimate losses to be expected under these programs.

The undiscounted ultimate losses of all the Company's self-insurance reserves at December 26, 2010, and December 27, 2009, were $20.4 million and $24.4 million, respectively. Based on historical payment patterns, the Company expects payments of undiscounted ultimate losses to be made as follows (in thousands):

Year	Amount
2011	$ 5,183
2012	3,566
2013	2,561
2014	1,953
2015	1,521
Thereafter	5,607
Total	$20,391

The Company discounts the ultimate losses above to present value using an approximate risk-free rate over the average life of its insurance claims. For the years ended December 26, 2010, and December 27, 2009, the discount rate used was 2.23% and 3.67%, respectively. The present value of all self-insurance reserves for the employee group health claims and

workers' compensation liability recorded at December 26, 2010, and December 27, 2009, was $19.9 million and $21.0 million, respectively.

The Company had letters of credit of $7.5 million outstanding at December 26, 2010, to collateralize its self-insurance obligations.

Investigations and Regulatory Action

1.120

HALLIBURTON COMPANY (DEC)

NOTES TO CONSOLIDATED FINANCIAL STATEMENTS

Note 8. Commitments and Contingencies (in part)

The Gulf of Mexico/Macondo Well Incident

Overview.—The semisubmersible drilling rig, Deepwater Horizon, sank on April 22, 2010 after an explosion and fire onboard the rig that began on April 20, 2010. The Deepwater Horizon was owned by Transocean Ltd. and had been drilling the Macondo exploration well in Mississippi Canyon Block 252 in the Gulf of Mexico for the lease operator, BP Exploration & Production, Inc. (BP Exploration), an indirect wholly owned subsidiary of BP p.l.c. We performed a variety of services for BP Exploration, including cementing, mud logging, directional drilling, measurement-while-drilling, and rig data acquisition services. Crude oil flowing from the well site spread across thousands of square miles of the Gulf of Mexico and reached the United States Gulf Coast. Numerous attempts at estimating the volume of oil spilled have been made by various groups, and on August 2, 2010 the federal government published an estimate that approximately 4.9 million barrels of oil were discharged from the well. Efforts to contain the flow of hydrocarbons from the well were led by the United States government and by BP p.l.c., BP Exploration, and their affiliates (collectively, BP). The flow of hydrocarbons from the well ceased on July 15, 2010, and the well was permanently capped on September 19, 2010. There were eleven fatalities and a number of injuries as a result of the Macondo well incident.

As of December 31, 2010, we had not accrued any amounts related to this matter because we do not believe that a loss is probable. We are currently unable to estimate the full impact the Macondo well incident will have on us. Further, an estimate of possible loss or range of loss related to this matter cannot be made. Considering the complexity of the Macondo well, however, and the number of investigations being conducted and lawsuits pending, as discussed below, new information or future developments may require us to adjust our liability assessment, and liabilities arising out of this matter could have a material adverse effect on our liquidity, consolidated results of operations, and consolidated financial condition.

Investigations and Regulatory Action.—The United States Department of Homeland Security and Department of the Interior are jointly investigating the cause of the Macondo well incident. The United States Coast Guard, a component of the United States Department of Homeland Security, and the Bureau of Ocean Energy Management, Regulation and Enforcement (formerly known as the Minerals Management Service), a bureau of the United States Department of the Interior, share jurisdiction over the investigation into the Macondo well incident and have formed a joint investigation team that continues to review information and hold hearings regarding the incident (Marine Board Investigation). We are named as one of the 16 parties-in-interest in the Marine Board Investigation. In addition, other investigations are underway by the Chemical Safety Board, the National Academy of Sciences, and the National Commission on the BP Deepwater Horizon Oil Spill and Offshore Drilling (National Commission) that the President of the United States has established to, among other things, examine the relevant facts and circumstances concerning the causes of the Macondo well incident and develop options for guarding against future oil spills associated with offshore drilling. We are assisting in efforts to identify the factors that led to the Macondo well incident and have participated and intend to continue participating in various hearings relating to the incident that are held by, among others, certain of the agencies referred to above and various committees and subcommittees of the House of Representatives and the Senate of the United States.

In May 2010, the United States Department of the Interior effectively suspended all offshore deepwater drilling projects in the United States Gulf of Mexico. The suspension was lifted in October 2010. Since that time, the Department of the Interior has issued guidance for drillers that intend to resume deepwater drilling activity. There has been no material increase, however, in the level of drilling activity in the Gulf of Mexico since the suspension was lifted, and we believe that the prospects for any significant increase will remain uncertain through the first half, and perhaps the full year, of 2011. For additional information, see Item 1(a), "Risk Factors" and "Management's Discussion and Analysis of Financial Condition and Results of Operations—Business Environment and Results of Operations."

DOJ Investigations and Actions.—On June 1, 2010, the United States Attorney General announced that the DOJ was launching civil and criminal investigations into the Macondo well incident to closely examine the actions of those involved, and that the DOJ was working with attorneys general of states affected by the Macondo well incident. The DOJ announced that it was reviewing, among other traditional criminal statutes, possible violations of and liabilities under The Clean Water Act (CWA), The Oil Pollution Act of 1990 (OPA), The Migratory Bird Treaty Act of 1918 (MBTA), and the Endangered Species Act of 1973 (ESA).

The CWA provides authority for civil and criminal penalties for discharges of oil into or upon navigable waters of the United States, adjoining shorelines, or in connection with the Outer Continental Shelf Lands Act in quantities that are deemed harmful. Criminal sanctions under the CWA can be assessed for negligent discharges (up to $50,000 per day of violation), for knowing discharges (up to $100,000 per day of violation), and for knowing endangerment (up to $2 million per violation), and federal agencies could be precluded from contracting with a company that is criminally sanctioned under the CWA. Civil proceedings under the CWA can be commenced against an "owner, operator or person in charge of any vessel or offshore facility that discharged oil or a hazardous substance." The civil penalties that can be imposed against responsible parties range from up to $1,100 per barrel of oil discharged in the case of those found strictly liable to $4,300 per barrel of oil discharged in the case of those found to have been grossly negligent.

The OPA establishes liability for discharges of oil from vessels, onshore facilities, and offshore facilities into or upon the navigable waters of the United States. Under the OPA, the "responsible party" for the discharging vessel or facility is liable for removal and response costs as well as for damages, including recovery costs to contain and remove discharged oil and compensation for injury to natural resources. The cap on liability under the OPA is the full cost of removal of the discharged oil plus up to $75 million for natural resources damages, except that the cap on natural resources damages does not apply in the event the damage was proximately caused by gross negligence or the violation of certain federal standards. The OPA defines the set of responsible parties differently depending on whether the source of the discharge is a vessel or an offshore facility. Liability for vessels is imposed on owners and operators; liability for offshore facilities is imposed on the holder of the permit or lessee of the area in which the facility is located.

The MBTA and the ESA provide penalties for injury and death to wildlife and bird species. The MBTA provides that violators are strictly liable and provides for fines of up to $15,000 per bird killed and imprisonment of up to six months. The ESA provides for civil penalties for knowing violations that can range up to $25,000 per violation and, in the case of criminal penalties, up to $50,000 per violation.

In addition, the Alternative Fines Act may be applied in lieu of the express amount of the criminal fines that may be imposed under the statutes described above in the amount of twice the gross economic loss suffered by third parties (or twice the gross economic gain realized by the defendant, if greater).

On December 15, 2010, the DOJ filed a civil action seeking damages and injunctive relief against BP, Anadarko, Transocean and others for violations of the CWA and the OPA. The DOJ's complaint seeks an action declaring that the defendants are strictly liable under the CWA as a result of harmful discharges of oil into the Gulf of Mexico and upon U.S. shorelines as a result of the Macondo well incident. The complaint also seeks an action declaring that the defendants are strictly liable under the OPA for the discharge of oil that has resulted in, among other things, injury to, loss of, loss of use of or destruction of natural resources and resource services in and around the Gulf of Mexico and the adjoining U.S. shorelines and resulting in removal costs and damages to the United States far exceeding $75 million. BP has been designated, and has accepted the designation, as a responsible party for the pollution under the CWA and the OPA. Others have also been named as responsible parties, and all responsible parties may be held jointly and severally liable for any damages under the OPA, although a responsible party may make a claim for contribution against any other "responsible party" it alleges contributed to the oil spill or any other person it alleges was the sole cause of the oil spill.

We were not named as a responsible party under the CWA or the OPA in the DOJ civil action, and we do not believe we are a "responsible party" under the CWA or the OPA. While we were not included in the DOJ's complaint, there can be no assurance that we will not be joined in the action or that the DOJ or other federal or state governmental authorities will not bring an action, whether civil or criminal, against us under other statutes or regulations. In connection with the DOJ's filing of the action, it announced that its criminal and civil investigations are continuing and that it will employ efforts to hold accountable those who are responsible for the incident.

As of February 17, 2011, no criminal proceedings have been commenced against us.

In June 2010, we received a letter from the DOJ requesting thirty days advance notice of any event that may involve substantial transfers of cash or other corporate assets outside of the ordinary course of business. In our reply to the June 2010 DOJ letter, we conveyed our interest in briefing the DOJ on the services we provided on the Deepwater Horizon but indicated that we would not bind ourselves to the DOJ request. Subsequently, we have had and expect to continue to have discussions with the DOJ regarding the Macondo well incident and the request contained in the June 2010 DOJ letter.

Investigative Reports.—On September 8, 2010, an incident investigation team assembled by BP issued the Deepwater Horizon Accident Investigation Report (BP Report). The BP Report outlines eight key findings of BP related to the possible causes of the Macondo well incident, including failures of cement barriers, failures of equipment provided by other service companies and the drilling contractor, and failures of judgment by BP and the drilling contractor. With respect to the BP Report's assessment that the cement barrier did not prevent hydrocarbons from entering the wellbore after cement placement, the BP Report concluded that, among other things, there were "weaknesses in cement design and testing." According to the BP Report, the BP incident investigation team did not review its analyses or conclusions with us or any other entity or governmental agency conducting a separate or independent investigation of the incident. In addition, the BP incident investigation team did not conduct any testing using our cementing products.

On January 11, 2011, the National Commission released "Deep Water—The Gulf Oil Disaster and the Future of Offshore Drilling," its investigation report (Investigation Report) to the President of the United States regarding, among other things, the National Commission's conclusions of the causes of the Macondo well incident. According to the Investigation Report, the "immediate causes" of the incident were the result of a series of missteps, oversights, miscommunications and failures to appreciate risk by BP, Transocean, and us, although the National Commission acknowledged that there were still many things it did not know about the incident, such as the role of the blowout preventer. The National Commission also acknowledged that it may never know the extent to which each mistake or oversight caused the Macondo well incident, but concluded that the immediate cause was "a failure to contain hydrocarbon pressures in the well," and pointed to three things that could have contained those pressures: "the cement at the bottom of the well, the mud in the well and in the riser, and the blowout preventer." In addition, the Investigation Report stated that "primary cement failure was a direct cause of the blowout" and that cement testing performed by an independent laboratory "strongly suggests" that the foam cement slurry used on the Macondo well was unstable. The Investigation Report, however, acknowledges a fact widely accepted by the industry that cementing wells is a complex endeavor utilizing an inherently uncertain process in which failures are not uncommon and that, as a result, the industry utilizes the negative pressure test and cement bond log test, among others, to identify cementing failures that require remediation before further work on a well is performed.

The Investigation Report also sets forth the National Commission's findings on certain missteps, oversights and other factors that may have caused, or contributed to the cause of, the incident, including BP's decision to use a long string cas-

ing instead of a liner casing, BP's decision to use only six centralizers, BP's failure to run a cement bond log, BP's reliance on the primary cement job as a barrier to a possible blowout, BP's and Transocean's failure to properly conduct and interpret a negative-pressure test, BP's temporary abandonment procedures, and the failure of the drilling crew and our surface data logging specialist to recognize that an unplanned influx of oil, gas or fluid into the well (known as a "kick") was occurring. With respect to the National Commission's finding that our surface data logging specialist failed to recognize a kick, the Investigation Report acknowledged that there were simultaneous activities and other monitoring responsibilities that may have prevented the surface data logging specialist from recognizing a kick.

The Investigation Report also identified two general root causes of the Macondo well incident: systemic failures by industry management, which the National Commission labeled "the most significant failure at Macondo," and failures in governmental and regulatory oversight. The National Commission cited examples of failures by industry management such as BP's lack of controls to adequately identify or address risks arising from changes to well design and procedures, the failure of BP's and our processes for cement testing, communication failures among BP, Transocean, and us, including with respect to the difficulty of our cement job, Transocean's failure to adequately communicate lessons from a recent near-blowout, and the lack of processes to adequately assess the risk of decisions in relation to the time and cost those decisions would save. With respect to failures of governmental and regulatory oversight, the National Commission concluded that applicable drilling regulations were inadequate, in part because of a lack of resources and political support of the Minerals Management Service (MMS), and a lack of expertise and training of MMS personnel to enforce regulations that were in effect.

We expect National Commission staff to issue a separate, more detailed report regarding the causes of the Macondo well incident sometime in the first quarter 2011.

The Cementing Job and Reaction to Reports. We disagree with the BP Report and the National Commission regarding many of their findings and characterizations with respect to the cementing and surface data logging services on the Deepwater Horizon. We have provided information to the National Commission and its staff that we believe has been overlooked or selectively omitted from the Investigation Report. We intend to continue to vigorously defend ourselves in any investigation relating to our involvement with the Macondo well that we believe inaccurately evaluates or depicts our services on the Deepwater Horizon.

The cement slurry on the Deepwater Horizon was designed and prepared pursuant to well condition data provided by BP. Regardless of whether alleged weaknesses in cement design and testing are or are not ultimately established, and regardless of whether the cement slurry was utilized in similar applications or was prepared consistent with industry standards, we believe that had BP and others properly interpreted a negative-pressure test, this test would have revealed any problems with the cement. In addition, had BP designed the Macondo well to allow a full cement bond log test or if BP had conducted even a partial cement bond log test, the test likely would have revealed any problems with the cement. BP, however, elected not to conduct any cement bond log test, and with others misinterpreted the negative-pressure test, both of which could have resulted in remedial action, if appropriate, with respect to the cementing services.

At this time we cannot predict the impact of the Investigation Report or the conclusions of future reports of the National Commission, the Marine Board Investigation, the Chemical Safety Board, the National Academy of Sciences, Congressional committees, or any other governmental or private entity. In addition, although we have not been served by the DOJ or any state agency, we cannot predict whether their investigations or any other report or investigation will have an influence on or result in our being named as a party in any action alleging violation of a statute or regulation, whether federal or state and whether criminal or civil.

We intend to continue to cooperate fully with all governmental hearings, investigations, and requests for information relating to the Macondo well incident. We cannot predict the outcome of, or the costs to be incurred in connection with, any of these hearings or investigations, and therefore we cannot predict the potential impact they may have on us.

Litigation.—Beginning on April 21, 2010, plaintiffs started filing lawsuits relating to the Macondo well incident. Generally, those lawsuits allege either (1) damages arising from the oil spill pollution and contamination (*e.g.*, diminution of property value, lost tax revenue, lost business revenue, lost tourist dollars, inability to engage in recreational or commercial activities) or (2) wrongful death or personal injuries. To date, we have been named along with other unaffiliated defendants in more than 330 complaints, most of which are alleged class actions, involving pollution damage claims and at least 28 personal injury lawsuits involving six decedents and 54 allegedly injured persons who were on the drilling rig at the time of the incident. Another six lawsuits naming us and others relate to alleged personal injuries sustained by those responding to the explosion and oil spill. Plaintiffs originally filed the lawsuits described above in federal and state courts throughout the United States, including Alabama, Delaware, Florida, Georgia, Kentucky, Louisiana, Mississippi, South Carolina, Tennessee, Texas, and Virginia. Except for approximately 25 lawsuits not yet consolidated, one lawsuit that is proceeding in Louisiana state court, and one lawsuit that is proceeding in Texas state court, the Judicial Panel on Multi-District Litigation ordered all of the lawsuits consolidated in a multi-district litigation (MDL) proceeding before Judge Carl Barbier in the U.S. Eastern District of Louisiana. The pollution complaints generally allege, among other things, negligence and gross negligence, property damages, taking of protected species, and potential economic losses as a result of environmental pollution and generally seek awards of unspecified economic, compensatory, and punitive damages, as well as injunctive relief. Plaintiffs in these pollution cases have brought suit under various legal provisions, including the OPA, the CWA, the MBTA, the ESA, the Outer Continental Shelf Lands Act, the Longshoremen and Harbor Workers Compensation Act, general maritime law, STATE COMMON LAW, and various state environmental and products liability statutes.

Furthermore, the pollution complaints include suits brought by governmental entities, including the State of Alabama, Plaquemines Parish, and three Mexican states. The wrongful death and other personal injury complaints generally allege negligence and gross negligence and seek awards of compensatory damages, including unspecified economic damages and punitive damages. We have retained counsel and are investigating and evaluating the claims, the theories of recovery, damages asserted, and our respective defenses to all of these claims.

According to case management and pre-trial orders, with respect to the MDL, the court may try one or more OPA "test cases" as early as third quarter 2011. These test cases, the number and specificity of which have not been determined, will consist of claims brought against BP as a responsible party under the OPA. The same judge is also presiding over a separate proceeding filed by Transocean under the Limitation of Liability Act (Limitation Action). In the Limitation Action, Transocean seeks to limit its liability for claims arising out of the Macondo well incident to the value of the rig and its freight. Although the Limitation Action is not consolidated in the MDL, to this point the judge is effectively treating the two proceedings as associated cases. Although we are not yet formally a party to the Limitation Action, we expect that Transocean will tender all defendants into the Limitation Action in February 2011. As a result of that anticipated tender, all defendants will be treated as direct defendants to the plaintiffs' claims as if the plaintiffs had sued each defendant directly.

In the Limitation Action, the judge intends to determine the allocation of liability among all defendants in the hundreds of lawsuits associated with the Macondo well incident that are pending in his court. More specifically, the court intends to try one or more "personal injury/wrongful death test cases" and one or more economic damage claim "test cases" in the first quarter 2012 in an attempt to determine liability, limitation, exoneration and fault allocation with regard to all of the defendants. We do not believe, however, that a single apportionment of liability in the Limitation Action is properly applied to the hundreds of lawsuits pending in the MDL Proceeding. Damages for the personal injury/wrongful death and economic damage claim "test cases" tried in the first quarter 2012, including punitive damages, are expected to be tried in a second phase of the Limitation Action. Under ordinary MDL procedures, such trials would, unless waived by the respective parties, be tried in the courts from which they were transferred into the MDL. It remains unclear, however, what impact the overlay of the Limitation Action will have on where these matters are tried.

Additional civil lawsuits may be filed against us. Document discovery and depositions among the parties to the MDL have begun. The deadline for defendants to file cross claims and third-party claims arising out of the Macondo well incident against other defendants is March 18, 2011.

We intend to vigorously defend any litigation, fines, and/or penalties relating to the Macondo well incident.

Shareholder derivative case.—In February 2011, a shareholder derivative lawsuit was filed in Harris County, Texas naming us as a nominal defendant and certain of our directors and officers as defendants. This case alleges that these defendants, among other things, breached fiduciary duties of good faith and loyalty by failing to properly exercise oversight responsibilities and establish adequate internal controls, including controls and procedures related to cement testing and the communication of test results, as they relate to the Deepwater Horizon incident. Due to the preliminary status of the lawsuit and uncertainties related to litigation, we are unable to evaluate the likelihood of either a favorable or unfavorable outcome.

Indemnification and Insurance.—Our contract with BP Exploration relating to the Macondo well provides for our indemnification for potential claims and expenses relating to the Macondo well incident, including those resulting from pollution or contamination (other than claims by our employees, loss or damage to our property, and any pollution emanating directly from our equipment). Also, under our contract with BP Exploration, we have, among other things, generally agreed to indemnify BP Exploration and other contractors performing work on the well for claims for personal injury of our employees and subcontractors, as well as for damage to our property. In turn, we believe that BP Exploration is obligated to obtain agreement by other contractors performing work on the well to indemnify us for claims for personal injury of their employees or subcontractors as well as for damages to their property.

In addition to the contractual indemnity, we have a general liability insurance program of $600 million. Our insurance is designed to cover claims by businesses and individuals made against us in the event of property damage, injury or death and, among other things, claims relating to environmental damage. To the extent we incur any losses beyond those covered by indemnification, there can be no assurance that our insurance policies will cover all potential claims and expenses relating to the Macondo well incident. Insurance coverage can be the subject of uncertainties and, particularly in the event of large claims, potential disputes with insurance carriers, as well as other potential parties claiming insured status under our insurance policies.

Given the potential amounts involved, BP Exploration and other indemnifying parties may seek to avoid their indemnification obligations. In particular, while we do not believe there is any justification to do so, BP Exploration, in response to our request for indemnification, on June 25, 2010 generally reserved all of its rights and stated that it is premature to conclude that it is obligated to indemnify us. In doing so, BP Exploration has asserted that the facts were not sufficiently developed to determine who is responsible, and cited a variety of possible legal theories based upon the contract and facts still to be developed. As indicated above, all cross claims among defendants must be filed by March 18, 2011. We expect that all defendants will make claims against each other and deny that they owe any indemnification or other obligations to any other defendant.

Indemnification for criminal fines or penalties, if any, may not be available if a court were to find such indemnification unenforceable as against public policy. We do not expect, however, public policy to limit substantially the enforceability of our contractual right to indemnification with respect to liabilities other than criminal fines and penalties, if any. We may not be insured with respect to civil or criminal fines or penalties, if any, pursuant to the terms of our insurance policies.

We believe the law likely to be held applicable to matters relating to the Macondo well incident does not allow for enforcement of indemnification of persons who are found to be grossly negligent, although we do not believe the performance of our services on the Deepwater Horizon constituted gross negligence. In addition, certain state laws, if deemed to apply, may not allow for enforcement of indemnification of persons who are found to be negligent with respect to personal injury claims. In addition, financial analysts and the press have speculated about the financial capacity of BP, and whether it might seek to avoid indemnification obligations in bankruptcy proceedings. We consider the likelihood of a BP bankruptcy to be remote.

Warranties

1.121

CISCO SYSTEMS, INC. (JUL)

NOTES TO CONSOLIDATED FINANCIAL STATEMENTS

11. Commitments and Contingencies (in part)

(e) Product Warranties and Guarantees

The following table summarizes the activity related to the product warranty liability during fiscal 2010 and 2009 (in millions):

	July 31, 2010	July 25, 2009
Balance at beginning of fiscal year	$321	$399
Provision for warranties issued	469	374
Payments	(437)	(452)
Fair value of warranty liability acquired	7	—
Balance at end of fiscal year	$360	$321

The Company accrues for warranty costs as part of its cost of sales based on associated material product costs, labor costs for technical support staff, and associated overhead. The Company's products are generally covered by a warranty for periods ranging from 90 days to five years, and for some products the Company provides a limited lifetime warranty.

In the normal course of business, the Company indemnifies other parties, including customers, lessors, and parties to other transactions with the Company, with respect to certain matters. The Company has agreed to hold the other parties harmless against losses arising from a breach of representations or covenants, or out of intellectual property infringement or other claims made against certain parties. These agreements may limit the time within which an indemnification claim can be made and the amount of the claim. In addition, the Company has entered into indemnification agreements with its officers and directors, and the Company's bylaws contain similar indemnification obligations to the Company's agents. It is not possible to determine the maximum potential amount under these indemnification agreements due to the Company's limited history with prior indemnification claims and the unique facts and circumstances involved in each particular agreement. Historically, payments made by the Company under these agreements have not had a material effect on the Company's operating results, financial position, or cash flows.

The Company also provides financing guarantees, which are generally for various third-party financing arrangements to channel partners and other end-user customers. See Note 6. The Company's other guarantee arrangements as of July 31, 2010 that are subject to recognition and disclosure requirements were not material.

Operating Loss Carryforward

1.122

LAM RESEARCH CORPORATION (JUN)

NOTES TO CONSOLIDATED FINANCIAL STATEMENTS

Note 14. Income Taxes (in part)

Deferred income taxes reflect the net tax effect of temporary differences between the carrying amounts of assets and liabilities for financial reporting purposes, and the amounts used for income tax purposes, as well as the tax effect of carryforwards. Significant components of the Company's net deferred tax assets are as follows:

(In thousands)	June 27, 2010	June 28, 2009
Deferred tax assets:		
Tax carryforwards	$ 50,182	$ 57,350
Allowances and reserves	63,143	72,037
Inventory valuation differences	7,764	11,656
Equity-based compensation	6,202	6,200
Capitalized R&D expenses	5,027	5,677
Other	5,088	4,095
Gross deferred tax assets	137,406	157,015
Valuation allowance	(36,957)	(35,518)
Net deferred tax assets	100,449	121,497
Deferred tax liabilities:		
Fixed assets depreciation and intangibles amortization	(20,188)	(25,632)
State cumulative temporary differences	(10,118)	(11,917)
Amortization of goodwill	(6,026)	(4,326)
Gross deferred tax liabilities	(36,332)	(41,875)
Net deferred tax assets	$ 64,117	$ 79,622

Realization of the Company's net deferred tax assets is based upon the weight of available evidence, including such factors as the recent earnings history and expected future taxable income. The Company believes it is more likely than not that such assets will be realized with the exception of $37.0 million related to certain California and foreign deferred tax assets. To the extent realization of the deferred tax assets becomes more-likely-than-not, the Company would recognize such deferred tax asset as an income tax benefit during the period the realization occurred. However, ultimate realization of deferred tax assets could be negatively impacted by market conditions and other variables not known or anticipated at this time.

The provisions related to the tax accounting for stock-based compensation prohibit the recognition of a deferred tax asset for an excess benefit that has not yet been realized. As a result, we will only recognize a benefit from stock-based compensation in additional paid-in-capital if an incremental tax benefit is realized or realizable after all other tax attributes currently available to us have been utilized. In addition, we have elected to account for the indirect benefits of stock-based compensation on the R&D tax credit through the consolidated statement of income (continuing operations) rather than through additional paid-in-capital.

As of June 27, 2010, the Company had California net operating loss carry-forwards of approximately $2.3 million. Unused net operating loss carry-forwards will expire in the year 2030. When recognized these net operating losses will result in a benefit to additional paid-in capital of approximately $0.1 million.

At June 27, 2010, the Company had federal and state tax credit carryforwards of approximately $182.5 million, of which approximately $66.8 million will expire in varying amounts between fiscal years 2026 and 2031. The remaining balance of $115.7 million of tax carryforwards may be carried forward indefinitely. The tax benefits relating to approximately $57.0 million of the tax credit carryforwards will be credited to additional paid-in-capital when recognized.

At June 27, 2010, the Company had foreign net operating loss carryforwards of approximately $68.9 million, of which approximately $25.9 million may be carried forward indefinitely and $43.0 million will begin to expire in fiscal year 2012.

A reconciliation of income tax expense provided at the federal statutory rate (35% in fiscal years 2010, 2009 and 2008) to actual income expense is as follows:

	Year Ended		
(In thousands)	June 27, 2010	June 28, 2009	June 29, 2008
Income tax expense computed at federal statutory rate	$150,549	$(92,083)	$201,942
State income taxes, net of federal tax benefit	4,754	(4,550)	3,712
Foreign income taxes at different rates	(84,081)	125,124	(84,077)
Tax credits	(4,410)	(9,273)	(6,745)
Valuation allowance, net of federal tax benefit	4,627	12,109	—
Equity-based compensation	11,847	10,985	10,717
Other, net	186	(3,257)	12,078
	$ 83,472	$ 39,055	$137,627

Tax Credits and Other Tax Carryforwards

1.123

EASTMAN KODAK COMPANY (DEC)

NOTES TO CONSOLIDATED FINANCIAL STATEMENTS

Note 15. Income Taxes (in part)

Deferred Tax Assets and Liabilities (in part)
The significant components of deferred tax assets and liabilities were as follows:

	As of December 31	
(In millions)	2010	2009
Deferred Tax Assets		
Pension and postretirement obligations	$ 809	$ 803
Restructuring programs	7	16
Foreign tax credit	477	350
Inventories	23	15
Investment tax credit	160	159
Employee deferred compensation	80	91
Depreciation	28	—
Research and development costs	184	146
Tax loss carryforwards	1,181	931
Other deferred revenue	—	32
Other	423	486
Total deferred tax assets	$3,372	$3,029
Deferred Tax Liabilities		
Depreciation	—	26
Leasing	47	51
Other deferred debt	15	—
Other	175	143
Total deferred tax liabilities	237	220
Net deferred tax assets before valuation allowance	3,135	2,809
Valuation allowance	2,335	2,092
Net deferred tax assets	$ 800	$ 717

Deferred tax assets (liabilities) are reported in the following components within the Consolidated Statement of Financial Position:

	As of December 31	
(In millions)	2010	2009
Deferred income taxes (current)	$120	$121
Other long-term assets	695	607
Accrued income taxes	(7)	—
Other long-term liabilities	(8)	(11)
Net deferred tax assets	$800	$717

As of December 31, 2010, the Company had available domestic and foreign net operating loss carryforwards for income tax purposes of approximately $3,690 million, of which approximately $609 million have an indefinite carryforward period. The remaining $3,081 million expire between the years 2011 and 2030. Utilization of these net operating losses may be subject to limitations in the event of significant changes in stock ownership of the Company. As of December 31, 2010, the Company had unused foreign tax credits and investment tax credits of $477 million and $160 million, respectively, with various expiration dates through 2030.

The Company has been granted a tax holiday in certain jurisdictions in China. The Company is eligible for a 50% reduction of the income tax rate as a tax holiday incentive. The tax rate currently varies by jurisdiction, due to the tax holiday, and will be 25% in all jurisdictions within China in 2013.

Alternative Minimum Tax Carryforward

1.124

PEABODY ENERGY CORPORATION (DEC)

NOTES TO CONSOLIDATED FINANCIAL STATEMENTS

(6) Income Taxes (in part)

The tax effects of temporary differences that give rise to significant portions of the deferred tax assets and liabilities consisted of the following:

	December 31	
(Dollars in millions)	2010	2009
Deferred tax assets:		
Tax credits and loss carryforwards	$ 425.2	$ 557.1
Postretirement benefit obligations	427.7	474.7
Intangible tax asset and purchased contract rights	15.1	30.9
Accrued reclamation and mine closing liabilities	97.8	57.0
Accrued long-term workers' compensation liabilities	15.5	23.1
Employee benefits	53.5	80.3
Hedge activities	30.6	—
Financial guarantee	18.8	20.1
Others	45.4	39.5
Total gross deferred tax assets	1,129.6	1,282.7
Deferred tax liabilities:		
Property, plant, equipment and mine development, leased coal interests and advance royalties, principally due to differences in depreciation, depletion and asset writedowns	1,241.5	1,221.0
Unamortized discount on Convertible Junior Subordinated Debentures	135.5	139.6
Hedge activities	—	29.2
Investments and other assets	107.0	64.8
Total gross deferred tax liabilities	1,484.0	1,454.6
Valuation allowance	(65.0)	(87.2)
Net deferred tax liability	$ (419.4)	$ (259.1)
Deferred taxes are classified as follows:		
Current deferred income taxes	$ 120.4	$ 40.0
Noncurrent deferred income taxes	(539.8)	(299.1)
Net deferred tax liability	$ (419.4)	$ (259.1)

The Company's tax credits and loss carryforwards included alternative minimum tax (AMT), foreign tax and general business credits of $317.0 million, state net operating loss (NOL) carryforwards of $23.8 million and foreign loss carryforwards of $84.4 million as of December 31, 2010. The AMT credits and foreign NOL and capital loss carryforwards have no expiration date. The foreign tax and general business credits begin to expire in 2020 and 2027, respectively. The state NOL carryforwards begin to expire in the year 2011. In assessing the near term use of NOLs and tax credits and corresponding valuation allowance adjustments, the Company evaluated the overall deferred tax position, available tax strategies and future taxable income. The $28.7 million change in the valuation allowance due to the 2010 assessment included a $48.8 million decrease on AMT credits, an $11.7 million increase on state NOLs and an $8.4 million increase on foreign deferred assets. The remaining valuation allowance at December 31, 2010 of $65.0 million represents a reserve for state NOLs and certain foreign deferred tax assets.

FINANCIAL INSTRUMENTS

RECOGNITION AND MEASUREMENT

1.125 FASB ASC 815 establishes accounting and reporting standards for derivative instruments, including certain derivative instruments embedded in other contracts (collectively referred to as derivatives), and hedging activities. FASB ASC 815 requires that an entity recognize all derivatives as either assets or liabilities in the statement of financial position and measure those instruments at fair value. In addition, paragraphs 4–6 of FASB ASC 815-15-25 simplify the accounting for certain hybrid financial instruments by permitting an entity to irrevocably elect to initially and subsequently measure that hybrid financial instrument in its entirety at fair value, with changes recognized in earnings. This election is also available when a previously-recognized financial instrument is subject to a remeasurement (new basis) event and the separate recognition of an embedded derivative.

1.126 FASB ASC 825, *Financial Instruments*, permits entities to choose to measure at fair value many financial instruments and certain other items that are not currently required to be measured at fair value. Further, under FASB ASC 825, a business entity should report unrealized gains and losses on eligible items for which the fair value option has been elected in earnings at each subsequent reporting date. The irrevocable election of the fair value option is made on an instrument-by-instrument basis, with certain exceptions, and applied to the entire instrument, not only to specified risks, specific cash flows, or portions of that instrument.

DISCLOSURE

1.127 The disclosures required by FASB ASC 815 for entities with derivative instruments or nonderivative instruments that are designated and qualify as hedging instruments are intended to enable users of financial statements to understand
- How and why an entity uses derivative or nonderivative instruments.
- How derivative instruments or such nonderivative instruments and related hedged items are accounted for under FASB ASC 815.
- How derivative instruments or such nonderivative instruments and related hedged items affect an entity's financial position, financial performance, and cash flows.

1.128 To meet those objectives, FASB ASC 815 requires qualitative disclosures about an entity's objectives and strategies for using derivatives and such nonderivative instruments. An entity that holds or issues derivative instruments or such nonderivative instruments should disclose all of the following for each interim and annual reporting period for which a statement of financial position and statement of financial performance are presented:
- Its objectives for holding or issuing those instruments.
- The context needed to understand those objectives. This should be disclosed in the context of each instrument's primary underlying risk exposure.
- Its strategies for achieving those objectives. This should be disclosed in the context of each instrument's primary underlying risk exposure.

1.129 These instruments should be disclosed in the context of each instrument's primary underlying risk exposure and should be distinguished among those used for risk management purposes, those used as economic hedges and other purposes related to risk exposure, and those used for other purposes. Those used for risk management purposes should be distinguished between those designated as hedging instruments and, further, whether they are fair value hedges, cash flow hedges, or foreign currency hedges. Information that would enable users of its financial statements to understand the volume of its activity in those instruments should also be disclosed for the same periods. An entity should select the format and specifics for this that are most relevant and practicable for its individual facts and circumstances. For any derivatives not designated as hedging instruments under FASB ASC 815-20, the description should include the purpose of the derivative activity.

1.130 FASB ASC 815 also requires quantitative disclosures about derivatives and such nonderivative instruments. For every annual and interim reporting period for which a statement of financial position and statement of financial performance are presented, an entity that holds or issues derivative instruments is required to disclose the location and fair value amounts of derivative instruments and such nonderivative instruments reported in the statement of financial position. The fair value of those instruments should be presented on a gross basis, even when those instruments are subject to master netting arrangements and qualify for net presentation in the statement of financial position. Cash collateral payables and receivables associated with these instruments should not be added to, or netted against, the fair value amounts.

1.131 Fair value amounts should be presented as separate asset and liability values segregated between derivatives that are designated and qualifying as hedging instruments presented separately by type of contract and those that are not. The disclosure should also identify the line item(s) in the statement of financial position in which the fair value amounts for these categories of derivative instruments are included. Also, disclosure of the location and amount of the gains and losses on derivative instruments and such nonderivative instruments and related hedged items in the statement of financial performance or statement of financial position (for example, in other comprehensive income) is required. These gain and loss disclosures should be presented separately by type of contract. These quantitative disclosures are required to be presented in tabular format, except for disclosures regarding hedged items that can be presented in either tabular or nontabular format.

1.132 For derivative instruments not designated or qualifying as hedging instruments under FASB ASC 815-20, if the entity's policy is to include them in its trading activities, the entity can elect not to separately disclose gains and losses, provided that the entity discloses certain other information. Additionally, FASB ASC 815 requires specific disclosures for derivative instruments that contain credit-risk-related features and credit derivatives.

1.133 FASB ASC 825 requires certain reporting entities to disclose the fair value of financial instruments and disclosure requirements of credit risk concentrations of all financial instruments, and it provides guidance on the fair value option. FASB ASC 825 also establishes presentation and disclosure requirements designed to facilitate comparison between entities that choose different measurement attributes for similar types of assets and liabilities.

1.134

TABLE 1-10: FINANCIAL INSTRUMENTS—FINANCIAL GUARANTEES/INDEMNIFICATIONS

Table 1-10 lists the frequencies of financial guarantees/indemnifications for the survey entities.

	Number of Entities		
	2010	2009	2008
Debt or line of credit	194	172	188
Lease payments	170	90	70
Contract performance	53	95	107
Employee related	19	53	47
Environmental	30	60	60
Tax	15	51	41
Intellectual property related	27	41	45
Product/service related	58	61	55
Other	28	47	37

1.135

TABLE 1-11: FINANCIAL INSTRUMENTS—INTEREST RATE CONTRACTS

Table 1-11 lists the frequencies of interest rate contracts for the survey entities.

	Number of Entities		
	2010	2009	2008
Swaps	247	N/C*	N/C*
Futures	3	N/C*	N/C*
Forward contracts	31	N/C*	N/C*
Caps	10	N/C*	N/C*
Collars	4	N/C*	N/C*
Swaption	2	N/C*	N/C*
Locks	23	N/C*	N/C*
Options	9	N/C*	N/C*
Other, described	3	N/C*	N/C*

* N/C = Not compiled. Line item was not included in the table for the year shown.

1.136

TABLE 1-12: FINANCIAL INSTRUMENTS—FOREIGN CURRENCY CONTRACTS

Table 1-12 lists the frequencies of foreign currency contracts for the survey entities.

	Number of Entities		
	2010	2009	2008
Forward contracts, foreign exchange contracts, or similar	302	N/C*	N/C*
Options	60	N/C*	N/C*
Swaps	43	N/C*	N/C*
Futures	7	N/C*	N/C*
Collars	7	N/C*	N/C*
Other, described	4	N/C*	N/C*

* N/C = Not compiled. Line item was not included in the table for the year shown.

1.137

TABLE 1-13: FINANCIAL INSTRUMENTS—COMMODITY CONTRACTS

Table 1-13 lists the frequencies of commodity contracts for the survey entities.

	Number of Entities		
	2010	2009	2008
Swaps	50	N/C*	N/C*
Futures	36	N/C*	N/C*
Forward contracts	85	N/C*	N/C*
Options	33	N/C*	N/C*
Collars	9	N/C*	N/C*
Other, described	4	N/C*	N/C*

* N/C = Not compiled. Line item was not included in the table for the year shown.

1.138

TABLE 1-14: FINANCIAL INSTRUMENTS—OTHER FINANCIAL INSTRUMENTS

Table 1-14 lists the frequencies of other financial instruments for the survey entities.

	Number of Entities		
	2010	2009	2008
Letters of credit.....................................	359	314	286
Sale of receivables with recourse............	12	11	20
Equity derivatives, put options, warrants, and forward contracts on stock............	40	N/C*	N/C*
Other, described.................................	11	N/C*	N/C*

* N/C = Not compiled. Line item was not included in the table for the year shown.

PRESENTATION AND DISCLOSURE EXCERPTS

Derivative Financial Instruments

1.139

LAM RESEARCH CORPORATION (JUN)

NOTES TO CONSOLIDATED FINANCIAL STATEMENTS

Note 2. Summary of Significant Accounting Policies (in part)

Derivative Financial Instruments: The Company's policy is to attempt to minimize short-term business exposure to foreign currency exchange rate risks using an effective and efficient method to eliminate or reduce such exposures. In the normal course of business, the Company's financial position is routinely subjected to market risk associated with foreign currency exchange rate fluctuations. The Company carries derivative financial instruments (derivatives) on the balance sheet at their fair values. The Company has a policy that allows the use of derivative financial instruments, specifically foreign currency forward exchange rate contracts, to hedge foreign currency exchange rate fluctuations on forecasted revenue transactions denominated in Japanese yen and net monetary assets or liabilities denominated in various foreign currencies. The Company does not use derivatives for trading or speculative purposes. The Company does not believe that it is or was exposed to more than a nominal amount of credit risk in its interest rate and foreign currency hedges, as counterparties are established and well-capitalized financial institutions. The Company's exposures are in liquid currencies (Japanese yen, Swiss francs, Euros, and Taiwanese dollars), so there is minimal risk that appropriate derivatives to maintain the Company's hedging program would not be available in the future.

To hedge foreign currency risks, the Company uses foreign currency exchange forward contracts, where possible and practical. These forward contracts are valued using standard valuation formulas with assumptions about future foreign currency exchange rates derived from existing exchange rates and interest rates observed in the market.

The Company considers its most current outlook in determining the level of foreign currency denominated intercompany revenue to hedge as cash flow hedges. The Company combines these forecasts with historical trends to establish the portion of its expected volume to be hedged. The revenue is hedged and designated as cash flow hedges to protect the Company from exposures to fluctuations in foreign currency exchange rates. If the underlying forecasted transaction does not occur, or it becomes probable that it will not occur, the related hedge gains and losses on the cash flow hedge are reclassified from accumulated other comprehensive income (loss) to interest and other income (expense) on the consolidated statement of operations at that time.

For further details related to the Company's derivatives, see Note 4 of the Notes to the Consolidated Financial Statements.

Note 4. Financial Instruments (in part)

Fair Value

Pursuant to the accounting guidance for fair value measurement and its subsequent updates, the Company defines fair value as the price that would be received from selling an asset or paid to transfer a liability in an orderly transaction between market participants at the measurement date. When determining the fair value measurements for assets and liabilities required or permitted to be recorded at fair value, the Company considers the principal or most advantageous market in which it would transact, and it considers assumptions that market participants would use when pricing the asset or liability.

The FASB has established a fair value hierarchy that prioritizes the inputs to valuation techniques used to measure fair value. An asset or liability's level in the hierarchy is based on the lowest level of input that is significant to the fair value measurement. Assets and liabilities carried at fair value are classified and disclosed in one of the following three categories:

Level 1: Valuations based on quoted prices in active markets for identical assets or liabilities with sufficient volume and frequency of transactions.

Level 2: Valuations based on observable inputs other than Level 1 prices such as quoted prices for similar assets or liabilities, quoted prices in markets that are not active, or model-derived valuations techniques for which all significant inputs are observable in the market or can be corroborated by, observable market data for substantially the full term of the assets or liabilities.

Level 3: Valuations based on unobservable inputs to the valuation methodology that are significant to the measurement of fair value of assets or liabilities and based on non-binding, broker-provided price quotes and may not have been corroborated by observable market data.

The following table sets forth the Company's financial assets and liabilities measured at fair value on a recurring basis as of June 27, 2010:

		Fair Value Measurement at June 27, 2010		
(In thousands)	Total	Quoted Prices in Active Markets for Identical Assets (Level 1)	Significant Other Observable Inputs (Level 2)	Significant Unobservable Inputs (Level 3)
Assets				
Fixed income				
Money market funds	$470,936	$470,936	$ —	$—
Municipal notes and bonds	103,903	—	103,903	—
US treasury & agencies	3,447	—	3,447	—
Government-sponsored enterprises	6,060	6,060	—	—
Foreign governments	1,008	—	1,008	—
Bank and corporate notes	289,437	169,723	119,636	78
Mortgage backed securities—residential	6,106	—	6,106	—
Mortgage backed securities—commercial	42,964	—	42,964	—
Total fixed income	$923,861	$646,719	$277,064	$78
Equities	7,636	7,636	—	—
Mutual funds	18,124	18,124	—	—
Derivatives assets	2,063	—	2,063	—
Total	$951,684	$672,479	$279,127	$78
Liabilities				
Derivative liabilities	$ 470	$ —	$ 470	$—

The amounts in the table above are reported in the consolidated balance sheet as of June 27, 2010 as follows:

(In thousands)	Total	(Level 1)	(Level 2)	(Level 3)
Reported as:				
Cash equivalents	$478,286	$477,279	$ 1,007	$—
Short-term investments	280,690	4,555	276,057	78
Restricted cash and investments	164,885	164,885	—	—
Prepaid expenses and other current assets	2,063	—	2,063	—
Other assets	25,760	25,760	—	—
	$951,684	$672,479	$279,127	$78
Accrued expenses and other current liabilities	$ 470	$ —	$ 470	$—

At June 27, 2010 the fair value of Level 3 assets measured on a recurring basis was $0.1 million and consisted of a corporate note security. Fair values were based on non-binding, broker-provided price quotes and may not have been corroborated by observable market data.

The following table sets forth the Company's financial assets and liabilities measured at fair value on a recurring basis as of June 28, 2009:

(In thousands)	Total	Quoted Prices in Active Markets for Identical Assets (Level 1)	Significant Other Observable Inputs (Level 2)	Significant Unobservable Inputs (Level 3)
		Fair Value Measurement at June 28, 2009		
Assets				
Fixed Income				
Money market funds	$273,439	$273,439	$ —	$—
Municipal notes and bonds	103,618	—	103,618	—
US treasury & agencies	24,184	24,184	—	—
Government-sponsored enterprises	6,323	—	6,323	—
Foreign governments	1,024	—	1,024	—
Bank and corporate notes	228,171	183,171	45,000	—
Mortgage backed securities—residential	11,630	—	11,630	—
Mortgage backed securities—commercial	13,442	—	13,442	—
Total fixed income	$661,831	$480,794	$181,037	$—
Equities	4,961	4,961	—	—
Mutual funds	—	—	—	—
Derivatives assets	74	—	74	—
Total	$666,866	$485,755	$181,111	$—
Liabilities				
Derivative liabilities	$ 69	$ —	$ 69	$—

The amounts in the table above are reported in the consolidated balance sheet as of June 28, 2009 as follows:

(In thousands)	Total	Level 1	Level 2	Level 3
Reported as:				
Cash equivalents	$278,304	$278,304	$ —	$—
Short-term investments	205,221	24,184	181,037	—
Restricted cash and investments	178,306	178,306	—	—
Prepaid expenses and other current assets	74	—	74	—
Other assets	4,961	4,961	—	—
	$666,866	$485,755	$181,111	$—
Accrued expenses and other current liabilities	$ 69	$ —	$ 69	$—

The Company's primary financial instruments include its cash, cash equivalents, short-term investments, restricted cash and investments, long-term investments, accounts receivable, accounts payable, long-term debt and capital leases, and foreign currency related derivatives. The estimated fair value of cash, accounts receivable and accounts payable approximates their carrying value due to the short period of time to their maturities. The estimated fair values of long-term debt and capital lease obligations approximate their carrying value as the substantial majority of these obligations have interest rates that adjust to market rates on a periodic basis. The fair value of cash equivalents, short-term investments, restricted cash and investments, long-term investments, and foreign currency related derivatives are based on quotes from brokers using market prices for similar instruments.

Derivative Instruments and Hedging

The Company carries derivative financial instruments ("derivatives") on its consolidated balance sheets at their fair values. The Company enters into foreign exchange forward contracts with financial institutions with the primary objective of reducing volatility of earnings and cash flows related to foreign currency exchange rate fluctuations. The counterparties to these foreign exchange forward contracts are creditworthy multinational financial institutions; therefore, we do not consider the risk of counterparty nonperformance to be material.

Cash Flow Hedges

The Company's policy is to attempt to minimize short-term business exposure to foreign currency exchange rate fluctuations using an effective and efficient method to eliminate or reduce such exposures. In the normal course of business, the Company's financial position is routinely subjected to market risk associated with foreign currency exchange rate fluctuations. To protect against a reduction in value of Japanese yen-denominated revenues, the Company has instituted a foreign currency cash flow hedging program. The Company enters into foreign exchange forward contracts that generally expire within 12 months and no later than 24 months. These foreign exchange forward contracts are designated as cash flow hedges and are carried on the Company's balance sheet at fair value with the effective portion of the contracts' gains or losses included in accumulated other comprehensive income (loss) and subsequently recognized in revenue in the same period the hedged revenue is recognized.

At inception and at each quarter end, hedges are tested for effectiveness using regression testing. Changes in the fair value of foreign exchange forward contracts due to changes in time value are excluded from the assessment of effectiveness and are recognized in revenue in the current period. The change in forward time value was not material for all reported periods. There were no gains or losses during the twelve months ended June 27, 2010 associated with ineffectiveness or forecasted transactions that failed to occur. There were $4.0 million of deferred net losses associated with ineffectiveness related to forecasted transactions that were no longer considered probable of occurring and were recognized in "Other income (expense), net" in the Company's consolidated statements of operations during twelve months ended June 28, 2009. There were no gains or losses during the twelve months ended June 29, 2008 associated with ineffectiveness or forecasted transactions that failed to occur. To qualify for hedge accounting, the hedge relationship must meet criteria relating both to the derivative instrument and the hedged item. These criteria include identification of the hedging instrument, the hedged item, the nature of the risk being hedged and how the hedging instrument's effectiveness in offsetting the exposure to changes in the hedged item's fair value or cash flows will be measured.

To receive hedge accounting treatment, all hedging relationships are formally documented at the inception of the hedge and the hedges must be highly effective in offsetting changes to future cash flows on hedged transactions. When derivative instruments are designated and qualify as effective cash flow hedges, the Company is able to defer effective changes in the fair value of the hedging instrument within accumulated other comprehensive income (loss) until the hedged exposure is realized. Consequently, with the exception of excluded time value and hedge ineffectiveness recognized, the Company's results of operations are not subject to fluctuation as a result of changes in the fair value of the

derivative instruments. If hedges are not highly effective or if the Company does not believe that the underlying hedged forecasted transactions will occur, the Company may not be able to account for its derivative instruments as cash flow hedges. If this were to occur, future changes in the fair values of the Company's derivative instruments would be recognized in earnings. Additionally, related amounts previously recorded in "Other comprehensive income" would be reclassified to income immediately. At June 27, 2010, the Company had a de minimis amount of losses accumulated in other comprehensive income.

Balance Sheet Hedges

The Company also enters into foreign exchange forward contracts to hedge the effects of foreign currency fluctuations associated with foreign currency denominated monetary assets and liabilities, primarily intercompany receivables and payables. These foreign exchange forward contracts are not designated for hedge accounting treatment. Therefore, the change in fair value of these derivatives is recorded as a component of other income (expense) and offsets the change in fair value of the foreign currency denominated assets and liabilities, recorded in other income (expense).

As of June 27, 2010, the Company had the following outstanding foreign currency forward contracts that were entered into to hedge forecasted revenues and purchases:

(In thousands)	Derivatives Designated as ASC 815 Hedging Instruments	Derivatives Not Designated as ASC 815 Hedging Instruments
Foreign Currency Forward Contracts		
Sell JPY	$73,349	$ —
Sell JPY		76,624
Buy CHF		189,158
Buy EUR		48,046
Sell EUR		9,882
Buy TWD		65,384
	$73,349	$389,094

The fair value of derivatives instruments in the Company's consolidated balance sheet as of June 27, 2010 was as follows:

	Fair Value of Derivative Instruments			
	Asset Derivatives		Liability Derivatives	
(In thousands)	Balance Sheet Location	Fair Value	Balance Sheet Location	Fair Value
Derivatives Designated as ASC 815 Hedging Instruments:				
Foreign exchange forward contracts	Prepaid expense and other assets	$ 30	Accrued liabilities	$ (52)
Derivatives Not Designated as Hedging Instruments Under ASC 815:				
Foreign exchange forward contracts	Prepaid expense and other assets	$2,033	Accrued liabilities	$(418)
Total derivatives		$2,063		$(470)

The fair value of derivatives instruments in the Company's consolidated balance sheet as of June 28, 2009 was as follows:

| | Fair Value of Derivative Instruments | | | |
| | Asset Derivatives | | Liability Derivatives | |
(In thousands)	Balance Sheet Location	Fair Value	Balance Sheet Location	Fair Value
Derivatives Designated as ASC 815 Hedging Instruments:				
Foreign exchange forward contracts	Prepaid expense and other assets	$ 6	Accrued liabilities	$ —
Derivatives Not Designated as Hedging Instruments Under ASC 815:				
Foreign exchange forward contracts	Prepaid expense and other assets	$68	Accrued liabilities	$(69)
Total derivatives		$74		$(69)

The effect of derivative instruments designated as cash flow hedges on the Company's consolidated statements of operations for the twelve months ended June 27, 2010 and June 28, 2009 was as follows:

| | Twelve Months Ended June 27, 2010 | | | |
(In thousands)	Gain (Loss) Recognized (Effective Portion)[1]	Gain (Loss) Recognized (Effective Portion)[2]	Gain (Loss) Recognized (Ineffective Portion)[3]	Gain (Loss) Recognized (Excluded from Effectiveness Testing)[4]
Derivatives Designated as ASC 815 Hedging Instruments:				
Foreign exchange forward contracts	$ 388	$ 404	$ —	$ 59

	Twelve Months Ended June 28, 2009			
Derivatives Designated as ASC 815 Hedging Instruments:				
Foreign exchange forward contracts	$(11,840)	$(3,485)	$(4,085)	$1,462

[1] Amount recognized in other comprehensive income (loss) (effective portion).
[2] Amount of gain (loss) reclassified from accumulated other comprehensive income into income (loss) (effective portion) located in revenue.
[3] Amount of gain (loss) recognized in income on derivative (ineffective portion) located in other income (expense), net.
[4] Amount of gain (loss) recognized in income on derivative (amount excluded from effectiveness testing) located in other income (expense), net.

The effect of derivative instruments not designated as cash flow hedges on the Company's consolidated statement of operations for the twelve months ended June 27, 2010 and June 28, 2009 was as follows:

| | Twelve Months Ended | |
| | June 27, 2010 Gain (Loss) Recognized[5] | June 28, 2009 Gain (Loss) Recognized[5] |
(In thousands)		
Derivatives Not Designated as ASC 815 Hedging Instruments:		
Foreign exchange forward contracts	$(17,367)	$(953)

[5] Amount of gain (loss) recognized in income located in other income (expense), net.

Concentrations of Credit Risk

Financial instruments that potentially subject the Company to concentrations of credit risk consist principally of cash equivalents, short term investments, restricted cash and investments, loans receivable, trade accounts receivable, and derivative financial instruments used in hedging activities. Cash is placed on deposit in major financial institutions in various countries throughout the world. Such deposits may be in excess of insured limits. Management believes that the financial institutions that hold the Company's cash are financially sound and, accordingly, minimal credit risk exists with respect to these balances.

The Company's available-for-sale securities, which are invested in taxable financial instruments, must have a minimum rating of A2 / A, as rated by two of the following three rating agencies: Moody's, Standard & Poor's (S&P), or Fitch. Available-for-sale securities that are invested in tax-exempt financial instruments must have a minimum rating of A2 / A, as rated by any one of the same three rating agencies. The Company's policy limits the amount of credit exposure with any one financial institution or commercial issuer.

The Company is exposed to credit losses in the event of nonperformance by counterparties on the foreign currency forward contracts that are used to mitigate the effect of exchange rate changes. These counterparties are large international financial institutions and to date no such counterparty has failed to meet its financial obligations to the Company. The Company does not anticipate nonperformance by these counterparties.

As of June 27, 2010, two customers accounted for approximately 24% and 22 % of accounts receivable. As of June 28, 2009, three customers accounted for approximately 17%, 15%, and 14% of accounts receivable.

Credit risk evaluations, including trade references, bank references and Dun & Bradstreet ratings, are performed on all new customers and the Company monitors its customers' financial statements and payment performance. In general, the Company does not require collateral on sales.

1.140

NOBLE ENERGY, INC. (DEC)

NOTES TO CONSOLIDATED FINANCIAL STATEMENTS

Note 1. Summary of Significant Accounting Policies (in part)

Derivative Instruments and Hedging Activities All derivative instruments (including certain derivative instruments embedded in other contracts) are recorded in our consolidated balance sheets as either an asset or liability and measured at fair value. Changes in the derivative instrument's fair value are recognized currently in earnings, unless the derivative instrument has been designated as a cash flow hedge and specific cash flow hedge accounting criteria are met. Under cash flow hedge accounting, unrealized gains and losses are reflected in shareholders' equity as accumulative other comprehensive loss (AOCL) until the forecasted transaction occurs. The derivative's gains or losses are then offset against related results on the hedged transaction in the statements of operations.

A company must formally document, designate and assess the effectiveness of transactions that receive hedge accounting. Only derivative instruments that are expected to be highly effective in offsetting anticipated gains or losses on the hedged cash flows and that are subsequently documented to have been highly effective can qualify for hedge accounting. Effectiveness must be assessed both at inception of the hedge and on an ongoing basis. Any ineffectiveness in hedging instruments whereby gains or losses do not exactly offset anticipated gains or losses of hedged cash flows is measured and recognized in earnings in the period in which it occurs. When using hedge accounting, we assess hedge effectiveness quarterly based on total changes in the derivative instrument's fair value by performing regression analysis. A hedge is considered effective if certain statistical tests are met. We record hedge ineffectiveness in (gain) loss on commodity derivative instruments.

Accounting for Commodity Derivative Instruments—We account for our commodity derivative instruments using mark-to-market accounting and recognize all gains and losses in earnings during the period in which they occur. Prior to January 1, 2008, we elected to designate certain of our commodity derivative instruments as cash flow hedges. Effective January 1, 2008, we voluntarily discontinued cash flow hedge accounting for our commodity derivative instruments. Net derivative gains and losses that were deferred in AOCL as of January 1, 2008, as a result of previous cash flow hedge accounting, were reclassified to earnings during the years ended December 31, 2008 through December 31, 2010 as the original transactions occurred.

We offset the fair value amounts recognized for derivative instruments and the fair value amounts recognized for the right to reclaim cash collateral or the obligation to return cash collateral. The cash collateral (commonly referred to as a "margin") must arise from derivative instruments recognized at fair value that are executed with the same counterparty under a master netting arrangement.

Accounting for Interest Rate Derivative Instruments We designate interest rate derivative instruments as cash flow hedges. Changes in fair value of interest rate swaps or interest rate "locks" used as cash flow hedges are reported in AOCL, to the extent the hedge is effective, until the forecasted transaction occurs, at which time they are recorded as adjustments to interest expense over the term of the related notes. See Note 10. Derivative Instruments and Hedging Activities.

Note 10. Derivative Instruments and Hedging Activities

Objective and Strategies for Using Derivative Instruments In order to reduce commodity price uncertainty and enhance the predictability of cash flows relating to the marketing of our crude oil and natural gas, we enter into crude oil and natural gas price hedging arrangements with respect to a portion of our expected production. The derivative instruments we use include variable to fixed price commodity swaps, two-way and three-way collars and basis swaps.

The fixed price swap, two-way collar, and basis swap contracts entitle us (floating price payor) to receive settlement from the counterparty (fixed price payor) for each calculation period in amounts, if any, by which the settlement price for the scheduled trading days applicable for each calculation period is less than the fixed strike price or floor price. We would pay the counterparty if the settlement price for the scheduled trading days applicable for each calculation period is more than the fixed strike price or ceiling price. The amount payable by us, if the floating price is above the fixed or ceiling price, is the product of the notional quantity per calculation period and the excess, if any, of the floating price over the fixed or ceiling price in respect of each calculation period. The amount payable by the counterparty, if the floating price is below the fixed or floor price, is the product of the notional quantity per calculation period and the excess, if any, of the fixed or floor price over the floating price in respect of each calculation period.

A three-way collar consists of a two-way collar contract combined with a put option contract sold by us with a strike price below the floor price of the two-way collar. We receive price protection at the purchased put option floor price of the two-way collar if commodity prices are above the sold put option strike price. If commodity prices fall below the sold put option strike price, we receive the cash market price plus the delta between the two put option strike prices. This type of instrument allows us to capture more value in a rising commodity price environment, but limits our benefits in a downward commodity price environment.

We also enter into forward contracts or swap agreements to hedge exposure to interest rate risk.

While these instruments mitigate the cash flow risk of future reductions in commodity prices or increases in interest rates, they may also curtail benefits from future increases in commodity prices or decreases in interest rates.

See Note 16. Fair Value Measurements and Disclosures for a discussion of methods and assumptions used to estimate the fair values of our derivative instruments.

Counterparty Credit Risk—Derivative instruments expose us to counterparty credit risk. Our commodity derivative instruments are currently with a diversified group of highly rated major banks or market participants, and we control our level of financial exposure. Our commodity derivative contracts are executed under master agreements which allow us, in the event of default, to elect early termination of all contracts with the defaulting counterparty. If we choose to elect early termination, all asset and liability positions with the defaulting counterparty would be net settled at the time of election.

We monitor the creditworthiness of our counterparties. However, we are not able to predict sudden changes in counterparties' creditworthiness. In addition, even if such changes are not sudden, we may be limited in our ability to mitigate an increase in counterparty credit risk. Possible actions would be to transfer our position to another counterparty or request a voluntary termination of the derivative contracts resulting in a cash settlement. Should one of these financial counterparties not perform, we may not realize the benefit of some of our derivative instruments under lower commodity prices or higher interest rates, and could incur a loss.

Unsettled Derivative Instruments

We have entered into the following crude oil derivative instruments:

| | | | | Swaps | Collars | | |
Period	Type of Contract	Index	Bbls Per Day	Weighted Average Fixed Price	Weighted Average Short Put Price	Weighted Average Floor Price	Weighted Average Ceiling Price
Instruments Entered Into Prior to December 31, 2010							
2011	Swaps	NYMEX WTI[1]	5,000	$85.52	$ —	$ —	$ —
2011	Two-Way Collars	NYMEX WTI	13,000	—	—	80.15	94.63
2011	Three-Way Collars	NYMEX WTI	12,000	—	58.33	78.33	100.71
2012	Swaps	NYMEX WTI	5,000	91.84	—	—	—
2012	Swaps	Dated Brent	5,000	83.09	—	—	—
2012	Three-Way Collars	NYMEX WTI	23,000	—	61.09	83.04	101.66
Instruments Entered Into During January 1–31, 2011							
2012	Swaps	Dated Brent	3,000	99.00	—	—	—
2012	Three-Way Collars	Dated Brent	3,000	—	70.00	95.83	105.00
2013	Swaps	Dated Brent	3,000	98.03	—	—	—
2013	Three-Way Collars	NYMEX WTI	5,000	—	65.00	85.00	113.63
2013	Three-Way Collars	Dated Brent	5,000	—	70.00	94.01	110.00

[1] West Texas Intermediate

We have entered into the following natural gas derivative instruments:

Period	Type of Contract	Index	MMBtu Per Day	Swaps Weighted Average Fixed Price	Collars Weighted Average Short Put Price	Weighted Average Floor Price	Weighted Average Ceiling Price
Instruments Entered Into Prior to December 31, 2010							
2011	Swaps	NYMEX HH[1]	25,000	$6.41	$ —	$ —	$ —
2011	Two-Way Collars	NYMEX HH	140,000	—	—	5.95	6.82
2011	Three-Way Collars	NYMEX HH	50,000	—	4.00	5.00	6.70
2012	Three-Way Collars	NYMEX HH	80,000	—	4.60	5.35	7.11
Instruments Entered Into During January 1–31, 2011							
2012	Swaps	NYMEX HH	30,000	5.10	—	—	—
2012	Three-Way Collars	NYMEX HH	30,000	—	4.00	5.00	5.48
2013	Swaps	NYMEX HH	30,000	5.25	—	—	—
2013	Three-Way Collars	NYMEX HH	50,000	—	4.00	5.25	5.59

[1] Henry Hub

As of December 31, 2010, we had entered into the following natural gas basis swaps:

Period	Index	Index Less Differential	MMBtu Per Day	Weighted Average Differential
2011	IFERC CIG[1]	NYMEX HH	140,000	$(0.70)
2012	IFERC CIG	NYMEX HH	150,000	(0.52)

[1] Colorado Interstate Gas—Northern System

Fair Value Amounts and Gains and Losses on Derivative Instruments—The fair values of derivative instruments in our consolidated balance sheets were as follows:

	Fair Value of Derivative Instruments							
	Asset Derivative Instruments				Liability Derivative Instruments			
	December 31				December 31			
	2010		2009		2010		2009	
(millions)	Balance Sheet Location	Fair Value	Balance Sheet Location	Fair Value	Balance Sheet Location	Fair Value	Balance Sheet Location	Fair Value
Commodity Derivative Instruments (Not Designated as Hedging Instruments)	Current Assets	$62	Current Assets	$13	Current Liabilities	$ 24	Current Liabilities	$100
	Noncurrent Assets	—	Noncurrent Assets	1	Noncurrent Liabilities	51	Noncurrent Liabilities	17
Interest Rate Derivative Instrument Designated as Hedging Instrument)[1]	Current Assets	—	Current Assets	—	Current Liabilities	63	Current Liabilities	—
	Total	$62	Total	$14	Total	$138	Total	$117

[1] In 2010, in anticipation of a long-term debt issuance, we entered into an interest rate forward starting swap to effectively fix the cash flows related to interest payments on the anticipated debt issuance. We are accounting for the instrument as a cash flow hedge against the variability of interest payments attributable to changes in interest rates on the forecasted issuance of fixed-rate debt. The swap is in the notional amount of $500 million and is based on a 30-year LIBOR swap rate.

The effect of derivative instruments on our consolidated statements of operations was as follows:

Commodity Derivative Instruments Not Designated as Hedging Instruments
Amount of (Gain) Loss on Derivative Instruments Recognized in Income

	Year Ended December 31		
(millions)	2010	2009	2008
Realized Mark-to-Market (Gain) Loss	$ (87)	$(496)	$ 82
Unrealized Mark-to-Market (Gain) Loss	(70)	606	(522)
Total (Gain) Loss on Commodity Derivative Instruments	$(157)	$ 110	$(440)

Derivative Instruments in Cash Flow Hedging Relationships

	Amount of (Gain) Loss on Derivative Instruments Recognized in Other Comprehensive (Income) Loss			Amount of (Gain) Loss on Derivative Instruments Reclassified from Accumulated Other Comprehensive Loss		
(millions)	2010	2009	2008	2010	2009	2008
Commodity Derivative Instruments in Previously Designated Cash Flow Hedging Relationships[1]						
Crude Oil	$ —	$—	$—	$19	$58	$365
Natural Gas	—	—	—	1	—	(34)
Interest Rate Derivative Instruments in Cash Flow Hedging Relationships	(63)	—	(1)	1	1	1
Total	$(63)	$—	$(1)	$21	$59	$332

[1] Includes effect of commodity derivative instruments previously accounted for as cash flow hedges. Net derivative gains and losses that were deferred in AOCL as of January 1, 2008, as a result of previous cash flow hedge accounting, were reclassified to oil, gas and NGL sales in our consolidated statements of operations in 2008, 2009 and 2010 as the original hedged transactions occurred.

AOCL—Commodity Derivative Instruments At December 31, 2010, AOCL included no further amounts related to commodity derivative instruments. At December 31, 2009, the balance in AOCL included net deferred losses of $12 million (net of deferred income tax benefits of $8 million) related to the fair value of crude oil and natural gas derivative instruments previously designated as cash flow hedges. The net deferred losses were reclassified to earnings during 2010 as the forecasted transactions occurred and recorded as a reduction in oil, gas and NGL sales of approximately $20 million before tax.

AOCL—Interest Rate Derivative Instruments At December 31, 2010, AOCL included deferred losses of $42 million, net of tax, related to interest rate derivative instruments. Of this amount, $1 million, net of tax, is currently being reclassified into earnings as adjustments to interest expense over the term of our Senior Notes due April 2014. Approximately $41 million will remain in AOCL until fixed-rate debt is issued, at which time we will begin amortizing it to interest expense over the life of the related debt issuance.

Note 16. Fair Value Measurements and Disclosures (in part)

Assets and Liabilities Measured at Fair Value on a Recurring Basis—Certain assets and liabilities are measured at fair value on a recurring basis in our consolidated balance sheets. The following methods and assumptions were used to estimate the fair values:

Commodity Derivative Instruments—Our commodity derivative instruments consist of variable to fixed price commodity swaps, two-way and three-way collars and basis swaps. We estimate the fair values of these instruments based on published forward commodity price curves as of the date of the estimate. The discount rate used in the discounted cash flow projections is based on published LIBOR rates, Eurodollar futures rates and interest swap rates. The fair values of commodity derivative instruments in an asset position include a measure of counterparty nonperformance risk, and the fair values of commodity derivative instruments in a liability position include a measure of our own nonperformance risk, each based on the current published credit default swap rates. In addition, for collars, we estimate the option values of the put options sold (for three-way collars) and the contract floors and ceilings (for two-way and three-way collars) using an option pricing model which takes into account market volatility, market prices and contract terms. See Note 10. Derivative Instruments and Hedging Activities.

Interest Rate Derivative Instrument—We estimate the fair value of our forward starting swap based on published interest rate yield curves as of the date of the estimate. The fair values of interest rate derivative instruments in an asset position include a measure of counterparty nonperformance risk, and the fair values of interest rate derivative instruments in a liability position include a measure of our own nonperformance risk, each based on the current published credit default swap rates. See Note 10. Derivative Instruments and Hedging Activities.

Measurement information for assets and liabilities that are measured at fair value on a recurring basis was as follows:

| (millions) | Fair Value Measurements Using | | | | |
	Quoted Prices in Active Markets (Level 1)[1]	Significant Other Observable Inputs (Level 2)[1]	Significant Unobservable Inputs (Level 3)[1]	Adjustment[2]	Fair Value Measurement
December 31, 2010					
Financial assets					
Mutual fund investments	$ 112	$ —	$—	$ —	$ 112
Commodity derivative instruments	—	106	—	(44)	62
Financial liabilities					
Commodity derivative instruments	—	(119)	—	44	(75)
Interest rate derivative instrument	—	(63)	—	—	(63)
Portion of deferred compensation					
Liability measured at fair value	(178)	—	—	—	(178)
December 31, 2009					
Financial assets					
Mutual fund investments	$ 108	$ —	$—	$ —	$ 108
Commodity derivative instruments	—	42	—	(28)	14
Financial liabilities					
Commodity derivative instruments	—	(145)	—	28	(117)
Portion of deferred compensation					
Liability measured at fair value	(168)	—	—	—	(168)

[1] See Note 1. Summary of Significant Accounting Policies—Fair Value Measurements for a description of the fair value hierarchy.
[2] Amount represents the impact of master netting agreements that allow us to settle asset and liability positions with the same counterparty.

1.141

SMITHFIELD FOODS, INC. (APR)

NOTES TO CONSOLIDATED FINANCIAL STATEMENTS

Note 7: Derivative Financial Instruments

Our meat processing and hog production operations use various raw materials, primarily live hogs, corn and soybean meal, which are actively traded on commodity exchanges. We hedge these commodities when we determine conditions are appropriate to mitigate price risk. While this hedging may limit our ability to participate in gains from favorable commodity fluctuations, it also tends to reduce the risk of loss from adverse changes in raw material prices. We attempt to closely match the commodity contract terms with the hedged item. We also enter into interest rate swaps to hedge exposure to changes in interest rates on certain financial instruments and foreign exchange forward contracts to hedge certain exposures to fluctuating foreign currency rates.

We record all derivatives in the balance sheet as either assets or liabilities at fair value. Accounting for changes in the fair value of a derivative depends on whether it qualifies and has been designated as part of a hedging relationship. For derivatives that qualify and have been designated as hedges for accounting purposes, changes in fair value have no net impact on earnings, to the extent the derivative is considered perfectly effective in achieving offsetting changes in fair value or cash flows attributable to the risk being hedged, until the hedged item is recognized in earnings (commonly referred to as the "hedge accounting" method). For derivatives that do not qualify or are not designated as hedging instruments for accounting purposes, changes in fair value are recorded in current period earnings (commonly referred to as the "mark-to-market" method). We may elect either method of accounting for our derivative portfolio, assuming all the necessary requirements are met. We have in the past, and will in the future, avail ourselves of either acceptable method. We believe all of our derivative instruments represent economic hedges against changes in prices and rates, regardless of their designation for accounting purposes.

We do not offset the fair value of derivative instruments with cash collateral held with or received from the same counterparty under a master netting arrangement. As of May 2, 2010, prepaid expenses and other current assets included $150.3 million representing cash on deposit with brokers to cover losses on our open derivative instruments. Changes in commodity prices could have a significant impact on cash deposit requirements under our broker and counterparty agreements. We have reviewed our derivative contracts and have determined that they do not contain credit contingent features which would require us to post additional collateral if we did not maintain a credit rating equivalent to what was in place at the time the contracts were entered into.

We are exposed to losses in the event of nonperformance or nonpayment by counterparties under financial instruments. Although our counterparties primarily consist of financial institutions that are investment grade, there is still a possibility that one or more of these companies could default. However, a majority of our financial instruments are exchange traded futures contracts held with brokers and counterparties with whom we maintain margin accounts that are settled on a daily basis, and therefore our credit risk is not significant. Determination of the credit quality of our counterparties is based upon a number of factors, including credit ratings and our evaluation of their financial condition. As of May 2, 2010, we had credit exposure of $4.5 million on non-exchange traded derivative contracts, excluding the effects of netting arrangements. As a result of netting arrangements, our credit exposure was reduced to $3.5 million. No significant concentrations of credit risk existed as of May 2, 2010.

The size and mix of our derivative portfolio varies from time to time based upon our analysis of current and future market conditions. The following table presents the fair values of our open derivative financial instruments in the consolidated balance sheets on a gross basis. All grain contracts, livestock contracts and foreign exchange contracts are recorded in prepaid expenses and other current assets or accrued expenses and other current liabilities within the consolidated condensed balance sheets, as appropriate. Interest rate contracts are recorded in accrued expenses and other current liabilities or other liabilities, as appropriate.

(In millions)	Assets		Liabilities	
	May 2, 2010	May 3, 2009	May 2, 2010	May 3, 2009
Derivatives using the "hedge accounting" method:				
Grain contracts	$11.5	$10.4	$ 3.4	$17.7
Livestock contracts	—	—	40.8	—
Interest rate contracts	—	0.6	8.1	10.3
Foreign exchange contracts	3.0	1.4	—	14.4
Total	14.5	12.4	52.3	42.4
Derivatives using the "mark-to-market" method:				
Grain contracts	5.5	10.2	6.5	16.2
Livestock contracts	5.8	21.9	87.6	6.3
Energy contracts	—	—	4.0	13.0
Foreign exchange contracts	0.5	1.7	0.2	1.6
Total	11.8	33.8	98.3	37.1
Total fair value of derivative instruments	$26.3	$46.2	$150.6	$79.5

Hedge Accounting Method

Cash Flow Hedges

We enter into derivative instruments, such as futures, swaps and options contracts, to manage our exposure to the variability in expected future cash flows attributable to commodity price risk associated with the forecasted sale of live hogs and the forecasted purchase of corn and soybean meal. In addition, we enter into interest rate swaps to manage our exposure to changes in interest rates associated with our variable interest rate debt, and we enter into foreign exchange contracts to manage our exposure to the variability in expected future cash flows attributable to changes in foreign exchange rates associated with the forecasted purchase or sale of assets denominated in foreign currencies. We generally do not hedge anticipated transactions beyond twelve months.

During fiscal 2010, the range of notional volumes associated with open derivative instruments designated in cash flow hedging relationships was as follows:

	Minimum	Maximum	Metric
Commodities:			
Corn	—	79,035,000	Bushels
Soybean meal	78,900	551,200	Tons
Lean Hogs	—	264,800,000	Pounds
Interest rate	200,000,000	200,000,000	U.S. Dollars
Foreign currency[1]	32,653,181	114,691,273	U.S. Dollars

[1] Amounts represent the U.S. dollar equivalent of various foreign currency contracts.

The following table presents the effects on our consolidated financial statements of pre-tax gains and losses on derivative instruments designated in cash flow hedging relationships for the fiscal years indicated:

(In millions)	Gain (Loss) Recognized in OCI on Derivative (Effective Portion)			Gain (Loss) Reclassified From Accumulated OCI into Earnings (Effective Portion)			Gain (Loss) Recognized in Earnings on Derivative (Ineffective Portion)		
	2010	2009	2008	2010	2009	2008	2010	2009	2008
Commodity contracts:									
Grain contracts	$ (4.0)	$(201.5)	$ —	$(85.4)	$(112.5)	$(29.3)	$(7.2)	$(4.6)	$—
Lean hog contracts	(22.8)	—	—	1.9	—	—	(0.5)	—	—
Interest rate contracts	(4.6)	(12.6)	—	(6.8)	(2.3)	—	—	—	—
Foreign exchange contracts	6.1	(37.5)	(1.4)	(8.0)	(21.7)	(2.6)	—	—	—
Total	$(25.3)	$(251.6)	$(1.4)	$(98.3)	$(136.5)	$(31.9)	$(7.7)	$(4.6)	$—

When cash flow hedge accounting is applied, derivative gains or losses from these cash flow hedges are recognized as a component of other comprehensive income (loss) and reclassified into earnings in the same period or periods during which the hedged transactions affect earnings. Derivative gains and losses, when reclassified into earnings, are recorded in cost of sales for grain contracts, sales for lean hog contracts, interest expense for interest rate contracts and selling, general and administrative expenses for foreign currency contracts.

As of May 2, 2010, there were deferred net losses of $24.5 million, net of tax of $15.5 million, in accumulated other comprehensive loss. We expect to reclassify $25.2 million ($15.4 million net of tax) of the deferred net losses on closed commodity contracts into earnings in fiscal 2011.

Fair Value Hedges

We enter into derivative instruments (primarily futures contracts) that are designed to hedge changes in the fair value of live hog inventories and firm commitments to buy grains. We also enter into interest rate swaps to manage interest rate risk associated with our fixed rate borrowings. When fair value hedge accounting is applied, derivative gains and losses from these fair value hedges are recognized in earnings currently along with the change in fair value of the hedged item attributable to the risk being hedged. The gains or losses on the derivative instruments and the offsetting losses or gains on the related hedged items are recorded in cost of sales for commodity contracts, interest expense for interest rate contracts and selling, general and administrative expenses for foreign currency contracts.

During fiscal 2010, the range of notional volumes associated with open derivative instruments designated in fair value hedging relationships was as follows:

	Minimum	Maximum	Metric
Commodities:			
Corn	2,070,000	11,610,000	Bushels
Lean Hogs	—	726,160,000	Pounds
Interest rate	—	50,000,000	U.S. Dollars
Foreign currency[1]	16,051,549	24,836,547	U.S. Dollars

[1] Amounts represent the U.S. dollar equivalent of various foreign currency contracts.

The following table presents the effects on our consolidated statements of income of gains and losses on derivative instruments designated in fair value hedging relationships and the related hedged items for the fiscal years indicated:

(In millions)	Gain (Loss) Recognized in Earnings on Derivative			Gain (Loss) Recognized in Earnings on Related Hedged Item		
	2010	2009	2008	2010	2009	2008
Commodity contracts	$(36.2)	$12.8	$4.3	$32.4	$(14.0)	$(4.3)
Interest rate contracts	0.6	0.7	(3.0)	(0.6)	(0.7)	3.0
Foreign exchange contracts	3.4	—	—	(1.5)	—	—
Total	$(32.2)	$13.5	$1.3	$30.3	$(14.7)	$(1.3)

Mark-to-Market Method

Derivative instruments that are not designated as a hedge, that have been de-designated from a hedging relationship, or do not meet the criteria for hedge accounting, are marked-to-market with the unrealized gains and losses together with actual realized gains and losses from closed contracts being recognized in current period earnings. Derivative gains and losses are recorded in cost of sales for commodity contracts, interest expense for interest rate contracts and selling, general and administrative expenses for foreign currency contracts.

During fiscal 2010, the range of notional volumes associated with open derivative instruments using the "mark-to-market" method was as follows:

	Minimum	Maximum	Metric
Commodities:			
Lean hogs	9,000,000	1,146,200,000	Pounds
Corn	3,125,000	63,304,300	Bushels
Soybean meal	—	516,421	Tons
Soybeans	10,000	595,000	Bushels
Wheat	—	360,000	Bushels
Live cattle	—	6,000,000	Pounds
Pork bellies	—	1,920,000	Pounds
Natural gas	2,145,000	5,040,000	Million BTU
Foreign currency[1]	55,909,712	152,889,945	U.S. Dollars

[1] Amounts represent the U.S. dollar equivalent of various foreign currency contracts.

The following table presents the amount of gains (losses) recognized in the consolidated statements of income on derivative instruments using the "mark-to-market" method by type of derivative contract for the fiscal years indicated:

	Fiscal Years		
(In millions)	2010	2009	2008
Commodity contracts	$ (92.4)	$104.0	$236.2
Interest rate contracts	—	2.3	(7.8)
Foreign exchange contracts	(11.1)	(3.1)	(0.2)
Total	$(103.5)	$103.2	$228.2

Financial Guarantees and Indemnifications

1.142

EASTMAN KODAK COMPANY (DEC)

NOTES TO FINANCIAL STATEMENTS

Note 11. Guarantees (in part)

The Company guarantees debt and other obligations of certain customers. The debt and other obligations are primarily due to banks and leasing companies in connection with financing of customers' purchases of equipment and product from the Company. At December 31, 2010, the maximum potential amount of future payments (undiscounted) that the Company could be required to make under these customer-related guarantees was $47 million. At December 31, 2010, the carrying amount of any liability related to these customer guarantees was not material.

The customer financing agreements and related guarantees, which mature between 2011 and 2016, typically have a term of 90 days for product and short-term equipment financing arrangements, and up to five years for long-term equipment financing arrangements. These guarantees would require payment from the Company only in the event of default on payment by the respective debtor. In some cases, particularly for guarantees related to equipment financing, the Company has collateral or recourse provisions to recover and sell the equipment to reduce any losses that might be incurred in connection with the guarantees. However, any proceeds received from the liquidation of these assets may not cover the maximum potential loss under these guarantees.

Eastman Kodak Company ("EKC") also guarantees potential indebtedness to banks and other third parties for some of its consolidated subsidiaries. The maximum amount guaranteed is $261 million, and the outstanding amount for those guarantees is $238 million with $109 million recorded within the Short-term borrowings and current portion of long-term debt, and Long-term debt, net of current portion components in the accompanying Consolidated Statement of Financial Position. These guarantees expire in 2010 through 2019. Pursuant to the terms of the Company's Amended Credit Agreement, obligations of the Borrowers to the Lenders under the Amended Credit Agreement, as well as secured agreements in an amount not to exceed $100 million, are guaranteed by the Company and the Company's U.S. subsidiaries and included in the above amounts. These secured agreements totaled $90 million as of December 31, 2010.

During the fourth quarter of 2007, EKC issued a guarantee to Kodak Limited (the "Subsidiary") and the Trustees (the "Trustees") of the Kodak Pension Plan of the United Kingdom (the "Plan"). Under that arrangement, EKC guaranteed to the Subsidiary and the Trustees the ability of the Subsidiary, only to the extent it becomes necessary to do so, to (1) make contributions to the Plan to ensure sufficient assets exist to make plan benefit payments, and (2) make contributions to the Plan such that it will achieve full funded status by the funding valuation for the period ending December 31, 2015. On October 12, 2010, the 2007 guarantee was replaced by a new guarantee from EKC to the Subsidiary and the Trustees. The new guarantee continues to guarantee the Subsidiary's ability to make contributions as set forth in the 2007 guarantee but extends the full funding date to December 31, 2022. The new guarantee expires (a) upon the conclusion of the funding valuation for the period ending December 31, 2022 if the Plan achieves full funded status or on payment of the balance if the Plan is underfunded by no more than 60 million British pounds by that date, (b) earlier in the event that the Plan achieves full funded status for two consecutive funding valuation cycles which are typically performed at least every three years, or (c) June 30, 2024 on payment of the balance in the event that the Plan is underfunded by more than 60 million British pounds upon conclusion of the funding valuation for the period ending December 31, 2022. The amount of potential future contributions is dependent on the funding status of the Plan as it fluctuates over the term of the guarantee and the United Kingdom Pension Regulator's approval of a funding plan agreed to by the Subsidiary and the Trustees to close the funding gap identified by the Plan's most recent local statutory funding valuation agreed to in March 2009. The funded status of the Plan (calculated in accordance with U.S. GAAP) is included in Pension and other postretirement liabilities presented in the Consolidated Statement of Financial Position.

1.143

NORTHROP GRUMMAN CORPORATION (DEC)

NOTES TO CONSOLIDATED FINANCIAL STATEMENTS

16. Commitments and Contingencies (in part)

Guarantees of Subsidiary Performance Obligations—From time to time in the ordinary course of business, the company guarantees performance obligations of its subsidiaries under certain contracts. In addition, the company's subsidiaries may enter into joint ventures, teaming and other business arrangements (collectively, Business Arrangements) to support the company's products and services in domestic and international markets. The company generally strives to limit its exposure under these arrangements to its subsidiary's investment in the Business Arrangements, or to the extent of such subsidiary's obligations under the applicable contract. In some cases, however, the company may be required to guarantee performance by the Business Arrangements and, in such cases, the company generally obtains cross-indemnification from the other members of the Business Arrangements. At December 31, 2010, the company is not aware of any existing event of default that would require it to satisfy any of these guarantees.

Financial Arrangements—In the ordinary course of business, the company uses standby letters of credit and guarantees issued by commercial banks and surety bonds issued principally by insurance companies to guarantee the performance on certain contracts and to support the company's self-insured workers' compensation plans. At December 31, 2010, there were $303 million of stand-by letters of credit, $192 million of bank guarantees, and $446 million of surety bonds outstanding.

The company has also guaranteed the remaining $22 million of bonds outstanding from the Gulf Opportunity Zone Industrial Revenue Development Bonds issued by the Mississippi Business Finance Corporation in December 2006. Under the guaranty, the company guaranteed the repayment of all payments due under the trust indenture and loan agreement. In addition, a subsidiary of the company has guaranteed Shipbuilding's outstanding $84 million Economic Development Revenue Bonds (Ingalls Shipbuilding, Inc. Project), Taxable Series 1999A.

Indemnifications—The company has retained certain warranty, environmental, income tax, and other potential liabilities in connection with certain of its divestitures. The settlement of these liabilities is not expected to have a material adverse effect on the company's consolidated financial position, results of operations or cash flows.

Standby Letters of Credit

1.144

HARSCO CORPORATION (DEC)

NOTES TO CONSOLIDATED FINANCIAL STATEMENTS

Note 13. Financial Instruments (in part)

Off-Balance Sheet Risk

As collateral for the Company's performance and to insurers, the Company is contingently liable under standby letters of credit, bonds and bank guarantees in the amounts of $286.1 million and $280.1 million at December 31, 2010 and 2009, respectively. These standby letters of credit, bonds and bank guarantees are generally in force for up to four years. Certain issues have no scheduled expiration date. The Company pays fees to various banks and insurance companies that range from 0.25 percent to 2.30 percent per annum of the instruments' face value. If the Company were required to obtain replacement standby letters of credit, bonds and bank guarantees at December 31, 2010 for those currently outstanding, it is the Company's opinion that the replacement costs would be within the present fee structure.

The Company has currency exposures in more than 50 countries. The Company's primary foreign currency exposures during 2010 were in the European Economic and Monetary Union, the United Kingdom, Brazil, Australia, South Africa and Canada.

FAIR VALUE

RECOGNITION AND MEASUREMENT

1.145 FASB ASC 820, *Fair Value Measurements and Disclosures*, defines fair value, establishes a framework for measuring fair value, and requires certain disclosures about fair value measurements. *Fair value* is defined as an exit price (that is, a price that would be received to sell, versus acquire, an asset or transfer a liability). Further, fair value is a market-based measurement. It establishes a fair value hierarchy that distinguishes between assumptions developed based on market data obtained from independent external sources and the reporting entity's own assumptions. Further, fair value measurement should consider adjustment for risk, such as the risk inherent in a valuation technique or its inputs.

1.146 FASB ASC 820-10-35-10 provides that a fair value measurement of an asset assumes the highest and best use of the asset by market participants, considering the use of the asset that is physically possible, legally permissible, and financially feasible at the measurement date. Highest and best use is determined based on the use of the asset by market participants, even if the intended use of the asset by the reporting entity is different. FASB ASC 820-10-35-10 states that the highest and best use for an asset is established by one of two valuation premises: value in use or value in exchange. The highest and best use of the asset is in use if the asset would provide maximum value to market participants principally through its use in combination with other assets as a group (as installed or otherwise configured for use). For example, value in use might be appropriate for certain nonfinancial assets. The highest and best use of the asset is in exchange if the asset would provide maximum value to market participants principally on a stand-alone basis. For example, value in exchange might be appropriate for a financial asset. According to paragraphs 12–13 of FASB ASC 820-10-35, an asset's value in use should be based on the price that would be received in a current transaction to sell the asset, assuming that the asset would be used with other assets as a group and that those other assets would be available to market participants. An asset's value in exchange is determined based on the price that would be received in a current transaction to sell the asset on a stand-alone basis.

1.147 According to paragraphs 16–16A of FASB ASC 820-10-35, a fair value measurement of a liability assumes that both (*a*) the liability is transferred to a market participant at the measurement date (the liability to the counterparty continues; it is not settled), and (*b*) the nonperformance risk relating to that liability is the same before and after its transfer. Certain liabilities, such as debt obligations, are traded in the marketplace as assets. However, liabilities are rarely transferred in the marketplace due to contractual or other legal restrictions. A reporting entity is permitted, as a practical expedient, to estimate the fair value of an investment within the scope of paragraphs 4–5 of FASB ASC 820-10-15 using the net asset value per share (or its equivalent) of the investment if the net asset value per share or its equivalent is calculated in a manner consistent with the measurement principles of FASB ASC 946, *Financial Services—Investment Companies*, as of the reporting entity's measurement date.

DISCLOSURE

1.148 For assets and liabilities measured at fair value, whether on a recurring or nonrecurring basis, FASB ASC 820-10-50 specifies the required disclosures concerning the inputs used to measure fair value. "Pending Content" in FASB ASC 820-10-50-1 explains that the reporting entity should disclose information that enables users of its financial statements to assess the following: (*a*) for assets and liabilities measured at fair value on a recurring basis in periods subsequent to initial recognition or measured on a nonrecurring basis in periods subsequent to initial recognition, the valuation techniques and inputs used to develop those measurements and (*b*) for recurring fair value measurements using significant unobservable inputs (level 3), the effect of the measurements on earnings for the period.

Author's Note

Separate disclosures about purchases, sales, issuances, and settlements relating to level 3 measurements, as discussed in FASB ASC 820-10-50-2(c)(2), will be required for fiscal years beginning after December 15, 2010, and for interim periods within those fiscal years. However, early adoption is permitted.

PRESENTATION AND DISCLOSURE EXCERPTS

Fair Value Measurements

1.149

SANDISK CORPORATION (DEC)

NOTES TO CONSOLIDATED FINANCIAL STATEMENTS

Note 1. Organization and Summary of Significant Accounting Policies (in part)

Fair Value of Financial Instruments. For certain of the Company's financial instruments, including accounts receivable, short-term marketable securities and accounts payable, the carrying amounts approximate fair value due to their short maturities.

The Company categorizes the fair value of its financial assets and liabilities according to the hierarchy established by the FASB, which prioritizes the inputs to valuation techniques used to measure fair value. The hierarchy gives the highest priority to unadjusted quoted prices in active markets for identical assets or liabilities (Level 1 measurements) and the lowest priority to unobservable inputs (Level 3 measurements). The three levels of the fair value hierarchy are described as follows:

Level 1 Valuations based on quoted prices in active markets for identical assets or liabilities that the Company has the ability to directly access.

Level 2 Valuations based on quoted prices for similar assets or liabilities; valuations for interest-bearing securities based on non-daily quoted prices in active markets; quoted prices in markets that are not active; or other inputs that are observable or can be corroborated by observable data for substantially the full term of the assets or liabilities.

Level 3 Valuations based on inputs that are supported by little or no market activity and that are significant to the fair value of the assets or liabilities.

A financial instrument's level within the fair value hierarchy is based on the lowest level of any input that is significant to the fair value measurement.

In circumstances in which a quoted price in an active market for the identical liability is not available, the Company is required to use the quoted price of the identical liability when traded as an asset, quoted prices for similar liabilities, or quoted prices for similar liabilities when traded as assets. If these quoted prices are not available, the Company is required to use another valuation technique, such as an income approach or a market approach.

The Company's financial assets are measured at fair value on a recurring basis. Instruments that are classified within Level 1 of the fair value hierarchy generally include money market funds, U.S. Treasury securities and equity securities. Level 1 securities represent quoted prices in active markets, and therefore do not require significant management judgment.

Instruments that are classified within Level 2 of the fair value hierarchy primarily include government agency securities, asset-backed securities, mortgage-backed securities, commercial paper, U.S. government-sponsored agency securities, and corporate/municipal notes and bonds. The Company's Level 2 securities are primarily valued using quoted market prices for similar instruments and nonbinding market prices that are corroborated by observable market data. The Company uses inputs such as actual trade data, benchmark yields, broker/dealer quotes, and other similar data, which are obtained from independent pricing vendors, quoted market prices, or other sources to determine the ultimate fair value of the Company's assets and liabilities. The inputs and fair value are reviewed for reasonableness and may be further validated by comparison to publicly available information or compared to multiple independent valuation sources.

Note 2. Investments and Fair Value Measurements

Financial assets and liabilities measured at fair value on a recurring basis as of January 2, 2011 were as follows (in thousands):

	Total	Quoted Prices in Active Markets for Identical Assets (Level 1)	Significant Other Observable Inputs (Level 2)	Significant Unobservable Inputs (Level 3)
Money market funds	$ 587,973	$587,973	$ —	$—
Fixed income securities	4,448,837	30,803	4,418,034	—
Equity securities	90,425	90,425	—	—
Derivative assets	19,462	—	19,462	—
Other	4,379	—	4,379	—
Total financial assets	$5,151,076	$709,201	$4,441,875	$—
Derivative liabilities	$ 76,762	$ —	$ 76,762	$—
Total financial liabilities	$ 76,762	$ —	$ 76,762	$—

Financial assets and liabilities measured at fair value on a recurring basis as of January 3, 2010 were as follows (in thousands):

	Total	Quoted Prices in Active Markets for Identical Assets (Level 1)	Significant Other Observable Inputs (Level 2)	Significant Unobservable Inputs (Level 3)
Money market funds	$ 869,643	$ 869,643	$ —	$—
Fixed income securities	1,831,360	61,129	1,770,231	—
Equity securities	85,542	85,542	—	—
Derivative assets	4,433	—	4,433	—
Other	3,395	—	3,395	—
Total financial assets	$2,794,373	$1,016,314	$1,778,059	$—
Derivative liabilities	$ 23,247	$ —	$ 23,247	$—
Total financial liabilities	$ 23,247	$ —	$ 23,247	$—

Financial assets and liabilities measured at fair value on a recurring basis as of January 2, 2011, were presented on the Company's Consolidated Balance Sheets as follows (in thousands):

	Total	Quoted Prices in Active Markets for Identical Assets (Level 1)	Significant Other Observable Inputs (Level 2)	Significant Unobservable Inputs (Level 3)
Cash equivalents[1]	$ 613,698	$587,973	$ 25,725	$—
Short-term marketable securities	2,018,565	112,906	1,905,659	—
Long-term marketable securities	2,494,972	8,322	2,486,650	—
Other current assets and other non-current assets	23,841	—	23,841	—
Total assets	$5,151,076	$709,201	$4,441,875	$—
Other current accrued liabilities	$ 33,606	$ —	$ 33,606	$—
Non-current liabilities	43,156	—	43,156	—
Total liabilities	$ 76,762	$ —	$ 76,762	$—

[1] Cash equivalents exclude cash of $215.5 million included in Cash and cash equivalents on the Consolidated Balance Sheets as of January 2, 2011.

Financial assets and liabilities measured at fair value on a recurring basis as of January 3, 2010, were presented on the Company's Consolidated Balance Sheets as follows (in thousands):

	Total	Quoted Prices in Active Markets for Identical Assets (Level 1)	Significant Other Observable Inputs (Level 2)	Significant Unobservable Inputs (Level 3)
Cash equivalents[1]	$ 871,173	$ 869,643	$ 1,530	$—
Short-term marketable securities	819,002	74,906	744,096	—
Long-term marketable securities	1,097,095	71,765	1,025,330	—
Other current assets and other non-current assets	7,103	—	7,103	—
Total assets	$2,794,373	$1,016,314	$1,778,059	$—
Other current accrued liabilities	$ 7,794	$ —	$ 7,794	$—
Non-current liabilities	15,453	—	15,453	—
Total liabilities	$ 23,247	$ —	$ 23,247	$—

[1] Cash equivalents exclude cash of $229.2 million included in Cash and cash equivalents on the Consolidated Balance Sheets as of January 3, 2010.

As of January 2, 2011, the Company did not elect the fair value option for any financial assets and liabilities for which such an election would have been permitted.

Available-for-Sale Investments. Available-for-sale investments as of January 2, 2011 were as follows (in thousands):

	Amortized Cost	Gross Unrealized Gain	Gross Unrealized Loss	Fair Value
Fixed income securities:				
U.S. Treasury and government agency securities	$ 36,015	$ 53	$ (33)	$ 36,035
U.S. government-sponsored agency securities	24,336	85	—	24,421
Corporate notes and bonds	401,182	2,689	(196)	403,675
Asset-backed securities	10,069	45	(5)	10,109
Mortgage-backed securities	6,500	35	—	6,535
Municipal notes and bonds	3,972,268	9,435	(13,641)	3,968,062
	4,450,370	12,342	(13,875)	4,448,837
Equity investments	68,525	21,900	—	90,425
Total available-for-sale investments	$4,518,895	$34,242	$(13,875)	$4,539,262

Available-for-sale investments as of January 3, 2010 were as follows (in thousands):

	Amortized Cost	Gross Unrealized Gain	Gross Unrealized Loss	Fair Value
Fixed income securities:				
U.S. Treasury and government agency securities	$ 66,984	$ 90	$(6)	$ 67,068
U.S. government-sponsored agency securities	37,211	20	(298)	36,933
Corporate notes and bonds	251,510	1,103	(664)	251,949
Asset-backed securities	27,719	175	—	27,894
Mortgage-backed securities	4,986	20	—	5,006
Municipal notes and bonds	1,422,126	20,581	(197)	1,442,510
	1,810,536	21,989	(1,165)	1,831,360
Equity investments	70,011	15,531	—	85,542
Total available-for-sale investments	$1,880,547	$37,520	$(1,165)	$1,916,902

The fair value and gross unrealized losses on the available-for-sale securities that have been in an unrealized loss position, aggregated by type of investment instrument, and the length of time that individual securities have been in a continuous unrealized loss position as of January 2, 2011, are summarized in the following table (in thousands). Available-for-sale securities that were in an unrealized gain position have been excluded from the table.

	Less Than 12 Months		Greater Than 12 Months	
	Fair Value	Gross Unrealized Loss	Fair Value	Gross Unrealized Loss
U.S. Treasury and government agency securities	$ 3,587	$ (33)	$ —	$—
Corporate notes and bonds	76,499	(190)	4,346	(6)
Asset-backed securities	6,003	(5)	—	—
Municipal notes and bonds	1,776,140	(13,641)	—	—
Total	$1,862,229	$(13,869)	$4,346	$(6)

Gross unrealized gains and losses related to publicly-traded equity investments are due to changes in market prices. The Company has cash flow hedges designated to substantially mitigate risks, of both gains and losses, from certain of these equity investments, as discussed in Note 3, "Derivatives and Hedging Activities." The gross unrealized loss related to U.S. Treasury and government agency securities, corporate and municipal notes and bonds and asset-backed securities was primarily due to changes in interest rates. The gross unrealized loss on all available-for-sale fixed income securities at January 2, 2011 was considered temporary in nature. Factors considered in determining whether a loss is temporary include the length of time and extent to which fair value has been less than the cost basis, the financial condition and near-term prospects of the investee, and the Company's intent and ability to hold an investment for a period of time sufficient to allow for any anticipated recovery in market value. For debt security investments, the Company considered additional factors including the Company's intent to sell the investments or whether it is more likely than not the Company will be required to sell the investments before the recovery of its amortized cost.

The following table shows the gross realized gains and (losses) on sales of available-for-sale securities (in thousands).

	Year Ended		
	January 2, 2011	January 3, 2010	December 28, 2008
Gross realized gains	$20,867	$13,997	$8,870
Gross realized (losses)	(344)	(576)	(640)

Fixed income securities by contractual maturity as of January 2, 2011 are shown below (in thousands). Actual maturities may differ from contractual maturities because issuers of the securities may have the right to prepay obligations.

	Amortized Cost	Fair Value
Due in one year or less	$1,951,220	$1,953,865
Due after one year through five years	2,499,150	2,494,972
Total	$4,450,370	$4,448,837

For certain of the Company's financial instruments, including accounts receivable, short-term marketable securities and accounts payable, the carrying amounts approximate fair value due to their short maturities. For those financial instruments where the carrying amounts differ from fair value, the following table represents the related carrying values and the fair values, which are based on quoted market prices (in thousands).

	As of January 2, 2011		As of January 3, 2010	
	Carrying Value	Fair Value	Carrying Value	Fair Value
1% Sr. Convertible notes due 2013	$993,199	$1,118,375	$934,722	$958,813
1.5% Sr. Convertible notes due 2017	717,833	1,132,500	—	—
1% Convertible notes due 2035	—	—	75,000	74,700

1.150

QWEST COMMUNICATIONS INTERNATIONAL INC. (DEC)

NOTES TO CONSOLIDATED FINANCIAL STATEMENTS

Note 2. Summary of Significant Accounting Policies (in part)

Fair Value of Financial Instruments

Our financial instruments consist of cash and cash equivalents, auction rate securities, accounts receivable, accounts payable, interest rate hedges and long-term notes including the current portion. The carrying values of cash and cash equivalents, auction rate securities, accounts receivable, accounts payable and interest rate hedges approximate their fair values. The carrying value of our long-term notes, including the current portion, reflects original cost net of unamortized discounts and other. See Note 3—Fair Value of Financial Instruments for a more detailed discussion of the fair value of our other financial instruments.

Pension and Post-Retirement Benefits

We sponsor a noncontributory defined benefit pension plan (referred to as our pension plan) for substantially all management and occupational employees. In addition to this tax qualified pension plan, we also maintain a non-qualified pension plan for certain eligible highly compensated employees. We maintain post-retirement benefit plans that provide health care and life insurance benefits for certain eligible retirees.

Pension and post-retirement health care and life insurance benefits attributed to eligible employees' service during the year, as well as interest on benefit obligations, are accrued currently. Prior service costs and actuarial gains and losses are generally recognized as a component of net periodic expense over one of the following periods: (i) the average remaining service period of the employees expected to receive benefits of approximately nine years; (ii) the average remaining life of the employees expected to receive benefits of approximately 18 years; or (iii) the term of the collective bargaining agreements, as applicable. Pension and post-retirement benefit expenses are recognized over the period in which the employee renders service and becomes eligible to receive benefits as determined using the projected unit credit method.

In computing the pension and post-retirement health care and life insurance benefits expenses and obligations, the most significant assumptions we make include discount rate, expected rate of return on plan assets, health care trend rates and our evaluation of the legal basis for plan amendments. The plan benefits covered by collective bargaining agreements as negotiated with our employees' unions can also significantly impact the amount of expense, benefit obligations and pension assets that we record.

The discount rate is the rate at which we believe we could effectively settle the benefit obligations as of the end of the year. We set our discount rates each year based upon the yields of high-quality fixed-income investments available at December 31 with maturities matching our future expected cash flows of the pension and post-retirement benefit plans. In making the determination of discount rates, we average the yields of various bond matching sources and the Citigroup Pension Discount Curve.

The expected rate of return on plan assets is the long-term rate of return we expect to earn on plan assets. The rate of return is determined by the strategic allocation of the plan assets and the long-term risk and return forecast for each asset class. The forecast for each asset class is generated primarily from an analysis of the long-term expectations of various third party investment management organizations. The expected rate of return on plan assets is reviewed annually and revised, as necessary, to reflect changes in the financial markets and our investment strategy.

To compute the expected return on pension and post-retirement benefit plan assets, we apply an expected rate of return to the market-related value of the pension plan assets and to the fair value of the post-retirement plan assets adjusted for projected benefit payments to be made from the plan assets. With respect to equity assets held by our pension plan, we have elected to recognize actual returns on these equity assets ratably over a five year period when computing our market-related value of pension plan assets; the unrecognized portion of actual returns on these equity assets is included in accumulated other comprehensive income. This method has the effect of reducing the impact on expenses of equity market volatility that may be experienced from year to year. With respect to bonds and other assets held by our pension plan and with respect to the assets held by our post-retirement benefit plans, we did not elect to recognize actual returns on these assets using this five-year ratable method. Therefore, the full impact of annual market volatility for these assets is reflected in the subsequent year's net periodic combined benefits expense.

The trusts for the pension and post-retirement benefits plans hold investments in equities, fixed income, real estate and other assets such as private equity assets. The assets held by these trusts are reflected at estimated fair value as of December 31. The fair value of certain assets held by the trusts is determined through use of observable inputs, such as quoted market prices for identical instruments in active markets or quoted prices for similar assets in active markets. For instance, the fair value of individual exchange traded equity securities is based on the last published price reported on the major market in which that individual security is traded and the fair value of certain individual fixed income securities is based on a spread to other more active fixed income securities last reported price on the major market in which that more active security is traded. Interests in commingled funds and limited partnerships are valued using the net asset value of each fund. The fair value of a significant amount of assets held by our trusts are not available by reference to a quoted market price or other significant observable inputs as of December 31. As a consequence, we believe there is a risk in reporting the fair value of these assets because the actual values of these assets could be significantly different from our estimates. The methods we use to value investments in the absence of observable market prices are described below.

Investments in partnerships (private equity, private debt and real estate) do not have observable market prices and are generally reported at fair value as determined by the partnership. Each partnership uses valuation methodologies that give consideration to a range of factors, including but not limited to the price at which the investment was acquired, the nature of the investments, market conditions, trading values on comparable public securities, current and projected operating performance and financing transactions subsequent to the acquisition of the investment. These valuation methodologies involve a significant degree of judgment. For some of these partnership investments, the fair value provided by the partnership is as of a date prior to our measurement date. In these situations, we adjust the fair value based on subsequent cash flows and review of the latest information provided by the partnership, including the impact of any significant events and changes in market conditions that have occurred since the last valuation date.

The assumptions and valuation methodologies of the pricing vendors, account managers, fund managers and partnerships are monitored and evaluated for reasonableness. See additional information about the valuation inputs used to value the assets in Note 11—Employee Benefits.

Note 3. Fair Value of Financial Instruments

Our financial instruments consisted of cash and cash equivalents, auction rate securities, accounts receivable, accounts payable, interest rate hedges, the embedded option in our previously outstanding convertible debt and long-term notes including the current portion. The carrying values of the following items approximate their fair values: cash and cash equivalents, auction rate securities, accounts receivable, accounts payable and interest rate hedges. The carrying value of our long-term notes, including the current portion, reflects original cost net of unamortized discounts and other and was $11.583 billion as of December 31, 2010. For additional information, see Note 8—Borrowings.

Fair value is defined as the price that would be received to sell an asset or paid to transfer a liability in an orderly transaction between independent and knowledgeable parties who are willing and able to transact for an asset or liability at the measurement date. We use valuation techniques that maximize the use of observable inputs and minimize the use of unobservable inputs when determining fair value and then we rank the estimated values based on the reliability of the inputs used following the fair value hierarchy set forth by the FASB.

The table below presents the fair values for auction rate securities, interest rate hedges and long-term notes including the current portion, as well as the input levels used to determine these fair values as of December 31, 2010 and 2009:

(Dollars in millions)	Level	Fair Value as of December 31 2010	2009
Assets:			
Auction rate securities	3	$ 92	$ 95
Fair value hedges	3	—	2
Total assets		$ 92	$ 97
Liabilities:			
Long-term notes, including the current portion	1 & 2	$12,480	$14,245
Cash flow hedges	3	—	3
Total liabilities		$12,480	$14,248

The three levels of the fair value hierarchy as defined by the FASB are as follows:

Input Level	Description of Input
Level 1	Inputs are based upon unadjusted quoted prices for identical instruments traded in active markets.
Level 2	Inputs are based upon quoted prices for similar instruments in active markets, quoted prices for identical or similar instruments in markets that are not active, and model-based valuation techniques for which all significant assumptions are observable in the market or can be corroborated by observable market data for substantially the full term of the assets or liabilities.
Level 3	Inputs are generally unobservable and typically reflect management's estimates of assumptions that market participants would use in pricing the asset or liability. The fair values are therefore determined using model-based techniques that include option pricing models, discounted cash flow models, and similar techniques.

We determined the fair value of our auction rate securities using a probability-weighted discounted cash flow model that takes into consideration the weighted average of the following factors:

- Coupon rate of 5.44%;
- Probability that we will be able to sell the securities in an auction or that the securities will be redeemed early of 75.23%;
- Probability that a default will occur of 20.98% with a related recovery rate of 55.00%; and
- Discount rate of 7.81%.

We determined the fair value of our interest rate hedges using projected future cash flows, discounted at the mid-market implied forward London Interbank Offered Rate ("LIBOR"). For additional information on our derivative financial instruments, see Note 9—Derivative Financial Instruments.

We determined the fair values of our long-term notes, including the current portion, based on quoted market prices where available or, if not available, based on discounted future cash flows using current market interest rates.

The table below presents a rollforward of the instruments valued using Level 3 inputs for the years ended December 31, 2010 and 2009:

(Dollars in millions)	Auction Rate Securities	Investment Fund	Fair Value Hedges	Cash Flow Hedges	Embedded Option in Convertible Debt
Balance at December 31, 2008	$90	$20	$—	$(8)	$ —
Transfers into (out of) Level 3	—	—	—	—	—
Additions	2	—	—	—	—
Dispositions and settlements	—	(21)	—	—	—
Realized and unrealized gains:					
Included in long-term borrowings—net	—	—	2	—	—
Included in other income (expense)—net	—	1	—	—	—
Included in other comprehensive income	3	—	—	5	—
Balance at December 31, 2009	95	—	2	(3)	—
Transfers into (out of) Level 3	—	—	—	—	—
Additions	—	—	—	—	—
Reclassification from equity	—	—	—	—	(165)
Dispositions and settlements	—	—	(7)	—	640
Realized and unrealized gains:					
Included in long-term borrowings—net	—	—	5	—	—
Included in other (expense) income—net	—	—	—	—	(475)
Included in other comprehensive (loss) income	(3)	—	—	3	—
Balance at December 31, 2010	$92	$—	$—	$—	$ —

Our 3.50% Convertible Senior Notes had previously been accounted for as two components: a debt component, and an equity component representing a written option on our stock. Our obligation under the CenturyLink merger agreement to redeem these notes for cash triggered a change in accounting to reclassify the equity component from equity to a liability. We therefore computed the fair value of the equity component to be $165 million as of April 21, 2010 (the date the merger agreement was signed) and reclassified this amount from additional paid-in capital to a current liability. We determined the stock price volatility considering the historical volatility of both our common stock and CenturyLink's common stock for a historical period equivalent to the expected remaining option term. Under the terms of these notes, the conversion price of the debt was adjusted based on dividend payments. The embedded option therefore effectively participated in dividends and the fair value of the embedded option was computed based upon the conversion price in effect on the valuation date and an assumed dividend yield of zero.

We determined the fair value of the embedded option in our convertible debt using a Black-Scholes option valuation model. The value was computed using the following assumptions as of April 21, 2010 (the date of the merger agreement).
- Stock price of $5.24;
- Stock price volatility of 28.7%;
- Exercise price of $4.92;
- Option term of approximately eight months; and
- Risk free rate of 0.29%.

See Note 8—Borrowings and Note 9—Derivative Financial Instruments for additional information.

By December 31, 2010 we had settled the outstanding liability for our embedded option for $640 million resulting in a loss of $475 million.

Note 4. Investments

As of December 31, 2010 and 2009, our investments included auction rate securities of $92 million and $95 million, respectively, which are classified as non-current, available-for-sale investments and are included in other non-current assets at their estimated fair value on our consolidated balance sheets.

Auction rate securities are generally long-term debt instruments that provide liquidity through a Dutch auction process that resets the applicable interest rate at pre-determined calendar intervals, generally every 28 days. This mechanism generally allows existing investors to rollover their holdings and continue to own their respective securities or liquidate their holdings by selling their securities at par value. Prior to August 2007, we invested in these securities for short periods of time as part of our cash management program. However, the uncertainties in the credit markets have prevented us and other investors from liquidating holdings of these securities in auctions since the third quarter of 2007. Because we are uncertain as to when the liquidity issues relating to these investments will improve, we continued to classify these securities as non-current as of December 31, 2010. These securities:
- Are structured obligations of special purpose reinsurance entities associated with life insurance companies and are referred to as "Triple X" securities;
- Currently pay interest every 28 days at one-month LIBOR plus 200 basis points;
- Are rated A;
- Are insured against loss of principal and interest by two bond insurers, one of which had a credit rating of B and the other of which was not rated and in the fourth quarter of 2009 was prohibited by its regulator from making any claim payments;
- Are collateralized by the issuers; and
- Mature between 2033 and 2036.

The following table summarizes the fair value of these auction rate securities, the cumulative net unrealized loss, net of deferred income taxes, and the cost basis of these securities as of December 31, 2010 and 2009:

(Dollars in millions)	December 31	
	2010	2009
Auction rate securities—fair value	$ 92	$ 95
Classification	Non-current, available-for-sale investments	
Balance sheet location (reported at estimated fair value)	Other non-current assets	
Cumulative net unrealized loss, net of deferred income taxes	$ 16	$ 15
Auction rate securities—cost basis	$120	$120

The following table summarizes the unrealized gains and losses, net of deferred income taxes included in comprehensive (loss) income, on our auction rate securities for the years ended December 31, 2010 and 2009:

(Dollars in millions)	December 31	
	2010	2009
Unrealized (loss) gain, net of deferred income taxes	$(1)	$2

These unrealized losses were recorded in accumulated other comprehensive loss on our consolidated balance sheets. We consider the decline in fair value to be a temporary impairment because we believe it is more likely than not that we will ultimately recover the entire $120 million cost basis, in part because the securities are rated investment grade, the securities are collateralized and the issuers continue to make required interest payments. At some point in the future, we may determine that the decline in fair value is other than temporary if, among other factors:

- The issuers cease making required interest payments;
- We believe it is more likely than not that we will be required to sell these securities before their values recover; or
- We change our intent to hold the securities due to events such as a change in the terms of the securities.

Note 11. Employee Benefits (in part)

Plan Assets

We maintain plan assets for our pension plan and certain post-retirement benefit plans. The pension plan assets are used for the payment of pension benefits and certain eligible plan expenses. The post-retirement benefit plan assets are used to pay health care benefits and premiums on behalf of eligible retirees who are former occupational plan participants and to pay certain eligible plan expenses. The following table summarizes the change in the fair value of plan assets for the pension and post-retirement benefit plans as of and for the years ended December 31, 2010 and 2009:

(Dollars in millions)	Pension Plan		Post-Retirement Benefit Plans	
	2010	2009	2010	2009
Fair value of plan assets at beginning of year	$7,326	$7,217	$863	$ 915
Actual gain on plan assets	1,094	793	124	141
Benefits paid from plan assets	(760)	(684)	(186)	(193)
Fair value of plan assets at end of year	$7,660	$7,326	$801	$ 863

Fair Value Measurements: Fair value is defined as the price that would be received to sell an asset or paid to transfer a liability in an orderly transaction between independent and knowledgeable parties who are willing and able to transact for an asset or liability at the measurement date. We use valuation techniques that maximize the use of observable inputs and minimize the use of unobservable inputs when determining fair value and then we rank the estimated values based on the reliability of the inputs used following the fair value hierarchy set forth by the FASB. For additional information on the fair value hierarchy, see Note 3—Fair Value of Financial Instruments.

The tables below presents the fair value of plan assets by category and the input levels used to determine those fair values as of December 31, 2010. It is important to note that the asset allocations do not include market exposures that are gained with derivatives.

(Dollars in millions)	Fair Value of Pension Plan Assets as of December 31, 2010			
	Level 1	Level 2	Level 3	Total
Investment grade bonds[a]	$ 453	$ 804	$ —	$1,257
High yield bonds[b]	—	520	114	634
Emerging market bonds[c]	—	191	—	191
Convertible bonds[d]	—	355	—	355
Diversified strategies[e]	—	444	—	444
U.S. stocks[f]	400	44	—	444
Non-U.S. stocks[g]	701	120	—	821
Emerging market stocks[h]	78	161	—	239
Private equity[i]	—	—	831	831
Private debt[j]	—	—	530	530
Market neutral hedge funds[k]	—	635	102	737
Directional hedge funds[k]	—	230	29	259
Real estate[l]	—	35	288	323
Derivatives[m]	8	(2)	—	6
Cash equivalents and short-term investments[n]	57	452	—	509
Securities lending collateral[o]	—	241	—	241
Total investments	1,697	4,230	1,894	7,821
Securities lending obligation[o]	—	(241)	—	(241)
Total investments, net of securities lending obligation	$1,697	$3,989	$1,894	7,580
Dividends and interest receivable				20
Pending trades receivable				83
Accrued expenses				(10)
Pending trades payable				(13)
Total pension plan assets				$7,660

(Dollars in millions)	Fair Value of Post-Retirement Plan Assets as of December 31, 2010			
	Level 1	Level 2	Level 3	Total
Investment grade bonds[a]	$ 10	$153	$ —	$163
High yield bonds[b]	—	123	—	123
Emerging market bonds[c]	—	38	—	38
Convertible bonds[d]	—	33	—	33
Diversified strategies[e]	—	6	—	6
U.S. stocks[f]	77	—	—	77
Non-U.S. stocks[g]	40	30	—	70
Emerging market stocks[h]	—	30	—	30
Private equity[i]	—	—	77	77
Private debt[j]	—	—	11	11
Market neutral hedge funds[k]	—	70	—	70
Directional hedge funds[k]	—	20	—	20
Real estate[l]	—	18	25	43
Derivatives[m]	—	1	—	1
Cash equivalents and short-term investments[n]	2	19	—	21
Securities lending collateral[o]	—	31	—	31
Total investments	129	572	113	814
Securities lending obligation[o]	—	(31)	—	(31)
Total investments, net of securities lending obligation	$129	$541	$113	783
Dividends and interest receivable				2
Pending trades receivable				17
Accrued expenses				(1)
Pending trades payable				—
Total post-retirement plan assets				$801

The tables below presents the fair value of plan assets by category and the input levels used to determine those fair values as of December 31, 2009. It is important to note that the asset allocations do not include market exposures that are gained with derivatives.

Fair Value of Pension Plan Assets as of December 31, 2009

(Dollars in millions)	Level 1	Level 2	Level 3	Total
Investment grade bonds[a]	$ 440	$ 844	$ —	$1,284
High yield bonds[b]	—	468	126	594
Emerging market bonds[c]	—	205	—	205
Convertible bonds[d]	—	426	—	426
Diversified strategies[e]	—	439	—	439
U.S. stocks[f]	445	89	—	534
Non-U.S. stocks[g]	668	105	—	773
Emerging market stocks[h]	74	138	—	212
Private equity[i]	—	—	741	741
Private debt[j]	—	—	524	524
Market neutral hedge funds[k]	—	839	58	897
Directional hedge funds[k]	—	161	4	165
Real estate[l]	—	—	294	294
Derivatives[m]	(7)	(36)	—	(43)
Cash equivalents and short-term investments[n]	96	173	—	269
Securities lending collateral[o]	—	289	—	289
Total investments	1,716	4,140	1,747	7,603
Securities lending obligation[o]	—	(289)	—	(289)
Total investments, net of securities lending obligation	$1,716	$3,851	$1,747	7,314
Dividends and interest receivable				22
Pending trades receivable				27
Accrued expenses				(12)
Pending trades payable				(25)
Total pension plan assets				$7,326

Fair Value of Post-retirement Plan Assets as of December 31, 2009

(Dollars in millions)	Level 1	Level 2	Level 3	Total
Investment grade bonds[a]	$ 12	$190	$ —	$202
High yield bonds[b]	—	143	—	143
Emerging market bonds[c]	—	33	—	33
Convertible bonds[d]	—	28	—	28
Diversified strategies[e]	—	5	—	5
U.S. stocks[f]	91	—	—	91
Non-U.S. stocks[g]	49	28	—	77
Emerging market stocks[h]	—	28	—	28
Private equity[i]	—	—	85	85
Private debt[j]	—	—	12	12
Market neutral hedge funds[k]	—	93	—	93
Directional hedge funds[k]	—	18	—	18
Real estate[l]	—	—	44	44
Cash equivalents and short-term investments[n]	2	14	—	16
Securities lending collateral[o]	—	29	—	29
Total investments	154	609	141	904
Securities lending obligation[o]	—	(29)	—	(29)
Total investments, net of securities lending obligation	$154	$580	$141	875
Dividends and interest receivable				3
Pending trades receivable				17
Accrued expenses				(19)
Pending trades payable				(13)
Total post-retirement plan assets				$863

The plans' assets are invested in various asset categories utilizing multiple strategies and investment managers. For several of the investments in the tables above and discussed below, the plans own units in commingled funds and limited partnerships that invest in various types of assets. Interests in commingled funds are valued using the net asset value (NAV) per unit of each fund. The NAV reported by the fund manager is based on the market value of the underlying investments owned by each fund, minus its liabilities, divided by the number of shares outstanding. All commingled funds held by the plans that can be redeemed at NAV within a year of the financial statement date are classified as Level 2, otherwise the fund is classified as Level 3. Investments in limited partnerships represent long-term commitments with a fixed maturity date, typically ten years. Valuation inputs for these limited partnership interests are generally based on assumptions and other information not observable in the market and are classified as Level 3 investments. The assumptions and valuation methodologies of the pricing vendors, account managers, fund managers, and partnerships are monitored and evaluated for reasonableness. Below is an overview of the asset categories, the underlying strategies, and valuation inputs used to value the assets in the preceding tables:

(a) *Investment grade bonds* represent stand-alone investments in U.S. Treasury securities as well as portfolios and commingled funds with characteristics similar to the Barclays Capital U.S. Aggregate Bond Index (the index). The index is comprised of U.S. Treasuries, agencies, corporate bonds, mortgage-backed securities, asset-backed securities, and commercial mortgage-backed securities. Treasury securities are valued at the bid price reported in the active market in which the security is traded and are classified as Level 1. Valuations of other investment grade bonds are based on a spread to U.S. Treasuries and consider yields available on comparable securities of issuers with similar credit ratings and are classified as Level 2. The commingled funds can be redeemed at NAV within a year of the financial statement date and are classified as Level 2.

(b) *High yield bonds* represent investments in fixed income securities below investment grade and bank loans. Investments are made in stand-alone portfolios and commingled funds. Valuations of publicly traded high yield bonds are based on a spread to U.S. Treasuries and consider yields available on comparable securities of issuers with similar credit ratings and are classified as Level 2. The commingled funds that can be redeemed at NAV within a year of the financial statement date are classified as Level 2. For the pension plan, all other high yield funds that cannot be redeemed at NAV or that cannot be redeemed at NAV within a year of the financial statement date are classified as Level 3.

(c) *Emerging market bonds* represent debt instruments issued by governments and other entities located in developing countries. Emerging market bonds are priced based on dealer quotes or a spread relative to the local government bonds and are classified as Level 2.

(d) *Convertible bonds* primarily represent investments in corporate debt securities that have features that allow the debt to be converted into equity securities under certain circumstances. Valuations of individual convertible bonds are based on a combination of a spread to U.S. Treasuries and the value and volatility of the underlying equity security. Convertible bonds are classified as Level 2.

(e) *Diversified strategies* represent investments in commingled funds that primarily have exposures to global government, corporate and inflation-linked bonds, but that also have exposures to global stocks and commodities. The funds can be redeemed at NAV within a year of the financial statement date and are classified as Level 2.

(f) *U.S. stocks* represent investments in securities that are held in stand-alone portfolios and commingled funds that track the broad U.S. stock markets. Individual U.S. stocks are valued at the last published price reported on the major market on which the individual securities are traded and are classified as Level 1. The commingled funds can be redeemed at NAV within a year of the financial statement date and are classified as Level 2.

(g) *Non-U.S. stocks* represent investments in securities, which are held in stand-alone portfolios, a registered mutual fund and commingled funds that track developed non-U.S. stock markets. Foreign currency exposure is hedged approximately 50% to the U.S. dollar. Individual non-U.S. stock securities and mutual funds are valued at the last published price reported on the major market on which the individual securities or mutual fund are traded and are classified as Level 1. The commingled funds can be redeemed at NAV within a year of the financial statement date and are classified as Level 2.

(h) *Emerging market stocks* represent investments in registered mutual funds and commingled funds for the pension plan and commingled funds for the post-retirement plan and are comprised of stocks of companies located in developing markets. Registered mutual funds are valued at the last published price reported on the major market on which the mutual funds are traded and are classified as Level 1. The commingled funds can be redeemed at NAV within a year of the financial statement date and are classified as Level 2.

(i) *Private equity* represents investments in nonpublicly traded domestic and foreign buy-out and venture capital funds. Private equity funds are structured as limited partnerships and are valued according to the valuation policy of each partnership, subject to prevailing accounting and other regulatory guidelines. The partnerships use valuation methodologies that give consideration to a range of factors, including but not limited to the price at which investments were acquired, the nature of the investments, market conditions, trading values on comparable public securities, current and projected operating performance, and financing transactions subsequent to the acquisition of the investments. These valuation methodologies involve a significant degree of judgment. For some investments, the fair value provided by the partnership is as of a date prior to our measurement date. In these situations, we adjust the value for subsequent cash flows and review the fair value based on the latest information provided by the partnership, including the impact of any significant events and changes in market conditions that have occurred since the last valuation date. Private equity investments are classified as Level 3.

(j) *Private debt* represents investments in nonpublicly traded funds that primarily invest in either distressed or mezzanine debt instruments. Mezzanine debt instruments are debt instruments that are subordinated to other debt issues and may include embedded equity instruments such as warrants. Private debt funds are structured as limited partnerships and are valued according to the valuation policy of each partnership, subject to prevailing accounting and other regulatory guidelines. The valuation of underlying fund investments are based on factors including the issuer's current and projected credit worthiness, the security's terms, reference to the securities of comparable companies, and other market factors. These valuation methodologies involve a significant degree of judgment. For some investments, the fair value provided by the partnership is as of a date prior to our measurement date. In these situations, we adjust the value for subsequent cash flows and review the fair value based on the latest information provided by the partnership, including the impact of any significant events and changes in market conditions that have occurred since the last valuation date. Private debt investments are classified as Level 3.

(k) *Hedge funds. Market neutral hedge funds* hold investments in a diversified mix of instruments that are intended in combination to exhibit low correlations to market fluctuations. For the pension plan, these investments are typically combined with futures to achieve uncorrelated excess returns over various markets. *Directional hedge funds* represent investments that may exhibit somewhat higher correlations to market fluctuations than the market neutral hedge funds. Investments in hedge funds include both direct investments and investments in diversified funds of funds. All hedge funds are valued at NAV. Hedge funds that can be redeemed at NAV within a year of the financial statement date are classified as Level 2. All other hedge fund investments that cannot be redeemed at NAV or that cannot be redeemed at NAV within a year of the financial statement date are classified as Level 3.

(l) *Real estate* represents investments in nonpublicly traded commingled funds and limited partnerships that invest in a diversified portfolio of real estate properties. Real estate investments are valued at NAV according to the valuation policy of each fund or partnership, subject to prevailing accounting and other regulatory guidelines. The valuation of specific properties is generally based on third-party appraisals that use comparable sales or a projection of future cash flows to determine fair value. Real estate investments that can be redeemed at NAV within a year of the financial statement date are classified as level 2. Real estate investments that cannot be redeemed at NAV or that cannot be redeemed at NAV within a year of the financial statement date are classified as Level 3.

(m) *Derivatives* include the market value of exchange-traded futures contracts which are classified as Level 1, as well as privately negotiated over-the-counter forwards and swaps that are valued based on changes in interest rates, currencies or a specific market index and classified as Level 2. The market values represent gains or losses that occur due to fluctuations in interest rates, foreign currency exchange rates, security prices, or other factors.

(n) *Cash equivalents and short-term investments* represent investments that are used in conjunction with derivatives positions or are used to provide liquidity for the payment of benefits or other purposes. U.S. Treasury Bills are valued at the bid price reported in the active market in which the security is traded and are classified as Level 1. Valuations of other securities are based on a spread to U.S. Treasury Bills, the Federal Funds Rate, or London Interbank Offered Rate and consider yields available on comparable securities of issuers with similar credit ratings and are classified as Level 2.

(o) *Securities lending obligation and collateral* represent securities lending transactions whereby the plans' lending agent lends stock and bond investments of the plan to other third-party investment firms in exchange for collateral. The stock and bond securities are generally loaned for a period of less than one month and can be recalled on a day's notice. Under the terms of its securities lending agreement, the plan typically requires collateral of a value in excess of the fair value of the loaned investments. Collateral received is then invested in certain collective investment vehicles maintained by the lending agent. Upon the maturity of the agreement, the borrower must return the same, or substantially the same, investments that were borrowed and the plan returns the collateral. The value of the obligation is a fixed amount based on the collateral received and is classified as Level 2. The collateral received is invested in collective investment vehicles that are comprised of short-term investment grade bonds and cash equivalents, the valuations of which are described above, and is classified as Level 2.

Concentrations of Risk: Investments, in general, are exposed to various risks, such as significant world events, interest rate, credit, foreign currency, and overall market volatility risk. These risks are managed by broadly diversifying assets across numerous asset classes and strategies with differing expected returns, volatilities, and correlations. Risk is also broadly diversified across numerous market sectors and individual companies. Financial instruments that potentially subject the plans to concentrations of counterparty risk consist principally of investment contracts with high quality financial institutions. These investment contracts are typically collateralized obligations and/or are actively managed, limiting the amount of counterparty exposure to any one financial institution. Although the investments are well diversified, the value of plan assets could change materially depending upon the overall market volatility, which could affect the funded status of the plans.

The table below presents a rollforward of the pension plan assets valued using Level 3 inputs for the years ended December 31, 2010 and 2009:

(Dollars in millions)	High Yield Bonds	Private Equity	Private Debt	Market Neutral Hedge Fund	Directional Hedge Funds	Real Estate	Total
Balance at December 31, 2008	$ 89	$686	$490	$ 70	$ 36	$421	$1,792
Net (dispositions) acquisitions	(44)	21	6	(22)	(30)	14	(55)
Actual return on plan assets:							
Gains (losses) relating to assets sold during the year	34	103	—	2	(5)	(7)	127
Gains (losses) relating to assets still held at year-end	47	(69)	28	8	3	(134)	(117)
Balance at December 31, 2009	126	741	524	58	4	294	1,747
Net transfers	—	—	—	—	—	(32)	(32)
Net (dispositions) acquisitions	(24)	(40)	(35)	41	25	6	(27)
Actual return on plan assets:							
(Losses) gains relating to assets sold during the year	(3)	146	25	—	—	23	191
Gains (losses) relating to assets still held at year-end	15	(16)	16	3	—	(3)	15
Balance at December 31, 2010	$114	$831	$530	$102	$ 29	$288	$1,894

The table below presents a rollforward of the post-retirement benefits plan assets valued using Level 3 inputs for the years ended December 31, 2010 and 2009:

(Dollars in millions)	Private Equity	Private Debt	Real Estate	Total
Balance at December 31, 2008	$ 85	$14	$ 72	$171
Net dispositions	(4)	(1)	(2)	(7)
Actual return on plan assets:				
Gains (losses) relating to assets sold during the year	13	(1)	(6)	6
Losses relating to assets still held at year-end	(9)	—	(20)	(29)
Balance at December 31, 2009	85	12	44	141
Net transfers	—	—	(17)	(17)
Net dispositions	(15)	(1)	(5)	(21)
Actual return on plan assets:				
Gains relating to assets sold during the year	21	—	1	22
(Losses) gains relating to assets still held at year-end	(14)	—	2	(12)
Balance at December 31, 2010	$ 77	$11	$ 25	$113

Certain gains and losses are allocated between assets sold during the year and assets still held at year-end based on transactions and changes in valuations that occurred during the year. These allocations also impact our calculation of net acquisitions and dispositions.

For the year ended December 31, 2010, the investment program produced actual gains on pension and post-retirement plan assets of $1.218 billion as compared to the expected returns of $617 million for a difference of $601 million. For the year ended December 31, 2009, the investment program produced actual gains on pension and post-retirement plan assets of $934 million as compared to the expected returns of $633 million for a difference of $301 million. The short-term annual returns on plan assets will almost always be different from the expected long-term returns, and the plans could experience net gains or losses, due primarily to the volatility occurring in the financial markets during any given year.

SUBSEQUENT EVENTS

RECOGNITION AND MEASUREMENT

1.151 The FASB ASC glossary defines *subsequent events* as events or transactions that occur subsequent to the balance sheet date but before financial statements are issued or available to be issued. The following are the two types of subsequent events: the first type existed at the balance sheet date and includes the estimates inherent in the process of preparing financial statements (recognized subsequent events); the second type did not exist at the balance sheet date but arose subsequent to that date (nonrecognized subsequent events). The first type of subsequent event should be recognized in the entity's financial statements. An entity that is either an SEC filer or a conduit bond obligor for conduit debt securities that are traded in a public market must evaluate subsequent events through the date the financial statements are issued. The SEC has indicated that issuance of financial statements generally is the earlier of when the annual or quarterly financial statements are widely distributed to all shareholders and other financial statement users or filed with the SEC.

DISCLOSURE

1.152 Some nonrecognized subsequent events may be of such a nature that they must be disclosed in order to keep the financial statements from being misleading. In that case, the entity should disclose the nature of the event and estimate of its financial effect or a statement that such an estimate cannot be made. For entities that are not SEC filers, the date through which subsequent events have been evaluated and whether that date is when the financial statements were issued or available to be issued must be disclosed. An entity that is an SEC filer is not required to disclose the date through which subsequent events have been evaluated.

1.153

TABLE 1-15: SUBSEQUENT EVENTS

Table 1-15 lists the subsequent events disclosed in the financial statements of the survey entities.

	Number of Entities		
	2010	2009	2008
Debt incurred, reduced or refinanced	24	56	73
Business combinations pending or consummated	66	44	46
Litigation	9	37	52
Discontinued operations or asset disposals	28	33	24
Employee benefit plan adopted, amended, or terminated	2	N/C*	N/C*
Capital stock issued or purchased	17	17	17
Reorganization, restructuring, realignment, recapitalization, or bankruptcy	13	16	26
Credit agreements	11	N/C*	N/C*
Tax matter resolution	3	N/C*	N/C*
Other, described	33	51	59

* N/C = Not compiled. Line item was not included in the table for the year shown.

PRESENTATION AND DISCLOSURE EXCERPTS

Periodic Fee Agreement

1.154

BOYD GAMING CORPORATION (DEC)

NOTES TO CONSOLIDATED FINANCIAL STATEMENTS

Note 22. Subsequent Events

We have evaluated all events or transactions that occurred after December 31, 2010. During this period, we had the following subsequent event, the effects of which did not require adjustment to our financial position or results of operations as of and for the year ended December 31, 2010.

Periodic Fee Agreement

On March 7, 2011, Echelon entered into the Periodic Fee Agreement with LVE. The Periodic Fee Agreement is effective from March 7, 2011 (the "Effective Date") until the earliest to occur of the following events (such earliest date, the "Termination Date"): (i) the date on which Echelon resumes construction of the Echelon resort and the parties agree to certain milestones with respect to the performance of the ESA; (ii) the date on which Echelon has purchased all or substantially all of the assets of LVE pursuant to the terms of the Purchase Option Agreement; and (iii) the date on which LVE draws down and receives the full amount available under the Letter of Credit (as defined below). On and after the Termination Date, the Periodic Fee Agreement shall be null and void and shall be deemed dissolved and of no effect, and the terms of the ESA shall be as they were prior to execution of the Periodic Fee Agreement.

The Periodic Fee Agreement provides for monthly payments by Echelon to LVE of approximately $1.0 million (subject to a reduction for Echelon's allocable share of reduced interest costs attributed to Tax-Exempt Bonds (as defined below) LVE redeems in excess of $27.0 million plus certain operation and maintenance fees (estimated by LVE not to exceed an aggregate of $0.6 million annually) on March 4, 2011 and the first day of each month, beginning on April 1, 2011 and ending on November 1, 2013. Monthly payments are also due on the first day of each month after November 1, 2013; however, the amount of the payments after such date will be based on the then-outstanding principal amount of LVE's obligation to its Lenders, the Tax-Exempt Bonds and certain advances from its members.

The Periodic Fee Agreement also provides that from the Effective Date through the Termination Date, neither LVE nor Echelon would give notice of, file or otherwise initiate any claim or cause of action, in or before any court, administrative agency, arbitrator, mediator or other tribunal, that arises under the ESA, subject to certain exceptions, and any statute of limitations or limitation periods for defenses, claims, causes of actions and counterclaims shall be tolled during such period (the "No-Litigation Period").

To secure Echelon's obligations under the Periodic Fee Agreement, Echelon also agreed to post a letter of credit in the amount of $6.0 million for the benefit of LVE (the "Letter of Credit"). LVE is entitled to draw down the Letter of Credit in the event that Echelon fails to make payments required pursuant to the Periodic Fee Agreement (a "Buyer Event of

Default"). LVE is obligated to reimburse Echelon for its reasonable substantiated third-party costs incurred in providing the Letter of Credit.

The Periodic Fee Agreement provides, among other things, for (i) LVE's maintenance of certain construction permits and certain assets; (ii) LVE's delivery of releases to Echelon from certain professional service contracts and its engagement of replacement professional service providers if the necessary releases are not obtained; (iii) LVE's delivery of recommendations to Echelon regarding certain aspects of the central energy center and energy distribution system at the Echelon resort (the "System"); (iv) the resolution of disputes between LVE and Echelon with respect to certain aspects of the System; (v) the possible sale of certain portions of the System; and (vi) LVE's agreement (subject to the consent of the applicable trustee) to use commercially reasonable efforts to redeem a portion of the tax-exempt bonds issued on behalf of LVE on December 20, 2007 (the "Tax-Exempt Bonds"), subject to certain exceptions.

Purchase Option

LVE also granted Echelon and the Company an option to purchase substantially all of the assets of LVE (the "Purchase Option") for a purchase price of approximately $195.1 million (subject to certain adjustments), which may be exercised from the Effective Date through the Termination Date, provided that no Buyer Event of Default has occurred and remains ongoing.

Future Commitments Related to LVE Agreements

Our future commitments with respect to the LVE agreements discussed above are as follows (in thousands):

For the Year Ending December 31

2011	$11,887
2012	11,887
2013	11,796
2014	10,800
2015	10,800
	$57,170

Litigation

1.155

CORN PRODUCTS INTERNATIONAL, INC. (DEC)

NOTES TO CONSOLIDATED FINANCIAL STATEMENTS

Note 13—Mexican Tax on Beverages Sweetened with HFCS

On January 1, 2002, a discriminatory tax on beverages sweetened with high fructose corn syrup ("HFCS") approved by the Mexican Congress late in 2001, became effective. In response to the enactment of the tax, which at the time effectively ended the use of HFCS for beverages in Mexico, the Company ceased production of HFCS 55 at its San Juan del Rio plant, one of its three plants in Mexico. Over time, the Company resumed production and sales of HFCS and by 2006 had returned to levels attained prior to the imposition

of the tax as a result of certain customers having obtained court rulings exempting them from paying the tax. The Mexican Congress repealed this tax effective January 1, 2007.

On October 21, 2003, the Company submitted, on its own behalf and on behalf of its Mexican affiliate, CPIngredientes, S.A. de C.V. (previously known as Compania Proveedora de Ingredientes), a Request for Institution of Arbitration Proceedings Submitted Pursuant to Chapter 11 of the North American Free Trade Agreement ("NAFTA") (the "Request"). The Request was submitted to the Additional Office of the International Centre for Settlement of Investment Disputes and was brought against the United Mexican States. In the Request, the Company asserted that the imposition by Mexico of a discriminatory tax on beverages containing HFCS in force from 2002 through 2006 breached various obligations of Mexico under the investment protection provisions of NAFTA. The case was bifurcated into two phases, liability and damages, and a hearing on liability was held before a Tribunal in July 2006. In a Decision dated January 15, 2008, the Tribunal unanimously held that Mexico had violated NAFTA Article 1102, National Treatment, by treating beverages sweetened with HFCS produced by foreign companies differently than those sweetened with domestic sugar. In July 2008, a hearing regarding the quantum of damages was held before the same Tribunal. The Company sought damages and pre- and post-judgment interest totaling $288 million through December 31, 2008.

In an award rendered August 18, 2009, the Tribunal awarded damages to CPIngredientes in the amount of $58.4 million, as a result of the tax and certain out-of-pocket expenses incurred by CPIngredientes, together with accrued interest. On October 1, 2009, the Company submitted to the Tribunal a request for correction of this award to avoid effective double taxation on the amount of the award in Mexico.

On March 26, 2010, the Tribunal issued a correction of its August 18, 2009 damages award. While the amount of damages had not changed, the decision made the damages payable to Corn Products International, Inc. instead of CPIngredientes.

On January 24 and 25, 2011, the Company received cash payments totaling $58.4 million from the Government of the United Mexican States pursuant to the corrected award. Mexico made these payments pursuant to an agreement with Corn Products International that provides for terminating pending post-award litigation and waiving post-award interest. The $58.4 million award will be recorded in the Company's first quarter 2011 consolidated financial statements.

1.156

THE KROGER CO. (JAN)

NOTES TO CONSOLIDATED FINANCIAL STATEMENTS

17. Subsequent Events (in part)

On March 9, 2010, the Company filed an action (The Kroger Co., et al. v. Excentus Corporation, Case No. 1:10-cv-00161-SSB, in the United States District Court for the Southern District of Ohio, Western Division at Cincinnati) seeking a declaration that the Company's actions related to fuel rewards programs do not infringe certain patents allegedly held by

Excentus Corporation and that certain patents allegedly held by Excentus Corporation are invalid. Shortly after the Company filed the action, on March 9, 2010, Excentus Corporation filed an action against the Company (Excentus Corporation v. The Kroger Co., Case No. 3:10-cv-00483, in the United States District Court for the Northern District of Texas, Dallas Division) seeking to recover damages from the Company for its alleged infringement of patents claimed to be held by Excentus Corporation, along with injunctive relief enjoining the Company from infringing the patents by reason of its actions related to fuel reward programs. Although these lawsuits are subject to uncertainties inherent in the litigation process and have only recently been filed, based on the information available to the Company, management does not expect that the ultimate resolution of these matters will have a material adverse effect on the Company's financial condition, results of operations, or cash flows.

Spin-offs

1.157

ITT CORPORATION (DEC)

NOTES TO CONSOLIDATED FINANCIAL STATEMENTS

Note 22—Subsequent Events

On January 12, 2011, the Company announced that its Board of Directors had unanimously approved a plan to separate the Company's businesses into three distinct, publicly traded companies. Following completion of the transaction, ITT will continue to trade on the New York Stock Exchange as an industrial company that supplies highly engineered solutions in the aerospace, transportation, energy and industrial markets. Under the plan, ITT shareholders will own shares in all three corporations following the completion of the transaction. The transaction is anticipated to be completed by the end of 2011.

Under the plan, ITT would execute tax-free spinoffs to shareholders of its water-related businesses and its Defense & Information Solutions segment. The water-related business will include the Water & Wastewater division and the Residential & Commercial Water division, as well as the Flow Control division that is currently reported within the Motion & Flow Control segment. The Industrial Process division, which is currently reported within the Fluid segment, will continue to operate as a subsidiary of the new ITT Corporation.

1.158

MARRIOTT INTERNATIONAL, INC. (DEC)

NOTES TO CONSOLIDATED FINANCIAL STATEMENTS

24. Subsequent Event

On February 14, 2011, we announced a plan to split the company's businesses into two separate, publicly traded compa-

nies. Under the plan, we expect to spin off our timeshare operations and development business as a new independent company through a special tax-free dividend to our shareholders in late 2011. The new company will focus on the timeshare business as the exclusive developer and operator of timeshare, fractional, and related products under the Marriott brand and the exclusive developer of fractional and related products under the Ritz-Carlton brand. After the split, we will concentrate on the lodging management and franchise business. We will receive franchise fees from the new timeshare company's use of the Marriott timeshare and Ritz-Carlton fractional brands.

As two separate public companies, Marriott and the new timeshare company will have separate boards of directors. William J. Shaw, who recently announced his retirement as vice chairman of Marriott and also resigned from its board, will become chairman of the board of the new timeshare company and Deborah Marriott Harrison, senior vice president of government affairs for Marriott, will serve as a board member of the new timeshare company. J.W. Marriott, Jr. will remain chairman of the board and chief executive officer of Marriott. Stephen P. Weisz, president of Marriott's timeshare business since 1997 and a 39-year Marriott veteran, will become chief executive officer of the new company. We expect that the common stock of the new timeshare company will be listed on the New York Stock Exchange. We do not expect that the new timeshare company will pay a quarterly cash dividend or be investment grade in the near term.

We expect that the new timeshare company will file a Form 10 registration statement with the SEC in the second quarter 2011. At that time, we will disclose additional details about the proposed transaction, including respective pro forma balance sheets and pro forma income statements of the two companies. The transaction is subject to the receipt of normal and customary regulatory approvals and third-party consents, the execution of inter-company agreements, receipt of a favorable ruling from the Internal Revenue Service, arrangement of adequate financing facilities, final approval by our board of directors, and other related matters. The transaction will not require shareholder approval and will have no impact on Marriott's contractual obligations to the existing securitizations. Subject to the completion of this ongoing work, and the receipt of regulatory approvals, the spin-off should be completed before year end 2011.

Restructuring

1.159

KIMBERLY-CLARK CORPORATION (DEC)

NOTES TO CONSOLIDATED FINANCIAL STATEMENTS

Note 19. Subsequent Events

On January 21, 2011, we initiated a pulp and tissue restructuring plan in order to exit our remaining integrated pulp manufacturing operations and improve the underlying profitability and return on invested capital of our consumer tissue and K-C Professional businesses. The restructuring is expected to be completed by the end of 2012 and will involve the streamlining, sale or closure of 5 to 6 of our manufacturing facilities around the world. In conjunction with these actions, we will be exiting certain non-strategic products, primarily non-branded offerings, and transferring some production to lower-cost facilities in order to improve overall profitability and returns. Facilities that will be impacted by the restructuring include our pulp and tissue facility in Everett, Washington and the two facilities in Australia that manufacture pulp and tissue.

The restructuring plan will commence in the first quarter of 2011 and is expected to be completed by December 31, 2012. The restructuring is expected to result in cumulative charges of approximately $400 million to $600 million before tax ($280 million to $420 million after tax) over that period. We anticipate that the charges will fall into the following categories and approximate dollar ranges: workforce reduction costs ($50 million to $100 million); incremental depreciation ($300 million to $400 million); and other associated costs ($50 million to $100 million). Cash costs related to the streamlining of operations, sale or closure, relocation of equipment, severance and other expenses are expected to account for approximately 25 percent to 50 percent of the charges. Noncash charges will consist primarily of incremental depreciation.

As a result of the restructuring, we expect that by 2013 annual net sales will be reduced by $250 million to $300 million and operating profit will increase by at least $75 million. Most of the restructuring will impact the consumer tissue business segment.

Assets Held for Sale

1.160

REYNOLDS AMERICAN INC. (DEC)

NOTES TO CONSOLIDATED FINANCIAL STATEMENTS

Note 3—Intangible Assets (in part)

During the fourth quarter of 2010, in order to facilitate its strategic focus on key brands in the cigarette, moist-snuff and modern smoke-free categories of the tobacco business, RAI determined that it was probable that it would dispose of the operations of Lane, which are included in the American Snuff segment. In accordance with accounting guidance, the assets of the disposal group were reclassified as assets held for sale, and liabilities held for sale were included in other current liabilities, in the consolidated balance sheet at December 31, 2010. See note 23 for additional information on the sale of Lane.

Note 23—Subsequent Event

On January 13, 2011, RAI reached an agreement to sell all the capital stock of Lane and certain other assets related to the Lane operations, to an affiliate of Scandinavian Tobacco Group A/S for approximately $200 million in cash. The transaction is expected to be completed in the first half of 2011, pending antitrust review and approval.

In accordance with accounting guidance, the assets of the disposal group were reclassified as assets held for sale, and liabilities held for sale that were included in other current liabilities, in the consolidated balance sheet at December 31,

2010. For further information related to goodwill and other intangible assets reclassified as held for sale, see note 3.

Purchase and Sale Agreement

1.161

IRON MOUNTAIN INCORPORATED (DEC)

NOTES TO CONSOLIDATED FINANCIAL STATEMENTS

15. Subsequent Events (in part; in thousands)

In January 2011, we acquired the remaining 80% interest of our joint venture in Poland (Iron Mountain Poland Holdings Limited) in a stock transaction for an estimated purchase price of $69,500, including an initial cash purchase price of $35,000. As a result, we now own 100% of our Polish operations, which provide storage and records management services. The terms of the purchase and sale agreement requires a second payment based upon the audited financial results of the joint venture for the period April 1, 2010 through March 31, 2011. This payment is based upon a formula defined in the purchase and sale agreement and is expected to be paid in the second quarter of 2011. Our current estimate of the second payment is approximately $32,000. Additionally, the purchase and sale agreement provides for the payment of up to a maximum of $2,500 of contingent consideration to be paid in July 2012 based upon meeting certain performance criteria. The carrying value of the 20% interest that we owned and accounted for under the equity method of accounting amounted to approximately $5,500 as of December 31, 2010. We will calculate the fair value of such interest on the date of the acquisition of the additional 80% interest and will record a gain during the first quarter of 2011 to other (income) expense, net included in the consolidated statement of operations. One of the members of our board of directors and several of his family members hold an indirect equity interest in one of the shareholders that will receive proceeds in connection with this transaction. As a result of this equity interest, our board member together with several of his family members will receive approximately 24% of the purchase price that we pay in connection with this transaction.

Business Combinations

1.162

COMCAST CORPORATION (DEC)

NOTES TO CONSOLIDATED FINANCIAL STATEMENTS

Note 21. Subsequent Events

NBCUniversal Transaction

On January 28, 2011, we closed our transaction with GE to form a new company named NBCUniversal, LLC ("NBCUniversal Holdings"). We now control and own 51% of NBCUniversal Holdings and GE owns the remaining 49%. As part of the NBCUniversal transaction, GE contributed the historical businesses of NBC Universal, which is now a wholly owned subsidiary of NBCUniversal Holdings. The NBCUniversal contributed businesses include its national cable programming networks, the NBC network and its owned NBC affiliated local television stations, the Telemundo network and its owned Telemundo affiliated local television stations, Universal Pictures filmed entertainment, the Universal Studios Hollywood theme park and other related assets. We contributed our national cable programming networks, our regional sports and news networks, certain of our Internet businesses, including DailyCandy and Fandango, and other related assets ("Comcast Content Business"). In addition to contributing the Comcast Content Business, we also made a cash payment of $6.2 billion at the closing. The cash paid will be adjusted subsequent to close to reflect final balances of certain working capital accounts and other closing adjustments. The transaction also calls for the payment to GE, in the future, of certain tax benefits to the extent realized. The combination of businesses creates a leading media and entertainment company capable of providing entertainment, news, sports and other content to a global audience across all platforms.

In connection with the NBCUniversal transaction, NBCUniversal issued $9.1 billion of senior debt securities with maturities ranging from 2014 to 2041 and repaid approximately $1.7 billion of existing debt during 2010. Immediately prior to the closing, NBCUniversal distributed approximately $7.4 billion to GE.

Under the terms of the operating agreement of NBCUniversal Holdings, during the six month period beginning on July 28, 2014 GE has the right to cause NBCUniversal Holdings to redeem half of GE's interest in NBCUniversal Holdings, and during the six month period beginning January 28, 2018, GE has the right to cause NBCUniversal Holdings to redeem GE's remaining interest, if any. If GE exercises its first redemption right, we have the immediate right to purchase the remainder of GE's interest. If GE does not exercise its first redemption right, during the six month period beginning on January 28, 2016, we have the right to purchase half of GE's interest in NBCUniversal Holdings. During the six month period beginning January 28, 2019, we have the right to purchase GE's remaining interest, if any, in NBCUniversal Holdings. The purchase price to be paid in connection with any purchase described in this paragraph will be equal to the ownership percentage being purchased multiplied by an amount equal to 120% of the fully distributed public market trading value of NBCUniversal Holdings (determined pursuant to an appraisal process if NBCUniversal Holdings is not then publicly traded), less 50% of an amount (not less than zero) equal to the excess of 120% of the fully distributed public market trading value over $28.4 billion. Subject to various limitations, we are committed to fund up to $2.875 billion in cash or our common stock for each of the two redemptions (up to an aggregate of $5.75 billion), with amounts not used in the first redemption to be available for the second redemption to the extent NBCUniversal Holdings cannot fund the redemptions.

Until July 28, 2014, GE may not directly or indirectly transfer its interest in NBCUniversal Holdings. Thereafter, GE may transfer its interest to a third party, subject to our right of first offer. The right of first offer would permit us to purchase all, but not less than all, of the interests proposed to be transferred. In the event that GE makes a registration request in accordance with certain registration rights that are granted to it under the agreement, we will have the right to purchase,

for cash at the market value (determined pursuant to an appraisal process if NBCUniversal Holdings is not then publicly traded), all of GE's interest in NBCUniversal Holdings that GE is seeking to register.

As a result of the NBCUniversal transaction, beginning in 2011 we expect to present five reportable segments, Cable Distribution (currently presented in our Cable segment), Cable Networks, Broadcast Networks, Filmed Entertainment and Theme Parks. Our Programming segment, our regional sports and news networks (currently presented in our Cable segment) and our contributed Comcast Interactive Media businesses (currently presented in Corporate and Other) will be presented with NBCUniversal's businesses in the new segments. The businesses of Comcast Interactive Media that were not contributed to NBCUniversal will be included in the Cable Distribution segment.

Acquisition-Related Expenses

In connection with the NBCUniversal transaction, we have incurred incremental expenses related to legal, accounting and valuation services, which are reflected in operating, selling, general and administrative expenses. We also incurred certain financing costs and other shared costs with GE associated with debt facilities that were entered into in December 2009 and with the issuance of NBCUniversal's senior notes in 2010, which are reflected in other income (expense) and interest expense. The table below presents the amounts related to these expenses included in our consolidated statement of operations.

Year Ended December 31, 2010 (In millions)

Operating, selling, general and administrative expenses	$ 80
Other expense	$129
Interest expense	$ 7

Additional fees paid in connection with the closing of the transaction will be recorded as expenses in the first quarter of 2011.

Preliminary Purchase Price Allocation and Unaudited Pro Forma Information

Since we now control NBCUniversal Holdings, we will apply acquisition accounting to the NBCUniversal contributed businesses and their results of operations will be included in our consolidated results of operations following the acquisition date. The NBCUniversal contributed businesses will be recorded at their estimated fair value. The Comcast Content Business will continue at its historical or carry-over basis. GE's interest in NBCUniversal Holdings will be recorded as a redeemable noncontrolling interest in our consolidated financial statements due to the redemption provisions outlined above.

Due to the limited time since the acquisition date and limitations on access to NBCUniversal information prior to the acquisition date, the initial accounting for the business combination is incomplete at this time. As a result, we are unable to provide amounts recognized as of the acquisition date for major classes of assets and liabilities acquired and resulting from the transaction, including the information required for indemnification assets, contingencies, noncontrolling interests and goodwill. Also, because the initial accounting for the transaction is incomplete, we are unable to provide the supplemental pro forma revenue and earnings of the combined entity. We will include this information in our Quarterly Report on Form 10-Q for the three months ended March 31, 2011.

Merger Agreements

1.163

ROBBINS & MYERS, INC. (AUG)

NOTES TO CONSOLIDATED FINANCIAL STATEMENTS

Note 14—Subsequent Events

On October 6, 2010, Robbins & Myers, Inc. ("R&M"), Triple Merger I, Inc., a Delaware corporation and a wholly-owned subsidiary of R&M ("Merger Sub I"), Triple Merger II, Inc., a Delaware corporation and a wholly-owned subsidiary of R&M ("Merger Sub II"), and T-3 Energy Services, Inc., a Delaware corporation ("T-3"), (NASDAQ: TTES), entered into an Agreement and Plan of Merger (the "Merger Agreement"). The Merger Agreement provides that, upon the terms and subject to the conditions set forth in the Merger Agreement, Merger Sub I will merge with and into T-3, with T-3 surviving as a wholly-owned subsidiary of R&M (the "Merger"). The Merger Agreement and the Merger have been unanimously approved by the Boards of Directors of both R&M and T-3.

T-3, located in Houston, Texas, provides oilfield and pipeline products and services and will operate under our Fluid Management segment. Under the Merger Agreement, T-3 stockholders will receive 0.894 common shares of R&M, without par value, plus $7.95 in cash, without interest, for each share of common stock of T-3, par value $0.001 per share, in a transaction valued at approximately $422 million as of the date of the announcement. Accordingly, T-3 stockholders are estimated to receive an aggregate of approximately 12 million of our common shares and $106 million in cash. Upon completion of the Merger Agreement, we expect T-3 stockholders to own approximately 27% of our outstanding common shares.

The exchange ratio is fixed and will not be adjusted in the event of any change in the price of R&M common shares or T-3 common stock between the date of the Merger Agreement and the closing. Because the exchange ratio is fixed, the value of the consideration paid for each share of T-3 common stock will vary based upon any changes in the market value of common shares of R&M. Changes in the market value of shares of T-3 common stock will have no effect upon the value of the consideration paid for each share of T-3 common stock.

Completion of the Merger is conditioned upon: (1) approval by R&M shareholders and T-3 stockholders; (2) the absence of any law or order prohibiting the closing; (3) regulatory approvals, including expiration or early termination of the applicable waiting period under the Hart-Scott Rodino Antitrust Improvements Act of 1976; (4) subject to certain exceptions, the accuracy of representations and warranties and the performance of covenants; (5) the effectiveness of a registration statement on Form S-4 that will be filed by R&M for the issuance of its common shares in the Merger and the authorization of the listing of those shares on the NYSE; (6) the delivery of customary opinions from counsel to Robbins & Myers and T-3 that the Merger will qualify as a tax-free re-

organization for U.S. federal income tax purposes; and (7) other closing conditions set forth in the Merger Agreement.

Annual revenues of T-3 for the years ended December 31, 2009 and 2008 were approximately $218 million and $285 million, respectively. Total assets of T-3 for the years ended December 31, 2009 and 2008 were approximately $280 million and $287 million, respectively.

1.164

SMURFIT-STONE CONTAINER CORPORATION (DEC)

NOTES TO CONSOLIDATED FINANCIAL STATEMENTS

26. Subsequent Events

On January 23, 2011, the Company and Rock-Tenn entered into the Merger Agreement pursuant to which the Company will merge with and into a subsidiary of Rock-Tenn (the "Merger"). This Merger, unanimously approved by the Boards of Directors of both companies, will create a leader in the North American paperboard packaging market with combined revenues of approximately $9 billion.

For each share of the Company's common stock, the Company's stockholders will be entitled to receive 0.30605 shares of Rock-Tenn common stock and $17.50 in cash, representing 50% cash and 50% stock on the date of the signing of the Merger Agreement. On January 23, 2011, the equity consideration was $35 per the Company's common share or approximately $3.5 billion, consisting of approximately $1.8 billion of cash and the issuance of approximately 30.9 million shares of Rock-Tenn common stock. In addition, Rock-Tenn will assume the Company's liabilities, including debt and underfunded pension liabilities, which were $1,194 million and $1,145 million, respectively, at December 31, 2010. Following the acquisition, Rock-Tenn stockholders will own approximately 56% and the Company's stockholders will own 44% of the combined company.

The transaction is expected to close in the second quarter of 2011 and is subject to customary closing conditions, regulatory approvals, as well as approval by both Rock-Tenn and the Company's stockholders.

Defined Benefit Plan

1.165

THE MCCLATCHY COMPANY (DEC)

NOTES TO CONSOLIDATED FINANCIAL STATEMENTS

Note 13. Subsequent Events (in part)

Contribution of Real Property to Qualified Defined Benefit Plan: On January 14, 2011, the Company contributed company-owned real property from seven locations to its qualified defined benefit pension plan. The pension plan obtained independent appraisals of the property, and based on these appraisals the plan recorded the contribution (the fair value of the property) at $49.6 million on January 14, 2011.

The Company has entered into leases for the contributed properties for 10 years at an annual rent of approximately $4.0 million and expects to continue to use the properties in its newspaper operations at the seven locations. The properties will be managed on behalf of the pension plan by an independent fiduciary, and the terms of the leases were negotiated with the fiduciary.

McClatchy expects its required pension contribution under the Employee Retirement Income Security Act to be approximately $51.2 million in 2011, and the contribution of real property is expected to satisfy virtually all of the Company's required pension contribution for fiscal 2011. The remaining required contribution, if any, will be made in cash.

The contribution and leaseback of the properties were treated as a financing transaction and accordingly, the Company will continue to depreciate the carrying value of the properties in its financial statements and no gain or loss is recognized. The $49.6 million will be recorded in other long-term obligations and will be reduced by a portion of lease payments made to the pension plan. The transaction will be recorded in the first fiscal quarter of 2011 and therefore the funded status of the Company's qualified pension plan disclosed in Note 7 and elsewhere in these financial statements does not reflect this transaction.

Taxable Investment Incentives

1.166

FIRST SOLAR, INC. (DEC)

NOTES TO CONSOLIDATED FINANCIAL STATEMENTS

Note 25. Subsequent Events (in part)

On February 11, 2011 we were approved to receive taxable investment incentives ("Investitionszuschüsse") of approximately €6.3 million ($8.4 million at the balance sheet close rate on December 31, 2010 of $1.33 /€1.00) from the State of Brandenburg, Germany. These funds will reimburse us for certain costs incurred building our expansion of our manufacturing plant in Frankfurt/Oder, Germany, including costs for the construction of buildings and the purchase of machinery and equipment. Receipt of these incentives is conditional upon the State of Brandenburg having sufficient funds allocated to this program to pay the reimbursements we claim. In addition, we are required to operate our facility for a minimum of five years. Our incentive approval expires on December 31, 2012.

Acquisition

1.167

NETAPP, INC. (APR)

NOTES TO CONSOLIDATED FINANCIAL STATEMENTS

20. Subsequent Event

On May 13, 2010, we completed the acquisition of Bycast Inc., a privately held company headquartered in Vancouver, British Columbia, Canada, for approximately $80 million in cash. This acquisition will extend our leadership position in unified storage by adding an object-based storage software offering which simplifies the task of large-scale object storage while improving the ability to quickly search and locate data objects. As of April 30, 2010, we had incurred $1.2 million in related expenses which is included in acquisition related income, net in our consolidated statements of operations.

Interest Rate Swap Agreement

1.168

TENET HEALTHCARE CORPORATION (DEC)

NOTES TO CONSOLIDATED FINANCIAL STATEMENTS

Note 22. Subsequent Events (in part)

Interest Rate Swap Agreement

In February 2011, we entered into an interest rate swap agreement for an aggregate notional amount of $600 million. The interest rate swap agreement has been designated as a fair value hedge and will be used to manage our exposure to future changes in interest rates. It has the effect of converting our 10% senior secured notes due 2018 from a fixed interest rate paid semi-annually to a variable interest rate paid semi-annually based on the one-month LIBOR plus a floating rate spread of approximately 6.60%. During the term of the interest rate swap agreement, changes in the fair value of the interest rate swap agreement and changes in the fair value of the 10% senior secured notes, which we anticipate should substantially offset each other, will be recorded in interest expense.

Research and Development

1.169

PFIZER INC. (DEC)

NOTES TO CONSOLIDATED FINANCIAL STATEMENTS

21. Subsequent Events (in part)

B. New Research and Development Productivity Initiative
On February 1, 2011, we announced that we are continuing to closely evaluate our global research and development function and will accelerate our current strategies to improve innovation and overall productivity by prioritizing areas with the greatest scientific and commercial promise, utilizing appropriate risk/return profiles and focusing on areas with the highest potential to deliver value in the near term and over time. In connection with these actions:

- We estimate that we will incur pre-tax employee-termination charges in the range of approximately $800 million to $1.1 billion and other pre-tax exit and implementation charges in the range of approximately $300 million to $500 million, all of which will result in future cash expenditures. We expect most of these charges to be incurred in 2011 and the balance to be incurred in 2012.
- We estimate that we will incur total pre-tax impairment and additional depreciation—asset restructuring charges in the range of approximately $1.1 billion to $1.3 billion, of which approximately $800 million to $900 million represent additional depreciation—asset restructuring charges. Most of these charges will be associated with our Sandwich, U.K. facility. We expect most of these non-cash charges to be incurred in 2011 and the balance to be incurred in 2012.

RELATED PARTY TRANSACTIONS

DISCLOSURE

1.170 FASB ASC 850, *Related Party Disclosures*, specifies the nature of information that should be disclosed in financial statements about related-party transactions and certain common control relationships. Financial statements should include disclosures of material related-party transactions, other than compensation arrangements, expense allowances, and other similar items in the ordinary course of business. The disclosures should include the nature of the relationship(s) involved, a description of the transactions, the dollar amounts of the transactions, and amounts due to or from related parties. For entities with separately-issued financial statements that are members of a consolidated tax return, additional disclosures are required. Further, if the reporting entity and one or more other companies are under common ownership or management control, and the existence of that control could result in operating results or a financial position of the reporting entity significantly different from those that would have been obtained if the companies were autonomous, the nature of the control relationship should be disclosed, even though there are no transactions between the entities.

PRESENTATION AND DISCLOSURE EXCERPTS

Related Party Receivables

1.171

CBS CORPORATION (DEC)

NOTES TO CONSOLIDATED FINANCIAL STATEMENTS

6) Related Parties

National Amusements, Inc. National Amusements, Inc. ("NAI") is the controlling stockholder of CBS Corp. Mr. Sumner M. Redstone, the controlling stockholder, chairman of the board of directors and chief executive officer of NAI, is the Executive Chairman of the Board of Directors and founder of both CBS Corp. and Viacom Inc. In addition, Ms. Shari Redstone, Mr. Sumner M. Redstone's daughter, is the president and a director of NAI and the vice chair of the board of directors of both CBS Corp. and Viacom Inc. Mr. David R. Andelman is a director of CBS Corp. and serves as a director of NAI. Mr. Frederic V. Salerno is a director of CBS Corp. and serves as a director of Viacom Inc. At December 31, 2010, NAI directly or indirectly owned approximately 79% of CBS Corp.'s voting Class A Common Stock and owned approximately 6% of CBS Corp.'s Class A Common Stock and non-voting Class B Common Stock on a combined basis.

Viacom Inc. CBS Corp., as part of its normal course of business, enters into transactions with Viacom Inc. and its subsidiaries. CBS Corp., through its Entertainment segment, licenses its television products to Viacom Inc., primarily MTV Networks and BET Networks. In addition, CBS Corp. recognizes advertising revenues for media spending placed by various subsidiaries of Viacom Inc., primarily Paramount Pictures. Paramount Pictures also distributes certain of the Company's television products in the home entertainment market. CBS Corp.'s total revenues from these transactions were $262.4 million, $243.3 million and $448.8 million for the years ended December 31, 2010, 2009 and 2008, respectively.

Showtime Networks licenses motion picture programming from Paramount Pictures under an exclusive output agreement which covered feature films initially theatrically released in the U.S. through 2007. Showtime Networks has exhibition rights to each film licensed under this agreement during three pay television exhibition windows over the course of several years after each such film's initial theatrical release. This agreement has not been renewed for new feature films initially theatrically released in the U.S. after 2007. In addition, CBS Corp. places advertisements with and purchases other goods and services from various subsidiaries of Viacom Inc. The total amounts purchased in connection with these transactions were $26.9 million, $23.0 million and $93.4 million for the years ended December 31, 2010, 2009 and 2008, respectively.

The following table presents the amounts due from or due to Viacom Inc. in the normal course of business as reflected on CBS Corp.'s Consolidated Balance Sheets.

| (In millions) | At December 31 | |
	2010	2009
Amounts Due From Viacom Inc.		
Receivables	$104.0	$164.4
Other assets (Receivables, noncurrent)	252.2	268.3
Total amounts due from Viacom Inc.	$356.2	$432.7
Amounts Due to Viacom Inc.		
Accounts payable	$ 5.6	$ 2.8
Program rights	4.1	18.4
Other liabilities (Program rights, noncurrent)	.5	3.8
Total amounts due to Viacom Inc.	$ 10.2	$ 25.0

Other Related Parties—The Company owns 50% of The CW, a television broadcast network, which is accounted for by the Company as an equity investment. CBS Corp. earns revenues from The CW, primarily from the licensing of the Company's television programming. Total revenues from The CW were $136.1 million, $130.5 million and $121.9 million for the years ended December 31, 2010, 2009 and 2008, respectively.

The Company, through the normal course of business, is involved in transactions with other related parties that have not been material in any of the periods presented.

Merger Agreement and Exchange Agreement

1.172

SPECTRUM BRANDS HOLDINGS, INC. (SEP)

NOTES TO CONSOLIDATED FINANCIAL STATEMENTS

(13) Related Party Transactions (in part; in thousands)

Merger Agreement and Exchange Agreement

On June 16, 2010 (the "Closing Date"), SB Holdings completed a business combination transaction pursuant to the Agreement and Plan of Merger (the "Mergers"), dated as of February 9, 2010, as amended on March 1, 2010, March 26, 2010 and April 30, 2010, by and among SB Holdings, Russell Hobbs, Spectrum Brands, Battery Merger Corp., and Grill Merger Corp. (the "Merger Agreement"). As a result of the Mergers, each of Spectrum Brands and Russell Hobbs became a wholly-owned subsidiary of SB Holdings. At the effective time of the Mergers, (i) the outstanding shares of Spectrum Brands common stock were canceled and converted into the right to receive shares of SB Holdings common stock, and (ii) the outstanding shares of Russell Hobbs common stock and preferred stock were canceled and converted into the right to receive shares of SB Holdings common stock.

Pursuant to the terms of the Merger Agreement, on February 9, 2010, Spectrum Brands entered into support agreements with Harbinger Capital Partners Master Fund I, Ltd. ("Harbinger Master Fund"), Harbinger Capital Partners Special Situations Fund, L.P. and Global Opportunities Break-

away Ltd. (collectively, the "Harbinger Parties") and Avenue International Master, L.P. and certain of its affiliates (the "Avenue Parties"), in which the Harbinger Parties and the Avenue Parties agreed to vote their shares of Spectrum Brands common stock acquired before the date of the Merger Agreement in favor of the Mergers and against any alternative proposal that would impede the Mergers.

Immediately following the consummation of the Mergers, the Harbinger Parties owned approximately 64% of the outstanding SB Holdings common stock and the stockholders of Spectrum Brands (other than the Harbinger Parties) owned approximately 36% of the outstanding SB Holdings common stock. Harbinger Group, Inc. ("HRG") and the Harbinger Parties are parties to a Contribution and Exchange Agreement (the "Exchange Agreement"), pursuant to the terms of which the Harbinger Parties will contribute 27,757 shares of SB Holdings common stock to HRG and received in exchange for such shares an aggregate of 119,910 shares of HRG common stock (the "Share Exchange"). Immediately following the consummation of the Share Exchange, (i) HRG will own 27,757 shares of SB Holdings common stock and the Harbinger Parties will own 6,500 shares of SB Holdings common stock, approximately 54.4% and 12.7% of the outstanding shares of SB Holdings common stock, respectively, and (ii) the Harbinger Parties will own 129,860 shares of HRG common stock, or approximately 93.3% of the outstanding HRG common stock.

In connection with the Mergers, the Harbinger Parties and SB Holdings entered into a stockholder agreement, dated February 9, 2010 (the "Stockholder Agreement"), which provides for certain protective provisions in favor of minority stockholders and provides certain rights and imposes certain obligations on the Harbinger Parties, including:

- For so long as the Harbinger Parties own 40% or more of the outstanding voting securities of SB Holdings, the Harbinger Parties and HRG will vote their shares of SB Holdings common stock to effect the structure of the SB Holdings board of directors as described in the Stockholder Agreement;
- The Harbinger Parties will not effect any transfer of equity securities of SB Holdings to any person that would result in such person and its affiliates owning 40% or more of the outstanding voting securities of SB Holdings, unless specified conditions are met; and
- The Harbinger Parties will be granted certain access and informational rights with respect to SB Holdings and its subsidiaries.

On September 10, 2010, the Harbinger Parties and HRG entered into a joinder to the Stockholder Agreement, pursuant to which, effective upon the consummation of the Share Exchange, HRG will become a party to the Stockholder Agreement, subject to all of the covenants, terms and conditions of the Stockholder Agreement to the same extent as the Harbinger Parties were bound thereunder prior to giving effect to the Share Exchange.

Certain provisions of the Stockholder Agreement terminate on the date on which the Harbinger Parties or HRG no longer constitutes a Significant Stockholder (as defined in the Stockholder Agreement). The Stockholder Agreement terminates when any person (including the Harbinger Parties or HRG) acquires 90% or more of the outstanding voting securities of SB Holdings.

Also in connection with the Mergers, the Harbinger Parties, the Avenue Parties and SB Holdings entered into a registration rights agreement, dated as of February 9, 2010 (the "SB

Holdings Registration Rights Agreement"), pursuant to which the Harbinger Parties and the Avenue Parties have, among other things and subject to the terms and conditions set forth therein, certain demand and so-called "piggy back" registration rights with respect to their shares of SB Holdings common stock. On September 10, 2010, the Harbinger Parties and HRG entered into a joinder to the SB Holdings Registration Rights Agreement, pursuant to which, effective upon the consummation of the Share Exchange, HRG will become a party to the SB Holdings Registration Rights Agreement, entitled to the rights and subject to the obligations of a holder thereunder.

(15) Acquisition

On June 16, 2010, the Company merged with Russell Hobbs. Headquartered in Miramar, Florida, Russell Hobbs is a designer, marketer and distributor of a broad range of branded small household appliances. Russell Hobbs markets and distributes small kitchen and home appliances, pet and pest products and personal care products. Russell Hobbs has a broad portfolio of recognized brand names, including Black & Decker, George Foreman, Russell Hobbs, Toastmaster, Litter-Maid, Farberware, Breadman and Juiceman. Russell Hobbs' customers include mass merchandisers, specialty retailers and appliance distributors primarily in North America, South America, Europe and Australia.

The results of Russell Hobbs operations since June 16, 2010 are included in the Company's Consolidated Statements of Operations. The financial results of Russell Hobbs are reported as a separate business segment, Small Appliances. Russell Hobbs contributed $237,576 in Net sales, and recorded Operating loss of $320 for the period from June 16, 2010 through the period ended September 30, 2010, which includes $13,400 of Acquisition and integration related charges.

In accordance with ASC Topic 805, *"Business Combinations"* ("ASC 805"), the Company accounted for the Merger by applying the acquisition method of accounting. The acquisition method of accounting requires that the consideration transferred in a business combination be measured at fair value as of the closing date of the acquisition. After consummation of the Merger, the stockholders of Spectrum Brands, inclusive of Harbinger, own approximately 60% of SB Holdings and the stockholders of Russell Hobbs own approximately 40% of SB Holdings. Inasmuch as Russell Hobbs is a private company and its common stock was not publicly traded, the closing market price of the Spectrum Brands common stock at June 15, 2010 was used to calculate the purchase price. The total purchase price of Russell Hobbs was approximately $597,579 determined as follows (in thousands, except per share data):

Spectrum Brands closing price per share on June 15, 2010	$ 28.15
Purchase price—Russell Hobbs allocation—20,704 shares[1][2]	$575,203
Cash payment to pay off Russell Hobbs' North American credit facility	22,376
Total purchase price of Russell Hobbs	$597,579

[1] Number of shares calculated based upon conversion formula, as defined in the Merger Agreement, using balances as of June 16, 2010.

[2] The fair value of 271 shares of unvested restricted stock units as they relate to post combination services will be recorded as operating expense over the remaining service period and were assumed to have no fair value for the purchase price.

Preliminary Purchase Price Allocation

The total purchase price for Russell Hobbs was allocated to the preliminary net tangible and intangible assets based upon their preliminary fair values at June 16, 2010 as set forth below. The excess of the purchase price over the preliminary net tangible assets and intangible assets was recorded as goodwill. The preliminary allocation of the purchase price was based upon a valuation for which the estimates and assumptions are subject to change within the measurement period (up to one year from the acquisition date). The primary areas of the preliminary purchase price allocation that are not yet finalized relate to the certain legal matters, amounts for income taxes including deferred tax accounts, amounts for uncertain tax positions, and net operating loss carryforwards inclusive of associated limitations, and the final allocation of goodwill. The Company expects to continue to obtain information to assist it in determining the fair values of the net assets acquired at the acquisition date during the measurement period. The preliminary purchase price allocation for Russell Hobbs is as follows (in thousands):

Current assets	$307,809
Property, plant and equipment	15,150
Intangible assets	363,327
Goodwill[A]	120,079
Other assets	15,752
Total assets acquired	$822,117
Current liabilities	142,046
Total debt	18,970
Long-term liabilities	63,522
Total liabilities assumed	$224,538
Net assets acquired	$597,579

[A] Consists of $25,426 of tax deductible Goodwill.

Preliminary Pre-Acquisition Contingencies Assumed

The Company has evaluated and continues to evaluate pre-acquisition contingencies relating to Russell Hobbs that existed as of the acquisition date. Based on the evaluation to date, the Company has preliminarily determined that certain pre-acquisition contingencies are probable in nature and estimable as of the acquisition date. Accordingly, the Company has preliminarily recorded its best estimates for these contingencies as part of the preliminary purchase price allocation for Russell Hobbs. The Company continues to gather information relating to all pre-acquisition contingencies that it has assumed from Russell Hobbs. Any changes to the pre-acquisition contingency amounts recorded during the measurement period will be included in the purchase price allocation. Subsequent to the end of the measurement period any adjustments to pre-acquisition contingency amounts will be reflected in the Company's results of operations.

Certain estimated values are not yet finalized and are subject to change, which could be significant. The Company will finalize the amounts recognized as it obtains the information necessary to complete its analysis during the measurement period. The following items are provisional and subject to change:

- Amounts for legal contingencies, pending the finalization of the Company's examination and evaluation of the portfolio of filed cases;

- Amounts for income taxes including deferred tax accounts, amounts for uncertain tax positions, and net operating loss carryforwards inclusive of associated limitations; and
- The final allocation of Goodwill.

ASC 805 requires, among other things, that assets acquired and liabilities assumed be recognized at their fair values as of the acquisition date. Accordingly, the Company performed a preliminary valuation of the assets and liabilities of Russell Hobbs at June 16, 2010. Significant adjustments as a result of that preliminary valuation are summarized as followed:

- Inventories—An adjustment of $1,721 was recorded to adjust inventory to fair value. Finished goods were valued at estimated selling prices less the sum of costs of disposal and a reasonable profit allowance for the selling effort.
- Deferred tax liabilities, net—An adjustment of $43,086 was recorded to adjust deferred taxes for the preliminary fair value allocations.
- Property, plant and equipment, net—An adjustment of $(455) was recorded to adjust the net book value of property, plant and equipment to fair value giving consideration to their highest and best use. Key assumptions used in the valuation of the Company's property, plant and equipment were based on the cost approach.
- Certain indefinite-lived intangible assets were valued using a relief from royalty methodology. Customer relationships and certain definite-lived intangible assets were valued using a multi-period excess earnings method. Certain intangible assets are subject to sensitive business factors of which only a portion are within control of the Company's management. The total fair value of indefinite and definite lived intangibles was $363,327 as of June 16, 2010. A summary of the significant key inputs were as follows:
  - —The Company valued customer relationships using the income approach, specifically the multi-period excess earnings method. In determining the fair value of the customer relationship, the multi-period excess earnings approach values the intangible asset at the present value of the incremental after-tax cash flows attributable only to the customer relationship after deducting contributory asset charges. The incremental after-tax cash flows attributable to the subject intangible asset are then discounted to their present value. Only expected sales from current customers were used which included an expected growth rate of 3%. The Company assumed a customer retention rate of approximately 93% which was supported by historical retention rates. Income taxes were estimated at 36% and amounts were discounted using a rate of 15.5%. The customer relationships were valued at $38,000 under this approach.
  - —The Company valued trade names and trademarks using the income approach, specifically the relief from royalty method. Under this method, the asset value was determined by estimating the hypothetical royalties that would have to be paid if the trade name was not owned. Royalty rates were selected based on consideration of several factors, including prior transactions of Russell Hobbs related trademarks and trade names, other similar trademark licensing and transaction agreements and the relative profitability and perceived contribution of the trade-

marks and trade names. Royalty rates used in the determination of the fair values of trade names and trademarks ranged from 2.0% to 5.5% of expected net sales related to the respective trade names and trademarks. The Company anticipates using the majority of the trade names and trademarks for an indefinite period as demonstrated by the sustained use of each subjected trademark. In estimating the fair value of the trademarks and trade names, Net sales for significant trade names and trademarks were estimated to grow at a rate of 1%–14% annually with a terminal year growth rate of 3%. Income taxes were estimated at a range of 30%–38% and amounts were discounted using rates between 15.5%–16.5%. Trade name and trademarks were valued at $170,930 under this approach.

- —The Company valued a trade name license agreement using the income approach, specifically the multi-period excess earnings method. In determining the fair value of the trade name license agreement, the multi-period excess earnings approach values the intangible asset at the present value of the incremental after-tax cash flows attributable only to the trade name license agreement after deducting contributory asset charges. The incremental after-tax cash flows attributable to the subject intangible asset are then discounted to their present value. In estimating the fair value of the trade name license agreement net sales were estimated to grow at a rate of (3)%–1% annually. The Company assumed a twelve year useful life of the trade name license agreement. Income taxes were estimated at 37% and amounts were discounted using a rate of 15.5%. The trade name license agreement was valued at $149,200 under this approach.

- —The Company valued technology using the income approach, specifically the relief from royalty method. Under this method, the asset value was determined by estimating the hypothetical royalties that would have to be paid if the technology was not owned. Royalty rates were selected based on consideration of several factors including prior transactions of Russell Hobbs related licensing agreements and the importance of the technology and profit levels, among other considerations. Royalty rates used in the determination of the fair values of technologies were 2% of expected net sales related to the respective technology. The Company anticipates using these technologies through the legal life of the underlying patent and therefore the expected life of these technologies was equal to the remaining legal life of the underlying patents ranging from 9 to 11 years. In estimating the fair value of the technologies, net sales were estimated to grow at a rate of 3%–12% annually. Income taxes were estimated at 37% and amounts were discounted using the rate of 15.5%. The technology assets were valued at $4,100 under this approach.

Supplemental Pro Forma Information (unaudited)

The following reflects the Company's pro forma results had the results of Russell Hobbs been included for all periods beginning after September 30, 2007.

	Successor Company		Predecessor Company	
	2010	Period From August 31, 2009 Through September 30, 2009	Period From October 1, 2008 Through August 30, 2009	2008
Net Sales:				
Reported Net sales	$2,567,011	$219,888	$2,010,648	$2,426,571
Russell Hobbs adjustment	543,952	64,641	711,046	909,426
Pro forma Net sales	$3,110,963	$284,529	$2,721,694	$3,335,997
(Loss) income from continuing operations:				
Reported (Loss) income from continuing operations	$ (187,020)	$ (71,193)	$1,100,743	$ (905,358)
Russell Hobbs adjustment	(5,504)	(2,284)	(25,121)	(43,480)
Pro forma Loss from continuing operations	$ (192,524)	$ (73,477)	$1,075,622	$ (948,838)

(A) The Company has not assumed the exercise of common stock equivalents as the impact would be antidilutive.

Major Stockholder Transactions

1.173

PILGRIM'S PRIDE CORPORATION (DEC)

NOTES TO CONSOLIDATED FINANCIAL STATEMENTS

16. Related Party Transactions

Upon the Effective Date, JBS USA became the holder of the majority of the common stock of the Company (the "Current Major Stockholder"). Prior to the Effective Date, Lonnie A. "Bo" Pilgrim and certain entities related to Mr. Pilgrim collectively owned a majority of the voting power of the common stock of the Company (the "Former Major Stockholder"). Mr. Pilgrim was also the Senior Chairman of the Company prior to the Effective Date. Mr. Pilgrim ceased being Senior Chairman on the Effective Date; however, he remains a director of the Company.

Transactions with the Current Major Stockholder and the Former Major Stockholder are summarized below:

(In thousands)	2010	Transition Period	2009	2008
Current Major Stockholder:				
Purchases from Current Major Stockholder[a][g]	$93,898	$ —	$ —	$ —
Expenditures paid by Current Major Stockholder on behalf of Pilgrim's Pride Corporation[f][g]	26,818	—	—	—
Sales to Current Major Stockholder[a][g]	5,422	—	—	—
Expenditures paid by Pilgrim's Pride Corporation on behalf of Current Major Stockholder[f][g]	482	—	—	—
Former Major Stockholder:				
Sale of airplane hangars and undeveloped land to Former Major Stockholder[e]	1,450	—	—	—
Purchase of commercial egg property from Former Major Stockholder[c]	12,000	—	—	—
Loan guaranty fees paid to Former Major Stockholder[b]	8,928	—	1,473	4,904
Contract grower pay paid to Former Major Stockholder	1,249	185	1,037	1,008
Consulting fee paid to Former Major Stockholder[d]	1,497	—	—	—
Board fees paid to Former Major Stockholder	105	—	—	—
Lease payments and operating expenses on air plane	—	—	68	456
Lease payments on commercial egg property paid to Former Major Stockholder	125	188	750	750
Sales to Former Major Stockholder	28	146	686	710

[a] JBS USA did not become the holder of the majority of the common stock of the Company until the Effective Date. Although transactions did occur between the Company and JBS USA during 2009, they were not related party transactions.

[b] Until the Effective Date, Pilgrim Interests, Ltd., an entity related to Lonnie A. "Bo" Pilgrim, guaranteed a portion of the Company's debt obligations. In consideration of such guarantees, the Company has paid Pilgrim Interests, Ltd. a quarterly fee equal to 0.25% of one-half of the average aggregate outstanding balance of such guaranteed debt. Pursuant to the terms of the DIP Credit Agreement, the Company could not pay any loan guarantee fees during the Chapter 11 case without the consent of the lenders party thereto. At December 27, 2009, the Company had accrued loan guaranty fees totaling $8.9 million. The Company paid these fees after emerging from bankruptcy on the Effective Date.

[c] On February 23, 2010, the Company purchased a commercial egg property from the Former Major Stockholder for $12.0 million. Prior to the purchase, the Company leased the commercial egg property including all of the ongoing costs of the operation from the Former Major Stockholder.

[d] In connection with the Plan, the Company and Lonnie A. "Bo" Pilgrim entered into a consulting agreement, which became effective on the Effective Date. The terms of the consulting agreement include, among other things, that (i) Mr. Pilgrim will provide services to the Company that are comparable in the aggregate with the services provided by him to the Company prior to the Effective Date, (ii) Mr. Pilgrim would be appointed to the Board of Directors of the Company and during the term of the consulting agreement will be nominated for subsequent terms on the board, (iii) Mr. Pilgrim will be compensated for services rendered to the Company at a rate of $1.5 million a year for a term of five years, (iv) Mr. Pilgrim will be subject to customary non-solicitation and non-competition provisions and (v) Mr. Pilgrim and his spouse will be provided with medical benefits (or will be compensated for medical coverage) that are comparable in the aggregate to the medical benefits afforded to employees of the Company.

[e] On June 9, 2010, the Company sold two airplane hangars and undeveloped land to the Former Major Stockholder for $1.45 million.

[f] On January 19, 2010, the Company entered into an agreement with JBS USA in order to allocate costs associated with JBS USA's procurement of SAP licenses and maintenance services for its combined companies. Under this agreement, the fees associated with procuring SAP licenses and maintenance services are allocated between the Company and JBS USA in proportion to the percentage of licenses used by each company. The agreement expires on the date of expiration, or earlier termination, of the underlying SAP license agreement. On May 5, 2010, the Company also entered into an agreement with JBS USA in order to allocate the costs of supporting the business operations by one consolidated corporate team, which have historically been supported by their respective corporate teams. Expenditures paid by the Current Major Stockholder on behalf of the Company will be reimbursed by the Company and expenditures paid by the Company on behalf of the Current Major Stockholder will be reimbursed by the Current Major Stockholder. This agreement expires on May 5, 2015.

[g] As of December 26, 2010, the outstanding payable to JBS USA was $7.2 million and the outstanding receivable from JBS USA was $0.5 million. As of December 26, 2010, approximately $3.9 million of goods from JBS USA were in transit and not reflected on our Consolidated Balance Sheet.

The Company is party to grower contracts involving farms owned by the Former Major Stockholder that provide for the placement of Company-owned flocks on these farms during the grow-out phase of production. These contracts are on terms substantially the same as contracts executed by the Company with unaffiliated parties and can be terminated by either party upon completion of the grow-out phase for each flock. The aggregate amounts paid by the Company to the Former Major Stockholder under these grower contracts were less than $1.3 million in each of the periods 2010, the Transition Period, 2009 and 2008.

The Company leased an airplane from its Former Major Stockholder under an operating lease agreement. The terms of the lease agreement required monthly payments of $33,000 plus operating expenses. The lease was terminated on November 18, 2008. Lease expense was $66,000 and $396,000 in 2009 and 2008, respectively. Operating expenses were $1,500 and $60,000 in 2009 and 2008, respectively.

The Company maintains depository accounts with a financial institution in which the Company's Former Major Stockholder is also a major stockholder. Fees paid to this bank in 2010, the Transition Period, 2009 and 2008 were insignificant.

The Company had account balances at this financial institution of approximately $4.2 million and $2.3 million at December 26, 2010 and September 26, 2009, respectively.

The Former Major Stockholder has deposited $0.3 million with the Company as an advance on miscellaneous expenditures.

A son of the Former Major Stockholder sold commodity feed products and a limited amount of other services to the Company totaling approximately $0.4 million in each of the years ended 2010, 2009 and 2008. We made no purchases during the Transition Period. He also leases an insignificant amount of land from the Company.

Transaction Between Reporting Entity and Officer/Director

1.174

TIFFANY & CO. (JAN)

NOTES TO CONSOLIDATED FINANCIAL STATEMENTS

M. Related Parties

The Company's Chairman of the Board and Chief Executive Officer is a member of the Board of Directors of The Bank of New York Mellon, which serves as the Company's lead bank for its Credit Facility, provides other general banking services and serves as the trustee and an investment manager for the Company's pension plan. BNY Mellon Shareowner Services serves as the Company's transfer agent and registrar. Fees paid to the bank for services rendered, interest on debt and premiums on derivative contracts amounted to $2,090,000, $1,666,000 and $1,534,000 in 2009, 2008 and 2007.

Transaction Between Reporting Entity and Variable Interest Entity

1.175

VIACOM INC. (SEP)

NOTES TO CONSOLIDATED FINANCIAL STATEMENTS

Note 3. Acquisitions & Investments (in part)

Variable Interest Entities

In the normal course of business, the Company enters into joint ventures or makes investments with business partners that support its underlying business strategy and provide it the ability to enter new markets to expand the reach of its brands, develop new programming and/or distribute its existing content. In certain instances, an entity in which the Company makes an investment may qualify as a VIE. In determining whether the Company is the primary beneficiary of a VIE, the Company assesses whether it has the power to direct matters that most significantly impact the activities of the VIE and has the obligation to absorb losses or the right to receive benefits from the VIE that could potentially be significant to the VIE.

Unconsolidated Variable Interest Entities

The Company has a number of unconsolidated investments in which it holds a non-controlling ownership interest, including but not limited to Rhapsody, EPIX and Viacom 18. These arrangements are typically entered into with strategic partners and generally contain the following governance provisions: (i) the funding of the venture is provided by the equity holders pro rata based on their ownership interest; (ii) the investments are initially funded to meet short-term working capital requirements with funding commitments provided by the partners to fund future operating needs; (iii) commercial arrangements between the Company, the venture and other related parties are negotiated between the parties and are believed to be at market rates; and (iv) voting rights are consistent with the equity holders' rights and obligations to share in the profits and losses of the variable interest entity. In connection with these investment arrangements the Company does not have the power to direct matters that most significantly impact the activities of the VIE and therefore does not qualify as the primary beneficiary. Accordingly, these investments are accounted for under the equity method of accounting and are included in *Other assets-noncurrent* in the Consolidated Balance Sheets. In these arrangements, the Company's risk of loss is typically limited to its carrying value and future funding commitments.

At September 30, 2010 and December 31, 2009, the Company's aggregate investment carrying value in unconsolidated VIEs was $98 million and $144 million, respectively. The impact of the Company's unconsolidated VIEs on its Consolidated Financial Statements, including related party transactions, is further described in Note 13.

Consolidated Variable Interest Entities

In April 2008, MTV Networks' Hispanic-oriented cable network MTV Tr3s acquired an interest in a television broadcaster to expand its reach to Hispanic audiences in the Los Angeles and other southwest markets where the target company held broadcast licenses. The Company acquired a non-voting equity interest in the broadcaster of approximately 32% and has certain rights and obligations related to its investment, including the guarantee of third-party bank debt. The Company has determined that it is the primary beneficiary as it has the power to direct certain matters that significantly impact the activities of the VIE and the obligation to absorb losses that could be potentially significant to the VIE through its equity interest and its guarantee of third-party bank debt. Accordingly, the Company consolidates the entity. As of September 30, 2010 and December 31, 2009, there are $37 million and $43 million of assets and $84 million and $85 million of liabilities, respectively, in respect of this entity included within the Company's Consolidated Balance Sheets. The operating results of this consolidated VIE in 2009 included a $60 million non-cash impairment charge related to certain broadcast licenses held by the entity. The impact to *Net earnings attributable to Viacom* in 2009 was a reduction of $19 million, with the remaining $41 million allocated to the noncontrolling interest. Except for the 2009 impairment charge, the revenues, expenses and operating income for the nine months ended September 30, 2010 and the years ended December 31, 2009 and 2008 were not significant to the Company.

Note 13. Related Party Transactions (in part)

Other Related Party Transactions

In the ordinary course of business, the Company is involved in related party transactions with equity investees, principally related to investments in unconsolidated VIEs as more fully described in Note 3. These related party transactions primarily relate to the provision of advertising services, licensing of film and programming content, distribution of films and provision of certain administrative support services, for which the impact on the Company's Consolidated Financial Statements is as follows:

Other Related Party Transactions	Nine Months Ended September 30, 2010	Year Ended December 31	
		2009	2008
(In millions)			
Consolidated Statements of Earnings			
Revenues	$168	$375	$408
Operating expenses	$ 53	$207	$249
Selling, general, and administrative	$ (24)	$ —	$ —
	September 30, 2010	December 31, 2009	
Consolidated Balance Sheets			
Accounts receivable	$ 88	$102	
Other assets	9	10	
Total due from other related parties	$ 97	$112	
Accounts payable	$ 26	$ 39	
Participants' share and residuals, current	—	47	
Other liabilities	29	55	
Debt, current	—	65	
Debt, noncurrent	—	33	
Total due to other related parties	$ 55	$239	

All other related party transactions are not material in the periods presented.

Transactions With Related Parties

1.176

WENDY'S/ARBY'S GROUP, INC. (DEC)

NOTES TO CONSOLIDATED FINANCIAL STATEMENTS

(24) Transactions with Related Parties (in part; in thousands)

The following is a summary of transactions between the Companies and their related parties:

(In thousands)	2010	2009	2008
Strategic Sourcing Group agreement[a]	$ 5,145	$ —	$ —
Wendy's Co-op Agreement[b]	—	15,500	—
Subleases with related parties[c]	(346)	(213)	(227)
Interest income on revolving credit facility[d]	(463)	(4)	—
AFA dues subsidy[e]	2,635	—	—
Advisory fees[g]	2,465	5,368	—
Charitable contributions to the Dave Thomas Foundation for Adoption[o]	—	—	1,000
Charitable contributions to Foundation[p]	500	500	500
(Wendy's/Arby's)			
Advisory fees[f]	$ 1,000	$ —	$ —
Services Agreement[h]	—	3,500	9,500
Sublease income[i]	(1,632)	(1,886)	(1,633)
Executive use of corporate aircraft[j]	(120)	(613)	(3,028)
Sale of helicopter interest[k]	—	—	(1,860)
Equities Account[l]	—	—	38
Withdrawal Agreement[m]	—	(37,401)	—
Liquidation Services Agreement[n]	441	239	—
Distributions to co-investment shareholders[q]	—	(795)	(2,014)

Transactions with Purchasing Cooperatives, Foundation, and AFA

[a] On April 5, 2010, the Wendy's independent purchasing cooperative Quality Supply Chain Co-op ("QSCC") and the Arby's independent purchasing cooperative ("ARCOP"), in consultation with Wendy's/Arby's Restaurants, established Strategic Sourcing Group Co-op, LLC ("SSG"). SSG was formed to manage and operate purchasing programs which combine the purchasing power of both Wendy's and Arby's company-owned and franchised restaurants to create buying efficiencies for certain non-perishable goods, equipment, and services.

   In order to facilitate the orderly transition of this purchasing function for the Companies' North America operations, Wendy's/Arby's Restaurants transferred certain contracts, assets and certain Wendy's/Arby's Restaurants purchasing employees to SSG in the second quarter of 2010. Wendy's/Arby's Restaurants had committed to pay approximately $5,145 of SSG expenses, which were expensed in 2010 and included in "General and administrative," and was to be paid over a 24 month period through March 2012. We made payments of $2,000 in 2010.

   Should a sale of Arby's occur as discussed in Note 1, under the change of control provisions in the agreement that established SSG, the activities of SSG would be wound up. In the wind up process, the assets, personnel and functions of SSG would be transferred to QSCC and ARCOP as such parties and Wendy's/Arby's Restaurants agree. In contemplation of a possible sale, the parties are in discussion regarding the dissolution of SSG and transferring SSG's assets, personnel and functions to QSCC and ARCOP.

[b] During the 2009 fourth quarter, Wendy's entered into a purchasing co-op relationship agreement (the "Co-op Agreement") to establish QSCC. QSCC manages food and related product purchases and distribution services for the Wendy's system in the United States and Canada. Through QSCC, Wendy's and Wendy's franchisees purchase food, proprietary paper and operating supplies under national contracts with pricing based upon total system volume.

   QSCC's supply chain management facilitates continuity of supply and provides consolidated purchasing efficiencies while monitoring and seeking to minimize possible obsolete inventory throughout the Wendy's North America supply chain. The system's purchasing function for 2009 and prior was performed and paid for by Wendy's. In order to facilitate the orderly transition of the 2010 purchasing function for North America operations, Wendy's transferred certain contracts, assets and certain Wendy's purchasing employees to QSCC in the first quarter of 2010. Pursuant to the terms of the Co-op Agreement, Wendy's was required to pay $15,500 to QSCC over an 18 month period through May 2011 in order to provide funding for start-up costs, operating expenses and cash reserves. The required payments by Wendy's under the Co-op Agreement were expensed in the fourth quarter of 2009 and included in "General and administrative." Wendy's made payments of $15,195 in 2010. In connection with the ongoing operations of QSCC during 2010, QSCC reimbursed Wendy's $913 for amounts Wendy's had paid primarily for payroll-related expenses for certain Canadian QSCC purchasing employees.

[c] ARCOP subleased approximately 4,500 square feet of the corporate headquarters office space from Arby's in 2010, and 2,680 square feet in 2009 and 2008. The Arby's Foundation, Inc. (the "Foundation"), a not-for-profit charitable foundation in which Arby's has non-controlling representation on the board of directors, subleased approximately 3,800 square feet of the corporate headquarters office space from Arby's in 2010, 2009 and 2008. Effective January 4, 2010, QSCC subleased approximately 9,333 square feet of office space from Wendy's. Effective April 5, 2010, the SSG leased 2,300 square feet of office space from Arby's. The Companies received $104, $106, and $111, of sublease income from ARCOP in 2010, 2009, and 2008, respectively, $105, $107 and $116 of sublease income from Foundation in 2010, 2009, and 2008, respectively, $113 of sublease income from QSCC in 2010, and $24 of sublease income from SSG in 2010.

(continued)

(continued)

(d) In December 2009, and as amended in February and August 2010, AFA entered into a revolving loan agreement with Arby's. The terms of this agreement allow AFA to have revolving loans of up to $14,000 outstanding with an expiration date of March 2012 and bearing interest at 7.5% per annum. In February 2011, the maximum principal amount of revolving loans was reduced to $11,000. As of January 2, 2011 and January 3, 2010, the outstanding revolving loan balance was $4,458 and $5,089, respectively. Arby's received interest income of $463 and $4 in 2010 and 2009, respectively, which is included in "Other income (expense)."

(e) Beginning in January 2010 and through March 2010, Arby's and most domestic Arby's franchisees paid 1.2% of sales as member dues to AFA. Beginning in April 2010 and for the remainder of 2010, the AFA Board approved a dues increase based on a tiered rate structure for the payment of the advertising and marketing service fee ranging between 1.4% and 3.6% of sales. As a result, the average Arby's advertising and marketing service fee percentage from April 2010 to the end of the 2010 fiscal year was approximately 2.3%. In addition, Arby's partially subsidized the top two rate tiers in 2010 thereby decreasing franchisees' effective advertising and marketing service fee percentages. This subsidy required payments by Arby's of $2,635 to AFA in 2010.

Transactions with the Management Company

(f) Wendy's/Arby's and the Management Company entered into a new services agreement (the "New Services Agreement"), which commenced on July 1, 2009 and will continue until June 30, 2011, unless sooner terminated. Under the New Services Agreement, the Management Company assists us with strategic merger and acquisition consultation, corporate finance and investment banking services and related legal matters. Pursuant to the terms of this agreement, Wendy's/Arby's is paying the Management Company a service fee of $250 per quarter, payable in advance commencing July 1, 2009. In addition, in the event the Management Company provides substantial assistance to us in connection with a merger or acquisition, corporate finance and/or similar transaction that is consummated at any time during the period commencing on the date the New Services Agreement was executed and ending six months following the expiration of its term, Wendy's/Arby's will negotiate a success fee to be paid to the Management Company which is reasonable and customary for such transactions. In addition, Wendy's/Arby's incurred service fees of $1,000 in 2010, which are included in "General and administrative."

(g) The Companies paid approximately $2,465 and $5,368 in 2010 and 2009, respectively, in fees for corporate finance advisory services under the New Services Agreement in connection with the negotiation and execution of the Credit Agreement in 2010 and the issuance of the Senior Notes in 2009.

(h) In connection with its 2007 restructuring, Wendy's/Arby's entered into an agreement with the Management Company for the provision of services under a two-year transition services agreement (the "Services Agreement"), effective June 30, 2007, pursuant to which the Management Company provided Wendy's/Arby's with a range of professional and strategic services. Under the Services Agreement, which expired on June 30, 2009 and was superseded by the New Services Agreement, Wendy's/Arby's paid the Management Company $3,000 per quarter for the first year of services and $1,750 per quarter for the second year of services. Wendy's/Arby's incurred $3,500 and $9,500 of such service fees for 2009 and 2008, respectively, which are included in "General and administrative."

(i) In July 2008 and July 2007, Wendy's/Arby's entered into agreements under which the Management Company is subleasing (the "Subleases") office space on two of the floors of the Company's former New York headquarters. Under the terms of the Subleases, the Management Company paid Wendy's/Arby's approximately $157 and $153 in 2009 and 2008, respectively, per month, which included an amount equal to the rent Wendy's/Arby's pays plus a fixed amount reflecting a portion of the increase in the then fair market value of Wendy's/Arby's leasehold interest, as well as amounts for property taxes and the other costs related to the use of the space. During the second quarter of 2010, Wendy's/Arby's and the Management Company entered into an amendment to the sublease, effective April 1, 2010, pursuant to which the Management Company's early termination right was cancelled in exchange for a reduction in rent. Under the terms of the amended sublease, the sublease is not cancelable prior to the expiration of the prime lease and the Management Company pays rent to Wendy's/Arby's in an amount that covers substantially all of the Company's rent obligations under the prime lease for the subleased space. Wendy's/Arby's recognized $1,632, $1,886, and $1,633 from the Management Company under the Subleases for 2010, 2009, and 2008, respectively, which has been recorded as a reduction of "General and administrative."

(j) In August 2007, Wendy's/Arby's entered into time share agreements under which the Chairman and then Chief Executive Officer and the Vice Chairman and then President and Chief Operating Officer of Wendy's/Arby's (the "Former Executives") and the Management Company used two Wendy's/Arby's corporate aircraft in exchange for payment of certain incremental flight and related costs of such aircraft. Those time share agreements expired during the second quarter of 2009 and, in the third quarter of 2009, one of the aircraft was sold to an unrelated third party. Such reimbursements for 2009 and 2008 amounted to $553 and $3,028 and have been recognized as a reduction of "General and administrative."

In June 2009, Wendy's/Arby's and TASCO, LLC (an affiliate of the Management Company) ("TASCO") entered into an aircraft lease agreement (the "Aircraft Lease Agreement") for the other aircraft that was previously under the time share agreement mentioned above. The Aircraft Lease Agreement originally provided that Wendy's/Arby's would lease such corporate aircraft to TASCO from July 1, 2009 until June 30, 2010. Under the Aircraft Lease Agreement, TASCO pays $10 per month for such aircraft plus substantially all operating costs of the aircraft including all costs of fuel, inspection, servicing and storage, as well as operational and flight crew costs relating to the operation of the aircraft, and all transit maintenance costs and other maintenance costs required as a result of TASCO's usage of the aircraft. Wendy's/Arby's continues to be responsible for calendar-based maintenance and any extraordinary and unscheduled repairs and/or maintenance for the aircraft, as well as insurance and other costs. The Aircraft Lease Agreement may be terminated by Wendy's/Arby's without penalty in the event it sells the aircraft to a third party, subject to a right of first refusal in favor of the Management Company with respect to such a sale.

On June 24, 2010, Wendy's/Arby's and TASCO renewed the Aircraft Lease Agreement for an additional one year period (expiring June 30, 2011). We received lease income of $120 and $60 in 2010 and 2009, respectively, under this agreement, which is included as an offset to "General and administrative."

(k) The Management Company assumed Wendy's/Arby's 25% fractional interest in a helicopter on October 1, 2008 for $1,860 which is the amount Wendy's/Arby's would have received under the relevant agreement, if it exercised its right to sell the helicopter interest on October 1, 2008, which is equal to the then fair value, less a remarketing fee. The Management Company paid the monthly management fee and all other costs related to the helicopter interest to the owner on behalf of Wendy's/Arby's from July 1, 2007 until October 1, 2008.

(l) In 2005, the Company invested $75,000 in brokerage accounts (the "Equities Account"), which were managed by the Management Company. The Equities Account was invested principally in equity securities, cash equivalents and equity derivatives of a limited number of publicly-traded companies. In addition, the Equities Account sold securities short and invested in market put options in order to lessen the impact of significant market downturns. On September 12, 2008, 251 shares of Wendy's common stock, which were included in the Equities Account, were sold to the Management Company at the closing market value as of the day the Company decided to sell the shares. The sale resulted in a loss of $38.

(continued)

(continued)

(m) On June 10, 2009, Wendy's/Arby's and the Management Company entered into a withdrawal agreement (the "Withdrawal Agreement") which provided that Wendy's/Arby's would be permitted to withdraw all amounts in the Equities Account on an accelerated basis (the "Early Withdrawal") effective no later than June 26, 2009. Prior to the Withdrawal Agreement and as a result of an investment management agreement with the Management Company which was terminated on June 26, 2009, Wendy's/Arby's had not been permitted to withdraw any amounts from the Equities Account until December 31, 2010, although $47,000 was released from the Equities Account in 2008 subject to an obligation to return that amount to the Equities Account by a specified date. In consideration for obtaining such Early Withdrawal right, Wendy's/Arby's agreed to pay the Management Company $5,500 (the "Withdrawal Fee"), was not required to return the $47,000 referred to above and was no longer obligated to pay investment management and incentive fees to the Management Company. The Equities Account investments were liquidated in June 2009 for $37,401 (the "Equities Sale"), of which $31,901 was received by Wendy's/Arby's, net of the Withdrawal Fee, and for which Wendy's/Arby's realized a gain of $2,280 in 2009, which are both included in "Investment income (expense), net."

(n) On June 10, 2009, Wendy's/Arby's and the Management Company entered into a liquidation services agreement (the "Liquidation Services Agreement") pursuant to which the Management Company assists us in the sale, liquidation or other disposition of our cost investments and DFR Notes, (the "Legacy Assets"), which are not related to the Equities Account. As of the date of the Liquidation Services Agreement, the Legacy Assets were valued at $36,600 (the "Target Amount"), of which $5,138 was owned by Wendy's/Arby's Restaurants. The Liquidation Services Agreement, which expires June 30, 2011, required Wendy's/Arby's to pay the Management Company a fee of $900 in two installments in June 2009 and 2010, which is being amortized over the term of the agreement. $441 and $239 were amortized and recorded in "General and administrative" in 2010 and 2009, respectively. In addition, in the event that any or all of the Legacy Assets are sold, liquidated or otherwise disposed of and the aggregate net proceeds to us are in excess of the Target Amount, we would be required to pay the Management Company a success fee equal to 10% of the aggregate net proceeds in excess of the Target Amount. Assuming a current liquidation of all remaining Legacy Assets, the aggregate proceeds ($32,209 as of January 2, 2011 primarily related to the cancellation and repayment of the DFR Notes) would not be expected to be in excess of the Target Amount.

Transactions with Other Related Parties

(o) In 2008, the Companies pledged $1,000 to be paid in equal annual installments over a five year period commencing in 2008 to be donated to the Dave Thomas Foundation for Adoption, a related party. The amount pledged was recorded in "General and administrative" in 2008.

(p) During the 2010, 2009, and 2008, the Companies made charitable contributions of $500 to Foundation, primarily utilizing funds reimbursed to it by one of the beverage companies used by Arby's as provided by their contract. Such payments are included in "General and administrative."

(q) As part of its overall retention efforts, Wendy's/Arby's provided certain of its Former Executives and current and former employees, the opportunity to co-invest with Wendy's/Arby's in certain investments. Wendy's/Arby's and certain of its former management have one remaining co-investment, 280 BT, which is a limited liability holding company principally owned by Wendy's/Arby's and former company management that, among other things, invested in operating companies. During 2009 and 2008, Wendy's/Arby's received distributions of $795 and $2,014, respectively, from the liquidation of certain of the investments owned by 280 BT. The minority portions of these distributions of $156 and $402 in 2009 and 2008, respectively, were further distributed to 280 BT's minority shareholders. No distributions were received in 2010. The ownership percentages as of January 2, 2011 were 80.1%, 11.2% and 8.7% for Wendy's/Arby's, the former officers of Wendy's/Arby's and other investors, respectively.

INFLATIONARY ACCOUNTING

DISCLOSURE

1.177 FASB ASC 255, *Changing Prices*, states that entities are encouraged to disclose supplementary information on the effects of changing prices (inflation). Entities are not discouraged from experimenting with other forms of disclosure.

1.178 However, the Item 303 of the SEC's Regulation S-K requires that registrants discuss in "Management's Discussion and Analysis of Financial Condition and Results of Operations" the effects of inflation and other changes in prices when considered material. The SEC also encourages experimentation with these disclosures in order to provide the most meaningful presentation of the impact of price changes on the registrant's financial statements. Accordingly, many of the survey entities include comments about inflation in MD&A.

PRESENTATION AND DISCLOSURE EXCERPT

Inflationary Accounting

1.179

H.J. HEINZ COMPANY (APR)

NOTES TO CONSOLIDATED FINANCIAL STATEMENTS

Item 7. Management's Discussion and Analysis of Financial Condition and Results of Operations

Venezuela-Foreign Currency and Inflation

Foreign Currency

The local currency in Venezuela is the VEF. A currency control board exists in Venezuela that is responsible for foreign exchange procedures, including approval of requests for exchanges of VEF for U.S. dollars at the official (government established) exchange rate. Our business in Venezuela has historically been successful in obtaining U.S. dollars at the official exchange rate for imports of ingredients, packaging, manufacturing equipment, and other necessary inputs, and for dividend remittances, albeit on a delay. While an unregulated parallel market exists for exchanging VEF for U.S dollars through securities transactions, our Venezuelan subsidiary has no recent history of entering into such exchange transactions.

The Company uses the official exchange rate to translate the financial statements of its Venezuelan subsidiary, since we expect to obtain U.S. dollars at the official rate for future dividend remittances. The official exchange rate in Venezuela had been fixed at 2.15 VEF to 1 U.S. dollar for several years, despite significant inflation. On January 8, 2010, the Venezuelan government announced the devaluation of its currency relative to the U.S. dollar. The official exchange rate for imported goods classified as essential, such as food and medicine, changed from 2.15 to 2.60, while payments for other non-essential goods moved to an exchange rate of 4.30. The majority, if not all, of our imported products in Venezuela are expected to fall into the essential classification and qualify for the 2.60 rate. However, our Venezuelan subsidiary's financial statements are translated using the 4.30 rate, as this is the rate expected to be applicable to dividend repatriations.

During Fiscal 2010, the Company recorded a $62 million currency translation loss as a result of the currency devaluation, which has been reflected as a component of accumulated other comprehensive loss within unrealized translation adjustment. The net asset position of our Venezuelan subsidiary has also been reduced as a result of the devaluation to approximately $81 million at April 28, 2010. While our future operating results in Venezuela will be negatively impacted by the currency devaluation, we plan to take actions to help mitigate these effects. Accordingly, we do not expect the devaluation to have a material impact on our operating results going forward.

Highly Inflationary Economy

An economy is considered highly inflationary under U.S. GAAP if the cumulative inflation rate for a three-year period meets or exceeds 100 percent. Based on the blended National Consumer Price Index, the Venezuelan economy exceeded the three-year cumulative inflation rate of 100 percent during the third quarter of Fiscal 2010. As a result, the financial statements of our Venezuelan subsidiary have been consolidated and reported under highly inflationary accounting rules beginning on January 28, 2010, the first day of our fiscal fourth quarter. Under highly inflationary accounting, the financial statements of our Venezuelan subsidiary are remeasured into the Company's reporting currency (U.S. dollars) and exchange gains and losses from the remeasurement of monetary assets and liabilities are reflected in current earnings, rather than accumulated other comprehensive loss on the balance sheet, until such time as the economy is no longer considered highly inflationary.

The impact of applying highly inflationary accounting for Venezuela on our consolidated financial statements is dependent upon movements in the applicable exchange rates (at this time, the official rate) between the local currency and the U.S. dollar and the amount of monetary assets and liabilities included in our subsidiary's balance sheet. At April 28, 2010, the U.S. dollar value of monetary assets, net of monetary liabilities, which would be subject to an earnings impact from exchange rate movements for our Venezuelan subsidiary under highly inflationary accounting was $42 million.

Section 2: Balance Sheet and Related Disclosures

GENERAL BALANCE SHEET CONSIDERATIONS

PRESENTATION

2.01 Financial Accounting Standards Board (FASB) *Accounting Standards Codification*™ (ASC) describes the benefits of presenting comparative financial statements instead of single-period financial statements and addresses the required disclosures and how the comparative information should be presented. Securities and Exchange Commission (SEC) Regulation S-X, together with Financial Reporting Releases and Staff Accounting Bulletins, prescribe the form and content of, and requirements for, financial statements filed with the SEC. However, those requirements are modified for smaller reporting companies, as defined by SEC Regulation S-K, in Article 8 of Regulation S-X.

2.02 FASB ASC 810, *Consolidation*, and Rule 3A-02 of Regulation S-X state that a presumption exists that consolidated financial statements are more meaningful than separate financial statements and that they are usually necessary for a fair presentation when one of the entities in the consolidated group directly or indirectly has a controlling financial interest in the other entities. Rule 3-01(a) of Regulation S-X requires an entity to present consolidated balance sheets as of the end of each of the two most recent fiscal years, unless the entity has been in existence for less than one year.

2.03 FASB ASC does not require an entity to present a classified balance sheet or mandate any particular ordering of balance sheet accounts. However, FASB ASC 210-10-05-4 states that entities usually present a classified balance sheet to facilitate calculation of working capital. FASB ASC 210-10-05-5 indicates that in the statements of manufacturing, trading, and service entities, assets and liabilities are generally classified and segregated. Financial institutions generally present unclassified balance sheets. The FASB ASC glossary includes definitions of *current assets* and *current liabilities* for when an entity presents a classified balance sheet. FASB ASC 210-10-45 provides additional guidance for determining these classifications.

DISCLOSURE

2.04 FASB ASC sets forth disclosure guidelines regarding capital structure and other balance sheet items. SEC regulations also contain additional requirements for disclosures that registrants should provide outside the financial statements.

2.05 FASB ASC 205-10-50 states that reclassifications or other changes in the manner of, or basis for, presenting corresponding items for two or more periods should be explained. This conforms with the well-recognized principle that any change that affects comparability of financial statements should be disclosed.

2.06

TABLE 2-1: BALANCE SHEET FORMAT AND CLASSIFICATION*

	Number of Entities		
	2010	2009	2008
Balance Sheet Format			
Account form	16	63	62
Report form	481	437	438
Other, described	3	—	—
Total Entities	**500**	**500**	**500**
Balance Sheet Classification			
Classified balance sheet	480	N/C^	N/C^
Unclassified balance sheet	18	N/C^	N/C^
Other, described	2	N/C^	N/C^
Total Entities	**500**	**500**	**500**

* Appearing in the balance sheet or notes to financial statements, or both.

^ N/C = Not compiled. Line item was not included in the table for the year shown.

PRESENTATION AND DISCLOSURE EXCERPTS

Reclassifications

2.07

COSTCO WHOLESALE CORPORATION (AUG)

NOTES TO CONSOLIDATED FINANCIAL STATEMENTS

(Dollars in millions, except share data)

Note 1—Summary of Significant Accounting Policies (in part)

Reclassifications

Certain reclassifications have been made to prior fiscal year amounts or balances to conform to the presentation in the current fiscal year. Additionally, as a result of the application of a new accounting pronouncement for noncontrolling interests in consolidated entities, as discussed below in Recently Adopted Accounting Pronouncements, the Company:

- Reclassified to noncontrolling interests, a component of total equity, $80 at August 31, 2009, which was previously reported as minority interest on our consolidated balance sheet, after the correction of an immaterial error of $6 relating to the noncontrolling interest component of accumulated other comprehensive income. A new subtotal, total Costco stockholders' equity, refers to the equity attributable to stockholders of Costco;

- Reported as separate captions within our consolidated statements of income, net income including noncontrolling interests, net income attributable to noncontrolling interests and net income attributable to Costco;
- Utilized net income including noncontrolling interests, as the starting point on our consolidated statements of cash flows in order to reconcile net income including noncontrolling interests to cash flows from operating activities; and
- Reported separately within our consolidated statements of equity and comprehensive income, distributions and cumulative balances attributable to noncontrolling interests.

These reclassifications did not have a material impact on the Company's previously reported consolidated financial statements.

2.08

BEST BUY CO., INC. (FEB)

NOTES TO CONSOLIDATED FINANCIAL STATEMENTS

($ in millions, except per share amounts or as otherwise noted)

1. Summary of Significant Accounting Policies (in part)

Reclassifications

To maintain consistency and comparability, certain amounts from previously reported consolidated financial statements have been reclassified to conform to the current-year presentation. As a result of our adoption of accounting guidance related to the treatment of noncontrolling interests in consolidated financial statements, as described below in *New Accounting Standards*, we:

- reclassified to noncontrolling interests, a component of shareholders' equity, $513 at February 28, 2009, which was previously reported as minority interests on our consolidated balance sheets;
- reported as separate captions within our consolidated statements of earnings, net earnings including noncontrolling interests, net earnings attributable to noncontrolling interests, and net earnings attributable to Best Buy Co., Inc. of $1,033, $(30) and $1,003, respectively, for the fiscal year ended February 28, 2009, and $1,410, $(3) and $1,407, respectively, for the fiscal year ended March 1, 2008;
- utilized net earnings including noncontrolling interests of $1,033 and $1,410 for the fiscal years ended February 28, 2009, and March 1, 2008, respectively, as the starting point on our consolidated statements of cash flows in order to reconcile net earnings to cash flows from operating activities, rather than beginning with net earnings, which was previously exclusive of noncontrolling interests; and

- reclassified $(146) from acquisition of businesses, net of cash acquired within the investing activities section of our consolidated statements of cash flows to acquisition of noncontrolling interests within the financing activities section for the fiscal year ended February 28, 2009.

These reclassifications had no effect on previously reported consolidated operating income, net earnings attributable to Best Buy Co., Inc., or net cash flows from operating activities. Also, earnings per share continues to be based on net earnings attributable to Best Buy Co., Inc.

CASH AND CASH EQUIVALENTS

PRESENTATION

2.09 Cash is commonly considered to consist of currency and demand deposits. The FASB ASC glossary defines *cash equivalents* as short-term, highly liquid investments that are both readily convertible into known amounts of cash and so near their maturity that they present an insignificant risk of changes in value because of changes in interest rates. Generally, only investments with original maturities of three months or less qualify under that definition.

DISCLOSURE

2.10 Rule 5-02.1 of Regulation S-X states that separate disclosure should be made of the cash and cash items that are restricted regarding withdrawal or usage. The provisions of any restrictions should be described in a note to the financial statements. Restrictions may include legally restricted deposits held as compensating balances against short-term borrowing arrangements, contracts entered into with others, or company statements of intention with regard to particular deposits; however, time deposits and short-term certificates of deposit are not generally included in legally restricted deposits. Compensating balance arrangements that do not legally restrict the use of cash should be described in the notes to the financial statements; the amount involved, if determinable, for the most recent audited balance sheet and any subsequent unaudited balance sheet should be disclosed. Compensating balances maintained under an agreement to assure future credit availability should be disclosed, along with the amount and terms of such agreement.

PRESENTATION AND DISCLOSURE EXCERPTS

Cash and Cash Equivalents

2.11

ORACLE CORPORATION (MAY)

CONSOLIDATED BALANCE SHEETS (in part)

As of May 31, 2010 and 2009

	May 31	
(In millions, except per share data)	2010	2009
Assets		
Current assets:		
Cash and cash equivalents	$ 9,914	$ 8,995
Marketable securities	8,555	3,629
Trade receivables, net of allowances for doubtful accounts of $305 and $270 as of May 31, 2010 and 2009, respectively	5,585	4,430
Inventories	259	—
Deferred tax assets	1,159	661
Prepaid expenses and other current assets	1,532	866
Total current assets	27,004	18,581

NOTES TO CONSOLIDATED FINANCIAL STATEMENTS

3. Cash, Cash Equivalents and Marketable Securities

Cash and cash equivalents primarily consist of deposits held at major banks, money market funds, Tier-1 commercial paper, U.S. Treasury obligations, U.S. government agency and government sponsored enterprise obligations, and other securities with original maturities of 90 days or less. Marketable securities primarily consist of time deposits held at major banks, Tier-1 commercial paper, corporate notes, U.S. Treasury obligations and U.S. government agency and government sponsored enterprise debt obligations and certain other securities.

The amortized principal amounts of our cash, cash equivalents and marketable securities approximated their fair values at May 31, 2010 and 2009. We use the specific identification method to determine any realized gains or losses from the sale of our marketable securities classified as available-for-sale. Such realized gains and losses were insignificant for fiscal 2010, 2009 and 2008. The following table summarizes the components of our cash equivalents and marketable securities held, substantially all of which were classified as available-for-sale:

	May 31	
(In millions)	2010	2009
Money market funds	$ 2,423	$ 467
U.S. Treasury, U.S. government and U.S. government agency debt securities	3,010	4,078
Commercial paper, corporate debt securities and other	5,634	2,700
Total investments	$11,067	$7,245
Investments classified as cash equivalents	$ 2,512	$3,616
Investments classified as marketable securities	$ 8,555	$3,629

Substantially all of our marketable security investments held as of May 31, 2010 mature within one year. Our investment portfolio is subject to market risk due to changes in interest rates. We place our investments with high credit quality issuers as described above and, by policy, limit the amount of credit exposure to any one issuer. As stated in our investment policy, we are averse to principal loss and seek to preserve our invested funds by limiting default risk, market risk and reinvestment risk.

2.12

APPLIED MATERIALS, INC. (OCT)

CONSOLIDATED BALANCE SHEETS (in part)

(In thousands, except per share amounts)	October 31, 2010	October 25, 2009
Assets		
Current assets:		
Cash and cash equivalents (Note 3)	$1,857,664	$1,576,381
Short-term investments (Note 3)	726,918	638,349
Accounts receivable, net (Note 6)	1,831,006	1,041,495
Inventories (Note 7)	1,547,378	1,627,457
Deferred income taxes, net (Note 15)	512,944	356,336
Income taxes receivable (Note 15)	857	184,760
Other current assets	288,548	264,169
Total current assets	6,765,315	5,688,947

NOTES TO CONSOLIDATED FINANCIAL STATEMENTS

Note 3. Cash, Cash Equivalents and Investments

Summary of Cash, Cash Equivalents and Investments
The following tables summarize Applied's cash, cash equivalents and investments by security type:

(In thousands)	October 31, 2010			
	Cost	Gross Unrealized Gains	Gross Unrealized Losses	Estimated Fair Value
Cash	$ 700,467	$ —	$ —	$ 700,467
Cash equivalents:				
Money market funds	1,138,770	—	—	1,138,770
Obligations of states and political subdivisions	18,427	—	—	18,427
Total cash equivalents	1,157,197	—	—	1,157,197
Total cash and cash equivalents	$1,857,664	$ —	$ —	$1,857,664
Short-term and long-term investments:				
U.S. Treasury and agency securities	$ 664,573	$ 8,697	$ 41	$ 673,229
Obligations of states and political subdivisions	500,392	5,039	65	505,366
U.S. commercial paper, corporate bonds and medium-term notes	501,686	6,611	40	508,257
Other debt securities*	261,335	2,317	382	263,270
Total fixed income securities	1,927,986	22,664	528	1,950,122
Publicly traded equity securities	9,119	16,067	—	25,186
Equity investments in privately-held companies	58,893	—	—	58,893
Total short-term and long-term investments	$1,995,998	$38,731	$528	$2,034,201
Total cash, cash equivalents and investments	$3,853,662	$38,731	$528	$3,891,865

(In thousands)	October 25, 2009			
	Cost	Gross Unrealized Gains	Gross Unrealized Losses	Estimated Fair Value
Cash	$ 341,127	$ —	$ —	$ 341,127
Cash equivalents:				
Money market funds	1,235,254	—	—	1,235,254
Total cash equivalents	1,235,254	—	—	1,235,254
Total cash and cash equivalents	$1,576,381	$ —	$ —	$1,576,381
Short-term and long-term investments:				
U.S. Treasury and agency securities	$ 653,627	$ 8,013	$170	$ 661,470
Obligations of states and political subdivisions	419,640	7,597	—	427,237
U.S. commercial paper, corporate bonds and medium-term notes	382,550	5,676	281	387,945
Other debt securities(*)	103,193	1,430	391	104,232
Total fixed income securities	1,559,010	22,716	842	1,580,884
Publicly traded equity securities	9,572	9,439	—	19,011
Equity investments in privately-held companies	90,619	—	—	90,619
Total short-term and long-term investments	$1,659,201	$32,155	$842	$1,690,514
Total cash, cash equivalents and investments	$3,235,582	$32,155	$842	$3,266,895

(*) Other debt securities consist primarily of investment grade asset-backed and mortgage-backed securities.

Maturities of Investments

The following table summarizes the contractual maturities of Applied's investments at October 31, 2010:

(In thousands)	Cost	Estimated Fair Value
Due in one year or less	$ 699,095	$ 701,494
Due after one through five years	964,098	981,459
Due after five years	3,457	3,899
No single maturity date(*)	329,348	347,349
	$1,995,998	$2,034,201

(*) Securities with no single maturity date include publicly-traded and privately-held equity securities, and asset-backed and mortgage-backed securities.

Gains and Losses on Investments

Gross realized gains and losses on sales of investments during fiscal 2010, 2009, and 2008 were as follows:

(In thousands)	2010	2009	2008
Gross realized gains	$6,184	$ 8,666	$13,483
Gross realized losses	1,622	10,486	14,690

At October 31, 2010, Applied had a gross unrealized loss of $1 million due to a decrease in the fair value of certain fixed income securities. Applied regularly reviews its investment portfolio to identify and evaluate investments that have indications of possible impairment. Factors considered in determining whether an unrealized loss is temporary, or other-than-temporary and therefore impaired, include: the length of time and extent to which fair value has been lower than the cost basis; the financial condition, credit quality and near-term prospects of the investee; and whether it is more likely than not that Applied will be required to sell the security prior to recovery. Generally, the contractual terms of investments in marketable securities do not permit settlement at prices less than the amortized cost of the investments. Applied has determined that the gross unrealized losses on its marketable securities at October 31, 2010 are temporary in nature and therefore it did not recognize any impairment of its marketable securities for fiscal 2010. During fiscal 2010, Applied determined that certain of its equity investments in privately-held companies were other-than-temporarily impaired and, accordingly, recognized impairment charges in the amounts of $13 million. Impairment charges associated with financial assets for fiscal 2009 totaled $84 million, consisting of the following: equity method investment, $45 million; publicly-traded equity securities, $20 million; equity investments in privately-held companies, $17 million; and marketable securities $2 million. Applied did not recognize any impairment of its financial assets for fiscal 2008.

The following table provides the fair market value of Applied's investments with unrealized losses that are not deemed to be other-than-temporarily impaired as of October 31, 2010.

(In thousands)	In Loss Position for Less Than 12 Months		In Loss Position for 12 Months or Greater		Total	
	Fair Value	Gross Unrealized Losses	Fair Value	Gross Unrealized Losses	Fair Value	Gross Unrealized Losses
U.S. Treasury and agency securities	$ 37,742	$ 31	$7,543	$ 10	$ 45,285	$ 41
Obligations of states and political subdivisions	66,024	65	—	—	66,024	65
U.S. commercial paper, corporate bonds and medium-term notes	54,127	40	—	—	54,127	40
Other debt securities	56,113	264	1,624	118	57,737	382
Total	$214,006	$400	$9,167	$128	$223,173	$528

Unrealized gains and temporary losses on investments classified as available-for-sale are included within accumulated other comprehensive income (loss), net of any related tax effect. Upon realization, those amounts are reclassified from accumulated other comprehensive income (loss) to results of operations.

MARKETABLE SECURITIES

RECOGNITION AND MEASUREMENT

2.13 FASB ASC 320, *Investments—Debt and Equity Securities*, provides guidance on accounting for and reporting investments in equity securities that have readily determinable fair values and all investments in debt securities.

2.14 FASB ASC 320-10-25 requires that at acquisition, entities classify certain debt and equity securities into one of three categories: held to maturity, trading, or available for sale. Investments in debt securities that the entity has the positive intent and ability to hold to maturity are classified as held to maturity and reported at amortized cost in the statement of financial position. Securities that are bought and held principally for the purpose of selling them in the near term (thus held for only a short period of time) are classified as trading securities and reported at fair value. Trading generally reflects active and frequent buying and selling, and trading securities are generally used to generate profit on short-term differences in price. Investments not classified as either held-to-maturity or trading securities are classified as available-for-sale securities and reported at fair value. Unrealized holding gains and losses are included in earnings for trading securities and other comprehensive income for available-for-sale securities.

2.15 FASB ASC 320 indicates when certain investments are considered impaired, whether that impairment is other than temporary, and the measurement and recognition of an impairment loss. FASB ASC 320 also provides guidance on accounting considerations for debt securities subsequent to the recognition of an other-than-temporary impairment and requires certain disclosures about unrealized losses that have not been recognized as other-than-temporary impairments.

PRESENTATION

2.16 Under FASB ASC 320-10-45-2, an entity that presents a classified balance sheet should report individual held-to-maturity securities, individual available-for-sale securities, and individual trading securities as either current or noncurrent.

DISCLOSURE

2.17 FASB ASC 320-10-50 includes detailed disclosure requirements for various marketable securities, including matters such as the nature and risks of the securities; cost, fair value, and transaction information; contractual maturities; impairment of securities; and certain transaction information.

2.18 By definition, investments in debt and equity securities are financial instruments. FASB ASC 825, *Financial Instruments*, requires disclosure of the fair value of those investments for which it is practicable to estimate that value, the methods and assumptions used in estimating the fair value of marketable securities, and a description of any changes in the methods and assumptions during the period. Under FASB ASC 825-10-50-3, the fair value disclosures are optional for certain nonpublic entities with assets less than $100 million.

2.19 FASB ASC 820, *Fair Value Measurement*, defines *fair value*, sets out a framework for measuring fair value, and requires certain disclosures about fair value measurements. FASB ASC 820 clarifies the definition of fair value as an exit price (that is, a price that would be received to sell, versus acquire, an asset or paid to transfer a liability). FASB ASC 820 emphasizes that fair value is a market-based measurement. It establishes a fair value hierarchy that distinguishes between assumptions developed based on market data obtained from independent external sources and the reporting entity's own assumptions. Further, FASB ASC 820 specifies that fair value measurement should consider adjustment for risk, such as the risk inherent in a valuation technique or its inputs. For assets measured at fair value, whether on a recurring or nonrecurring basis, FASB ASC 820 specifies the required disclosures concerning the inputs used to measure fair value.

2.20 FASB Accounting Standards Update (ASU) No. 2010-06, *Fair Value Measurements and Disclosures (Topic 820): Improving Disclosures about Fair Value Measurements*, requires more robust disclosures about different classes of assets and liabilities measured at fair value; the valuation techniques and inputs used; the activity in level 3 fair value measurements; and the transfers between levels 1, 2, and 3. FASB ASU No. 2010-06 is effective for fiscal years beginning after December 15, 2009, except for disclosures about certain level 3 activity. Those disclosures are effective for fiscal years beginning after December 15, 2010.

2.21 FASB ASC 825 permits entities to choose to measure many financial instruments and certain other items at fair value that are not currently required to be measured at fair value. Further, under FASB ASC 825, a business entity shall report unrealized gains and losses on eligible items for which the fair value option has been elected in earnings at each subsequent reporting date. The irrevocable election of the fair value option is made on an instrument-by-instrument basis and applied to the entire instrument, not just a portion of it. FASB ASC 825 also establishes presentation and disclosure requirements designed to facilitate comparison between entities that choose different measurement attributes for similar types of assets and liabilities. The required disclosures are optional for certain nonpublic entities.

2.22

TABLE 2-2: MARKETABLE SECURITIES—FAIR VALUE INPUTS

Table 2-2 lists the level of input for the fair value of marketable securities.

	Number of Entities		
	2010	2009	2008
Available for Sale Securities			
No available for sale securities............	245	N/C*	N/C*
Debt securities: fair value level 1 inputs.................................	109	N/C*	N/C*
Debt securities: fair value level 2 inputs.................................	107	N/C*	N/C*
Debt securities: fair value level 3 inputs.................................	39	N/C*	N/C*
Debt securities: other, described........	2	N/C*	N/C*
Equity securities: fair value level 1 inputs.................................	155	N/C*	N/C*
Equity securities: fair value level 2 inputs.................................	67	N/C*	N/C*
Equity securities: fair value level 3 inputs.................................	19	N/C*	N/C*
Equity securities: other, described.......	2	N/C*	N/C*
Held to Maturity Securities			
No held to maturity securities.............	461	N/C*	N/C*
Debt securities: amortized cost...........	9	N/C*	N/C*
Debt securities: fair value level 1 inputs.................................	12	N/C*	N/C*
Debt securities: fair value level 2 inputs.................................	6	N/C*	N/C*
Debt securities: fair value level 3 inputs.................................	2	N/C*	N/C*
Debt securities: other, described........	1	N/C*	N/C*
Trading Securities			
No trading securities..........................	448	N/C*	N/C*
Debt securities: fair value level 1 inputs.................................	10	N/C*	N/C*
Debt securities: fair value level 2 inputs.................................	9	N/C*	N/C*
Debt securities: fair value level 3 inputs.................................	2	N/C*	N/C*
Debt securities: other, described........	1	N/C*	N/C*
Equity securities: fair value level 1 inputs.................................	31	N/C*	N/C*
Equity securities: fair value level 2 inputs.................................	11	N/C*	N/C*
Equity securities: fair value level 3 inputs.................................	2	N/C*	N/C*
Equity securities: other, described.......	1	N/C*	N/C*

* N/C = Not compiled. Line item was not included in the table for the year shown.

PRESENTATION AND DISCLOSURE EXCERPTS

Marketable Securities

2.23

STARBUCKS CORPORATION (SEP)

CONSOLIDATED BALANCE SHEETS (in part)

(In millions, except per share data)	Oct 3, 2010	Sep 27, 2009
Assets		
Current assets:		
Cash and cash equivalents	$1,164.0	$ 599.8
Short-term investments— available-for-sale securities	236.5	21.5
Short-term investments—trading securities	49.2	44.8
Accounts receivable, net	302.7	271.0
Inventories	543.3	664.9
Prepaid expenses and other current assets	156.5	147.2
Deferred income taxes, net	304.2	286.6
Total current assets	2,756.4	2,035.8
Long-term investments— available-for-sale securities	191.8	71.2
Equity and cost investments	341.5	352.3
Property, plant and equipment, net	2,416.5	2,536.4
Other assets	346.5	253.8
Other intangible assets	70.8	68.2
Goodwill	262.4	259.1
Total assets	$6,385.9	$5,576.8

NOTES TO CONSOLIDATED FINANCIAL STATEMENTS

Note 1. Summary of Significant Accounting Policies (in part)

Short-Term and Long-Term Investments

Our short-term and long-term investments consist primarily of investment grade debt securities, all of which are classified as available-for-sale. We have investments in auction rate securities within the long-term investment portfolio. Our trading portfolio is primarily comprised of equity mutual funds and equity exchange-traded funds. Trading securities are recorded at fair value with unrealized holding gains and losses included in net earnings. Available-for-sale securities are recorded at fair value, and unrealized holding gains and losses are recorded, net of tax, as a component of accumulated other comprehensive income. Available-for-sale securities with remaining maturities of less than one year and those identified by management at time of purchase for funding operations in less than one year are classified as short term, and all other available-for-sale securities are classified as long term. Unrealized losses are charged against net earnings when a decline in fair value is determined to be other than temporary. Management reviews several factors to determine whether a loss is other than temporary, such as the length and extent of the fair value decline, the financial condition and near term prospects of the issuer, and for equity investments, our intent and ability to hold the security for a period of time sufficient to allow for any anticipated recovery in fair value. For debt securities, management also evaluates whether we have the intent to sell or will likely be required to sell before their anticipated recovery, which may be at maturity. Realized gains and losses are accounted for using the specific identification method. Purchases and sales are recorded on a trade date basis.

Fair Value of Financial Instruments and Equity and Cost Investments

The carrying value of cash and cash equivalents approximates fair value because of the short-term maturity of those instruments. The fair value of our investments in marketable debt and equity securities, equity mutual funds and equity exchange-traded funds is based upon the quoted market price on the last business day of the fiscal year. Where an observable quoted market price for a security does not exist,

we estimate fair value using a variety of valuation methodologies, which include observable inputs for comparable instruments and unobservable inputs. The specific methodologies include comparing the security with securities of publicly traded companies in similar lines of business, applying revenue multiples to estimated future operating results and estimating discounted cash flows. The fair value of our long-term debt is estimated based on the quoted market prices for the same or similar issues or on the current rates offered to us for debt of the same remaining maturities.

We measure our equity and cost method investments at fair value on a nonrecurring basis when they are determined to be other-than temporarily impaired. Fair values are determined using available quoted market prices or standard valuation techniques, including discounted cash flows, comparable transactions, and comparable company analyses.

Note 3. Investments (In millions)

	Amortized Cost	Gross Unrealized Holding Gains	Gross Unrealized Holding Losses	Fair Value
October 3, 2010				
Short-Term Investments:				
Available-for-sale securities—Agency obligations	$ 30.0	$0.0	$ 0.0	$ 30.0
Available-for-sale securities—Corporate debt securities	15.0	0.0	0.0	15.0
Available-for-sale securities—State and local government obligations	0.7	0.0	0.0	0.7
Available-for-sale securities—Government treasury securities	190.7	0.1	0.0	190.8
Trading securities	58.8			49.2
Total short-term investments	$295.2	$0.1		$285.7
Long-Term Investments:				
Available-for-sale securities—Agency obligations	$ 27.0	$0.0	$ 0.0	$ 27.0
Available-for-sale securities—Corporate debt securities	121.4	2.1	0.0	123.5
Available-for-sale securities—State and local government obligations	44.8	0.0	(3.5)	41.3
Total long-term investments	$193.2	$2.1	$(3.5)	$191.8
September 27, 2009				
Short-Term Investments:				
Available-for-sale securities—Corporate debt securities	$ 2.5	$0.0	$ 0.0	$ 2.5
Available-for-sale securities—Government treasury securities	19.0	0.0	0.0	19.0
Trading securities	58.5			44.8
Total short-term investments	$ 80.0			$ 66.3
Long-Term Investments:				
Available-for-sale securities—State and local government obligations	$ 57.8	$0.0	$(2.1)	$ 55.7
Available-for-sale securities—Corporate debt securities	14.7	0.8	0.0	15.5
Total long-term investments	$ 72.5	$0.8	$(2.1)	$ 71.2

Available-for-Sale Securities

Proceeds from sales of available-for-sale securities were $1.1 million, $5.0 million and $75.9 million in fiscal years 2010, 2009 and 2008, respectively. For fiscal years 2010, 2009 and 2008, realized gains and losses on sales and maturities were immaterial.

As of October 3, 2010, long-term available-for-sale securities of $191.8 million included $41.3 million invested in auction rate securities ("ARS"). As of September 27, 2009, long-term available-for-sale securities of $71.2 million included $55.7 million invested in ARS. ARS have long-dated maturities but provide liquidity through a Dutch auction process that resets the applicable interest rate at pre-determined calendar intervals. Due to the auction failures that began in 2008,

these securities became illiquid and were classified as long-term investments. The investment principal associated with the failed auctions will not be accessible until:

- Successful auctions resume;
- An active secondary market for these securities develops;
- The issuers replace these securities with another form of financing; or
- Final payments are made according to the contractual maturities of the debt issues which range from 20 to 35 years.

We do not intend to sell the ARS, nor is it likely we will be required to sell the ARS before their anticipated recovery, which may be at maturity. In fiscal 2010, two ARS were fully called at par value of $6.1 million and three ARS were partially called at par value of $6.0 million.

The gross unrealized holding losses on our state and local government obligations as of October 3, 2010 and September 27, 2009 are all related to our ARS investments. Our ARS are collateralized by portfolios of student loans, substantially all of which are guaranteed by the United States Department of Education.

Long-term investments (except for ARS) generally mature within three years.

Trading securities

Trading securities are comprised of marketable equity mutual funds and equity exchange-traded funds that approximate a

portion of the liability under the Management Deferred Compensation Plan ("MDCP"), a defined contribution plan. The corresponding deferred compensation liability of $82.7 million and $68.3 million as of October 3, 2010 and September 27, 2009, respectively, is included in accrued compensation and related costs on the consolidated balance sheets. The changes in net unrealized holding gains/losses in the trading portfolio included in earnings for fiscal years 2010 and 2009 were a net gain of $4.1 million and a net loss of $4.9 million, respectively.

Note 5. Fair Value Measurements (in part)

Fair value accounting guidance defines fair value, establishes a framework for measuring fair value under GAAP and expands disclosures about fair value measurements, for both financial and non-financial assets. It also establishes a fair value hierarchy that prioritizes the inputs used to measure fair value.

Assets and Liabilities Measured at Fair Value on a Recurring Basis (in millions):

		Fair Value Measurements at Reporting Date Using		
	Balance at Oct 3, 2010	Quoted Prices in Active Markets for Identical Assets (Level 1)	Significant Other Observable Inputs (Level 2)	Significant Unobservable Inputs (Level 3)
Assets:				
Trading securities	$ 49.2	$ 49.2	$ 0.0	$ 0.0
Available-for-sale securities	428.3	190.8	196.2	41.3
Derivatives	0.1	0.0	0.1	0.0
Total	$477.6	$240.0	$196.3	$41.3
Liabilities:				
Derivatives	$ 34.7	$ 0.0	$ 34.7	$ 0.0

		Fair Value Measurements at Reporting Date Using		
	Balance at Sept 27, 2009	Quoted Prices in Active Markets for Identical Assets (Level 1)	Significant Other Observable Inputs (Level 2)	Significant Unobservable Inputs (Level 3)
Assets:				
Trading securities	$ 44.8	$44.8	$ 0.0	$ 0.0
Available-for-sale securities	92.7	19.0	18.0	55.7
Derivatives	13.2	0.0	13.2	0.0
Total	$150.7	$63.8	$31.2	$55.7
Liabilities:				
Derivatives	$ 33.2	$ 0.0	$33.2	$ 0.0

Trading securities include equity mutual funds and exchange-traded funds. For these securities, we use quoted prices in active markets for identical assets to determine their fair value, thus they are considered to be Level 1 instruments.

Available-for-sale securities include government treasury securities, corporate and agency bonds and ARS. For government treasury securities, we use quoted prices in active markets for identical assets to determine their fair value, thus they are considered to be Level 1 instruments. We use ob-

servable direct and indirect inputs for corporate and agency bonds, which are considered Level 2 instruments. Level 3 instruments are comprised solely of ARS, all of which are considered to be illiquid due to the auction failures that began in 2008. We value ARS using an internally developed valuation model, using inputs that include interest rate curves, credit and liquidity spreads, and effective maturity.

2.24

PAYCHEX, INC. (MAY)

CONSOLIDATED BALANCE SHEETS (in part)

In thousands, except per share amount

As of May 31	2010	2009
Assets		
Cash and cash equivalents	$ 284,316	$ 472,769
Corporate investments	82,496	19,710
Interest receivable	28,672	27,722
Accounts receivable, net of allowance for doubtful accounts	186,587	177,958
Deferred income taxes	3,799	10,180
Prepaid income taxes	6,653	2,198
Prepaid expenses and other current assets	25,540	27,913
Current assets before funds held for clients	618,063	738,450
Funds held for clients	3,541,054	3,501,376
Total current assets	4,159,117	4,239,826
Long-term corporate investments	290,106	82,234
Property and equipment, net of accumulated depreciation	267,583	274,530
Intangible assets, net of accumulated amortization	63,262	76,641
Goodwill	421,559	433,316
Deferred income taxes	21,080	16,487
Other long-term assets	3,592	4,381
Total assets	$5,226,299	$5,127,415

NOTES TO CONSOLIDATED FINANCIAL STATEMENTS

Note A —Description of Business and Significant Accounting Policies (in part)

Funds held for clients and corporate investments: Marketable securities included in funds held for clients and corporate investments consist primarily of securities classified as available-for-sale and are recorded at fair value obtained from an independent pricing service. The funds held for clients portfolio also includes cash, money market securities, and short-term investments. Unrealized gains and losses, net of applicable income taxes, are reported as comprehensive income in the Consolidated Statements of Stockholders' Equity. Realized gains and losses on the sale of available-for-sale securities are determined by specific identification of the cost basis of each security. On the Consolidated Statements of Income, realized gains and losses from their respective portfolios are included in interest on funds held for clients and investment income, net.

Note D—Funds Held for Clients and Corporate Investments

Funds held for clients and corporate investments are as follows:

(In thousands)	Amortized Cost	Gross Unrealized Gains	Gross Unrealized Losses	Fair Value
		May 31, 2010		
Type of issue:				
Money market securities and other cash equivalents	$1,754,545	$ —	$ —	$1,754,545
Available-for-sale securities:				
General obligation municipal bonds	951,085	33,653	(248)	984,490
Pre-refunded municipal bonds[1]	539,809	19,545	(26)	559,328
Revenue municipal bonds	368,075	13,726	(121)	381,680
Variable rate demand notes[2]	226,280	—	—	226,280
Other equity securities	20	49	—	69
Total available-for-sale securities	2,085,269	66,973	(395)	2,151,847
Other	7,484	15	(235)	7,264
Total funds held for clients and corporate investments	$3,847,298	$66,988	$(630)	$3,913,656

(In thousands)	Amortized Cost	Gross Unrealized Gains	Gross Unrealized Losses	Fair Value
May 31, 2009				
Type of issue:				
Money market securities and other cash equivalents	$1,816,278	$ —	$ —	$1,816,278
Available-for-sale securities:				
General obligation municipal bonds	849,594	32,698	(136)	882,156
Pre-refunded municipal bonds(1)	527,864	21,334	(24)	549,174
Revenue municipal bonds	336,675	12,818	(32)	349,461
Variable rate demand notes	—	—	—	—
Other equity securities	20	42	—	62
Total available-for-sale securities	1,714,153	66,892	(192)	1,780,853
Other	7,477	—	(1,288)	6,189
Total funds held for clients and corporate investments	$3,537,908	$66,892	$(1,480)	$3,603,320

(1) Pre-refunded municipal bonds are secured by an escrow fund of U.S. government obligations.

(2) Beginning in November 2009, the Company began to invest in variable rate demand notes ("VRDNs") for the first time since September 2008.

Included in money market securities and other cash equivalents as of May 31, 2010 and May 31, 2009 are U.S. agency discount notes, government money market funds, and bank demand deposit accounts.

Classification of investments on the Consolidated Balance Sheets is as follows:

(In thousands)	May 31 2010	2009
Funds held for clients	$3,541,054	$3,501,376
Corporate investments	82,496	19,710
Long-term corporate investments	290,106	82,234
Total funds held for clients and corporate investments	$3,913,656	$3,603,320

The Company is exposed to credit risk in connection with these investments through the possible inability of borrowers to meet the terms of their bonds. In addition, the Company is exposed to interest rate risk, as rate volatility will cause fluctuations in the fair value of held investments and in the earnings potential of future investments. The Company follows a conservative investment strategy of optimizing liquidity and protecting principal. The Company invests primarily in high credit quality securities with AAA and AA ratings and short-term securities with A-1/P-1 ratings. It limits the amounts that can be invested in any single issuer, and invests in short- to intermediate-term instruments whose fair value is less sensitive to interest rate changes. All the investments held as of May 31, 2010 are traded in active markets. The Company has not and does not utilize derivative financial instruments to manage interest rate risk.

The Company's available-for-sale securities reflected a net unrealized gain of $66.6 million as of May 31, 2010 compared with a net unrealized gain of $66.7 million as of May 31, 2009. The gross unrealized losses of $0.4 million, included in the net unrealized gain as of May 31, 2010, were comprised of 23 available-for-sale securities, which had a total fair value of $73.6 million. The gross unrealized losses of $0.2 million, included in the net unrealized gain as of May 31, 2009, were comprised of 14 available-for-sale securities with a total fair value of $39.4 million. The securities in an unrealized loss position were as follows as of May 31, 2010 and May 31, 2009:

The securities in an unrealized loss position were as follows:

(In thousands)	Less Than Twelve Months Gross Unrealized Losses	Less Than Twelve Months Fair Value	More Than Twelve Months Gross Unrealized Losses	More Than Twelve Months Fair Value	Total Gross Unrealized Losses	Total Fair Value
May 31, 2010						
Type of issue:						
General obligation municipal bonds	$(248)	$44,025	$—	$—	$(248)	$44,025
Pre-refunded municipal bonds	(26)	4,135	—	—	(26)	4,135
Revenue municipal bonds	(121)	25,469	—	—	(121)	25,469
Total	$(395)	$73,629	$—	$—	$(395)	$73,629

(In thousands)	May 31, 2009					
	Less Than Twelve Months		More Than Twelve Months		Total	
	Gross Unrealized Losses	Fair Value	Gross Unrealized Losses	Fair Value	Gross Unrealized Losses	Fair Value
Type of issue:						
General obligation municipal bonds	$(136)	$28,915	$ —	$ —	$(136)	$28,915
Pre-refunded municipal bonds	(24)	4,490	—	—	(24)	4,490
Revenue municipal bonds	(21)	2,943	(11)	3,010	(32)	5,953
Total	$(181)	$36,348	$(11)	$3,010	$(192)	$39,358

The Company regularly reviews its investment portfolios to determine if any investment is other-than-temporarily impaired due to changes in credit risk or other potential valuation concerns. The Company believes that the investments held as of May 31, 2010 were not other-than-temporarily impaired. While $73.6 million of available-for-sale securities had fair values that were below amortized cost, the Company believes that it is probable that the principal and interest will be collected in accordance with contractual terms, and that the decline in the fair value to $0.4 million below amortized cost was due to changes in interest rates and was not due to increased credit risk or other valuation concerns. All of the securities in an unrealized loss position as of May 31, 2010 and the majority of the securities in an unrealized loss position as of May 31, 2009 held an AA rating or better. The Company intends to hold these investments until the recovery of their amortized cost basis or maturity, and further believes that it is more likely than not that it will not be required to sell these investments prior to that time. The Company's assessment that an investment is not other-than-temporarily impaired could change in the future due to new developments or changes in the Company's strategies or assumptions related to any particular investment.

Realized gains and losses from the sale of available-for-sale securities were as follows:

(In thousands)	Year Ended May 31		
	2010	2009	2008
Gross realized gains	$3,235	$1,269	$7,161
Gross realized losses	(3)	(134)	(711)
Net realized gains	$3,232	$1,135	$6,450

The amortized cost and fair value of available-for-sale securities that had stated maturities as of May 31, 2010 are shown below by contractual maturity. Expected maturities can differ from contractual maturities because borrowers may have the right to prepay obligations without prepayment penalties.

(In thousands)	May 31, 2010	
	Amortized Cost	Fair Value
Maturity date:		
Due in one year or less	$ 320,289	$ 323,966
Due after one year through three years	756,267	783,097
Due after three years through five years	499,530	526,116
Due after five years	509,163	518,599
Total	$2,085,249	$2,151,778

VRDNs are primarily categorized as due after five years in the table above as the contractual maturities on these securities are typically 20 to 30 years. Although these securities are issued as long-term securities, they are priced and traded as short-term instruments because of the liquidity provided through the tender feature.

Note E—Fair Value Measurements

The carrying values of cash and cash equivalents, accounts receivable, net of allowance for doubtful accounts, and accounts payable approximate fair value due to the short maturities of these instruments. Marketable securities included in funds held for clients and corporate investments consist primarily of securities classified as available-for-sale and are recorded at fair value on a recurring basis.

The accounting standards related to fair value measurements include a hierarchy for information and valuations used in measuring fair value that is broken down into three levels based on reliability, as follows:

- Level 1 valuations are based on quoted prices in active markets for identical instruments that the Company has the ability to access.
- Level 2 valuations are based on quoted prices for similar, but not identical, instruments in active markets; quoted prices for identical or similar instruments in markets that are not active; or other than quoted prices observable inputs.
- Level 3 valuations are based on information that is unobservable and significant to the overall fair value measurement.

The Company's financial assets and liabilities measured at fair value on a recurring basis were as follows:

| (In thousands) | May 31, 2010 | | | |
	Carrying Value (Fair Value)	Quoted Prices in Active Markets (Level 1)	Significant Other Observable Inputs (Level 2)	Significant Unobservable Inputs (Level 3)
Assets:				
Available-for-sale securities:				
General obligation municipal bonds	$ 984,490	$ —	$ 984,490	$—
Pre-refunded municipal bonds	559,328	—	559,328	—
Revenue municipal bonds	381,680	—	381,680	—
Variable rate demand notes	226,280	—	226,280	—
Other equity securities	69	69	—	—
Total available-for-sale securities	2,151,847	69	2,151,778	—
Other securities	7,264	7,264	—	—
Liabilities:				
Other long-term liabilities	7,254	7,254	—	—

| (In thousands) | May 31, 2009 | | | |
	Carrying Value (Fair Value)	Quoted Prices in Active Markets (Level 1)	Significant Other Observable Inputs (Level 2)	Significant Unobservable Inputs (Level 3)
Assets:				
Available-for-sale securities:				
General obligation municipal bonds	$ 882,156	$ —	$ 882,156	$—
Pre-refunded municipal bonds	549,174	—	549,174	—
Revenue municipal bonds	349,461	—	349,461	—
Variable rate demand notes	—	—	—	—
Other equity securities	62	62	—	—
Total available-for-sale securities	1,780,853	62	1,780,791	—
Other securities	6,189	6,189	—	—
Liabilities:				
Other long-term liabilities	6,197	6,197	—	—

In determining the fair value of its assets and liabilities, the Company predominately uses the market approach. In determining the fair value of its available-for-sale securities, the Company utilizes the Interactive Data Pricing service. Other securities are comprised of mutual fund investments, which are valued based on quoted market prices. Other long-term liabilities include the liability for the Company's non-qualified and unfunded deferred compensation plans, and are valued based on the quoted market prices for various mutual fund investment choices.

The preceding methods described may produce a fair value calculation that may not be indicative of net realizable value or reflective of future fair values. Furthermore, although the Company believes its valuation methods are appropriate and consistent with other market participants, the use of different methodologies or assumptions to determine the fair value of certain financial instruments could result in a different fair value measurement at the reporting date.

2.25

GENERAL DYNAMICS CORPORATION (DEC)

CONSOLIDATED BALANCE SHEET (in part)

| (Dollars in millions) | December 31 | |
	2009	2010
Assets		
Current assets:		
Cash and equivalents	$ 2,263	$ 2,613
Accounts receivable	3,678	3,848
Contracts in process	4,449	4,873
Inventories	2,126	2,158
Other current assets	733	694
Total current assets	13,249	14,186
Noncurrent assets:		
Property, plant and equipment, net	2,912	2,971
Intangible assets, net	2,098	1,992
Goodwill	12,269	12,649
Other assets	549	747
Total noncurrent assets	17,828	18,359
Total assets	$31,077	$32,545

NOTES TO CONSOLIDATED FINANCIAL STATEMENTS

A. Summary of Significant Accounting Policies (in part)

Cash and Equivalents and Investments in Debt and Equity Securities (in part). We consider securities with a maturity of three months or less to be cash equivalents. We report our investments in available-for-sale securities at fair value. Changes in the fair value of available-for-sale securities are recognized as a component of accumulated other comprehensive income within shareholders' equity on the Consolidated Balance Sheet. We report our held-to-maturity securities at amortized cost. The interest income on these securities is a component of our net interest expense in the Consolidated Statement of Earnings. We had marketable securities and other investments totaling $482 on December 31, 2009, and $325 on December 31, 2010. These investments are included in other current and noncurrent assets on the Consolidated Balance Sheet (see note D). We had no trading securities at the end of either period.

D. Fair Value of Financial Instruments

Our financial instruments include cash and equivalents, marketable securities and other investments; accounts receivable and accounts payable; short- and long-term debt; and derivative financial instruments. We did not have any significant non-financial assets or liabilities measured at fair value on December 31, 2009 or 2010.

Fair value is defined as the price that would be received to sell an asset or paid to transfer a liability in the principal or most advantageous market in an orderly transaction between marketplace participants. Various valuation approaches can be used to determine fair value, each requiring different valuation inputs.

The following hierarchy classifies the inputs used to determine fair value into three levels:

- Level 1—quoted prices in active markets for identical assets or liabilities;
- Level 2—inputs, other than quoted prices, observable by a marketplace participant either directly or indirectly and
- Level 3—unobservable inputs significant to the fair value measurement.

The carrying values of cash and equivalents, accounts receivable and payable, and short-term debt (commercial paper) on the Consolidated Balance Sheet approximate their fair value. The following tables present the fair values of our other financial assets and liabilities on December 31, 2009 and 2010, and the basis for determining their fair values:

Financial Assets (Liabilities)[b]	Carrying Value	Fair Value	Quoted Prices in Active Markets for Identical Assets (Level 1)	Significant Other Observable Inputs (Level 2)[a]
December 31, 2009				
Marketable securities:				
Available-for-sale	$ 24	$ 24	$ 24	$ —
Held-to-maturity	336	336	—	336
Other investments	122	122	122	—
Derivatives	28	28	—	28
Long-term debt, including current portion	(3,864)	(4,079)	—	(4,079)
December 31, 2010				
Marketable securities:				
Available-for-sale	$ 47	$ 47	$ 47	$ —
Held-to-maturity	165	165	—	165
Other investments	113	113	113	—
Derivatives	130	130	—	130
Long-term debt, including current portion	(3,203)	(3,436)	—	(3,436)

[a] Determined under a market approach using valuation models that incorporate observable inputs such as interest rates, bond yields and quoted prices for similar assets and liabilities.
[b] We had no Level 3 financial instruments on December 31, 2009 or 2010.

CURRENT RECEIVABLES

PRESENTATION

2.26 FASB ASC 310, *Receivables*, indicates that loans or trade receivables may be presented on the balance sheet as aggregate amounts. However, major categories of loans or trade receivables should be presented separately either in the balance sheet or notes to the financial statements. Also, any such receivables held for sale should be a separate balance sheet category. Receivables from officers, employees, or affiliated companies should be shown separately and not included under a general heading, such as "Accounts Receivable." Valuation allowance for credit losses or doubtful accounts and any unearned income included in the face amount of receivables should be shown as a deduction from the related receivables.

DISCLOSURE

2.27 FASB ASC 310 states that allowances for doubtful accounts should be deducted from the related receivables and appropriately disclosed. FASB ASC 310-10-50-4 requires, as applicable, any unearned income, unamortized premiums and discounts, and net unamortized deferred fees and costs be disclosed in the financial statements. Under FASB ASC 825, fair value disclosure is not required for trade receivables when the carrying amount of the trade receivable approximates its fair value.

PRESENTATION AND DISCLOSURE EXCERPTS

Receivables from Related Parties

2.28

CONOCOPHILLIPS (DEC)

CONSOLIDATED BALANCE SHEET (in part)

	At December 31	
Millions of Dollars	**2010**	**2009**
Assets		
Cash and cash equivalents	$ 9,454	$ 542
Short-term investments	973	—
Accounts and notes receivable (net of allowance of $32 million in 2010 and $76 million in 2009)	13,787	11,861
Accounts and notes receivable—related parties	2,025	1,354
Investment in LUKOIL	1,083	—
Inventories	5,197	4,940
Prepaid expenses and other current assets	2,141	2,470
Total current assets	$34,660	$21,167

NOTES TO CONSOLIDATED FINANCIAL STATEMENTS

Note 6—Investments, Loans and Long-Term Receivables (in part)

Components of investments, loans and long-term receivables at December 31 were:

Millions of Dollars	**2010**	**2009**
Equity investments[*]	$30,055	$34,280
Loans and advances—related parties	2,180	2,352
Long-term receivables	922	1,009
Other investments	604	453
	$33,761	$38,094

[*] 2009 recast to reflect a change in accounting principle. See Note 2—Changes in Accounting Principles, for more information.

Loans and Long-Term Receivables

As part of our normal ongoing business operations and consistent with industry practice, we enter into numerous agreements with other parties to pursue business opportunities. Included in such activity are loans and long-term receivables to certain affiliated and non-affiliated companies. Loans are recorded when cash is transferred or seller financing is provided to the affiliated or non-affiliated company pursuant to a loan agreement. The loan balance will increase as interest is earned on the outstanding loan balance and will decrease as interest and principal payments are received. Interest is earned at the loan agreement's stated interest rate. Loans and long-term receivables are assessed for impairment when events indicate the loan balance may not be fully recovered.

At December 31, 2010, significant loans to affiliated companies include the following:

- $653 million in loan financing to Freeport LNG Development, L.P. for the construction of an LNG receiving terminal that became operational in June 2008. Freeport began making repayments in 2008 and is required to continue making repayments through full repayment of the loan in 2026. Repayment by Freeport is supported by "process-or-pay" capacity service payments made by us to Freeport under our terminal use agreement.

- $1,118 million of project financing and an additional $96 million of accrued interest to Qatar Liquefied Gas Company Limited (3) (QG3), which is an integrated project to produce and liquefy natural gas from Qatar's North Field. We own a 30 percent interest in QG3, for which we use the equity method of accounting. The other participants in the project are affiliates of Qatar Petroleum (68.5 percent) and Mitsui & Co., Ltd. (1.5 percent). QG3 secured project financing of $4.0 billion in December 2005, consisting of $1.3 billion of loans from export credit agencies (ECA), $1.5 billion from commercial banks, and $1.2 billion from ConocoPhillips. The ConocoPhillips loan facilities have substantially the same terms as the ECA and commercial bank facilities. Prior to project completion certification, all loans, including the ConocoPhillips loan facilities, are guaranteed by the participants based on their respective ownership interests. Accordingly, our maximum exposure to this financing structure is $1.2 billion. Upon completion certification, which is expected in 2011, all project loan facilities, including the ConocoPhillips loan facilities, will become nonrecourse to the project participants. At December 31, 2010, QG3 had approximately $4.0 billion outstanding under all the loan facilities. Bi-annual repayments began in January 2011 and will extend through July 2022.

- $550 million of loan financing to WRB Refining LP to assist it in meeting its operating and capital spending requirements. We have certain creditor rights in case of default or insolvency.

The long-term portion of these loans are included in the "Loans and advances—related parties" line on the consolidated balance sheet, while the short-term portion is in "Accounts and notes receivable—related parties."

At September 30, 2010, the Varandey Terminal Company was no longer considered a related party. Accordingly, the long-term portion of this loan is included in the "Investments and long-term receivables" line of the consolidated balance sheet, while the short-term portion is in "Prepaid expenses and other current assets."

At December 31, 2010, significant long-term receivables and loans to non-affiliated companies included $372 million related to seller financing of U.S. retail marketing assets. In January 2009, we closed on the sale of a large part of our U.S. retail marketing assets which included a five-year note to finance the sale of certain assets. The note is collateralized by the underlying assets related to the sale.

Long-term receivables and the long-term portion of these loans are included in the "Investments and long-term receivables" line on the consolidated balance sheet, while the short-term portion related to non-affiliate loans is in "Accounts and notes receivable."

Finance Receivables

2.29

PITNEY BOWES INC. (DEC)

CONSOLIDATED BALANCE SHEETS (in part)

(In thousands, except per share data)	December 31, 2010	December 31, 2009
Assets		
Current assets:		
Cash and cash equivalents	$ 484,363	$ 412,737
Short-term investments	30,609	14,682
Accounts receivables, gross	824,015	859,633
Allowance for doubtful accounts receivables	(31,880)	(42,781)
Accounts receivables, net	792,135	816,852
Finance receivables	1,370,305	1,417,708
Allowance for credit losses	(48,709)	(46,790)
Finance receivables, net	1,321,596	1,370,918
Inventories	168,967	156,502
Current income taxes	103,542	101,248
Other current assets and prepayments	107,029	98,297
Total current assets	$3,008,241	$2,971,236

NOTES TO CONSOLIDATED FINANCIAL STATEMENTS

(Tabular dollars in thousands, except per share data)

17. Finance Assets

Finance Receivables

Finance receivables are comprised of sales-type lease receivables and unsecured revolving loan receivables. Sales-type leases are generally due in monthly, quarterly or semi-annual installments over periods ranging from three to five years. Loan receivables arise primarily from financing services offered to our customers for postage and related supplies. Loan receivables are generally due each month; however, customers may rollover outstanding balances. The components of sales-type lease and loan receivables at December 31, 2010 and 2009 were as follows:

	U.S.	International	Total
December 31, 2010			
Sales-type lease receivables			
Gross finance receivables	$1,669,963	$ 745,765	$2,415,728
Unguaranteed residual values	217,394	38,331	255,725
Unearned income	(357,970)	(165,513)	(523,483)
Allowance for credit losses	(24,261)	(16,849)	(41,110)
Net investment in sales-type lease receivables	1,505,126	601,734	2,106,860
Loan receivables			
Loan receivables	432,137	55,418	487,555
Allowance for credit losses	(25,552)	(2,768)	(28,320)
Net investment in loan receivables	406,585	52,650	459,235
Net investment in finance receivables	$1,911,711	$ 654,384	$2,566,095
December 31, 2009			
Sales-type lease receivables			
Gross finance receivables	$1,836,899	$ 774,971	$2,611,870
Unguaranteed residual values	245,086	37,122	282,208
Unearned income	(423,290)	(178,141)	(601,431)
Allowance for credit losses	(26,629)	(17,453)	(44,082)
Net investment in sales-type lease receivables	1,632,066	616,499	2,248,565
Loan receivables			
Loan receivables	456,308	49,563	505,871
Allowance for credit losses	(25,889)	(2,187)	(28,076)
Net investment in loan receivables	430,419	47,376	477,795
Net investment in finance receivables	$2,062,485	$ 663,875	$2,726,360

Maturities of gross sales-type lease and loan receivables at December 31, 2010 were as follows:

	Sales-Type Lease Receivables			Loan Receivables		
	U.S.	International	Total	U.S.	International	Total
2011	$ 723,567	$233,509	$ 957,076	$432,137	$55,418	$487,555
2012	461,222	191,822	653,044	—	—	—
2013	291,280	156,570	447,850	—	—	—
2014	147,509	118,566	266,075	—	—	—
2015	41,614	40,649	82,263	—	—	—
Thereafter	4,771	4,649	9,420	—	—	—
Total	$1,669,963	$745,765	$2,415,728	$432,137	$55,418	$487,555

Activity in the allowance for credit losses for sales-type lease and loan receivables for each of the three years ended December 31, 2010, 2009 and 2008 is as follows:

	Allowance for Credit Losses				
	Sales-Type Lease Receivables		Loan Receivables		
	U.S.	International	U.S.	International	Total
Balance January 1, 2008	$ 31,173	$ 21,384	$ 23,110	$ 2,704	$ 78,371
Amounts charged to expense	10,015	6,592	32,117	3,012	51,736
Accounts written off	(14,481)	(11,269)	(29,782)	(2,785)	(58,317)
Balance December 31, 2008	26,707	16,707	25,445	2,931	71,790
Amounts charged to expense	15,304	12,437	31,894	2,120	61,755
Accounts written off	(15,382)	(11,691)	(31,450)	(2,864)	(61,387)
Balance December 31, 2009	26,629	17,453	25,889	2,187	72,158
Amounts charged to expense	12,076	7,854	19,360	2,710	42,000
Accounts written off	(14,444)	(8,458)	(19,697)	(2,129)	(44,728)
Balance December 31, 2010	$ 24,261	$ 16,849	$ 25,552	$ 2,768	$ 69,430

The aging of sales-type lease and loan receivables at December 31, 2010 and 2009 was as follows:

	Sales-Type Lease Receivables		Loan Receivables		
	U.S.	International	U.S.	International	Total
December 31, 2010					
< 31 days past due	$1,575,968	$703,146	$409,583	$52,848	$2,741,545
> 30 days and < 61 days	40,129	15,123	11,586	1,644	68,482
> 60 days and < 91 days	27,052	7,071	4,517	519	39,159
> 90 days and < 121 days	8,109	4,530	2,650	254	15,543
> 120 days	18,705	15,895	3,801	153	38,554
Total	$1,669,963	$745,765	$432,137	$55,418	$2,903,283
Past due amounts > 90 days					
Still accruing interest	$ 8,109	$ 4,530	$ —	$ —	$ 12,639
Not accruing interest	18,705	15,895	6,451	407	41,458
Total	$ 26,814	$ 20,425	$ 6,451	$ 407	$ 54,097
December 31, 2009					
< 31 days past due	$1,730,355	$725,643	$428,769	$47,009	$2,931,776
> 30 days and < 61 days	45,946	16,006	13,783	1,254	76,989
> 60 days and < 91 days	28,872	7,547	5,207	495	42,121
> 90 days and < 121 days	8,139	7,441	3,261	253	19,094
> 120 days	23,587	18,334	5,288	552	47,761
Total	$1,836,899	$774,971	$456,308	$49,563	$3,117,741
Past due amounts > 90 days					
Still accruing interest	$ 8,139	$ 7,441	$ —	$ —	$ 15,580
Not accruing interest	23,587	18,334	8,549	805	51,275
Total	$ 31,726	$ 25,775	$ 8,549	$ 805	$ 66,855

Credit Quality

We use credit scores as one of many data elements in making the decision to grant credit at inception, setting credit lines at inception, managing credit lines through the life of the customer, and to assist in collections strategy.

We use a third party to score the majority of the North American portfolio on a quarterly basis using a commercial credit score. Accounts may not receive a score because of data issues related to SIC information, customer identification mismatches between the various data sources and other reasons. We do not currently score the portfolios outside of North America because the cost to do so is prohibitive, it is a fragmented process and there is no single credit score model that covers all countries. However, credit policies are similar to those in North America.

The table below shows the portfolio at December 31, 2010 and December 31, 2009 by relative risk class (low, medium and high) based on the relative scores of the accounts within each class. A fourth class is shown for accounts that are not scored. The degree of risk, as defined by the third party, refers to the likelihood that an account in the next 12 month period

may become delinquent. Absence of a score is not indicative of the credit quality of the account.
- Low risk accounts are companies with very good credit risk
- Medium risk accounts are companies with average to good credit risk
- High risk accounts are companies with poor credit risk, are delinquent, or are at risk of becoming delinquent

Although the relative score of accounts within each class is used as a factor for determining the establishment of a customer credit limit, it is not indicative of our actual history of losses due to the business essential nature of our products and services.

The aging schedule included above, showing approximately 1.9% of the portfolio as greater than 90 days past due, and the roll-forward schedule of the allowance for credit losses, showing the actual history of losses for the three most recent years ended December 31, 2010 are more representative of the potential loss performance of our portfolio than relative risk based on scores, as defined by the third party.

	U.S.	International	December 31, 2010 Total	U.S.	International	Total
Sales-Type Lease Receivables						
Risk level						
Low	$1,001,663	$190,018	$1,191,681	60.0%	25.5%	49.3%
Medium	443,139	69,280	512,419	26.5%	9.3%	21.2%
High	49,183	11,572	60,755	2.9%	1.6%	2.5%
Not scored	175,978	474,895	650,873	10.5%	63.7%	26.9%
Total	$1,669,963	$745,765	$2,415,728	100%	100%	100%
Loan Receivables						
Risk level						
Low	$ 21,808	$ 12,002	$ 33,810	5.0%	21.7%	6.9%
Medium	260,708	7,640	268,348	60.3%	13.8%	55.0%
High	147,975	1,406	149,381	34.2%	2.5%	30.6%
Not scored	1,646	34,370	36,016	0.4%	62.0%	7.4%
Total	$ 432,137	$ 55,418	$ 487,555	100%	100%	100%
Total						
Risk level						
Low	$1,023,471	$202,020	$1,225,491	48.7%	25.2%	42.2%
Medium	703,847	76,920	780,767	33.5%	9.6%	26.9%
High	197,158	12,978	210,136	9.4%	1.6%	7.2%
Not scored	177,624	509,265	686,889	8.4%	63.6%	23.7%
Total	$2,102,100	$801,183	$2,903,283	100%	100%	100%

	U.S.	International	December 31, 2009 Total	U.S.	International	Total
Sales-Type Lease Receivables						
Risk level						
Low	$1,142,945	$207,214	$1,350,159	62.2%	26.7%	51.7%
Medium	466,616	89,606	556,222	25.4%	11.6%	21.3%
High	51,211	3,042	54,253	2.8%	0.4%	2.1%
Not scored	176,127	475,109	651,236	9.6%	61.3%	24.9%
Total	$1,836,899	$774,971	$2,611,870	100%	100%	100%
Loan Receivables						
Risk level						
Low	$ 20,688	$ 10,382	$ 31,070	4.5%	20.9%	6.1%
Medium	288,062	5,675	293,737	63.1%	11.5%	58.1%
High	147,558	201	147,759	32.3%	0.4%	29.2%
Not scored	—	33,305	33,305	0.0%	67.2%	6.6%
Total	$ 456,308	$ 49,563	$ 505,871	100%	100%	100%
Total						
Risk level						
Low	$1,163,633	$217,596	$1,381,229	50.7%	26.4%	44.3%
Medium	754,678	95,281	849,959	32.9%	11.6%	27.3%
High	198,769	3,243	202,012	8.7%	0.4%	6.5%
Not scored	176,127	508,414	684,541	7.7%	61.7%	22.0%
Total	$2,293,207	$824,534	$3,117,741	100%	100%	100%

Pitney Bowes Bank

At December 31, 2010, PBB had assets of $675 million and liabilities of $626 million. The bank's assets consist of finance receivables, short and long-term investments and cash. PBB's key product offering, Purchase Power, is a revolving credit solution, which enables customers to finance their postage costs when they refill their meter. PBB earns revenue through transaction fees, finance charges on outstanding balances, and other fees for services. The bank's liabilities consist primarily of PBB's deposit solution, Reserve Account, which provides value to large-volume mailers who prefer to prepay postage and earn interest on their deposits. PBB is regulated by the Federal Deposit Insurance Corporation (FDIC) and the Utah Department of Financial Institutions.

Leveraged Leases

Our investment in leveraged lease assets consists of the following:

	December 31	
	2010	2009
Rental receivables	$1,802,107	$1,747,811
Unguaranteed residual values	14,141	13,399
Principal and interest on non-recourse loans	(1,373,651)	(1,341,820)
Unearned income	(191,591)	(186,031)
Investment in leveraged leases	251,006	233,359
Less: deferred taxes related to leveraged leases	(192,128)	(175,329)
Net investment in leveraged leases	$ 58,878	$ 58,030

The following is a summary of the components of income from leveraged leases:

	December 31		
	2010	2009	2008
Pre-tax leveraged lease income	$8,334	$ 918	$ 316
Income tax effect	(863)	6,676	7,063
Income from leveraged leases	$7,471	$7,594	$7,379

Income from leveraged leases was positively impacted by $2.2 million, $2.8 million and $2.6 million in 2010, 2009 and 2008, respectively, due to changes in statutory tax rates.

Retained Interest

2.30

AIRGAS, INC. (MAR)

CONSOLIDATED BALANCE SHEETS (in part)

	March 31	
(In thousands, except per share amounts)	2010	2009
Assets		
Current assets		
Cash	$ 47,001	$ 47,188
Trade receivables, less allowances for doubtful accounts of $25,359 in 2010 and $27,572 in 2009 (Note 4)	186,804	184,739
Inventories, net (Note 5)	333,961	390,445
Deferred income tax asset, net (Note 6)	48,591	45,692
Prepaid expenses and other current assets	94,978	76,679
Total current assets	$711,335	$744,743

NOTES TO CONSOLIDATED FINANCIAL STATEMENTS

(4) Trade Receivables Securitization

The Company participates in the Securitization Agreement with three commercial banks to which it sells qualifying trade receivables on a revolving basis. Upon its renewal in March 2010, the maximum amount of the facility was established at $295 million, down from $345 million at March 31, 2009. The Securitization Agreement expires in March 2012 and contains customary events of termination, including standard cross default provisions with respect to outstanding debt. During the year ended March 31, 2010, the Company sold approximately $3.5 billion of trade receivables and remitted to bank conduits, pursuant to a servicing agreement, approximately $3.5 billion in collections on those receivables. The amount of receivables sold under the securitization agreements was $295 million at March 31, 2010 and $311 million at March 31, 2009.

The transaction has been accounted for as a sale, as control of the receivables has been surrendered. Under the Securitization Agreement, trade receivables are sold to bank conduits through a bankruptcy-remote special purpose entity, which is consolidated for financial reporting purposes. The difference between the proceeds from the sale and the carrying value of the receivables is recognized as "Discount on securitization of trade receivables" in the accompanying Consolidated Statements of Earnings and varies on a monthly basis depending on the amount of trade receivables sold and market rates. The Company retains a subordinated interest in the trade receivables sold, which is recorded at the trade receivables' previous carrying value. Accordingly, the Company is exposed to credit risk associated with its retained interest in the trade receivables. The Company is not exposed to interest rate risk due to the short-term nature of the trade receivables and their general collectability.

Subordinated retained interests of approximately $142 million, net of an allowance for doubtful accounts of $23 million, and $148 million, net of an allowance for doubtful accounts of $26 million, are included in trade receivables in the accompanying Consolidated Balance Sheets at March 31, 2010 and 2009, respectively. At March 31, 2010 and 2009, approximately 2.8% and 6.4%, respectively, of the accounts included in the retained interest were delinquent, as defined under the Securitization Agreement. Credit losses for the years ended March 31, 2010 and 2009 were $13 million and $22 million, respectively. On a monthly basis, management calculates the fair value of the retained interest based on management's best estimate of the undiscounted expected future cash collections on the trade receivables. Changes in the fair value are recognized as bad debt expense. Actual cash collections may differ from these estimates and would directly affect the fair value of the retained interest. In accordance with the servicing agreement, the Company continues to service, administer and collect the trade receivables on behalf of the bank conduits. The servicing fees charged to the bank conduits approximate the costs of collections. Accordingly, the net servicing asset is immaterial. The Company does not provide any financial guarantees of the bank conduits' obligations.

On April 1, 2010, the Company adopted new guidance establishing revised standards on accounting for the transfers of financial assets. These standards apply to the Company's Securitization Agreement and effectively require the Company to recognize the trade receivables sold under the Securitization Agreement and the related proceeds as debt on its Consolidated Balance Sheet. The Securitization Agreement will be reflected as such on the Company's Consolidated Balance Sheet for the fiscal quarter ending on June 30, 2010.

Insurance Claims

2.31

D.R. HORTON, INC. (SEP)

CONSOLIDATED BALANCE SHEETS (in part)

	September 30	
(In millions)	2010	2009
Assets		
Homebuilding:		
Cash and cash equivalents	$1,282.6	$1,922.8
Marketable securities, available-for-sale	297.7	—
Restricted cash	53.7	55.2
Inventories:		
Construction in progress and finished homes	1,286.0	1,446.6
Residential land and lots—developed and under development	1,406.1	1,643.3
Land held for development	749.3	562.5
Land inventory not owned	7.6	14.3
	3,449.0	3,666.7
Income taxes receivable	16.0	293.1
Deferred income taxes, net of valuation allowance of $902.6 million and $1,073.9 million at September 30, 2010 and 2009, respectively	—	—
Property and equipment, net	60.5	57.8
Other assets	434.8	433.0
Goodwill	15.9	15.9
	5,610.2	6,444.5
Financial services:		
Cash and cash equivalents	26.7	34.5
Mortgage loans held for sale	253.8	220.8
Other assets	47.9	57.0
	328.4	312.3
Total assets	$5,938.6	$6,756.8

NOTES TO CONSOLIDATED FINANCIAL STATEMENTS

Note A—Summary of Significant Accounting Policies (in part)

Insurance and Legal Claims

The Company has, and requires the majority of the subcontractors it uses to have, general liability insurance which includes construction defect coverage. The Company's general liability insurance policies protect it against a portion of its risk of loss from construction defect and other claims and lawsuits, subject to self-insured retentions and other coverage limits. For policy years ended June 30, 2004 through 2010, the Company is self-insured for up to $22.5 million of the aggregate claims incurred, at which point the excess loss insurance begins, depending on the policy year. Once the Company has satisfied the annual aggregate limits, it is self-insured for the first $250,000 to $1.0 million for each claim occurrence, depending on the policy year. For policy years 2010 and 2011, the Company is self-insured for up to $20.0 million and $15.0 million, respectively, of the aggregate claims incurred and for up to $0.5 million of each claim occurrence thereafter.

In some states where the Company believes it is too difficult or expensive for its subcontractors to obtain general liability insurance, the Company has waived its traditional subcontractor general liability insurance requirements to obtain lower costs from subcontractors. In these states, the Company purchases insurance policies from either third-party carriers or its wholly-owned captive insurance subsidiary, and names certain subcontractors as additional insureds. The policies issued by the captive insurance subsidiary represent self insurance of these risks by the Company and are considered in the self-insured amounts above. For policy years after April 2007, the captive insurance subsidiary has acquired $15.0 million of reinsurance coverage with a third-party insurer.

The Company is self-insured for the deductible amounts under its workers' compensation insurance policies. The deductibles vary by policy year, but in no years exceed $0.5 million per occurrence. The deductible for the 2010 and 2011 policy years was $0.5 million per occurrence.

The Company records expenses and liabilities related to the costs for exposures related to construction defects and claims and lawsuits incurred in the ordinary course of business, including employment matters, personal injury claims, land development issues and contract disputes. Also, the Company records expenses and liabilities for any estimated costs of potential construction defect claims and lawsuits (including expected legal costs), based on an analysis of the Company's historical claims, which includes an estimate of construction defect claims incurred but not yet reported. Related to the exposures for actual construction defect claims and estimates of construction defect claims incurred but not yet reported and other legal claims and lawsuits incurred in the ordinary course of business, the Company estimates and records insurance receivables for these matters under applicable insurance policies when recovery is probable. Additionally, the Company may have the ability to recover a portion of its legal expenses from its subcontractors when the Company has been named as an additional insured on their insurance policies. The expenses, liabilities and receivables related to these claims are subject to a high degree of variability due to uncertainties such as trends in construction defect claims relative to the Company's markets, the types of products it builds, claim settlement patterns, insurance industry practices and legal interpretations, among others. See Note M.

Note M—Commitments and Contingencies (in part)

Insurance and Legal Claims

The Company has been named as defendant in various claims, complaints and other legal actions including construction defect claims on closed homes and other claims and lawsuits incurred in the ordinary course of business, including employment matters, personal injury claims, land development issues, contract disputes and claims related to its mortgage activities. The Company has established reserves for these contingencies, based on the expected costs of the claims. The Company's estimates of such reserves are based on the facts and circumstances of individual pending claims and historical data and trends, including costs relative to revenues, home closings and product types, and include estimates of the costs of construction defect claims incurred but not yet reported. These reserve estimates are subject to ongoing revision as the circumstances of individual pending claims and historical data and trends change. Adjustments to estimated reserves are recorded in the accounting period in which the change in estimate occurs. The Company's liabilities for these items were $571.3 million and $534.0 million at September 30, 2010 and 2009, respectively, and are included in homebuilding accrued expenses and other liabilities in the consolidated balance sheets. Related to the contingencies for construction defect claims and estimates of construction defect claims incurred but not yet reported, and other legal claims and lawsuits incurred in the ordinary course of business, the Company estimates and records insurance receivables for these matters under applicable insurance policies when recovery is probable. Additionally, the Company may have the ability to recover a portion of its legal expenses from its subcontractors when the Company has been named as an additional insured on their insurance policies. Estimates of the Company's insurance receivables related to these matters totaled $251.5 million and $234.6 million at September 30, 2010 and 2009, respectively, and are included in homebuilding other assets in the consolidated balance sheets. Expenses related to these items were approximately $43.2 million, $58.3 million and $53.8 million in fiscal 2010, 2009 and 2008, respectively.

Management believes that, while the outcome of such contingencies cannot be predicted with certainty, the liabilities arising from these matters will not have a material adverse effect on the Company's consolidated financial position, results of operations or cash flows. To the extent the liability arising from the ultimate resolution of any matter exceeds management's estimates reflected in the recorded reserves relating to these matters, the Company would incur additional charges that could be significant.

Note N — Other Assets and Accrued Expenses and Other Liabilities (in part)

The Company's homebuilding other assets at September 30, 2010 and 2009 were as follows:

	September 30	
(In millions)	2010	2009
Insurance receivables	$251.5	$234.6
Accounts and notes receivable	18.5	50.7
Prepaid assets	28.9	39.0
Other assets	135.9	108.7
	$434.8	$433.0

Vendors and Suppliers

2.32

COSTCO WHOLESALE CORPORATION (AUG)

CONSOLIDATED BALANCE SHEETS (in part)

(Dollars in millions, except par value and share data)	August 29, 2010	August 30, 2009
Assets		
Current assets		
Cash and cash equivalents	$ 3,214	$ 3,157
Short-term investments	1,535	570
Receivables, net	884	834
Merchandise inventories	5,638	5,405
Deferred income taxes and other current assets	437	371
Total current assets	$11,708	$10,337

NOTES TO CONSOLIDATED FINANCIAL STATEMENTS

(dollars in millions, except share data)

Note 1—Summary of Significant Accounting Policies (in part)

Receivables, Net (in part)

Receivables consist of the following at the end of 2010 and 2009:

	2010	2009
Vendor receivables, and other	$448	$418
Reinsurance receivables	196	169
Other receivables	103	82
Third-party pharmacy receivables	75	73
Receivables from governmental entities	64	95
Allowance for doubtful accounts	(2)	(3)
Receivables, net	$884	$834

Vendor receivable balances are generally presented on a gross basis separate from any related payable due. In certain circumstances, these receivables may be settled against the related payable to that vendor.

Vendor Receivables and Allowances

Periodic payments from vendors in the form of volume rebates or other purchase discounts that are evidenced by signed agreements are reflected in the carrying value of the inventory when earned or as the Company progresses towards earning the rebate or discount and as a component of merchandise costs as the merchandise is sold. Other consideration received from vendors is generally recorded as a reduction of merchandise costs upon completion of contractual milestones, terms of the related agreement, or by other systematic approach.

RECEIVABLES SOLD OR COLLATERALIZED

RECOGNITION AND MEASUREMENT

2.33 FASB ASC 860, *Transfers and Servicing*, establishes criteria for determining whether a transfer of financial assets in exchange for cash or other consideration should be accounted for as a sale or pledge of collateral in a secured borrowing. FASB ASC 860 also establishes the criteria for accounting for securitizations and other transfers of financial assets and collateral and requires certain disclosures.

2.34 FASB ASC 860 requires that all separately recognized servicing assets and liabilities be initially measured at fair value. Further, FASB ASC 860 permits, but does not require, the subsequent measurement of servicing assets and liabilities at fair value.

2.35 ASU No. 2009-16, *Transfers and Servicing (Topic 860): Accounting for Transfers of Financial Assets*, eliminated the exceptions for qualifying special-purpose entities from the consolidation guidance. Further, ASU No. 2009-16 provides clarifications of the requirements for isolation and limitations on portions of financial assets that are eligible for sale accounting. ASU No. 2009-16 was effective for fiscal years beginning after November 15, 2009.

DISCLOSURE

2.36 FASB ASC 860 requires additional disclosures and separate balance sheet presentation of the carrying amounts of servicing assets and liabilities that are subsequently measured at fair value. ASU No. 2009-16 requires enhanced disclosures about (*a*) the risks that a transferor continues to be exposed to because of its continuing involvement in transferred financial assets and (*b*) any restrictions on the assets of the entity.

2.37

TABLE 2-3: RECEIVABLES SOLD OR COLLATERALIZED

	2010	2009	2008
Receivables sold with recourse	8	2	13
Receivables sold with limited recourse	6	9	7
Receivables sold without recourse	29	45	39
Receivables sold, recourse not discussed	N/C*	46	51
Receivables sold, other	19	N/C*	N/C*
Receivables sold, factoring agreement	6	N/C*	N/C*
Receivables transferred to a special-purpose entity	18	N/C*	N/C*
Receivables pledged as collateral	22	21	13
No reference to receivables sold or collateralized	410	377	377

* N/C = Not compiled. Line item was not included in the table for the year shown.

PRESENTATION AND DISCLOSURE EXCERPTS

Receivables Sold or Collateralized

2.38

CROWN HOLDINGS, INC. (DEC)

CONSOLIDATED BALANCE SHEETS (in part)

(In millions, except share data)

December 31	2010	2009
Assets		
Current assets		
Cash and cash equivalents	$ 463	$ 459
Receivables, net . . . *Note C*	936	714
Inventories . . . *Note D*	1,060	960
Prepaid expenses and other current assets	190	109
Total current assets	$2,649	$2,242

NOTES TO CONSOLIDATED FINANCIAL STATEMENTS

(In millions, except share, per share, employee and statistical data)

C. Receivables

	2010	2009
Accounts and notes receivable	$829	$598
Less: allowance for doubtful accounts	(40)	(40)
Net trade receivables	789	558
Miscellaneous receivables	147	156
	$936	$714

Following are the changes in the allowance for doubtful accounts for the years ended December 31, 2010, 2009 and 2008.

	Balance at Beginning of Year	Expense	Write Offs	Translation	Balance at End of Year
2008	$28	$ 1	$(4)	$(1)	$24
2009	24	17	(3)	2	40
2010	40	4	(3)	(1)	40

The Company utilizes receivable securitization facilities in the normal course of business as part of its management of cash flows. Under its committed $200 North American facility, the Company sells receivables, on a revolving basis, to a wholly-owned, bankruptcy-remote subsidiary. The subsidiary was formed for the sole purpose of buying and selling receivables generated by the Company and, in turn, sells undivided percentage ownership interests in the pool of purchased receivables to a syndicate of financial institutions. The Company generally retains an ownership interest in the pool of receivables that is subordinated to the ownership interests in the pool of receivables that are sold to third parties. Accordingly, the Company has determined that these transactions do not qualify for sale accounting and has therefore accounted for the transactions as secured borrowings.

Under the Company's committed €120 European securitization facility, certain subsidiaries in the U.K. and France sell receivables to an entity formed in France for the sole purpose of buying receivables from the selling subsidiaries. The buying entity finances the purchase of receivables through the issuance of senior units to a third party. Since the units issued to the third party are senior to the interests retained by the Company, the Company has determined that these transactions do not qualify for sale accounting and has therefore accounted for the transactions as secured borrowings.

In addition, the Company utilizes receivables factoring arrangements in the normal course of business as part of managing cash flows for its European operations. Under the arrangements, the Company sells its entire interest in specified receivables to various third parties. Where the Company has surrendered control over factored receivables, the Company has accounted for the transfers as sales.

The Company's continuing involvement in factored receivables accounted for as sales is limited to servicing the receivables. The Company receives adequate compensation for servicing the receivables; therefore, no servicing asset or liability was recorded.

At December 31, 2010, the Company's Consolidated Balance Sheet included $208 of receivables that were securitized or factored and $208 of associated liabilities. In addition, at December 31, 2010, the Company derecognized receivables of $210 related to factoring arrangements accounted for as sales. At December 31, 2009, receivables of $392 securitized or factored under the Company's facilities were accounted for as sales and reported as a reduction of receivables in the Company's Consolidated Balance Sheet.

In 2010, 2009 and 2008, the Company recorded expenses related to securitization and factoring facilities of $10, $10 and $23 as interest expense, respectively.

Collections from customers on securitized or factored receivables and related fees and costs are included in operating activities in the Consolidated Statements of Cash Flows. Proceeds and repayments from issuances of ownership interests in the consolidated entity that buys and sells the Company's receivables under its securitization facilities as well as amounts received from factors for transactions that do not qualify for sale accounting are included in financing activities in the Consolidated Statements of Cash Flows.

2.39

TENNECO INC. (DEC)

CONSOLIDATED BALANCE SHEETS (in part)

	December 31	
(millions)	2010	2009
Assets		
Current assets:		
Cash and cash equivalents	$ 233	$ 167
Receivables—		
Customer notes and accounts, net	796	572
Other	30	24
Inventories	547	428
Deferred income taxes	38	35
Prepayments and other	146	167
Total current assets	1,790	1,393
Other assets:		
Long-term receivables, net	9	8
Goodwill	89	89
Intangibles, net	32	30
Deferred income taxes	92	100
Other	105	111
	327	338
Plant, property, and equipment, at cost	3,109	3,099
Less—Accumulated depreciation and amortization	(2,059)	(1,989)
	1,050	1,110
	$ 3,167	$ 2,841

NOTES TO CONSOLIDATED FINANCIAL STATEMENTS

5. Long-Term Debt, Short-Term Debt, and Financing Arrangements (in part)

Accounts Receivable Securitization. We also securitize some of our accounts receivable on a limited recourse basis in North America and Europe. As servicer under these accounts receivable securitization programs, we are responsible for performing all accounts receivable administration functions for these securitized financial assets including collections and processing of customer invoice adjustments. In North America, we have an accounts receivable securitization program with three commercial banks. We securitize original equipment and aftermarket receivables on a daily basis under the bank program. We had no outstanding third party investments in our securitized accounts receivable bank program as of December 31, 2010 and $62 million at December 31, 2009. In February 2010, the North American program was amended and extended to February 18, 2011, at a maximum facility size of $100 million. As part of this renewal, the margin we pay to our banks decreased. In March 2010, the North American program was further amended to extend the revolving terms of the program to March 25, 2011, add an additional bank and increase the available financing under the facility by $10 million to a new maximum of $110 million. In addition, we added a second priority facility to the North American program, which provides up to an additional $40 million of financing against accounts receivable generated in the U.S. or Canada that would otherwise be ineligible under the existing securitization facility. This new second priority facility also expires on March 25, 2011, and is subordinated to the existing securitization facility.

Each facility contains customary covenants for financings of this type, including restrictions related to liens, payments, mergers or consolidation and amendments to the agreements underlying the receivables pool. Further, each facility may be terminated upon the occurrence of customary events (with customary grace periods, if applicable), including breaches of covenants, failure to maintain certain financial ratios, inaccuracies of representations and warranties, bankruptcy and insolvency events, certain changes in the rate of default or delinquency of the receivables, a change of control and the entry or other enforcement of material judgments. In addition, each facility contains cross-default provisions, where the facility could be terminated in the event of non-payment of other material indebtedness when due and any other event which permits the acceleration of the maturity of material indebtedness.

We also securitize receivables in our European operations with regional banks in Europe. The amount of outstanding third party investments in our securitized accounts receivable in Europe was $91 million and $75 million at December 31, 2010 and December 31, 2009, respectively. The arrangements to securitize receivables in Europe are provided under seven separate facilities provided by various financial institutions in each of the foreign jurisdictions. The commitments for these arrangements are generally for one year, but some may be cancelled with notice 90 days prior to renewal. In some instances, the arrangement provides for cancellation by the applicable financial institution at any time upon 15 days, or less, notification.

If we were not able to securitize receivables under either the North American or European securitization programs, our borrowings under our revolving credit agreements might increase. These accounts receivable securitization programs provide us with access to cash at costs that are generally favorable to alternative sources of financing, and allow us to reduce borrowings under our revolving credit agreements.

We adopted the amended accounting guidance under ASC Topic 860, Accounting for Transfers of Financial Assets effective January 1, 2010. Prior to the adoption of this new guidance, we accounted for activities under our North American and European accounts receivable securitization programs as sales of financial assets to our banks. The new accounting guidance changed the conditions that must be met for the transfer of financial assets to be accounted for as a sale. The new guidance adds additional conditions that must be satisfied for transfers of financial assets to be accounted for as sales when the transferor has not transferred the entire original financial asset, including the requirement that no partial interest holder have rights in the transferred asset that are subordinate to the rights of other partial interest holders. In our North American accounts receivable securitization programs we transfer a partial interest in a pool of receivables and the interest that we retain is subordinate to the transferred interest. Accordingly, beginning January 1, 2010, we account for our North American securitization program as a secured borrowing. In our European programs we transfer accounts receivables in their entirety to the acquiring entities and satisfy all of the conditions established under amended ASC Topic 860 to report the transfer of financial assets in their entirety as a sale. The fair value of assets received as proceeds in exchange for the transfer of accounts receivable under our European securitization programs approximates

the fair value of such receivables. We recognized $4 million in interest expense in 2010 relating to our North American securitization program which effective January 1, 2010, is accounted for as a secured borrowing arrangement under the amended accounting guidance for transfers of financial assets. In addition, we recognized a loss of $3 million, $9 million and $10 million for the years ended 2010, 2009 and 2008, respectively, on the sale of trade accounts receivable in both the North American and European accounts receivable securitization programs, representing the discount from book values at which these receivables were sold to our banks. The discount rate varies based on funding costs incurred by our banks, which averaged approximately four percent during 2010.

The impact of the new accounting rules on our consolidated financial statements includes an increase of $4 million in interest expense and a corresponding decrease in loss on sale of receivables on our income statement in 2010. In 2010, there was no cash flow impact as a result of the new accounting rules. Funding levels provided by our European securitization programs continue to be reflected as a change in receivables and included in net cash provided (used) by operating activities as under the previous accounting rules. Had the new accounting rules been in effect prior to 2010, reported receivables and short-term debt would both have been $62 million higher as of December 31, 2009. The loss on sale of receivables would have been $5 million lower, offset by a corresponding $5 million increase to interest expense for 2009. The loss on sales of receivables would have been $4 million lower, offset by a corresponding $4 million increase to interest expense for 2008. Additionally, our cash provided (used) by operations would have decreased by $62 million with a corresponding increase in cash provided by financing activities for the same amount for 2009.

2.40

STANLEY BLACK & DECKER, INC. (DEC)

CONSOLIDATED BALANCE SHEETS (in part)

January 1, 2011 and January 2, 2010

(Millions of dollars)	2010	2009
Assets		
Current Assets		
Cash and cash equivalents	$ 1,745.4	$ 400.7
Accounts and notes receivable, net	1,417.1	532.0
Inventories, net	1,272.0	366.2
Prepaid expenses	224.0	73.2
Other current assets	157.1	39.8
Total Current Assets	4,815.6	1,411.9
Property, plant and equipment, net	1,166.5	575.9
Goodwill	5,941.9	1,818.4
Customer relationships, net	889.8	413.4
Trade names, net	1,839.4	331.1
Other intangible assets, net	143.0	31.9
Other assets	343.2	186.5
Total Assets	$15,139.4	$4,769.1

NOTES TO CONSOLIDATED FINANCIAL STATEMENTS

B. Accounts and Financing Receivable

(Millions of dollars)	2010	2009
Trade accounts receivable	$1,333.2	$486.4
Trade notes receivable	61.9	45.7
Other accounts receivables	78.3	31.8
Gross accounts and notes receivable	1,473.4	563.9
Allowance for doubtful accounts	(56.3)	(31.9)
Accounts and notes receivable, net	$1,417.1	$532.0
Long-term trade notes receivable, net	$ 114.9	$ 93.2

Trade receivables are dispersed among a large number of retailers, distributors and industrial accounts in many countries. Adequate reserves have been established to cover anticipated credit losses. Long-term trade financing receivables are reported within Other assets in the Consolidated Balance Sheets. Financing receivables and long-term financing receivables are predominately related to certain security equipment leases with commercial businesses. Generally, the Company retains legal title to any equipment leases and bears the right to repossess such equipment in an event of default. All financing receivables are interest bearing and the Company has not classified any financing receivables as held-for-sale.

In December 2009, the Company entered into an accounts receivable sale program that was scheduled to expire on December 28, 2010. On December 13, 2010, the Company extended the term of that program for one year and the program is now scheduled to expire on December 12, 2011. According to the terms of that program the Company is required to sell certain of its trade accounts receivables at fair value to a wholly owned, bankruptcy-remote special purpose subsidiary ("BRS"). The BRS, in turn, must sell such receivables to a third-party financial institution ("Purchaser") for cash and a deferred purchase price receivable. The Purchaser's maximum cash investment in the receivables at any time is $100.0 million. The purpose of the program is to provide liquidity to the Company. The Company accounts for these transfers as sales under ASC 860 "Transfers and Servicing." The Company has no retained interests in the transferred receivables, other than collection and administrative responsibilities and its right to the deferred purchase price receivable. At January 1, 2011 the Company did not record a servicing asset or liability related to its retained responsibility, based on its assessment of the servicing fee, market values for similar transactions and its cost of servicing the receivables sold.

As of January 1, 2011 and January 2, 2010, $31.5 million and $35.2 million of net receivables were derecognized. Gross receivables sold amounted to $552.1 million ($492.9 million, net) for the year ended January 1, 2011. These sales resulted in a pre-tax loss of $1.4 million for the year ended January 1, 2011. Proceeds from transfers of receivables to the Purchaser totaled $495.3 million for the year ended January 1, 2011. Collections of previously sold receivables, including deferred purchase price receivables, and all fees, which are settled one month in arrears, resulted in payments to the Purchaser of $498.8 million for the year ended January 1, 2011. Servicing fees amounted to $0.3 million for the year ended January 1, 2011. The Company's risk of loss following the sale of the receivables is limited to the deferred purchase price, which was $13.8 million at January 1, 2011 and $17.7 million at January 2, 2010. The deferred purchase price receivable will be repaid in cash as receivables are collected, generally within 30 days, and as such the carrying value of the receivable recorded approximates fair value. Delinquencies and credit losses on receivables sold in 2010 were less than $0.2 million for the year ended January 1, 2011. Cash inflows related to the deferred purchase price receivable totaled $174.4 million for the year ended January 1, 2011. All cash flows under the program are reported as a component of changes in accounts receivable within operating activities in the consolidated statements of cash flows since all the cash from the Purchaser is either: 1) received upon the initial sale of the receivable; or 2) from the ultimate collection of the underlying receivables and the underlying receivables are not subject to significant risks, other than credit risk, given their short-term nature.

2.41

HANESBRANDS INC. (DEC)

CONSOLIDATED BALANCE SHEETS (in part)

(In thousands, except share and per share amounts)

	January 1, 2011	January 2, 2010
Assets		
Cash and cash equivalents	$ 43,671	$ 38,943
Trade accounts receivable less allowances of $19,192 at January 1, 2011 and $25,776 at January 2, 2010	503,243	450,541
Inventories	1,322,719	1,049,204
Deferred tax assets	149,431	139,836
Other current assets	128,607	144,033
Total current assets	2,147,671	1,822,557
Property, net	631,254	602,826
Trademarks and other identifiable intangibles, net	178,622	136,214
Goodwill	430,144	322,002
Deferred tax assets	319,798	357,103
Other noncurrent assets	82,513	85,862
Total assets	$3,790,002	$3,326,564

NOTES TO CONSOLIDATED FINANCIAL STATEMENTS

(Amounts in thousands, except per share data)

(5) Trade Accounts Receivable (in part)

Sales of Accounts Receivable

The Company has entered into agreements to sell selected trade accounts receivable to financial institutions. After the sale, the Company does not retain any interests in the receivables and the applicable financial institution services and collects these accounts receivable directly from the customer. Net proceeds of these accounts receivable sale programs are recognized in the Consolidated Statements of Cash Flows as part of operating cash flows. The Company recognized funding fees of $3,464 and $163 in 2010 and 2009, respectively, for sales of accounts receivable to financial institutions in the "Other expenses" line in the Consolidated Statements of Income.

2.42

TARGET CORPORATION (JAN)

CONSOLIDATED STATEMENTS OF FINANCIAL POSITION (in part)

(Millions, except footnotes)	January 30, 2010	January 31, 2009
Assets		
Cash and cash equivalents, including marketable securities of $1,617 and $302	$ 2,200	$ 864
Credit card receivables, net of allowance of $1,016 and $1,010	6,966	8,084
Inventory	7,179	6,705
Other current assets	2,079	1,835
Total current assets	18,424	17,488
Property and equipment		
Land	5,793	5,767
Buildings and improvements	22,152	20,430
Fixtures and equipment	4,743	4,270
Computer hardware and software	2,575	2,586
Construction-in-progress	502	1,763
Accumulated depreciation	(10,485)	(9,060)
Property and equipment, net	25,280	25,756
Other noncurrent assets	829	862
Total assets	$ 44,533	$44,106
Liabilities and shareholders' investment		
Accounts payable	$ 6,511	$ 6,337
Accrued and other current liabilities	3,120	2,913
Unsecured debt and other borrowings	796	1,262
Nonrecourse debt collateralized by credit card receivables	900	—
Total current liabilities	11,327	10,512
Unsecured debt and other borrowings	10,643	12,000
Nonrecourse debt collateralized by credit card receivables	4,475	5,490
Deferred income taxes	835	455
Other noncurrent liabilities	1,906	1,937
Total noncurrent liabilities	17,859	19,882
Shareholders' investment		
Common stock	62	63
Additional paid-in-capital	2,919	2,762
Retained earnings	12,947	11,443
Accumulated other comprehensive loss	(581)	(556)
Total shareholders' investment	15,347	13,712
Total liabilities and shareholders' investment	$ 44,533	$44,106

NOTES TO CONSOLIDATED FINANCIAL STATEMENTS

10. Credit Card Receivables (in part)

As a method of providing funding for our credit card receivables, we sell on an ongoing basis all of our consumer credit card receivables to Target Receivables Corporation (TRC), a wholly owned, bankruptcy remote subsidiary. TRC then transfers the receivables to the Target Credit Card Master Trust (the Trust), which from time to time will sell debt securities to third parties either directly or through a related trust. These debt securities represent undivided interests in the Trust assets. TRC uses the proceeds from the sale of debt securities and its share of collections on the receivables to pay the purchase price of the receivables to the Corporation.

We consolidate the receivables within the Trust and any debt securities issued by the Trust, or a related trust, in our Consolidated Statements of Financial Position based upon the applicable accounting guidance. The receivables transferred to the Trust are not available to general creditors of the Corporation. The payments to the holders of the debt securities issued by the Trust or the related trust are made solely from the assets transferred to the Trust or the related trust and are nonrecourse to the general assets of the Corporation. Upon termination of the securitization program and repayment of all debt securities, any remaining assets could be distributed to the Corporation in a liquidation of TRC.

In the second quarter of 2008, we sold an interest in our credit card receivables to JPMC. The interest sold represented 47 percent of the receivables portfolio at the time of the transaction. This transaction was accounted for as a secured borrowing, and accordingly, the credit card receivables within the Trust and the note payable issued are reflected in our Consolidated Statements of Financial Position. Notwithstanding this accounting treatment, the accounts receivable assets that collateralize the note payable supply the cash flow to pay principal and interest to the note holder; the receivables are not available to general creditors of the Corporation; and the payments to JPMC are made solely from the Trust and are nonrecourse to the general assets of the Corporation. Interest and principal payments due on the note are satisfied provided the cash flows from the Trust assets are sufficient. If the cash flows are less than the periodic interest, the available amount, if any, is paid with respect to interest. Interest shortfalls will be paid to the extent subsequent cash flows from the assets in the Trust are sufficient. Future principal payments will be made from JPMC's prorata share of cash flows from the Trust assets.

In the event of a decrease in the receivables principal amount such that JPMC's interest in the entire portfolio would exceed 47 percent for three consecutive months, TRC (using the cash flows from the assets in the Trust) would be required to pay JPMC a prorata amount of principal collections such that the portion owned by JPMC would not exceed 47 percent, unless JPMC provides a waiver. Conversely, at the option of the Corporation, JPMC may be required to fund an increase in the portfolio to maintain their 47 percent interest up to a maximum JPMC principal balance of $4.2 billion. If a three-month average of monthly finance charge excess (JPMC's prorata share of finance charge collections less write-offs and specified expenses) is less than 2 percent of the outstanding principal balance of JPMC's interest, the Corporation must implement mutually agreed upon underwriting strategies. If the three-month average finance charge excess falls below 1 percent of the outstanding principal balance of JPMC's interest, JPMC may compel the Corporation to implement underwriting and collections activities, provided those activities are compatible with the Corporation's systems, as well as consistent with similar credit card receivable portfolios managed by JPMC. If the Corporation fails to implement the activities, JPMC would cause the accelerated repayment of the note payable issued in the transaction. As noted in the preceding paragraph, payments would be made solely from the Trust assets.

19. Notes Payable and Long-Term Debt (in part)

As further explained in Note 10, we maintain an accounts receivable financing program through which we sell credit card receivables to a bankruptcy remote, wholly owned subsidiary, which in turn transfers the receivables to a Trust. The Trust, either directly or through related trusts, sells debt securities to third parties. The following summarizes this activity for fiscal 2008 and 2009.

Nonrecourse Debt Collateralized by Credit Card Receivables (millions)	Amount
At February 2, 2008	$2,400
Issued, net of $268 discount	3,557
Accretion(a)	33
Repaid	(500)
At January 31, 2009	5,490
Issued	—
Accretion(a)	48
Repaid	(163)
At January 30, 2010	$5,375

(a) Represents the accretion of the 7 percent discount on the 47 percent interest in credit card receivables sold to JPMC.

Other than debt backed by our credit card receivables and other immaterial borrowings, all of our outstanding borrowings are senior, unsecured obligations.

INVENTORY

RECOGNITION AND MEASUREMENT

2.43   FASB ASC 330, *Inventory*, states that the primary basis of accounting for inventories is cost, but a departure from the cost basis of pricing the inventory is required when the utility of the goods is no longer as great as their cost.

2.44   FASB ASC 330-10-35-14 states that if inventories are written down below cost at the close of a fiscal year, such reduced amount is to be considered the cost for subsequent accounting purposes. Similarly, the Topic 5(BB), "Inventory Valuation Allowances," of the SEC's *Codification of Staff Accounting Bulletins* indicates that a write-down of inventory creates a new cost basis that subsequently cannot be marked up.

PRESENTATION

2.45   Rule 5-02.6 of Regulation S-X requires separate presentation in the balance sheet or notes of the amounts of major classes of inventory, such as finished goods, work in process, raw materials, and supplies. Additional disclosures are required for amounts related to long-term contracts or programs.

DISCLOSURE

2.46   FASB ASC 330 requires disclosure of the basis for stating inventories. Rule 5-02.6 of Regulation S-X requires disclosure of the method by which amounts are removed from inventory (for example, average cost; first in, first out (FIFO); last in, first out (LIFO); estimated average cost per unit). Table 2-4 summarizes the methods used by the survey entities to determine inventory costs and indicates the portion of inventory cost determined by LIFO.

2.47   Rule 5-02.6c of Regulation S-X requires that registrants using LIFO disclose the excess of replacement or current cost over stated LIFO value, if material. 325 survey entities disclosed the effect of income from using LIFO, rather than FIFO or average cost, to determine inventory cost.

2.48

TABLE 2-4: INVENTORY COST DETERMINATION

	Number of Entities		
	2010	**2009**	**2008**
Methods			
Not disclosed	55	N/C*	N/C*
First in, first out (FIFO)	316	325	323
Last in, first out (LIFO)	166	176	179
Average cost	113	147	146
Standard costs	15	N/C*	N/C*
Retail method	21	N/C*	N/C*
Other	74	18	17
Use of LIFO			
All inventories	4	4	7
50% or more of inventories	83	82	86
Less than 50% of inventories	54	78	72
Not determinable	25	12	14
Additional LIFO Information			
LIFO discontinued for all or portion of inventories	1	N/C*	N/C*
LIFO liquidation	28	N/C*	N/C*
Effect on income from using LIFO instead of FIFO or average cost	50	N/C*	N/C*
Dollar value LIFO used to calculate LIFO inventory cost	1	N/C*	N/C*

* N/C = Not compiled. Line item was not included in the table for the year shown.

PRESENTATION AND DISCLOSURE EXCERPTS

First-In First-Out

2.49

KOHL'S CORPORATION (JAN)

CONSOLIDATED BALANCE SHEETS (in part)

(Dollars In Millions, Except Per Share Data)

	January 30, 2010	January 31, 2009
Assets		
Current assets:		
Cash and cash equivalents	$ 2,267	$ 643
Merchandise inventories	2,923	2,799
Deferred income taxes	73	74
Other	222	212
Total current assets	5,485	3,728
Property and equipment, net	7,018	6,984
Long-term investments	321	333
Favorable lease rights, net	204	201
Other assets	132	117
Total assets	$13,160	$11,363

NOTES TO CONSOLIDATED FINANCIAL STATEMENTS

1. Business and Summary of Accounting Policies (in part)

Merchandise Inventories

Merchandise inventories are valued at the lower of cost or market with cost determined on the first-in, first-out ("FIFO") basis using the retail inventory method ("RIM"). Under RIM, the valuation of inventory at cost and the resulting gross margins are calculated by applying a cost-to-retail ratio to the retail value inventory. RIM is an averaging method that has been widely used in the retail industry due to its practicality. The use of RIM will result in inventory being valued at the lower of cost or market since permanent markdowns are currently taken as a reduction of the retail value of inventory. We record an additional reserve when the future estimated selling price is less than cost.

2.50

SNAP-ON INCORPORATED (DEC)

CONSOLIDATED BALANCE SHEETS (in part)

	Year End	
(Amounts in millions, except share data)	2010	2009
Assets		
Current assets		
Cash and cash equivalents	$ 572.2	$ 699.4
Trade and other accounts receivable—net	443.3	414.4
Finance receivables—net	215.3	122.3
Contract receivables—net	45.6	32.9
Inventories—net	329.4	274.7
Deferred income tax assets	87.0	69.5
Prepaid expenses and other assets	72.7	62.9
Total current assets	1,765.5	1,676.1
Property and equipment—net	344.0	347.8
Deferred income tax assets	91.5	88.2
Long-term finance receivables—net	345.7	177.9
Long-term contract receivables—net	119.3	70.7
Goodwill	798.4	814.3
Other intangibles—net	192.8	206.2
Other assets	72.2	66.2
Total assets	$3,729.4	$3,447.4

NOTES TO CONSOLIDATED FINANCIAL STATEMENTS

Note 1. Summary of Accounting Policies (in part)

Inventories: Snap-on values its inventory at the lower of cost or market and adjusts for the value of inventory that is estimated to be excess, obsolete or otherwise unmarketable. Snap-on records allowances for excess and obsolete inventory based on historical and estimated future demand and market conditions. Allowances for raw materials are largely based on an analysis of raw material age and actual physical inspection of raw material for fitness for use. As part of evaluating the adequacy of allowances for work-in-progress and finished goods, management reviews individual product stock-keeping units (SKUs) by product category and product life cycle. Cost adjustments for each product category/product life-cycle state are generally established and maintained based on a combination of historical experience, forecasted sales and promotions, technological obsolescence, inventory age and other actual known conditions and circumstances. Should actual product marketability and raw material fitness for use be affected by conditions that are different from management estimates, further adjustments to inventory allowances may be required.

Snap-on adopted the "last-in, first-out" ("LIFO") inventory valuation method in 1973 for its U.S. locations. Snap-on's U.S. inventories accounted for on a LIFO basis consist of purchased product and inventory manufactured at the company's heritage U.S. manufacturing facilities (primarily hand tools and tool storage). As Snap-on began acquiring businesses in the 1990's, the company retained the "first-in, first-out" ("FIFO") inventory valuation methodology used by the predecessor businesses prior to their acquisition by Snap-on; the company does not adopt the LIFO inventory valuation methodology for new acquisitions. See Note 4 for further information on inventories.

Note 4. Inventories

Inventories by major classification as of 2010 and 2009 year end are as follows:

(Amounts in millions)	2010	2009
Finished goods	$308.7	$254.3
Work in progress	25.0	28.3
Raw materials	64.1	60.5
Total FIFO value	397.8	343.1
Excess of current cost over LIFO cost	(68.4)	(68.4)
Total inventories—net	$329.4	$274.7

Inventories accounted for using the FIFO method as of 2010 and 2009 year end approximated 64% and 66%, respectively, of total inventories. The company accounts for its non-U.S. inventory on the FIFO method. As of 2010 year end, approximately 27% of the company's U.S. inventory was accounted for using the FIFO method and 73% was accounted for using the LIFO method. LIFO inventory liquidations resulted in a reduction of "Cost of goods sold" on the accompanying Consolidated Statements of Earnings of $9.5 million in 2009; there were no LIFO inventory liquidations in 2010 or 2008.

Last-In First-Out

2.51

THE SHERWIN-WILLIAMS COMPANY (DEC)

CONSOLIDATED BALANCE SHEETS (in part)

	December 31		
(Thousands of dollars)	2010	2009	2008
Assets			
Current assets:			
Cash and cash equivalents	$ 58,585	$ 69,329	$ 26,212
Accounts receivable, less allowance	916,661	696,055	769,985
Inventories:			
Finished goods	743,953	630,683	749,405
Work in process and raw materials	173,748	107,805	114,795
	917,701	738,488	864,200
Deferred income taxes	127,348	121,276	97,568
Other current assets	193,427	144,871	151,240
Total current assets	$2,213,722	$1,770,019	$1,909,205

NOTES TO CONSOLIDATED FINANCIAL STATEMENTS

Note 4—Inventories

Inventories were stated at the lower of cost or market with cost determined principally on the last-in, first-out (LIFO) method. The following presents the effect on inventories, net income and net income per common share had the Company used the first-in, first-out (FIFO) inventory valuation method adjusted for income taxes at the statutory rate and assuming no other adjustments. Management believes that the use of LIFO results in a better matching of costs and revenues. This information is presented to enable the reader to make comparisons with companies using the FIFO method of inventory valuation. During 2009, certain inventories accounted for on the LIFO method were reduced, resulting in the liquidation of certain quantities carried at costs prevailing in prior years. The impact on Net income of such liquidations was $8,634.

	2010	2009	2008
Percentage of total inventories on LIFO	76%	83%	86%
Excess of FIFO over LIFO	$277,164	$250,454	$321,280
(Decrease) increase in net income due to LIFO	(16,394)	43,650	(49,184)
(Decrease) increase in net income per common share due to LIFO	(.15)	.38	(.41)

2.52

THE BON-TON STORES, INC. (JAN)

CONSOLIDATED BALANCE SHEETS (in part)

(In thousands except share and per share data)	January 30, 2010	January 31, 2009
Assets		
Current assets:		
Cash and cash equivalents	$ 18,922	$ 19,719
Merchandise inventories	659,399	666,081
Prepaid expenses and other current assets	87,690	113,441
Total current assets	$766,011	$799,241

NOTES TO CONSOLIDATED FINANCIAL STATEMENTS

(In thousands except share and per share data)

1. Summary of Significant Accounting Policies (in part)

Merchandise Inventories

For financial reporting and tax purposes, merchandise inventories are determined by the retail method. As of January 30, 2010 and January 31, 2009, approximately 32% of the Company's merchandise inventories were valued using a first-in, first-out ("FIFO") cost basis and approximately 68% of merchandise inventories were valued using a last-in, first-out ("LIFO") cost basis. There was no effect on costs of merchandise sold for LIFO valuations in 2009, 2008 and 2007. If the FIFO method of inventory valuation had been used for all inventories, the Company's merchandise inventories would have been lower by $6,837 at January 30, 2010 and January 31, 2009.

Costs for merchandise purchases, product development and distribution are included in costs of merchandise sold.

2.53

J. C. PENNEY COMPANY, INC. (JAN)

CONSOLIDATED BALANCE SHEETS (in part)

($ in millions, except per share data)	2009	2008
Assets		
Current assets		
Cash in banks and in transit	$ 163	$ 167
Cash short-term investments	2,848	2,185
Cash and cash equivalents	3,011	2,352
Merchandise inventory	3,024	3,259
Income taxes receivable	395	352
Prepaid expenses and other	222	257
Total current assets	6,652	6,220
Property and equipment, net	5,357	5,367
Other assets	572	424
Total assets	$12,581	$12,011

NOTES TO CONSOLIDATED FINANCIAL STATEMENTS

1) Nature of Operations and Summary of Significant Accounting Policies (in part)

Use of Estimates

The preparation of financial statements, in conformity with generally accepted accounting principles in the United States of America (GAAP), requires us to make assumptions and use estimates that affect the reported amounts of assets and liabilities and disclosure of contingent liabilities at the date of the financial statements and the reported amounts of revenues and expenses during the reporting period. The most significant estimates relate to: inventory valuation under the retail method, specifically permanent reductions to retail prices (markdowns) and adjustments for shortages (shrinkage); valuation of long-lived assets; valuation allowances and reserves for workers' compensation and general liability, environmental contingencies, income taxes and litigation; and pension accounting. While actual results could differ from these estimates, we do not expect the differences, if any, to have a material effect on the consolidated financial statements.

Merchandise Inventory

In the fourth quarter of 2009, we elected to change our method of valuing inventory to the FIFO method from the LIFO method. We believe that the FIFO method is preferable as it better reflects current and future operations with respect to the sourcing of merchandise, more accurately reflects the current value of our inventory presented in our con-

solidated balance sheet, and provides a better matching of cost of goods sold with revenue. The cumulative effect of the change was a $1.8 million increase to gross margin recorded in the fourth quarter of 2009. The change was not applied retrospectively to prior periods, as the effect of the change was immaterial to the consolidated financial statements of all prior periods, including interim periods.

The table below presents the results, in the period of the change, with and without the change in accounting principle on inventory and cost of sales.

	Determined by	
($ in millions)	LIFO Method	FIFO Method
January 30, 2010		
Merchandise inventory	$ 2,999	$ 3,024
Cost of goods sold	$10,671	$10,646

For the year ended January 30, 2010, without the accounting change, income from continuing operations before income taxes would have been $23 million lower, net income would have been $14 million lower and EPS would have been $0.06 lower; however, this would not have been reflective of our 2009 operating results, as described above.

Inventories are valued at the lower of cost or market. For department stores, regional warehouses and store distribution centers, we value inventories using the retail method. Lower of cost or market for Direct (Internet/catalog) is determined by standard cost, representing average vendor cost.

Standard Cost

2.54

JDS UNIPHASE CORPORATION (JUN)

CONSOLIDATED BALANCE SHEETS (in part)

(In millions, except share and par value data)

	July 3, 2010	June 27, 2009
Assets		
Current assets:		
Cash and cash equivalents	$ 340.2	$ 286.9
Short-term investments	227.4	398.3
Restricted cash	32.5	10.3
Accounts receivable, less reserves and allowances of $3.0 at July 3, 2010 and $2.4 at June 27, 2009	271.8	187.3
Inventories, net	125.7	144.8
Refundable income taxes	4.0	14.4
Other current assets	73.0	65.8
Total current assets	$1,074.6	$1,107.8

NOTES TO CONSOLIDATED FINANCIAL STATEMENTS

Note 1. Description of Business and Summary of Significant Accounting Policies (in part)

Inventories

Inventory is valued at standard cost, which approximates actual cost computed on a first-in, first-out basis, not in excess of net realizable market value. The Company assesses the valuation on a quarterly basis and writes down the value for estimated excess and obsolete inventory based upon estimates of future demand, including warranty requirements.

Note 5. Balance Sheet and Other Details (in part)

Inventories

Inventories are stated at the lower of cost or market, and include material, labor, and manufacturing overhead costs. The components of inventories were as follows (*in millions*):

| | Years Ended | |
	July 3, 2010	June 27, 2009
Deferred cost of sales	$ 17.0	$ 11.5
Finished goods	43.7	52.3
Work in process	25.4	33.6
Raw materials and purchased parts	39.6	47.4
Total inventories	$125.7	$144.8

During fiscal 2010, 2009, and 2008, the Company recorded write-downs of inventories of $14.6 million, $12.9 million, and $24.6 million respectively.

The Company also sold previously written-down inventories of $10.4 million, $13.8 million, and $17.2 million during fiscal 2010, 2009, and 2008, respectively. In addition, the Company has an active scrap program and typically disposes of inventory that has been written down through the use of scrap dealers or physical disposal/destruction. During fiscal 2010, 2009, and 2008, the Company scrapped $5.8 million, $38.5 million, and $31.2 million of previously written-down inventory, respectively.

The inventory write-downs were predominantly the result of changes in forecasted customer demand and technological changes in the Company's products. The majority of the inventory written down consisted of raw material and finished goods. The major elements of the written down raw material consists of components and items that had not entered into production. The finished goods inventory includes the cost of raw material inputs, labor, and overhead.

The Company operates in markets with relatively few customers and has historically experienced variability in product demand driven by the buying behavior of these customers. In addition, the Company's products utilize long-lead time parts which are available from a limited set of vendors. The combined effects of a limited customer base, variability of demand among the customer base and significant long-lead time or single sourced materials has historically contributed to significant inventory write-downs. The Company routinely reviews inventory for usage potential, including fulfillment of customer warranty obligations and spare part requirements. The Company writes down to zero the value of excess and obsolete ("E&O") inventory that is not expected to be consumed through operations generally within 12 months. Excess is written down to zero value in large part due to the Company's history of changes in customer demand and inherent product obsolescence concerns.

For any written down inventory items retained, the Company evaluates the future realizable value of inventories and impact on gross margins, taking into consideration product life cycles, technological and product changes, demand visibility and other market conditions. The Company believes its current process for writing down inventory appropriately balances the risk in the marketplace with a fair representation of the realizable value of the Company's inventory.

OTHER CURRENT ASSETS

PRESENTATION

2.55 Rule 5-02.8 of Regulation S-X requires that any amounts in excess of 5 percent of total current assets be stated separately on the balance sheet or disclosed in the notes.

TABLE 2-5: OTHER CURRENT ASSET CAPTIONS*

| | Number of Entities | | |
	2010	2009	2008
Nature of Asset			
Deferred and prepaid income taxes.....	331	381	371
Derivatives...	142	232	55
Property held for sale...........................	56	79	80
Advances or deposits...........................	25	8	22
Current assets of discontinued operations.....................................	22	N/C^	N/C^
Unbilled costs or costs in excess of related billings................................	16	N/C^	N/C^
Program/broadcast rights....................	7	N/C^	N/C^

* Other than cash, marketable securities, inventories, and prepaid expenses and appearing in the balance sheet or notes to financial statements, or both.
^ N/C = Not compiled. Line item was not included in the table for the year shown.

PRESENTATION AND DISCLOSURE EXCERPTS

Deferred Taxes

2.56

TRW AUTOMOTIVE HOLDINGS CORP. (DEC)

CONSOLIDATED BALANCE SHEETS (in part)

	As of December 31	
(Dollars in millions)	**2010**	**2009**
Assets		
Current assets:		
Cash and cash equivalents	$1,078	$ 788
Accounts receivable—net	2,087	1,943
Inventories	760	660
Prepaid expenses and other current assets	126	135
Deferred income taxes	89	66
Total current assets	$4,140	$3,592

NOTES TO CONSOLIDATED FINANCIAL STATEMENTS

7. Income Taxes (in part)

Deferred tax assets and liabilities result from differences in the bases of assets and liabilities for tax and financial statement purposes. The approximate tax effect of each type of temporary difference and carryforward that gives rise to a significant portion of the deferred tax assets and liabilities follows:

	As of December 31	
(Dollars in millions)	**2010**	**2009**
Deferred tax assets:		
Pensions and postretirement benefits other than pensions	$ 180	$ 302
Inventory	39	46
Reserves and accruals	226	220
Net operating loss and credit carryforwards	795	904
Fixed assets and intangibles	56	56
Other	54	47
Total deferred tax assets	1,350	1,575
Valuation allowance for deferred tax assets	(775)	(1,011)
Net deferred tax assets	575	564
Deferred tax liabilities:		
Pensions and postretirement benefits other than pensions	(109)	(59)
Fixed assets and intangibles	(189)	(169)
Undistributed earnings of foreign subsidiaries	(59)	(11)
Deferred gain	(75)	(79)
Other	(92)	(101)
Total deferred tax liabilities	(524)	(419)
Net deferred taxes	$ 51	$ 145

The Company has separately reflected the current deferred tax asset and the long term deferred tax assets and liabilities on the consolidated balance sheets for December 31, 2010 and 2009. However, the current deferred tax liability of $26 million as of December 31, 2010 and $25 million as of December 31, 2009 is included in other current liabilities on the consolidated balance sheets.

2.57

THE L.S. STARRETT COMPANY (JUN)

CONSOLIDATED BALANCE SHEETS (in part)

(In thousands except share data)

	June 26, 2010	June 27, 2009
Assets		
Current assets:		
Cash (Note 4)	$ 20,478	$ 10,248
Investments (Note 4)	1,250	1,791
Accounts receivable (less allowance for doubtful accounts of $607 and $678, respectively)	33,707	27,233
Inventories:		
Raw materials and supplies	14,939	19,672
Goods in process and finished parts	16,794	20,265
Finished goods	14,423	20,289
Total inventories	46,156	60,226
Current deferred income tax asset (Note 10)	3,300	5,170
Prepaid expenses and other current assets	5,510	8,054
Total current assets	$110,401	$112,722

NOTES TO CONSOLIDATED FINANCIAL STATEMENTS

10. Income Taxes (in part)

Deferred income taxes at June 26, 2010 and June 27, 2009 are attributable to the following (in thousands):

	2010	2009
Deferred assets (current):		
Inventories	$ (1,816)	$ (3,396)
Employee benefits (other than pension)	(276)	(525)
Book reserves	(1,208)	(1,249)
	$ (3,300)	$ (5,170)
Deferred assets (long-term):		
Federal NOL, carried forward	$ (9,820)	$ (7,347)
State NOL, various carryforward periods	(962)	(865)
Foreign NOL, various carried forward periods	(914)	(752)
Foreign tax credit carryforward, expiring 2010–16	(1,194)	(1,194)
Pension benefit	(5,589)	(1,439)
Retiree medical benefits	(4,562)	(4,228)
Intangibles	(3,553)	(2,983)
Other	(1,389)	(558)
	$(27,983)	$(19,366)
Valuation reserve for state NOL, foreign NOL and foreign tax credits	$ 1,868	$ 1,687
Long-term deferred assets	$(26,115)	$(17,679)
Deferred liabilities (long-term):		
Depreciation	2,436	2,467
	$ 2,436	$ 2,467
Net deferred tax assets	$(26,979)	$(20,382)

As of June 26, 2010 and June 27, 2009, the net long-term deferred tax asset and deferred tax liability respectively, on the balance sheet are as follows:

	2010	2009
Long-term liabilities	$ 2,436	$ 2,467
Long-term assets	(26,115)	(17,679)
	$(23,679)	$(15,212)

Foreign operations deferred assets (current) relate primarily to book reserves.

Foreign operations net deferred assets (long-term) relate primarily to foreign NOL and foreign tax credits carryforwards.

Amounts related to foreign operations included in the long-term portion of deferred liabilities relate primarily to depreciation.

Property Held for Sale

2.58

PULTEGROUP, INC. (DEC)

CONSOLIDATED BALANCE SHEETS (in part)

December 31, 2010 and 2009
  ($000's omitted, except per share data)

	2010	2009
Assets		
Cash and equivalents	$1,470,625	$ 1,858,234
Restricted cash	24,601	32,376
Unfunded settlements	12,765	2,153
House and land inventory	4,781,813	4,940,358
Land held for sale	71,055	58,645
Land, not owned, under option agreements	50,781	174,132
Residential mortgage loans available-for-sale	176,164	166,817
Investments in unconsolidated entities	46,313	73,815
Goodwill	240,541	895,918
Intangible assets, net	175,448	188,548
Other assets	567,963	705,040
Income taxes receivable	81,307	955,186
	$7,699,376	$10,051,222

NOTES TO CONSOLIDATED FINANCIAL STATEMENTS

5. Inventory and Land Held for Sale (in part)

Net Realizable Value Adjustments—Land Held for Sale

The Company acquires land primarily for the construction of homes for sale to customers but periodically sells select parcels of land to third parties for commercial or other development. Additionally, the Company may determine that certain of its land assets no longer fit into its strategic operating plans. In such instances, the Company classifies the land asset as land held for sale, assuming the criteria in ASC 360 are met.

The Company values land held for sale at the lower of carrying value or fair value less costs to sell. In determining the fair value of land held for sale, the Company considers recent legitimate offers received, prices for land in recent comparable sales transactions, and other factors. As a result of changing market conditions in the real estate industry, a portion of the Company's land held for sale was written down to net realizable value. During 2010, 2009, and 2008, the Company recognized net realizable value adjustments related to land held for sale of $39.1 million, $113.7 million, and $271.1 million, respectively. The Company records these net realizable value adjustments in its Consolidated Statements of Operations within Homebuilding land cost of revenues.

The Company's land held for sale at December 31, 2010 and 2009 was as follows ($000's omitted):

	2010	2009
Land held for sale, gross	$124,919	$ 84,495
Net realizable value reserves	(53,864)	(25,850)
Land held for sale, net	$ 71,055	$ 58,645

Current Assets of Discontinued Operations

2.59

MEADWESTVACO CORPORATION (DEC)

CONSOLIDATED BALANCE SHEETS (in part)

	December 31	
(In millions, except share and per share data)	2010	2009
Assets		
Cash and cash equivalents	$ 790	$ 850
Accounts receivable, net	827	839
Inventories	642	523
Other current assets	131	148
Current assets of discontinued operations	56	170
Current assets	$2,446	$2,530

NOTES TO CONSOLIDATED FINANCIAL STATEMENTS

R. Dispositions (in part)

On February 1, 2011, the company completed the sale of its envelope products business for cash proceeds of $55 million. During 2010, the company recorded pre-tax charges of $19 million ($15 million after taxes) comprised of impairment of long-lived assets of $6 million, impairment of allocated goodwill of $7 million and a pension curtailment loss of $6 million. For 2010 and prior years, the operating results of this business, as well as the charges noted above, are reported in discontinued operations in the consolidated statements of operations on an after-tax basis. The results of operations and assets and liabilities of the envelope products business were previously included in the Consumer & Office Products segment.

On September 30, 2010, the company completed the sale of its media and entertainment packaging business for cash proceeds of $68 million. The sale resulted in a pre-tax loss of $153 million ($126 million after taxes). For 2010 and prior years, the operating results of this business, as well as the loss on disposition, are reported in discontinued operations in the consolidated statements of operations on an after-tax basis. The results of operations and assets and liabilities of the media and entertainment packaging business were previously included in the Consumer Solutions segment.

On July 1, 2008, the company completed the sale of its Kraft business for net cash proceeds of $466 million. The sale resulted in a pre-tax gain of $13 million ($8 million after taxes). For 2008, the operating results of this business, as well as the gain on sale, are reported as discontinued operations in the consolidated statements of operations on an after-tax basis. The results of operations and assets and liabilities of the Kraft business were previously included in the Packaging Resources segment.

Below are amounts attributed to the above dispositions included in discontinued operations in the consolidated statements of operations.

	Year Ended December 31		
(In millions, except per share amounts)	2010	2009	2008
Net sales	$ 475	$643	$1,081
Cost of sales[(1),(4)]	459	584	980
Selling, general and administrative expenses[(2),(4)]	52	69	100
Interest expense	6	8	18
Other expense (income), net[(3)]	152	(1)	(17)
Loss before income taxes	(194)	(17)	0
Income tax (benefit) provision	(38)	(2)	1
Net loss	$(156)	$ (15)	$ (1)

[(1)] For the years ended December 31, 2010, 2009, and 2008, cost of sales includes restructuring charges of $1 million, $13 million and $10 million, respectively.

[(2)] For the years ended December 31, 2010, 2009, and 2008, selling, general and administrative expenses include restructuring charges of $2 million, $3 million and $7 million, respectively.

[(3)] Other expense in 2010 includes a loss on sale of the media and entertainment packaging business of $153 million.

[(4)] For the year ended December 31, 2010 pursuant to the sale of the envelope products business that closed on February 1, 2011, cost of sales includes an impairment charge of allocated goodwill of $7 million, an impairment charge of long-lived assets of $6 million and a pension curtailment charge of $5 million; selling, general and administrative expenses include a pension curtailment charge of $1 million.

The following table shows the major categories of assets and liabilities that are classified as discontinued operations in the consolidated balance sheet at December 31, 2010 and 2009:

(In millions)	December 31, 2010	December 31, 2009
Accounts receivable, net	$30	$97
Inventories	25	67
Other current assets	1	6
Current assets	56	170
Property, plant and equipment, net	24	141
Other assets	1	54
Non-current assets	25	195
Accounts payable	11	49
Accrued expenses	12	42
Current liabilities	23	91
Other long-term liabilities	$ 3	$ 5

Costs and Estimated Earnings in Excess of Billings

2.60

THE SHAW GROUP INC. (AUG)

CONSOLIDATED BALANCE SHEETS (in part)

As of August 31, 2010 and 2009
(In thousands, except share amounts)

	2010	2009
Assets		
Current assets:		
Cash and cash equivalents	$ 912,736	$1,029,138
Restricted and escrowed cash and cash equivalents	33,926	81,925
Short-term investments	551,960	342,219
Restricted short-term investments	321,056	80,000
Accounts receivable, including retainage, net	833,574	815,862
Inventories	228,891	262,284
Costs and estimated earnings in excess of billings on uncompleted contracts, including claims	637,651	599,741
Deferred income taxes	319,712	270,851
Investment in Westinghouse	967,916	1,008,442
Prepaid expenses and other current assets	64,468	62,786
Total current assets	$4,871,890	$4,553,248

NOTES TO CONSOLIDATED FINANCIAL STATEMENTS

Note 1—Description of Business and Summary of Significant Accounting Policies (in part)

Costs and Estimated Earnings in Excess of Billings on Uncompleted Contracts, Including Claims, and Advanced Billings and Billings in Excess of Costs and Estimated Earnings on Uncompleted Contracts

In accordance with normal practice in the construction industry, we include in current assets and current liabilities amounts related to construction contracts realizable and payable over a period in excess of one year. Costs and estimated earnings in excess of billings on uncompleted contracts represent the excess of contract costs and profits recognized to date using the percentage-of-completion method over billings to date on certain contracts. Billings in excess of costs and estimated earnings on uncompleted contracts represents the excess of billings to date over the amount of contract costs and profits recognized to date using the percentage-of-completion method on certain contracts.

Note 5—Accounts Receivable, Concentrations of Credit Risk, and Inventories (in part)

Concentrations of Credit

Amounts due from U.S. government agencies or entities were $72.1 million and $110.3 million at August 31, 2010, and August 31, 2009, respectively. Costs and estimated earnings in excess of billings on uncompleted contracts include $309.3 million and $217.1 million at August 31, 2010, and August 31, 2009, respectively, related to the U.S. government agencies and related entities.

Additionally, at August 31, 2010 and August 31, 2009, respectively, we had approximately $110.0 million and $94.6 million in retention and approximately $74.8 million and $13.3 million in trade receivables related to one customer.

Derivatives

2.61

EBAY INC. (DEC)

CONSOLIDATED BALANCE SHEET (in part)

(In thousands, except par value amounts)	December 31, 2009	December 31, 2010
Assets		
Current assets:		
Cash and cash equivalents	$ 3,999,818	$ 5,577,411
Short-term investments	943,986	1,045,403
Accounts receivable, net	407,507	454,366
Loans and interest receivable, net	622,846	956,189
Funds receivable and customer accounts	2,157,945	2,550,731
Other current assets	328,106	481,238
Total current assets	8,460,208	11,065,338
Long-term investments	1,381,765	2,492,012
Property and equipment, net	1,314,328	1,523,333
Goodwill	6,143,086	6,193,163
Intangible assets, net	767,812	540,711
Other assets	341,121	189,205
Total assets	$18,408,320	$22,003,762

NOTES TO CONSOLIDATED FINANCIAL STATEMENTS

Note 1—The Company and Summary of Significant Accounting Policies (in part)

Derivative Instruments

We have significant international revenues as well as costs denominated in foreign currencies, subjecting us to foreign currency risk. We purchase foreign currency exchange contracts that qualify as cash flow hedges, generally with maturities of 15 months or less, to reduce the volatility of cash flows primarily related to forecasted revenue and intercompany transactions denominated in certain foreign currencies. All outstanding designated derivatives that qualify for hedge accounting are recognized on the balance sheet at fair value. The effective portion of the designated derivative's gain or loss is initially reported as a component of accumulated other comprehensive income and is subsequently reclassified into the financial statement line item in which the hedged item is recorded in the same period the forecasted transaction affects earnings. We also economically hedge our exposure to foreign currency denominated monetary assets and liabilities with foreign currency contracts. The gains and losses on the foreign exchange contracts economically offset transaction gains and losses on certain foreign currency denominated monetary assets and liabilities recognized in earnings. Accordingly, these outstanding non-designated derivatives are recognized on the balance sheet at fair value and changes in fair value from these contracts are recorded in interest and other income (expense), net, in the consolidated statement of income. Our derivatives program is not designed or operated for trading or speculative purposes.

Our derivative instruments expose us to credit risk to the extent that our counterparties may be unable to meet the terms of the agreements. We seek to mitigate this risk by limiting our counterparties to major financial institutions and by spreading the risk across several major financial institutions. In addition, the potential risk of loss with any one counterparty resulting from this type of credit risk is monitored on an ongoing basis. See "Note 9—Derivative Instruments" for additional information related to our derivative instruments.

Note 8—Fair Value Measurement of Assets and Liabilities (in part)

The following table summarizes our financial assets and liabilities measured at fair value on a recurring basis as of December 31, 2009 (in thousands):

Description	Balance as of December 31, 2009	Quoted Prices in Active Markets for Identical Assets (Level 1)	Significant Other Observable Inputs (Level 2)
Assets:			
Cash and cash equivalents	$3,999,818	$3,999,818	$ —
Short-term investments:			
Restricted cash	29,123	29,123	—
Corporate debt securities	73,140	—	73,140
Government and agency securities	109,807	—	109,807
Time deposits	310,418	—	310,418
Equity instruments	421,498	421,498	—
Total short-term investments	943,986	450,621	493,365
Derivatives	362	—	362
Long-term investments:			
Restricted cash	985	985	—
Corporate debt securities	457,183	—	457,183
Government and agency securities	249,360	—	249,360
Time deposits and other	1,583	—	1,583
Total long-term assets	709,111	985	708,126
Total financial assets	$5,653,277	$4,451,424	$1,201,853
Liabilities:			
Derivatives	$ 5,710	$ —	$ 5,710

The following table summarizes our financial assets and liabilities measured at fair value on a recurring basis as of December 31, 2010 (in thousands):

Description	Balance as of December 31, 2010	Quoted Prices in Active Markets for Identical Assets (Level 1)	Significant Other Observable Inputs (Level 2)
Assets:			
Cash and cash equivalents	$5,577,411	$5,577,411	$ —
Short-term investments:			
Restricted cash	20,351	20,351	—
Corporate debt securities	372,225	—	372,225
Government and agency securities	66,534	—	66,534
Time deposits	44,772	—	44,772
Equity instruments	541,521	541,521	—
Total short-term investments	1,045,403	561,872	483,531
Derivatives	37,196	—	37,196
Long-term assets:			
Restricted cash	1,332	1,332	—
Corporate debt securities	1,605,770	—	1,605,770
Government and agency securities	150,966	—	150,966
Time deposits and other	4,541	—	4,541
Total long-term assets	1,762,609	1,332	1,761,277
Total financial assets	$8,422,619	$6,140,615	$2,282,004
Liabilities:			
Derivatives	$ 4,963	$ —	$ 4,963

Our financial assets and liabilities are valued using market prices on both active markets (level 1) and less active markets (level 2). Level 1 instrument valuations are obtained from real-time quotes for transactions in active exchange markets involving identical assets. Level 2 instrument valuations are obtained from readily available pricing sources for comparable instruments. As of December 31, 2010, we did not have any assets or liabilities requiring measurement at fair value without observable market values that would require a high level of judgment to determine fair value (level 3). Our derivative instruments are valued using pricing models that take into account the contract terms as well as multiple inputs where applicable, such as equity prices, interest rate yield curves, option volatility and currency rates. Our derivative instruments are short-term in nature, typically one month to fifteen months in duration. We maintain our customer account balances in interest bearing bank deposits (including time deposits with maturity dates of less than a year), which are valued using market prices on active markets (level 1). As of December 31, 2010, our customer account balances were approximately $1.9 billion.

Note 9—Derivative Instruments (in part)

The notional amounts associated with our foreign currency contracts at December 31, 2009 and December 31, 2010 were $298.6 million and $1.8 billion, respectively. Derivative transactions are measured in terms of the notional amount, but this amount is not recorded on the balance sheet and is not, when viewed in isolation, a meaningful measure of the risk profile of the instruments. The notional amount is generally not exchanged, but is used only as the basis on which the value of foreign exchange payments are determined.

Fair Value of Derivative Contracts: Derivative instruments are reported at fair value as follows (in thousands):

	December 31, 2009		December 31, 2010	
	Derivative Assets Reported in Other Current Assets	**Derivative Liabilities Reported in Other Current Liabilities**	**Derivative Assets Reported in Other Current Assets**	**Derivative Liabilities Reported in Other Current Liabilities**
Foreign exchange contracts designated as cash flow hedges	$ 27	$4,848	$35,853	$4,162
Foreign exchange contracts not designated as hedging instruments	335	862	1,343	801
Total fair value of derivative instruments	$362	$5,710	$37,196	$4,963

2.62

PFIZER INC. (DEC)

CONSOLIDATED BALANCE SHEETS (in part)

	As of December 31	
(Millions, except preferred stock issued and per common share data)	**2010**	**2009**
Assets		
Cash and cash equivalents	$ 1,735	$ 1,978
Short-term investments	26,277	23,991
Accounts receivable, less allowance for doubtful accounts: 2010—$217; 2009—$176	14,612	14,645
Short-term loans	467	1,195
Inventories	8,405	12,403
Taxes and other current assets	8,411	6,962
Assets held for sale	561	496
Total current assets	$60,468	$61,670

NOTES TO CONSOLIDATED FINANCIAL STATEMENTS

9. Financial Instruments (in part)

A. Selected Financial Assets and Liabilities (in part)
Information about certain of our financial assets and liabilities follows:

(Millions of dollars)	As of December 31	
	2010	**2009**
Selected financial assets measured at fair value on a recurring basis[a]:		
Trading securities[b]	$ 173	$ 184
Available-for-sale debt securities[c]	32,699	32,338
Available-for-sale money market funds[d]	1,217	2,569
Available-for-sale equity securities, excluding money market funds[c]	230	281
Derivative financial instruments in receivable positions[e]:		
Interest rate swaps	603	276
Foreign currency forward-exchange contracts	494	502
Foreign currency swaps	128	798
Total	35,544	36,948
Other selected financial assets[f]:		
Held-to-maturity debt securities, carried at amortized cost[c]	1,178	812
Private equity securities, carried at cost or equity method[g]	1,135	811
Short-term loans, carried at cost[h]	467	1,195
Long-term loans, carried at cost[h]	299	784
Total	3,079	3,602
Total selected financial assets[i]	$38,623	$40,550

[a] Fair values are determined based on valuation techniques categorized as follows: Level 1 means the use of quoted prices for identical instruments in active markets; Level 2 means the use of quoted prices for similar instruments in active markets or quoted prices for identical or similar instruments in markets that are not active or are directly or indirectly observable; Level 3 means the use of unobservable inputs. All of our financial assets and liabilities measured at fair value on a recurring basis use Level 2 inputs in the calculation of fair value, except that included in available-for-sale equity securities, excluding money market funds, are $105 million as of December 31, 2010 and $77 million as of December 31, 2009 of investments that use Level 1 inputs in the calculation of fair value. None of our financial assets and liabilities measured at fair value on a recurring basis are valued using Level 3 inputs at December 31, 2010 or 2009.

[b] Trading securities are held in trust for legacy business acquisition severance benefits.

[c] Gross unrealized gains and losses are not significant.

[d] Includes approximately $625 million as of December 31, 2010 and approximately $1.2 billion as of December 31, 2009 of money market funds held in escrow to secure certain of Wyeth's payment obligations under its 1999 Nationwide Class Action Settlement Agreement, which relates to litigation against Wyeth concerning its former weight-loss products, Redux and Pondimin (see *Note 9G. Financial Instruments: Guarantee*).

[e] Designated as hedging instruments, except for certain foreign currency contracts used as offsets; namely, foreign currency forward-exchange contracts with fair values of $326 million and foreign currency swaps with fair values of $17 million at December 31, 2010; and foreign currency swaps with fair values of $106 million and foreign currency forward-exchange contracts with fair values of $100 million at December 31, 2009.

[f] The differences between the estimated fair values and carrying values of our financial assets and liabilities not measured at fair value on a recurring basis were not significant as of December 31, 2010 or December 31, 2009.

[g] Our private equity securities represent investments in the life sciences sector.

[h] Our short-term and long-term loans are due from companies with highly rated securities (Standard & Poor's (S&P) ratings of mostly AA or better).

[i] The decrease in selected financial assets is primarily due to the use of proceeds of short-term investments for repayment of short-term borrowings and for tax payments made in the first quarter of 2010, primarily associated with certain business decisions executed to finance the Wyeth acquisition, partially offset by cash flows from operations.

The following methods and assumptions were used to estimate the fair value of our financial assets and liabilities:
- Trading equity securities—quoted market prices.
- Trading debt securities—observable market interest rates.
- Available-for-sale debt securities—third-party matrix-pricing model that uses significant inputs derived from or corroborated by observable market data and credit-adjusted interest rate yield curves.
- Available-for-sale money market funds—observable Net Asset Value prices.

- Available-for-sale equity securities, excluding money market funds—third-party pricing services that principally use a composite of observable prices.
- Derivative financial instruments (assets and liabilities)—third-party matrix-pricing model that uses significant inputs derived from or corroborated by observable market data. Where applicable, these models discount future cash flow amounts using market-based observable inputs, including interest rate yield curves, and forward and spot prices for currencies. The credit risk impact to our derivative financial instruments was not significant.

- Held-to-maturity debt securities—third-party matrix-pricing model that uses significant inputs derived from or corroborated by observable market data and credit-adjusted interest rate yield curves.
- Private equity securities, excluding equity-method investments—application of the implied volatility associated with an observable biotech index to the carrying amount of our portfolio and, to a lesser extent, performance multiples of comparable securities adjusted for company-specific information.
- Short-term and long-term loans—third-party model that discounts future cash flows using current interest rates at which similar loans would be made to borrowers with similar credit ratings and for the same remaining maturities.
- Short-term borrowings and long-term debt—third-party matrix-pricing model that uses significant inputs derived from or corroborated by observable market data and our own credit rating.

In addition, we have long-term receivables where the determination of fair value employs discounted future cash flows, using current interest rates at which similar loans would be made to borrowers with similar credit ratings and for the same remaining maturities.

A single estimate of fair value for these financial instruments relies heavily on estimates and assumptions (see *Note 1C. Significant Accounting Polices: Estimates and Assumptions*).

These selected financial assets and liabilities are presented in our Consolidated Balance Sheets as follows (*in part*):

	As of December 31	
(Millions of dollars)	2010	2009
Assets		
Cash and cash equivalents	$ 906	$ 666
Short-term investments	26,277	23,991
Short-term loans	467	1,195
Long-term investments and loans	9,748	13,122
Taxes and other current assets[(a)]	515	526
Taxes and other noncurrent assets[(b)]	710	1,050
Total	$38,623	$40,550

[(a)] As of December 31, 2010, derivative instruments at fair value include foreign currency forward-exchange contracts ($494 million) and foreign currency swaps ($21 million) and, as of December 31, 2009, include foreign currency forward-exchange contracts ($503 million) and foreign currency swaps ($23 million).

[(b)] As of December 31, 2010, derivative instruments at fair value include interest rate swaps ($603 million) and foreign currency swaps ($107 million) and, as of December 31, 2009, include foreign currency swaps ($774 million) and interest rate swaps ($276 million).

E. Derivative Financial Instruments and Hedging Activities (in part)

Foreign Exchange Risk—A significant portion of our revenues, earnings and net investments in foreign affiliates is exposed to changes in foreign exchange rates. We seek to manage our foreign exchange risk, in part, through operational means, including managing expected same-currency revenues in relation to same-currency costs and same-currency assets in relation to same-currency liabilities. Depending on market conditions, foreign exchange risk also is managed through the use of derivative financial instruments and for-eign currency debt. These financial instruments serve to protect net income and net investments against the impact of the translation into U.S. dollars of certain foreign exchange-denominated transactions. The aggregate notional amount of foreign exchange derivative financial instruments hedging or offsetting foreign currency exposures is $47.6 billion. The derivative financial instruments primarily hedge or offset exposures in the euro, Japanese yen and U.K. pound. The maximum length of time over which we are hedging future foreign exchange cash flows relates to our $2.3 billion U.K. pound debt maturing in 2038.

All derivative contracts used to manage foreign currency risk are measured at fair value and are reported as assets or liabilities on the consolidated balance sheet. Changes in fair value are reported in earnings or deferred, depending on the nature and purpose of the financial instrument (offset or hedge relationship) and the effectiveness of the hedge relationships, as follows:

- We defer on the balance sheet the effective portion of the gains or losses on foreign currency forward-exchange contracts and foreign currency swaps that are designated as cash flow hedges and reclassify those amounts, as appropriate, into earnings in the same period or periods during which the hedged transaction affects earnings.
- We recognize the gains and losses on forward-exchange contracts and foreign currency swaps that are used to offset the same foreign currency assets or liabilities immediately into earnings along with the earnings impact of the items they generally offset. These contracts essentially take the opposite currency position of that reflected in the month-end balance sheet to counterbalance the effect of any currency movement.
- We recognize the gain and loss impact on foreign currency swaps designated as hedges of our net investments in earnings in three ways: over time—for the periodic net swap payments; immediately—to the extent of any change in the difference between the foreign exchange spot rate and forward rate; and upon sale or substantial liquidation of our net investments—to the extent of change in the foreign exchange spot rates.
- We defer on the balance sheet foreign exchange gains and losses related to foreign exchange-denominated debt designated as a hedge of our net investments in foreign subsidiaries and reclassify those amounts into earnings upon the sale or substantial liquidation of our net investments.

Any ineffectiveness is recognized immediately into earnings. There was no significant ineffectiveness in 2010, 2009 or 2008.

Interest Rate Risk—Our interest-bearing investments, loans and borrowings are subject to interest rate risk. We seek to invest and loan primarily on a short-term or variable-rate basis; however, in light of current market conditions, we currently borrow primarily on a long-term, fixed-rate basis. From time to time, depending on market conditions, we will change the profile of our outstanding debt by entering into derivative financial instruments like interest rate swaps.

We entered into derivative financial instruments to hedge or offset the fixed interest rates on the hedged item, matching the amount and timing of the hedged item. The aggregate notional amount of interest rate derivative financial instruments is $11.6 billion. The derivative financial instruments hedge U.S. dollar and euro fixed-rate debt.

All derivative contracts used to manage interest rate risk are measured at fair value and reported as assets or liabilities on the consolidated balance sheet. Changes in fair value are reported in earnings, as follows:

- We recognize the gains and losses on interest rate swaps that are designated as fair value hedges in earnings upon the recognition of the change in fair value of the hedged risk. We recognize the offsetting earnings impact of fixed-rate debt attributable to the hedged risk also in earnings.

Any ineffectiveness is recognized immediately into earnings. There was no significant ineffectiveness in 2010, 2009 or 2008.

PROPERTY, PLANT, AND EQUIPMENT

RECOGNITION AND MEASUREMENT

2.63 *Property, plant, and equipment* are the long-lived, physical assets of the entity acquired for use in the entity's normal business operations and not intended for resale by the entity. FASB ASC 360, *Property, Plant, and Equipment*, states that these assets are initially recorded at historical cost, which includes the costs necessarily incurred to bring them to the condition and location necessary for their intended use. FASB ASC 835-20 establishes standards for capitalizing interest cost as part of the historical cost of acquiring assets constructed by an entity for its own use or produced for the entity by others for which deposits or progress payments have been made.

2.64 An entity may acquire or develop computer software either for internal use or for sale or lease to others. If for internal use, FASB ASC 350-40 provides guidance on accounting for the costs of computer software and for determining whether the software is for internal use. Under FASB ASC 350-40, internal and external costs incurred to develop internal-use software during the application development stage should be capitalized and amortized over the software's estimated useful life. Accounting for software acquired or developed for sale or lease is addressed by FASB ASC 985-20. Whether for internal use or sale or lease, FASB ASC refers to capitalized software costs as amortizable intangible assets.

PRESENTATION

2.65 FASB ASC 210-10-45-4 indicates that property, plant, and equipment should be classified as noncurrent when a classified balance sheet is presented. Under FASB ASC 805-20-55-37, some use rights acquired in a business combination may have characteristics of tangible, rather than intangible, assets. An example is mineral rights.

2.66 Under FASB ASC 985-20-45-2, capitalized costs related to software for sale or lease having a life of more than one year or one operating cycle should be presented as an other asset. Under FASB ASC 985-20, amortization expense should be on a product-by-product basis and charged to cost of sales or a similar expense category because it relates to a software product that is marketed to others. Presentations of capitalized computer software costs by survey entities vary.

DISCLOSURE

2.67 FASB ASC 360-10-50 requires the following disclosures in the financial statements or notes thereto:

a. Depreciation expense for the period
b. Balance of major classes of depreciable assets, by nature or function, at the balance sheet date
c. Accumulated depreciation, either by major classes of depreciable assets or in total, at the balance sheet date
d. A general description of the method(s) used in computing depreciation with respect to major classes of depreciable assets.

FASB ASC 360 also provides accounting and disclosure guidance for the long-lived assets that are impaired or held for disposal. Rule 5-02 of Regulation S-X requires that registrants state the basis of determining the amounts of property, plant, and equipment.

2.68

TABLE 2-6: LAND CAPTIONS*

	Number of Entities		
	2010	2009	2008
Land	281	282	289
Land and improvements	117	111	104
Land and buildings	43	47	50
Land combined with other identified assets	7	7	6
No caption with term land	34	42	39
Lines of business classification	11	11	12
Other, described	7	N/C^	N/C^
Total Entities	**500**	**500**	**500**

* Appearing in the balance sheet or notes to financial statements, or both.

^ N/C = Not compiled. Line item was not included in the table for the year shown.

2.69

TABLE 2-7: DEPRECIABLE ASSET CAPTIONS*

	Number of Entities		
	2010	2009	2008
Capital Leases			
Leased assets	277	N/C^	N/C^
No leased assets	208	N/C^	N/C^
Buildings			
Buildings/plant	136	137	144
Buildings and improvements	245	235	235
Buildings combined with land or other identified assets	61	74	75
No caption with term buildings	41	41	37
Line of business classification	4	13	9
Other	13	N/C^	N/C^
Total Entities	500	500	500
Machinery and Equipment			
Machinery or equipment, or both	310	308	304
Machinery or equipment, or both, combined with other assets	112	115	104
Information technology equipment	52	59	64
Transportation	33	N/C^	N/C^
Specific type of machinery or equipment	47	N/C^	N/C^
Other Property Items			
Construction in progress	265	262	250
Leasehold improvements	132	112	103
Furniture and/or fixtures	106	82	89
Software	105	74	75
Assets leased to others	9	12	14
Other, identified	84	N/C^	N/C^

* Appearing in the balance sheet or notes to financial statements, or both.

^ N/C = Not compiled. Line item was not included in the table for the year shown.

PRESENTATION AND DISCLOSURE EXCERPTS

Property, Plant, and Equipment

2.70

CLIFFS NATURAL RESOURCES INC. (DEC)

NOTES TO CONSOLIDATED FINANCIAL STATEMENTS

Note 9—Lease Obligations

We lease certain mining, production and other equipment under operating and capital leases. The leases are for varying lengths, generally at market interest rates and contain purchase and/or renewal options at the end of the terms. Our operating lease expense was $24.2 million, $25.5 million and $20.8 million in 2010, 2009 and 2008, respectively. Capital lease assets were $283.2 million and $167.1 million at December 31, 2010 and 2009, respectively. Corresponding accumulated amortization of capital leases included in respective allowances for depreciation were $92.7 million and $41.5 million at December 31, 2010 and 2009, respectively.

In December 2010, our North American Coal segment entered into a sale-leaseback arrangement. Under the arrangement, we sold the new longwall plow system at our Pinnacle mine in West Virginia and leased it back for a period of five years. The sale-leaseback arrangement was specific to the assets at the time of the agreement and does not include the longwall plow system assets pending delivery. The leaseback has been accounted for as a capital lease. We recorded assets and liabilities under the capital lease of $57.3 million, reflecting the lower of the present value of the minimum lease payments or the fair value of the asset.

Future minimum payments under capital leases and noncancellable operating leases at December 31, 2010 are as follows:

(In millions)	Capital Leases	Operating Leases
2011	$ 46.5	$21.3
2012	43.5	17.1
2013	37.6	17.0
2014	37.1	12.4
2015	41.3	5.7
2016 and thereafter	47.7	8.0
Total minimum lease payments	253.7	$81.5
Amounts representing interest	51.8	
Present value of net minimum lease payments	$201.9[1]	

[1] The total is comprised of $33.7 million and $168.2 million classified as *Other current liabilities* and *Other liabilities*, respectively, on the Statements of Consolidated Financial Position at December 31, 2010.

Total minimum capital lease payments of $253.7 million include $166.4 million for our Asia Pacific Iron Ore segment, $64.1 million for our North American Coal segment, $21.9 million for our North American Iron Ore segment and $1.3 million for our Corporate segment, respectively. Total minimum operating lease payments of $81.5 million include $52.3 million for our North American Iron Ore segment, $18.4 million for our Corporate segment, and $10.8 million for our Asia Pacific Iron Ore, North American Coal and Other segments.

2.71

AK STEEL HOLDING CORPORATION (DEC)

CONSOLIDATED BALANCE SHEETS (in part)

December 31, 2010 and 2009
(Dollars in millions, except per share amounts)

	2010	2009
Assets		
Current assets:		
Cash and cash equivalents	$ 216.8	$ 461.7
Accounts receivable, net	482.8	463.1
Inventory, net	448.7	416.7
Deferred tax asset, current	225.7	223.9
Other current assets	30.1	64.7
Total current assets	1,404.1	1,630.1
Property, plant and equipment	5,668.2	5,385.1
Accumulated depreciation	(3,635.0)	(3,409.1)
Property, plant and equipment, net	$ 2,033.2	$ 1,976.0

NOTES TO CONSOLIDATED FINANCIAL STATEMENTS

(Dollars in millions, except per share amounts)

Note 1—Summary of Significant Accounting Policies (in part)

Property, Plant and Equipment: Plant and equipment are depreciated under the straight-line method over their estimated lives. Estimated lives are as follows: land improvements over 20 years, leaseholds over the life of the lease, buildings over 40 years and machinery and equipment over two to 20 years. The estimated weighted-average life of the Company's machinery and equipment is 17.7 years. The Company recognizes costs associated with major maintenance activities at its operating facilities in the period in which they occur. The Company's property, plant and equipment balances as of December 31, 2010 and 2009 are as follows:

	2010	2009
Land, land improvements and leaseholds	$ 154.7	$ 149.3
Buildings	363.8	366.2
Machinery and equipment	4,688.8	4,714.3
Construction in progress	460.9	155.3
Total	5,668.2	5,385.1
Less accumulated depreciation	(3,635.0)	(3,409.1)
Property, plant and equipment, net	$ 2,033.2	$ 1,976.0

The amount of interest on capital projects capitalized in 2010, 2009 and 2008 was $10.1, $7.8 and $4.4, respectively. The Company reviews the carrying value of long-lived assets to be held and used and long-lived assets to be disposed of when events and circumstances warrant such a review. The carrying value of a long-lived asset is not recoverable if it exceeds the sum of the undiscounted cash flows expected to result from the use and eventual disposition of the asset. If the carrying value of a long-lived asset exceeds its fair value an impairment has occurred and a loss is recognized based on the amount by which the carrying value exceeds the fair market value less cost to dispose for assets to be sold or

abandoned. Fair market value is determined using quoted market prices, estimates based on prices of similar assets or anticipated cash flows discounted at a rate commensurate with risk. During December 2010, the Company announced that it was permanently closing its Ashland, Kentucky coke plant during the first half of 2011 and recognized an approximate $45.9 impairment charge for the coke plant assets in the fourth quarter of 2010.

The Company has historically considered the Ashland coke plant as a part of a collective asset grouping which included the operations of all the Company's steelmaking facilities. The Ashland coke plant produces coke, a commodity that is readily obtainable in the market. In 2010, the Company concluded that it could purchase coke at a price significantly below the cost to produce such coke at Ashland. As a result, the Company decided in late 2010 to permanently close the Ashland coke plant. Effectively, the Company viewed this as a make-versus-buy decision and decided to buy because it concluded that it is more beneficial to the Company to buy coke rather than continue to produce it at Ashland. As such, the Company has determined that the Ashland coke facility is no longer a part of the "integrated process," as the product produced there can be replaced cost-effectively in the market. The change that led to this determination was the added cost to produce coke resulting from increased maintenance cost due to age and more stringent environmental regulations. As it relates to asset groupings, the Company views this as an isolated situation that stemmed from the change in the cost-competitiveness of the Ashland coke plant. The Company has not changed its view of its other facilities from an integrated-process perspective.

2.72

REPUBLIC SERVICES, INC. (DEC)

CONSOLIDATED BALANCE SHEETS (in part)

(In millions, except per share amounts)	December 31, 2010	December 31, 2009
Assets		
Current assets:		
Cash and cash equivalents	$ 88.3	$ 48.0
Accounts receivable, less allowance for doubtful accounts of $50.9 and $55.2, respectively	828.9	865.1
Prepaid expenses and other current assets	207.4	156.5
Deferred tax assets	121.5	195.3
Total current assets	1,246.1	1,264.9
Restricted cash and marketable securities	172.8	240.5
Property and equipment, net	6,698.5	6,657.7
Goodwill, net	10,655.3	10,667.1
Other intangible assets, net	451.3	500.0
Other assets	237.9	210.1
Total assets	$19,461.9	$19,540.3

NOTES TO CONSOLIDATED FINANCIAL STATEMENTS

2. Summary of Significant Accounting Policies (in part)

Property and Equipment

Property and equipment are recorded at cost. Expenditures for major additions and improvements to facilities are capitalized, while maintenance and repairs are charged to expense as incurred. When property is retired or otherwise disposed of, the related cost and accumulated depreciation are removed from the accounts and any resulting gain or loss is reflected in the consolidated statements of income.

We revise the estimated useful lives of property and equipment acquired through business acquisitions to conform with our policies. Depreciation is provided over the estimated useful lives of the assets involved using the straight-line method. We assume no salvage value for our depreciable property and equipment. The estimated useful lives of our property and equipment are as follows:

	Estimated Useful Lives
Buildings and improvements	7–40 years
Vehicles	5–12 years
Landfill equipment	7–10 years
Other equipment	3–15 years
Furniture and fixtures	5–12 years

Landfill development costs are also included in property and equipment. Landfill development costs include direct costs incurred to obtain landfill permits and direct costs incurred to acquire, construct and develop sites as well as final capping, closure and post-closure assets. These costs are amortized or depleted based on consumed airspace. All indirect landfill development costs are expensed as incurred. (For additional information, see Note 8, *Landfill and Environmental Costs*.)

4. Property and Equipment, Net

A summary of property and equipment as of December 31 is as follows:

	2010	2009
Other land	$ 391.9	$ 418.7
Non-depletable landfill land	158.0	142.7
Landfill development costs	4,575.2	4,230.9
Vehicles and equipment	4,142.1	3,792.4
Buildings and improvements	768.5	741.6
Construction-in-progress—landfill	133.2	245.1
Construction-in-progress—other	27.2	23.0
	10,196.1	9,594.4
Less: accumulated depreciation, depletion and amortization:		
Landfill development costs	(1,504.6)	(1,275.4)
Vehicles and equipment	(1,820.6)	(1,518.2)
Buildings and improvements	(172.4)	(143.1)
	(3,497.6)	(2,936.7)
Property and equipment, net	$ 6,698.5	$ 6,657.7

EQUITY METHOD AND JOINT VENTURES

RECOGNITION AND MEASUREMENT

2.73 FASB ASC 323, *Investments—Equity Method and Joint Ventures*, stipulates that the equity method should be used to account for investments in corporate joint ventures and certain other noncontrolled entities when an investor has the ability to exercise significant influence over operating and financial policies of an investee, even though the investor holds 50 percent or less of the common stock. FASB ASC 323 considers an investor to have the ability to exercise significant influence when it owns 20 percent or more of the voting stock of an investee. FASB ASC 323 specifies the criteria for applying the equity method of accounting to 50 percent or less owned entities and lists circumstances under which, despite 20 percent ownership, an investor may not be able to exercise significant influence.

PRESENTATION

2.74 Under the equity method, FASB ASC 323-10-45-1 requires that an investment in common stock be shown in the balance sheet of an investor as a single amount.

DISCLOSURE

2.75 Under FASB ASC 323-10-50-2, the significance of an equity method investment to the investor's financial position and results of operations should be considered in evaluating the extent of disclosures of the financial position and results of operations of an investee. If the investor has more than one investment in common stock, disclosures wholly or partly on a combined basis may be appropriate. FASB ASC 323-10-50-3 details disclosures required for equity method investments, including name and percentage of ownership of the investee, investor accounting policies, any difference between the amount at which an investment is carried and the amount of underlying equity in net assets, and the accounting treatment of the difference.

2.76

TABLE 2-8: NONCURRENT INVESTMENTS—CARRYING BASES*

	Number of Entities		
	2010	2009	2008
Equity method	111	237	262
Valued at cost	36	88	100
Fair value	135	131	120
Other, described	7	2	3

* Appearing in the balance sheet or notes to financial statements, or both.

PRESENTATION AND DISCLOSURE EXCERPTS

Equity Method

2.77

THE COCA-COLA COMPANY (DEC)

CONSOLIDATED BALANCE SHEETS (in part)

December 31	2010	2009
Assets		
Current assets		
Cash and cash equivalents	$ 8,517	$ 7,021
Short-term investments	2,682	2,130
Total cash, cash equivalents and short-term investments	11,199	9,151
Marketable securities	138	62
Trade accounts receivable, less allowances of $48 and $55, respectively	4,430	3,758
Inventories	2,650	2,354
Prepaid expenses and other assets	3,162	2,226
Total current assets	21,579	17,551
Equity method investments	6,954	6,217
Other investments, principally bottling companies	631	538
Other assets	2,121	1,976
Property, plant and equipment—net	14,727	9,561
Trademarks with indefinite lives	6,356	6,183
Bottlers' franchise rights with indefinite lives	7,511	1,953
Goodwill	11,665	4,224
Other intangible assets	1,377	468
Total assets	$72,921	$48,671

NOTES TO CONSOLIDATED FINANCIAL STATEMENTS

Note 6. Equity Method Investments

Our consolidated net income includes our Company's proportionate share of the net income or loss of our equity method investees. When we record our proportionate share of net income, it increases equity income (loss)—net in our consolidated statements of income and our carrying value in that investment. Conversely, when we record our proportionate share of a net loss, it decreases equity income (loss)—net in our consolidated statements of income and our carrying value in that investment. The Company's proportionate share of the net income or loss of our equity method investees includes significant operating and nonoperating items recorded by our equity method investees. These items can have a significant impact on the amount of equity income (loss)—net in our consolidated statements of income and our carrying value in those investments. Refer to Note 17 for additional information related to significant operating and nonoperating items recorded by our equity method investees. The carrying values of our equity method investments are also impacted by our proportionate share of items impacting the equity investee's AOCI.

We eliminate from our financial results all significant intercompany transactions, including the intercompany portion of transactions with equity method investees.

Coca-Cola Enterprises Inc.

On October 2, 2010, we completed our acquisition of CCE's North American business and relinquished our indirect ownership interest in CCE's European operations. As a result of this transaction, the Company does not own any interest in New CCE. Refer to Note 2 for additional information related to this acquisition.

We accounted for our investment in CCE under the equity method of accounting until our acquisition of CCE's North American business was completed on October 2, 2010. Therefore, our consolidated net income for the year ended December 31, 2010, included equity income from CCE during the first nine months of 2010. The Company owned 33 percent of the outstanding common stock of CCE immediately prior to the acquisition. The following table provides summarized financial information for CCE for the nine months ended October 1, 2010, and for the years ended December 31, 2009 and 2008 (in millions):

	Nine Months Ended October 1, 2010	Year Ended December 31	
		2009	2008
Net operating revenues	$16,464	$21,645	$21,807
Cost of goods sold	10,028	13,333	13,763
Gross profit	$ 6,436	$ 8,312	$ 8,044
Operating income (loss)	$ 1,369	$ 1,527	$(6,299)
Net income (loss)	$ 677	$ 731	$(4,394)

The following table provides a summary of our significant transactions with CCE for the nine months ended October 1, 2010, and for the years ended December 31, 2009 and 2008 (in millions):

	Nine Months Ended October 1, 2010	Year Ended December 31	
		2009	2008
Concentrate, syrup and finished product sales to CCE	$4,737	$6,032	$6,431
Syrup and finished product purchases from CCE	263	351	344
CCE purchases of sweeteners through our company	251	419	357
Marketing payments made by us directly to CCE	314	415	626
Marketing payments made to third parties on behalf of CCE	106	174	131
Local media and marketing program reimbursements from CCE	268	330	316
Payments made to CCE for dispensing equipment repair services	64	87	84
Other payments—net	$ 19	$ 66	$ 75

Syrup and finished product purchases from CCE represent purchases of fountain syrup in certain territories that have been resold by our Company to major customers and purchases of bottle and can products. Marketing payments made by us directly to CCE represent support of certain marketing activities and our participation with CCE in cooperative advertising and other marketing activities to promote the sale of Company trademark products within CCE territories. These programs were agreed to on an annual basis. Marketing payments made to third parties on behalf of CCE represent support of certain marketing activities and programs to promote the sale of Company trademark products within CCE's territories in conjunction with certain of CCE's customers. Pursuant to cooperative advertising and trade agreements with CCE, we received funds from CCE for local media and marketing program reimbursements. Payments made to CCE for dispensing equipment repair services represent reimbursement to CCE for its costs of parts and labor for repairs on cooler, dispensing or post-mix equipment owned by us or our customers. The other payments—net line in the table above represents payments made to and received from CCE that are individually not significant.

Our Company had previously entered into programs with CCE designed to help develop cold-drink infrastructure. Under these programs, we paid CCE for a portion of the cost of developing the infrastructure necessary to support accelerated placements of cold-drink equipment. These payments supported a common objective of increased sales of Company Trademark Beverages from increased availability and consumption in the cold-drink channel. The amortizable carrying value of our investment in these infrastructure programs with CCE was $307 million as of December 31, 2009.

Preexisting Relationships

The Company evaluated all of our preexisting relationships with CCE prior to the close of the transaction. Based on these evaluations, the Company recognized a charge of $265 million related to preexisting relationships with CCE. This charge primarily related to the write-off of our investment in cold-drink infrastructure programs with CCE. This charge was recorded in the line item other income (loss)—net and impacted the Corporate operating segment. Refer to Note 17.

Other Equity Method Investments

Our other equity method investments include our ownership interests in Coca-Cola Hellenic, Coca-Cola FEMSA and Coca-Cola Amatil. As of December 31, 2010, we owned approximately 23 percent, 32 percent and 30 percent, respectively, of these companies' common shares. As of December 31, 2010, our investment in our equity method investees in the aggregate exceeded our proportionate share of the net assets of these equity method investees by approximately $1,337 million. This difference is not amortized.

A summary of financial information for our equity method investees in the aggregate, other than CCE, is as follows (in millions):

Year Ended December 31	2010	2009	2008
Net operating revenues	$38,663	$34,292	$34,482
Cost of goods sold	23,053	20,205	19,974
Gross profit	$15,610	$14,087	$14,508
Operating income	$ 4,134	$ 3,657	$ 3,687
Consolidated net income (loss)	$ 2,659	$ 2,269	$ 1,950
Less: Net income (loss) attributable to noncontrolling interests	$ 89	$ 78	$ 53
Net income (loss) attributable to common shareowners	$ 2,570	$ 2,191	$ 1,897

December 31	2010	2009
Current assets	$12,223	$10,848
Noncurrent assets	26,524	25,397
Total assets	$38,747	$36,245
Current liabilities	$ 9,039	$ 8,578
Noncurrent liabilities	11,175	10,945
Total liabilities	$20,214	$19,523
Shareowners' equity	$18,046	$16,232
Noncontrolling interest	$ 487	$ 490
Total equity (deficit)	$18,533	$16,722
Company equity investment	$ 6,954	$ 6,192

Net sales to equity method investees other than CCE, the majority of which are located outside the United States, were approximately $6.2 billion, $5.6 billion and $9.4 billion in 2010, 2009 and 2008, respectively. Total payments, primarily marketing, made to equity method investees other than CCE were approximately $1,034 million, $878 million and $659 million in 2010, 2009 and 2008, respectively. In addition, purchases of finished products from equity method investees were approximately $205 million, $152 million and $228 million in 2010, 2009 and 2008, respectively.

If valued at the December 31, 2010, quoted closing prices of shares actively traded on stock markets, the value of our equity method investments in publicly traded bottlers would have exceeded our carrying value by approximately $6.8 billion.

Net Receivables and Dividends from Equity Method Investees

Total net receivables due from equity method investees was approximately $899 million and $949 million as of December 31, 2010 and 2009, respectively. The total amount of dividends received from equity method investees was approximately $354 million, $422 million and $254 million for the years ended December 31, 2010, 2009 and 2008, respectively. Dividends received in 2009 included the receipt of a $183 million special dividend from Coca-Cola Hellenic, which was incremental to its normal quarterly dividend. We classified the receipt of this cash dividend in cash flows from operating activities due to the fact that our cumulative equity in earnings from Coca-Cola Hellenic exceeded the cumulative distributions received; therefore, the dividend was deemed to be a return on our investment and not a return of our investment.

2.78

CORNING INCORPORATED (DEC)

CONSOLIDATED BALANCE SHEETS (in part)

(In millions, except share and per share amounts)	2010	2009
Assets		
Current assets:		
Cash and cash equivalents	$ 4,598	$ 2,541
Short-term investments, at fair value (Note 3)	1,752	1,042
Total cash, cash equivalents and short-term investments	6,350	3,583
Trade accounts receivable, net of doubtful accounts and allowances—$20 and $20	973	753
Inventories (Note 5)	738	579
Deferred income taxes (Note 6)	431	235
Other current assets	367	371
Total current assets	8,859	5,521
Investments (Note 7)	4,372	3,992
Property, net of accumulated depreciation—$6,420 and $5,503 (Note 9)	8,943	7,995
Goodwill and other intangible assets, net (Note 10)	716	676
Deferred income taxes (Note 6)	2,790	2,982
Other assets	153	129
Total assets	$25,833	$21,295

NOTES TO CONSOLIDATED FINANCIAL STATEMENTS

7. Investments

Investments comprise the following (dollars in millions):

	Ownership Interest[1]	2010	2009
Affiliated companies accounted for under the equity method:			
Samsung Corning Precision Materials Co., Ltd.	50%	$2,943	$2,772
Dow Corning Corporation	50%	1,186	992
All other	20%–50%	240	224
		4,369	3,988
Other investments		3	4
Total		$4,372	$3,992

[1] Amounts reflect Corning's direct ownership interests in the respective affiliated companies. Corning does not control any of such entities.

Affiliated Companies at Equity

The results of operations and financial position of the investments accounted for under the equity method follow (in millions):

	2010	2009	2008
Statement of Operations:			
Net sales	$11,717	$10,211	$10,049
Gross profit	6,107	5,043	4,752
Net income	3,901	2,944	2,724
Corning's equity in earnings of affiliated companies[1]	1,958	1,435	1,358
Related Party Transactions:			
Corning sales to affiliated companies	27	50	41
Corning purchases from affiliated companies	59	56	46
Corning transfers of assets, at cost, to affiliated companies[2]	121	78	173
Dividends received from affiliated companies	1,712	755	546
Royalty income from affiliated companies	268	234	188
Corning services to affiliates	37	22	—

	2010	2009
Balance sheet:		
Current Assets	$ 8,418	$ 7,236
Noncurrent assets	12,253	11,081
Short-term borrowings, including current portion of long-term debt	842	690
Other current liabilities	2,465	2,145
Long-term debt	868	745
Other long-term liabilities	6,297	5,362
Non-controlling interest	728	588
Related Party Transactions:		
Balances due from affiliated companies	101	122
Balances due to affiliated companies	7	2

[1] In 2010, amounts include the following items:
- In 2009, equity in earnings of affiliated companies included a charge of $29 million ($27 million after-tax) for our share of the restructuring charges and a credit of $29 million ($27 million after-tax) primarily for excess foreign tax credits that Dow Corning generated from foreign dividends.
- In 2008, Dow Corning recorded an other-than-temporary impairment for certain securities of Fannie Mae and Freddie Mac, which reduced Corning's equity earnings by $18 million.

[2] Corning purchases machinery and equipment on behalf of Samsung Corning Precision to support its capital expansion initiatives. The machinery and equipment are transferred to Samsung Corning Precision at our cost basis, resulting in no revenue or gain being recognized on the transaction.

We have contractual agreements with several of our equity affiliates which include sales, purchasing, licensing and technology agreements.

At December 31, 2010, approximately $4.4 billion of equity in undistributed earnings of equity companies was included in our retained earnings.

A discussion and summarized results of Corning's significant affiliates at December 31, 2010 follows:

Samsung Corning Precision Materials Co., Ltd. (Samsung Corning Precision)

Samsung Corning Precision is a South Korea-based manufacturer of liquid crystal display glass for flat panel displays. In 2010, they changed their name from Samsung Corning Precision Glass Co., Ltd. to Samsung Corning Precision Materials Co., Ltd.

Samsung Corning Precision's financial position and results of operations follow (in millions):

	Years Ended December 31		
	2010	2009	2008
Statement of Operations:			
Net sales	$4,856	$4,250	$3,636
Gross profit	$3,731	$3,053	$2,521
Net income	$2,946	$2,212	$1,874
Corning's equity in earnings of Samsung Corning Precision	$1,473	$1,115	$ 927
Related Party Transactions:			
Corning sales to Samsung Corning Precision		$ 30	$ 9
Corning purchases from Samsung Corning Precision	$ 33	$ 37	$ 30
Corning transfer of machinery and equipment to Samsung Corning Precision at cost[1]	$ 121	$ 78	$ 173
Dividends received from Samsung Corning Precision	$1,474	$ 490	$ 278
Royalty income from Samsung Corning Precision	$ 265	$ 231	$ 184

	December 31	
	2010	2009
Balance Sheet:		
Current assets	$3,122	$2,963
Noncurrent assets	$3,791	$3,409
Short-term borrowings, including current portion of long-term debt		
Other current liabilities	$ 696	$ 565
Long-term debt		
Other long-term liabilities	$ 252	$ 189
Non-controlling interest	$ 35	$ 31

[1] Corning purchases machinery and equipment on behalf of Samsung Corning Precision to support its capital expansion initiatives. The machinery and equipment are transferred to Samsung Corning Precision at our cost basis, resulting in no revenue or gain being recognized on the transaction.

In 2010, Samsung Corning Precision's earnings were positively impacted from a revised tax holiday calculation agreed to by the Korean National Tax service. Corning's share of this adjustment was $61 million.

Balances due from Samsung Corning Precision were $29 million at December 31, 2010. Balances due to Samsung Corning Precision were $5 million at December 31, 2010. Balances due from Samsung Corning Precision were $36 million at December 31, 2009. Balances due to Samsung Corning Precision were $14 million at December 31, 2009.

Corning owns 50% of Samsung Corning Precision. Samsung Electronics Co., Ltd. owns 43% and other shareholders own the remaining 7%.

On December 31, 2007, Samsung Corning Precision acquired all of the outstanding shares of Samsung Corning Co., Ltd. (Samsung Corning). After the transaction, Corning retained its 50% interest in Samsung Corning Precision. Samsung Corning Precision accounted for the transaction at fair value, while Corning accounted for the transaction at historical cost.

Prior to their merger, Samsung Corning Precision and Samsung Corning were two of approximately thirty co-defendants in a lawsuit filed by Seoul Guarantee Insurance Co. and thirteen other creditors (SGI and Creditors) for alleged breach of an agreement that approximately twenty-eight affiliates of the Samsung group (Samsung Affiliates) entered into with SGI and Creditors on August 24, 1999 (the Agreement). The lawsuit is pending in the courts of South Korea. Under the Agreement it is alleged that the Samsung Affiliates agreed to sell certain shares of Samsung Life Insurance Co., Ltd. (SLI), which had been transferred to SGI and Creditors in connection with the petition for court receivership of Samsung Motor Inc. In the lawsuit, SGI and Creditors allege a breach of the Agreement by the Samsung Affiliates and are seeking the loss of principal (approximately $1.95 billion) for loans extended to Samsung Motors Inc., default interest and a separate amount for breach. On January 31, 2008, the Seoul District Court ordered the Samsung Affiliates: to pay approximately $1.30 billion by disposing of 2,334,045 shares of SLI less 1,165,955 shares of SLI previously sold by SGI and Creditors and paying the proceeds to SGI and Creditors; to satisfy any shortfall by participating in the purchase of equity or subordinate debentures issued by them; and pay default interest of 6% per annum. The ruling has been appealed. On November 10, 2009, the Appellate Court directed the parties to attempt to resolve this matter through mediation. The parties agreed not to accept the court's attempt at mediation. A portion of an escrow account established upon completion of SLI's initial public offering ("IPO") on May 7, 2010 was used to pay court ordered interest for the delay of the IPO. Samsung Corning Precision has concluded that no provision for loss should be reflected in its financial statements. Possible appeals are being considered. Other than as described above, no claim in these matters has been asserted against Corning or any of its affiliates.

In connection with an investigation by the Commission of the European Communities, Competition DG, of alleged anticompetitive behavior relating to the worldwide production of LCD glass, Corning and Samsung Corning Precision received a request on March 30, 2009, for certain information from the Competition DG. Corning and Samsung Corning Precision have responded to those requests for information. On October 9, 2009, in connection with its investigation, the Competition DG made a further request for information from both Corning and Samsung Corning Precision to which each party has responded. Samsung Corning Precision has also responded to the Competition DG and authorities in other jurisdictions, including the United States in connection with similar investigations of alleged anticompetitive behavior relating to worldwide production of cathode ray tube glass.

In September 2009, Corning and Samsung Corning Precision formed Corsam Technologies LLC (Corsam), a new equity affiliate established to provide glass technology research for future product applications. Samsung Corning Precision invested $124 million in cash and Corning contributed intellectual property with a corresponding value. Corning and Samsung Corning Precision each own 50% of the common stock of Corsam, and Corning has agreed to provide research and development services at arms length to Corsam. Corning does not control Corsam because Samsung Corning Precision's other investors maintain significant participating voting rights. In addition, Corsam has sufficient equity to finance its activities, the voting rights of investors in Corsam are considered substantive, and the risks and rewards of Corsam's research are shared only by those investors noted. As a result, Corsam is accounted for under the equity method of accounting for investments.

Dow Corning Corporation (Dow Corning)

Dow Corning is a U.S.-based manufacturer of silicone products. Corning and the Dow Chemical Company (Dow Chemical) each own half of Dow Corning.

Dow Corning's financial position and results of operations follow (in millions):

	Years Ended December 31		
	2010	2009	2008
Statement of Operations:			
Net sales	$5,997	$5,093	$5,450
Gross profit	$2,135	$1,760	$1,953
Net income attributable to Dow Corning	$ 887	$ 573	$ 739
Corning's equity in earnings of Dow Corning	$ 444	$ 287	$ 369
Related Party Transactions:			
Corning purchases from Dow Corning	$ 19	$ 17	$ 14
Dividends received from Dow Corning	$ 222	$ 222	$ 206

	December 31	
	2010	2009
Balance Sheet:		
Current assets	$4,625	$3,581
Noncurrent assets	$8,024	$7,203
Short-term borrowings, including current portion of long-term debt	$ 842	$ 683
Other current liabilities	$1,446	$1,230
Long-term debt	$ 867	$ 742
Other long-term liabilities	$5,996	$5,108
Non-controlling interest	$ 625	$ 558

At December 31, 2010, Dow Corning's marketable securities included approximately $535 million of auction rate securities, net of impairments of $36 million. As a result of a temporary impairment, unrealized losses of $29 million, net of $8 million for a minority interests' share, were included in accumulated other comprehensive income in Dow Corning's consolidated balance sheet. Corning's share of this unrealized loss was $14 million and is included in Corning's accumulated other comprehensive income.

In January 2010, Dow Corning received approval for U.S. Federal Advanced Energy Manufacturing Tax Credits of approximately $169 million. The tax credits were granted as part of the American Reinvestment and Recovery Act of 2009, and

are focused on job creation from U.S. manufacturing capacity which supplies clean and renewable energy products.

In response to economic challenges, Dow Corning incurred restructuring charges associated with a global workforce reduction in 2009. Our share of these charges was $29 million.

In 2008, Dow Corning recorded an other-than-temporary impairment of $37 million, net of $14 million for a minority interests' share, which was included in Dow Corning's net income for certain securities of Fannie Mae and Freddie Mac. Corning's share of this loss was $18 million and is included in equity earnings in Corning's consolidated statements of income. No additional impairment on the Fannie Mae and Freddy Mac securities was recorded during the year ended December 31, 2009. The majority of Dow Corning's securities are collateralized by portfolios of student loans that are guaranteed by the U.S. government. Auctions for these securities have failed since the first quarter of 2008, reducing the immediate liquidity of these investments. Since Dow Corning does not know when a market will return or develop for these securities, Dow Corning has classified these securities as non-current. Market conditions could result in additional unrealized or realized losses for Dow Corning. Corning's equity earnings from Dow Corning would be reduced by our 50% share of any future impairment that is considered to be other-than-temporary.

In 2008, Dow Corning changed its depreciation method and the estimated useful lives of certain fixed assets. These changes were accounted for as a change in estimate resulting in increased net income of $40 million of which Corning's share was $20 million.

Dow Corning has borrowed the full amount under its $500 million revolving credit facility and believes it has adequate liquidity to fund operations, its capital expenditure plan, breast implant settlement liabilities, and shareholder dividends.

In 1995, Corning fully impaired its investment of Dow Corning upon its entry into bankruptcy proceedings and did not recognize net equity earnings from the second quarter of 1995 through the end of 2002. Corning began recognizing equity earnings in the first quarter of 2003, when management concluded that Dow Corning's emergence from bankruptcy protection was probable. Dow Corning emerged from bankruptcy in 2004. See discussion below for additional information and for a history of this matter. Corning considers the $249 million difference between the carrying value of its investment in Dow Corning and its 50% share of Dow Corning's equity to be permanent.

Corning and Dow Chemical each own 50% of the common stock of Dow Corning. In May 1995, Dow Corning filed for bankruptcy protection to address pending and claimed liabilities arising from many thousands of breast implant product lawsuits. On June 1, 2004, Dow Corning emerged from Chapter 11 with a Plan of Reorganization (the Plan), which provided for the settlement or other resolution of implant claims. The Plan also includes releases for Corning and Dow Chemical as shareholders in exchange for contributions to the Plan.

Under the terms of the Plan, Dow Corning has established and is funding a Settlement Trust and a Litigation Facility to provide a means for tort claimants to settle or litigate their claims. Inclusive of insurance, Dow Corning has paid approximately $1.7 billion to the Settlement Trust. As of December 31, 2010, Dow Corning had recorded a reserve for breast implant litigation of $1.6 billion and anticipates insurance receivables of $3 million. As a separate matter arising from the bankruptcy proceedings, Dow Corning is defending claims asserted by a number of commercial creditors who claim additional interest at default rates and enforcement costs, during the period from May 1995 through June 2004. As of December 31, 2010, Dow Corning has estimated the liability to commercial creditors to be within the range of $81 million to $267 million. As Dow Corning management believes no single amount within the range appears to be a better estimate than any other amount within the range, Dow Corning has recorded the minimum liability within the range. Should Dow Corning not prevail in this matter, Corning's equity earnings would be reduced by its 50% share of the amount in excess of $81 million, net of applicable tax benefits. In addition, the London Market Insurers (the LMI Claimants) have claimed a reimbursement right with respect to a portion of insurance proceeds previously paid by the LMI Claimants to Dow Corning. This claim is based on a theory that the LMI Claimants overestimated Dow Corning's liability for the resolution of implant claims pursuant to the Plan. The LMI Claimants offered two calculations of their claim amount: $54 million and $93 million, plus minimum interest of $67 million and $116 million, respectively. These estimates were explicitly characterized as preliminary and subject to change. Litigation regarding this claim is in the discovery stage. Dow Corning disputes the claim. Based on settlement negotiations, Dow Corning has estimated that the most likely outcome will result in payment to the LMI Claimants in a range of $10 million to $20 million. Dow Corning has recorded a liability for an amount within this range as of December 31, 2010. There are a number of other claims in the bankruptcy proceedings against Dow Corning awaiting resolution by the U.S. District Court, and it is reasonably possible that Dow Corning may record bankruptcy-related charges in the future. The remaining tort claims against Corning relating to breast implant products are expected be channeled by the Plan into facilities established by the Plan or otherwise defended by the Litigation Facility.

Pittsburgh Corning Corporation (PCC)

Corning and PPG Industries, Inc. (PPG) each own 50% of the capital stock of Pittsburgh Corning Corporation (PCC). Over a period of more than two decades, PCC and several other defendants have been named in numerous lawsuits involving claims alleging personal injury from exposure to asbestos. On April 16, 2000, PCC filed for Chapter 11 reorganization in the U.S. Bankruptcy Court for the Western District of Pennsylvania. At the time PCC filed for bankruptcy protection, there were approximately 11,800 claims pending against Corning in state court lawsuits alleging various theories of liability based on exposure to PCC's asbestos products and typically requesting monetary damages in excess of one million dollars per claim. Corning has defended those claims on the basis of the separate corporate status of PCC and the absence of any facts supporting claims of direct liability arising from PCC's asbestos products. Corning is also currently involved in approximately 10,300 other cases (approximately 38,700 claims) alleging injuries from asbestos and similar amounts of monetary damages per case. Those cases have been covered by insurance without material impact to Corning to date. As described below, several of Corning's insurance carriers have filed a legal proceeding concerning the extent of any insurance coverage for these claims. Asbestos litigation is inherently difficult, and past trends in resolving these claims may not be indicators of future outcomes.

On March 28, 2003, Corning announced that it had reached agreement with the representatives of asbestos claimants for the resolution of all current and future asbestos claims against it and PCC, which might arise from PCC products or operations (the 2003 Plan). The 2003 Plan would have required Corning to relinquish its equity interest in PCC, contribute its equity interest in Pittsburgh Corning Europe N.V. (PCE), a Belgian corporation, contribute 25 million shares of Corning common stock, and pay a total of $140 million in six annual installments (present value $131 million at March 2003), beginning one year after the plan's effective date, with 5.5 percent interest from June 2004. In addition, the 2003 Plan provided that Corning would assign certain insurance policy proceeds from its primary insurance and a portion of its excess insurance.

On December 21, 2006, the Bankruptcy Court issued an order denying confirmation of the 2003 Plan for reasons it set out in a memorandum opinion. Several parties, including Corning, filed motions for reconsideration. These motions were argued on March 5, 2007, and the Bankruptcy Court reserved decision. On January 29, 2009, a proposed plan of reorganization (the Amended PCC Plan) resolving issues raised by the Court in denying confirmation of the 2003 Plan was filed with the Bankruptcy Court.

As a result, Corning believes the Amended PCC Plan, modified as indicated below, now represents the most probable outcome of this matter and expects that the Amended PCC Plan will be confirmed by the Court. At the same time, Corning believes the 2003 Plan no longer serves as the basis for the Company's best estimate of liability. Key provisions of the Amended PCC Plan address the concerns expressed by the Bankruptcy Court. Accordingly, in the first quarter of 2008, Corning adjusted its asbestos litigation liability to reflect components of the Amended PCC Plan. The proposed resolution of PCC asbestos claims under the Amended PCC Plan requires Corning to contribute its equity interests in PCC and PCE and to contribute a fixed series of payments, recorded at present value. Corning will have the option to use its shares rather than cash to make these payments, but the liability is fixed by dollar value and not the number of shares. The Amended PCC Plan originally required Corning to make (1) one payment of $100 million one year from the date the Amended PCC Plan becomes effective and certain conditions are met and (2) five additional payments of $50 million, on each of the five subsequent anniversaries of the first payment, the final payment of which is subject to reduction based on the application of credits under certain circumstances. Documents were filed with the Bankruptcy Court further modifying the Amended PCC Plan by reducing Corning's initial payment by $30 million and reducing its second and fourth payments by $15 million each. In return, Corning will relinquish its claim for reimbursement of its payments and contributions under the Amended PCC Plan from the insurance carriers involved in the bankruptcy proceeding with certain exceptions. These modifications are expected to resolve objections to the Amended PCC Plan filed by some of the insurance carriers. Confirmation hearings on the Amended PCC Plan were held in June 2010 and briefs discussing the legal issues have been filed. The Bankruptcy Court's opinion on the Amended Plan is pending.

The Amended PCC Plan does not include non-PCC asbestos claims that may be or have been raised against Corning. Corning has recorded an additional $150 million for such claims in its estimated asbestos litigation liability. The liability for non-PCC claims was estimated based upon industry data for asbestos claims since Corning does not have recent claim history due to the injunction issued by the Bankruptcy Court. The estimated liability represents the undiscounted projection of claims and related legal fees over the next 20 years. The amount may need to be adjusted in future periods as more data becomes available.

The liability for the Amended PCC Plan and the non-PCC asbestos claims was estimated to be $633 million at December 31, 2010, compared with an estimate of liability of $682 million at December 31, 2009. For the years ended December 31, 2010 and 2009, Corning recorded asbestos litigation expense of $5 million and $20 million, respectively. In the first quarter of 2010, Corning recorded a credit of $54 million to reflect the change in terms of Corning's proposed payments under the Amended Plan. The entire obligation is classified as a non-current liability as installment payments for the cash portion of the obligation are not planned to commence until more than 12 months after the Amended PCC Plan becomes effective and the PCE portion of the obligation will be fulfilled through the direct contribution of Corning's investment in PCE (currently recorded as a non-current other equity method investment).

In the first quarter of 2008, Corning recorded a credit to asbestos settlement expense of $327 million as a result of the increase in likelihood of a settlement under the Amended PCC Plan and a corresponding decrease in the likelihood of a settlement under the 2003 Plan. For the year ended December 31, 2008, after the first quarter adjustment to the settlement amount, Corning recorded a benefit of $13 million to reflect the change in value of the estimated liability under an Amended PCC Plan.

The Amended PCC Plan is subject to a number of contingencies. Payment of the amounts required to fund the Amended PCC Plan from insurance and other sources are subject to a number of conditions that may not be achieved. The approval of the Amended PCC Plan by the Bankruptcy Court is not certain and faces objections by some parties. Any approval of the Amended PCC Plan by the Bankruptcy Court is subject to appeal. For these and other reasons, Corning's liability for these asbestos matters may be subject to changes in subsequent quarters. The estimate of the cost of resolving the non-PCC asbestos claims may also be subject to change as developments occur. Management continues to believe that the likelihood of the uncertainties surrounding these proceedings causing a material adverse impact to Corning's financial statements is remote.

Several of Corning's insurers have commenced litigation for a declaration of the rights and obligations of the parties under insurance policies, including rights that may be affected by the potential resolutions described above. Corning is vigorously contesting these cases. Management is unable to predict the outcome of this insurance litigation and therefore cannot estimate the range of any possible loss.

At December 31, 2010 and 2009, the fair value of PCE significantly exceeded its carrying value of $129 million and $125 million, respectively. There have been no impairment indicators for our investment in PCE and we continue to recognize equity earnings of this affiliate. PCC filed for Chapter 11 reorganization in the U.S. Bankruptcy Court on April 16, 2000. At that time, Corning determined it lacked the ability to recover the carrying amount of its investment in PCC and its investment was other than temporarily impaired. As a result, we reduced our investment in PCC to zero.

Cost Method

2.79

AMERON INTERNATIONAL CORPORATION (NOV)

CONSOLIDATED BALANCE SHEETS (in part)

	As of November 30	
(Dollars in thousands)	2010	2009
Assets		
Current assets		
Cash and cash equivalents	$ 236,737	$ 181,114
Receivables, less allowances of $3,848 in 2010 and $5,351 in 2009	129,855	151,210
Inventories	69,381	62,700
Deferred income taxes	22,441	19,795
Prepaid expenses and other current assets	10,862	11,585
Total current assets	469,276	426,404
Investments		
Equity method affiliate	—	30,626
Cost method affiliates	3,784	3,784
Property, plant and equipment		
Land	46,132	46,029
Buildings	103,438	100,583
Machinery and equipment	371,153	345,604
Construction in progress	31,048	32,306
Total property, plant and equipment at cost	551,771	524,522
Accumulated depreciation	(307,573)	(286,014)
Total property, plant and equipment, net	244,198	238,508
Deferred income taxes	11,289	14,321
Goodwill and intangible assets, net of accumulated amortization of $1,293 in 2010 and $1,257 in 2009	2,061	2,088
Other assets	50,961	46,818
Total assets	$ 781,569	$ 762,549

NOTES TO CONSOLIDATED FINANCIAL STATEMENTS

Note 1—Summary of Significant Accounting Policies (in part)

Affiliates

Investments in unconsolidated affiliates over which the Company has significant influence are accounted for under the equity method of accounting, whereby the investment is carried at the cost of acquisition, including subsequent capital contributions and loans from the Company, plus the Company's equity in undistributed earnings or losses since acquisition. Investments in affiliates which the Company does not have the ability to exert significant influence over the investees' operating and financing activities are accounted for under the cost method of accounting. The Company's investment in TAMCO, a steel mini-mill in California, was accounted for under the equity method. On October 21, 2010, the Company completed the sale of its 50% ownership interest in TAMCO. Investments in Ameron Saudi Arabia, Ltd. and Bondstrand, Ltd. are accounted for under the cost method due to Management's current assessment of the Company's influence over these affiliates.

Note 6—Affiliates (in part)

Investments, advances and equity in undistributed earnings of affiliates were as follows at November 30:

(In thousands)	2010	2009
Investment—equity method affiliate	—	$30,626
Investments—cost method affiliates	$3,784	3,784
	$3,784	$34,410

The Company's ownership of affiliates at November 30, 2010 is summarized below:

Products	Affiliates	Ownership Interest
Fiberglass pipe	Bondstrand, Ltd.	40%
Concrete pipe	Ameron Saudi Arabia, Ltd.	30%

On October 21, 2010 the Company completed the sale of its 50% ownership interest in TAMCO. The Company sold its TAMCO investment and extinguished all outstanding debt owed by TAMCO to the Company under a shareholder loan for gross proceeds of $78,067,000 after estimated working capital adjustments of $697,000 and before closing costs of approximately $2,128,000, recognizing an estimated pretax gain of $48,401,000. Under the terms of the sale, an additional $5,000,000 is to be held in escrow for a period of time to cover potential working capital adjustments and potential indemnification obligations related to the transaction.

Investments in affiliates and the amount of undistributed earnings were as follows:

(In thousands)	Fiberglass Pipe	Concrete Pipe	TAMCO	Total
Cost	$3,784	$—	$ —	$ 3,784
Investment, November 30, 2010	$3,784	$—	$ —	$ 3,784
2010 Dividends	$1,899	$—	$ —	$ 1,899
Cost and outstanding loans	$3,784	$—	$33,482	$37,266
Accumulated comprehensive loss from affiliate	—	—	(4,849)	(4,849)
Accumulated equity in undistributed earnings	—	—	1,993	1,993
Investment, November 30, 2009	$3,784	$—	$30,626	$34,410
2009 Dividends	$4,764	$—	$ —	$ 4,764

Fair Value

2.80

INTEL CORPORATION (DEC)

CONSOLIDATED BALANCE SHEETS (in part)

December 25, 2010 and December 26, 2009

(In millions, except par value)	2010	2009
Assets		
Current assets:		
Cash and cash equivalents	$ 5,498	$ 3,987
Short-term investments	11,294	5,285
Trading assets	5,093	4,648
Accounts receivable, net of allowance for doubtful accounts of $28 ($19 in 2009)	2,867	2,273
Inventories	3,757	2,935
Deferred tax assets	1,488	1,216
Other current assets	1,614	813
Total current assets	31,611	21,157
Property, plant and equipment, net	17,899	17,225
Marketable equity securities	1,008	773
Other long-term investments	3,026	4,179
Goodwill	4,531	4,421
Other long-term assets	5,111	5,340
Total assets	$63,186	$53,095

NOTES TO CONSOLIDATED FINANCIAL STATEMENTS

Note 2. Accounting Policies (in part)

Fair Value

Fair value is the price that would be received from selling an asset or paid to transfer a liability in an orderly transaction between market participants at the measurement date. When determining fair value, we consider the principal or most advantageous market in which we would transact, and we consider assumptions that market participants would use when pricing the asset or liability. Our financial instruments are measured and recorded at fair value, except for equity method investments, cost method investments, cost method loans receivable, and most of our liabilities.

Fair Value Hierarchy

The three levels of inputs that may be used to measure fair value are as follows:

Level 1. Quoted prices in active markets for identical assets or liabilities.

Level 2. Observable inputs other than Level 1 prices, such as quoted prices for similar assets or liabilities, quoted prices in markets with insufficient volume or infrequent transactions (less active markets), or model-derived valuations in which all significant inputs are observable or can be derived principally from or corroborated with observable market data for substantially the full term of the assets or liabilities. Level 2 inputs also include non-binding market consensus prices that can be corroborated with observable market data, as well as quoted prices that were adjusted for security-specific restrictions.

Level 3. Unobservable inputs to the valuation methodology that are significant to the measurement of the fair value of assets or liabilities. Level 3 inputs also include non-binding market consensus prices or non-binding broker quotes that we were unable to corroborate with observable market data.

For further discussion of fair value, see "Note 5: Fair Value" and "Note 22: Retirement Benefit Plans."

Non-Marketable and Other Equity Investments

Our non-marketable equity and other equity investments are included in other long-term assets. We account for non-marketable equity and other equity investments for which we do not have control over the investee as:

- *Equity method investments* when we have the ability to exercise significant influence, but not control, over the investee. Gains (losses) on equity method investments, net may be recorded with up to a one-quarter lag. Equity method investments include marketable and non-marketable investments.
- *Non-marketable cost method investments* when the equity method does not apply. We record the realized gains or losses on the sale of non-marketable cost method investments in gains (losses) on other equity investments, net.

Note 5. Fair Value (in part)

Assets/Liabilities Measured and Recorded at Fair Value on a Recurring Basis (in part)

Assets and liabilities measured and recorded at fair value on a recurring basis, excluding accrued interest components, consisted of the following types of instruments as of December 25, 2010 and December 26, 2009:

(In millions)	December 25, 2010 Fair Value Measured and Recorded at Reporting Date Using				December 26, 2009 Fair Value Measured and Recorded at Reporting Date Using			
	Level 1	Level 2	Level 3	Total	Level 1	Level 2	Level 3	Total
Assets								
Cash equivalents:								
Commercial paper	$ —	$ 2,600	$ —	$ 2,600	$ —	$ 2,919	$ —	$ 2,919
Government bonds	1,279	505	—	1,784	—	—	—	—
Bank deposits	—	560	—	560	—	459	—	459
Money market fund deposits	34	—	—	34	48	—	—	48
Short-term investments:								
Government bonds	4,890	1,320	—	6,210	—	250	—	250
Commercial paper	—	2,712	—	2,712	—	2,525	—	2,525
Corporate bonds	121	1,378	1	1,500	133	1,560	76	1,769
Bank deposits	—	858	—	858	—	697	—	697
Asset-backed securities	—	—	14	14	—	—	27	27
Money market fund deposits	—	—	—	—	—	17	—	17
Trading assets:								
Government bonds	311	2,115	—	2,426	—	1,351	—	1,351
Corporate bonds	199	916	—	1,115	80	1,005	45	1,130
Commercial paper	—	488	—	488	—	882	—	882
Marketable equity securities	388	—	—	388	—	—	—	—
Municipal bonds	—	375	—	375	—	390	—	390
Asset-backed securities	—	—	190	190	—	—	618	618
Bank deposits	—	108	—	108	—	264	—	264
Money market fund deposits	3	—	—	3	13	—	—	13
Other current assets:								
Derivative assets	—	330	—	330	—	136	—	136
Marketable equity securities	785	223	—	1,008	676	97	—	773
Other long-term investments:								
Government bonds	83	2,002	—	2,085	17	1,948	—	1,965
Corporate bonds	104	601	50	755	366	1,329	248	1,943
Bank deposits	—	133	—	133	—	162	—	162
Asset-backed securities	—	—	53	53	—	—	109	109
Other long-term assets:								
Loans receivable	—	642	—	642	—	249	—	249
Derivative assets	—	19	31	50	—	1	31	32
Total assets measured and recorded at fair value	$8,197	$17,885	$339	$26,421	$1,333	$16,241	$1,154	$18,728

2.81

TIME WARNER INC. (DEC)

CONSOLIDATED BALANCE SHEET (in part)

(Millions, except per share amounts)	December 31, 2010	December 31, 2009
Assets		
Current assets		
Cash and equivalents	$ 3,663	$ 4,733
Receivables, less allowances of $2,161 and $2,247	6,413	5,070
Securitized receivables	—	805
Inventories	1,920	1,769
Deferred income taxes	581	670
Prepaid expenses and other current assets	561	645
Total current assets	13,138	13,692
Noncurrent inventories and film costs	5,985	5,754
Investments, including available-for-sale securities	1,796	1,542
Property, plant and equipment, net	3,874	3,922
Intangible assets subject to amortization, net	2,492	2,676
Intangible assets not subject to amortization	7,827	7,734
Goodwill	29,994	29,639
Other assets	1,418	1,100
Total assets	$66,524	$66,059

NOTES TO CONSOLIDATED FINANCIAL STATEMENTS

1. Description of Business, Basis of Presentation and Summary of Significant Accounting Policies (in part)

Asset Impairments

Investments

The Company's investments consist of (i) fair-value investments, including available-for-sale securities and deferred compensation-related investments, (ii) investments accounted for using the cost method of accounting and (iii) investments accounted for using the equity method of accounting. The Company regularly reviews its investments for impairment, including when the carrying value of an investment exceeds its related market value. If it has been determined that an investment has sustained an other-than-temporary decline in its value, the investment is written down to its fair value by a charge to earnings. Factors that are considered by the Company in determining whether an other-than-temporary decline in value has occurred include the (i) market value of the security in relation to its cost basis, (ii) financial condition of the investee and (iii) the Company's intent and ability to retain the investment for a sufficient period of time to allow for recovery in the market value of the investment.

In evaluating the factors described above for available-for-sale securities, the Company presumes a decline in value to be other-than-temporary if the quoted market price of the security is 20% or more below the investment's cost basis for a period of six months or more (the "20% criterion") or the quoted market price of the security is 50% or more below the security's cost basis at any quarter end (the "50% criterion"). However, the presumption of an other-than-temporary decline in these instances may be overcome if there is persuasive evidence indicating that the decline is temporary in nature (e.g., the investee's operating performance is strong, the market price of the investee's security is historically volatile, etc.). Additionally, there may be instances in which impairment losses are recognized even if the 20% and 50% criteria are not satisfied (e.g., there is a plan to sell the security in the near term and the fair value is below the Company's cost basis).

For investments accounted for using the cost or equity method of accounting, the Company evaluates information (e.g., budgets, business plans, financial statements, etc.) in addition to quoted market prices, if any, in determining whether an other-than-temporary decline in value exists. Factors indicative of an other-than-temporary decline include recurring operating losses, credit defaults and subsequent rounds of financing at an amount below the cost basis of the Company's investment. For more information, see Note 4.

4. Investments (in part)

The Company's investments consist of equity-method investments, fair-value and other investments, including available-for-sale securities, and cost-method investments. Time Warner's investments, by category, consist of (millions):

	December 31	
	2010	2009
Equity-method investments	$ 883	$ 641
Fair-value and other investments, including available-for-sale securities	600	578
Cost-method investments	313	323
Total	$1,796	$1,542

Fair-Value and Other Investments, Including Available-for-Sale Securities

Fair-value and other investments include deferred compensation-related investments and available-for-sale securities of $547 million and $53 million, respectively, as of December 31, 2010 and $544 million and $33 million respectively, as of December 31, 2009. Equity derivative instruments were $1 million as of December 31, 2009.

Deferred compensation-related investments included $248 million and $238 million at December 31, 2010 and 2009, respectively, which were recorded at fair value, and $299 million and $306 million at December 31, 2010 and 2009, respectively, of life insurance-related investments, which were recorded at cash surrender value.

Equity derivative instruments and available-for-sale securities are recorded at fair value in the consolidated balance sheet, and the realized gains and losses are included as a component of Other income, net.

The cost basis, unrealized gains, unrealized losses and fair market value of available-for-sale securities are set forth below (millions):

	December 31	
	2010	2009
Cost basis	$39	$21
Gross unrealized gain	14	14
Gross unrealized loss	—	(2)
Fair value	$53	$33
Deferred tax liability	$ 5	$ 5

During 2010, 2009 and 2008, $(2) million, $20 million and $6 million, respectively, of net unrealized gains (losses) were reclassified from Accumulated other comprehensive income, net, to Other income, net, in the consolidated statement of operations, based on the specific identification method.

5. Fair Value Measurements (in part)

A fair value measurement is determined based on the assumptions that a market participant would use in pricing an asset or liability. A three-tiered hierarchy draws distinctions between market participant assumptions based on (i) observable inputs such as quoted prices in active markets (Level 1), (ii) inputs other than quoted prices in active markets that are observable either directly or indirectly (Level 2) and (iii) unobservable inputs that require the Company to use present value and other valuation techniques in the determination of fair value (Level 3). The following tables present information about assets and liabilities required to be carried at fair value on a recurring basis as of December 31, 2010 and December 31, 2009, respectively (millions):

Fair Value Measurements

Description	December 31, 2010				December 31, 2009			
	Level 1	Level 2	Level 3	Total	Level 1	Level 2	Level 3	Total
Assets:								
Trading securities:								
Diversified equity securities	$261	$ 4	$ —	$265	$243	$ 4	$ —	$247
Available-for-sale securities:								
Equity securities	12	—	—	12	11	—	—	11
Debt securities	—	41	—	41	—	22	—	22
Derivatives:								
Foreign exchange contracts	—	17	—	17	—	8	—	8
Other	4	—	19	23	5	—	32	37
Liabilities:								
Derivatives:								
Foreign exchange contracts	—	(20)	—	(20)	—	(91)	—	(91)
Other	—	—	(28)	(28)	—	—	(12)	(12)
Total	$277	$ 42	$ (9)	$310	$259	$(57)	$ 20	$222

NONCURRENT RECEIVABLES

PRESENTATION

2.82   FASB ASC 210, *Balance Sheet*, states that the concept of current assets excludes receivables arising from unusual transactions that are not expected to be collected within 12 months, such as the sale of capital assets or loans or advances to affiliates, officers, or employees.

2.83   FASB ASC 825 includes noncurrent receivables as financial instruments. FASB ASC 820 requires disclosure of both the fair value and bases for estimating the fair value of noncurrent receivables, unless it is not practicable to estimate that value. However, FASB ASC 825-10-50-14 indicates that for trade receivables and payables, fair value disclosure is not required if the carrying amount approximates fair value.

PRESENTATION AND DISCLOSURE EXCERPTS

Insurance Receivable

2.84

CRANE CO. (DEC)

CONSOLIDATED BALANCE SHEETS (in part)

(In thousands, except shares and per share data)	Balance at December 31	
	2010	**2009**
Assets		
Current assets:		
Cash and cash equivalents	$ 272,941	$ 372,714
Current insurance receivable—asbestos	33,000	35,300
Accounts receivable, net	301,918	282,463
Inventories, net	319,077	284,552
Current deferred tax assets	44,956	58,856
Other current assets	16,769	12,461
Total current assets	988,661	1,046,346
Property, plant and equipment, net	280,746	285,224
Insurance receivable—asbestos	180,689	213,004
Long-term deferred tax assets	182,832	204,386
Other assets	100,848	83,229
Intangible assets, net	162,636	118,731
Goodwill	810,285	761,978
Total assets	$2,706,697	$2,712,898

NOTES TO CONSOLIDATED FINANCIAL STATEMENTS

Note 1—Nature of Operations and Significant Accounting Policies (in part)

Use of Estimates—The Company's consolidated financial statements are prepared in conformity with accounting principles generally accepted in the United States of America ("U.S. GAAP"). These accounting principles require management to make estimates and assumptions that affect the reported amounts of assets and liabilities at the date of the financial statements and the reported amounts of revenue and expense during the reporting period. Actual results may differ from those estimated. Estimates and assumptions are reviewed periodically, and the effects of revisions are reflected in the financial statements in the period in which they are determined to be necessary. Estimates are used when accounting for such items as asset valuations, allowance for doubtful accounts, depreciation and amortization, impairment assessments, restructuring provisions, employee benefits, taxes, asbestos liability and related insurance receivable, environmental liability and contingencies.

Note 10—Commitments and Contingencies Leases (in part)

Asbestos Liability (in part)

Insurance Coverage and Receivables. Prior to 2005, a significant portion of the Company's settlement and defense costs were paid by its primary insurers. With the exhaustion of that primary coverage, the Company began negotiations with its excess insurers to reimburse the Company for a portion of its settlement and/or defense costs as incurred. To date, the Company has entered into agreements providing for such reimbursements, known as "coverage-in-place," with eleven of its excess insurer groups. Under such coverage-in-place agreements, an insurer's policies remain in force and the insurer undertakes to provide coverage for the Company's present and future asbestos claims on specified terms and conditions that address, among other things, the share of asbestos claims costs to be paid by the insurer, payment terms, claims handling procedures and the expiration of the insurer's obligations. The most recent such agreement became effective July 7, 2010, between the Company and Travelers Casualty & Surety Company. On March 3, 2008, the Company reached agreement with certain London Market Insurance Companies, North River Insurance Company and TIG Insurance Company, confirming the aggregate amount of available coverage under certain London policies and setting forth a schedule for future reimbursement payments to the Company based on aggregate indemnity and defense payments made. In addition, with six of its excess insurer groups, the Company entered into policy buyout agreements, settling all asbestos and other coverage obligations for an agreed sum, totaling $79.5 million in aggregate. The most recent of these buyouts was reached with Munich Reinsurance America, Inc. and involved certain historical policies issued by American Re-Insurance Company and American Excess Insurance Company. Reimbursements from insurers for past and ongoing settlement and defense costs allocable to their policies have been made as coverage-in-place and other agreements are reached with such insurers. All of these agreements include provisions for mutual releases, indemnification of the insurer and, for coverage-in-place, claims handling procedures. With the agreements referenced above, the Company has concluded settlements with all but one of its solvent excess insurers whose policies are expected to respond to the aggregate costs included in the updated liability estimate. That insurer, which issued a single applicable policy, has agreed to pay the shares of defense and indemnity costs the Company has allocated to it, subject to a reservation of rights, pending negotiation of a formal settlement agreement with the Company. If the Company is not successful in concluding an agreement with that insurer, then the Company anticipates that it would pursue litigation to enforce its rights under such insurer's policy. There are no pending legal proceedings between the Company and any insurer contesting the Company's asbestos claims under its insurance policies.

In conjunction with developing the aggregate liability estimate referenced above, the Company also developed an estimate of probable insurance recoveries for its asbestos liabilities. In developing this estimate, the Company considered its coverage-in-place and other settlement agreements described above, as well as a number of additional factors. These additional factors include the financial viability of the insurance companies, the method by which losses will be allocated to the various insurance policies and the years covered by those policies, how settlement and defense costs will be covered by the insurance policies and interpretation of the effect on coverage of various policy terms and limits and their interrelationships. In addition, the timing and amount of reimbursements will vary because the Company's insurance coverage for asbestos claims involves multiple insurers, with different policy terms and certain gaps in coverage. In addition to consulting with legal counsel on these insurance matters, the Company retained insurance consultants to assist management in the estimation of probable insurance recoveries based upon the aggregate liability estimate described above and assuming the continued viability of all solvent insurance carriers. Based upon the analysis of policy terms and other factors noted above by the Company's legal counsel, and incorporating risk mitigation judgments by the Company where policy terms or other factors were not certain, the Company's insurance consultants compiled a model indicating how the Company's historical insurance policies would respond to varying levels of asbestos settlement and defense costs and the allocation of such costs between such insurers and the Company. Using the estimated liability as of September 30, 2007 (for claims filed through 2017), the insurance consultant's model forecasted that approximately 33% of the liability would be reimbursed by the Company's insurers. An asset of $351 million was recorded as of September 30, 2007 representing the probable insurance reimbursement for such claims. The asset is reduced as reimbursements and other payments from insurers are received. The asset was $214 million as of December 31, 2010.

The Company reviews the aforementioned estimated reimbursement rate with its insurance consultants on a periodic basis in order to confirm its overall consistency with the Company's established reserves. The reviews encompass consideration of the performance of the insurers under coverage-in-place agreements, the effect of any additional lump-sum payments under policy buyout agreements, and, following consultation with legal counsel, the consistency of any new coverage-in-place agreements with the assumptions in the model. Since September 2007, there have been no developments that have caused the Company to change the estimated 33% rate, although actual insurance reimbursements vary from period to period, and will decline over time, for the reasons cited above. While there are overall limits on the aggregate amount of insurance available to the Company with respect to asbestos claims, those overall limits were not reached by the total estimated liability currently recorded by the Company, and such overall limits did not influence the Company in its determination of the asset amount to record. The proportion of the asbestos liability that is allocated to certain insurance coverage years, however, exceeds the limits of available insurance in those years. The Company allocates to itself the amount of the asbestos liability (for claims filed through 2017) that is in excess of available insurance coverage allocated to such years.

Uncertainties. Estimation of the Company's ultimate exposure for asbestos-related claims is subject to significant uncertainties, as there are multiple variables that can affect the timing, severity and quantity of claims. The Company cautions that its estimated liability is based on assumptions with respect to future claims, settlement and defense costs based on recent experience during the last few years that may not prove reliable as predictors. A significant upward or downward trend in the number of claims filed, depending on the nature of the alleged injury, the jurisdiction where filed and the quality of the product identification, or a significant upward or downward trend in the costs of defending claims, could change the estimated liability, as would substantial adverse verdicts at trial. A legislative solution or a revised structured settlement transaction could also change the estimated liability.

The same factors that affect developing estimates of probable settlement and defense costs for asbestos-related liabilities also affect estimates of the probable insurance reimbursements, as do a number of additional factors. These additional factors include the financial viability of the insurance companies, the method by which losses will be allocated to the various insurance policies and the years covered by those policies, how settlement and defense costs will be covered by the insurance policies and interpretation of the effect on coverage of various policy terms and limits and their interrelationships. In addition, due to the uncertainties inherent in litigation matters, no assurances can be given regarding the outcome of any litigation, if necessary, to enforce the Company's rights under its insurance policies.

Many uncertainties exist surrounding asbestos litigation, and the Company will continue to evaluate its estimated asbestos-related liability and corresponding estimated insurance reimbursement as well as the underlying assumptions and process used to derive these amounts. These uncertainties may result in the Company incurring future charges or increases to income to adjust the carrying value of recorded liabilities and assets, particularly if the number of claims and settlement and defense costs change significantly or if legislation or another alternative solution is implemented; however, the Company is currently unable to estimate such future changes and, accordingly, while it is probable that the Company will incur additional charges for asbestos liabilities and defense costs in excess of the amounts currently provided, the Company does not believe that any such amount can be reasonably determined. Although the resolution of these claims may take many years, the effect on the results of operations, financial position and cash flow in any given period from a revision to these estimates could be material.

Financing Receivables

2.85

DELL INC. (JAN)

CONSOLIDATED STATEMENTS OF FINANCIAL POSITION (in part)

(In millions)	January 29, 2010	January 30, 2009
Assets		
Current assets:		
Cash and cash equivalents	$10,635	$ 8,352
Short-term investments	373	740
Accounts receivable, net	5,837	4,731
Financing receivables, net	2,706	1,712
Inventories, net	1,051	867
Other current assets	3,643	3,749
Total current assets	24,245	20,151
Property, plant, and equipment, net	2,181	2,277
Investments	781	454
Long-term financing receivables, net	332	500
Goodwill	4,074	1,737
Purchased intangible assets, net	1,694	724
Other non-current assets	345	657
Total assets	$33,652	$26,500

NOTES TO CONSOLIDATED FINANCIAL STATEMENTS

Note 1—Description of Business and Summary of Significant Accounting Policies (in part)

Financing Receivables—Financing receivables consist of customer receivables, residual interest and retained interest in securitized receivables. Customer receivables include revolving loans and fixed-term leases and loans resulting from the sale of Dell products and services. Financing receivables are presented net of the allowance for losses. See Note 4 of Notes to Consolidated Financial Statements for additional information.

Note 4—Financial Services (in part)

Financing Receivables

The following table summarizes the components of Dell's financing receivables:

(In millions)	January 29, 2010	January 30, 2009
Financing Receivables, Net		
Customer receivables		
Revolving loans, gross	$2,046	$ 963
Fixed-term leases and loans	824	723
Subtotal	2,870	1,686
Allowances for losses	(237)	(149)
Customer receivables, net	2,633	1,537
Residual interest	254	279
Retained interest	151	396
Financing receivables, net	$3,038	$2,212
Short-term	$2,706	$1,712
Long-term	332	500
Financing receivables, net	$3,038	$2,212

Customer Receivables

The following is the description of the components of Dell's customer receivables:
- Revolving loans offered under private label credit financing programs provide qualified customers with a revolving credit line for the purchase of products and services offered by Dell. Revolving loans bear interest at a variable annual percentage rate that is tied to the prime rate. Based on historical payment patterns, revolving loan transactions are typically repaid on average within 12 months. Revolving loans are included in short-term financing receivables in the table above. From time to time, account holders may have the opportunity to finance their Dell purchases with special programs during which, if the outstanding balance is paid in full by a specific date, no interest is charged. These special programs generally range from 3 to 12 months. At January 29, 2010, and January 30, 2009, receivables under these special programs were $442 million and $352 million, respectively.
- Revolving loans includes customer receivables that were previously securitized and held by a nonconsolidated qualifying special purpose entity. In the second quarter of Fiscal 2010, the beneficial interest in the securitization conduit held by third parties fell below 10% and the special purpose entity was consolidated.

Upon consolidation, these customer receivables were recorded at fair value and the associated retained interest was eliminated. The balance of these customer receivables was $435 million as of January 29, 2010.
- Dell enters into sales-type lease arrangements with customers who desire lease financing. Leases with business customers have fixed terms of two to five years. Future maturities of minimum lease payments at January 29, 2010, for Dell are as follows: Fiscal 2011—$303 million; Fiscal 2012—$188 million; Fiscal 2013—$76 million; and Fiscal 2014—$4 million. Fixed-term loans are offered to qualified small businesses, large commercial accounts, governmental organizations, and educational entities.

Delinquency and charge-off statistics for customer receivables are:
- As of January 29, 2010, and January 30, 2009, customer financing receivables 60 days or more delinquent were $127 million and $58 million, respectively. These amounts represent 4.4% and 3.7% of the ending gross customer financing receivables balance for the respective periods.
- Net principal write-offs charged to the allowance for Fiscal 2010 and Fiscal 2009, were $130 million and $86 million, respectively. These amounts represent 6.2% and 5.5% of the average quarterly gross outstanding customer financing receivables balance (including accrued interest) for the respective periods.

Residual Interest

Dell retains a residual interest in equipment leased under its fixed-term lease programs. The amount of the residual interest is established at the inception of the lease based upon estimates of the value of the equipment at the end of the lease term using historical studies, industry data, and future value-at-risk demand valuation methods. On a quarterly basis, Dell assesses the carrying amount of its recorded residual values for impairment. Anticipated declines in specific future residual values that are considered to be other-than-temporary are recorded currently in earnings.

Retained Interest

Certain transfers of financial assets to nonconsolidated qualified special purpose entities are accounted for as a sale. Upon the sale of the customer receivables to nonconsolidated qualifying special purpose entities, Dell recognizes a gain on the sale and retains a residual beneficial interest in the pool of assets sold, referred to as retained interest. The retained interest represents Dell's right to receive collections for assets securitized exceeding the amount required to pay interest, principal, and other fees and expenses.

Retained interest is stated at the present value of the estimated net beneficial cash flows after payment of all senior interests. Dell values the retained interest at the time of each receivable transfer and at the end of each reporting period. The fair value of the retained interest is determined using a discounted cash flow model with various key assumptions, including payment rates, credit losses, discount rates, and the remaining life of the receivables sold. These assumptions are supported by both Dell's historical experience and anticipated trends relative to the particular receivable pool. The key valuation assumptions for retained interest can be affected by many factors, including repayment terms and the credit quality of receivables securitized.

The following table summarizes the activity in retained interest balances:

(In millions)	January 29, 2010	January 30, 2009	February 1, 2008
Retained Interest:			
Retained interest at beginning of period	$ 396	$ 223	$ 159
Issuances	322	427	173
Distributions from conduits	(91)	(246)	(132)
Net accretion	31	16	31
Change in fair value for the period	(5)	(24)	(8)
Impact of special purpose entity consolidation	(502)	—	—
Retained interest at end of the period	$ 151	$ 396	$ 223

The following table summarizes the key assumptions used to measure the fair value of the retained interest of the fixed term leases and loans at time of transfer within the period and at January 29, 2010, the balance sheet date:

	Monthly Payment Rates	Credit Losses (Lifetime)	Discount Rates (Annualized)	Life (Months)
Time of transfer valuation of retained interest	5%	1%	12%	20
Valuation of retained interest	8%	3%	12%	14

The impact of adverse changes to the key valuation assumptions to the fair value of retained interest at January 29, 2010 is shown in the following table:

(In millions)	January 29, 2010
Adverse Change of:	
Expected prepayment speed: 10%	$(0.1)
Expected prepayment speed: 20%	$(0.2)
Expected credit losses: 10%	$(1.1)
Expected credit losses: 20%	$(2.2)
Discount rate: 10%	$(1.7)
Discount rate: 20%	$(3.4)

The analysis above utilized 10% and 20% adverse variation in assumptions to assess the sensitivities in the fair value of the retained interest. However, these changes generally cannot be extrapolated because the relationship between a change in one assumption to the resulting change in fair value may not be linear. For the above sensitivity analyses, each key assumption was isolated and evaluated separately. Each assumption was adjusted by 10% and 20% while holding the other key assumptions constant. Assumptions may be interrelated, and changes to one assumption may impact others and the resulting fair value of the retained interest. For example, increases in market interest rates may result in lower prepayments and increases in credit losses. The effect of multiple assumption changes were not considered in the analysis.

During Fiscal 2010 and Fiscal 2009, $784 million and $1.4 billion, respectively, of customer receivables were funded via securitization through nonconsolidated qualified special purpose entities. The principal balance of securitized receivables reported off-balance sheet as of January 29, 2010, and January 30, 2009, were $774 million and $1.4 billion, respectively. Dell's risk of loss related to securitized receivables is limited to the amount of its retained interest.

Lease and loan receivables transferred to the nonconsolidated qualified special purpose entities exceed the level of debt issued. As of January 29, 2010, the nonconsolidated securitized receivables were $774 million, and the associated debt was $624 million. Upon consolidation of these customer receivables and associated debt in the first quarter of Fiscal 2011 as previously discussed, Dell's retained interest in securitized receivables of $151 million at January 29, 2010, will be eliminated.

Delinquency and charge-off statistics for securitized receivables held by nonconsolidated qualified special purpose entities are:

- As of January 29, 2010, and January 30, 2009, securitized financing receivables 60 days or more delinquent were $11 million and $63 million, respectively. These amounts represent 1.5% and 4.6% of the ending securitized financing receivables balances for the respective periods.
- Net principal chargeoffs for Fiscal 2010 and Fiscal 2009, were $72 million and $114 million, respectively. These amounts represent 6.9% and 8.2% of the average quarterly outstanding securitized financing receivables balance (including accrued interest) for the respective years.

INTANGIBLE ASSETS

RECOGNITION AND MEASUREMENT

2.86 FASB ASC 350, *Intangibles—Goodwill and Other*, specifies that goodwill and intangible assets that have indefinite lives are not subject to amortization but, rather, should be tested at least annually for impairment. In addition, FASB ASC 350 provides specific guidance on how to determine and measure impairment of goodwill and intangible assets not subject to amortization. Intangible assets that have finite useful lives should be amortized over their useful lives.

2.87 FASB ASC 350 also provides guidance on accounting for the cost of computer software developed or obtained for internal use and website development costs.

PRESENTATION

2.88 FASB ASC 350-20-45-1 requires that the aggregate amount of goodwill be presented as a separate line item in the balance sheet. Under FASB ASC 350-30-45-1, at minimum, all intangible assets should be aggregated and presented as a separate line item in the balance sheet. However, that requirement does not preclude the presentation of individual intangible assets or classes of intangible assets as separate line items. Rule 5-02 of Regulation S-X also calls for separately stating each class of intangible assets in excess of 5 percent of total assets and for separate presentation of the amount of accumulated amortization of intangible assets.

DISCLOSURE

2.89 FASB ASC 350 requires additional disclosures for each period for which a balance sheet is presented, including information about gross carrying amounts and changes therein of goodwill and other intangible assets, accumulated amortization for amortizable assets, and estimates about intangible asset amortization expense for each of the five succeeding fiscal years. For intangibles, the balance sheet disclosures should be in total and by major intangible asset class.

2.90

TABLE 2-9: INTANGIBLE ASSETS*

Table 2-9 lists those intangible assets, amortized or not, which are most frequently disclosed by the survey entities.

	Number of Entities		
	2010	2009	2008
Goodwill recognized in a business combination	443	434	444
Trademarks, brand names, copyrights....	300	307	295
Customer lists/relationships	288	277	272
Technology	156	148	138
Licenses, franchises, memberships	104	96	96
Research and development acquired in a business combination	19	12	N/C^
Other, described	267	380	332

* Appearing in the balance sheet or notes to financial statements, or both.
^ N/C = Not compiled. Line item was not included in the table for the year shown.

PRESENTATION AND DISCLOSURE EXCERPTS

Goodwill

2.91

THE SHERWIN-WILLIAMS COMPANY (DEC)

CONSOLIDATED BALANCE SHEETS (in part)

	December 31		
(Thousands of dollars)	2010	2009	2008
Assets			
Current assets:			
Cash and cash equivalents	$ 58,585	$ 69,329	$ 26,212
Accounts receivable, less allowance	916,661	696,055	769,985
Inventories:			
Finished goods	743,953	630,683	749,405
Work in process and raw materials	173,748	107,805	114,795
	917,701	738,488	864,200
Deferred income taxes	127,348	121,276	97,568
Other current assets	193,427	144,871	151,240
Total current assets	2,213,722	1,770,019	1,909,205
Goodwill	1,102,458	1,014,825	1,006,712
Intangible assets	320,504	279,413	299,963
Deferred pension assets	248,333	245,301	215,637
Other assets	332,100	195,612	124,117
Property, plant and equipment:			
Land	106,101	85,166	85,485
Buildings	668,506	600,687	580,216
Machinery and equipment	1,617,530	1,512,218	1,564,221
Construction in progress	34,038	23,086	26,560
	2,426,175	2,221,157	2,256,482
Less allowances for depreciation	1,474,057	1,402,472	1,396,357
	952,118	818,685	860,125
Total assets	$5,169,235	$4,323,855	$4,415,759

NOTES TO CONSOLIDATED FINANCIAL STATEMENTS

(Thousands of dollars unless otherwise indicated)

Note 1—Significant Accounting Policies (in part)

Goodwill. Goodwill represents the cost in excess of fair value of net assets acquired in business combinations accounted for by the purchase method. In accordance with the Impairments Topic of the ASC, goodwill is tested for impairment on an annual basis and in between annual tests if events or circumstances indicate potential impairment. See Note 5.

Note 5—Goodwill, Intangible and Long-Lived Assets (in part)

During 2010, the Company recognized $79,909 of goodwill and $18,007 of trademarks in the acquisitions of Sayerlack, Acroma and Pinturas Condor. Customer relationships valued at $35,886 recognized in the acquisitions of Acroma and Pinturas Condor are being amortized over periods of 15 and 19 years, respectively, from the date of acquisition.

During 2009, the Company recognized $4,147 of goodwill, $3,211 of trademarks and $2,643 of other intangibles in the acquisition of Altax. Customer relationships valued at $1,572 and intellectual property valued at $1,071 are being amortized over 10 and 8 years, respectively, from the date of acquisition.

During 2008, the Company recognized $24,383 of goodwill in the acquisitions of Euronavy, Inchem, Becker and Columbia. There was no goodwill recognized in the acquisition of Wagman Primus. Trademarks of $10,265 were recognized in the acquisition valuation of Inchem and Euronavy. Covenants not to compete of $3,000, obtained in the acquisitions of Inchem, Becker and Wagman Primus, are being amortized over five years from the date of acquisition. Customer lists valued at $6,950, recognized in the acquisitions of Inchem and Becker, are being amortized over periods of 4.5 years and 10 years, respectively. A value for formulations acquired of $300, recognized in the acquisition of Becker, is being amortized over 5 years. No significant residual value was estimated for any of the acquired identified intangible assets.

In accordance with the Goodwill and Other Intangibles Topic of the ASC, goodwill and indefinite-lived intangible assets are tested for impairment annually, and interim impairment tests are performed whenever an event occurs or circumstances change that indicate an impairment has more likely than not occurred. October 1 has been established for the annual impairment review. At the time of impairment testing, values are estimated separately for goodwill and trademarks with indefinite lives using a discounted cash flow valuation model, incorporating discount rates commensurate with the risks involved for each group of assets. Impairments of goodwill and trademarks with indefinite lives have been reported as a separate line in the Statements of Consolidated Income.

The annual impairment review performed as of October 1, 2010 resulted in a trademark impairment in the Paint Stores Group of $120 and no goodwill impairment. The trademark impairment related primarily to lower-than-anticipated sales of an acquired brand.

The annual impairment review performed as of October 1, 2009 resulted in trademark impairments of $14,144 ($10,998 in the Paint Stores Group, $86 in the Consumer Group and $3,060 in the Global Finishes Group), and no goodwill impairment. The trademark impairments related primarily to lower-than-anticipated sales of certain acquired brands.

The annual impairment review performed as of October 1, 2008 resulted in reductions in the carrying values of goodwill of $8,113 and trademarks with indefinite lives of $22,579. The goodwill impairment was included in the Consumer Group. The trademark impairments were in the Paint Stores Group ($22,474) and the Consumer Group ($105). The goodwill and trademark impairments related primarily to lower-than-anticipated cash flow in a certain acquired business and lower-than-anticipated sales of certain acquired brands, respectively.

During the second quarter of 2008, the Company performed an interim impairment review of its goodwill and indefinite-lived intangible assets. Soft domestic architectural paint sales in the new residential, residential repaint, DIY and commercial markets indicated that certain domestic indefinite-lived trademarks might be impaired. In addition, continued low cash flow projections in one foreign business unit indicated that goodwill impairment might be likely. The interim impairment review resulted in reductions in the carrying values of certain trademarks with indefinite lives of $23,121. The trademark impairments were charged to the Paint Stores Group ($20,364) and the Consumer Group ($2,757). The goodwill impairment of a foreign business unit aggregated $791 and was charged to the Global Finishes Group.

Amortization of finite-lived intangible assets is as follows for the next five years: $24,187 in 2011, $22,645 in 2012, $18,402 in 2013 and $15,222 in 2014 and $12,375 in 2015.

A summary of changes in the Company's carrying value of goodwill by reportable operating segment is as follows:

Goodwill	Paint Stores Group	Consumer Group	Global Finishes Group	Consolidated Totals
Balance at January 1, 2008	$274,250	$689,635	$ 32,728	$ 996,613
Acquisitions	10,133		14,250	24,383
Impairment charged to operations		(8,113)	(791)	(8,904)
Currency and other adjustments	1,042	1,842	(8,264)	(5,380)
Balance at December 31, 2008[a]	285,425	683,364	37,923	1,006,712
Acquisitions		4,147		4,147
Currency and other adjustments	20	(899)	4,845	3,966
Balance at December 31, 2009[a]	285,445	686,612	42,768	1,014,825
Acquisitions			79,909	79,909
Currency and other adjustments	1,299	2,776	3,649	7,724
Balance at December 31, 2010[a]	$286,744	$689,388	$126,326	$1,102,458

[a] Net of accumulated impairment losses of $8,904 ($8,113 in the Consumer Group and $791 in the Global Finishes Group).

A summary of the Company's carrying value of intangible assets is as follows:

	Finite-Lived Intangible Assets			Trademarks With Indefinite Lives	Total Intangible Assets
	Software	All other	Subtotal		
December 31, 2010					
Weighted-average amortization period	8 years	13 years	11 years		
Gross	$107,141	$ 254,462	$ 361,603		
Accumulated amortization	(57,480)	(171,153)	(228,633)		
Net value	$ 49,661	$ 83,309	$ 132,970	$187,534	$320,504
December 31, 2009					
Weighted-average amortization period	9 years	10 years	9 years		
Gross	$ 90,263	$ 218,621	$ 308,884		
Accumulated amortization	(47,140)	(152,552)	(199,692)		
Net value	$ 43,123	$ 66,069	$ 109,192	$170,221	$279,413
December 31, 2008					
Weighted-average amortization period	9 years	9 years	9 years		
Gross	$ 81,236	$ 199,746	$ 280,982		
Accumulated amortization	(35,856)	(129,710)	(165,566)		
Net value	$ 45,380	$ 70,036	$ 115,416	$184,547	$299,963

2.92

EATON CORPORATION (DEC)

CONSOLIDATED BALANCE SHEETS (in part)

	December 31	
(In millions)	2010	2009
Assets		
Current assets		
Cash	$ 333	$ 340
Short-term investments	838	433
Accounts receivable-net	2,239	1,899
Inventory	1,564	1,326
Deferred income taxes	303	377
Prepaid expenses and other current assets	229	149
Total current assets	5,506	4,524
Property, plant and equipment		
Land and buildings	1,494	1,459
Machinery and equipment	4,485	4,241
Gross property, plant and equipment	5,979	5,700
Accumulated depreciation	(3,502)	(3,255)
Net property, plant and equipment	2,477	2,445
Other noncurrent assets		
Goodwill	5,454	5,435
Other intangible assets	2,272	2,441
Deferred income taxes	1,001	973
Other assets	542	464
Total assets	$17,252	$16,282

NOTES TO CONSOLIDATED FINANCIAL STATEMENTS

Amounts are in millions or shares unless indicated otherwise (per share data assume dilution).

Note 1. Summary of Significant Accounting Policies (in part)

Goodwill and Indefinite Life Intangible Assets

Goodwill and indefinite life intangible assets are tested annually for impairment as of July 1 using a discounted cash flow model and other valuation techniques. Additionally, goodwill and indefinite life intangible assets are evaluated for impairment whenever events or circumstances indicate there may be a possible permanent loss of value.

Goodwill is tested for impairment at the reporting unit level, which is equivalent to Eaton's operating segments, and based on the net assets for each segment, including goodwill and intangible assets. Goodwill is assigned to each operating segment, as this represents the lowest level that constitutes a business and for which discrete financial information is available and is the level which management regularly reviews the operating results. A discounted cash flow model is used to estimate the fair value of each operating segment, which considers forecasted cash flows discounted at an estimated weighted-average cost of capital. The Company selected the discounted cash flow methodology as it believes that it is comparable to what would be used by market participants. The forecasted cash flows are based on the Company's long-term operating plan, and a terminal value is used to estimate the operating segment's cash flows beyond the period covered by the operating plan. The weighted-average cost of capital is an estimate of the overall after-tax rate of return required by equity and debt market participants of a business enterprise. These analyses require the exercise of significant judgments, including judgments about appropriate discount rates, perpetual growth rates and the timing of expected future cash flows. Discount rate assumptions are based on an assessment of the risk inherent in the future cash flows of the respective operating segment. Sensitivity analyses are performed around these assumptions in order to assess the reasonableness of the assumptions and the resulting estimated fair values.

Indefinite life intangible assets primarily consist of trademarks. The fair value of these assets is determined using a royalty relief methodology similar to that employed when the associated assets were acquired, but using updated estimates of future sales, cash flows and profitability.

For 2010, the fair value of Eaton's reporting units and indefinite life intangible assets substantially exceeded the respective carrying values. For additional information about goodwill and other intangible assets, see Note 4.

Note 4. Goodwill and Other Intangible Assets (in part)

A summary of goodwill follows:

	2010	2009
Electrical Americas	$2,061	$2,003
Electrical Rest of World	985	1,005
Hydraulics	1,007	1,016
Aerospace	1,037	1,047
Truck	151	147
Automotive	213	217
Total goodwill	$5,454	$5,435

The increase in goodwill in 2010 was due to businesses acquired during 2010, the finalization of purchase price allocations related to businesses acquired in 2009, and foreign currency translation. For additional information regarding acquired businesses, see Note 2.

Tradenames and Other Intangibles

2.93

CHURCH & DWIGHT CO., INC. (DEC)

CONSOLIDATED BALANCE SHEETS (in part)

(Dollars in thousands, except share and per share data)	December 31, 2010	December 31, 2009
Assets		
Current Assets		
Cash and cash equivalents	$ 189,202	$ 447,143
Accounts receivable, less allowances of $5,496 and $5,782	231,055	222,158
Inventories	195,401	216,870
Deferred income taxes	16,298	20,432
Other current assets	17,525	21,662
Total current assets	649,481	928,265
Property, plant and equipment, net	468,324	455,636
Equity investment in affiliates	9,192	12,815
Tradenames and other intangibles	872,460	794,891
Goodwill	857,361	838,078
Other assets	88,376	88,761
Total assets	$2,945,194	$3,118,446

NOTES TO CONSOLIDATED FINANCIAL STATEMENTS

6. Acquisition of Assets

On June 4, 2010, the Company acquired the Simply Saline brand from Blairex Laboratories ("Simply Saline Acquisition") for cash consideration of $70.0 million. Simply Saline annual net sales are approximately $20.0 million. The Simply Saline brand will be managed principally within the Consumer Domestic segment.

On September 2, 2010, the Company acquired certain oral care technology ("Technology Acquisition") for cash consideration of $10.0 million. The new oral care technology will be managed principally within the Consumer Domestic segment.

On December 21, 2010, the Company acquired the Feline Pine cat litter brand from Nature's Earth Products, Inc. ("Feline Pine Acquisition") for cash consideration of $46.0 million. Feline Pine annual net sales are approximately $20.0 million. The acquired brand will complement the existing Arm & Hammer's cat litter business. The Feline Pine brand will be managed within the Consumer Domestic segment.

The fair values of the assets acquired in 2010 are as follows:

(In thousands)	Fair Value of Assets Acquired in 2010			
	Simply Saline	Technology	Feline Pine	Total
Inventory/current assets	$ 1,725	$ 0	$ 1,417	$ 3,142
Tradenames and other intangibles	55,635	10,000	38,500	104,135
Goodwill	12,665	0	6,083	18,748
Total assets	70,025	10,000	46,000	126,025
Liabilities	0	0	0	0
Purchase price	$70,025	$10,000	$46,000	$126,025

The asset allocation of the Feline Pine Acquisition is based on a preliminary valuation. Pro forma results reflecting the Simply Saline and Feline Pine Acquisitions are not presented because they did not have a material effect on the Company's consolidated financial results.

The weighted average life of the amortizable intangible assets recognized from the Simply Saline Acquisition was 15 years and from the Technology Acquisition was 10 years.

On July 7, 2008, the Company purchased substantially all of the assets and certain liabilities of Del Pharmaceuticals, Inc. from Coty, Inc. (the "Orajel Acquisition") for cash consideration of $383.4 million including fees. Products acquired from Del Pharmaceuticals, Inc. include the Orajel brand of oral analgesics and various other over-the-counter brands.

7. Goodwill and Other Intangibles (in part)

The following table provides information related to the carrying value of all intangible assets, other than goodwill:

| (In thousands) | December 31, 2010 | | | | December 31, 2009 | | |
	Gross Carrying Amount	Accumulated Amortization	Net	Amortization Period (Years)	Gross Carrying Amount	Accumulated Amortization	Net
Amortizable Intangible Assets:							
Tradenames	$117,077	$ (53,871)	$ 63,206	3–20	$118,373	$ (46,721)	$ 71,652
Customer relationships	250,540	(50,496)	200,044	15–20	241,640	(37,205)	204,435
Patents/Formulas	38,520	(21,049)	17,471	4–20	27,370	(18,084)	9,286
Non compete agreement	1,378	(1,059)	319	5–10	1,143	(918)	225
Total	$407,515	$(126,475)	$281,040		$388,526	$(102,928)	$285,598
Indefinite Lived Intangible Assets—Carrying Value							
Tradenames	$591,420				$509,293		

Intangible amortization expense amounted to $23.7 million for 2010, $24.2 million for 2009 and $21.8 million in 2008. The Company estimates that intangible amortization expense will be approximately $24.8 million in 2011 and $22.0 to $24.0 million in each of the next four years.

Other intangible assets increased in 2010 due to the Simply Saline, Technology and Feline Pine Acquisitions. The acquired intangible assets reflect their allocable purchase price as of their respective purchase dates.

The Company recognized tradename impairment charges within selling, general and administrative expenses during the three year period ended December 31, 2010 as follows:

(In thousands)	2010	2009	2008
Segments:			
Consumer domestic	$0	$0	$1,910
Consumer international	0	0	3,764
Total	$0	$0	$5,674

The tradename impairment charges recorded in 2008 were a result of management's decision to exit a business, a potential change of a brand's name, lost distribution at key customer accounts and reduced profitability. The amount of the impairment charge was determined by comparing the estimated fair value of the asset to its carrying amount. Fair value was estimated based on a "relief from royalty" discounted cash flow method. Under this method, the owner of an intangible asset must determine the arm's length royalty that likely would have been charged if the owner had to license that asset from a third party. Estimates under the relief from royalty method involve numerous variables that are subject to change as business conditions change, and therefore could impact fair values in the future. The Company determined that the remaining carrying value of all tradenames was recoverable based upon the forecasted cash flows and profitability of the related brands.

Trademarks

2.94

DEAN FOODS COMPANY (DEC)

CONSOLIDATED BALANCE SHEETS (in part)

	December 31	
(Dollars in thousands, except share data)	2010	2009
Assets		
Current assets:		
Cash and cash equivalents	$ 92,007	$ 45,190
Receivables, net of allowance of $15,347 and $16,888	891,019	871,833
Income tax receivable	71,337	19,434
Inventories, net	425,576	436,061
Deferred income taxes	141,653	154,927
Prepaid expenses and other current assets	77,510	90,061
Assets held for sale	117,114	30,088
Total current assets	1,816,216	1,647,594
Property, plant and equipment, net	2,113,391	2,102,253
Goodwill	3,179,192	3,272,814
Identifiable intangible and other assets	847,868	821,280
Total	$7,956,667	$7,843,941

NOTES TO CONSOLIDATED FINANCIAL STATEMENTS

1. Summary of Significant Accounting Policies (in part)

Intangible and Other Assets—Identifiable intangible assets, other than trademarks that have indefinite lives, are typically amortized over the following range of estimated useful lives:

Asset	Useful Life
Customer relationships	5 to 15 years
Certain finite lived trademarks	5 to 15 years
Customer supply contracts	Over the terms of the agreements
Noncompetition agreements	Over the terms of the agreements
Deferred financing costs	Over the terms of the related debt

In accordance with Accounting Standards related to "Goodwill and Other Intangible Assets", we do not amortize goodwill and other intangible assets determined to have indefinite useful lives. Instead, we conduct impairment tests on our goodwill, trademarks and other intangible assets with indefinite lives annually and when circumstances indicate that the carrying value may not be recoverable. To determine whether impairment exists, we primarily utilize a discounted future cash flow analysis.

6. Goodwill and Intangible Assets (in part)

The gross carrying amount and accumulated amortization of our intangible assets other than goodwill as of December 31, 2010 and 2009 are as follows:

	December 31					
	2010			2009		
(In thousands)	Gross Carrying Amount	Accumulated Amortization	Net Carrying Amount	Gross Carrying Amount	Accumulated Amortization	Net Carrying Amount
Intangible assets with indefinite lives:						
Trademarks[1][2]	$593,387	$ —	$593,387	$608,339	$ —	$608,339
Intangible assets with finite lives:						
Customer-related and other	133,829	(44,622)	89,207	135,993	(35,737)	100,256
Trademarks	18,614	(4,474)	14,140	10,146	(1,940)	8,206
Total	$745,830	$(49,096)	$696,734	$754,478	$(37,677)	$716,801

[1] A trademark with a gross carrying amount of $7.5 million was moved from indefinite lived intangible assets to finite lived intangible assets in the first quarter of 2010. The remaining decrease in the gross carrying amount of intangible assets with indefinite lives is the result of foreign currency translation adjustments.

[2] In the third quarter of 2010, $2.1 million of indefinite lived intangible assets attributable to Rachel's were sold. Amounts at December 31, 2009 have been moved to assets held for sale to reflect this change.

Amortization expense on intangible assets for the years ended December 31, 2010, 2009 and 2008 was $11.3 million, $9.6 million and $9.8 million, respectively. Estimated aggregate intangible asset amortization expense for the next five years is as follows:

2011	$11.2 million
2012	9.9 million
2013	9.8 million
2014	9.1 million
2015	9.0 million

Our goodwill and intangible assets have resulted from acquisitions. Upon acquisition, the purchase price is first allocated to identifiable assets and liabilities, including trademarks and customer-related intangible assets, with any remaining purchase price recorded as goodwill. Goodwill and trademarks with indefinite lives are not amortized.

A trademark is recorded with an indefinite life if it has a history of strong sales and cash flow performance that we expect to continue for the foreseeable future. If these perpetual trademark criteria are not met, the trademarks are amortized over their expected useful lives. Determining the expected life of a trademark is based on a number of factors including the competitive environment, trademark history and anticipated future trademark support.

We conduct impairment tests of goodwill and intangible assets with indefinite lives annually in the fourth quarter or when circumstances arise that indicate a possible impairment might exist. If the fair value of an evaluated asset is less than its book value, an impairment charge is recorded. Our reporting units are Fresh Dairy Direct, WhiteWave, Morningstar and Alpro. We did not recognize any impairment charges related to goodwill during 2010, 2009 or 2008.

Considerable management judgment is necessary to evaluate goodwill for impairment. We determine fair value using widely acceptable valuation techniques including discounted cash flows, market multiples analyses and relief from royalty analyses. Increasing our discount rates assumed in these analyses by 0.25% would not have resulted in an impairment charge. Assumptions used in our valuations, such as forecasted growth rates and our cost of capital, are consistent with our internal projections and operating plans. The terminal growth rates utilized in calculating the fair value of our reporting units (ranging from 1.8% to 3.5%) is also dependent upon meeting our internal projections and operating plans, as well as other factors and assumptions. A 0.25% reduction in the terminal growth rate assumptions could result in a material impairment charge.

Based on our analysis performed in the fourth quarter of 2010, each of our reporting units tested had fair values in excess of book values by approximately $229 million or 6.4%, $367 million or 65.1%, $856 million or 80.4% and $33 million or 7.8% for Fresh Dairy Direct, Morningstar, WhiteWave and Alpro, respectively. The sum of the fair values of our reporting units was in excess of our market capitalization. We believe that the difference between the fair value and market capitalization is reasonable (in the context of assessing whether any asset impairment exists) when market-based control premiums are taken into consideration. While the results of our testing indicate that each of our reporting units has a fair value in excess of its carrying value and no impairment charge was required; the excess of the reporting unit fair values over carrying values, specifically with respect to our Fresh Dairy Direct reporting unit, is significantly less than in prior years. We can provide no assurance that we will not have an impairment charge in future periods as a result of changes in our operating results or our assumptions.

While the results of our testing indicate that each of our reporting units has a fair value in excess of its carrying value and no impairment charge was required; the excess of the reporting unit fair values over carrying values, specifically with respect to our Fresh Dairy Direct reporting unit, is significantly less than in prior years. While testing results do not indicate an impairment charge, we can provide no assurance that we will not have an impairment charge in future periods as a result of changes in our operating results.

The sum of the fair values of our reporting units was in excess of our market capitalization. We believe that the difference between the fair value and market capitalization is reasonable (in the context of assessing whether any asset impairment exists) when market-based control premiums are taken into consideration.

In 2009, we recognized an impairment charge of $0.5 million in Fresh Dairy Direct related to a perpetual trademark for a regional brand due to projected declining annualized sales volumes and profitability. This trademark was no longer deemed to have a perpetual life and therefore is amortized over its estimated remaining life. In 2008, we recognized an impairment charge of $2.3 million related to three perpetual trademarks for regional brands in Fresh Dairy Direct. The write-downs were the result of lower annualized sales volumes from certain facilities partly related to movement of production between regional brands. These trademarks were no longer deemed to have a perpetual life and are being amortized over their respective estimated remaining lives.

Amortizable intangible assets are only evaluated for impairment upon a significant change in the operating environment. If an evaluation of the undiscounted cash flows indicates impairment, the asset is written down to its estimated fair value, which is generally based on discounted future cash flows.

Customer Contracts and Relationships

2.95

ADOBE SYSTEMS INCORPORATED (NOV)

CONSOLIDATED BALANCE SHEETS (in part)

(In thousands, except par value)	December 3, 2010	November 27, 2009
Assets		
Current assets:		
Cash and cash equivalents	$ 749,891	$ 999,487
Short-term investments	1,718,124	904,986
Trade receivables, net of allowances for doubtful accounts of $15,233 and $15,225, respectively	554,328	410,879
Deferred income taxes	83,247	77,417
Prepaid expenses and other current assets	110,460	80,855
Total current assets	3,216,050	2,473,624
Property and equipment, net	448,881	388,132
Goodwill	3,641,844	3,494,589
Purchased and other intangibles, net	457,263	527,388
Investment in lease receivable	207,239	207,239
Other assets	169,871	191,265
Total assets	$8,141,148	$7,282,237

NOTES TO CONSOLIDATED FINANCIAL STATEMENTS

Note 1. Basis of Presentation and Significant Accounting Policies (in part)

Goodwill, Purchased Intangibles and Other Long-Lived Assets (in part)

We amortize intangible assets with finite lives over their estimated useful lives and review them for impairment whenever an impairment indicator exists. We continually monitor events and changes in circumstances that could indicate carrying amounts of our long-lived assets, including our intangible assets may not be recoverable. When such events or changes in circumstances occur, we assess recoverability by determining whether the carrying value of such assets will be recovered through the undiscounted expected future cash flows. If the future undiscounted cash flows are less than the carrying amount of these assets, we recognize an impairment loss based on the excess of the carrying amount over the fair value of the assets. We did not recognize any intangible asset impairment charges in fiscal 2010, 2009 or 2008.

Our intangible assets are amortized over their estimated useful lives of 1 to 13 years as shown in the table below. Amortization is based on the pattern in which the economic benefits of the intangible asset will be consumed.

	Weighted Average Useful Life (Years)
Purchased technology	6
Localization	1
Trademarks	8
Customer contracts and relationships	10
Other intangibles	2

Note 2. Acquisitions (in part)

Fiscal 2010 Acquisitions (in part)

On October 28, 2010, we completed our acquisition of Day Software Holding AG ("Day"). Under the terms of the agreement, we completed our public tender offer to acquire all of the publicly held registered shares of Day for 139 Swiss Francs per share in cash in a transaction valued at approximately $248.3 million on a fully diluted equity-value basis. In order to hedge the economic exposure related to this acquisition, we entered into a forward contract to purchase 254.7 million Swiss Francs for $242.5 million U.S. dollars maturing near the expected closing date of the acquisition. Upon maturity of the forward contract, we recorded a $20.8 million gain to interest and other income (expense), net. This forward contract is accounted for as a separate transaction apart from the acquisition.

Under the acquisition method, the total preliminary purchase price was allocated to Day's net tangible and intangible assets based upon their estimated fair values as of October 28, 2010. The excess purchase price over the value of the net tangible and identifiable intangible assets was recorded as goodwill. Goodwill represents the excess of the purchase price over the fair value of the underlying acquired net tangible and intangible assets. The factors that contributed to the recognition of goodwill included securing buyer-specific synergies to increase revenue and profits and are not otherwise available to a marketplace participant in addition to acquiring a talented workforce.

The total preliminary purchase price for Day was approximately $248.3 million of which approximately $159.9 million was allocated to goodwill, $79.2 million for substantially all of the identifiable intangible assets, and $6.1 million to net tangible assets. The impact of this acquisition was not material to our consolidated balance sheets and results of operations.

Fiscal 2009 Acquisitions

On October 23, 2009, we completed the acquisition of Omniture, Inc. ("Omniture"), an industry leader in Web analytics and online business optimization based in Orem, Utah, for approximately $1.8 billion. Under the terms of the agreement, we completed our tender offer to acquire all of the outstanding shares of Omniture common stock at a price of $21.50 per share, net to the seller in cash, without interest. Acquiring

Omniture accelerates our strategy of delivering more effective solutions for creating, delivering, measuring and optimizing Web content and applications. The transaction was accounted for using the purchase method of accounting. We have included the financial results of Omniture in our Consolidated Financial Statements beginning on the acquisition date. Following the closing, we disclosed Omniture as a new segment for financial reporting purposes.

Assets acquired and liabilities assumed were recorded at their fair values as of October 23, 2009. The total $1.8 billion purchase price was comprised of the following (in thousands):

Acquisition of approximately 79 million shares of outstanding common stock of Omniture at $21.50 per share in cash	$1,698,926
Estimated fair value of earned stock options and restricted stock units assumed and converted	84,968
Estimated direct transaction costs	14,365
Total purchase price	$1,798,259

Purchase Price Allocation

Under the purchase accounting method, the total purchase price was allocated to Omniture's net tangible and intangible assets based upon their estimated fair values as of October 23, 2009. The excess purchase price over the value of the net tangible and identifiable intangible assets was recorded as goodwill.

The table below summarizes the allocation of the purchase price to the acquired net assets of Omniture based on their estimated fair values as of October 23, 2009 and the associated estimated useful lives at that date. During the first half of fiscal 2010, we finalized our purchase accounting after adjustments were made to the preliminary purchase price allocation to reflect the finalization of the valuation of intangible assets and deferred revenue. Additional adjustments were also made to restructuring liabilities, taxes and residual goodwill.

(In thousands)	Amount	Weighted Average Useful Life (Years)
Net tangible assets	$ 33,397	
Identifiable intangible assets:		
Existing technology	176,200	6
Customer contracts and relationships	168,600	11
Contract backlog	44,800	2
Non-competition agreements	900	2
Trademarks	41,000	8
In-process research and development	4,600	N/A
Goodwill	1,340,021	
Restructuring liability	(11,259)	
Total purchase price allocation	$1,798,259	

Note 7. Goodwill and Purchased and Other Intangibles (in part)

Purchased and other intangible assets, net by reportable segment as of December 3, 2010 and November 27, 2009 were as follows (in thousands):

	2010	2009
Creative Solutions	$ 20,617	$124,178
Knowledge Worker	9,455	23,041
Enterprise	80,092	6,588
Omniture	344,059	358,204
Platform	1,208	9,159
Print and Publishing	1,832	6,218
Purchased and other intangible assets, net	$457,263	$527,388

Purchased and other intangible assets subject to amortization as of December 3, 2010 and November 27, 2009 were as follows (in thousands):

	2010			2009		
	Cost	Accumulated Amortization	Net	Cost	Accumulated Amortization	Net
Purchased technology	$260,198	$ (61,987)	$198,211	$ 586,952	$(387,731)	$199,221
Localization	$ 14,768	$ (9,355)	$ 5,413	$ 20,284	$ (15,222)	$ 5,062
Trademarks	172,019	(136,480)	35,539	172,030	(104,953)	67,077
Customer contracts and relationships	398,421	(197,459)	200,962	363,922	(159,450)	204,472
Other intangibles	51,265	(34,127)	17,138	54,535	(2,979)	51,556
Total other intangible assets	$636,473	$(377,421)	$259,052	$ 610,771	$(282,604)	$328,167
Purchased and other intangible assets	$896,671	$(439,408)	$457,263	$1,197,723	$(670,335)	$527,388

During the first half of fiscal 2010, purchased and other intangible assets from prior acquisitions, primarily Macromedia, became fully amortized and were removed from the balance sheet. Amortization expense related to purchased and other intangible assets was $156.7 million, $151.3 million and $184.4 million for fiscal 2010, 2009 and 2008, respectively. Of these amounts, for fiscal 2010, 2009 and 2008, $84.5 million, $88.3 million and $116.1 million, respectively, was included in cost of sales.

Purchased and other intangible assets are amortized over their estimated useful lives of 1 to 13 years. As of December 3, 2010, we expect amortization expense in future periods to be as follows (in thousands):

Fiscal Year	Purchased Technology	Other Intangible Assets
2011	$ 44,306	$ 57,980
2012	42,699	29,374
2013	38,691	27,029
2014	35,801	26,191
2015	30,938	25,777
Thereafter	5,776	92,701
Total expected amortization expense	$198,211	$259,052

2.96

SPRINT NEXTEL CORPORATION (DEC)

CONSOLIDATED BALANCE SHEETS (in part)

	December 31	
(In millions, except share and per share data)	2010	2009
Assets		
Current assets		
Cash and cash equivalents	$ 5,173	$ 3,819
Short-term investments	300	105
Accounts and notes receivable, net	3,036	2,996
Device and accessory inventory	670	628
Deferred tax assets	185	295
Prepaid expenses and other current assets	516	750
Total current assets	9,880	8,593
Investments	3,389	4,624
Property, plant and equipment, net	15,214	18,280
Intangible assets		
Goodwill	359	373
FCC licenses and other	20,336	19,911
Definite-lived intangible assets, net	2,009	3,178
Other assets	467	465
	$51,654	$55,424

NOTES TO CONSOLIDATED FINANCIAL STATEMENTS

Note 2. Summary of Significant Accounting Policies and Other Information (in part)

Summary of Significant Accounting Policies (in part)

Long-Lived Asset Impairment

Sprint evaluates long-lived assets, including intangible assets subject to amortization, for impairment whenever events or changes in circumstances indicate that the carrying amount of an asset group may not be recoverable. Asset groups are determined at the lowest level for which identifiable cash flows are largely independent of cash flows of other groups of assets and liabilities. When it is probable that undiscounted future cash flows will not be sufficient to recover an asset group's carrying amount, an impairment is determined by the excess of the asset group's net carrying value over the estimated fair value. Refer to note 8 for additional information on asset impairments.

Certain assets that have not yet been deployed in the business, including network equipment, cell site development costs and software in development, are periodically assessed to determine recoverability. Network equipment and cell site development costs are expensed whenever events or changes in circumstances cause the Company to conclude the assets are no longer needed to meet management's strategic network plans and will not be deployed. Software development costs are expensed when it is no longer probable that the software project will be deployed. Network equipment that has been removed from the network is also periodically assessed to determine recoverability. If we continue to have operational challenges, including obtaining and retaining subscribers, future cash flows of the Company may not be sufficient to recover the carrying value of our wireless asset group, and we could record asset impairments that are material to Sprint's consolidated results of operations and financial condition.

During 2010, we assessed the recoverability of the wireless asset group, which includes tangible and intangible long-lived assets subject to amortization as well as indefinite-lived intangible assets. We included cash flow projections from wireless operations along with cash flows associated with the eventual disposition of the long-lived assets, which included estimated proceeds from the assumed sale of FCC licenses, trademarks and customer relationships. The estimated undiscounted future cash flows of the wireless long-lived assets exceeded their carrying amount and, as a result, no impairment charge was recorded. In addition, we re-assessed the remaining useful lives of these long-lived assets and concluded they were appropriate.

Note 6. Intangible Assets (in part)

Intangible Assets Subject to Amortization

Sprint's customer relationships are amortized using the sum of the years' digits method. As customer relationships amortize and reach the end of their amortization period, we remove the gross and accumulated amounts associated with these fully amortized intangible assets. During 2010, we reduced the gross carrying value and accumulated amortization by $10.3 billion associated with fully amortized intangible assets primarily related to customer relationships associated with the Nextel acquisition in 2005. Other intangible assets primarily include certain rights under affiliation agreements that were reacquired in connection with the acquisitions of Affiliates and Nextel Partners, Inc., which are being amortized over the remaining terms of those affiliation agreements on a straight-line basis, and the Nextel, Direct Connect and Virgin Mobile trade names, which are being amortized on a straight-line basis.

(In millions)	Useful Lives	December 31, 2010			December 31, 2009		
		Gross Carrying Value	Accumulated Amortization	Net Carrying Value	Gross Carrying Value	Accumulated Amortization	Net Carrying Value
Customer relationships	2 to 5 years	$1,925	$(1,717)	$ 208	$12,224	$(11,093)	$1,131
Other intangible assets							
Trademarks	10 to 37 years	1,169	(490)	679	1,169	(394)	775
Reacquired rights	9 to 14 years	1,571	(519)	1,052	1,572	(386)	1,186
Other	9 to 16 years	116	(46)	70	126	(40)	86
Total other intangible assets		2,856	(1,055)	1,801	2,867	(820)	2,047
Total definite lived intangible assets		$4,781	$(2,772)	$2,009	$15,091	$(11,913)	$3,178

(In millions)	2011	2012	2013	2014	2015
Estimated amortization expense	$ 403	$ 279	$ 242	$ 238	$ 197

Technology

2.97

CACI INTERNATIONAL INC (JUN)

CONSOLIDATED BALANCE SHEETS (in part)

(Amounts in thousands, except per share data)	June 30	
	2010	2009 (As Adjusted[1])
Assets		
Current assets:		
Cash and cash equivalents	$ 254,543	$ 208,488
Accounts receivable, net	531,033	477,025
Deferred income taxes	12,641	18,191
Prepaid expenses and other current assets	42,529	21,128
Total current assets	840,746	724,832
Goodwill	1,161,861	1,083,750
Intangible assets, net	108,298	97,829
Property and equipment, net	58,666	30,923
Supplemental retirement savings plan assets	51,736	40,791
Accounts receivable, long-term	9,291	8,677
Other long-term assets	14,168	19,277
Total assets	$2,244,766	$2,006,079

NOTES TO CONSOLIDATED FINANCIAL STATEMENTS

Note 3. Summary of Significant Accounting Policies (in part)

Goodwill

Goodwill represents the excess of costs over the fair value of assets of businesses acquired. Goodwill and intangible assets acquired in a purchase business combination and determined to have an indefinite useful life are not amortized, but instead tested for impairment at least annually or if impairment indicators are present. The evaluation includes comparing the fair value of the relevant reporting unit to the carrying value, including goodwill, of such unit. If the fair value exceeds the carrying value, no impairment loss is recognized. However, if the carrying value of the reporting unit exceeds its fair value, the goodwill of the reporting unit may be impaired. Impairment is measured by comparing the derived fair value of the goodwill to its carrying value. Separately identifiable intangible assets with estimable useful lives are amortized over their respective estimated useful lives to their estimated residual values, and reviewed for impairment at least annually or if impairment indicators are present.

The Company has two reporting units—domestic operations and international operations. Its reporting units are the same as its operating segments. Approximately 95 percent of the Company's goodwill is attributable to its domestic operations. The Company estimates the fair value of its reporting units using both an income approach and a market approach. The valuation process considers management's estimates of the future operating performance of each reporting unit. Companies in similar industries are researched and analyzed and management considers the domestic and international economic and financial market conditions, both in general and specific to the industry in which the Company operates,

prevailing as of the valuation date. The income approach utilizes discounted cash flows. The Company calculates a weighted average cost of capital for each reporting unit in order to estimate the discounted cash flows. The Company performs its annual testing for impairment of goodwill and other intangible assets as of June 30 of each year. The fair value of each of the Company's reporting units as of June 30, 2010 exceeded its carrying value by more than 50 percent.

Note 5. Acquisitions (in part)

Year Ended June 30, 2010 (in part)

The Company has completed its detailed valuations of the assets acquired and liabilities assumed, including recognizing a liability of $35.8 million for the fair value as of the acquisition date of Contingent Consideration. See Note 23 for additional information on the valuation of Contingent Consideration. Based on its valuations, the total consideration of $129.1 million has been allocated to assets acquired, including identifiable intangible assets and goodwill, and liabilities assumed, as follows (in thousands):

Cash	$ 4,843
Accounts receivable	6,980
Prepaid expenses and other current assets	6,950
Property and equipment	2,220
Customer contracts, customer relationships, acquired technologies	48,245
Goodwill	83,049
Other assets	93
Accounts payable	(705)
Accrued expenses and other current liabilities	(8,662)
Long-term deferred taxes	(13,944)
Total consideration paid	$129,069

The value attributed to customer contracts, customer relationships and acquired technologies is being amortized on an accelerated basis over periods ranging from two to 10 years.

Note 9. Intangible Assets

Intangible assets consisted of the following (in thousands):

	June 30	
	2010	2009
Customer contracts and related customer relationships	$ 253,031	$ 233,531
Acquired technologies	27,177	—
Covenants not to compete	2,373	2,409
Other	1,631	851
Intangible assets	284,212	236,791
Less accumulated amortization	(175,914)	(138,962)
Total intangible assets, net	$ 108,298	$ 97,829

Intangible assets are primarily amortized on an accelerated basis over periods ranging from 12 to 120 months. The weighted-average period of amortization for customer contracts and related customer relationships as of June 30, 2010 is 8.3 years, and the weighted-average remaining period of amortization is 5.6 years. The weighted-average period of amortization for acquired technologies as of June 30, 2010 is 6.7 years, and the weighted-average remaining period of amortization is 6.3 years.

Amortization expense for the years ended June 30, 2010, 2009 and 2008 was $37.2 million, $32.1 million, and $31.8 million, respectively. Expected amortization expense for each of the fiscal years through June 30, 2015 and for periods thereafter is as follows (in thousands):

	Amount
Year ending June 30, 2011	$ 35,141
Year ending June 30, 2012	23,467
Year ending June 30, 2013	15,938
Year ending June 30, 2014	12,801
Year ending June 30, 2015	9,003
Thereafter	11,948
Total intangible assets, net	$108,298

Franchise License

2.98

COCA-COLA ENTERPRISES INC. (DEC)

CONSOLIDATED BALANCE SHEETS (in part)

	December 31	
(In millions)	2010	2009
Assets		
Current:		
Cash and cash equivalents	$ 321	$ 404
Trade accounts receivable, less allowances of $16 and $13, respectively	1,329	1,309
Amounts receivable from The Coca-Cola Company	86	78
Amounts due from Coca-Cola Enterprises Inc.	0	153
Inventories	367	288
Prepaid expenses and other current assets	127	124
Total current assets	2,230	2,356
Amounts due from Coca-Cola Enterprises Inc.	0	193
Property, plant, and equipment, net	2,220	1,883
Franchise license intangible assets, net	3,828	3,487
Goodwill	131	0
Other noncurrent assets, net	187	53
Total assets	$8,596	$7,972

NOTES TO CONSOLIDATED FINANCIAL STATEMENTS

Note 2—Franchise License Intangible Assets and Goodwill

The following table summarizes the changes in our net franchise license intangible assets and goodwill for the periods presented (in millions):

	Franchise License Intangible Assets	Goodwill
Balance at December 31, 2007	$4,075	$ 0
Currency translation adjustments	(845)	0
Balance at December 31, 2008	3,230	0
Currency translation adjustments	257	0
Balance at December 31, 2009	3,487	0
Acquisition of the bottling operations in Norway and Sweden	496	131
Currency translation adjustments	(155)	0
Balance at December 31, 2010	$3,828	$131

Our franchise license agreements contain performance requirements and convey to us the rights to distribute and sell products of the licensor within specified territories. Our license agreements with TCCC for each of our territories have terms of 10 years each and expire on October 2, 2020, with each containing the right for us to request a 10-year renewal. While these agreements contain no automatic right of renewal beyond that date, we believe that our interdependent relationship with TCCC and the substantial cost and disruption to TCCC that would be caused by nonrenewals ensure that these agreements will continue to be renewed and, therefore, are essentially perpetual. We have never had a franchise license agreement with TCCC terminated due to nonperformance of the terms of the agreement or due to a decision by TCCC to terminate an agreement at the expiration of a term. After evaluating the contractual provisions of our franchise license agreements, our mutually beneficial relationship with TCCC, and our history of renewals, we have assigned indefinite lives to all of our franchise license intangible assets.

We do not amortize our franchise license intangible assets and goodwill. Instead, we test these assets for impairment annually, or more frequently if facts or circumstances indicate they may be impaired. The annual testing date for impairment purposes is the last reporting day of October, which was established upon discontinuing the amortization of our franchise license intangible assets and goodwill in 2002. The impairment tests for our franchise license intangible assets involves comparing the estimated fair value of franchise license intangible assets for a reporting unit to its carrying amount to determine if a write down to fair value is required. If the carrying amount of the franchise license intangible assets exceeds its estimated fair value, an impairment charge is recognized in an amount equal to the excess, not to exceed the carrying amount. The impairment test for our goodwill involves comparing the fair value of a reporting unit to its carrying amount, including goodwill, and after adjusting for any franchise license impairment charges (net of tax). If the carrying amount of the reporting unit exceeds its fair value, a second step is required to measure the goodwill impairment loss. This step compares the implied fair value of the reporting unit's goodwill to the carrying amount of that goodwill. If the carrying amount of the reporting unit's goodwill exceeds the implied fair value of the goodwill, an impairment loss is recognized in an amount equal to the excess, not to exceed the carrying amount. Any subsequent recoveries in the estimated fair values of our franchise license intangible assets or goodwill are not recorded. The fair values calculated in these impairment tests are determined using discounted cash flow models involving assumptions that are based upon what we believe a hypothetical marketplace participant would use in estimating fair value on the measurement date. In developing these assumptions, we compare the resulting estimated enterprise value to our observable market enterprise value.

2010 Impairment Analysis

Based on our review of the facts and circumstances and updated assumptions, we did not perform a full annual impairment analysis of our franchise license intangible assets or goodwill during 2010 since we concluded it was remote that changes in the facts and circumstances would have caused the fair value of these assets to fall below their carrying amounts. This conclusion was based on the following factors: (1) the fair value of our franchise license intangible assets exceeded its carrying amount by a substantial margin in the most recent annual impairment analysis performed; (2) our business performance during 2010 exceeded the forecast used to estimate fair value in the most recent impairment analysis performed; (3) our outlook for 2011 and beyond is greater than the forecast used to estimate fair value in the most recent impairment analysis performed; (4) other significant assumptions used in estimating fair value, such as our weighted average cost of capital, have improved since the most recent impairment analysis performed; and (5) we have experienced significant appreciation in our market capitalization.

2009 and 2008 Impairment Analyses

During 2009 and 2008, our franchise license intangible assets were included as part of Legacy CCE's impairment testing. Legacy CCE performed its impairment tests at its operating segment level, which were Legacy CCE's reporting units. The results of the impairment tests performed by Legacy CCE during these periods indicated that the fair value of our franchise license intangible assets (Legacy CCE's Europe operating segment) exceeded their carrying amounts by a substantial margin.

Note 17—Acquisition of Norway and Sweden Bottling Operations (in part)

On October 2, 2010, two indirect, wholly owned subsidiaries of CCE acquired TCCC's bottling operations in Norway and Sweden, pursuant to the Norway-Sweden SPA, for a purchase price of $822 million plus a working capital adjustment of $55 million (of which $6 million, representing the final working capital settlement, is owed to TCCC as of December 31, 2010 and has been recorded in Amounts payable to TCCC on our Consolidated Balance Sheets; refer to Note 1). These operations serve approximately 14 million people across Norway and Sweden and allow us to further expand our operations across Western Europe.

The following table summarizes the allocation of the purchase price based on the fair value of the acquired assets and liabilities assumed (in millions):

Assets & liabilities[a]	Amounts
Current assets[b]	$210
Property, plant, and equipment	357
Franchise license intangible assets[c]	496
Customer relationships[d]	23
Other noncurrent assets	1
Current liabilities	(183)
Noncurrent liabilities	(158)
Net assets acquired	746
Goodwill[e]	131
Total purchase price	$877

[a] amounts are subject to change based on the final determination of the fair value of the assets acquired and liabilities assumed.

[b] current assets include cash and cash equivalents of $72 million, trade accounts receivable of $73 million, inventories of $48 million, and other current assets of $17 million.

[b] we have assigned the acquired franchise license intangible assets an indefinite life. While our franchise license agreements contain no automatic right of renewal, we believe that our interdependent relationship with TCCC and the substantial cost and disruption to TCCC that would be caused by nonrenewals ensure that these agreements will continue to be renewed and, therefore, are essentially perpetual. Refer to Note 2.

[d] the value assigned to customer relationships is being amortized over a period of 20 years, beginning on the date of acquisition.

[e] goodwill represents the excess of the purchase price (including the working capital adjustment) over the net tangible and intangible assets acquired, and is not deductible for tax purposes. This goodwill is primarily attributable to additional company-specific synergies we expect to be able to achieve by integrating Norway and Sweden into our existing operations. Additionally, a portion of the goodwill is attributable to future cash flows we expect to generate by expanding certain non-TCCC brands, such as Monster Energy drinks, into these territories.

Research and Development Acquired

2.99

BAKER HUGHES INCORPORATED (DEC)

CONSOLIDATED BALANCE SHEETS (in part)

	December 31	
(In millions, except par value)	2010	2009
Assets		
Current assets:		
Cash and cash equivalents	$ 1,456	$ 1,595
Short-term investments	250	—
Accounts receivable—less allowance for doubtful accounts (2010—$162; 2009—$157)	3,942	2,331
Inventories, net	2,594	1,836
Deferred income taxes	234	268
Other current assets	231	195
Total current assets	8,707	6,225
Property, plant and equipment—less accumulated depreciation (2010—$4,367; 2009—$3,668)	6,310	3,161
Goodwill	5,869	1,418
Intangible assets, net	1,569	195
Other assets	531	440
Total assets	$22,986	$11,439

NOTES TO CONSOLIDATED FINANCIAL STATEMENTS

Basis of Presentation (in part)

In the Notes to Consolidated Financial Statements, all dollar and share amounts in tabulations are in millions of dollars and shares, respectively, unless otherwise indicated.

Note 2. Acquisitions (in part)

Acquisition of BJ Services (in part)

On April 28, 2010, we acquired 100% of the outstanding common stock of BJ Services Company (including its successor, "BJ Services") in a cash and stock transaction valued at $6,897 million. BJ Services is a leading provider of pressure pumping and other oilfield services and was acquired to expand our suite of service and product offerings. Revenues and net income of BJ Services from the acquisition date included in our consolidated statement of operations for 2010 were $3,686 million and $290 million, respectively.

Recording of Assets Acquired and Liabilities Assumed (in part)

The transaction has been accounted for using the acquisition method of accounting which requires that, among other things, assets acquired and liabilities assumed be recorded at their fair values as of the acquisition date. The excess of the consideration transferred over those fair values is recorded as goodwill. While we have substantially completed the determination of the fair values of the assets acquired and liabilities assumed, some of the estimated fair values set forth below are subject to adjustment once the valuations are completed. We will finalize these items as we obtain the information necessary to complete the analysis, which we expect to be completed during the first quarter of 2011. Under U.S. generally accepted accounting principles, companies have one year from the date of an acquisition to finalize the acquisition accounting. The following table summarizes the estimated amounts recognized for assets acquired and liabilities assumed as of the acquisition date.

	Estimated Fair Value
Assets:	
Cash and cash equivalents	$ 113
Accounts receivable	951
Inventories	419
Other current assets	125
Property, plant and equipment	2,757
Intangible assets	1,404
Goodwill	4,336
Other long-term assets	109
Liabilities:	
Liabilities for change in control and transaction fees	(210)
Current liabilities	(759)
Deferred income taxes and other tax liabilities	(1,455)
Debt	(531)
Pension and other postretirement liabilities	(154)
Other long-term liabilities	(29)
Noncontrolling interests	(179)
Net assets acquired	$ 6,897

Intangible Assets

We identified intangible assets including trade names, technology, in-process research and development ("IPR&D"), and customer relationships. We consider the BJ Services trade name to be an indefinite life intangible asset, which will not be amortized and will be subject to an annual impairment test. We account for IPR&D as an indefinite-lived intangible asset until completion or abandonment of the associated project. Therefore, such assets would not be amortized but would be tested for impairment. Once the research and development activities are completed, the assets would be amortized over the related product's useful life. If the project is abandoned, the assets would be written off if they have no alternative future use.

The following table summarizes the fair values recorded for the identifiable intangible assets and their estimated useful lives:

	Fair Value	Estimated Useful Life
Customer relationships	$ 428	3–16 years
Technology	451	5–15 years
BJ Services trade name	360	Indefinite
Other trade names	38	5–12 years
IPR&D	127	Indefinite
Total identifiable intangible assets	$1,404	

Note 10. Goodwill and Intangible Assets (in part)

Intangible assets are comprised of the following at December 31:

	2010			2009		
	Gross Carrying Amount	Accumulated Amortization	Net	Gross Carrying Amount	Accumulated Amortization	Net
Definite lived intangibles:						
Technology	$ 760	$(181)	$ 579	$278	$(141)	$137
Contract-based	20	(11)	9	13	(9)	4
Trade names	84	(18)	66	36	(13)	23
Customer relationships	495	(39)	456	41	(10)	31
Subtotal	1,359	(249)	1,110	368	(173)	195
Indefinite lived intangibles:						
Trade name	360	—	360	—	—	—
IPR&D	99	—	99	—	—	—
Total	$1,818	$(249)	$1,569	$368	$(173)	$195

Intangible assets are amortized either on a straight-line basis with estimated useful lives ranging from 1 to 20 years, or on a basis that reflects the pattern in which the economic benefits of the intangible assets are expected to be realized, which range from 15 to 30 years. As a result of the acquisition of BJ Services, we recognized intangible assets of $1,404 million (See Note 2—Acquisitions).

Amortization expense included in net income for the years ended December 31, 2010, 2009 and 2008 was $76 million, $31 million and $20 million, respectively. Estimated amortization expense for each of the subsequent five fiscal years is expected to be as follows: 2011—$100 million; 2012—$107 million; 2013—$108 million; 2014—$107 million; and 2015—$99 million.

Other Intangible Assets

2.100

QUANTUM CORPORATION (MAR)

CONSOLIDATED BALANCE SHEETS (in part)

(In thousands, except par value)	March 31, 2010	March 31, 2009
Assets		
Current assets:		
Cash and cash equivalents	$114,947	$ 85,532
Restricted cash	1,896	1,773
Accounts receivable, net of allowance for doubtful accounts of $798 and $1,999, respectively	103,397	107,851
Manufacturing inventories, net	54,080	61,237
Service parts inventories, net	53,217	63,029
Deferred income taxes	7,907	9,935
Other current assets	14,500	24,745
Total current assets	349,944	354,102
Long-term assets:		
Property and equipment, less accumulated depreciation	24,528	28,553
Intangible assets, less accumulated amortization	73,092	109,236
Goodwill	46,770	46,770
Other long-term assets	9,809	10,708
Total long-term assets	154,199	195,267
	$504,143	$549,369

NOTES TO CONSOLIDATED FINANCIAL STATEMENTS

Note 2. Financial Statement Presentation and Summary of Significant Accounting Policies (in part)

Amortizable Intangible and Other Long-Lived Assets

We review amortizable intangible and other long-lived assets ("long-lived assets") for impairment whenever events or changes in circumstances indicate the carrying amount of such assets may not be recoverable. Indicators we consider include adverse changes in the business climate that could affect the value of our long-lived assets, changes in our stock price and resulting market capitalization relative to book value, downward revisions in our revenue outlook, decreases or slower than expected growth in sales of products and relative weakness in customer channels.

A long-lived asset or asset group that is held for use is required to be grouped with other assets and liabilities at the lowest level for which identifiable cash flows are largely independent of the cash flows of other assets and liabilities. When an asset or asset group does not have identifiable cash flows that are largely independent of the cash flows of other assets and liabilities, the asset group for that long-lived asset includes all assets and liabilities of the entity.

We evaluate the company as a single reporting unit for business and operating purposes. We have attempted to identify cash flows at levels lower than the consolidated company; however, this is not possible because many of our revenue streams are generated by technology related to more than a single long-lived asset, and individual long-lived assets support more than one of our three reported revenue categories. In addition, the majority of our costs are, by their nature, shared costs that are not specifically identifiable with a particular long-lived asset or product line but relate to multiple products. As a result, there is a high degree of interdependency among our cash flows for levels below the consolidated company, and we do not have identifiable cash flows for an asset group separate from the consolidated company. Therefore, we consider the consolidated company as a single asset group for purposes of impairment testing.

We evaluate the recoverability of the asset group using an undiscounted cash flow approach. Estimates of future cash flows incorporate company forecasts and our expectations of future use of our long-lived assets, and these factors are impacted by market conditions. We determine the remaining useful life of an asset group based on the remaining useful life of the primary asset of the group, where the primary asset is defined as the asset with the greatest cash flow generating ability. Our primary long-lived asset is an intangible technology asset supporting disk products and software license revenue. If the primary asset of the asset group does not have the longest remaining life in the group, then a sale of the asset group is assumed at the end of life of the primary asset. Our primary long-lived asset does not have the longest remaining life of long-lived assets in our asset group; therefore, for purposes of impairment testing, we assume the asset group is sold after the end of the primary asset's useful life, or our first quarter of fiscal 2015.

If the undiscounted cash flows, including residual value, exceed the carrying value of the consolidated company asset group we conclude no impairment of our long-lived assets exists. If the carrying value of the consolidated company asset group exceeds the undiscounted cash flows, including residual value, then we measure the impairment charge for the excess of the carrying value over the fair value of the asset group. We monitor relevant market and economic conditions on a quarterly basis, and perform impairment reviews when there are indicators of impairment.

Note 5. Goodwill and Intangible Assets (in part)

Net goodwill and intangible assets as of March 31, 2010 and 2009 represented approximately 24% and 28% of total assets, respectively. The goodwill and intangible asset balances, net of amortization, as of March 31, 2010 and 2009 were $119.9 million and $156.0 million, respectively.

Intangible Assets

Acquired intangible assets are amortized over their estimated useful lives, which generally range from one to eight years. In estimating the useful lives of intangible assets, we considered the following factors:

- The cash flow projections used to estimate the useful lives of the intangible assets showed a trend of growth that was expected to continue for an extended period of time;
- Our tape automation products, disk backup products and software, in particular, have long development cycles; these products have experienced long product life cycles; and
- Our ability to leverage core technology into backup, recovery and archive solutions and, therefore, to extend the lives of these technologies.

Following is the weighted average amortization period for our intangible assets:

	Amortization (Years)
Purchased technology	6.2
Trademarks	7.5
Non-compete agreements	5.0
Customer lists	7.0
All intangible assets	6.6

Intangible amortization within our Consolidated Statements of Operations for the years ended March 31, 2010, 2009 and 2008 follows (in thousands):

	For the Year Ended March 31		
	2010	2009	2008
Purchased technology	$22,469	$25,067	$31,857
Trademarks	810	2,018	3,457
Non-compete agreements	100	100	100
Customer lists	12,765	13,018	13,297
	$36,144	$40,203	$48,711

The following tables provide a summary of the carrying amount of intangible assets that will continue to be amortized (in thousands):

	As of March 31, 2010			As of March 31, 2009		
	Gross Amount	Accumulated Amortization	Net Amount	Gross Amount	Accumulated Amortization	Net Amount
Purchased technology	$188,167	$(161,488)	$26,679	$188,167	$(139,019)	$ 49,148
Trademarks	27,260	(25,506)	1,754	27,260	(24,696)	2,564
Non-compete agreements	500	(368)	132	500	(268)	232
Customer lists	106,419	(61,892)	44,527	108,219	(50,927)	57,292
	$322,346	$(249,254)	$73,092	$324,146	$(214,910)	$109,236

The total expected future amortization related to intangible assets is provided in the table below (in thousands):

	Amortization
Fiscal 2011	$28,381
Fiscal 2012	20,385
Fiscal 2013	12,834
Fiscal 2014	8,400
Fiscal 2015	3,092
Total as of March 31, 2010	$73,092

We did not have impairment indicators for our long-lived assets in fiscal 2010 and fiscal 2008. In fiscal 2009, we had impairment indicators and performed an impairment analysis of our long-lived assets. The result of our fiscal 2009 impairment analysis was that the undiscounted cash flows exceeded the carrying value of the asset group and we concluded no impairment of our long-lived assets.

OTHER NONCURRENT ASSETS

RECOGNITION AND MEASUREMENT

2.101 FASB ASC 210 indicates that the concept of current assets excludes resources such as the following:
- Cash restricted regarding withdrawal or use for other than current operations, designated for expenditure in the acquisition or construction of noncurrent assets, or segregated for the liquidation of long-term debts
- Investments or advances for the purposes of control, affiliation, or other continuing business advantage
- Certain receivables (see the "Noncurrent Receivables" section)
- Cash surrender value of life insurance
- Land and other natural resources
- Long-term prepayments chargeable to operations over several years

DISCLOSURE

2.102 Rule 5-02 of Regulation S-X requires that any item not classed in another Regulation S-X caption and in excess of 5 percent of total assets be stated separately on the balance sheet or disclosed in the notes.

2.103

TABLE 2-10: OTHER NONCURRENT ASSETS*

Table 2-10 summarizes the nature of assets (other than property, investments, noncurrent receivables, and intangible assets) classified as noncurrent assets on the balance sheet of the survey entities.

	Number of Entities		
	2010	2009	2008
Deferred income taxes	232	277	261
Pension asset	106	160	169
Derivatives	95	150	47
Advances/deposits/prepayments	40	N/C^	N/C^
Segregated cash or securities	41	103	100
Software	25	87	98
Debt issue costs	70	68	79
Property held for sale	33	43	45
Cash surrender value of life insurance	37	42	32
Assets of nonhomogeneous operations	5	9	10
Contracts	7	8	10
Estimated insurance recoveries	12	5	6
Assets leased to others	4	5	4
Property held for future development	6	N/C^	N/C^
Other	177	58	62

* Appearing in the balance sheet or notes to financial statements, or both.

^ N/C = Not compiled. Line item was not included in the table for the year shown.

PRESENTATION AND DISCLOSURE EXCERPTS

Long-Term Assets Held for Sale

2.104

DEVON ENERGY CORPORATION (DEC)

CONSOLIDATED BALANCE SHEETS (in part)

	December 31	
(In millions, except share data)	2010	2009
Current assets:		
Cash and cash equivalents	$ 2,866	$ 646
Accounts receivable	1,202	1,208
Current assets held for sale	563	657
Other current assets	924	481
Total current assets	5,555	2,992
Property and equipment, at cost:		
Oil and gas, based on full cost accounting:		
Subject to amortization	56,012	52,352
Not subject to amortization	3,434	4,078
Total oil and gas	59,446	56,430
Other	4,429	4,045
Total property and equipment, at cost	63,875	60,475
Less accumulated depreciation, depletion and amortization	(44,223)	(41,708)
Property and equipment, net	19,652	18,767
Goodwill	6,080	5,930
Long-term assets held for sale	859	1,250
Other long-term assets	781	747
Total assets	$32,927	$29,686

NOTES TO CONSOLIDATED FINANCIAL STATEMENTS

1. Summary of Significant Accounting Policies (in part)

Discontinued Operations

As a result of the November 2009 plan to divest Devon's offshore assets, all amounts related to Devon's International operations are classified as discontinued operations. The Gulf of Mexico properties that were divested in 2010 do not qualify as discontinued operations under accounting rules. As such, amounts in these notes and the accompanying consolidated financial statements that pertain to continuing operations include amounts related to Devon's offshore Gulf of Mexico operations. See Note 5 for additional details of the offshore divestiture program.

The captions assets held for sale and liabilities associated with assets held for sale in the accompanying consolidated balance sheets present the assets and liabilities associated with Devon's discontinued operations. Devon measures its assets held for sale at the lower of its carrying amount or estimated fair value less costs to sell. Additionally, Devon does not recognize depreciation, depletion and amortization on its long-lived assets held for sale.

18. Discontinued Operations (in part)

For the three-year period ended December 31, 2010, Devon's discontinued operations include amounts related to its assets in Azerbaijan, Brazil, China, Angola and other minor International properties. Additionally, during 2008, Devon's discontinued operations included amounts related to its assets in Egypt and West Africa, including Equatorial Guinea, Cote d'Ivoire, Gabon and other countries in the region, until they were sold.

The following table presents the main classes of assets and liabilities associated with Devon's discontinued operations.

	December 31	
(In millions)	2010	2009
Cash and cash equivalents	$424	$ 365
Accounts receivable	43	165
Other current assets	96	127
Current assets	$563	$ 657
Property and equipment, net	$848	$1,099
Goodwill	—	68
Other long-term assets	11	83
Total long-term assets	$859	$1,250
Accounts payable	$260	$ 158
Other current liabilities	45	76
Current liabilities	$305	$ 234
Asset retirement obligations	$ 24	$ 109
Deferred income taxes	2	101
Other liabilities	—	3
Long-term liabilities	$ 26	$ 213

Reductions of Carrying Value of Oil and Gas Properties

During 2009 and 2008, Devon reduced the carrying values of certain of its oil and gas properties that are now held for sale. These reductions primarily resulted from full cost ceiling limitations. A summary of these reductions and additional discussion is provided below.

	Year Ended December 31			
	2009		2008	
(In millions)	Gross	After Taxes	Gross	After Taxes
Brazil	$103	$103	$437	$437
Other	6	2	57	28
Total	$109	$105	$494	$465

Brazil's 2009 reduction resulted largely from an exploratory well drilled at the BM-BAR-3 block in the offshore Barreirinhas Basin. After drilling this well in the first quarter of 2009, Devon concluded that the well did not have adequate reserves for commercial viability. As a result, the seismic, leasehold and drilling costs associated with this well contributed to the reduction recognized in the first quarter of 2009.

Brazil's 2008 reduction was recognized in the fourth quarter of 2008 and resulted primarily from a significant decrease in its full cost ceiling. The lower ceiling value largely resulted from the effects of sharp declines in oil prices compared to previous quarter-end prices.

Pension Asset

2.105

EASTMAN KODAK COMPANY (DEC)

CONSOLIDATED STATEMENT OF FINANCIAL POSITION (in part)

	As of December 31	
(In millions, except share and per share data)	2010	2009
Assets		
Current assets		
Cash and cash equivalents	$1,624	$2,024
Receivables, net	1,259	1,395
Inventories, net	696	679
Deferred income taxes	120	121
Other current assets	100	84
Total current assets	3,799	4,303
Property, plant and equipment, net	1,037	1,254
Goodwill	294	907
Other long-term assets	1,109	1,227
Total assets	$6,239	$7,691

NOTES TO FINANCIAL STATEMENTS

Note 6. Other Long-Term Assets

	As of December 31	
(In millions)	2010	2009
Overfunded pension plans	$ 48	$ 169
Deferred income taxes, net of valuation allowance	695	607
Intangible assets	124	184
Other	242	267
Total	$1,109	$1,227

The Other component above consists of other miscellaneous long-term assets that, individually, were less than 5% of the Company's total assets in the accompanying Consolidated Statement of Financial Position, and therefore, have been aggregated in accordance with Regulation S-X.

2.106

W. R. GRACE & CO. (DEC)

CONSOLIDATED BALANCE SHEETS (in part)

(In millions, except par value and shares)	December 31, 2010	December 31, 2009
Assets		
Current assets		
Cash and cash equivalents	$1,015.7	$ 893.0
Restricted cash and cash equivalents	97.8	—
Trade accounts receivable, less allowance of $7.0 (2009—$7.9)	380.8	365.8
Accounts receivable— unconsolidated affiliates	5.3	7.4
Inventories	259.3	220.6
Deferred income taxes	54.7	61.5
Other current assets	90.6	80.4
Total current assets	1,904.2	1,628.7
Properties and equipment, net of accumulated depreciation and amortization of $1,675.2 (2009—$1,611.3)	702.5	690.1
Goodwill	125.5	118.6
Deferred income taxes	845.0	843.4
Asbestos-related insurance	500.0	500.0
Overfunded defined benefit pension plans	35.6	36.7
Investments in unconsolidated affiliates	56.4	45.7
Other assets	102.5	105.0
Total assets	$4,271.7	$3,968.2

NOTES TO CONSOLIDATED FINANCIAL STATEMENTS

11. Pension Plans and Other Postretirement Benefit Plans (in part)

Pension Plans The following table presents the funded status of Grace's fully-funded, underfunded, and unfunded pension plans:

(In millions)	December 31, 2010	December 31, 2009
Overfunded defined benefit pension plans	$ 35.6	$ 36.7
Underfunded defined benefit pension plans	(383.9)	(372.2)
Unfunded defined benefit pension plans	(155.9)	(158.2)
Total underfunded and unfunded defined benefit pension plans	(539.8)	(530.4)
Unfunded defined benefit pension plans included in liabilities subject to compromise	(113.8)	(105.4)
Pension liabilities included in other current liabilities	(12.9)	(12.9)
Net funded status	$(630.9)	$(612.0)

Fully-funded plans include several advance-funded plans where the fair value of the plan assets exceeds the projected benefit obligation ("PBO"). This group of plans was overfunded by $35.6 million as of December 31, 2010, and the overfunded status is reflected as "overfunded defined benefit pension plans" in the Consolidated Balance Sheets. Underfunded plans include a group of advance-funded plans that are underfunded on a PBO basis. Unfunded plans include several plans that are funded on a pay-as-you-go basis, and therefore, the entire PBO is unfunded. The combined balance of the underfunded and unfunded plans was $666.5 million as of December 31, 2010 and is presented as a liability on the Consolidated Balance Sheets as follows: $12.9 million in "other current liabilities;" $539.8 million included in "underfunded and unfunded defined benefit pension plans," of which $383.9 million relates to underfunded plans and $155.9 million relates to unfunded plans; and $113.8 million in "liabilities subject to compromise."

Grace maintains defined benefit pension plans covering current and former employees of certain business units and divested business units who meet age and service requirements. Benefits are generally based on final average salary and years of service. Grace funds its U.S. qualified pension plans ("U.S. qualified pension plans") in accordance with U.S. federal laws and regulations. Non-U.S. pension plans ("non-U.S. pension plans") are funded under a variety of methods, as required under local laws and customs.

Grace also provides, through nonqualified plans, supplemental pension benefits in excess of U.S. qualified pension plan limits imposed by federal tax law. These plans cover officers and higher-level employees and serve to increase the combined pension amount to the level that they otherwise would have received under the U.S. qualified pension plans in the absence of such limits. The nonqualified plans are un-

funded and Grace pays the costs of benefits as they are due to the participants.

At the December 31, 2010 measurement date for Grace's defined benefit pension plans, the PBO was approximately $1,616 million as measured under U.S. GAAP compared with $1,531 million as of December 31, 2009. The PBO basis reflects the present value (using a 5.25% discount rate for U.S. plans and a 5.45% weighted average discount rate for non-U.S. plans as of December 31, 2010) of vested and nonvested benefits earned from employee service to date, based upon current services and estimated future pay increases for active employees.

On a quarterly basis, Grace analyzes pension assets and pension liabilities along with the resulting funded status and updates its estimate of these measures. Funded status is adjusted for contributions, benefit payments, actual return on assets, current discount rates, and other identifiable and material actuarial changes. A full remeasurement is performed annually.

Restricted Cash

2.107

LAM RESEARCH CORPORATION (JUN)

CONSOLIDATED BALANCE SHEETS (in part)

(In thousands, except per share data)	June 27, 2010	June 28, 2009
Assets		
Cash and cash equivalents	$ 545,767	$ 374,167
Short-term investments	280,690	205,221
Accounts receivable, less allowance for doubtful accounts of $10,609 as of June 27, 2010 and $10,719 as of June 28, 2009	499,890	253,585
Inventories	318,479	233,410
Deferred income taxes	46,158	69,043
Prepaid expenses and other current assets	65,677	101,714
Total current assets	1,756,661	1,237,140
Property and equipment, net	200,336	215,666
Restricted cash and investments	165,234	178,439
Deferred income taxes	26,218	17,007
Goodwill	169,182	169,182
Intangible assets, net	67,724	91,605
Other assets	102,037	84,145
Total assets	$2,487,392	$1,993,184

NOTES TO CONSOLIDATED FINANCIAL STATEMENTS

Note 4. Financial Instruments (in part)

Fair Value

Pursuant to the accounting guidance for fair value measurement and its subsequent updates, the Company defines fair value as the price that would be received from selling an asset or paid to transfer a liability in an orderly transaction between market participants at the measurement date. When determining the fair value measurements for assets and liabilities required or permitted to be recorded at fair value, the Company considers the principal or most advantageous market in which it would transact, and it considers assumptions that market participants would use when pricing the asset or liability.

The FASB has established a fair value hierarchy that prioritizes the inputs to valuation techniques used to measure fair value. An asset or liability's level in the hierarchy is based on the lowest level of input that is significant to the fair value measurement. Assets and liabilities carried at fair value are classified and disclosed in one of the following three categories:

Level 1: Valuations based on quoted prices in active markets for identical assets or liabilities with sufficient volume and frequency of transactions.

Level 2: Valuations based on observable inputs other than Level 1 prices such as quoted prices for similar assets or liabilities, quoted prices in markets that are not active, or model-derived valuations techniques for which all significant inputs are observable in the market or can be corroborated by, observable market data for substantially the full term of the assets or liabilities.

Level 3: Valuations based on unobservable inputs to the valuation methodology that are significant to the measurement of fair value of assets or liabilities and based on non-binding, broker-provided price quotes and may not have been corroborated by observable market data.

The following table sets forth the Company's financial assets and liabilities measured at fair value on a recurring basis as of June 27, 2010:

| | | Fair Value Measurement at June 27, 2010 | | |
(In thousands)	Total	Quoted Prices in Active Markets for Identical Assets (Level 1)	Significant Other Observable Inputs (Level 2)	Significant Unobservable Inputs (Level 3)
Assets				
Fixed income				
Money market funds	$470,936	$470,936	$ —	$—
Municipal notes and bonds	103,903	—	103,903	—
US treasury & agencies	3,447	—	3,447	—
Government-sponsored enterprises	6,060	6,060	—	—
Foreign governments	1,008	—	1,008	—
Bank and corporate notes	289,437	169,723	119,636	78
Mortgage backed securities—residential	6,106	—	6,106	—
Mortgage backed securities—commercial	42,964	—	42,964	—
Total fixed income	$923,861	$646,719	$277,064	$78
Equities	7,636	7,636	—	—
Mutual funds	18,124	18,124	—	—
Derivatives assets	2,063	—	2,063	—
Total	$951,684	$672,479	$279,127	$78
Liabilities				
Derivative liabilities	$ 470	$ —	$ 470	$—

The amounts in the table above are reported in the consolidated balance sheet as of June 27, 2010 as follows:

(In thousands)	Total	(Level 1)	(Level 2)	(Level 3)
Reported as:				
Cash equivalents	$478,286	$477,279	$ 1,007	$—
Short-term investments	280,690	4,555	276,057	78
Restricted cash and investments	164,885	164,885	—	—
Prepaid expenses and other current assets	2,063	—	2,063	—
Other assets	25,760	25,760	—	—
	$951,684	$672,479	$279,127	$78
Accrued expenses and other current liabilities	$ 470	$ —	$ 470	$—

At June 27, 2010 the fair value of Level 3 assets measured on a recurring basis was $0.1 million and consisted of a corporate note security. Fair values were based on non-binding, broker-provided price quotes and may not have been corroborated by observable market data.

The following table sets forth the Company's financial assets and liabilities measured at fair value on a recurring basis as of June 28, 2009:

| | | Fair Value Measurement at June 28, 2009 | | |
(In thousands)	Total	Quoted Prices in Active Markets for Identical Assets (Level 1)	Significant Other Observable Inputs (Level 2)	Significant Unobservable Inputs (Level 3)
Assets				
Fixed income				
Money market funds	$273,439	$273,439	$ —	$—
Municipal notes and bonds	103,618	—	103,618	—
US treasury & agencies	24,184	24,184	—	—
Government-sponsored enterprises	6,323	—	6,323	—
Foreign governments	1,024	—	1,024	—
Bank and corporate notes	228,171	183,171	45,000	—
Mortgage backed securities—residential	11,630	—	11,630	—
Mortgage backed securities—commercial	13,442	—	13,442	—
Total fixed income	$661,831	$480,794	$181,037	$—
Equities	4,961	4,961	—	—
Mutual funds	—	—	—	—
Derivatives assets	74	—	74	—
Total	$666,866	$485,755	$181,111	$—
Liabilities				
Derivative liabilities	$ 69	$ —	$ 69	$—

The amounts in the table above are reported in the consolidated balance sheet as of June 28, 2009 as follows:

(In thousands)	Total	(Level 1)	(Level 2)	(Level 3)
Reported as:				
Cash equivalents	$278,304	$278,304	$ —	$—
Short-term investments	205,221	24,184	181,037	—
Restricted cash and investments	178,306	178,306	—	—
Prepaid expenses and other current assets	74	—	74	—
Other assets	4,961	4,961	—	—
	$666,866	$485,755	$181,111	$—
Accrued expenses and other current liabilities	$ 69	$ —	$ 69	$—

The Company's primary financial instruments include its cash, cash equivalents, short-term investments, restricted cash and investments, long-term investments, accounts receivable, accounts payable, long-term debt and capital leases, and foreign currency related derivatives. The estimated fair value of cash, accounts receivable and accounts payable approximates their carrying value due to the short period of time to their maturities. The estimated fair values of long-term debt and capital lease obligations approximate their carrying value as the substantial majority of these obligations have interest rates that adjust to market rates on a periodic basis. The fair value of cash equivalents, short-term investments, restricted cash and investments, long-term investments, and foreign currency related derivatives are based on quotes from brokers using market prices for similar instruments.

Investments

The following tables summarize the Company's investments (in thousands):

	June 27, 2010				June 28, 2009			
	Cost	Unrealized Gain	Unrealized (Loss)	Fair Value	Cost	Unrealized Gain	Unrealized (Loss)	Fair Value
Cash	$ 67,830	$ —	$ —	$ 67,830	$ 95,996	$ —	$ —	$ 95,996
Fixed income money market funds	470,936	—	—	470,936	273,439	—	—	273,439
Municipal notes and bonds	102,130	1,784	(11)	103,903	101,587	2,069	(38)	103,618
US treasury & agencies	3,437	10	—	3,447	23,828	387	(31)	24,184
Government-sponsored enterprises	5,976	84	—	6,060	6,177	146	—	6,323
Foreign governments	1,007	1	—	1,008	1,024	—	—	1,024
Bank and corporate notes	287,922	1,608	(93)	289,437	227,244	1,025	(98)	228,171
Mortgage backed securities—residential	5,825	323	(42)	6,106	11,328	385	(83)	11,630
Mortgage backed securities—commercial	42,765	275	(76)	42,964	13,465	166	(189)	13,442
Total cash and short—term investments	$ 987,828	$4,085	$ (222)	$ 991,691	$754,088	$4,178	$ (439)	$757,827
Publicly traded equity securities	$ 9,471	$ —	$(1,835)	$ 7,636	$ 8,359	$ —	$(3,398)	$ 4,961
Mutual funds	19,043	—	(919)	18,124	—	—	—	—
Total financial instruments	$1,016,342	$4,085	$(2,976)	$1,017,451	$762,447	$4,178	$(3,837)	$762,788
As reported								
Cash and cash equivalents	$ 545,766	$ 1	$ —	$ 545,767	$374,167	$ —	$ —	$374,167
Short-term investments	276,828	4,084	(222)	280,690	201,482	4,178	(439)	205,221
Restricted cash and investments	165,234	—	—	165,234	178,439	—	—	178,439
Other assets	28,514	—	(2,754)	25,760	8,359	—	(3,398)	4,961
Total	$1,016,342	$4,085	$(2,976)	$1,017,451	$762,447	$4,178	$(3,837)	$762,788

The Company accounts for its investment portfolio at fair value. Realized gains (losses) for investments sold are specifically identified. Management assesses the fair value of investments in debt securities that are not actively traded through consideration of interest rates and their impact on the present value of the cash flows to be received from the investments. The Company also considers whether changes in the credit ratings of the issuer could impact the assessment of fair value. Net realized gains (losses) on investments included other-than-temporary impairment charges of $0.9 million, $0.3 million and $1.0 million in fiscal years 2010, 2009 and 2008, respectively. Additionally, realized gains (losses) from sales of investments were approximately $0.8 million and $(0.2) million in fiscal year 2010, $2.2 million and $(1.9) million in fiscal year 2009 and $3.3 million and $(1.3) million in fiscal year 2008, respectively.

The following is an analysis of the Company's fixed income securities in unrealized loss positions as of June 27, 2010 (in thousands):

	June 27, 2010					
	Unrealized Losses Less Than 12 Months		Unrealized Losses 12 Months or Greater		Total	
	Fair Value	Gross Unrealized Loss	Fair Value	Gross Unrealized Loss	Fair Value	Gross Unrealized Loss
Fixed income securities						
Municipal notes and bonds	$ 6,567	$ (11)	$ —	$ —	$ 6,567	$ (11)
Bank and corporate bonds	24,996	(92)	204	(1)	25,200	(93)
Mortgage backed securities—residential	—	—	395	(42)	395	(42)
Mortgage backed securities—commercial	15,558	(76)	—	—	15,558	(76)
Total fixed income	$47,121	$(179)	$599	$(43)	$47,720	$(222)

The amortized cost and fair value of cash equivalents and short-term investments and restricted cash and investments with contractual maturities are as follows:

	June 27, 2010		June 28, 2009	
(In thousands)	Cost	Estimated Fair Value	Cost	Estimated Fair Value
Due in less than one year	$723,143	$723,707	$504,359	$504,597
Due in more than one year	196,855	200,154	153,732	157,233
	$919,998	$923,861	$658,091	$661,830

Management has the ability, if necessary, to liquidate any of its investments in order to meet the Company's liquidity needs in the next 12 months. Accordingly, those investments with contractual maturities greater than one year from the date of purchase nonetheless are classified as short-term on the accompanying consolidated balance sheets.

Note 13. Commitments (in part)

Operating Leases (in part)

The Company is required, pursuant to the terms of the Operating Leases and associated documents, to maintain collateral in an aggregate of approximately $164.9 million in separate interest-bearing accounts as security for the Company's obligations under the Operating Leases. As of June 27, 2010, the Company had $164.9 million recorded as restricted cash in its consolidated balance sheet as collateral required under the Operating Leases related to the amounts currently outstanding on the facilities.

Deferred Taxes

2.108

THE GOODYEAR TIRE & RUBBER COMPANY (DEC)

CONSOLIDATED BALANCE SHEETS (in part)

	December 31	
(In millions)	2010	2009
Assets		
Current assets:		
Cash and cash equivalents (Note 1)	$ 2,005	$ 1,922
Accounts receivable (Note 5)	2,736	2,540
Inventories (Note 6)	2,977	2,443
Prepaid expenses and other current assets (Note 8)	327	320
Total current assets	8,045	7,225
Goodwill (Note 7)	683	706
Intangible assets (Note 7)	161	164
Deferred income taxes (Note 15)	58	43
Other assets (Note 8)	518	429
Property, plant and equipment (Note 9)	6,165	5,843
Total assets	$15,630	$14,410

NOTES TO CONSOLIDATED FINANCIAL STATEMENTS

Note 15. Income Taxes (in part)

Temporary differences and carryforwards giving rise to deferred tax assets and liabilities at December 31 follow:

(In millions)	2010	2009
Postretirement benefits and pensions	$ 1,044	$ 1,088
Tax loss carryforwards and credits	1,151	1,126
Capitalized expenditures	501	455
Accrued expenses deductible as paid	496	440
Alternative minimum tax credit carryforwards[1]	100	120
Vacation and sick pay	42	40
Rationalizations and other provisions	72	50
Other	95	79
	3,501	3,398
Valuation allowance	(3,113)	(3,056)
Total deferred tax assets	388	342
Tax on undistributed subsidiary earnings	(17)	(16)
Property basis differences	(383)	(352)
Total net deferred tax liabilities	$ (12)	$ (26)

[1] Primarily unlimited carryforward period.

At December 31, 2010, we had $372 million of tax assets for net operating loss, capital loss and tax credit carryforwards related to certain international subsidiaries that are primarily from countries with unlimited carryforward periods. A valuation allowance totaling $542 million has been recorded against these and other deferred tax assets where recovery of the asset or carryforward is uncertain. In addition, we had $708 million of Federal and $107 million of state tax assets for net operating loss and tax credit carryforwards. The state carryforwards are subject to expiration from 2011 to 2031. The Federal carryforwards consist of $454 million of Federal tax net operating losses that expire in 2028 and 2030, $231 million of foreign tax credits which are subject to expiration in 2016 and 2018, and $23 million of tax assets related to research and development credits that are subject to expiration from 2027 to 2030. The amount of tax credit and loss carryforwards reflected in the table above has been reduced by $36 million related to unrealized stock option deductions. A full valuation allowance has also been recorded against these deferred tax assets as recovery is uncertain.

At December 31, 2010, we had unrecognized tax benefits of $87 million that if recognized, would have a favorable impact on our tax expense of $81 million. We had accrued interest of $13 million as of December 31, 2010. If not favorably settled, $23 million of the unrecognized tax benefits and $13 million of the accrued interest would require the use of our cash.

During 2010, our European entities have settled various tax years, resulting in a $48 million reduction of our unrecognized tax benefits. It is reasonably possible that the total amount of unrecognized tax benefits will change during the next 12 months. However, we do not expect those changes to have a significant impact on our financial position or results of operations.

2.109

EATON CORPORATION (DEC)

CONSOLIDATED BALANCE SHEETS (in part)

	December 31	
(In millions)	**2010**	**2009**
Assets		
Current assets		
Cash	$ 333	$ 340
Short-term investments	838	433
Accounts receivable—net	2,239	1,899
Inventory	1,564	1,326
Deferred income taxes	303	377
Prepaid expenses and other current assets	229	149
Total current assets	5,506	4,524
Property, plant and equipment		
Land and buildings	1,494	1,459
Machinery and equipment	4,485	4,241
Gross property, plant and equipment	5,979	5,700
Accumulated depreciation	(3,502)	(3,255)
Net property, plant and equipment	2,477	2,445
Other noncurrent assets		
Goodwill	5,454	5,435
Other intangible assets	2,272	2,441
Deferred income taxes	1,001	973
Other assets	542	464
Total assets	$17,252	$16,282

NOTES TO CONSOLIDATED FINANCIAL STATEMENTS

Amounts are in millions or shares unless indicated otherwise
(per share data assume dilution).

Note 8. Income Taxes (in part)

Deferred Income Tax Assets and Liabilities

Components of current and long-term deferred income taxes
follow:

	2010		2009	
	Current Assets	**Long-Term Assets and Liabilities**	**Current Assets**	**Long-Term Assets and Liabilities**
Accruals and other adjustments				
Employee benefits	$ 94	$ 681	$ 78	$ 773
Depreciation and amortization	(1)	(567)	3	(642)
Other accruals and adjustments	224	90	293	103
Other items	—	(6)	—	(5)
United States federal income tax loss carryforwards[1]	—	5	13	38
United States federal income tax credit carryforwards	—	253	—	165
United States state and local tax loss carryforwards and tax credit carryforwards	—	74	—	72
Non-United States tax loss carryforwards	—	360	—	291
Non-United States income tax credit carryforwards	—	72	—	66
Valuation allowance for income tax loss and income tax credit carryforwards	—	(421)	—	(360)
Other valuation allowances	(14)	(27)	(10)	(78)
Total deferred income taxes	$303	$ 514	$377	$ 423

[1] United States deferred income tax assets of $37 for income tax loss carryforwards were reduced by $32 for the excess income tax benefit related to the exercise of stock options. A tax benefit and a credit to Capital in excess of par value for the excess benefit will not be recognized until the deduction reduces income taxes payable. The net income tax loss carryforward of $37 in the table below reflects the $32 related to the excess income tax benefit.

Recoverability of Deferred Income Tax Assets

Eaton is subject to the income tax laws in the jurisdictions in which it operates. In order to determine its income tax provision for financial statement purposes, Eaton must make significant estimates and judgments about its business operations in these jurisdictions. These estimates and judgments are also used in determining the deferred income tax assets and liabilities that have been recognized for differences between the financial statement and income tax basis of assets and liabilities, and income tax loss carryforwards and income tax credit carryforwards.

Management evaluates the realizability of deferred income tax assets for each of the jurisdictions in which it operates. If the Company experiences cumulative pretax income in a particular jurisdiction in the three-year period including the current and prior two years, management normally concludes that the deferred income tax assets will more likely than not be realizable and no valuation allowance is recognized, unless known or planned operating developments would lead management to conclude otherwise. However, if the Company experiences cumulative pretax losses in a particular jurisdiction in the three-year period including the current and prior two years, management then considers a series of significant factors in the determination of whether the deferred income tax assets can be realized. The significant factors include historical operating results, known or planned operating developments, the period of time over which certain temporary differences will reverse, consideration of the utilization of certain deferred income tax liabilities, tax law carryback capability in the particular country, and feasible tax planning strategies, and estimates of future earnings and taxable income using the same assumptions as the Company's goodwill and other impairment testing. After evaluation of these factors, if the deferred income tax assets are expected to be realized within the tax carryforward period allowed for that specific country, management would conclude that no valuation allowance would be required. To the extent that the deferred income tax assets exceed the amount that is expected to be realized within the tax carryforward period for a particular jurisdiction, management would conclude that a valuation allowance is required.

As of December 31, 2010, United States federal deferred income tax assets were $1.3 billion. The largest component of the deferred income tax assets is due to timing differences between revenue and expense recognition for income tax versus financial statement purposes. In addition, the Company had a tax net operating loss in the United States in 2010 and possesses certain income tax credit carryforwards that comprise the remainder of the balance. Over the 20 year carryforward period available for net operating losses and general business credits, taxable income of approximately $3.7 billion would need to be realized to utilize all deferred income tax assets. As of December 31, 2010, management believes that, with a couple of very limited exceptions totaling $24, it is more likely than not that the entire United States federal deferred income tax assets will be realized.

Applying the above methodology, valuation allowances have been established for certain United States federal, state and local income, as well as certain non-United States, deferred income tax assets to the extent they are not expected to be realized within the particular tax carryforward period.

Cash Surrender Value of Life Insurance

2.110

WOLVERINE WORLD WIDE, INC. (DEC)

CONSOLIDATED BALANCE SHEETS (in part)

(Thousands of dollars, except share and per share data)	As of Fiscal Year End	
	2010	2009
Assets		
Current assets:		
Cash and cash equivalents	$ 150,400	$ 160,439
Accounts receivable, less allowances (2010—$(11,413); 2009—$(13,946))	196,457	163,755
Inventories		
Finished products	188,647	140,124
Raw materials and work-in-process	20,008	17,941
	208,655	158,065
Deferred income taxes	13,225	12,475
Prepaid expenses and other current assets	11,397	12,947
Total current assets	580,134	507,681
Property, plant and equipment:		
Land	826	881
Buildings and improvements	71,724	80,511
Machinery and equipment	129,707	147,197
Software	79,307	74,559
	281,564	303,148
Accumulated depreciation	(207,167)	(229,196)
	74,397	73,952
Other assets:		
Goodwill	39,014	39,972
Other non-amortizable intangibles	16,464	16,226
Cash surrender value of life insurance	36,042	35,405
Deferred income taxes	37,602	35,094
Other	2,922	3,746
	132,044	130,443
Total assets	$ 786,575	$ 712,076

NOTES TO CONSOLIDATED FINANCIAL STATEMENTS

All amounts are in thousands of dollars except share and per share data and elsewhere as noted.

6. Retirement Plans (in part)

The Company has two non-contributory, defined benefit pension plans covering a majority of its domestic employees. The Company's principal defined benefit pension plan provides benefits based on the employee's years of service and final average earnings (as defined in the plan), while the other plan provides benefits at a fixed rate per year of service.

The Company has a Supplemental Executive Retirement Plan (the "SERP") for certain current and former employees that entitles a participating employee to receive payments from the Company following retirement based on the employee's years of service and final average earnings (as defined in the SERP). Under the SERP, the employees can elect early retirement with a corresponding reduction in benefits. The Company also has individual deferred compensation agreements with certain former employees that entitle these employees to receive payments from the Company for a period of fifteen to eighteen years following retirement. The Company maintains life insurance policies with a cash surrender value of $36,042 at January 1, 2011 and $35,405 at January 2, 2010 that are intended to fund deferred compensation benefits under the SERP and deferred compensation agreements.

Derivatives

2.111

KIMBALL INTERNATIONAL, INC. (JUN)

CONSOLIDATED BALANCE SHEETS (in part)

(Amounts in thousands, except for share and per share data)	June 30, 2010	June 30, 2009
Assets		
Current assets:		
Cash and cash equivalents	$ 65,342	$ 75,932
Short-term investments	2,496	25,376
Receivables, net of allowances of $3,349 and $4,366, respectively	154,343	143,398
Inventories	146,406	127,004
Prepaid expenses and other current assets	43,776	35,720
Assets held for sale	1,160	1,358
Total current assets	413,523	408,788
Property and equipment, net of accumulated depreciation of $337,251 and $338,001, respectively	186,999	200,474
Goodwill	2,443	2,608
Other intangible assets, net of accumulated amortization of $63,595 and $62,481, respectively	8,113	10,181
Other assets	25,673	20,218
Total assets	$636,751	$642,269

NOTES TO CONSOLIDATED FINANCIAL STATEMENTS

Note 1 Summary of Significant Accounting Policies (in part)

Derivative Instruments and Hedging Activities: Derivative financial instruments are recognized on the balance sheet as assets and liabilities and are measured at fair value. Changes in the fair value of derivatives are recorded each period in earnings or Accumulated Other Comprehensive Income (Loss), depending on whether a derivative is designated and effective as part of a hedge transaction, and if it is, the type of hedge transaction. Hedge accounting is utilized when a derivative is expected to be highly effective upon execution and continues to be highly effective over the duration of the hedge transaction. Hedge accounting permits gains and losses on derivative instruments to be deferred in Accumulated Other Comprehensive Income (Loss) and subsequently included in earnings in the periods in which earnings are affected by the hedged item, or when the derivative is determined to be ineffective. The Company's use of derivatives is generally limited to forward purchases of foreign currency to manage exposure to the variability of cash flows, primarily related to the foreign exchange rate risks inherent in forecasted transactions denominated in foreign currency. See Note 12—Derivative Instruments of Notes to Consolidated Financial Statements for more information on derivative instruments and hedging activities.

Note 11 Fair Value (in part)

The Company categorizes assets and liabilities measured at fair value into three levels based upon the assumptions (inputs) used to price the assets or liabilities. Level 1 provides the most reliable measure of fair value, whereas level 3 generally requires significant management judgment. The three levels are defined as follows:

- Level 1: Unadjusted quoted prices in active markets for identical assets and liabilities.
- Level 2: Observable inputs other than those included in level 1. For example, quoted prices for similar assets or liabilities in active markets or quoted prices for identical assets or liabilities in inactive markets.
- Level 3: Unobservable inputs reflecting management's own assumptions about the inputs used in pricing the asset or liability.

Financial Instruments Recognized at Fair Value

The following methods and assumptions were used to measure fair value:

Financial Instrument	Valuation Technique/Inputs Used
Cash Equivalents	Market—Quoted market prices
Available-for-sale securities: Municipal securities	Market—Based on market data which use evaluated pricing models and incorporate available trade, bid, and other market information
Available-for-sale securities: Convertible debt securities	Market—Fair value approximated using the amortized cost basis of promissory notes, with the discount amortized to interest income over the term of the notes
Derivative Assets: Foreign exchange contracts	Market—Based on observable market inputs using standard calculations, such as time value, forward interest rate yield curves, and current spot rates, considering counterparty credit risk
Derivative Assets: Stock warrants	Market—Based on a Black-Scholes valuation model with the following inputs: risk-free interest rate, volatility, expected life, and estimated stock price
Trading securities: Mutual funds held by nonqualified supplemental employee retirement plan	Market—Quoted market prices
Derivative Liabilities: Foreign exchange contracts	Market—Based on observable market inputs using standard calculations, such as time value, forward interest rate yield curves, and current spot rates adjusted for the Company's non-performance risk

Recurring Fair Value Measurements (in part)

As of June 30, 2010 and 2009, the fair values of financial assets and liabilities that are measured at fair value on a recurring basis using the market approach are categorized as follows:

(Amounts in thousands)	June 30, 2010			
	Level 1	Level 2	Level 3	Total
Assets				
Cash equivalents	$32,706	$ -0-	$ -0-	$32,706
Available-for-sale securities: Convertible debt securities	-0-	-0-	2,496	2,496
Derivatives: Foreign exchange contracts	-0-	2,223	-0-	2,223
Derivatives: Stock warrants	-0-	-0-	395	395
Trading securities: Mutual funds held by nonqualified supplemental employee retirement plan	13,071	-0-	-0-	13,071
Total assets at fair value	$45,777	$ 2,223	$2,891	$50,891
Liabilities				
Derivatives: Foreign exchange contracts	$ -0-	$ 392	$ -0-	$ 392
Total liabilities at fair value	$ -0-	$ 392	$ -0-	$ 392

(Amounts in thousands)	June 30, 2009			
	Level 1	Level 2	Level 3	Total
Assets				
Cash equivalents	$42,114	$ -0-	$ -0-	$42,114
Available-for-sale securities: Municipal securities	-0-	25,376	-0-	25,376
Derivatives: Foreign exchange contracts	-0-	784	-0-	784
Trading securities: Mutual funds held by nonqualified supplemental employee retirement plan	10,992	-0-	-0-	10,992
Total assets at fair value	$53,106	$26,160	$ -0-	$79,266
Liabilities				
Derivatives: Foreign exchange contracts	$ -0-	$ 3,407	$ -0-	$ 3,407
Total liabilities at fair value	$ -0-	$ 3,407	$ -0-	$ 3,407

During fiscal year 2010, the Company purchased convertible debt securities of $2.3 million and stock warrants of $0.4 million. See Note 13—Short-Term Investments of Notes to Consolidated Financial Statements for further information regarding the convertible debt securities. See Note 12—Derivative Instruments of Notes to Consolidated Financial Statements for further information regarding the stock warrants. The changes in fair value of Level 3 investment assets during fiscal year 2010 were immaterial. There were no Level 3 investments as of June 30, 2009.

Note 12. Derivative Instruments (in part)

Foreign Exchange Contracts

The Company operates internationally and is therefore exposed to foreign currency exchange rate fluctuations in the normal course of its business. The Company's primary means of managing this exposure is to utilize natural hedges, such as aligning currencies used in the supply chain with the sale currency. To the extent natural hedging techniques do not fully offset currency risk, the Company uses derivative instruments with the objective of reducing the residual exposure to certain foreign currency rate movements. Factors considered in the decision to hedge an underlying market exposure include the materiality of the risk, the volatility of the market, the duration of the hedge, the degree to which the underlying exposure is committed to, and the availability, effectiveness, and cost of derivative instruments. Derivative instruments are only utilized for risk management purposes and are not used for speculative or trading purposes.

The Company uses forward contracts designated as cash flow hedges to protect against foreign currency exchange rate risks inherent in forecasted transactions denominated in a foreign currency. Foreign exchange contracts are also used to hedge against foreign currency exchange rate risks related to intercompany balances denominated in currencies other than the functional currencies. As of June 30, 2010, the Company had outstanding foreign exchange contracts to hedge currencies against the U.S. dollar in the aggregate notional amount of $13.1 million and to hedge currencies against the Euro in the aggregate notional amount of 28.4 million EUR. The notional amounts are indicators of the volume of derivative activities but are not indicators of the potential gain or loss on the derivatives.

In limited cases due to unexpected changes in forecasted transactions, cash flow hedges may cease to meet the criteria to be designated as cash flow hedges. Depending on the type of exposure hedged, the Company may either purchase a derivative contract in the opposite position of the undesignated hedge or may retain the hedge until it matures if the hedge continues to provide an adequate offset in earnings against the currency revaluation impact of foreign currency denominated liabilities.

The fair value of outstanding derivative instruments is recognized on the balance sheet as a derivative asset or liability. When derivatives are settled with the counterparty, the derivative asset or liability is relieved and cash flow is impacted for the net settlement. For derivative instruments that meet the criteria of hedging instruments under FASB guidance, the effective portions of the gain or loss on the derivative instrument are initially recorded net of related tax effect in Accumulated Other Comprehensive Income (Loss), a component of Share Owners' Equity, and are subsequently reclassified into earnings in the period or periods during which the hedged transaction is recognized in earnings. The ineffective portion of the derivative gain or loss is reported in the Non-operating income or expense line item on the Consolidated Statements of Income immediately. The gain or loss associated with derivative instruments that are not designated as hedging instruments or that cease to meet the criteria for hedging under FASB guidance is also reported in the Non-operating income or expense line item on the Consolidated Statements of Income immediately. Based on fair values as of June 30, 2010, the Company estimates that $0.1 million of pre-tax derivative losses deferred in Accumulated Other Comprehensive Income (Loss) will be reclassified into earnings, along with the earnings effects of related forecasted transactions, within the fiscal year ending June 30, 2011. Losses on foreign exchange contracts are generally offset by gains in operating costs in the income statement when the underlying hedged transaction is recognized in earnings. Because gains or losses on foreign exchange contracts fluctuate partially based on currency spot rates, the future effect on earnings of the cash flow hedges alone is not determinable, but in conjunction with the underlying hedged transactions, the result is expected to be a decline in currency risk. The maximum length of time the Company had hedged its exposure to the variability in future cash flows was 11 and 15 months as of June 30, 2010 and June 30, 2009, respectively.

Stock Warrants:

In conjunction with the Company's investments in convertible debt securities of a privately-held company during fiscal year 2010, the Company received common and preferred stock warrants which provide the right to purchase the privately-held company's equity securities at a specified exercise price. Specifically, the Company received stock warrants to purchase 2,750,000 shares of common stock at a $0.15 per share exercise price and received stock warrants to purchase a number of shares of preferred stock based on the latest preferred stock offering price (1,833,000 shares of preferred stock at a $1.50 per share exercise price, based on the last offering price of outstanding preferred stock). The value of the stock warrants will fluctuate primarily in relation to the value of the privately-held company's underlying securities, either providing an appreciation in value or potentially expiring with no value. Gains and losses on the revaluation of stock warrants are recognized in the Non-operating income or expense line item on the Consolidated Statements of Income.

See Note 11—Fair Value of Notes to Consolidated Financial Statements for further information regarding the fair value of derivative assets and liabilities and Note 17—Comprehensive Income of Notes to Consolidated Financial Statements for the amount and changes in derivative gains and losses deferred in Accumulated Other Comprehensive Income (Loss). Information on the location and amounts of derivative fair values in the Consolidated Balance Sheets and derivative gains and losses in the Consolidated Statements of Income are presented below.

Fair Values of Derivative Instruments on the Consolidated Balance Sheets

| | Asset Derivatives | | | Liability Derivatives | | |
| | Balance Sheet | Fair Value As of | | Balance Sheet | Fair Value As of | |
(Amounts in thousands)	Location	June 30, 2010	June 30, 2009	Location	June 30, 2010	June 30, 2009
Derivatives designated as hedging instruments:						
Foreign exchange contracts	Prepaid expenses and other current assets	$ 525	$742	Accrued expenses	$339	$2,581
Derivatives not designated as hedging instruments:						
Foreign exchange contracts	Prepaid expenses and other current assets	1,698	42	Accrued expenses	53	631
Foreign exchange contracts				Other liabilities (long-term)	-0-	195
Stock warrants	Other assets (long-term)	395	-0-			
Total derivatives		$2,618	$784		$392	$3,407

Software

2.112

CACI INTERNATIONAL INC (JUN)

CONSOLIDATED BALANCE SHEETS (in part)

(Amounts in thousands, except per share data)	June 30	
	2010	2009 (As Adjusted[1])
Assets		
Current assets:		
Cash and cash equivalents	$ 254,543	$ 208,488
Accounts receivable, net	531,033	477,025
Deferred income taxes	12,641	18,191
Prepaid expenses and other current assets	42,529	21,128
Total current assets	840,746	724,832
Goodwill	1,161,861	1,083,750
Intangible assets, net	108,298	97,829
Property and equipment, net	58,666	30,923
Supplemental retirement savings plan assets	51,736	40,791
Accounts receivable, long-term	9,291	8,677
Other long-term assets	14,168	19,277
Total assets	$2,244,766	$2,006,079

[1] Certain balances as of June 30, 2009 have been adjusted to reflect the retroactive application of new accounting standards. See Note 2.

NOTES TO CONSOLIDATED FINANCIAL STATEMENTS

Note 3. Summary of Significant Accounting Policies (in part)

External Software Development Costs

Costs incurred in creating a software product to be sold or licensed for external use are charged to expense when incurred as indirect costs and selling expenses until technological feasibility has been established for the software. Technological feasibility is established upon completion of a detailed program design or, in its absence, completion of a working software version. Thereafter, all such software development costs are capitalized and subsequently reported at the lower of unamortized cost or estimated net realizable value. Capitalized costs are amortized on a straight-line basis over the remaining estimated economic life of the product.

Note 11. Capitalized External Software Development Costs (in part)

A summary of changes in capitalized external software development costs, including costs capitalized and amortized during each of the years in the three-year period ended June 30, 2010, is as follows (in thousands):

	Year Ended June 30		
	2010	2009	2008
Capitalized software development costs, beginning of year	$ 2,001	$ 5,165	$ 9,452
Costs capitalized	1,230	171	—
Amortization	(1,916)	(3,335)	(4,287)
Capitalized software development costs, end of year	$ 1,315	$ 2,001	$ 5,165

Capitalized software development costs are presented within other current assets and other long-term assets in the accompanying consolidated balance sheets.

Debt Issuance Costs

2.113

SEALY CORPORATION (NOV)

CONSOLIDATED BALANCE SHEETS (in part)

(In thousands, except per share amounts)	November 28, 2010	November 29, 2009
Assets		
Current assets:		
Cash and equivalents	$ 109,255	$ 131,427
Accounts receivable (net of allowance for doubtful accounts, discounts and returns, 2010—$25,812; 2009—$26,675)	140,778	156,850
Inventories	57,178	56,810
Prepaid expenses and other current assets	19,543	21,080
Deferred income taxes	19,127	20,222
	345,881	386,389
Property, plant and equipment—at cost:		
Land	7,414	10,555
Buildings and improvements	126,645	147,415
Machinery and equipment	241,766	284,468
Construction in progress	9,645	4,551
	385,470	446,989
Less accumulated depreciation	(217,398)	(239,508)
	168,072	207,481
Other assets:		
Goodwill	361,958	360,583
Other intangibles—net of accumulated amortization (2010—$3,201; 2009—$18,900)	1,387	1,937
Deferred income taxes	6,140	6,874
Debt issuance costs, net, and other assets	53,319	52,206
	422,804	421,600
Total assets	$ 936,757	$1,015,470

NOTES TO CONSOLIDATED FINANCIAL STATEMENTS

Note 1. Basis of Presentation and Significant Accounting Policies (in part)

Supply Agreements

The Company from time to time enters into long term supply agreements with its customers to sell its branded products to customers in exchange for minimum sales volume or a minimum percentage of the customer's sales or space on the retail floor. Such agreements generally cover a period of two to five years. In these long term agreements, the Company reserves the right to pass on its cost increases to its customers. Other costs such as transportation and warranty costs are factored into the wholesale price of the Company's products and passed on to the customer. Initial cash outlays by the Company for such agreements are capitalized and amortized generally as a reduction of sales over the life of the contract. The majority of these cash outlays are ratably recoverable upon contract termination. Such capitalized amounts are included in "Prepaid expenses and other current assets" and "Debt issuance costs, net, and other assets" in the Company's Consolidated Balance Sheets.

Debt Issuance Costs

The Company capitalizes costs associated with the issuance of debt and amortizes them as additional interest expense over the lives of the debt on a straight-line basis which approximates the effective interest method. Upon the prepayment of the related debt, the Company accelerates the recognition of an appropriate amount of the costs as refinancing and extinguishment of debt and interest rate derivatives. Additional expense arising from such prepayments during fiscal 2010, 2009 and 2008 was $2.7 million, $0.1 million and $0.0 million, respectively.

In connection with the refinancing of the Company's senior secured credit facilities in May 2009, the Company recorded fees in the amount of $27.6 million which were deferred and will be amortized over the life of the new agreements. Since the old senior secured term loans are considered terminated, the remaining unamortized debt issuance costs of $2.1 million were expensed and recognized as a component of refinancing and extinguishment of debt and interest rate derivatives in the Consolidated Statements of Operations. The remaining unamortized debt issuance costs associated with the old senior revolving credit facility will continue to be amortized over the life of the Company's new asset-based revolving credit facility as such credit facility met the criteria for modification treatment rather than extinguishment.

In connection with the Second Amendment to the Third Amended and Restated Credit Agreement entered into in November 2008, the Company paid fees to the creditor in the amount of $5.4 million, which were recorded as a component of refinancing and extinguishment of debt and interest rate derivatives in the Consolidated Statements of Operations. In accordance with the FASB's authoritative guidance surrounding a debtor's accounting for a modification or exchange of debt instruments, these costs were expensed as incurred. The Company also paid approximately $0.1 million of fees to third parties that were deferred and will be amortized over the life of the amended agreement. The Company has the following amounts recorded in debt issuance costs, net, and other assets (in thousands):

	November 28, 2010	November 29, 2009
Gross cost	$27,744	$34,008
Accumulated amortization	(5,603)	(4,783)
Net deferred debt issuance costs	$22,141	$29,225

Prepaid Expenses

2.114

ADMINISTAFF, INC. (DEC)

CONSOLIDATED BALANCE SHEETS (in part)

(In thousands)	December 31, 2010	December 31, 2009
Assets		
Current assets:		
Cash and cash equivalents	$ 234,829	$ 227,085
Restricted cash	41,204	36,436
Marketable securities	43,367	6,037
Accounts receivable, net:		
Trade	1,194	2,899
Unbilled	134,187	106,601
Other	6,726	13,092
Prepaid insurance	24,978	14,484
Other current assets	8,528	6,317
Income taxes receivable	1,808	2,692
Deferred income taxes	1,267	2,578
Total current assets	498,088	418,221
Property and equipment:		
Land	3,260	3,260
Buildings and improvements	64,953	64,692
Computer hardware and software	67,714	65,980
Software development costs	27,482	25,372
Furniture and fixtures	35,164	35,499
Aircraft	31,524	31,524
	230,097	226,327
Accumulated depreciation and amortization	(154,070)	(145,153)
Total property and equipment, net	76,027	81,174
Other assets:		
Prepaid health insurance	9,000	9,000
Deposits—health insurance	2,640	2,785
Deposits—workers' compensation	51,731	55,744
Goodwill and other intangible assets, net	21,251	8,487
Other assets	1,108	1,059
Total other assets	85,730	77,075
Total assets	$ 659,845	$ 576,470

NOTES TO CONSOLIDATED FINANCIAL STATEMENTS

1. Accounting Policies (in part)

Health Insurance Costs

The Company provides group health insurance coverage to its worksite employees through a national network of carriers including UnitedHealthcare ("United"), PacifiCare, Kaiser Permanente, Blue Shield of California, Hawaii Medical Service Association, Unity Health Plans and Tufts, all of which provide fully insured policies or service contracts.

The policy with United provides the majority of the Company's health insurance coverage. As a result of certain contractual terms, the Company has accounted for this plan since its inception using a partially self-funded insurance accounting model. Accordingly, Administaff records the costs of the United plan, including an estimate of the incurred claims, taxes and administrative fees (collectively the "Plan Costs") as benefits expense in the Consolidated Statements of Operations. The estimated incurred claims are based upon: (i) the level of claims processed during each quarter; (ii) estimated completion rates based upon recent claim development patterns under the plan; and (iii) the number of participants in the plan, including both active and COBRA enrollees. Each reporting period, changes in the estimated ultimate costs resulting from claim trends, plan design and migration, participant demographics and other factors are incorporated into the benefits costs.

Additionally, since the plan's inception, under the terms of the contract, United establishes cash funding rates 90 days in advance of the beginning of a reporting quarter. If the Plan Costs for a reporting quarter are greater than the premiums paid and owed to United, a deficit in the plan would be incurred and a liability for the excess costs would be accrued in the Company's Consolidated Balance Sheet. On the other hand, if the Plan Costs for the reporting quarter are less than the premiums paid and owed to United, a surplus in the plan would be incurred and the Company would record an asset for the excess premiums in its Consolidated Balance Sheet. The terms of the arrangement require Administaff to maintain an accumulated cash surplus in the plan of $9.0 million, which is reported as long-term prepaid insurance. As of December 31, 2010, Plan Costs were less than the net premiums paid and owed to United by $28.9 million. As this amount is in excess of the agreed-upon $9.0 million surplus maintenance level, the $19.9 million balance is included in prepaid insurance, a current asset, in the Company's Consolidated Balance Sheet. The premiums owed to United at December 31, 2010, were $12.1 million, which is included in accrued health insurance costs, a current liability in the Company's Consolidated Balance Sheet.

SHORT-TERM DEBT

PRESENTATION

2.115 FASB ASC 470, *Debt*, addresses classification determination for specific debt obligations, such as the following:
- Short-term obligations expected to be refinanced on a long-term basis
- Due-on-demand loan arrangements
- Callable debt
- Sales of future revenue
- Increasing-rate debt
- Debt that includes covenants
- Revolving credit agreements subject to lock-box arrangements and subjective acceleration clauses

DISCLOSURE

2.116 Rule 5-02 of Regulation S-X calls for disclosure of the amount and terms of unused lines of credit for short-term financing, if significant. The weighted average interest rate on short-term borrowings outstanding as of the date of each balance sheet presented should be furnished. Further, the amount of these lines of credit that support commercial paper or similar borrowing arrangements should be separately identified.

2.117 By definition, *short-term notes payable, loans payable,* and *commercial paper* are financial instruments. FASB ASC 825 requires disclosure of both the fair value and bases for estimating the fair value of short-term notes payable, loans payable, and commercial paper, unless it is not practicable to estimate that value.

2.118

TABLE 2-11: SHORT-TERM DEBT*

Table 2-11 lists the captions used by the survey entities to describe short-term notes payable, loans payable and commercial paper. By definition, such short-term obligations are financial instruments.

	2010	2009	2008
Payee indicated	69	22	19
Payee not indicated	74	61	60
Short-term debt or borrowings	84	113	138
Commercial paper	56	39	43
Credit agreements	64	39	43
Other	35	14	19
	Number of Entities		
Showing short-term debt	266	243	263
Not showing short-term debt	234	257	237
Total Entities	**500**	**500**	**500**

* Appearing in the balance sheet or notes to financial statements, or both.

PRESENTATION AND DISCLOSURE EXCERPTS

Short-Term Debt

2.119

WAL-MART STORES, INC. (JAN)

CONSOLIDATED BALANCE SHEETS (in part)

	January 31	
(Amounts in millions except per share data)	2010	2009
Current liabilities:		
Short-term borrowings	$ 523	$ 1,506
Accounts payable	30,451	28,849
Accrued liabilities	18,734	18,112
Accrued income taxes	1,365	677
Long-term debt due within one year	4,050	5,848
Obligations under capital leases due within one year	346	315
Current liabilities of discontinued operations	92	83
Total current liabilities	$55,561	$55,390

NOTES TO CONSOLIDATED FINANCIAL STATEMENTS

Note 4. Short-Term Borrowings and Long-Term Debt (in part)

Information on short-term borrowings and interest rates is as follows:

	Fiscal Year Ended January 31		
(Dollar amounts in millions)	2010	2009	2008
Maximum amount outstanding at any month-end	$4,536	$7,866	$9,176
Average daily short-term borrowings	1,596	4,520	5,657
Weighted-average interest rate	0.5%	2.1%	4.9%

Short-term borrowings consist of commercial paper and lines of credit. Short term borrowings outstanding at January 31, 2010 and 2009 were $523 million and $1.5 billion, respectively. The company has certain lines of credit totaling $9.0 billion, most of which were undrawn as of January 31, 2010. Of the $9.0 billion in lines of credit, $8.6 billion is committed with 34 financial institutions. In conjunction with these lines of credit, the company has agreed to observe certain covenants, the most restrictive of which relates to maximum amounts of secured debt and long-term leases. Committed lines of credit are primarily used to support commercial paper. The portion of committed lines of credit used to support commercial paper remained undrawn as of January 31, 2010. The committed lines of credit mature at various times starting between June 2010 and June 2012, carry interest rates in some cases equal to the company's one-year credit default swap mid-rate spread and in other cases LIBOR plus 15 basis points and incur commitment fees of 4.0 to 10.0 basis points on undrawn amounts.

The company had trade letters of credit outstanding totaling $2.4 billion at January 31, 2010 and 2009. At January 31, 2010 and 2009, the company had standby letters of credit outstanding totaling $2.4 billion and $2.0 billion, respectively. These letters of credit were issued primarily for the purchase of inventory and self-insurance purposes.

2.120

BADGER METER, INC. (DEC)

CONSOLIDATED BALANCE SHEETS (in part)

	December 31	
(Dollars in thousands except share and per share amounts)	2010	2009
Current liabilities:		
Short-term debt	$12,878	$ 2,574
Current portion of long-term debt	—	5,429
Payables	11,159	10,773
Accrued compensation and employee benefits	7,143	6,071
Warranty and after-sale costs	889	907
Income and other taxes	610	507
Total current liabilities	$32,679	$26,261

NOTES TO CONSOLIDATED FINANCIAL STATEMENTS

Note 1 Summary of Significant Accounting Policies (in part)

Fair Value Measurements of Financial Instruments

The carrying amounts of cash, receivables and payables in the financial statements approximate their fair values due to the short-term nature of these financial instruments. Short-term debt is comprised of notes payable drawn against the Company's lines of credit and commercial paper. Because of its short-term nature, the carrying amount of the short-term debt also approximates fair value. Included in other assets is insurance policies on various individuals that were associated with the Company. The carrying amounts of these insurance policies approximates their fair value.

Note 4 Short-Term Debt and Credit Lines (in part)

Short-term debt at December 31, 2010 and 2009 consisted of:

(In thousands)	2010	2009
Notes payable to banks	$ 2,278	$2,574
Commercial paper	10,600	—
Total short-term debt	$12,878	$2,574

Included in notes payable to banks was $2.3 million and $2.5 million outstanding in 2010 and 2009, respectively, under a 4.0 million euro-based revolving loan facility (U.S. dollar equivalent of $5.4 million and $5.7 million at December 31, 2010 and 2009, respectively) that does not expire and which bore interest at 2.37% and 2.01% during 2010 and 2009, respectively. Included in 2009 was also $0.1 million borrowed under a 3.4 million euro-based revolving loan facility (U.S. dollar equivalent of $4.9 million at December 31, 2009) that bore interest at 2.41% and expired in October 2010. The Company has $61.5 million of short-term credit lines with domestic and foreign banks, which includes a $50.0 million line of credit that can also support the issuance of commercial paper.

2.121

EMC CORPORATION (DEC)

CONSOLIDATED BALANCE SHEETS (in part)

	December 31	
(In thousands, except per share amounts)	2010	2009
Current liabilities:		
Accounts payable	$1,062,600	$ 899,298
Accrued expenses	2,090,035	1,944,210
Income taxes payable	199,735	41,691
Convertible debt	3,214,771	—
Deferred revenue	2,810,873	2,262,968
Total current liabilities	$9,378,014	$5,148,167

NOTES TO CONSOLIDATED FINANCIAL STATEMENTS

E. Convertible Debt

In November 2006, we issued our Notes for total gross proceeds of $3.45 billion. The Notes are senior unsecured obligations and rank equally with all other existing and future senior unsecured debt. Holders may convert their Notes at their option on any day prior to the close of business on the scheduled trading day immediately preceding (i) September 1, 2011, with respect to the 2011 Notes, and (ii) September 1, 2013, with respect to the 2013 Notes, in each case only under the following circumstances: (1) during the five business-day period after any five consecutive trading-day period (the "measurement period") in which the price per Note of the applicable series for each day of that measurement period was less than 98% of the product of the last reported sale price of our common stock and the conversion rate on each such day; (2) during any calendar quarter, if the last reported sale price of our common stock for 20 or more trading days in a period of 30 consecutive trading days ending on the last trading day of the immediately preceding calendar quarter exceeds 130% of the applicable conversion price in effect on the last trading day of the immediately preceding calendar quarter; or (3) upon the occurrence of certain events specified in the Notes. Additionally, the Notes will become convertible during the last three months prior to the respective maturities of the 2011 Notes and the 2013 Notes.

Upon conversion, we will pay cash up to the principal amount of the debt converted. With respect to any conversion value in excess of the principal amount of the Notes converted, we have the option to settle the excess with cash, shares of our common stock, or a combination of cash and shares of our common stock based on a daily conversion value, determined in accordance with the indenture, calculated on a proportionate basis for each day of the relevant 20-day observation period. The initial conversion rate for the Notes will be 62.1978 shares of our common stock per one thousand dollars of principal amount of Notes, which represents a 27.5% conversion premium from the date the Notes were issued and is equivalent to a conversion price of approximately $16.08 per share of our common stock. The conversion price is subject to adjustment in some events as set forth in the indenture. In addition, if a "fundamental change" (as defined in the indenture) occurs prior to the maturity date, we will in some cases increase the conversion rate for a holder of Notes that elects to convert its Notes in connection with such fundamental change.

Based upon the closing price of our common stock for the prescribed measurement period during the three months ended December 31, 2010, the contingent conversion thresholds on the Notes were exceeded. As a result, the Notes are convertible at the option of the holder through March 31, 2011. Accordingly, since the terms of the Notes require the principal to be settled in cash, we reclassified from equity the portion of the Notes attributable to the conversion feature which had not yet been accreted to its face value and the Notes have been classified as a current liability. Contingencies continue to exist regarding the holders' ability to convert such Notes in future quarters. The determination of whether the Notes are convertible will be performed on a quarterly basis. Consequently, the Notes might not be convertible in future quarters and therefore the 2013 Notes may be reclassified as long-term debt, if the contingent conversion thresholds are not met.

The carrying amount reported in the consolidated balance sheet as of December 31, 2010 for our convertible debt was $3,450.0 million and the fair value was $5,102.8 million. The carrying amount of the equity component was $433.9 million at December 31, 2010.

The Notes pay interest in cash at a rate of 1.75% semi-annually in arrears on December 1 and June 1 of each year.

The following table represents the key components of our convertible debt (table in thousands):

	For the Twelve Months Ended		
	2010	2009	2008
Contractual interest expense on the coupon	$ 60,375	$ 60,375	$ 60,375
Amortization of the discount component recognized as interest expense	114,481	108,347	102,581
Total interest expense on the convertible debt	$174,856	$168,722	$162,956

As of December 31, 2010, the unamortized discount consists of $58.4 million which will be amortized over 2011 and an unamortized discount of $176.8 million which will be amortized over 3 years. The effective interest rate on the Notes was 5.6% for the years ended December 31, 2010, 2009 and 2008.

In connection with the sale of the Notes, we entered into separate convertible note hedge transactions with respect to our common stock (the "Purchased Options"). The Purchased Options allow us to receive shares of our common stock and/or cash related to the excess conversion value that we would pay to the holders of the Notes upon conversion. The Purchased Options will cover, subject to customary anti-dilution adjustments, approximately 215 million shares of our common stock. Half of the Purchased Options expire on December 1, 2011 and the remaining half of the Purchased Options expire on December 1, 2013. We paid an aggregate amount of $669.1 million of the proceeds from the sale of the Notes for the Purchased Options that was recorded as additional paid-in-capital in Shareholders' Equity.

We also entered into separate transactions in which we sold warrants to acquire, subject to customary anti-dilution adjustments, approximately 215 million shares of our common stock at an exercise price of approximately $19.55 per share of our common stock. Half of the associated warrants have expiration dates between February 15, 2012 and March 15, 2012 and the remaining half of the associated warrants have expiration dates between February 18, 2014 and March 18, 2014. We received aggregate proceeds of $391.1 million from the sale of the associated warrants. Upon exercise, the value of the warrants is required to be settled in shares.

The Purchased Options and associated warrants will generally have the effect of increasing the conversion price of the Notes to approximately $19.55 per share of our common stock, representing an approximate 55% conversion premium based on the closing price of $12.61 per share of our common stock on November 13, 2006.

TRADE ACCOUNTS PAYABLE

RECOGNITION AND MEASUREMENT

2.122 FASB ASC 210 states that current liabilities generally include obligations for items that have entered into the operating cycle, such as payables incurred in the acquisition of materials and supplies to be used in the production of goods or in providing services to be offered for sale.

PRESENTATION

2.123 Rule 5.02 of Regulation S-X requires that amounts payable to trade creditors be separately stated.

DISCLOSURE

2.124 Under FASB ASC 825, fair value disclosure is not required for trade payables when the carrying amount of the trade payable approximates its fair value.

PRESENTATION AND DISCLOSURE EXCERPTS

Trade Accounts Payable

2.125

DILLARD'S, INC. (JAN)

CONSOLIDATED BALANCE SHEETS (in part)

(Dollars in thousands)	January 30, 2010	January 31, 2009
Current liabilities:		
Trade accounts payable and accrued expenses	$676,501	$642,940
Current portion of long-term debt	1,719	25,535
Current portion of capital lease obligations	1,775	1,704
Other short-term borrowings	—	200,000
Federal and state income taxes including current deferred taxes	89,027	43,486
Total current liabilities	$769,022	$913,665

NOTES TO CONSOLIDATED FINANCIAL STATEMENTS

1. Description of Business and Summary of Significant Accounting Policies (in part)

Operating Leases (in part)

To account for construction allowance reimbursements from landlords and rent holidays, the Company records a deferred rent liability included in trade accounts payable and accrued expenses and other liabilities on the consolidated balance sheets and amortizes the deferred rent over the lease term, as a reduction to rent expense on the consolidated income statements. For leases containing rent escalation clauses, the Company records minimum rent expense on a straight-line basis over the lease term on the consolidated income statement. The lease term used for lease evaluation includes renewal option periods only in instances in which the exercise of the option period can be reasonably assured and failure to exercise such options would result in an economic penalty.

Gift Card Revenue Recognition—The Company establishes a liability upon the sale of a gift card. The liability is relieved and revenue is recognized when gift cards are redeemed for merchandise. The Company uses a homogeneous pool to recognize gift card breakage and will recognize income over the period when the likelihood of the gift card being redeemed is remote and the Company determines that it does not have a legal obligation to remit the value of unredeemed gift cards to the relevant jurisdiction as abandoned property. The Company determines gift card breakage income based upon historical redemption patterns. At that time, the Company will recognize breakage income over the performance period for those gift cards (i.e. 60 months) as a reduction of cost of sales. As of January 30, 2010 and January 31, 2009, gift card liabilities of $58.5 million and $65.1 million, respectively, were included in trade accounts payable and accrued expenses and other liabilities.

7. Trade Accounts Payable and Accrued Expenses

Trade accounts payable and accrued expenses consist of the following:

(In thousands of dollars)	January 30, 2010	January 31, 2009
Trade accounts payable	$494,372	$457,062
Accrued expenses:		
Taxes, other than income	59,791	62,885
Salaries, wages and employee benefits	50,421	43,244
Liability to customers	43,197	49,750
Interest	16,957	18,503
Rent	3,435	5,048
Other	8,328	6,448
	$676,501	$642,940

EMPLOYEE-RELATED LIABILITIES

PRESENTATION

2.126 FASB ASC 715, *Compensation—Retirement Benefits*, requires that an entity recognize the overfunded or underfunded status of a single-employer defined benefit postretirement plan as an asset or a liability in its statement of financial position. FASB ASC 715 also requires that an employer that presents a classified balance sheet should classify the liability for an underfunded plan as a current liability, a noncurrent liability, or a combination of both. The current portion (determined on a plan-by-plan basis) is the amount by which the actuarial present value of benefits included in the benefit obligation that is payable in the next 12 months, or operating cycle if longer, exceeds the fair value of plan assets. The asset for an overfunded plan shall be classified as a noncurrent asset in a classified balance sheet. The amount classified as a current liability is limited to the amount of the plan's unfunded status recognized in the employer's balance sheet.

DISCLOSURE

2.127 FASB ASC 715 requires that employers recognize changes in that funded status in comprehensive income and disclose in the notes to financial statements additional information about plan assets, the benefit obligation, reconciliations of beginning and ending balances of both plan assets and obligations, and net periodic benefit cost.

PRESENTATION AND DISCLOSURE EXCERPTS

Employee-Related Liabilities

2.128

THE BRINK'S COMPANY (DEC)

CONSOLIDATED BALANCE SHEETS (in part)

	December 31	
(In millions, except per share amounts)	2010	2009
Current liabilities:		
Short-term borrowings	$ 36.5	$ 7.2
Current maturities of long-term debt	29.0	16.1
Accounts payable	141.5	127.2
Accrued liabilities	469.0	369.8
Total current liabilities	676.0	520.3
Long-term debt	323.7	172.3
Accrued pension costs	266.8	192.1
Retirement benefits other than pensions	218.6	198.3
Deferred income taxes	30.6	30.5
Other	171.7	170.5
Total liabilities	$1,687.4	$1,284.0

NOTES TO CONSOLIDATED FINANCIAL STATEMENTS

Note 1—Summary of Significant Accounting Policies (in part)

Retirement Benefit Plans

We account for retirement benefit obligations under FASB ASC Topic 715, *Compensation—Retirement Benefits*. We derive the discount rates used to measure the present value of our benefit obligations using the cash flow matching method. Under this method, we compare the plan's projected payment obligations by year with the corresponding yields on the Mercer Yield Curve. Each year's projected cash flows are then discounted back to their present value at the measurement date and an overall discount rate is determined. The overall discount rate is then rounded to the nearest tenth of a percentage point. We use a similar approach to select the discount rates for major non-U.S. plans. For other non-U.S. plans, discount rates are developed based on a bond index within the country of domicile.

We select the expected long-term rate of return assumption for our U.S. pension plan and retiree medical plans using advice from an investment advisor and an actuary. The selected rate considers plan asset allocation targets, expected overall investment manager performance and long-term historical average compounded rates of return.

Benefit plan experience gains and losses are recognized in other comprehensive income (loss). Accumulated net benefit plan experience gains and losses that exceed 10% of the greater of a plan's benefit obligation or plan assets at the beginning of the year are amortized into earnings from other comprehensive income (loss) on a straight-line basis. The amortization period for pension plans is the average remaining service period of employees expected to receive benefits under the plans. The amortization period for other retirement plans is primarily the average remaining life expectancy of inactive participants.

Note 3—Retirement Benefits (in part)

Defined-benefit Pension Plans (in part)

Summary

We have various defined-benefit pension plans covering eligible current and former employees. Benefits under most plans are based on salary and years of service. There are limits to the amount of benefits which can be paid to participants from a U.S. qualified pension plan. We maintain a nonqualified U.S. plan to pay benefits for those eligible current and former employees in the U.S. whose benefits exceed the regulatory limits.

Obligations and Funded Status

Changes in the projected benefit obligation ("PBO") and plan assets for our pension plans are as follows:

| | Years Ended December 31 | | | | | |
| | U.S. Plans | | Non-U.S. Plans | | Total | |
(In millions)	2010	2009	2010	2009	2010	2009
PBO at beginning of year	$ 810.5	$ 769.3	$223.4	$196.3	$1,033.9	$ 965.6
Service cost	—	—	6.6	6.1	6.6	6.1
Interest cost	46.5	47.7	13.4	12.2	59.9	59.9
Plan participant contributions	—	—	2.9	2.8	2.9	2.8
Plan settlements	—	(3.5)	(0.5)	—	(0.5)	(3.5)
Acquisition	—	—	39.0	—	39.0	—
Benefits paid	(38.0)	(36.1)	(8.8)	(8.9)	(46.8)	(45.0)
Actuarial (gains) losses	71.1	33.1	15.7	(0.6)	86.8	32.5
Foreign currency exchange effects	—	—	(2.1)	15.5	(2.1)	15.5
PBO at end of year	$ 890.1	$ 810.5	$289.6	$223.4	$1,179.7	$1,033.9
Fair value of plan assets at beginning of year	$ 658.2	$ 440.1	$188.9	$147.9	$ 847.1	$ 588.0
Return on assets—actual	77.4	103.5	22.2	19.2	99.6	122.7
Plan participant contributions	—	—	2.9	2.8	2.9	2.8
Employer contributions:						
Primary U.S. plan[a]	—	150.0	—	—	—	150.0
Other plans	0.8	4.2	15.3	14.8	16.1	19.0
Plan settlements	—	(3.5)	(0.5)	—	(0.5)	(3.5)
Acquisition	—	—	0.6	—	0.6	—
Benefits paid	(38.0)	(36.1)	(8.8)	(8.9)	(46.8)	(45.0)
Foreign currency effects	—	—	(2.0)	13.1	(2.0)	13.1
Fair value of plan assets at end of year	$ 698.4	$ 658.2	$218.6	$188.9	$ 917.0	$ 847.1
Funded status	$(191.7)	$(152.3)	$ (71.0)	$ (34.5)	$ (262.7)	$ (186.8)
Included in:						
Noncurrent asset	$ —	—	(8.6)	(8.2)	(8.6)	(8.2)
Current liability, included in accrued liabilities	1.4	1.7	3.1	1.2	4.5	2.9
Noncurrent liability	190.3	150.6	76.5	41.5	266.8	192.1
Net pension liability	$ 191.7	$ 152.3	$ 71.0	$ 34.5	$ 262.7	$ 186.8

[a] Comprised of $92.4 million of cash and $57.6 million of shares of Brink's common stock.

Retirement Benefits Other than Pensions (in part)

Summary

We provide retirement health care benefits for eligible current and former U.S. and Canadian employees, including former employees of our former U.S. coal operation. Retirement benefits related to our former coal operation include medical benefits provided by the Pittston Coal Group Companies Employee Benefit Plan for UMWA Represented Employees (the "UMWA plans") as well as costs related to Black Lung obligations.

Obligations and Funded Status

Changes in the APBO and plan assets related to retirement health care benefits are as follows:

| | Years Ended December 31 | | | | | |
| | UMWA Plans | | Black Lung and Other Plans | | Total | |
(In millions)	2010	2009	2010	2009	2010	2009
APBO at beginning of year	$ 465.5	$ 483.6	$ 47.1	$ 48.6	$ 512.6	$ 532.2
Interest cost	27.1	25.8	2.9	2.8	30.0	28.6
Plan amendments	—	—	19.3	—	19.3	—
Benefits paid	(37.8)	(39.6)	(5.9)	(7.6)	(43.7)	(47.2)
Medicare subsidy received	3.2	3.2	—	—	3.2	3.2
Actuarial (gain) loss, net	16.3	(7.5)	(1.3)	4.5	15.0	(3.0)
Foreign currency exchange effects and other	—	—	0.1	(1.2)	0.1	(1.2)
APBO at end of year	$ 474.3	$ 465.5	$ 62.2	$ 47.1	$ 536.5	$ 512.6
Fair value of plan assets at beginning of year	$ 308.0	$ 276.1	$ —	$ —	$ 308.0	$ 276.1
Employer contributions	—	—	5.9	7.6	5.9	7.6
Return on assets—actual	37.1	67.8	—	—	37.1	67.8
Benefits paid	(38.1)	(39.1)	(5.9)	(7.6)	(44.0)	(46.7)
Medicare subsidy received	3.2	3.2	—	—	3.2	3.2
Fair value of plan assets at end of year	$ 310.2	308.0	—	—	310.2	308.0
Funded status	$(164.1)	$(157.5)	$(62.2)	$(47.1)	$(226.3)	$(204.6)
Included in:						
Current, included in accrued liabilities	$ —	$ —	$ 7.7	$ 6.3	$ 7.7	$ 6.3
Noncurrent	164.1	157.5	54.5	40.8	218.6	198.3
Retirement benefits other than pension liability	$ 164.1	$ 157.5	$ 62.2	$ 47.1	$ 226.3	$ 204.6

2.129

JOHNSON & JOHNSON (DEC)

CONSOLIDATED BALANCE SHEETS (in part)

At January 2, 2011 and January 3, 2010
(Dollars in Millions Except Share and Per Share Data) (Note 1)

	2010	2009
Current liabilities		
Loans and notes payable (Note 7)	$ 7,617	6,318
Accounts payable	5,623	5,541
Accrued liabilities	4,100	4,625
Accrued rebates, returns and promotions	2,512	2,028
Accrued compensation and employee related obligations	2,642	2,777
Accrued taxes on income	578	442
Total current liabilities	23,072	21,731
Long-term debt (Note 7)	9,156	8,223
Deferred taxes on income (Note 8)	1,447	1,424
Employee related obligations (Notes 9 and 10)	6,087	6,769
Other liabilities	6,567	5,947
Total liabilities	$46,329	44,094

NOTES TO CONSOLIDATED FINANCIAL STATEMENTS

9. Employee Related Obligations

At the end of 2010 and 2009, employee related obligations recorded on the Consolidated Balance Sheet were:

(Dollars in millions)	2010	2009
Pension benefits	$2,175	2,792
Postretirement benefits	2,359	2,245
Postemployment benefits	1,379	1,504
Deferred compensation	820	790
Total employee obligations	6,733	7,331
Less current benefits payable	646	562
Employee related obligations—non-current	$6,087	6,769

Prepaid employee related obligations of $615 million and $266 million for 2010 and 2009, respectively, are included in other assets on the consolidated balance sheet.

10. Pensions and Other Benefit Plans (in part)

The Company sponsors various retirement and pension plans, including defined benefit, defined contribution and termination indemnity plans, which cover most employees worldwide. The Company also provides postretirement benefits, primarily health care, to all U.S. retired employees and their dependents.

Many international employees are covered by government-sponsored programs and the cost to the Company is not significant.

Retirement plan benefits are primarily based on the employee's compensation during the last three to five years before retirement and the number of years of service. International subsidiaries have plans under which funds are deposited with trustees, annuities are purchased under group contracts, or reserves are provided.

The Company does not fund retiree health care benefits in advance and has the right to modify these plans in the future.

The Company uses the date of its consolidated financial statements (January 2, 2011 and January 3, 2010, respectively) as the measurement date for all U.S. and international retirement and other benefit plans.

In accordance with U.S. GAAP, the Company has adopted the recent standards related to employers' accounting for defined benefit pension and other postretirement plans.

The following table sets forth information related to the benefit obligation and the fair value of plan assets at year-end 2010 and 2009 for the Company's defined benefit retirement plans and other postretirement plans:

(Dollars in millions)	Retirement Plans		Other Benefit Plans	
	2010	2009	2010	2009
Change in benefit obligation				
Projected benefit obligation—beginning of year	$13,449	$11,923	$ 3,590	$ 2,765
Service cost	550	511	134	137
Interest cost	791	746	202	174
Plan participant contributions	42	50	—	—
Amendments	—	3	—	—
Actuarial losses	815	412	115	51
Divestitures & acquisitions	—	15	—	13
Curtailments & settlements & restructuring	(10)	(3)	—	748
Benefits paid from plan	(627)	(570)	(476)	(313)
Effect of exchange rates	(17)	362	7	15
Projected benefit obligation—end of year*	$14,993	$13,449	$ 3,572	$ 3,590
Change in plan assets				
Plan assets at fair value—beginning of year	$10,923	7,677	$ 16	17
Actual return on plan assets	1,466	2,048	2	4
Company contributions	1,611	1,354	472	308
Plan participant contributions	42	50	—	—
Settlements	(7)	—		
Benefits paid from plan assets	(627)	(570)	(476)	(313)
Effect of exchange rates	25	364	—	—
Plan assets at fair value—end of year	$13,433	$10,923	$ 14	$ 16
Funded status at—end of year*	$ (1,560)	$ (2,526)	$(3,558)	$(3,574)
Amounts recognized in the company's balance sheet consist of the following:				
Non-current assets	$ 615	266	$ —	—
Current liabilities	(54)	(53)	(576)	(484)
Non-current liabilities	(2,121)	(2,739)	(2,982)	(3,090)
Total recognized in the consolidated balance sheet—end of year	$ (1,560)	$ (2,526)	$(3,558)	$(3,574)
Amounts recognized in accumulated other comprehensive income consist of the following:				
Net actuarial loss	$ 3,539	3,415	$ 1,017	924
Prior service cost (credit)	39	47	(21)	(23)
Unrecognized net transition obligation	4	5	—	—
Total before tax effects	$ 3,582	$ 3,467	$ 996	$ 901
Accumulated benefit obligations—end of year(*)	$13,134	11,687		
Changes in plan assets and benefit obligations recognized in other comprehensive income				
Net periodic benefit cost	$ 584	$ 481	$ 379	$ 359
Net actuarial loss (gain)	354	(704)	134	48
Amortization of net actuarial loss	(242)	(134)	(46)	(131)
Prior service cost	—	3	—	—
Amortization of prior service (cost) credit	(10)	(13)	4	5
Effect of exchange rates	13	57	3	2
Total recognized in other comprehensive income, before tax	$ 115	$ (791)	$ 95	$ (76)
Total recognized in net periodic benefit cost and other comprehensive income	$ 699	$ (310)	$ 474	$ 283

(*) The Company does not fund certain plans, as funding is not required. $1.3 billion and $1.2 billion of the 2010 and 2009 projected benefit obligation and $1.3 billion and $1.2 billion of the underfunded status for each of the fiscal years 2010 and 2009, respectively, relates to the unfunded pension plans. $1.1 billion and $1.0 billion of the accumulated benefit obligation for the fiscal years 2010 and 2009, respectively, relate to these unfunded pension plans.

Plans with accumulated benefit obligations in excess of plan assets consist of the following:

(Dollars in millions)	Retirement Plans	
	2010	2009
Accumulated benefit obligation	$(2,361)	(4,065)
Projected benefit obligation	(2,771)	(4,663)
Plan assets at fair value	817	2,564

2.130

ARKANSAS BEST CORPORATION (DEC)

CONSOLIDATED BALANCE SHEETS (in part)

($ thousands, except share data)	December 31	
	2010	2009
Current liabilities		
Bank overdraft and drafts payable	$ 13,023	$ 21,941
Accounts payable	62,134	59,386
Income taxes payable	196	826
Accrued expenses	144,543	150,799
Current portion of long-term debt	14,001	3,603
Total current liabilities	233,897	236,555
Long-term debt, less current portion	42,657	13,373
Pension and postretirement liabilities	65,421	67,445
Other liabilities	19,827	20,254
Deferred income taxes	$ 19,405	$ 31,023

NOTES TO CONSOLIDATED FINANCIAL STATEMENTS

Note I—Employee Benefit Plans (in part)

Nonunion Defined Benefit Pension, Supplemental Benefit Pension and Postretirement Health Benefit Plans

The Company has a noncontributory defined benefit pension plan covering substantially all noncontractual employees hired before January 1, 2006. Noncontractual employees hired after 2005 participate in a defined contribution plan (see Defined Contribution Plans within this note). Benefits under the defined benefit pension plan are generally based on years of service and employee compensation. The Company's contributions to the defined benefit pension plan are based upon the minimum funding levels required under provisions of the Employee Retirement Income Security Act of 1974 and the Pension Protection Act of 2006 (the "PPA"), with the maximum contributions not to exceed deductible limits under the U.S. Internal Revenue Code ("IRC").

The Company also has an unfunded supplemental benefit plan ("SBP") for the purpose of supplementing benefits under the Company's defined benefit pension plan. Under the SBP, the Company will pay sums in addition to amounts payable under the defined benefit plan to eligible participants. Participation in the SBP is limited to employees of the Company who are participants in the Company's defined benefit plan and who are designated as participants in the SBP by the Company's Board of Directors. The SBP provides for a lump-sum payment following termination made in accordance with the six month delay provision for key employees as required by Section 409A of the IRC. The Compensation Committee of the Company's Board of Directors ("Compensation Committee") elected to close the SBP to new entrants and to place a cap on the maximum payment per participant to existing participants in the SBP effective January 1, 2006. In place of the SBP, eligible officers of the Company appointed after 2005 participate in a long-term cash incentive plan (see Long-Term Cash Incentive Plan within this note).

Effective December 31, 2009, the Compensation Committee elected to freeze the accrual of benefits for remaining participants under the SBP, resulting in a plan curtailment. The Compensation Committee provided the SBP participants an option to freeze their SBP benefits without early retirement penalties and continue participation in the deferred salary agreement program (see Deferred Compensation Plans within this note) or to freeze their benefits in both the SBP and deferred salary agreement program and begin participation in the Company's long-term cash incentive plan. With the exception of early retirement penalties that may apply in certain cases, the valuation inputs for calculating the frozen SBP benefits to be paid to participants, including final average salary and the interest rate, were established at December 31, 2009. The curtailment decreased the projected benefit obligation resulting in a curtailment gain of $0.1 million, which was netted with the unrecognized actuarial loss at December 31, 2009, to be amortized over the remaining service period of the SBP participants.

The Company also sponsors an insured postretirement health benefit plan that provides supplemental medical benefits and dental benefits primarily to certain officers of the Company and certain subsidiaries. Effective January 1, 2011, retirees pay a portion of the premiums under the plan according to age and coverage levels. The amendment to the plan to implement retiree premiums resulted in an unrecognized prior service credit which is included in accumulated other comprehensive loss as of December 31, 2010.

Amounts recognized in the consolidated balance sheets at December 31 consist of the following:

($ thousands)	Nonunion Defined Benefit Pension Plan		Supplemental Benefit Pension Plan		Postretirement Health Benefit Plan	
	2010	2009	2010	2009	2010	2009
Current liabilities (included in accrued expenses)	$ —	$ —	$ —	$ (7,753)	$ (600)	$ (600)
Noncurrent liabilities (included in pension and postretirement liabilities)	(42,750)	(45,795)	(9,341)	(8,790)	(13,330)	(12,860)
Liabilities recognized	$(42,750)	$(45,795)	$(9,341)	$(16,543)	$(13,930)	$(13,460)

2.131

ADMINISTAFF, INC. (DEC)

CONSOLIDATED BALANCE SHEETS (in part)

(In thousands)	December 31, 2010	December 31, 2009
Current liabilities:		
Accounts payable	$ 3,309	$ 1,857
Payroll taxes and other payroll deductions payable	145,096	127,597
Accrued worksite employee payroll cost	109,697	93,138
Accrued health insurance costs	15,419	6,374
Accrued workers' compensation costs	42,081	37,049
Accrued corporate payroll and commissions	23,743	16,178
Other accrued liabilities	14,264	8,401
Total current liabilities	353,609	290,594
Noncurrent liabilities:		
Accrued workers' compensation costs	55,730	52,014
Other accrued liabilities	1,261	—
Deferred income taxes	8,850	10,702
Total noncurrent liabilities	$ 65,841	$ 62,716

NOTES TO CONSOLIDATED FINANCIAL STATEMENTS

1. Accounting Policies (in part)

Workers' Compensation Costs

The Company's workers' compensation coverage has been provided through an arrangement with the ACE Group of Companies ("the ACE Program") since 2007. The ACE Program is fully insured in that ACE has the responsibility to pay all claims incurred regardless of whether the Company satisfies its responsibilities. Through September 30, 2010, the Company bore the economic burden for the first $1 million layer of claims per occurrence, and the insurance carrier was and remains responsible for the economic burden for all claims in excess of such first $1 million layer.

Effective for the ACE Program year beginning on October 1, 2010, in addition to the Company bearing the economic burden for the first $1 million layer of claims per occurrence, the Company will also bear the economic burden for those claims exceeding $1 million, up to a maximum aggregate amount of $5 million per policy year.

Because the Company bears the economic burden for claims up to the levels noted above, such claims, which are the primary component of the Company's workers' compensation costs, are recorded in the period incurred. Workers' compensation insurance includes ongoing health care and indemnity coverage whereby claims are paid over numerous years following the date of injury. Accordingly, the accrual of related incurred costs in each reporting period includes estimates, which take into account the ongoing development of claims and therefore requires a significant level of judgment.

The Company employs a third party actuary to estimate its loss development rate, which is primarily based upon the nature of worksite employees' job responsibilities, the lo-

cation of worksite employees, the historical frequency and severity of workers compensation claims, and an estimate of future cost trends. Each reporting period, changes in the actuarial assumptions resulting from changes in actual claims experience and other trends are incorporated into the Company's workers' compensation claims cost estimates. During the year ended December 31, Administaff reduced accrued workers' compensation costs by $6.2 million and $5.7 million, respectively, in 2010 and 2009, for changes in estimated losses related to prior reporting periods. Workers' compensation cost estimates are discounted to present value at a rate based upon the U.S. Treasury rates that correspond with the weighted average estimated claim payout period (the average discount rates utilized in 2010 and 2009 were 1.4% and 1.8%, respectively) and are accreted over the estimated claim payment period and included as a component of direct costs in the Company's Consolidated Statements of Operations.

The following table provides the activity and balances related to incurred but not reported workers' compensation claims for the years ended December 31, 2010 and 2009 (in thousands):

	Year Ended	
	2010	2009
Beginning balance	$ 88,450	$ 83,055
Accrued claims	34,345	35,525
Present value discount	(1,675)	(2,203)
Paid claims	(24,186)	(27,927)
Ending balance	$ 96,934	$ 88,450
Current portion of accrued claims	$ 41,204	$ 36,436
Long-term portion of accrued claims	55,730	52,014
	$ 96,934	$ 88,450

The current portion of accrued workers' compensation costs at December 31, 2010 and 2009, includes $877,000 and $613,000, respectively, of workers' compensation administrative fees.

As of December 31, the undiscounted accrued workers' compensation costs were $111.5 million in 2010 and $103.8 million in 2009.

At the beginning of each policy period, the insurance carrier establishes monthly funding requirements comprised of premium costs and funds to be set aside for payment of future claims ("claim funds"). The level of claim funds is primarily based upon anticipated worksite employee payroll levels and expected workers compensation loss rates, as determined by the insurance carrier. Monies funded into the program for incurred claims expected to be paid within one year are recorded as restricted cash, a short-term asset, while the remainder of claim funds are included in deposits, a long-term asset in the Company's Consolidated Balance Sheets. In 2010, the Company received $15.6 million for the return of excess claim funds related to the ACE program, which reduced deposits. As of December 31, 2010, the Company had restricted cash of $41.2 million and deposits of $51.7 million.

The Company's estimate of incurred claim costs expected to be paid within one year are recorded as accrued workers' compensation costs and included in short-term liabilities, while its estimate of incurred claim costs expected to be paid beyond one year are included in long-term liabilities on the Company's Consolidated Balance Sheets.

INCOME TAX LIABILITY

PRESENTATION

2.132 FASB ASC 210 provides general guidance for classification of accounts in balance sheets. FASB 740-10-45 addresses classification matters applicable to income tax accounts and is incremental to the general guidance.

DISCLOSURE

2.133 FASB 740-10-50 provides detailed disclosures for income taxes, including the components of the net deferred tax liability or asset recognized in an entity's balance sheet.

PRESENTATION AND DISCLOSURE EXCERPTS

Income Taxes Payable

2.134

XILINX, INC. (MAR)

CONSOLIDATED BALANCE SHEETS (in part)

(In thousands, except par value amounts)	April 3, 2010	March 28, 2009(*)
Current liabilities:		
Accounts payable	$ 96,169	$ 48,201
Accrued payroll and related liabilities	114,663	89,918
Income taxes payable	14,452	10,171
Deferred income on shipments to distributors	80,132	62,364
Other accrued liabilities	51,745	22,412
Total current liabilities	$357,161	$233,066

(*) As adjusted for the retrospective adoption of the accounting standard for convertible debentures in the first quarter of fiscal 2010 (see Note 2).

NOTES TO CONSOLIDATED FINANCIAL STATEMENTS

Note 2. Summary of Significant Accounting Policies and Concentrations of Risk (in part)

Income Taxes

All income tax amounts reflect the use of the liability method under the accounting for income taxes, as interpreted by FASB authoritative guidance for measuring uncertain tax positions. Under this method, deferred tax assets and liabilities are determined based on the expected future tax consequences of temporary differences between the carrying amounts of assets and liabilities for financial and income tax reporting purposes.

2.135

APPLIED MATERIALS, INC. (OCT)

CONSOLIDATED BALANCE SHEETS (in part)

(In thousands, except per share amounts)	October 31, 2010	October 25, 2009
Current liabilities:		
Current portion of long-term debt	$ 1,258	$ 1,240
Accounts payable and accrued expenses (Note 7)	1,765,966	1,061,502
Customer deposits and deferred revenue (Note 7)	847,231	864,280
Income taxes payable (Note 15)	273,421	12,435
Total current liabilities	2,887,876	1,939,457
Long-term debt (Note 11)	204,271	200,654
Employee benefits and other liabilities (Note 14)	315,085	339,524
Total liabilities	$3,407,232	$2,479,635

NOTES TO CONSOLIDATED FINANCIAL STATEMENTS

Note 15 Income Taxes (in part)

For fiscal 2010, U.S. income taxes have not been provided for approximately $652 million of cumulative undistributed earnings of several non-U.S. subsidiaries. Applied intends to reinvest these earnings indefinitely in operations outside of the U.S. If these earnings were distributed to the United States in the form of dividends or otherwise, or if the shares of the relevant foreign subsidiaries were sold or otherwise transferred, the Company would be subject to additional U.S. income taxes (subject to an adjustment for foreign tax credits) and foreign withholding taxes. Determination of the amount of unrecognized deferred income tax liability related to these earnings is not practicable.

At October 31, 2010, Applied's state net operating loss carryforwards were $55 million. The carryforwards expire between fiscal 2021 and fiscal 2031. Applied has a California research and development tax credit carryforward of $31 million which has an unlimited life. Applied also has net operating loss carryforwards in foreign jurisdictions of $105 million. The carryforwards have lives ranging from five years to indefinite. Management believes it is more likely than not that all loss and tax credit carryforwards at October 31, 2010 will be utilized in future periods.

Applied's income taxes payable have been reduced by the tax benefits associated with employee stock option transactions. These benefits, credited directly to stockholders' equity, amounted to $2 million for fiscal 2010, $1 million for fiscal 2009, and $7 million for fiscal 2008 with a corresponding reduction to taxes payable of $2 million in fiscal 2010, $1 million in fiscal 2009, and $7 million for fiscal 2008.

CURRENT AMOUNT OF LONG-TERM DEBT

PRESENTATION

2.136   FASB ASC 470 addresses classification determination for specific debt obligations, such as the following:
- Short-term obligations expected to be refinanced on a long-term basis
- 'Due-on-demand loan arrangements
- Callable debt
- Sales of future revenue
- Increasing rate debt
- Debt that includes covenants
- Revolving credit agreements subject to lock-box arrangements and subjective acceleration clauses

DISCLOSURE

2.137   FASB ASC 470 includes disclosures required for long-term debt (see the "Long-Term Debt" section). FASB ASC 825 requires disclosure of both the fair value and bases for estimating the fair value of the current amount of long-term debt, unless it is not practicable to estimate that value.

PRESENTATION AND DISCLOSURE EXCERPTS

Current Amount of Long-Term Debt

2.138

WELLPOINT, INC. (DEC)

CONSOLIDATED BALANCE SHEETS (in part)

	December 31	
(In millions, except share data)	2010	2009
Liabilities		
Current liabilities:		
Policy liabilities:		
Medical claims payable	$ 4,852.4	$ 5,450.5
Reserves for future policy benefits	56.4	62.6
Other policyholder liabilities	1,909.1	1,617.6
Total policy liabilities	6,817.9	7,130.7
Unearned income	891.4	1,050.0
Accounts payable and accrued expenses	2,942.2	2,994.1
Income tax payable	—	1,228.7
Security trades pending payable	33.3	37.6
Securities lending payable	901.5	396.6
Short-term borrowings	100.0	—
Current portion of long-term debt	705.9	60.8
Other current liabilities	1,617.3	1,775.2
Total current liabilities	14,009.5	14,673.7
Long-term debt, less current portion	8,147.8	8,338.3
Reserves for future policy benefits, noncurrent	646.7	664.6
Deferred tax liabilities, net	2,586.9	2,470.4
Other noncurrent liabilities	963.4	1,115.1
Total liabilities	$26,354.3	$27,262.1

NOTES TO CONSOLIDATED FINANCIAL STATEMENTS

(In Millions, Except Per Share Data or Otherwise Stated Herein)

13. Debt

Short-Term Borrowings

We are a member of the Federal Home Loan Bank of Indianapolis and the Federal Home Loan Bank of Cincinnati, collectively, the FHLBs, and as a member we have the ability to obtain cash advances subject to certain requirements. In order to obtain cash advances, we are required to pledge securities as collateral to the FHLBs, initially equal to a certain percentage of the cash borrowings, depending on the type of securities pledged as collateral. The market value of the collateral is monitored daily by the FHLBs, and if it falls below the required percentage of the cash borrowings, we are required to pledge additional securities as collateral or repay a portion of the outstanding cash advance balance. In addition, our borrowings may be limited based on the amount of our investment in the FHLBs' common stock. Our investment in the FHLBs' common stock at December 31, 2010 totaled $11.4, which is reported in "Investments available-for-sale—Equity securities" on the consolidated balance sheets. On December 21, 2010, we borrowed $100.0 from the FHLBs with a one-month term at a fixed interest rate of 0.120%, which was outstanding at December 31, 2010 and was repaid on January 18, 2011. On January 18, 2011, we borrowed another $100.0 for a two-month period at 0.200%, with a maturity date of March 21, 2011. In addition, on April 12, 2010, we borrowed $100.0 from the FHLBs with a two-year term at a fixed interest rate of 1.430%, which is reported with "Long-term debt, less current portion" on the consolidated balance sheets. Securities, primarily certain U.S. government sponsored mortgage-backed securities, with a fair value of $237.9 at December 31, 2010, have been pledged as collateral. The securities pledged are reported in "Investments available-for-sale—Fixed maturity securities" on the consolidated balance sheets.

Long-Term Debt

The carrying value of long-term debt at December 31 consists of the following:

	2010	2009
Senior unsecured notes:		
5.000%, face amount of $700.0, due 2011	$ 701.8	$ 698.7
6.375%, face amount of $350.0, due 2012	354.4	358.5
6.800%, face amount of $800.0, due 2012	842.0	846.2
6.000%, face amount of $400.0, due 2014	397.6	396.8
5.000%, face amount of $500.0, due 2014	547.5	532.9
5.250%, face amount of $1,100.0, due 2016	1,093.4	1,092.1
5.875%, face amount of $700.0, due 2017	693.0	692.1
7.000%, face amount of $600.0, due 2019	595.2	594.7
4.350%, face amount of $700.0, due 2020	693.3	—
5.950%, face amount of $500.0, due 2034	494.9	494.7
5.850%, face amount of $900.0, due 2036	889.7	889.3
6.375%, face amount of $800.0, due 2037	789.7	789.4
5.800%, face amount of $300.0, due 2040	293.5	—
Surplus notes:		
9.125%, face amount of $42.0, due 2010	—	42.0
9.000%, face amount of $25.1, due 2027	24.9	24.8
Variable rate debt:		
Commercial paper program	336.2	500.6
Senior term loan	—	433.1
Fixed rate 1.430% FHLBs secured loan, due 2012	100.0	—
Capital leases, stated or imputed rates from 4.860% to 26.030% due through 2012	6.6	13.2
Total long-term debt	8,853.7	8,399.1
Current portion of long-term debt	(705.9)	(60.8)
Long-term debt, less current portion	$8,147.8	$8,338.3

At maturity on January 15, 2011, we repaid the $700.0 outstanding balance of our 5.000% senior unsecured notes.

On September 30, 2010, we entered into a senior credit facility, or the facility, with certain lenders for general corporate purposes. The facility provides credit up to $2,000.0 and matures on September 30, 2013. The interest rate on the facility is based on either, (i) the LIBOR rate plus a predetermined percentage rate based on our credit rating at the date of utilization, or (ii) a base rate as defined in the facility agreement plus a predetermined percentage rate based on our credit rating at the date of utilization. Our ability to borrow under the facility is subject to compliance with certain covenants. Commitment and legal fees paid for the facility were $7.6 and there are no conditions that are probable of occurring under which the facility may be withdrawn. There were no amounts outstanding under the facility as of or during the three months ended December 31, 2010, or under a previous facility during the nine months ended September 30, 2010. At December 31, 2010, we had $2,000.0 available under the facility. This facility replaced our previous senior credit facility, which provided credit up to $2,392.0.

On August 12, 2010, we issued $700.0 of 4.350% notes due 2020 and $300.0 of 5.800% notes due 2040 under our shelf registration statement. We used the proceeds from this debt issuance to repay the remaining outstanding balance of our variable rate senior term loan and for general corporate purposes. The notes have a call feature that allows us to repurchase the notes at any time at our option and a put feature that allows a note holder to require us to repurchase the notes upon the occurrence of both a change of control event and a downgrade of the notes.

Surplus notes are unsecured obligations of Anthem Insurance Companies, Inc., or Anthem Insurance, a wholly owned subsidiary, and are subordinate in right of payment to all of Anthem Insurance's existing and future indebtedness. Any payment of interest or principal on the surplus notes may be made only with the prior approval of the Indiana Department of Insurance, or IDOI, and only out of capital and surplus funds of Anthem Insurance that the IDOI determines to be available for the payment under Indiana insurance laws. During April 2010, we repaid the remaining $42.0 outstanding balance of our 9.125% surplus notes.

In July 2009, May 2009 and March 2009, we repurchased $390.0, $300.0 and $400.0, respectively, of our $1,090.0 face value due at maturity zero coupon notes. The notes were issued in August 2007 in a private placement transaction. We paid cash totaling $553.8 to repurchase the notes, which had a remaining carrying value of zero at December 31, 2009.

On February 5, 2009, we issued $400.0 of 6.000% notes due 2014 and $600.0 of 7.000% notes due 2019 under our shelf registration statement. The proceeds from this debt issuance were used for general corporate purposes, including, but not limited to, repayment of short-term debt and repurchasing shares of our common stock. The notes have a call feature that allows us to repurchase the notes at any time at our option and a put feature that allows a note holder to require us to repurchase the notes upon the occurrence of both a change of control event and a downgrade of the notes.

We have an authorized commercial paper program of up to $2,500.0, the proceeds of which may be used for general corporate purposes. The weighted-average interest rate on commercial paper borrowings at December 31, 2010 and 2009 was 0.359% and 0.340%, respectively. Commercial paper borrowings have been classified as long-term debt at December 31, 2010 and 2009 as our practice and intent is to replace short-term commercial paper outstanding at expiration with additional short-term commercial paper for an uninterrupted period extending for more than one year or our ability to redeem our commercial paper with borrowings under the senior credit facility described above.

Interest paid during 2010, 2009 and 2008 was $419.6, $409.2 and $443.4, respectively.

We were in compliance with all applicable covenants under our outstanding debt agreements.

Future maturities of debt, including capital leases, are as follows: 2011, $1,043.9; 2012, $1,297.1; 2013, $0.0; 2014, $945.1; 2015, $0.0 and thereafter, $5,567.6.

2.139

NATIONAL OILWELL VARCO, INC. (DEC)

CONSOLIDATED BALANCE SHEETS (in part)

(In millions, except share data)

	December 31	
	2010	2009
Current liabilities:		
Accounts payable	$ 628	$ 584
Accrued liabilities	2,105	2,267
Billings in excess of costs	511	1,090
Current portion of long-term debt and short-term borrowings	373	7
Accrued income taxes	468	226
Deferred income taxes	451	340
Total current liabilities	$4,536	$4,514

NOTES TO CONSOLIDATED FINANCIAL STATEMENTS

9. Long-Term Debt

Debt consists of (in millions):

	December 31	
	2010	2009
Senior notes, interest at 6.5% payable semiannually, principal due on March 15, 2011	$150	$150
Senior notes, interest at 7.25% payable semiannually, principal due on May 1, 2011	201	205
Senior notes, interest at 5.65% payable semiannually, principal due on November 15, 2012	200	200
Senior notes, interest at 5.5% payable semiannually, principal due on November 19, 2012	151	151
Senior notes, interest at 6.125% payable semiannually, principal due on August 15, 2015	151	151
Other	34	26
Total debt	887	883
Less current portion	373	7
Long-term debt	$514	$876

Principal payments of debt for years subsequent to 2010 are as follows (in millions):

2011	$373
2012	355
2013	5
2014	2
2015	151
Thereafter	1
	$887

Revolving Credit Facilities

On April 21, 2008, the Company replaced its existing $500 million unsecured revolving credit facility with an aggregate of $3 billion of unsecured credit facilities and borrowed $2 billion to finance the cash portion of the Grant Prideco acquisition. These facilities consisted of a $2 billion, five-year revolving credit facility and a $1 billion, 364-day revolving credit facility which was terminated early in February 2009. At December 31, 2010, there were no borrowings against the remaining credit facility, and there were $477 million in outstanding letters of credit issued under this facility, resulting in $1,523 million of funds available under this revolving credit facility. Interest under this multicurrency facility is based upon LIBOR, NIBOR or EURIBOR plus 0.26% subject to a ratings-based grid, or the prime rate.

The Company also had $1,366 million of additional outstanding letters of credit at December 31, 2010, primarily in Norway, that are essentially under various bilateral committed letter of credit facilities. Other letters of credit are issued as bid bonds and performance bonds. The Senior Notes contain reporting covenants and the credit facility contains a financial covenant regarding maximum debt to capitalization. The Company was in compliance with all covenants at December 31, 2010.

OTHER CURRENT LIABILITIES

PRESENTATION

2.140   Rule 5-02 of Regulation S-X requires that any items in excess of 5 percent of total current liabilities be stated separately on the balance sheet or disclosed in the notes. In addition, registrants should state separately amounts payable to the following:
- Banks for borrowings
- Factors or other financial institutions for borrowings
- Holders of commercial paper
- Trade creditors
- Related parties
- Underwriters, promoters, and employees (other than related parties)
- Others

Amounts applicable to the first three categories may be stated separately in the balance sheet or in a note thereto.

2.141

TABLE 2-12: OTHER CURRENT LIABILITIES*

Table 2-12 summarizes other identified current liabilities. The most common types of other current liabilities are liabilities related to derivatives, discontinued operations, deferred revenue, accrued interest, and deferred taxes.

	Number of Entities		
	2010	2009	2008
Derivatives	129	253	88
Costs related to discontinued operations/restructuring	116	158	148
Deferred revenue	150	140	150
Interest	96	123	128
Deferred taxes	138	118	122
Taxes other than federal income taxes	138	116	122
Guarantees or warranties	83	99	101
Insurance	87	86	83
Advertising	59	64	63
Dividends	54	59	62
Environmental costs	48	59	58
Rebates/discounts/incentives	63	55	54
Customer advances, deposits	54	54	57
Litigation	30	43	39
Tax uncertainties	38	33	29
Billings on uncompleted contracts	18	26	26
Due to affiliated companies	4	23	25
Royalties	15	19	20
Asset retirement obligations	15	15	18
Unrecognized tax (benefit) liability	37	N/C^	N/C^
Outstanding checks	18	N/C^	N/C^
Merger/acquisition	8	N/C^	N/C^
Professional fees	11	N/C^	N/C^
Accrued rent/lease payments	13	N/C^	N/C^
Other—described	193	135	127

* Appearing in the balance sheet or notes to financial statements, or both.
^ N/C = Not compiled. Line item was not included in the table for the year shown.

PRESENTATION AND DISCLOSURE EXCERPTS

Dividends

2.142

PALL CORPORATION (JUL)

CONSOLIDATED BALANCE SHEETS (in part)

(In thousands, except per share data)

	July 31, 2010	July 31, 2009
Current liabilities:		
Notes payable	$ 40,072	$ 42,371
Accounts payable	186,407	171,956
Accrued liabilities	270,244	250,838
Income taxes payable	120,051	137,846
Current portion of long-term debt	1,956	97,432
Dividends payable	18,475	16,947
Total current liabilities	$637,205	$717,390

Item 7. Management's Discussion and Analysis of Financial Condition and Results of Operations

Liquidity and Capital Resources (in part)

In fiscal year 2010, the Company paid dividends of $71,284 compared to $64,914 in fiscal year 2009, an increase of approximately 10%. The Company increased its quarterly dividend by 10.3% from 14.5 cents to 16 cents per share, effective with the dividend declared on January 21, 2010.

Deposits or Advances

2.143

LOCKHEED MARTIN CORPORATION (DEC)

CONSOLIDATED BALANCE SHEETS (in part)

	December 31	
(In millions, except per share data)	2010	2009
Current liabilities		
Accounts payable	$ 1,627	$ 2,030
Customer advances and amounts in excess of costs incurred	5,719	5,049
Salaries, benefits and payroll taxes	1,870	1,648
Liabilities of discontinued operation held for sale	204	—
Other current liabilities	1,737	1,976
Total current liabilities	$11,157	$10,703

NOTES TO CONSOLIDATED FINANCIAL STATEMENTS

Note 1—Significant Accounting Policies (in part)

Customer advances and amounts in excess of cost incurred—We receive advances, performance-based payments, and progress payments from customers that may exceed costs incurred on certain contracts, including contracts with agencies of the U.S. Government. We classify such advances, other than those reflected as a reduction of receivables or inventories as discussed above, as Current Liabilities.

Note 5—Information on Business Segments (in part)

Selected Financial Data by Business Segment (in part)

(In millions)	2010	2009
Assets[a]		
Aeronautics	$ 5,230	$ 4,356
Electronic Systems	9,972	10,080
Information Systems & Global Solutions	5,524	6,443
Space Systems	3,014	3,097
Total business segments	23,740	23,976
Corporate assets[b]	10,928	11,135
Assets of discontinued operation held for sale	399	—
Total	$35,067	$35,111
Goodwill		
Aeronautics	$ 148	$ 148
Electronic Systems	5,601	5,595
Information Systems & Global Solutions	3,363	3,712
Space Systems	493	493
Total	$ 9,605	$ 9,948
Customer Advances and Amounts in Excess of Costs Incurred		
Aeronautics	$ 2,773	$ 2,389
Electronic Systems	2,408	2,297
Information Systems & Global Solutions	195	172
Space Systems	343	191
Total	$ 5,719	$ 5,049

[a] We have no significant long-lived assets located in foreign countries.

[b] Corporate assets primarily include cash and cash equivalents, short-term investments, deferred income taxes, the prepaid pension asset, deferred environmental assets, and investments held in a Rabbi Trust.

Tax Uncertainties

2.144

LAM RESEARCH CORPORATION (JUN)

CONSOLIDATED BALANCE SHEETS (in part)

(In thousands, except per share data)

	June 27, 2010	June 28, 2009
Trade accounts payable	$121,099	$ 49,606
Accrued expenses and other current liabilities	309,397	281,335
Deferred profit	123,194	45,787
Current portion of long-term debt and capital leases	4,967	5,348
Total current liabilities	$558,657	$382,076

NOTES TO CONSOLIDATED FINANCIAL STATEMENTS

Note 7. Accrued Expenses and Other Current Liabilities

Accrued expenses and other current liabilities consist of the following:

(In thousands)	June 27, 2010	June 28, 2009
Accrued compensation	$164,579	$171,609
Warranty reserves	31,756	21,185
Income and other taxes payable	54,874	31,970
Other	58,188	56,571
	$309,397	$281,335

Following a voluntary independent review of the Company's historical employee stock option grant process, the Company considered whether Section 409A ("Section 409A") of the Internal Revenue Code of 1986, as amended ("IRC") and similar provisions of state law would apply to certain stock option grants that were found to have intrinsic value at the time of their respective measurement dates. If a stock option is not considered as issued with an exercise price of at least the fair market value of the underlying stock on the date of grant, it may be subject to penalty taxes under Section 409A and similar provisions of state law. In such a case, such taxes may be assessed not only on the intrinsic value increase, but on the entire stock option gain as measured at various times. On March 30, 2008, the Board of Directors of the Company authorized the Company to assume potential tax liabilities of certain employees, including the Company's Chief Executive Officer and certain other executive officers, relating to options that might be subject to Section 409A and similar provisions of state law. The assumed Section 409A liability was $53.7 million as of June 28, 2009 and is included in accrued compensation in the table above.

During fiscal year 2010, the Company reached a final settlement with respect to its Section 409A liabilities, which resulted in a reduction of the liability and net credits recognized in the statements of operations of $(5.8) million recorded in cost of goods sold and $(38.6) million recorded in operating expenses.

Product Warranty

2.145

JOHNSON CONTROLS, INC. (SEP)

NOTES TO CONSOLIDATED FINANCIAL STATEMENTS

6. Product Warranties

The Company offers warranties to its customers depending upon the specific product and terms of the customer purchase agreement. A typical warranty program requires that the Company replace defective products within a specified time period from the date of sale. The Company records an estimate for future warranty-related costs based on actual historical return rates and other known factors. Based on analysis of return rates and other factors, the adequacy of the Company's warranty provisions are adjusted as necessary. While the Company's warranty costs have historically been within its calculated estimates, the Company monitors its warranty activity and adjusts its reserve estimates when it is probable that future warranty costs will be different than those estimates. Accruals related to pre-existing warranties includes incremental warranty charges of $105 million recorded in the fourth quarter of fiscal 2009 by the building efficiency North America unitary products segment, of which $76 million was due to a specific product issue and $29 million was a result of the Company's periodic warranty review process and analysis of return rates. The portion of the incremental charge due to a specific product issue related to the anticorrosive film applied to certain coils used in residential indoor heating, ventilating and air conditioning units as a means to promote flow of condensation and adding to the efficiency of the units.

The Company's product warranty liability is recorded in the consolidated statement of financial position in other current liabilities if the warranty is less than one year and in other noncurrent liabilities if the warranty extends longer than one year.

The changes in the carrying amount of the Company's total product warranty liability for the fiscal years ended September 30, 2010 and 2009 were as follows (in millions):

	Year Ended September 30	
	2010	2009
Balance at beginning of period	$ 344	$ 204
Accruals for warranties issued during the period	260	238
Accruals from acquisitions	1	—
Accruals related to pre-existing warranties (including changes in estimates)	(18)	115
Settlements made (in cash or in kind) during the period	(245)	(214)
Currency translation	(5)	1
Balance at end of period	$ 337	$ 344

Billings in Excess of Costs

2.146

JACOBS ENGINEERING GROUP INC. (SEP)

CONSOLIDATED BALANCE SHEETS (in part)

(In thousands, except share information)
At October 1, 2010 and October 2, 2009

	2010	2009
Current liabilities:		
Notes payable	$ 79,399	$ 17,495
Accounts payable	303,877	340,651
Accrued liabilities	661,278	679,109
Billings in excess of costs	194,899	252,149
Income taxes payable	—	6,497
Total current liabilities	$1,239,453	$1,295,901

NOTES TO CONSOLIDATED FINANCIAL STATEMENTS

2. Significant Accounting Policies (in part)

"Billings in excess of costs" represent cash collected from clients, and billings to clients in advance of work performed. We anticipate that substantially all such amounts will be earned over the next twelve months.

Held for Sale

2.147

VIACOM INC. (SEP)

CONSOLIDATED BALANCE SHEETS (in part)

(In millions, except par value)	September 30, 2010	December 31, 2009
Current liabilities:		
Accounts payable	$ 210	$ 247
Accrued expenses	1,000	1,148
Participants' share and residuals	1,059	1,063
Program rights obligations	390	404
Deferred revenue	256	286
Current portion of debt	31	123
Other liabilities	435	394
Liabilities held for sale	117	86
Total current liabilities	$3,498	$3,751

NOTES TO CONSOLIDATED FINANCIAL STATEMENTS

Note 19. Discontinued Operations (in part)

In September 2010, the Company's Board of Directors authorized management to proceed with a sale of Harmonix. Management is actively marketing Harmonix for sale and is committed to a plan that management believes will result in the sale of the business within twelve months. Accordingly, the results of operations of Harmonix, which were previously included in the *Media Networks* segment, are presented as discontinued operations in all periods presented.

Assets and liabilities classified as held for sale as of September 30, 2010 and December 31, 2009 are related to Harmonix and are as follows:

Harmonix Net Assets (In millions)	September 30, 2010	December 31, 2009
Assets/(Liabilities):		
Current assets	$ 76	$137
Goodwill	64	294
Other assets	10	20
Accounts payable and other liabilities	(103)	(54)
Deferred revenue	(14)	(37)
Net assets	$ 33	$360

Self-Insurance Reserves

2.148

AVIS BUDGET GROUP, INC. (DEC)

NOTES TO CONSOLIDATED FINANCIAL STATEMENTS

(Unless otherwise noted, all dollar amounts are in millions, except per share amounts)

2. Summary of Significant Accounting Policies (in part)

Self-Insurance Reserves

The Consolidated Balance Sheets include $305 million and $308 million of liabilities with respect to self-insured public liability and property damage as of December 31, 2010 and 2009, respectively. Such liabilities relate to supplemental liability insurance, personal effects protection insurance, public liability, property damage and personal accident insurance claims for which the Company is self-insured. These obligations represent an estimate for both reported claims not yet paid and claims incurred but not yet reported. The Company estimates the required reserve for such claims on an undiscounted basis utilizing an actuarial method that is based upon various assumptions which include, but are not limited to, the Company's historical loss experience and projected loss development factors. The required liability is also subject to adjustment in the future based upon the changes in claims experience, including changes in the number of incidents and changes in the ultimate cost per incident. These amounts are included within accounts payable and other current liabilities and other non-current liabilities.

The Consolidated Balance Sheets also include liabilities of approximately $56 million and $65 million as of December 31, 2010 and 2009, respectively, related to health and welfare, workers' compensation and other benefits the Company provides to its employees. The Company estimates the liability required for such benefits based on actual claims outstanding and the estimated cost of claims incurred as of the balance sheet date. These amounts are included within accounts payable and other current liabilities.

Advertising

2.149

BURGER KING HOLDINGS, INC. (JUN)

CONSOLIDATED BALANCE SHEETS (in part)

(In millions, except share data)

	As of June 30	
	2010	2009
Current liabilities:		
Accounts and drafts payable	$106.9	$127.0
Accrued advertising	71.9	67.8
Other accrued liabilities	200.9	220.0
Current portion of long term debt and capital leases	93.3	67.5
Total current liabilities	$473.0	$482.3

NOTES TO CONSOLIDATED FINANCIAL STATEMENTS

Note 2. Summary of Significant Accounting Policies (in part)

Advertising and Promotional Costs

The Company expenses the production costs of advertising when the advertisements are first aired or displayed. All other advertising and promotional costs are expensed in the period incurred.

Franchise restaurants and Company restaurants contribute to advertising funds managed by the Company in the United States and certain international markets where Company restaurants operate. Under the Company's franchise agreements, contributions received from franchisees must be spent on advertising, marketing and related activities, and result in no gross profit recognized by the Company. Advertising expense, net of franchisee contributions, totaled $91.3 million for the year ended June 30, 2010, $93.3 million for the year ended June 30, 2009, and $91.5 million for the year ended June 30, 2008, and is included in selling, general and administrative expenses in the accompanying consolidated statements of income.

To the extent that contributions received exceed advertising and promotional expenditures, the excess contributions are accounted for as a deferred liability and are recorded in accrued advertising in the accompanying consolidated balance sheets.

Franchisees in markets where no Company restaurants operate contribute to advertising funds not managed by the Company. Such contributions and related fund expenditures are not reflected in the Company's results of operations or financial position.

Deferred Revenue

2.150

REYNOLDS AMERICAN INC. (DEC)

CONSOLIDATED BALANCE SHEETS (in part)

(Dollars in millions)

	December 31	
	2010	2009
Current liabilities:		
Accounts payable	$ 179	$ 196
Tobacco settlement accruals	2,589	2,611
Due to related party	4	3
Deferred revenue, related party	53	57
Current maturities of long-term debt	400	300
Other current liabilities	1,147	1,173
Total current liabilities	$4,372	$4,340

Note 19—Related Party Transactions (in part)

RAI and its operating subsidiaries engage in transactions with affiliates of BAT. The following is a summary of balances and transactions with such BAT affiliates as of and for the years ended December 31:
Balances: (Dollars in millions)

	2010	2009
Accounts receivable	$48	$96
Accounts payable	(4)	(3)
Deferred revenue	(53)	(57)

Significant transactions: (Dollars in Millions)

	2010	2009	2008
Net sales	$381	$404	$468
Purchases	12	16	12
RAI common stock purchases from B&W	—	—	75
Research and development services billings	4	2	3

RAI's operating subsidiaries sell contract-manufactured cigarettes, processed strip leaf, pipe tobacco and little cigars to BAT affiliates. During the second quarter of 2010, RJR Tobacco and BAT concluded their negotiations over certain contract manufacturing arrangements, which resulted in the termination of a prior contract manufacturing agreement between RJR Tobacco and an affiliate of BAT and entering into a new contract manufacturing agreement with pricing based on negotiated cost plus 10% for 2010. For contract years 2011 through 2014, prices will increase or decrease by a multiple equal to changes in the Producer Price Index, reported by the U.S. Bureau of Labor Statistics. Net sales, primarily of cigarettes, to BAT affiliates represented approximately 4.0% of RAI's total net sales in 2010 and 5.0% in each of 2009 and 2008.

RJR Tobacco recorded deferred sales revenue relating to leaf sold to BAT affiliates that had not been delivered as of December 31, given that RJR Tobacco had a legal right to bill the BAT affiliates. Leaf sales revenue to BAT affiliates will be recognized when the product is shipped to the customer.

Environment

2.151

SCHNITZER STEEL INDUSTRIES, INC. (AUG)

CONSOLIDATED BALANCE SHEETS (in part)

(In thousands)

	August 31	
	2010	2009
Current liabilities:		
Long-term debt and capital lease obligations	$ 1,189	$ 1,317
Accounts payable	91,879	72,289
Accrued payroll and related liabilities	34,162	23,636
Environmental liabilities	2,588	3,148
Accrued income taxes	1,816	776
Other accrued liabilities	28,479	38,963
Total current liabilities	$160,113	$140,129

NOTES TO CONSOLIDATED FINANCIAL STATEMENTS

Note 2—Summary of Significant Accounting Policies (in part)

Environmental Liabilities

The Company estimates future costs for known environmental remediation requirements and accrues for them on an undiscounted basis when it is probable that the Company has incurred a liability and the related costs can be reasonably estimated but the timing of incurring the estimated costs is unknown. The Company considers various factors when estimating its environmental liabilities. Adjustments to the liabilities are made when additional information becomes available that affects the estimated costs to study or remediate any environmental issues or when expenditures are made for which reserves were established. Legal costs incurred in connection with environmental contingencies are expensed as incurred.

When only a wide range of estimated amounts can be reasonably established and no other amount within the range is better than another, the low end of the range is recorded in the financial statements. In a number of cases, it is possible that the Company may receive reimbursement through insurance or from other potentially responsible parties for a site. In these situations, recoveries of environmental remediation costs from other parties are recognized when the claim for recovery is actually realized. The amounts recorded for environmental liabilities are reviewed periodically as site assessment and remediation progresses at individual sites and adjusted to reflect additional information that becomes available. Due to evolving remediation technology, changing regulations, possible third party contributions, the inherent shortcomings of the estimation process and other factors, amounts accrued could vary significantly from amounts paid.

Note 12—Commitments and Contingencies (in part)

Contingencies—Environmental

The Company evaluates the adequacy of its environmental liabilities on a quarterly basis in accordance with Company policy. Adjustments to the liabilities are made when additional information becomes available that affects the estimated costs to study or remediate any environmental issues or expenditures are made for which reserves were established.

Changes in the Company's environmental liabilities for the years ended August 31, 2010 and 2009 were as follows (in thousands):

Reporting Segment	Balance 9/1/2008	Reserves Released, Net[1]	Payments	Ending Balance 8/31/2009	Reserves Established (Released), Net[2]	Payments	Ending Balance 8/31/2010	Short-Term	Long-Term
Metals Recycling Business	$26,704	$ (519)	$(577)	$25,608	$ 710	$(944)	$25,374	$2,034	$23,340
Auto Parts Business	17,000	(700)	0	16,300	(1,800)	0	14,500	554	13,946
Total	$43,704	$(1,219)	$(577)	$41,908	$(1,090)	$(944)	$39,874	$2,588	$37,286

[1] During fiscal 2009, the Company released $4 million in environmental reserves, primarily related to the resolution of the Hylebos Waterway litigation, which was partially offset by $2 million in environmental liabilities recorded in purchase accounting related to acquisitions completed in fiscal 2009 and $1 million in new reserves.

[2] During fiscal 2010, the Company released $2 million in environmental reserves through discontinued operations related to the full-service auto parts operation, which was partially offset by $1 million in environmental liabilities recorded in purchase accounting.

Metals Recycling Business

As of August 31, 2010, MRB had environmental reserves of $25 million for the potential remediation of locations where it has conducted business and has environmental liabilities from historical or recent activities.

Portland Harbor

The Company has been notified by the US Environmental Protection Agency ("EPA") under the Comprehensive Environmental Response, Compensation and Liability Act ("CERCLA") that it is one of at least 100 potentially responsible parties ("PRPs") that own or operate or formerly owned or operated sites adjacent to the Portland Harbor Superfund site (the "Site"). The precise nature and extent of any cleanup of the Site, the parties to be involved, the process to be followed for any cleanup and the allocation of the costs for any cleanup among responsible parties have not yet been determined, but the process of identifying additional PRPs and beginning allocation of costs is underway. It is unclear to what extent the Company will be liable for environmental costs or natural resource damage claims or third party contribution or damage claims with respect to the Site. While the Company participated in certain preliminary Site study efforts, it is not party to the consent order entered into by the EPA with certain other PRPs, referred to as the "Lower Willamette Group" ("LWG"), for a remedial investigation/feasibility study ("RI/FS").

During fiscal 2007, the Company and certain other parties agreed to an interim settlement with the LWG under which the Company made a cash contribution to the LWG RI/FS. The Company has also joined with more than 80 other PRPs, including the LWG, in a voluntary process to establish an allocation of costs at the Site. These parties have selected an allocation team and are finalizing an allocation process design agreement. The LWG has also commenced federal court litigation, which has been stayed, seeking to bring additional parties into the allocation process.

In January 2008, the Natural Resource Damages Trustee Council ("Trustees") for Portland Harbor invited the Company and other PRPs to participate in funding and implementing the Natural Resource Injury Assessment for the Site. Following meetings among the Trustees and the PRPs, a funding and participation agreement was negotiated under which the participating PRPs agreed to fund the first phase of natural resource damage assessment. The Company joined in that Phase I agreement and paid a portion of those costs. The Company did not participate in funding the second phase of the natural resource damage assessment.

The cost of the investigations and any remediation associated with the Site will not be reasonably estimable until completion of the data review and further investigations now being conducted by the LWG and the Trustees and the selection and approval of a remedy by the EPA. However, given the size of the Site and the nature of the conditions identified to date, the total cost of the investigations and remediation is likely to be substantial. In addition, because there has not been a determination of the total cost of the investigations, the remediation that will be required, the amount of natural resource damages or how the costs of the ongoing investigations and any remedy and natural resource damages will be allocated among the PRPs, it is not possible to estimate the costs which the Company might incur in connection with the Site, although such costs could be material to the Company's financial position or results of operations. The Company has insurance policies that we believe will provide reimbursement for costs we incur for defense and remediation in connection with the Site, although there is no assurance that those policies will cover all of the costs which we may incur. In fiscal 2006, the Company recorded a liability for its then estimated share of the costs of the investigation incurred by the LWG to date. As of August 31, 2010 and 2009, the Company's reserve for third party investigation costs of the Site was $1 million.

The Oregon Department of Environmental Quality is separately providing oversight of voluntary investigation by the Company involving the Company's sites adjacent to the Portland Harbor which are focused on controlling any current "uplands" releases of contaminants into the Willamette River. No reserves have been established in connection with these investigations because the extent of contamination (if any) and the Company's responsibility for the contamination (if any) has not yet been determined.

Other Metals Recycling Business Sites

As of August 31, 2010, the Company had environmental reserves related to various MRB sites of $24 million. The reserves, which range in amounts from less than $1 million to $2 million per site, relate to the potential future remediation of soil contamination, groundwater contamination and storm water runoff issues. No material environmental compliance enforcement proceedings are currently pending related to these sites.

Auto Parts Business

As of August 31, 2010, the Company had environmental reserves related to various APB sites of $15 million. The reserves, which range in amounts from less than $1 million to $2 million per site, relate to the potential future remediation of soil contamination, groundwater contamination and storm water runoff issues. No material environmental compliance enforcement proceedings are currently pending related to these sites.

Steel Manufacturing Business

SMB's electric arc furnace generates dust ("EAF dust") that is classified as hazardous waste by the EPA because of its zinc and lead content. As a result, the Company captures the EAF dust and ships it in specialized rail cars to a domestic firm that applies a treatment that allows the EAF dust to be delisted as hazardous waste so it can be disposed of as a non-hazardous solid waste.

SMB has an operating permit issued under Title V of the Clean Air Act Amendments of 1990, which governs certain air quality standards. The permit was first issued in 1998 and has since been renewed through 2012. The permit is based on an annual production capacity of 950 thousand tons.

SMB had no environmental reserves as of August 31, 2010.

Other than Portland Harbor, which is discussed above, management currently believes that adequate provision has been made in the financial statements for the potential impact of these issues and that the outcomes will not significantly impact the financial position or the results of operations of the Company, although they may have a material impact on earnings for a particular quarter. Historically, the amounts the Company has ultimately paid for such remediation activities have not been material.

Litigation

2.152

PPG INDUSTRIES, INC. (DEC)

CONSOLIDATED BALANCE SHEET (in part)

	December 31	
(millions)	2010	2009
Current liabilities		
Short-term debt and current portion of long-term debt (See Note 9)	$ 28	$ 272
Asbestos settlement (See Note 16)	578	534
Accounts payable and accrued liabilities (See Note 4)	3,002	2,648
Business restructuring (See Note 8)	17	123
Total current liabilities	$3,625	$3,577

NOTES TO CONSOLIDATED FINANCIAL STATEMENTS

16. Commitments and Contingent Liabilities (in part)

PPG is involved in a number of lawsuits and claims, both actual and potential, including some that it has asserted against others, in which substantial monetary damages are sought. These lawsuits and claims, the most significant of which are described below, relate to contract, patent, environmental, product liability, antitrust and other matters arising out of the conduct of PPG's current and past business activities. To the extent that these lawsuits and claims involve personal injury and property damage, PPG believes it has adequate insurance; however, certain of PPG's insurers are contesting coverage with respect to some of these claims, and other insurers, as they had prior to the asbestos settlement described below, may contest coverage with respect to some of the asbestos claims if the settlement is not implemented. PPG's lawsuits and claims against others include claims against insurers and other third parties with respect to actual and contingent losses related to environmental, asbestos and other matters.

The results of any future litigation and the above lawsuits and claims are inherently unpredictable. However, management believes that, in the aggregate, the outcome of all lawsuits and claims involving PPG, including asbestos-related claims in the event the settlement described below does not become effective, will not have a material effect on PPG's consolidated financial position or liquidity; however, such outcome may be material to the results of operations of any particular period in which costs, if any, are recognized.

Asbestos Matters

For over 30 years, PPG has been a defendant in lawsuits involving claims alleging personal injury from exposure to asbestos. Most of PPG's potential exposure relates to allegations by plaintiffs that PPG should be liable for injuries involving asbestos-containing thermal insulation products, known as Unibestos, manufactured and distributed by Pittsburgh Corning Corporation ("PC"). PPG and Corning Incorporated are each 50% shareholders of PC. PPG has denied responsibility for, and has defended, all claims for any injuries caused by PC products. As of the April 16, 2000 order which stayed and enjoined asbestos claims against PPG (as discussed below), PPG was one of many defendants in numerous asbestos-related lawsuits involving approximately 114,000 claims served on PPG. During the period of the stay, PPG generally has not been aware of the dispositions, if any, of these asbestos claims.

Background of PC Bankruptcy Plan of Reorganization

On April 16, 2000, PC filed for Chapter 11 Bankruptcy in the U.S. Bankruptcy Court for the Western District of Pennsylvania located in Pittsburgh, Pa. Accordingly, in the first quarter of 2000, PPG recorded an after-tax charge of $35 million for the write-off of all of its investment in PC. As a consequence of the bankruptcy filing and various motions and orders in that proceeding, the asbestos litigation against PPG (as well as against PC) has been stayed and the filing of additional asbestos suits against them has been enjoined, until 30 days after the effective date of a confirmed plan of reorganization for PC substantially in accordance with the settlement arrangement among PPG and several other parties discussed below. The stay may be terminated if the Bankruptcy Court determines that such a plan will not be confirmed, or the settlement arrangement set forth below is not likely to be consummated.

On May 14, 2002, PPG announced that it had agreed with several other parties, including certain of its insurance carriers, the official committee representing asbestos claimants in the PC bankruptcy, and the legal representatives of future asbestos claimants appointed in the PC bankruptcy, on the terms of a settlement arrangement relating to certain asbestos claims against PPG and PC (the "2002 PPG Settlement Arrangement").

On March 28, 2003, Corning Incorporated announced that it had separately reached its own arrangement with the representatives of asbestos claimants for the settlement of certain asbestos claims against Corning and PC (the "2003 Corning Settlement Arrangement").

The terms of the 2002 PPG Settlement Arrangement and the 2003 Corning Settlement Arrangement were incorporated into a bankruptcy reorganization plan for PC along with a disclosure statement describing the plan, which PC filed with the Bankruptcy Court on April 30, 2003. Amendments to the plan and disclosure statement were subsequently filed. On November 26, 2003, after considering objections to the second amended disclosure statement and plan of reorganization, the Bankruptcy Court entered an order approving such disclosure statement and directing that it be sent to creditors, including asbestos claimants, for voting. In March 2004, the second amended PC plan of reorganization (the "second amended PC plan of reorganization") received the required votes to approve the plan with a channeling injunction for present and future asbestos claimants under §524(g) of the Bankruptcy Code. After voting results for the second amended PC plan of reorganization were received, the Bankruptcy Court judge conducted a hearing regarding the fairness of the settlement, including whether the plan would be fair with respect to present and future claimants, whether such claimants would be treated in substantially the same manner, and whether the protection provided to PPG and its participating insurers would be fair in view of the assets they would convey to the asbestos settlement trust (the "Trust") to be established as part of the second amended PC plan of reorganization. At that hearing, creditors and other parties in interest raised objections to the second amended PC plan of reorganization. Following that hearing, the Bankruptcy Court scheduled oral arguments for the contested items.

The Bankruptcy Court heard oral arguments on the contested items on November 17-18, 2004. At the conclusion of the hearing, the Bankruptcy Court agreed to consider certain post-hearing written submissions. In a further development, on February 2, 2005, the Bankruptcy Court established a briefing schedule to address whether certain aspects of a decision of the U.S. Third Circuit Court of Appeals in an unrelated case had any applicability to the second amended PC plan of reorganization. Oral arguments on these matters were subsequently held in March 2005. During an omnibus hearing on February 28, 2006, the Bankruptcy Court judge stated that she was prepared to rule on the PC plan of reorganization in the near future, provided certain amendments were made to the plan. Those amendments were filed, as directed, on March 17, 2006. After further conferences and supplemental briefings, in December 2006, the court denied confirmation of the second amended PC plan of reorganization, on the basis that the plan was too broad in the treatment of allegedly independent asbestos claims not associated with PC.

Terms of 2002 PPG Settlement Arrangement

PPG had no obligation to pay any amounts under the 2002 PPG Settlement Arrangement until 30 days after the second amended PC plan of reorganization was finally approved by an appropriate court order that was no longer subject to appellate review (the "Effective Date"). If the second amended PC plan of reorganization had been approved as proposed, PPG and certain of its insurers (along with PC) would have made payments on the Effective Date to the Trust, which would have provided the sole source of payment for all present and future asbestos bodily injury claims against PPG, its subsidiaries or PC alleged to be caused by the manufacture, distribution or sale of asbestos products by these companies. PPG would have conveyed the following assets to the Trust: (i) the stock it owns in PC and Pittsburgh Corning Europe, (ii) 1,388,889 shares of PPG's common stock and (iii) aggregate cash payments to the Trust of approximately $998 million, payable according to a fixed payment schedule over 21 years, beginning on June 30, 2003, or, if later, the Effective Date. PPG would have had the right, in its sole discretion, to prepay these cash payments to the Trust at any time at a discount rate of 5.5% per annum as of the prepayment date. In addition to the conveyance of these assets, PPG would have paid $30 million in legal fees and expenses on behalf of the Trust to recover proceeds from certain historical insurance assets, including policies issued by certain insurance carriers that were not participating in the settlement, the rights to which would have been assigned to the Trust by PPG.

Under the proposed 2002 PPG Settlement Arrangement, PPG's participating historical insurance carriers would have made cash payments to the Trust of approximately $1.7 billion between the Effective Date and 2023. These payments could also have been prepaid to the Trust at any time at a discount rate of 5.5% per annum as of the prepayment date. In addition, as referenced above, PPG would have assigned to the Trust its rights, insofar as they related to the asbestos claims to have been resolved by the Trust, to the proceeds of policies issued by certain insurance carriers that were not participating in the 2002 PPG Settlement Arrangement and from the estates of insolvent insurers and state insurance guaranty funds.

Under the proposed 2002 PPG Settlement Arrangement, PPG would have granted asbestos releases to all participating insurers, subject to a coverage-in-place agreement with certain insurers for the continuing coverage of premises claims (discussed below). PPG would have granted certain participating insurers full policy releases on primary policies and full product liability releases on excess coverage policies. PPG would have also granted certain other participating excess insurers credit against their product liability coverage limits.

If the second amended PC plan of reorganization incorporating the terms of the 2002 PPG Settlement Arrangement and the 2003 Corning Settlement Arrangement had been approved by the Bankruptcy Court, the Court would have entered a channeling injunction under §524(g) and other provisions of the Bankruptcy Code, prohibiting present and future claimants from asserting bodily injury claims after the Effective Date against PPG or its subsidiaries or PC relating to the manufacture, distribution or sale of asbestos-containing products by PC or PPG or its subsidiaries. The injunction would have also prohibited codefendants in those cases from asserting claims against PPG for contribution, indemnification or other recovery. All such claims would have been filed with the Trust and only paid from the assets of the Trust.

Modified Third Amended PC Plan of Reorganization

To address the issues raised by the Bankruptcy Court in its December 2006 ruling, the interested parties engaged in extensive negotiations regarding the terms of a third amended PC plan of reorganization, including modifications to the 2002 PPG Settlement Arrangement. A modified third amended PC plan of reorganization (the "third amended PC plan of reorganization"), including a modified PPG settlement arrangement (the "2009 PPG Settlement Arrangement"), was filed with the Bankruptcy Court on January 29, 2009. The parties also filed a disclosure statement describing the third amended PC plan of reorganization with the court. The third amended PC plan of reorganization also includes a modified settlement arrangement of Corning Incorporated.

Several creditors and other interested parties filed objections to the disclosure statement. Those objections were overruled by the Bankruptcy Court by order dated July 6, 2009 approving the disclosure statement. The third amended PC plan of reorganization and disclosure statement were then sent to creditors, including asbestos claimants, for voting. The report of the voting agent, filed on February 18, 2010, reveals that all voting classes, including asbestos claimants, voted overwhelmingly in favor of the third amended PC plan of reorganization, which included the 2009 PPG Settlement Arrangement. In light of the favorable vote on the third amended PC plan of reorganization, the Bankruptcy Court conducted a hearing regarding the fairness of the proposed plan, including whether (i) the plan would be fair with respect to present and future claimants, (ii) such claimants would be treated in substantially the same manner, and (iii) the protection provided to PPG and its participating insurers would be fair in view of the assets they would convey to the Trust to be established as part of the third amended PC plan of reorganization. The hearing was held in June of 2010. The remaining objecting parties (a number of objections were resolved through plan amendments and stipulations filed before the hearing) appeared at the hearing and presented their cases. At the conclusion of the hearing, the Bankruptcy Court established a briefing schedule for its consideration of confirmation of the plan and the objections to confirmation. That briefing was completed and final oral arguments held in October 2010. Following those arguments, the Bankruptcy Court, after considering the objections to the third amended PC plan of reorganization, will enter a confirmation order if all requirements to confirm a plan of reorganization under the Bankruptcy Code have been satisfied. Such an order could be appealed to the U.S. District Court for the Western District of Pennsylvania. Assuming that the District Court approves a confirmation order, interested parties could appeal the order to the U.S. Third Circuit Court of Appeals and subsequently could seek review by the U.S. Supreme Court.

The 2009 PPG Settlement Arrangement will not become effective until the third amended PC plan of reorganization is finally approved by an appropriate court order that is no longer subject to appellate review, and PPG's initial contributions will not be due until 30 business days thereafter (the "Funding Effective Date").

Asbestos Claims Subject to Bankruptcy Court's Channeling Injunction

If the third amended PC plan of reorganization is approved by the Bankruptcy Court and becomes effective, a channeling injunction will be entered under §524(g) of the Bankruptcy Code prohibiting present and future claimants from asserting asbestos claims against PC. With regard to PPG, the channeling injunction by its terms will prohibit present and future claimants from asserting claims against PPG that arise, in whole or in part, out of exposure to Unibestos, or any other asbestos or asbestos-containing products manufactured, sold and/or distributed by PC, or asbestos on or emanating from any PC premises. The injunction by its terms will also prohibit codefendants in these cases that are subject to the channeling injunction from asserting claims against PPG for contribution, indemnification or other recovery. Such injunction will also preclude the prosecution of claims against PPG arising from alleged exposure to asbestos or asbestos-containing products to the extent that a claimant is alleging or seeking to impose liability, directly or indirectly, for the conduct of, claims against or demands on PC by reason of PPG's: (i) ownership of a financial interest in PC; (ii) involvement in the management of PC, or service as an officer, director or employee of PC or a related party; (iii) provision of insurance to PC or a related party; or (iv) involvement in a financial transaction affecting the financial condition of PC or a related party. The foregoing PC related claims are referred to as "PC Relationship Claims" and constitute, in PPG management's opinion, the vast majority of the pending asbestos personal injury claims against PPG. All claims channeled to the Trust will be paid only from the assets of the Trust.

Asbestos Claims Retained by PPG

The channeling injunction provided for under the third amended PC plan of reorganization will not extend to any claim against PPG that arises out of exposure to any asbestos or asbestos-containing products manufactured, sold and/or distributed by PPG or its subsidiaries that is not a PC Relationship Claim, and in this respect differs from the channeling injunction contemplated by the second amended PC plan of reorganization filed in 2003. While management believes that the vast majority of the approximately 114,000 claims against PPG alleging personal injury from exposure to asbestos relate to products manufactured, distributed or sold by PC, the potential liability for any non-PC Relationship Claims will be retained by PPG. Because a determination of whether an asbestos claim is a non-PC Relationship Claim would typically not be known until shortly before trial and because the filing and prosecution of asbestos claims (other than certain premises claims) against PPG has been enjoined since April 2000, the actual number of non-PC Relationship Claims that may be pending at the expiration of the stay or the number of additional claims that may be filed against PPG in the future cannot be determined at this time. PPG does not expect the Bankruptcy Court to lift the stay until after confirmation or rejection of the third amended PC plan of reorganization. PPG intends to defend against all such claims vigorously and their ultimate resolution in the court system is expected to occur over a period of years.

In addition, similar to what was contemplated by the second amended PC plan of reorganization, the channeling injunction will not extend to claims against PPG alleging personal injury caused by asbestos on premises owned, leased or occupied by PPG (so called "premises claims"), which generally have been subject to the stay imposed by the Bankruptcy Court. Historically, a small proportion of the claims against PPG and its subsidiaries have been premises claims, and based upon review and analysis, PPG believes that the number of premises claims currently comprises less than 2% of the total asbestos related claims against PPG. Beginning in late 2006, the Bankruptcy Court lifted the stay with respect to certain premises claims against PPG. As a result, PPG and its primary insurers have settled approximately 500 premises claims. PPG's insurers agreed to provide insurance coverage for a major portion of the payments made in connection with the settled claims, and PPG accrued the portion of the settlement amounts not covered by insurance. PPG, in conjunction with its primary insurers as appropriate, evaluates the factual, medical, and other relevant information pertaining to additional claims as they are being considered for potential settlement. The number of such claims under consideration for potential settlement, currently approximately 300, varies from time to time. Premises claims remain subject to the stay, as outlined above, although certain claimants have requested the Court to lift the stay with respect to these claims and the stay has been lifted as to some claims. PPG believes that any financial exposure resulting from such premises claims, taking into account available insurance coverage, will not have a material adverse effect on PPG's consolidated financial position, liquidity or results of operations.

PPG's Funding Obligations

PPG has no obligation to pay any amounts under the third amended PC plan of reorganization until the Funding Effective Date. If the third amended PC plan of reorganization is approved, PPG and certain of its insurers will make the following contributions to the Trust. On the Funding Effective Date, PPG will relinquish any claim to its equity interest in PC, convey the stock it owns in Pittsburgh Corning Europe and transfer 1,388,889 shares of PPG's common stock or cash equal to the fair value of such shares as defined in the 2009 PPG Settlement Arrangement. PPG will make aggregate cash payments to the Trust of approximately $825 million, payable according to a fixed payment schedule over a period ending in 2023. The first payment is due on the Funding Effective Date. PPG would have the right, in its sole discretion, to prepay these cash payments to the Trust at

any time at a discount rate of 5.5% per annum as of the prepayment date. PPG's historical insurance carriers participating in the third amended PC plan of reorganization will also make cash payments to the Trust of approximately $1.7 billion between the Funding Effective Date and 2027. These payments could also be prepaid to the Trust at any time at a discount rate of 5.5% per annum as of the prepayment date. PPG will grant asbestos releases and indemnifications to all participating insurers, subject to amended coverage-in-place arrangements with certain insurers for remaining coverage of premises claims. PPG will grant certain participating insurers full policy releases on primary policies and full product liability releases on excess coverage policies. PPG will also grant certain other participating excess insurers credit against their product liability coverage limits.

PPG's obligation under the 2009 PPG Settlement Arrangement at December 31, 2008 was $162 million less than the amount that would have been due under the 2002 PPG Settlement Arrangement. This reduction is attributable to a number of negotiated provisions in the 2009 PPG Settlement Arrangement, including the provisions relating to the channeling injunction under which PPG retains liability for any non-PC Relationship Claims. PPG will retain such amount as a reserve for asbestos-related claims that will not be channeled to the Trust, as this amount represents PPG's best estimate of its liability for these claims. PPG does not have sufficient current claim information or settlement history on which to base a better estimate of this liability, in light of the fact that the Bankruptcy Court's stay has been in effect since 2000. As a result, PPG's reserve at December 31, 2010 and 2009 for asbestos-related claims that will not be channeled to the Trust is $162 million. In addition, under the 2009 PPG Settlement Arrangement, PPG will retain for its own account rights to recover proceeds from certain historical insurance assets, including policies issued by non-participating insurers. Rights to recover these proceeds would have been assigned to the Trust by PPG under the 2002 PPG Settlement Arrangement.

Following the effective date of the third amended PC plan of reorganization and the lifting of the Bankruptcy Court stay, PPG will monitor the activity associated with asbestos claims which are not channeled to the Trust pursuant to the third amended PC plan of reorganization, and evaluate its estimated liability for such claims and related insurance assets then available to the Company as well as underlying assumptions on a periodic basis to determine whether any adjustment to its reserve for these claims is required.

Of the total obligation of $821 million and $772 million under the 2009 PPG Settlement Arrangement at December 31, 2010 and 2009, respectively, $578 million and $534 million are reported as a current liabilities and the present value of the payments due in the years 2012 to 2023 totaling $243 and 2011 to 2023 totaling $238 million are reported as a non-current liability in the accompanying consolidated balance sheet as of December 31, 2010 and 2009. The future accretion of the non-current portion of the liability will total $136 million at December 31, 2010, and be reported as expense in the consolidated statement of income over the period through 2023, as follows (in millions):

2011	$ 14
2012	14
2013–2023	108
Total	$136

The following table summarizes the impact on PPG's financial statements for the three years ended December 31, 2010 resulting from the 2009 PPG Settlement Arrangement including the change in fair value of the stock to be transferred to the Trust and the equity forward instrument (see Note 12, "Derivative Financial Instruments and Hedge Activities") and the increase in the net present value of the future payments to be made to the Trust.

	Consolidated Balance Sheet			
	Asbestos Settlement Liability		Equity Forward (Asset) Liability	Pretax Charge
(Millions)	Current	Long-Term		
Balance as of January 1, 2008	$ 593	$324	$(18)	$ 24
Change in fair value:				
PPG stock	(39)	—	—	(39)
Equity forward instrument	—	—	24	24
Accretion of asbestos liability	—	19	—	19
Reclassification	38	(38)	—	—
Impact of 2009 PPG settlement arrangement[1]	(101)	(61)	—	—
Balance as of and activity for the year ended December 31, 2008	$ 491	$244	$ 6	$ 4
Change in fair value:				
PPG stock	23	—	—	23
Equity forward instrument	—	—	(24)	(24)
Accretion of asbestos liability	—	14	—	14
Reclassification	20	(20)	—	—
Balance as of and activity for the year ended December 31, 2009	$ 534	$238	$(18)	$ 13
Change in fair value:				
PPG stock	35	—	—	35
Equity forward instrument	—	—	(37)	(37)
Accretion of asbestos liability	—	14	—	14
Reclassification	9	(9)	—	—
Balance as of and activity for the year ended December 31, 2010	$ 578	$243	$(55)	$ 12

[1] Amounts have been reclassified to Other liabilities and retained as a reserve for asbestos-related claims that will not be channeled to the Trust. The balance in this reserve at December 31, 2010 remains $162 million.

The fair value of the equity forward instrument is included as an Other current asset as of December 31, 2010 and 2009 in the accompanying consolidated balance sheet. Payments under the fixed payment schedule require annual payments that are due each June. The current portion of the asbestos settlement liability included in the accompanying consolidated balance sheet as of December 31, 2010, consists of all such payments required through June 2011, the fair value of PPG's common stock and the value of PPG's investment in Pittsburgh Corning Europe. The amount due June 30, 2012 of $16 million and the net present value of the remaining payments is included in the long-term asbestos settlement liability in the accompanying consolidated balance sheet as of December 31, 2010.

Derivatives

2.153

RETAIL VENTURES, INC. (JAN)

CONSOLIDATED BALANCE SHEET (in part)

January 30, 2010 and January 31, 2009
(In thousands, except share amounts)

	January 30, 2010	January 31, 2009
Accounts payable	$120,038	$ 93,088
Accounts payable to related parties	1,239	3,125
Accrued expenses:		
Compensation	27,056	12,632
Taxes	29,682	14,857
Gift cards and merchandise credits	17,774	15,491
Guarantees from discontinued operations	2,800	2,909
Other	36,162	31,175
Warrant liability	23,068	6,292
Current maturities of long-term debt		250
Current liabilities held for sale		76,030
Total current liabilities	$257,819	$255,849

NOTES TO CONSOLIDATED FINANCIAL STATEMENTS

12. Warrants

Warrants

The detached warrants with dual optionality issued in connection with previously paid credit facilities qualified as derivatives under ASC 815, *Derivatives and Hedging*. The fair values of the warrants have been recorded on the balance sheet within current liabilities. As of January 30, 2010, the Company had outstanding 3,683,959 and as of January 31, 2009, the Company had outstanding 12,017,292 warrants. On June 10, 2009, the 8,333,333 outstanding Conversion Warrants expired and Retail Ventures repaid in full the $250,000 remaining balance along with the related accrued interest on the Senior Non-Convertible Loan, as amended and restated on August 16, 2006, made by Schottenstein Stores Corporation in favor of Value City, which loan was assumed by RVI in connection with the disposition of its 81% ownership interest in the Value City operations on January 23, 2008. The warrants outstanding as of January 30, 2010 expire on June 11, 2012.

During fiscal 2007, Retail Ventures issued 1,333,333 of its Common Shares at an exercise price of $4.50 per share to Cerberus in connection with Cerberus' exercise of its remaining Conversion Warrants. In connection with this exercise, Retail Ventures received $6.0 million and reclassified $19.6 million from the warrant liability to paid in capital during fiscal 2007.

For fiscal 2009, the Company recorded a non-cash charge of $16.8 million for the change in fair value of warrants, of which the portion held by related parties was a non-cash charge of $6.9 million. For fiscal 2008 and fiscal 2007, the Company recorded a non-cash reduction of expense of $35.9 million and $154.6 million, respectively, for the change in fair value of warrants, of which the portion held by related parties was a non-cash reduction of expenses of $30.0 million and $151.9 million, respectively. No tax benefit has been recognized in connection with this charge. These derivative instruments do not qualify for hedge accounting under ASC 815, *Derivatives and Hedging*, therefore, changes in the fair values are recognized in earnings in the period of change.

Retail Ventures estimates the fair values of derivatives based on the Black-Scholes Pricing Model using current market rates and records all derivatives on the balance sheet at fair value. The fair market value of the warrants was $23.1 million and $6.3 million at January 30, 2010 and January 31, 2009 and, respectively. The values ascribed to warrants were estimated using the Black-Scholes Pricing Model with the following assumptions.

	Term Warrants		Conversion Warrants
	January 30, 2010	January 31, 2009	January 31, 2009
Assumptions:			
Risk-free interest rate	0.8%	1.3%	0.3%
Expected volatility of common shares	123.0%	95.9%	114.3%
Expected option term	2.4 years	3.4 years	0.4 years
Expected dividend yield	0.0%	0.0%	0.0%

VCHI Acquisition Co. Warrants

On January 23, 2008, Retail Ventures disposed of an 81% ownership interest in its Value City Department Stores business to VCHI Acquisition Co., a newly formed entity owned by VCDS Acquisition Holdings, LLC, Emerald Capital Management LLC and Crystal Value, LLC. As part of the transaction, Retail Ventures issued VCHI Warrants to VCHI Acquisition Co. to purchase 150,000 RVI Common Shares, at an exercise price of $10.00 per share, and exercisable within 18 months of January 23, 2008. The VCHI Warrants expired in the quarter ended August 1, 2009.

An update to ASC 815-40, *Derivatives and Hedging, Contracts in Entity's Own Equity*, resulted in the redesignation and reclassification of the VCHI Warrants from Equity to Liabilities within the balance sheets during the quarter ended May 2, 2009. In addition, the VCHI Warrants were marked to market and continued to be marked to market through their expiration date. A charge of $0.1 million was recorded in other comprehensive income as of February 1, 2009, which represented the change in fair value of the VCHI Warrants from the date of issuance to the date of adoption of ASC 815-40. During fiscal 2009, the Company recorded an immaterial non-cash charge related to the change in fair value of the VCHI warrants.

Rebates and Incentives

2.154

PENTAIR, INC. (DEC)

CONSOLIDATED BALANCE SHEET (in part)

(In thousands, except share and per-share data)	December 31, 2010	December 31, 2009
Current liabilities		
Short-term borrowings	$ 4,933	$ 2,205
Current maturities of long-term debt	18	81
Accounts payable	262,357	207,661
Employee compensation and benefits	107,995	74,254
Current pension and post-retirement benefits	8,733	8,948
Accrued product claims and warranties	42,295	34,288
Income taxes	5,964	5,659
Accrued rebates and sales incentives	33,559	27,554
Other current liabilities	80,942	85,629
Total current liabilities	$546,796	$446,279

NOTES TO CONSOLIDATED FINANCIAL STATEMENTS

1. Summary of Significant Accounting Policies (in part)

Revenue Recognition (in part)

Pricing and Sales Incentives

We record estimated reductions to revenue for customer programs and incentive offerings including pricing arrangements, promotions and other volume-based incentives at the later of the date revenue is recognized or the incentive is offered. Sales incentives given to our customers are recorded as a reduction of revenue unless we (1) receive an identifiable benefit for the goods or services in exchange for the consideration and (2) we can reasonably estimate the fair value of the benefit received. The following represents a description of our pricing arrangements, promotions and other volume-based incentives:

Pricing Arrangements

Pricing is established up front with our customers and we record sales at the agreed-upon net selling price. However, one of our businesses allows customers to apply for a refund of a percentage of the original purchase price if they can demonstrate sales to a qualifying OEM customer. At the time of sale, we estimate the anticipated refund to be paid based on historical experience and reduce sales for the probable cost of the discount. The cost of these refunds is recorded as a reduction in gross sales.

Promotions

Our primary promotional activity is what we refer to as cooperative advertising. Under our cooperative advertising programs, we agree to pay the customer a fixed percentage of sales as an allowance that may be used to advertise and promote our products. The customer is generally not required to provide evidence of the advertisement or promotion. We recognize the cost of this cooperative advertising at the time of sale. The cost of this program is recorded as a reduction in gross sales.

Volume-Based Incentives

These incentives involve rebates that are negotiated up front with the customer and are redeemable only if the customer achieves a specified cumulative level of sales or sales increase. Under these incentive programs, at the time of sale, we reforecast the anticipated rebate to be paid based on forecasted sales levels. These forecasts are updated at least quarterly for each customer and sales are reduced for the anticipated cost of the rebate. If the forecasted sales for a customer changes, the accrual for rebates is adjusted to reflect the new amount of rebates expected to be earned by the customer.

Asset Retirement Obligation

2.155

JDS UNIPHASE CORPORATION (JUN)

CONSOLIDATED BALANCE SHEET (in part)

(In millions, except share and par value data)

	July 3, 2010	June 27, 2009
Current liabilities:		
Accounts payable	$137.4	$106.6
Current portion of long-term debt	0.2	0.2
Accrued payroll and related expenses	62.9	45.7
Income taxes payable	19.8	20.3
Deferred income taxes	2.1	5.6
Restructuring accrual	7.1	16.6
Warranty accrual	7.3	7.3
Accrued expenses	47.7	56.0
Other current liabilities	66.4	51.6
Total current liabilities	$350.9	$309.9

NOTES TO CONSOLIDATED FINANCIAL STATEMENTS

Note 1. Description of Business and Summary of Significant Accounting Policies (in part)

Asset Retirement Obligations

Asset retirement obligations ("ARO") are legal obligations associated with the retirement of long-lived assets. These liabilities are initially recorded at fair value and the related asset retirement costs are capitalized by increasing the carrying amount of the related assets by the same amount as the liability. Asset retirement costs are subsequently depreciated over the useful lives of the related assets. Subsequent to initial recognition, the Company records period-to-period changes in the ARO liability resulting from the passage of time and revisions to either the timing or the amount of the original estimate of undiscounted cash flows. The Company derecognizes ARO liabilities when the related obligations are settled. At July 3, 2010 and June 27, 2009, $0.5 million and $7.3 million of ARO was included in the Consolidated Balance Sheets in "Other current liabilities" and the remainder of $7.4 million and $6.6 million was included in "Other non-current liabilities."

(In millions)	Balance at Beginning of Period	Liabilities Incurred	Liabilities Settled	Accretion Expense	Revisions to Estimates	Balance at End of Period
Asset retirement obligations:						
Year ended July 3, 2010	$13.9	0.7	(7.2)	0.5	—	$ 7.9
Year ended June 27, 2009	$13.1	0.4	(0.4)	0.5	0.3	$13.9

LONG-TERM DEBT

PRESENTATION

2.156 FASB ASC 470 addresses classification determination for specific debt obligations. FASB ASC 470-10-45-11 states that the current liability classification is intended to include long-term obligations that are or will be callable by the creditor either because the debtors' violation of a provision of the debt agreement at the balance sheet date makes the obligation callable, or the violation, if not cured within a specified grace period, will make the obligation callable. Accordingly, such callable obligations should be classified as current liabilities, unless one of the following conditions is met:

- The creditor has waived or subsequently lost the right to demand payment for more than one year, or operating cycle if longer, from the balance sheet date. For example, the debtor may have cured the violation after the balance sheet date, and the obligation is not callable at the time the financial statements are issued or available to be issued.
- For long-term obligations containing a grace period within which the debtor may cure the violation, it is probable that the violation will be cured within that period, thus preventing the obligation from becoming callable.

DISCLOSURE

2.157 FASB ASC 470 requires, for each of the five years following the date of the latest balance sheet presented, disclosure of the combined aggregate amount of maturities and sinking fund requirements for all long-term borrowings. In addition, FASB ASC 440, *Commitments*, requires disclosure of terms and conditions provided in loan agreements, such as assets pledged as collateral and covenants to limit additional debt, maintain working capital, and restrict dividends. Regulation S-X has similar or expanded requirements for matters such as debt details, assets subject to lien, defaults, dividend restrictions, and changes in long-term debt.

2.158 FASB ASC 825 requires disclosure of both the fair value and bases for estimating the fair value of long-term debt, unless it is not practicable to estimate the value.

2.159

TABLE 2-13: LONG-TERM DEBT*

Table 2-13 summarizes the types of long-term debt most frequently disclosed by the survey companies.

	Number of Entities 2010
Unsecured	
Notes	360
Credit agreement/revolving credit	180
Debentures	91
Loans	77
Foreign borrowing	30
Commercial paper	24
Bonds	31
Employee stock ownership plan loans	4
Other, described	26
Collateralized	
Notes	70
Credit agreements	62
Loans	32
Mortgages	24
Industrial revenue/development bonds	31
Pollution control bonds	3
Leases	101
Receivable financing/securitization	24
Other, described	6
Convertible	
Debentures	19
Notes	64
Debt exchangeable into stock of another company...	2
Other, described	3

* Appearing in the balance sheet or notes to financial statements, or both.
Note: Classification of long-term debt changed for this edition, so no prior year data are available.

PRESENTATION AND DISCLOSURE EXCERPTS

Unsecured

2.160

PILGRIM'S PRIDE CORPORATION (DEC)

CONSOLIDATED BALANCE SHEETS (in part)

(In thousands, except shares and per share data)	December 26, 2010	September 26, 2009
Liabilities and stockholders' equity:		
Accounts payable	$ 329,780	$ 182,173
Accounts payable to JBS USA, LLC	7,212	—
Accrued expenses	297,594	309,259
Pre-petition obligations	346	—
Income taxes payable	6,814	—
Current deferred tax liabilities	38,745	16,732
Current maturities of long-term debt	58,144	—
Total current liabilities	738,635	508,164
Long-term debt, less current maturities	1,281,160	41,062
Deferred tax liabilities	3,476	22,213
Other long-term liabilities	117,031	98,783
Total liabilities not subject to compromise	2,140,302	670,222
Liabilities subject to compromise	$ —	$2,233,161

NOTES TO CONSOLIDATED FINANCIAL STATEMENTS

12. Long-Term Debt and Other Borrowing Arrangements

Long-term debt consisted of the following components:

(In thousands)	Maturity	December 26, 2010	September 26, 2009
Senior notes, at 7 7/8%, net of unaccreted discounts	2018	$ 496,393	$ —
Senior unsecured notes, at 7 5/8%	2015	116	400,000
Senior subordinated unsecured notes, at 8 3/8%	2017	3,517	250,000
The Exit Credit Facility with two term notes payable at 5.313% and one term note payable at 9.00%	2014	632,500	—
The Exit Credit Facility with one revolving note payable on which the Company had funds borrowed at 4.183% and 6.75%	2012	205,300	—
Pre-petition BMO Facility with notes payable at LIBOR plus 1.25% to LIBOR plus 2.75%	2013	—	218,936
ING Credit Agreement (defined below) with notes payable at LIBOR plus 1.65% to LIBOR plus 3.125%	2011	—	41,062
Pre-petition CoBank Facility with four notes payable at LIBOR plus a spread, one note payable at 7.34% and one note payable at 7.56%	2016	—	1,126,398
Other	Various	1,478	8,698
Long-term debt		1,339,304	2,045,094
Less: Current maturities of long-term debt		(58,144)	—
Less: Long-term debt subject to compromise		—	(2,004,032)
Long-term debt, less current maturities		$1,281,160	$ 41,062

Debt Obligations

Senior and Subordinated Notes. On December 15, 2010, the Company closed on the sale of $500.0 million of 7 7/8% Senior Notes due 2018 (the "2018 Notes"). The 2018 Notes are unsecured obligations of the Company and are guaranteed by one of the Company's subsidiaries. Interest is payable on December 15 and June 15 of each year, commencing on June 15, 2011. The proceeds from the sale of the notes, after initial purchasers' discounts and expenses, were used to (i) repay all indebtedness outstanding under the Term A loan commitments of our Exit Credit Facility and (ii) repay a portion of the indebtedness outstanding under the Term B-1 loans commitments of our Exit Credit Facility. The indenture governing the 2018 Notes contains various covenants that may adversely affect our ability, among other things, to incur additional indebtedness, incur liens, pay dividends or make certain restricted payments, consummate certain asset sales, enter into certain transactions with JBS USA and our other affiliates, merge, consolidate and/or sell or dispose of all or substantially all of our assets. Additionally, we have $3.6 million of 7 5/8% senior unsecured notes and 8 3/8% senior subordinated unsecured notes outstanding in the aggregate.

Exit Credit Facility. Upon exiting from bankruptcy, the Company and certain of its subsidiaries, consisting of To-Ricos, Ltd. and To-Ricos Distribution, Ltd. (collectively, the "To-Ricos Borrowers"), entered into the Exit Credit Facility, which provides for an aggregate commitment of $1.75 billion consisting of (i) a revolving loan commitment of $600.0 million, (ii) a Term A loans commitment of $375.0 million and (iii) a Term B loans commitment of $775.0 million. The Exit Credit Facility also includes an accordion feature that allows us at any time to increase the aggregate revolving loan commitment by up to an additional $250 million and to increase the aggregate Term B loans commitment by up to an additional $400 million, in each case subject to the satisfaction of certain conditions, including an aggregate cap on all commitments under the Exit Credit Facility of $1.85 billion. The proceeds received from the Exit Credit Facility and sale of common stock to JBS USA were used to repay prepetition notes and bank debt as well as fund distributions to holders of other allowed claims. On January 13, 2011, we increased the amount of the revolving loan commitments under the Exit Credit Facility to $700.0 million. The Term A loan was repaid on December 15, 2010 with proceeds from the 2018 Notes. The revolving loan commitment and the Term B loans will mature on December 28, 2014.

On December 26, 2010, a principal amount of $632.5 million under the Term B loans commitment and $205.3 million under the revolving loan commitment were outstanding. On December 28, 2009, the Company also paid loan costs totaling $50.0 million related to the Exit Credit Facility that it recognized as an asset on its balance sheet. The Company amortizes these capitalized costs to expense over the life of the Exit Credit Facility.

Subsequent to the end of each fiscal year, a portion of our cash flow must be used to repay outstanding principal amounts under the Term B loans. With respect to 2010, the Company must pay approximately $46.3 million of its cash flow toward the outstanding principal under the Term B loans. After giving effect to this prepayment and other prepayments of the Term B Loans, the Term B Loans must be repaid in 16 quarterly installments of approximately $3.9 million beginning on April 15, 2011, with the final installment due on December 28, 2014. The Exit Credit Facility also requires us to use the proceeds we receive from certain asset sales and specified debt or equity issuances and upon the occurrence of other events to repay outstanding borrowings under the Exit Credit Facility.

The Exit Credit Facility includes a $50.0 million sub-limit for swingline loans and a $200.0 million sub-limit for letters of credit. Outstanding borrowings under the revolving loan commitment bear interest at a per annum rate equal to 3.00% plus the greater of (i) the US prime rate as published by the *Wall Street Journal*, (ii) the average federal funds rate plus 0.5%, and (iii) the one-month LIBOR rate plus 1.0%, in the case of alternate base rate loans, or 4.00% plus the one, two, three or six month LIBOR rate adjusted by the applicable statutory reserve, in the case of Eurodollar loans. Outstanding Term B-1 loans bear interest at a per annum rate equal to 3.50% plus greater of (i) the US prime rate, as published by the *Wall Street Journal*, (ii) the average federal funds rate plus 0.5%, and (iii) the one month LIBOR rate plus 1.0%, in the case of alternate base rate loans, or 4.50%, plus the one, two, three or six month LIBOR Rate adjusted by the applicable statutory reserve, in the case of Eurodollar loans. Outstanding Term B-2 loans bear interest at a per annum rate equal to 9.00%. Commitment fees charged on the revolving commitments under the Exit Credit Facility accrue at a per annum rate equal to 0.50%.

Actual borrowings by the Company under the revolving credit commitment part of the Exit Credit Facility are subject to a borrowing base, which is a formula based on certain eligible inventory, eligible receivables and restricted cash under the control of CoBank ACB, as administrative agent under the Exit Credit Facility. The borrowing base formula is reduced by the sum of (i) inventory reserves, (ii) rent and collateral access reserves, and (iii) any amount more than 15 days past due that is owed by the Company or its subsidiaries to any person on account of the purchase price of agricultural products or services (including poultry and livestock) if that person is entitled to any grower's or producer's lien or other security arrangement. Revolving loan availability under the borrowing base is also limited to an aggregate of $25.0 million with respect to the To-Ricos Borrowers. As of December 26, 2010, the applicable borrowing base was $600.0 million, the amount available for borrowing under the revolving loan commitment was $354.2 million and outstanding borrowings and letters of credit under the revolving loan commitment totaled $245.8 million.

The Exit Credit Facility provides that the Company may not incur capital expenditures in excess of $275.0 million in 2011 and $350.0 million per fiscal year thereafter. The Company must also maintain a minimum fixed charge coverage ratio and a minimum level of tangible net worth and may not exceed a maximum senior secured leverage ratio. The Company must maintain compliance with these covenants at the following levels:

Minimum fixed charge coverage ratio[a]	At least 1.05 to 1.00 on or before December 31, 2012 and at least 1.10 to 1.00 after January 1, 2013.
Maximum senior secured leverage ratio[b]	No greater than (i) 4.00 to 1.00 on or before December 31, 2012, (ii) 3.75 to 1.00 for the period from January 1, 2013 to December 31, 2013 and (iii) 3.50 to 1.00 for any period after January 1, 2014.
Minimum consolidated tangible net worth[c]	At least $656.1 million plus 50.0% of the cumulative net income (excluding any losses) of the Company and its subsidiaries from the Effective Date through the date of calculation.

[a] Fixed charge coverage ratio means the ratio of (i) EBITDA, as adjusted, minus the unfinanced portion of capital expenditures, minus taxes paid in cash, in each case for the period of eight consecutive fiscal quarters ending as of such date; to (ii) Fixed Charges as of such date, all calculated for the Company on a consolidated basis. EBITDA, as adjusted, means (i) net income (loss) for such period plus interest, taxes, depreciation and amortization, plus (ii) cash (if taken in connection with or during the bankruptcy of the Company) and non-cash tangible and intangible asset impairment charges, lease termination costs, severance costs, facility shutdown costs, and other related restructuring charges for such period related to a permanent reduction in capacity, plant or facility closures/cut-backs or a significant reconfiguration of a plant or facility and extraordinary, unusual or non-recurring non-cash charges or losses (other than for write-down or write-off of inventory); minus (iii) any extraordinary, unusual or nonrecurring income or gains; provided however, that aggregate principal amount of Plan Sponsor Subordinated Indebtedness included in the calculating EBITDA shall not exceed $100.0 million. Plan Sponsor Subordinated Indebtedness means additional unsecured Indebtedness owed to JBS USA Holdings, Inc., a Delaware corporation, or any wholly-owned subsidiary thereof that is (i) organized under the laws of the United States, any state thereof or the District of Columbia, and (ii) has been formed for the purpose of acquiring a majority of the equity interests of the Company, or merging or consolidating with the Company for the purpose of acquiring a majority of the equity interests of the Company. Fixed Charges means all amounts that are required to be paid by the Company during an eight fiscal quarter period for scheduled principal payments on indebtedness and capital lease obligations; plus all amounts that were paid in cash by the Company during the preceding eight fiscal quarter period in respect of interest, dividends, contributions to certain employee pension benefit plans and non-cancellable operating lease payments not included in the calculation of EBITDA.

[b] Senior secured leverage ratio means the ratio of Senior Secured Indebtedness on such date to EBITDA, as adjusted, during the preceding four consecutive fiscal quarters. Senior Secured Indebtedness means, at any date, the aggregate principal amount of all Indebtedness (other than unsecured Indebtedness) of the Company at such date, determined on a consolidated basis, to the extent required to be reflected in the "Liabilities" section of the Consolidated Balance Sheet of the Company. Indebtedness means the aggregate principal amount of all (i) borrowed money and capital lease obligations, (ii) deposits or advances owed by the Company, (iii) obligations evidenced by bonds, debentures, notes or similar instruments, (iv) obligations under conditional sale or other title retention agreements, (v) obligations related to the deferred purchase price of property or services, (vi) all indebtedness of others secured by liens on property of the Company, (vii) guarantor obligations, (viii) obligations in respect to letters of credit, letters of guaranty, bankers' acceptances and liquidated earn-outs and (ix) any other off-balance sheet liability, each to the extent required to be reflected in the Liabilities section of our Consolidated Balance Sheets.

[c] Consolidated tangible net worth means shareholders' equity minus intangible assets.

The Company is currently in compliance with these covenants. However, chicken prices, commodity prices, access to export markets and other factors could affect the Company's ability to maintain compliance with its financial covenants.

Under the Exit Credit Facility, JBS USA, the Company's majority stockholder, or its affiliates may make loans to the Company on a subordinated basis on terms reasonably satisfactory to the agents under the Exit Credit Facility and up to $100 million of such subordinated indebtedness may be included in the calculation of EBITDA (as defined in the Exit Credit Facility).

The Exit Credit Facility contains various covenants that may adversely affect our ability to, among other things, incur additional indebtedness, incur liens, pay dividends or make certain restricted payments, consummate certain assets sales, enter into certain transactions with JBS USA and our other affiliates, merge, consolidate and/or sell or dispose of all or substantially all of our assets.

All obligations under the Exit Credit Facility are unconditionally guaranteed by certain of the Company's subsidiaries and are secured by a first priority lien on (i) the domestic (including Puerto Rico) accounts and inventory of the Company and its subsidiaries, (ii) 100% of the equity interests in the To-Ricos Borrowers and the Company's domestic subsidiaries and 65% of the equity interests in the Company's direct foreign subsidiaries, (iii) substantially all of the personal property and intangibles of the Company, the To-Ricos Borrowers and the guarantor subsidiaries, and (iv) substantially all of the real estate and fixed assets of the Company and the subsidiary guarantors.

ING Credit Agreement. On September 25, 2006, a subsidiary of the Company, Avícola Pilgrim's Pride de México, S. de R.L. de C.V. (the "Mexico Borrower"), entered into a secured revolving credit agreement (the "ING Credit Agreement") with ING Capital, LLC, as agent (the "Mexico Agent") and the lenders party thereto (the "Mexico Lenders"). The ING Credit Agreement has a final maturity date of September 25, 2011 and a revolving commitment of 557.4 million Mexican pesos, a US dollar-equivalent $45.1 million at December 26, 2010. There were no outstanding borrowings under the ING Credit Agreement at December 26, 2010. Outstanding amounts under the ING Credit Agreement bear interest at a rate per annum equal to: the LIBOR Rate, the Base Rate, or the Interbank Equilibrium Interest Rate (the "TIIE Rate"), as applicable, plus the Applicable Margin (as those terms are defined in the ING Credit Agreement). While the Company was operating in Chapter 11, the Applicable Margin for LIBOR loans, Base Rate loans, and TIIE loans was 6.0%, 4.0%, and 5.8%, respectively. Following the Effective Date, the Applicable Margin for LIBOR loans and Base Rate loans is 0.375% higher than the highest applicable interest rate margin under the Exit Credit Facility and for TIIE loans is 0.20% less than the Applicable Margin for LIBOR loans.

The ING Credit Agreement requires the Company to make a mandatory prepayment of the revolving loans, in an aggregate amount equal to 100.0% of the net cash proceeds received by any Mexican subsidiary of the Company (a "Mexico

Subsidiary"), as applicable, in excess of thresholds specified in the ING Credit Agreement (i) from the occurrence of certain asset sales by the Mexico Subsidiaries; (ii) from the occurrence of any casualty or other insured damage to, or any taking under power of eminent domain or by condemnation or similar proceedings of, any property or asset of any Mexico Subsidiary; or (iii) from the incurrence of certain indebtedness by a Mexico Subsidiary. Any such mandatory prepayments will permanently reduce the amount of the commitment under the ING Credit Agreement. The Mexico Subsidiaries have pledged substantially all of their receivables, inventory, and equipment and certain fixed assets. The Mexico Subsidiaries were excluded from the US bankruptcy proceedings.

Other Disclosures

Most of our domestic inventories and domestic fixed assets are pledged as collateral on our long-term debt and credit facilities.

Annual maturities of long-term debt for the five years subsequent to December 26, 2010 are as follows:

(In thousands)	Debt Maturities
For the fiscal years ending December:	
2011	$ 58,144
2012	15,612
2013	15,886
2014	749,027
2015	263
Thereafter	503,979
Total maturities	1,342,911
Less: amount representing original issue discount, net of accretion	(3,607)
Total long-term debt	$1,339,304

Total interest expense was $105.6 million, $44.7 million, $161.9 million and $134.2 million in 2010, the Transition Period, 2009 and 2008, respectively. Interest related to new construction capitalized in 2010, the Transition Period, 2009 and 2008 was $1.3 million, $1.1 million, $2.6 million and $5.3 million, respectively.

Collateralized

2.161

GENCORP INC. (NOV)

CONSOLIDATED BALANCE SHEETS (in part)

(In millions, except per share amounts)	November 30, 2010	November 30, 2009
Current liabilities		
Short-term borrowings and current portion of long-term debt	$ 66.0	$ 17.8
Accounts payable	27.1	18.4
Reserves for environmental remediation costs	40.7	44.5
Postretirement medical and life benefits	7.1	7.2
Advance payments on contracts	110.0	66.0
Other current liabilities	110.3	107.5
Total current liabilities	361.2	261.4
Noncurrent liabilities		
Senior debt	50.6	51.2
Senior subordinated notes	75.0	97.5
Convertible subordinated notes	200.0	254.4
Other debt	1.1	0.7
Deferred income taxes	7.6	9.6
Reserves for environmental remediation costs	177.0	178.2
Pension benefits	175.5	210.3
Postretirement medical and life benefits	71.8	75.7
Other noncurrent liabilities	66.8	68.8
Total noncurrent liabilities	825.4	946.4
Total Liabilities	$1,186.6	$1,207.8

NOTES TO CONSOLIDATED FINANCIAL STATEMENTS

5. Long-Term Debt (in part)

(In millions)	As of November 30	
	2010	2009
Senior debt	$ 51.1	$ 68.3
Senior subordinated notes	75.0	97.5
Convertible subordinated notes, net of $4.0 million and $17.0 million of debt discount as of November 30, 2010 and 2009, respectively	264.6	254.4
Other debt	2.0	1.4
Total debt, carrying amount	392.7	421.6
Less: Amounts due within one year		
Senior debt	0.5	17.1
Other debt	65.5	0.7
Total long-term debt, carrying amount	$326.7	$403.8

As of November 30, 2010, the Company's annual fiscal year debt contractual principal maturities are summarized as follows (in millions):

2011[1]	$ 69.9
2012	0.7
2013	125.3
2014	200.2
2015	0.2
Thereafter	0.4
Total debt	$396.7

[1] Includes the $68.6 million of principal 2 ¼% Debentures due November 2024 that can be put to us in November 2011 at a price equal to 100% of the principal amount plus accrued and unpaid interest, including liquidated damages, if any, payable in cash, to but not including the repurchase date, plus, in certain circumstances, a make-whole premium, payable in common stock.

a. Senior Debt

(In millions)	As of November 30	
	2010	2009
Term loan, bearing interest at various rates (rate of 3.55% as of November 30, 2010), payable in quarterly installments of $0.1 million plus interest, maturing in April 2013	$51.1	$68.3

Senior Credit Facility

The Company's Senior Credit Facility provides for a $65.0 million revolving credit facility ("Revolver") and a $175.0 million credit-linked facility, consisting of a $100.0 million letter of credit subfacility and a $75.0 million term loan subfacility. On March 17, 2010, the Company executed an amendment (the "Second Amendment") to the Company's existing Amended and Restated Credit Agreement, originally entered into as of June 21, 2007, by and among the Company, as borrower, the subsidiaries of the Company from time to time

party thereto, as guarantors, the lenders from time to time party thereto and Wachovia Bank, National Association, as administrative agent for the lenders, as amended to date (the "Credit Agreement"). The Second Amendment, among other things, (i) permits the Company to repurchase its outstanding convertible subordinated notes and senior subordinated notes, subject to certain conditions; (ii) permits the Company to incur additional senior unsecured or subordinated indebtedness, subject to specified limits and other conditions; (iii) permits the Company to conduct a rescission offer, using stock and/or cash up to $15.0 million, with respect to certain units issued under the GenCorp Savings Plan; (iv) permits the Company to repurchase its stock, subject to certain conditions; (v) limits the circumstances under which the Company would have to mandatorily prepay loans under the Senior Credit Facility with the proceeds from equity issuances; and (vi) amends the definitions of the leverage ratio and net cash proceeds from permitted real estate sales. The Second Amendment reduced the Revolver capacity from $80.0 million to $65.0 million and the letter of credit subfacility capacity from $125.0 million to $100.0 million. Under the Second Amendment, the interest rate on LIBOR rate borrowings is LIBOR plus 325 basis points, an increase of 100 basis points, and the letter of credit subfacility commitment fee has been similarly amended. The Second Amendment also provides for a commitment fee on the unused portion of the Revolver in the amount of 62.5 basis points, an increase of 12.5 basis points.

As of November 30, 2010, the borrowing limit under the Revolver was $65.0 million, of which $50.0 million can be utilized for letters of credit, with all of it available. Also, as of November 30, 2010, the Company had $69.4 million outstanding letters of credit under the $100.0 million letter of credit subfacility and had permanently reduced the amount of its term loan subfacility to the $51.1 million outstanding.

During the first quarter of fiscal 2010, the Company made a required principal payment of $16.6 million on the term loan subfacility due to the excess cash flow prepayment provisions of the Credit Agreement.

The Senior Credit Facility is collateralized by a substantial portion of the Company's real property holdings and substantially all of the Company's other assets, including the stock and assets of its material domestic subsidiaries that are guarantors of the facility. The Company is subject to certain limitations including the ability to: incur additional senior debt, release collateral, retain proceeds from asset sales and issuances of debt or equity, make certain investments and acquisitions, grant additional liens, and make restricted payments, including stock repurchases and dividends. In addition, the Credit Agreement contains certain restrictions surrounding the ability of the Company to refinance its subordinated debt, including provisions that, except on terms no less favorable to the Credit Agreement, the Company's subordinated debt cannot be refinanced prior to maturity. Furthermore, provided that the Company has cash and cash equivalents of at least $25.0 million after giving effect thereto, the Company may redeem (with funds other than Senior Credit Facility proceeds) the subordinated notes to the extent required by the mandatory redemption provisions of the subordinated note indenture. The Company is also subject to the following financial covenants:

Financial Covenant	Actual Ratios as of November 30, 2010	Required Ratios December 1, 2009 and thereafter
Interest coverage ratio, as defined under the Credit Agreement	4.56 to 1.00	Not less than: 2.25 to 1.00
Leverage ratio, as defined under the Credit Agreement[(1)]	1.67 to 1.00	Not greater than: 5.50 to 1.00

[(1)] As a result of the March 17, 2010 amendment, the leverage ratio calculation was amended to allow for all cash and cash equivalents to reduce funded debt in the calculation as long as there are no loans outstanding under the Revolver.

The Company was in compliance with its financial and non-financial covenants as of November 30, 2010.

2.162

ALLIANCE ONE INTERNATIONAL, INC. (MAR)

CONSOLIDATED BALANCE SHEETS (in part)

(In thousands)	March 31, 2010	March 31, 2009
Current liabilities		
Notes payable to banks	$188,981	$261,468
Accounts payable	146,395	120,214
Due to related parties	20,275	27,488
Advances from customers	102,286	44,440
Accrued expenses and other current liabilities	113,048	97,644
Current derivative liability	—	25,670
Income taxes	16,281	16,659
Long-term debt current	457	17,842
Total current liabilities	587,723	611,425
Long-term debt	788,880	652,584
Deferred income taxes	4,399	8,230
Liability for unrecognized tax benefits	20,168	58,135
Pension, postretirement and other long-term liabilities	115,107	97,365
	$928,554	$816,314

NOTES TO CONSOLIDATED FINANCIAL STATEMENTS

(In thousands)

Note H—Long-Term Debt (in part)

The Company completed a number of refinancing transactions, which are described below.

Senior Secured Credit Facility

On July 2, 2009, the Company entered into a Credit Agreement (the "Credit Agreement"), with a syndicate of banks that replaced the Company's $305,000 Amended and Restated Credit Agreement dated March 30, 2007 and provides for a senior secured credit facility (the "Credit Facility") that consists of:

- A three and one-quarter year $270,000 revolver (the "Revolver") which initially accrues interest at a rate of LIBOR plus 2.50%.

The interest rate for the Revolver may increase or decrease according to a consolidated interest coverage ratio pricing matrix as defined in the Credit Agreement. The Credit Agreement permits the Company to add $55,000 in commitments from existing or additional lenders which would increase the amount of the Revolver to $325,000. As of April 7, 2010, the Company exercised $20,000 of the $55,000 incremental borrowing to increase the amount of the Revolver to $290,000.

First Amendment. On August 24, 2009, the Company closed the First Amendment to the Credit Agreement which included the following modifications effective August 24, 2009:

- Amended the definition for Senior Notes to allow for the issuance of up to an additional $100,000 of Senior Notes due 2016 within 90 days of the First Amendment Effective Date;
- Amended the definition of Consolidated Total Senior Debt to exclude the Existing Senior Notes 2005;
- Amended the definition of Applicable Percentage to clarify the effective date of the change in the Applicable Percentage;
- Modifications to several schedules within the Credit Agreement.

Second Amendment. Effective June 9, 2010, the Company closed the Second Amendment to the Credit Agreement. See Note U "Subsequent Event" to the "Notes to Consolidated Financial Statements" for further information.

Borrowers and Guarantors. One of the Company's primary foreign holding companies, Intabex Netherlands B.V. ("Intabex"), is co-borrower under the Revolver, and the Company's portion of the borrowings under the Revolver is limited to $200,000 outstanding at any one time. One of the Company's primary foreign trading companies, Alliance One International AG ("AOIAG"), is a guarantor of Intabex's obligations under the Credit Agreement. Such obligations are also guaranteed by the Company and must be guaranteed by any of its material direct or indirect domestic subsidiaries of which the Company has none.

Collateral. The Company's borrowings under the Credit Facility are secured by a first priority pledge of:

- 100% of the capital stock of any domestic subsidiary held directly by the Company or by any material domestic subsidiary;
- 100% of the capital stock of any material domestic subsidiary;
- 100% of the capital stock of any material foreign subsidiary held directly by the Company or any domestic subsidiary; provided that not more than 65% of the voting stock of any material foreign subsidiary is required to be pledged to secure obligations of the Company or any domestic subsidiary;
- U.S. accounts receivable and U.S. inventory owned by the Company or its material domestic subsidiaries (other than inventory the title of which has passed to a customer and inventory financed through customer advances and certain other exceptions); and
- Intercompany notes evidencing loans or advances the Company makes to subsidiaries.

In addition, Intabex's borrowings under the Credit Facility are secured by a pledge of 100% of the capital stock of Intabex,

AOIAG, certain of the Company's and Intabex's material and other foreign subsidiaries and the collateral described above for the Company's borrowings.

Financial Covenants. The Credit Facility includes certain financial covenants and required financial ratios, including:

- A minimum consolidated interest coverage ratio of not less than 1.90 to 1.00;
- A maximum consolidated leverage ratio in an amount not more than a ratio specified for each fiscal quarter, which ratio is 5.50 to 1.00 for the fiscal quarter ended March 31, 2010;
- A maximum consolidated total senior debt to working capital amount ratio of not more than 0.80 to 1.00; and
- A maximum amount of annual capital expenditures of $75,000 during fiscal year ending March 31, 2010 and $40,000 during any fiscal year thereafter, with a one-year carry-forward for capital expenditures in any fiscal year below the maximum amount.

Certain of these financial covenants and required financial ratios adjust over time in accordance with schedules in the Credit Agreement.

The Credit Agreement also contains certain customary affirmative and negative covenants, including, without limitation, restrictions on additional indebtedness, guarantees, liens and asset sales.

The Company continuously monitors its compliance with these covenants. If the Company fails to comply with any of these covenants and is unable to obtain the necessary amendments or waivers under the Credit Agreement, the lenders under the Credit Agreement have the right to accelerate the outstanding loans thereunder and demand repayment in full and to terminate their commitment to make any further loans under the Credit Facility. Certain defaults under the Credit Facility would result in a cross default under the indentures governing the Company's senior notes and convertible senior subordinated notes and could impair access to its seasonal operating lines of credit in local jurisdictions. A default under the Credit Agreement would have a material adverse effect on the Company's liquidity and financial condition. At March 31, 2010, the Company is in compliance with these covenants. The Company records all fees and third-party costs associated with the Credit Agreement, including amendments thereto, in accordance with accounting guidance for changes in line of credit or revolving debt arrangements.

As a result of terminating the $305,000 Amended and Restated Credit Agreement dated March 30, 2007, the Company accelerated approximately $5,741 of deferred financing costs.

Summary of Debt

The carrying value and estimated fair value of the Company's long-term debt are $789,337 and $845,642, respectively, as of March 31, 2010 and $670,426 and $613,336, respectively, as of March 31, 2009.

The following table summarizes the Company's debt financing as of March 31, 2010:

| | Outstanding | | March 31, 2010 | | Long Term Debt Repayment Schedule | | | | | |
	March 31, 2009	March 31, 2010	Lines and Letters Available	Interest Rate	2011	2012	2013	2014	2015	Later
Senior secured credit facility:										
Revolver	$120,000	$ —	$270,000		$ —	$ —	$ —	$—	$ —	$ —
Senior notes:										
10% senior notes due 2016[4]	—	642,225	—	10.0% [4]	—	—	—	—	—	642,225
11% senior notes due 2012	264,381	—	—	11.0%	—	—	—	—	—	—
8½% senior notes due 2012[5]	149,520	29,568	—	8.5%	—	—	29,568	—	—	—
Other[1]	10,157	—	—		—	—	—	—	—	—
	424,058	671,793	—		—	—	29,568	—	—	642,225
5½% convertible senior subordinated notes due 2014	—	115,000	—	5.5%	—	—	—	—	115,000	—
12¼% senior subordinated notes due 2012	83,999	—	—	12.8%	—	—	—	—	—	—
Other long-term debt	42,369	2,544	—	9.0% [2]	457	1,638	63	68	30	288
Notes payable to banks[3]	261,468	188,981	416,131	7.5% [2]	—	—	—	—	—	—
Total debt	$931,894	$978,318	$686,131		$457	$1,638	$29,631	$68	$115,030	$642,513
Short term	$261,468	$188,981								
Long term:										
Long term debt current	$ 17,842	$ 457								
Long term debt	652,584	788,880								
	$670,426	$789,337								
Letters of credit	$ 3,814	$ 5,346	8,836							
Total credit available			$694,967							

[1] Notes redeemed in total as of December 4, 2009
[2] Weighted average rate for the twelve months ended March 31, 2010
[3] Primarily foreign seasonal lines of credit
[4] Repayment of $642,225 is net of original issue discount of $27,775. Total repayment will be $670,000. On March 29, 2010, the interest rate increased to 10.5% pending completion of a registered exchange offer for these notes.
[5] Repayment of $29,568 is net of original issue discount of $67. Total repayment will be $29,635.

Convertible

2.163

PRICELINE.COM INCORPORATED (DEC)

CONSOLIDATED BALANCE SHEETS (in part)

(In thousands, except share and per share data)

	December 31	
	2010	2009
Current liabilities:		
Accounts payable	$ 90,311	$ 60,568
Accrued expenses and other current liabilities	243,767	127,561
Deferred merchant bookings	136,915	60,758
Convertible debt (see Note 11)	175	159,878
Total current liabilities	471,168	408,765
Deferred income taxes	56,440	43,793
Other long-term liabilities	42,990	24,052
Convertible debt (See Note 11)	476,230	—
Total liabilities	1,046,828	476,610
Commitments and contingencies (see Note 16)		
Redeemable noncontrolling interests (see Note 13)	45,751	—
Convertible debt (see Note 11)	$ 38	$ 35,985

NOTES TO CONSOLIDATED FINANCIAL STATEMENTS

11. Debt (in part)

Convertible Debt

Convertible debt as of December 31, 2010 consists of the following (in thousands):

December 31, 2010	Outstanding Principal Amount	Unamortized Debt Discount	Carrying Value
1.25% Convertible senior notes due March 2015	$575,000	$(98,770)	$476,230
0.75% Convertible senior notes due September 2013	213	(38)	175
Outstanding convertible debt	$575,213	$(98,808)	$476,405

Convertible debt as of December 31, 2009 consisted of the following (in thousands):

December 31, 2009	Outstanding Principal Amount	Unamortized Debt Discount	Carrying Value
0.50% Convertible senior notes due September 2011	$ 39,990	$ (4,730)	$ 35,260
0.75% Convertible senior notes due September 2013	133,000	(31,151)	101,849
2.25% Convertible senior notes due January 2025	22,873	(104)	22,769
Outstanding convertible debt	$195,863	$(35,985)	$159,878

Based upon the closing price of the Company's common stock for the prescribed measurement periods during the three months ended December 31, 2010 and 2009, the contingent conversion thresholds of the 2013 Notes were exceeded as of December 31, 2010 and the contingent conversion thresholds of the 2013 Notes, the 2011 Notes and the 2.25% Convertible Notes due 2025 (the "2025 Notes") were exceeded as of December 31, 2009. Accordingly, the carrying value of the aforementioned notes was classified as a current liability at those dates. Since the notes are convertible at the option of the holder and the principal amount is required to be paid in cash, the difference between the principal amount and the carrying value of these notes is reflected as convertible debt in mezzanine on the Company's Balance Sheets as of those dates. The determination of whether or not the notes are convertible must continue to be performed on a quarterly basis. Consequently, the 2013 Notes may not be convertible in future quarters, and therefore may again be classified as long-term debt, if the contingent conversion thresholds are not met in such quarters. The contingent conversion threshold on the 2015 Notes was not exceeded at December 31, 2010, and therefore that debt is reported as a non-current liability. The determination of whether or not the 2015 Notes are convertible must also continue to be performed on a quarterly basis.

If the note holders exercise their option to convert, the Company delivers cash to repay the principal amount of the notes and delivers shares of common stock or cash, at its option, to satisfy the conversion value in excess of the principal amount. In cases where holders decide to convert prior to the maturity date or the first stated put date, the Company writes off the proportionate amount of remaining debt issuance costs to interest expense. In the year ended December 31, 2010, $39.9 million aggregate principal amount of 2011 Notes, $132.8 million aggregate principal amount of 2013 Notes and $22.9 million of the 2025 Notes were converted. The Company delivered cash of $195.6 million to repay the principal amount and issued 3,457,828 shares and delivered $99.8 million in cash in satisfaction of the conversion value in excess of the principal amount for the year ended December 31, 2010.

As of December 31, 2010 and 2009, the estimated market value of the outstanding senior notes was approximately $0.9 billion and $1.1 billion, respectively. Fair value was estimated based upon actual trades at the end of the reporting period or the most recent trade available as well as the Company's stock price at the end of the reporting period. A substantial portion of the market value of the Company's debt in excess of the carrying value relates to the conversion premium on the bonds.

Description of Senior Notes

In March 2010, the Company issued in a private placement $575.0 million aggregate principal amount of Convertible Senior Notes due March 15, 2015, with an interest rate of 1.25% (the "2015 Notes"). The Company paid $13.3 million in debt financing costs associated with the 2015 Notes for the year ended December 31, 2010. The 2015 Notes are convertible, subject to certain conditions, into the Company's common stock at a conversion price of approximately $303.06 per share. The 2015 Notes are convertible, at the option of the holder, prior to March 15, 2015 upon the occurrence of specified events, including, but not limited to a change in control, or if the closing sales price of the Company's common stock for at least 20 consecutive trading days in the period of the 30 consecutive trading days ending on the last trading day of the immediately preceding calendar quarter is more than 150% of the applicable conversion price in effect for the notes on the last trading day of the immediately preceding quarter. In the event that all or substantially all of the Company's common stock is acquired on or prior to the maturity of the 2015 Notes in a transaction in which the consideration paid to holders of the Company's common stock consists of all or substantially all cash, the Company would be required to make additional payments in the form of additional shares of common stock to the holders of the 2015 Notes in aggregate value ranging from $0 to approximately $132.7 million depending upon the date of the transaction and the then current stock price of the Company. As of December 15, 2014, holders will have the right to convert all or any portion of the 2015 Notes. The 2015 Notes may not be redeemed by the Company prior to maturity. The holders may require the Company to repurchase the 2015 Notes for cash in certain circumstances. Interest on the 2015 Notes is payable on March 15 and September 15 of each year.

In 2006, the Company issued in a private placement $172.5 million aggregate principal amount of Convertible Senior Notes due September 30, 2011, with an interest rate of 0.50% (the "2011 Notes"), and $172.5 million aggregate principal amount of Convertible Senior Notes due September 30, 2013, with an interest rate of 0.75% (the "2013 Notes"). The 2011 Notes and the 2013 Notes were convertible, subject to certain conditions, into the Company's common stock at a conversion price of approximately $40.38 per share. The 2011 Notes and the 2013 Notes were convertible, at the option of the holder, prior to June 30, 2011 in the case of the 2011 Notes, and prior to June 30, 2013 in the case of the 2013 Notes, upon the occurrence of specified events, including, but not limited to a change in control, or if the closing sale price of the Company's common stock for at least 20 consecutive trading days in the period of the 30 consecutive trading days ending on the last trading day of the immediately preceding calendar quarter was more than 120% of the applicable conversion price in effect for the notes on the last trading day of the immediately preceding quarter. Neither the 2011 Notes nor the 2013 Notes could be redeemed by the Company prior to maturity.

In 2006, the Company entered into hedge transactions relating to potential dilution of the Company's common stock upon conversion of the 2011 Notes and the 2013 Notes (the "Conversion Spread Hedges"). Under the Conversion Spread Hedges, the Company is entitled to purchase from Goldman Sachs and Merrill Lynch approximately 8.5 million shares of the Company's common stock (4.27 million shares underlying each of the 2011 Notes and the 2013 Notes) at a strike price of $40.38 per share (subject to adjustment in certain circumstances) in 2011 and 2013, and the counterparties are entitled to purchase from the Company approximately 8.5 million shares of the Company's common stock at a strike price of $50.47 per share (subject to adjustment in certain circumstances) in 2011 and 2013. The Conversion Spread Hedges increase the effective conversion price of the 2011 Notes and the 2013 Notes to $50.47 per share from the Company's perspective and were designed to reduce the potential dilution upon conversion of the 2011 Notes and the 2013 Notes. If the market value per share of the Company's common stock at maturity is above $40.38, the Conversion Spread Hedges entitle the Company to receive from

the counterparties net shares of the Company's common stock based on the excess of the then current market price of the Company's common stock over the strike price of the hedge (up to $50.47). The Conversion Spread Hedges are separate transactions entered into by the Company with the counterparties and were not part of the terms of the Notes. The Conversion Spread Hedges were designed to be exercisable at dates coinciding with the scheduled maturities of the 2011 Notes and 2013 Notes. The Conversion Spread Hedges did not immediately hedge against the associated dilution from conversions of the Notes prior to their stated maturities. Therefore, upon early conversion of the 2011 Notes or the 2013 Notes, the Company has delivered any related conversion premium in shares of common stock or a combination of cash and shares. However, the hedging counterparties were not obligated to deliver the Company shares or cash that would offset the dilution associated with the early conversion activity. Because of this timing difference, the number of shares, if any, that the Company receives from its Conversion Spread Hedges can differ materially from the number of shares that it was required to deliver to holders of the Notes upon their early conversion. The actual number of shares to be received will depend upon the Company's stock price on the date the Conversion Spread Hedges are exercisable, which coincides with the scheduled maturity of the 2013 Notes. During the year ended December 31, 2010, the Company and the counterparties agreed to terminate the Conversion Spread Hedges associated with 4.27 million shares underlying the 2011 Notes. The Company recorded the $43 million received as an increase to additional paid-in capital.

Accounting guidance requires that cash-settled convertible debt, such as the Company's convertible senior notes, be separated into debt and equity at issuance and each be assigned a value. The value assigned to the debt component is the estimated fair value, as of the issuance date, of a similar bond without the conversion feature. The difference between the bond cash proceeds and this estimated fair value, representing the value assigned to the equity component, is recorded as a debt discount. Debt discount is amortized using the effective interest method over the period from origination or modification date through the earlier of the first stated put date or the stated maturity date.

The Company estimated the straight debt borrowing rates at debt origination to be 5.89% for the 2015 Notes and 8.0% for the 2013 Notes. The yield to maturity was estimated at an at-market coupon priced at par.

Debt discount after tax of $69.1 million ($115.2 million before tax) partially offset by financing costs associated with the equity component of convertible debt of $1.6 million were recorded in additional paid-in capital related to the 2015 Notes at December 31, 2010.

For the years ended December 31, 2010, 2009 and 2008, the Company recognized interest expense of $27.6 million, $22.1 million and $33.4 million, respectively, related to convertible notes, comprised of $5.8 million, $2.9 million and $4.6 million, respectively, for the contractual coupon interest, $20.1 million, $18.2 million and $26.7 million, respectively, related to the amortization of debt discount and $1.7 million, $1.0 million and $2.1 million, respectively, related to the amortization of debt issuance costs. In addition, unamortized debt issuance costs written off to interest expense related to debt conversions in 2010, 2009 and 2008 was $1.4 million, $1.2 million, and $0.3 million, respectively. The remaining period for amortization of debt discount and debt issuance costs is the stated maturity dates for the respective debt. The effective interest rates for the years ended December 31, 2010, 2009, and 2008 are 6.7%, 8.5% and 8.5%, respectively.

In addition, if the Company's convertible debt is redeemed or converted prior to maturity, a gain or loss on extinguishment will be recognized. The gain or loss is the difference between the fair value of the debt component immediately prior to extinguishment and its carrying value. To estimate the fair value at each conversion date, the Company used an applicable LIBOR rate plus an applicable credit default spread based upon the Company's credit rating at the respective conversion dates. In the years ended December 31, 2010, 2009 and 2008, the Company recognized a loss of $11.3 million ($6.8 million after tax), a loss of $1.0 million ($0.6 million after tax) and a gain of $6.0 million ($3.6 million after tax), respectively, in "Foreign currency transactions and other" in the Consolidated Statements of Operations.

Covenants

2.164

TEXTRON INC. (DEC)

CONSOLIDATED BALANCE SHEETS (in part)

(In millions, except share data)	January 1, 2011	January 2, 2010
Liabilities		
Manufacturing group		
Current portion of long-term debt	$ 19	$ 134
Accounts payable	622	569
Accrued liabilities	2,016	2,039
Total current liabilities	2,657	2,742
Other liabilities	2,993	3,253
Long-term debt	2,283	3,450
Total Manufacturing group liabilities	7,933	9,445
Finance group		
Other liabilities	391	564
Due to Manufacturing group	326	438
Debt	3,660	5,667
Total Finance group liabilities	4,377	6,669
Total liabilities	$12,310	$16,114

NOTES TO CONSOLIDATED FINANCIAL STATEMENTS

Note 8. Debt and Credit Facilities (in part)

Our debt and credit facilities are summarized below:

(In millions)	January 1, 2011	January 2, 2010
Manufacturing group		
Current portion of long-term debt	$ 19	$ 134
Long-term senior debt:		
Medium-term notes due 2010 to 2011 (weighted-average rate of 9.83%)	13	13
4.50% due 2010	—	128
Credit line borrowings due 2012 (weighted-average rate of 0.93% and 0.96%, respectively)	—	1,167
6.50% due 2012	154	154
3.875% due 2013	315	345
4.50% convertible senior notes due 2013	504	471
6.20% due 2015	350	350
5.60% due 2017	350	350
7.25% due 2019	250	250
6.625% due 2020	231	240
Other (weighted-average rate of 3.12% and 3.65%, respectively)	135	116
	2,302	3,584
Less: current portion of long-term debt	(19)	(134)
Total long-term debt	2,283	3,450
Total Manufacturing group debt	$2,302	$3,584
Finance group		
Medium-term fixed-rate and variable-rate notes[*]:		
Due 2010 (weighted-average rate of 2.09%)	$ —	$1,635
Due 2011 (weighted-average rate of 3.07% and 2.94%, respectively)	374	419
Due 2012 (weighted-average rate of 4.43%)	52	52
Due 2013 (weighted-average rate of 4.46% and 4.49%, respectively)	553	578
Due 2014 (weighted-average rate of 5.07%)	111	111
Due 2015 (weighted-average rate of 3.59% and 4.59%, respectively)	14	10
Due 2016 and thereafter (weighted-average rate of 3.37% and 4.04%, respectively)	252	222
Credit line borrowings due 2012 (weighted-average rate of 0.91%)	1,440	1,740
Securitized debt (weighted-average rate of 2.01% and 1.45%, respectively)	530	559
6% Fixed-to-Floating Rate Junior Subordinated Notes	300	300
Fair value adjustments and unamortized discount	34	41
Total Finance group debt	$3,660	$5,667

[*] Variable-rate notes totaled $0.3 billion and $1.4 billion at January 1, 2011 and January 2, 2010, respectively.

Financial Covenants

Under a Support Agreement, Textron Inc. is required to ensure that TFC maintains fixed charge coverage of no less than 125% and consolidated shareholder's equity of no less than $200 million. In addition, TFC has lending agreements that contain provisions restricting additional debt, which is not to exceed nine times consolidated net worth and qualifying subordinated obligations. Due to certain charges as discussed in Note 11, on December 29, 2008, Textron Inc. made a cash payment of $625 million to TFC, which was reflected as a capital contribution, to maintain compliance with the fixed charge coverage ratio required by the Support Agreement and to maintain the leverage ratio required by its credit facility. Cash payments of $383 million in 2010 and $270 million in 2009 were paid to TFC to maintain compliance with the fixed charge coverage ratio. In addition, we paid $63 million on January 11, 2011 related to 2010.

2.165

VALASSIS COMMUNICATIONS, INC. (DEC)

CONSOLIDATED BALANCE SHEETS (in part)

	December 31	
(U.S. dollars in thousands)	2010	2009
Current liabilities:		
Current portion long-term debt (Note 3)	$ 7,058	$ 6,197
Accounts payable	329,602	338,418
Progress billings	53,001	40,532
Accrued expenses (Note 4)	99,612	127,658
Total current liabilities	489,273	512,805
Long-term debt (Note 3)	699,169	1,004,875
Deferred income taxes (Note 5)	78,764	87,914
Other non-current liabilities	49,568	40,567
Total liabilities	$1,316,774	$1,646,161

NOTES TO CONSOLIDATED FINANCIAL STATEMENTS

3. Long-Term Debt (in part)

Long-term debt is summarized as follows:

	December 31	
(In thousands of U.S. dollars)	2010	2009
Senior Secured Revolving Credit Facility	$ —	$ —
Senior Secured Convertible Notes due 2033, net of discount	58	58
8 ¼% Senior Notes due 2015	242,224	540,000
Senior Secured Term Loan B	347,723	353,624
Senior Secured Delayed Draw Term Loan	116,222	117,390
	$706,227	$1,011,072
Less current portion	7,058	6,197
Total long-term debt	$699,169	$1,004,875

Credit Facility and Other Debt (in part)

Our Senior Secured Credit Facility (in part)

Covenants—Subject to customary and otherwise agreed upon exceptions, our senior secured credit facility contains affirmative and negative covenants, including, but not limited to:

- The payment of other obligations;
- The maintenance of organizational existences, including, but not limited to, maintaining our property and insurance;
- Compliance with all material contractual obligations and requirements of law;
- Limitations on the incurrence of indebtedness;
- Limitations on creation and existence of liens;

- Limitations on certain fundamental changes to our corporate structure and nature of our business, including mergers;
- Limitations on asset sales;
- Limitations on restricted payments, including certain dividends and stock repurchases;
- Limitations on capital expenditures;
- Limitations on any investments, provided that certain "permitted acquisitions" and strategic investments are allowed;

- Limitations on optional prepayments and modifications of certain debt instruments;
- Limitations on modifications to material agreements;
- Limitations on transactions with affiliates;
- Limitations on entering into certain swap agreements;
- Limitations on negative pledge clauses or clauses restricting subsidiary distributions;
- Limitations on sale-leaseback and other lease transactions; and
- Limitations on changes to our fiscal year.

Our senior secured credit facility also requires us to comply with a maximum senior secured leverage ratio, as defined in our senior secured credit facility (generally, the ratio of our consolidated senior secured indebtedness to consolidated earnings before interest, taxes, depreciation and amortization, or EBITDA, for the most recent four quarters), of 3.50:1.00 and a minimum consolidated interest coverage ratio, as defined in our senior secured credit facility (generally, the ratio of our consolidated EBITDA for such period to consolidated interest expense for such period), of 2.00:1.00. For purposes of calculating the minimum consolidated interest coverage ratio, the First Amendment permits us to exclude from the definition of "consolidated interest expense" in our senior secured credit facility swap termination and cancellation costs incurred in connection with any purchase, repurchase, payments or repayment of any loans under our senior secured credit facility, including pursuant to a modified Dutch auction. The table below shows the required and actual financial ratios under our senior secured credit facility as of December 31, 2010.

	Required Ratio	Actual Ratio
Maximum senior secured leverage ratio	No greater than 3.50:1.00	0.59:1.00
Minimum consolidated interest coverage ratio	No less than 2.00:1.00	12.44:1.00

In addition, we are required to give notice to the administrative agent and the lenders under our senior secured credit facility of defaults under the facility documentation and other material events, make any new wholly-owned restricted domestic subsidiary (other than an immaterial subsidiary) a subsidiary guarantor and pledge substantially all after-acquired property as collateral to secure our and our subsidiary guarantors' obligations in respect of the facility.

CREDIT AGREEMENTS

DISCLOSURE

2.166   Regulation S-X requires disclosure of the amounts and terms, including commitment fees and conditions for drawdowns, of unused commitments for short-term and long-term financing.

PRESENTATION AND DISCLOSURE EXCERPTS

Credit Agreements

2.167

WYNDHAM WORLDWIDE CORPORATION (DEC)

NOTES TO CONSOLIDATED FINANCIAL STATEMENTS

(Unless otherwise noted, all amounts are in millions, except per share amounts)

13. Long-Term Debt and Borrowing Arrangements (in part)

The Company's indebtedness consisted of:

	December 31, 2010	December 31, 2009
Securitized Vacation Ownership Debt:[a]		
Term notes	$1,498	$1,112
Bank conduit facility[b]	152	395
Total securitized vacation ownership debt	1,650	1,507
Less: Current portion of securitized vacation ownership debt	223	209
Long-term securitized vacation ownership debt	$1,427	$1,298

(continued)

	December 31, 2010	December 31, 2009
Long-Term Debt:		
6.00% senior unsecured notes (due December 2016)[(c)]	$ 798	$ 797
Term loan[(d)]	—	300
Revolving credit facility (due October 2013)[(e)]	154	—
9.875% senior unsecured notes (due May 2014)[(f)]	241	238
3.50% convertible notes (due May 2012)[(g)]	266	367
7.375% senior unsecured notes (due March 2020)[(h)]	247	—
5.75% senior unsecured notes (due February 2018)[(i)]	247	—
Vacation ownership bank borrowings[(j)]	—	153
Vacation rentals capital leases[(k)]	115	133
Other	26	27
Total long-term debt	2,094	2,015
Less: Current portion of long-term debt	11	175
Long-term debt	$2,083	$1,840

[(a)] Represents debt that is securitized through bankruptcy remote SPEs, the creditors of which have no recourse to the Company for principal and interest.

[(b)] Represents a 364-day, $600 million, non-recourse vacation ownership bank conduit facility, with a term through September 2011 whose capacity is subject to the Company's ability to provide additional assets to collateralize the facility. As of December 31, 2010, the total available capacity of the facility was $448 million.

[(c)] The balance as of December 31, 2010 represents $800 million aggregate principal less $2 million of unamortized discount.

[(d)] The term loan facility was fully repaid during March 2010.

[(e)] The revolving credit facility has a total capacity of $970 million, which includes availability for letters of credit. As of December 31, 2010, the Company had $28 million of letters of credit outstanding and, as such, the total available capacity of the revolving credit facility was $788 million.

[(f)] Represents senior unsecured notes issued by the Company during May 2009. The balance at December 31, 2010 represents $250 million aggregate principal less $9 million of unamortized discount.

[(g)] Represents convertible notes issued by the Company during May 2009, which includes debt principal, less unamortized discount, and a liability related to a bifurcated conversion feature. During the third and fourth quarters of 2010, the Company repurchased a portion of its 3.50% convertible notes. The following table details the components of the convertible notes:

	December 31, 2010	December 31, 2009
Debt principal	$116	$230
Unamortized discount	(12)	(39)
Debt less discount	104	191
Fair value of bifurcated conversion feature[(*)]	162	176
Convertible notes	$266	$367

[(*)] The Company also has an asset with a fair value equal to the bifurcated conversion feature, which represents cash-settled call options that the Company purchased concurrent with the issuance of the convertible notes.

[(h)] Represents senior unsecured notes issued by the Company during February 2010. The balance as of December 31, 2010 represents $250 million aggregate principal less $3 million of unamortized discount.

[(i)] Represents senior unsecured notes issued by the Company during September 2010. The balance as of December 31, 2010 represents $250 million aggregate principal less $3 million of unamortized discount.

[(j)] Represents a 364-day, AUD 213 million, secured, revolving foreign credit facility, which was paid down and terminated during March 2010.

[(k)] Represents capital lease obligations with corresponding assets classified within property and equipment on the Company's Consolidated Balance Sheets.

Covenants

The revolving credit facility is subject to covenants including the maintenance of specific financial ratios. The financial ratio covenants consist of a minimum consolidated interest coverage ratio of at least 3.0 to 1.0 as of the measurement date and a maximum consolidated leverage ratio not to exceed 3.75 to 1.0 on the measurement date. The consolidated interest coverage ratio is calculated by dividing consolidated EBITDA (as defined in the credit agreement) by consolidated interest expense (as defined in the credit agreement), both as measured on a trailing 12 month basis preceding the measurement date. Consolidated interest expense excludes, among other things, interest expense on any securitization indebtedness (as defined in the credit agreement). The consolidated leverage ratio is calculated by dividing consolidated total indebtedness (as defined in the credit agreement and which excludes, among other things, securitization indebtedness) as of the measurement date by consolidated EBITDA as measured on a trailing 12 month basis preceding the measurement date. Covenants in this credit facility also include limitations on indebtedness of material subsidiaries; liens; mergers, consolidations, liquidations and dissolutions; sale of all or substantially all of the Company's assets; and sale and leaseback transactions. Events of default in this credit facility include failure to pay interest, principal and fees when due; breach of a covenant or warranty; acceleration of or failure to pay other debt in excess of $50 million (excluding securitization indebtedness); insolvency matters; and a change of control.

The 6.00% senior unsecured notes, 9.875% senior unsecured notes, 7.375% senior unsecured notes and 5.75% senior unsecured notes contain various covenants including limitations on liens, limitations on potential sale and leaseback transactions and change of control restrictions. In addition, there are limitations on mergers, consolidations and potential sale of all or substantially all of the Company's assets. Events of default in the notes include failure to pay interest and principal when due, breach of a covenant or warranty, acceleration of other debt in excess of $50 million and insolvency matters. The Convertible Notes do not contain affirmative or negative covenants; however, the limitations on mergers, consolidations and potential sale of all or substantially all of the Company's assets and the events of default for the Company's senior unsecured notes are applicable to such notes. Holders of the Convertible Notes have the right to require the Company to repurchase the Convertible Notes at 100% of principal plus accrued and unpaid interest in the event of a fundamental change, defined to include, among other things, a change of control, certain recapitalizations and if the Company's common stock is no longer listed on a national securities exchange.

As of December 31, 2010, the Company was in compliance with all of the financial covenants described above.

Each of the Company's non-recourse, securitized term notes and the bank conduit facility contain various triggers relating to the performance of the applicable loan pools. For example, if the vacation ownership contract receivables pool that collateralizes one of the Company's securitization notes fails to perform within the parameters established by the contractual triggers (such as higher default or delinquency rates), there are provisions pursuant to which the cash flows for that pool will be maintained in the securitization as extra collateral for the note holders or applied to accelerate the repayment of outstanding principal to the noteholders. As of December 31, 2010, all of the Company's securitized loan pools were in compliance with applicable contractual triggers.

2.168

R.R. DONNELLEY & SONS COMPANY (DEC)

NOTES TO CONSOLIDATED FINANCIAL STATEMENTS

(In millions, except per share data and unless otherwise indicated)

Note 13. Debt (in part)

The Company's debt at December 31, 2010 and 2009 consists of the following:

	2010	2009
Credit facility borrowings	$ 120.0	$ —
4.95% senior notes due May 15, 2010	—	325.7
5.625% senior notes due January 15, 2012	158.6	158.5
4.95% senior notes due April 1, 2014	599.2	599.0
5.50% senior notes due May 15, 2015	499.6	499.6
8.60% senior notes due August 15, 2016	346.0	345.3
6.125% senior notes due January 15, 2017	622.0	621.5
11.25% senior notes due February 1, 2019	400.0	400.0
7.625% senior notes due June 15, 2020	400.0	—
8.875% debentures due April 15, 2021	80.9	80.9
6.625% debentures due April 15, 2029	199.3	199.3
8.820% debentures due April 15, 2031	68.9	68.9
Other, including capital leases	35.5	23.7
Total debt	3,530.0	3,322.4
Less: current portion	(131.4)	(339.9)
Long-term debt	$3,398.6	$2,982.5

The fair values of the senior notes and debentures, which were based upon interest rates available to the Company for borrowings with similar teams and maturities, were determined to be Level 2 under the fair value hierarchy. The fair value of the Company's debt was greater than its book value by approximately $259.3 million and $177.9 million at December 31, 2010 and 2009, respectively.

On December 17, 2010, the Company entered into a $1.75 billion unsecured and committed revolving credit agreement (the "Credit Agreement") which expires December 17, 2013, subject to a possible one-year extension if agreed to by the lending financial institutions. Borrowings under the Credit Agreement bear interest at a rate dependent on the Company's credit ratings at the time of borrowing that will be calculated according to a base Eurocurrency rate plus an applicable margin. The Company will pay annual commitment fees at rates dependent on the Company's credit ratings. The Credit Agreement replaced the Company's previous $2.0 billion unsecured and committed revolving credit facility (the "previous Facility"). All amounts outstanding under the previous Facility were repaid with borrowings under the Credit Agreement. The Credit Agreement will be used for general corporate purposes, including letters of credit and as a backstop for the Company's commercial paper program. The Credit Agreement is subject to a number of financial covenants that, in part, may limit the use of proceeds, and the ability of the Company to create liens on assets, incur subsidiary debt, engage in mergers and consolidations, or dispose of assets. The financial covenants require a minimum interest coverage ratio and maximum leverage ratio.

On June 21, 2010, the Company issued $400.0 million of 7.625% senior notes due June 15, 2020. Interest on the notes is payable semi-annually on June 15 and December 15 of each year, commencing on December 15, 2010. The net proceeds from the offering were used to repay borrowings under the previous Facility and for general corporate purposes.

On August 26, 2009, the Company issued $350.0 million of 8.60% senior notes due August 15, 2016. Interest on the notes is payable semi-annually on February 15 and August 15 of each year, commencing on February 15, 2010. The net proceeds from the offering, along with borrowings under the previous Facility and cash on hand, were used to repurchase $466.4 million of the 5.625% senior notes due January 15, 2012 and $174.2 million of the 4.95% senior notes due May 15, 2010. These repurchases resulted in a pre-tax loss on debt extinguishment of $10.3 million, which is reflected in investment and other expense on the Consolidated Statements of Operations for the year ended December 31, 2009.

On January 14, 2009, the Company issued $400.0 million of 11.25% senior notes due February 1, 2019. Interest on the notes is payable semi-annually on February 1 and August 1 of each year, commencing on August 1, 2009. The net proceeds from the offering were used to pay down short-term debt. If the Company experiences certain downgrades in its credit ratings, these notes would be subject to a coupon step-up resulting in higher interest payments.

As of December 31, 2010, the Company had $120.0 million of borrowings outstanding under the Credit Agreement. The proceeds from these borrowings were used to repay borrowings under the previous Facility. The borrowings under the previous Facility, along with cash on hand, were used to fund the acquisition of Bowne. The weighted average interest rate on borrowings during the year ended December 31, 2010 was 1.27% per annum.

Additionally, the Company had $107.4 million in credit facilities (the "Foreign Facilities") at its foreign locations, most of which are uncommitted. As of December 31, 2010 and 2009, total borrowings under the Credit Agreement, the previous Facility and the Foreign Facilities (the "Combined Facilities") were $129.1 million and $12.7 million, respectively. As of December 31, 2010, the Company had $57.0 million in outstanding letters of credit. At December 31, 2010, approximately $1.7 billion was available under the Company's Combined Facilities, of which the Company may borrow approximately $1.4 billion, as borrowings above $1.4 billion would cause the Company to violate certain debt covenants in the Facility.

The Company was in compliance with its debt covenants as of December 31, 2010, and is expected to remain in compliance based on management's estimates of operating and financial results for 2011 and the foreseeable future.

LONG-TERM LEASES

RECOGNITION AND MEASUREMENT

2.169 FASB ASC 840 establishes standards of financial accounting and reporting for leases on the financial statements of lessees and lessors. FASB ASC 840 classifies leases as capital or operating. Capital leases are accounted for as the acquisition of

an asset and the incurrence of an obligation by the lessee and as a sale or financing by the lessor. All other leases are accounted for as operating leases.

PRESENTATION

2.170 Under FASB ASC 840-30, lessees should separately identify on the balance sheet or notes thereto assets recorded under capital leases, the accumulated amortization thereon, and obligations. Capital lease obligations are subject to the same considerations as other obligations in classifying them with current and noncurrent liabilities in classified balance sheets. Similarly, a lessor's net investment in a sales-type or direct financing lease is also subject to the same considerations as other assets in classification as current or noncurrent assets.

2.171 FASB ASC 840-20 requires that lessors include property subject to operating leases with or near property, plant, and equipment in the balance sheet. Accumulated depreciation should be deducted by lessors from the investments in the leased property.

DISCLOSURE

2.172 FASB ASC 840-20-50 and 840-30-50 contain detailed disclosure requirements for lessors and lessees under operating and capital leases, respectively.

PRESENTATION AND DISCLOSURE EXCERPTS

Lessee Leases

2.173

WINN-DIXIE STORES, INC. (JUN)

CONSOLIDATED BALANCE SHEETS (in part)

(Dollar amounts in thousands except share data)	June 30, 2010	June 24, 2009
Current liabilities:		
Current obligations under capital leases	$ 9,397	$ 10,888
Accounts payable	345,955	333,471
Reserve for self-insurance liabilities	73,661	71,744
Accrued wages and salaries	65,417	80,796
Deferred tax liabilities	48,667	45,792
Accrued expenses	118,094	116,514
Total current liabilities	661,191	659,205
Reserve for self-insurance liabilities	109,240	117,396
Unfavorable leases	99,049	110,936
Obligations under capital leases	20,075	24,378
Other liabilities	24,775	24,036
Total liabilities	$914,330	$935,951

NOTES TO CONSOLIDATED FINANCIAL STATEMENTS

(Dollar amounts in thousands except per share data, unless otherwise stated.)

12. Leases (in part)

The Company leases substantially all of its stores and other facilities, as well as certain information technology equipment and transportation equipment. The majority of the Company's lease obligations relate to real properties with remaining terms ranging from less than one year to twenty-one years. Many of the Company's leases contain renewal options after the initial term. In addition to minimum rents, certain store leases require contingent rental payments if sales volumes exceed specified amounts.

Lease Commitments

As of June 30, 2010, future contractual minimum lease payments under both capital and operating leases that have remaining terms in excess of one year are:

	Capital	Operating	Subleases	Net
Fiscal Year:				
2011	$11,171	$209,231	$(1,658)	$218,744
2012	8,536	192,371	(1,397)	199,510
2013	6,780	176,927	(1,126)	182,581
2014	5,122	163,944	(311)	168,755
2015	917	142,506	(41)	143,382
Thereafter	2,019	540,829	(30)	542,818
Total minimum lease payments	34,545	1,425,808	(4,563)	1,455,790
Less: amount representing interest	5,073			
Present value of net minimum lease payments	$29,472			

The carrying amount of the Company's capital lease obligations of $29.5 million and $35.3 million approximates fair value as of June 30, 2010, and June 24, 2009, respectively.

2.174

YUM! BRANDS, INC. (DEC)

NOTES TO CONSOLIDATED FINANCIAL STATEMENTS

(Tabular amounts in millions, except share data)

Note 2—Summary of Significant Accounting Policies (in part)

Leases and Leasehold Improvements. The Company leases land, buildings or both for more than 6,000 of its restaurants worldwide. Lease terms, which vary by country and often include renewal options, are an important factor in determining the appropriate accounting for leases including the initial classification of the lease as capital or operating and the tim-

ing of recognition of rent expense over the duration of the lease. We include renewal option periods in determining the term of our leases when failure to renew the lease would impose a penalty on the Company in such an amount that a renewal appears to be reasonably assured at the inception of the lease. The primary penalty to which we are subject is the economic detriment associated with the existence of leasehold improvements which might be impaired if we choose not to continue the use of the leased property. Leasehold improvements, which are a component of buildings and improvements described above, are amortized over the shorter of their estimated useful lives or the lease term. We generally do not receive leasehold improvement incentives upon opening a store that is subject to a lease.

We expense rent associated with leased land or buildings while a restaurant is being constructed whether rent is paid or we are subject to a rent holiday. Additionally, certain of the Company's operating leases contain predetermined fixed escalations of the minimum rent during the lease term. For leases with fixed escalating payments and/or rent holidays, we record rent expense on a straight-line basis over the lease term, including any option periods considered in the determination of that lease term. Contingent rentals are generally based on sales levels in excess of stipulated amounts, and thus are not considered minimum lease payments and are included in rent expense when attainment of the contingency is considered probable.

Note 11—Leases (in part)

At December 25, 2010 we operated more than 7,200 restaurants, leasing the underlying land and/or building in more than 6,000 of those restaurants with the vast majority of our commitments expiring within 20 years from the inception of the lease. Our longest lease expires in 2151. We also lease office space for headquarters and support functions, as well as certain office and restaurant equipment. We do not consider any of these individual leases material to our operations. Most leases require us to pay related executory costs, which include property taxes, maintenance and insurance.

Future minimum commitments and amounts to be received as lessor or sublessor under non-cancelable leases are set forth below:

	Commitments		Lease Receivables	
	Capital	Operating	Direct Financing	Operating
2011	$ 26	$ 550	$ 12	$ 49
2012	63	514	12	42
2013	23	483	17	38
2014	23	447	16	37
2015	23	405	13	34
Thereafter	222	2,605	58	151
	$380	$5,004	$128	$351

At December 25, 2010 and December 26, 2009, the present value of minimum payments under capital leases was $236 million and $249 million, respectively. At December 25, 2010 and December 26, 2009, unearned income associated with direct financing lease receivables was $50 million and $61 million, respectively.

2.175

BRINKER INTERNATIONAL, INC. (JUN)

NOTES TO CONSOLIDATED FINANCIAL STATEMENTS

1. Nature of Operations and Summary of Significant Accounting Policies (in part)

(j) Operating Leases

Rent expense for leases that contain scheduled rent increases is recognized on a straight-line basis over the lease term, including cancelable option periods where failure to exercise such options would result in an economic penalty such that the renewal appears reasonably assured. The straight-line rent calculation and rent expense includes the rent holiday period, which is the period of time between taking control of a leased site and the rent commencement date.

Contingent rents are generally amounts due as a result of sales in excess of amounts stipulated in certain restaurant leases and are included in rent expense as they are incurred. Landlord contributions are recorded when received as a deferred rent liability and amortized as a reduction of rent expense on a straight-line basis over the lesser of the lease term, including renewal options, or 20 years.

10. Leases (in part)

(b) Operating Leases

We lease restaurant facilities, office space, and certain equipment under operating leases having terms expiring at various dates through fiscal 2093. The restaurant leases have renewal clauses of 1 to 35 years at our option and, in some cases, have provisions for contingent rent based upon a percentage of sales in excess of specified levels, as defined in the leases. Rent expense for fiscal 2010, 2009, and 2008 was $102.5 million, $117.5 million, and $131.9 million, respectively. Contingent rent included in rent expense for fiscal 2010, 2009, and 2008 was $4.7 million, $6.5 million, and $8.8 million, respectively.

(c) Commitments

As of June 30, 2010, future minimum lease payments on capital and operating leases were as follows (in thousands):

Fiscal Year	Capital Leases	Operating Leases
2011	$ 5,262	$100,152
2012	5,367	94,049
2013	5,473	86,810
2014	5,581	77,337
2015	5,692	65,562
Thereafter	59,205	178,836
Total minimum lease payments(a)	86,580	$602,746
Imputed interest (average rate of 7%)	(34,608)	
Present value of minimum lease payments	51,972	
Less current installments	(1,866)	
	$ 50,106	

(a) Future minimum lease payments have not been reduced by minimum sublease rentals due in the future under non-cancelable subleases. Sublease rentals are approximately $34.5 million and $66.8 million for capital and operating subleases, respectively.

2.176

WENDY'S/ARBY'S GROUP, INC. (DEC)

COMBINED NOTES TO CONSOLIDATED FINANCIAL STATEMENTS

(In thousands except per share amounts)

(1) Summary of Significant Accounting Policies (in part)

Leases

We operate restaurants that are located on sites owned by us and sites leased by us from third parties. At inception, each lease is evaluated to determine whether the lease will be accounted for as an operating or capital lease based on lease terms. When determining the lease term, we include option periods for which failure to renew the lease imposes a significant economic detriment. The primary penalty to which we may be subject is the economic detriment associated with the existence of unamortized leasehold improvements which might be impaired if we choose not to exercise the available renewal options.

For operating leases, minimum lease payments, including minimum scheduled rent increases, are recognized as rent expense on a straight line basis ("Straight-Line Rent") over the applicable lease terms. Lease terms are generally initially for 20 years and, in most cases, provide for rent escalations and renewal options. The term used for Straight-Line Rent expense is calculated initially from the date we obtain possession of the leased premises through the expected lease termination date. We expense rent from possession date to the restaurant opening date. There is a period under certain lease agreements referred to as a rent holiday ("Rent Holiday") that generally begins on the possession date and ends on the rent commencement date. During the Rent Holiday period, no cash rent payments are typically due under the terms of the lease; however, expense is recorded for that period on a straight-line basis consistent with the Straight-Line Rent policy.

For leases that contain rent escalations, we record the rent payable during the lease term, as determined above, on the straight-line basis over the term of the lease (including the rent holiday period beginning upon possession of the premises), and record the excess of the Straight-Line Rent over the minimum rents paid as a deferred lease liability included in "Other liabilities." Certain leases contain provisions, referred to as contingent rent ("Contingent Rent"), that require additional rental payments based upon restaurant sales volume. Contingent Rent is expensed each period as the liability is incurred.

Favorable and unfavorable lease amounts, when we purchase restaurants, are recorded as components of "Other intangible assets" and "Other liabilities," respectively, and are amortized to "Cost of sales"—both on a straight-line basis over the remaining term of the leases. When the expected term of a lease is determined to be shorter than the original amortization period, the favorable or unfavorable lease balance associated with the lease is adjusted to reflect the revised lease term and a gain or loss recognized.

Management makes certain estimates and assumptions regarding each new lease agreement, lease renewal, and lease amendment, including, but not limited to, property values, market rents, property lives, discount rates, and probable term, all of which can impact (1) the classification and accounting for a lease as capital or operating, (2) the rent holiday and escalations in payment that are taken into consideration when calculating straight-line rent, (3) the term over which leasehold improvements for each restaurant are amortized, and (4) the values and lives of favorable and unfavorable leases. Different amounts of depreciation and amortization, interest and rent expense would be reported if different estimates and assumptions were used.

(22) Lease Commitments (in part)

The Companies lease real property, leasehold interests, and restaurant, transportation, and office equipment. Some leases which relate to restaurant operations provide for contingent rentals based on sales volume.

The Companies' future minimum rental payments and rental receipts, for non-cancelable leases, including rental receipts for leased properties owned by the Companies, having an initial lease term in excess of one year as of January 2, 2011, are as follows:

| | Rental Payments | | | Rental Receipts | | | |
	Sale-Leaseback Obligations	Capitalized Leases	Operating Leases[a]	Sale-Leaseback Obligations	Capitalized Leases	Operating Leases[a]	Owned Properties
Fiscal Year							
2011	$ 14,948	$ 15,856	$ 150,465	$ 966	$ 291	$12,501	$ 7,064
2012	15,406	12,372	140,592	966	291	11,271	7,001
2013	14,824	12,729	131,518	946	291	9,541	6,590
2014	14,814	12,899	120,996	931	291	8,493	6,393
2015	15,640	13,912	112,363	887	291	7,551	6,113
Thereafter	137,459	108,766	1,032,878	3,440	1,279	36,175	45,731
Total minimum payments	213,091	176,534	$1,688,812	$8,136	$2,734	$85,532	$78,892
Less amounts representing interest, with interest rates of between 3% and 22%	(91,207)	(89,864)					
Present value of minimum sale leaseback and capitalized lease payments	$121,884	$ 86,670					

[a] In addition to the amounts presented in the table above, Wendy's/Arby's has rental payments of $1,605 and $673, and rental receipts of $1,360 and $567 in 2011 and 2012, both respectively, under the lease for Wendy's/Arby's former corporate headquarters and of the sublease for office space on two of the floors covered under the lease to personnel from a management company formed by our Chairman, who was our former Chief Executive Officer, and our Vice Chairman, who was our former President and Chief Operating Officer, and a director, who was our former Vice Chairman (the "Management Company").

Lessor Leases

2.177

BURGER KING HOLDINGS, INC. (JUN)

NOTES TO CONSOLIDATED FINANCIAL STATEMENTS

Note 18. Leases (in part)

As of June 30, 2010, the Company leased or subleased 1,145 restaurant properties to franchisees and non-restaurant properties to third parties under capital and operating leases. The building and leasehold improvements of the leases with franchisees are usually accounted for as direct financing leases and recorded as a net investment in property leased to franchisees, while the land is recorded as operating leases. Most leases to franchisees provide for fixed payments with contingent rent when sales exceed certain levels. Lease terms generally range from 10 to 20 years. The franchisees bear the cost of maintenance, insurance and property taxes.

Property and equipment, net leased to franchisees and other third parties under operating leases was as follows (in millions):

| | As of June 30 | |
	2010	2009
Land	$198.3	$195.8
Buildings and improvements	79.6	114.0
Restaurant equipment	8.1	5.1
	$286.0	$314.9
Accumulated depreciation	(70.5)	(40.9)
	$215.5	$274.0)

Net investment in property leased to franchisees and other third parties under direct financing leases was as follows (in millions):

	As of June 30	
	2010	2009
Future minimum rents to be received	$ 316.6	$ 306.4
Estimated unguaranteed residual value	3.7	4.0
Unearned income	(172.3)	(166.2)
Allowance on direct financing leases	(0.6)	(0.2)
	$ 147.4	$ 144.0
Current portion included within trade receivables	(8.9)	(8.7)
Net investment in property leased to franchisees	$ 138.5	$ 135.3

As of June 30, 2010, future minimum lease receipts and commitments were as follows (in millions):

	Lease Receipts		Lease Commitments[a]	
	Direct Financing Leases	Operating Leases	Capital Leases	Operating Leases
2011	$ 29.9	$ 67.8	$ (15.2)	$ (161.7)
2012	29.3	62.9	(14.9)	(156.9)
2013	28.8	60.3	(14.8)	(144.7)
2014	27.6	58.2	(14.8)	(136.5)
2015	27.0	51.3	(12.8)	(125.6)
Thereafter	174.0	335.3	(61.6)	(729.6)
Total	$316.6	$635.8	$(134.1)	$(1,455.0)

[a] Lease commitments under operating leases have not been reduced by minimum sublease rentals of $343.1 due in the future under noncancelable subleases.

2.178

AIR PRODUCTS AND CHEMICALS, INC. (SEP)

CONSOLIDATED BALANCE SHEETS (in part)

	30 September	
(Millions of dollars, except for share data)	2010	2009
Assets		
Current assets		
Cash and cash items	$ 374.3	$ 488.2
Trade receivables, less allowances for doubtful accounts of $99.3 in 2010 and $65.0 in 2009	1,481.9	1,363.2
Inventories	571.6	509.6
Contracts in progress, less progress billings	163.6	132.3
Prepaid expenses	70.3	99.7
Other receivables and current assets	372.1	404.8
Total current assets	3,033.8	2,997.8
Investment in net assets of and advances to equity affiliates	912.8	868.1
Plant and equipment, at cost	16,309.7	15,751.3
Less: accumulated depreciation	9,258.4	8,891.7
Plant and equipment, net	7,051.3	6,859.6
Goodwill	914.6	916.0
Intangible assets, net	285.7	262.6
Noncurrent capital lease receivables	770.4	687.0
Other noncurrent assets	537.3	438.0
Total noncurrent assets	10,472.1	10,031.3
Total assets	$13,505.9	$13,029.1

NOTES TO CONSOLIDATED FINANCIAL STATEMENTS

(Millions of dollars, except for share data)

1. Major Accounting Policies (in part)

Revenue Recognition (in part)

Certain contracts associated with facilities that are built to provide product to a specific customer are required to be accounted for as leases. In cases where operating lease treatment is necessary, there is no difference in revenue recogni-

tion over the life of the contract as compared to accounting for the contract as product sales. In cases where capital lease treatment is necessary, the timing of revenue and expense recognition is impacted. Revenue and expense are recognized up front for the sale of equipment component of the contract as compared to revenue recognition over the life of the arrangement under contracts not qualifying as capital leases. Additionally, a portion of the revenue representing interest income from the financing component of the lease receivable is reflected as sales over the life of the contract.

12. Leases (in part)

Lessor Accounting

As discussed under Revenue Recognition in Note 1, Major Accounting Policies, certain contracts associated with facilities that are built to provide product to a specific customer are required to be accounted for as leases. Lease receivables, net, were included principally in noncurrent capital lease receivables on the Company's consolidated balance sheets. The components of lease receivables were as follows:

30 September	2010	2009
Gross minimum lease payments receivable	$1,195.5	$1,068.9
Unearned interest income	(386.0)	(349.3)
Net lease receivable	$ 809.5	$ 719.6

Lease payments collected in 2010, 2009, and 2008 were $68.0, $53.6, and $33.7, respectively.

At 30 September 2010, minimum lease payments to be collected are as follows:

2011	$ 93.2
2012	95.6
2013	93.9
2014	92.3
2015	90.0
Thereafter	730.5
	$1,195.5

OTHER NONCURRENT LIABILITIES

PRESENTATION

2.179 FASB ASC 210 indicates that liabilities classified as noncurrent (that is, beyond the operating cycle) include long-term deferments of the delivery of goods or services, such as the issuance of a long-term warranty or the advance receipt by a lessor of rental for the final period of a 10-year lease. Similarly, a loan on a life insurance policy with the intent that it will not be paid but will be liquidated by deduction from the proceeds of the policy upon maturity or cancellation should be excluded from current liabilities.

2.180 FASB ASC 480, *Distinguishing Liabilities from Equity*, requires that an issuer classify certain financial instruments with characteristics of both liabilities and equity as liabilities. Some issuances of stock, such as mandatorily redeemable preferred stock, impose unconditional obligations requiring the issuer to transfer assets or issue its equity shares. FASB ASC 480 requires an issuer to classify such financial instruments as liabilities, not present them between the "Liabilities" and "Equity" sections of the balance sheet. Rule 5-02 of Regulation S-X includes matters related to redeemable preferred stocks to be stated on the face of the balance sheet or included in the notes.

2.181 Rule 5-02 of Regulation S-X requires that any item not classed in another Regulation S-X liability caption and in excess of 5 percent of total liabilities be stated separately on the balance sheet or disclosed in the notes. Regulation S-X also requires that deferred income taxes, deferred tax credits, and deferred income be stated separately in the balance sheet.

2.182 Rule 5-02 of Regulation S-X includes a balance sheet caption for commitments and contingent liabilities. When commitments or contingent liabilities exist and are disclosed in footnotes, registrants customarily include a caption on the balance sheet without an amount but with a reference to the related footnote.

2.183

TABLE 2-14: OTHER NONCURRENT LIABILITIES*

Table 2-14 summarizes the nature of such noncurrent liabilities and deferred credits.

	Number of Entities		
	2010	2009	2008
Noncurrent Employee Liabilities			
Pension accruals	295	311	327
Benefits	255	268	203
Deferred compensation	77	65	71
Workers' compensation	22	N/C^	N/C^
Other, described	32	24	22
Deferred Credits			
Deferred profit, income, gain, revenue from sale of assets	14	N/C^	N/C^
Described deferred profit, income, gain, revenue—other than sale of assets	36	N/C^	N/C^
Deferred profit/credit/income/revenue—nature not disclosed	40	N/C^	N/C^
Deferred subscription revenue	4	N/C^	N/C^
Deferred service contract income	9	N/C^	N/C^
Grants	2	N/C^	N/C^
Deferred rent revenue	22	N/C^	N/C^
Other, described	9	N/C^	N/C^
Other			
Redeemable noncontrolling/minority interest	15	65	154
Deferred income taxes	314	340	346
Tax uncertainties	120	155	151
Interest/penalties on tax uncertainties	34	33	N/C^
Insurance	46	46	43
Discontinued operations/restructuring	52	58	55
Preferred stock	2	13	14
Warranties	30	28	24
Guarantees	9	N/C^	N/C^
Environmental	62	70	70
Asset retirement obligations	37	43	38
Litigation	16	23	25
Derivatives	87	152	58
Other, described	87	72	63

* Appearing in the balance sheet or notes to financial statements, or both.

^ N/C = Not compiled. Line item was not included in the table for the year shown.

PRESENTATION AND DISCLOSURE EXCERPTS

Deferred Income Taxes

2.184

FEDEX CORPORATION (MAY)

CONSOLIDATED BALANCE SHEETS (in part)

	May 31	
(In millions, except share data)	2010	2009
Liabilities and Stockholders' Investment		
Current Liabilities		
Current portion of long-term debt	$ 262	$ 653
Accrued salaries and employee benefits	1,146	861
Accounts payable	1,522	1,372
Accrued expenses	1,715	1,638
Total current liabilities	4,645	4,524
Long-term debt, less current portion	1,668	1,930
Other Long-Term Liabilities		
Deferred income taxes	891	1,071
Pension, postretirement healthcare and other		
benefit obligations	1,705	934
Self-insurance accruals	960	904
Deferred lease obligations	804	802
Deferred gains, principally related to aircraft		
transactions	267	289
Other liabilities	151	164
Total other long-term liabilities	$4,778	$4,164

NOTES TO CONSOLIDATED FINANCIAL STATEMENTS

Note 1. Description of Business and Summary of Significant Accounting Policies (in part)

Income Taxes. Deferred income taxes are provided for the tax effect of temporary differences between the tax basis of assets and liabilities and their reported amounts in the financial statements. The liability method is used to account for income taxes, which requires deferred taxes to be recorded at the statutory rate expected to be in effect when the taxes are paid.

We recognize liabilities for uncertain income tax positions based on a two-step process. The first step is to evaluate the tax position for recognition by determining if the weight of available evidence indicates that it is more likely than not that the position will be sustained on audit, including resolution of related appeals or litigation processes, if any. The second step requires us to estimate and measure the tax benefit as the largest amount that is more than 50% likely to be realized upon ultimate settlement. It is inherently difficult and subjective to estimate such amounts, as we must determine the probability of various possible outcomes. We reevaluate these uncertain tax positions on a quarterly basis or when new information becomes available to management. These reevaluations are based on factors including, but not limited to, changes in facts or circumstances, changes in tax law, successfully settled issues under audit and new audit activity. Such a change in recognition or measurement could result in the recognition of a tax benefit or an increase to the related provision.

We classify interest related to income tax liabilities as interest expense, and if applicable, penalties are recognized as a component of income tax expense. The income tax liabilities and accrued interest and penalties that are due within one year of the balance sheet date are presented as current liabilities. The remaining portion of our income tax liabilities and accrued interest and penalties are presented as noncurrent liabilities because payment of cash is not anticipated within one year of the balance sheet date. These noncurrent income tax liabilities are recorded in the caption "Other liabilities" in our consolidated balance sheets.

Note 10. Income Taxes (in part)

The significant components of deferred tax assets and liabilities as of May 31 were as follows (in millions):

	2010		2009	
	Deferred Tax Assets	Deferred Tax Liabilities	Deferred Tax Assets	Deferred Tax Liabilities
Property, equipment, leases and intangibles	$ 377	$2,157	$ 406	$1,862
Employee benefits	783	36	384	143
Self-insurance accruals	416	—	392	—
Other	490	238	491	222
Net operating loss/credit carryforwards	142	—	131	—
Valuation allowances	(139)	—	(137)	—
	$2,069	$2,431	$1,667	$2,227

The net deferred tax liabilities as of May 31 have been classified in the balance sheets as follows (in millions):

	2010	2009
Current deferred tax asset	$ 529	$ 511
Noncurrent deferred tax liability	(891)	(1,071)
	$(362)	$ (560)

2.185

VALASSIS COMMUNICATIONS, INC. (DEC)

CONSOLIDATED BALANCE SHEETS (in part)

	December 31	
(U.S. dollars in thousands)	2010	2009
Current liabilities:		
Current portion long-term debt (Note 3)	$ 7,058	$ 6,197
Accounts payable	329,602	338,418
Progress billings	53,001	40,532
Accrued expenses (Note 4)	99,612	127,658
Total current liabilities	489,273	512,805
Long-term debt (Note 3)	699,169	1,004,875
Deferred income taxes (Note 5)	78,764	87,914
Other non-current liabilities	49,568	40,567
Total liabilities	$1,316,774	$1,646,161

NOTES TO CONSOLIDATED FINANCIAL STATEMENTS

1. Basis of Presentation and Significant Accounting Policies (in part)

Significant Accounting Policies (in part)

Income Taxes

Deferred income tax assets and liabilities are computed annually for differences between the consolidated financial statement and tax bases of assets and liabilities that will result in taxable or deductible amounts in the future based on enacted tax laws and rates applicable to the periods in which the differences are expected to affect taxable income. Valuation allowances are established when necessary to reduce deferred tax assets to the amount more likely than not to be realized. Income tax expense is the tax payable or refundable for the period plus or minus the change during the period in deferred tax assets and liabilities.

5. Income Taxes (in part)

Significant components of our deferred tax assets and liabilities are as follows:

	December 31	
(In thousands of U.S. dollars)	2010	2009
Long-Term Deferred Income Tax (Liabilities) Assets:		
Intangibles	$(85,538)	$(88,147)
Depreciation on plant and equipment	(36,826)	(40,236)
Deferred compensation	17,537	11,041
Cancellation of indebtedness income	(3,858)	(3,812)
Loss and tax credit carryforwards	5,957	10,012
Stock compensation	3,510	518
Partnership losses	2,849	1,980
Investment impairments	5,663	5,905
Foreign	285	248
Acquisition costs	13,778	13,837
Interest rate swaps	1,752	6,288
Allowance for uncollectible accounts	1,397	1,335
Other reserves	10,334	10,606
Long-term deferred income tax liabilities	(63,160)	(70,425)
Valuation allowance	(15,604)	(17,489)
Net long-term deferred income tax (liabilities)	$(78,764)	$(87,914)
Current Deferred Income Tax (Liabilities) Assets:		
Inventory	$ 894	$ 883
Accrued expense	5,501	3,558
Allowance for uncollectible accounts	9,306	7,225
Other reserves	(794)	376
Prepaid expense	(4,487)	(7,100)
Intangibles	(3,560)	(4,964)
Current deferred income tax (liabilities) assets:	6,860	(22)
Valuation allowance	(2,278)	—
Net current deferred income tax assets (liabilities)	$ 4,582	$ (22)

Our net current deferred income tax asset of $4.6 million as of December 31, 2010 is recorded in Prepaid expenses and other in the consolidated balance sheet. Our net current deferred income tax liability of $22,000 as of December 31, 2009 is recorded in Accrued expenses in the consolidated balance sheet.

Our net deferred tax assets and liabilities are summarized as follows (in thousands):

	December 31	
(In thousands of U.S. dollars)	2010	2009
Total deferred tax assets	$ 76,432	$ 75,379
Total deferred tax liabilities	(150,614)	(163,315)
Net deferred income tax liabilities	$ (74,182)	$ (87,936)

For financial statement purposes, the tax benefits of net operating/capital loss and tax credit carryforwards are recognized as deferred tax assets, subject to appropriate valuation allowances, when we determine that the likelihood of recovering the deferred tax asset falls below the "more likely than not" threshold. We evaluate our net operating loss and credit carryforwards on an ongoing basis. As of December 31, 2010, the expiration periods for $6.0 million of deferred tax assets related to net operating/capital loss and tax credit carryforwards are as follows: $0.7 million between calendar years 2011 and 2015; $0.4 million between calendar years 2016 and 2025; $0.9 million between calendar years 2026 and 2030 and $4.0 million can be carried forward indefinitely. We have provided valuation allowances on these deferred tax assets of approximately $0.4 million for deferred tax assets expiring between calendar years 2011 and 2015, $0.2 million between calendar years 2016 and 2025, $0.8 million between calendar years 2026 and 2030 and $3.2 million for deferred tax assets with an indefinite life. A valuation allowance of $13.3 million exists for capitalized costs associated with the ADVO acquisition.

We recognize tax benefits only for tax positions that are more-likely-than-not to be sustained based solely on its technical merits as of the reporting date. The more-likely-than-not threshold represents a positive assertion by management that a company is entitled to the economic benefit of a tax position. If a tax position is not considered more-likely-than-not to be sustained based solely on its technical merits, the company cannot recognize any benefit for the tax position. In addition, the tax position must continue to meet the more-likely-than-not threshold in each reporting period after initial recognition in order to support continued recognition of a benefit.

Taxes Payable

2.186

PFIZER INC. (DEC)

CONSOLIDATED BALANCE SHEETS (in part)

(Millions, except preferred stock issued and per common share data)	As of December 31	
	2010	2009
Short-term borrowings, including current portion of long-term debt: 2010—$3,502; 2009—$27	$ 5,623	$ 5,469
Accounts payable	4,026	4,370
Dividends payable	1,601	1,454
Income taxes payable	946	10,107
Accrued compensation and related items	2,108	2,242
Other current liabilities	14,305	13,583
Total current liabilities	28,609	37,225
Long-term debt	38,410	43,193
Pension benefit obligations	6,201	6,392
Postretirement benefit obligations	3,035	3,243
Noncurrent deferred tax liabilities	18,648	17,839
Other taxes payable	6,245	9,000
Other noncurrent liabilities	5,601	5,611
Total liabilities	$106,749	$122,503

NOTES TO CONSOLIDATED FINANCIAL STATEMENTS

3. Other Significant Transactions and Events (in part)

A. Tax Audit Settlements

During the fourth quarter of 2010, we reached a settlement with the U.S. Internal Revenue Service (IRS) related to issues we had appealed with respect to the audits of the Pfizer Inc. tax returns for the years 2002 through 2005, as well as the Pharmacia audit for the year 2003 through the date of merger with Pfizer (April 16, 2003). The IRS concluded its examination of the aforementioned tax years and issued a final Revenue Agent's Report (RAR). We agreed with all of the adjustments and computations contained in the RAR. As a result of settling these audit years, in the fourth quarter of 2010, we reduced our unrecognized tax benefits by approximately $1.4 billion and reversed the related interest accruals by approximately $600 million. During 2010, we also recognized $320 million in tax benefits and reversed the related interest accruals of $140 million resulting from the resolution of certain tax positions pertaining to prior years with various foreign tax authorities as well as from the expiration of the statute of limitations. The aforementioned amounts had been classified in *Other taxes payable*, and the corresponding tax benefit was recorded in *Provision for taxes on Income* (see *Note 7. Taxes on Income*). In the second quarter of 2008, we effectively settled certain issues common among multinational corporations with various foreign tax authorities primarily relating to tax years 2000 to 2005. As a result, we recognized $305 million in tax benefits in *Provision for taxes on income*.

7. Taxes on Income (in part)

D. Tax Contingencies (in part)

A reconciliation of the beginning and ending amounts of gross unrecognized tax benefits is as follows:

(Millions of dollars)	2010	2009
Balance, January 1	$(7,657)	$(5,372)
Acquisition of Wyeth	(49)	(1,785)
Increases based on tax positions taken during a prior period[a]	(513)	(79)
Decreases based on tax positions taken during a prior period[a],[b]	2,384	38
Decreases based on cash payments for a prior period	280	—
Increases based on tax positions taken during the current period[a]	(1,396)	(941)
Decreases based on tax positions taken during the current period	—	712
Impact of foreign exchange	104	(284)
Other, net[c]	88	54
Balance, December 31[d]	$(6,759)	$(7,657)

[a] Primarily included in *Provision for taxes on income*.

[b] Decreases are primarily a result of effectively settling certain issues with the U.S. and foreign tax authorities for a net benefit of $1.7 billion, reflecting the reversal of the related tax assets associated with the competent authority process and state and local taxes and are primarily included in *Provision for taxes on income*.

[c] Primarily includes decreases as a result of a lapse of applicable statutes of limitations.

[d] In 2010, included in Income taxes payable ($421 million), *Taxes and other current assets* ($279 million), *Taxes and other noncurrent assets* ($169 million), *Noncurrent deferred tax liabilities* ($369 million) and *Other taxes payable* ($5.5 billion). In 2009, included in *Income taxes payable* ($144 million), *Taxes and other current assets* ($78 million), *Noncurrent deferred tax liabilities* ($208 million) and *Other taxes payable* ($7.2 billion).

- Interest related to our unrecognized tax benefits is recorded in accordance with the laws of each jurisdiction and is recorded in *Provision for taxes on income* in our Consolidated Statements of Income. In 2010, we recorded net interest income of $545 million, primarily as a result of settling certain issues with the U.S. and various foreign tax authorities, which are discussed below. In 2009 and 2008, we recorded net interest expense of $191 million and $106 million. Gross accrued interest totaled $952 million as of December 31, 2010 and $1.9 billion as of December 31, 2009 (including $300 million recorded upon the acquisition of Wyeth). In 2010, these amounts were included in *Income taxes payable* ($112 million), *Taxes and other current assets* ($122 million) and *Other taxes payable* ($718 million). In 2009, these amounts were included in *Income taxes payable* ($90 million), *Taxes and other current assets* ($55 million) and *Other taxes payable* ($1.8 billion). Accrued penalties are not significant.

Tax Uncertainties

2.187

PITNEY BOWES INC. (DEC)

CONSOLIDATED BALANCE SHEETS (in part)

(In thousands, except per share data)	December 31, 2010	December 31, 2009
Current liabilities:		
Accounts payable and accrued liabilities	$1,825,261	$1,748,254
Current income taxes	192,924	144,385
Notes payable and current portion of long-term obligations	53,494	226,022
Advance billings	481,900	447,786
Total current liabilities	2,553,579	2,566,447
Deferred taxes on income	261,118	347,402
Tax uncertainties and other income tax liabilities	536,531	525,253
Long-term debt	4,239,248	4,213,640
Other non-current liabilities	653,758	625,079
Total liabilities	$8,244,234	$8,277,821

NOTES TO CONSOLIDATED FINANCIAL STATEMENTS

(Tabular dollars in thousands, except per share data)

9. Income Taxes (in part)

Uncertain Tax Positions

A reconciliation of the amount of unrecognized tax benefits at December 31, 2010, 2009 and 2008 is as follows:

	2010	2009	2008
Balance at beginning of year	$515,565	$434,164	$398,878
Increases from prior period positions	17,775	65,540	21,623
Decreases from prior period positions	(27,669)	(7,741)	(8,899)
Increases from current period positions	43,804	42,696	33,028
Decreases from current period positions	(8,689)	—	—
Decreases relating to settlements with tax authorities	(1,434)	(3,173)	(7,426)
Reductions as a result of a lapse of the applicable statute of limitations	(7,562)	(15,921)	(3,040)
Balance at end of year	$531,790	$515,565	$434,164

The amount of the unrecognized tax benefits at December 31, 2010, 2009 and 2008 that would affect the effective tax rate if recognized was $434 million, $411 million and $371 million, respectively.

Tax authorities continually examine our tax filings. On a regular basis, we conclude tax return examinations, statutes of limitations expire, and court decisions interpret tax law. We regularly assess tax uncertainties in light of these developments. As a result, it is reasonably possible that the amount of our unrecognized tax benefits will decrease in the next 12 months, and we expect this change could be up to one-third of our unrecognized tax benefits. Any such change will likely be arising from the completion of tax return examinations, including the resolution of certain issues related to our former Capital Services third party leasing business. We recognize interest and penalties related to uncertain tax positions in our provision for income taxes or discontinued operations as appropriate. During the years ended December 31, 2010, 2009 and 2008, we recorded $9 million, $23 million and $26 million, respectively, in interest and penalties primarily in discontinued operations. We had $202 million and $186 million accrued for the payment of interest and penalties at December 31, 2010 and 2009, respectively.

Insurance

2.188

SNYDER'S-LANCE, INC. (DEC)

CONSOLIDATED BALANCE SHEETS (in part)

January 1, 2011 and December 26, 2009

(In thousands, except share data)	2010	2009^(*)
Current Liabilities		
Accounts payable	$ 39,938	$ 29,777
Accrued compensation	31,564	26,604
Accrued profit-sharing retirement plan	9,884	6,285
Accrual for casualty insurance claims	6,477	4,840
Accrued selling costs	15,521	9,235
Other payables and accrued liabilities	32,118	19,625
Current portion of long-term debt	57,767	—
Total current liabilities	193,269	96,366
Long-term debt	227,462	113,000
Deferred income taxes	180,812	35,515
Accrual for casualty insurance claims	9,195	8,287
Other long-term liabilities	15,003	8,436
Total liabilities	$625,741	$261,604

^(*) 2009 amounts have been revised to reflect the change in accounting for inventory. See Note 2 for more information.

NOTES TO CONSOLIDATED FINANCIAL STATEMENTS

Note 1. Operations and Summary of Significant Accounting Policies (in part)

Self-Insurance Reserves

We maintain reserves for the self-funded portions of employee medical insurance benefits. The employer's portion of employee medical claims is limited by stop-loss insurance coverage each year to $0.3 million per person for Lance. At January 1, 2011 and December 26, 2009, the accruals for our portion of medical insurance benefits were $3.1 million and $2.9 million, respectively. As part of the Merger, we also assumed additional reserves of $1.9 million. Snyder's portion of employee medical claims is limited by stop-loss coverage each year to $0.2 million per person, and the accrual at January 1, 2011 was $1.9 million.

For certain casualty insurance obligations, we maintain self-insurance reserves for workers' compensation and auto liability for individual losses up to the $0.3 million insurance deductible, and in some cases, up to a $0.5 million insurance deductible. In addition, certain general and product liability claims are self-funded for individual losses up to the $0.1 million insurance deductible. Claims in excess of the deductible are fully insured up to $100 million per individual claim. We evaluate input from a third-party actuary in the estimation of the casualty insurance obligation on an annual basis. In determining the ultimate loss and reserve requirements, we use various actuarial assumptions including compensation trends, healthcare cost trends and discount rates. We also use historical information for claims frequency and severity in order to establish loss development factors. The esti-

mate of discounted loss reserves ranged from $14.3 million to $19.3 million in 2010. In 2009, the estimate of discounted loss reserves ranged from $11.6 million to $14.4 million. This increase was the result of assuming Snyder's workers' compensation liabilities and other factors as described below.

During 2010, we determined that no other point within the range of loss reserves was more probable than another. Accordingly, we selected the midpoint of the range as our estimated liability. In 2009, we estimated the claims liability to be at the 75 th percentile. This change decreased the estimated claims liability by approximately $0.5 million. In addition, we lowered the discount rate from 3.5% in 2009 to 2.5% in 2010 based on projected investment returns over the estimated future payout period, which increased the estimated claims liability by approximately $0.2 million.

In December 2010, we assumed a liability for workers' compensation relating to claims that had originated prior to 1992 and been insured by a third-party insurance company. Due to the uncertainty of that insurer's ability to continue paying claims, we entered into an agreement where we assumed the full liability of approximately $3.6 million of insurance claims under the pre-existing workers' compensation policies and received $1.5 million in cash consideration to be placed in an escrow account to pay these specific claims. Therefore, we have recognized the net liability of $2.1 million as of January 1, 2011.

Discontinued Operations

2.189

FMC CORPORATION (DEC)

CONSOLIDATED BALANCE SHEETS (in part)

	December 31	
(In millions, except share and par value data)	2010	2009
Current Liabilities		
Short-term debt	$ 18.5	$ 33.4
Current portion of long-term debt	116.4	22.5
Accounts payable, trade and other	389.3	290.5
Accrued and other liabilities	223.0	180.8
Accrued payroll	66.3	52.2
Accrued customer rebates	100.9	67.3
Guarantees of vendor financing	24.1	49.5
Accrued pension and other postretirement benefits, current	9.5	9.4
Income taxes	15.4	3.6
Total current liabilities	963.4	709.2
Long-term debt, less current portion	503.0	588.0
Accrued pension and other postretirement benefits, long-term	307.5	364.8
Environmental liabilities, continuing and discontinued	209.9	167.0
Reserve for discontinued operations	38.6	41.7
Other long-term liabilities	108.3	132.4
Commitments and contingent liabilities (Note 18)		

NOTES TO CONSOLIDATED FINANCIAL STATEMENTS

Note 9: Discontinued Operations (in part)

Reserve for Discontinued Operations at December 31, 2010 and 2009

The reserve for discontinued operations totaled $38.6 million and $41.7 million at December 31, 2010 and 2009, respectively. The liability at December 31, 2010, was comprised of $6.0 million for workers' compensation and product liability, $10.8 million for other postretirement medical and life insurance benefits provided to former employees of discontinued businesses and $21.8 million of reserves for legal proceedings associated with discontinued operations. The discontinued postretirement medical and life insurance benefits liability equals the accumulated postretirement benefit obligation. Associated with this liability is a net pretax actuarial gain and prior service credit of $14.0 million ($9.1 million after-tax) and $15.4 million ($10.3 million after-tax) at December 31, 2010 and 2009, respectively. The estimated net actuarial gain and prior service credit that will be amortized from accumulated other comprehensive income into discontinued operations during 2011 are $1.7 million and $0.1 million, respectively.

The liability at December 31, 2009, was comprised of $7.3 million for workers' compensation and product liability, $11.8 million for other postretirement medical and life insurance benefits provided to former employees of discontinued businesses and $22.6 million of reserves for legal proceedings associated with discontinued operations.

We use actuarial methods, to the extent practicable, to monitor the adequacy of product liability, workers' compensation and other postretirement benefit reserves on an ongoing basis. While the amounts required to settle our liabilities for discontinued operations could ultimately differ materially from the estimates used as a basis for recording these liabilities, we believe that changes in estimates or required expenditures for any individual cost component will not have a material adverse effect on our liquidity or financial condition in any single year and that, in any event, such costs will be satisfied over the course of several years.

Spending in 2010, 2009 and 2008 was $0.7 million, $1.1 million and $0.6 million, respectively, for workers' compensation, product liability and other claims; $1.6 million, $1.2 million and $1.5 million, respectively, for other postretirement benefits; and $25.8 million, $17.6 million and $15.5 million, respectively, related to reserves for legal proceedings associated with discontinued operations.

Warranty

2.190

DELL INC. (JAN)

NOTES TO CONSOLIDATED FINANCIAL STATEMENTS

Note 7—Warranty and Deferred Extended Warranty Revenue

Dell records liabilities for its standard limited warranties at the time of sale for the estimated costs that may be incurred. The liability for standard warranties is included in accrued and other current and other non-current liabilities on Dell's Consolidated Statements of Financial Position. Revenue from the sale of extended warranties is recognized over the term of the contract or when the service is completed, and the costs associated with these contracts are recognized as incurred. Deferred extended warranty revenue is included in deferred services revenue on Dell's Consolidated Statements of Financial Position. Changes in Dell's liabilities for standard limited warranties and deferred services revenue related to extended warranties are presented in the following tables:

	Fiscal Year Ended		
(In millions)	January 29, 2010	January 30, 2009	February 1, 2008
Warranty Liability:			
Warranty liability at beginning of period	$ 1,035	$ 929	$ 958
Costs accrued for new warranty contracts and changes in estimates for pre-existing warranties[a][b]	987	1,180	1,176
Service obligations honored	(1,110)	(1,074)	(1,205)
Warranty liability at end of period	$ 912	$ 1,035	$ 929
Current portion	$ 593	$ 721	$ 690
Non-current portion	319	314	239
Warranty liability at end of period	$ 912	$ 1,035	$ 929

	Fiscal Year Ended		
(In millions)	January 29, 2010	January 30, 2009	February 1, 2008
Deferred Extended Warranty Revenue:			
Deferred extended warranty revenue at beginning of period	$ 5,587	$ 5,233	$ 4,194
Revenue deferred for new extended warranties[b]	3,481	3,470	3,806
Revenue recognized	(3,158)	(3,116)	(2,767)
Deferred extended warranty revenue at end of period	$ 5,910	$ 5,587	$ 5,233
Current portion	$ 2,906	$ 2,601	$ 2,459
Non-current portion	3,004	2,986	2,774
Deferred extended warranty revenue at end of period	$ 5,910	$ 5,587	$ 5,233

[a] Changes in cost estimates related to pre-existing warranties are aggregated with accruals for new standard warranty contracts. Dell's warranty liability process does not differentiate between estimates made for pre-existing warranties and new warranty obligations.

[b] Includes the impact of foreign currency exchange rate fluctuations.

Environmental

2.191

MUELLER INDUSTRIES, INC. (DEC)

CONSOLIDATED BALANCE SHEETS (in part)

As of December 25, 2010 and December 26, 2009

(In thousands, except share data)	2010	2009
Liabilities		
Current liabilities:		
Current portion of debt	$ 32,020	$ 24,325
Accounts payable	67,849	73,837
Accrued wages and other		
Currentemployee costs	33,338	24,829
Other current liabilities	61,920	60,379
Total current liabilities	195,127	183,370
Long-term debt, less current portion	158,226	158,226
Pension liabilities	18,249	20,715
Postretirement benefits other than		
pensions	22,690	23,605
Environmental reserves	23,902	23,268
Deferred income taxes	24,081	31,128
Other noncurrent liabilities	824	887
Total liabilities	$443,099	$441,199

NOTES TO CONSOLIDATED FINANCIAL STATEMENTS

Note 1—Summary of Significant Accounting Policies (in part)

Environmental Reserves

The Company recognizes an environmental liability when it is probable the liability exists and the amount is reasonably estimable. The Company estimates the duration and extent of its remediation obligations based upon reports of outside consultants; internal analyses of clean-up costs, and ongoing monitoring costs; communications with regulatory agencies; and changes in environmental law. If the Company were to determine that its estimates of the duration or extent of its environmental obligations were no longer accurate, the Company would adjust its environmental liabilities accordingly in the period that such determination is made. Estimated future expenditures for environmental remediation are not discounted to their present value. Accrued environmental liabilities are not reduced by potential insurance reimbursements.

Environmental expenses that relate to ongoing operations are included as a component of cost of goods sold. Environmental expenses related to non-operating properties are included in other (expense) income, net in the Consolidated Statements of Income.

Note 10—Commitments and Contingencies (in part)

Environmental

The Company is subject to environmental standards imposed by federal, state, local, and foreign environmental laws and regulations. For all properties, the Company has provided and charged to expense $5.4 million in 2010, $1.1 million in 2009, and $15.4 million in 2008 for pending environmental matters. Environmental costs related to non-operating properties are classified as a component of other (expense) in-

come, net and costs related to operating properties are classified as cost of goods sold. Environmental reserves totaled $23.9 million at December 25, 2010 and $23.3 million at December 26, 2009. As of December 25, 2010, the Company expects to spend on existing environmental matters $1.6 million in 2011, $1.0 million in 2012, $1.0 million in 2013, $1.0 million in 2014, $0.5 million in 2015, and $9.3 million thereafter. The timing of a potential payment for a $9.5 million settlement offer has not yet been determined.

Asset Retirement Obligations

2.192

EASTMAN KODAK COMPANY (DEC)

NOTES TO FINANCIAL STATEMENTS

Note 9. Other Long-Term Liabilities

	As of December 31	
(In millions)	2010	2009
Non-current tax-related liabilities	$160	$ 477
Environmental liabilities	103	102
Asset retirement obligations	57	62
Deferred compensation	29	39
Other	276	325
Total	$625	$1,005

The Other component above consists of other miscellaneous long-term liabilities that, individually, were less than 5% of the total liabilities component in the accompanying Consolidated Statement of Financial Position, and therefore, have been aggregated in accordance with Regulation S-X.

Note 10. Commitments and Contingencies (in part)

Asset Retirement Obligations

As of December 31, 2010 and 2009, the Company has recorded approximately $57 million and $62 million, respectively, of asset retirement obligations within Other long-term liabilities in the accompanying Consolidated Statement of Financial Position. The Company's asset retirement obligations primarily relate to asbestos contained in buildings that the Company owns. In many of the countries in which the Company operates, environmental regulations exist that require the Company to handle and dispose of asbestos in a special manner if a building undergoes major renovations or is demolished. Otherwise, the Company is not required to remove the asbestos from its buildings. The Company records a liability equal to the estimated fair value of its obligation to perform asset retirement activities related to the asbestos, computed using an expected present value technique, when sufficient information exists to calculate the fair value. The Company does not have a liability recorded related to every building that contains asbestos because the Company cannot estimate the fair value of its obligation for certain buildings due to a lack of sufficient information about the range of time over which the obligation may be settled through demolition, renovation or sale of the building.

The following table provides asset retirement obligation activity:

(In millions)	For the Year Ended December 31		
	2010	2009	2008
Asset retirement obligations as of January 1	$62	$ 67	$64
Liabilities incurred in the current period	—	4	9
Liabilities settled in the current period	(8)	(13)	(9)
Accretion expense	3	3	3
Other	—	1	—
Asset retirement obligations as of December 31	$57	$ 62	$67

Litigation

2.193

AMPCO-PITTSBURGH CORPORATION (DEC)

CONSOLIDATED BALANCE SHEETS (in part)

(In thousands, except par value)	December 31	
	2010	2009
Current Liabilities:		
Accounts payable	$ 20,137	$ 15,799
Accrued payrolls and employee benefits	11,690	10,497
Industrial Revenue Bond debt	13,311	13,311
Asbestos liability—current portion	25,000	30,000
Other current liabilities	19,582	19,898
Total current liabilities	89,720	89,505
Employee benefit obligations	44,114	52,373
Asbestos liability	193,603	147,093
Other noncurrent liabilities	2,749	3,652
Total liabilities	$330,186	$292,623
Commitments and contingent liabilities (Note 8)		

NOTES TO CONSOLIDATED FINANCIAL STATEMENTS

Note 17—Litigation: (claims not in thousands) (in part)

Litigation (in part)

The Corporation and its subsidiaries are involved in various claims and lawsuits incidental to their businesses. In addition, it is also subject to asbestos litigation as described below.

Asbestos Litigation

Claims have been asserted alleging personal injury from exposure to asbestos-containing components historically used in some products of predecessors of the Corporation's Air & Liquid Systems Corporation subsidiary ("Asbestos Liability") and of an inactive subsidiary in dissolution and another former division of the Corporation. Those subsidiaries, and in some cases the Corporation, are defendants (among a number of defendants, typically over 50) in cases filed in various state and federal courts.

Asbestos Claims

The following table reflects approximate information about the claims for Asbestos Liability against the subsidiaries and the Corporation, along with certain asbestos claims asserted against the inactive subsidiary in dissolution and the former division, for the three years ended December 31, 2010, 2009 and 2008:

	2010	2009	2008
Open claims at end of period	8,081[1]	8,168[1]	9,354[1]
Gross settlement and defense costs (in 000's)	$18,085	$28,744	$19,102
Claims resolved	1,377	3,336	1,015

[1] Included as "open claims" are approximately 1,791 claims in 2010, 1,938 claims in 2009 and 3,243 claims in 2008 classified in various jurisdictions as "inactive" or transferred to a state or federal judicial panel on multi-district litigation, commonly referred to as the MDL.

A substantial majority of the settlement and defense costs reflected in the above table were reported and paid by insurers. Because claims are often filed and can be settled or dismissed in large groups, the amount and timing of settlements, as well as the number of open claims, can fluctuate significantly from period to period. In 2006, for the first time, a claim for Asbestos Liability against one of the Corporation's subsidiaries was tried to a jury. The trial resulted in a defense verdict. Plaintiffs appealed that verdict and in 2008 the California Court of Appeals reversed the jury verdict and remanded the case back to the trial court.

Asbestos Insurance

Certain of the Corporation's subsidiaries and the Corporation have an arrangement (the "Coverage Arrangement") with insurers responsible for historical primary and some first-layer excess insurance coverage for Asbestos Liability (the "Paying Insurers"). Under the Coverage Arrangement, the Paying Insurers accept financial responsibility, subject to the limits of the policies and based on fixed defense percentages and specified indemnity allocation formulas, for pending and future claims for Asbestos Liability. The claims against the Corporation's inactive subsidiary that is in dissolution proceedings, numbering approximately 400 as of December 31, 2010, are not included within the Coverage Arrangement. The one claim filed against the former division also is not included within the Coverage Arrangement. The Corporation believes that the claims against the inactive subsidiary in dissolution and the former division are immaterial.

The Coverage Arrangement includes an acknowledgement that Howden North America, Inc. ("Howden") is entitled to coverage under policies covering Asbestos Liability for claims arising out of the historical products manufactured or distributed by Buffalo Forge, a former subsidiary of the Corporation (the "Products"). The Coverage Arrangement does not provide for any prioritization on access to the applicable policies or monetary cap other than the limits of the policies, and, accordingly, Howden may access the policies at any time for any covered claim arising out of a Product. In general, access by Howden to the policies covering the Products will erode the coverage under the policies available to the Corporation and the relevant subsidiaries for Asbestos Liability alleged to arise out of not only the Products but also other historical products of the Corporation and its subsidiaries covered by the applicable policies.

On August 4, 2009, Howden filed a lawsuit in the United States District Court for the Western District of Pennsylvania. In the lawsuit, Howden raised claims against certain insurance companies that allegedly issued policies to Howden that do not cover the Corporation or its subsidiaries, and also raised claims against the Corporation and two other insurance companies that issued excess insurance policies covering certain subsidiaries of the Corporation (the "Excess Policies"), but that were not part of the Coverage Arrangement. In the lawsuit, Howden seeks, as respects the Corporation, a declaratory judgment from the court as to the respective rights and obligations of Howden, the Corporation and the insurance carriers under the Excess Policies. One of the excess carriers and the Corporation filed cross-claims against each other seeking declarations regarding their respective rights and obligations under Excess Policies issued by that carrier. The Corporation's cross-claim also sought damages for the carrier's failure to pay certain defense and indemnity costs. The Corporation and that carrier concluded a settlement generally consistent with the Coverage Arrangement, and all claims between that carrier and the Corporation were dismissed with prejudice on December 8, 2010. The litigation remains pending with respect to the other carrier that issued one of the Excess Policies.

On February 24, 2011, the Corporation and its Air & Liquid Systems Corporation subsidiary filed a lawsuit in the United States District Court for the Western District of Pennsylvania against thirteen domestic insurance companies, certain underwriters at Lloyd's, London and certain London market insurance companies, and Howden. The lawsuit seeks a declaratory judgment regarding the respective rights and obligations of the parties under excess insurance policies not included within the Coverage Arrangement that were issued to the Corporation from 1981 through 1984 as respects claims against the Corporation and its subsidiary for Asbestos Liability and as respects asbestos bodily-injury claims against Howden arising from the Products.

Asbestos Valuations

In 2006, the Corporation retained Hamilton, Rabinovitz & Associates, Inc. ("HR&A"), a nationally recognized expert in the valuation of asbestos liabilities, to assist the Corporation in estimating the potential liability for pending and unasserted future claims for Asbestos Liability. HR&A was not requested to estimate asbestos claims against the inactive subsidiary in dissolution or the former division, which the Corporation believes are immaterial. Based on this analysis, the Corporation recorded a reserve for Asbestos Liability claims pending or projected to be asserted through 2013 as at December 31, 2006. HR&A's analysis was updated in 2008, and additional reserves were established by the Corporation as at December 31, 2008 for Asbestos Liability claims pending or projected to be asserted through 2018. HR&A's analysis was most recently updated in 2010, and additional reserves were established by the Corporation as at December 31, 2010 for Asbestos Liability claims pending or projected to be asserted through 2020. The methodology used by HR&A in its projection in 2010 of the operating subsidiaries' liability for pending and unasserted potential future claims for Asbestos Liability, which is substantially the same as the methodology employed by HR&A in the 2006 and 2008 estimates, relied upon and included the following factors:

- HR&A's interpretation of a widely accepted forecast of the population likely to have been exposed to asbestos;
- Epidemiological studies estimating the number of people likely to develop asbestos-related diseases;
- HR&A's analysis of the number of people likely to file an asbestos-related injury claim against the subsidiaries and the Corporation based on such epidemiological data and relevant claims history from January 1, 2008 to August 30, 2010;
- An analysis of pending cases, by type of injury claimed and jurisdiction where the claim is filed;
- An analysis of claims resolution history from January 1, 2008 to August 30, 2010 to determine the average settlement value of claims, by type of injury claimed and jurisdiction of filing; and
- An adjustment for inflation in the future average settlement value of claims, at an annual inflation rate based on the Congressional Budget Office's ten year forecast of inflation.

Using this information, HR&A estimated in 2010 the number of future claims for Asbestos Liability that would be filed through the year 2020, as well as the settlement or indemnity costs that would be incurred to resolve both pending and future unasserted claims through 2020. This methodology has been accepted by numerous courts.

In conjunction with developing the aggregate liability estimate referenced above, the Corporation also developed an estimate of probable insurance recoveries for its Asbestos Liabilities. In developing the estimate, the Corporation considered HR&A's projection for settlement or indemnity costs for Asbestos Liability and management's projection of associated defense costs (based on the current defense to indemnity cost ratio), as well as a number of additional factors. These additional factors included the Coverage Arrangement, self-insured retentions, policy exclusions, policy limits, policy provisions regarding coverage for defense costs, attachment points, prior impairment of policies and gaps in the coverage, policy exhaustions, insolvencies among certain of the insurance carriers, the nature of the underlying claims for Asbestos Liability asserted against the subsidiaries and the Corporation as reflected in the Corporation's asbestos claims database, as well as estimated erosion of insurance limits on account of claims against Howden arising out of the Products. In addition to consulting with the Corporation's outside legal counsel on these insurance matters, the Corporation retained in 2010 a nationally-recognized insurance consulting firm to assist the Corporation with certain policy allocation matters that also are among the several factors considered by the Corporation when analyzing potential recoveries from relevant historical insurance for Asbestos Liabilities. Based upon all of the factors considered by the Corporation, and taking into account the Corporation's analysis of publicly available information regarding the credit-worthiness of various insurers, the Corporation estimated the probable insurance recoveries for Asbestos Liability and defense costs through 2020. Although the Corporation believes that the assumptions employed in the insurance valuation were reasonable and previously consulted with its outside legal counsel and insurance consultant regarding those assumptions, there are other assumptions that could have been employed that would have resulted in materially lower insurance recovery projections.

Based on the analyses described above, the Corporation's reserve at December 31, 2010 for the total costs, including defense costs, for Asbestos Liability claims pending or projected to be asserted through 2020 was $218,303 of which approximately 85% was attributable to settlement costs for unasserted claims projected to be filed through 2020 and future defense costs. While it is reasonably possible that the Corporation will incur additional charges for Asbestos Liability and defense costs in excess of the amounts currently reserved, the Corporation believes that there is too much uncertainty to provide for reasonable estimation of the number of future claims, the nature of such claims and the cost to resolve them beyond 2020. Accordingly, no reserve has been recorded for any costs that may be incurred after 2020.

The Corporation's receivable at December 31, 2010 for insurance recoveries attributable to the claims for which the Corporation's Asbestos Liability reserve has been established, including the portion of incurred defense costs covered by the Coverage Arrangement, and the probable payments and reimbursements relating to the estimated indemnity and defense costs for pending and unasserted future Asbestos Liability claims, was $141,839 ($115,430 as of December 31, 2009). The insurance receivable recorded by the Corporation does not assume any recovery from insolvent carriers, and substantially all of the insurance recoveries deemed probable were from insurance companies rated A—(excellent) or better by A.M. Best Corporation. There can be no assurance, however, that there will not be further insolvencies among the relevant insurance carriers, or that the assumed percentage recoveries for certain carriers will prove correct. The $76,464 million difference between insurance recoveries and projected costs at December 31, 2010 is not due to exhaustion of all insurance coverage for Asbestos Liability. The Corporation and the subsidiaries have substantial additional insurance coverage which the Corporation expects to be available for Asbestos Liability claims and defense costs the subsidiaries and it may incur after 2020. However, this insurance coverage also can be expected to have gaps creating significant shortfalls of insurance recoveries as against claims expense, which could be material in future years.

The amounts recorded by the Corporation for Asbestos Liabilities and insurance receivables rely on assumptions that are based on currently known facts and strategy. The Corporation's actual expenses or insurance recoveries could be significantly higher or lower than those recorded if assumptions used in the Corporation's or HR&A's calculations vary significantly from actual results. Key variables in these assumptions are identified above and include the number and type of new claims to be filed each year, the average cost of disposing of each such new claim, average annual defense costs, the resolution of coverage issues with insurance carriers, and the solvency risk with respect to the relevant insurance carriers. Other factors that may affect the Corporation's Asbestos Liability and ability to recover under its insurance policies include uncertainties surrounding the litigation process from jurisdiction to jurisdiction and from case to case, reforms that may be made by state and federal courts, and the passage of state or federal tort reform legislation.

The Corporation intends to evaluate its estimated Asbestos Liability and related insurance receivables as well as the underlying assumptions on a regular basis to determine whether any adjustments to the estimates are required. Due to the uncertainties surrounding asbestos litigation and insurance, these regular reviews may result in the Corporation incurring future charges; however, the Corporation is currently unable to estimate such future charges. Adjustments, if any, to the Corporation's estimate of its recorded Asbestos Liability and/or insurance receivables could be material to operating results for the periods in which the adjustments to the liability or receivable are recorded, and to the Corporation's liquidity and consolidated financial position.

Derivatives

2.194

CRACKER BARREL OLD COUNTRY STORE, INC. (JUL)

CONSOLIDATED BALANCE SHEETS (in part)

(In thousands except share data)	July 30, 2010	July 31, 2009
Current Liabilities:		
Accounts payable	$116,218	$ 92,168
Current maturities of long-term debt and capital lease obligations	6,765	7,422
Taxes withheld and accrued	32,987	32,081
Income taxes payable	7,624	—
Accrued employee compensation	59,874	49,994
Accrued employee benefits	30,937	32,633
Deferred revenues	27,544	22,528
Accrued interest expense	10,535	10,379
Other accrued expenses	17,064	17,757
Total current liabilities	309,548	264,962
Long-term debt	573,744	638,040
Capital lease obligations	41	60
Interest rate swap liability	66,281	61,232
Other long-term obligations	93,781	89,610
Deferred income taxes	$ 57,055	$ 55,655

NOTES TO CONSOLIDATED FINANCIAL STATEMENTS

(In thousands except share data)

2. Summary of Significant Accounting Policies (in part)

Fair value measurements—Fair value is defined as the price that would be received to sell an asset or paid to transfer a liability in an orderly transaction between market participants at the measurement date. In determining fair value, a three level hierarchy for inputs is used. These levels are:

- Level 1—quoted prices (unadjusted) for an identical asset or liability in an active market.
- Level 2—quoted prices for a similar asset or liability in an active market or model-derived valuations in which all significant inputs are observable for substantially the full term of the asset or liability.
- Level 3—unobservable and significant to the fair value measurement of the asset or liability.

The fair values of cash equivalents and deferred compensation plan assets (included in other assets) are based on quoted market prices. The fair values of accounts receivable and accounts payable at July 30, 2010 and July 31, 2009, approximate their carrying amounts due to their short duration. The fair value of the Company's variable-rate term loans and revolving credit facility, based on quoted market prices, totaled approximately $566,510 and $619,200 on July 30, 2010 and July 31, 2009, respectively. The estimated fair value of the Company's interest rate swap is the present value of the expected cash flows, which is calculated by using the replacement fixed rate in the then-current market, and incorporates the Company's own non-performance risk. See Note 3 for additional information on the Company's fair value measurements.

Derivative instruments and hedging activities (in part)—The Company is exposed to market risk, such as changes in interest rates and commodity prices. The Company has interest rate risk relative to its outstanding borrowings under its Credit Facility (see Note 5). Loans under the Credit Facility bear interest, at the Company's election, either at the prime rate or LIBOR plus a percentage point spread based on certain specified financial ratios. The Company uses derivative instruments to mitigate its interest rate risk. The Company's policy has been to manage interest cost using a mix of fixed and variable rate debt (see Note 5). To manage this risk in a cost efficient manner, the Company entered into an interest rate swap on May 4, 2006 in which it agreed to exchange with a counterparty, at specified intervals effective August 3, 2006, the difference between fixed and variable interest amounts calculated by reference to an agreed-upon notional principal amount.

The swapped portion of the outstanding debt or notional amount of the interest rate swap is as follows:

From August 3, 2006 to May 2, 2007	$525,000
From May 3, 2007 to May 5, 2008	650,000
From May 6, 2008 to May 4, 2009	625,000
From May 5, 2009 to May 3, 2010	600,000
From May 4, 2010 to May 2, 2011	575,000
From May 3, 2011 to May 2, 2012	550,000
From May 3, 2012 to May 3, 2013	525,000

The interest rate swap was accounted for as a cash flow hedge. The swapped portion of the Company's outstanding debt is fixed at a rate of 5.57% plus the Company's credit spread over the 7-year life of the interest rate swap. The Company's weighted average credit spreads at July 30, 2010 and July 31, 2009 were 1.90% and 1.50%, respectively.

Additionally, the Company entered into an interest rate swap on August 10, 2010 in which it agreed to exchange with a counterparty, effective May 3, 2013, the difference between fixed and variable interest amounts calculated by reference to the notional principal amount of $200,000. The interest rate swap was accounted for as a cash flow hedge. The swapped portion of the Company's outstanding debt will be fixed at a rate of 2.73% plus the Company's credit spread over the 2-year life of the interest rate swap.

The Company does not hold or use derivative instruments for trading purposes. The Company also does not have any derivatives not designated as hedging instruments and has not designated any non-derivatives as hedging instruments. See Note 6 for additional information on the Company's derivative and hedging activities.

3. Fair Value Measurements (in part)

The Company's assets and liabilities measured at fair value on a recurring basis at July 30, 2010 were as follows:

(In thousands, except share data)	Quoted Prices in Active Markets for Identical Assets (Level 1)	Significant Other Observable Inputs (Level 2)	Significant Unobservable Inputs (Level 3)	Fair Value as of July 30, 2010
Cash equivalents[*]	$35,250	$ —	$—	$35,250
Deferred compensation plan assets[**]	25,935	—	—	25,935
Total assets at fair value	$61,185	$ —	$—	$61,185
Interest rate swap liability (see Note 6)	$ —	$66,281	$—	$66,281
Total liabilities at fair value	$ —	$66,281	$—	$66,281

The Company's assets and liabilities measured at fair value on a recurring basis at July 31, 2009 were as follows:

(In thousands, except share data)	Quoted Prices in Active Markets for Identical Assets (Level 1)	Significant Other Observable Inputs (Level 2)	Significant Unobservable Inputs (Level 3)	Fair Value as of July 31, 2009
Cash equivalents[*]	$ 48	$ —	$—	$ 48
Deferred compensation plan assets[**]	22,583	—	—	22,583
Total assets at fair value	$22,631	$ —	$—	$22,631
Interest rate swap liability (see Note 6)	$ —	$61,232	$—	$61,232
Total liabilities at fair value	$ —	$61,232	$—	$61,232

[*] Consists of money market fund investments.
[**] Represents plan assets invested in mutual funds established under a Rabbi Trust for the Company's non-qualified savings plan and is included in the Consolidated Balance Sheet as other assets (see Note 13).

6. Derivative Instruments and Hedging Activities (in part)

The estimated fair values of the Company's derivative instrument were as follows:

(In thousands, except share data)	Balance Sheet Location	July 31, 2009 Fair Value	July 30, 2010 Fair Value
Interest rate swap (See Note 3)	Interest rate swap liability	$61,232	$66,281

The estimated fair value of the Company's interest rate swap liability incorporates the Company's own non-performance risk. The adjustment related to the Company's non-performance risk at July 30, 2010 and July 31, 2009 resulted in reductions of $3,915 and $5,372, respectively, in the fair value of the interest rate swap liability. The offset to the interest rate swap liability is recorded in accumulated other comprehensive loss ("AOCL"), net of the deferred tax asset, and will be reclassified into earnings over the term of the underlying debt. As of July 30, 2010, the estimated pre-tax portion of AOCL that is expected to be reclassified into earnings over the next twelve months is $29,270. Cash flows related to the interest rate swap are included in interest expense and in operating activities.

Deferred Credits

2.195

LAS VEGAS SANDS CORP. (DEC)

CONSOLIDATED BALANCE SHEETS (in part)

(In thousands, except share data)	December 31 2010	December 31 2009
Current liabilities:		
Accounts payable	$ 113,505	$ 82,695
Construction payables	516,981	778,771
Accrued interest payable	42,625	18,332
Other accrued liabilities	1,160,234	786,192
Current maturities of long-term debt	767,068	173,315
Total current liabilities	2,600,413	1,839,305
Other long-term liabilities	78,240	81,959
Deferred income taxes	115,219	—
Deferred proceeds from sale of The Shoppes at The Palazzo	243,928	243,928
Deferred gain on sale of The Grand Canal Shoppes	50,808	54,272
Deferred rent from mall transactions	147,378	149,074
Long-term debt	9,373,755	10,852,147
Total liabilities	12,609,741	13,220,685

NOTES TO CONSOLIDATED FINANCIAL STATEMENTS

Note 13—Mall Sales

The Grand Canal Shoppes at The Venetian Las Vegas

In April 2004, the Company entered into an agreement to sell The Grand Canal Shoppes and lease certain restaurant and other retail space at the casino level of The Venetian Las Vegas (the "Master Lease") to GGP for approximately $766.0 million (the "Mall Sale"). The Mall Sale closed in May 2004, and the Company realized a gain of $417.6 million in connection with the Mall Sale. Under the Master Lease agreement, The Venetian Las Vegas leased nineteen spaces on its casino level currently occupied by various tenants to GGP for 89 years with annual rent of one dollar and GGP assumed the various leases. Under generally accepted accounting principles, the Master Lease agreement does not qualify as a sale of the real property assets, which real property was not separately legally demised. Accordingly, $109.2 million of the transaction has been deferred as prepaid operating lease payments to The Venetian Las Vegas, which will amortize into income on a straight-line basis over the 89-year lease term. During each of the years ended December 31, 2010, 2009 and 2008, $1.2 million of this deferred item was amortized and is included in convention, retail and other revenue. In addition, the Company agreed with GGP to: (i) continue to be obligated to fulfill certain lease termination and asset purchase agreements as further described in "—Note 14—Commitments and Contingencies—Other Ventures and Commitments"; (ii) lease the Blue Man Group theater space located within The Grand Canal Shoppes from GGP for a period of 25 years with fixed minimum rent of $3.3 million per year with cost of living adjustments; (iii) operate the Gondola ride under an operating agreement for a period of 25 years for an annual fee of $3.5 million; and (iv) lease certain office space from GGP for a period of 10 years, subject to extension options for a period of up to 65 years, with annual rent of approximately $0.9 million. The lease payments under clauses (ii) through (iv) above are subject to automatic increases beginning on the sixth lease year. The net present value of the lease payments under clauses (ii) through (iv) on the closing date of the sale was $77.2 million. Under generally accepted accounting principles, a portion of the transaction must be deferred in an amount equal to the present value of the minimum lease payments set forth in the lease back agreements. This deferred gain will be amortized to reduce lease expense on a straight-line basis over the life of the leases. During each of the years ended December 31, 2010, 2009 and 2008, $3.5 million of this deferred item was amortized as an offset to convention, retail and other expense.

As of December 31, 2010, the Company was obligated under (ii), (iii), and (iv) above to make future payments as follows (in thousands):

2011	$ 8,043
2012	8,043
2013	8,043
2014	7,725
2015	7,497
Thereafter	106,302
	$145,653

The Shoppes at The Palazzo

The Shoppes at The Palazzo opened on January 18, 2008, with some tenants not yet open and with construction of certain portions of the mall not yet completed. Pursuant to the Amended Agreement, the Company contracted to sell The Shoppes at The Palazzo to GGP. The Final Purchase Price for The Shoppes at The Palazzo is determined by taking The Shoppes at The Palazzo's NOI, as defined in the Amended Agreement, for months 19 through 30 of its operations (assuming that the fixed rent and other fixed periodic payments due from all tenants in month 30 was actually due in each of months 19 through 30, provided that this 12-month period can be delayed if certain conditions are satisfied) divided by a capitalization rate. The capitalization rate is 0.06 for every dollar of NOI up to $38.0 million and 0.08 for every dollar of NOI above $38.0 million. On the closing date of the sale, February 29, 2008, GGP made its initial purchase price payment of $290.8 million based on projected net operating income for the first 12 months of operations (only taking into account tenants open for business or paying rent as of February 29, 2008). Pursuant to the Amended Agreement, periodic adjustments to the purchase price (up or down, but never to less than $250.0 million) were to be made based on projected NOI for the then upcoming 12 months. Pursuant to the Amended Agreement, the Company received an additional $4.6 million in June 2008, representing the adjustment payment at the fourth month after closing. During the years ended December 31, 2010 and 2009, the Company and GGP agreed to suspend the scheduled purchase price adjustments, subsequent to the June 2008 payment, except for the Final Purchase Price payment. Subject to adjustments for certain audit and other issues, the final adjustment to the purchase price was to be made on the 30-month anniversary of the closing date (or later if certain conditions are satisfied) based on the previously described formula. For all purchase price and purchase price adjustment calculations, NOI will be calculated by using the "accrual" method of accounting. Additionally, given the economic and market conditions facing retailers on a national and local level, tenants are facing economic challenges that have had an effect on the calculation of NOI. During the year ended December 31, 2010, the Company and GGP deferred the time to reach agreement on the Final Purchase Price as both parties were continuing to work on various matters related to the calculation of NOI.

In April 2009, GGP and its subsidiary that owns The Shoppes at The Palazzo filed voluntary petitions under Chapter 11 of the U.S. Bankruptcy Code (the "Chapter 11 Cases"). The United States Bankruptcy Court for the Southern District of New York entered orders approving the plans of reorganization of GGP and the subsidiary that owns The Shoppes at The Palazzo on October 21 and April 29, 2010, respectively, and the effective date of such plans of reorganization occurred on November 9 and May 28, 2010, respectively. Under the confirmed plans of reorganization, the only impaired creditors were mortgage holders. The Company will continue to review the Chapter 11 Cases and will adjust the estimates of NOI and capitalization rates as additional information is received.

In the Amended Agreement, the Company agreed to lease certain restaurant and retail space on the casino level of The Palazzo to GGP pursuant to a master lease agreement ("The Palazzo Master Lease"). Under The Palazzo Master Lease, which was executed concurrently with, and as a part of, the closing on the sale of The Shoppes at The Palazzo to GGP on February 29, 2008, The Palazzo leased nine restaurant and retail spaces on the casino level of The Palazzo, currently occupied by various tenants, to GGP for 89 years with annual rent of one dollar and GGP assumed the various tenant operating leases for those spaces. Under generally accepted accounting principles, The Palazzo Master Lease does not qualify as a sale of the real property, which real property was not separately legally demised. Accordingly, $41.8 million of the mall sale transaction has been deferred as prepaid operating lease payments to The Palazzo, which is amortized into income on a straight-line basis over the 89-year lease term. An additional $7.0 million of the total proceeds from the mall sale transaction has been deferred as unearned revenues as of December 31, 2010. This balance will be adjusted upon resolution of the Final Purchase Price.

In addition, the Company agreed with GGP to lease certain spaces located within The Shoppes at The Palazzo for a period of 10 years with total fixed minimum rents of $0.7 million per year, subject to extension options for a period of up to 10 years and automatic increases beginning on the second lease year. As of December 31, 2009, the Company was obligated to make future payments of approximately $0.8 million annually for the five years ended December 31, 2014, and $3.2 million thereafter. Under generally accepted accounting principles, a gain on the sale has not been recorded as the Company has continuing involvement in the transaction related to the certain activities to be performed on behalf of GGP and the uncertainty of the final sales price, which will be determined as previously described. Therefore, $243.9 million of the mall sale transaction has been recorded as deferred proceeds from the sale as of December 31, 2010, which accrued interest at an imputed interest rate offset by (i) imputed rental income and (ii) rent payments made to GGP related to those spaces leased back from GGP. The property sold to GGP will continue to be recorded in the Company's consolidated financial statements until the Final Purchase Price has been determined.

ACCUMULATED OTHER COMPREHENSIVE INCOME

PRESENTATION

2.196 FASB ASC 220, *Comprehensive Income*, requires that a separate caption for accumulated other comprehensive income be presented in the "Equity" section of a balance sheet. An entity should disclose accumulated balances for each classification in that separate component of equity on the face of a balance sheet, in a statement of changes in equity, or in notes to the financial statements.

2.197

TABLE 2-15: ACCUMULATED OTHER COMPREHENSIVE INCOME—PRESENTATION OF COMPONENT BALANCES

Table 2-15 shows where accumulated component balances are presented.

	2010	2009	2008
Notes to financial statements..................	105	298	327
Statement of changes in stockholders' equity...	232	90	68
"Stockholders' Equity" section of the balance sheet..	123	27	30
Statement of comprehensive income......	12	1	1
Component balances not presented.......	19	73	63
	491	489	489
No accumulated other comprehensive income...	9	11	11
Total Entities...	**500**	**500**	**500**

PRESENTATION AND DISCLOSURE EXCERPTS

Accumulated Other Comprehensive Income—Equity Section of Balance Sheet

2.198

NACCO INDUSTRIES, INC. (DEC)

CONSOLIDATED BALANCE SHEETS (in part)

	December 31	
(In millions, except share data)	2010	2009
Stockholders' Equity		
Common stock:		
Class A, par value $1 per share, 6,737,199 shares outstanding (2009—6,694,380 shares outstanding)	$ 6.8	$ 6.7
Class B, par value $1 per share, convertible into Class A on a one-for-one basis, 1,596,093 shares outstanding (2009—1,599,356 shares outstanding)	1.6	1.6
Capital in excess of par value	22.6	16.1
Retained earnings	475.4	413.3
Accumulated other comprehensive income (loss):		
Foreign currency translation adjustment	28.1	34.8
Deferred gain (loss) on cash flow hedging	(9.0)	3.5
Pension and postretirement plan adjustment	(78.1)	(79.4)
Total Stockholders' equity	447.4	396.6
Noncontrolling interest	0.8	0.5
Total equity	$448.2	$397.1

2.199

DEERE & COMPANY (OCT)

CONSOLIDATED BALANCE SHEET (in part)

As of October 31, 2010 and 2009
  (In millions of dollars except per share amounts)

	2010	2009
Stockholders' Equity		
Common stock, $1 par value (authorized—1,200,000,000 shares; issued—536,431,204 shares in 2010 and 2009), at paid-in amount	3,106.3	2,996.2
Common stock in treasury, 114,250,815 shares in 2010 and 113,188,823 shares in 2009, at cost	(5,789.5)	(5,564.7)
Retained earnings	12,353.1	10,980.5
Accumulated other comprehensive income (loss):		
Retirement benefits adjustment	(3,797.0)	(3,955.0)
Cumulative translation adjustment	436.0	400.2
Unrealized loss on derivatives	(29.2)	(44.1)
Unrealized gain on investments	10.6	5.6
Accumulated other comprehensive income (loss)	(3,379.6)	(3,593.3)
Total Deere & Company stockholders' equity	6,290.3	4,818.7
Noncontrolling interests	13.1	4.1
Total stockholders' equity	6,303.4	4,822.8

Accumulated Other Comprehensive Income—Statement of Changes in Equity

2.200

HONEYWELL INTERNATIONAL INC. (DEC)

CONSOLIDATED STATEMENT OF SHAREOWNERS EQUITY

(In millions)	Years Ended December 31					
	2010		2009		2008	
	Shares	$	Shares	$	Shares	$
Common stock, par value	957.6	958	957.6	958	957.6	958
Additional paid-in capital						
Beginning balance		3,823		3,994		4,014
Issued for employee savings and option plans		(35)		(99)		(56)
Contributed to pension plans		32		(190)		(90)
Stock-based compensation expense		157		118		128
Other owner changes		—		—		(2)
Ending balance		3,977		3,823		3,994
Treasury stock						
Beginning balance	(193.4)	(8,995)	(223.0)	(10,206)	(211.0)	(9,479)
Reacquired stock or repurchases of common stock	—	—	—	—	(27.4)	(1,459)
Issued for employee savings and option plans	8.9	328	6.6	281	9.0	427
Contributed to pension plans	9.9	368	23.0	930	6.1	290
Other owner changes	—	—	—	—	0.3	15
Ending balance	(174.6)	(8,299)	(193.4)	(8,995)	(223.0)	(10,206)
Retained earnings						
Beginning balance		14,023		13,391		13,400
Net income attributable to Honeywell		2,022		1,548		806
Dividends paid on common stock		(948)		(916)		(815)
Ending balance		15,097		14,023		13,391
Accumulated other comprehensive income (loss)						
Beginning balance		(948)		(1,078)		329
Foreign exchange translation adjustment		(249)		259		(614)
Pensions and other post retirement benefit adjustments		44		(271)		(718)
Changes in fair value of available for sale investments		90		112		(51)
Changes in fair value of effective cash flow hedges		(4)		30		(24)
Ending balance		(1,067)		(948)		(1,078)
Non controlling interest						
Beginning balance		110		82		71
Acquisitions		2		5		4
Interest sold (bought)		4		—		(3)
Net income attributable to non controlling interest		13		36		20
Foreign exchange translation adjustment		2		(1)		(2)
Dividends paid		(10)		(9)		(7)
Other owner changes		—		(3)		(1)
Ending balance		121		110		82
Total shareowners equity	783.0	10,787	764.2	8,971	734.6	7,141
Comprehensive income						
Net income		2,035		1,584		826
Foreign exchange translation adjustment		(249)		259		(614)
Pensions and other post retirement benefit adjustments		44		(271)		(718)
Changes in fair value of available for sale investments		90		112		(51)
Changes in fair value of effective cash flow hedges		(4)		30		(24)
Total comprehensive income		1,916		1,714		(581)
Comprehensive income attributable to non controlling interest		(15)		(36)		(20)
Comprehensive income (loss) attributable to Honeywell		1,901		1,678		(601)

The Notes to Financial Statements are integral part of this statement.

ATT-SEC 2.200

2.201

CLIFFS NATURAL RESOURCES INC. (DEC)

STATEMENTS OF CONSOLIDATED CHANGES IN EQUITY

(In millions)	Number of Common Shares	Common Shares	Capital in Excess of Par Value of Shares	Retained Earnings	Common Shares in Treasury	Accumulated Other Comprehensive Income (Loss)	Non-Controlling Interest	Total
Cliffs Shareholders								
January 1, 2008	87.2	$16.8	$116.6	$1,316.2	$(255.6)	$ (30.3)	$ 117.8	$1,281.5
Comprehensive income								
Net income	—	—	—	515.8	—	—	21.2	537.0
Other comprehensive income								
Pension and OPEB liability	—	—	—	—	—	(188.5)	(8.0)	(196.5)
Unrealized net loss on marketable securities	—	—	—	—	—	(10.3)	(1.4)	(11.7)
Unrealized net loss on foreign currency translation	—	—	—	—	—	(165.1)	(13.7)	(178.8)
Unrealized loss on interest rate swap	—	—	—	—	—	(0.8)	—	(0.8)
Unrealized gain on derivative instruments	—	—	—	—	—	0.4	0.8	1.2
Total comprehensive income	—	—	—	—	—	—	(1.1)	150.4
Equity purchase of noncontrolling interest	4.3	—	141.8	—	23.2	—	—	165.0
Purchase of subsidiary shares from noncontrolling interest	—	—	—	—	—	—	(111.2)	(111.2)
Undistributed losses to noncontrolling interest	—	—	—	—	—	—	(2.9)	(2.9)
Capital contribution by noncontrolling interest to subsidiary	—	—	—	—	—	—	0.7	0.7
PinnOak settlement	4.0	—	131.5	—	21.5	—	—	153.0
Stock and other incentive plans	—	—	19.2	—	0.8	—	—	20.0
Conversion of preferred stock	18.0	—	33.1	5.1	96.3	—	—	134.5
Preferred stock dividends	—	—	—	(1.1)	—	—	—	(1.1)
Common stock dividends	—	$ —	$ —	$ (36.1)	$ —	$ —	$ —	$ (36.1)
December 31, 2008	113.5	16.8	442.2	1,799.9	(113.8)	(394.6)	3.3	1,753.8
Comprehensive income								
Net income	—	—	—	205.1	—	—	(0.8)	204.3
Other comprehensive income								
Pension and OPEB liability	—	—	—	—	—	24.2	(2.4)	21.8
Unrealized net gain on marketable securities	—	—	—	—	—	29.5	—	29.5
Unrealized net gain on foreign currency translation	—	—	—	—	—	231.7	—	231.7
Unrealized gain on interest rate swap	—	—	—	—	—	1.7	—	1.7
Reclassification of net gains on derivative financial instruments into net income	—	—	—	—	—	(15.1)	—	(15.1)
Total comprehensive income	—	—	—	—	—	—	(3.2)	473.9
Purchase of subsidiary shares from noncontrolling interest	—	—	—	—	—	—	0.1	0.1
Undistributed losses to noncontrolling interest	—	—	—	—	—	—	(6.7)	(6.7)
Capital contribution by noncontrolling interest to subsidiary	—	—	—	—	—	—	0.7	0.7
Issuance of common shares	17.3	—	254.5	—	92.8	—	—	347.3
Purchase of additional noncontrolling interest	—	—	(5.4)	—	—	—	—	(5.4)
Stock and other incentive plans	0.2	—	4.1	—	0.9	—	—	5.0
Conversion of preferred stock	—	—	—	—	0.2	—	—	0.2
Common stock dividends	—	—	—	(31.9)	—	—	—	(31.9)
December 31, 2009	131.0	16.8	695.4	1,973.1	(19.9)	(122.6)	(5.8)	2,537.0

(continued)

(In millions)	Cliffs Shareholders							
	Number of Common Shares	Common Shares	Capital in Excess of Par Value of Shares	Retained Earnings	Common Shares in Treasury	Accumulated Other Comprehensive Income (Loss)	Non-Controlling Interest	Total
Comprehensive income								
Net income	—	$ —	$ —	$1,019.9	$ —	$ —	$(0.2)	$1,019.7
Other comprehensive income								
Pension and OPEB liability	—	—	—	—	—	14.0	0.8	14.8
Unrealized net gain on marketable securities	—	—	—	—	—	4.2	—	4.2
Unrealized net gain on foreign currency translation	—	—	—	—	—	151.6	—	151.6
Reclassification of net gains on derivative financial instruments into net income	—	—	—	—	—	(3.2)	—	(3.2)
Unrealized gain on derivative instruments	—	—	—	—	—	1.9	—	1.9
Total comprehensive income							0.6	1,189.0
Purchase of subsidiary shares from noncontrolling interest	—	—	—	—	—	—	(0.5)	(0.5)
Undistributed losses to noncontrolling interest	—	—	—	—	—	—	(4.5)	(4.5)
Capital contribution by noncontrolling interest to subsidiary	—	—	—	—	—	—	3.0	3.0
Purchase of additional noncontrolling interest	—	—	(1.6)	—	—	—	—	(1.6)
Acquisition of controlling interest	4.2	0.5	172.6	—	—	—	—	173.1
Stock and other incentive plans	0.3	—	19.4	—	(7.3)	—	—	12.1
Common stock dividends	—	—	—	(68.9)	—	—	—	(68.9)
Other	—	—	10.5	—	(10.5)	—	—	—
December 31, 2010	135.5	$17.3	$896.3	$2,924.1	$(37.7)	$45.9	$(7.2)	$3,838.7

See notes to consolidated financial statements.

Accumulated Other Comprehensive Income—Notes to Consolidated Financial Statements

2.202

ALLIANT TECHSYSTEMS INC. (MAR)

NOTES TO CONSOLIDATED FINANCIAL STATEMENTS

1. Summary of Significant Accounting Policies (in part)

Comprehensive Income. The components of comprehensive income for fiscal 2010, 2009, and 2008 are as follows (amounts in thousands):

	Years Ended March 31		
	2010	2009	2008
Income before noncontrolling interest	$ 278,944	$ 140,953	$209,377
Other comprehensive (loss) income (OCI):			
Change in fair value of derivatives, net of income taxes of $(25,386), (365), and $(336), respectively	39,706	550	600
Pension and other postretirement benefit liabilities, net of income taxes of $131,654, $177,118, and $641, respectively	(211,513)	(274,601)	(508)
Change in fair value of available-for-sale securities, net of income taxes of $(1,517), $643, and $183, respectively	2,373	(965)	(229)
Total OCI	(169,434)	(275,016)	(137)
Comprehensive income (loss)	109,510	(134,063)	209,240
Comprehensive income attributable to noncontrolling interest	230	187	376
Comprehensive income (loss) attributable to Alliant Techsystems Inc.	$ 109,280	$(134,250)	$208,864

The components of accumulated OCI, net of income taxes, are as follows:

	March 31	
	2010	**2009**
Derivatives	$ 39,706	$ —
Pension and other postretirement benefit liabilities	(862,356)	(650,843)
Available-for-sale securities	1,564	(809)
Total accumulated other comprehensive loss	$(821,086)	$(651,652)

2.203

RPM INTERNATIONAL INC. (MAY)

NOTES TO CONSOLIDATED FINANCIAL STATEMENTS

6) Accumulated Other Comprehensive Income (Loss)

Accumulated other comprehensive income (loss) consists of the following components:

(In thousands)	Foreign Currency Translation Adjustments	Pension and Other Postretirement Benefit Liability Adjustments, Net of Tax	Unrealized Gain (Loss) on Derivatives, Net of Tax	Unrealized Gain (Loss) on Securities, Net of Tax	Total
Balance at June 1, 2007	$ 70,999	$ (46,156)	$ 3,311	$ 8,644	$ 36,798
Reclassification adjustments for (gains) losses included in net income				(882)	(882)
Other comprehensive income (loss)	55,857	(1,433)	7,195	7,842	69,461
Deferred taxes		946	(2,404)	(2,757)	(4,215)
Balance at May 31, 2008	126,856	(46,643)	8,102	12,847	101,162
Reclassification adjustments for losses included in net income, net of tax of $3,989				9,682	9,682
Other comprehensive (loss)	(99,458)	(26,401)	(6,871)	(32,475)	(165,205)
Deferred taxes		9,842	2,283	10,679	22,804
Balance at May 31, 2009	27,398	(63,202)	3,514	733	(31,557)
Reclassification adjustments for losses included in net income, net of tax of $783				(1,399)	(1,399)
Other comprehensive income (loss)	(44,082)	(69,791)	(3,239)	17,574	(99,538)
Deferred taxes		22,442	1,072	(6,031)	17,483
Adjustment due to deconsolidation of SPHC	222	7,286	(288)		7,220
Balance at May 31, 2010	$(16,462)	$(103,265)	$ 1,059	$10,877	$(107,791)

Section 3: Income Statement

INCOME STATEMENT FORMAT

PRESENTATION

3.01 Either a single-step or multistep form is acceptable for preparing a statement of income. In a single-step format, income tax is shown as a separate last item. In a multistep format, either costs are deducted from sales to show the gross margin, or costs and expenses are deducted from sales to show operating income. Further, net income should reflect all items of profit and loss recognized during the period, except for certain entities (investment companies, insurance entities, and certain not-for-profit entities) and with the sole exception of error corrections, as discussed in Financial Accounting Standards Board (FASB) *Accounting Standards Codification* (ASC) 250, *Accounting Changes and Error Corrections*.

3.02 FASB ASC 220, *Comprehensive Income*, requires that comprehensive income and its components be reported in a financial statement. Comprehensive income and its components can be reported in an income statement, a separate statement of comprehensive income, or a statement of changes in stockholders' equity.

3.03

TABLE 3-1: INCOME STATEMENT FORMAT

	2010	2009	2008
Income tax shown as separate last item.....................	87	76	82
Costs deducted from sales to show gross margin..........................	265	247	235
Costs and expenses deducted from sales to show operating income.......	146	177	183
Other..	2	N/C*	N/C*
Total Entities...............................	**500**	**500**	**500**

* N/C = Not compiled. The line item was not included in the table for the year shown.

PRESENTATION AND DISCLOSURE EXCERPTS

Reclassifications

3.04

QWEST COMMUNICATIONS INTERNATIONAL INC. (DEC)

NOTES TO CONSOLIDATED FINANCIAL STATEMENTS

Note 2. Summary of Significant Accounting Policies (in part)

Reclassifications

During the first quarter of 2010, we changed the definitions we use to classify expenses as cost of sales, selling expenses or general, administrative and other operating expenses and, as a result, certain expenses in our consolidated statements of operations for the prior year have been reclassified to conform to the current year presentation. Our new definitions of these expenses are as follows:

- *Cost of sales (exclusive of depreciation and amortization)* are expenses incurred in providing products and services to our customers. These expenses include: facilities expenses (which are third-party telecommunications expenses we incur for using other carriers' networks to provide services to our customers); employee-related expenses directly attributable to operating and maintaining our network (such as salaries, wages and certain benefits); equipment sales expenses (such as data integration and modem expenses); rents and utilities expenses incurred by our network operations and data centers; fleet expenses; and other expenses directly related to our network operations (such as professional fees and outsourced services).

- *Selling expenses* are expenses incurred in selling products and services to our customers. These expenses include: employee-related expenses directly attributable to selling products or services (such as salaries, wages, internal commissions and certain benefits); marketing and advertising; external commissions; bad debt expense; and other selling expenses (such as professional fees and outsourced services).

- *General, administrative and other operating expenses* are corporate overhead and other operating expenses. These expenses include: employee-related expenses for administrative functions (such as salaries, wages and certain benefits); taxes and fees (such as property and other taxes and universal service funds ("USF") charges); rents and utilities expenses incurred by our administrative offices; and other general, administrative and other operating expenses (such as professional fees). These expenses also include our combined net periodic pension and post-retirement benefits expenses for all eligible employees and retirees.

These definitions reflect changes primarily to reclassify expenses for: rent and utilities incurred by our network operations and data centers; fleet; network and supply chain management; and insurance and risk management from general, administrative and other operating expenses to cost of sales, where these expenses are more aligned with how we now manage our segments. We believe these changes allow users of our financial statements to better understand our expense structure. These expense classifications may not be comparable to those of other companies. These changes had no impact on total operating expenses or net income for any period. These changes resulted in the reclassification of $370 million and $371 million from the general, administrative and other operating expenses and selling expenses categories to cost of sales for the years ended December 31, 2009 and 2008, respectively.

We have also reclassified certain other prior year amounts in our Annual Report on Form 10-K for the year ended December 31, 2009 to conform to the current year presentation.

3.05

EL PASO CORPORATION (DEC)

CONSOLIDATED STATEMENTS OF COMPREHENSIVE INCOME

(In millions)	Year Ended December 31		
	2010	2009	2008
Net income (loss)	$ 924	$(474)	$ (789)
Pension and postretirement obligations:			
Unrealized actuarial gains (losses) arising during period (net of income taxes of $24 in 2010, $11 in 2009 and $288 in 2008)	(46)	36	(527)
Reclassifications of actuarial gains during period (net of income taxes of $25 in 2010, $16 in 2009 and $8 in 2008)	46	27	16
Cash flow hedging activities:			
Unrealized mark-to-market gains (losses) arising during period (net of income taxes of $24 in 2010, $6 in 2009 and $106 in 2008)	(40)	11	191
Reclassification adjustments for changes in initial value to the settlement date (net of income taxes of $4 in 2010, $146 in 2009 and $31 in 2008)	7	(260)	57
Other comprehensive (loss)	(33)	(186)	(263)
Comprehensive income (loss)	891	(660)	(1,052)
Comprehensive income attributable to noncontrolling interests	(166)	(65)	(34)
Comprehensive income (loss) attributable to El Paso Corporation	$ 725	$(725)	$(1,086)

See accompanying notes.

NOTES TO CONSOLIDATED FINANCIAL STATEMENTS

7. Financial Instruments (in part)

Below are the impacts of our commodity-based and interest rate derivatives to our income statement and statement of comprehensive income (loss) for the years ended December 31, 2010 and 2009:

(In millions)	2010				2009			
	Operating Revenues	Interest Expense	Other Income	Other Comprehensive Income (Loss)	Operating Revenues	Interest Expense	Other Income	Other Comprehensive Income (Loss)
Production-related derivatives[1]	$390	$—	$—	$ 11	$687	$—	$ —	$(406)
Other natural gas and power derivatives not designated as hedges	(45)	—	—	—	41	—	—	—
Total interest rate derivatives[2]	—	18	—	(52)	—	14	(26)	9
Total[3]	$345	$18	$—	$(41)	$728	$14	$(26)	$(397)

[1] We reclassified $11 million of accumulated other comprehensive loss and $406 million of accumulated other comprehensive income for the years ended December 31, 2010 and 2009 into operating revenues related to derivatives for which we removed the cash-flow hedging designation in 2008. Approximately $11 million of our accumulated other comprehensive loss will be reclassified to operating revenues over the next twelve months.

[2] Included in interest expense is $7 million representing the amount of accumulated other comprehensive income that was reclassified into income related to these interest rate derivatives designated as cash flow hedges for each of the years ended December 31, 2010 and 2009. Also included in interest expense is $11 million and $7 million related to our fair value interest rate derivatives for the years ended December 31, 2010 and 2009. We anticipate that $24 million of our accumulated other comprehensive income will be reclassified to interest expense during the next twelve months. No ineffectiveness was recognized on our interest rate hedges for the year ended December 31, 2010 and 2009.

[3] Excludes approximately $3 million of losses and $21 million of gains for the year ended December 31, 2010 and 2009 recognized in operating expenses related to other derivative instruments not associated with our price risk management activities.

REVENUES AND GAINS

RECOGNITION AND MEASUREMENT

3.06 As explained by FASB ASC 605-10-25-1, the recognition of revenue and gains of an entity during a period involves consideration of the following two factors, with sometimes one and sometimes the other being the more important consideration:

- *Being realized or realizable.* Revenue and gains generally are not recognized until realized or realizable. Paragraph 83(a) of FASB Concepts Statement No. 5, *Recognition and Measurement in Financial Statements of Business Enterprises,* states that revenue and gains are realized when products (goods or services), merchandise, or other assets are exchanged for cash or claims to cash. That paragraph states that revenue and gains are realizable when related assets received or held are readily convertible to known amounts of cash or claims to cash.
- *Being earned.* Paragraph 83(b) of FASB Concepts Statement No. 5 states that revenue is not recognized until earned. That paragraph states that an entity's revenue-earning activities involve delivering or producing goods, rendering services, or other activities that constitute its ongoing major or central operations, and revenues are considered to have been earned when the entity has substantially accomplished what it must do to be entitled to the benefits represented by the revenues. That paragraph states that gains commonly result from transactions and other events that involve no earning process, and for recognizing gains, being earned is generally less significant than being realized or realizable.

3.07

TABLE 3-2: FREQUENTLY DISCLOSED GAINS AND OTHER INCOME*

Gains and other income most frequently shown on the face of the income statement or disclosed by the survey entities are listed in Table 3-2. Excluded from Table 3-2 are credits shown after the income tax caption, segment disposals, and extraordinary credits.

	Number of Entities		
	2010	2009	2008
Interest	285	318	327
Change in fair value of derivatives	77	202	90
Sale of assets	121	149	200
Equity in earnings of investees	107	108	111
Dividends	28	60	70
Liability accruals reduced	19	60	43
Foreign currency transactions	51	59	76
Debt extinguishments	14	33	26
Royalty, franchise and license fees	31	32	34
Litigation settlements	16	26	14
Insurance recoveries	13	15	22
Change in fair value of financial assets/liabilities	29	12	3
Employee benefit/pension related	16	8	5
Rentals	5	6	4
Noncontrolling interest in investee loss	13	6	4
Business combination adjustment gain	16	6	—
Other	95	N/C^	N/C^

* Appearing in the income statement or notes to the financial statements, or both.
^ N/C = Not compiled. The line item was not included in the table for the year shown.

PRESENTATION AND DISCLOSURE EXCERPTS

Revenues

3.08

APPLE INC. (SEP)

CONSOLIDATED STATEMENTS OF OPERATIONS (in part)

(In millions, except share amounts which are reflected in thousands and per share amounts)

Three Years Ended September 25, 2010	2010	2009	2008
Net sales	$65,225	$42,905	$37,491
Cost of sales	39,541	25,683	24,294
Gross margin	25,684	17,222	13,197
Operating expenses:			
Research and development	1,782	1,333	1,109
Selling, general and administrative	5,517	4,149	3,761
Total operating expenses	7,299	5,482	4,870
Operating income	18,385	11,740	8,327

NOTES TO CONSOLIDATED FINANCIAL STATEMENTS

Note 1—Summary of Significant Accounting Policies (in part)

Revenue Recognition

Net sales consist primarily of revenue from the sale of hardware, software, digital content and applications, peripherals, and service and support contracts. The Company recognizes revenue when persuasive evidence of an arrangement exists, delivery has occurred, the sales price is fixed or determinable, and collection is probable. Product is considered delivered to the customer once it has been shipped and title and risk of loss have been transferred. For most of the Company's product sales, these criteria are met at the time the product is shipped. For online sales to individuals, for some sales to education customers in the U.S., and for certain other sales, the Company defers revenue until the customer receives the product because the Company legally retains a portion of the risk of loss on these sales during transit. The Company recognizes revenue from the sale of hardware products (e.g., Macs, iPhones, iPads, iPods and peripherals), software bundled with hardware that is essential to the functionality of the hardware, and third-party digital content sold on the iTunes Store in accordance with general revenue recognition accounting guidance. The Company recognizes revenue in accordance with industry specific software accounting guidance for the following types of sales transactions: (i) standalone sales of software products, (ii) sales of software upgrades and (iii) sales of software bundled with hardware not essential to the functionality of the hardware.

The Company sells software and peripheral products obtained from other companies. The Company generally establishes its own pricing and retains related inventory risk, is the primary obligor in sales transactions with its customers, and assumes the credit risk for amounts billed to its customers. Accordingly, the Company generally recognizes revenue for the sale of products obtained from other companies based on the gross amount billed. For certain sales made through the iTunes Store, including sales of third-party software applications for the Company's iOS devices, the Company is not the primary obligor to users of the software, and third-party developers determine the selling price of their software. Therefore, the Company accounts for such sales on a net basis by recognizing only the commission it retains from each sale and including that commission in net sales in the Consolidated Statements of Operations. The portion of the sales price paid by users that is remitted by the Company to third-party developers is not reflected in the Company's Consolidated Statement of Operations.

The Company records deferred revenue when it receives payments in advance of the delivery of products or the performance of services. This includes amounts that have been deferred related to embedded unspecified and specified software upgrades rights. The Company sells gift cards redeemable at its retail and online stores, and also sells gift cards redeemable on the iTunes Store for the purchase of content and software. The Company records deferred revenue upon the sale of the card, which is relieved upon redemption of the card by the customer. Revenue from AppleCare service and support contracts is deferred and recognized ratably over the service coverage periods. AppleCare service and support contracts typically include extended phone support, repair services, web-based support resources and diagnostic tools offered under the Company's standard limited warranty.

The Company records reductions to revenue for estimated commitments related to price protection and for customer incentive programs, including reseller and end-user rebates, and other sales programs and volume-based incentives. The estimated cost of these programs is recognized in the period the Company has sold the product and committed to a plan. The Company also records reductions to revenue for expected future product returns based on the Company's historical experience. Revenue is recorded net of taxes collected from customers that are remitted to governmental authorities, with the collected taxes recorded as current liabilities until remitted to the relevant government authority.

Revenue Recognition for Arrangements with Multiple Deliverables

For multi-element arrangements that include tangible products that contain software that is essential to the tangible product's functionality and undelivered software elements that relate to the tangible product's essential software, the Company allocates revenue to all deliverables based on their relative selling prices. In such circumstances, the Company uses a hierarchy to determine the selling price to be used for allocating revenue to deliverables: (i) vendor-specific objective evidence of fair value ("VSOE"), (ii) third-party evidence of selling price ("TPE"), and (iii) best estimate of the selling price ("ESP"). VSOE generally exists only when the Company sells the deliverable separately and is the price actually charged by the Company for that deliverable. ESPs reflect the Company's best estimates of what the selling prices of elements would be if they were sold regularly on a stand-alone basis.

As described in more detail below, for all past and current sales of iPhone, iPad, Apple TV and for sales of iPod touch beginning in June 2010, the Company has indicated it may from time-to-time provide future unspecified software upgrades and features free of charge to customers. The Company has identified two deliverables in arrangements involving the sale of these devices. The first deliverable is the hardware and software essential to the functionality of the hardware device delivered at the time of sale. The second deliverable is the embedded right included with the purchase of iPhone, iPad, iPod touch and Apple TV to receive on a when-and-if-available basis, future unspecified software upgrades and features relating to the product's essential software. The Company has allocated revenue between these two deliverables using the relative selling price method. Because the Company has neither VSOE nor TPE for the two deliverables, the allocation of revenue has been based on the Company's ESPs. Amounts allocated to the delivered hardware and the related essential software are recognized at the time of sale provided the other conditions for revenue recognition have been met. Amounts allocated to the embedded unspecified software upgrade rights are deferred and recognized on a straight-line basis over the 24-month estimated life of each of these devices. All product cost of sales, including estimated warranty costs, are recognized at the time of sale. Costs for engineering and sales and marketing are expensed as incurred.

The Company's process for determining its ESP for deliverables without VSOE or TPE considers multiple factors that may vary depending upon the unique facts and circumstances related to each deliverable. The Company believes its customers, particularly consumers, would be reluctant to buy unspecified software upgrade rights related to iPhone, iPad, iPod touch and Apple TV. This view is primarily based on the fact that unspecified upgrade rights do not obligate the Company to provide upgrades at a particular time or at all, and do not specify to customers which upgrades or features will be delivered. Therefore, the Company has concluded that if it were to sell upgrade rights on a standalone basis, including those rights associated with iPhone, iPad, iPod touch and Apple TV, the selling price would be relatively low. Key factors considered by the Company in developing the ESPs for these upgrade rights include prices charged by the Company for similar offerings, the Company's historical pricing practices, the nature of the upgrade rights (e.g., unspecified and when-and-if-available), and the relative ESP of the upgrade rights as compared to the total selling price of the product. The Company may also consider, when appropriate, the impact of other products and services, including advertising services, on selling price assumptions when developing and reviewing its ESPs for software upgrade rights and related deliverables. The Company may also consider additional factors as appropriate, including the pricing of competitive alternatives if they exist, and product-specific business objectives.

Beginning in the third quarter of 2010 in conjunction with the announcement of iOS 4, the Company's ESPs for the embedded software upgrade rights included with iPhone, iPad and iPod touch reflect the positive financial impact expected by the Company as a result of its introduction of a mobile advertising platform for these devices and the expectation of customers regarding software that includes or supports an advertising component. iOS 4 supports iAd, the Company's new mobile advertising platform, which enables applications on iPhone, iPad and iPod touch to embed media-rich advertisements.

For all periods presented, the Company's ESP for the embedded software upgrade right included with each Apple TV sold is $10. The Company's ESP for the software upgrade right included with each iPhone sold through the Company's second quarter of 2010 was $25. Beginning in April 2010 in conjunction with the Company's announcement of iOS 4 for iPhone, the Company lowered its ESP for the software upgrade right included with each iPhone to $10.

Beginning with initial sales of iPad in April 2010, the Company has also indicated it may from time-to-time provide future unspecified software upgrades and features free of charge to iPad customers. The Company's ESP for the embedded software upgrade right included with the sale of each iPad is $10. In June 2010, the Company announced that certain previously sold iPod touch models would receive an upgrade to iOS 4 free of charge and indicated iPod touch devices running on iOS 4 may from time-to-time receive future unspecified software upgrades and features free of charge. The Company's ESP for the embedded software upgrade right included with each iPod touch sold beginning in June 2010 is $5.

The Company accounts for multiple element arrangements that consist only of software or software-related products, including the sale of upgrades to previously sold software, in accordance with industry specific accounting guidance for software and software-related transactions. For such transactions, revenue on arrangements that include multiple elements is allocated to each element based on the relative fair value of each element, and fair value is determined by VSOE. If the Company cannot objectively determine the fair value of any undelivered element included in such multiple-element arrangements, the Company defers revenue until all elements are delivered and services have been performed, or until fair value can objectively be determined for any remaining undelivered elements. When the fair value of a delivered element has not been established, but fair value exists for the undelivered elements, the Company uses the residual method to recognize revenue. Under the residual method, the fair value of the undelivered elements is deferred and the remaining portion of the arrangement fee is allocated to the delivered elements and is recognized as revenue.

Except as described for iPhone, iPad, iPod touch and Apple TV, the Company generally does not offer unspecified upgrade rights to its customers in connection with software sales or the sale of AppleCare extended warranty and support contracts. A limited number of the Company's software products are available with maintenance agreements that grant customers rights to unspecified future upgrades over the maintenance term on a when and if available basis. Revenue associated with such maintenance is recognized ratably over the maintenance term.

3.09

ORACLE CORPORATION (MAY)

CONSOLIDATED STATEMENTS OF OPERATIONS
(in part)

For the Years Ended May 31, 2010, 2009 and 2008

(In millions, except per share data)	Year Ended May 31		
	2010	2009	2008
Revenues:			
New software licenses	$ 7,533	$ 7,123	$ 7,515
Software license updates and product support	13,092	11,754	10,328
Software revenues	20,625	18,877	17,843
Hardware systems products	1,506	—	—
Hardware systems support	784	—	—
Hardware systems revenues	2,290	—	—
Services	3,905	4,375	4,587
Total revenues	26,820	23,252	22,430
Operating Expenses:			
Sales and marketing	5,080	4,638	4,679
Software license updates and product support	1,063	1,088	997
Hardware systems products	880	—	—
Hardware systems support	423	—	—
Services	3,398	3,706	3,984
Research and development	3,254	2,767	2,741
General and administrative	911	785	808
Amortization of intangible assets	1,973	1,713	1,212
Acquisition related and other	154	117	124
Restructuring	622	117	41
Total operating expenses	17,758	14,931	14,586
Operating income	9,062	8,321	7,844

NOTES TO CONSOLIDATED FINANCIAL STATEMENTS

1. Organization and Significant Accounting Policies (in part)

Revenue Recognition

Our sources of revenues include: (1) software, which includes new software license revenues and software license updates and product support revenues; (2) hardware systems, which includes the sale of hardware systems products including computer servers and storage products, and hardware systems support revenues; and (3) services, which include software and hardware related services including consulting, On Demand and education revenues.

Revenue Recognition for Software Products and Software Related Services (Software Elements)

New software license revenues represent fees earned from granting customers licenses to use our database, middleware and applications software, and exclude revenues derived from software license updates, which are included in software license updates and product support revenues. While the basis for software license revenue recognition is substantially governed by the accounting guidance contained in ASC 985-605, *Software-Revenue Recognition*, we exercise judgment and use estimates in connection with the determination of the amount of software and services revenues to be recognized in each accounting period.

For software license arrangements that do not require significant modification or customization of the underlying software, we recognize new software license revenues when: (1) we enter into a legally binding arrangement with a customer for the license of software; (2) we deliver the products; (3) customer payment is deemed fixed or determinable and free of contingencies or significant uncertainties; and (4) collection is probable. Substantially all of our new software license revenues are recognized in this manner.

Substantially all of our software license arrangements do not include acceptance provisions. However, if acceptance provisions exist as part of public policy, for example, in agreements with government entities where acceptance periods are required by law, or within previously executed terms and conditions that are referenced in the current agreement and are short-term in nature, we generally recognize revenues upon delivery provided the acceptance terms are perfunctory and all other revenue recognition criteria have been met. If acceptance provisions are not perfunctory (for example, acceptance provisions that are long-term in nature or are not included as standard terms of an arrangement), revenues are recognized upon the earlier of receipt of written customer acceptance or expiration of the acceptance period.

The vast majority of our software license arrangements include software license updates and product support contracts, which are entered into at the customer's option and are recognized ratably over the term of the arrangement, typically one year. Software license updates provide customers with rights to unspecified software product upgrades, maintenance releases and patches released during the term of the support period. Product support includes internet access to technical content, as well as internet and telephone access to technical support personnel. Software license updates and product support contracts are generally priced as a percentage of the net new software license fees. Substantially all of our customers renew their software license updates and product support contracts annually.

Revenue Recognition for Multiple-Element Arrangements— Software Products and Software Related Services (Software Arrangements)

We often enter into arrangements with customers that purchase both software related products and services from us at the same time, or within close proximity of one another (referred to as software related multiple-element arrangements). Such software related multiple-element arrangements include the sale of our software products, software license updates and product support contracts and other software related services whereby software license delivery is followed by the subsequent or contemporaneous delivery of the other elements. For those software related multiple-element arrangements, we have applied the residual method to determine the amount of license revenues to be recognized pursuant to ASC 985-605. Under the residual method, if fair value exists for undelivered elements in a multiple-element arrangement, such fair value of the undelivered elements is deferred with the remaining portion of the arrangement consideration recognized upon delivery of the software license or services arrangement. We allocate the fair value of each element of a software related multiple-element arrangement based upon its fair value as determined by our vendor specific objective evidence (VSOE—described further below), with any remaining amount allocated to the software license.

Revenue Recognition for Hardware Systems Products and Hardware Systems Related Services (Nonsoftware Elements)

Revenues from the sale of hardware systems products represent amounts earned primarily from the sale of computer servers and storage products. Our revenue recognition policy for these nonsoftware deliverables is based upon the accounting guidance contained in ASC 605, *Revenue Recognition*, and we exercise judgment and use estimates in connection with the determination of the amount of hardware systems products and hardware systems related services revenues to be recognized in each accounting period.

Revenues from the sales of hardware products are recognized when: (1) persuasive evidence of an arrangement exists; (2) we deliver the products and passage of the title to the buyer occurs; (3) the sale price is fixed or determinable; and (4) collection is reasonably assured. Revenues that are not recognized at the time of sale because the foregoing conditions are not met are recognized when those conditions are subsequently met. When applicable, we reduce revenues for estimated returns or certain other incentive programs where we have the ability to sufficiently estimate the effects of these

items. Where an arrangement is subject to acceptance criteria and the acceptance provisions are not perfunctory (for example, acceptance provisions that are long-term in nature or are not included as standard terms of an arrangement), revenues are recognized upon the earlier of receipt of written customer acceptance or expiration of the acceptance period.

Our hardware systems support offerings generally provide customers with software updates for the software components that are essential to the functionality of our systems and storage products and can also include product repairs, maintenance services, and technical support services. Hardware systems support contracts are entered into at the customer's option and are recognized ratably over the contractual term of the arrangements.

Revenue Recognition for Multiple-Element Arrangements—Hardware Systems Products and Hardware Systems Related Services (Nonsoftware Arrangements)

In the third quarter of fiscal 2010, we early adopted the provisions of Accounting Standards Update No. 2009-13, *Revenue Recognition (Topic 605) Multiple-Deliverable Revenue Arrangements* (ASU 2009-13) and Accounting Standards Update 2009-14, *Software (Topic 985)—Certain Revenue Arrangements that Include Software Elements* (ASU 2009-14). ASU 2009-13 amended existing accounting guidance for revenue recognition for multiple-element arrangements. To the extent a deliverable within a multiple-element arrangement is not accounted for pursuant to other accounting standards, including ASC 985-605, *Software-Revenue Recognition,* ASU 2009-13 establishes a selling price hierarchy that allows for the use of an estimated selling price (ESP) to determine the allocation of arrangement consideration to a deliverable in a multiple element arrangement where neither VSOE nor third-party evidence (TPE) is available for that deliverable. ASU 2009-14 modifies the scope of ASC 985-605 to exclude tangible products containing software components and nonsoftware components that function together to deliver the product's essential functionality. In addition, ASU 2009-14 provides guidance on how a vendor should allocate arrangement consideration to nonsoftware and software deliverables in an arrangement where the vendor sells tangible products containing software components that are essential in delivering the tangible product's functionality.

As a result of our early adoption of ASU 2009-13 and ASU 2009-14, we applied the provisions of these accounting standards updates as of the beginning of fiscal 2010. The impact of our adoption of ASU 2009-13 and ASU 2009-14 was not material to our results of operations for fiscal 2010.

We enter into arrangements with customers that purchase both nonsoftware related products and services from us at the same time, or within close proximity of one another (referred to as nonsoftware multiple-element arrangements). Each element within a nonsoftware multiple-element arrangement is accounted for as a separate unit of accounting provided the following criteria are met: the delivered products or services have value to the customer on a standalone basis; and for an arrangement that includes a general right of return relative to the delivered products or services, delivery or performance of the undelivered product or service is considered probable and is substantially controlled by us. We consider a deliverable to have standalone value if the product or service is sold separately by us or another vendor or could be resold by the customer. Further, our revenue arrangements generally do not include a general right of return relative to the delivered products. Where the aforementioned criteria for a separate unit of accounting are not met, the deliverable is combined with the undelivered element(s) and treated as a single unit of accounting for the purposes of allocation of the arrangement consideration and revenue recognition. For those units of accounting that include more than one deliverable but are treated as a single unit of accounting, we generally recognize revenues over the delivery period. For the purposes of revenue classification of the elements that are accounted for as a single unit of accounting, we allocate revenue to hardware systems and services based on a rational and consistent methodology utilizing our best estimate of fair value of such elements.

For our nonsoftware multiple-element arrangements, we allocate revenue to each element based on a selling price hierarchy at the arrangement inception. The selling price for each element is based upon the following selling price hierarchy: VSOE if available, TPE if VSOE is not available, or ESP if neither VSOE nor TPE is available (a description as to how we determine VSOE, TPE and ESP is provided below). If a tangible hardware systems product includes software, we determine whether the tangible hardware systems product and the software work together to deliver the product's essential functionality and, if so, the entire product is treated as a nonsoftware deliverable. The total arrangement consideration is allocated to each separate unit of accounting for each of the nonsoftware deliverables using the relative selling prices of each unit based on the aforementioned selling price hierarchy. We limit the amount of revenue recognized for delivered elements to an amount that is not contingent upon future delivery of additional products or services or meeting of any specified performance conditions.

To determine the selling price in multiple-element arrangements, we establish VSOE of selling price using the price charged for a deliverable when sold separately and for software license updates and product support and hardware systems support, based on the renewal rates offered to customers. For nonsoftware multiple element arrangements, TPE is established by evaluating similar and interchangeable competitor products or services in standalone arrangements with similarly situated customers. If we are unable to determine the selling price because VSOE or TPE doesn't exist, we determine ESP for the purposes of allocating the arrangement by considering several external and internal factors including, but not limited to, pricing practices, margin objectives, competition, geographies in which we offer our products and services, internal costs and stage of the product lifecycle. The determination of ESP is made through consultation with and approval by our management, taking into consideration our go-to-market strategy. As our, or our competitors', pricing and go-to-market strategies evolve, we may modify our pricing practices in the future, which could result in changes to our determination of VSOE, TPE and ESP. As a result, our future revenue recognition for multiple-element arrangements could differ materially from our results in the current period. Selling prices are analyzed on an annual basis or more frequently if we experience significant changes in our selling prices.

Revenue Recognition Policies Applicable to both Software and Nonsoftware Elements

Revenue Recognition for Multiple-Element Arrangements—Arrangements with Software and Nonsoftware Elements

We also enter into multiple-element arrangements that may include a combination of our various software related and nonsoftware related products and services offerings including hardware systems products, hardware systems support, new software licenses, software license updates and product support, consulting, On Demand and education. In such arrangements, we first allocate the total arrangement consideration based on the relative selling prices of the software group of elements as a whole and to the nonsoftware elements. We then further allocate consideration within the software group to the respective elements within that group following the guidance in ASC 985-605 and our policies described above. After the arrangement consideration has been allocated to the elements, we account for each respective element in the arrangement as described above.

Other Revenue Recognition Policies Applicable to Software and Nonsoftware Elements

Many of our software arrangements include consulting implementation services sold separately under consulting engagement contracts and are included as a part of our services business. Consulting revenues from these arrangements are generally accounted for separately from new software license revenues because the arrangements qualify as services transactions as defined in ASC 985-605. The more significant factors considered in determining whether the revenues should be accounted for separately include the nature of services (i.e. consideration of whether the services are essential to the functionality of the licensed product), degree of risk, availability of services from other vendors, timing of payments and impact of milestones or acceptance criteria on the realizability of the software license fee. Revenues for consulting services are generally recognized as the services are performed. If there is a significant uncertainty about the project completion or receipt of payment for the consulting services, revenues are deferred until the uncertainty is sufficiently resolved. We estimate the proportional performance on contracts with fixed or "not to exceed" fees on a monthly basis utilizing hours incurred to date as a percentage of total estimated hours to complete the project. If we do not have a sufficient basis to measure progress towards completion, revenues are recognized when we receive final acceptance from the customer. When total cost estimates exceed revenues, we accrue for the estimated losses immediately using cost estimates that are based upon an average fully burdened daily rate applicable to the consulting organization delivering the services. The complexity of the estimation process and factors relating to the assumptions, risks and uncertainties inherent with the application of the proportional performance method of accounting affects the amounts of revenues and related expenses reported in our consolidated financial statements. A number of internal and external factors can affect our estimates, including labor rates, utilization and efficiency variances and specification and testing requirement changes.

On Demand is comprised of Oracle On Demand and Advanced Customer Services and is a part of our services business. Oracle On Demand services are offered as standalone arrangements or as a part of arrangements to customers buying new software licenses or hardware systems products and services. Our On Demand services provide multi-featured software and hardware management and maintenance services for our software and hardware systems products delivered at our data center facilities, select partner data centers or customer facilities. Advanced Customer Services provide customers with services to architect, implement and manage customer IT environments including software and hardware systems product management services, industry-specific solution support centers and remote and on-site expert services. Depending upon the nature of the arrangement, revenues from On Demand services are recognized as services are performed or ratably over the term of the service period, which is generally one year or less.

Education revenues are a part of our services business and include instructor-led, media-based and internet-based training in the use of our software and hardware products. Education revenues are recognized as the classes or other education offerings are delivered.

If an arrangement contains multiple elements and does not qualify for separate accounting for the product and service transactions, then new software license revenues and/or hardware systems products revenues, including the costs of hardware systems products, are generally recognized together with the services based on contract accounting using either the percentage-of-completion or completed-contract method. Contract accounting is applied to any bundled software, hardware systems and services arrangements: (1) that include milestones or customer specific acceptance criteria that may affect collection of the software license or hardware systems product fees; (2) where consulting services include significant modification or customization of the software or hardware systems product; (3) where significant consulting services are provided for in the software license contract or hardware systems product contract without additional charge or are substantially discounted; or (4) where the software license or hardware systems product payment is tied to the performance of consulting services. For the purposes of revenue classification of the elements that are accounted for as a single unit of accounting, we allocate revenues to software and nonsoftware elements based on a rational and consistent methodology utilizing our best estimate of fair value of such elements.

We also evaluate arrangements with governmental entities containing "fiscal funding" or "termination for convenience" provisions, when such provisions are required by law, to determine the probability of possible cancellation. We consider multiple factors, including the history with the customer in similar transactions, the "essential use" of the software or hardware systems products and the planning, budgeting and approval processes undertaken by the governmental entity. If we determine upon execution of these arrangements that the likelihood of cancellation is remote, we then recognize revenues once all of the criteria described above have been met. If such a determination cannot be made, revenues are recognized upon the earlier of cash receipt or approval of the applicable funding provision by the governmental entity.

We assess whether fees are fixed or determinable at the time of sale and recognize revenues if all other revenue recognition requirements are met. Our standard payment terms are net 30 days. However, payment terms may vary based on the country in which the agreement is executed. Payments that are due within six months are generally deemed to be fixed or determinable based on our successful collection history on such arrangements, and thereby satisfy the required criteria for revenue recognition.

While most of our arrangements for sales within our software and hardware systems businesses include short-term payment terms, we have a standard practice of providing long-term financing to creditworthy customers through our financing division. Since fiscal 1989, when our financing division was formed, we have established a history of collection, without concessions, on these receivables with payment terms that generally extend up to five years from the contract date. Provided all other revenue recognition criteria have been met, we recognize new software license revenues and hardware systems products revenues for these arrangements upon delivery, net of any payment discounts from financing transactions. We have generally sold receivables financed through our financing division on a non-recourse basis to third party financing institutions and we classify the proceeds from these sales as cash flows from operating activities in our consolidated statements of cash flows. We account for the sales of these receivables as "true sales" as defined in ASC 860, *Transfers and Servicing*.

In addition, we sell hardware products to leasing companies that, in turn, lease these products to end-users. In transactions where the leasing companies have no recourse to us in the event of default by the end-user, we recognize revenue at point of shipment or point of delivery, depending on the shipping terms and if all the other revenue recognition criteria have been met. In arrangements where the leasing companies have more than insignificant recourse to us in the event of default by the end-user (defined as recourse leasing), we recognize both the product revenue and the related cost of the product as the payments are made to the leasing company by the end-user, generally ratably over the lease term.

Our customers include several of our suppliers and on rare occasion, we have purchased goods or services for our operations from these vendors at or about the same time that we have sold our products to these same companies (Concurrent Transactions). Software license agreements or sales of hardware systems that occur within a three-month time period from the date we have purchased goods or services from that same customer are reviewed for appropriate accounting treatment and disclosure. When we acquire goods or services from a customer, we negotiate the purchase separately from any sales transaction, at terms we consider to be at arm's length, and settle the purchase in cash. We recognize new software license revenues or hardware systems product revenues from Concurrent Transactions if all of our revenue recognition criteria are met and the goods and services acquired are necessary for our current operations.

Interest

3.10

OCCIDENTAL PETROLEUM CORPORATION (DEC)

CONSOLIDATED STATEMENTS OF INCOME (in part)

(In millions, except per-share amounts)	For the Years Ended December 31		
	2010	2009	2008
Revenues and Other Income			
Net sales	$19,045	$14,814	$23,713
Interest, dividends and other income	111	118	236
Gains on disposition of assets, net	1	10	27
	$19,157	$14,942	$23,976

Dividends

3.11

ALTRIA GROUP, INC. (DEC)

NOTES TO CONSOLIDATED FINANCIAL STATEMENTS

Note 1—Background and Basis of Presentation (in part)

Background (in part): At December 31, 2010, Altria Group, Inc.'s wholly-owned subsidiaries included Philip Morris USA Inc. ("PM USA"), which is engaged in the manufacture and sale of cigarettes and certain smokeless products in the United States; UST LLC ("UST"), which through its subsidiaries is engaged in the manufacture and sale of smokeless products and wine; and John Middleton Co. ("Middleton"), which is engaged in the manufacture and sale of machine-made large cigars and pipe tobacco. Philip Morris Capital Corporation ("PMCC"), another wholly-owned subsidiary of Altria Group, Inc., maintains a portfolio of leveraged and direct finance leases. In addition, Altria Group, Inc. held a 27.1% economic and voting interest in SABMiller plc ("SABMiller") at December 31, 2010. Altria Group, Inc.'s access to the operating cash flows of its wholly-owned subsidiaries consists of cash received from the payment of dividends and distributions, and the payment of interest on intercompany loans by its subsidiaries. In addition, Altria Group, Inc. receives cash dividends on its interest in SABMiller, if and when SABMiller pays cash dividends on their stock.

Note 8—Investment in SABMiller:

At December 31, 2010, Altria Group, Inc. held a 27.1% economic and voting interest in SABMiller. Altria Group, Inc.'s investment in SABMiller is being accounted for under the equity method.

Pre-tax earnings from Altria Group, Inc.'s equity investment in SABMiller consisted of the following:

(In millions)	For the Years Ended December 31		
	2010	2009	2008
Equity earnings	$578	$407	$467
Gains resulting from issuances of common stock by SABMiller	50	193	
	$628	$600	$467

Summary financial data of SABMiller is as follows:

(In millions)	At December 31	
	2010	2009
Current assets	$ 4,518	$ 4,495
Long-term assets	$34,744	$33,841
Current liabilities	$ 6,625	$ 5,307
Long-term liabilities	$11,270	$13,199
Non-controlling interests	$ 766	$ 672

(In millions)	For the Years Ended December 31		
	2010	2009	2008
Net revenues	$18,981	$17,020	$20,466
Operating profit	$ 2,821	$ 2,173	$ 2,854
Net earnings	$ 2,133	$ 1,473	$ 1,635

The fair value, based on market quotes, of Altria Group, Inc.'s equity investment in SABMiller at December 31, 2010, was $15.1 billion, as compared with its carrying value of $5.4 billion. The fair value, based on market quotes, of Altria Group, Inc.'s equity investment in SABMiller at December 31, 2009, was $12.7 billion, as compared with its carrying value of $5.0 billion.

Licensing

3.12

AVIS BUDGET GROUP, INC. (DEC)

CONSOLIDATED STATEMENTS OF OPERATIONS
(in part)

	Year Ended December 31		
(In millions, except per share data)	2010	2009	2008
Revenues			
Vehicle rental	$3,882	$3,906	$4,564
Other	1,303	1,225	1,420
Net revenues	$5,185	$5,131	$5,984

NOTES TO CONSOLIDATED FINANCIAL STATEMENTS

5. Licensing Activities

Revenues from licensing, which are recorded within other revenues on the accompanying Consolidated Statements of Operations, amounted to $46 million, $43 million and $40 million during 2010, 2009 and 2008, respectively. The Company renews licensee agreements in the normal course of business and occasionally terminates, purchases or sells licensee agreements. In connection with ongoing fees the Company receives from its licensees pursuant to the license agreements, the Company is required to provide certain services, such as training, marketing and the operation of reservation systems.

Equity in Earnings of Investees

3.13

ALLIANCE ONE INTERNATIONAL, INC. (MAR)

*STATEMENTS OF CONSOLIDATED OPERATIONS AND
COMPREHENSIVE INCOME (in part)*

	Years Ended March 31		
(In thousands, except per share data)	2010	2009	2008
Sales and other operating revenues	$2,308,299	$2,258,219	$2,011,503
Cost of goods and services sold	1,911,849	1,897,380	1,761,111
Gross profit	396,450	360,839	250,392
Selling, administrative and general expenses	155,376	156,000	157,405
Other income (expense)	(17,260)	214	20,188
Restructuring and asset impairment charges	—	591	19,580
Operating income	223,814	204,462	93,595
Debt retirement expense	40,353	954	5,909
Interest expense	113,819	97,984	101,885
Interest income	4,550	3,808	16,245
Income before income taxes and other items	74,192	109,332	2,046
Income tax benefit	(3,791)	(22,020)	(5,499)
Equity in net income of investee companies	1,963	1,478	1,829
Income from continuing operations	79,946	132,830	9,374
Income from discontinued operations, net of tax	—	407	7,855
Net income	79,946	133,237	17,229
Less: Net income attributable to noncontrolling interests	779	679	368
Net income attributable to Alliance One International, Inc.	$ 79,167	$ 132,558	$ 16,861
Other comprehensive income:			
Net income	$ 79,946	$ 133,237	$ 17,229
Currency translation adjustment	(1,837)	(7,207)	6,530
Pension adjustment, net of tax $(5,107) in 2010, $(3,378) in 2009 and $(3,450) in 2008	(6,383)	(13,165)	(6,949)
Total comprehensive income	71,726	112,865	16,810
Comprehensive income attributable to noncontrolling interests	763	496	402
Total comprehensive income attributable to Alliance One International, Inc.	$ 70,963	$ 112,369	$ 16,408

NOTES TO CONSOLIDATED FINANCIAL STATEMENTS

(In thousands)

*Note J—Equity in Net Assets of Investee Companies
(in part)*

The Company has equity basis investments in companies located in Asia which purchase and process tobacco. The

Asia investees and ownership percentages are as follows: Transcontinental Leaf Tobacco India Private Ltd. (India) 49%, Siam Tobacco Export Company (Thailand) 49%, Adams International Ltd. (Thailand) 49%. Summarized financial information for these investees for fiscal years ended March 31, 2010, 2009 and 2008 follows:

	Years Ended March 31		
Operations Statement Information	**2010**	**2009**	**2008**
Sales	$105,123	$122,000	$109,636
Gross Profit	14,947	12,111	13,095
Net Income	$ 3,994	$ 3,023	$ 3,852

Gain on Asset Disposals

3.14

LOCKHEED MARTIN CORPORATION (DEC)

CONSOLIDATED STATEMENTS OF EARNINGS

	Year Ended December 31		
(In millions, except per share data)	**2010**	**2009**	**2008**
Net Sales			
Products	$36,448	$35,763	$34,091
Services	9,355	8,232	7,281
Total Net Sales	45,803	43,995	41,372
Cost of Sales			
Products	(32,655)	(31,756)	(30,220)
Services	(8,350)	(7,376)	(6,517)
Voluntary executive separation and other charges	(220)	—	—
Other unallocated corporate costs	(742)	(671)	(61)
Total Cost of Sales	(41,967)	(39,803)	(36,798)
Gross Profit	3,836	4,192	4,574
Other Income, Net	261	223	475
Operating Profit	4,097	4,415	5,049
Interest Expense	(345)	(308)	(332)
Other Non-Operating Income (Expense), Net	74	123	(91)
Earnings from Continuing Operations Before Income Taxes	3,826	4,230	4,626
Income Tax Expense	(1,181)	(1,231)	(1,459)
Earnings from Continuing Operations	2,645	2,999	3,167
Earnings from Discontinued Operations	281	25	50
Net Earnings	$ 2,926	$ 3,024	$ 3,217
Earnings Per Common Share			
Basic			
Continuing Operations	$ 7.26	$ 7.79	$ 7.92
Discontinued Operations	.77	.07	.13
Basic Earnings Per Common Share	$ 8.03	$ 7.86	$ 8.05
Diluted			
Continuing Operations	$ 7.18	$ 7.71	$ 7.74
Discontinued Operations	.76	.07	.12
Diluted Earnings Per Common Share	$ 7.94	$ 7.78	$ 7.86

See accompanying Notes to Consolidated Financial Statements.

NOTES TO CONSOLIDATED FINANCIAL STATEMENTS

Note 2—Discontinued Operations

In June 2010, we announced plans to divest Pacific Architects and Engineers, Inc. (PAE) and most of our Enterprise Integration Group (EIG), two businesses within our Information Systems & Global Solutions (IS&GS) reporting segment. On November 22, 2010, we closed on the sale of EIG for $815 million and recognized a gain, net of tax, of $184 million ($.50 per share) in the fourth quarter of 2010 which is included in discontinued operations. We received proceeds, net of $17 million in transaction costs, of $798 million related to the sale, which are included in investing activities on our Statement of Cash Flows. We made a $260 million tax payment related to the sale which is included in operating activities on our Statement of Cash Flows. EIG's operating results are included in discontinued operations on our Statements of Earnings for all periods presented. Our decision to divest EIG was based on our analysis of the U.S. Government's increased concerns about perceived organizational conflicts of interest within the defense contracting community. EIG provides systems engineering, architecture, and integration services and support to a broad range of government customers.

As a result of our decision in 2010 to sell PAE, we recorded a $182 million deferred tax asset which reflects the federal and state tax benefits that we expect to realize on the sale of the PAE business because our tax basis is higher than our book basis. We also recorded a $109 million impairment charge which reduced the carrying value of PAE to equal the expected net proceeds from the transaction. The net result increased earnings from discontinued operations by $73 million ($.20 per share). PAE's operating results are included in discontinued operations on our Statements of Earnings for all periods presented, and its assets and liabilities are classified as held for sale on our 2010 Balance Sheet. On February 22, 2011, we announced that we entered into a definitive agreement to sell PAE. We expect the transaction will close in the second quarter of 2011, subject to satisfaction of closing conditions.

The plan to divest PAE is a result of changes in customer priorities. When we acquired the business, we envisioned it as an entry point to a new customer set that would need additional services, primarily in the areas of information technology and systems integration. Those customers, however, are seeking a different mix of services, such as the construction of facilities and provision of physical security, which does not fit with our long-term strategy.

In the following table of financial information, we have combined the results of operations of PAE and EIG as the amounts for the individual businesses are not material. Summary financial information related to discontinued operations is as follows:

(In millions)	2010	2009	2008
Net sales	$1,087	$1,195	$1,359
Earnings before income taxes	44	54	76
Earnings after income taxes	$ 24	$ 25	$ 50
Gain on sale of EIG	184	—	—
Adjustments from planned sale of PAE	73	—	—
Earnings from discontinued operations	$ 281	$ 25	$ 50

The major classes of assets and liabilities related to PAE and classified as held for sale on our Balance Sheet as of December 31, 2010 are listed in the table below.

(In millions)	December 31, 2010
Assets	
Receivables	$267
Goodwill and other assets	132
Assets of discontinued operation held for sale	$399
Liabilities	
Accounts payable and accrued expenses	$122
Other liabilities	82
Liabilities of Discontinued Operation Held for Sale	$204

Reversal of Accrued Amounts (Reserves)

3.15

NACCO INDUSTRIES, INC. (DEC)

CONSOLIDATED STATEMENTS OF OPERATIONS (in part)

	Years Ended December 31		
(In millions, except per share data)	2010	2009	2008
Revenues	$2,687.5	$2,310.6	$3,665.1
Cost of sales	2,161.3	1,902.5	3,174.0
Gross profit	526.2	408.1	491.1
Earnings of unconsolidated mines	43.4	38.6	39.4
Operating Expenses			
Selling, general and administrative expenses	425.3	388.3	475.3
Goodwill and other intangible assets impairment charges	—	—	435.7
Restructuring charges (reversals)	(1.9)	9.3	9.1
Loss on sale of businesses	4.0	—	—
(Gain) loss on sale of assets	1.9	(10.0)	(0.1)
	429.3	387.6	920.0
Operating Profit (Loss)	$ 140.3	$ 59.1	$ (389.5)

NOTES TO CONSOLIDATED FINANCIAL STATEMENTS

Note 2—Significant Accounting Policies (in part)

Restructuring Reserves: Restructuring reserves reflect estimates related to employee-related costs, lease termination costs and other exit costs. Lease termination costs include remaining payments due under existing lease agreements after the cease-use date, less estimated sublease income and any lease termination fees. Other costs include costs to move equipment and costs incurred to close a facility. Actual costs could differ from management estimates, resulting in additional expense or the reversal of previously recorded expenses.

Note 3—Restructuring and Related Programs (in part)

During 2009, NMHG's management approved a plan to close its facility in Modena, Italy and consolidate its activities into NMHG's facility in Masate, Italy. These actions are being taken to further reduce NMHG's manufacturing capacity to more appropriate levels. As a result, NMHG recognized a charge of approximately $5.6 million during 2009, which is classified in the Consolidated Statement of Operations on the line "Restructuring charges (reversals)." Of this amount, $5.3

million related to severance and $0.3 million related to lease impairment. During 2010, $1.9 million of the accrual was reversed as a result of a reduction in the expected amount to be paid to former employees due to the finalization of an agreement with the Italian government. Payments of $1.4 million and $0.3 million were made for severance and lease termination, respectively, during 2010. Severance payments of $0.3 million were made during 2009. Payments related to this restructuring program are expected to continue through 2012. No further charges related to this plan are expected.

Rental Income

3.16

ALLEGHENY TECHNOLOGIES INCORPORATED (DEC)

CONSOLIDATED STATEMENTS OF INCOME (in part)

(In millions, except per share amounts)

For the Years Ended December 31	2010	2009	2008
Sales	$4,047.8	$3,054.9	$5,309.7
Costs and expenses:			
Cost of sales	3,557.5	2,646.5	4,157.8
Selling and administrative expenses	304.9	315.7	282.7
Income before interest, other income and income taxes	185.4	92.7	869.2
Interest expense, net	(62.7)	(19.3)	(3.5)
Debt extinguishment costs	—	(9.2)	—
Other income, net	3.0	0.7	2.0
Income before income taxes	125.7	64.9	867.7

NOTES TO CONSOLIDATED FINANCIAL STATEMENTS

*Note 5. Supplemental Financial Statement Information
(in part)*

Other income (expense) for the years ended December 31, 2010, 2009, and 2008 was as follows:

(In millions)	2010	2009	2008
Rent, royalty income and other income	$ 1.4	$ 0.9	$1.6
Gain on insured event	2.0	—	—
Net gains (losses) on property and investments	—	(0.2)	0.1
Other	(0.4)	—	0.3
Total other income	$ 3.0	$ 0.7	$2.0

Litigation

3.17

VALASSIS COMMUNICATIONS, INC. (DEC)

CONSOLIDATED STATEMENTS OF INCOME (in part)

	Years Ended December 31		
(U.S. dollars in thousands, except per share data)	2010	2009	2008
Revenues	$2,333,512	$2,244,248	$2,381,907
Costs and expenses:			
Cost of sales	1,724,606	1,693,652	1,855,894
Selling, general and administrative	371,264	354,933	385,826
Amortization expense	12,624	12,624	9,223
Impairment charge	—	—	245,700
Total costs and expenses	2,108,494	2,061,209	2,496,643
Gain from litigation settlement, net (Note 8)	490,085	—	—
Earnings (loss) from operations	715,103	183,039	(114,736)
Other expenses and income:			
Interest expense	64,904	87,041	98,903
Interest income	(653)	(546)	(2,913)
Loss (gain) on extinguishment of debt (Note 3)	23,873	(10,028)	—
Other (income) expense, net	(5,676)	(4,371)	5,111
Total other expenses, net	82,448	72,096	101,101
Earnings (loss) before income taxes	$ 632,655	$ 110,943	$ (215,837)

NOTES TO CONSOLIDATED FINANCIAL STATEMENTS

8. Gain from Litigation Settlement

On January 30, 2010, we announced that we had reached an agreement to settle our outstanding lawsuits against News America Incorporated, a/k/a News America Marketing Group, News America Marketing, FSI, Inc. a/k/a News America Marketing FSI, LLC and News America Marketing In-Store Services, Inc. a/k/a News America Marketing In-Store Services, LLC (collectively "News"). The operative complaint alleged violations of the Sherman Act and various state competitive statutes and the commission of torts by News in connection with the marketing and sale of FSI space and in-store promotion and advertising services.

On February 4, 2010, we executed a settlement agreement and release (the "Settlement Agreement") with News, and pursuant to the terms of the Settlement Agreement, News paid us $500.0 million. News America, Inc. also entered into a 10-year shared mail distribution agreement with our subsidiary, Valassis Direct Mail, Inc., which provides for our sale of certain shared mail services to News on specified terms.

In connection with the settlement, the parties are working with the United States District Court for the Eastern District of Michigan (the "Court"), under the Honorable Arthur J. Tarnow, on a set of procedures to handle future disputes among the parties with respect to conduct at issue in the litigation. The precise timing and form of the relief rests with the Court.

The settlement resolves all outstanding claims between us and News as of February 4, 2010. As a result, the parties agreed to dismiss all outstanding litigation between them and release all existing and potential claims against each other that were or could have been asserted in the litigation as of the date of the Settlement Agreement.

During the first quarter of 2010, in connection with the successful settlement of these lawsuits, we made $9.9 million in related payments, including special bonuses to certain of our employees (including our executive officers identified as the "named executive officers" in our proxy statement filed with the SEC on March 30, 2010) in an aggregate amount of $8.1 million. These expenses were netted against the $500.0 million of proceeds received, and the net proceeds of $490.1 million have been recorded as a separate line item "Gain from litigation settlement" in our consolidated statement of income for the year ended December 31, 2010.

Employee Benefits

3.18

KIMBALL INTERNATIONAL, INC. (JUN)

CONSOLIDATED STATEMENTS OF INCOME (in part)

		Year Ended June 30	
(Amounts in thousands, except for per share data)	**2010**	**2009**	**2008**
Net sales	$1,122,808	$1,207,420	$1,351,985
Cost of sales	946,275	1,004,901	1,103,511
Gross profit	176,533	202,519	248,474
Selling and administrative expenses	181,771	192,711	232,131
Other general income	(9,980)	(33,417)	-0-
Restructuring expense	2,051	2,981	21,911
Goodwill impairment	-0-	14,559	-0-
Operating income (loss)	2,691	25,685	(5,568)
Other income (Expense):			
Interest income	1,188	2,499	3,362
Interest expense	(142)	(1,565)	(1,967)
Non-operating income	2,980	2,663	3,512
Non-operating expense	(749)	(3,956)	(1,703)
Other income (expense), net	3,277	(359)	3,204
Income (Loss) from continuing operations before taxes on income	5,968	25,326	(2,364)
Provision (Benefit) for income taxes	(4,835)	7,998	(2,442)
Income from continuing operations	10,803	17,328	78
Loss from discontinued operation, net of tax	-0-	-0-	(124)
Net income (Loss)	$ 10,803	$ 17,328	$ (46)

NOTES TO CONSOLIDATED FINANCIAL STATEMENTS

Note 1—Summary of Significant Accounting Policies (in part)

Non-operating Income and Expense: Non-operating income and expense include the impact of such items as foreign currency rate movements and related derivative gain or loss, fair value adjustments on Supplemental Employee Retirement Plan (SERP) investments, non-production rent income, bank charges, and other miscellaneous non-operating income and expense items that are not directly related to operations.

Note 13—Short-Term Investments (in part)

Supplemental Employee Retirement Plan Investments:
The Company maintains a self-directed supplemental employee retirement plan (SERP) for executive employees. The SERP utilizes a rabbi trust, and therefore assets in the SERP portfolio are subject to creditor claims in the event of bankruptcy. The Company recognizes SERP investment assets on the balance sheet at current fair value. A SERP liability of the same amount is recorded on the balance sheet representing the Company's obligation to distribute SERP funds

to participants. The SERP investment assets are classified as trading, and accordingly, realized and unrealized gains and losses are recognized in income in the Other Income (Expense) category. Adjustments made to revalue the SERP liability are also recognized in income as selling and administrative expenses and exactly offset valuation adjustments on SERP investment assets. The change in net unrealized holding gains and (losses) for the fiscal years ended June 30, 2010, 2009, and 2008 was, in thousands, $1,385, ($2,739), and ($2,385), respectively. SERP asset and liability balances were as follows:

	June 30	
(Amounts in thousands)	**2010**	**2009**
SERP investment—current asset	$ 4,822	$ 3,536
SERP investment—other long-term asset	8,249	7,456
Total SERP investment	$13,071	$10,992
SERP obligation—current liability	$ 4,822	$ 3,536
SERP obligation—other long-term liability	8,249	7,456
Total SERP obligation	$13,071	$10,992

Derivatives

3.19

ANADARKO PETROLEUM CORPORATION (DEC)

CONSOLIDATED STATEMENTS OF INCOME (in part)

	Years Ended December 31		
(Millions except per-share amounts)	**2010**	**2009**	**2008**
Revenues and other			
Natural-gas sales	$ 3,420	$2,924	$ 5,770
Oil and condensate sales	5,592	4,022	6,425
Natural-gas liquids sales	997	536	802
Gathering, processing and marketing sales	833	728	1,082
Gains (losses) on divestitures and other, net	142	133	1,083
Reversal of accrual for DWRRA dispute (Note 15)	—	657	—
Total	10,984	9,000	15,162
Costs and expenses			
Oil and gas operating	830	859	1,036
Oil and gas transportation and other	816	664	621
Exploration	974	1,107	1,369
Gathering, processing and marketing	615	617	800
General and administrative	982	983	866
Depreciation, depletion and amortization	3,714	3,532	3,194
Other taxes	1,068	746	1,452
Impairments	216	115	223
Total	9,215	8,623	9,561
Operating income (Loss)	1,769	377	5,601
Other (Income) Expense			
Interest expense	855	702	732
(Gains) losses on commodity derivatives, net	(893)	408	(561)
(Gains) losses on other derivatives, net	285	(582)	7
Other (income) expense, net	(119)	(43)	55
Total	128	485	233
Income (Loss) from continuing operations before income taxes	$ 1,641	$ (108)	$ 5,368

NOTES TO CONSOLIDATED FINANCIAL STATEMENTS

9. Derivative Instruments

Interest-Rate Derivatives—In 2008 and 2009, Anadarko entered into interest-rate swap agreements to mitigate the risk of rising interest rates on up to $3.0 billion of debt originally expected to be refinanced in 2011 and 2012, over a reference term of either 10 years or 30 years. The Company locked in a fixed interest rate in exchange for a floating interest rate indexed to the three-month LIBOR. The swap instruments include a provision that requires both the termination of the swaps and cash settlement in full at the start of the reference period.

(Gains) losses on other derivatives, net for 2010 and 2009 includes unrealized (gains) losses of $284 million and $(57) million, respectively, and realized (gains) losses of zero and $(552) million, respectively, on these swap agreements. The realized gain in 2009 resulted from revising the contractual terms of this swap portfolio to increase the weighted-average interest rate from approximately 3.25% to approximately 4.80%.

A summary of the swaps outstanding at December 31, 2010, including the outstanding notional principal amounts and the associated reference periods, is presented below.

Notional Principal Amount:	Reference Period		Weighted-Average Interest
(Millions except percentages)	**Start**	**End**	**Rate**
$750	October 2011	October 2021	4.72%
$1,250	October 2011	October 2041	4.83%
$250	October 2012	October 2022	4.91%
$750	October 2012	October 2042	4.80%

Effect of Derivative Instruments—Balance Sheet. The fair value of all derivative instruments is included in the table below.

Derivatives (Millions)	Balance Sheet Classification	Gross Derivative Assets		Gross Derivative Liabilities	
		December 31, 2010	December 31, 2009	December 31, 2010	December 31, 2009
Commodity					
	Other Current Assets	$444	$140	$(274)	$ (63)
	Other Assets	242	82	(56)	(6)
	Accrued Expenses	89	195	(131)	(417)
	Other Liabilities	26	25	(28)	(52)
		801	442	(489)	(538)
Interest Rate and Other					
	Other Assets	—	53	—	—
	Accrued Expenses	—	—	(190)	—
	Other Liabilities	—	—	(45)	(3)
		—	53	(235)	(3)
Total Derivatives		$801	$495	$(724)	$(541)

Effect of Derivative Instruments—Statement of Income. The unrealized and realized gain or loss amounts and classification related to derivative instruments for the respective years ended December 31 are as follows:

Derivatives (Millions)	Classification of (Gain) Loss Recognized	(Gain) Loss		
		Realized	Unrealized	Total
2010				
Commodity	Gathering, Processing and Marketing Sales[1]	$ 3	$ (4)	$ (1)
	(Gains) Losses on Commodity Derivatives, net	(498)	(395)	(893)
Interest Rate and Other	(Gains) Losses on Other Derivatives, net	—	285	285
Derivative (Gain) Loss, net		$(495)	$(114)	$(609)
2009				
Commodity	Gathering, Processing and Marketing Sales[1]	$ (2)	$ 39	$ 37
	(Gains) Losses on Commodity Derivatives, net	(327)	735	408
Interest Rate	(Gains) Losses on Other Derivatives, net	(525)	(57)	(582)
Derivative (Gain) Loss, net		$(854)	$ 717	$(137)
2008				
Commodity	Gathering, Processing and Marketing Sales[1]	$ 26	$ (29)	$ (3)
	(Gains) Losses on Commodity Derivatives, net	339	(900)	(561)
Interest Rate	(Gains) Losses on Other Derivatives, net	—	7	7
Derivative (Gain) Loss, net		$ 365	$(922)	$(557)

[1] Represents the effect of marketing and trading derivative activities.

Change in Fair Value

3.20

AMKOR TECHNOLOGY, INC. (DEC)

CONSOLIDATED STATEMENTS OF OPERATIONS
(in part)

(In thousands, except per share data)	For the Year Ended December 31		
	2010	2009	2008
Net sales	$2,939,483	$2,179,109	$2,658,602
Cost of sales	2,275,727	1,698,713	2,096,864
Gross profit	663,756	480,396	561,738
Operating expenses:			
Selling, general and administrative	242,424	210,907	251,756
Research and development	47,534	44,453	56,227
Goodwill impairment	—	—	671,117
Gain on sale of real estate	—	(281)	(9,856)
Total operating expenses	289,958	255,079	969,244
Operating income (loss)	373,798	225,317	(407,506)
Other (income) expense:			
Interest expense	85,595	102,396	118,729
Interest expense, related party	15,250	13,000	6,250
Interest income	(2,950)	(2,367)	(8,749)
Foreign currency loss (gain)	13,756	3,339	(61,057)
Loss (gain) on debt retirement, net	18,042	(15,088)	(35,987)
Equity in earnings of unconsolidated affiliate	(6,435)	(2,373)	—
Other income, net	(619)	(113)	(1,004)
Total other expense, net	122,639	98,794	18,182
Income (loss) before income taxes	$ 251,159	$ 126,523	$ (425,688)

NOTES TO CONSOLIDATED FINANCIAL STATEMENTS

10. Investments (in part)

Investments consist of the following:

(In thousands)	December 31			
	2010		2009	
	Carrying Value	Ownership Percentage	Carrying Value	Ownership Percentage
Investment in unconsolidated affiliate	$28,215	30.0%	$19,108	30.0%
Total investments	$28,215		$19,108	

J-Devices Corporation

On October 30, 2009, Amkor and Toshiba Corporation ("Toshiba") invested in Nakaya Microdevices Corporation ("NMD") and formed a joint venture to provide semiconductor assembly and final testing services in Japan. As a result of the transaction, NMD is now owned 60% by the existing shareholders of NMD, 30% by Amkor and 10% by Toshiba and has changed its name to J-Devices.

J-Devices purchased an assembly and test business from Toshiba. J-Devices has also entered into various other agreements with Toshiba including a supply agreement, license agreement, support services agreements and employee secondment agreements.

We invested 1.5 billion Japanese yen (approximately $16.7 million at inception) for our 30% equity interest and call options to acquire additional equity interest. The call options were valued at $1.7 million, and, at our discretion, permit us to subscribe to new or existing J-Devices' shares until our maximum ownership ratio is 60%, 66% and 80% beginning in 2012, 2014 and 2015, respectively. In 2014 and beyond, Toshiba has at its discretion, a put option which allows Toshiba to sell shares to us if we have exercised any of our call options. The exercise price for all options is determined using a contractual pricing formula based primarily upon the financial position of J-Devices at the time of exercise.

J-Devices is a separate business and is not integrated with our existing Japan-based businesses. We account for our investment in J-Devices using the equity method of accounting. J-Devices is a variable interest entity, but we are not the primary beneficiary as of December 31, 2010.

Under the equity method of accounting, we recognize our 30% share of J-Devices' net income or loss during each accounting period. J-Devices' financial information is converted to U.S. GAAP and translated into U.S. dollars using the Japanese yen as the functional currency. In addition to our proportionate share of J-Devices' income or loss, we record equity method adjustments for the amortization of a $1.9 million difference as our carrying value exceeded our equity in the net assets of J-Devices at the date of investment and other adjustments required by the equity method. As of December 31, 2010 and 2009, our equity earnings in J-Devices were $6.4 million and $2.4 million, respectively, net of J-Devices' income taxes in Japan.

Insurance Recoveries

3.21

MUELLER INDUSTRIES, INC. (DEC)

CONSOLIDATED STATEMENTS OF INCOME (in part)

Years Ended December 25, 2010, December 26, 2009, and December 27, 2008

(In thousands, except per share data)	2010	2009	2008
Net sales	$2,059,797	$1,547,225	$2,558,448
Cost of goods sold	1,774,811	1,327,022	2,233,123
Depreciation and amortization	40,364	41,568	44,345
Selling, general, and administrative expense	131,211	116,660	136,884
Insurance settlements	(22,736)	—	—
Impairment charges	—	29,755	18,000
Operating income	136,147	32,220	126,096
Interest expense	(11,647)	(9,963)	(19,050)
Other (expense) income, net	(2,650)	872	13,896
Income before income taxes	121,850	23,129	120,942

FINANCIAL REVIEW (in part)

Results of Operations (in part)

2010 Performance Compared with 2009 (in part)

During 2010, the Company recognized insurance settlements of $22.7 million related to the reimbursement for losses claimed as a result of fires at the U.K. copper tube mill in November 2008, and the Fulton, Mississippi copper tube mill in July 2009, the results of which are not impacted by daily operations and are not expected to recur in future periods.

Gains on Extinguishment of Debt

3.22

DOMINO'S PIZZA, INC. (DEC)

CONSOLIDATED STATEMENTS OF INCOME (in part)

	For the Years Ended		
(In thousands, except per share amounts)	December 28, 2008	January 3, 2010	January 2, 2011
Revenues:			
Domestic company-owned stores	$ 357,703	$ 335,779	$ 345,636
Domestic franchise	153,858	157,780	173,345
Domestic supply chain	771,106	763,733	875,517
International	142,447	146,765	176,396
Total revenues	1,425,114	1,404,057	1,570,894
Cost of sales:			
Domestic company-owned stores	298,857	274,474	278,297
Domestic supply chain	699,669	680,427	778,510
International	63,327	62,180	75,498
Total cost of sales	1,061,853	1,017,081	1,132,305
Operating margin	363,261	386,976	438,589
General and administrative	168,231	197,467	210,887
Income from operations	195,030	189,509	227,702
Interest income	2,746	683	244
Interest expense	(114,906)	(110,945)	(96,810)
Other	—	56,275	7,809
Income before provision for income taxes	82,870	135,522	138,945

NOTES TO CONSOLIDATED FINANCIAL STATEMENTS

(4) Recapitalization and Financing Arrangements (in part)

Repurchases of Long-Term Debt

During 2009, the Company repurchased and retired approximately $189.2 million in principal amount of its Class A-2 Notes for a total purchase price of approximately $133.9 million, including approximately $1.0 million of accrued interest that resulted in pre-tax gains of approximately $56.3 million in 2009. The pre-tax gains were recorded in Other in the Company's consolidated statements of income. In connection with the aforementioned transactions, the Company wrote-off deferred financing fees of approximately $2.3 million in 2009, which were recorded in interest expense in the Company's consolidated statements of income.

During 2010, the Company repurchased and retired $100.0 million in principal amount of its Class A-2 Notes and approximately $23.9 million in principal amount of its Class M-1 Notes for a total purchase price of approximately $116.6 million, including approximately $0.5 million of accrued interest that resulted in pre-tax gains of approximately $7.8 million. The net pre-tax gains were recorded in Other in the Company's consolidated statements of income. In connection with the aforementioned transactions, the Company wrote-off deferred financing fees and prepaid insurance fees totaling approximately $1.7 million in 2010, which were recorded in interest expense in the Company's consolidated statements of income.

Gain on Involuntary Conversion

3.23

THOR INDUSTRIES, INC. (JUL)

CONSOLIDATED STATEMENTS OF INCOME

For the Years Ended July 31, 2010, 2009 and 2008
(Amounts in thousands except per share data)

	2010	2009	2008
Net sales	$2,276,557	$1,521,896	$2,640,680
Cost of products sold	1,969,471	1,369,359	2,318,254
Gross profit	307,086	152,537	322,426
Selling, general and administrative expenses	147,407	124,578	177,068
Impairment of goodwill and trademarks	500	10,281	7,535
Amortization of intangibles	510	476	813
Gain on sale of property	0	373	2,308
Gain on involuntary conversion (Note R)	7,593	0	0
Interest income	5,515	5,530	11,511
Interest expense	395	525	1,315
Other income	11	815	2,893
Income before income taxes	171,393	23,395	152,407
Income taxes (Note F)	61,329	6,252	59,701
Net income	$ 110,064	$ 17,143	$ 92,706
Earnings per common share (Note A)			
Basic	$ 2.08	$ 0.31	$ 1.67
Diluted	$ 2.07	$ 0.31	$ 1.66

NOTES TO CONSOLIDATED FINANCIAL STATEMENTS

(All amounts presented in thousands except share and per share data)

R. Fire at Bus Production Facility

On February 14, 2010, a fire occurred at the northern production facility (the "Facility") at the Company's manufacturing site located near Imlay City, Michigan. The Facility is one of the Company's principal manufacturing locations for its Champion and General Coach America bus lines. The fire resulted in the destruction of a significant portion of the work in process, raw materials and equipment contained in the Facility. There were no reported injuries and the origin of the fire is undetermined. The southern production plant, paint facility and other buildings at the site were not affected by the fire and remain intact. The Company resumed limited production activities for its Champion and General Coach America buses in the southern manufacturing facility. In addition, the Company addressed equipment and staffing reallocation. Many employees continued to work out of the southern manufacturing facility and an office building on this site on a temporary basis.

The Company maintains a property and business interruption insurance policy that it believes will provide substantial coverage for the currently foreseeable losses arising from this incident, less up to the first $5,000 representing the Company's deductible per the policy.

The Company received $13,313 of insurance proceeds as of July 31, 2010. Of these proceeds, $13,079 represents recognized insurance recoveries, net of the deductible, and $234 represents advances recorded as deferred revenue in other liabilities. Through July 31, 2010, the cost incurred and insurance recoveries recognized, including $6,087 for business interruption ($4,121 net of applied deductible), are reflected in the Company's consolidated statements of income as follows:

Gain on Involuntary Conversion:

Insurance recoveries recognized	$18,079
Deductible	(5,000)
WIP and raw material destroyed	(4,305)
Property and equipment destroyed	(578)
Clean up and other costs	(603)
Gain on involuntary conversion	$ 7,593

The costs incurred to date of reconstructing the Facility and replacing inventory have been accounted for in the normal course of business. The costs incurred as of July 31, 2010 to reconstruct the Facility totaled $1,483, and the Facility is substantially completed and operational as of September 28, 2010. The Company expects that a.) the replacement cost of the property and equipment will substantially exceed the current carrying costs, and b.) lost profits covered under business interruption and future clean-up and related costs will be reimbursed under the policy, however, an accurate estimate of the remaining potential gain resulting from the involuntary conversion cannot be made at this time.

EXPENSES AND LOSSES

PRESENTATION

3.24 Paragraphs 80 and 83 of FASB Concepts Statement No. 6, *Elements of Financial Statements—a replacement of FASB Concepts Statement No. 3 (incorporating an amendment of FASB Concepts Statement No. 2)*, define expenses and losses as follows:

80. Expenses are outflows or other using up of assets or incurrences of liabilities (or a combination of both) from delivering or producing goods, rendering services, or carrying out other activities that constitute the entity's ongoing major or central operations.

83. Losses are decreases in equity (net assets) from peripheral or incidental transactions of an entity and from all other transactions and other events and circumstances affecting the entity except those that result from expenses or distributions to owners.

3.25

TABLE 3-3: EXPENSES AND LOSSES—OTHER THAN COST OF GOODS SOLD*

Table 3-3 summarizes the nature of expenses and losses most frequently disclosed by the survey entities, other than cost of goods sold. Excluded from Table 3-3 are rent, employee benefits, depreciation, income taxes, losses shown after the caption for income taxes, segment disposals, and extraordinary losses.

	Number of Entities		
	2010	2009	2008
Selling, general and administrative	296	300	298
Selling and administrative	56	70	70
General and/or administrative	71	98	94
Selling	15	40	33
Interest	265	453	457
Interest and penalty on income taxes	14	24	21
Research, development, engineering, and so on	170	229	222
Advertising	99	173	188
Provision for doubtful accounts	39	122	130
Warranty	15	99	99
Shipping	41	62	58
Asset retirement obligation accretion	9	43	39
Taxes other than income taxes	18	17	18
Maintenance and repairs	25	14	12
Exploration, dry holes, abandonments	10	7	9
Intangible asset amortization	168	276	280
Write-down of assets	139	248	234
Restructuring of operations	205	242	226
Change in fair value of derivatives	78	239	94
Impairment of intangibles	93	166	155
Foreign currency transactions	88	101	82
Sale of assets	41	84	75
Debt extinguishment	70	68	35
Litigation	27	49	52
Equity in losses of investees	27	47	40
Environmental cleanup	25	37	32
Sale of receivables	8	33	35
Merger costs	29	33	15
Software amortization	29	32	32
Fair value adjustments	18	23	8
Minority interests	6	14	48
Start-up costs	1	11	8
Purchased research and development	3	10	15
Royalties	5	10	9
Business combination adjustment loss	3	4	N/C^
Distributions on preferred securities of subsidiary trust	—	—	1

* Appearing in the income statement or notes to the financial statements, or both
^ N/C = Not compiled. The line item was not included in the table for the year shown.

PRESENTATION AND DISCLOSURE EXCERPTS

Selling, General, and Administrative

3.26

CONAGRA FOODS, INC. (MAY)

CONSOLIDATED STATEMENTS OF EARNINGS (in part)

Dollars in millions except per share amounts

	For the Fiscal Years Ended May		
	2010	2009	2008
Net sales	$12,079.4	$12,426.1	$11,248.2
Costs and expenses:			
Cost of goods sold	9,014.2	9,644.1	8,595.9
Selling, general and administrative expenses	1,820.0	1,683.6	1,747.6
Interest expense, net	160.4	186.0	252.9
Income from continuing operations before income taxes and equity method investment earnings	1,084.8	912.4	651.8
Income tax expense	362.1	318.6	210.4
Equity method investment earnings	22.1	24.0	49.7
Income from continuing operations	744.8	617.8	491.1
Income (loss) from discontinued operations, net of tax	(21.5)	361.2	439.5
Net income	$ 723.3	$ 979.0	$ 930.6

NOTES TO CONSOLIDATED FINANCIAL STATEMENTS

Columnar Amounts in Millions Except Per Share Amounts

1. Summary of Significant Accounting Policies (in part)

Marketing Costs—We promote our products with advertising, consumer incentives, and trade promotions. Such programs include, but are not limited to, discounts, coupons, rebates, and volume-based incentives. Advertising costs are expensed as incurred. Consumer incentives and trade promotion activities are recorded as a reduction of revenue or as a component of cost of goods sold based on amounts estimated as being due to customers and consumers at the end of the period, based principally on historical utilization and redemption rates. Advertising and promotion expenses totaled $409.3 million, $380.7 million, and $376.7 million in fiscal 2010, 2009, and 2008, respectively, and are included in selling, general and administrative expenses.

Foreign Currency Transaction Gains and Losses—We recognized net foreign currency transaction gains (losses) from continuing operations of $(6.2) million, $0.7 million, and $(8.1) million in fiscal 2010, 2009, and 2008, respectively, in selling, general and administrative expenses.

2. Discontinued Operations and Divestitures (in part)

Other Divestitures

In February 2010, we completed the sale of our *Luck's®* brand for proceeds of approximately $22.0 million, resulting in a pre-tax gain of approximately $14.3 million ($9.0 million after-tax), reflected in selling, general and administrative expenses.

In July 2008, we completed the sale of our *Pemmican®* beef jerky business for proceeds of approximately $29.4 million in cash, resulting in a pre-tax gain of approximately $19.4 million ($10.6 million after-tax), reflected in selling, general and administrative expenses. Due to our continuing involvement with the business, the results of operations of the *Pemmican®* business have not been reclassified as discontinued operations.

5. Garner, North Carolina Accident

On June 9, 2009, an accidental explosion occurred at our manufacturing facility in Garner, North Carolina. This facility was the primary production facility for our *Slim Jim®* branded meat snacks. On June 13, 2009, the U.S. Bureau of Alcohol, Tobacco, Firearms and Explosives announced its determination that the explosion was the result of an accidental natural gas release, and not a deliberate act.

We maintain comprehensive property (including business interruption), workers' compensation, and general liability insurance policies with very significant loss limits that we believe will provide substantial and broad coverage for the anticipated losses arising from this accident.

The costs incurred and insurance recoveries recognized, to date, are reflected in our consolidated financial statements, as follows:

Fiscal Year Ended May 30, 2010

(In millions)	Consumer Foods	Corporate	Total
Cost of goods sold: Inventory write-downs and other costs	$ 11.9	$ —	$ 11.9
Selling, general and administrative expenses: Fixed asset impairments, clean-up costs, etc.	$ 47.5	$2.6	$ 50.1
Insurance recoveries recognized	(58.1)	—	(58.1)
Total selling, general and administrative expenses	$(10.6)	$2.6	$ (8.0)
Net loss	$ 1.3	$2.6	$ 3.9

The amounts in the table, above, exclude lost profits due to the interruption of the business, as well as any related business interruption insurance recoveries.

Through May 30, 2010, we had received payment advances from the insurers of approximately $85.0 million for our initial insurance claims for this matter, $58.1 million of which has been recognized as a reduction to selling, general and administrative expenses. We anticipate final settlement of the claim will occur in fiscal 2011. Based on management's current assessment of production options, the expected level of insurance proceeds, and the estimated potential amount of losses and impact on the *Slim Jim®* brand, we do not believe that the accident will have a material adverse effect on our results of operations, financial condition, or liquidity.

In the fourth quarter of fiscal 2010, we determined that certain additional equipment located in the facility, with a book value of approximately $12 million, was impaired (included in the table above). We expect to be reimbursed by our insurers for the cost of replacing these assets, and we have recognized a $12 million insurance recovery in fiscal 2010 (included in the table above), representing the carrying value of these destroyed assets.

6. Restructuring Activities (in part)

2010 Restructuring Plan

During the fourth quarter of fiscal 2010, our board of directors approved a plan recommended by executive management related to the long-term production of our meat snack products. The plan provides for the closure of our meat snacks production facility in Garner, North Carolina, and the movement of production to our existing facility in Troy, Ohio. Since the accident at Garner, in June 2009, the Troy facility has been producing a portion of our meat snack products. Upon completion of the plan's implementation, which is expected to be in the second quarter of fiscal 2012, the Troy facility will be our primary meat snacks production facility. The plan is expected to result in the termination of approximately 500 employee positions in Garner and the creation of approximately 200 employee positions in Troy.

In May 2010, we made a decision to move certain administrative functions from Edina, Minnesota, to Naperville, Illinois. We expect to complete the transition of these functions in the first half of fiscal 2011. This plan, together with the plan to move production of our meat snacks from Garner, North Carolina to Troy, Ohio, are collectively referred to as the 2010 restructuring plan ("2010 plan").

In connection with the 2010 plan, we expect to incur pre-tax cash and non-cash charges for asset impairments, accelerated depreciation, severance, relocation, and site closure costs estimated to be approximately $67.5 million, of which $39.2 million was recognized in fiscal 2010. We have recorded expenses associated with this restructuring plan, including but not limited to, impairments of property, plant and equipment, accelerated depreciation, severance and related costs, and plan implementation costs (e.g., consulting, employee relocation, etc.). We anticipate that we will recognize the following pre-tax expenses associated with the 2010 plan in the fiscal 2010 to 2012 timeframe (amounts include charges recognized in fiscal 2010):

	Consumer Foods	Corporate	Total
Accelerated depreciation	$20.6	$ —	$20.6
Total cost of goods sold	20.6	—	20.6
Asset impairment	16.5	—	16.5
Severance and related costs	16.2	—	16.2
Other, net	10.7	3.5	14.2
Total selling, general and administrative expenses	43.4	3.5	46.9
Consolidated total	$64.0	$3.5	$67.5

Included in the above estimates are $25.5 million of charges which have resulted or will result in cash outflows and $42.0 million of non-cash charges.

During fiscal 2010, the Company recognized the following pre-tax charges in its consolidated statement of earnings for the fiscal 2010 plan:

	Consumer Foods	Corporate	Total
Accelerated depreciation	$ 3.4	$ —	$ 3.4
Total cost of goods sold	3.4	—	3.4
Asset impairment	16.5	—	16.5
Severance and related costs	14.2	—	14.2
Other, net	1.6	3.5	5.1
Total selling, general and administrative expenses	32.3	3.5	35.8
Consolidated total	$35.7	$3.5	$39.2

We also recognized income tax expense of $1.2 million related to tax credits we will no longer be able to realize related to the 2010 plan.

Liabilities recorded for the various initiatives and changes therein for fiscal 2010 under the 2010 plan were as follows:

	Balance at May 31, 2009	Costs Incurred and Charged to Expense	Costs Paid or Otherwise Settled	Changes in Estimates	Balance at May 30, 2010
Severance and related costs	$—	$14.2	$ —	$—	$14.2
Plan implementation costs	—	1.1	(0.1)	—	1.0
Other costs	—	3.5	—	—	3.5
Total	$—	$18.8	$(0.1)	$—	$18.7

2008–2009 Restructuring Plan

During fiscal 2008, our board of directors approved a plan ("2008-2009 plan") recommended by executive management to improve the efficiency of our Consumer Foods operations and related functional organizations and to streamline our international operations to reduce our manufacturing and selling, general, and administrative costs. This plan includes the reorganization of the Consumer Foods operations, the integration of the international headquarters functions into our domestic business, and exiting a number of international markets. These plans were substantially completed by the end of fiscal 2009. The total cost of the 2008-2009 plan was $36.3 million, of which $8.5 million was recorded in fiscal 2009 and $27.8 million was recorded in fiscal 2008. We have recorded expenses associated with the 2008-2009 plan, including but not limited to, inventory write-downs, severance and related costs, and plan implementation costs (e.g., consulting, employee relocation, etc.).

During fiscal 2009, we recognized the following pre-tax charges in our consolidated statement of earnings for the 2008-2009 plan:

	Consumer Foods	Corporate	Total
Severance and related costs	$(0.4)	$0.4	$ —
Contract termination	(1.3)	—	(1.3)
Plan implementation costs	1.9	1.5	3.4
Other, net	6.4	—	6.4
Total selling, general and administrative expenses	6.6	1.9	8.5
Consolidated total	$ 6.6	$1.9	$8.5

We recognized the following cumulative (plan inception to May 31, 2009) pre-tax charges related to the 2008-2009 plan in our consolidated statements of earnings:

	Consumer Foods	Corporate	Total
Inventory write-downs	$ 2.4	$ —	$ 2.4
Total cost of goods sold	2.4	—	2.4
Asset impairment	0.8	—	0.8
Severance and related costs	16.4	3.5	19.9
Contract termination	1.0	—	1.0
Plan implementation costs	2.2	2.8	5.0
Goodwill/brand impairment	0.2	—	0.2
Other, net	7.0	—	7.0
Total selling, general and administrative expenses	27.6	6.3	33.9
Consolidated total	$30.0	$6.3	$36.3

Included in the above amounts are $26.4 million of charges which have resulted in cash outflows and $9.9 million of non-cash charges.

No material liabilities remain in connection with the 2008-2009 plan at May 30, 2010.

2006–2008 Restructuring Plan

In February 2006, our board of directors approved a plan recommended by executive management to simplify our operating structure and reduce our manufacturing and selling, general, and administrative costs ("2006–2008 plan"). The plan included supply chain rationalization initiatives, the relocation of a divisional headquarters from Irvine, California to Naperville, Illinois, the centralization of shared services, salaried headcount reductions, and other cost-reduction initiatives. The plan was completed during fiscal 2009. No material expenses were recognized in fiscal 2009 or 2008 in connection with this plan.

As part of the 2006-2008 restructuring plan, we began construction of a new production facility in fiscal 2007. We determined that we will divest this facility. Accordingly, in the fourth quarter of fiscal 2010, we recognized an impairment charge of $33.3 million to write-down the asset to its expected sales value. This charge is reflected in selling, general and administrative expenses within the Consumer Foods segment.

3.27

TARGET CORPORATION (JAN)

CONSOLIDATED STATEMENTS OF OPERATIONS (in part)

(Millions, except per share data)	2009	2008	2007
Sales	$63,435	$62,884	$61,471
Credit card revenues	1,922	2,064	1,896
Total revenues	65,357	64,948	63,367
Cost of sales	44,062	44,157	42,929
Selling, general and administrative expenses	13,078	12,954	12,670
Credit card expenses	1,521	1,609	837
Depreciation and amortization	2,023	1,826	1,659
Earnings before interest expense and income taxes	4,673	4,402	5,272
Net interest expense			
Nonrecourse debt collateralized by credit card receivables	97	167	133
Other interest expense	707	727	535
Interest income	(3)	(28)	(21)
Net interest expense	801	866	647
Earnings before income taxes	3,872	3,536	4,625
Provision for income taxes	1,384	1,322	1,776
Net earnings	$ 2,488	$ 2,214	$ 2,849

NOTES TO CONSOLIDATED FINANCIAL STATEMENTS

3. Cost of Sales and Selling, General and Administrative Expenses

The following table illustrates the primary costs classified in each major expense category:

Cost of Sales	Selling, General and Administrative Expenses
Total cost of products sold including • Freight expenses associated with moving merchandise from our vendors to our distribution centers and our retail stores, and among our distribution and retail facilities • Vendor income that is not reimbursement of specific, incremental and identifiable costs Inventory shrink Markdowns Outbound shipping and handling expenses associated with sales to our guests Terms cash discount Distribution center costs, including compensation and benefits costs	Compensation and benefit costs including • Stores • Headquarters Occupancy and operating costs of retail and headquarters facilities Advertising, offset by vendor income that is a reimbursement of specific, incremental and identifiable costs Preopening costs of stores and other facilities Other administrative costs

The classification of these expenses varies across the retail industry.

Research, Development, and Engineering

3.28

JOHNSON & JOHNSON (DEC)

CONSOLIDATED STATEMENTS OF EARNINGS
(in part)

(Dollars in millions except per share figures) (Note 1)

	2010	2009	2008
Sales to customers	$61,587	$61,897	$63,747
Cost of products sold	18,792	18,447	18,511
Gross profit	42,795	43,450	45,236
Selling, marketing and administrative expenses	19,424	19,801	21,490
Research and development expense	6,844	6,986	7,577
Purchased in-process research and development (Note 20)	—	—	181
Interest income	(107)	(90)	(361)
Interest expense, net of portion capitalized (Note 4)	455	451	435
Other (income) expense, net	(768)	(526)	(1,015)
Restructuring (Note 22)	—	1,073	—
Earnings before provision for taxes on income	16,947	15,755	16,929
Provision for taxes on income (Note 8)	3,613	3,489	3,980
Net earnings	$13,334	$12,266	$12,949

NOTES TO CONSOLIDATED FINANCIAL STATEMENTS

1. Summary of Significant Accounting Policies (in part)

Research and Development

Research and development expenses are expensed as incurred. Upfront and milestone payments made to third-parties in connection with research and development collaborations are expensed as incurred up to the point of regulatory approval. Payments made to third parties subsequent to regulatory approval are capitalized and amortized over the remaining useful life of the related product. Amounts capitalized for such payments are included in other intangibles, net of accumulated amortization.

The Company enters into collaborative arrangements, typically with other pharmaceutical or biotechnology companies, to develop and commercialize drug candidates or intellectual property. These arrangements typically involve two (or more) parties who are active participants in the collaboration and are exposed to significant risks and rewards dependent on the commercial success of the activities. These collaborations usually involve various activities by one or more parties, including research and development, marketing and selling and distribution. Often, these collaborations require upfront, milestone and royalty or profit share payments, contingent upon the occurrence of certain future events linked to the success of the asset in development. Amounts due from collaborative partners related to development activities are generally reflected as a reduction of research and development expense because the performance of contract development services is not central to the Company's operations. In general, the income statement presentation for these collaborations is as follows:

Nature/Type of Collaboration	Statement of Earnings Presentation
Third-party sale of product	Sales to customers
Royalties/milestones paid to collaborative partner (post-regulatory approval)[*]	Cost of goods sold
Royalties received from collaborative partner	Other income (expense), net
Upfront payments & milestones paid to collaborative partner (pre-regulatory approval)	Research and development expense
Research and development payments to collaborative partner	Research and development expense
Research and development payments received from collaborative partner	Reduction of research and development expense

[*] Milestones are capitalized as intangible assets and amortized to cost of goods sold over the useful life.

3.29

STRYKER CORPORATION (DEC)

Item 1. Business (in part)

Product Development

Most of the Company's products and product improvements have been developed internally. The Company maintains close working relationships with physicians and medical personnel in hospitals and universities who assist in product research and development. New and improved products play a critical role in the Company's sales growth. The Company continues to place emphasis on the development of proprietary products and product improvements to complement and expand its existing product lines. The Company has a decentralized research and development focus, with manufacturing locations responsible for new product development and product improvements. Research, development and engineering personnel at the various manufacturing locations maintain relationships with staff at distribution locations and with customers to understand changes in the market and product needs.

Total expenditures for product research, development and engineering were $393.9 million in 2010, $336.2 million in 2009 and $367.8 million in 2008. Research, development and engineering expenses represented 5.4% of sales in 2010, compared to 5.0% in 2009 and 5.5% in 2008. The spending level in 2010 increased due to the Company's increased focus on new product development for anticipated future product launches and investments in new technologies. Recent new product introductions in the Orthopaedic Implants and MedSurg Equipment segments are more fully described under the caption *Product Sales*.

In addition to internally developed products, the Company invests in technologies developed by third parties that have the potential to expand the markets in which the Company operates. In 2010 the Company acquired the Sonopet Ultrasonic Aspirator control consoles, handpieces and accessories from Mutoh Co., Ltd. and Synergetics USA, Inc., Gaymar Industries, a manufacturer of specialized support surface and pressure ulcer management solutions, and the bioimplantable porous polyethylene (PPE) product line from Porex Surgical, Inc. for use primarily in reconstructive surgery of the head and face. In December 2009 the Company acquired Ascent, the market leader in the reprocessing and remanufacturing of medical devices in the U.S. During 2010 and 2009, the Company acquired certain additional companies all of which are expected to enhance the Company's product offerings to its customers within its Orthopaedic Implants and MedSurg Equipment business segments.

CONSOLIDATED STATEMENTS OF EARNINGS
(in part)

(In millions, except per share amounts)	Years Ended December 31		
	2010	**2009**	**2008**
Net sales	$7,320.0	$6,723.1	$6,718.2
Cost of sales	2,285.7	2,183.7	2,131.4
Gross profit	5,034.3	4,539.4	4,586.8
Research, development and engineering expenses	393.9	336.2	367.8
Selling, general and administrative expenses	2,707.3	2,506.3	2,625.1
Intangible asset amortization	58.2	35.5	40.0
Property, plant and equipment impairment	123.5	—	—
Restructuring charges	—	67.0	34.9
Total operating expenses	3,282.9	2,945.0	3,067.8
Operating income	1,751.4	1,594.4	1,519.0

Exploration

3.30

NOBLE ENERGY, INC. (DEC)

CONSOLIDATED STATEMENTS OF OPERATIONS
(in part)

(In millions, except per share amounts)	Year Ended December 31		
	2010	**2009**	**2008**
Revenues			
Oil, Gas and NGL Sales	$2,832	$2,060	$3,651
Income from Equity Method Investees	118	84	174
Other Revenues	72	169	76
Total Revenues	3,022	2,313	3,901
Costs and Expenses			
Production Expense	570	525	594
Exploration Expense	245	144	217
Depreciation, Depletion and Amortization	883	816	791
General and Administrative	277	237	236
Net Gain on Asset Sales	(113)	(22)	(5)
Asset Impairments	144	604	294
Other Operating Expense, Net	64	67	139
Total Operating Expenses	2,070	2,371	2,266
Operating Income (Loss)	952	(58)	1,635
Other (Income) Expense			
(Gain) Loss on Commodity Derivative Instruments	(157)	110	(440)
Interest, Net of Amount Capitalized	72	84	69
Other Non-Operating (Income) Expense, Net	6	12	(55)
Total Other (Income) Expense	(79)	206	(426)
Income (Loss) Before Income Taxes	1,031	(264)	2,061

NOTES TO CONSOLIDATED FINANCIAL STATEMENTS

Note 1. Summary of Significant Accounting Policies (in part)

Property, Plant and Equipment (in part)—Significant accounting policies for our property, plant and equipment are as follows:

Successful Efforts Method—We account for crude oil and natural gas properties under the successful efforts method of accounting. Under this method, costs to acquire mineral interests in crude oil and natural gas properties, drill and equip exploratory wells that find proved reserves, and drill and equip development wells are capitalized. Capitalized costs of producing crude oil and natural gas properties, along with support equipment and facilities, are amortized to expense by the unit-of-production method based on proved crude oil and natural gas reserves on a field-by-field basis as estimated by our qualified petroleum engineers. Our policy is to use quarter-end reserves and add back current period production to compute quarterly DD&A expense. Costs of certain gathering facilities or processing plants serving a number of properties or used for third-party processing are depreciated using the straight-line method over the useful lives of the assets ranging from five to 14 years. Upon sale or retirement of depreciable or depletable property, the cost and related accumulated DD&A are eliminated from the accounts and the resulting gain or loss is recognized. Repairs and maintenance are expensed as incurred.

Proved Property Impairment—We review proved oil and gas properties and other long-lived assets for impairment when events and circumstances indicate a decline in the recoverability of the carrying values of such properties, such as a negative revision of reserves estimates or sustained decrease in commodity prices. We estimate future cash flows expected in connection with the properties and compare such future cash flows to the carrying amount of the properties to determine if the carrying amount is recoverable. When the carrying amount of a property exceeds its estimated undiscounted future cash flows, the carrying amount is reduced to estimated fair value. Fair value may be estimated using comparable market data, a discounted cash flow method, or a combination of the two. In the discounted cash flow method, estimated future cash flows are based on management's expectations for the future and include estimates of future oil and gas production, commodity prices based on published forward commodity price curves as of the date of the estimate, operating and development costs, and a risk-adjusted discount rate.

We recorded proved property impairment charges in 2010, 2009, and 2008. It is reasonably possible that other proved oil and gas properties could become impaired in the future if commodity prices decline. See Note 4. Asset Impairments.

Unproved Property Impairment—We assess individually significant unproved properties for impairment of value on a quarterly basis and recognize a loss at the time of impairment by providing an impairment allowance. In determining whether a significant unproved property is impaired we consider numerous factors including, but not limited to, current exploration plans, favorable or unfavorable exploration activity on the property being evaluated and/or adjacent properties, our geologists' evaluation of the property, and the remaining months in the lease term for the property.

When we have allocated significant fair value to an unproved property as the result of a transaction accounted for as a business combination, we use a future cash flow analysis to assess the unproved property for impairment. Cash flows used in the impairment analysis are determined based on management's estimates of crude oil and natural gas reserves, future commodity prices and future costs to extract the reserves. Cash flow estimates related to probable and possible reserves are reduced by additional risk-weighting factors. Other individually insignificant unproved properties are amortized on a composite method based on our experience of successful drilling and average holding period.

We recorded unproved property impairment charges in 2008. It is reasonably possible that other unproved oil and gas properties could become impaired in the future if commodity prices decline. See Note 4. Asset Impairments.

Properties Acquired in Business Combinations—If sufficient market data is not available, we determine the fair values of proved and unproved properties acquired in transactions accounted for as business combinations by preparing our own estimates of crude oil and natural gas reserves. We estimate future prices to apply to the estimated reserves quantities acquired, and estimate future operating and development costs, to arrive at estimates of future net cash flows. For the fair value assigned to proved reserves, future net cash flows are discounted using a market-based weighted average cost of capital rate determined appropriate at the time of the business combination. To compensate for the inherent risk of estimating and valuing unproved reserves, discounted future net cash flows of probable and possible reserves are reduced by additional risk-weighting factors. See Note 3. Acquisitions and Divestitures.

Exploration Costs—Geological and geophysical costs, delay rentals, amortization of unproved leasehold costs, and costs to drill exploratory wells that do not find proved reserves are expensed as oil and gas exploration. We carry the costs of an exploratory well as an asset if the well finds a sufficient quantity of reserves to justify its capitalization as a producing well and as long as we are making sufficient progress assessing the reserves and the economic and operating viability of the project. For certain capital-intensive deepwater Gulf of Mexico or international projects, it may take us more than one year to evaluate the future potential of the exploration well and make a determination of its economic viability. Our ability to move forward on a project may be dependent on gaining access to transportation or processing facilities or obtaining permits and government or partner approval, the timing of which is beyond our control. In such cases, exploratory well costs remain suspended as long as we are actively pursuing access to necessary facilities and access to such permits and approvals and believe they will be obtained. We assess the status of suspended exploratory well costs on a quarterly basis. See Note 7. Capitalized Exploratory Well Costs.

Note 7. Capitalized Exploratory Well Costs

We capitalize exploratory well costs until a determination is made that the well has found proved reserves or is deemed noncommercial. If a well is deemed to be noncommercial, the well costs are immediately charged to exploration expense.

Changes in capitalized exploratory well costs are as follows and exclude amounts that were capitalized and subsequently expensed in the same period:

(Millions)	Year Ended December 31		
	2010	2009	2008
Capitalized Exploratory Well Costs, Beginning of Period	$ 432	$ 501	$249
Additions to Capitalized Exploratory Well Costs Pending Determination of Proved Reserves	143	136	253
Reclassified to Proved Oil and Gas Properties Based on Determination of Proved Reserves	(146)	(198)	—
Capitalized Exploratory Well Costs Charged to Expense	(3)	(7)	(1)
Capitalized Exploratory Well Costs, End of Period	$ 426	$ 432	$501

The following table provides an aging of capitalized exploratory well costs (suspended well costs) based on the date the drilling was completed and the number of projects for which exploratory well costs have been capitalized for a period greater than one year since the completion of drilling:

(Millions)	December 31		
	2010	2009	2008
Exploratory Well Costs Capitalized for a Period of One Year or Less	$148	$158	$256
Exploratory Well Costs Capitalized for a Period Greater Than One Year After Completion of Drilling	278	274	245
Balance at End of Period	$426	$432	$501
Number of Projects with Exploratory Well Costs That Have Been Capitalized for a Period Greater Than One Year After Completion of Drilling	8	5	6

The following table provides a further aging of those exploratory well costs that have been capitalized for a period greater than one year since the completion of drilling as of December 31, 2010:

(Millions)	Total	Suspended Since		
		2009	2008	2007 & Prior
Project				
Blocks O and I (West Africa)	$133	$14	$ 9	$110
Dalit (Israel)	20	20	—	—
Gunflint (Deepwater Gulf of Mexico)	52	3	49	—
Redrock (Deepwater Gulf of Mexico)	17	—	—	17
Deep Blue (Deepwater Gulf of Mexico)	19	19	—	—
Flyndre (North Sea)	13	—	—	13
Selkirk (North Sea)	20	—	—	20
Other	4	1	3	—
Total Exploratory Well Costs Capitalized for a Period Greater Than One Year After Completion of Drilling	$278	$57	$61	$160

Blocks O and I (West Africa)—The West Africa project includes Blocks O and I offshore Equatorial Guinea and the YoYo mining concession and Tilapia PSC offshore Cameroon. In December 2010, we and our partners sanctioned the development plan for Alen, which was subsequently approved by the government of Equatorial Guinea in January 2011. Approximately $61 million of capitalized costs were reclassified to proved oil and gas properties. In 2009, we sanctioned the Aseng development project and reclassified $76 million of capitalized costs to proved oil and gas properties. We are evaluating future oil projects and planning to drill an appraisal well at Diega/Carmen, offshore Equatorial Guinea. In Cameroon, we recently completed a 3-D seismic acquisition, and results are being processed for future drilling potential.

Dalit (Israel)—Dalit is a 2009 natural gas discovery located offshore Israel. We are currently working with our partners on a cost-effective development plan. In 2010, we sanctioned the Tamar development project and reclassified $77 million of capitalized costs to proved oil and gas properties.

Gunflint (Deepwater Gulf of Mexico)—Gunflint (Mississippi Canyon Block 948) is a 2008 crude oil discovery. Our plans to drill one or two appraisal wells in 2010 were delayed by the Deepwater Moratorium. Once a drilling permit is approved, we plan to drill one or two appraisal wells. We are also reviewing host platform options including: subsea tieback to an existing third-party host, procurement and modification of an existing platform, and new construction. If we are able to connect to an existing third-party host, the project could have an accelerated completion schedule, thereby potentially absorbing time lost due to the drilling delay caused by the Deepwater Moratorium.

Redrock (Deepwater Gulf of Mexico)—Redrock (Mississippi Canyon Block 204) was a 2006 natural gas/condensate discovery and is currently considered a co-development candidate with Raton South (Mississippi Canyon Block 292). We are in the process of tying back Raton South to a host platform at Viosca Knoll Block 900. We plan to tie back Redrock after Raton South commences production, which is currently expected to occur by the end of 2011.

Deep Blue (Deepwater Gulf of Mexico)—Deep Blue (Green Canyon Block 723) was a significant test well, which began drilling during 2009. When the Deepwater Moratorium was announced in May 2010, we were required to suspend sidetrack drilling activities at the Deep Blue prospect. Once a drilling permit is approved, we plan to resume exploration activities at Deep Blue.

Flyndre (North Sea)—The Flyndre project is located in the UK sector of the North Sea and we successfully completed an exploratory appraisal well in 2007. We are currently working with the project operator and other partners to finalize the field development plan and relevant operating agreements.

Selkirk (North Sea)—The Selkirk project is also located in the UK sector of the North Sea. Capitalized costs to date primarily consist of the cost of drilling an exploratory well. We are currently working with our partners on a cost-effective development plan, including selection of a host facility.

Advertising

3.31

KOHL'S CORPORATION (JAN)

CONSOLIDATED STATEMENTS OF INCOME (in part)

(In millions, except per share data)	2009	2008	2007
Net sales	$17,178	$16,389	$16,474
Cost of merchandise sold (exclusive of depreciation shown separately below)	10,680	10,334	10,460
Gross margin	6,498	6,055	6,014
Operating expenses:			
Selling, general, and administrative	4,144	3,936	3,697
Depreciation and amortization	590	541	452
Preopening expenses	52	42	61
Operating income	1,712	1,536	1,804
Other expense (income):			
Interest expense	134	132	82
Interest income	(10)	(21)	(20)
Income before income taxes	1,588	1,425	1,742

NOTES TO CONSOLIDATED FINANCIAL STATEMENTS

1. Business and Summary of Accounting Policies (in part)

Cost of Merchandise Sold and Selling, General and Administrative Expenses

The following table illustrates the primary costs classified in Cost of Merchandise Sold and Selling, General and Administrative Expenses:

Cost of Merchandise Sold	Selling, General and Administrative Expenses

• Total cost of products sold including product development costs, net of vendor payments other than reimbursement of specific, incremental and identifiable costs
• Inventory shrink
• Markdowns
• Freight expenses associated with moving merchandise from our vendors to our distribution centers
• Shipping and handling expenses of e-commerce sales
• Terms cash discount
	• Compensation and benefit costs including:
	  — Stores
	  — Corporate headquarters, including buying and merchandising
	  — Distribution centers
	• Occupancy and operating costs of our retail, distribution and corporate facilities
	• Net revenues from the Kohl's credit card agreement with JPMorgan Chase
	• Freight expenses associated with moving merchandise from our distribution centers to our retail stores, and among distribution and retail facilities
	• Advertising expenses, offset by vendor payments for reimbursement of specific, incremental and identifiable costs
	• Other administrative costs

The classification of these expenses varies across the retail industry.

Advertising

Advertising costs, which include primarily television and radio broadcast, direct mail, and newspaper circulars, are expensed when the advertisement is first seen. Advertising costs, net of related vendor allowances, were as follows:

(In millions)	2009	2008	2007
Gross advertising costs	$988	$1,037	$981
Vendor allowances	142	147	142
Net advertising costs	$846	$ 890	$839

Taxes Other Than Income Taxes

3.32

CHEVRON CORPORATION (DEC)

CONSOLIDATED STATEMENT OF INCOME (in part)

	Year Ended December 31		
(Millions of dollars, except per-share amounts)	2010	2009	2008
Revenues and Other Income			
Sales and other operating revenues(*)	$198,198	$167,402	$264,958
Income from equity affiliates	5,637	3,316	5,366
Other income	1,093	918	2,681
Total Revenues and Other Income	204,928	171,636	273,005
Costs and Other Deductions			
Purchased crude oil and products	116,467	99,653	171,397
Operating expenses	19,188	17,857	20,795
Selling, general and administrative expenses	4,767	4,527	5,756
Exploration expenses	1,147	1,342	1,169
Depreciation, depletion and amortization	13,063	12,110	9,528
Taxes other than on income(*)	18,191	17,591	21,303
Interest and debt expense	50	28	—
Total Costs and Other Deductions	172,873	153,108	229,948
Income Before Income Tax Expense	32,055	18,528	43,057
Income Tax Expense	12,919	7,965	19,026
Net Income	19,136	10,563	24,031

NOTES TO THE CONSOLIDATED FINANCIAL STATEMENTS

Note 1—Summary of Significant Accounting Policies (in part)

Revenue Recognition—Revenues associated with sales of crude oil, natural gas, coal, petroleum and chemicals products, and all other sources are recorded when title passes to the customer, net of royalties, discounts and allowances, as applicable. Revenues from natural gas production from properties in which Chevron has an interest with other producers are generally recognized on the entitlement method. Excise, value-added and similar taxes assessed by a governmental authority on a revenue-producing transaction between a seller and a customer are presented on a gross basis. The associated amounts are shown as a footnote to the Consolidated Statement of Income on page FS-27. Purchases and sales of inventory with the same counterparty that are entered into in contemplation of one another (including buy/sell arrangements) are combined and recorded on a net basis and reported in "Purchased crude oil and products" on the Consolidated Statement of Income.

Provision for Doubtful Accounts

3.33

FRONTIER COMMUNICATIONS CORPORATION (DEC)

CONSOLIDATED STATEMENTS OF OPERATIONS (in part)

($ in thousands, except for per-share amounts)	2010	2009	2008
Revenue	$3,797,675	$2,117,894	$2,237,018
Operating expenses:			
Network access expenses	383,679	225,907	222,013
Other operating expenses	1,611,137	781,097	810,748
Depreciation and amortization	893,719	476,391	561,801
Acquisition and integration costs	137,142	28,334	—
Total operating expenses	3,025,677	1,511,729	1,594,562
Operating income	771,998	606,165	642,456
Investment income	6,848	6,285	16,118
Other income (loss), net	13,690	(41,127)	(5,170)
Interest expense	521,820	378,214	362,634
Income before income taxes	270,716	193,109	290,770
Income tax expense	114,999	69,928	106,496
Net income	$ 155,717	$ 123,181	$ 184,274

NOTES TO CONSOLIDATED FINANCIAL STATEMENTS

(5) Accounts Receivable

The components of accounts receivable, net at December 31, 2010 and 2009 are as follows:

($ in thousands)	2010	2009
End user	$627,573	$205,384
Other	14,306	15,532
Less: Allowance for doubtful accounts	(73,571)	(30,171)
Accounts receivable, net	$568,308	$190,745

An analysis of the activity in the allowance for doubtful accounts for the years ended December 31, 2010, 2009 and 2008 is as follows ($ in thousands):

		Additions			
Allowance for Doubtful Accounts	Balance at Beginning of Period	Charged to Bad Debt Expense[*]	Charged to Other Accounts— Revenue	Deductions	Balance at End of Period
2008	$32,748	$31,700	$ 2,352	$(26,675)	$40,125
2009	40,125	33,682	(6,181)	(37,455)	30,171
2010	30,171	55,161	14,873	(26,634)	73,571

[*] Such amounts are included in bad debt expense and for financial reporting purposes are classified as a reduction to other revenue.

We maintain an allowance for estimated bad debts based on our estimate of our ability to collect accounts receivable. Bad debt expense is recorded as a reduction to revenue.

Warranty

3.34

HARRIS CORPORATION (JUN)

CONSOLIDATED STATEMENT OF INCOME (in part)

	Fiscal Years Ended		
(In millions, except per share amounts)	2010	2009	2008
Revenue from product sales and services			
Revenue from product sales	$ 3,935.2	$ 3,915.3	$ 3,544.2
Revenue from services	1,270.9	1,089.7	1,051.9
	5,206.1	5,005.0	4,596.1
Cost of product sales and services			
Cost of product sales	(2,268.7)	(2,498.0)	(2,289.7)
Cost of services	(1,065.7)	(922.2)	(855.9)
	(3,334.4)	(3,420.2)	(3,145.6)
Engineering, selling and administrative expenses	(958.9)	(791.3)	(746.5)
Impairment of goodwill and other long-lived assets	—	(255.5)	—
Non-operating income (loss)	(1.9)	(3.1)	11.4
Interest income	1.5	3.2	5.2
Interest expense	(72.1)	(52.8)	(53.1)
Income from continuing operations before income taxes	840.3	485.3	667.5
Income taxes	(278.7)	(172.9)	(214.0)
Income from continuing operations	561.6	312.4	453.5

NOTES TO CONSOLIDATED FINANCIAL STATEMENTS

Note 1. Significant Accounting Policies (in part)

Warranties—On development and production contract sales in our Government Communications Systems and RF Communications segments, the value or price of our warranty is generally included in the contract and funded by the customer. A provision for warranties is built into the estimated program costs when determining the profit rate to accrue when applying the cost-to-cost percentage-of-completion revenue recognition method. Warranty costs, as incurred, are charged to the specific program's cost, and both revenue and cost are recognized at that time. Factors that affect the estimated program cost for warranties include terms of the contract, complexity of the delivered product or service, number of installed units, historical experience and management's judgment regarding anticipated rates of warranty claims and cost per claim.

On product sales in our RF Communications, Broadcast Communications and Government Communications Systems segments, we provide for future warranty costs upon product delivery. The specific terms and conditions of those warranties vary depending upon the product sold, customer and country in which we do business. In the case of products sold by us, our warranties start from the shipment, delivery or customer acceptance date and continue as follows:

Segment	Warranty Periods
RF Communications	One to twelve years
Broadcast Communications	Less than one year to five years
Government Communications Systems	One to two years

Because our products are manufactured, in many cases, to customer specifications and their acceptance is based on meeting those specifications, we historically have experienced minimal warranty costs. Factors that affect our warranty liability include the number of installed units, historical experience and management's judgment regarding anticipated rates of warranty claims and cost per claim. We assess the adequacy of our recorded warranty liabilities every quarter and make adjustments to the liability as necessary.

Automation software products sold by our Broadcast Communications segment generally carry a 90-day warranty from the date of shipment. Our liability under these warranties is either to provide a corrected copy of any portion of the software found not to be in substantial compliance with the specifications or, if we are unable to do so, to provide a full refund.

Software license agreements and sales contracts for products in our Broadcast Communications segment generally include provisions for indemnifying customers against certain specified liabilities should that segment's products infringe certain intellectual property rights of third parties. Certain of our Broadcast Communications transmission systems customers have notified us of potential claims against us based on these standard indemnification provisions included in sales contracts between us and these customers. These indemnification claims arise from litigation brought by a third-party patent licensing company asserting alleged technology rights against these customers. We are cooperating with these customers in efforts to mitigate their litigation exposure. To date, we have not incurred material costs as a result of such indemnification and have not accrued any liabilities related to such obligations in our Consolidated Financial Statements. See *Note 10: Accrued Warranties* for additional information regarding warranties.

Note 10. Accrued Warranties

Changes in our warranty liability, which is included as a component of the "Other accrued items" line item in our Consolidated Balance Sheet, during fiscal 2010 and 2009, are as follows:

(In millions)	2010	2009
Balance at beginning of the fiscal year	$ 65.5	$ 41.6
Warranty provision for sales made during the year	28.4	26.4
Settlements made during the year	(43.4)	(19.4)
Other adjustments to the warranty liability, including those for acquisitions and foreign currency translation, during the year	22.6	16.9
Balance at end of the fiscal year	$ 73.1	$ 65.5

Interest

3.35

ANADARKO PETROLEUM CORPORATION (DEC)

CONSOLIDATED STATEMENTS OF INCOME (in part)

	Years Ended December 31		
(Millions except per-share amounts)	2010	2009	2008
Revenues and Other			
Natural-gas sales	$ 3,420	$2,924	$ 5,770
Oil and condensate sales	5,592	4,022	6,425
Natural-gas liquids sales	997	536	802
Gathering, processing and marketing sales	833	728	1,082
Gains (losses) on divestitures and other, net	142	133	1,083
Reversal of accrual for DWRRA dispute (Note 15)	—	657	—
Total	10,984	9,000	15,162
Costs and Expenses			
Oil and gas operating	830	859	1,036
Oil and gas transportation and other	816	664	621
Exploration	974	1,107	1,369
Gathering, processing and marketing	615	617	800
General and administrative	982	983	866
Depreciation, depletion and amortization	3,714	3,532	3,194
Other taxes	1,068	746	1,452
Impairments	216	115	223
Total	9,215	8,623	9,561
Operating Income (Loss)	1,769	377	5,601
Other (Income) Expense			
Interest expense	855	702	732
(Gains) losses on commodity derivatives, net	(893)	408	(561)
(Gains) losses on other derivatives, net	285	(582)	7
Other (income) expense, net	(119)	(43)	55
Total	128	485	233
Income (Loss) from Continuing Operations Before Income Taxes	1,641	(108)	5,368
Income Tax Expense (Benefit)	820	(5)	2,148
Income (Loss) from Continuing Operations	821	(103)	3,220

NOTES TO CONSOLIDATED FINANCIAL STATEMENTS

11. Debt and Interest Expense (in part)

Debt—The following table presents the Company's outstanding debt and capital lease obligation at December 31, 2010 and 2009. See Note 8 for disclosure regarding Anadarko's notes payable related to its ownership of certain noncontrolling mandatorily redeemable interests that are not included in the Company's reported debt balance and do not affect consolidated interest expense.

(Millions)	December 31, 2010			December 31, 2009		
	Principal	Carrying Value	Fair Value	Principal	Carrying Value	Fair Value
6.750% Senior Notes due 2011	$ —	$ —	$ —	$ 950	$ 940	$ 1,004
6.875% Senior Notes due 2011	285	287	296	675	688	726
6.125% Senior Notes due 2012	131	131	138	170	169	180
5.000% Senior Notes due 2012	39	39	40	82	82	85
5.750% Senior Notes due 2014	275	274	289	275	274	296
7.625% Senior Notes due 2014	500	499	561	500	499	571
5.950% Senior Notes due 2016	1,750	1,745	1,880	1,750	1,744	1,893
6.375% Senior Notes due 2017	2,000	2,000	2,179	—	—	—
7.050% Debentures due 2018	114	108	125	114	108	120
6.950% Senior Notes due 2019	300	297	334	300	297	340
8.700% Senior Notes due 2019	600	598	733	600	598	749
6.950% Senior Notes due 2024	650	672	706	650	673	704
7.500% Debentures due 2026	112	106	123	112	106	115
7.000% Debentures due 2027	54	54	55	54	54	54
7.125% Debentures due 2027	150	157	161	150	157	152
6.625% Debentures due 2028	17	17	17	17	17	17
7.150% Debentures due 2028	235	216	244	235	215	233
7.200% Debentures due 2029	135	135	138	135	135	139
7.950% Debentures due 2029	117	117	126	117	117	127
7.500% Senior Notes due 2031	900	858	995	900	858	1,010
7.875% Senior Notes due 2031	500	578	573	500	580	583
Zero-Coupon Senior Notes due 2036	2,360	607	704	2,360	591	623
6.450% Senior Notes due 2036	1,750	1,742	1,745	1,750	1,742	1,827
7.950% Senior Notes due 2039	325	324	372	325	324	398
6.200% Senior Notes due 2040	750	745	743	—	—	—
7.730% Debentures due 2096	61	61	61	61	60	66
7.500% Debentures due 2096	78	72	75	78	72	74
7.250% Debentures due 2096	49	49	46	49	49	47
WES borrowings	299	299	299	—	—	—
Midstream subsidiary note payable to a related party	—	—	—	1,599	1,599	1,599
Total borrowings	$14,536	$12,787	$13,758	$14,508	$12,748	$13,732
Capital lease obligation	226	226	N/A	—	—	N/A
Less: Current portion of long-term debt	289	291	296	—	—	—
Total long-term debt	$14,473	$12,722	$13,462	$14,508	$12,748	$13,732

Carrying values in the table above include net unamortized debt discount of $1.7 billion and $1.8 billion at December 31, 2010 and 2009, respectively, which is amortized to interest expense over the terms of the related debt.

In a 2006 private offering, Anadarko received $500 million of loan proceeds upon issuing Zero-Coupon Senior Notes (the Zero Coupons) maturing October 2036. The Zero Coupons have an aggregate principal amount due at maturity of $2.4 billion, reflecting a yield to maturity of 5.24%. The holder has the right to cause the Company to repay up to 100% of the then-accreted value of the Zero Coupons in October of each year starting in 2012.

All of the Company's outstanding debt is senior unsecured. WES's borrowings under its senior unsecured revolving credit facility (the RCF) and its senior unsecured term loan (the Term Loan) are not guaranteed by Anadarko or any of its wholly owned subsidiaries.

Midstream Subsidiary Note Payable to a Related Party—In 2007, Anadarko, and an entity formed by a group of unrelated third-party investors (the Investor), formed Trinity Associates LLC (Trinity), a variable interest entity. Trinity was initially capitalized with a $100 million cash contribution by Anadarko in exchange for Class A member and managing member interests in Trinity, and a $2.2 billion cash contribution by the Investor in exchange for a Class B member cu-

mulative preferred interest. Trinity invested $100 million in a United States Government securities money market fund (the Fund) and loaned $2.2 billion to a wholly owned midstream subsidiary of Anadarko (Midstream Holding). The outstanding balance, described in the accompanying Consolidated Balance Sheets as Midstream Subsidiary Note Payable to a Related Party (Midstream Subsidiary Note), was repaid in full in 2010.

Proceeds from repayment of the Midstream Subsidiary Note were distributed by Trinity to the Investor. Proceeds from Trinity's liquidation of its investment in the Fund were distributed to Anadarko. Anadarko accounted for its investment in Trinity using the equity method of accounting, and the $100 million distribution received reduced the carrying amount of that investment to zero.

Anadarko Revolving Credit Facility—In September 2010, the Company entered into the $5.0 billion Facility, and terminated its $1.3 billion revolving credit agreement, scheduled to mature in 2013. At December 31, 2010, the $5.0 billion Facility was undrawn with available capacity of $4.6 billion ($5.0 billion undrawn capacity less $377 million in outstanding letters of credit).

Borrowings under the $5.0 billion Facility will bear interest, at the Company's election, at (i) LIBOR plus a margin ranging from 2.75% to 3.75%, based on the Company's credit rating, or (ii) the greatest of (a) the JPMorgan Chase Bank prime rate, (b) the federal funds rate plus 0.50%, or (c) one-month LIBOR plus 1%, plus in each case, an applicable margin.

Obligations incurred under the $5.0 billion Facility, as well as obligations Anadarko has to lenders or their affiliates pursuant to certain derivative instruments (as discussed in Note 9), are guaranteed by certain of the Company's wholly owned domestic subsidiaries, and are secured by a perfected first-priority security interest in certain exploration and production assets located in the United States and 65% of the capital stock of certain wholly owned foreign subsidiaries. The $5.0 billion Facility contains various customary covenants with which Anadarko must comply, including, but not limited to, limitations on incurrence of indebtedness, liens on assets, and asset sales. Anadarko is also required to maintain, at the end of each quarter, (i) a Consolidated Leverage Ratio of no more than 4.5 to 1.0 (relative to Consolidated EBITDAX for the most recent period of four calendar quarters), (ii) a ratio of Current Assets to Current Liabilities of no less than 1.0 to 1.0, and (iii) a Collateral Coverage Ratio of no less than 1.75 to 1.0, in each case, as defined in the $5.0 billion Facility. The Collateral Coverage Ratio is the ratio of an annually redetermined value of pledged assets to outstanding loans under the $5.0 billion Facility. Additionally, to borrow from the $5.0 billion Facility, the Collateral Coverage Ratio must be no less than 1.75 to 1.0 after giving pro forma effect to the requested borrowing. The Company was in compliance with all applicable covenants at December 31, 2010, and there were no restrictions on its ability to utilize the available capacity of the $5.0 billion Facility.

WES Revolving Credit Facility—At December 31, 2010, the WES RCF had outstanding borrowings of $49 million, with $401 million of available borrowing capacity. The RCF matures in October 2012 and bears interest at LIBOR plus an applicable margin ranging from 2.375% to 3.250%, for a rate of 3.26% at December 31, 2010.

WES Term Loan—In August 2010, WES borrowed $250 million under the Term Loan, which matures in 2013, from a group of banks. The Term Loan bears interest at LIBOR plus an applicable margin ranging from 2.50% to 3.50% (for a rate of 3.26% at December 31, 2010) depending on WES's Consolidated Leverage Ratio, as defined in the agreement governing the Term Loan.

Interest Expense—The following table summarizes the amounts included in interest expense.

(Millions)	Years Ended December 31		
	2010	2009	2008
Current debt, long-term debt and other[1]	$ 856	$734	$ 762
Midstream subsidiary note payable to a related party	24	39	109
(Gain) loss on early debt retirements and commitment termination	103	(2)	(16)
Capitalized interest	(128)	(69)	(123)
Interest expense	$ 855	$702	$ 732

[1] Included in 2009 is the reversal of the $78 million liability for unpaid interest related to the DWRRA dispute. See Note 15.

Interest and Penalties Related to Unrecognized Tax Benefits

3.36

KIMBALL INTERNATIONAL, INC. (JUN)

CONSOLIDATED STATEMENTS OF INCOME (in part)

(Amounts in thousands, except for per share data)	Year Ended June 30		
	2010	2009	2008
Net Sales	$1,122,808	$1,207,420	$1,351,985
Cost of Sales	946,275	1,004,901	1,103,511
Gross Profit	176,533	202,519	248,474
Selling and Administrative Expenses	181,771	192,711	232,131
Other General Income	(9,980)	(33,417)	-0-
Restructuring Expense	2,051	2,981	21,911
Goodwill Impairment	-0-	14,559	-0-
Operating Income (Loss)	2,691	25,685	(5,568)
Other Income (Expense):			
Interest income	1,188	2,499	3,362
Interest expense	(142)	(1,565)	(1,967)
Non-operating income	2,980	2,663	3,512
Non-operating expense	(749)	(3,956)	(1,703)
Other income (expense), net	3,277	(359)	3,204
Income (Loss) from Continuing Operations Before Taxes on Income	5,968	25,326	(2,364)
Provision (Benefit) for Income Taxes	(4,835)	7,998	(2,442)
Income from Continuing Operations	10,803	17,328	78
Loss from Discontinued Operation, Net of Tax	-0-	-0-	(124)
Net Income (Loss)	$ 10,803	$ 17,328	$ (46)

NOTES TO CONSOLIDATED FINANCIAL STATEMENTS

Note 1. Summary of Significant Accounting Policies (in part)

Change in Accounting Policy: During the third quarter of fiscal year 2010, the Company changed its classification of interest and penalties related to unrecognized tax benefits, reflected in the Consolidated Statements of Income. Interest related to unrecognized tax benefits was previously classified on either the Interest income line or the Interest expense line. Penalties related to unrecognized tax benefits were previously classified as Non-operating expense. In accordance with the guidance for accounting for uncertainty in income taxes, based on an accounting policy election, interest related to unrecognized tax benefits may either be classified as income taxes or interest, and penalties related to unrecognized tax benefits may either be classified as income taxes or another expense classification. Beginning January 1, 2010, the Company revised its accounting policy and now classifies interest and penalties related to unrecognized tax benefits in the Provision (Benefit) for Income Taxes line of the Consolidated Statements of Income. The Company believes that the classification of interest and penalties in the Provision (Benefit) for Income Taxes line is preferable because it is management's belief that interest and penalties related to unrecognized tax benefits are costs of managing taxes payable (as opposed to, for example, interest as a cost of debt). Also, this presentation is more consistent with the practice followed by most of the Company's competitors. As a result of reclassifying interest related to unrecognized tax benefits, the Company's interest coverage ratio, which is a debt covenant in its revolving credit facility, will change. This change does not impact the Company's compliance with this debt covenant. Interest and penalties related to unrecognized tax benefits were not material during the period subsequent to the change in ac-

counting policy. Prior periods were not adjusted retrospectively due to immateriality. This change had no impact on Operating Income, Income from Continuing Operations, Net Income, or Earnings Per Share. This change had an impact on Income from Continuing Operations Before Taxes on Income, however the impact was not material.

Note 9. Income Taxes (in part)

Beginning January 1, 2010, the Company recognizes interest and penalties related to unrecognized tax benefits in the Provision (Benefit) for Income Taxes line of the Consolidated Statements of Income. See *Note 1—Summary of Significant Accounting Policies* of Notes to Consolidated Financial Statements, under the caption Change in Accounting Policy, regarding the change in accounting policy for the classification of interest and penalties. Amounts accrued for interest and penalties were as follows:

(Amounts in thousands)	As of June 30, 2010	As of June 30, 2009	As of June 30, 2008
Accrued Interest and Penalties:			
Interest	$311	$344	$341
Penalties	117	146	159

Accrued interest and penalties are not included in the tabular roll forward of unrecognized tax benefits above. Interest and penalties recognized for fiscal years 2010, 2009, and 2008 were, in thousands, income of $72, $10, and $325, respectively.

Interest and Penalties Related to Income Tax

3.37

POLARIS INDUSTRIES INC. (DEC)

CONSOLIDATED STATEMENTS OF INCOME (in part)

(In thousands, except per share data)	For the Years Ended December 31		
	2010	2009	2008
Sales	$1,991,139	$1,565,887	$1,948,254
Cost of sales	1,460,926	1,172,668	1,502,546
Gross profit	530,213	393,219	445,708
Operating expenses:			
Selling and marketing	142,353	111,137	137,035
Research and development	84,940	62,999	77,472
General and administrative	99,055	71,184	69,607
Total operating expenses	326,348	245,320	284,114
Income from financial services	16,856	17,071	21,205
Operating income	220,721	164,970	182,799
Non-operating expense (Income):			
Interest expense	2,680	4,111	9,618
Gain (Loss) on securities available for sale	(825)	8,952	—
Other expense (income), net	325	733	(3,881)
Income before income taxes	218,541	151,174	177,062
Provision for income taxes	71,403	50,157	59,667
Net Income	$ 147,138	$ 101,017	$ 117,395

NOTES TO CONSOLIDATED FINANCIAL STATEMENTS

Note 4. Income Taxes (in part)

Polaris' Income before income taxes was generated from its United States and foreign operations as follows:

(In thousands)	For the Years Ended December 31		
	2010	2009	2008
United States	$210,155	$143,483	$163,322
Foreign	8,386	7,691	13,740
Income before income taxes	$218,541	$151,174	$177,062

Components of Polaris' Provision for income taxes are as follows:

(In thousands)	For the Years Ended December 31		
	2010	2009	2008
Current:			
Federal	$ 73,597	$27,104	$48,370
State	7,381	3,723	5,520
Foreign	6,783	5,757	6,744
Deferred	(16,358)	13,573	(967)
Total	$ 71,403	$50,157	$59,667

Polaris had liabilities recorded related to unrecognized tax benefits totaling $5,509,000 and $4,988,000 at December 31, 2010 and 2009, respectively. The liabilities were classified as Long-term income taxes payable in the accompanying consolidated balance sheets in accordance with ASC Topic 740. Polaris recognizes potential interest and penalties related to income tax positions as a component of the Provision for income taxes on the consolidated statements of income. Polaris had reserves related to potential interest of $331,000 and $612,000 recorded as a component of the liabilities at December 31, 2010 and 2009, respectively. The entire balance of unrecognized tax benefits at December 31, 2010, if recognized, would affect the Company's effective tax rate. The Company does not anticipate that total unrecognized tax benefits will materially change in the next twelve months. Tax years 2006 through 2009 remain open to examination by certain tax jurisdictions to which the Company is subject. A reconciliation of the beginning and ending amount of unrecognized tax benefits is as follows:

(In thousands)	For the Years Ended December 31	
	2010	2009
Balance at January 1	$ 4,988	$5,103
Gross increases for tax positions of prior years	1,259	94
Gross decreases for tax positions of prior years	—	(275)
Gross increases for tax positions of current year	1,345	985
Decreases due to settlements	—	(171)
Decreases for lapse of statute of limitations	(2,083)	(748)
Balance at December 31	$ 5,509	$4,988

Accretion on Asset Retirement Obligation

3.38

APACHE CORPORATION (DEC)

STATEMENT OF CONSOLIDATED OPERATIONS (in part)

(In millions, except per common share data)	For the Year Ended December 31		
	2010	2009	2008
Revenues and Other:			
Oil and gas production revenues	$12,183	$8,574	$12,328
Other	(91)	41	62
	12,092	8,615	12,390
Operating Expenses:			
Depreciation, depletion and amortization			
Recurring	3,083	2,395	2,516
Additional	—	2,818	5,334
Asset retirement obligation accretion	111	105	101
Lease operating expenses	2,032	1,662	1,910
Gathering and transportation	178	143	157
Taxes other than income	690	580	985
General and administrative	380	344	289
Merger, acquisitions & transition	183	—	—
Financing costs, net	229	242	166
	6,886	8,289	11,458
Income before income taxes	5,206	326	932

NOTES TO CONSOLIDATED FINANCIAL STATEMENTS

1. Summary of Significant Accounting Policies (in part)

Asset Retirement Obligation

The initial estimated asset retirement obligation (ARO) related to properties is recognized as a liability, with an associated increase in property and equipment for the asset retirement cost. Accretion expense is recognized over the estimated productive life of the related assets. If the fair value of the estimated ARO changes, an adjustment is recorded to both the ARO and the asset retirement cost. Revisions in estimated liabilities can result from changes in estimated inflation rates, changes in service and equipment costs and changes in the estimated timing of settling ARO.

4. Asset Retirement Obligation

The following table describes changes to the Company's ARO liability for the years ended December 31, 2010 and 2009:

(In millions)	2010	2009
Asset retirement obligation at beginning of year	$1,784	$1,895
Liabilities incurred	270	213
Liabilities acquired	847	5
Liabilities settled	(329)	(508)
Accretion expense	111	105
Revisions in estimated liabilities	189	74
Asset retirement obligation at end of year	2,872	1,784
Less current portion	(407)	(147)
Asset retirement obligation, long-term	$2,465	$1,637

The ARO liability reflects the estimated present value of the amount of dismantlement, removal, site reclamation and similar activities associated with Apache's oil and gas properties. The Company utilizes current retirement costs to estimate the expected cash outflows for retirement obligations. The Company estimates the ultimate productive life of the properties, a risk-adjusted discount rate and an inflation factor in order to determine the current present value of this obligation. To the extent future revisions to these assumptions impact the present value of the existing ARO liability, a corresponding adjustment is made to the oil and gas property balance.

During 2010, the Company recorded additional abandonment liabilities of $847 million related to the properties acquired in the BP, Devon and Mariner transactions. Apache also recorded additional abandonment liabilities of $270 million associated with its drilling and development program during the year.

Liabilities settled in 2010 relate to individual properties, platforms and facilities plugged and abandoned during the period. The Company has an active abandonment program with a majority of the activity in the Gulf of Mexico and Canada. In September 2010 the Bureau of Ocean Management, Regulation and Enforcement (BOEMRE, formerly known as the Minerals Management Service), a division of the U.S. Department of the Interior, issued Notice to Lessees (NTL) No. 2010-G05, which includes guidelines for decommissioning idle infrastructure on active leases in the Gulf of Mexico within a specified period of time. The Company has reviewed its Gulf of Mexico abandonment program in light of these new regulations and adjusted the timing of its abandonment program accordingly.

Write-down of Assets

3.39

THE MCCLATCHY COMPANY (DEC)

CONSOLIDATED STATEMENT OF OPERATIONS
(in part)

(In thousands, except for per share amounts)	Year Ended		
	December 26, 2010	December 27, 2009	December 28, 2008
Revenues—Net:			
Advertising	$1,049,964	$1,143,129	$1,568,766
Circulation	272,776	278,256	265,584
Other	52,492	50,199	66,106
	1,375,232	1,471,584	1,900,456
Operating Expenses:			
Compensation	519,179	582,241	822,771
Newsprint and supplements	136,642	167,164	252,599
Depreciation and amortization	133,404	142,889	142,948
Other operating expenses	347,124	380,778	460,973
Masthead impairment	—	—	59,563
	1,136,349	1,273,072	1,738,854
Operating income	238,883	198,512	161,602
Non-Operating (Expenses) Income:			
Interest expense	(177,641)	(127,276)	(157,385)
Interest income	550	47	1,429
Equity income (loss) in unconsolidated companies—net	11,752	2,130	(14,021)
Write-down of investments and land	(24,297)	(28,322)	(26,462)
Gain on sale of SP Newsprint Company	—	208	34,417
Gain (loss) on extinguishment of debt	(10,661)	44,117	21,026
Gain (loss) on non-operating items and other—net	265	(5)	1,479
	(200,032)	(109,101)	(139,517)
Income from continuing operations before income taxes	38,851	89,411	22,085

NOTES TO CONSOLIDATED FINANCIAL STATEMENTS

Note 3. Investments in Unconsolidated Companies and Miami Land

The following is the Company's ownership interest and investment in unconsolidated companies and joint ventures as of December 26, 2010, and December 27, 2009, (dollars in thousands):

Company	% Ownership Interest	December 26, 2010	December 27, 2009
CareerBuilder, LLC	14.4	$220,777	$218,736
Classified Ventures, LLC	25.6	66,976	81,538
HomeFinder, LLC	33.3	3,061	5,048
Seattle Times Company (C-Corporation)	49.5	—	—
Ponderay (general partnership)	27.0	13,320	13,754
Other	Various	2,747	3,033
		$306,881	$322,109

The Company uses the equity method of accounting for a majority of investments.

HomeFinder, LLC, formerly a division of Classified Ventures, LLC (CV), operates the real estate website HomeFinder.com. It was spun off in the first quarter of 2009 into a separate limited liability corporation in which the Company has a one-third ownership interest. The initial carrying value of the Company's investment in HomeFinder primarily represented its proportionate ownership of HomeFinder which was previously reflected in the Company's value of CV.

In fiscal 2010 CV paid the Company a dividend totaling $24.3 million that was recorded as a return of capital and reduced the carrying value of the Company's investment in CV.

Also in 2010, a less-than-50% owned company identified goodwill impairment at a reporting unit and as a result, the Company recognized $3.0 million as its portion of the charge related to this write-down in fiscal 2010. In fiscal 2008, a less-than-50% owned company identified goodwill impairment at a reporting unit and as a result, the Company recognized its portion of the charge related to this write-down. The total non-cash pre-tax charges related to impairments of internet investments recorded in fiscal 2008 were $26.5 million.

On March 31, 2008, McClatchy and its partners, affiliates of Cox Enterprises, Inc. and Media General, Inc., completed the sale of SP Newsprint Company (SP), of which McClatchy was a one-third owner. The Company recorded a gain on the transaction of approximately $34.4 million. The Company used the $55.0 million of sales proceeds it received in the second fiscal quarter of 2008 and an additional $5.0 million it received in 2009 to reduce debt.

The Company has an annual purchase commitment for 109,730 metric tons of newsprint from SP. The Company is required to purchase 56,800 metric tons of newsprint of annual production from Ponderay on a "take-if-tendered" basis at prevailing market prices.

At the end of 2008, the Seattle Times Company (STC) recorded a comprehensive loss related to its retirement plan liabilities. The Company recorded its share of the compre-

hensive loss in the Company's comprehensive income (loss) in stockholders' equity to the extent that it had a carrying value in its investment in STC. As a result, the Company's investment in STC at December 27, 2008, was zero, and no future income or losses from STC will be recorded until the Company's carrying value on its balance sheet is restored through future earnings by STC.

The Company also incurred expense related to the purchase of products and services provided by these companies, for the uploading and hosting of online advertising on behalf of the Company's newspapers' advertisers.

The following table summarizes expenses incurred for products provided by its less-than 50% owned companies and is recorded in operating expenses in fiscal 2010, 2009 and 2008 (in thousands):

	Career-Builder	Classified Ventures	Ponderay	Other
2010	$1,272	$11,073	$23,048	NA
2009	1,241	10,250	27,413	NA
2008	2,670	11,561	15,703	$353

As of December 26, 2010, and December 27, 2009, the Company had approximately $3.6 million and $3.9 million, respectively, included in amounts payable to CareerBuilder, CV and Ponderay.

The table below presents the summarized financial information for the Company's investments in unconsolidated companies on a combined basis (dollars in thousands):

	2010	2009
Current assets	$473,765	$393,914
Noncurrent assets	603,216	664,876
Current liabilities	298,229	269,501
Noncurrent liabilities	280,184	269,546
Equity	498,568	519,743

	2010	2009	2008
Net revenues	$1,195,755	$1,142,551	$1,334,372
Operating income (loss)	102,863	67,442	(52,579)
Net income (loss)	95,855	66,524	(50,722)

On January 31, 2011, the contract to sell certain land in Miami terminated because the buyer did not consummate the transaction by the closing deadline in the contract. Under the terms of an agreement with the developer, McClatchy is now entitled to receive a $7.0 million termination fee. McClatchy previously received approximately $16.5 million in nonrefundable deposits, which it used to repay debt.

The Company obtained an independent appraisal to determine the fair value of the land at December 26, 2010. The valuation process incorporated the income capitalization valuation technique and the market data or direct sales comparison approach. Based on the appraisal, the carrying value was written down by $21.4 million to $116.0 million in 2010 (net of the $16.5 million of nonrefundable deposits received) and is included in other assets on the Company's Balance Sheet.

The Company wrote down the value of the land by $26.3 million in the fourth quarter of 2009 after extending the deadline on the contract to January 31, 2011, and receipt of an additional $6.0 million nonrefundable deposit from the buyer.

The fair value analysis performed in 2009 incorporated an independent appraisal and consideration of the existing contract to sell the land.

Fair value measurement requires three classifications of investments based on the nature of available fair value inputs and the valuation methodologies used to measure these investments at fair value. Under the fair value guidance, the Company classified the land as a Level 3 classification. Level 3 classifications are based on input to the valuation methodology that are unobservable inputs in situations where there is little or no market activity for the asset or liability and the reporting entity makes estimates and assumptions related to the pricing of the asset or liability.

Restructuring

3.40

CARDINAL HEALTH, INC. (JUN)

CONSOLIDATED STATEMENTS OF EARNINGS
(in part)

(In millions, except per common share amounts)	Fiscal Year Ended June 30		
	2010	2009	2008
Revenue	$98,502.8	$95,991.5	$87,408.2
Cost of products sold	94,722.1	92,244.0	83,631.1
Gross margin	3,780.7	3,747.5	3,777.1
Operating expenses			
Distribution, selling, general and administrative expenses	2,408.0	2,333.5	2,340.6
Restructuring and employee severance	90.7	104.7	55.3
Acquisition related costs	8.4	2.8	2.6
Impairments and (gain)/loss on sale of assets	29.1	13.9	(33.3)
Litigation (credits)/charges, net	(62.4)	5.2	19.5
Operating earnings	1,306.9	1,287.4	1,392.4
Other (income)/expense, net	(13.5)	13.2	(38.8)
Interest expense, net	113.5	114.4	136.1
Loss on extinguishment of debt	39.9	0.0	0.0
Gain on sale of CareFusion common stock	(44.6)	0.0	0.0
Earnings before income taxes and discontinued operations	1,211.6	1,159.8	1,295.1

NOTES TO CONSOLIDATED FINANCIAL STATEMENTS

3. Restructuring and Employee Severance

Restructuring Policy

We consider restructuring activities as programs whereby we fundamentally change our operations such as closing facilities, moving manufacturing of a product to another location or outsourcing the production of a product. Restructuring activities may also involve substantial re-alignment of the management structure of a business unit in response to changing market conditions. A liability for a cost associated with an exit or disposal activity is recognized and measured initially at its fair value in the period in which it is incurred except for a liability for a one-time termination benefit, which is recognized over its future service period.

Restructuring and Employee Severance

The following table summarizes activity related to our restructuring and employee severance costs during fiscal 2010, 2009 and 2008:

(In millions)	Fiscal Year Ended June 30		
	2010	2009	2008
Employee related costs[1]	$32.9	$ 33.8	$30.0
Facility exit and other costs[2]	57.8	70.9	25.3
Total restructuring and employee severance	$90.7	$104.7	$55.3

[1] *Employee-Related Costs.* These costs primarily consist of one-time termination benefits provided to employees who have been involuntarily terminated and duplicate payroll costs during transition periods.

[2] *Facility Exit and Other Costs.* Facility exit and other costs consist of accelerated depreciation, equipment relocation costs, project consulting fees and costs associated with restructuring our delivery of information technology infrastructure services.

Restructuring and employee severance for fiscal 2010, 2009 and 2008 included costs related to the following significant projects:

(In millions)	Fiscal Year Ended June 30		
	2010	2009	2008
Spin-off[1]	$64.5	$73.8	$ 0.0
Segment Realignment[2]	2.0	15.7	0.2
Medical Headquarters Relocation[3]	0.1	1.0	28.3

[1] During fiscal 2009 and fiscal 2010, we incurred restructuring expenses related to the Spin-Off consisting of employee-related costs, share-based compensation, costs to evaluate and execute the transaction, costs to separate certain functions and information technology systems and other one-time transaction related costs. See Note 17 for further information regarding share-based compensation incurred in connection with the Spin-Off. Also included within these costs is $18.6 million of costs related to the retirement of our former Chairman and Chief Executive Officer upon completion of the Spin-Off.

[2] During fiscal 2009, we consolidated our businesses into two primary operating and reportable segments to reduce costs and align resources with the needs of each segment ("Segment Realignment"). In connection with the Spin-Off, these reportable segments have since been reorganized. Refer to Notes 1 and 16 for additional information regarding our current reportable segments.

[3] In April 2007, we announced a plan to move our medical products distribution headquarters and certain corporate functions from Waukegan, Illinois to our corporate headquarters in Dublin, Ohio.

In addition to the significant restructuring programs discussed above, from time to time we incur costs to implement smaller restructuring efforts for specific operations within our segments. These restructuring plans focus on various aspects of operations, including closing and consolidating certain manufacturing and distribution operations, rationalizing headcount and aligning operations in the most strategic and cost-efficient structure.

We estimate that we will incur additional costs in future periods associated with currently anticipated restructuring activities totaling $14.5 million. These additional costs are primarily associated with the Spin-Off.

Restructuring and Employee Severance Accrual Rollforward

The following table summarizes activity related to liabilities associated with our restructuring and employee severance activities during fiscal 2010, 2009 and 2008:

(In millions)	Employee Related Costs	Facility Exit and Other Costs	Total
Balance at June 30, 2007	$ 14.1	$ 1.8	$ 15.9
Additions	30.0	25.3	55.3
Payments and other adjustments	(21.6)	(26.7)	(48.3)
Balance at June 30, 2008	22.5	0.4	22.9
Additions	33.8	70.9	104.7
Payments and other adjustments	(43.1)	(59.0)	(102.1)
Balance at June 30, 2009	13.2	12.3	25.5
Additions	32.9	57.8	90.7
Payments and other adjustments	(36.9)	(62.7)	(99.6)
Balance at June 30, 2010	$ 9.2	$ 7.4	$ 16.6

Intangible Asset Amortization

3.41

PPG INDUSTRIES, INC. (DEC)

CONSOLIDATED STATEMENT OF INCOME (in part)

	For the Year		
(Millions, except per share amounts)	2010	2009	2008
Net sales	$13,423	$12,239	$15,849
Cost of sales, exclusive of depreciation and amortization (See Note 2)	8,214	7,539	10,155
Selling, general and administrative (See Note 3)	2,979	2,936	3,432
Depreciation (See Note 3)	346	354	428
Amortization (See Note 7)	124	126	135
Research and development—net (See Note 23)	394	388	451
Interest	189	193	254
Asbestos settlement—net (See Notes 12 and 16)	12	13	4
In-process research and development (See Note 2)	—	—	23
Business restructuring (See Note 8)	—	186	163
Other charges (See Note 16)	84	65	61
Other earnings (See Note 20)	(214)	(178)	(165)
Income before income taxes	1,295	617	908
Income tax expense (See Note 14)	415	191	284
Net income attributable to the controlling and noncontrolling interests (See Note 1)	880	426	624
Less: net income attributable to noncontrolling interests (See Note 1)	111	90	86
Net income (attributable to PPG)	$ 769	$ 336	$ 538

NOTES TO CONSOLIDATED FINANCIAL STATEMENTS

7. Goodwill and Other Identifiable Intangible Assets

The change in the carrying amount of goodwill attributable to each reportable business segment for the years ended December 31, 2010 and 2009 was as follows:

(Millions)	Performance Coatings	Industrial Coatings	Architectural Coatings— EMEA	Optical and Specialty Materials	Glass	Commodity Chemicals	Total
Balance, Jan. 1, 2009	$1,078	$482	$ 976	$50	$55	$—	$2,641
Goodwill from acquisitions	—	9	5	—	—	3	17
Currency translation	65	18	40	1	2	—	126
Balance, Dec. 31, 2009	$1,143	$509	$1,021	$51	$57	$ 3	$2,784
Goodwill from acquisitions	—	7	8	—	—	3	18
Currency translation	8	(21)	(63)	(2)	(5)	—	(83)
Balance, Dec. 31, 2010	$1,151	$495	$ 966	$49	$52	$ 6	$2,719

The carrying amount of acquired trademarks with indefinite lives as of December 31, 2010 and 2009 totaled $323 million and $334 million, respectively.

The Company's identifiable intangible assets with finite lives are being amortized over their estimated useful lives and are detailed below.

(Millions)	Dec. 31, 2010			Dec. 31, 2009		
	Gross Carrying Amount	Accumulated Amortization	Net	Gross Carrying Amount	Accumulated Amortization	Net
Acquired technology	$ 515	$(273)	$242	$ 519	$(234)	$ 285
Customer-related intangibles	974	(355)	619	990	(286)	704
Tradenames	120	(44)	76	122	(35)	87
Other	31	(23)	8	28	(22)	6
Balance	$1,640	$(695)	$945	$1,659	$(577)	$1,082

Aggregate amortization expense was $ 124 million, $126 million and $135 million in 2010, 2009 and 2008, respectively. The estimated future amortization expense of identifiable intangible assets is approximately $130 million during 2011 and 2012, and approximately $115-$120 million during 2013, 2014 and 2015.

Foreign Currency

3.42

THE GOODYEAR TIRE & RUBBER COMPANY (DEC)

CONSOLIDATED STATEMENTS OF OPERATIONS (in part)

(In millions, except per share amounts)	Year Ended December 31		
	2010	2009	2008
Net Sales	$18,832	$16,301	$19,488
Cost of Goods Sold	15,452	13,676	16,139
Selling, Administrative and General Expense	2,630	2,404	2,600
Rationalizations (Note 2)	240	227	184
Interest Expense (Note 16)	316	311	320
Other Expense (Note 3)	186	40	59
Income (Loss) Before Income Taxes	8	(357)	186
United States and Foreign Taxes (Note 15)	172	7	209
Net Loss	(164)	(364)	(23)
Less: Minority Shareholders' Net Income	52	11	54
Goodyear Net Loss	$ (216)	$ (375)	$ (77)

NOTES TO CONSOLIDATED FINANCIAL STATEMENTS

Note 3. Other Expense (in part)

(In millions)	2010	2009	2008
Expense (Income)			
Net foreign currency exchange losses	$159	$ 7	$ 57
Financing fees and financial instruments	95	39	97
Net (gains) losses on asset sales	(73)	30	(53)
Royalty income	(30)	(28)	(32)
Interest income	(11)	(17)	(68)
General and product liability—discontinued products	11	9	30
Subsidiary liquidation loss	—	18	16
Miscellaneous	35	(18)	12
	$186	$ 40	$ 59

Net foreign currency exchange losses in 2010 were $159 million, compared to $7 million and $57 million of losses in 2009 and 2008, respectively. Losses in 2010 included a first quarter loss of $110 million resulting from the January 8, 2010 devaluation of the Venezuelan bolivar fuerte against the U.S. dollar and the establishment of a two-tier exchange rate structure, and a fourth quarter foreign currency exchange loss of $24 million in connection with the January 1, 2011 elimination of the two-tier exchange rate structure. Foreign currency exchange also reflected net gains and losses resulting from the effect of exchange rate changes on various foreign currency transactions worldwide.

Effective January 1, 2010, Venezuela's economy was considered to be highly inflationary under U.S. generally accepted accounting principles since it experienced a rate of general inflation in excess of 100% over the latest three year period, based upon the blended Consumer Price Index and National Consumer Price Index. Accordingly, the U.S. dollar was determined to be the functional currency of our Venezuelan subsidiary. All gains and losses resulting from the remeasurement of its financial statements since January 1, 2010 were determined using official exchange rates.

On January 8, 2010, Venezuela established a two-tier exchange rate structure for essential and non-essential goods. For essential goods the official exchange rate was 2.6 bolivares fuertes to the U.S. dollar and for non-essential goods the official exchange rate was 4.3 bolivares fuertes to the U.S. dollar. As announced by the Venezuelan government in December 2010, on January 1, 2011, the two-tier exchange rate structure was eliminated and the exchange rate for essential goods cannot be used for our unsettled amounts at December 31, 2010. Effective January 1, 2011, the official exchange rate of 4.3 bolivares fuertes to the U.S. dollar was established for substantially all goods.

The $110 million foreign currency exchange loss in the first quarter of 2010 primarily consisted of a $157 million remeasurement loss on bolivar-denominated net monetary assets and liabilities, including deferred taxes, at the time of the January 2010 devaluation. The loss was primarily related to cash deposits in Venezuela that were remeasured at the official exchange rate of 4.3 bolivares fuertes applicable to non-essential goods, and was partially offset by $47 million subsidy receivable related to U.S. dollar-denominated payables that were expected to be settled at the official subsidy exchange rate of 2.6 bolivares fuertes applicable to essential goods. Since we expected these payables to be settled at the subsidy essential goods rate, we established a subsidy receivable to reflect the expected benefit to be received in the form of the difference between the essential and non-essential goods exchange rates. Throughout 2010, we periodically assessed our ability to realize the benefit of the subsidy receivable, and a substantial portion of purchases by our Venezuelan subsidiary had qualified and settled at the official exchange rate for essential goods.

As a result of the elimination of the official subsidy exchange rate for essential goods, we no longer expect our Venezuelan subsidiary to settle payables at that exchange rate. Accordingly, we recorded a foreign exchange loss of $24 million in the fourth quarter of 2010 related to the reversal of the subsidy receivable at December 31, 2010.

Net foreign currency exchange losses decreased in 2009 compared to 2008, due primarily to the weakening of various currencies against the U.S. dollar in 2008.

Sale of Assets

3.43

THE DOW CHEMICAL COMPANY (DEC)

CONSOLIDATED STATEMENTS OF INCOME (in part)

	For the Years Ended December 31		
(In millions, except per share amounts)	**2010**	**2009**	**2008**
Net sales	$53,674	$44,875	$57,361
Cost of sales	45,780	39,148	51,913
Research and development expenses	1,660	1,492	1,310
Selling, general and administrative expenses	2,609	2,487	1,966
Amortization of intangibles	509	399	92
Goodwill impairment losses	—	7	239
Restructuring charges	26	689	839
Purchased in-process research and development charges	—	7	44
Acquisition and integration related expenses	143	166	49
Asbestos-related credits	54	—	54
Equity in earnings of nonconsolidated affiliates	1,112	630	787
Sundry income—net	125	891	89
Interest income	37	39	86
Interest expense and amortization of debt discount	1,473	1,571	648
Income from continuing operations before income taxes	2,802	469	1,277
Provision (Credit) for income taxes	481	(97)	651
Net income from continuing operations	2,321	566	626

NOTES TO CONSOLIDATED FINANCIAL STATEMENTS

Note O—Transfers of Financial Assets

On January 1, 2010, the Company adopted ASU 2009-16, "Transfers and Servicing (Topic 860): Accounting for Transfers of Financial Assets." This ASU is intended to improve the information provided in financial statements concerning transfers of financial assets, including the effects of transfers on financial position, financial performance and cash flows, and any continuing involvement of the transferor with the transferred financial assets. The Company evaluated the impact of adopting the guidance and the terms and conditions in place at January 1, 2010 and determined that certain sales of accounts receivable would be classified as secured borrowings. Under the Company's sale of accounts receivable arrangements, $915 million was outstanding at January 1, 2010. The maximum amount of receivables available for participation in these programs was $1,939 million at January 1, 2010.

In January 2010, the Company terminated the North American arrangement and replaced it with a new arrangement that qualified for treatment as a sale under ASU 2009-16. The arrangement related to $294 million of the $915 million outstanding at January 1, 2010 and $1,100 million of the $1,939 million maximum participation.

In June 2010, the Company terminated the European arrangement and replaced it with a new arrangement that qualified for treatment as a sale under ASU 2009-16. The arrangement related to $584 million of the $915 million outstanding at January 1, 2010 and $721 million of the $1,939 million maximum participation.

Sale of Trade Accounts Receivable in North America

In January 2010, the Company terminated its previous facilities used in North America for the transfers of trade accounts receivable by entering into an agreement to repurchase the outstanding receivables for $264 million and replacing it with a new arrangement. During the year ended December 31, 2010, under the new arrangement, the Company sold the trade accounts receivable of select North America entities on a revolving basis to certain multi-seller commercial paper conduit entities. The Company maintains servicing responsibilities and the related costs are insignificant. The proceeds received are comprised of cash and interests in specified assets (the receivables sold by the Company) of the conduits that entitle the Company to the residual cash flows of such specified assets in the conduits after the commercial paper has been repaid. Neither the conduits nor the investors in those entities have recourse to other assets of the Company in the event of nonpayment by the debtors.

During the year ended December 31, 2010, the Company recognized a loss of $19 million on the sale of these receivables, which is classified as "Interest expense and amortization of debt discount" in the consolidated statements of income. The Company classifies its interests in the conduits as "Accounts and notes receivable—Other" on the consolidated balance sheets and those interests are carried at fair value. Fair value of the interests is determined by calculating the expected amount of cash to be received and is based on unobservable inputs (a Level 3 measurement). The key input in the valuation is percentage of anticipated credit losses, which was 1.42 percent, in the portfolio of receivables sold that have not yet been collected. Given the short-term nature of the underlying receivables, discount rates and prepayments are not factors in determining the fair value of the interests. At December 31, 2010, the carrying value of the interests held was $1,110 million, which is the Company's maximum exposure to loss related to the receivables sold.

The sensitivity of the fair value of the interests held to hypothetical adverse changes in the anticipated credit losses are as follows (amounts shown are the corresponding hypothetical decreases in the carrying value of the interests):

Impact to Carrying Value
(In millions)

10% adverse change	$2
20% adverse change	$5

Following is an analysis of certain cash flows between the Company and the North American conduits:

Cash Proceeds
(In millions)

	2010
Sale of receivables	$ 264
Collections reinvested in revolving receivables	$18,952
Interests in conduits[1]	$ 974

[1] Presented in operating activities in the consolidated statements of cash flows.

Delinquencies on the sold receivables that were still outstanding at December 31, 2010 were $127 million. Trade accounts receivable outstanding and derecognized from the Company's consolidated balance sheet at December 31, 2010 were $1,930 million. Credit losses, net of any recoveries, on receivables sold during the year ended December 31, 2010 were $2 million. During 2010, the Company repurchased $13 million of previously sold receivables related to a divestiture.

Sale of Trade Accounts Receivable in Europe

In June 2010, the Company terminated its previous facility used in Europe for the transfers of trade accounts receivable by entering into an agreement to repurchase the outstanding receivables for $11 million and replacing it with a new arrangement. Since June 2010, under the new arrangement, the Company sold qualifying trade accounts receivable of select European entities on a revolving basis to certain multi-seller commercial paper conduit entities. The Company maintains servicing responsibilities and the related costs are insignificant. The proceeds received are comprised of cash and interests in specified assets (the receivables sold by the Company) of the conduits that entitle the Company to the residual cash flows of such specified assets in the conduits after the commercial paper has been repaid. Neither the conduits nor the investors in those entities have recourse to other assets of the Company in the event of nonpayment by the debtors.

During the period from the June 2010 inception of the new arrangement through December 31, 2010, the Company recognized a loss of $7 million on the sale of these receivables, which is classified as "Interest expense and amortization of debt discount" in the consolidated statements of income. The Company classifies its interests in the conduits as "Accounts and notes receivable—Other" on the consolidated balance sheets and those interests are carried at fair value. Fair value of the interests is determined by calculating the expected amount of cash to be received and is based on unobserv-

able inputs (a Level 3 measurement). The key input in the valuation is percentage of anticipated credit losses, which was zero, in the portfolio of receivables sold that have not yet been collected. Given the short-term nature of the underlying receivables, discount rates and prepayments are not factors in determining the fair value of the interests. At December 31, 2010, the carrying value of the interests held was $157 million, which is the Company's maximum exposure to loss related to the receivables sold.

Following is an analysis of certain cash flows between the Company and the European conduits:

Cash Proceeds
(In millions)

	2010
Sale of receivables	$ 554
Collections reinvested in revolving receivables	$3,914
Interests in conduits[1]	$ 64

[1] Presented in operating activities in the consolidated statements of cash flows.

Delinquencies on the sold receivables still outstanding at December 31, 2010 were $42 million. Trade accounts receivable outstanding and derecognized from the Company's consolidated balance sheet at December 31, 2010 were $405 million. There were no credit losses on receivables sold since June 2010.

Sale of Trade Accounts Receivable in Asia Pacific

During the year ended December 31, 2010, the Company sold participating interests in trade accounts receivable of select Asia Pacific entities for which the Company received cash. The Company maintains servicing responsibilities for the participating interests sold and the related costs are insignificant. The third-party holders of the participating interests do not have recourse to the Company's assets in the event of nonpayment by the debtors.

During the year ended December 31, 2010, the Company recognized a loss of less than $1 million on the sale of the participating interests in the receivables, which is classified as "Interest expense and amortization of debt discount" in the consolidated statements of income.

Following is an analysis of certain cash flows between the Company and the third-party holders of the participating interests:

Cash Proceeds
(In millions)

	2010
Sale of participating interests	$218
Collections reinvested in revolving receivables	$195

Following is additional information related to the sale of participating interests in the receivables under this facility:

Trade Accounts Receivable
(In millions)

	Dec. 31, 2010
Derecognized from the consolidated balance sheet	$ 25
Outstanding in the consolidated balance sheet	281
Total accounts receivable in select Asia Pacific entities	$306

There were no credit losses on receivables relating to the participating interests sold during the year ended December

31, 2010. There were no delinquencies on the outstanding receivables related to the participating interests sold at December 31, 2010.

Software Amortization

3.44

FIDELITY NATIONAL INFORMATION SERVICES, INC. (DEC)

CONSOLIDATED STATEMENTS OF EARNINGS (in part)

Years ended December 31, 2010, 2009 and 2008

(In millions, except per share amounts)	2010	2009	2008
Processing and services revenues (for related party activity see note 4)	$5,269.5	$3,711.1	$3,359.5
Cost of revenues (for related party activity see note 4)	3,637.7	2,741.5	2,616.1
Gross profit	1,631.8	969.6	743.4
Selling, general, and administrative expenses (for related party activity see note 4)	675.8	547.1	381.0
Impairment charges	154.9	136.9	26.0
Operating income	801.1	285.6	336.4
Other income (expense):			
Interest income	6.4	3.4	6.3
Interest expense	(179.7)	(134.0)	(163.4)
Other income, net	(11.5)	8.7	1.5
Total other income (expense)	(184.8)	(121.9)	(155.6)
Earnings from continuing operations before income taxes and equity in losses of unconsolidated entities	616.3	163.7	180.8
Provision for income taxes	215.3	54.7	57.6
Equity in losses of unconsolidated entities	—	—	(0.2)
Earnings from continuing operations, net of tax	401.0	109.0	123.0
Earnings (loss) from discontinued operations, net of tax	(43.1)	(0.5)	96.5
Net earnings	357.9	108.5	219.5
Net (earnings) loss attributable to noncontrolling interest	46.6	(2.6)	(4.7)
Net earnings attributable to FIS	$ 404.5	$ 105.9	$ 214.8

NOTES TO CONSOLIDATED FINANCIAL STATEMENTS

(2) Summary of Significant Accounting Policies (in part)

(o) Cost of Revenue and Selling, General and Administrative Expenses

Cost of revenue includes payroll, employee benefits, occupancy costs and other costs associated with personnel employed in customer service roles, including program design and development and professional services. Cost of revenue also includes data processing costs, amortization of software, customer relationship intangible assets and depreciation on operating assets.

Selling, general and administrative expenses include payroll, employee benefits, occupancy and other costs associated with personnel employed in sales, marketing, human resources, finance and other administrative roles. Selling, general and administrative expenses also include depreciation on non-operating corporate assets, advertising costs and other marketing-related programs.

(10) Computer Software

Computer software as of December 31, 2010 and 2009 consisted of the following (in millions):

	2010	2009
Software from business acquisitions	$ 653.7	$ 646.7
Capitalized software development costs	690.9	662.6
Purchased software	76.5	72.3
Computer software	1,421.1	1,381.6
Accumulated amortization	(512.1)	(448.9)
Computer software, net of accumulated amortization	$ 909.0	$ 932.7

Amortization expense for computer software was $180.5 million, $149.8 million and $149.9 million for the years ended December 31, 2010, 2009 and 2008, respectively. Included in discontinued operations in the Consolidated Statements of Earnings was amortization expense on computer software of $3.3 million, $0.7 million and $15.3 million for the years ended December 31, 2010, 2009 and 2008, respectively. During the year ended December 31, 2010, as a result of Banco Santander's exit from the Brazilian Venture, we recorded a $14.6 million charge pertaining to capitalized software development costs incurred exclusively for use in processing Banco Santander's card activity. The write-off was included in the ISG segment. During the year ended December 31, 2009, we recorded a $12.9 million charge to write-off the carrying value of impaired software resulting from the rationalization of FIS and Metavante product lines. Of this total, $6.8 million related to FSG and $6.1 million related to PSG. The impairment was recorded in the Corporate and Other Segment.

Litigation

3.45

AMPCO-PITTSBURGH CORPORATION (DEC)

CONSOLIDATED STATEMENTS OF OPERATIONS
(in part)

	For the Year Ended December 31		
(In thousands, except per share amounts)	2010	2009	2008
Net sales	$326,886	$299,177	$394,513
Operating costs and expenses:			
Costs of products sold (excluding depreciation)	229,528	202,769	280,091
Selling and administrative	44,168	39,722	42,867
Depreciation	8,565	7,150	6,988
Goodwill impairment charge	—	2,694	—
Charge for asbestos litigation	19,980	—	51,018
(Gain) loss on disposition of assets	(82)	111	(59)
	302,159	252,446	380,905
Income from operations	24,727	46,731	13,608
Other (expense) income:			
Investment-related income	1,183	1,039	2,263
Interest expense	(324)	(312)	(511)
Other—net	(964)	(2,569)	(545)
	(105)	(1,842)	1,207
Income before income taxes and equity losses in Chinese joint venture	24,622	44,889	14,815
Income tax provision	(8,687)	(17,050)	(2,240)
Equity losses in Chinese joint venture	(479)	(162)	—
Net income	$ 15,456	$ 27,677	$ 12,575

NOTES TO CONSOLIDATED FINANCIAL STATEMENTS

Note 17—Litigation: (claims not in thousands)

Litigation

The Corporation and its subsidiaries are involved in various claims and lawsuits incidental to their businesses. In addition, it is also subject to asbestos litigation as described below.

Asbestos Litigation

Claims have been asserted alleging personal injury from exposure to asbestos-containing components historically used in some products of predecessors of the Corporation's Air & Liquid Systems Corporation subsidiary ("Asbestos Liability") and of an inactive subsidiary in dissolution and another former division of the Corporation. Those subsidiaries, and in some cases the Corporation, are defendants (among a number of defendants, typically over 50) in cases filed in various state and federal courts.

Asbestos Claims

The following table reflects approximate information about the claims for Asbestos Liability against the subsidiaries and the Corporation, along with certain asbestos claims asserted against the inactive subsidiary in dissolution and the former division, for the three years ended December 31, 2010, 2009 and 2008:

	2010	2009	2008
Open claims at end of period	8,081[1]	8,168[1]	9,354[1]
Gross settlement and defense costs (in 000's)	$18,085	$28,744	$19,102
Claims resolved	1,377	3,336	1,015

[1] Included as "open claims" are approximately 1,791 claims in 2010, 1,938 claims in 2009 and 3,243 claims in 2008 classified in various jurisdictions as "inactive" or transferred to a state or federal judicial panel on multi-district litigation, commonly referred to as the MDL.

A substantial majority of the settlement and defense costs reflected in the above table were reported and paid by insurers. Because claims are often filed and can be settled or dismissed in large groups, the amount and timing of settlements, as well as the number of open claims, can fluctuate significantly from period to period. In 2006, for the first time, a claim for Asbestos Liability against one of the Corporation's subsidiaries was tried to a jury. The trial resulted in a defense verdict. Plaintiffs appealed that verdict and in 2008 the California Court of Appeals reversed the jury verdict and remanded the case back to the trial court.

Asbestos Insurance

Certain of the Corporation's subsidiaries and the Corporation have an arrangement (the "Coverage Arrangement") with insurers responsible for historical primary and some first-layer excess insurance coverage for Asbestos Liability (the "Paying Insurers"). Under the Coverage Arrangement, the Paying Insurers accept financial responsibility, subject to the limits of the policies and based on fixed defense percentages and specified indemnity allocation formulas, for pending and future claims for Asbestos Liability. The claims against the Corporation's inactive subsidiary that is in dissolution proceedings, numbering approximately 400 as of December 31, 2010, are not included within the Coverage Arrangement. The one claim filed against the former division also is not included within the Coverage Arrangement. The Corporation believes that the claims against the inactive subsidiary in dissolution and the former division are immaterial.

The Coverage Arrangement includes an acknowledgement that Howden North America, Inc. ("Howden") is entitled to coverage under policies covering Asbestos Liability for claims arising out of the historical products manufactured or distributed by Buffalo Forge, a former subsidiary of the Corporation (the "Products"). The Coverage Arrangement does not provide for any prioritization on access to the applicable policies or monetary cap other than the limits of the policies, and, accordingly, Howden may access the policies at any time for any covered claim arising out of a Product. In general, access by Howden to the policies covering the Products will erode the coverage under the policies available to the Corporation and the relevant subsidiaries for Asbestos Liability alleged to arise out of not only the Products but also other historical products of the Corporation and its subsidiaries covered by the applicable policies.

On August 4, 2009, Howden filed a lawsuit in the United States District Court for the Western District of Pennsylva-

nia. In the lawsuit, Howden raised claims against certain insurance companies that allegedly issued policies to Howden that do not cover the Corporation or its subsidiaries, and also raised claims against the Corporation and two other insurance companies that issued excess insurance policies covering certain subsidiaries of the Corporation (the "Excess Policies"), but that were not part of the Coverage Arrangement. In the lawsuit, Howden seeks, as respects the Corporation, a declaratory judgment from the court as to the respective rights and obligations of Howden, the Corporation and the insurance carriers under the Excess Policies. One of the excess carriers and the Corporation filed cross-claims against each other seeking declarations regarding their respective rights and obligations under Excess Policies issued by that carrier. The Corporation's cross-claim also sought damages for the carrier's failure to pay certain defense and indemnity costs. The Corporation and that carrier concluded a settlement generally consistent with the Coverage Arrangement, and all claims between that carrier and the Corporation were dismissed with prejudice on December 8, 2010. The litigation remains pending with respect to the other carrier that issued one of the Excess Policies.

On February 24, 2011, the Corporation and its Air & Liquid Systems Corporation subsidiary filed a lawsuit in the United States District Court for the Western District of Pennsylvania against thirteen domestic insurance companies, certain underwriters at Lloyd's, London and certain London market insurance companies, and Howden. The lawsuit seeks a declaratory judgment regarding the respective rights and obligations of the parties under excess insurance policies not included within the Coverage Arrangement that were issued to the Corporation from 1981 through 1984 as respects claims against the Corporation and its subsidiary for Asbestos Liability and as respects asbestos bodily-injury claims against Howden arising from the Products.

Asbestos Valuations

In 2006, the Corporation retained Hamilton, Rabinovitz & Associates, Inc. ("HR&A"), a nationally recognized expert in the valuation of asbestos liabilities, to assist the Corporation in estimating the potential liability for pending and unasserted future claims for Asbestos Liability. HR&A was not requested to estimate asbestos claims against the inactive subsidiary in dissolution or the former division, which the Corporation believes are immaterial. Based on this analysis, the Corporation recorded a reserve for Asbestos Liability claims pending or projected to be asserted through 2013 as at December 31, 2006. HR&A's analysis was updated in 2008, and additional reserves were established by the Corporation as at December 31, 2008 for Asbestos Liability claims pending or projected to be asserted through 2018. HR&A's analysis was most recently updated in 2010, and additional reserves were established by the Corporation as at December 31, 2010 for Asbestos Liability claims pending or projected to be asserted through 2020. The methodology used by HR&A in its projection in 2010 of the operating subsidiaries' liability for pending and unasserted potential future claims for Asbestos Liability, which is substantially the same as the methodology employed by HR&A in the 2006 and 2008 estimates, relied upon and included the following factors:
- HR&A's interpretation of a widely accepted forecast of the population likely to have been exposed to asbestos;
- Epidemiological studies estimating the number of people likely to develop asbestos-related diseases;

- HR&A's analysis of the number of people likely to file an asbestos-related injury claim against the subsidiaries and the Corporation based on such epidemiological data and relevant claims history from January 1, 2008 to August 30, 2010;
- An analysis of pending cases, by type of injury claimed and jurisdiction where the claim is filed;
- An analysis of claims resolution history from January 1, 2008 to August 30, 2010 to determine the average settlement value of claims, by type of injury claimed and jurisdiction of filing; and
- An adjustment for inflation in the future average settlement value of claims, at an annual inflation rate based on the Congressional Budget Office's ten year forecast of inflation.

Using this information, HR&A estimated in 2010 the number of future claims for Asbestos Liability that would be filed through the year 2020, as well as the settlement or indemnity costs that would be incurred to resolve both pending and future unasserted claims through 2020. This methodology has been accepted by numerous courts.

In conjunction with developing the aggregate liability estimate referenced above, the Corporation also developed an estimate of probable insurance recoveries for its Asbestos Liabilities. In developing the estimate, the Corporation considered HR&A's projection for settlement or indemnity costs for Asbestos Liability and management's projection of associated defense costs (based on the current defense to indemnity cost ratio), as well as a number of additional factors. These additional factors included the Coverage Arrangement, self-insured retentions, policy exclusions, policy limits, policy provisions regarding coverage for defense costs, attachment points, prior impairment of policies and gaps in the coverage, policy exhaustions, insolvencies among certain of the insurance carriers, the nature of the underlying claims for Asbestos Liability asserted against the subsidiaries and the Corporation as reflected in the Corporation's asbestos claims database, as well as estimated erosion of insurance limits on account of claims against Howden arising out of the Products. In addition to consulting with the Corporation's outside legal counsel on these insurance matters, the Corporation retained in 2010 a nationally-recognized insurance consulting firm to assist the Corporation with certain policy allocation matters that also are among the several factors considered by the Corporation when analyzing potential recoveries from relevant historical insurance for Asbestos Liabilities. Based upon all of the factors considered by the Corporation, and taking into account the Corporation's analysis of publicly available information regarding the creditworthiness of various insurers, the Corporation estimated the probable insurance recoveries for Asbestos Liability and defense costs through 2020. Although the Corporation believes that the assumptions employed in the insurance valuation were reasonable and previously consulted with its outside legal counsel and insurance consultant regarding those assumptions, there are other assumptions that could have been employed that would have resulted in materially lower insurance recovery projections.

Based on the analyses described above, the Corporation's reserve at December 31, 2010 for the total costs, including defense costs, for Asbestos Liability claims pending or projected to be asserted through 2020 was $218,303 of which approximately 85% was attributable to settlement costs for unasserted claims projected to be filed through 2020 and future defense costs. While it is reasonably possible that the Corporation will incur additional charges for Asbestos Liability and defense costs in excess of the amounts currently reserved, the Corporation believes that there is too much uncertainty to provide for reasonable estimation of the number of future claims, the nature of such claims and the cost to resolve them beyond 2020. Accordingly, no reserve has been recorded for any costs that may be incurred after 2020.

The Corporation's receivable at December 31, 2010 for insurance recoveries attributable to the claims for which the Corporation's Asbestos Liability reserve has been established, including the portion of incurred defense costs covered by the Coverage Arrangement, and the probable payments and reimbursements relating to the estimated indemnity and defense costs for pending and unasserted future Asbestos Liability claims, was $141,839 ($115,430 as of December 31, 2009). The insurance receivable recorded by the Corporation does not assume any recovery from insolvent carriers, and substantially all of the insurance recoveries deemed probable were from insurance companies rated A—(excellent) or better by A.M. Best Corporation. There can be no assurance, however, that there will not be further insolvencies among the relevant insurance carriers, or that the assumed percentage recoveries for certain carriers will prove correct. The $76,464 million difference between insurance recoveries and projected costs at December 31, 2010 is not due to exhaustion of all insurance coverage for Asbestos Liability. The Corporation and the subsidiaries have substantial additional insurance coverage which the Corporation expects to be available for Asbestos Liability claims and defense costs the subsidiaries and it may incur after 2020. However, this insurance coverage also can be expected to have gaps creating significant shortfalls of insurance recoveries as against claims expense, which could be material in future years.

The amounts recorded by the Corporation for Asbestos Liabilities and insurance receivables rely on assumptions that are based on currently known facts and strategy. The Corporation's actual expenses or insurance recoveries could be significantly higher or lower than those recorded if assumptions used in the Corporation's or HR&A's calculations vary significantly from actual results. Key variables in these assumptions are identified above and include the number and type of new claims to be filed each year, the average cost of disposing of each such new claim, average annual defense costs, the resolution of coverage issues with insurance carriers, and the solvency risk with respect to the relevant insurance carriers. Other factors that may affect the Corporation's Asbestos Liability and ability to recover under its insurance policies include uncertainties surrounding the litigation process from jurisdiction to jurisdiction and from case to case, reforms that may be made by state and federal courts, and the passage of state or federal tort reform legislation.

The Corporation intends to evaluate its estimated Asbestos Liability and related insurance receivables as well as the underlying assumptions on a regular basis to determine whether any adjustments to the estimates are required. Due to the uncertainties surrounding asbestos litigation and insurance, these regular reviews may result in the Corporation incurring future charges; however, the Corporation is currently unable to estimate such future charges. Adjustments, if any, to the Corporation's estimate of its recorded Asbestos Liability and/or insurance receivables could be material to operating results for the periods in which the adjustments to the liability or receivable are recorded, and to the Corporation's liquidity and consolidated financial position.

Equity in Losses of Investees

3.46

VIACOM INC. (SEP)

CONSOLIDATED STATEMENTS OF EARNINGS
(in part)

(In millions, except per share amounts)	Nine Months Ended September 30, 2010	Year Ended December 31 2009	Year Ended December 31 2008
Revenues	$9,337	$13,257	$13,947
Expenses:			
Operating	4,883	7,191	8,167
Selling, general and administrative	2,025	2,642	2,824
Depreciation and amortization	222	379	394
Total expenses	7,130	10,212	11,385
Operating income	2,207	3,045	2,562
Interest expense, net	(320)	(430)	(482)
Equity in net losses of investee companies	(67)	(77)	(74)
Loss on extinguishment of debt	—	(84)	—
Other items, net	(8)	(37)	(112)
Earnings from continuing operations before provision for income taxes	1,812	2,417	1,894
Provision for income taxes	(627)	(762)	(620)
Net earnings from continuing operations	1,185	1,655	1,274
Discontinued operations, net of tax	(321)	(67)	(6)
Net earnings (Viacom and noncontrolling interests)	864	1,588	1,268
Net losses (earnings) attributable to noncontrolling interests	(10)	23	(17)
Net earnings attributable to Viacom	$ 854	$ 1,611	$ 1,251
Amounts attributable to Viacom:			
Net earnings from continuing operations	$1,175	$ 1,678	$ 1,257
Discontinued operations, net of tax	(321)	(67)	(6)
Net earnings attributable to Viacom	$ 854	$ 1,611	$ 1,251

NOTES TO CONSOLIDATED FINANCIAL STATEMENTS

Note 2. Summary of Significant Accounting Policies (in part)

Principles of Consolidation
The consolidated financial statements of the Company include the accounts of Viacom Inc., its subsidiaries and VIEs where the Company is considered the primary beneficiary, after elimination of intercompany accounts and transactions. Investments in business entities in which the Company lacks control but does have the ability to exercise significant influence over operating and financial policies are accounted for using the equity method. The Company's proportionate share of net income or loss of the entity is recorded in *Equity in net losses of investee companies* in the Consolidated Statements of Earnings. Related party transactions between the Company and CBS Corporation ("CBS"), National Amusements Inc. ("NAI") and Midway Games, Inc. ("Midway"), which ceased to be a related party on November 28, 2008, have not been eliminated.

Environmental

3.47

ITT CORPORATION (DEC)

CONSOLIDATED INCOME STATEMENTS (in part)

	Year Ended December 31		
(In millions, except per share amounts)	**2010**	**2009**	**2008**
Product revenue	$ 8,494	$ 8,244	$ 9,181
Service revenue	2,501	2,430	2,295
Total revenue	10,995	10,674	11,476
Costs of product revenue	5,624	5,528	6,255
Costs of service revenue	2,196	2,122	2,007
Total costs of revenue	7,820	7,650	8,262
Gross profit	3,175	3,024	3,214
Selling, general and administrative expenses	1,584	1,555	1,689
Research and development expenses	253	258	236
Asbestos-related costs, net	385	238	14
Restructuring and asset impairment charges, net	53	79	77
Operating income	900	894	1,198
Interest expense	100	99	140
Interest income	16	24	31
Miscellaneous (income) expense, net	(2)	9	13
Income from continuing operations before income tax expense	818	810	1,076
Income tax expense	164	169	308
Income from continuing operations	654	641	768
Income from discontinued operations, including tax (expense) benefit of $(8), $(1) and $2, respectively	144	3	27
Net income	$ 798	$ 644	$ 795

NOTES TO CONSOLIDATED FINANCIAL STATEMENTS

(Dollars and share amounts in millions, unless otherwise stated)

Note 1—Summary of Significant Accounting Policies (in part)

Use of Estimates

The preparation of financial statements in conformity with GAAP requires management to make estimates and assumptions that affect the reported amounts of assets and liabilities, the disclosure of contingent assets and liabilities at the date of the financial statements, and the reported amounts of revenue and expenses during the reporting period. Estimates are revised as additional information becomes available. Estimates and assumptions are used for, but not limited to, asbestos-related liabilities and recoveries from insurers and other responsible parties, postretirement obligations and assets, revenue recognition, income tax contingency accruals and valuation allowances, goodwill impairment testing and contingent liabilities. Actual results could differ from these estimates.

Note 19—Commitments and Contingencies (in part)

2010 Charge

In the third quarter of 2010, we conducted our annual detailed study with the assistance of outside consultants to review and update the underlying assumptions used in our liability and asset estimates. During this study, the underlying assumptions were updated based on our actual experience since our last detailed review in the third quarter of 2009, a reassessment of the appropriate reference period of years of experience used in determining each assumption and our expectations regarding future conditions, including inflation. Based on the results of this study, we increased our estimated undiscounted asbestos liability, including legal fees, by $691, reflecting costs that the Company is estimated to incur to resolve all pending claims, as well as unasserted claims estimated to be filed over the next 10 years. The increase in our estimated liability is a result of several developments, including higher settlement costs and significantly increased activity in several higher-cost jurisdictions, increasing the number of cases to be adjudicated and the expected legal costs.

Further, in the third quarter of 2010, the Company recorded a $372 increase in its asbestos-related assets based on the results of this study. These assets comprise an insurance asset, as well as receivables from other responsible parties. See discontinued operations discussion below for further information about receivables from parties other than insurers.

For the full year 2010 and 2009, the net asbestos charge can be summarized as follows:

	2010		2009	
	Pre-Tax	After-Tax	Pre-Tax	After-Tax
Continuing operations	$385	$247	$238	$148
Discontinued operations	(10)	(6)	9	6
Total	$375	$241	$247	$154

Environmental

In the ordinary course of business, we are subject to federal, state, local, and foreign environmental laws and regulations. We are responsible, or are alleged to be responsible, for ongoing environmental investigation and remediation of sites in various countries. These sites are in various stages of investigation and/or remediation and in many of these proceedings our liability is considered de minimis. We have received notification from the U.S. Environmental Protection Agency, and from similar state and foreign environmental agencies, that a number of sites formerly or currently owned and/or operated by ITT, and other properties or water supplies that may be or have been impacted from those operations, contain disposed or recycled materials or wastes and require environmental investigation and/or remediation. These sites include instances where we have been identified as a potentially responsible party under federal and state environmental laws and regulations.

Accruals for environmental matters are recorded on a site by site basis when it is probable that a liability has been incurred and the amount of the liability can be reasonably estimated, based on current law and existing technologies. Our accrued liabilities for these environmental matters represent the best estimates related to the investigation and remediation of environmental media such as water, soil, soil vapor, air and structures, as well as related legal fees. These estimates, and related accruals, are reviewed periodically and updated for progress of investigation and remediation efforts and changes in facts and legal circumstances. Liabilities for these environmental expenditures are recorded on an undiscounted basis.

It is difficult to estimate the final costs of investigation and remediation due to various factors, including incomplete information regarding particular sites and other potentially responsible parties, uncertainty regarding the extent of investigation or remediation and our share, if any, of liability for such conditions, the selection of alternative remedial approaches, and changes in environmental standards and regulatory requirements. In our opinion, the total amount accrued is appropriate based on existing facts and circumstances. We do not anticipate these liabilities will have a material adverse effect on our consolidated financial position, results of operations or cash flows.

The following table illustrates the activity related to our accrued liabilities for these environmental matters.

	2010	2009
Environmental liability—1/1	$140	$135
Accruals added during the period	—	1
Change in estimates for pre-existing accruals	14	18
Payments	(15)	(14)
Environmental liability—12/31	$139	$140

The following table illustrates the reasonably possible low- and high end range of estimated liability, and number of active sites for these environmental matters.

	2010	2009
Low-end range	$117	$113
High end range	$251	$249
Number of active environmental investigation and remediation sites	99	98

Sale of Receivables

3.48

ALLIANCE ONE INTERNATIONAL, INC. (MAR)

STATEMENTS OF CONSOLIDATED OPERATIONS AND COMPREHENSIVE INCOME (in part)

	Years Ended March 31		
(In thousands, except per share data)	2010	2009	2008
Sales and other operating revenues	$2,308,299	$2,258,219	$2,011,503
Cost of goods and services sold	1,911,849	1,897,380	1,761,111
Gross profit	396,450	360,839	250,392
Selling, administrative and general expenses	155,376	156,000	157,405
Other income (expense)	(17,260)	214	20,188
Restructuring and asset impairment charges	—	591	19,580
Operating income	223,814	204,462	93,595
Debt retirement expense	40,353	954	5,909
Interest expense	113,819	97,984	101,885
Interest income	4,550	3,808	16,245
Income before income taxes and other items	74,192	109,332	2,046
Income tax benefit	(3,791)	(22,020)	(5,499)
Equity in net income of investee companies	1,963	1,478	1,829
Income from continuing operations	79,946	132,830	9,374
Income from discontinued operations, net of tax	—	407	7,855
Net income	79,946	133,237	17,229
Less: Net income attributable to noncontrolling interests	779	679	368
Net income attributable to Alliance One International, Inc.	$ 79,167	$ 132,558	$ 16,861

NOTES TO CONSOLIDATED FINANCIAL STATEMENTS

(In thousands)

Note A—Significant Accounting Policies (in part)

Other Income (Expense)

Other Income (Expense) consists primarily of gains on sales of property, plant and equipment and assets held for sale. This caption also includes expenses related to the Company's sale of receivables. See Note Q "Sale of Receivables" to the "Notes to Consolidated Financial Statements" for further information. In 2010, an estimate of a probable loss in connection with a Foreign Corrupt Practices Act ("FCPA") investigation has been recorded. See Note P "Contingencies and Other Information" to the "Notes to Consolidated Financial Statements" for further information. The following table summarizes the significant components of Other Income (Expense) *(in thousands):*

	Years Ending March 31		
	2010	2009	2008
Malawi factory and other property sales	$ 1,677	$ —	$ 9,500
Turkey storage and other property sales	2,567	—	—
Greece factory and other property sales	647	—	6,990
Brazil factory and other property sales	822	—	2,815
Other sales of assets and expenses	(573)	3,762	4,182
FCPA loss	(19,450)	—	—
Losses on sale of receivables	(2,950)	(3,548)	(3,299)
	$(17,260)	$ 214	$20,188

Sale of Accounts Receivable

The Company is engaged in a revolving trade accounts receivable securitization arrangement to sell receivables to a third party limited liability company. The Company records the transaction as a sale of receivables, removes such receivables from its financial statements and records a receivable for the retained interest in such receivables. The losses on the sale of receivables are recognized in Other Income (Expense). As of March 31, 2010 and 2009, respectively, accounts receivable sold and outstanding were $105,579 and $100,611. See Note Q "Sale of Receivables" and Note R "Fair Value Measurements" to the "Notes to Consolidated Financial Statements" for further information.

Note Q—Sale of Receivables

Alliance One International, A.G., a wholly owned subsidiary of the Company is engaged in a revolving trade accounts receivable securitization arrangement to sell receivables to a third party limited liability company ("LLC"). The agreement, which matures March 26, 2013, is funded through third-party loans to the LLC which is committed up to a maximum of $100,000 in funding at any time. To the extent that the balance of the loan is less than $100,000 the Company is subject to a 0.25% fee on the unused amount. The Company is currently working on modifications to the agreements, including to add Alliance One International, Inc. as an additional seller.

Proceeds consist of 90% of the face value in cash, less contractual dilutions which limit the amount that may be outstanding from any one particular customer and insurance reserves that also have the effect of limiting the risk attributable to any one customer. Upon sale, the Company reduces the carrying value of the receivable sold and records the fair value of the retained interest in the receivable in accounts receivable. The fair value of the retained interest is calculated by applying the commercial paper rate and the servicing rate to the balance of the outstanding receivables in the facility. The Company receives a 0.5% per annum servicing fee on receivables sold and outstanding which is recorded as a reduction of selling, administrative and general expenses. This fee is compensatory and no servicing asset or liability has resulted from the sale. The receivables sold are non-interest bearing. This in conjunction with the short life of the receivables sold and outstanding causes the effects of any prepayments on the value of assets recorded to be inconsequential. Losses on sale of receivables are recorded as a component of other income (expense) in the statement of operations.

Receivables sold to the LLC are insured against loss. The Company provides no guarantee as to the value of the sold receivables and its retained interest in any receivable may also be recovered under the terms of the insurance.

The following table summarizes the Company's accounts receivable securitization information as of March 31 *(in thousands)*:

	2010	2009
Receivables Outstanding in Facility:		
As of April 1	$ 100,611	$ 70,862
Sold	859,062	732,889
Collected	(854,094)	(703,140)
As of March 31	$ 105,579	$ 100,611
Retained interest as of March 31	$ 25,125	$ 26,833
Decreases in Retained Interest Resulting from Changes in Discount Rate:		
10%	$ 83	$ 107
20%	$ 165	$ 214
Criteria to Determine Retained Interest as of March 31:		
Weighted average life in days	95	85
Discount rate (inclusive of 0.5% servicing fee)	3.00%	4.71%
Unused balance fee	0.25%	0.25%
Cash Proceeds for the Twelve Months Ended March 31:		
Current purchase price	$ 606,772	$ 476,523
Deferred purchase price	232,101	235,880
Service fees	517	501
Total	$ 839,390	$ 712,904
Loss on sale of receivables	$ 2,950	$ 3,548

It is the Company's intention to maximize the receivables sold under the revolving agreement meaning that amounts collected by the pool would be reinvested in the purchase of additional eligible receivables. Since April 1, 2009, the average outstanding balance of the facility utilized has been $76,711 with a minimum outstanding balance of $47,174 and a maximum of $99,712.

Mergers and Acquisitions

3.49

PEPSICO, INC. (DEC)

CONSOLIDATED STATEMENT OF INCOME (in part)

Fiscal years ended December 25, 2010, December 26, 2009
and December 27, 2008

(In millions except per share amounts)	2010	2009	2008
Net Revenue	$57,838	$43,232	$43,251
Cost of sales	26,575	20,099	20,351
Selling, general and administrative expenses	22,814	15,026	15,877
Amortization of intangible assets	117	63	64
Operating Profit	8,332	8,044	6,959
Bottling equity income	735	365	374
Interest expense	(903)	(397)	(329)
Interest income	68	67	41
Income before income taxes	8,232	8,079	7,045
Provision for income taxes	1,894	2,100	1,879
Net income	6,338	5,979	5,166
Less: Net income attributable to noncontrolling interests	18	33	24
Net Income Attributable to PepsiCo	$ 6,320	$ 5,946	$ 5,142

NOTES TO CONSOLIDATED FINANCIAL STATEMENTS

Note 3—Restructuring, Impairment and Integration Charges

In 2010, we incurred merger and integration charges of $799 million related to our acquisitions of PBG and PAS, as well as advisory fees in connection with our acquisition of WBD. $467 million of these charges were recorded in the PAB segment, $111 million recorded in the Europe segment, $191 million recorded in corporate unallocated expenses and $30 million recorded in interest expense. All of these charges, other than the interest expense portion, were recorded in selling, general and administrative expenses. The merger and integration charges related to our acquisitions of PBG and PAS are being incurred to help create a more fully integrated supply chain and go-to-market business model, to improve the effectiveness and efficiency of the distribution of our brands and to enhance our revenue growth. These charges also include closing costs, one-time financing costs and advisory fees related to our acquisitions of PBG and PAS. In addition, we recorded $9 million of merger–related charges, representing our share of the respective merger costs of PBG and PAS,

in bottling equity income. Substantially all cash payments related to the above charges are expected to be paid by the end of 2011. In total, these charges had an after-tax impact of $648 million or $0.40 per share.

In 2009, we incurred $50 million of charges related to the merger of PBG and PAS, of which substantially all was paid in 2009. In 2009, we also incurred charges of $36 million ($29 million after-tax or $0.02 per share) in conjunction with our Productivity for Growth program that began in 2008. The program includes actions in all divisions of the business, including the closure of six plants that we believe will increase cost competitiveness across the supply chain, upgrade and streamline our product portfolio, and simplify the organization for more effective and timely decision-making. These charges were recorded in selling, general and administrative expenses. These initiatives were completed in the second quarter of 2009 and substantially all cash payments related to these charges were paid by the end of 2010.

In 2008, we incurred charges of $543 million ($408 million after-tax or $0.25 per share) in conjunction with our Productivity for Growth program. Approximately $455 million of the charge was recorded in selling, general and administrative expenses, with the remainder recorded in cost of sales.

A summary of our merger and integration activity in 2010 is as follows:

	Severance and Other Employee Costs[a]	Asset Impairment	Other Costs	Total
2010 merger and integration charges	$ 396	$ 132	$ 280	$ 808
Cash payments	(114)	—	(271)	(385)
Non-cash charges	(103)	(132)	16	(219)
Liability as of December 25, 2010	$ 179	$ —	$ 25	$ 204

[a] Primarily reflects termination costs for approximately 2,370 employees.

A summary of our restructuring and impairment charges in 2009 is as follows:

	Severance and Other Employee Costs[a]	Other Costs	Total
FLNA	$—	$ 2	$ 2
QFNA	—	1	1
LAF	3	—	3
PAB	6	10	16
Europe	1	—	1
AMEA	7	6	13
	$17	$19	$36

[a] Primarily reflects termination costs for approximately 410 employees.

A summary of our restructuring and impairment charges in 2008 is as follows:

	Severance and Other Employee Costs	Asset Impairments	Other Costs	Total
FLNA	$ 48	$ 38	$ 22	$108
QFNA	14	3	14	31
LAF	30	8	2	40
PAB	68	92	129	289
Europe	39	6	5	50
AMEA	11	2	2	15
Corporate	2	—	8	10
	$212	$149	$182	$543

Severance and other employee costs primarily reflect termination costs for approximately 3,500 employees. Asset impairments relate to the closure of six plants and changes to our beverage product portfolio. Other costs include contract exit costs and third-party incremental costs associated with upgrading our product portfolio and our supply chain.

A summary of our Productivity for Growth program activity is as follows:

	Severance and Other Employee Costs	Asset Impairments	Other Costs	Total
2008 restructuring and impairment charges	$ 212	$ 149	$ 182	$ 543
Cash payments	(50)	—	(109)	(159)
Non-cash charge	(27)	(149)	(9)	(185)
Currency translation	(1)	—	—	(1)
Liability as of December 27, 2008	134	—	64	198
2009 restructuring and impairment charges	17	12	7	36
Cash payments	(128)	—	(68)	(196)
Currency translation	(14)	(12)	25	(1)
Liability as of December 26, 2009	9	—	28	37
Cash payments	(6)	—	(25)	(31)
Non-cash charge	(2)	—	(1)	(3)
Currency translation	—	—	(1)	(1)
Liability as of December 25, 2010	$ 1	$ —	$ 1	$ 2

Change in Fair Value of Derivatives

3.50

HANESBRANDS INC. (DEC)

CONSOLIDATED STATEMENTS OF INCOME (in part)

(In thousands, except per share amounts)

	Years Ended		
	January 1, 2011	January 2, 2010	January 3, 2009
Net sales	$4,326,713	$3,891,275	$4,248,770
Cost of sales	2,911,944	2,626,001	2,871,420
Gross profit	1,414,769	1,265,274	1,377,350
Selling, general and administrative expenses	1,010,581	940,530	1,009,607
Restructuring	—	53,888	50,263
Operating profit	404,188	270,856	317,480
Other expense (income)	20,221	49,301	(634)
Interest expense, net	150,236	163,279	155,077
Income before income tax expense	233,731	58,276	163,037
Income tax expense	22,438	6,993	35,868
Net income	$ 211,293	$ 51,283	$ 127,169

NOTES TO CONSOLIDATED FINANCIAL STATEMENTS

(Amounts in thousands, except per share data)

(13) Financial Instruments and Risk Management (in part)

Net Derivative Gain or Loss

The effect of cash flow hedge derivative instruments on the Consolidated Statements of Income and Accumulated Other Comprehensive Loss is as follows:

	Amount of Gain (Loss) Recognized in Accumulated Other Comprehensive Loss (Effective Portion) Year Ended		
	January 1, 2011	January 2, 2010	January 3, 2009
Interest rate contracts	$ (516)	$20,559	$(66,088)
Foreign exchange contracts	(2,180)	(1,560)	756
Commodity contracts	—	—	(208)
Total	$(2,696)	$18,999	$(65,540)

	Amount of Gain (Loss) Reclassified from Accumulated Other Comprehensive Loss Into Income (Effective Portion) Year Ended			Location of Gain (Loss) Reclassified from Accumulated Other Comprehensive Loss Into Income (Effective Portion)
	January 1, 2011	January 2, 2010	January 3, 2009	
Interest rate contracts	$(17,964)	$ (1,820)	$(1,176)	Interest expense, net
Interest rate contracts	—	(26,029)	—	Other income (expense)
Foreign exchange contracts	(1,715)	721	(2,025)	Cost of sales
Commodity contracts	—	(95)	473	Cost of sales
Total	$(19,679)	$(27,223)	$(2,728)	

The Company expects to reclassify into earnings during the next 12 months a net loss from Accumulated Other Comprehensive Loss of approximately $10,171.

As disclosed in Note 9, in connection with the amendment and restatement of the 2006 Senior Secured Credit Facility and repayment of the Second Lien Credit Facility in December 2009, all outstanding interest rate hedging instruments which were hedging these underlying debt instruments along with the interest rate hedge instrument related to the Floating Rate Senior Notes were settled for $62,256, of which $40,391 was paid in December 2009 and the remaining $21,865 was included in the "Accounts Payable" line of the Consolidated Balance Sheet at January 2, 2010. The amounts deferred in Accumulated Other Comprehensive Loss associated with the 2006 Senior Secured Credit Facility and Second Lien Credit Facility were released to earnings as the underlying forecasted interest payments were no longer probable of occurring, which resulted in recognition of losses totaling $26,029 that are included in the "Other Expense (Income)" line of the Consolidated Statement of Income. The amounts deferred in Accumulated Other Comprehensive Loss associated with the Floating Rate Senior Notes interest rate hedge were frozen at the termination date and will be amortized over the original remaining term of the interest rate hedge instrument. The unamortized balance in Accumulated Other Comprehensive Loss was $17,043 as of January 1, 2011.

In the first quarter of 2010, the Company entered into two interest rate caps to hedge the risks associated with fluctuations in the 6-month LIBOR rate for the Floating Rate Senior Notes. The terms of the interest rate caps include: a total notional amount of $490,735, consisting of $240,735 and $250,000, respectively, an expiration date of December 2011, and a capped 6-month LIBOR interest rate of 4.26%.

The changes in fair value of derivatives excluded from the Company's effectiveness assessments and the ineffective portion of the changes in the fair value of derivatives used as cash flow hedges are reported in the "Selling, general and administrative expenses" line in the Consolidated Statements of Income. The Company recognized gains (losses) related to ineffectiveness of hedging relationships in 2010 of $6 related to interest rate contracts. The Company recognized gains (losses) related to ineffectiveness of hedging relationships in 2009 of $161, consisting of $152 for interest rate contracts and $9 for foreign exchange contracts. The Company recognized gains (losses) related to ineffectiveness of hedging relationships in 2008 of $(323), consisting of $(149) for interest rate contracts and $(174) for foreign exchange contracts.

The effect of mark to market hedge derivative instruments on the Consolidated Statements of Income is as follows:

	Location of Gain (Loss) Recognized in Income on Derivative	Amount of Gain (Loss) Recognized in Income Year Ended		
		January 1, 2011	January 2, 2010	January 3, 2009
Foreign exchange contracts	Selling, general and administrative expenses	$(2,073)	$3,846	$(6,691)
Total		$(2,073)	$3,846	$(6,691)

Change in Fair Value

3.51

ADVANCED MICRO DEVICES, INC. (DEC)

CONSOLIDATED STATEMENTS OF OPERATIONS
(in part)

	Year Ended		
(In millions, except per share amounts)	December 25, 2010	December 26, 2009	December 27, 2008
Net revenue	$6,494	$ 5,403	$ 5,808
Cost of sales	3,533	3,131	3,488
Gross margin	2,961	2,272	2,320
Research and development	1,405	1,721	1,848
Marketing, general and administrative	934	994	1,304
Legal settlement	(283)	(1,242)	—
Amortization of acquired intangible assets	61	70	137
Impairment of goodwill and acquired intangible assets	—	—	1,089
Restructuring charges (reversals)	(4)	65	90
Gain on sale of 200 millimeter equipment	—	—	(193)
Operating income (loss)	848	664	(1,955)
Interest income	11	16	39
Interest expense	(199)	(438)	(391)
Other income (expense), net	311	166	(37)
Income (loss) before equity in net loss of investees and income taxes	971	408	(2,344)
Provision for income taxes	38	112	68
Equity in net loss of investee	(462)	—	—
Income (loss) from continuing operations	471	296	(2,412)
Loss from discontinued operations, net of tax	—	(3)	(684)
Net income (loss)	$ 471	$ 293	$(3,096)

Item 7. Management's Discussion and Analysis of Financial Condition and Results of Operations (in part)

Equity in Net Loss of Investee

During the time that we applied the equity method of accounting for our ownership interest in GF, our equity in net loss of investee primarily consisted of our proportionate share of GF's losses for the period based on our ownership percentage of GF's Class A Preferred Shares, our portion of the non-cash accretion on GF's Class B Preferred Shares, the elimination of intercompany profit, reflecting the mark-up on inventory that remained on our consolidated balance sheet at the end of the period, the amortization of basis differences identified from the purchase price allocation process, based on the fair value of GF upon deconsolidation and, to the extent applicable, the gain or loss on dilution of our ownership interest as a result of the capital infusion into GF by ATIC.

NOTES TO CONSOLIDATED FINANCIAL STATEMENTS

Note 3. Globalfoundries (in part)

Equity Method

In applying the equity method of accounting for 2010, the equity in net loss of investee primarily consists of the Company's proportionate share of GF's losses for the period based on the Company's ownership percentage of GF's Class A Preferred Shares, the Company's portion of the non-cash accretion on GF's Class B Preferred Shares, the elimination of intercompany profit, reflecting the mark-up on inventory that remains

on the Company's consolidated balance sheet at the end of the period, the amortization of basis differences identified from the purchase price allocation process based on the fair value of GF upon deconsolidation, and, to the extent applicable, the gain or loss on dilution of the Company's ownership interest as a result of capital infusions into GF by ATIC.

GF consolidated Chartered in 2010 because it was deemed to be the primary beneficiary of Chartered (GLOBALFOUNDRIES Singapore Pte. Ltd. or GFS). For the purposes of the Company's application of the equity method of accounting, the Company recorded its share of the GF results excluding the results of Chartered because GF did not have an equity ownership interest in Chartered in 2010.

As of December 25, 2010, the Company's investment in GF is reflected as a liability in the consolidated balance sheet with a balance of $7 million. This amount primarily reflects the accumulated loss that the Company has recognized in excess of the value of its investment in GF since the Company began accounting for GF under the equity method of accounting. Based on the current structure of the Company's Wafer Supply Agreement, its guarantee of certain GF indebtedness, its ownership interest in GF and governance relationship with GF, the Company concluded that it was required to continue to record its share of the equity loss in excess of the carrying amount of its investment balance throughout 2010.

Impairment of Intangibles

3.52

FURNITURE BRANDS INTERNATIONAL, INC. (DEC)

CONSOLIDATED STATEMENTS OF OPERATIONS (in part)

	Year Ended December 31		
(In thousands except per share data)	2010	2009	2008
Net sales	$1,159,934	$1,224,370	$1,743,176
Cost of sales	883,620	994,370	1,428,641
Gross profit	276,314	230,000	314,535
Selling, general, and administrative expenses	320,226	363,636	524,457
Impairment of goodwill	—	—	166,680
Impairment of trade names	1,100	39,050	35,271
Operating loss	(45,012)	(172,686)	(411,873)
Interest expense	3,172	5,342	12,510
Other income, net	264	1,549	5,425
Loss from continuing operations before income tax benefit	(47,920)	(176,479)	(418,958)
Income tax benefit	(8,894)	(67,793)	(3,157)
Net loss from continuing operations	(39,026)	(108,686)	(415,801)
Net earnings from discontinued operations	—	—	29,920
Net loss	$ (39,026)	$ (108,686)	$ (385,881)

NOTES TO CONSOLIDATED FINANCIAL STATEMENTS

(Dollars in thousands except per share data)

7. Trade Names

Trade name activity is as follows:

	December 31, 2010	December 31, 2009
Beginning balance	$87,608	$127,300
Impairment	(1,100)	(39,050)
Income tax benefit of deductible goodwill	—	(642)
Ending balance	$86,508	$ 87,608

Our trade names are tested for impairment annually, in the fourth fiscal quarter. Trade names, and long-lived assets, are also tested for impairment whenever events or changes in circumstances indicate that the asset may be impaired. Each quarter, we assess whether events or changes in circumstances indicate a potential impairment of these assets considering many factors, including significant changes in market capitalization, cash flow or projected cash flow, the condition of assets, and the manner in which assets are used.

Trade names are tested by comparing the carrying value and fair value of each trade name to determine the amount, if any, of impairment. The fair value of trade names is calculated using a "relief from royalty payments" methodology. This approach involves two steps: (i) estimating royalty rates for each trademark and (ii) applying these royalty rates to a net sales stream and discounting the resulting cash flows to determine fair value.

In the fourth quarter of 2010, we tested our trade names for impairment and recorded an impairment charge of $1,100, resulting in the carrying value of one of our trade names being reduced, and thus equal, to the estimated fair value. The

decrease in the fair value of this trade name was primarily caused by a decrease in projected sales. In total, the fair value of our trade names exceed the carrying value by $4,294 or 4.9% as of December 31, 2010. Any future decrease in the fair value of our trade names could result in a corresponding impairment charge. The estimated fair value of our trade names is highly contingent upon sales trends and assumptions including royalty rates, net sales streams, and a discount rate. Lower sales trends, decreases in projected net sales, decreases in royalty rates, or increases in the discount rate would cause additional impairment charges and a corresponding reduction in our earnings.

We determine royalty rates for each trademark considering contracted rates and industry benchmarks. Royalty rates generally are not volatile and do not fluctuate significantly with short term changes in economic conditions.

Weighted average net sales streams are calculated for each trademark based on a probability weighting assigned to each reasonably possible future net sales stream. The probability weightings are determined considering historical performance, management forecasts and other factors such as economic conditions and trends. Estimated net sales streams could fluctuate significantly based on changes in the economy, actual sales, or forecasted sales.

The discount rate is a calculated weighted average cost of capital determined by observing typical rates and proportions of interest-bearing debt, preferred equity, and common equity of publicly traded companies engaged in lines of business similar to our company. The discount rate could fluctuate significantly with changes in the risk profile of our industry or in the general economy.

Loss on Extinguishment of Debt

3.53

PALL CORPORATION (JUL)

CONSOLIDATED STATEMENTS OF EARNINGS
(in part)

	Years Ended		
(In thousands, except per share data)	July 31, 2010	July 31, 2009	July 31, 2008
Net sales	$2,401,932	$2,329,158	$2,571,645
Cost of sales	1,195,830	1,228,468	1,360,810
Gross profit	1,206,102	1,100,690	1,210,835
Selling, general and administrative expenses	739,936	699,832	749,519
Research and development	74,944	71,213	71,647
Restructuring and other charges, net	17,664	30,723	31,538
Interest expense, net	14,324	28,136	32,576
Loss on extinguishment of debt	31,513	—	—
Earnings before income taxes	327,721	270,786	325,555
Provision for income taxes	86,473	75,167	108,276
Net earnings	$ 241,248	$ 195,619	$ 217,279

NOTES TO CONSOLIDATED FINANCIAL STATEMENTS

(In thousands, except per share data)

Note 8—Notes Payable and Long-Term Debt (in part)

Notes payable is comprised of overdraft borrowings from a financial institution of $39,728, and borrowings under various short-term unsecured credit facilities of $344 as of July 31, 2010. The Company had available unsecured credit facilities which require no compensating balances, totaling approxi-

mately $140,227. In addition to providing short-term liquidity and overdraft protection, these facilities also support various programs (such as guarantee, performance bond and warranty) mandated by customers. At July 31, 2010, borrowings under these facilities were included in notes payable and an additional $46,702 was committed to various other programs. The weighted average interest rates on notes payable at the end of fiscal years 2010 and 2009 were 0.2% and 0.3%, respectively. The weighted average interest rates on the senior revolving credit facilities at the end of fiscal years 2010 and 2009 were 2.3% and 0.6%, respectively.

Long-term debt consists of:

	2010	2009
Senior revolving credit facility, due in fiscal year 2015[a]	$250,000	$ —
Senior revolving credit facility, due in fiscal year 2011[a]	—	280,000
5% Senior Notes, due in fiscal year 2020, net of discount[b]	373,027	—
Private placement senior notes, due in fiscal year 2013[b]	—	280,000
Japanese Yen ("JPY") denominated loan, due in fiscal year 2015[c]	104,166	—
JPY denominated loan, due in fiscal year 2010[c]	—	95,121
Other	16,116	19,897
	743,309	675,018
Fair value adjustment, net[d]	—	80
Total long-term debt	743,309	675,098
Current portion	(1,956)	(97,432)
Long-term debt, net of current portion	$741,353	$577,666

[a] On July 13, 2010, the Company entered into a five-year $500,000 unsecured senior revolving credit facility (the "New Facility") with a syndicate of banks, which expires on July 13, 2015. The Company terminated the existing $500,000 senior revolving credit facility, which was due in fiscal year 2011 (the "Prior Facility"). Simultaneous with entry into the New Facility, the Company borrowed approximately $295,000, principally to: (1) redeem all $280,000 outstanding of the 6.00% Senior Notes due in fiscal year 2013 (the "Prior Notes") and, (2) pay a portion of the redemption premium on the Prior Notes of $28,268 (other funds were used to pay the balance of approximately $13,268). In connection with the New Facility, the Company incurred deferred financing costs of $2,856, which will be amortized to interest expense over the term of the New Facility. In addition, the Company wrote-off approximately $139 of unamortized deferred financing costs related to the Prior Facility, which has been reflected as a loss on the extinguishment of debt. Letters of credit outstanding against the New Facility as of July 31, 2010 were approximately $12,606.

Borrowings under the new facility bear interest at either a variable rate based upon the London InterBank Offered Rate (U.S. dollar, British Pound, Euro, Swiss Franc and Japanese Yen borrowings) or the European Union Banking Federation Rate (Euro borrowings) or at the prime rate of the Facility Agent (U.S. dollar borrowing only). The New Facility contains customary affirmative and negative covenants, financial covenants, representations and warranties and events of defaults. The financial covenants are as follows:

   i. Minimum interest coverage ratio: The Ratio of Earnings Before Net Interest, Taxes, Depreciation, Amortization and the Non-Cash Portion of Non-Recurring Charges and Income ("EBITDA") to Net Interest Expense shall not be less than 3.50 to 1.00, computed on the basis of cumulative results for the most recently ended four consecutive quarters.

   ii. Maximum funded debt ratio: The Ratio of Consolidated Funded Debt to EBITDA shall not exceed 3.50 to 1.00, EBITDA computed on the basis of cumulative results for the most recently ended four consecutive quarters.

In addition, the New Facility includes other covenants that under certain circumstances can restrict the Company's ability to incur additional indebtedness, make investments and other restricted payments, enter into sale and leaseback transactions, create liens and sell assets. As of July 31, 2010, the Company was in compliance with all related financial and other restrictive covenants, including limitations on indebtedness.

[b] On June 18, 2010, the Company issued $375,000 of publicly traded notes with an aggregate principal amount of its 5.00% Senior Notes, due 2020 (the "New Notes"). After the closing of the New Notes, the Company received proceeds (net of the discount on the New Notes of $2,006 and underwriting fees of $2,438) of $370,556. The Company used the net proceeds from this offering principally (1) to repay its then outstanding balance on the Prior Facility, and (2) for general corporate purposes. The Prior Notes, originally due August 1, 2012, were fully redeemed in July 2010 after the satisfaction of a 30-day notice period. In connection with this redemption, the Company recorded a loss on extinguishment of debt totaling $31,374, primarily comprised of the aforementioned redemption premium and the recognition of previously deferred financing costs related to the Prior Notes. In connection with the New Notes, the Company incurred deferred financing costs of $3,455, which will be amortized to interest expense over the term of the New Notes.

The notes are unsecured and unsubordinated obligations of the Company and rank pari passu to its other outstanding unsecured and unsubordinated indebtedness.

[c] On May 26, 2010, the Company refinanced its loan of JPY 9 billion (approximately $104,166 as of July 31, 2010), which was due on June 20, 2010, to May 26, 2015. Under the new financing agreement, interest is fixed at a rate of 2.33%. Previously, the interest payments were at a variable rate based upon Yen LIBOR. The Company designated this borrowing as a non-derivative hedge of a portion of its net JPY investment in a Japanese subsidiary.

[d] Refer to Note 10, Financial Instruments and Risks & Uncertainties, for further discussion of the Company's derivative financial instruments and hedging activities.

The aggregate annual maturities of long-term debt during fiscal years 2011 through 2015 are approximately as follows:

2011	$ 1,956
2012	1,568
2013	1,590
2014	1,639
2015	355,887

Business Combination Adjustment Loss

3.54

ZIMMER HOLDINGS, INC. (DEC)

CONSOLIDATED STATEMENTS OF EARNINGS
(in part)

(In millions, except per share amounts)	For the Years Ended December 31		
	2010	2009	2008
Net Sales	$4,220.2	$4,095.4	$4,121.1
Cost of products sold	1,012.4	990.7	997.3
Gross Profit	3,207.8	3,104.7	3,123.8
Research and development	220.0	205.7	192.3
Selling, general and administrative	1,757.4	1,729.0	1,704.0
Certain claims (Note 19)	75.0	35.0	69.0
Goodwill impairment (Note 9)	204.0	73.0	—
Net curtailment and settlement (Note 14)	—	(32.1)	—
Special items (Note 2)	34.7	75.3	68.5
Operating expenses	2,291.1	2,085.9	2,033.8
Operating Profit	916.7	1,018.8	1,090.0
Interest and other income (expense), net	(56.5)	(20.6)	31.8
Earnings before income taxes	860.2	998.2	1,121.8
Provision for income taxes	263.3	280.8	272.3
Net earnings	596.9	717.4	849.5
Less: Net earnings attributable to noncontrolling interest	—	—	(0.9)
Net Earnings of Zimmer Holdings, Inc.	$ 596.9	$ 717.4	$ 848.6

NOTES TO CONSOLIDATED FINANCIAL STATEMENTS

2. Significant Accounting Policies (in part)

Special Items—We recognize expenses resulting directly from our business combinations and other items as "Special items" in our consolidated statement of earnings. Expenses in the "Special items" line for the years ended December 31, 2010, 2009 and 2008, included (in millions):

	2010	2009	2008
Adjustment or impairment of assets and obligations, net	$11.4	$ (1.5)	$(10.4)
Consulting and professional fees	4.9	11.7	13.2
Employee severance and retention, including share-based compensation acceleration	6.7	19.0	0.2
Information technology integration	0.1	1.1	0.7
In-process research & development	—	—	38.5
Vacated facilities	0.2	1.4	—
Facility and employee relocation	2.0	5.4	7.5
Distributor acquisitions	1.9	1.1	6.9
Certain litigation matters	(0.3)	23.4	—
Contract terminations	3.9	9.4	5.7
Other	3.9	4.3	6.2
Special items	$34.7	$75.3	$ 68.5

Adjustment or impairment of assets and obligations relates to impairment on assets that were acquired in business combinations, impairment of assets related to a transformation of our global information technology infrastructure or adjustments to certain liabilities of acquired companies due to changes in circumstances surrounding those liabilities subsequent to the related measurement period.

PENSIONS AND OTHER POSTRETIREMENT BENEFITS

RECOGNITION AND MEASUREMENT

3.55 FASB ASC 715, *Compensation—Retirement Benefits*, requires that an entity recognize the overfunded or underfunded status of a single-employer defined benefit postretirement plan as an asset or a liability in its statement of financial position, recognize changes in that funded status in comprehensive income, and disclose in the notes to the financial statements additional information about net periodic benefit cost. FASB ASC 715 requires an entity to recognize as components of other comprehensive income the gains or losses and prior service costs or credits that arise during a period but are not recognized in the income statement as components of net periodic benefit cost of a period. Those amounts recognized in accumulated other comprehensive income are adjusted as they are subsequently recognized in the income statement as components of net periodic benefit cost. Additionally, FASB ASC 715 requires that an entity measure plan assets and benefit obligations as of the date of its fiscal year-end statement of financial position. An employer whose equity securities are publicly traded is required to initially recognize the funded status of a defined benefit postretirement plan.

DISCLOSURE

3.56 FASB ASC 715 states the disclosure requirements for pensions and other postretirement benefits, including disclosures about the assets, obligations, cash flows, investment strategy, and net periodic benefit cost of defined pension and postretirement plans. FASB ASC 715 also includes disclosures related to multiemployer plans. FASB ASC 715-20 calls for different disclosures about defined benefit plans for public and nonpublic entities.

3.57 The disclosure requirements of FASB ASC 715 include, but are not limited to, the actuarial gains and losses, the assumed health care cost trend rate for other postretirement benefits, the allocation by major category of plan assets, the inputs and valuation techniques used to measure the fair value of plan assets, the effect of fair value measurements using significant unobservable inputs (level 3) on changes in plan assets for the period, and significant concentrations of risk within plan assets.

PRESENTATION AND DISCLOSURE EXCERPTS

Defined Benefit Plans

3.58

INTERNATIONAL PAPER COMPANY (DEC)

NOTES TO CONSOLIDATED FINANCIAL STATEMENTS

Note 15. Retirement Plans

U.S. Defined Benefit Plans

International Paper sponsors and maintains the Retirement Plan of International Paper Company (the "Pension Plan"), a tax-qualified defined benefit pension plan that provides retirement benefits to substantially all U.S. salaried employees and hourly employees (receiving salaried benefits) hired prior to July 1, 2004, and substantially all other U.S. hourly and union employees who work at a participating business unit regardless of hire date. These employees generally are eligible to participate in the Pension Plan upon attaining 21 years of age and completing one year of eligibility service. U.S. salaried employees and hourly employees (receiving salaried benefits) hired after June 30, 2004, are not eligible to participate in the Pension Plan, but receive a company contribution to their individual savings plan accounts (see "Other U.S. Plans" on page 85). The Pension Plan provides defined pension benefits based on years of credited service and either final average earnings (salaried employees and hourly employees receiving salaried benefits), hourly job rates or specified benefit rates (hourly and union employees).

Former Weyerhaeuser Company salaried and hourly employees acquired by International Paper in the CBPR acquisition became participants in the Pension Plan if they were hired by Weyerhaeuser prior to July 1, 2004. Acquired salaried employees and hourly employees (receiving salaried benefits) hired by Weyerhaeuser after June 30, 2004 are not eligible to participate in the Pension Plan and instead receive a company contribution to their savings plan accounts.

In connection with the CBPR acquisition, International Paper assumed sponsorship in 2008 of the Western Kraft, Albany, Oregon, Hourly Employees' Retirement Plan, a defined benefit pension plan covering hourly employees at the Albany, Oregon mill. The assets and liabilities of that plan were merged into the Pension Plan as of December 31, 2009.

The Company's funding policy for the Pension Plan is to contribute amounts sufficient to meet legal funding requirements, plus any additional amounts that the Company may determine to be appropriate considering the funded status of the plans, tax deductibility, cash flow generated by the Company, and other factors. The Company continually reassesses the amount and timing of any discretionary contributions. Voluntary contributions totaling $1.15 billion were made by the Company in 2010. No contributions were made in 2009 or 2008.

The Company also has two unfunded nonqualified defined benefit pension plans: a Pension Restoration Plan available to employees hired prior to July 1, 2004 that provides retirement benefits based on eligible compensation in excess of limits set by the Internal Revenue Service, and a supplemental retirement plan for senior managers (SERP), which is an alternative retirement plan for salaried employees who are senior vice presidents and above or who are designated by the chief executive officer as participants. These nonqualified plans are only funded to the extent of benefits paid, which totaled $37 million, $35 million and $24 million in 2010, 2009 and 2008, respectively, and which are expected to be $36 million in 2011.

Net Periodic Pension Expense

Service cost is the actuarial present value of benefits attributed by the plans' benefit formula to services rendered by employees during the year. Interest cost represents the increase in the projected benefit obligation, which is a discounted amount, due to the passage of time. The expected return on plan assets reflects the computed amount of current-year earnings from the investment of plan assets using an estimated long-term rate of return.

Net periodic pension expense for qualified and nonqualified U.S. defined benefit plans comprised the following:

(In millions)	2010	2009	2008
Service cost	$ 116	$ 120	$ 105
Interest cost	541	537	540
Expected return on plan assets	(631)	(634)	(672)
Actuarial loss	174	160	121
Amortization of prior service cost	31	30	29
Net periodic pension expense[a]	$ 231	$ 213	$ 123

[a] Excludes $1.1 million in 2008 in curtailment losses, and $83.2 million and $13.9 million in 2009 and 2008, respectively, of termination benefits, in connection with cost reduction programs and facility rationalizations that were recorded in Restructuring and other charges in the consolidated statement of operations.

The increase in 2010 pension expense reflects a decrease in the assumed discount rate to 5.80% in 2010 from 6.00% in 2009 and higher amortization of unrecognized actuarial losses. International Paper evaluates its actuarial assumptions annually as of December 31 (the measurement date) and considers changes in these long-term factors based upon market conditions and the requirements for employers' accounting for pensions. These assumptions are used to calculate benefit obligations as of December 31 of the current year and pension expense to be recorded in the following year (i.e., the discount rate used to determine the benefit obligation as of December 31, 2010 was also the discount rate used to determine net pension expense for the 2011 year).

Weighted average assumptions used to determine net pension expense for 2010, 2009 and 2008 were as follows:

	2010	2009	2008
Discount rate	5.80%	6.00%	6.20%
Expected long-term rate of return on plan assets	8.25%	8.25%	8.50%
Rate of compensation increase	3.75%	3.75%	3.75%

Weighted average assumptions used to determine benefit obligations as of December 31, 2010 and 2009, were as follows:

	2010	2009
Discount rate	5.60%	5.80%
Rate of compensation increase	3.75%	3.75%

The expected long-term rate of return on plan assets is based on projected rates of return for current and planned asset classes in the plan's investment portfolio. Projected rates of return are developed through an asset/liability study in which projected returns for each of the plan's asset classes are determined after analyzing historical experience and future expectations of returns and volatility of the various asset classes. Based on the target asset allocation for each asset class, the overall expected rate of return for the portfolio is developed considering the effects of active portfolio management and expenses paid from plan assets. The discount rate assumption was determined based on a yield curve that incorporates approximately 500 Aa-graded bonds. The plan's projected cash flows were then matched to the yield curve to develop the discount rate. To calculate pension expense for 2011, the Company will use an expected long-term rate of return on plan assets of 8.25%, a discount rate of 5.60% and an assumed rate of compensation increase of 3.75%. The Company estimates that it will record net pension expense of approximately $179 million for its U.S. defined benefit plans in 2011, with the decrease from expense of $231 million in 2010 reflecting increased plan assets and higher than expected asset returns in 2010, partially offset by a decrease in the discount rate.

The following illustrates the effect on pension expense for 2011 of a 25 basis point decrease in the above assumptions:

(In millions)	2011
Expense/(income):	
Discount rate	$29
Expected long-term rate of return on plan assets	22
Rate of compensation increase	$ (4)

Investment Policy/Strategy

International Paper's Board of Directors has appointed a Fiduciary Review Committee that is responsible for fiduciary oversight of the Pension Plan, approving investment policy and reviewing the management and control of plan assets. Pension Plan assets are invested to maximize returns within prudent levels of risk. The Pension Plan maintains a strategic asset allocation policy that designates target allocations by asset class. Investments are diversified across classes and within each class to minimize the risk of large losses. Derivatives, including swaps, forward and futures contracts, may be used as asset class substitutes or for hedging or other risk management purposes. Periodic reviews are made of investment policy objectives and investment manager performance.

International Paper's pension allocations by type of fund at December 31, and target allocations were as follows:

Asset Class	2010	2009	Target Allocations
Equity accounts	49%	49%	40%–51%
Fixed income accounts	31%	32%	30%–40%
Real estate accounts	8%	7%	7%–13%
Other	12%	12%	9%–18%
Total	100%	100%	

The fair values of International Paper's pension plan assets at December 31, 2010 by asset class are shown below. Plan assets included an immaterial amount of International Paper common stock at December 31, 2010. No International Paper shares were included in plan assets in 2009. Hedge funds disclosed in the following table are allocated equally between equity and fixed income accounts for target allocation purposes. Cash and cash equivalent portfolios are allocated to the types of account from which they originated. Mortgage backed securities were transferred from significant unobservable inputs (Level 3) in 2009 to significant observable inputs (Level 2) in 2010 as a result of identifying observable market data for the securities.

Asset Class (In millions)		Fair Value Measurement at December 31, 2010		
	Total	Quoted Prices in Active Markets for Identical Assets (Level 1)	Significant Observable Inputs (Level 2)	Significant Unobservable Inputs (Level 3)
Equities—domestic	$1,921	$ 860	$1,057	$ 4
Equities—international	1,317	1,005	312	0
Common collective funds-fixed income	305	0	291	14
Corporate bonds	817	0	817	0
Government securities	936	0	936	0
Mortgage backed securities	194	0	194	0
Other fixed income	30	0	25	5
Commodities	264	0	30	234
Hedge funds	681	0	19	662
Private equity	415	0	0	415
Real estate	650	0	0	650
Derivatives	349	10	1	338
Cash and cash equivalents	465	5	460	0
Total investments	$8,344	$1,880	$4,142	$2,322

Equity securities consist primarily of publicly traded U.S. companies and international companies and common collective funds. Publicly traded equities are valued at the closing prices reported in the active market in which the individual securities are traded. Common collective funds are valued at the net asset value per share multiplied by the number of shares held as of the measurement date.

Fixed income consists of corporate bonds, government securities, and common collective funds. Government securities are valued by third-party pricing sources. Corporate bonds are valued using either the yields currently available on comparable securities of issuers with similar credit ratings or using a discounted cash flows approach that utilizes observable inputs, such as current yields of similar instruments, but includes adjustments for certain risks that may not be observable, such as credit and liquidity risks. Common collective funds are valued at the net asset value per share multiplied by the number of shares held as of the measurement date.

Commodities consist of commodity-linked notes and commodity-linked derivatives. Commodities are valued at closing prices determined by calculation agents for outstanding transactions.

Hedge funds are investment structures that pursue a diverse array of investment strategies with a wide range of different securities and derivative instruments. These investments are made through funds-of-funds (commingled, multi-manager fund structures) and through direct investments in individual hedge funds. Hedge funds are primarily valued by each fund's third party administrator based upon the valuation of the underlying securities and instruments and primarily by applying a market or income valuation methodology as appropriate depending on the specific type of security or instrument held. Funds-of-funds are valued based upon the net asset values of the underlying investments in hedge funds.

Private equity consists of interests in partnerships that invest in U.S. and non-U.S. debt and equity securities. Partnership interests are valued using the most recent general partner statement of fair value, updated for any subsequent partnership interest cash flows.

Real estate includes commercial properties, land and timberland, and generally includes, but is not limited to, retail, office, industrial, multifamily and hotel properties. Real estate holdings, taken together, are intended to have characteristics similar to, but not necessarily equal to, the National Council of Real Estate Investment Fiduciaries (NCREIF) Property Index. Real estate fund values are primarily reported by the fund manager and are based on valuation of the underlying investments which include inputs such as cost, discounted cash flows, independent appraisals and market based comparable data.

Derivative investments such as futures, forward contracts, options, and swaps are used to help manage risks. Derivatives are generally employed as asset class substitutes (such as when employed within a portable alpha strategy), for managing asset/liability mismatches, or bona fide hedging or other appropriate risk management purposes. Derivative instruments are generally valued by the investment managers or in certain instances by third party pricing sources.

The fair value measurements using significant unobservable inputs (Level 3) at December 31, 2010 were as follows:

Fair Value Measurements Using Significant Unobservable Inputs (Level 3)

(In millions)	Equities-Domestic	Equities-International	Fixed Income Common Collective Funds	Corporate Bonds	Government Securities	Mortgage Backed Securities	Other Fixed Income	Commodities	Hedge Funds	Private Equity	Real Estate	Derivatives	Total
Beginning balance at December 31, 2009	$4	$1	$29	$2	$3	$175	$24	$174	$668	$344	$457	$269	$2,150
Actual return on plan assets:													
Relating to assets still held at the reporting date	3	0	0	0	(1)	0	(3)	37	33	30	43	68	210
Relating to assets sold during the period	(2)	0	3	0	0	0	2	0	6	(4)	0	65	70
Purchases, sales and settlements	(1)	0	(18)	(2)	(2)	0	(18)	23	(45)	45	150	(64)	68
Transfers in and/or out of Level 3[a]	0	(1)	0	0	0	(175)	0	0	0	0	0	0	(176)
Ending balance at December 31, 2010	$4	$0	$14	$0	$0	$ 0	$ 5	$234	$662	$415	$650	$338	$2,322

[a] Transferred out of Level 3 to Level 2 because market data for these securities was observable.

At December 31, 2010, projected future pension benefit payments, excluding any termination benefits, were as follows:

(In millions)	
2011	$ 628
2012	622
2013	624
2014	630
2015	639
2016–2020	3,348

Pension Plan Asset/Liability

As required by ASC 715, "Compensation—Retirement Benefits," the pension plan funded status must be recorded on the consolidated balance sheet. Therefore, pension plan gains or losses and prior service costs not yet recognized in net periodic cost are recognized on a net-of-tax basis in OCI. These amounts will be subject to amortization in the future.

At December 31, 2010, the fair value of plan assets for the Pension Plan was less than the projected benefit obligation (PBO). However, the deficit was lower than at December 31, 2009, resulting in a decrease in the recorded minimum pension obligation of $1.3 billion and an after-tax credit to OCI of $92 million. An after-tax credit to OCI of $318 million and an after-tax charge to OCI of $1.8 billion had been recorded for 2009 and 2008, respectively. For the unfunded nonqualified plans, changes in the liabilities resulted in after-tax charges to OCI of $19 million, $9 million and $5 million in 2010, 2009 and 2008, respectively. In 2008, in conjunction with the CBPR business acquisition, the Company acquired a small overfunded pension plan covering hourly employees at the Albany, Oregon mill. For this plan, the Company recorded an after-tax charge to OCI of $13 million at December 31, 2008.

The accumulated benefit obligation for all defined benefit plans was $9.6 billion and $9.3 billion at December 31, 2010 and 2009, respectively.

The following table summarizes information for pension plans with an accumulated benefit obligation in excess of plan assets at December 31, 2010 and 2009.

(In millions)	2010	2009
Projected benefit obligation	$9,824	$9,544
Accumulated benefit obligation	9,594	9,312
Fair value of plan assets	8,344	6,784

Unrecognized Actuarial Losses

ASC 715, "Compensation—Retirement Benefits" provides for delayed recognition of actuarial gains and losses, including amounts arising from changes in the estimated projected plan benefit obligation due to changes in the assumed discount rate, differences between the actual and expected return on plan assets and other assumption changes. These net gains and losses are recognized prospectively over a period that approximates the average remaining service period of active employees expected to receive benefits under the plans (approximately 9 years as of December 31, 2010) to the extent that they are not offset by gains in subsequent years. The estimated net loss and prior service cost that will be amortized from AOCI into net periodic pension cost during the next fiscal year are expected to be $204 million and $31 million, respectively.

The following table shows the changes in the benefit obligation and plan assets for 2010 and 2009, and the plans' funded status. The benefit obligation as of December 31, 2010 increased by $281 million, principally as a result of a decrease in the discount rate assumption used in computing the estimated benefit obligation. Plan assets increased by $1.6 billion, reflecting favorable investment results and the $1.15 billion voluntary contribution.

(In millions)	2010	2009
Change in Projected Benefit Obligation:		
Benefit obligation, January 1	$ 9,544	$ 9,275
Service cost	116	120
Interest cost	541	537
Actuarial loss	264	134
Benefits paid	(646)	(617)
Restructuring	(2)	2
Special termination benefits	0	83
Plan amendments	7	10
Benefit obligation, December 31	$ 9,824	$ 9,544
Change in Plan Assets:		
Fair value of plan assets, January 1	$ 6,784	$ 6,079
Actual return on plan assets	1,019	1,287
Company contributions	1,187	35
Benefits paid	(646)	(617)
Fair value of plan assets, December 31	$ 8,344	$ 6,784
Funded status, December 31	$(1,480)	$(2,760)

(In millions)	2010	2009
Amounts Recognized in the Consolidated Balance Sheet:		
Current liability	$ (36)	$ (41)
Non-current liability	(1,444)	(2,719)
	$(1,480)	$(2,760)
Amounts Recognized in Accumulated Other Comprehensive Income Under ASC 715 (Pre-Tax):		
Net actuarial loss	$ 3,412	$ 3,712
Prior service cost	183	206
	$ 3,595	$ 3,918

The components of the $323 million decrease in the amounts recognized in OCI during 2010 consisted of:

(In millions)	
Curtailment effects	$ (2)
Current year actuarial gain	(123)
Amortization of actuarial loss	(174)
Current year prior service cost	7
Amortization of prior service cost	(31)
	$(323)

The portion of the change in the funded status that was recognized either in net periodic benefit costs or OCI was $(92) million, $(483) million and $3 billion for 2010, 2009 and 2008, respectively.

Non-U.S. Defined Benefit Plans

Generally, International Paper's non-U.S. pension plans are funded using the projected benefit as a target, except in certain countries where funding of benefit plans is not required. Net periodic pension expense for non-U.S. plans was as follows:

(In millions)	2010	2009	2008
Service cost	$ 3	$ 4	$ 7
Interest cost	12	12	11
Expected return on plan assets	(11)	(10)	(13)
Actuarial gain	0	(2)	(1)
Curtailment gain	(2)	(1)	0
Settlement gain	(2)	0	0
Net periodic pension expense	$ 0	$ 3	$ 4

Weighted average assumptions used to determine net pension expense for 2010, 2009 and 2008 were as follows:

	2010	2009	2008
Discount rate	6.45%	6.37%	6.40%
Expected long-term rate of return on plan assets	8.20%	8.88%	8.87%
Rate of compensation increase	4.06%	3.81%	3.55%

Weighted average assumptions used to determine benefit obligations as of December 31, 2010 and 2009, were as follows:

	2010	2009
Discount rate	6.01%	6.45%
Rate of compensation increase	3.07%	4.06%

The following table shows the changes in the benefit obligation and plan assets for 2010 and 2009, and the plans' funded status as of December 31, 2010 and 2009.

(In millions)	2010	2009
Change in Projected Benefit Obligation:		
Benefit obligation, January 1	$186	$168
Service cost	3	4
Interest cost	12	12
Curtailments	(3)	(5)
Settlements	(14)	0
Actuarial loss	11	0
Benefits paid	(7)	(12)
Effect of foreign currency exchange rate movements	(5)	19
Benefit obligation, December 31	$183	$186
Change in Plan Assets:		
Fair value of plan assets, January 1	$150	$115
Actual return on plan assets	21	20
Company contributions	8	7
Benefits paid	(7)	(12)
Settlements	(14)	0
Effect of foreign currency exchange rate movements	(2)	20
Fair value of plan assets, December 31	$156	$150
Funded status, December 31	$ (27)	$ (36)
Amounts Recognized in the Consolidated Balance Sheet:		
Non-current asset	$ 13	$ 12
Current liability	(2)	(2)
Non-current liability	(38)	(46)
	$ (27)	$ (36)
Amounts Recognized in Accumulated Other Comprehensive Income (Pre-Tax):		
Prior service cost	$ 0	$ 0
Net actuarial loss (gain)	1	(1)
	$ 1	$ (1)

The components of the $2 million increase in the amounts recognized in OCI during 2010 consisted of:

(In millions)	
Current year actuarial loss	$ 1
Curtailment effects	(1)
Settlements	2
	$ 2

The portion of the change in the funded status that was recognized in either net periodic benefit cost or OCI was $1 million, $(11) million and $40 million for 2010, 2009 and 2008, respectively. For non-U.S. plans with accumulated benefit obligations in excess of plan assets, the projected benefit obligations, accumulated benefit obligations and fair values of plan assets totaled $42 million, $34 million and $2 million, respectively, at December 31, 2010. Plan assets consist principally of common stock and fixed income securities.

3.59

DEAN FOODS COMPANY (DEC)

NOTES TO CONSOLIDATED FINANCIAL STATEMENTS

14. Employee Retirement and Profit Sharing Plans (in part)

We sponsor various defined benefit and defined contribution retirement plans, including various employee savings and profit sharing plans, and contribute to various multi-employer pension plans on behalf of our employees. Substantially all full-time union and non-union employees who have completed one or more years of service and have met other requirements pursuant to the plans are eligible to participate in one or more of these plans. On July 2, 2009, we acquired Alpro, including its defined benefit pension plans. During 2010, 2009 and 2008, our retirement and profit sharing plan expenses were as follows:

	Year Ended December 31		
(In thousands)	2010	2009	2008
Defined benefit plans	$12,975	$21,053	$ 4,398
Defined contribution plans	27,182	28,300	23,331
Multi-employer pension and certain union plans	28,768	29,604	28,295
Total	$68,925	$78,957	$56,024

Defined Benefit Plans—The benefits under our defined benefit plans are based on years of service and employee compensation. Our funding policy is to contribute annually the minimum amount required under ERISA regulations plus additional amounts as we deem appropriate.

Included in accumulated other comprehensive income at December 31, 2010 and 2009 are the following amounts that have not yet been recognized in net periodic pension cost: unrecognized transition obligation of $225,000 ($138,000 net of tax) and $337,000 ($206,000 net of tax), unrecognized prior service costs of $5.6 million ($3.5 million net of tax) and $7.1 million ($4.4 million net of tax) and unrecognized actuarial losses of $124.1 million ($76.0 million net of tax) and $120.4 million ($73.7 million net of tax). The transition obligation, prior service costs, and actuarial losses included in accumulated other comprehensive income and expected to be recognized in net periodic pension cost during the year

ended December 31, 2011 are $112,000 ($69,000 net of tax), $763,000 ($467,000 net of tax), and $9.0 million ($5.5 million net of tax), respectively.

The reconciliation of the beginning and ending balances of the projected benefit obligation and the fair value of plans assets for the years ended December 31, 2010 and 2009 and the funded status of the plans at December 31, 2010 and 2009 is as follows:

	December 31	
(In thousands)	2010	2009
Change in Benefit Obligation:		
Benefit obligation at beginning of year	$294,569	$276,355
Service cost	3,699	3,147
Interest cost	16,941	16,947
Plan participants' contributions	66	48
Actuarial (gain) loss	16,619	10,330
Benefits paid	(20,822)	(18,873)
Plan amendments	—	—
Plan settlements	(2,914)	(1,769)
Acquisition	—	8,605
Exchange rate changes	(627)	(221)
Benefit obligation at end of year	307,531	294,569
Change in Plan Assets:		
Fair value of plan assets at beginning of year	223,369	181,027
Actual return on plan assets	22,240	34,062
Employer contribution	10,277	24,517
Plan participants' contributions	66	48
Benefits paid	(20,822)	(18,873)
Plan settlements	(2,914)	(1,769)
Acquisition	—	4,496
Exchange rate changes	(394)	(139)
Fair value of plan assets at end of year	231,822	223,369
Funded status at end of year	$ (75,709)	$ (71,200)

The underfunded status of the plans of $75.7 million at December 31, 2010 is recognized in our Consolidated Balance Sheet and includes $845,000 classified as a current accrued pension liability. We do not expect any plan assets to be returned to us during the year ended December 31, 2011. We expect to contribute approximately $12.1 million to the pension plans in 2011.

A summary of our key actuarial assumptions used to determine benefit obligations as of December 31, 2010 and 2009 follows:

	December 31	
	2010	2009
Weighted average discount rate[1]	5.28%	6.00%
Rate of compensation increase[1]	4.00%	4.00%

[1] Assumptions in this table represent the assumptions utilized for our domestic pension plans as they represented more than 90% of our total benefit obligation as of December 31, 2010 and 2009.

A summary of our key actuarial assumptions used to determine net periodic benefit cost for 2010, 2009 and 2008 follows:

	Year Ended December 31		
	2010	2009	2008
Weighted average discount rate[1]	6.00%	6.32%	6.40%
Expected return on plan assets[1]	7.70%	7.70%	8.00%
Rate of compensation increase[1]	4.00%	4.00%	4.00%

[1] Assumptions in this table represent the assumptions utilized for our domestic pension plans as they represented more than 90% of our total net periodic benefit cost during the years ended December 31, 2010, 2009 and 2008.

	Year Ended December 31		
(In thousands)	2010	2009	2008
Components of net periodic benefit cost:			
Service cost	$ 3,699	$ 3,147	$ 2,727
Interest cost	16,941	16,947	16,160
Expected return on plan assets	(16,584)	(14,017)	(19,185)
Amortizations:			
Unrecognized transition obligation	112	112	112
Prior service cost	716	921	890
Unrecognized net loss	5,594	12,093	2,038
Effect of curtailment	790	945	—
Effect of settlement	1,707	905	1,656
Net periodic benefit cost	$ 12,975	$ 21,053	$ 4,398

The overall expected long-term rate of return on plan assets is a weighted-average expectation based on the targeted and expected portfolio composition. We consider historical performance and current benchmarks to arrive at expected long-term rates of return in each asset category.

The amortization of unrecognized net loss represents the amortization of investment losses incurred. In 2010, we closed a plant in South Carolina and also carried out a broad-based workforce reduction plan within our Fresh Dairy Direct-Morningstar segment. The effect of curtailment cost in 2010 represents the recognition of net periodic pension service costs associated with these activities. In 2009, we closed a plant in Michigan. The effect of curtailment cost in 2009 represents the recognition of net periodic pension service costs associated with the closure of that plant. The effect of settlement costs in 2010, 2009 and 2008 represents the recognition of net periodic benefit cost related to pension settlements reached as a result of plant closures.

Pension plans with an accumulated benefit obligation in excess of plan assets follows:

	December 31	
(In millions)	2010	2009
Projected benefit obligation	$299.6	$286.0
Accumulated benefit obligation	290.2	283.2
Fair value of plan assets	226.3	217.0

The accumulated benefit obligation for all defined benefit plans was $295.0 million and $289.0 million at December 31, 2010 and 2009, respectively.

Almost 90% of our defined benefit plan obligations are frozen as to future participants or increases in accumulated benefits. Many of these obligations were acquired in prior strategic transactions. As an alternative to defined benefit plans, we offer defined contribution plans for eligible employees.

The weighted average discount rate reflects the rate at which our defined benefit plan obligations could be effectively settled. The rate, which is updated annually with the assistance of an independent actuary, uses a model that reflects rates of a hypothetical portfolio of zero-coupon, high quality corporate bonds that mirror our forecasted benefit plan payments in the future. The weighted average discount rate was decreased from 6.00% at December 31, 2009 to 5.28% at December 31, 2010, which will increase the net periodic benefit cost in 2011.

Substantially all of our qualified pension plans are consolidated into one master trust. The investments held in the master trust are managed by an established Investment Committee with assistance from independent investment advisors. On July 1, 2009, the Investment Committee adopted a new long-term investment policy for the master trust that decreases the expected relative holdings of equity securities that targets investments in equity securities at 59% of the portfolio, fixed income at 37%, cash equivalents at 3% and other investments of 1%. Policy objectives include maximizing long-term return at acceptable risk levels, diversifying among asset classes, if appropriate, and among investment managers, as well as establishing relevant risk parameters within each asset class. The investment policies permit variances from the targets within certain parameters. The investment policy prohibits investments in non-marketable or exotic securities, such as short-sale contracts; letter stock; commodities and private placements, without the Investment Committee's prior approval. At December 31, 2010, our master trust was invested as follows: investments in equity securities were at 62%; investments in fixed income were at 34%; cash equivalents were less than 1% and other investments were at 4%. Given meaningful equity returns in the fourth quarter of 2010, these investment percentages were slightly different from the Investment Committee targets noted above, and our master trust investments were rebalanced accordingly during the first quarter of 2011 in order to be consistent with those targets. Equity securities of the plan did not include any investment in our common stock at December 31, 2010 or 2009.

Estimated pension plan benefit payments to participants for the next ten years are as follows:

2011	$ 19.8 million
2012	19.2 million
2013	19.7 million
2014	20.4 million
2015	19.8 million
Next five years	106.0 million

Fair value is an exit price, representing the amount that would be received to sell an asset or paid to transfer a liability in an orderly transaction between market participants. As such, fair value is a market-based measurement that should be determined based on assumptions that market participants would use in pricing an asset or liability. As a basis for considering assumptions, we follow a three-tier fair value hierarchy, which prioritizes the inputs used in measuring fair value of our defined benefit plans' consolidated assets as follows:

- Level 1—Quoted prices for identical instruments in active markets.
- Level 2—Quoted prices for similar instruments in active markets, quoted prices for identical or similar instruments in markets that are not active and model-derived valuations, in which all significant inputs are observable in active market.
- Level 3—Unobservable inputs in which there is little or no market data, which require the reporting entity to develop its own assumptions.

The fair values by category of inputs as of December 31, 2010 were as follows (in thousands):

	Fair Value as of December 31, 2010	Level 1	Level 2	Level 3
Equity Securities:				
Common Stock	$ 17	$17	$ —	$ —
Index Funds:				
U.S. Equities[a]	114,232	—	114,232	—
International Equities[b]	22,933	—	22,933	—
Equity Funds[c]	5,722	—	5,722	—
Total Equity Securities	142,904	17	142,887	—
Fixed Income:				
Bond Funds[d]	74,322	—	74,322	—
Diversified Funds[e]	4,353	—	—	4,353
Total Fixed Income	78,675	—	74,322	4,353
Cash Equivalents:				
Short-Term Investment Funds[f]	1,783	—	1,783	—
Total Cash Equivalents	1,783	—	1,783	—
Other Investments:				
Insurance Contracts[g]	6,169	—	—	6,169
Partnerships/Joint Ventures[h]	1,913	—	—	1,913
Insurance Reserves	378	—	—	378
Total Other Investments	8,460	—	—	8,460
Total	$231,822	$17	$218,992	$12,813

[a] Represents a pooled/separate account that tracks the Dow Jones U.S. Total Stock Market Index.

[b] Represents a pooled/separate account that tracks the MSCI EAFE Index.

[c] Represents a pooled/separate account comprised of approximately 90% U.S. large-cap stocks and 10% in international stocks.

[d] Represents a pooled/separate account which tracks the overall performance of the Barclays Capital Long Term Government/Credit Index.

[e] Represents a pooled/separate account investment in the General Investment Accounts of two investment managers. The accounts primarily invest in fixed income debt securities, such as high grade corporate bonds, government bonds and asset-backed securities.

[f] Investment is comprised of high grade money market instruments with short-term maturities and high liquidity.

[g] Approximately 90% of the insurance contracts are financed by employer premiums with the insurer managing the reserves as calculated using an actuarial model. The remaining 10% of the insurance contracts are financed by employer and employee contributions with the insurer managing the reserves collectively with other pension plans.

[h] The majority of the total partnership balance is a partnership comprised of a portfolio of two limited partnership funds that invest in public and private equity.

The fair values by category of inputs as of December 31, 2009 were as follows (in thousands):

	Fair Value as of December 31, 2009	Level 1	Level 2	Level 3
Equity Securities:				
Common Stock	$ 28	$ 28	$ —	$ —
Index Funds:				
U.S. Equities[a]	103,535	—	103,535	—
International Equities[b]	21,219	—	21,219	—
Equity Funds[c]	6,560	—	6,560	—
Total Equity Securities	131,342	28	131,314	—
Fixed Income:				
Bond Funds[d]	73,142	—	73,142	—
Diversified Funds[e]	4,674	—	—	4,674
Total Fixed Income	77,816	—	73,142	4,674
Cash Equivalents:				
Cash and Cash Equivalents	2,000	2,000	—	—
Short-term Investment Funds[f]	4,562	—	4,562	—
Total Cash Equivalents	6,562	2,000	4,562	—
Other Investments:				
Insurance Contracts[g]	5,197	—	—	5,197
Partnerships/Joint Ventures[h]	2,092	—	—	2,092
Insurance Reserves	360	—	—	360
Total Other Investments	7,649	—	—	7,649
Total	$223,369	$2,028	$209,018	$12,323

[a] Represents a pooled/separate account that tracks the Dow Jones U.S. Total Stock Market Index.

[b] Represents a pooled/separate account that tracks the MSCI EAFE Index.

[c] Represents a pooled/separate account comprised of approximately 90% U.S. large-cap stocks and 10% in international stocks.

[d] Approximately 60% of investment represents a pooled/separate account that tracks the overall performance of the Barclays Capital U.S. Aggregate Bond Index. The remaining 40% represents a pooled/separate account invested in government and investment grade corporate securities.

[e] Represents a pooled/separate account investment in the General Investment Accounts of two investment managers. The accounts primarily invest in fixed income debt securities, such as high grade corporate bonds, government bonds and asset-backed securities.

[f] Investment is comprised of high grade money market instruments with short-term maturities and high liquidity.

[g] Approximately 90% of the insurance contracts are financed by employer premiums with the insurer managing the reserves as calculated using an actuarial model. The remaining 10% of the insurance contracts are financed by employer and employee contributions with the insurer managing the reserves collectively with other pension plans.

[h] The majority of the total partnership balance is a partnership comprised of a portfolio of three limited partnership funds that invest in public and private equity.

A reconciliation of the change in the fair value measurement of the defined benefit plans' consolidated assets using significant unobservable inputs (Level 3) during the years ended December 31, 2010 and 2009 is as follows (in thousands):

	Diversified Funds	Insurance Contracts	Partnerships/ Joint Ventures	Insurance Reserves	Total
Balance at December 31, 2008	$4,770	$ —	$2,937	$361	$ 8,068
Actual return on plan assets:					
Relating to instruments still held at reporting date	58	—	(845)	(1)	(788)
Acquisitions[1]	—	5,197	—	—	5,197
Purchases, sales and settlements (net)	(2,265)	—	—	—	(2,265)
Transfers in and/or out of Level 3	2,111	—	—	—	2,111
Balance at December 31, 2009	$4,674	$5,197	$2,092	$360	$12,323
Actual return on plan assets:					
Relating to instruments still held at reporting date	226	284	(179)	18	65
Purchases, sales and settlements (net)	(3,410)	688	—	—	(3,410)
Transfers in and/or out of Level 3	2,863	—	—	—	3,835
Balance at December 31, 2010	$4,353	$6,169	$1,913	$378	$12,813

[1] Represents the plan assets transferred in as part of the Alpro acquisition on July 2, 2009.

Defined Contribution Plans

3.60

VULCAN MATERIALS COMPANY (DEC)

NOTES TO CONSOLIDATED FINANCIAL STATEMENTS

Note 10. Benefit Plans (in part)

Pension Plans (in part)

We sponsor three funded, noncontributory defined benefit pension plans. These plans cover substantially all employees hired prior to July 15, 2007, other than those covered by union-administered plans. Normal retirement age is 65, but the plans contain provisions for earlier retirement. Benefits for the Salaried Plan and a plan we assumed from Florida Rock are generally based on salaries or wages and years of service; the Construction Materials Hourly Plan and the Chemicals Hourly Plan provide benefits equal to a flat dollar amount for each year of service. Effective July 15, 2007, we amended our defined benefit pension plans and our then existing defined contribution 401(k) plans to no longer accept new participants. Existing participants continue to accrue benefits under these plans. Salaried and non-union hourly employees hired on or after July 15, 2007 are eligible for a new single defined contribution 401(k)/Profit-Sharing plan established on that date.

Defined Contribution Plans

We sponsor three defined contribution plans. Substantially all salaried and nonunion hourly employees are eligible to be covered by one of these plans. As stated above, effective July 15, 2007, we amended our defined benefit pension plans and our defined contribution 401(k) plans to no longer accept new participants. Existing participants continue to accrue benefits under these plans. Salaried and nonunion hourly employees hired on or after July 15, 2007 are eligible for a single defined contribution 401(k)/Profit-Sharing plan. Expense recognized in connection with these plans totaled $15,273,000 in 2010, $13,361,000 in 2009 and $16,930,000 in 2008.

Note 13. Shareholders' Equity (in part)

We periodically issue shares of common stock to the trustee of our 401(k) savings and retirement plan to satisfy the plan participants' elections to invest in our common stock. The resulting cash proceeds provide a means of improving cash flow, increasing shareholders' equity and reducing leverage. Under this arrangement, the stock issuances and resulting cash proceeds for the years ended December 31 were as follows: 2010—issued 882,131 shares for cash proceeds of $41,734,000; and 2009—issued 1,135,510 shares for cash proceeds of $52,691,000.

Supplemental Retirement Plans (SERP)

3.61

ARROW ELECTRONICS, INC. (DEC)

NOTES TO CONSOLIDATED FINANCIAL STATEMENTS

(Dollars in thousands except per share data)

13. Employee Benefit Plans (in part)

Supplemental Executive Retirement Plans ("SERP")

The company maintains an unfunded Arrow SERP under which the company will pay supplemental pension benefits to certain employees upon retirement. There are 11 current and 14 former corporate officers participating in this plan.

The Board determines those employees who are eligible to participate in the Arrow SERP.

The Arrow SERP, as amended, provides for the pension benefits to be based on a percentage of average final compensation, based on years of participation in the Arrow SERP. The Arrow SERP permits early retirement, with payments at a reduced rate, based on age and years of service subject to a minimum retirement age of 55. Participants whose accrued rights under the Arrow SERP, prior to the 2002 amendment, which were adversely affected by the amendment, will continue to be entitled to such greater rights.

The company acquired Wyle Electronics ("Wyle") in 2000. Wyle also sponsored an unfunded SERP for certain of its executives. Benefit accruals for the Wyle SERP were frozen as of December 31, 2000. There are 19 participants in this plan.

The company uses a December 31 measurement date for the Arrow SERP and the Wyle SERP. Pension information for the years ended December 31 is as follows:

	2010	2009
Accumulated benefit obligation	$ 53,980	$ 49,058
Changes in Projected Benefit Obligation:		
Projected benefit obligation at beginning of year	$ 57,052	$ 53,885
Service cost (Arrow SERP)	1,642	2,320
Interest cost	3,202	3,017
Actuarial (gain)/loss	2,961	848
Benefits paid	(3,298)	(3,018)
Projected benefit obligation at end of year	$ 61,559	$ 57,052
Funded status	$(61,559)	$(57,052)
Components of Net Periodic Pension Cost:		
Service cost (Arrow SERP)	$ 1,642	$ 2,320
Interest cost	3,202	3,017
Amortization of net loss	744	(174)
Amortization of prior service cost (Arrow SERP)	80	591
Amortization of transition obligation (Arrow SERP)	29	410
Net periodic pension cost	$ 5,697	$ 6,164
Weighted Average Assumptions Used to Determine Benefit Obligation:		
Discount rate	5.50%	5.50%
Rate of compensation increase (Arrow SERP)	5.00%	5.00%
Weighted Average Assumptions Used to Determine Net Periodic Pension Cost:		
Discount rate	5.50%	6.00%
Rate of compensation increase (Arrow SERP)	5.00%	5.00%

The amounts reported for net periodic pension cost and the respective benefit obligation amounts are dependent upon the actuarial assumptions used. The company reviews historical trends, future expectations, current market conditions, and external data to determine the assumptions. The discount rate represents the market rate for a high-quality corporate bond. The rate of compensation increase is determined by the company, based upon its long-term plans for such increases. The actuarial assumptions used to determine the net periodic pension cost are based upon the prior year's assumptions used to determine the benefit obligation.

Benefit payments are expected to be paid as follows:

2011	$ 3,638
2012	3,767
2013	3,798
2014	3,758
2015	3,712
2016–2020	23,761

Multi-Employer Plans

3.62

SYSCO CORPORATION (JUN)

NOTES TO CONSOLIDATED FINANCIAL STATEMENTS

12. Employee Benefit Plans (in part)

Sysco has defined benefit and defined contribution retirement plans for its employees. Also, the company contributes to various multi-employer plans under collective bargaining agreements and provides certain health care benefits to eligible retirees and their dependents.

Sysco maintains a qualified pension plan (Retirement Plan) that pays benefits to employees at retirement, using formulas based on a participant's years of service and compensation.

The company's defined contribution 401(k) plan provides that under certain circumstances the company may make matching contributions of up to 50% of the first 6% of a participant's compensation. Sysco's expense related to this plan was $22.8 million in fiscal 2010, $30.2 million in fiscal 2009, and $36.2 million in fiscal 2008.

Sysco's contributions to multi-employer pension plans, which include payments for voluntary withdrawals, were $51.5 million, $48.0 million, and $36.9 million in fiscal 2010, 2009 and 2008, respectively. Payments for voluntary withdrawals included in contributions were approximately $17.4 million and $15.0 million in fiscal 2010 and fiscal 2009, respectively. See further discussion of Sysco's participation in multi-employer pension plans in Note 18, "Commitments and Contingencies."

In addition to receiving benefits upon retirement under the company's Retirement Plan, participants in the Management Incentive Plan (see "Management Incentive Compensation" in Note 15, "Share-Based Compensation") will receive benefits under a Supplemental Executive Retirement Plan (SERP). This plan is a nonqualified, unfunded supplementary retirement plan.

Funded Status (in part)

The funded status of Sysco's company-sponsored defined benefit plans is presented in the table below. The caption "Pension Benefits" in the tables below includes both the Retirement Plan and the SERP.

(In thousands)	Pension Benefits		Other Postretirement Plans	
	July 3, 2010	June 27, 2009	July 3, 2010	June 27, 2009
Change in benefit obligation:				
Benefit obligation at beginning of year	$1,551,944	$1,634,987	$ 7,197	$ 9,155
Service cost	66,650	80,899	328	490
Interest cost	119,593	113,715	562	624
Amendments	—	26,752	—	527
Recognized net actuarial loss (gain)	523,432	(262,164)	734	(3,813)
Total disbursements	(49,315)	(42,245)	(360)	214
Benefit obligation at end of year	2,212,304	1,551,944	8,461	7,197
Change in plan assets:				
Fair value of plan assets at beginning of year	1,244,085	1,526,572	—	—
Actual return on plan assets	174,269	(336,018)	—	—
Employer contribution	297,933	95,776	360	(214)
Total disbursements	(49,315)	(42,245)	(360)	214
Fair value of plan assets at end of year	1,666,972	1,244,085	—	—
Funded status at end of year	$ (545,332)	$ (307,859)	$(8,461)	$(7,197)

In order to meet a portion of its obligations under the SERP, Sysco maintains life insurance policies on the lives of the participants with carrying values of $149.5 million as of July 3, 2010 and $130.2 million as of June 27, 2009. These policies are not included as plan assets or in the funded status amounts in the tables above and below. Sysco is the sole owner and beneficiary of such policies. The projected benefit obligation for the SERP of $363.5 million and $334.6 million as of July 3, 2010 and June 27, 2009, respectively, was included in Other long-term liabilities on the balance sheet.

During fiscal 2009, the company merged participants from an under-funded multi-employer pension plan into its Retirement Plan and assumed $26.7 million of liabilities as part of its withdrawal agreement from this plan. These liabilities are due to the assumption of prior service costs related to the participants and their accrued benefits which were previously included in this multi-employer plan. This amount is reflected in the change in benefit obligation for Pension Benefits as of June 27, 2009 in the table above. See further discussion of this withdrawal under Multi-Employer Pension Plans in Note 18, "Commitments and Contingencies."

18. Commitments and Contingencies (in part)

Multi-Employer Pension Plans

Sysco contributes to several multi-employer defined benefit pension plans based on obligations arising under collective bargaining agreements covering union-represented employees. Approximately 11% of Sysco's current employees are participants in such multi-employer plans. In fiscal 2010, total contributions to these plans were approximately $51.5 million.

Sysco does not directly manage these multi-employer plans, which are generally managed by boards of trustees, half of whom are appointed by the unions and the other half by other employers contributing to the plan. Based upon the information available from plan administrators, management believes that several of these multi-employer plans are underfunded. In addition, the Pension Protection Act, enacted in August 2006, requires underfunded pension plans to improve their funding ratios within prescribed intervals based on the level of their underfunding. As a result, Sysco expects its contributions to these plans to increase in the future.

Under current law regarding multi-employer defined benefit plans, a plan's termination, Sysco's voluntary withdrawal, or the mass withdrawal of all contributing employers from any underfunded multi-employer defined benefit plan would require Sysco to make payments to the plan for Sysco's proportionate share of the multi-employer plan's unfunded vested liabilities. Generally, Sysco does not have the greatest share of liability among the participants in any of these plans. Based on the information available from plan administrators, which has valuation dates ranging from January 31, 2008 to June 30, 2009, Sysco estimates its share of withdrawal liability on most of the multi-employer plans in which it participates could have been as much as $183.0 million as of July 3, 2010, based on a voluntary withdrawal. The majority of the plans we participate in have a valuation date of calendar year-end. As such, the majority of the estimated withdrawal liability results from plans for which the valuation date was December 31, 2008; therefore, the company's estimated liability reflects the asset losses incurred by the financial markets as of that date. In general, the financial markets have improved since December 31, 2008; therefore, management believes Sysco's current share of the withdrawal liability could differ from this estimate. In addition, if a multi-employer defined benefit plan fails to satisfy certain minimum funding requirements, the IRS may impose a nondeductible excise tax of 5% on the amount of the accumulated funding deficiency for those employers contributing to the fund. As of July 3, 2010, Sysco had approximately $0.9 million in liabilities recorded in total related to certain multi-employer defined benefit plans for which Sysco's voluntary withdrawal had already occurred.

During fiscal 2008, the company obtained information that a multi-employer pension plan it participated in failed to satisfy minimum funding requirements for certain periods and concluded that it was probable that additional funding would be required as well as the payment of excise tax. As a result, during fiscal 2008, Sysco recorded a liability of approximately $16.5 million related to its share of the minimum funding requirements and related excise tax for these periods. During the first quarter of fiscal 2009, Sysco effectively withdrew from this multi-employer pension plan in an effort to secure benefits for Sysco's employees that were participants in the plan and to manage the company's exposure to this under-funded plan. Sysco agreed to pay $15.0 million to the plan, which included the minimum funding requirements.

In connection with this withdrawal agreement, Sysco merged participants from this plan into its company-sponsored Retirement Plan and assumed $26.7 million in liabilities. The payment to the plan was made in the second quarter of fiscal 2009. If this plan were to undergo a mass withdrawal, as defined by the Pension Benefit Guaranty Corporation, prior to September 2010, the company could have additional liability. The company does not currently believe a mass withdrawal from this plan prior to September 2010 is probable.

Sysco has experienced other instances triggering voluntary withdrawal from multi-employer pension plans. Total withdrawal liability provisions recorded include $2.9 million in fiscal 2010, $9.6 million in fiscal 2009 and $22.3 million in fiscal 2008.

Plan Amendment and Termination

3.63

KIMBERLY-CLARK CORPORATION (DEC)

NOTES TO CONSOLIDATED FINANCIAL STATEMENTS

Note 11. Employee Postretirement Benefits (in part)

Pension Plans (in part)

Substantially all regular employees in North America and the U.K. are covered by defined benefit pension plans (the "Principal Plans") and/or defined contribution retirement plans. Certain other subsidiaries have defined benefit pension plans or, in certain countries, termination pay plans covering substantially all regular employees. The funding policy for the qualified defined benefit plans in North America and the defined benefit plans in the U.K. is to contribute assets at least equal in amount to regulatory minimum requirements. Nonqualified U.S. plans providing pension benefits in excess of limitations imposed by the U.S. income tax code are not funded. Funding for the remaining defined benefit plans outside the U.S. is based on legal requirements, tax considerations, investment opportunities, and customary business practices in these countries.

In 2009, we took action with respect to our U.S. defined benefit pension and supplemental benefit plans to provide that no future compensation and benefit service will be accrued under these plans, other than for certain employees subject to collective bargaining agreements, for plan years after December 31, 2009 ("U.S. DB Pension Freeze").

The U.S. DB Pension Freeze resulted in a pension curtailment charge aggregating $21 million in 2009 due to the write-off of applicable unamortized prior service costs. In addition, the average remaining life expectancy of inactive participants rather than the average remaining service lives of active employees must be used in the amortization of actuarial gains and losses as a result of the freeze.

POSTEMPLOYMENT BENEFITS

RECOGNITION AND MEASUREMENT

3.64 FASB ASC 712, *Compensation—Nonretirement Postemployment Benefits*, requires that entities providing postemployment benefits to their employees accrue the cost of such benefits. FASB ASC 712 does not require that the amount of other postemployment benefits be disclosed.

PRESENTATION AND DISCLOSURE EXCERPTS

Postemployment Benefits

3.65

AIR PRODUCTS AND CHEMICALS, INC. (SEP)

NOTES TO THE CONSOLIDATED FINANCIAL STATEMENTS

(Millions of dollars, except for share data)

1. Major Accounting Policies (in part)

Postemployment Benefits

The Company has substantive ongoing severance arrangements. Termination benefits provided to employees as part of the global cost reduction plan (discussed in Note 5, Global Cost Reduction Plan) are consistent with termination benefits in previous, similar arrangements. Because the Company's plan met the definition of an ongoing benefit arrangement, a liability was recognized for termination benefits when probable and estimable. These criteria are met when management, with the appropriate level of authority, approves and commits to its plan of action for termination; the plan identifies the employees to be terminated and their related benefits; and the plan is to be completed within one year. During periods of operations where terminations are made on an as-needed basis, absent a detailed committed plan, terminations are accounted for on an individual basis and a liability is recognized when probable and estimable.

5. Global Cost Reduction Plan

2009 Plan

The 2009 results from continuing operations included a total charge of $298.2 ($200.3 after-tax, or $.94 per share) for the global cost reduction plan. In the first quarter of 2009, the Company announced the global cost reduction plan designed to lower its cost structure and better align its businesses to reflect rapidly declining economic conditions around the world. The 2009 first-quarter results included a charge of $174.2 ($116.1 after-tax, or $.55 per share). In the third quarter 2009, due to the continuing slow economic recovery, the Company committed to additional actions associated with its global cost reduction plan that resulted in a charge of $124.0 ($84.2 after-tax, or $.39 per share).

The total 2009 charge included $210.0 for severance and other benefits, including pension-related costs, associated with the elimination of approximately 2,550 positions from the Company's global workforce. The reductions were targeted at reducing overhead and infrastructure costs, reducing and refocusing elements of the Company's technology and business development spending, lowering its plant operating costs, and the closure of certain manufacturing facilities. The remainder of this charge, $88.2, was for business exits and asset management actions. Assets held for sale were written down to net realizable value, and an environmental liability of $16.0 was recognized. This environmental liability resulted from a decision to sell a production facility.

Business Segments

The global cost reduction plan charge recorded in 2009 was excluded from segment operating profit. The table below displays how this charge related to the businesses at the segment level *(in millions)*:

	Severance and Other Benefits	Asset Impairments/ Other Costs	Total
Merchant Gases	$127.5	$ 7.2	$134.7
Tonnage Gases	14.2	—	14.2
Electronics and Performance Materials	30.6	58.9	89.5
Equipment and Energy	37.7	22.1	59.8
2009 Charge	$210.0	$88.2	$298.2

During 2010, the Company revised its estimate of the costs associated with the 2009 global cost reduction plan. The unfavorable impact of additional severance and other benefits was primarily offset by favorable variances related to completed business exits and asset management actions. These adjustments to the charge were excluded from segment operating profit and did not have a material impact on any individual segment.

As of 30 September 2010, the planned actions associated with the global cost reduction plan were substantially completed with the exception of certain benefit payments associated with a small number of position eliminations. In addition, as part of the asset management actions included in the plan, the Company anticipates completing the sale of a facility by the end of calendar year 2010.

Accrual Balance

The following table summarizes changes to the carrying amount of the accrual for the global cost reduction plan *(in millions)*:

	Severance and Other Benefits	Asset Impairments/ Other Costs	Total
First quarter 2009 charge	$ 120.0	$ 54.2	$ 174.2
Third quarter 2009 charge	90.0	34.0	124.0
Environmental charge[A]	—	(16.0)	(16.0)
Noncash items	(33.8)[B]	(66.1)	(99.9)
Cash expenditures	(75.3)	(.9)	(76.2)
Currency translation adjustment	4.3	—	4.3
30 September 2009	$ 105.2	$ 5.2	$ 110.4
Adjustment to charge	7.6	(6.6)	1.0
Environmental charge[A]	—	1.5	1.5
Noncash items	(2.8)[B]	.1	(2.7)
Cash expenditures	(102.8)	(.2)	(103.0)
Currency translation adjustment	(5.3)	—	(5.3)
30 September 2010	$ 1.9	$ —	$ 1.9

[A] Reflected in accrual for environmental obligations. See Note 17, Commitments and Contingencies.
[B] Primarily pension-related costs, which are reflected in the accrual for pension benefits.

EMPLOYEE COMPENSATORY PLANS

RECOGNITION AND MEASUREMENT

3.66 FASB ASC 718, *Compensation—Stock Compensation*, establishes accounting and reporting standards for share-based payment transactions with employees, including awards classified as equity, awards classified as liabilities, employee stock ownership plans, and employee stock purchase plans. FASB ASC 718 requires that share-based payment transactions be accounted for using a fair-value-based method. Thus, entities are required to recognize the cost of employee services received in exchange for award of equity instruments based on the grant-date fair value of those awards or the fair value of the liabilities incurred. FASB ASC 718 provides clarification and expanded guidance in several areas, including measuring fair value, classifying an award as equity or a liability, and attributing compensation cost to reporting periods.

PRESENTATION AND DISCLOSURE EXCERPTS

Stock Option Plans

3.67

J. C. PENNEY COMPANY, INC. (JAN)

NOTES TO CONSOLIDATED FINANCIAL STATEMENTS

14) Stock-Based Compensation (in part)

At our Annual Meeting of Stockholders on May 15, 2009, our stockholders approved the J. C Penney Company, Inc. 2009 Long-Term Incentive Plan (2009 Plan), reserving 13.1 million shares for future grants (8.5 million newly authorized shares, plus up to 4.6 million reserved but unissued shares from our prior 2005 Equity Compensation Plan (2005 Plan)). In addition, shares underlying any outstanding stock award or stock option grant canceled prior to vesting or exercise become available for use under the 2009 Plan. The 2005 Plan was terminated on May 15, 2009, except for outstanding awards. Subsequent awards have been and will be granted under the 2009 Plan.

The 2009 Plan allows for grants of stock options, stock appreciation rights and stock awards (collectively, Equity Awards) and cash incentive awards (together, Awards) to employees (associates) and Equity Awards to our non-employee members of the Board of Directors. Under the Plan, Awards to associates are subject to such conditions as continued employment, qualifying termination, passage of time and/or satisfaction of performance criteria as specified in the Plan or set by the Human Resources and Compensation Committee of the Board. As of January 30, 2010, 14.2 million shares of stock were available for future grant under the 2009 Plan, which includes approximately 1.3 million shares from awards cancelled subsequent to May 15, 2009.

Associate stock options and restricted stock awards typically vest over periods ranging from one to three years. The exercise price of stock options and the market value of restricted stock awards are determined based on the closing market price of our common stock on the date of grant. The 2009 Plan does not permit awarding stock options below grant-date market value nor does it allow any repricing subsequent to the date of grant. Associate stock options have a maximum term of 10 years.

Over the past three years, our stock option and restricted stock award grants have averaged about 1.8% of total outstanding stock. We issue new shares upon the exercise of stock options, granting of restricted shares and vesting of restricted stock units.

Stock-Based Compensation Cost

($ in millions)	2009	2008	2007
Stock options	$28	$29	$23
Stock awards (shares and units)	12	18	22
Total stock-based compensation cost	$40	$47	$45
Total income tax benefit recognized for stock-based compensation arrangements	$15	$18	$18

Stock Options

On March 16, 2009, we made our annual grant of stock options covering approximately 3,873,000 shares to associates at an option price of $16.09, with a fair value of $6.27 per option.

As of January 30, 2010, options to purchase approximately 13.6 million shares of common stock were outstanding. If all options were exercised, common stock outstanding would increase by 5.7%. Additional information regarding options outstanding as of January 30, 2010 follows:

(Shares in thousands; price is weighted-average exercise price)	Exercisable			Unexercisable			Total Outstanding		
	Shares	%	Price	Shares	%	Price	Shares	%	Price
In-the-money	588	8%	$19	4,244	65%	$16	4,832	36%	$16
Out-of-the-money[1]	6,465	92%	49	2,264	35%	44	8,729	64%	48
Total options outstanding	7,053	100%	47	6,508	100%	25	13,561	100%	36

[1] Out-of-the-money options are those with an exercise price above the closing price of JCPenney common stock of $24.83 as of January 30, 2010.

The following table summarizes stock options outstanding as of January 30, 2010, as well as activity during the year then ended:

	Shares (In Thousands)	Weighted-Average Exercise Price Per Share	Weighted-Average Remaining Contractual Term (In Years)	Aggregate Intrinsic Value ($ in Millions)[1]
Outstanding at January 31, 2009	11,862	$42		
Granted	3,882	16		
Exercised	(199)	24		
Forfeited/canceled	(1,984)	33		
Outstanding at January 30, 2010	13,561	36	6.9	$42
Exercisable at January 30, 2010	7,053	47	5.1	4

[1] The intrinsic value of a stock option is the amount by which the market value of the underlying stock exceeds the exercise price of the option at year end.

Cash proceeds, tax benefits and intrinsic value related to total stock options exercised are provided in the following table:

($ in millions)	2009	2008	2007
Proceeds from stock options exercised	$ 4	$4	$45
Intrinsic value of stock options exercised	1	2	47
Tax benefit related to stock-based compensation	2	2	18
Excess tax benefits realized on stock-based compensation	—	1	17

As of January 30, 2010, we had $34 million of unrecognized and unearned compensation expense, net of estimated forfeitures, for stock options not yet vested, which will be recognized as expense over the remaining weighted-average vesting period of approximately one year.

Stock Option Valuation

Valuation Method. We estimate the fair value of stock option awards on the date of grant using a binomial lattice model. We believe that the binomial lattice model is a more accurate model for valuing employee stock options since it better reflects the impact of stock price changes on option exercise behavior.

Expected Term. Our expected option term represents the average period that we expect stock options to be outstanding and is determined based on our historical experience, giving consideration to contractual terms, vesting schedules, anticipated stock prices and expected future behavior of option holders.

Expected Volatility. Our expected volatility is based on a blend of the historical volatility of JCPenney stock combined with an estimate of the implied volatility derived from exchange traded options. Beginning in 2008, we increased the weighting of the historical volatility component of our expected volatility assumption due to historical volatility being more representative of our current business model. Our historical volatility no longer reflects the volatility associated with the Eckerd drugstore business, which was sold in mid-2004.

Risk-Free Interest Rate. Our risk-free interest rate is based on zero-coupon U.S. Treasury yields in effect at the date of grant with the same period as the expected option life.

Expected Dividend Yield. The dividend assumption is based on our current expectations about our dividend policy.

Our weighted-average fair value of stock options at grant date was $6.29 in 2009, $11.74 in 2008 and $19.85 in 2007 using the binomial lattice valuation model and the following assumptions:

	2009	2008	2007
Weighted-average expected option term	4.5 years	4.6 years	4.5 years
Weighted-average expected volatility	57.0%	44.7%	25.0%
Weighted-average risk-free interest rate	1.8%	2.7%	4.5%
Weighted-average expected dividend yield	3.3%	2.0%	0.9%
Expected dividend yield range	1.8%–5.0%	1.2%–5.6%	—

3.68

JOHNSON CONTROLS, INC. (SEP)

(In millions, except per share data)

NOTES TO CONSOLIDATED FINANCIAL STATEMENTS

12. Stock-Based Compensation (in part)

Effective October 1, 2005, the Company adopted ASC 718, "Stock Compensation," using the modified prospective method. The modified prospective method requires compensation cost to be recognized beginning on the effective date (a) for all share-based payments granted after the effective date and (b) for all awards granted to employees prior to the effective date of ASC 718 that remain unvested on the effective date. The cumulative impact of adopting ASC 718 was not significant to the Company's operating results since the Company had previously adopted certain provisions of this guidance.

The Company has three share-based compensation plans, which are described below. The compensation cost charged against income for those plans was approximately $52 million, $27 million and $29 million for the fiscal years ended September 30, 2010, 2009 and 2008, respectively. The total income tax benefit recognized in the consolidated statements of income for share-based compensation arrangements was approximately $21 million, $11 million and $11 million for the fiscal years ended September 30, 2010, 2009 and 2008, respectively.

Prior to the adoption of ASC 718, the Company applied a nominal vesting approach for employee stock-based compensation awards with retirement eligible provisions. Under the nominal vesting approach, the Company recognized compensation cost over the vesting period and, if the employee retired before the end of the vesting period, the Company recognized any remaining unrecognized compensation cost at the date of retirement. For stock-based payments issued after the adoption of ASC 718, the Company applies a non-substantive vesting period approach whereby expense is accelerated for those employees that receive awards and are eligible to retire prior to the award vesting. Had the Company applied the non-substantive vesting period approach prior to the adoption of ASC 718, an approximate $2 million reduction of pre-tax compensation cost would have been recognized for the year ended September 30, 2008. There would have been no impact for the years ended September 30, 2010 and 2009.

Stock Option Plan

The Company's 2007 Stock Option Plan, as amended (the Plan), which is shareholder-approved, permits the grant of stock options to its employees for up to approximately 41 million shares of new common stock as of September 30, 2010. Option awards are granted with an exercise price equal to the market price of the Company's stock at the date of grant; those option awards vest between two and three years after the grant date and expire ten years from the grant date (approximately 25 million shares of common stock remained available to be granted at September 30, 2010).

The fair value of each option award is estimated on the date of grant using a Black-Scholes option valuation model that uses the assumptions noted in the following table. Expected volatilities are based on the historical volatility of the Company's stock and other factors. The Company uses historical data to estimate option exercises and employee terminations within the valuation model. The expected term of options represents the period of time that options granted are expected to be outstanding. The risk-free rate for periods during the contractual life of the option is based on the U.S. Treasury yield curve in effect at the time of grant.

	Year Ended September 30		
	2010	2009	2008
Expected life of option (years)	4.3–5.0	4.2–4.5	4.5–5.25
Risk-free interest rate	1.91%–2.20%	2.57%–2.68%	4.06%–4.23%
Expected volatility of the company's stock	40.00%	28.00%	22.00%
Expected dividend yield on the company's stock	1.73%	1.52%	1.55%

A summary of stock option activity at September 30, 2010, and changes for the year then ended, is presented below:

	Weighted Average Option Price	Shares Subject to Option	Weighted Average Remaining Contractual Life (Years)	Aggregate Intrinsic Value (In Millions)
Outstanding, September 30, 2009	$23.62	33,244,637		
Granted	24.89	5,382,100		
Exercised	18.97	(3,095,823)		
Forfeited or expired	28.58	(372,805)		
Outstanding, September 30, 2010	$24.17	35,158,109	5.8	$253
Exercisable, September 30, 2010	$22.23	24,386,551	4.6	$217

The weighted-average grant-date fair value of options granted during the fiscal years ended September 30, 2010, 2009 and 2008 was $7.70, $6.68 and $9.08, respectively.

The total intrinsic value of options exercised during the fiscal years ended September 30, 2010, 2009 and 2008 was approximately $33 million, $4 million and $45 million, respectively.

In conjunction with the exercise of stock options granted, the Company received cash payments for the fiscal years ended September 30, 2010, 2009 and 2008 of approximately $52 million, $8 million and $34 million, respectively.

The Company has elected to utilize the alternative transition method for calculating the tax effects of stock-based compensation. The alternative transition method includes computational guidance to establish the beginning balance of the additional paid-in capital pool (APIC Pool) related to the tax effects of employee stock-based compensation, and a simplified method to determine the subsequent impact on the APIC Pool for employee stock-based compensation awards that are vested and outstanding upon adoption of ASC 718. The tax benefit from the exercise of stock options, which is recorded in capital in excess of par value, was $7 million, $1 million and $19 million for the fiscal years ended September 30, 2010, 2009 and 2008. The Company does not settle equity instruments granted under share-based payment arrangements for cash.

At September 30, 2010, the Company had approximately $26 million of total unrecognized compensation cost related to nonvested share-based compensation arrangements granted under the Plan. That cost is expected to be recognized over a weighted-average period of 0.8 years.

Stock Award Plans

3.69

CATERPILLAR INC. (DEC)

NOTES TO CONSOLIDATED FINANCIAL STATEMENTS

2. Stock-Based Compensation

Our stock-based compensation plans primarily provide for the granting of stock options, stock-settled stock appreciation rights (SARs) and restricted stock units (RSUs) to Officers and other key employees, as well as non-employee Directors. Stock options permit a holder to buy Caterpillar stock at the stock's price when the option was granted. SARs permit a holder the right to receive the value in shares of the appreciation in Caterpillar stock that occurred from the date the right was granted up to the date of exercise. A restricted stock unit (RSU) is an agreement to issue shares of Caterpillar stock at the time of vesting.

Our long-standing practices and policies specify all stock-based compensation awards are approved by the Compensation Committee (the Committee) of the Board of Directors on the date of grant. The stock-based award approval process specifies the number of awards granted, the terms of the award and the grant date. The same terms and conditions are consistently applied to all employee grants, including Officers. The Committee approves all individual Officer grants. The number of stock-based compensation awards included in an individual's award is determined based on the methodology approved by the Committee. In 2007, under the terms of the Caterpillar Inc. 2006 Long-Term Incentive Plan (approved by stockholders in June of 2006), the Compensation Committee approved the exercise price methodology to be the closing price of the Company stock on the date of the grant.

Common stock issued from Treasury stock under the plans totaled 12,612,514 for 2010, 3,571,268 for 2009 and 4,807,533 for 2008.

The 2010, 2009 and 2008 awards generally vest three years after the date of grant. At grant, SARs and option awards have a term life of ten years. Upon separation from service, if the participant is 55 years of age or older with more than ten years of service, the participant meets the criteria for a "Long Service Separation." If the "Long Service Separation" criteria are met, the vested options/SARs will have a life that is the lesser of 10 years from the original grant date or five years from the separation date.

Our stock-based compensation plans allow for the immediate vesting upon separation for employees who meet the criteria for a "Long Service Separation" and who have fulfilled the requisite service period of six months. Compensation expense is recognized over the period from the grant date to the end date of the requisite service period for employees who meet the immediate vesting upon retirement requirements. For those employees who become eligible for immediate vesting upon retirement subsequent to the requisite service period and prior to the completion of the vesting period, compensation expense is recognized over the period from grant date to the date eligibility is achieved.

Accounting guidance on share-based payments requires companies to estimate the fair value of options/SARs on the date of grant using an option-pricing model. The fair value of the option/SAR grant was estimated using a lattice-based option-pricing model. The lattice-based option-pricing model considers a range of assumptions related to volatility, risk-free interest rate and historical employee behavior. Expected volatility was based on historical and current implied volatilities from traded options on our stock. The risk-free rate was based on U.S. Treasury security yields at the time of grant. The weighted-average dividend yield was based on historical information. The expected life was determined from the lattice-based model. The lattice-based model incorporated exercise and post vesting forfeiture assumptions based on analysis of historical data. The following table provides the assumptions used in determining the fair value of the stock-based awards for the years ended December 31, 2010, 2009 and 2008, respectively.

	Grant Year		
	2010	**2009**	**2008**
Weighted-average dividend yield	2.3%	3.1%	1.9%
Weighted-average volatility	36.4%	36.0%	27.1%
Range of volatilities	35.2–51.8%	35.8–61.0%	27.1–29.0%
Range of risk-free interest rates	0.32–3.61%	0.17–2.99%	1.60–3.64%
Weighted-average expected lives	7 years	8 years	8 years

The fair value of the RSU grant was determined by reducing the stock price on the day of grant by the present value of the estimated dividends to be paid during the vesting period. The estimated dividends are based on Caterpillar's weighted-average dividend yield.

The amount of stock-based compensation expense capitalized for the years ended December 31, 2010, 2009 and 2008 did not have a significant impact on our financial statements.

At December 31, 2010, there was $134 million of total unrecognized compensation cost from stock-based compensation arrangements granted under the plans, which is related to non-vested stock-based awards. The compensation expense is expected to be recognized over a weighted-average period of approximately 1.9 years.

Please refer to Tables I and II below for additional information on our stock-based awards.

Table I—Financial Information Related to Stock-based Compensation

	2010		2009		2008	
	Shares	Weighted-Average Exercise Price	Shares	Weighted-Average Exercise Price	Shares	Weighted-Average Exercise Price
Stock options/SARs activity:						
Outstanding at beginning of year	63,082,787	$44.24	60,398,074	$45.68	60,855,854	$42.18
Granted to officers and key employees[1]	7,556,481	$57.85	6,823,227	$22.17	4,886,601	$73.20
Exercised	(12,568,232)	$32.83	(3,906,785)	$28.13	(5,006,435)	$30.04
Forfeited/expired	(188,038)	$43.64	(231,729)	$38.05	(337,946)	$46.45
Outstanding at end of year	57,882,998	$48.50	63,082,787	$44.24	60,398,074	$45.68
Exercisable at year-end	41,658,033	$48.23	48,256,847	$43.14	43,083,319	$35.81
RSUs activity:						
Outstanding at beginning of year	4,531,545		2,673,474		1,253,326	
Granted to officers and key employees	1,711,771		2,185,674		1,490,645	
Granted to outside directors	—		—		20,878	
Vested	(1,538,047)		(286,413)		(61,158)	
Forfeited	(55,028)		(41,190)		(30,217)	
Outstanding at end of year	4,650,241		4,531,545		2,673,474	

Stock options/SARs outstanding and exercisable:

	Outstanding				Exercisable			
Exercise Prices	# Outstanding at 12/31/10	Weighted-Average Remaining Contractual Life (Years)	Weighted-Average Exercise Price	Aggregate Intrinsic Value[2]	# Outstanding at 12/31/10	Weighted-Average Remaining Contractual Life (Years)	Weighted-Average Exercise Price	Aggregate Intrinsic Value[2]
$22.17–25.36	8,716,831	6.49	$22.96	$ 616	3,189,844	3.58	$24.32	$ 221
$26.03–29.43	5,614,162	2.23	27.11	373	5,614,162	2.23	27.11	373
$38.63–40.64	9,355,978	3.44	38.65	514	9,355,978	3.44	38.65	514
$44.90–57.85	16,257,410	6.47	51.28	688	9,244,580	4.42	46.30	437
$63.04–73.20	17,938,617	5.92	70.22	420	14,253,469	5.60	69.45	344
	57,882,998		$48.50	$2,611	41,658,033		$48.23	$1,889

[1] Of the 7,556,481 awards granted during the year ended December 31, 2010, 7,125,210 were SARs. Of the 6,823,227 awards granted during the year ended December 31, 2009, 6,260,647 were SARs. Of the 4,886,601 awards granted during the year ended December 31, 2008, 4,476,095 were SARs.

[2] The difference between a stock award's exercise price and the underlying stock's market price at December 31, 2010, for awards with market price greater than the exercise price. Amounts are in millions of dollars.

The computations of weighted-average exercise prices and aggregate intrinsic values are not applicable to RSUs since an RSU represents an agreement to issue shares of stock at the time of vesting. At December 31, 2010, there were 4,650,241 outstanding RSUs with a weighted average remaining contractual life of 1.2 years.

Table II—Additional Stock-based Award Information

(Dollars in millions except per share data)	2010	2009	2008
Stock Options/SARs Activity:			
Weighted-average fair value per share of stock awards granted	$22.31	$ 7.10	$22.32
Intrinsic value of stock awards exercised	$ 518	$ 77	$ 232
Fair value of stock awards vested	$ 119	$ 213	$ 18
Cash received from stock awards exercised	$ 325	$ 89	$ 130
RSUs activity:			
Weighted-average fair value per share of stock awards granted	$53.35	$20.22	$69.17
Fair value of stock awards vested	$ 99	$ 10	$ 4

Before tax, stock-based compensation expense for 2010, 2009 and 2008 was $226 million, $132 million and $194 million, respectively, with a corresponding income tax benefit of $73 million, $42 million and $62 million, respectively. Included in the 2010 pre-tax stock-based compensation expense was $19 million relating to the modification of awards resulting from separations due to the streamlining of our corporate structure as announced in the second quarter.

In accordance with guidance on share-based payments, we classify stock-based compensation within cost of goods sold, selling, general and administrative expenses and research and development expenses corresponding to the same line item as the cash compensation paid to respective employees, officers and non-employee directors.

We currently use shares in treasury stock to satisfy share award exercises.

The cash tax benefits realized from stock awards exercised for December 31, 2010, 2009 and 2008 were $188 million, $26 million and $60 million, respectively. We use the direct only method and tax law ordering approach to calculate the tax effects of stock-based compensation. In certain jurisdictions, tax deductions for exercises of stock-based awards did not generate a cash benefit. A tax benefit of approximately $30 million will be recorded in APIC when these deductions reduce our future income taxes payable.

Savings and Investment Plans

3.70

DELL INC. (JAN)

NOTES TO CONSOLIDATED FINANCIAL STATEMENTS

Note 13—Stock-Based Compensation and Benefit Plans (in part)

Employee Benefits

401(k) Plan—Dell has a defined contribution retirement plan (the "401(k) Plan") that complies with Section 401(k) of the Internal Revenue Code. Substantially all employees in the U.S.

are eligible to participate in the 401(k) Plan. Effective January 1, 2008, Dell matches 100% of each participant's voluntary contributions, subject to a maximum contribution of 5% of the participant's compensation, and participants vest immediately in all Dell contributions to the 401(k) Plan. Dell's contributions during Fiscal 2010, 2009, and 2008 were $91 million, $93 million, and $76 million, respectively. Dell's contributions are invested according to each participant's elections in the investment options provided under the Plan. Investment options include Dell common stock, but neither participant nor Dell contributions are required to be invested in Dell common stock. During Fiscal 2010, Dell also contributed $4.2 million to Perot Systems' 401(k) Plan after the acquisition of the company on November 3, 2009.

Employee Stock Purchase Plans (ESPP)

3.71

COMCAST CORPORATION (DEC)

NOTES TO CONSOLIDATED FINANCIAL STATEMENTS

Note 15. Share-Based Compensation (in part)

Our approach to long-term incentive compensation includes the awarding of stock options and RSUs to certain employees and directors. We grant these awards under various plans. Additionally, through our employee stock purchase plan, employees are able to purchase shares of Comcast Class A common stock at a discount through payroll deductions.

Recognized Share-Based Compensation Expense (in part)

(In millions)	Year Ended December 31		
	2010	2009	2008
Stock options	$103	$103	$ 99
Restricted share units	136	93	96
Employee stock purchase plan	12	13	13
Total	$251	$209	$208
Tax benefit	$ 89	$ 73	$ 71

Employee Stock Purchase Plan

We maintain an employee stock purchase plan that offers employees the opportunity to purchase shares of Class A common stock at a 15% discount. We recognize the fair value of the discount associated with shares purchased under the plan as share-based compensation expense. The employee cost associated with participation in the plan was satisfied with payroll deductions of approximately $50 million, $48 million and $50 million in 2010, 2009 and 2008, respectively.

Deferred Compensation Plans

3.72

GENERAL CABLE CORPORATION (DEC)

NOTES TO CONSOLIDATED FINANCIAL STATEMENTS

13. Total Equity (in part)

The Company maintains a deferred compensation plan ("Deferred Compensation Plan"). This plan is available to directors and certain officers and managers of the Company. The plan allows participants to defer all or a portion of their directors' fees and/or salary and annual bonuses, as applicable, and it permits participants to elect to contribute and defer all or any portion of their nonvested stock, restricted stock and stock awards. All deferrals to the participants' accounts vest immediately; Company contributions vest according to the vesting schedules in the qualified plan and nonvested stock and restricted stock vests according to the schedule designated by the award. The Company makes matching and retirement contributions (currently equal to 6%) of compensation paid over the maximum allowed for qualified pension benefits, whether or not the employee elects to defer any compensation. The Deferred Compensation Plan does not have dollar limits on tax-deferred contributions. The assets of the Deferred Compensation Plan are held in a Rabbi Trust ("Trust") and, therefore, are available to satisfy the claims of the Company's creditors in the event of bankruptcy or insolvency of the Company. Participants have the right to request that their account balance be determined by reference to specified investment alternatives (with the exception of the portion of the account which consists of deferred nonvested and subsequently vested stock and restricted stock). With certain exceptions, these investment alternatives are the same alternatives offered to participants in the General Cable Retirement and Savings Plan for Salaried Associates. In addition, participants have the right to request that the Plan Administrator re-allocate the deferral among available investment alternatives; provided, however that the Plan Administrator is not required to honor such requests. Distributions from the plan are generally made upon the participants' termination as a director and/or employee, as applicable, of the Company. Participants receive payments from the plan in cash, either as a lump sum payment or through equal annual installments from between one and ten years, except for the nonvested and subsequently vested stock and restricted stock, which the participants receive in shares of General Cable stock.

The Company accounts for its Deferred Compensation Plan in accordance with ASC 710 *Compensation—General*, as it relates to arrangements where amounts earned are held in rabbi trusts. Assets of the Trust, other than the nonvested and subsequently vested stock and restricted stock of the Company, are invested in funds covering a variety of securities and investment strategies, approximately 87% are invested in mutual funds and the remaining 13% are invested in a General Cable stock fund. Mutual funds available to participants are publicly quoted and reported at market value. The Company accounts for these investments as trading securities in accordance with ASC 320 *Investments—Debt and Equity Securities*. The Trust also holds nonvested and subsequently vested stock and restricted stock shares of the Company. The Company's nonvested and subsequently vested and restricted stock that are held by the Trust are accounted for in additional paid-in capital as discussed in ASC 718 *Compensation—Stock Compensation*.

The market value of mutual fund investments, nonvested and subsequently vested stock and restricted stock in the Trust was $39.3 million and $33.6 million as of December 31, 2010 and 2009, respectively. The market value of the assets held by the Trust, exclusive of the market value of the shares of the Company's nonvested and subsequently vested restricted stock, restricted stock units held in the deferred compensation plan and Company stock investments by participants' elections, at December 31, 2010 and December 31, 2009 was $16.0 million and $14.2 million, respectively, and is classified as "other non-current assets" in the consolidated balance sheets. Amounts payable to the plan participants at December 31, 2010 and 2009, excluding the market value of the shares of the Company's nonvested and subsequently vested restricted stock and restricted stock units held, was $18.3 million and $16.0 million, respectively, and is classified as "other liabilities" in the consolidated balance sheets.

In accordance with ASC 710, all market value fluctuations of the Trust assets, exclusive of the shares of nonvested and subsequently vested stock and restricted stock of the Company, are effectively offset by changes in the market value of the deferred compensation liability held by the Trust, which are included as compensation expense in the consolidated statements of operations. Prior to 2009, management had classified the mutual fund assets as available for sale; as such, changes in the value of these investments were recorded in accumulated other comprehensive income. The total aggregate net gain in other comprehensive income was $7.3 million for the year ended December 31, 2009.

Incentive Compensation Plans

3.73

QUANTUM CORPORATION (MAR)

NOTES TO CONSOLIDATED FINANCIAL STATEMENTS

Note 2. Financial Statement Presentation and Summary of Significant Accounting Policies (in part)

Share-Based Compensation

We account for share-based compensation using the Black-Scholes option pricing model to estimate the fair value of share-based awards at the date of grant. The Black-Scholes model requires the use of highly subjective assumptions, including expected life, expected volatility and expected risk-free rate of return. Other reasonable assumptions could provide differing results. We calculate a forfeiture rate to estimate the share-based awards that will ultimately vest based on types of awards and historical experience. Additionally, for awards which are performance based, we make estimates as to the probability of the underlying performance being achieved.

Note 10. Stock Incentive Plans and Share-Based Compensation (in part)

Description of Stock Incentive Plans

Long-Term Incentive Plan

We have a Long-Term Incentive Plan (the "Plan") that provides for the issuance of stock options, stock appreciation rights, stock purchase rights and long-term performance awards to our employees, officers and affiliates. The Plan has authorized 76.5 million shares of stock of which 13.3 million shares of stock were available for grant as of March 31, 2010. There are 29.7 million options and restricted shares outstanding under the Long-Term Incentive Plan.

Beginning in the first quarter of fiscal 2007, under the Plan we began granting restricted stock units with a zero purchase price in place of stock options in most cases to our existing employees. We continued to grant stock options to our existing employees in certain circumstances. Newly hired employees are typically granted stock options under the Plan. In fiscal 2010, due to a combination of factors including our share price at the beginning of the fiscal year, we primarily granted stock options to our existing employees. Stock options granted to existing employees in fiscal 2010 and fiscal 2009 generally vest annually over three years and have contractual terms of seven years. Stock options granted to newly hired employees in fiscal 2010 and fiscal 2009 generally vest 25% on the first anniversary of the grant date with the remainder vesting monthly at the rate of 1/48th over the following three years and have contractual terms of seven years. Grants in prior fiscal years typically had four year vesting terms and contractual terms of seven years while grants prior to fiscal 2004 had contractual terms of ten years. Options under the Plan are granted at prices determined by the Board of Directors, but at not less than the fair market value. The majority of restricted stock units granted in fiscal 2010 and 2009 vest over two years and restricted stock awards and units ("restricted stock") granted prior to fiscal 2009 generally vest over two to four years. Both options and restricted stock granted under the Plan are subject to forfeiture if employment terminates. In fiscal 2007, we granted restricted stock with both market and service vesting conditions that, upon meeting certain market conditions over one and two year periods from initial grant, vested over the two years following the grant date.

Supplemental Stock Plan

We have a Supplemental Stock Plan (the "SSOP"), which was not approved by our stockholders, that provided for the issuance of stock options and stock purchase rights to our employees and consultants. The SSOP was terminated effective April 1, 2003, from which time no new stock options or stock purchase rights have been or will be granted under the SSOP. Outstanding stock options and stock purchase rights granted under the SSOP prior to April 1, 2003 remained outstanding and continue to be governed by the terms and conditions of the SSOP. Options under the SSOP generally vested over two to four years and expire ten years after the grant date. Options granted under the SSOP are subject to forfeiture if employment terminates. There are 0.9 million options outstanding under the SSOP as of March 31, 2010, which expire at various times through January 2013.

Assumed Stock Option Plans

During the second quarter of fiscal 2007, in connection with our acquisition of ADIC, we assumed 14.7 million outstanding stock options granted under the four stock option plans of ADIC ("assumed option plans"). Outstanding options are governed by the Agreement and Plan of Merger ("Merger Agreement") and generally vest over four years from initial ADIC grant. No additional options will be granted under these assumed option plans. There are 4.3 million options outstanding under the assumed stock option plans as of March 31, 2010 which expire at various times through May 2015.

Other Stock Option Plans

We have other stock option plans (the "Other Plans") under which stock options, stock appreciation rights, stock purchase rights, restricted stock awards and long-term performance awards to our employees, consultants, officers and affiliates have been authorized. Restricted stock granted under the Other Plans generally vests over two to three years. Options granted under the Other Plans generally vest over one to four years and expire seven years after the grant date. Many of the Other Plans have been terminated. Outstanding stock options and stock purchase rights granted under those certain Other Plans that have been terminated remain outstanding and continue to be governed by the terms and conditions of the respective other stock option plan. Terminated plans included in Other Plans typically granted options which generally expire ten years from grant date. Options and restricted stock granted under all of the Other Plans are subject to forfeiture if employment terminates. Options under the Other Plans are granted at prices determined by the Board of Directors, but at not less than the fair market value. We have 6.1 million shares authorized under the Other Plans, of which 1.5 million options and restricted shares are outstanding, and 1.1 million shares were available for grant.

Stock Purchase Plan

We have an employee stock purchase plan (the "Purchase Plan") that allows for the purchase of stock at 85% of fair market value at the date of grant or the exercise date, whichever value is less. The Purchase Plan is qualified under Section 423 of the Internal Revenue Code. Under the Purchase Plan, rights to purchase shares are granted during the second and fourth quarter of each fiscal year. There were 9.2 million shares available for issuance as of March 31, 2010.

During fiscal 2009, our Board of Directors cancelled rights to purchase shares under our Purchase Plan for the fourth quarter of fiscal 2009 and for fiscal 2010. On January 1, 2010, the Purchase Plan was reinstated and amended to set the maximum number of shares available in any one offering period to no more than two million shares. Employees purchased 1.9 million shares and 2.6 million shares of common stock under the Purchase Plan in fiscal 2009 and 2008, respectively. The weighted-average price of stock purchased under the Purchase Plan was $1.37 and $2.08 in fiscal 2009 and 2008, respectively.

Determining Fair Value

Stock Options

We use the Black-Scholes option valuation model for estimating fair value of stock options granted under our plans and rights to acquire stock granted under our Purchase Plan.

We amortize the fair value of stock options on a ratable basis over the requisite service periods, which are generally the vesting periods. The expected life of awards granted represents the period of time that they are expected to be outstanding. We determine the expected life based on historical experience with similar awards, giving consideration to the contractual terms, exercise patterns and post-vesting forfeitures. We estimate volatility based on the historical volatility of our common stock over the most recent period corresponding with the estimated expected life of the award. We base the risk-free interest rate used in the Black-Scholes option valuation model on the implied yield currently available on U.S. Treasury zero-coupon issues with an equivalent term equal to the expected life of the award. We have not paid any cash dividends on our common stock and do not anticipate paying any cash dividends in the foreseeable future. Consequently, we use an expected dividend yield of zero. We use historical data to estimate pre-vesting option forfeitures and record share-based compensation for those awards that are expected to vest. We adjust share-based compensation for changes to the estimate of expected equity award forfeitures based on actual forfeiture experience. The effect of adjusting the forfeiture rate is recognized in the period the forfeiture estimate is changed.

The weighted-average estimated fair values and the assumptions used in calculating such values for stock options during each fiscal period are as follows:

	For the Year Ended March 31		
	2010	2009	2008
Option life (in years)	3.9	4.0	3.8
Risk-free interest rate	2.05%	2.54%	4.51%
Stock price volatility	107.67%	56.59%	44.54%
Dividend yield	—	—	—
Weighted-average grant date fair value	$ 0.73	$ 0.66	$ 1.24

The above assumptions were used to calculate the fair value of options granted under the Long-Term Incentive Plan and Other Plans.

Restricted Stock

The fair value of our restricted stock is the intrinsic value as of the grant date.

Stock Purchase Plan

Under the Purchase Plan, rights to purchase shares are granted during the second and fourth quarter of each fiscal year. Due to reinstatement of the Purchase Plan on January 1, 2010, rights to purchase shares were granted in February 2010 and such shares will be purchased in August 2010, or the second quarter of fiscal 2011. The weighted-average fair values and the assumptions used in calculating fair values during each fiscal period are as follows:

	For the Year Ended March 31		
	2010	2009	2008
Option life (in years)	0.50	0.50	0.50
Risk-free interest rate	0.15%	2.84%	3.93%
Stock price volatility	69.14%	60.98%	48.49%
Dividend yield	—	—	—
Weighted-average grant date fair value	$ 0.82	$ 0.81	$ 0.79

Share-Based Compensation Expense

The following tables summarize share-based compensation expense (in thousands):

	For the Year Ended March 31		
	2010	2009	2008
Share-based compensation expense included in operations:			
Cost of revenue	$1,366	$ 1,419	$ 1,929
Research and development	2,373	2,722	3,778
Sales and marketing	2,581	2,695	3,269
General and administrative	3,469	3,756	5,022
Total share-based compensation expense	$9,789	$10,592	$13,998

	For the Year Ended March 31		
	2010	2009	2008
Share-based compensation by type of award:			
Stock options	$3,633	$ 3,450	$ 5,911
Restricted stock	5,878	6,447	6,318
Stock purchase plan	278	695	1,769
Total share-based compensation expense	$9,789	$10,592	$13,998

The total share-based compensation cost capitalized as part of inventory as of March 31, 2010 and 2009 was not material. During fiscal 2010, 2009 and 2008, no tax benefit was realized for the tax deduction from option exercises and other awards due to our net operating losses and tax benefit carryforwards.

As of March 31, 2010, there was $6.9 million of total unrecognized compensation cost related to stock options granted under our plans. This unrecognized compensation cost is expected to be recognized over a weighted-average period of 2.0 years. Total intrinsic value of options exercised for the years ended March 31, 2010, 2009 and 2008 was $1.9 million, $26,000 and $5.4 million, respectively. We settle stock option exercises by issuing additional common shares.

As of March 31, 2010, there was $4.3 million of total unrecognized compensation cost related to nonvested restricted stock granted under our plans. The unrecognized compensation cost for restricted stock is expected to be recognized over a weighted-average period of 1.0 years. Total fair value of awards released during the years ended March 31, 2010, 2009 and 2008 was $3.1 million, $2.6 million and $4.3 million, respectively, based on the fair value of our common stock on the date of award release. We issue additional common shares upon vesting of restricted stock units.

Stock Activity

Stock Options

A summary of activity relating to all of our stock option plans is as follows (options and intrinsic value in thousands):

	Options	Weighted-Average Exercise Price	Weighted-Average Remaining Contractual Term	Aggregate Intrinsic Value
Outstanding as of March 31, 2007	36,259	$ 3.62		
Granted	4,985	3.15		
Exercised	(5,847)	2.21		
Forfeited	(6,947)	5.54		
Expired	(283)	11.42		
Outstanding as of March 31, 2008	28,167	3.27		
Granted	2,597	1.60		
Exercised	(61)	1.41		
Forfeited	(4,159)	3.28		
Expired	(918)	5.64		
Outstanding as of March 31, 2009	25,626	3.02		
Granted	9,655	1.01		
Exercised	(1,883)	1.51		
Forfeited	(1,778)	3.32		
Expired	(291)	11.08		
Outstanding as of March 31, 2010	31,329	$ 2.40	4.11	$23,624
Vested and expected to vest at March 31, 2010	30,008	$ 2.46	4.02	$21,544
Exercisable as of March 31, 2010	20,049	$ 3.02	3.10	$ 7,952

The following table summarizes information about options outstanding and exercisable as of March 31, 2010 (options in thousands):

Range of Exercise Prices	Options Outstanding	Weighted-Average Exercise Price	Weighted-Average Remaining Contractual Life (Years)	Options Exercisable	Weighted-Average Exercise Price
$ 0.11–$ 0.75	150	$ 0.32	5.74	41	$ 0.31
$ 0.77–$ 1.13	8,793	0.98	6.13	263	0.90
$ 1.14–$ 1.68	3,725	1.40	3.39	3,078	1.44
$ 1.69–$ 2.53	7,513	2.08	3.58	6,628	2.07
$ 2.54–$ 3.80	9,189	3.21	3.37	8,179	3.21
$ 3.82–$ 5.70	326	3.99	4.34	227	3.99
$ 6.70–$ 8.55	604	6.76	2.07	604	6.76
$ 8.72–$12.82	963	10.40	0.93	963	10.40
$13.25–$15.00	66	13.46	0.72	66	13.46
	31,329	$ 2.40	4.11	20,049	$ 3.02

Expiration dates ranged from May 2010 to March 2017 for options outstanding at March 31, 2010. Prices for options exercised during the three-year period ended March 31, 2010, ranged from $0.11 to $3.44.

Restricted Stock

A summary of activity relating to our restricted stock follows (shares in thousands):

	Shares	Weighted-Average Grant Date Fair Value
Nonvested at March 31, 2007	3,714	$1.69
Granted	3,471	3.01
Vested	(1,355)	2.28
Forfeited	(922)	1.61
Nonvested at March 31, 2008	4,908	2.48
Granted	3,870	1.41
Vested	(1,887)	2.71
Forfeited	(633)	2.17
Nonvested at March 31, 2009	6,258	1.78
Granted	2,526	1.45
Vested	(2,853)	2.01
Forfeited	(796)	0.83
Nonvested at March 31, 2010	5,135	$1.64

Employee Stock Ownership Plans (ESOP)

3.74

THE DOW CHEMICAL COMPANY (DEC)

NOTES TO CONSOLIDATED FINANCIAL STATEMENTS

Note D—Acquisitions (in part)

Pursuant to the terms and conditions of the Merger Agreement, each outstanding share of Rohm and Haas common stock was converted into the right to receive cash of $78 per share, plus additional cash consideration of $0.97 per share. The additional cash consideration represented 8 percent per annum on the $78 per share consideration from January 10, 2009 to the closing of the Merger, less dividends declared by Rohm and Haas with a dividend record date between January 10, 2009 and the closing of the Merger. All options to purchase shares of common stock of Rohm and Haas granted under the Rohm and Haas stock option plans and all other Rohm and Haas equity-based compensation awards, whether vested or unvested as of April 1, 2009, became fully vested and converted into the right to receive cash of $78.97 per share, less any applicable exercise price. Total cash consideration paid to Rohm and Haas shareholders was $15,681 million. As part of the purchase price, $552 million in cash was paid to the Rohm and Haas Company Employee Stock Ownership Plan ("Rohm and Haas ESOP") on April 1, 2009 for 7.0 million shares of Rohm and Haas common stock held by the Rohm and Haas ESOP.

Note X—Stockholders' Equity (in part)

Employee Stock Ownership Plan

The Company has the Dow Employee Stock Ownership Plan (the "ESOP"), which is an integral part of The Dow Chemical Company Employees' Savings Plan (the "Plan"). A significant majority of full-time employees in the United States are eligible to participate in the Plan. The Company uses the ESOP to provide the Company's matching contribution in the form of the Company's stock to Plan participants.

In connection with the acquisition of Rohm and Haas (see Note D), $552 million in cash was paid to the Rohm and Haas Company Employee Stock Ownership Plan (the "Rohm and Haas ESOP") for 7.0 million shares of Rohm and Haas common stock held by the Rohm and Haas ESOP on April 1, 2009. On the date of the acquisition, the Rohm and Haas ESOP was merged into the Plan, and the Company assumed the $78 million balance of debt at 9.8 percent interest with final maturity in 2020 that was used to finance share purchases by the Rohm and Haas ESOP in 1990. The outstanding balance of the debt was $64 million at December 31, 2010.

On May 11, 2009, the Company sold 36.7 million shares of common stock (from treasury stock) to the ESOP at a price of $15.0561 per share for a total of $553 million. The treasury stock was carried at an aggregate historical cost of $1,529 million.

Dividends on unallocated shares held by the ESOP are used by the ESOP to make debt service payments. Dividends on allocated shares are used by the ESOP to make debt service payments to the extent needed; otherwise, they are paid to the Plan participants. Shares are released for allocation to participants based on the ratio of the current year's debt service to the sum of the principal and interest payments over the life of the loan. The shares are allocated to Plan participants in accordance with the terms of the Plan.

Compensation expense for allocated shares is recorded at the fair value of the shares on the date of allocation. ESOP shares that have not been released or committed to be released are not considered outstanding for purposes of computing basic and diluted earnings per share.

Compensation expense for ESOP shares allocated to plan participants was $81 million for the year ended December 31, 2010 ($48 million for the year ended December 31, 2009); no shares were allocated to plan participants in 2008. At December 31, 2010, 14.4 million shares out of a total 46.0 million shares held by the ESOP had been allocated to participants' accounts; 0.9 million shares were released but unallocated; and 30.7 million shares, at a fair value of $1,050 million, were considered unearned.

Profit Sharing Plans

3.75

TIFFANY & CO. (JAN)

NOTES TO CONSOLIDATED FINANCIAL STATEMENTS

P. Employee Benefit Plans (in part)

Effective February 1, 2006, the Qualified Plan was amended to exclude all employees hired on or after January 1, 2006. Instead, employees hired on or after January 1, 2006 will be eligible to receive a defined contribution retirement benefit under the Employee Profit Sharing and Retirement Savings ("EPSRS") Plan (see "Employee Profit Sharing and Retirement Savings Plan" below). Employees hired before January 1, 2006 will continue to be eligible for and accrue benefits under the Qualified Plan.

Employee Profit Sharing and Retirement Savings Plan

The Company maintains an EPSRS Plan that covers substantially all U.S.-based employees. Under the profit-sharing feature of the EPSRS Plan, the Company makes contributions, in the form of newly-issued Company Common Stock, to the employees' accounts based on the achievement of certain targeted earnings objectives established by, or as otherwise determined by, the Company's Board of Directors. The Company recorded expense of $5,000,000 and $4,750,000 in 2009 and 2007. The Company did not meet its targeted earnings objectives in 2008 and, therefore, did not record any expense. Under the retirement savings feature of the EPSRS Plan, employees who meet certain eligibility requirements may participate by contributing up to 15% of their annual compensation, and the Company may provide up to a 50% matching cash contribution up to 6% of each participant's total compensation. The Company recorded expense of $5,506,000, $7,440,000 and $6,940,000 in 2009, 2008 and 2007. Contributions to both features of the EPSRS Plan are made in the following year.

Under the profit-sharing feature of the EPSRS Plan, the Company's stock contribution is required to be maintained in such stock until the employee has two or more years of service, at which time the employee may diversify his or her Company stock account into other investment options provided under the plan. Under the retirement savings portion of the EPSRS Plan, the employees have the ability to elect to invest their contribution and the matching contribution in Company stock. At January 31, 2010, investments in Company stock represented 26% of total EPSRS Plan assets.

Effective as of February 1, 2006, the EPSRS Plan was amended to provide a defined contribution retirement benefit ("DCRB") to eligible employees hired on or after January 1, 2006 (see "Pensions and Other Postretirement Benefits" above). Under the DCRB, the Company makes contributions each year to each employee's account at a rate based upon age and years of service. These contributions are deposited into individual accounts set up in each employee's name to be invested in a manner similar to the retirement savings portion of the EPSRS Plan. The Company recorded expense of $1,685,000, $1,606,000 and $1,032,000 in 2009, 2008 and 2007.

Multi-Employer Pension Plan (MEPP)

3.76

SARA LEE CORPORATION (JUN)

NOTES TO FINANCIAL STATEMENTS

Note 14—Contingencies and Commitments (in part)

Multi-Employer Pension Plans

The corporation participates in various multi-employer pension plans that provide retirement benefits to certain employees covered by collective bargaining agreements (MEPP). Participating employers in a MEPP are jointly responsible for any plan underfunding. MEPP contributions are established by the applicable collective bargaining agreements; however, the MEPPs may impose increased contribution rates and sur-

charges based on the funded status of the plan and the provisions of the Pension Protection Act, which requires substantially underfunded MEPPs to implement rehabilitation plans to improve funded status. Factors that could impact funded status of a MEPP include investment performance, changes in the participant demographics, financial stability of contributing employers and changes in actuarial assumptions.

In addition to regular contributions, the corporation could be obligated to pay additional contributions (known as a complete or partial withdrawal liability) if a MEPP has unfunded vested benefits. These withdrawal liabilities, which would be triggered if the corporation ceases to make contributions to a MEPP with respect to one or more collective bargaining units, would equal the corporation's proportionate share of the unfunded vested benefits based on the year in which the liability is triggered. The corporation believes that certain of the MEPPs in which it participates have unfunded vested benefits, and some are significantly underfunded. Withdrawal liability triggers could include the corporation's decision to close a plant or the dissolution of a collective bargaining unit. Due to uncertainty regarding future withdrawal liability triggers, we are unable to determine the amount and timing of the corporation's future withdrawal liability, if any, or whether the corporation's participation in these MEPPs could have any material adverse impact on its financial condition, results of operations or liquidity. Disagreements over potential withdrawal liability may lead to legal disputes. The corporation currently is involved in litigation with one MEPP and it is probable that the outcome of this litigation may result in a partial withdrawal liability of approximately $22 million.

The corporation's regular scheduled contributions to MEPPs totaled $50 million in 2010, $49 million in 2009 and $48 million in 2008. The corporation recognized charges for partial withdrawal liabilities of approximately $23 million in 2010, $31 million in 2009, and an immaterial amount in 2008.

Note 16—Defined Benefit Pension Plans (in part)

Multi-Employer Plans

The corporation participates in multi-employer plans that provide defined benefits to certain employees covered by collective bargaining agreements. Such plans are usually administered by a board of trustees composed of the management of the participating companies and labor representatives. The net pension cost of these plans is equal to the annual contribution determined in accordance with the provisions of negotiated labor contracts. These contributions were $50 million in 2010, $49 million in 2009 and $48 million in 2008. Assets contributed to such plans are not segregated or otherwise restricted to provide benefits only to the employees of the corporation. The future cost of these plans is dependent on a number of factors including the funded status of the plans and the ability of the other participating companies to meet ongoing funding obligations.

In addition to regular contributions, the corporation could be obligated to pay additional contributions (known as complete or partial withdrawal liabilities) if a multi-employer pension plan (MEPP) has unfunded vested benefits. The corporation recognized a partial withdrawal liability in 2010 of $22 million related to one collective bargaining agreement, all of which was recognized in Selling, general and administrative expenses in the Consolidated Statements of Income. The corporation also recognized a partial withdrawal liability of $31 million in 2009 as a result of the cessation of contributions to a MEPP with respect to one collective bargaining unit. Of the total charge to income in 2009, $13 million was recognized in Cost of sales and $18 million was recognized in Selling, general and administrative expenses in the Consolidated Statements of Income. The charges for both years was recognized in the results of the North American Fresh Bakery segment.

DEPRECIATION EXPENSE

RECOGNITION AND MEASUREMENT

3.77 FASB ASC 360, *Property, Plant, and Equipment*, defines *depreciation accounting* (the process of allocating the cost of productive facilities over the expected useful lives of the facilities) as a system of accounting that aims to distribute the cost or other basic value of tangible capital assets, less salvage (if any), over the estimated useful life of the unit, which may be a group of assets, in a systematic and rational manner. It is a process of allocation, not valuation.

3.78 FASB ASC 250 requires that a change in depreciation, amortization, or depletion method for long-lived, nonfinancial assets be accounted for as a change in accounting estimate effected by a change in accounting principle. Changes in accounting estimate are accounted for prospectively, not retrospectively as is required for changes in accounting principle.

DISCLOSURE

3.79 FASB ASC 360 stipulates that both the amount of depreciation expense and method(s) of depreciation should be disclosed in the financial statements or notes thereto.

3.80

TABLE 3-4: DEPRECIATION METHODS

Table 3-4 summarizes the methods of depreciation used to allocate the cost of depreciable assets.

	Number of Entities		
	2010	2009	2008
Straight line	492	488	494
Declining balance	10	10	10
Sum of the years' digits	2	3	3
Accelerated method—not specified	13	17	21
Units of production	15	16	14
Group/composite	4	10	7

PRESENTATION AND DISCLOSURE EXCERPTS

Straight-Line Method

3.81

ADMINISTAFF, INC. (DEC)

CONSOLIDATED STATEMENTS OF OPERATIONS
(in part)

(In thousands, except per share amounts)

	Year Ended December 31		
	2010	2009	2008
Revenues (gross billings of $10.169 billion, $9.856 billion and $10.372 billion, less worksite employee payroll cost of $8.449 billion, $8.203 billion and $8.648 billion, respectively)	$1,719,752	$1,653,096	$1,724,434
Direct costs:			
Payroll taxes, benefits and workers' compensation costs	1,421,216	1,365,129	1,380,695
Gross profit	298,536	287,967	343,739
Operating expenses:			
Salaries, wages and payroll taxes	146,901	144,086	153,538
Stock-based compensation	8,126	10,064	9,970
General and administrative expenses	63,214	62,381	69,348
Commissions	11,881	11,800	12,665
Advertising	16,447	16,011	17,666
Depreciation and amortization	14,907	16,592	15,570
	261,476	260,934	278,757
Operating income	37,060	27,033	64,982

NOTES TO CONSOLIDATED FINANCIAL STATEMENTS

1. Accounting Policies (in part)

Property and Equipment

Property and equipment are recorded at cost and are depreciated over the estimated useful lives of the related assets using the straight-line method. The estimated useful lives of property and equipment for purposes of computing depreciation are as follows:

Buildings and improvements	5–30 years
Computer hardware and software, and acquired technologies	1–5 years
Software development costs	3 years
Furniture and fixtures	5–7 years
Aircraft	20 years

Software development costs relate primarily to software coding, system interfaces and testing of the Company's proprietary professional employer information systems and are accounted for in accordance with ASC 350-40, *Internal Use Software*. Capitalized software development costs are amortized using the straight-line method over the estimated useful lives of the software, generally three years.

The Company accounts for its software products in accordance with ASC 985-20, *Costs of Software to be Sold*. This Topic establishes standards of financial accounting and reporting for the costs of computer software to be sold, leased, or otherwise marketed as a separate product or as part of a product or process, whether internally developed and produced or purchased.

The Company periodically evaluates its long-lived assets for impairment in accordance with ASC 360-10, *Property, Plant, and Equipment*. ASC 360-10 requires that an impairment loss be recognized for assets to be disposed of or held-for-use when the carrying amount of an asset is deemed to not be recoverable. If events or circumstances were to indicate that any of the Company's long-lived assets might be impaired, the Company would assess recoverability based on the estimated undiscounted future cash flows to be generated from the applicable asset. In addition, the Company may record an impairment loss to the extent that the carrying value of the asset exceeded the fair value of the asset. Fair value is generally determined using an estimate of discounted future net cash flows from operating activities or upon disposal of the asset.

3.82

HILL-ROM HOLDINGS, INC. (SEP)

NOTES TO CONSOLIDATED FINANCIAL STATEMENTS

(Dollars in millions except per share data)

Note 1. Summary of Significant Accounting Policies (in part)

Property, Plant and Equipment

Property, plant and equipment is recorded at cost and depreciated over the estimated useful life of the assets using principally the straight-line method. Ranges of estimated useful lives are as follows:

	Useful Life
Land improvements	6–25 years
Buildings and building equipment	20–40 years
Machinery and equipment	3–10 years
Equipment leased to others	2–10 years

When property, plant and equipment is retired from service or otherwise disposed of, the cost and related amount of depreciation or amortization are eliminated from the asset and accumulated depreciation accounts. The difference, if any, between the net asset value and the proceeds on sale are charged or credited to income. Total depreciation expense included within continuing operations on the Statements of Consolidated Income (Loss) for fiscal years 2010, 2009 and 2008 was $72.8 million, $74.3 million and $81.0 million. The major components of property and the related accumulated depreciation at September 30, were as follows:

	September 30, 2010		September 30, 2009	
	Cost	Accumulated Depreciation	Cost	Accumulated Depreciation
Land and land improvements	$ 12.5	$ 3.7	$ 12.0	$ 3.5
Buildings and building equipment	112.8	75.7	112.7	74.5
Machinery and equipment	257.1	192.2	269.9	199.0
Equipment leased to others	422.6	289.7	426.6	271.8
Total	$805.0	$561.3	$821.2	$548.8

Accelerated Methods

3.83

GENERAL DYNAMICS CORPORATION (DEC)

NOTES TO CONSOLIDATED FINANCIAL STATEMENTS

(Dollars in millions, except per-share amounts or unless otherwise noted)

I. Property, Plant and Equipment, Net

Property, plant and equipment are carried at historical cost, net of accumulated depreciation. The major classes of property, plant and equipment were as follows:

December 31	2009	2010
Machinery and equipment	$ 3,195	$ 3,388
Buildings and improvements	2,069	2,084
Land and improvements	270	283
Construction in process	143	204
Total property, plant and equipment(*)	5,677	5,959
Accumulated depreciation	(2,765)	(2,988)
Property, plant and equipment, net	$ 2,912	$ 2,971

(*) Our government customers provide certain facilities; we do not include these facilities above.

We depreciate most of our assets using the straight-line method and the remainder using accelerated methods. Buildings and improvements are depreciated over periods up to 50 years. Machinery and equipment are depreciated over periods up to 30 years.

3.84

THE HERSHEY COMPANY (DEC)

NOTES TO CONSOLIDATED FINANCIAL STATEMENTS

3. Business Realignment and Impairment Charges (in part)

Charges (credits) associated with business realignment initiatives and impairment recorded during 2010, 2009 and 2008 were as follows:

(In thousands of dollars)	For the Years Ended December 31		
	2010	2009	2008
Cost of Sales			
Next Century program	$13,644	$ —	$ —
Global supply chain transformation program	—	10,136	77,767
Total cost of sales	13,644	10,136	77,767
Selling, Marketing and Administrative			
Next Century program	1,493	—	—
Global supply chain transformation program	—	6,120	8,102
Total selling, marketing and administrative	1,493	6,120	8,102
Business Realignment and Impairment Charges, Net			
Next Century program:			
Fixed asset impairment and plant closure expenses	5,516	—	—
Employee separation costs	33,225	—	—
2007 business realignment initiatives:			
Global supply chain transformation program:			
Net gain on sale of fixed assets	—	(3,418)	(4,882)
Plant closure expense	—	22,157	23,415
Employee separation costs	—	2,474	11,469
Pension settlement loss	—	60,431	12,501
Contract termination costs	—	1,231	1,637
Brazilian business realignment:			
Employee separation costs	—	—	1,581
Fixed asset impairment charges	—	—	754
Contract termination and other exit costs	—	—	2,587
2008 impairment of trademarks	—	—	45,739
Godrej Hershey Ltd. goodwill impairment	44,692	—	—
Total business realignment and impairment charges, net	83,433	82,875	94,801
Total net charges associated with business realignment initiatives and impairment	$98,570	$99,131	$180,670

Next Century Program

The charge of $13.6 million recorded in cost of sales during 2010 related primarily to accelerated depreciation of fixed assets over a reduced estimated remaining useful life associated with the Next Century program. A charge of $1.5 million was recorded in selling, marketing and administrative expenses during 2010 for project administration. Fixed asset impairment charges of $5.5 million were recorded during 2010. In determining the costs related to fixed asset impairments, fair value was estimated based on the expected sales proceeds. Employee separation costs of $33.2 million during 2010 were related to expected voluntary and involuntary terminations at the two manufacturing facilities.

Global Supply Chain Transformation Program

The charge of $10.1 million recorded in cost of sales during 2009 related to start-up costs and the accelerated depreciation of fixed assets over the estimated remaining useful life. The $6.1 million recorded in selling, marketing and administrative expenses was associated with project administration. The $3.4 million net gain on sale of fixed assets resulted from higher proceeds received from the sale of equipment. The $22.2 million of plant closure expenses for 2009 pertained to the preparation of plants for sale and equipment removal costs. The global supply chain transformation program had

identified six manufacturing facilities which would be closed. As of December 31, 2009, manufacturing facilities located in Dartmouth, Nova Scotia; Oakdale, California; and Montreal, Quebec had been closed and sold. The facilities located in Naugatuck, Connecticut; Reading, Pennsylvania; and Smiths Falls, Ontario had been closed and were being held for sale. The global supply chain transformation program employee separation costs were primarily related to involuntary terminations at the manufacturing facilities of Artisan Confections Company which have been closed. The higher pension settlement loss in 2009 compared to 2008 resulted from an increase in actuarial losses associated with the significant decline in the fair value of pension assets in 2008, along with the increased level of lump sum withdrawals from a defined benefit pension plan related to employee departures.

The 2008 charge of $77.8 million recorded in cost of sales related primarily to the accelerated depreciation of fixed assets over a reduced estimated remaining useful life and start-up costs. The $8.1 million recorded in selling, marketing and administrative expenses was associated with project administration. The $4.9 million of gains on sale of fixed assets resulted from the receipt of proceeds in excess of the carrying value primarily from the sale of a warehousing and distribution facility. The $23.4 million of plant closure expenses for 2008 resulted from the preparation of plants for sale and production line removal costs. Employee separation costs were related to involuntary terminations at the North American manufacturing facilities which were being closed.

Units-of-Production Method

3.85

EXXON MOBIL CORPORATION (DEC)

CONSOLIDATED STATEMENT OF INCOME (in part)

(Millions of dollars)	Note Reference Number	2010	2009	2008
Revenues and Other Income				
Sales and other operating revenue[(1)]		$370,125	$301,500	$459,579
Income from equity affiliates	6	10,677	7,143	11,081
Other income[(2)]		2,419	1,943	6,699
Total revenues and other income		$383,221	$310,586	$477,359
Costs and Other Deductions				
Crude oil and product purchases		$197,959	$152,806	$249,454
Production and manufacturing expenses		35,792	33,027	37,905
Selling, general and administrative expenses		14,683	14,735	15,873
Depreciation and depletion		14,760	11,917	12,379
Exploration expenses, including dry holes		2,144	2,021	1,451
Interest expense		259	548	673
Sales-based taxes[(1)]	18	28,547	25,936	34,508
Other taxes and duties	18	36,118	34,819	41,719
Total costs and other deductions		$330,262	$275,809	$393,962
Income before income taxes		$ 52,959	$ 34,777	$ 83,397

[(1)] Sales and other operating revenue includes sales-based taxes of $28,547 million, $25,936 million for 2009 and $34,508 million for 2008.
[(2)] Other income for 2008 includes a $62 million gain from the sale of a non-U.S. investment and a related $143 million foreign exchange loss.

NOTES TO CONSOLIDATED FINANCIAL STATEMENTS

1. Summary of Accounting Policies (in part)

Property, Plant and Equipment. Depreciation, depletion and amortization, based on cost less estimated salvage value of the asset, are primarily determined under either the unit-of-production method or the straight-line method, which is based on estimated asset service life taking obsolescence into consideration. Maintenance and repairs, including planned major maintenance, are expensed as incurred. Major renewals and improvements are capitalized and the assets replaced are retired.

Interest costs incurred to finance expenditures during the construction phase of multiyear projects are capitalized as part of the historical cost of acquiring the constructed assets. The project construction phase commences with the development of the detailed engineering design and ends when the constructed assets are ready for their intended use. Capitalized interest costs are included in property, plant and equipment and are depreciated over the service life of the related assets.

The Corporation uses the "successful efforts" method to account for its exploration and production activities. Under this method, costs are accumulated on a field-by-field basis with certain exploratory expenditures and exploratory dry holes being expensed as incurred. Costs of productive wells and development dry holes are capitalized and amortized on the unit-of-production method.

The Corporation carries as an asset exploratory well costs when the well has found a sufficient quantity of reserves to justify its completion as a producing well and where the Corporation is making sufficient progress assessing the reserves and the economic and operating viability of the project. Exploratory well costs not meeting these criteria are charged to expense.

Acquisition costs of proved properties are amortized using a unit-of-production method, computed on the basis of total proved oil and gas reserves. Significant unproved properties are assessed for impairment individually and valuation allowances against the capitalized costs are recorded based on the estimated economic chance of success and the length of time that the Corporation expects to hold the properties. Properties that are not individually significant are aggregated by groups and amortized based on development risk and average holding period. The valuation allowances are reviewed at least annually. Other exploratory expenditures, including geophysical costs, other dry hole costs and annual lease rentals, are expensed as incurred.

Unit-of-production depreciation is applied to property, plant and equipment, including capitalized exploratory drilling and development costs, associated with productive depletable extractive properties in the Upstream segment. Unit-of-production rates are based on the amount of proved developed reserves of oil, gas and other minerals that are estimated to be recoverable from existing facilities using current operating methods.

Under the unit-of-production method, oil and gas volumes are considered produced once they have been measured through meters at custody transfer or sales transaction points at the outlet valve on the lease or field storage tank.

Production costs are expensed as incurred. Production involves lifting the oil and gas to the surface and gathering, treating, field processing and field storage of the oil and gas. The production function normally terminates at the outlet valve on the lease or field production storage tank. Production costs are those incurred to operate and maintain the Corporation's wells and related equipment and facilities. They become part of the cost of oil and gas produced. These costs, sometimes referred to as lifting costs, include such items as labor costs to operate the wells and related equipment; repair and maintenance costs on the wells and equipment; materials, supplies and energy costs required to operate the wells and related equipment; and administrative expenses related to the production activity.

Gains on sales of proved and unproved properties are only recognized when there is no uncertainty about the recovery of costs applicable to any interest retained or where there is no substantial obligation for future performance by the Corporation. Losses on properties sold are recognized when incurred or when the properties are held for sale and the fair value of the properties is less than the carrying value.

Proved oil and gas properties held and used by the Corporation are reviewed for impairment whenever events or changes in circumstances indicate that the carrying amounts may not be recoverable. Assets are grouped at the lowest level for which there are identifiable cash flows that are largely independent of the cash flows of other groups of assets.

The Corporation estimates the future undiscounted cash flows of the affected properties to judge the recoverability of carrying amounts. Cash flows used in impairment evaluations are developed using annually updated corporate plan investment evaluation assumptions for crude oil commodity prices and foreign currency exchange rates. Annual volumes are based on individual field production profiles, which are also updated annually. Prices for natural gas and other products are based on corporate plan assumptions developed annually by major region and also for investment evaluation purposes. Cash flow estimates for impairment testing exclude derivative instruments.

Impairment analyses are generally based on proved reserves. Where probable reserves exist, an appropriately risk-adjusted amount of these reserves may be included in the impairment evaluation. Impairments are measured by the amount the carrying value exceeds the fair value.

8. Property, Plant and Equipment and Asset Retirement Obligations (in part)

Property, Plant and Equipment (Millions of dollars)	Dec. 31, 2010		Dec. 31, 2009	
	Cost	Net	Cost	Net
Upstream	$264,136	$148,152	$198,036	$ 88,319
Downstream	68,652	30,095	68,092	30,499
Chemical	29,524	14,255	28,464	13,511
Other	11,626	7,046	11,314	6,787
Total	$373,938	$199,548	$305,906	$139,116

In the Upstream segment, depreciation is generally on a unit-of production basis, so depreciable life will vary by field. In the Downstream segment, investments in refinery and lubes basestock manufacturing facilities are generally depreciated on a straight-line basis over a 25-year life and service station buildings and fixed improvements over a 20-year life. In the Chemical segment, investments in process equipment are generally depreciated on a straight-line basis over a 20-year life.

Accumulated depreciation and depletion totaled $174,390 million at the end of 2010 and $166,790 million at the end of 2009. Interest capitalized in 2010, 2009 and 2008 was $532 million, $425 million and $510 million, respectively.

INCOME TAXES

RECOGNITION AND MEASUREMENT

3.86 FASB ASC 740, *Income Taxes*, clarifies the accounting for tax positions in an entity's financial statements. FASB ASC 740 prescribes a more-likely-than-not recognition threshold and measurement attribute for the financial statement recognition and measurement of a tax position taken or expected to be taken. Under FASB ASC 740, tax positions will be evaluated for recognition, derecognition, and measurement using consistent criteria. In addition, FASB ASC 740 provides guidance on classification and disclosure. FASB ASC 740 requires, except in certain specified situations, that undistributed earnings of a subsidiary included in consolidated income be accounted for as a temporary difference. Finally, the provisions of FASB ASC 740 provide more information about the uncertainty in income tax assets and liabilities.

DISCLOSURE

3.87 FASB ASC 740 sets forth standards for financial presentation and disclosure of income tax liabilities or assets and expense. These requirements vary for public and nonpublic entities. FASB ASC 740 states that amounts and expiration dates of operating loss and tax credit carryforwards for tax purposes should be disclosed. Any portion of the valuation allowance for deferred tax assets for which subsequently recognized tax benefits will be credited directly to contributed capital should also be disclosed. An entity's temporary difference and carryforward information requires additional disclosure, which differs for public and nonpublic entities.

PRESENTATION AND DISCLOSURE EXCERPTS

Expense Provision

3.88

YAHOO! INC. (DEC)

CONSOLIDATED STATEMENTS OF INCOME (in part)

	Years Ended December 31		
(In thousands, except per share amounts)	2008	2009	2010
Revenue	$7,208,502	$6,460,315	$6,324,651
Cost of revenue	3,023,362	2,871,746	2,627,545
Gross profit	4,185,140	3,588,569	3,697,106
Operating expenses:			
Sales and marketing	1,563,313	1,245,350	1,264,491
Product development	1,221,787	1,210,168	1,082,176
General and administrative	705,136	580,352	488,332
Amortization of intangibles	87,550	39,106	31,626
Restructuring charges, net	106,854	126,901	57,957
Goodwill impairment charge	487,537	—	—
Total operating expenses	4,172,177	3,201,877	2,924,582
Income from operations	12,963	386,692	772,524
Other income, net	73,750	187,528	297,869
Income before income taxes and earnings in equity interests	86,713	574,220	1,070,393
Provision for income taxes	(259,006)	(219,321)	(221,523)
Earnings in equity interests	596,979	250,390	395,758
Net income	$ 424,686	$ 605,289	$1,244,628

NOTES TO CONSOLIDATED FINANCIAL STATEMENTS

Note 9. Income Taxes

The components of income before income taxes and earnings in equity interests are as follows (in thousands):

	Years Ended December 31		
	2008	2009	2010
United States	$ 448,175	$387,212	$ 872,042
Foreign(*)	(361,462)	187,008	198,351
Income before provision for income taxes and earnings in equity interests	$ 86,713	$574,220	$1,070,393

(*) Includes a $488 million goodwill impairment charge in 2008.

The provision (benefit) for income taxes is composed of the following (in thousands):

	Years Ended December 31		
	2008	2009	2010
Current:			
United States federal	$228,209	$191,845	$ 26,342
State	16,603	51,662	39,258
Foreign	53,229	66,376	43,341
Total current provision for income taxes	298,041	309,883	108,941
Deferred:			
United States federal	8,987	(32,385)	67,621
State	(35,064)	(58,660)	37,438
Foreign	(12,958)	483	7,523
Total deferred provision (benefit) for income taxes	(39,035)	(90,562)	112,582
Provision for income taxes	$259,006	$219,321	$221,523

The provision for income taxes differs from the amount computed by applying the federal statutory income tax rate to income before provision for income taxes and earnings in equity interests as follows (in thousands):

	Years Ended December 31		
	2008	2009	2010
Income tax at the U.S. federal statutory rate of 35 percent	$ 30,349	$200,976	$374,638
State income taxes, net of federal benefit	(8,925)	(4,549)	54,268
Change in valuation allowance	25,674	13,521	(1,315)
Stock-based compensation expense	44,938	28,322	4,404
Research tax credits	(13,954)	(11,046)	(10,345)
Effect of non-U.S. operations	18,403	20,126	(17,344)
Resolution with tax authorities	(5,245)	—	(159,168)
Tax gain in excess of book gain from sales of Zimbra, Inc. and HotJobs due to basis differences	—	—	23,184
Nondeductible goodwill	170,644	—	—
Tax restructuring	—	(25,583)	(43,361)
Other	(2,878)	(2,446)	(3,438)
Provision for income taxes	$259,006	$219,321	$221,523

The 2010 differences above are further explained as follows:
- State taxes are higher in 2010 than in prior years due to a reduction of deferred tax assets associated with an effective tax rate reduction in California starting in 2011.
- Stock-based compensation increases the Company's effective tax rate to the extent that stock-based compensation expense recorded in the Company's financial statements is non-deductible for tax purposes. This primarily occurs with regard to options granted outside the U.S. The 2010 effective tax rate increase is lower than in prior years due to recently granted stock-based compensation awards having a lower grant date fair value than stock-based compensation awards from

prior years. That effect results in a lower non-deductible expense for financial statement purposes and a lower increase to the Company's effective tax rate. Additionally, in 2010 there is a lower effective tax rate impact associated with non-deductible stock-based compensation awards related to prior year acquisitions to the extent such awards became vested or forfeited in 2010.

- The Company's effective tax rate in all periods is the result of the mix of income earned in various tax jurisdictions that apply a broad range of income tax rates. Operating losses in some non-U.S. jurisdictions cannot be used to offset profits and thus increase the overall effective tax rate. The impact of those losses in 2010 was lower than in prior years. Additionally, in 2010, the Company benefited from increased profit in lower tax jurisdictions, primarily in Asia.

- In 2010, the Company had a favorable resolution of certain issues in an IRS examination of its 2005 and 2006 U.S. federal income tax returns resulting in a reduction of reserves for tax uncertainties and the availability of capital loss carryforwards to offset the tax on the gain from the sales of Zimbra, Inc. and HotJobs.

- During 2010, in connection with tax restructuring activities, the Company reached a formal agreement with the IRS through a pre-filing agreement to treat certain intercompany bad debts as deductible business expenses on the 2009 federal income tax return.

The 2008 provision for income taxes reflects a $488 million goodwill impairment charge, the majority of which was non-deductible for tax purposes. In addition, the 2008 effective tax rate also included the cumulative tax benefit of a favorable state tax ruling granted in 2008 and retroactive to 2007.

Deferred income taxes reflect the tax effects of temporary differences between the carrying amounts of assets and liabilities for financial reporting purposes and the amounts used for income tax purposes. The components of deferred income tax assets and liabilities are as follows (in thousands):

| | December 31 | |
	2009	2010
Deferred Income Tax Assets:		
Net operating loss and tax credit carryforwards	$ 171,883	$ 152,138
Stock-based compensation expense	234,108	178,294
Non-deductible reserves and expenses	268,015	166,015
Intangible assets	14,336	9,283
Gross deferred income tax assets	688,342	505,730
Valuation allowance	(63,364)	(60,176)
Deferred income tax assets	$ 624,978	$ 445,554
Deferred Income Tax Liabilities:		
Unrealized investment gains	$ 4,404	$ 3,192
Purchased intangible assets	(9,684)	(11,050)
Investments in equity interests	(405,880)	(447,022)
Deferred income tax liabilities	$(411,160)	$(454,880)
Net deferred income tax assets (liabilities)	$ 213,818	$ (9,326)

As of December 31, 2010, the Company's federal and state net operating loss carryforwards for income tax purposes

were approximately $211 million and $26 million, respectively. If not utilized, the federal and state net operating loss carryforwards will begin to expire in 2021. The Company's federal and state research tax credit carryforwards for income tax purposes are approximately $115 million and $183 million, respectively. If not utilized, the federal research tax credit carryforwards will begin to expire in 2019. The state research tax credit carryforwards will not expire. Federal and state net operating loss and tax credit carryforwards that result from the exercise of employee stock options are not recorded on the Company's consolidated balance sheets. Federal and state net operating loss and tax credit carryforwards that result from the exercise of employee stock options are accounted for as a credit to additional paid-in capital if and when realized through a reduction in income taxes payable.

The Company has a valuation allowance of approximately $60 million as of December 31, 2010 against certain deferred income tax assets that are not more likely than not to be realized in future periods. In evaluating the Company's ability to realize its deferred income tax assets, the Company considers all available positive and negative evidence, including operating results, ongoing tax planning, and forecasts of future taxable income on a jurisdiction by jurisdiction basis. The valuation allowance as of December 31, 2010 relates primarily to foreign net operating loss and credit carryforwards that will reduce the provision for income taxes if and when recognized.

The Company provides U.S. income taxes on the earnings of foreign subsidiaries unless the subsidiaries' earnings are considered indefinitely reinvested outside the U.S. As of December 31, 2010, U.S. income taxes were not provided for on a cumulative total of $2.6 billion of undistributed earnings for certain foreign subsidiaries and a corporate joint venture. If these earnings were to be repatriated, the Company would be subject to additional U.S. income taxes (subject to an adjustment for foreign tax credits). It is not practicable to determine the income tax liability that might be incurred if these earnings were to be repatriated.

The total amount of gross unrecognized tax benefits was $597 million as of December 31, 2010, of which up to $437 million would affect the Company's effective tax rate if realized. A reconciliation of the beginning and ending amount of unrecognized tax benefits in 2009 and 2010 is as follows (in thousands):

	2009	2010
Unrecognized tax benefits balance at January 1	$798,057	$ 893,475
Gross increase for tax positions of prior years	18,027	44,978
Gross decrease for tax positions of prior years	(16,044)	(370,363)
Gross increase for tax positions of current year	102,855	48,570
Gross decrease for tax positions of current year	—	—
Settlements	(9,420)	(19,293)
Lapse of statute of limitations	—	(312)
Unrecognized tax benefits balance at December 31	$893,475	$597,055

The total unrecognized tax benefits as of December 31, 2009 and 2010 include approximately $420 million and $193 million, respectively, of unrecognized tax benefits that have been netted against the related deferred tax assets. The remaining balances are recorded on the Company's consolidated balance sheets as follows (in thousands):

	December 31	
	2009	2010
Total unrecognized tax benefits balance	$ 893,475	$ 597,055
Amounts netted against related deferred tax assets	(419,782)	(193,275)
Unrecognized tax benefits recorded on consolidated balance sheets	$ 473,693	$ 403,780
Amounts classified as accrued expenses and other current liabilities	$ 53,858	$ 111,997
Amounts classified as deferred and other long-term tax liabilities, net	419,835	291,783
Unrecognized tax benefits recorded on consolidated balance sheets	$ 473,693	$ 403,780

The Company recognizes interest and/or penalties related to uncertain tax positions in income tax expense. To the extent accrued interest and penalties do not ultimately become payable, amounts accrued will be reduced and reflected as a reduction of the overall income tax provision in the period that such determination is made. During 2009 and 2010, interest and penalties recorded in the consolidated statements of income were $3 million and $4 million, respectively. The amounts of accrued interest and penalties recorded on the consolidated balance sheets as of December 31, 2009 and 2010 were approximately $15 million and $16 million, respectively.

The Company's gross amount of unrecognized tax benefits as of December 31, 2010 is $597 million, of which $420 million is recorded on the consolidated balance sheets. The agreements reached in 2010 with the IRS resulted in a reduction to the Company's gross unrecognized tax benefits of $357 million. Of this $357 million reduction in unrecognized tax benefits, $202 million resulted in an effective tax rate benefit. The reduction to the gross unrecognized tax benefits has been partially offset by increases from current year tax positions. In total, the gross unrecognized tax benefits as of December 31, 2010 decreased by $296 million from the recorded balance as of December 31, 2009.

The Company files income tax returns in the U.S. federal jurisdiction and in many U.S. states and foreign jurisdictions. The tax years 1995 to 2009 remain open to examination by the major taxing jurisdictions in which the Company is subject to tax.

During the year ended December 31, 2010, the IRS completed its field examination of the Company's 2005 and 2006 tax returns and issued notices of proposed adjustment. The Company reached an agreement with the IRS in connection with several of the adjustments and adjusted its reserves accordingly. There are other proposed adjustments, including an intercompany transfer pricing matter which could have a significant impact on its tax liability in future years if not resolved favorably. The Company has not agreed to these other proposed adjustments and is contesting them through the administrative process. In the third quarter of 2010, the Company completed a Fast Track Settlement process with the IRS related to certain capital losses that became available for use. In the fourth quarter of 2010, the Company reached a formal agreement through a pre-filing agreement with the IRS to treat certain bad debt expense as a deductible business

expense on the 2009 federal income tax return. The Company has recognized a benefit in 2010 for both capital loss and bad debt expense as a result of the resolution with the IRS.

During the year ended December 31, 2010, the IRS commenced an examination of the Company's 2007 and 2008 tax returns. The Company is also under audit by the California Franchise Tax Board for its 2005 and 2006 tax returns. The Company believes its existing reserves for all tax matters are adequate. The Company also filed with the IRS amended federal tax returns for its fiscal years 2000 to 2008, to elect foreign tax credits for foreign taxes paid versus the previous election to deduct foreign taxes from taxable income, reducing income taxes payable by $102 million. The Company's tax provisions for all years had been computed on the basis of foreign tax credits, and differences between book and tax treatment were charged to additional paid-in capital due to the interaction of stock option deductions and the foreign tax credit computations. Accordingly, the $102 million was recorded as a credit to additional paid-in capital with a corresponding reduction of $49 million in current year income taxes payable and a $53 million receivable from the IRS for taxes paid in prior years.

The Company is in various stages of the examination and appeals process in connection with all of its tax audits worldwide and it is difficult to determine when these examinations will be settled. It is reasonably possible that over the next twelve-month period the Company may experience an increase or decrease in its unrecognized tax benefits. It is not possible to determine either the magnitude or the range of any increase or decrease at this time.

3.89

THE PROCTER & GAMBLE COMPANY (JUN)

CONSOLIDATED STATEMENTS OF EARNINGS
(in part)

(Amounts in millions except per share amounts)	Years Ended June 30		
	2010	2009	2008
Net sales	$78,938	$76,694	$79,257
Cost of products sold	37,919	38,690	39,261
Selling, general and administrative expense	24,998	22,630	24,017
Operating income	16,021	15,374	15,979
Interest expense	946	1,358	1,467
Other non-operating income/(expense), net	(28)	397	373
Earnings from continuing operations before income taxes	15,047	14,413	14,885
Income taxes on continuing operations	4,101	3,733	3,594
Net earnings from continuing operations	10,946	10,680	11,291
Net earnings from discontinued operations	1,790	2,756	784
Net earnings	$12,736	$13,436	$12,075

NOTES TO CONSOLIDATED FINANCIAL STATEMENTS

Amounts in millions of dollars except per share amounts or as otherwise specified.

Note 9—Income Taxes

Income taxes are recognized for the amount of taxes payable for the current year and for the impact of deferred tax liabilities and assets, which represent future tax consequences of events that have been recognized differently in the financial statements than for tax purposes. Deferred tax assets and liabilities are established using the enacted statutory tax rates and are adjusted for any changes in such rates in the period of change.

Earnings from continuing operations before income taxes consisted of the following:

Years ended June 30	2010	2009	2008
United States	$ 8,368	$ 8,409	$ 8,167
International	6,679	6,004	6,718
Total	15,047	14,413	14,885

Income taxes on continuing operations consisted of the following:

Years ended June 30	2010	2009	2008
Current Tax Expense			
U.S. federal	$2,154	$1,619	$ 670
International	1,616	1,268	1,515
U.S. state and local	295	229	188
	4,065	3,116	2,373
Deferred Tax Expense			
U.S. federal	253	595	1,272
International and other	(217)	22	(51)
	36	617	1,221
Total tax expense	4,101	3,733	3,594

A reconciliation of the U.S. federal statutory income tax rate to our actual income tax rate on continuing operations is provided below:

Years ended June 30	2010	2009	2008
U.S. federal statutory income tax rate	35.0%	35.0%	35.0%
Country mix impacts of foreign operations	−7.5%	−7.1%	−6.8%
Income tax reserve adjustments	−0.4%	−1.3%	−3.4%
Patient Protection and Affordable Care Act	1.0%	0.0%	0.0%
Other	−0.8%	−0.7%	−0.7%
Effective income tax rate	27.3%	25.9%	24.1%

Income tax reserve adjustments represent changes in our net liability for uncertain tax positions related to prior year tax positions.

In March 2010, the Patient Protection and Affordable Care Act (PPACA) was signed into law. One of the provisions of the PPACA changed the taxability of federal subsidies received by plan sponsors that provide retiree prescription drug benefits at least equivalent to Medicare Part D coverage. As a result of the change in taxability of the federal subsidy, we were required to make adjustments to deferred tax asset balances, resulting in a $152 charge to income tax expense.

Tax benefits credited to shareholders' equity totaled $5 and $556 for the years ended June 30, 2010 and 2009, respectively. These primarily relate to the tax effects of net investment hedges, excess tax benefits from the exercise of stock options and the impacts of certain adjustments to pension and other retiree benefit obligations recorded in shareholders' equity.

We have undistributed earnings of foreign subsidiaries of approximately $30 billion at June 30, 2010, for which deferred taxes have not been provided. Such earnings are considered indefinitely invested in the foreign subsidiaries. If such earnings were repatriated, additional tax expense may result, although the calculation of such additional taxes is not practicable.

On July 1, 2007, we adopted accounting guidance on the accounting for uncertainty in income taxes. The adoption of the guidance resulted in a decrease to retained earnings as of July 1, 2007 of $232, which was reflected as a cumulative effect of a change in accounting principle with a corresponding increase to the net liability for uncertain tax positions. The impact primarily reflects the accrual of additional statutory interest and penalties as required by accounting guidance, partially offset by adjustments to existing balances for uncertain tax positions to comply with measurement principles. The implementation of the guidance also resulted in a reduction in our net tax liabilities for uncertain tax positions related to prior acquisitions accounted for under purchase accounting, resulting in an $80 decrease to goodwill.

A reconciliation of the beginning and ending liability for uncertain tax positions is as follows:

	2010	2009	2008
Beginning of year	$2,003	$2,582	$2,971
Increases in tax positions for prior years	128	116	164
Decreases in tax positions for prior years	(146)	(485)	(576)
Increases in tax positions for current year	193	225	375
Settlements with taxing authorities	(216)	(172)	(260)
Lapse in statute of limitations	(45)	(68)	(200)
Currency translation	(120)	(195)	108
End of year	1,797	2,003	2,582

The Company is present in over 150 taxable jurisdictions and, at any point in time, has 50–60 audits underway at various stages of completion. We evaluate our tax positions and establish liabilities for uncertain tax positions that may be challenged by local authorities and may not be fully sustained, despite our belief that the underlying tax positions are fully supportable. Uncertain tax positions are reviewed on an ongoing basis and are adjusted in light of changing facts and circumstances, including progress of tax audits, developments in case law and closing of statute of limitations. Such adjustments are reflected in the tax provision as appropriate. The Company is making a concerted effort to bring its audit inventory to a more current position. We have done this by working with tax authorities to conduct audits for several open years at once. We have tax years open ranging from 1997 and forward. We are generally not able to reliably estimate the ultimate settlement amounts until the close of the audit. While we do not expect material changes, it is possible that the amount of unrecognized benefit with respect to our uncertain tax positions will significantly increase or decrease within the next 12 months related to the audits described above. At this time, we are not able to make a reasonable estimate of the range of impact on the balance of uncertain tax positions or the impact on the effective tax rate related to these items.

Included in the total liability for uncertain tax positions at June 30, 2010 is $1,318 that, depending on the ultimate resolution, could impact the effective tax rate in future periods.

We recognize accrued interest and penalties related to uncertain tax positions in income tax expense. As of June 30, 2010 and 2009, we had accrued interest of $622 and $636 and penalties of $89 and $100, respectively, that are not included in the above table. During the fiscal years ended June 30, 2010 and 2009, we recognized $38 and $119 in interest and $(8) and $(4) in penalties, respectively.

Deferred income tax assets and liabilities were comprised of the following:

June 30	2010	2009
Deferred Tax Assets		
Pension and postretirement benefits	$ 1,717	$ 1,395
Stock-based compensation	1,257	1,182
Loss and other carryforwards	595	439
Goodwill and other intangible assets	312	331
Accrued marketing and promotion	216	167
Fixed assets	102	114
Unrealized loss on financial and foreign exchange transactions	88	577
Accrued interest and taxes	88	120
Advance payments	16	15
Inventory	35	97
Other	757	885
Valuation allowances	(120)	(104)
Total	5,063	5,218
Deferred Tax Liabilities		
Goodwill and other intangible assets	11,760	11,922
Fixed assets	1,642	1,654
Other	269	146
Total	13,671	13,722

Net operating loss carryforwards were $1,875 and $1,428 at June 30, 2010 and 2009, respectively. If unused, $567 will expire between 2011 and 2030. The remainder, totaling $1,308 at June 30, 2010, may be carried forward indefinitely.

Credit Provision

3.90

WINNEBAGO INDUSTRIES, INC. (AUG)

STATEMENTS OF OPERATIONS (in part)

	Year Ended		
(In thousands, except per share data)	August 28, 2010	August 29, 2009	August 30, 2008
Net revenues	$449,484	$211,519	$604,352
Cost of goods sold	423,217	242,265	569,580
Gross profit (deficit)	26,267	(30,746)	34,772
Operating expenses:			
Selling	12,724	12,616	18,482
General and administrative	13,023	15,298	21,359
Asset impairment	—	855	4,686
Total operating expenses	25,747	28,769	44,527
Operating income (loss)	520	(59,515)	(9,755)
Financial income	222	1,452	4,314
Income (loss) before income taxes	742	(58,063)	(5,441)
(Benefit) provision for taxes	(9,505)	20,703	(8,225)
Net income (loss)	$ 10,247	$ (78,766)	$ 2,784

NOTES TO FINANCIAL STATEMENTS

Note 10. Income Taxes

The components of the (benefit) provision for income taxes are as follows:

	Year Ended[1]		
(In thousands)	August 28, 2010	August 29, 2009	August 30, 2008
Current			
Federal	$ (7,694)	$(17,882)	$(2,132)
State	(3,255)	(1,049)	(4,212)
Total current benefit	(10,949)	(18,931)	(6,344)
Deferred			
Federal	1,260	34,559	(1,630)
State	184	5,075	(251)
Total deferred provision (benefit)	1,444	39,634	(1,881)
Total (benefit) provision	$ (9,505)	$ 20,703	$(8,225)

[1] Fiscal year ended August 30, 2008 contained 53 weeks; all other fiscal years contained 52 weeks.

Current Benefit

Of the current federal benefit of $7.7 million for Fiscal 2010 reflected in the table above, $5.8 million relates to the carryback of our Fiscal 2009 losses and the remaining benefit relates to settlements of uncertain tax positions as a result of our federal audit. On November 6, 2009, the President of the United States signed into law the Worker, Homeownership, and Business Assistance Act of 2009, which expanded the NOL carryback period from two to five years, allowing us to carryback all Fiscal 2009 NOLs. We filed our original tax return and carryback claim in December 2009 and received our federal refund of $21.9 million during our second quarter of Fiscal 2010. During the third quarter of Fiscal 2010, we filed a superseding federal tax return and amended our original carryback request, recording an additional benefit of approximately $1.0 million. As a result, we recorded a total tax benefit of $5.8 million in Fiscal 2010 related to the portion of the 2009 NOL that was previously not able to be carried back and reduced the associated valuation allowance. The current federal benefit recorded in Fiscal 2009 was primarily the amount of tax benefit that we were able to carryback under the then current legislation for taxable losses incurred during Fiscal 2009. The federal benefit recorded in Fiscal 2008 was primarily a result of tax planning initiatives recorded during the year.

The state benefit recorded in Fiscal 2010 and Fiscal 2009 is primarily a result of tax planning initiatives recorded during those years. The state benefit recorded during Fiscal 2008 is primarily a result of settlements of uncertain tax positions with various jurisdictions occurring during the year.

Deferred Provision (Benefit)

The deferred federal tax expense recorded during Fiscal 2010 is primarily the result of tax planning initiatives and changes in the valuation allowance recorded during the year. The deferred federal tax expense reported during Fiscal 2009 is primarily a result of establishing a full valuation allowance on all deferred tax assets during the year.

The deferred state tax expense reported during Fiscal 2009 is primarily a result of recording a full valuation allowance on all deferred tax assets during the year.

The following is a reconciliation of the U.S. statutory income tax rate to our effective tax rate:

(A percentage)	Year Ended[1]		
	August 28, 2010	August 29, 2009	August 30, 2008
U.S. federal statutory rate	35.0%	(35.0)%	(35.0)%
Tax-free and dividend income	(136.5)%	(2.0)%	(69.6)%
Other permanent items	187.2%	—%	—%
State taxes, net of federal benefit	4.2%	(2.5)%	1.3%
Valuation allowance	(735.3)%	77.5%	6.0%
Amended state returns	(193.4)%	—%	—%
Incentive stock options	—%	—%	2.1%
Uncertain tax positions settlements & adjustments	(430.6)%	(0.9)%	(52.2)%
Other	(11.6)%	(1.5)%	(3.8)%
Effective tax (benefit) provision rate	(1,281.0)%	35.6%	(151.2)%

[1] Fiscal year ended August 30, 2008 contained 53 weeks; all other fiscal years contained 52 weeks.

Significant items comprising our net deferred tax assets are as follows:

(In thousands)	August 28, 2010			August 29, 2009		
	Assets	Liabilities	Total	Assets	Liabilities	Total
Current						
Warranty reserves	$ 2,592	$ —	$ 2,592	$ 2,393	$ —	$ 2,393
Self-insurance reserve	1,657	—	1,657	1,752	—	1,752
Accrued vacation	1,658	—	1,658	1,842	—	1,842
Miscellaneous reserves	3,816	(262)	3,554	4,087	(1,147)	2,940
Total current	9,723	(262)	9,461	10,074	(1,147)	8,927
Noncurrent						
Deferred compensation	13,879	—	13,879	14,439	—	14,439
Postretirement health care benefits	14,688	—	14,688	12,940	—	12,940
Unrecognized tax benefit	1,756	—	1,756	2,249	—	2,249
Tax credits and NOL carryforwards	3,217	—	3,217	8,370	—	8,370
Depreciation	—	(2,160)	(2,160)	—	(2,766)	(2,766)
Other	988	—	988	1,142	—	1,142
Total noncurrent	34,528	(2,160)	32,368	39,140	(2,766)	36,374
Total gross deferred tax assets	44,251	(2,422)	41,829	49,214	(3,913)	45,301
Valuation allowance	(44,251)	2,422	(41,829)	(49,214)	3,913	(45,301)
Total deferred tax assets	$ —	$ —	$ —	$ —	$ —	$ —

Deferred income taxes reflect the net tax effects of temporary differences between the carrying amounts of assets and liabilities for financial reporting purposes and the amounts used for income tax purposes. At August 28, 2010, our deferred tax assets included $1.8 million of unused tax credits, of which $365,000 can be carried forward 20 years and $1.4 million will expire in Fiscal 2014. In addition, at August 28, 2010, our deferred tax assets also included $1.5 million of NOL carryforwards, $115,000 of which is Federal NOLs that can be carried forward 20 years, and state NOLs in the amount of $1.3 million that will begin to expire in Fiscal 2013, if not otherwise used by us. A valuation allowance of $(41.8) million has been recognized to offset the related deferred tax assets due to the uncertainty of realizing the deferred tax assets.

Unrecognized Tax Benefits

At the beginning of Fiscal 2008, we adopted ASC 740 *Income Taxes*. ASC 740 prescribes criteria for the financial statement recognition and measurement of tax positions taken or expected to be taken in a tax return, among other items. In addition, ASC 740 provides guidance on classification of tax liabilities, interest and penalties, accounting interim periods, disclosure and transition with respect to the application of the new accounting standard. As a result of this adoption, we recognized a cumulative effect adjustment of $8.5 million as a reduction to the balance of retained earnings, an increase of $7.1 million in deferred tax assets, and an increase of $15.6 million in tax liabilities. The amount of unrecognized tax benefits totaled $21.8 million, of which $8.3 million was accrued for interest and penalties. It is our policy to recognize interest and penalties accrued relative to unrecognized tax benefits into tax expense.

Changes in the unrecognized tax benefits are as follows:

(In thousands)	Fiscal 2010	Fiscal 2009	Fiscal 2008
Unrecognized tax benefits—beginning balance	$(9,012)	$(9,469)	$(21,807)
Gross increases—tax positions in a prior period	(254)	(57)	(979)
Gross decreases—tax positions in a prior period	2,900[1]	677	7,218[3]
Gross increases—current period tax positions	(57)	(163)	(1,862)
Settlements	546[1]	—	7,961[3]
Unrecognized tax benefits—ending balance	$(5,877)	$(9,012)	$ (9,469)

[1] The $2.9 million decrease in unrecognized benefit reserves is primarily a reduction of reserves associated with positive settlements of uncertain tax positions related to the finalization of the IRS examination of our federal income tax returns for Fiscal 2006 through Fiscal 2008.
[2] The $546,000 reduction in reserves is actual cash payments as result of settlements of uncertain tax positions in various taxing jurisdictions.
[3] During Fiscal 2008, there were favorable settlements of uncertain tax positions with various taxing jurisdictions. The original unrecognized tax benefit associated with these positions was $14.6 million, of which $8.0 million was paid in cash and included in "Settlements." The $6.6 million balance of this reserve, inclusive of related deferred taxes, is included in "Gross decreases-tax positions in a prior period."

If the remaining uncertain positions are ultimately resolved, all of the $5.9 million could have a positive impact on our effective tax rate, as the deferred tax assets associated with these positions have a full valuation allowance established against them. Currently, $2.5 million is accrued for interest and penalties.

We file tax returns in the U.S. federal jurisdiction, as well as various international and state jurisdictions. Our federal income tax returns for Fiscal 2006 through Fiscal 2008 were under examination by the IRS and finalized during the third quarter of Fiscal 2010. Although certain years are no longer subject to examinations by the IRS and various state taxing authorities, NOL carryforwards generated in those years may still be adjusted upon examination by the IRS or state taxing authorities if they either have been or will be used in a future period. A number of years may elapse before an uncertain tax position is audited and finally resolved, and it is often very difficult to predict the outcome of such audits. Periodically, various state and local jurisdictions conduct audits, therefore, a variety of years are subject to state and local jurisdiction review.

We do not believe within the next twelve months there will be a significant change in the total amount of unrecognized tax benefits as of August 28, 2010.

Operating Loss and Tax Credit Carryforwards

3.91

SPECTRUM BRANDS HOLDINGS, INC. (SEP)

NOTES TO CONSOLIDATED FINANCIAL STATEMENTS

(In thousands, except per share amounts)

(8) Income Taxes (in part)

The Company, as of September 30, 2010, has U.S. federal and state net operating loss carryforwards of approximately $1,087,489 and $936,208, respectively. These net operating loss carryforwards expire through years ending in 2031. The Company has foreign loss carryforwards of approximately $195,456 which will expire beginning in 2011. Certain of the foreign net operating losses have indefinite carryforward periods. The Company is subject to an annual limitation on the use of its net operating losses that arose prior to its emergence from bankruptcy. The Company has had multiple changes of ownership, as defined under IRC Section 382, that subject the Company's U.S. federal and state net operating losses and other tax attributes to certain limitations. The annual limitation is based on a number of factors including the value of the Company's stock (as defined for tax purposes) on the date of the ownership change, its net unrealized built in gain position on that date, the occurrence of realized built in gains in years subsequent to the ownership change, and the effects of subsequent ownership changes (as defined for tax purposes) if any. Based on these factors, the Company projects that $296,160 of the total U.S. federal and $462,837 of the state net operating loss carryforwards will expire unused. In addition, separate return year limitations apply to limit the Company's utilization of the acquired Russell Hobbs U.S. federal and state net operating losses to future income of the Russell Hobbs subgroup. The Company also projects that $37,542 of the total foreign loss carryforwards will expire unused. The Company has provided a full valuation allowance against those deferred tax assets.

The Predecessor Company recognized income tax expense of approximately $124,054 related to the gain on the settlement of liabilities subject to compromise and the modification of the senior secured credit facility in the period from October 1, 2008 through August 30, 2009. The Company, has, in accordance with the IRC Section 108 reduced its net operating loss carryforwards for cancellation of debt income that arose from its emergence from Chapter 11 of the Bankruptcy Code, under IRC Section 382(1)(6).

3.92

DELL INC. (JAN)

NOTES TO CONSOLIDATED FINANCIAL STATEMENTS

Note 10—Income and Other Taxes

Income before income taxes included approximately $1.8 billion, $2.7 billion, and $3.3 billion related to foreign operations in Fiscal 2010, 2009, and 2008, respectively.

The provision for income taxes consisted of the following:

	Fiscal Year Ended		
(In millions)	January 29, 2010	January 30, 2009	February 1, 2008
Current:			
Domestic	$527	$465	$ 901
Foreign	116	295	287
Current	643	760	1,188
Deferred:			
Domestic	(12)	15	(230)
Foreign	(40)	71	(78)
Deferred	(52)	86	(308)
Provision for income taxes	$591	$846	$ 880

Deferred tax assets and liabilities for the estimated tax impact of temporary differences between the tax and book basis of assets and liabilities are recognized based on the enacted statutory tax rates for the year in which Dell expects the differences to reverse. A valuation allowance is established against

a deferred tax asset when it is more likely than not that the asset or any portion thereof will not be realized. Based upon all the available evidence including expectation of future taxable income, Dell has provided a valuation allowance of $41 million and $31 million for Fiscal 2010 and 2009, respectively, related to state income credit carryforwards, and $22 million related to net operating losses for Fiscal 2010. Dell has determined that it will be able to realize the remainder of its deferred tax assets.

The components of Dell's net deferred tax asset are as follows:

(In millions)	January 29, 2010	January 30, 2009
Deferred Tax Assets:		
Deferred revenue	$ 610	$ 633
Inventory and warranty provisions	13	36
Provisions for product returns and doubtful accounts	60	53
Leasing and financing	191	242
Credit carryforwards	51	47
Loss carryforwards	173	88
Stock-based and deferred compensation	225	233
Operating accruals	25	33
Compensation related accruals	25	48
Other	56	85
Deferred tax assets	1,429	1,498
Valuation allowance	(63)	(31)
Deferred tax assets, net of valuation allowance	1,366	1,467
Deferred Tax Liabilities:		
Property and equipment	(142)	(160)
Acquired intangibles	(478)	(167)
Unrealized gains	—	(14)
Other	(65)	(59)
Deferred tax liabilities	(685)	(400)
Net deferred tax asset	$ 681	$1,067
Current portion (included in other current assets)	$ 444	$ 499
Non-current portion (included in other non-current assets)	237	568
Net deferred tax asset	$ 681	$1,067

During Fiscal 2010, Dell recorded $26 million of deferred tax assets related to acquired net operating loss and credit carryforwards, net of valuation allowances of $17 million. The offset for recording the acquired net operating loss and credit carryforwards was $9 million to goodwill. During Fiscal 2009, Dell recorded $76 million of deferred tax assets related to net operating loss and credit carryforwards acquired during the year. The offset for recording the acquired net operating loss and credit carryforwards was $56 million to goodwill and $20 million to additional paid in capital. Utilization of the acquired carryforwards is subject to limitations due to ownership changes that may delay the utilization of a portion of the acquired carryforwards. No additional valuation allowances have been placed on the acquired net operating loss and credit carryforwards. The carryforwards for significant taxing jurisdictions expire beginning in Fiscal 2017.

Deferred taxes have not been recorded on the excess book basis in the shares of certain foreign subsidiaries because these basis differences are not expected to reverse in the foreseeable future and are expected to be permanent in duration. These basis differences in the amount of approximately $11.3 billion arose primarily from the undistributed book earnings of substantially all of the subsidiaries in which Dell intends to reinvest indefinitely. The basis differences could reverse through a sale of the subsidiaries or the receipt of dividends from the subsidiaries, as well as various other events. Net of available foreign tax credits, residual income tax of approximately $3.7 billion would be due upon reversal of this excess book basis as of January 29, 2010.

A portion of Dell's operations is subject to a reduced tax rate or is free of tax under various tax holidays that expire in whole or in part during Fiscal 2011 through 2019. Many of these tax holidays and reduced tax rates may be extended when certain conditions are met or may be terminated early if certain conditions are not met. The income tax benefits attributable to the tax status of these subsidiaries were estimated to be approximately $149 million ($0.08 per share) in Fiscal 2010, $338 million ($0.17 per share) in Fiscal 2009, and $502 million ($0.23 per share) in Fiscal 2008.

The effective tax rate differed from the statutory U.S. federal income tax rate as follows:

	Fiscal Year Ended		
	January 29, 2010	January 30, 2009	February 1, 2008
U.S. federal statutory rate	35.0%	35.0%	35.0%
Foreign income taxed at different rates	(7.5)	(9.8)	(12.5)
In-process research and development	—	—	0.8
Other	1.7	0.2	(0.3)
Total	29.2%	25.4%	23.0%

At the beginning of Fiscal 2008, Dell adopted the accounting guidance for uncertain tax positions, which requires that a tax benefit from an uncertain tax position not be recognized in the financial statements unless it is more likely than not that the position will be sustained upon examination. The cumulative effect of adoption of this standard was a $62 million increase in tax liabilities and a corresponding decrease in stockholders' equity.

A reconciliation of the beginning and ending amount of unrecognized tax benefits is as follows:

(In millions)	Total
Balance at February 3, 2007 (adoption)	$1,096
Increases related to tax positions of the current year	390
Increases related to tax positions of prior years	34
Reductions for tax positions of prior years	(13)
Lapse of statute of limitations	(6)
Settlements	(18)
Balance at February 1, 2008	1,483
Increases related to tax positions of the current year	298
Increases related to tax positions of prior years	19
Reductions for tax positions of prior years	(217)
Lapse of statute of limitations	(7)
Settlements	(38)
Balance at January 30, 2009	1,538
Increases related to tax positions of the current year	298
Increases related to tax positions of prior years	32
Reductions for tax positions of prior years	(69)
Lapse of statute of limitations	(3)
Settlements	(3)
Balance at January 29, 2010	$1,793

Fiscal 2009 reductions for tax positions of prior years in the table above include $163 million of items that did not impact Dell's effective tax rate for Fiscal 2009. These items include foreign currency translation, withdrawal of positions expected to be taken for prior year tax filings, and a reduction that is included in the deferred tax asset valuation allowance at January 30, 2009. There were no significant items of a similar nature in Fiscal 2010.

Associated with the unrecognized tax benefits of $1.8 billion, $1.5 billion, and $1.5 billion at January 29, 2010, January 30, 2009, and February 1, 2008, respectively, are interest and penalties as well as $209 million, $166 million and $171 million of offsetting tax benefits associated with estimated transfer pricing, the benefit of interest deductions, and state income tax benefits. The net amount of $2.1 billion, if recognized, would favorably affect Dell's effective tax rate.

Interest and penalties related to income tax liabilities are included in income tax expense. The balance of gross accrued interest and penalties recorded in the Consolidated Statements of Financial Position at January 29, 2010, January 30, 2009, and February 1, 2008 was $507 million, $400 million, and $288 million, respectively. During Fiscal 2010, 2009, and 2008, $107 million, $112 million, and $88 million, respectively, related to interest and penalties were included in income tax expense.

Dell is currently under income tax audits in various jurisdictions, including the United States. The tax periods open to examination by the major taxing jurisdictions to which Dell is subject include fiscal years 1997 through 2010. As a result of these audits, Dell maintains ongoing discussions and negotiations relating to tax matters with the taxing authorities in these various jurisdictions. Dell's U.S. federal income tax returns for fiscal years 2007 through 2009 are currently under examination by the Internal Revenue Service ("IRS"). In April 2009, the IRS issued a Revenue Agent's Report ("RAR") for fiscal years 2004 through 2006 proposing certain assessments primarily related to transfer pricing matters. Dell disagrees with certain of the proposed assessments, primarily related to transfer pricing matters, contained in the RAR and has contested them through the IRS administrative appeals procedures. The first meeting between Dell and the IRS Appeals Division is scheduled for early 2010. Dell anticipates the appeals process will involve multiple meetings and could take several years to complete. Dell believes that adequate reserves have been provided related to all matters contained in tax periods open to examination. However, should Dell experience an unfavorable outcome in this matter, such outcome could have a material impact on its results of operations, financial position, and cash flows. Although the timing of income tax audit resolutions and negotiations with taxing authorities are highly uncertain, Dell does not anticipate a significant change to the total amount of unrecognized income tax benefits within the next 12 months.

Dell takes certain non-income tax positions in the jurisdictions in which it operates and has received certain non-income tax assessments from various jurisdictions. Dell believes its positions in these non-income tax litigation matters are supportable, that a liability is not probable, and that it will ultimately prevail. In the normal course of business, Dell's positions and conclusions related to its non-income taxes could be challenged and assessments may be made. To the extent new information is obtained and Dell's views on its positions, probable outcomes of assessments, or litigation change, changes in estimates to Dell's accrued liabilities would be recorded in the period in which such determination is made.

Taxes on Undistributed Earnings

3.93

GOOGLE INC. (DEC)

NOTES TO CONSOLIDATED FINANCIAL STATEMENTS

Note 15. Income Taxes (in part)

Income before income taxes included income from domestic operations of $2,059 million, $3,579 million, and $4,948 million for 2008, 2009, and 2010, and income from foreign operations of $3,794 million, $4,802 million, and $5,848 million for 2008, 2009, and 2010. Substantially all of the income from foreign operations was earned by an Irish subsidiary.

The provision for income taxes consists of the following (in millions):

	Year Ended December 31		
	2008	**2009**	**2010**
Current:			
Federal	$1,348	$1,531	$1,657
State	468	450	458
Foreign	91	148	167
Total	1,907	2,129	2,282
Deferred:			
Federal	(198)	(273)	(25)
State	(63)	13	47
Foreign	(20)	(8)	(13)
Total	(281)	(268)	9
Provision for income to	$1,626	$1,861	$2,291

The reconciliation of federal statutory income tax rate to our effective income tax rate is as follows (in millions):

	Year Ended December 31		
	2008	**2009**	**2010**
Expected provision at federal statutory tax rate (35%)	$ 2,049	$ 2,933	$ 3,779
State taxes, net of federal benefit	263	302	322
Stock-based compensation expense	91	63	79
Change in valuation allowance	313	(41)	(34)
Foreign rate differential	(1,020)	(1,339)	(1,769)
Federal research credit	(52)	(56)	(84)
Tax exempt interest	(52)	(15)	(12)
Other permanent differences	34	14	10
Provision for income taxes	$ 1,626	$ 1,861	$ 2,291

We have not provided U.S. income taxes and foreign withholding taxes on the undistributed earnings of foreign subsidiaries as of December 31, 2010 because we intend to permanently reinvest such earnings outside the U.S. If these foreign earnings were to be repatriated in the future, the related U.S. tax liability may be reduced by any foreign income taxes previously paid on these earnings. As of December 31, 2010, the cumulative amount of earnings upon which U.S. income taxes have not been provided is approximately $17.5 billion. Determination of the amount of unrecognized deferred tax liability related to these earnings is not practicable.

3.94

TUPPERWARE BRANDS CORPORATION (DEC)

NOTES TO THE CONSOLIDATED FINANCIAL STATEMENTS

Note 13. Income Taxes (in part)

As of December 25, 2010 and December 26, 2009, the Company's gross unrecognized tax benefit was $27.3 million and $53.1 million, respectively. The Company expects to settle one or more foreign audits in the next twelve months that will result in a decrease in the amount of accrual for uncertain tax positions of up to $2.0 million. For the remaining balance as of December 25, 2010, the Company is not able to reliably estimate the timing or ultimate settlement amount. While the Company does not currently expect material changes, it is possible that the amount of unrecognized benefit with respect to the uncertain tax positions will significantly increase or decrease related to audits in various foreign jurisdictions that may conclude during that period or new developments that could also in turn impact the Company's assessment relative to the establishment of valuation allowances against certain existing deferred tax assets. At this time, the Company is not able to make a reasonable estimate of the range of impact on the balance of unrecognized tax benefits or the impact on the effective tax rate related to these items.

As of December 25, 2010, the Company had $845.8 million of undistributed earnings of international subsidiaries. The Company has not provided for U.S. deferred income taxes on these undistributed earnings because of its intention to indefinitely reinvest these earnings. The determination of the amount of unrecognized deferred U.S. income tax liability is not practicable because of the complexities associated with its hypothetical calculation.

CONSTRUCTION-TYPE AND PRODUCTION-TYPE CONTRACTS

RECOGNITION AND MEASUREMENT

3.95 Accounting and disclosure requirements for construction-type and production-type contracts are discussed in FASB ASC 605–35. In accounting for contracts, the basic accounting policy decision is the choice between the percentage-of-completion method and the completed-contract method. The determination of which is preferable is based on an evaluation of the circumstances.

3.96

TABLE 3-5: METHOD OF ACCOUNTING FOR CONSTRUCTION-TYPE AND PROUDCTION-TYPE CONTRACTS

Table 3-5 shows that usually the percentage of completion method or a modification of this method is used to recognize revenue on long-term contracts.

	Number of Entities		
	2010	2009	2008
Percentage of completion: input based..........	43	63	56
Percentage of completion: output based........	32	41	40
Completed contract...	8	20	17

PRESENTATION AND DISCLOSURE EXCERPTS

Construction and Production Type Contracts

3.97

CACI INTERNATIONAL INC (JUN)

NOTES TO CONSOLIDATED FINANCIAL STATEMENTS

Note 3. Summary of Significant Accounting Policies (in part)

Revenue Recognition

The Company generates almost all of its revenue from three different types of contractual arrangements: cost-plus-fee contracts, time-and-materials contracts, and fixed price contracts. Revenue on cost-plus-fee contracts is recognized to the extent of costs incurred plus an estimate of the applicable fees earned. The Company considers fixed fees under cost-plus-fee contracts to be earned in proportion to the allowable costs incurred in performance of the contract. For cost-plus-

fee contracts that include performance based fee incentives, and that are subject to the provisions of ASC 605-35, *Revenue Recognition—Construction-Type and Production-Type Contracts* (ASC 605-35), the Company recognizes the relevant portion of the expected fee to be awarded by the customer at the time such fee can be reasonably estimated, based on factors such as the Company's prior award experience and communications with the customer regarding performance. For such cost-plus-fee contracts subject to the provisions of ASC 605-10-S99, *Revenue Recognition—SEC Materials* (ASC 605-10-S99), the Company recognizes the relevant portion of the fee upon customer approval. Revenue on time-and-material contracts is recognized to the extent of billable rates times hours delivered for services provided, to the extent of material cost for products delivered to customers, and to the extent of expenses incurred on behalf of the customers. Shipping and handling fees charged to the customers are recognized as revenue at the time products are delivered to the customers.

The Company has four basic categories of fixed price contracts: fixed unit price, fixed price-level of effort, fixed price-completion, and fixed price-license. Revenue on fixed unit price contracts, where specified units of output under service arrangements are delivered, is recognized as units are delivered based on the specified price per unit. Revenue on fixed unit price maintenance contracts is recognized ratably over the length of the service period. Revenue for fixed price-level of effort contracts is recognized based upon the number of units of labor actually delivered multiplied by the agreed rate for each unit of labor.

A significant portion of the Company's fixed price-completion contracts involve the design and development of complex client systems. For these contracts that are within the scope of ASC 605-35, revenue is recognized on the percentage-of-completion method using costs incurred in relation to total estimated costs. For fixed price-completion contracts that are not within the scope of ASC 605-35, revenue is generally recognized ratably over the service period. The Company's fixed price-license agreements and related services contracts are primarily executed in its international operations. As the agreements to deliver software require significant production, modification or customization of software, revenue is recognized using the contract accounting guidance of ASC 605-35. For agreements to deliver data under license and related services, revenue is recognized as the data is delivered and services are performed. Except for losses on contracts accounted for under ASC 605-10-S99, provisions for estimated losses on uncompleted contracts are recorded in the period such losses are determined. Losses on contracts accounted for under ASC 605-10-S99 are recognized as the services and materials are provided.

The Company's contracts may include the provision of more than one of its services. In these situations, and for applicable arrangements, revenue recognition includes the proper identification of separate units of accounting and the allocation of revenue across all elements based on relative fair values, with proper consideration given to the guidance provided by other authoritative literature.

Contract accounting requires judgment relative to assessing risks, estimating contract revenue and costs, and making assumptions for schedule and technical issues. Due to the size and nature of many of the Company's contracts, the estimation of total revenue and cost at completion is complicated and subject to many variables. Contract costs include material, labor, subcontracting costs, and other direct costs, as well as an allocation of allowable indirect costs. Assumptions have to be made regarding the length of time to complete the contract because costs also include expected increases in wages and prices for materials. For contract change orders, claims or similar items, the Company applies judgment in estimating the amounts and assessing the potential for realization. These amounts are only included in contract value when they can be reliably estimated and realization is considered probable. Incentives or penalties related to performance on contracts are considered in estimating sales and profit rates, and are recorded when there is sufficient information for the Company to assess anticipated performance. Estimates of award fees for certain contracts are also a factor in estimating revenue and profit rates based on actual and anticipated awards.

Long-term development and production contracts make up a large portion of the Company's business, and therefore the amounts recorded in the Company's financial statements using contract accounting methods are material. For federal government contracts, the Company follows U.S. government procurement and accounting standards in assessing the allowability and the allocability of costs to contracts. Due to the significance of the judgments and estimation processes, it is likely that materially different amounts could be recorded if the Company used different assumptions or if the underlying circumstances were to change. The Company closely monitors compliance with, and the consistent application of, its critical accounting policies related to contract accounting. Business operations personnel conduct thorough periodic contract status and performance reviews. When adjustments in estimated contract revenue or costs are required, any changes from prior estimates are generally included in earnings in the current period. Also, regular and recurring evaluations of contract cost, scheduling and technical matters are performed by management personnel who are independent from the business operations personnel performing work under the contract. Costs incurred and allocated to contracts with the U.S. government are scrutinized for compliance with regulatory standards by Company personnel, and are subject to audit by the Defense Contract Audit Agency (DCAA).

From time to time, the Company may proceed with work based on client direction prior to the completion and signing of formal contract documents. The Company has a formal review process for approving any such work. Revenue associated with such work is recognized only when it can be reliably estimated and realization is probable. The Company bases its estimates on previous experiences with the client, communications with the client regarding funding status, and its knowledge of available funding for the contract or program.

The Company's U.S. government contracts (94.8 percent of total revenue in the year ended June 30, 2010) are subject to subsequent government audit of direct and indirect costs. Incurred cost audits have been completed through June 30, 2005. Management does not anticipate any material adjustment to the consolidated financial statements in subsequent periods for audits not yet completed.

3.98

LOCKHEED MARTIN CORPORATION (DEC)

NOTES TO CONSOLIDATED FINANCIAL STATEMENTS

Note 1—Significant Accounting Policies (in part)

Sales and earnings—We record net sales and estimated profits on a percentage-of-completion (POC) basis for cost-reimbursable and fixed-price design, development, and production (DD&P) contracts. Revenue is recorded on time-and-materials contracts as the work is performed based on agreed-upon hourly rates and allowable costs. The POC method for DD&P contracts depends on the nature of the products provided under the contract. For example, for contracts that require us to perform a significant level of development effort in comparison to the total value of the contract and/or to deliver less than substantial quantities of similar items, sales are recorded using the cost-to-cost method to measure progress toward completion. Under the cost-to-cost method of accounting, we recognize sales and an estimated profit as costs are incurred based on the proportion that the incurred costs bear to total estimated costs. For contracts that require us to provide a substantial number of similar items without a significant level of development effort, we record sales and profit on a percentage-of-completion basis using units-of-delivery as the basis to measure progress toward completing the contract.

When adjustments in estimated contract revenues or estimated costs at completion are required on DD&P contracts, any changes from prior estimates are recognized in the current period for the inception-to-date effect of the changes. When estimates of total costs to be incurred on a contract exceed total estimates of revenue to be earned, a provision for the entire loss on the contract is recorded in the period in which the loss is determined.

Award fees and incentives, as well as penalties related to contract performance, are considered in estimating sales and profit rates on DD&P contracts. We consider estimates of award fees in estimating sales and profit rates based on past experience and anticipated performance. We record incentives or penalties when there is sufficient information to assess anticipated contract performance. We do not recognize incentive provisions that increase or decrease earnings based solely on a single significant event until the event occurs. We only include amounts representing contract change orders, claims, or other items in contract value when they can be reliably estimated and realization is probable.

For cost-reimbursable contracts for services that provide for award and incentive fees, we record net sales as services are performed, except for the award and incentive fees. Award and incentive fees are recorded when they are fixed or determinable, generally at the date the amount is communicated to us by the customer. This approach results in the recognition of such fees at contractual intervals (typically every six months) throughout the contract and is dependent on the customer's processes for notification of awards and issuance of formal notifications. Under a fixed-price service contract, we get paid a predetermined fixed amount for a specified scope of work and generally have full responsibility for the costs associated with the contract and the resulting profit or loss. We record net sales under fixed-price service contracts on a straight-line basis over the period of contract performance, unless evidence suggests that net sales are earned or the obligations are fulfilled in a different pattern. Costs for all service contracts are expensed as incurred.

Change in Accounting Principle—Effective January 1, 2011, we changed our methodology for recognizing net sales for service contracts with the U.S. Government. We will recognize sales on those contracts using the POC method similar to our DD&P contracts as described above. As such, we expect that approximately 95% of our consolidated net sales will be recognized using the POC method. We believe the POC method is preferable, as consistent revenue recognition application across all contracts with the U.S. Government better reflects the underlying economics of those contracts and aligns our financial reporting with others in our industry. Beginning with our first quarter 2011 financial statements, all prior periods presented will be retrospectively adjusted to apply the new method of accounting. The effect of this change is expected to be less than one percent of net sales and segment operating profit in 2011, and was not material to prior periods.

3.99

TEXTRON INC. (DEC)

NOTES TO THE CONSOLIDATED FINANCIAL STATEMENTS

Note 1. Summary of Significant Accounting Policies (in part)

Revenue Recognition (in part)

We generally recognize revenue for the sale of products, which are not under long-term contracts, upon delivery. For commercial aircraft, delivery is upon completion of manufacturing, customer acceptance, and the transfer of the risk and rewards of ownership. Taxes collected from customers and remitted to government authorities are recorded on a net basis.

When a sale arrangement involves multiple deliverables, such as sales of products that include customization and other services, we evaluate the arrangement to determine whether there are separate items that are required to be delivered under the arrangement that qualify as separate units of accounting. These arrangements typically involve the customization services we offer to customers who purchase Bell helicopters, and the services generally are provided within the first six months after the customer accepts the aircraft and assumes risk of loss. We consider the aircraft and the customization services to be separate units of accounting and allocate contract price between the two on a relative selling price basis using the best evidence of selling price for each of the arrangement deliverables, typically by reference to the price charged when the same or similar items are sold separately by us, taking into consideration any performance, cancellation, termination or refund-type provisions. We recognize revenue when the recognition criteria for each unit of accounting are met.

Long-Term Contracts—Revenues under long-term contracts are accounted for under the percentage-of-completion method of accounting. Under this method, we estimate profit as the difference between the total estimated revenues and cost of a contract. We then recognize that estimated profit over the contract term based on either the units-of-delivery method or the cost-to-cost method (which typically is used for development effort as costs are incurred), as appropriate under the circumstances. Revenues under fixed-price contracts generally are recorded using the units-of-delivery method. Revenues under cost-reimbursement contracts are recorded using the cost-to-cost method.

Our long-term contract profits are based on estimates of total contract cost and revenues utilizing current contract specifications, expected engineering requirements and the achievement of contract milestones, including product deliveries. Certain contracts are awarded with fixed-price incentive fees that also are considered when estimating revenues and profit rates. Contract costs typically are incurred over a period of several years, and the estimation of these costs requires substantial judgment. We review and revise these estimates periodically throughout the contract term. Revisions to contract profits are recorded when the revisions to estimated revenues or costs are made. Anticipated losses on contracts are recognized in full in the period in which the losses become probable and estimable.

Collaborative Arrangements—Our Bell segment has a strategic alliance agreement with The Boeing Company (Boeing) to provide engineering, development and test services related to the V-22 aircraft, as well as to produce the V-22 aircraft, under a number of separate contracts with the U.S. Government (V-22 Contracts). The alliance created by this agreement is not a legal entity and has no employees, no assets and no true operations. This agreement creates contractual rights and does not represent an entity in which we have an equity interest. We account for this alliance as a collaborative arrangement with Bell and Boeing reporting costs incurred and revenue generated from transactions with the U.S. Government in each company's respective income statement. Neither Bell nor Boeing is considered to be the principal participant for the transactions recorded under this agreement. Profits on cost-plus contracts are allocated between Bell and Boeing on a 50%-50% basis. Negotiated profits on fixed-price contracts are also allocated 50%-50%; however, Bell and Boeing are each responsible for their own cost overruns and are entitled to retain any cost underruns. Based on the contractual arrangement established under the alliance, Bell accounts for its rights and obligations under the specific requirements of the V-22 Contracts allocated to Bell under the work breakdown structure. We account for all of our rights and obligations, including warranty, product and any contingent liabilities, under the specific requirements of the V-22 Contracts allocated to us under the agreement. Revenues and cost of sales reflect our performance under the V-22 Contracts with revenues recognized using the units-of-delivery method. We include all assets used in performance of the V-22 Contracts that we own, including inventory and unpaid receivables and all liabilities arising from our obligations under the V-22 Contracts in our Consolidated Balance Sheets.

DISCONTINUED OPERATIONS

RECOGNITION AND MEASUREMENT

3.100 FASB ASC 205-20 sets forth the financial accounting and reporting requirements for discontinued operations of a component of an entity. A *component of an entity* comprises operations and cash flows that can be clearly distinguished, operationally and for financial reporting purposes, from the rest of the entity. A component of an entity may be a reportable or an operating segment, a reporting unit, a subsidiary, or an asset group.

3.101 FASB ASC 205-20 uses a single accounting model to account for all long-lived assets to be disposed of (by sale, abandonment, or distribution to owners). This includes asset disposal groups meeting the criteria for presentation as a discontinued operation, as specified in FASB ASC 205-20. A long-lived asset group classified as held for sale should be measured at the lower of its carrying amount or fair value less cost to sell. Additionally, in accordance with FASB ASC 360, a loss shall be recognized for any write-down to fair value less cost to sell. A gain shall be recognized for any subsequent recovery of cost. Lastly, a gain or loss not previously recognized that results from the sale of the asset disposal group should be recognized at the date of sale.

PRESENTATION

3.102 The conditions for determining whether discontinued operations treatment is appropriate and the required income statement presentation are stated in FASB ASC 205-20-45-1, as follows:

The results of operations of a component of an entity that either has been disposed of or is classified as held for sale . . . [should] be reported in discontinued operations . . . if both of the following conditions are met:

a. The operations and cash flow of the component have been (or will be) eliminated from the ongoing operations of the entity as a result of the disposal transaction.

b. The entity will not have any significant continuing involvement in the operations of the component after the disposal transaction.

3.103 In a period in which a component of an entity either has been disposed of or is classified as held for sale, the income statement of a business entity or statement of activities of a not-for-profit entity for current and prior periods should report the results of operations of the component, including any gain or loss recognized from the sale or write-down, in discontinued operations. The results of operations of a component classified as held for sale should be reported in discontinued operations in the period(s) in which they occur. The results of discontinued operations, less applicable income taxes (benefit), should be reported as a separate component of income before extraordinary items (if applicable). For example, the results of discontinued operations may be reported in the income statement of a business entity as follows:

Income from continuing operations before income taxes	$XXXX
Income taxes	XXX
Income from continuing operations	$XXXX
Discontinued operations (Note X):	
Loss from operations of discontinued component X (including loss on disposal of $XXX)	$XXXX
Income tax benefit	XXXX
Loss on discontinued operations	XXXX
Net income	$XXXX

A gain or loss recognized on the disposal should be disclosed either on the face of the income statement or in the notes to the financial statements.

3.104 Illustrations of transactions that should and should not be accounted for as business segment disposals are presented in the implementation guidance and illustrations of FASB ASC 205-20-55.

PRESENTATION AND DISCLOSURE EXCERPTS

Business Component Disposals

3.105

DEAN FOODS COMPANY (DEC)

CONSOLIDATED STATEMENTS OF INCOME

	Year Ended December 31		
(Dollars in thousands, except share data)	**2010**	**2009**	**2008**
Net sales	$ 12,122,887	$ 11,113,782	$ 12,361,311
Cost of sales	9,116,965	8,008,561	9,438,593
Gross profit	3,005,922	3,105,221	2,922,718
Operating costs and expenses:			
Selling and distribution	1,904,526	1,818,833	1,802,214
General and administrative	629,656	623,835	482,392
Amortization of intangibles	11,295	9,637	9,836
Facility closing and reorganization costs	30,761	30,162	22,758
Other expense	30,000	—	—
Total operating costs and expenses	2,606,238	2,482,467	2,317,200
Operating income	399,684	622,754	605,518
Other (income) expense:			
Interest expense	248,301	246,510	308,178
Other (income) expense, net	161	(4,221)	1,123
Total other expense	248,462	242,289	309,301
Income from continuing operations before income taxes	151,222	380,465	296,217
Income taxes	73,482	151,845	114,330
Income from continuing operations	77,740	228,620	181,887
Gain (loss) on sale of discontinued operations, net of tax	7,521	89	(1,275)
Income (loss) from discontinued operations, net of tax	(2,505)	(862)	3,158
Net Income	82,756	227,847	183,770
Net loss attributable to non-controlling interest	8,735	12,461	—
Net income attributable to Dean Foods Company	$ 91,491	$ 240,308	$ 183,770
Average common shares:			
Basic	181,799,306	170,986,886	149,266,519
Diluted	182,861,802	173,858,303	153,395,746
Basic earnings per common share:			
Income from continuing operations attributable to Dean Foods Company	$ 0.48	$ 1.41	$ 1.22
Income from discontinued operations attributable to Dean Foods Company	0.02	—	0.01
Net income attributable to Dean Foods Company	$ 0.50	$ 1.41	$ 1.23
Diluted earnings per common share:			
Income from continuing operations attributable to Dean Foods Company	$ 0.47	$ 1.39	$ 1.19
Income (loss) from discontinued operations attributable to Dean Foods Company	0.03	(0.01)	0.01
Net income attributable to Dean Foods Company	$ 0.50	$ 1.38	$ 1.20

See Notes to Consolidated Financial Statements.

NOTES TO CONSOLIDATED FINANCIAL STATEMENTS

2. Discontinued Operations, Divestitures and Acquisitions (in part)

Discontinued Operations

During the second quarter of 2010, we committed to a plan to sell the business operations of Rachel's, which provides organic branded dairy-based chilled yogurt, milk and related dairy products primarily in the United Kingdom. We completed the sale of our Rachel's business on August 4, 2010 and recognized a gain of $5.7 million, net of tax. Our Rachel's operations, previously reported within the WhiteWave-Alpro segment, have been reclassified as discontinued operations in our Consolidated Financial Statements for the twelve-month periods ended December 31, 2010, 2009 and 2008 and as of December 31, 2009.

The following is a summary of Rachel's assets and liabilities held for sale as of December 31, 2009:

(In thousands)	December 31, 2009
Assets	
Current assets	$11,514
Property, plant and equipment, net	6,626
Goodwill, identifiable intangibles and other assets	11,948
Assets of discontinued operations held for sale	$30,088
Liabilities	
Accounts payable and accrued expenses	$ 5,156
Other liabilities	3,889
Liabilities of discontinued operations held for sale	$ 9,045

The following is a summary of Rachel's operating results, which are included in discontinued operations:

	Year Ended December 31		
(In thousands)	2010	2009	2008
Operations:			
Net sales	$26,319	$44,606	$93,302
Income (loss) before income taxes	(3,783)	(642)	3,460
Income tax	1,399	(220)	(507)
Net income (loss)	$ (2,384)	$ (862)	$ 2,953

In 2010 and 2008, we recognized expense of $121,000 and income of $205,000, respectively, related to prior discontinued operations. In 2010, 2009 and 2008, we recognized a gain of $1.8 million, a gain of $89,000 and a loss of $1.3 million, respectively, on the sale of prior discontinued operations.

Divestitures

In the fourth quarter of 2010, we entered into two separate agreements to sell our Mountain High and private label yogurt operations, which are part of our Fresh Dairy Direct-Morningstar segment. We expect to record a gain related to the sale of both of these operations. On February 1, 2011, we completed the sale of our Mountain High yogurt operations. We expect our private label operations sale to close in the first half of 2011. These operations did not meet the requirement to be accounted for as discounted operations. We intend to use the proceeds from the sale of our yogurt operations to pay down outstanding debt under our senior secured credit facility. See Note 9.

The following is a summary of our Mountain High and private label yogurt operations' assets and liabilities held for sale as of December 31, 2010:

(In thousands)	December 31, 2010
Assets	
Current assets	$ 8,329
Property, plant and equipment, net	26,346
Goodwill, identifiable intangibles and other assets	82,439
Assets held for sale	$117,114
Liabilities	
Accounts payable and accrued expenses	$ 3,839

3.106

VULCAN MATERIALS COMPANY (DEC)

CONSOLIDATED STATEMENTS OF EARNINGS AND
COMPREHENSIVE INCOME

	For the Years Ended December 31		
(In thousands, except per share data)	2010	2009	2008
Net sales	$2,405,916	$2,543,707	$3,453,081
Delivery revenues	152,946	146,783	198,357
Total revenues	2,558,862	2,690,490	3,651,438
Cost of goods sold	2,105,190	2,097,745	2,703,369
Delivery costs	152,946	146,783	198,357
Cost of revenues	2,258,136	2,244,528	2,901,726
Gross profit	300,726	445,962	749,712
Selling, administrative and general expenses	327,537	321,608	342,584
Gain on sale of property, plant & equipment and businesses, net	59,302	27,104	94,227
Goodwill impairment	0	0	252,664
Charge for legal settlement	40,000	0	0
Other operating income (expense), net	(7,031)	(3,006)	411
Operating earnings (loss)	(14,540)	148,452	249,102
Other income (expense), net	3,074	5,307	(4,357)
Interest income	863	2,282	3,126
Interest expense	181,603	175,262	172,813
Earnings (loss) from continuing operations before income taxes	(192,206)	(19,221)	75,058
Provision (benefit) for income taxes			
Current	(37,805)	6,106	92,346
Deferred	(51,858)	(43,975)	(20,655)
Total provision (benefit) for income taxes	(89,663)	(37,869)	71,691
Earnings (loss) from continuing operations	(102,543)	18,648	3,367
Earnings (loss) on discontinued operations, net of income taxes (Note 2)	6,053	11,666	(2,449)
Net earnings (loss)	$ (96,490)	$ 30,314	$ 918
Other comprehensive income (loss), net of tax			
Fair value adjustments to cash flow hedge	(481)	(2,748)	(2,640)
Reclassification adjustment for cash flow hedges included in net earnings (loss)	10,709	9,902	1,968
Adjustment for funded status of pension and postretirement benefit plans	3,201	(17,367)	(154,099)
Amortization of pension and postretirement plan actuarial loss and prior service cost	3,590	1,138	724
Other comprehensive income (loss)	17,019	(9,075)	(154,047)
Comprehensive income (loss)	$ (79,471)	$ 21,239	$ (153,129)
Basic earnings (loss) per share			
Continuing operations	$ (0.80)	$ 0.16	$ 0.03
Discontinued operations	$ 0.05	$ 0.09	$ (0.02)
Net earnings (loss) per share	$ (0.75)	$ 0.25	$ 0.01
Diluted earnings (loss) per share			
Continuing operations	$ (0.80)	$ 0.16	$ 0.03
Discontinued operations	$ 0.05	$ 0.09	$ (0.02)
Net earnings (loss) per share	$ (0.75)	$ 0.25	$ 0.01
Dividends declared per share	$ 1.00	$ 1.48	$ 1.96
Weighted-average common shares outstanding	128,050	118,891	109,774
Weighted-average common shares outstanding, assuming dilution	128,050	119,430	110,954

The accompanying Notes to Consolidated Financial Statements are an integral part of these statements.

NOTES TO CONSOLIDATED FINANCIAL STATEMENTS

Note 2. Discontinued Operations

In 2005, we sold substantially all the assets of our Chemicals business to Basic Chemicals, a subsidiary of Occidental Chemical Corporation. In addition to the initial cash proceeds, Basic Chemicals was required to make payments under two earn-out agreements subject to certain conditions. During 2007, we received the final payment under the ECU (electrochemical unit) earn-out, bringing cumulative cash receipts to its $150,000,000 cap.

Proceeds under the second earn-out agreement are based on the performance of the hydrochlorocarbon product HCC-240fa (commonly referred to as 5CP) from the closing of the transaction through December 31, 2012 (5CP earn-out). The primary determinant of the value for this earn-out is the level of growth in 5CP sales volume. At the June 7, 2005 closing date, the value assigned to the 5CP earn-out was limited to an amount that resulted in no gain on the sale of the business, as the gain was contingent in nature. A gain on disposal of the Chemicals business is recognized to the extent cumulative cash receipts under the 5CP earn-out exceed the initial value recorded.

During 2010, we received a payment of $8,794,000 (recorded as gain on disposal of discontinued operations) under the 5CP earn-out related to performance during the year ended December 31, 2009. Any future payments received pursuant to the 5CP earn-out will be recorded as additional gain on disposal of discontinued operations. During 2009 and 2008, we received payments of $11,625,000 and $10,014,000, respectively, under the 5CP earn- out related to the respective years ended December 31, 2008 and December 31, 2007. Through December 31, 2010, we have received a total of $42,707,000 under the 5CP earn-out, a total of $9,606,000 in excess of the receivable recorded on the date of disposition.

We are liable for a cash transaction bonus payable to certain former key Chemicals employees. This transaction bonus is payable if cash receipts realized from the two earn-out agreements described above exceed an established minimum threshold. The bonus is payable annually based on the prior year's results. Payments for the transaction bonus were $882,000 during 2010, $521,000 during 2009 and $0 during 2008.

The financial results of the Chemicals business are classified as discontinued operations in the accompanying Consolidated Statements of Earnings and Comprehensive Income for all periods presented. There were no net sales or revenues from discontinued operations for the years presented. Results from discontinued operations are as follows:

(In thousands)	2010	2009	2008
Discontinued Operations			
Pretax earnings (loss) from results	$ 2,103	$18,872	$(4,059)
Gain on disposal, net of transaction bonus	7,912	584	0
Income tax (provision) benefit	(3,962)	(7,790)	1,610
Earnings (loss) on discontinued operations, net of income taxes	$ 6,053	$11,666	$(2,449)

The 2010 pretax earnings from results of discontinued operations of $2,103,000 are due primarily to a $6,000,000 pretax gain recognized on recovery from an insurer in lawsuits involving perchloroethylene. This gain was offset in part by general and product liability costs, including legal defense costs, and environmental remediation costs associated with our former Chemicals business. The 2009 pretax earnings from results of discontinued operations relate primarily to settlements with two of our insurers in lawsuits involving perchloroethylene. These settlements resulted in pretax gains of $23,500,000. The insurance proceeds and associated gains represent a partial recovery of legal and settlement costs recognized in prior years. The 2008 pretax loss from discontinued operations and the remaining results from 2009 reflect charges primarily related to general and product liability costs, including legal defense costs and environmental remediation costs associated with our former Chemicals business.

In January 2011, we recovered an additional $7,500,000 from an insurer in lawsuits involving perchlorethylene. This recovery will be recorded as earnings from results of discontinued operations in the first quarter of 2011.

Adjustment of Gain or Loss

3.107

THE BRINK'S COMPANY (DEC)

NOTES TO CONSOLIDATED FINANCIAL STATEMENTS

Note 17—Income from Discontinued Operations

	Year Ended December 31		
(In millions)	2010	2009	2008
Brink's Home Security Holdings, Inc. ("BHS"):			
Income from operations before tax[a]	$ —	$ —	$105.4
Expense associated with the spin-off	—	—	(13.0)
Adjustments to contingencies of former operations:			
Gain from FBLET refunds	—	19.7	—
BAX Global indemnification	1.7	(13.2)	—
Insurance recoveries related to BAX Global indemnification	1.6	—	—
Workers' compensation	(7.2)	(1.5)	(1.0)
Other	0.8	1.8	5.9
Income (loss) from discontinued operations before income taxes	(3.1)	6.8	97.3
Provision (credit) for income taxes	(3.4)	2.3	45.8
Income from discontinued operations, net of tax	$ 0.3	$ 4.5	$ 51.5

[a] Revenues of BHS were $442.4 million in 2008 (partial year).

Federal Black Lung Excise Tax ("FBLET") Refunds

The Energy Improvement and Extension Act of 2008 enabled taxpayers to file claims for FBLET refunds for periods prior to those open under the previously applicable statute of limitations. In 2009, we received FBLET refunds and recognized a pre-tax gain of $19.7 million.

BAX Global

BAX Global, a former business unit, had been defending a claim related to the apparent diversion by a third party of goods being transported for a customer. On April 23, 2010, the Dutch Supreme Court denied the final appeal of BAX Global, letting stand the lower court ruling that BAX Global is liable for this claim. We had contractually indemnified the purchaser of BAX Global for this contingency. We recognized €9 million ($13.2 million) related to this matter in discontinued operations in 2009 and made an $11.5 million payment in 2010 in satisfaction of the judgment. We have insurance coverage applicable to this matter and we have collected $1.6 million from insurance companies in 2010.

BHS Spin-Off

On October 31, 2008, we distributed all of our interest in BHS to our shareholders of record as of the close of business on October 21, 2008, in a tax-free distribution. We distributed one share of BHS common stock for every share of our common stock outstanding. We contributed $50 million in cash to BHS at the time of the spin-off. We also forgave all the existing intercompany debt owed by BHS to us as of the distribution date.

BHS offered monitored security services in North America primarily for owner-occupied, single-family residences. To a lesser extent, BHS offered security services for commercial and multi-family properties. BHS typically installed and owned the on-site security systems and charged fees to monitor and service the systems.

In connection with the spin-off, we entered into a Tax Matters Agreement with BHS which provided a basis for the preparation and filing of tax returns for pre-spin and post-spin operations of BHS in 2008. As authorized by the Tax Matters Agreement, we made certain elections related to BHS' operations for our U.S. federal and state 2008 consolidated tax returns in 2009. These elections have the effect of decreasing the net deferred tax assets allocated to BHS at the time of the spin-off. As a result, we increased the amount of our current income tax receivable during 2009 by $26.8 million, with an offsetting increase in retained earnings to adjust the amount of the spin-off distribution.

After the spin-off, we reclassified BHS' results of operations, including previously reported results and non-segment income (expense) directly related to the spin-off, within discontinued operations.

Interest Expense

Interest expense included in discontinued operations was $0.3 million in 2008. Interest expense recorded in discontinued operations includes only interest on third-party borrowings made directly by BHS.

EXTRAORDINARY ITEMS

RECOGNITION AND MEASUREMENT

3.108 FASB ASC 225-20 defines *extraordinary items* as events and transactions that are distinguished by their unusual nature and the infrequency of their occurrence. Both of the following criteria should be met to classify an event or a transaction as an extraordinary item:

- *Unusual nature.* The underlying event or transaction should possess a high degree of abnormality and be of a type clearly unrelated to or only incidentally related to the ordinary and typical activities of the entity, taking into account the environment in which the entity operates.

- *Infrequency of occurrence.* The underlying event or transaction should be of a type that would not reasonably be expected to recur in the foreseeable future, taking into account the environment in which the entity operates.

PRESENTATION

3.109 FASB ASC 225-20 also addresses the presentation and disclosure of unusual and infrequently occurring items that do not meet the extraordinary criteria. Such items are reported as a separate component of continuing operations either on the face of the income statement or in the notes. FASB ASC 225-20-55 illustrates events and transactions that should and should not be classified as extraordinary items.

3.110

TABLE 3-6: UNUSUAL ITEMS

	2010
Impairment losses	16
Environmental	3
Investment losses	3
Litigation costs due to takeover attempt	1
Other	26
Total Unusual Items	**49**
No unusual items	451
Total Entities	**500**

NOTE: Because unusual items were not tracked in previous editions, no prior year data are available.

3.111

TABLE 3-7: EXTRAORDINARY ITEMS

Table 3-7 shows the nature of items classified as extraordinary by the survey entities.

	2010	2009	2008
Nature			
Early retirement of debt	11	N/C*	N/C*
Litigation settlement	1	N/C*	N/C*
Recharacterization of debt	—	—	1
Negative goodwill	—	—	—
Expropriation	—	—	—
Other	12	3	1
Total Extraordinary Items	**24**	**3**	**2**
Number of Entities			
Presenting extraordinary items	24	3	2
Not presenting extraordinary items	476	497	498
Total Entities	**500**	**500**	**500**

* N/C = Not compiled. The line item was not included in the table for the year shown.

PRESENTATION AND DISCLOSURE EXCERPTS

Extraordinary Items

3.112

HUNTSMAN CORPORATION (DEC)

*CONSOLIDATED STATEMENTS OF OPERATIONS AND
COMPREHENSIVE INCOME (LOSS) (in part)*

	Year Ended December 31		
(In millions, except per share amounts)	**2010**	**2009**	**2008**
(Loss) income from continuing operations	(9)	125	512
Income (loss) from discontinued operations, (including gain (loss) on disposal of $1 in 2009 and $11 in 2008), net of tax	42	(19)	84
Income before extraordinary gain	33	106	596
Extraordinary (loss) gain on the acquisition of a business, net of tax of nil	(1)	6	14
Net income	32	112	610
Net (income) loss attributable to noncontrolling interests	(5)	2	(1)
Net income attributable to Huntsman Corporation	$ 27	$ 114	$ 609
Net income	$ 32	$ 112	$ 610
Other comprehensive (loss) income	(11)	203	(749)
Comprehensive income (loss)	21	315	(139)
Comprehensive (income) loss attributable to noncontrolling interests	(4)	1	2
Comprehensive income (loss) attributable to Huntsman Corporation	$ 17	$ 316	$(137)
Basic income (loss) per share:			
(Loss) income from continuing operations attributable to Huntsman Corporation common stockholders	$(0.06)	$0.54	$2.20
Income (loss) from discontinued operations attributable to Huntsman Corporation common stockholders, net of tax	0.17	(0.08)	0.36
Extraordinary gain on the acquisition of a business attributable to Huntsman Corporation common stockholders, net of tax	—	0.03	0.06
Net income attributable to Huntsman Corporation common stockholders	$ 0.11	$0.49	$2.62
Weighted average shares	236.0	233.9	232.0
Diluted income (loss) per share:			
(Loss) income from continuing operations attributable to Huntsman Corporation common stockholders	$(0.06)	$0.53	$2.18
Income (loss) from discontinued operations attributable to Huntsman Corporation common stockholders, net of tax	0.17	(0.08	0.36
Extraordinary gain on the acquisition of a business attributable to Huntsman Corporation common stockholders, net of tax	—	0.03	0.06
Net income attributable to Huntsman Corporation common stockholders	$ 0.11	$0.48	$2.60
Weighted average shares	236.0	238.3	234.3
Amounts attributable to Huntsman Corporation common stockholders:			
(Loss) income from continuing operations	$ (14)	$ 127	$ 511
Income (loss) from discontinued operations, net of tax	42	(19)	84
Extraordinary (loss) gain on the acquisition of a business	(1)	6	14
Net income	$ 27	$ 114	$ 609
Dividends per share	$ 0.40	$0.40	$0.40

See accompanying notes to consolidated financial statements.

NOTES TO CONSOLIDATED FINANCIAL STATEMENTS

3. Business Combinations (in part)

Textile Effects Acquisition

On June 30, 2006, we acquired Ciba's textile effects business and accounted for the Textile Effects Acquisition using the purchase method. As such, we analyzed the fair value of tangible and intangible assets acquired and liabilities assumed and we determined the excess of fair value of net assets over cost. Because the fair value of the acquired assets and liabilities assumed exceeded the purchase price, the valuation of the long-lived assets acquired was reduced to zero. Accordingly, no basis was assigned to property, plant and equipment or any other non-current nonfinancial assets and the remaining excess was recorded as an extraordinary gain, net of taxes (which were not applicable because the gain was recorded in purchase accounting). During 2010, 2009 and 2008, we recorded an additional extraordinary (loss) gain on the acquisition of $(1) million, $6 million and $14 million, respectively, related to settlement of contingent purchase price consideration, the reversal of accruals for certain restructuring and employee termination costs recorded in connection with the Textile Effects Acquisition and a reimbursement by Ciba of certain costs pursuant to the acquisition agreements.

Unusual Items

3.113

THE COCA-COLA COMPANY (DEC)

NOTES TO CONSOLIDATED FINANCIAL STATEMENTS

Note 17. Significant Operating and Nonoperating Items (in part)

Other Nonoperating Items (in part)

Equity Income (Loss)—Net

In 2010, the Company recorded a net charge of $66 million in equity income (loss)—net. This net charge primarily represents the Company's proportionate share of unusual tax charges, asset impairments, restructuring charges and transaction costs recorded by equity method investees. The unusual tax charges primarily relate to an additional tax liability recorded by Coca-Cola Hellenic Bottling Company S.A. as a result of the Extraordinary Social Contribution Tax levied by the Greek government. The transaction costs represent our proportionate share of certain costs incurred by CCE in connection with our acquisition of CCE's North American business and the sale of our Norwegian and Swedish bottling operations to New CCE. Refer to Note 2 for additional information related to these transactions. These charges were partially offset by our proportionate share of a foreign currency remeasurement gain recorded by an equity method investee. The components of the net charge were individually insignificant. Refer to Note 19 for the impact these charges had on our operating segments.

3.114

GENCORP INC. (NOV)

CONSOLIDATED STATEMENTS OF OPERATIONS (in part)

(In millions, except per share amounts)	Year Ended		
	2010	2009	2008
Net sales	$857.9	$795.4	$742.3
Operating costs and expenses:			
Cost of sales (exclusive of items shown separately below)	753.9	674.0	645.4
Selling, general and administrative	26.7	10.2	1.9
Depreciation and amortization	27.9	25.7	25.5
Other expense, net	8.5	2.9	7.6
Unusual items			
Shareholder agreement and related costs	—	—	16.8
Executive severance agreements	1.4	3.1	—
Defined benefit pension plan amendment	—	—	14.6
Loss on legal matters and settlements	2.8	1.3	2.9
Loss on bank amendment	0.7	0.2	—
Loss on debt repurchased	1.2	—	—
Gain on legal settlement and insurance recoveries	(2.7)	—	(1.2)
Total operating costs and expenses	820.4	717.4	713.5
Operating income	37.5	78.0	28.8

NOTES TO CONSOLIDATED FINANCIAL STATEMENTS

13. Unusual Items

Charges and gains associated with unusual items are summarized as follows:

(In millions)	Year Ended		
	2010	2009	2008
Aerospace and Defense:			
Loss on legal matters and settlements	$2.8	$1.3	$ 2.9
Defined benefit pension plan amendment	—	—	13.6
Aerospace and defense unusual items	2.8	1.3	16.5
Corporate:			
Executive severance agreements	1.4	3.1	—
Loss on debt repurchased	1.2	—	—
Loss on bank amendment	0.7	0.2	—
Gain on legal settlement and insurance recoveries	(2.7)	—	(1.2)
Defined benefit pension plan amendment	—	—	1.0
Shareholder agreement and related costs	—	—	16.8
Corporate unusual items	0.6	3.3	16.6
Total unusual items	$3.4	$4.6	$33.1

In fiscal 2010, the Company recorded $1.4 million associated with executive severance. In addition, the Company recorded a charge of $1.9 million related to the estimated unrecoverable costs of legal matters and $0.9 million for realized losses and interest associated with the failure to register with the

SEC the issuance of certain of its common shares under the defined contribution 401(k) employee benefit plan. Further, the Company recorded a $2.7 million gain related to a legal settlement.

In addition, during fiscal 2010, the Company recorded $0.7 million of losses related to an amendment to the Senior Credit Facility.

A summary of the Company's losses on the $2\frac{1}{4}$% Debentures repurchased during fiscal 2010 is as follows (in millions):

Principal amount repurchased	$ 77.8
Cash repurchase price	(74.3)
	3.5
Write-off of the associated debt discount	(6.3)
Portion of the $2\frac{1}{4}$% Debentures repurchased attributed to the equity component	2.9
Write-off of the deferred financing costs	(0.4)
Loss on $2\frac{1}{4}$% Debentures repurchased	$ (0.3)

A summary of the Company's losses on the $9\frac{1}{2}$% Notes repurchased during fiscal 2010 is as follows (in millions):

Principal amount repurchased	$ 22.5
Cash repurchase price	(23.0)
Write-off of the deferred financing costs	(0.4)
Loss on $9\frac{1}{2}$% Notes repurchased	$ (0.9)

In fiscal 2009, the Company recorded a charge of $1.3 million for realized losses and interest associated with its failure to register with the SEC the issuance of certain of the Company's common shares under its defined contribution 401(k) employee benefit plan. During fiscal 2009, the Company also incurred a charge of $3.1 million associated with executive severance agreements. Additionally, the Company recorded costs of $0.2 million related to a bank amendment.

On November 25, 2008, the Company decided to amend the defined benefit pension and benefits restoration plans to freeze future accruals under such plans. Effective February 1, 2009 and July 31, 2009, future benefit accruals for all current salaried employees and collective bargaining unit employees were discontinued, respectively. No employees lost their previously earned pension benefits. As a result of the amendment and freeze, the Company incurred a curtailment charge of $14.6 million in the fourth quarter of fiscal 2008 primarily due to the immediate recognition of unrecognized prior service costs.

On March 5, 2008, the Company entered the Shareholder Agreement which resulted in a charge of $16.8 million in fiscal 2008 comprised of the following (in millions):

Increases in pension benefits	$ 5.3
Executive severance charges	7.1
Accelerated vesting of stock appreciation rights	1.1
Accelerated vesting of restricted stock, service-based	0.6
Accelerated vesting of restricted stock, performance-based	0.7
Professional fees and other	2.0
	$16.8

As a result of the Shareholder Agreement, the executive severance agreements required the Company to fund into a grantor trust on March 12, 2008, an amount equal to $34.8 million, which represents liabilities associated with the benefits restoration plans and amounts payable to certain officers of the Company party to executive severance agreements in the event of qualifying terminations of employment following a change in control (as defined in the benefits restoration plan and the executive severance agreements) of the Company. In addition, as a result of the resignation of three additional Board members on May 16, 2008, the Company was required to fund $0.4 million into a grantor trust on May 22, 2008, which primarily represents the amount payable to an officer party to an executive severance agreement in the event of a qualifying termination of employment.

In fiscal 2008, the Company recorded a charge of $2.9 million related to the estimated unrecoverable costs of legal matters, including $1.7 million associated with the failure to register with the SEC the issuance of certain of its common shares under its defined contribution 401(k) employee benefit plan and $1.2 million related to a legal settlement and other legal matters. The Company recorded a $1.2 million gain related to an insurance settlement for an environmental claim.

EARNINGS PER SHARE

PRESENTATION

3.115 The computation, presentation, and disclosure requirements for earnings per share (EPS) for entities with publicly held common stock or potential common stock are stated in FASB ASC 260, *Earnings Per Share*. The objective of basic EPS is to measure the performance of an entity over the reporting period. The objective of diluted EPS is to measure the performance of an entity over the reporting period while giving effect to all dilutive potential common shares that were outstanding during the period. FASB ASC 260 also discusses the application of EPS guidance to master limited partnerships.

PRESENTATION AND DISCLOSURE EXCERPTS

Earnings per Share

3.116

PEABODY ENERGY CORPORATION (DEC)

CONSOLIDATED STATEMENTS OF OPERATIONS
(in part)

	Year Ended December 31		
(Dollars in millions, except per share data)	**2010**	**2009**	**2008**
Income from continuing operations before income taxes	$1,113.2	$651.7	$1,179.3
Income tax provision	308.1	193.8	191.4
Income from continuing operations, net of income taxes	805.1	457.9	987.9
Income (loss) from discontinued operations, net of income taxes	(2.9)	5.1	(28.8)
Net income	802.2	463.0	959.1
Less: Net income attributable to noncontrolling interests	28.2	14.8	6.2
Net income attributable to common stockholders	$ 774.0	$448.2	$ 952.9
Income From Continuing Operations			
Basic earnings per share	$ 2.89	$ 1.66	$ 3.63
Diluted earnings per share	$ 2.86	$ 1.64	$ 3.60
Net Income Attributable to Common Stockholders			
Basic earnings per share	$ 2.88	$ 1.68	$ 3.52
Diluted earnings per share	$ 2.85	$ 1.66	$ 3.50
Dividends declared per share	$ 0.295	$0.250	$ 0.240

NOTES TO CONSOLIDATED FINANCIAL STATEMENTS

(17) Earnings per Share

The Company's restricted stock awards are considered participating securities. As such, the Company uses the two-class method to compute basic and diluted EPS. The following illustrates the earnings allocation method utilized in the calculation of basic and diluted EPS. Diluted EPS includes any dilutive impact of share-based compensation and the Debentures.

	Year Ended December 31		
(In millions, except per share amounts)	**2010**	**2009**	**2008**
EPS numerator:			
Income from continuing operations, net of income taxes	$805.1	$457.9	$987.9
Less: Net income attributable to noncontrolling interests	28.2	14.8	6.2
Income from continuing operations attributable to common stockholders before allocation of earnings to participating securities	776.9	443.1	981.7
Less: Earnings allocated to participating securities	(5.6)	(2.9)	(5.5)
Income from continuing operations attributable to common stockholders, after earnings allocated to participating securities[1]	771.3	440.2	976.2
Income (loss) from discontinued operations, net of income taxes	(2.9)	5.1	(28.8)
Net income attributable to common stockholders, after earnings allocated to participating securities[1]	$768.4	$445.3	$947.4
EPS denominator:			
Weighted average shares outstanding—basic	267.0	265.5	268.9
Impact of dilutive securities	2.9	2.0	1.8
Weighted average shares outstanding—diluted[2]	269.9	267.5	270.7
Basic EPS attributable to common stockholders:			
Income from continuing operations	$ 2.89	$ 1.66	$ 3.63
Income (loss) from discontinued operations	(0.01)	0.02	(0.11)
Net income	$ 2.88	$ 1.68	$ 3.52
Diluted EPS attributable to common stockholders:			
Income from continuing operations	$ 2.86	$ 1.64	$ 3.60
Income (loss) from discontinued operations	(0.01)	0.02	(0.10)
Net income	$ 2.85	$ 1.66	$ 3.50

[1] The reallocation adjustment for participating securities to arrive at the numerator used to calculate diluted EPS was less than $0.1 million for the periods presented.

[2] Weighted average shares outstanding excludes anti-dilutive shares that totaled 0.2 million for the years ended December 31, 2010 and 2009 and 0.1 million for the year ended December 31, 2008.

3.117

GOOGLE INC. (DEC)

CONSOLIDATED STATEMENTS OF INCOME (in part)

	Year Ended December 31		
(In millions, except per share amounts)	**2008**	**2009**	**2010**
Income from operations	6,632	8,312	10,381
Impairment of equity investments	(1,095)	0	0
Interest and other income, net	316	69	415
Income before income taxes	5,853	8,381	10,796
Provision for income taxes	1,626	1,861	2,291
Net income	$4,227	$6,520	$ 8,505
Net income per share of Class A and Class B common stock:			
Basic	$13.46	$20.62	$ 26.69
Diluted	$13.31	$20.41	$ 26.31

NOTES TO CONSOLIDATED FINANCIAL STATEMENTS

Note 2. Net Income Per Share of Class A and Class B Common Stock

We compute net income per share of Class A and Class B common stock using the two-class method. Basic net income per share is computed using the weighted-average number of common shares outstanding during the period except that it does not include unvested common shares subject to repurchase or cancellation. Diluted net income per share is computed using the weighted-average number of common shares and, if dilutive, potential common shares outstanding during the period. Potential common shares consist of the incremental common shares issuable upon the exercise of stock options, warrants, restricted shares, restricted stock units, and unvested common shares subject to repurchase or cancellation. The dilutive effect of outstanding stock options, restricted shares, restricted stock units, and warrants is reflected in diluted earnings per share by application of the treasury stock method. The computation of the diluted net income per share of Class A common stock assumes the conversion of Class B common stock, while the diluted net income per share of Class B common stock does not assume the conversion of those shares.

The rights, including the liquidation and dividend rights, of the holders of our Class A and Class B common stock are identical, except with respect to voting. Further, there are a number of safeguards built into our certificate of incorporation, as well as Delaware law, which preclude our board of directors from declaring or paying unequal per share dividends on our Class A and Class B common stock. Specifically, Delaware law provides that amendments to our certificate of incorporation which would have the effect of adversely altering the rights, powers, or preferences of a given class of stock (in this case the right of our Class A common stock to receive an equal dividend to any declared on our Class B common stock) must be approved by the class of stock adversely affected by the proposed amendment. In addition, our certificate of incorporation provides that before any such amendment may be put to a stockholder vote, it must be approved by the unanimous consent of our Board of Directors. As a result, the undistributed earnings for each year are allocated based on the contractual participation rights of the Class A and Class B common shares as if the earnings for the year had been distributed. As the liquidation and dividend rights are identical, the undistributed earnings are allocated on a proportionate basis. Further, as we assume the conversion of Class B common stock in the computation of the diluted net income per share of Class A common stock, the undistributed earnings are equal to net income for that computation.

The following table sets forth the computation of basic and diluted net income per share of Class A and Class B common stock (in millions, except share amounts which are reflected in thousands and per share amounts):

| | Year Ended December 31 | | | | | |
| | 2008 | | 2009 | | 2010 | |
	Class A	Class B	Class A	Class B	Class A	Class B
Basic Net Income Per Share:						
Numerator						
Allocation of undistributed earnings	$ 3,209	$ 1,018	$ 4,981	$ 1,539	$ 6,569	$ 1,936
Denominator						
Weighted-average common shares outstanding	238,473	75,614	241,575	74,651	246,168	72,534
Less: Weighted-average unvested common shares subject to repurchase or cancellation	(120)	(8)	(5)	0	0	0
Number of shares used in per share computation	238,353	75,606	241,570	74,651	246,168	72,534
Basic net income per share	$ 13.46	$ 13.46	$ 20.62	$ 20.62	$ 26.69	$ 26.69
Diluted Net Income Per Share:						
Numerator						
Allocation of undistributed earnings for basic computation	$ 3,209	$ 1,018	$ 4,981	$ 1,539	$ 6,569	$ 1,936
Reallocation of undistributed earnings as a result of conversion of Class B to Class A shares	1,018	0	1,539	0	1,936	0
Reallocation of undistributed earnings to Class B shares	0	(8)	0	(13)	0	(26)
Allocation of undistributed earnings	$ 4,227	$ 1,010	$ 6,520	$ 1,526	$ 8,505	$ 1,910
Denominator						
Number of shares used in basic computation	238,353	75,606	241,570	74,651	246,168	72,534
Weighted-average effect of dilutive securities						
Add:						
Conversion of Class B to Class A common shares outstanding	75,606	0	74,651	0	72,534	0
Unvested common shares subject to repurchase or cancellation	128	8	5	0	0	0
Employee stock options, including warrants issued under transferable stock option program	2,810	223	2,569	114	3,410	71
Restricted shares and RSUs	617	0	621	0	1,139	0
Number of shares used in per share computation	317,514	75,837	319,416	74,765	323,251	72,605
Diluted net income per share	$ 13.31	$ 13.31	$ 20.41	$ 20.41	$ 26.31	$ 26.31

The net income per share amounts are the same for Class A and Class B common stock because the holders of each class are legally entitled to equal per share distributions whether through dividends or in liquidation.

Section 4: Comprehensive Income

COMPREHENSIVE INCOME IN ANNUAL FILINGS

RECOGNITION AND MEASUREMENT

4.01 Financial Accounting Standards Board (FASB) *Accounting Standards Codification* (ASC) 220, *Comprehensive Income,* requires that items included in other comprehensive income should be classified based on their nature. Other comprehensive income includes the following: foreign currency items, changes in the fair value of certain derivatives, unrealized gains and losses on certain securities, and certain pension or other postretirement benefit items.

PRESENTATION

4.02 FASB ASC 220 requires entities that provide a full set of general-purpose financial statements (that is, financial position, results of operations, and cash flows) report comprehensive income and its components. The FASB ASC glossary defines *comprehensive income* as the change in equity (net assets) of a business entity during a period from transactions and other events and circumstances from nonowner sources. It includes all changes in equity during a period, except those resulting from investments by owners and distributions to owners. *Other comprehensive income* is defined as revenues, expenses, gains, and losses that under generally accepted accounting principles are included in comprehensive income but excluded from net income. If an entity has only net income, it is not required to report comprehensive income. All items that meet the definition of *components of comprehensive income* must be reported in a financial statement for the period in which they are recognized. Further, a total amount for comprehensive income should be displayed in the financial statement when the components of other comprehensive income are reported. No specific required format exists for displaying comprehensive income and its components. However, an entity is encouraged to display the components of other comprehensive income and total comprehensive income below the total for net income in a statement that reports results of operations or in a separate statement of comprehensive income that begins with net income.

4.03 FASB ASC 220 also states that an entity should disclose the amount of income tax expense or benefit allocated to each component of other comprehensive income, including reclassification adjustments, either on the face of the statement in which those components are displayed or in the notes thereto. Also, FASB ASC 810, *Consolidation,* states that if an entity has an outstanding noncontrolling interest (minority interest), the components of other comprehensive income attributable to the parent and noncontrolling interest in a less-than-wholly-owned subsidiary are required to be reported on the face of the financial statement in which comprehensive income is presented, in addition to presenting consolidated comprehensive income.

4.04 FASB ASC 220 also requires that adjustments should be made to avoid double counting in comprehensive income items that are displayed as part of net income for a period that also had been displayed as part of other comprehensive income in that period or earlier periods. For example, gains on investment securities that were realized and included in net income of the current period that also had been included in other comprehensive income as unrealized holding gains in the period in which they arose must be deducted through other comprehensive income of the period in which they are included in net income to avoid including them in comprehensive income twice. These adjustments are called *reclassification adjustments.* An entity may display reclassification adjustments on the face of the financial statement in which comprehensive income is reported, or it may disclose them in the notes to the financial statements (that is, either a gross display on the face of the financial statement or a net display on the face of the financial statement and disclosure of the gross change in the notes to the financial statements).

4.05

TABLE 4-1: COMPREHENSIVE INCOME—REPORTING STATEMENT

Table 4-1 shows the statement in which comprehensive income was presented.

Reporting Format:	2010	2009	2008
Included in statement of changes in stockholders' equity	409	405	415
Separate statement of comprehensive income	75	76	62
Combined statement of income and comprehensive income	7	11	15
	486	492	492
No comprehensive income reported	9	8	8
Total Entities	**500**	**500**	**500**

4.06

TABLE 4-2: OTHER COMPREHENSIVE INCOME—COMPONENTS*

Table 4-2 lists the components of other comprehensive income disclosed by survey entities in the statement used to present comprehensive income for the period reported.

	2010
Foreign currency translation	405
Defined benefit postretirement plan adjustments	379
Gains and losses on derivatives held as cash flow hedges	286
Unrealized gains/losses on securities	200
Reclassification adjustments (includes realized gains/losses)	83
Outstanding noncontrolling interest	17
Share of investee other comprehensive income	7
Other	31

* Appearing in the statement used to present comprehensive income.
Note: Classification of the components of other comprehensive income changed for this edition, so no prior year data are available.

4.07

TABLE 4-3: COMPREHENSIVE INCOME—TAX EFFECT DISCLOSURE

Tax Effect Disclosure in Any Statement:			
Amount of tax effect allocated to each component	175	109	120
Amount of tax effect allocated to some but not all components	84	136	133
Total amount of tax effect	61	9	11
	320	254	264
Tax Effect Disclosure in Notes:			
Amount of tax effect allocated to each component	47	76	77
Amount of tax effect allocated to some but not all components	21	41	25
Total amount of tax effect	6	7	11
	74	124	113
Tax effect not disclosed in any statement	97	114	115
	491	492	492
No comprehensive income reported	9	8	8
Total Entities	**500**	**500**	**500**

PRESENTATION AND DISCLOSURE EXCERPTS

Combined Statement of Income and Comprehensive Income

4.08

ENERGIZER HOLDINGS, INC. (SEP)

CONSOLIDATED STATEMENTS OF EARNINGS AND COMPREHENSIVE INCOME

(Dollars in millions, except per share data)	Years Ended September 30		
Statement of Earnings	**2010**	**2009**	**2008**
Net sales	$4,248.3	$3,999.8	$4,331.0
Cost of products sold	2,229.0	2,141.2	2,293.3
Gross profit	2,019.3	1,858.6	2,037.7
Selling, general and administrative expense	765.7	742.6	794.0
Advertising and promotion expense	461.3	414.5	486.8
Research and development expense	97.1	90.5	91.7
Interest expense	125.4	144.7	181.3
Other financing expense, net	26.4	21.0	10.7
Earnings before income taxes	543.4	445.3	473.2
Income taxes	140.4	147.5	143.9
Net earnings	$ 403.0	$ 297.8	$ 329.3
Earnings Per Share			
Basic net earnings per share	$ 5.76	$ 4.77	$ 5.71
Diluted net earnings per share	$ 5.72	$ 4.72	$ 5.59
Statement of Comprehensive Income			
Net earnings	$ 403.0	$ 297.8	$ 329.3
Other comprehensive (loss)/income, net of tax			
Foreign currency translation adjustments	(43.2)	12.7	3.8
Pension/postretirement activity, net of tax of $(19.8) in 2010, $(45.9) in 2009 and $(17.8) in 2008	(47.5)	(78.6)	(46.5)
Deferred (loss)/gain on hedging activity, net of tax of $(6.9) in 2010, $0.9 in 2009 and $1.7 in 2008	(11.7)	3.1	3.8
Comprehensive income	$ 300.6	$ 235.0	$ 290.4

The above financial statements should be read in conjunction with the Notes to Consolidated Financial Statements.

Separate Statement of Comprehensive Income

4.09

EXXON MOBIL CORPORATION (DEC)

CONSOLIDATED STATEMENT OF COMPREHENSIVE INCOME

(Millions of dollars)	2010	2009	2008
Net income including noncontrolling interests	$31,398	$19,658	$46,867
Other comprehensive income (net of income taxes)			
Foreign exchange translation adjustment	1,034	3,629	(7,298)
Adjustment for foreign exchange translation loss included in net income	25	—	155
Postretirement benefits reserves adjustment (excluding amortization)	(1,161)	(340)	(6,077)
Amortization of postretirement benefits reserves adjustment included in net periodic benefit costs	1,040	1,461	759
Change in fair value of cash flow hedges	184	—	—
Realized (gain)/ loss from settled cash flow hedges included in net income	(129)	—	—
Comprehensive income including noncontrolling interests	32,391	24,408	34,406
Comprehensive income attributable to noncontrolling interests	1,293	658	1,106
Comprehensive income attributable to ExxonMobil	$31,098	$23,750	$33,300

The information in the Notes to Consolidated Financial Statements is an integral part of these statements.

4.10

CF INDUSTRIES HOLDINGS, INC. (DEC)

CONSOLIDATED STATEMENTS OF COMPREHENSIVE INCOME

(In millions)	Year Ended December 31		
	2010	2009	2008
Net earnings	$440.7	$448.5	$801.5
Other comprehensive income (loss):			
Foreign currency translation adjustment	24.2	7.3	(10.1)
Unrealized gain (loss) on securities—net of taxes	(14.6)	23.7	(14.5)
Defined benefit plans—net of taxes	(18.3)	4.3	(34.1)
	(8.7)	35.3	(58.7)
Comprehensive income	432.0	483.8	742.8
Less: Comprehensive income attributable to the noncontrolling interest	92.9	86.2	112.2
Comprehensive income attributable to common stockholders	$339.1	$397.6	$630.6

See Accompanying Notes to Consolidated Financial Statements.

Statement of Comprehensive Income Included With Statement of Changes in Stockholders' Equity

4.11

TIFFANY & CO. (JAN)

CONSOLIDATED STATEMENTS OF STOCKHOLDERS' EQUITY AND COMPREHENSIVE EARNINGS

(In thousands)	Total Stockholders' Equity	Retained Earnings	Accumulated Other Comprehensive Gain (Loss)	Common Stock Shares	Common Stock Amount	Additional Paid-In Capital
Balances, January 31, 2007	$1,863,937	$1,328,982	$ (2,590)	135,875	$1,358	$536,187
Implementation effect of uncertain tax positions guidance	(4,299)	(4,299)	—	—	—	—
Balances, February 1, 2007	1,859,638	1,324,683	(2,590)	135,875	1,358	536,187
Exercise of stock options and vesting of restricted stock units ("RSUs")	68,830	—	—	3,200	32	68,798
Tax effect of exercise of stock options and vesting of RSUs	20,802	—	—	—	—	20,802
Share-based compensation expense	38,343	—	—	—	—	38,343
Issuance of common stock under employee profit sharing and retirement savings ("EPSRS") Plan	2,450	—	—	52	1	2,449
Purchase and retirement of common stock	(574,608)	(540,577)	—	(12,374)	(123)	(33,908)
Cash dividends on common stock	(69,921)	(69,921)	—	—	—	—
Deferred hedging loss, net of tax	(1,157)	—	(1,157)	—	—	—
Unrealized loss on marketable securities, net of tax	(799)	—	(799)	—	—	—
Foreign currency translation adjustments, net of tax	30,271	—	30,271	—	—	—
Net unrealized gain on benefit plans, net of tax	18,788	—	18,788	—	—	—
Net earnings	323,478	323,478	—	—	—	—
Balances, January 31, 2008	1,716,115	1,037,663	44,513	126,753	1,268	632,671
Implementation effect of change in employee benefit plans' measurement date, net of tax	(1,073)	(1,114)	41	—	—	—
Exercise of stock options and vesting of RSUs	30,357	—	—	2,342	23	30,334
Tax effect of exercise of stock options and vesting of RSUs	10,317	—	—	—	—	10,317
Share-based compensation expense	24,507	—	—	—	—	24,507
Issuance of common stock under EPSRS plan	4,750	—	—	124	1	4,749
Purchase and retirement of common stock	(218,379)	(203,014)	—	(5,375)	(54)	(15,311)
Cash dividends on common stock	(82,258)	(82,258)	—	—	—	—
Deferred hedging loss, net of tax	(9,873)	—	(9,873)	—	—	—
Unrealized loss on marketable securities, net of tax	(5,519)	—	(5,519)	—	—	—
Foreign currency translation adjustments, net of tax	(68,355)	—	(68,355)	—	—	—
Net unrealized loss on benefit plans, net of tax	(32,240)	—	(32,240)	—	—	—
Net earnings	220,022	220,022	—	—	—	—
Balances, January 31, 2009	1,588,371	971,299	(71,433)	123,844	1,238	687,267
Exercise of stock options and vesting of RSUs	71,485	—	—	2,493	25	71,460
Tax effect of exercise of stock options and vesting of RSUs	1,896	—	—	—	—	1,896
Share-based compensation expense	23,995	—	—	—	—	23,995
Purchase and retirement of common stock	(467)	(434)	—	(11)	—	(33)
Purchase of noncontrolling interests	(20,453)	—	—	—	—	(20,453)
Cash dividends on common stock	(84,579)	(84,579)	—	—	—	—
Deferred hedging gain, net of tax	6,377	—	6,377	—	—	—
Unrealized gain on marketable securities, net of tax	4,241	—	4,241	—	—	—
Foreign currency translation adjustments, net of tax	42,750	—	42,750	—	—	—
Net unrealized loss on benefit plans, net of tax	(15,200)	—	(15,200)	—	—	—
Net earnings	264,823	264,823	—	—	—	—
Balances, January 31, 2010	$1,883,239	$1,151,109	$(33,265)	126,326	$1,263	$764,132

Years Ended January 31	2010	2009	2008
Comprehensive earnings are as follows:			
Net earnings	$264,823	$220,022	$323,478
Deferred hedging gain (loss), net of tax expense (benefit) of $3,388, ($6,307) and ($110)	6,377	(9,873)	(1,157)
Foreign currency translation adjustments, net of tax expense of $716, $1,015 and $4,714	42,750	(68,355)	30,271
Unrealized gain (loss) on marketable securities, net of tax expense (benefit) of $2,302, ($3,248) and ($283)	4,241	(5,519)	(799)
Net unrealized (loss) gain on benefit plans, net of tax (benefit) expense of ($10,525), ($19,907) and $14,352	(15,200)	(32,240)	18,788
Comprehensive earnings	$302,991	$104,035	$370,581

See notes to consolidated financial statements.

4.12

WAL-MART STORES, INC. (JAN)

CONSOLIDATED STATEMENTS OF SHAREHOLDERS' EQUITY

(Amounts in millions except per share data)	Number of Shares	Common Stock	Capital in Excess of Par Value	Retained Earnings	Accumulated Other Comprehensive Income (Loss)	Total Walmart Shareholders' Equity	Noncontrolling Interest	Total Equity
Balances—February 1, 2007	4,131	$413	$2,834	$55,818	$ 2,508	$61,573	$2,160	$63,733
Consolidated net income				12,731		12,731	406	13,137
Other comprehensive income					1,356	1,356	8	1,364
Cash dividends ($0.88 per share)				(3,586)		(3,586)		(3,586)
Purchase of company stock	(166)	(17)	(190)	(7,484)		(7,691)		(7,691)
Other	8	1	384			385	(635)	(250)
Adoption of accounting for uncertainty in income taxes				(160)		(160)		(160)
Balances—January 31, 2008	3,973	$397	$3,028	$57,319	$ 3,864	$64,608	$1,939	$66,547
Consolidated net income				13,400		13,400	499	13,899
Other comprehensive income					(6,552)	(6,552)	(371)	(6,923)
Cash dividends ($0.95 per share)				(3,746)		(3,746)		(3,746)
Purchase of company stock	(61)	(6)	(95)	(3,315)		(3,416)		(3,416)
Other	13	2	987	2		991	(273)	718
Balances—January 31, 2009	3,925	$393	$3,920	$63,660	$(2,688)	$65,285	$1,794	$67,079
Consolidated net income (excludes redeemable noncontrolling interest)				14,335		14,335	499	14,834
Other comprehensive income					2,618	2,618	64	2,682
Cash dividends ($1.09 per share)				(4,217)		(4,217)		(4,217)
Purchase of Company stock	(145)	(15)	(246)	(7,136)		(7,397)		(7,397)
Purchase of redeemable noncontrolling interest			(288)			(288)		(288)
Other	6		417	(4)		413	(177)	236
Balances—January 31, 2010	3,786	$378	$3,803	$66,638	$ (70)	$70,749	$2,180	$72,929

Fiscal Years Ended January 31	2010	2009	2008
Comprehensive Income:			
Consolidated net income[1]	$14,848	$13,899	$13,137
Other comprehensive income:			
Currency translation[2]	2,854	(6,860)	1,226
Net change in fair values of derivatives	94	(17)	—
Minimum pension liability	(220)	(46)	138
Total comprehensive income	17,576	6,976	14,501
Less amounts attributable to the noncontrolling interest:			
Net income[1]	(513)	(499)	(406)
Currency translation[2]	(110)	371	(8)
Amounts attributable to the noncontrolling interest	(623)	(128)	(414)
Comprehensive income attributable to Walmart	$16,953	$ 6,848	$14,087

[1] Includes $14 million in fiscal 2010 that is related to the redeemable noncontrolling interest.
[2] Includes $46 million in fiscal 2010 that is related to the redeemable noncontrolling interest.

See accompanying notes.

Tax Effect Disclosure in the Notes

4.13

PERKINELMER, INC. (DEC)

CONSOLIDATED STATEMENTS OF STOCKHOLDERS'
EQUITY AND COMPREHENSIVE INCOME

For the Three Fiscal Years Ended January 2, 2011 (amounts
in thousands)

	Comprehensive Income	Common Stock Amount	Capital in Excess of Par	Retained Earnings	Accumulated Other Comprehensive Income (Loss)	Total Stockholders' Equity
Balance, December 30, 2007		$117,585	$257,850	$1,142,135	$ 57,707	$1,575,277
Comprehensive income:						
Net income	$126,409	—	—	126,409	—	126,409
Other comprehensive loss						
Foreign currency translation adjustments	(29,067)	—	—	—	(29,067)	(29,067)
Unrecognized losses and prior service costs, net of tax	(57,220)	—	—	—	(57,220)	(57,220)
Unrealized and realized losses on derivatives, net of tax	(2,338)	—	—	—	(2,338)	(2,338)
Unrealized losses on securities arising during the period, net of tax	(321)	—	—	—	(321)	(321)
Other comprehensive loss	(88,946)					
Comprehensive income	$ 37,463					
Dividends		—	—	(33,023)	—	(33,023)
Exercise of employee stock options and related income tax benefits		2,251	41,832	—	—	44,083
Issuance of common stock for employee benefit plans		85	2,095	—	—	2,180
Purchases of common stock		(2,997)	(72,517)	—	—	(75,514)
Issuance of common stock for long-term incentive program		188	6,730	—	—	6,918
Stock compensation		—	10,559	—	—	10,559
Balance, December 28, 2008		$117,112	$246,549	$1,235,521	$(31,239)	$1,567,943
Comprehensive income:						
Net income	$ 85,599	—	—	85,599	—	85,599
Other comprehensive income (loss)						
Foreign currency translation adjustments	4,937	—	—	—	4,937	4,937
Unrecognized losses and prior service costs, net of tax	(2,349)	—	—	—	(2,349)	(2,349)
Reclassification adjustments for losses on derivatives included in net income, net of tax	1,196	—	—	—	1,196	1,196
Unrealized gains on securities arising during the period, net of tax	204	—	—	—	204	204
Other comprehensive income	3,988					
Comprehensive income	$ 89,587					
Dividends		—	—	(32,534)	—	(32,534)
Exercise of employee stock options and related income tax benefits		460	2,875	—	—	3,335
Issuance of common stock for employee benefit plans		195	2,941	—	—	3,136
Purchases of common stock		(1,030)	(13,589)	—	—	(14,619)
Issuance of common stock for long-term incentive program		286	3,245	—	—	3,531
Stock compensation		—	8,578	—	—	8,578
Balance, January 3, 2010		$117,023	$250,599	$1,288,586	$(27,251)	$1,628,957

The accompanying notes are an integral part of these consolidated financial statements.

	Comprehensive Income	Common Stock Amount	Capital in Excess of Par	Retained Earnings	Accumulated Other Comprehensive Income (Loss)	Total Stockholders' Equity
Balance, January 3, 2010		$117,023	$250,599	$1,288,586	$(27,251)	$1,628,957
Comprehensive income:						
Net income	$383,919	—	—	$ 383,919	—	$ 383,919
Other comprehensive (loss) income						
Foreign currency translation adjustments	(34,086)	—	—	—	(34,086)	(34,086)
Reclassification of foreign currency translation gains to earnings upon sale of subsidiaries	394	—	—	—	394	394
Unrecognized gains and prior service costs, net of tax	6,192	—	—	—	6,192	6,192
Reclassification adjustments for losses on derivatives included in net income, net of tax	1,196	—	—	—	1,196	1,196
Unrealized gains on securities arising during the period, net of tax	64	—	—	—	64	64
Other comprehensive loss	(26,240)					
Comprehensive income	$357,679					
Dividends		—	—	(32,924)	—	(32,924)
Exercise of employee stock options and related income tax benefits		1,543	29,714	—	—	31,257
Issuance of common stock for employee benefit plans		86	1,780	—	—	1,866
Purchases of common stock		(3,058)	(69,710)	—	—	(72,768)
Issuance of common stock for long-term incentive program		121	5,126	—	—	5,247
Stock compensation		—	6,504	—	—	6,504
Balance, January 2, 2011		$115,715	$224,013	$1,639,581	$(53,491)	$1,925,818

The accompanying notes are an integral part of these consolidated financial statements.

NOTES TO CONSOLIDATED FINANCIAL STATEMENTS

Note 18. Stockholders' Equity (in part)

Comprehensive (Loss) Income

The components of accumulated other comprehensive loss consist of the following:

(In thousands)	Foreign Currency Translation Adjustment	Unrecognized Losses and Prior Service Costs, Net of Tax	Unrealized (Losses) Gains on Securities, Net of Tax	Unrealized and Realized (Losses) Gains on Derivatives, Net of Tax	Accumulated Other Comprehensive (Loss) Income
Balance, December 30, 2007	$112,172	$ (49,080)	$ (47)	$(5,338)	$ 57,707
Current year change	(29,067)	(57,220)	(321)	(2,338)	(88,946)
Balance, December 28, 2008	83,105	(106,300)	(368)	(7,676)	(31,239)
Current year change	4,937	(2,349)	204	1,196	3,988
Balance, January 3, 2010	88,042	(108,649)	(164)	(6,480)	(27,251)
Current year change	(33,692)	6,192	64	1,196	(26,240)
Balance, January 2, 2011	$ 54,350	$(102,457)	$(100)	$(5,284)	$(53,491)

The tax effects on the foreign currency translation component of other comprehensive (loss) income are minimal due to the Company's previous position that undistributed earnings of foreign subsidiaries are permanently reinvested. As a result of the sale of the IDS and Photoflash businesses, the Company concluded that the remaining operations within those foreign subsidiaries previously containing IDS and Photoflash

operations did not require the same level of capital as previously required, and therefore the Company plans to repatriate $250.0 million of cash and has provided for the taxes on the related previously unremitted earnings. Taxes have not been provided for unremitted earnings that the Company continues to consider permanently reinvested, which is based on its future operational and capital requirements. The components of other comprehensive (loss) income were as follows:

(In thousands)	After-Tax Amount
2010	
Foreign currency translation adjustments	$(34,086)
Reclassification of foreign currency translation gains to earnings upon sale of subsidiaries	394
Unrecognized gains and prior service costs, net of income taxes	6,192
Unrealized net gains on securities, net of income taxes	64
Reclassification adjustments for losses on derivatives included in net income	1,196
Other comprehensive loss	$(26,240)
2009	
Foreign currency translation adjustments	$ 4,937
Unrecognized losses and prior service costs, net of income taxes	(2,349)
Unrealized net gains on securities, net of income taxes	204
Reclassification adjustments for losses on derivatives included in net income	1,196
Other comprehensive income	$ 3,988
2008	
Foreign currency translation adjustments	$(29,067)
Unrecognized losses and prior service costs, net of income taxes	(57,220)
Unrealized net losses on securities, net of income taxes	(321)
Reclassification adjustments for losses on derivatives included in net income	3,268
Unrealized and realized losses on derivatives, net of income taxes	(5,606)
Other comprehensive loss	$(88,946)

4.14

STARBUCKS CORPORATION (SEP)

CONSOLIDATED STATEMENTS OF EQUITY

(In millions)	Common Stock Shares	Common Stock Amount	Additional Paid-In Capital	Other Additional Paid-In Capital	Retained Earnings	Accumulated Other Comprehensive Income/(Loss)	Shareholders' Equity	Noncontrolling Interest	Total
Balance, September 30, 2007	738.3	$0.7	$ 0.0	$39.4	$2,189.4	$54.6	$2,284.1	$17.3	$2,301.4
Cumulative impact of adoption of accounting requirements for uncertain tax positions	0.0	0.0	(1.6)	0.0	(1.7)	0.0	(3.3)	0.0	(3.3)
Net earnings	0.0	0.0	0.0	0.0	315.5	0.0	315.5	(3.8)	311.7
Unrealized holding gain, net	0.0	0.0	0.0	0.0	0.0	0.8	0.8	0.0	0.8
Translation adjustment, net of tax	0.0	0.0	0.0	0.0	0.0	(7.0)	(7.0)	0.0	(7.0)
Comprehensive income							309.3	(3.8)	305.5
Stock-based compensation expense	0.0	0.0	76.8	0.0	0.0	0.0	76.8	0.0	76.8
Exercise of stock options, including tax benefit of $8.4	6.6	0.0	77.4	0.0	0.0	0.0	77.4	0.0	77.4
Sale of common stock, including tax benefit of $0.1	2.8	0.0	41.9	0.0	0.0	0.0	41.9	0.0	41.9
Repurchase of common stock	(12.2)	0.0	(194.5)	0.0	(100.8)	0.0	(295.3)	0.0	(295.3)
Net contributions from noncontrolling interests	0.0	$0.0	$ 0.0	$ 0.0	$ 0.0	$ 0.0	$ 0.0	$ 4.8	$ 4.8

(continued)

(In millions)	Common Stock Shares	Common Stock Amount	Additional Paid-In Capital	Other Additional Paid-In Capital	Retained Earnings	Accumulated Other Comprehensive Income/(Loss)	Shareholders' Equity	Noncontrolling Interest	Total
Balance, September 28, 2008	735.5	$0.7	$ 0.0	$39.4	$2,402.4	$ 48.4	$2,490.9	$18.3	$2,509.2
Net earnings	0.0	0.0	0.0	0.0	390.8	0.0	390.8	0.7	391.5
Unrealized holding gain, net	0.0	0.0	0.0	0.0	0.0	1.8	1.8	0.0	1.8
Translation adjustment, net of tax	0.0	0.0	0.0	0.0	0.0	15.2	15.2	0.0	15.2
Comprehensive income							407.8	0.7	408.5
Stock-based compensation expense	0.0	0.0	84.3	0.0	0.0	0.0	84.3	0.0	84.3
Exercise of stock options, including tax benefit of $5.3	4.9	0.0	35.9	0.0	0.0	0.0	35.9	0.0	35.9
Sale of common stock, including tax benefit of $0.1	2.5	0.0	26.8	0.0	0.0	0.0	26.8	0.0	26.8
Net distributions to noncontrolling interests	0.0	0.0	0.0	0.0	0.0	0.0	0.0	(7.8)	(7.8)
Balance, September 27, 2009	742.9	$0.7	$ 147.0	$39.4	$2,793.2	$65.4	$3,045.7	$11.2	$3,056.9
Net earnings	0.0	0.0	0.0	0.0	945.6	0.0	945.6	2.7	948.3
Unrealized holding loss, net	0.0	0.0	0.0	0.0	0.0	(17.0)	(17.0)	0.0	(17.0)
Translation adjustment, net of tax	0.0	0.0	0.0	0.0	0.0	8.8	8.8	0.0	8.8
Comprehensive income							937.4	2.7	940.1
Stock-based compensation expense	0.0	0.0	115.6	0.0	0.0	0.0	115.6	0.0	115.6
Exercise of stock options, including tax benefit of $27.7	10.1	0.0	137.5	0.0	0.0	0.0	137.5	0.0	137.5
Sale of common stock, including tax benefit of $0.1	0.8	0.0	18.5	0.0	0.0	0.0	18.5	0.0	18.5
Repurchase of common stock	(11.2)	0.0	(285.6)	0.0	0.0	0.0	(285.6)	0.0	(285.6)
Net distributions to noncontrolling interests	0.0	0.0	0.0	0.0	0.0	0.0	0.0	(0.8)	(0.8)
Cash dividend	0.0	0.0	0.0	0.0	(267.6)	0.0	(267.6)	0.0	(267.6)
Purchase of noncontrolling interests	0.0	0.0	(26.8)	0.0	0.0	0.0	(26.8)	(5.5)	(32.3)
Balance, October 3, 2010	742.6	$0.7	$ 106.2	$39.4	$3,471.2	$ 57.2	$3,674.7	$ 7.6	$3,682.3

NOTES TO CONSOLIDATED FINANCIAL STATEMENTS

Note 13: Shareholders' Equity (in part)

Comprehensive Income

Comprehensive income includes all changes in equity during the period, except those resulting from transactions with shareholders of the Company. It has two components: net earnings and other comprehensive income. Accumulated other comprehensive income reported on our consolidated balance sheets consists of foreign currency translation adjustments and the unrealized gains and losses, net of applicable taxes, on available-for-sale securities and on derivative instruments designated and qualifying as cash flow and net investment hedges.

Comprehensive income, net of related tax effects (in millions):

Fiscal Year Ended	Oct 3, 2010	Sep 27, 2009	Sep 28, 2008
Net earnings attributable to Starbucks	$945.6	$390.8	$315.5
Unrealized holding gains/(losses) on available-for-sale securities, net of tax (provision)/benefit of $0.1, $(1.9) and $2.4, respectively	(0.2)	3.3	(4.0)
Unrealized holding gains/(losses) on cash flow hedging instruments, net of tax (provision)/benefit of $6.6, $(2.4) and $(0.4), respectively	(11.3)	4.0	0.7
Unrealized holding losses on net investment hedging instruments, net of tax benefit of $4.0, $4.0 and $0.6, respectively	(6.8)	(6.8)	(0.9)
Reclassification adjustment for net losses realized in net earnings for cash flow hedges, net of tax benefit of $0.8, $0.8 and $3.0, respectively	1.3	1.3	5.0
Net unrealized gain/(loss)	(17.0)	1.8	0.8
Translation adjustment, net of tax (provision)/benefit of $(3.2), $6.0 and $0.3, respectively	8.8	15.2	(7.0)
Total comprehensive income	$937.4	$407.8	$309.3

The favorable translation adjustment change during fiscal 2010 was primarily due to the weakening of the US dollar against several currencies including the Japanese yen and Canadian dollar, partially offset by the strengthening of the US dollar against the euro. The favorable translation adjustment change during fiscal 2009 was primarily due to the weakening of the US dollar against the Japanese yen, Australian dollar and the euro. The unfavorable translation adjustment change during fiscal 2008 was primarily due to the strengthening of the US dollar against several currencies including the Australian dollar, Korean won and Canadian dollar.

Components of accumulated other comprehensive income, net of tax *(in millions)*:

Fiscal Year Ended	Oct 3, 2010	Sep 27, 2009
Net unrealized gains/(losses) on available-for-sale securities	$ (0.9)	$ (0.8)
Net unrealized gains/(losses) on hedging instruments	(40.5)	(23.7)
Translation adjustment	98.6	89.9
Accumulated other comprehensive income	$ 57.2	$ 65.4

As of October 3, 2010, the translation adjustment was net of tax provisions of $4.2 million. As of September 27, 2009, the translation adjustment was net of tax provisions of $1.0 million.

Tax Effect Disclosure on the Face of the Financial Statements

4.15

CORN PRODUCTS INTERNATIONAL, INC. (DEC)

CONSOLIDATED STATEMENTS OF COMPREHENSIVE INCOME (LOSS)

(In millions)	Years Ended December 31		
	2010	2009	2008
Net income	$176	$ 47	$ 275
Other comprehensive income (loss):			
Gains (losses) on cash flow hedges, net of income tax effect of $12, $28 and $77, respectively	20	(45)	(127)
Reclassification adjustment for losses (gains) on cash flow hedges included in net income, net of income tax effect of $34, $117 and $63, respectively	54	199	(105)
Actuarial loss on pension and other postretirement obligations, settlements and plan amendments, net of income tax	(7)	(5)	(15)
Losses related to pension and other postretirement obligations reclassified to earnings, net of income tax	3	2	2
Unrealized loss on investment, net of income tax	—	—	(3)
Currency translation adjustment	48	135	(231)
Comprehensive income (loss)	$294	$333	$(204)
Less: Comprehensive income attributable to non-controlling interests	7	6	8
Comprehensive income (loss) attributable to CPI	$287	$327	$(212)

See notes to the consolidated financial statements.

Foreign Currency Translation

4.16

THE SHAW GROUP INC. (AUG)

*CONSOLIDATED STATEMENTS OF SHAREHOLDERS'
EQUITY*

(In thousands, except share amounts)	Common Stock Shares	Treasury Stock Shares	Common Stock Amount	Treasury Stock Amount	Accumulated Other Comprehensive Income (Loss)	Retained Earnings	Total Shaw Equity	Noncontrolling Equity	Total Equity
Balance, September 1, 2007	86,711,957	(5,514,484)	$1,104,633	$(105,048)	$(17,073)	$273,602	$1,256,114	$ 18,825	$1,274,939
Net income	—	—	—	—	—	140,717	140,717	26,070	166,787
FIN 48 adjustment	—	—	—	—	—	(4,943)	(4,943)	—	(4,943)
Other comprehensive income:									
Foreign currency translation adjustments	—	—	—	—	6,837	—	6,837	—	6,837
Change in unrealized net gains (losses) on hedging activities, net of tax of $775	—	—	—	—	(1,360)	—	(1,360)	—	(1,360)
Equity in Westinghouse's pre-tax other comprehensive income, net of Shaw's tax of $4,206	—	—	—	—	6,467	—	6,467	—	6,467
Pension liability, not yet recognized in net periodic pension expense, net of tax benefit of $736	—	—	—	—	(4,480)	—	(4,480)	—	(4,480)
Comprehensive income	—	—	—	—	—	—	143,238	26,070	169,308
Exercise of options	2,492,602	—	41,816	—	—	—	41,816	—	41,816
Tax benefits from stock based compensation	—	—	37,464	—	—	—	37,464	—	37,464
Stock-based compensation	(8,658)	(145,976)	21,001	(9,903)	—	—	11,098	—	11,098
Contributions to noncontrolling interests	—	—	—	—	—	—	—	1,050	1,050
Distributions to noncontrolling interests	—	—	—	—	—	—	—	(16,863)	(16,863)
Balance, August 31, 2008	89,195,901	(5,660,460)	$1,204,914	$(114,951)	$ (9,609)	$409,376	$1,489,730	$ 29,082	$1,518,812
Net income	—	—	—	—	—	14,995	14,995	16,733	31,728
Other comprehensive income (loss):									
Foreign currency translation adjustments	—	—	—	—	(10,339)	—	(10,339)	—	(10,339)
Change in unrealized net gains (losses) on hedging activities, net of tax benefit of $8,711	—	—	—	—	(13,857)	—	(13,857)	—	(13,857)
Equity in Westinghouse's pre-tax other comprehensive income, net of Shaw's tax benefit of $50,744	—	—	—	—	(80,717)	—	(80,717)	—	(80,717)
Pension liability, not yet recognized in net periodic pension expense, net of tax benefit of $6,422	—	—	—	—	(7,444)	—	(7,444)	—	(7,444)
Comprehensive income (loss)	—	—	—	—	—	—	(97,362)	16,733	(80,629)
Adjustment for Westinghouse's cumulative effect upon initial adoption of SFAS 158 (codified in ASC 715), net of tax benefit of $462	—	—	—	—	—	(720)	(720)	—	(720)
Exercise of options	76,828	—	1,233	—	—	—	1,233	—	1,233
Shares exchanged for taxes on stock based compensation	(13,106)	(48,789)	(315)	(1,162)	—	—	(1,477)	—	(1,477)
Tax benefits from stock based compensation	—	—	(1,472)	—	—	—	(1,472)	—	(1,472)
Stock-based compensation	56,434	—	33,367	—	—	—	33,367	—	33,367
Contributions to noncontrolling interests	—	—	—	—	—	—	—	—	—
Distributions to noncontrolling interests	—	—	$ —	$ —	$ —	$ —	$ —	$ (21,124)	$ (21,124)

(continued)

(In thousands, except share amounts)	Common Stock Shares	Treasury Stock Shares	Common Stock Amount	Treasury Stock Amount	Accumulated Other Comprehensive Income (Loss)	Retained Earnings	Total Shaw Equity	Noncontrolling Equity	Total Equity
Balance, August 31, 2009	89,316,057	(5,709,249)	$1,237,727	$(116,113)	$(121,966)	$423,651	$1,423,299	$ 24,691	$1,447,990
Net income	—	—	—	—	—	92,714	92,714	18,185	110,899
Other comprehensive income (loss):									
Foreign currency translation adjustments	—	—	—	—	(5,610)	—	(5,610)	—	(5,610)
Change in unrealized net gains (losses) on hedging activities, net of tax of $729	—	—	—	—	(1,144)	—	(1,144)	—	(1,144)
Equity in Westinghouse's pre-tax other comprehensive income, net of Shaw's tax of $7,411	—	—	—	—	(11,640)	—	(11,640)	—	(11,640)
Pension liability, not yet recognized in net periodic pension expense, net of tax of $2,258	—	—	—	—	(2,831)	—	(2,831)	—	(2,831)
Unrealized loss on securities, net of tax of $348	—	—	—	—	546	—	546	—	546
Comprehensive income	—	—	—	—	—	—	72,035	18,185	90,220
Exercise of options	784,124	—	16,226	—	—	—	16,226	—	16,226
Shares exchanged for taxes on stock based compensation	(225,018)	(46,700)	(6,576)	(1,340)	—	—	(7,916)	—	(7,916)
Tax benefits from stock based compensation	—	—	1,590	—	—	—	1,590	—	1,590
Stock-based compensation	793,848	—	34,923	—	—	—	34,923	—	34,923
Acquisition of noncontrolling interests	—	—	—	—	—	—	—	10,030	10,030
Contributions to noncontrolling interests	—	—	—	—	—	—	—	8,975	8,975
Distributions to noncontrolling interests	—	—	—	—	—	—	—	(14,757)	(14,757)
Balance, August 31, 2010	90,669,011	(5,755,949)	$1,283,890	$(117,453)	$(142,645)	$516,365	$1,540,157	$ 47,124	$1,587,281

See accompanying notes to consolidated financial statements.

NOTES TO CONSOLIDATED FINANCIAL STATEMENTS

Note 1—Description of Business and Summary of Significant Accounting Policies (in part)

Other Comprehensive Income

ASC 220, Comprehensive Income, establishes standards for reporting and displaying comprehensive income and its components in the consolidated financial statements. We report, net of tax, foreign currency translation adjustments, unrealized gains and losses on derivative instruments accounted for as cash flow hedges, changes in our net pension liabilities, our equity in Westinghouse's pre-tax other comprehensive income, and unrealized gains and losses on securities as components of other comprehensive income.

Foreign Currency Translation

Our significant foreign subsidiaries maintain their accounting records in their local currency (primarily British pounds, Mexican pesos, and Canadian dollars). All of the assets and liabilities of these subsidiaries (including long-term assets, such as goodwill) are converted to U.S. dollars at the exchange rate in effect at the balance sheet date, income and expense accounts are translated at average rates for the period, and shareholders' equity accounts are translated at historical rates. The net effect of foreign currency translation adjustments is included in stockholders' equity as a component of accumulated other comprehensive income in the accompanying Consolidated Balance Sheets. See Note 19—Other Comprehensive Income (Loss) for additional information.

Foreign currency transaction gains or losses are credited or charged to income as incurred. Transaction gains reflected in income were $3.3 million, $1.0 million, and $6.6 million for the fiscal years 2010, 2009, and 2008, respectively. Additionally, during fiscal years 2010, 2009 and 2008, we incurred foreign currency translation losses on the Westinghouse Bonds associated with our investment in Westinghouse of $131.6 million, $198.1 million, and $69.7 million, respectively.

4.17

VIAD CORP (DEC)

CONSOLIDATED STATEMENTS OF COMPREHENSIVE INCOME

	Year Ended December 31		
(In thousands)	2010	2009	2008
Net income (loss)	$ 1,079	$(104,129)	$ 43,923
Other comprehensive income (loss):			
Unrealized gains (losses) on investments:			
Holding gains (losses) arising during the period, net of tax expense (benefit) of $82, $137 and $(347)	128	216	(543)
Unrealized foreign currency translation adjustments	7,696	25,050	(41,672)
Pension and postretirement benefit plans:			
Amortization of net actuarial loss, net of tax expense (benefit) of $1,433, $(2,859) and $(755)	(2,109)	(4,164)	(1,219)
Amortization of prior service credit, net of tax expense (benefit) of $17, $(353) and $(483)	84	(548)	(757)
Total other comprehensive income (loss)	5,799	20,554	(44,191)
Comprehensive income (loss)	6,878	(83,575)	(268)
Comprehensive income attributable to noncontrolling interest	(636)	(582)	(550)
Comprehensive income (loss) attributable to Viad	$ 6,242	$ (84,157)	$ (818)

See Notes to Consolidated Financial Statements.

NOTES TO CONSOLIDATED FINANCIAL STATEMENTS

Note 1. Summary of Significant Accounting Policies (in part)

Foreign Currency Translation. Viad conducts its foreign operations primarily in Canada and the United Kingdom, and to a lesser extent in certain other countries. The functional currency of Viad's foreign subsidiaries is their local currency. Accordingly, for purposes of consolidation, Viad translates the assets and liabilities of its foreign subsidiaries into U.S. dollars at the foreign exchange rates in effect at the balance sheet date. The unrealized gains or losses resulting from the translation of these foreign denominated assets and liabilities are included as a component of accumulated other comprehensive income in Viad's consolidated balance sheets. In addition, for purposes of consolidation, the revenues, expenses and gains and losses related to Viad's foreign operations are translated into U.S. dollars at the average foreign exchange rates for the period.

Pension and Postretirement Adjustments

4.18

CHURCH & DWIGHT CO., INC. (DEC)

NOTES TO CONSOLIDATED FINANCIAL STATEMENTS

13. Benefit Plans (in part)

U.S. Pension Plan Termination (in part)

On January 27, 2010, the Company's Board of Directors approved the termination, effective April 15, 2010, of The Church & Dwight Co., Inc. Retirement Plan for Hourly Employees (the "U.S. Pension Plan"), under which approxi-

mately 766 participants, including 46 active employees, have accrued benefits. On December 1, 2010, the Company as plan sponsor of the U.S. Pension Plan, purchased a non participating group annuity contract from the Principal Life Insurance Company for the benefit of certain former and current employees with vested benefits in, and retired participants currently receiving benefits from, the U.S. Pension Plan. In addition, effective December 1, 2010, an existing participating annuity contract with Aetna Insurance Company was changed to a non-participating annuity contract.

The purchase price of the contracts was approximately $63 million, which was funded from the assets of the U.S. Pension Plan on December 1, 2010 (considered the measurement date for accounting purposes) and a one-time payment by the Company of approximately $14 million ($9 million after taxes). The transactions resulted in the transfer and settlement of the U.S. pension benefit obligation, thus relieving the Company of any responsibility for the U.S. Pension Plan obligations.

As a result of the transfer of the U.S. Pension Plan obligations and assets described above, the Company recorded a charge to earnings in the fourth quarter of 2010 of approximately $24 million pre-tax or $0.21 per share. This charge is included in selling, general and administrative expenses.

15. Comprehensive Income

Comprehensive income is defined as net income and other changes in stockholders' equity from transactions and other events from sources other than stockholders.

Consolidated Statement of Comprehensive Income

The following table provides information related to the Company's comprehensive income for the three years ended December 31, 2010:

(In thousands)	Twelve Months Ended December 31		
	2010	**2009**	**2008**
Net Income	$270,694	$243,521	$195,182
Other comprehensive income, net of tax:			
Foreign exchange translation adjustments	(2,469)	34,129	(47,518)
Derivative agreements			
Gains (losses) from derivative agreements	753	1,138	(3,451)
Reclassification adjustments for interest rate collar net loss included in net income	2,616	0	0
Defined benefit plan adjustments			
Net periodic benefit cost	(3,195)	(4,726)	(8,623)
Reclassification adjustments for pension plan termination net loss included in net income	8,528	0	0
Comprehensive income	276,927	274,062	135,590
Comprehensive income attributable to the noncontrolling interest	19	3	2
Comprehensive income attributable to Church & Dwight Co., Inc.	$276,946	$274,065	$135,592

Accumulated Other Comprehensive Income

The components of changes in accumulated other comprehensive income are as follows:

(In thousands)	Foreign Currency Adjustments	Defined Benefit Plans	Derivative Agreements	Accumulated Other Comprehensive Income (Loss)
Balance January 1, 2008	$ 40,335	$ 56	$(1,263)	$ 39,128
Comprehensive income changes during the year (net of taxes of $7,935)	(47,508)	(8,623)	(3,451)	(59,582)
Balance December 31, 2008	(7,173)	(8,567)	(4,714)	(20,454)
Comprehensive income changes during the year (net of taxes of $51)	34,120	(4,726)	1,138	30,532
Balance December 31, 2009	26,947	(13,293)	(3,576)	10,078
Comprehensive income changes during the year (net of taxes of $6,525)	(2,473)	5,333	3,369	6,229
Balance December 31, 2010	$ 24,474	$ (7,960)	$ (207)	$ 16,307

The 2010 change in comprehensive income related to derivatives reflects $4.3 million ($2.6 million after tax) reclassified to interest expense as a result of the termination of the Company's interest rate collar and swap cash flow hedge agreements. The 2010 Defined Benefit Plan Adjustments includes $14 million ($8.5 million after tax) reclassified to earnings as a result of the termination of the U.S. Pension Plan.

4.19

HARLEY-DAVIDSON, INC. (DEC)

NOTES TO CONSOLIDATED FINANCIAL STATEMENTS

12. Comprehensive Income

The following table sets forth the reconciliation of net income (loss) to comprehensive income for the years ended December 31 (in thousands):

	2010		2009		2008	
Net income (loss)		$146,545		$(55,116)		$ 654,718
Other comprehensive income, net of tax:						
Foreign currency translation adjustment		9,449		30,932		(44,012)
Investment in retained securitization interest:						
Unrealized net gains (losses) arising during the period	—		9,760		(18,838)	
Less: net losses reclassified into net income	—	—	(3,840)	13,600	—	(18,838)
Derivative financial instruments:						
Unrealized net losses arising during period	(7,852)		(4,242)		(6,060)	
Less: net losses reclassified into net income	(4,880)	(2,972)	(3,003)	(1,239)	(17,616)	11,556
Marketable securities						
Unrealized losses on marketable securities	(133)		—		—	
Less: net losses reclassified into net income	—	(133)	—	—	(76)	76
Pension and postretirement healthcare plans:						
Amortization of net prior service cost	925		2,679		3,116	
Amortization of actuarial loss	20,944		11,761		7,376	
Pension and postretirement healthcare funded status adjustment	18,431		37,504		(347,165)	
Less: actuarial loss reclassified into net income due to settlement	(2,942)		(884)		—	
Less: net prior service credit (cost) reclassified into net income due to curtailment	1,393	41,849	(22,920)	75,748	—	(336,673)
Comprehensive income		$194,738		$ 63,925		$ 266,827

15. Employee Benefit Plans and Other Postretirement Benefits (in part)

The Company has several defined benefit pension plans and several postretirement healthcare benefit plans, which cover substantially all employees of the Motorcycles segment. The Company also has unfunded supplemental employee retirement plan agreements (SERPA) with certain employees which were instituted to replace benefits lost under the Tax Revenue Reconciliation Act of 1993.

Pension benefits are based primarily on years of service and, for certain plans, levels of compensation. Employees are eligible to receive postretirement healthcare benefits upon attaining age 55 after rendering at least 10 years of service to the Company. Some of the plans require employee contributions to partially offset benefit costs.

Obligations and Funded Status

The following table provides the changes in the benefit obligations, fair value of plan assets and funded status of the Company's pension, SERPA and postretirement healthcare plans as of the Company's December 31, 2010 and 2009 measurement dates (in thousands):

	Pension and SERPA Benefits		Postretirement Healthcare Benefits	
	2010	2009	2010	2009
Change in Benefit Obligation				
Benefit obligation, beginning of period	$1,284,722	$1,178,283	$ 377,283	$ 372,631
Service cost	42,889	47,308	9,957	11,390
Interest cost	77,996	74,578	20,774	22,449
Plan amendments	1,855	620	(22,282)	(9,559)
Actuarial losses (gains)	46,035	12,774	(231)	(7,279)
Plan participant contributions	3,840	5,593	1,431	991
Benefits paid, net of Medicare Part D subsidy	(81,188)	(52,224)	(23,729)	(18,341)
Net curtailments and settlements	14,225	17,790	15,138	5,001
Benefit obligation, end of period	1,390,374	1,284,722	378,341	377,283
Change in Plan Assets:				
Fair value of plan assets, beginning of period	1,026,124	690,558	109,143	96,606
Actual return on plan assets	136,711	159,153	15,151	21,166
Company contributions	20,000	223,044	19,957	10,180
Plan participant contributions	3,840	5,593	1,431	991
Benefits paid	(81,188)	(52,224)	(24,618)	(19,800)
Fair value of plan assets, end of period	1,105,487	1,026,124	121,064	109,143
Funded status of the plans, December 31	$ (284,887)	$ (258,598)	$(257,277)	$(268,140)
Amounts Recognized in the Consolidated Balance Sheets, December 31:				
Accrued benefit liability (other current liabilities)	$ (2,802)	$ (13,266)	$ (2,515)	$ (3,668)
Accrued benefit liability (other long-term liabilities)	(282,085)	(245,332)	(254,762)	(264,472)
Net amount recognized	$ (284,887)	$ (258,598)	$(257,277)	$(268,140)

Benefit Costs

Components of net periodic benefit costs for the years ended December 31 (in thousands):

	Pension and SERPA Benefits			Postretirement Healthcare Benefits		
	2010	2009	2008	2010	2009	2008
Service cost	$ 42,889	$ 47,308	$ 51,363	$ 9,957	$ 11,390	$ 13,078
Interest cost	77,996	74,578	68,592	20,774	22,449	21,640
Expected return on plan assets	(97,376)	(86,225)	(88,061)	(9,781)	(11,175)	(11,232)
Amortization of unrecognized:						
Prior service cost (credit)	4,383	5,553	6,158	(2,914)	(1,299)	(1,123)
Net loss	23,872	12,755	6,414	9,394	5,924	5,501
Net curtailment loss	15,508	29,390	—	11,643	7,014	—
Settlement loss	4,673	1,411	—	—	—	—
Special retiree benefits	—	—	—	—	—	4,881
Net periodic benefit cost	$ 71,945	$ 84,770	$ 44,466	$39,073	$ 34,303	$ 32,745

As discussed in Note 4, the Company recorded restructuring expense of $163.5 million during 2010. The restructuring actions resulted in a pension and postretirement healthcare plan net curtailment loss of $27.1 million, which is included in the $163.5 million restructuring expense. The net curtailment loss of $27.1 million consists of a $28.2 million curtailment loss related to the 2010 Restructuring Plan and a $1.1 million curtailment gain related to the 2009 Restructuring Plan.

During 2009, the Company recorded a curtailment charge of $36.4 million on its pension and post-retirement healthcare plans in connection with the 2009 Restructuring Plan. During 2010, the Company incurred a $4.7 million settlement loss on its SERPA plans compared to a $1.4 million settlement loss on its SERPA plans during 2009. The settlement losses were the result of benefit payments made to former executives who departed the Company during 2009 and 2010.

As discussed in Note 4, the Company recorded a restructuring reserve of $4.8 million in 2008 related to postretirement healthcare benefits which is included as special retiree benefits in the table above.

Amounts included in accumulated other comprehensive income, net of tax, at December 31, 2010 which have not yet been recognized in net periodic benefit cost are as follows (in thousands):

	Pension and SERPA Benefits	Postretirement Healthcare Benefits	Total
Prior service cost (credit)	$ 7,229	$(20,789)	$ (13,560)
Net actuarial loss	339,251	84,037	423,288
	$346,480	$ 63,248	$409,728

Amounts expected to be recognized in net periodic benefit cost, net of tax, during the year ended December 31, 2011 are as follows (in thousands):

	Pension and SERPA Benefits	Postretirement Healthcare Benefits	Total
Prior service cost (credit)	$ 1,877	$(2,442)	$ (565)
Net actuarial loss	19,050	4,528	23,578
	$20,927	$ 2,086	$23,013

Net Change in Unrealized Gains and Losses on Available-for-Sale Securities

4.20

THE COCA-COLA COMPANY (DEC)

NOTES TO CONSOLIDATED FINANCIAL STATEMENTS

Note 3. Investments (in part)

Investments in debt and marketable securities, other than investments accounted for under the equity method, are classified as trading, available-for-sale or held-to-maturity. Our marketable equity investments are classified as either trading or available-for-sale with their cost basis determined by the specific identification method. Realized and unrealized gains and losses on trading securities and realized gains and losses on available-for-sale securities are included in net income. Unrealized gains and losses, net of deferred taxes, on available-for-sale securities are included in our consolidated balance sheets as a component of AOCI.

Our investments in debt securities are carried at either amortized cost or fair value. Investments in debt securities that the Company has the positive intent and ability to hold to maturity are carried at amortized cost and classified as held-to-maturity. Investments in debt securities that are not classified as held-to-maturity are carried at fair value and classified as either trading or available-for-sale.

Available-for-Sale and Held-to-Maturity Securities

As of December 31, 2010 and 2009, available-for-sale and held-to-maturity securities consisted of the following (in millions):

	Cost	Gross Unrealized Gains	Gross Unrealized Losses	Estimated Fair Value
2010				
Available-for-sale securities:[1]				
Equity securities	$209	$267	$ (5)	$471
Other securities	14	—	—	14
	$223	$267	$ (5)	$485
Held-to-maturity securities:				
Bank and corporate debt	$111	$ —	$ —	$111
2009				
Available-for-sale securities:[1]				
Equity securities	$231	$176	$(18)	$389
Other securities	12	—	(3)	9
	$243	$176	$(21)	$398
Held-to-maturity securities:				
Bank and corporate debt	$199	$ —	$ —	$199

[1] Refer to Note 16 for additional information related to the estimated fair value.

In 2010, the Company had several investments classified as available-for-sale securities in which our cost basis exceeded the fair value of the investment. Management assessed each of these investments on an individual basis to determine if the decline in fair value was other than temporary. Based on these assessments, management determined that the decline in fair value of each investment was other than temporary. As a result, the Company recognized other-than-temporary impairment charges of $26 million. These impairment charges were recorded in other income (loss)—net. Refer to Note 16 and Note 17. The Company did not sell any available-for-sale securities during 2010.

In 2009, the Company divested certain available-for-sale securities. These divestitures were the result of both sales and a charitable donation. The sales of available-for-sale securities resulted in cash proceeds of $157 million, gross realized gains of $44 million and gross realized losses of $2 million. In addition to the sale of available-for-sale securities, the Company donated certain available-for-sale securities to

The Coca-Cola Foundation. The donated investments had a cost basis of $7 million and a fair value of $106 million at the date of donation. The net impact of this donation was an expense equal to our cost basis in the securities, which was recorded in other income (loss)—net.

In 2008, the Company realized losses of $81 million due to other-than-temporary impairments of certain available-for-sale securities. These impairment charges were recorded in other income (loss)—net. Refer to Note 17. The Company did not sell any available-for-sale securities during 2008.

The Company's available-for-sale and held-to-maturity securities were included in the following captions in our consolidated balance sheets (in millions):

| | December 31, 2010 | | December 31, 2009 | |
	Available-for-Sale Securities	Held-to-Maturity Securities	Available-for-Sale Securities	Held-to-Maturity Securities
Cash and cash equivalents	$ —	$110	$ —	$198
Marketable securities	5	1	—	1
Other investments, principally bottling companies	471	—	389	—
Other assets	9	—	9	—
	$485	$111	$398	$199

The contractual maturities of these investments as of December 31, 2010, were as follows (in millions):

| | Available-for-Sale Securities | | Held-to-Maturity Securities | |
	Cost	Fair Value	Amortized Cost	Fair Value
Within 1 year	$ 5	$ 5	$111	$111
After 1 year through 5 years	—	—	—	—
After 5 years through 10 years	2	2	—	—
After 10 years	7	7	—	—
Equity securities	209	471	—	—
	$223	$485	$111	$111

Note 15. Other Comprehensive Income

AOCI attributable to shareowners of The Coca-Cola Company is separately presented on our consolidated balance sheets as a component of The Coca-Cola Company's shareowners' equity, which also includes our proportionate share of equity method investees' AOCI. Other comprehensive income (loss) ("OCI") attributable to noncontrolling interests is allocated to, and included in, our balance sheets as part of the line item equity attributable to noncontrolling interests. AOCI attributable to the shareowners of The Coca-Cola Company consisted of the following (in millions):

December 31	2010	2009
Foreign currency translation adjustment	$ (805)	$ 130
Accumulated derivative net losses	(198)	(78)
Unrealized net gain on available-for-sale securities	167	65
Adjustment to pension and other benefit liabilities	(614)	(874)
Accumulated other comprehensive income (loss)	$(1,450)	$(757)

OCI attributable to shareowners of The Coca-Cola Company, including our proportionate share of equity method investees' OCI, for the years ended December 31, 2010, 2009 and 2008, is as follows (in millions):

	Before-Tax Amount	Income Tax	After-Tax Amount
2010			
Net foreign currency translation adjustment	$ (966)	$ 31	$ (935)
Net gain (loss) on derivatives[1]	(222)	102	(120)
Net change in unrealized gain on available-for-sale securities	133	(31)	102
Net change in pension and other benefit liabilities	396	(136)	260
Other comprehensive income (loss)	$ (659)	$ (34)	$ (693)
2009			
Net foreign currency translation adjustment	$ 1,968	$(144)	$ 1,824
Net gain (loss) on derivatives[1]	58	(24)	34
Net change in unrealized gain on available-for-sale securities[2]	(39)	(13)	(52)
Net change in pension and other benefit liabilities	173	(62)	111
Other comprehensive income (loss)	$ 2,160	$(243)	$ 1,917
2008			
Net foreign currency translation adjustment	$(2,626)	$ 341	$(2,285)
Net gain (loss) on derivatives	2	(1)	1
Net change in unrealized gain on available-for-sale securities	(56)	12	(44)
Net change in pension and other benefit liabilities	(1,561)	589	(972)
Other comprehensive income (loss)	$(4,241)	$ 941	$(3,300)

[1] Refer to Note 5 for information related to the net gain or loss on derivative instruments designated and qualifying as cash flow hedging instruments.

[2] Includes reclassification adjustments related to divestitures of certain available-for-sale securities. Refer to Note 3 for additional information related to these divestitures.

4.21

CARDINAL HEALTH, INC. (JUN)

CONSOLIDATED STATEMENTS OF SHAREHOLDERS' EQUITY

(In millions)	Common Shares — Shares Issued	Common Shares — Amount	Retained Earnings	Treasury Shares — Shares	Treasury Shares — Amount	Accumulated Other Comprehensive Income/(Loss)	Total Shareholders' Equity
Balance June 30, 2007	493.0	$ 3,931.3	$11,539.9	(124.9)	$(8,215.3)	$121.0	$ 7,376.9
Comprehensive income:							
Net earnings			1,300.6				1,300.6
Foreign currency translation adjustments						93.2	93.2
Unrealized loss on derivatives, net of tax						(5.3)	(5.3)
Net change in minimum pension liability, net of tax						1.9	1.9
Total comprehensive income							1,390.4
Impact of adopting income tax guidance (see Note 9)			(139.3)				(139.3)
Employee stock plans activity, including tax benefits of $42.1 million	(0.3)	97.8		6.1	293.2		391.0
Treasury shares acquired				(16.8)	(1,091.6)		(1,091.6)
Retirement of treasury shares	(128.0)	(1,027.9)	(7,505.1)	128.0	8,533.0		0.0
Dividends declared			$ (179.9)				$ (179.9)

(continued)

(In millions)	Common Shares		Retained Earnings	Treasury Shares		Accumulated Other Comprehensive Income/(Loss)	Total Shareholders' Equity
	Shares Issued	Amount		Shares	Amount		
Balance June 30, 2008	364.7	$3,001.2	$5,016.2	(7.6)	$(480.7)	$210.8	$7,747.5
Comprehensive income:							
Net earnings			1,151.6				1,151.6
Foreign currency translation adjustments						(122.5)	(122.5)
Unrealized loss on derivatives, net of tax						(0.8)	(0.8)
Net change in pension liability, net of tax						(5.3)	(5.3)
Total comprehensive income							1,023.0
Employee stock plans activity, including tax expense of $2.9 million	(1.0)	30.4		3.9	137.7		168.1
Dividends declared			(213.9)				(213.9)
Balance June 30, 2009	363.7	3,031.6	5,953.9	(3.7)	(343.0)	82.2	8,724.7
Comprehensive income:							
Net earnings			642.2				642.2
Foreign currency translation adjustments						(97.2)	(97.2)
Unrealized gain on derivatives, net of tax						23.8	23.8
Unrealized gain on investment in CareFusion, net of tax						61.2	61.2
Total comprehensive income							630.0
Employee stock plans activity, including tax expense of $16.1 million	(0.1)	(141.7)		3.9	261.9		120.2
Treasury shares acquired				(7.4)	(249.9)		(249.9)
Dividends declared			(259.5)				(259.5)
Non-cash dividend issued in connection with Spin-off			(3,689.4)				(3,689.4)
Balance June 30, 2010	363.6	$2,889.9	$ 2,647.2	(7.2)	$(331.0)	$ 70.0	$ 5,276.1

The accompanying notes are an integral part of these consolidated statements.

NOTES TO CONSOLIDATED FINANCIAL STATEMENTS

7. Investment in Carefusion

The following table provides a summary of our investment in CareFusion, which is classified as available-for-sale, as of June 30, 2010:

(In millions)	Available-for-Sale Securities			
	Cost[2]	Gross Unrealized Gains	Gross Unrealized Losses	Estimated Fair Value
Equity securities[1]	$630.3	$61.2	$0.0	$691.5
Total	$630.3	$61.2	$0.0	$691.5

[1] Equity securities consist of our remaining ownership of 30.5 million shares of the 41.4 million shares of CareFusion common stock that we held immediately after the Spin-Off. These securities are stated at fair value with unrealized gains and losses reported in other comprehensive income. Realized gains and losses and declines in fair value deemed to be other-than-temporary are recognized in net earnings immediately. During fiscal 2010, we disposed of 10.9 million shares of CareFusion common stock, resulting in cash proceeds of $270.7 million and a pre-tax realized gain of $44.6 million.

[2] Represents our cost investment in the net book value of CareFusion's assets immediately following the Spin-Off adjusted for the sale of securities during fiscal 2010.

Gains and Losses on Derivatives Held as Cash Flow Hedges

4.22

APACHE CORPORATION (DEC)

STATEMENT OF CONSOLIDATED SHAREHOLDERS' EQUITY

(In millions)	Comprehensive Income (Loss)	Series B Preferred Stock	Series D Preferred Stock	Common Stock	Paid-In Capital	Retained Earnings	Treasury Stock	Accumulated Other Comprehensive Income (Loss)	Total Shareholders' Equity
Balance at December 31, 2007		$ 98	$ —	$213	$4,367	$11,458	$(238)	$(520)	$15,378
Comprehensive income:									
Net income	$ 712	—	—	—	—	712	—	—	712
Postretirement, net of income tax benefit of $7	(8)	—	—	—	—	—	—	(8)	(8)
Commodity hedges, net of income tax expense of $301	550	—	—	—	—	—	—	550	550
Comprehensive income	$1,254								
Cash dividends:									
Preferred		—	—	—	—	(6)	—	—	(6)
Common ($.70 per share)		—	—	—	—	(234)	—	—	(234)
Common shares issued		—	—	1	37	—	—	—	38
Treasury shares issued, net		—	—	—	—	—	10	—	10
Compensation expense		—	—	—	94	—	—	—	94
Other		—	—	—	(25)	—	—	—	(25)
Balance at December 31, 2008		98	—	214	4,473	11,930	(228)	22	16,509
Comprehensive loss:									
Net loss	$ (285)	—	—	—	—	(285)	—	—	(285)
Postretirement, net of income tax benefit of $5	(4)	—	—	—	—	—	—	(4)	(4)
Commodity hedges, net of income tax benefit of $171	(308)	—	—	—	—	—	—	(308)	(308)
Comprehensive loss	$ (597)								
Cash dividends:									
Preferred		—	—	—	—	(7)	—	—	(7)
Common ($.60 per share)		—	—	—	—	(201)	—	—	(201)
Preferred stock redemption		(98)	—	—	—	—	—	—	(98)
Common shares issued		—	—	1	15	—	—	—	16
Treasury shares issued, net		—	—	—	(5)	—	11	—	6
Compensation expense		—	—	—	128	—	—	—	128
Other		—	—	—	23	—	—	—	23
Balance at December 31, 2009		—	—	215	4,634	11,437	(217)	(290)	15,779
Comprehensive income:									
Net income	$3,032	—	—	—	—	3,032	—	—	3,032
Postretirement, net of income tax expense of $2	(2)	—	—	—	—	—	—	(2)	(2)
Commodity hedges, net of income tax expense of $62	151	—	—	—	—	—	—	151	151
Comprehensive income	$3,181								
Cash dividends:									
Preferred		—	—	—	—	(32)	—	—	(32)
Common ($.60 per share)		—	—	—	—	(214)	—	—	(214)
Mandatory convertible preferred stock issued		—	1,227	—	—	—	—	—	1,227
Common stock issuance		—	—	24	3,969	—	170	—	4,163
Common stock activity, net		—	—	1	26	—	—	—	27
Treasury stock activity, net		—	—	—	1	—	11	—	12
Compensation expense		—	—	—	225	—	—	—	225
Other		—	—	—	9	—	—	—	9
Balance at December 31, 2010		$ —	$1,227	$240	$8,864	$14,223	$ (36)	$(141)	$24,377

The accompanying notes to consolidated financial statements are an integral part of this statement.

NOTES TO CONSOLIDATED FINANCIAL STATEMENTS

1. Summary of Significant Accounting Policies (in part)

Derivative Instruments and Hedging Activities

Apache periodically enters into derivative contracts to manage its exposure to commodity price risk. These derivative contracts, which are generally placed with major financial institutions that the Company believes are minimal credit risks, may take the form of forward contracts, futures contracts, swaps or options. The oil and gas reference prices, upon which the commodity derivative contracts are based, reflect various market indices that have a high degree of historical correlation with actual prices received by the Company for its oil and gas production.

Apache accounts for its derivative instruments in accordance with ASC Topic 815, "Derivatives and Hedging," which requires that all derivative instruments, other than those that meet the normal purchases and sales exception, be recorded on the balance sheet as either an asset or liability measured at fair value. Changes in fair value are recognized currently in earnings unless specific hedge accounting criteria are met. Hedge accounting treatment allows unrealized gains and losses on cash flow hedges to be deferred in other comprehensive income. Realized gains and losses from the Company's oil and gas cash flow hedges, including terminated

contracts, are generally recognized in oil and gas production revenues when the forecasted transaction occurs. Gains and losses from the change in fair value of derivative instruments that do not qualify for hedge accounting are reported in current-period income as "Other" under Revenues and Other in the statement of consolidated operations. If at any time the likelihood of occurrence of a hedged forecasted transaction ceases to be "probable," hedge accounting treatment will cease on a prospective basis, and all future changes in the fair value of the derivative will be recognized directly in earnings. Amounts recorded in other comprehensive income prior to the change in the likelihood of occurrence of the forecasted transaction will remain in other comprehensive income until such time as the forecasted transaction impacts earnings. If it becomes probable that the original forecasted production will not occur, then the derivative gain or loss would be reclassified from accumulated other comprehensive income into earnings immediately. Hedge effectiveness is measured at least quarterly based on the relative changes in fair value between the derivative contract and the hedged item over time, and any ineffectiveness is immediately reported as "Other" under Revenues and Other in the statement of consolidated operations.

3. Derivative Instruments and Hedging Activities (in part)

Commodity Derivative Activity in Accumulated Other Comprehensive Income (Loss)

As of December 31, 2010, the Company's derivative instruments were designated as cash flow hedges in accordance with ASC Topic 815. A reconciliation of the components of accumulated other comprehensive income (loss) in the statement of consolidated shareholders' equity related to Apache's cash flow hedges is presented in the table below:

(In millions)	2010		2009		2008	
	Before Tax	After Tax	Before Tax	After Tax	Before Tax	After Tax
Unrealized gain (loss) on derivatives at beginning of year	$(267)	$(170)	$ 212	$ 138	$(639)	$(412)
Realized (gain) loss reclassified into earnings	(165)	(106)	(181)	(123)	436	282
Net change in derivative fair value	376	256	(297)	(184)	415	268
Ineffectiveness reclassified into earnings	2	1	(1)	(1)	—	—
Unrealized gain (loss) on derivatives at end of year	$ (54)	$ (19)	$(267)	$(170)	$ 212	$ 138

Gains and losses on existing hedges will be realized in future earnings through mid-2014, in the same period as the related sales of natural gas and crude oil production applicable to specific hedges. Included in accumulated other comprehensive loss as of December 31, 2010 is a net loss of approximately $45 million ($24 million after tax) that applies to the next 12 months; however, estimated and actual amounts are likely to vary materially as a result of changes in market conditions.

7. Capital Stock (in part)

Accumulated Other Comprehensive Income (Loss)

Components of accumulated other comprehensive income (loss) consist of the following:

	For the Year Ended December 31		
(In millions)	2010	2009	2008
Currency translation adjustment[1]	$(109)	$(109)	$(109)
Unrealized gain (loss) on derivatives (Note 3)	(19)	(170)	138
Unfunded pension and postretirement benefit plan	(13)	(11)	(7)
Accumulated other comprehensive income (loss)	$(141)	$(290)	$ 22

[1] Prior to October 1, 2002, the Company's Canadian subsidiaries' functional currency was the Canadian dollar. Translation adjustments resulting from translating the Canadian subsidiaries' financial statements into U.S. dollar equivalents were reported separately and accumulated in other comprehensive income (loss). Currency translation adjustments held in other comprehensive income (loss) on the balance sheet will remain there indefinitely unless there is a substantially complete liquidation of the Company's Canadian operations.

4.23

GENERAL DYNAMICS CORPORATION (DEC)

CONSOLIDATED STATEMENT OF SHAREHOLDERS' EQUITY

	Common Stock		Retained	Treasury	Accumulated Other Comprehensive	Total Shareholders'	Comprehensive
(Dollars in millions)	Par	Surplus	Earnings	Stock	Income (Loss)	Equity	Income
Balance, December 31, 2007	$482	$1,141	$11,379	$(1,881)	$ 647	$11,768	
Net earnings	—	—	2,459	—	—	2,459	$ 2,459
Cash dividends declared	—	—	(551)	—	—	(551)	—
Stock-based awards	—	205	—	62	—	267	
Shares purchased	—	—	—	(1,530)	—	(1,530)	—
Net loss on cash flow hedges	—	—	—	—	(24)	(24)	(24)
Unrealized losses on securities	—	—	—	—	(5)	(5)	(5)
Foreign currency translation adjustments	—	—	—	—	(153)	(153)	(153)
Change in retirement plans' funded status	—	—	—	—	(2,178)	(2,178)	(2,178)
Balance, December 31, 2008	482	1,346	13,287	(3,349)	(1,713)	10,053	$ 99
Net earnings	—	—	2,394	—	—	2,394	$ 2,394
Cash dividends declared	—	—	(588)	—	—	(588)	—
Stock-based awards	—	172	—	86	—	258	
Shares purchased	—	—	—	(200)	—	(200)	—
Net gain on cash flow hedges	—	—	—	—	45	45	45
Unrealized gains on securities	—	—	—	—	3	3	3
Foreign currency translation adjustments	—	—	—	—	290	290	290
Change in retirement plans' funded status	—	—	—	—	168	168	168
Balance, December 31, 2009	482	1,518	15,093	(3,463)	(1,207)	12,423	$ 2,900
Net earnings	—	—	2,624	—	—	2,624	$ 2,624
Cash dividends declared	—	—	(641)	—	—	(641)	—
Stock-based awards	—	211	—	191	—	402	—
Shares purchased	—	—	—	(1,263)	—	(1,263)	—
Net gain on cash flow hedges	—	—	—	—	66	66	66
Unrealized gains on securities	—	—	—	—	1	1	1
Foreign currency translation adjustments	—	—	—	—	279	279	279
Change in retirement plans' funded status	—	—	—	—	(575)	(575)	(575)
Balance, December 31, 2010	$482	$1,729	$17,076	$(4,535)	$(1,436)	$13,316	$ 2,395

The accompanying Notes to Consolidated Financial Statements are an integral part of this statement.

NOTES TO CONSOLIDATED FINANCIAL STATEMENTS

L. Shareholders' Equity

Authorized Stock. Our authorized capital stock consists of 500 million shares of $1 per share par value common stock and 50 million shares of $1 per share par value preferred stock. The preferred stock is issuable in series, with the rights, preferences and limitations of each series to be determined by our board of directors.

Shares Issued and Outstanding. We had 481,880,634 shares of common stock issued on December 31, 2009 and 2010. We had 385,704,691 shares of common stock outstanding on December 31, 2009 and 372,052,313 shares of common stock outstanding on December 31, 2010. No shares of our preferred stock were outstanding on either date. The only changes in our shares outstanding during 2010 resulted from shares issued under our equity compensation plans (see Note O for further discussion) and share repurchases in the open market. In 2010, we repurchased 18.9 million shares at an average price of $67 per share. On February 2, 2011, our board of directors authorized our management to repurchase up to an additional 10 million shares, about 3 percent of our total shares outstanding.

Dividends per Share. Dividends declared per share were $1.40 in 2008, $1.52 in 2009 and $1.68 in 2010.

Accumulated Other Comprehensive Income. Accumulated other comprehensive income (loss) (AOCI) consisted of the following:

	December 31, 2009		
	Gross Balance	Deferred Taxes[a]	Net Balance
Unrealized gains on securities	$ 5	$ (2)	$ 3
Foreign currency translation adjustment	732	(118)	614
Pension plans[b]	(2,756)	936	(1,820)
Other post-retirement plans[b]	(33)	11	(22)
Gains on cash flow hedges	23	(5)	18
Total AOCI	$(2,029)	$ 822	$(1,207)

	December 31, 2010		
	Gross Balance	Deferred Taxes	Net Balance
Unrealized gains on securities	$ 6	$ (2)	$ 4
Foreign currency translation adjustment	1,040	(147)	893
Pension plans[b]	(3,457)	1,178	(2,279)
Other post-retirement plans[b]	(210)	72	(138)
Gains on cash flow hedges	112	(28)	84
Total AOCI	$(2,509)	$1,073	$(1,436)

[a] The amount of income tax expense (benefit) reported in other comprehensive income was ($1,330) in 2008, $244 in 2009 and ($251) in 2010.

[b] We recognize an asset or liability on the balance sheet for the full funded status of our defined-benefit retirement plans. The difference between the cumulative benefit cost recognized and the full funded status of these plans is recorded directly to AOCI, net of tax. See Note P for further discussion.

M. Derivative Instruments and Hedging Activities (in part)

Hedging Activities

We had $1.8 billion in notional forward foreign exchange contracts outstanding on December 31, 2009, and $4.2 billion on December 31, 2010. The increase in the amount of outstanding foreign currency forward contracts is due to significant international contract awards in 2010. We recognize derivative financial instruments on the Consolidated Balance Sheet at fair value (see Note D). The fair value of these derivative contracts consisted of the following:

December 31	2009	2010
Other Current Assets:		
Designated as cash flow hedges	$ 37	$128
Not designated as cash flow hedges	12	35
Other Current Liabilities:		
Designated as cash flow hedges	(14)	(16)
Not designated as cash flow hedges	(7)	(17)
Total	$ 28	$130

We had no material derivative financial instruments designated as fair value or net investment hedges on December 31, 2009 or 2010.

We record changes in the fair value of derivative financial instruments in operating costs and expenses in the Consolidated Statement of Earnings or in AOCI within shareholders' equity on the Consolidated Balance Sheet depending on whether the derivative is designated and qualifies for hedge accounting. Gains and losses related to derivatives that qualify as cash flow hedges are deferred in AOCI until the underlying transaction is reflected in earnings. We adjust derivative financial instruments not designated as cash flow hedges to market value each period and record the gain or loss in the Consolidated Statement of Earnings. The gains and losses on these instruments generally offset losses and gains on the assets, liabilities and other transactions being hedged.

Gains and losses resulting from hedge ineffectiveness are recognized in the Consolidated Statement of Earnings for all derivative financial instruments, regardless of designation.

Net gains and losses recognized in earnings and AOCI, including gains and losses related to hedge ineffectiveness, were not material in 2010. We do not expect the amount of gains and losses in AOCI that will be reclassified to earnings in 2011 to be material.

Reclassification Adjustments

4.24

ALCOA INC. (DEC)

STATEMENT OF CONSOLIDATED COMPREHENSIVE INCOME (LOSS)

	For the Year Ended December 31								
	Alcoa Inc.			**Noncontrolling Interests**			**Total**		
(In millions)	**2010**	**2009**	**2008**	**2010**	**2009**	**2008**	**2010**	**2009**	**2008**
Net income (loss)	$ 254	$(1,151)	$ (74)	$138	$ 61	$ 221	$ 392	$(1,090)	$ 147
Other comprehensive income (loss), net of tax:									
Change in unrecognized net actuarial loss and prior service cost/benefit related to pension and other postretirement benefit plans (W)	(140)	(110)	(1,382)	(4)	8	(52)	(144)	(102)	(1,434)
Foreign currency translation adjustments (A)	441	1,377	(1,457)	334	320	(311)	775	1,697	(1,768)
Unrealized (losses) gains on available-for-sale securities (I):									
Unrealized holding (losses) gains	(5)	49	(432)	—	—	—	(5)	49	(432)
Net amount reclassified to earnings	4	381	—	—	—	—	4	381	—
Net change in unrealized (losses) gains on available-for-sale securities	(1)	430	(432)	—	—	—	(1)	430	(432)
Unrecognized gains (losses) on derivatives (X):									
Net change from periodic revaluations	(21)	(609)	282	4	(5)	3	(17)	(614)	285
Net amount reclassified to earnings	138	(11)	157	—	—	(2)	138	(11)	155
Net unrecognized gains (losses) on derivatives	117	(620)	439	4	(5)	1	121	(625)	440
Total other comprehensive income (loss), net of tax	417	1,077	(2,832)	334	323	(362)	751	1,400	(3,194)
Comprehensive income (loss)	$ 671	$ (74)	$(2,906)	$472	$384	$(141)	$1,143	$ 310	$(3,047)

The accompanying notes are an integral part of the consolidated financial statements.

NOTES TO CONSOLIDATED FINANCIAL STATEMENTS

A. Summary of Significant Accounting Policies (in part)

Derivatives and Hedging. Derivatives are held for purposes other than trading and are part of a formally documented risk management program. For derivatives designated as fair value hedges, Alcoa measures hedge effectiveness by for-

mally assessing, at least quarterly, the historical high correlation of changes in the fair value of the hedged item and the derivative hedging instrument. For derivatives designated as cash flow hedges, Alcoa measures hedge effectiveness by formally assessing, at least quarterly, the probable high correlation of the expected future cash flows of the hedged item and the derivative hedging instrument. The ineffective portions of both types of hedges are recorded in sales or other income or expense in the current period. If the hedging relationship ceases to be highly effective or it becomes probable that an expected transaction will no longer occur, future gains or losses on the derivative are recorded in other income or expense.

Alcoa accounts for interest rate swaps related to its existing long-term debt and hedges of firm customer commitments for aluminum as fair value hedges. As a result, the fair values of the derivatives and changes in the fair values of the underlying hedged items are reported in other current and noncurrent assets and liabilities in the Consolidated Balance Sheet. Changes in the fair values of these derivatives and underlying hedged items generally offset and are recorded each period in sales or interest expense, consistent with the underlying hedged item.

Alcoa accounts for hedges of foreign currency exposures and certain forecasted transactions as cash flow hedges. The fair values of the derivatives are recorded in other current and noncurrent assets and liabilities in the Consolidated Balance Sheet. The effective portions of the changes in the fair values of these derivatives are recorded in other comprehensive income and are reclassified to sales, cost of goods sold, or other income or expense in the period in which earnings are impacted by the hedged items or in the period that the transaction no longer qualifies as a cash flow hedge. These contracts cover the same periods as known or expected exposures, generally not exceeding five years.

If no hedging relationship is designated, the derivative is marked to market through earnings.

Cash flows from derivatives are recognized in the Statement of Consolidated Cash Flows in a manner consistent with the underlying transactions.

X. Derivatives and Other Financial Instruments (in part)

Cash Flow Hedges (in part)

For derivative instruments that are designated and qualify as cash flow hedges, the effective portion of the gain or loss on the derivative is reported as a component of other comprehensive income (OCI) and reclassified into earnings in the same period or periods during which the hedged transaction affects earnings. Gains and losses on the derivative representing either hedge ineffectiveness or hedge components excluded from the assessment of effectiveness are recognized in current earnings.

Derivatives in Cash Flow Hedging Relationships	Amount of Gain or (Loss) Recognized in OCI on Derivatives (Effective Portion)			Location of Gain or (Loss) Reclassified from Accumulated OCI Into Earnings (Effective Portion)	Amount of Gain or (Loss) Reclassified from Accumulated OCI Into Earnings (Effective Portion)[*]			Location of Gain or (Loss) Recognized in Earnings on Derivatives (Ineffective Portion and Amount Excluded from Effectiveness Testing)	Amount of Gain or (Loss) Recognized in Earnings on Derivatives (Ineffective Portion and Amount Excluded from Effectiveness Testing)[**]		
	2010	2009	2008		2010	2009	2008		2010	2009	2008
Aluminum contracts	$ (6)	$(589)	$232	Sales	$(106)	$ (4)	$(136)	Other income, net	$—	$3	$(2)
Aluminum contracts	—	13	90	Other income, net	—	49	(35)	Other income, net	—	—	—
Energy contracts	(10)	(29)	(41)	Cost of goods sold	(25)	(37)	(16)	Other income, net	—	—	—
Foreign exchange contracts	(3)	(2)	1	Sales	(6)	3	46	Other income, net	—	—	—
Foreign exchange contracts	—	—	—	Cost of goods sold	—	—	(16)	Other income, net	—	—	—
Interest rate contracts	(1)	—	—	Interest expense	(1)	—	—	Other income, net	—	—	—
Interest rate contracts	(1)	(2)	—	Other income, net	—	—	—	Other income, net	—	—	—
Total	$(21)	$(609)	$282		$(138)	$ 11	$(157)		$—	$3	$(2)

[*] Assuming market rates remain constant with the rates at December 31, 2010, a loss of $86 is expected to be recognized in earnings over the next 12 months.

[**] In 2010, 2009, and 2008, the amount of gain or (loss) recognized in earnings represents less than $1, $3, and $(1), respectively, related to the ineffective portion of the hedging relationships. There was also (1) related to the amount excluded from the assessment of hedge effectiveness in 2008.

Aluminum and Energy. Alcoa anticipates the continued requirement to purchase aluminum and other commodities, such as electricity, natural gas, and fuel oil, for its operations. Alcoa enters into futures and forward contracts to reduce volatility in the price of these commodities. Alcoa has also entered into power supply and other contracts that contain pricing provisions related to the LME aluminum price. The LME-linked pricing features are considered embedded derivatives. A majority of these embedded derivatives have been designated as cash flow hedges of future sales of aluminum.

In 2010, Alcoa entered into contracts to hedge the anticipated power requirements at two smelters in Australia. These derivatives hedge forecasted power purchases through December 2036.

On March 31, 2009, Alcoa acquired an embedded derivative in a power contract, which is linked to the LME, in the Elkem transaction.

Interest Rates. Alcoa had no outstanding cash flow hedges of interest rate exposures as of December 31, 2010, 2009, or 2008. An investment accounted for on the equity method by Alcoa has entered into interest rate contracts, which are designated as cash flow hedges.

Foreign Exchange. Alcoa is subject to exposure from fluctuations in foreign currency exchange rates. These contracts may be used from time to time to hedge the variability in cash flows from the forecasted payment or receipt of currencies other than the functional currency. These contracts cover periods consistent with known or expected exposures through 2011. On March 31, 2009, Alcoa acquired foreign currency derivatives in the Elkem transaction which cover anticipated foreign currency exposures through 2011.

4.25

THE BRINK'S COMPANY (DEC)

*CONSOLIDATED STATEMENTS OF COMPREHENSIVE
INCOME (LOSS)*

	Years Ended December 31		
(In millions)	2010	2009	2008
Net income	$ 72.8	231.9	223.1
Other Comprehensive Income (Loss):			
Benefit plan adjustments:			
Net experience gains (losses) arising during the year	(67.8)	68.2	(501.2)
Deferred profit sharing	(0.4)	—	—
Tax benefit (provision) related to net experience gains and losses arising during the year	24.1	(0.3)	32.7
Reclassification adjustment for amortization of prior net experience loss included in net income	37.8	28.2	11.8
Tax benefit related to reclassification adjustment	(13.5)	(9.5)	(0.7)
Prior service cost (credit) from plan amendment during the year	(19.3)	—	3.1
Tax benefit (provision) related to prior service cost (credit) from plan amendment during the year	7.1	—	(0.5)
Reclassification adjustment for amortization of prior service cost (credit) included in net income	2.7	1.2	(0.3)
Tax provision (benefit) related to reclassification adjustment	(0.9)	(0.1)	0.6
Benefit plan adjustments, net of tax	(30.2)	87.7	(454.5)
Foreign Currency:			
Translation adjustments arising during the year	4.6	(92.4)	(47.0)
Reclassification from available-for-sale securities	(0.6)	—	—
Tax benefit (provision) related to translation adjustments	(0.1)	(0.7)	0.8
Reclassification adjustment for deconsolidation of a former subsidiary	(2.0)	—	—
Foreign currency translation adjustments, net of tax	1.9	(93.1)	(46.2)
Available-for-Sale Securities:			
Unrealized net gains (losses) on available-for-sale securities arising during the year	5.4	2.1	(7.2)
Reclassification to foreign currency	0.6	—	—
Tax benefit (provision) related to unrealized net gains and losses on available-for-sale securities	(1.7)	—	2.6
Reclassification adjustment for net (gains) losses realized in net income	(3.8)	—	6.2
Tax provision (benefit) related to reclassification adjustment	1.1	—	(2.2)
Unrealized net gains (losses) on available-for-sale securities, net of tax	1.6	2.1	(0.6)
Other comprehensive income (loss)	(26.7)	(3.3)	(501.3)
Comprehensive income (loss)	$ 46.1	228.6	(278.2)
Amounts Attributable to Brink's:			
Net income	$ 57.1	200.2	183.3
Benefit plan adjustments	(30.2)	87.7	(454.5)
Foreign currency	(3.3)	(40.3)	(43.9)
Available-for-sale securities	1.2	2.6	(0.6)
Other comprehensive income (loss)	(32.3)	50.0	(499.0)
Comprehensive income (loss) attributable to Brink's	24.8	250.2	(315.7)
Amounts Attributable to Noncontrolling Interests:			
Net income	15.7	31.7	39.8
Foreign currency	5.2	(52.8)	(2.3)
Available-for-sale securities	0.4	(0.5)	—
Other comprehensive income (loss)	5.6	(53.3)	(2.3)
Comprehensive income (loss) attributable to noncontrolling interests	21.3	(21.6)	37.5
Comprehensive income (loss)	$ 46.1	228.6	(278.2)

See accompanying notes to consolidated financial
statements.

NOTES TO CONSOLIDATED FINANCIAL STATEMENTS

Note 3—Retirement Benefits (in part)

Defined-benefit Pension Plans (in part)
Other Changes in Plan Assets and Benefit Recognized in
Other Comprehensive Income (in part)

(In millions) Years Ended December 31	U.S. Plans		Non-U.S. Plans		Total	
	2010	2009	2010	2009	2010	2009
Benefit Plan Experience Loss Recognized in Accumulated Other Comprehensive Income (Loss):						
Beginning of year	$(367.4)	(385.7)	(17.4)	(30.2)	(384.8)	(415.9)
Net experience gains (losses) arising during the year	(60.5)	9.2	(4.1)	10.8	(64.6)	20.0
Reclassification adjustment for amortization of experience loss included in net income	19.5	9.1	1.9	2.0	21.4	11.1
End of year	$(408.4)	(367.4)	(19.6)	(17.4)	(428.0)	(384.8)
Benefit Plan Prior Service Cost Recognized in Accumulated Other Comprehensive Income (Loss):						
Beginning of year	$ —	—	(8.9)	(10.4)	(8.9)	(10.4)
Reclassification adjustment for amortization of prior service cost included in net income	—	—	1.3	1.5	1.3	1.5
End of year	$ —	—	(7.6)	(8.9)	(7.6)	(8.9)

Retirement Benefits Other Than Pensions (in part)

Other Changes in Plan Assets and Benefit Recognized in
Other Comprehensive Income (in part)

Changes in accumulated other comprehensive income (loss) of our retirement benefit plans other than pensions are as follows:

(In millions) Years Ended December 31	UMWA Plans		Black Lung and Other Plans		Total	
	2010	2009	2010	2009	2010	2009
Benefit Plan Experience Gain (Loss) Recognized in Accumulated Other Comprehensive Income (Loss):						
Beginning of year	$(251.6)	(321.0)	$ (9.3)	(5.2)	$(260.9)	(326.2)
Net experience gains (losses) arising during the year	(4.5)	52.7	1.3	(4.5)	(3.2)	48.2
Reclassification adjustment for amortization of experience losses included in net income	16.0	16.7	0.4	0.4	16.4	17.1
End of year	$(240.1)	(251.6)	$(7.6)	(9.3)	$(247.7)	(260.9)
Benefit Plan Prior Service (Cost) Credit Recognized in Accumulated Other Comprehensive Income (Loss):						
Beginning of year	$ —	—	$ 2.6	2.9	$ 2.6	2.9
Prior service cost from plan amendments during the year	—	—	(19.3)	—	(19.3)	—
Reclassification adjustment for amortization or curtailment recognition of prior service credit included in net income	—	—	1.4	(0.3)	1.4	(0.3)
End of year	$ —	—	$(15.3)	2.6	$ (15.3)	2.6

ATT-SEC 4.25

4.26

WELLPOINT, INC. (DEC)

CONSOLIDATED STATEMENTS OF SHAREHOLDERS' EQUITY

(In millions)	Common Stock		Additional Paid-In Capital	Retained Earnings	Accumulated Other Comprehensive (Loss) Income	Total Shareholders' Equity
	Number of Shares	Par Value				
January 1, 2008	556.2	$ 5.6	$18,441.1	$ 4,387.6	$ 156.1	$22,990.4
Net income	—	—	—	2,490.7	—	2,490.7
Change in net unrealized gains/losses on investments	—	—	—	—	(662.4)	(662.4)
Change in net unrealized gains/losses on cash flow hedges	—	—	—	—	(0.5)	(0.5)
Change in net periodic pension and postretirement costs	—	—	—	—	(388.1)	(388.1)
Adoption of FASB measurement date provisions	—	—	—	—	(0.8)	(0.8)
Comprehensive income						1,438.9
Repurchase and retirement of common stock	(56.4)	(0.6)	(1,879.1)	(1,396.5)	—	(3,276.2)
Issuance of common stock under employee stock plans, net of related tax benefit	3.4	—	281.0	—	—	281.0
Adoption of FASB retirement benefits guidance	—	—	—	(1.3)	—	(1.3)
Adoption of FASB measurement date provisions	—	—	—	(1.1)	—	(1.1)
December 31, 2008	503.2	$ 5.0	$16,843.0	$ 5,479.4	$ (895.7)	$21,431.7
Cumulative effect of adoption of FASB OTTI guidance, net of taxes	—	—	—	88.9	(88.9)	—
Net income	—	—	—	4,745.9	—	4,745.9
Change in net unrealized gains/losses on investments	—	—	—	—	1,055.2	1,055.2
Non-credit component of other-than-temporary impairment losses on investments, net of taxes	—	—	—	—	(20.7)	(20.7)
Change in net unrealized gains/losses on cash flow hedges	—	—	—	—	(2.3)	(2.3)
Change in net periodic pension and postretirement costs	—	—	—	—	19.3	19.3
Foreign currency translation adjustments	—	—	—	—	1.2	1.2
Comprehensive income						5,798.6
Repurchase and retirement of common stock	(57.3)	(0.5)	(1,922.2)	(715.7)	—	(2,638.4)
Issuance of common stock under employee stock plans, net of related tax benefit	3.9	—	271.4	—	—	271.4
December 31, 2009	449.8	$ 4.5	$15,192.2	$ 9,598.5	$ 68.1	$24,863.3
Net income	—	—	—	2,887.1	—	2,887.1
Change in net unrealized gains/losses on investments	—	—	—	—	125.1	125.1
Change in non-credit component of other-than-temporary impairment losses on investments, net of taxes	—	—	—	—	14.7	14.7
Change in net unrealized gains/losses on cash flow hedges	—	—	—	—	(14.5)	(14.5)
Change in net periodic pension and postretirement costs	—	—	—	—	32.9	32.9
Foreign currency translation adjustments	—	—	—	—	(1.7)	(1.7)
Comprehensive income						3,043.6
Repurchase and retirement of common stock	(76.7)	(0.7)	(2,595.6)	(1,764.0)	—	(4,360.3)
Issuance of common stock under employee stock plans, net of related tax benefit	4.6	—	266.0	—	—	266.0
December 31, 2010	377.7	$ 3.8	$12,862.6	$10,721.6	$ 224.6	$23,812.6

See accompanying notes.

NOTES TO CONSOLIDATED FINANCIAL STATEMENTS

16. Accumulated Other Comprehensive Income (Loss)

A reconciliation of the components of accumulated other comprehensive income at December 31 is as follows:

	2010	2009
Investments:		
Gross unrealized gains	$1,048.0	$896.5
Gross unrealized losses	(134.5)	(153.7)
Net pretax unrealized gains	913.5	742.8
Deferred tax liability	(320.5)	(274.9)
Net unrealized gains on investments	593.0	467.9
Non-credit component of OTTI on investments:		
Unrealized losses	(9.1)	(32.8)
Deferred tax asset	3.1	12.1
Net unrealized non-credit component of OTTI on investments	(6.0)	(20.7)
Cash flow hedges:		
Gross unrealized losses	(39.1)	(16.5)
Deferred tax asset	13.8	5.7
Net unrealized losses on cash flow hedges	(25.3)	(10.8)
Defined benefit pension plans:		
Deferred net actuarial loss	(460.7)	(555.1)
Deferred prior service credits	5.5	6.3
Deferred tax asset	184.3	222.1
Net unrecognized periodic benefit costs for defined benefit pension plans	(270.9)	(326.7)
Postretirement benefit plans:		
Deferred net actuarial loss	(191.8)	(162.9)
Deferred prior service credits	81.4	91.0
Deferred tax asset	44.7	29.1
Net unrecognized periodic benefit costs for postretirement benefit plans	(65.7)	(42.8)
Foreign currency translation adjustments:		
Gross unrealized (losses) gains	(0.9)	1.6
Deferred tax asset (liability)	0.4	(0.4)
Net unrealized (losses) gains on foreign currency translation adjustment	(0.5)	1.2
Accumulated other comprehensive income	$ 224.6	$ 68.1

Other comprehensive income (loss) reclassification adjustments for the years ended December 31 are as follows:

	2010	2009	2008
Investments:			
Net holding gain on investment securities arising during the period, net of tax (benefit) expense of $(8.9), $690.8 and $40.8, respectively	$ 24.9	$1,310.4	$ 97.2
Reclassification adjustment for net realized gain (loss) on investment securities, net of tax expense (benefit) of $54.5, $(138.6) and $(419.6), respectively	100.2	(255.2)	(759.6)
Total reclassification adjustment on investments	125.1	1,055.2	(662.4)
Non-credit component of OTTI on investments:			
Cumulative effect of adoption of FASB OTTI guidance, net of tax benefit of $0, $54.2 and $0, respectively	—	(88.9)	—
Non-credit component of OTTI on investments, net of tax expense (benefit) of $9.0, $(12.1) and $0, respectively	14.7	(20.7)	—
Cash flow hedges:			
Holding loss, net of tax benefit of $8.1, $1.0 and $0.2, respectively	(14.5)	(2.3)	(0.5)
Other:			
Net change in unrecognized periodic benefit costs for defined benefit pension and postretirement benefit plans, net of tax expense (benefit) of $22.3, $15.0 and $(266.1), respectively	32.9	19.3	(388.9)
Foreign currency translation adjustment, net of tax (benefit) expense of $(0.8), $0.4 and $0, respectively	(1.7)	1.2	—
Net gain (loss) recognized in other comprehensive income, net of tax expense (benefit) of $68.0, $500.3 and $(645.1), respectively	$156.5	$ 963.8	$(1,051.8)

ATT-SEC 4.26

Section 5: Stockholders' Equity

FORMAT OF STOCKHOLDERS' EQUITY IN ANNUAL FILINGS

PRESENTATION

5.01 *Equity* (sometimes referred to as net assets) is the residual interest in the assets of an entity that remains after deducting its liabilities. As discussed in Financial Accounting Standards Board (FASB) *Accounting Standards Codification* (ASC) 505, *Equity*, if both financial position and results of operations are presented, disclosure of changes in (*a*) the separate accounts comprising stockholders' equity (in addition to retained earnings) and (*b*) the number of shares of equity securities during at least the most recent annual fiscal period and any subsequent interim period presented is required in order to make the financial statements sufficiently informative. Disclosure of such changes may take the form of separate statements or may be made in the basic financial statements or notes thereto. Most public entities present a statement of stockholders' equity to conform with Rule 3-04 of Securities and Exchange Commission (SEC) Regulation S-X. As shown in Table 5-1, which summarizes the presentation formats used by the survey entities to present changes in retained earnings, changes in retained earnings are most frequently presented in a Statement of Stockholders' Equity.

5.02 FASB ASC 505 explains that additional paid-in capital, however created, should not be used to relieve income of the current or future years of charges that would otherwise be made to the income statement. In accounting for a stock dividend, a corporation should transfer from retained earnings to the category of capital stock and additional paid-in capital an amount equal to the fair value of the additional shares issued.

5.03 Rule 5-02 of Regulation S-X requires separate captions for additional paid-in capital, other additional capital, and retained earnings. If appropriate, additional paid-in capital and other additional capital may be combined with the stock caption to which it applies.

DISCLOSURE

5.04 FASB ASC 505, *Equity*, states that an entity should explain the pertinent rights and privileges of the various securities outstanding. Examples are dividend and liquidation preferences; contractual rights of security holders to receive dividends or returns from the security issuer's profits, cash flows, or returns on investments; participation rights; call prices and dates; conversion or exercise prices or rates and pertinent dates; sinking-fund requirements; unusual voting rights; and significant terms of contracts to issue additional shares.

5.05 FASB ASC 505 also requires disclosure of changes in the separate accounts comprising shareholders' equity (in addition to retained earnings) and of the changes in the number of shares of equity securities during at least the most recent annual fiscal period. Disclosure of such changes may take the form of separate statements or may be made in the basic financial statements or notes thereto.

5.06

TABLE 5-1: FORMAT OF CHANGES IN STOCKHOLDERS' EQUITY

	2010	2009	2008
Statement of stockholders' equity	489	490	490
Separate statement of retained earnings	5	2	3
Combined statement of income and retained earnings	1	2	2
Schedule in notes	5	6	5
Total Entities	**500**	**500**	**500**

5.07

TABLE 5-2: PRESENTATION OF CHANGES IN ADDITIONAL PAID-IN CAPITAL

Table 5-2 summarizes the presentation formats used by the survey entities to present changes in additional paid-in capital.

	2010	2009	2008
Statement of stockholders' equity	455	446	449
Schedule in notes	8	8	7
Statement of additional paid-in capital only	1	N/C*	N/C*
Balance unchanged during the year	—	1	3
	464	455	459
Additional paid-in capital account not presented	36	45	41
Total Entities	**500**	**500**	**500**

* N/C = Not compiled. The line item was not included in the table for the year shown.

5.08

TABLE 5-3: CREDITS AND CHARGES TO ADDITIONAL PAID-IN CAPITAL*

Table 5-3 summarizes credits and charges to additional paid-in capital.

	Number of Entities		
	2010	2009	2008
Credits			
Common stock issued......................................			
Employee benefits..	272	303	369
Public offerings..	20	38	27
Business combinations...............................	24	20	27
Debt conversions/extinguishments............	12	14	15
Preferred stock conversions.......................	5	8	9
Compensation recognized.............................	344	310	291
Stock compensation tax benefits..................	138	137	201
Warrants issued or exercised........................	30	6	—
Treasury stock purchased or retired.............	13	N/C^	N/C^
Market value adjustment for employee benefit trust.....	2	N/C^	N/C^
Other—described..	86	70	59
Charges			
Treasury stock issued for less than cost........	58	86	79
Purchase or retirement of capital stock..........	112	84	120
Stock compensation tax benefits...................	22	66	N/C^
Restricted stock...	52	64	61
Other employee benefits................................	31	52	48
Conversion of preferred stock.......................	6	4	4
Stock issue expense......................................	25	N/C^	N/C^
Business combination consummated in current year.....	9	N/C^	N/C^
Stock splits..	2	N/C^	N/C^
Dividends...	15	N/C^	N/C^
Other—described..	100	59	50

* Appearing in the statement of stockholders' equity or notes to the financial statements, or both.
^ N/C = Not compiled. The line item was not included in the table for the year shown.

PRESENTATION AND DISCLOSURE EXCERPTS

Stock Issued Under Employee Stock Option Plan (ESOP) and Employee Stock Purchase Plan (ESPP)

5.09

COHERENT, INC. (SEP)

CONSOLIDATED STATEMENTS OF STOCKHOLDERS' EQUITY

Three Years in the Period Ended October 2, 2010
  (In thousands)

	Common Stock Shares	Common Stock Par Value	Add. Paid-In Capital	Accum. Other Comp. Income	Retained Earnings	Total
Balances, September 29, 2007	31,552	$313	$380,516	$70,672	$319,485	$770,986
Components of comprehensive income:						
Net income	—	—	—	—	23,403	23,403
Translation adjustment, net of tax	—	—	—	8,247	—	8,247
Unrealized gain on available for sale securities, net of tax	—	—	—	165	—	165
Net loss realized on derivative instruments, net of tax	—	—	—	5	—	5
Total comprehensive income						31,820
Amortization, issuance and forfeitures of restricted stock	(32)	1	(884)	—	—	(883)
Sales of shares under Employee Stock Option Plan	643	7	16,501	—	—	16,508
Stock-based compensation	—	—	8,982	—	—	8,982
Tax benefit from employee stock options	—	—	665	—	—	665
Repurchases of Common Stock	(7,972)	(80)	(228,134)	—	—	(228,214)
Cumulative effect of adoption of tax accounting standard	—	—	—	—	(1,429)	(1,429)
Balances, September 27, 2008	24,191	$241	$177,646	$79,089	$341,459	$598,435
Components of comprehensive income:						
Net loss	—	—	—	—	(35,319)	(35,319)
Translation adjustment, net of tax	—	—	—	1,156	—	1,156
Unrealized gain on available for sale securities, net of tax	—	—	—	16	—	16
Net loss realized on derivative instruments, net of tax	—	—	—	8	—	8
Total comprehensive loss						(34,139)
Amortization, issuance and forfeitures of restricted stock	31	1	(725)	—	—	(724)
Sales of shares under Employee Stock Option Plan	9	—	226	—	—	226
Sales of shares under Employee Stock Purchase Plan	224	2	4,445	—	—	4,447
Stock-based compensation	—	—	7,326	—	—	7,326
Balances, October 3, 2009	24,455	$244	$188,918	$80,269	$306,140	$575,571
Components of comprehensive income:						
Net income	—	—	—	—	36,916	36,916
Translation adjustment, net of tax	—	—	—	(18,259)	—	(18,259)
Unrealized loss on available for sale securities, net of tax	—	—	—	(11)	—	(11)
Net loss realized on derivative instruments, net of tax	—	—	—	85	—	85
Total comprehensive income						18,731
Amortization, issuance and forfeitures of restricted stock	60	1	(1,212)	—	—	(1,211)
Sales of shares under Employee Stock Option Plan	1,005	10	29,189	—	—	29,199
Sales of shares under Employee Stock Purchase Plan	230	2	4,237	—	—	4,239
Repurchases of Common Stock	(1,196)	(12)	(43,323)	—	—	(43,335)
Stock-based compensation	—	—	8,269	—	—	8,269
Balances, October 2, 2010	24,554	$245	$186,078	$62,084	$343,056	$591,463

See accompanying Notes to Consolidated Financial Statements.

NOTES TO CONSOLIDATED FINANCIAL STATEMENTS *(in part)*

14. Employee Stock Option and Benefit Plans

Deferred Compensation Plans

Under our deferred compensation plans ("plans"), eligible employees are permitted to make compensation deferrals up to established limits set under the plans and accrue income on these deferrals based on reference to changes in a limited number of investment options. While not required by the plan, the Company chooses to invest in insurance contracts and mutual funds in order to approximate the changes in the liability to the employees. These investments and the liability to the employees were as follows (in thousands):

	Fiscal Year-End	
	2010	2009
Cash surrender value of life insurance contracts	$17,047	$16,758
Fair value of mutual funds	6,711	7,067
Total assets	$23,758	$23,825
Total assets, included in:		
Prepaid expenses and other assets	$ 2,340	$ 2,196
Other assets	21,418	21,629
Total assets	$23,758	$23,825

	Fiscal Year-End	
	2010	2009
Total deferred compensation liability, included in:		
Other current liabilities	$ 2,340	$ 2,196
Other long-term liabilities	21,927	22,723
Total deferred compensation liability	$24,267	$24,919

Life insurance premiums loads, policy fees and cost of insurance that are paid from the asset investments and gains and losses from the asset investments for these plans are recorded as components of other income or expense; such amounts were a net gain of $0.7 million in fiscal year 2010, a net loss of $4.3 million in fiscal year 2009 and a net loss of $1.1 million in fiscal year 2008. Changes in the obligation to plan participants are recorded as a component of operating expenses and cost of sales; such amounts were an expense of $1.6 million in fiscal year 2010, a benefit of $3.6 million in fiscal year 2009 and a benefit of $1.4 million in fiscal year 2008. Liabilities associated with participant balances under our deferred compensation plans are affected by individual contributions and distributions made, as well as gains and losses on the participant's investment allocation election.

Coherent Employee Retirement and Investment Plan

Under the Coherent Employee Retirement and Investment Plan, we match employee contributions to the plan up to a maximum of 4% of the employee's individual earnings. Employees become eligible for participation on their first day of employment and for Company matching contributions after completing one year of service. The Company matching contribution percentage was decreased from 6% to 4% during fiscal 2009. Our contributions (net of forfeitures) during fiscal

2010, 2009, and 2008 were $2.6 million, $3.4 million and $4.8 million, respectively.

Employee Stock Purchase Plan

We have an Employee Stock Purchase Plan ("ESPP") whereby eligible employees may authorize payroll deductions of up to 10% of their regular base salary to purchase shares at the lower of 85% of the fair market value of the common stock on the date of commencement of the offering or on the last day of the six-month offering period. During fiscal 2010, 2009 and 2008, a total of 229,172 shares, 224,226 shares and zero shares, respectively, were purchased by and distributed to employees at an average price of $18.50, $19.83 and zero per share, respectively. At fiscal 2010 year-end, we had 371,138 shares of our common stock reserved for future issuance under the plan.

In the second quarter of fiscal 2007, the ESPP was suspended and employee contributions made to the ESPP were returned while a voluntary review of our historical stock option practices was conducted. The ESPP was reopened on March 2, 2008 with an 8 month offering period ending October 31, 2008 and employees began making contributions during the second quarter of fiscal 2008.

Stock Option Plans

We have two Stock Option Plans for which employees and service providers are eligible participants and a non-employee Directors' Stock Option Plan for which only non-employee directors are eligible participants. The Directors' Stock Option Plan is designed to work automatically without administration, however to the extent administration is necessary, it will be performed by the Board of Directors (or an independent committee thereof). Under these plans, Coherent may grant options to purchase up to an aggregate of 5,500,000, 6,300,000 and 689,000 shares of common stock, respectively, of which zero, 2,388,066 and 132,000, respectively, remain available for grant at fiscal 2010 year-end. Employee options are generally exercisable between two and four years from the grant date at a price equal to the fair market value of the common stock on the date of the grant and generally vest 25% to 50% annually. The Company settles stock option exercises with newly issued shares of common stock. Grants under employee plans generally expire six years from the original grant date. Director options are automatically granted to our non-employee directors. Such directors initially receive a stock option for 24,000 shares exercisable over a three-year period and an award of restricted stock units of 2,000 shares. Currently, the non-employee directors receive an annual stock option grant of 6,000 shares exercisable as to 50% of the shares on the day prior to each of the next two annual stockholder meetings. Grants under director plans expire ten years from the original grant date. In addition, currently each non-employee director receives an annual grant of 2,000 shares of restricted stock units that vest on the day prior to the annual stockholder meeting held in the third calendar year following the date of grant. Beginning with our next annual meeting of stockholders in 2011, the annual grant for non-employee directors will be 3,500 shares of restricted stock units that will vest on February 15 of the calendar year following the grant.

In the second quarter of fiscal 2007, the Company stopped granting stock options while a voluntary review of our historical stock option practices was conducted. The Company resumed granting stock options in the first quarter of fiscal 2008.

In April 2008, we initiated a tender offer for non-executive officer employees related to certain discount options discovered during our voluntary review of our historical stock option practices. Discount options are options with an exercise price that is less than the fair market value of the shares underlying the option at the time of grant. The discounted options included in this offer were certain options which vested after December 31, 2004. During the tender offer period, employees had the ability to amend the exercise price per share for eligible options to the fair market value of the underlying option as of the measurement date of that option, and receive a cash payment for the difference between the discounted share price and the amended share price. This amendment was designed to allow holders of discount options to avoid certain adverse tax consequences associated with discount options. The offer expired on May 9, 2008. The incremental stock compensation expense resulting from the offer was $0.4 million which was recognized immediately as all eligible options were fully vested. During fiscal 2010, 2009 and 2008, we also recorded expense of $0.2 million, $0.5 million and $2.5 million, respectively, for tax payments to be made to United States and United Kingdom tax authorities on behalf of employees in connection with these amended shares.

Fair Value of Stock Compensation

We recognize compensation expense for all share-based payment awards based on the fair value of such awards. The expense is recognized on a straight-line basis over the respective requisite service period of the awards.

Determining Fair Value

Valuation and amortization method—We estimate the fair value of stock options granted using the Black-Scholes-Merton option-pricing formula and a single option award approach. This fair value is then amortized on a straight-line basis over the requisite service periods of the awards, which is generally the vesting period.

Expected Term—The expected term represents the period that our stock-based awards are expected to be outstanding and was determined based on historical experience of similar awards, giving consideration to the contractual terms of the stock-based awards, vesting schedules and expectations of future employee behavior as influenced by changes to the terms of its stock-based awards.

Expected Volatility—Our process for computing expected volatility considers both historical volatility and market-based implied volatility; however our estimate of expected forfeitures is based on historical employee data and could differ from actual forfeitures.

Risk-Free Interest Rate—The risk-free interest rate used in the Black-Scholes-Merton valuation method is based on the implied yield currently available on U.S. Treasury zero-coupon issues with an equivalent remaining term.

Expected Dividend—The expected dividend assumption is based on our current expectations about our anticipated dividend policy.

The fair values of the Company's stock options granted to employees and shares purchased under the stock purchase plan for fiscal 2010, 2009 and 2008 were estimated using the following weighted-average assumptions:

| | Employee Stock Option Plans | | | Employee Stock Purchase Plans | | |
| | Fiscal | | | Fiscal | | |
	2010	2009	2008	2010	2009	2008
Expected life in years	4.6	4.2	3.5	0.5	0.5	0.7
Expected volatility	33.0%	48.0%	29.5%	33.5%	50.7%	31.9%
Risk-free interest rate	2.0%	2.0%	3.9%	0.2%	0.8%	1.8%
Expected dividends	none	none	none	none	none	none
Weighted average fair value per share	$8.27	$8.95	$8.78	$7.27	$6.50	$7.31

Stock Compensation Expense

The following table shows total stock-based compensation expense included in the Consolidated Statements of Operations for fiscal 2010, 2009 and 2008 (in thousands):

	Fiscal 2010	Fiscal 2009	Fiscal 2008
Cost of sales	$ 949	$ 753	$1,893
Research and development	1,174	933	1,970
Selling, general and administrative	6,333	5,199	9,062
Income tax benefit	(1,610)	(1,084)	(3,919)
	$6,846	$5,801	$9,006

Total stock-based compensation cost capitalized as part of inventory during fiscal 2010 was $0.9 million. $0.9 million was amortized into income during fiscal 2010, which includes amounts capitalized in fiscal 2010 and amounts carried over from fiscal 2009. Total stock-based compensation cost capitalized as part of inventory during fiscal 2009 was $0.8 million. $0.9 million was amortized into income during fiscal 2009, which includes amounts capitalized in fiscal 2009 and amounts carried over from fiscal 2008. Management has made an estimate of expected forfeitures and is recognizing compensation costs only for those equity awards expected to vest.

At fiscal 2010 year-end, the total compensation cost related to unvested stock-based awards granted to employees under the Company's stock option and award plans but not yet recognized was approximately $10.1 million, net of estimated forfeitures of $1.4 million. This cost will be amortized on a straight-line basis over a weighted-average period of approximately 1.3 years and will be adjusted for subsequent changes in estimated forfeitures.

At fiscal 2010 year-end, the total compensation cost related to options to purchase common shares under the ESPP but not yet recognized was approximately $0.1 million. This cost will be amortized on a straight-line basis over a weighted-average period of approximately one month.

The stock option exercise tax benefits reported in the statement of cash flows results from the excess tax benefits arising from tax deductions in excess of the stock-based compensation cost recognized, determined on a grant-by-grant basis. During fiscal 2010 and fiscal 2009, we recorded approximately $0.9 million and $0.0 million, respectively, of excess tax benefits as cash flows from financing activities.

During fiscal 2008, our Board of Directors approved an extension of the exercise period to August 25, 2009 for 397,500 fully vested stock options previously granted by the Company to employees. As a result, we recorded approximately $0.5 million in compensation expense related to the stock option modification during fiscal 2008. There were no extensions granted during fiscal 2010 or 2009.

During fiscal 2010 and fiscal 2008, we recorded cash-based compensation expense of $0.3 million and $0.6 million, respectively for cash payments to employees for options that were not able to be exercised due to the internal stock option investigation. In addition, we recorded compensation expense of $0.5 million and $1.6 million, respectively, in fiscal 2009 and fiscal 2008 for tax payments to be made to United States and United Kingdom tax authorities on behalf of employees in connection with discounted options previously exercised, for the adverse tax consequences associated with these discount options. We also recorded $0.4 million in fiscal 2008 for tax payments to be made to United States tax authorities on behalf of employees in connection with shares amended to allow the holders of unexercised discount options to avoid certain adverse tax consequences associated with those discount options.

Stock Options & Awards Activity

The following is a summary of option activity for our Stock Option Plans for fiscal 2010, 2009 and 2008 (in thousands, except per share amounts and remaining contractual term in years):

	Number of Shares	Weighted Average Exercise Price Per Share	Weighted Average Remaining Contractual Term in Years	Aggregate Intrinsic Value
Outstanding at September 29, 2007	3,196	$29.00		
Granted	851	32.50		
Exercised	(643)	25.67		
Forfeitures	(75)	32.99		
Expirations	(449)	31.36		
Outstanding at September 27, 2008	2,880	$30.31	3.0	$13,496
Vested and expected to vest at September 27, 2008	2,873	$30.31	3.0	$13,475
Exercisable at September 27, 2008	2,442	$29.99	2.6	$12,218
Outstanding at September 28, 2008	2,880	$30.31		
Granted	499	22.30		
Exercised	(9)	25.37		
Forfeitures	(26)	25.94		
Expirations	(850)	28.34		
Outstanding at October 3, 2009	2,494	$29.44	3.4	$ 562
Vested and expected to vest at October 3, 2009	2,458	$29.54	3.4	$ 547
Exercisable at October 3, 2009	1,968	$31.23	2.7	$ 147
Outstanding at October 3, 2009	2,494	$29.44		
Granted	476	26.59		
Exercised	(1,004)	29.09		
Forfeitures	(38)	24.66		
Expirations	(35)	31.95		
Outstanding at October 2, 2010	1,893	$28.96	4.0	$21,279
Vested and expected to vest at October 2, 2010	1,862	$29.02	4.0	$20,820
Exercisable at October 2, 2010	1,118	$31.69	2.8	$ 9,520

The aggregate intrinsic value is calculated as the difference between the exercise price of the underlying options and the quoted price of our common stock for in-the-money options. During fiscal 2010, 2009 and 2008, the aggregate intrinsic value of options exercised under the Company's stock option plans were $6.0 million, $0.1 million and $6.0 million, respectively, determined as of the date of option exercise.

Under our 2001 Stock Plan, employees and non-employee directors are eligible for grants of restricted stock awards and/or restricted stock units. Restricted stock awards and restricted stock units are independent of option grants and are typically subject to vesting restrictions—either time-based or performance-based conditions for vesting. Until restricted stock vests, shares (including those issuable upon vesting of the applicable restricted stock unit) are subject to forfeiture if employment terminates prior to the release of restrictions and cannot be transferred.

- The service based restricted stock awards generally vest three years from the date of grant.
- The service based restricted stock unit awards are generally subject to annual vesting over three years from the date of grant.
- The performance-based restricted stock unit award grants are generally subject to a single vest measurement three years from the date of grant, depending upon achievement of performance measurements ("Performance RSUs").

The Company granted Performance RSUs during the second quarter of fiscal 2008 which have a single vesting measurement date of November 14, 2010. These RSUs vest as to anywhere between 0% and 300% of the targeted amount based upon achievement by the Company of (a) an annual revenue threshold amount and (b) adjusted EBITDA percentage targets. The Company has determined that the performance target has not been met and these awards were cancelled in fiscal 2011 with no shares vesting. For the purposes of calculating potentially dilutive shares, performance RSUs have not been included.

The cost of the restricted stock awards and units, determined to be the fair market value of the shares at the date of grant, is expensed ratably over the period the restrictions lapse. We had 480,931 units of restricted stock outstanding at fiscal 2010 year-end and 356,528 shares and units of restricted stock outstanding at fiscal 2009 year-end.

The following table summarizes our restricted stock award and restricted stock unit activity for fiscal 2010, 2009 and 2008 (in thousands, except per share amounts):

	Number of Shares[2]	Weighted Average Grant Date Fair Value
Nonvested stock at September 29, 2007	261	$33.02
Granted	262	28.72
Vested[1]	(79)	33.35
Forfeited	(103)	32.80
Nonvested stock at September 27, 2008	341	$29.70
Granted	178	22.38
Vested[1]	(112)	30.72
Forfeited	(50)	30.22
Nonvested stock at October 3, 2009	357	$25.66
Granted	245	26.73
Vested[1]	(104)	25.87
Forfeited	(17)	23.87
Nonvested stock at October 2, 2010	481	$26.22

[1] Service-based restricted stock vested during each fiscal year.
[2] Performance-based awards and units included at 100% of target goal.

At fiscal 2010 year-end, 2,520,066 options were available for future grant under all plans. At fiscal 2010 year-end, all outstanding stock options have been issued under plans approved by our shareholders.

The following table summarizes information about stock options outstanding at fiscal 2010 year-end:

	Options Outstanding			Options Exercisable	
Range of Exercise Prices	Number of Shares	Weighted Average Exercise Price per Share	Weighted Average Remaining Contractual Life (Years)	Number of Shares	Weighted Average Exercise Price per Share
$15.21–$22.98	58,867	$18.21	7.61	18,800	$17.85
$23.16–$23.16	353,684	23.16	4.13	92,248	23.16
$26.16–$26.16	433,550	26.16	6.13	1,125	26.16
$26.41–$32.10	247,100	30.37	3.68	209,100	30.22
$32.23–$32.23	3,000	32.23	2.08	3,000	32.23
$32.95–$32.95	580,000	32.95	2.99	580,000	32.95
$33.18–$35.01	132,430	34.28	2.05	132,430	34.28
$35.03–$35.03	78,560	35.03	0.68	78,560	35.03
$35.36–$35.36	3,000	35.36	6.67	—	—
$37.91–$37.91	3,000	37.91	1.60	3,000	37.91
$15.21–$37.91	1,893,191	$28.96	4.00	1,118,263	$31.69

There were 1,967,520 and 2,442,162 options exercisable as of fiscal 2009 and 2008 year-ends with weighted average exercise prices of $31.23 per share and $29.99 per share, respectively.

Common Stock Issued to Employees

5.10

QWEST COMMUNICATIONS INTERNATIONAL INC.
(DEC)

CONSOLIDATED STATEMENTS OF STOCKHOLDERS' (DEFICIT) EQUITY AND COMPREHENSIVE (LOSS) INCOME

(Shares in thousands, dollars in millions)	Shares of Common Stock	Common Stock and Additional Paid-in Capital	Treasury Stock at Cost	Accumu- lated Deficit	AOCI(L)[1]	Total	Compre- hensive (Loss) Income
Balance as of December 31, 2007	1,787,287	$42,526	$ (18)	$(43,156)	$1,303	$655	
Net income	—	—	—	652	—	652	$ 652
Other comprehensive loss—net of taxes:							
Pension—net of deferred taxes of $950	—	—	—	—	(1,501)	(1,501)	(1,501)
Other post-retirement benefit obligations, net of deferred taxes of $142	—	—	—	—	(267)	(267)	(267)
Unrealized loss on derivative instruments, net of deferred taxes of $3	—	—	—	—	(6)	(6)	(6)
Unrealized loss on auction rate securities and other, net of deferred taxes of $10	—	—	—	—	(16)	(16)	(16)
Total comprehensive loss—net							$(1,138)
Dividends declared	—	—	—	(550)	—	(550)	
Common stock repurchases	(95,386)	(430)	—	—	—	(430)	
Common stock issuances:							
Stock options exercised	703	3	—	—	—	3	
Employee stock purchase plan	3,409	12	—	—	—	12	
401(k) plan trustee discretionary purchases	7,527	27	—	—	—	27	
Other	3,213	46	(2)	(9)	—	35	
Balance as of December 31, 2008	1,706,753	42,184	(20)	(43,063)	(487)	(1,386)	
Net income	—	—	—	662	—	662	$ 662
Other comprehensive income—net of taxes:							
Pension—net of deferred taxes of $23	—	—	—	—	36	36	36
Other post-retirement benefit obligations, net of deferred taxes of $33	—	—	—	—	(47)	(47)	(47)
Unrealized gain on derivative instruments, net of deferred taxes of $4	—	—	—	—	7	7	7
Unrealized gain on auction rate securities and other, net of deferred taxes of $1	—	—	—	—	2	2	2
Total comprehensive income—net							$ 660
Dividends declared	—	—	—	(552)	—	(552)	
Common stock issuances:							
Stock options exercised	1,043	4	—	—	—	4	
Employee stock purchase plan	3,490	11	—	—	—	11	
401(k) plan trustee discretionary purchases	11,607	42	—	—	—	42	
Other	6,353	45	(2)	—	—	43	
Balance as of December 31, 2009	1,729,246	42,286	(22)	(42,953)	(489)	(1,178)	
Net loss	—	—	—	(55)	—	(55)	$ (55)
Other comprehensive income—net of taxes:							
Pension—net of deferred taxes of $100	—	—	—	—	155	155	155
Other post-retirement benefit obligations, net of deferred taxes of $21	—	—	—	—	(40)	(40)	(40)
Unrealized loss on derivative instruments, net of deferred taxes of $1	—	—	—	—	(1)	(1)	(1)
Unrealized loss on auction rate securities and other, net of deferred taxes of $1	—	—	—	—	(1)	(1)	(1)
Total comprehensive income—net							$ 58
Dividends declared	—	—	—	(417)	—	(417)	
Common stock issuances:							
Stock options exercised	10,498	50	—	—	—	50	
Purchase of treasury stock	(18,359)	—	(136)	—	—	(136)	
Employee stock purchase plan	2,324	11	—	—	—	11	
401(k) plan trustee discretionary purchases	1,554	8	—	—	—	8	
Stock-based compensation	39,439	115	—	—	—	115	
Embedded option in convertible debt	—	(165)	—	—	—	(165)	
Other	(398)	(2)	1	—	—	(1)	
Balance as of December 31, 2010	1,764,304	$42,303	$(157)	$(43,425)	$(376)	$(1,655)	

[1] Accumulated Other Comprehensive Income (Loss).

The accompanying notes are an integral part of these consolidated financial statements.

NOTES TO CONSOLIDATED FINANCIAL STATEMENTS (in part)

Note 11. Employee Benefits (in part)

Other Benefit Plans (in part)

401(k) Plan

We sponsor a qualified defined contribution benefit plan covering substantially all management and occupational employees. Under this plan, employees may contribute a percentage of their annual compensation to the plan up to certain maximums, as defined by the plan and by the Internal Revenue Service ("IRS"). Currently, we match a percentage of employee contributions in cash. As of December 31, 2010 and 2009, the assets of the plan included approximately 42 million and 44 million shares of our common stock, respectively, as a result of the combination of our employer match and participant directed contributions. We recognized $56 million, $59 million and $64 million in expense related to this plan for the years ended December 31, 2010, 2009 and 2008, respectively.

Deferred Compensation Plans

We sponsor non-qualified unfunded deferred compensation plans for various groups that include certain of our current and former highly compensated employees. One of these plans is open to new participants. Participants in these plans may, at their discretion, invest their deferred compensation in various investment choices including our common stock. Shares of our common stock owned by rabbi trusts, such as those established for our deferred compensation plans, are treated as treasury stock and are included at cost on our consolidated balance sheets. The values of assets and liabilities related to these plans are not significant.

Note 15. Stock-Based Compensation

Equity Incentive Plan

We adopted an Equity Incentive Plan ("EIP") on June 23, 1997. The EIP was most recently amended and restated on May 23, 2007. The EIP permits the grant of non-qualified stock options, incentive stock options, stock appreciation rights, restricted stock, stock units and other stock grants to selected eligible employees, consultants and non-employee members of our Board of Directors. The Compensation and Human Resources Committee of our Board of Directors, or its delegate, approves the granting and terms of all awards under the EIP (including the exercise prices for stock options). The maximum number of shares of our common stock that may be issued under the EIP at any time pursuant to awards is equal to 10% of the aggregate number of our common shares issued and outstanding reduced by the aggregate number of options and other awards then outstanding under the EIP or otherwise. Issued and outstanding shares are determined as of the close of trading on the New York Stock Exchange on the preceding trading day. As of December 31, 2010, approximately 176 million shares of our common stock were authorized for grant under the EIP and approximately 122 million shares were available for future issuance under the EIP.

In general, the awards that we grant under our EIP include either service-based vesting terms (generally with ratable vesting over three to five years) or market- or performance-based vesting terms. Unless otherwise provided by the Compensation and Human Resources Committee of our Board of Directors, the EIP provides that, upon a "change in control," all awards granted under the EIP will vest immediately. From September 2002 to October 2008, awards granted to our employees at the vice president level and above typically provide for accelerated vesting and an extended exercise period upon a change in control, and awards granted to all other employees typically provide for accelerated vesting if the optionee is terminated without cause following a change in control. Since October 2008, awards granted to our employees at the executive vice president level and above typically provide for accelerated vesting and an extended exercise period if the optionee is terminated without cause following a change in control, awards granted to our employees at the vice president level provide for accelerated vesting and an extended exercise period upon a change in control, and awards granted to all other employees typically provide for accelerated vesting if the optionee is terminated without cause following a change in control.

On December 21, 2010, we accelerated the vesting of certain restricted stock and performance share awards issued under our EIP in order to preserve certain economic benefits to our stockholders that otherwise would have been lost in connection with our pending merger with CenturyLink. As a result, we recorded an increase to stock-based compensation expense of $63 million. There was no incremental compensation cost for this modification. This modification affected approximately 80 employees.

Awards Without Market-Based Conditions

Stock Options

Options generally have an exercise price that is at least equal to the fair market value of the common stock on the date of grant, subject to certain restrictions. Options have ten-year terms.

Our stock option activity for the three-year period ended December 31, 2010 is summarized below:

	Number of Shares (In Thousands)	Weighted Average Exercise Price	Weighted Average Grant Date Fair Value
Outstanding as of December 31, 2007	69,253	$17.20	
Granted	15,138	4.92	$1.44
Exercised	(703)	4.08	
Canceled or forfeited	(2,446)	6.28	
Expired	(10,854)	22.77	
Outstanding as of December 31, 2008	70,388	$14.21	
Granted	346	3.45	$0.67
Exercised	(1,043)	3.37	
Canceled or forfeited	(2,019)	5.26	
Expired	(13,044)	28.90	
Outstanding as of December 31, 2009	54,628	$11.17	
Granted	11,630	4.66	$1.15
Exercised	(10,498)	4.73	
Canceled or forfeited	(1,514)	4.56	
Expired	(9,790)	35.55	
Outstanding as of December 31, 2010	44,456	$5.84	

The aggregate intrinsic values of the options exercised during the years ended December 31, 2010, 2009 and 2008, totaled approximately $16 million, $1 million and $1 million, respectively.

The outstanding options as of December 31, 2010 have the following characteristics:

	Outstanding Options			Exercisable Options	
Range of Exercise Price	Number Outstanding (In Thousands)	Weighted Average Remaining Life (Years)	Weighted Average Exercise Price	Number Exercisable (In Thousands)	Weighted Average Exercise Price
$0.01–$4.00	6,389	4.24	$ 3.63	5,690	$ 3.63
$4.01–$4.50	5,173	3.62	$ 4.17	5,076	$ 4.17
$4.51–$5.00	13,453	7.93	$ 4.67	2,733	$ 4.70
$5.01–$6.00	11,511	5.02	$ 5.26	8,656	$ 5.24
$6.01–$7.50	2,203	4.74	$ 6.20	2,196	$ 6.20
$7.51–$50.00	5,727	4.23	$13.62	5,726	$13.62
Total	44,456	5.51	$ 5.84	30,077	$ 6.37

The aggregate intrinsic value for outstanding options that were in-the-money was approximately $113 million as of December 31, 2010. The exercisable options as of December 31, 2010 had remaining contractual terms with a weighted average of 3.99 years. Options that were both exercisable and in-the-money on December 31, 2010 had an aggregate intrinsic value of approximately $72 million on that date.

We use the Black-Scholes model to estimate the fair value of new stock option grants and establish that fair value at the date of grant. The Black-Scholes option valuation model was developed for use in estimating the fair value of traded options, which have no vesting restrictions and are fully transferable. Additionally, all option valuation models require the input of highly subjective assumptions including the expected life of the options and the expected stock price volatility. Because our stock options have characteristics significantly different from traded options, and changes in the input assumptions can materially affect the fair value estimate, estimates of the fair value of our stock options are subjective.

Following are the weighted-average assumptions used with the Black-Scholes option-pricing model to determine the fair value estimates of options granted in the years ended December 31, 2010, 2009 and 2008:

	Years Ended December 31		
	2010	2009	2008
Black-Scholes assumptions:			
Risk-free interest rate	2.3%	1.8%	2.7%
Expected dividend yield	6.6%	8.9%	6.4%
Expected option life (years)	4.8	4.8	4.9
Expected stock price volatility	48%	47%	38%

We believe the two most significant assumptions used in our estimates of fair value are the expected option life and the expected stock price volatility, both of which we estimate based on historical information.

Restricted Stock

Restricted stock activity as of and for the three-year period ended December 31, 2010 is summarized below:

	Number of Shares (In Thousands)	Weighted Average Grant Date Fair Value
Restricted stock:		
Unvested balance as of December 31, 2007	4,526	$7.43
Granted	4,759	4.99
Vested	(1,505)	7.44
Forfeited	(960)	6.32
Unvested balance as of December 31, 2008	6,820	$5.88
Granted	8,669	3.19
Vested	(2,792)	6.16
Forfeited	(1,437)	4.27
Unvested balance as of December 31, 2009	11,260	$3.95
Granted	9,020	5.78
Vested	(16,472)	4.19
Forfeited	(420)	3.89
Unvested balance as of December 31, 2010	3,388	$7.65

Based on our stock price on the vesting dates, the fair value of restricted stock that vested during the years ended December 31, 2010, 2009 and 2008 totaled $112 million, $10 million and $8 million, respectively. We use the closing price of our common stock on the date of grant as the fair value of our restricted stock awards for expense recognition purposes.

Awards with Market-Based Conditions

In 2007, we granted certain non-qualified options and restricted stock with vesting conditions tied in part to the market value of our common stock. Only one of these option awards and one of these restricted stock awards remain outstanding, and the option has a ten-year term.

In 2008, we began granting what we call "performance share awards." For performance share awards that were granted in 2008, all of which have either vested or been forfeited, a grantee could elect to receive payout in cash. All other performance share awards payout in shares of our common stock, and the number of shares that a grantee ultimately receives is based on a formula that utilizes our total shareholder return as compared to the total shareholder return of a basket of our peers. We value these awards using Monte-Carlo simulations because our standard valuation models do not accurately estimate their fair value. We believe the most significant assumption used in our estimate of fair value is the expected volatility, which we estimated based on historical information.

Stock Options

Stock options with market-based conditions activity as of and for the three-year period ended December 31, 2010 is summarized below:

	Number of Shares (In Thousands)	Weighted Average Exercise Price	Weighted Average Grant Date Fair Value
Stock options with market-based conditions:			
Outstanding as of December 31, 2007	2,340	$8.39	$4.17
Canceled or forfeited	(257)	8.52	4.49
Outstanding as of December 31, 2008	2,083	$8.37	$4.13
Canceled or forfeited	—	—	—
Outstanding as of December 31, 2009	2,083	$8.37	$4.13
Canceled or forfeited	—	—	—
Outstanding as of December 31, 2010	2,083	$8.37	$4.13

Restricted Stock

Restricted stock with market-based conditions activity as of and for the three-year period ended December 31, 2010 is summarized below:

	Number of Shares (In Thousands)	Weighted Average Grant Date Fair Value
Restricted stock with market-based conditions:		
Unvested balance as of December 31, 2007	1,011	$5.73
Forfeited	(115)	6.32
Unvested balance as of December 31, 2008	896	$5.65
Forfeited	—	—
Unvested balance as of December 31, 2009	896	$5.65
Forfeited	—	—
Unvested balance as of December 31, 2010	896	$5.65

Performance Share Awards

The payout under performance share awards can range from 0% to 200% of the award and is based on our total shareholder return as compared to the total shareholder return of a basket of our peers over the service period of three years. As such, these awards are considered to have market-based conditions.

Performance share awards activity as of and for the three-year period ended December 31, 2010 is summarized below:

	Number of Original Awards (In Thousands)	Performance Adjustment (In Thousands)	Total Number of Awards (In Thousands)	Weighted Average Grant Date Fair Value
Performance share awards:				
Ending balance as of December 31, 2007	—			—
Granted	1,713			$4.90
Vested	—			—
Forfeited	(192)			4.90
Ending balance as of December 31, 2008	1,521			4.90
Granted	11,090			2.64
Vested	—			—
Forfeited	(1,278)			2.88
Ending balance as of December 31, 2009	11,333	9,920	21,253	2.85
Granted	6,943	5,912	12,855	3.89
Vested	(15,900)	(15,832)	(31,732)[1]	3.29
Forfeited	(566)	—	(566)	2.94
Ending balance as of December 31, 2010	1,810	—	1,810	$3.28

[1] Of the 31,732,000 shares, 1,312,000 shares vested to employees who selected a cash payout option. No actual shares of our common stock were issued for these performance share awards.

Based on our stock price on the vesting dates, the fair value of the performance share awards that vested during the year ended December 31, 2010 totaled $244 million. We settled $21 million of share-based liabilities for $11 million of stock and $10 million of cash during the year ended December 31, 2010.

If the service period had ended on December 31, 2010, we would have paid out 3,620,000 shares of our common stock for the unvested performance share awards. Our compensation expense relating to the unvested awards was approximately $1 million for the year ended December 31, 2010 and $1 million for the year ended December 31, 2009.

The weighted-average assumptions used to estimate the grant date fair values of the market-based condition awards granted during the years ended December 31, 2010, 2009 and 2008 are summarized below.

	For the Years Ended December 31		
	2010	2009	2008
Monte-Carlo simulation assumptions:			
Risk-free interest rate	1.43%	1.31%	2.10%
Expected dividend yield	6.9%	10.1%	6.8%
Expected stock price volatility	57%	53%	32%

Employee Stock Purchase Plan

We have an Employee Stock Purchase Plan ("ESPP") under which we are authorized to issue 50 million shares of our common stock to eligible employees. Under the terms of our ESPP, eligible employees may authorize payroll deductions of up to 15% of their base compensation, as defined, to purchase our common stock at a price of 85% of the fair market value of our common stock on the last trading day of the month in which our common stock is purchased. For the years ended December 31, 2010, 2009 and 2008, approximately 2.3 million, 3.5 million and 3.4 million shares, respectively, were purchased under this plan at weighted-average purchase prices of $4.76, $3.15 and $3.50 per share, respectively.

Stock-Based Compensation Expense

Stock-based compensation expense is included in cost of sales, selling expenses and general, administrative and other operating expenses in our consolidated statements of operations. We recognize compensation expense relating to our service-based and certain of our market-based awards under our EIP using the straight-line method over the applicable vesting periods. Some of our market-based performance share awards were accounted for as liability awards because the employees can choose to receive the award payout in stock or cash. We estimate the fair value of these liability awards throughout their vesting period and record an expense representing the cumulative portion of the award earned through that period. We recognize compensation expense related to employee purchases under our ESPP for the difference between the employees' purchase prices and the fair market values of the stock. While we have recorded deferred income tax benefits relative to our stock compensation expense, we have not realized any income tax benefits resulting from deductions on our tax returns for the year ended December 31, 2010 due to our NOL carryforwards.

As of December 31, 2010, there was $39 million of total unrecognized compensation expense related to unvested stock options, restricted stock and performance shares under our EIP. We expect to recognize this amount over the remaining weighted average service period of 1.8 years. There is no unrecognized compensation expense related to the ESPP. Included in the stock-based compensation below, there was an immaterial amount of stock compensation awarded as a severance benefit to certain employees whose employment was terminated during the year.

Stock-based compensation capitalized during the year was not material.

The following table presents details of our stock-based compensation for the years ended December 31, 2010, 2009 and 2008:

(Dollars in millions, except per share amounts)	Years Ended December 31		
	2010	2009	2008
Stock-based compensation expense:			
EIP awards (excluding market-based conditions):			
Stock options	$ 9	$ 12	$ 24
Restricted stock	51	22	18
EIP awards with market-based conditions:			
Stock options	2	3	2
Restricted stock	1	1	2
Performance share awards	58	9	—
ESPP	2	2	2
Total stock-based compensation expense	$ 123	$ 49	$ 48
Impact on (loss) earnings per common share:			
Basic	$(0.07)	$(0.02)	$(0.02)
Diluted	$(0.07)	$(0.02)	$(0.02)

We recognized an income tax benefit of $31 million, $19 million and $17 million associated with our stock compensation expense during the years ended December 31, 2010, 2009 and 2008, respectively.

Proceeds From EIP and Employee Stock Purchase Plan

We issue new shares of our common stock upon: the exercise of stock options; grants of restricted stock; vesting and payout of performance share awards; and employee purchases of our stock under our ESPP. The cash received upon exercise of stock options and from employee purchases under our ESPP was $61 million, $15 million and $15 million for the years ended December 31, 2010, 2009 and 2008, respectively.

Deferred Compensation Plan for Non-Employee Directors

We sponsor a deferred compensation plan for current and former non-employee members of our Board of Directors. Under this plan, participants may, at their discretion, elect to defer all or any portion of the directors' fees for the upcoming year for services they perform. Participants in the plan are fully vested in their plan accounts. Subject to the terms of the plan, participants can suspend or change their election to defer fees in future calendar years.

Quarterly, we credit each participant's account with a number of "phantom units" having a value equal to his or her deferred directors' fees. Each phantom unit has a value equal to one share of our common stock and is subject to adjustment for cash dividends payable to our stockholders as well as stock dividends and splits, consolidations and the like that affect shares of our common stock outstanding. Non-employee directors participating in the plan held approximately 860,000 and 937,000 phantom units as of December 31, 2010 and 2009, respectively. Subject to the terms of the plan, each participant's account will be distributed as a lump sum as soon as practicable following the end of his or her services as a director. Amounts deferred before 2005 and earnings on those amounts are subject to the distribution options elected in advance by the participant and may be in the form of: (i) a lump-sum payment; (ii) annual cash installments over periods up to 10 years; or (iii) some other form selected by our chief human resources officer (or his or her designee). A change in our stock price of one dollar would not result in a significant expense impact to our consolidated financial statements.

Investment earnings, administrative expenses and increases or decreases in the deferred compensation liability resulting from changes in the value of our common stock are recorded in our consolidated statements of operations. The deferred compensation liability is recorded in other long-term liabilities. The expense associated with this plan did not have a significant impact on our consolidated financial statements for the periods presented. However, depending on the extent of appreciation in the value of our common stock, expenses incurred under this plan could become significant in subsequent years.

Common Stock Issued in a Public Offering

5.11

SMITHFIELD FOODS, INC. (APR)

CONSOLIDATED STATEMENTS OF SHAREHOLDERS' EQUITY

(In millions)	Common Stock (Shares)	Common Stock (Amount)	Additional Paid-In Capital	Stock Held in Trust	Retained Earnings	Accumulated Other Comprehensive Income (Loss)	Total Shareholders' Equity	Noncontrolling Interests	Total Equity
Balance at April 29, 2007	112.4	$56.2	$510.1	$(52.5)	$1,724.8	$2.2	$2,240.8	$3.5	$2,244.3
Common stock issued	21.7	10.8	609.4	—	—	—	620.2	—	620.2
Exercise of stock options	0.3	0.2	2.7	—	—	—	2.9	—	2.9
Stock compensation expense	—	—	2.0	—	—	—	2.0	—	2.0
Tax benefit of stock option exercises	—	—	1.3	—	—	—	1.3	—	1.3
Equity method investee acquisitions of treasury shares	—	—	4.7	—	—	—	4.7	—	4.7
Purchase of stock for trust	—	—	—	(0.6)	—	—	(0.6)	—	(0.6)
Adoption of new accounting guidance on income tax	—	—	—	—	(15.2)	—	(15.2)	—	(15.2)
Change in ownership of noncontrolling interest	—	—	—	—	—	—	—	2.5	2.5
Distributions to noncontrolling interest	—	—	—	—	—	—	—	(0.4)	(0.4)
Comprehensive income (loss):									
Net income (loss)	—	—	—	—	128.9	—	128.9	—	128.9
Hedge accounting	—	—	—	—	—	(18.5)	(18.5)	—	(18.5)
Pension accounting	—	—	—	—	—	(4.0)	(4.0)	—	(4.0)
Foreign currency translation	—	—	—	—	—	85.7	85.7	—	85.7
Total comprehensive income (loss)	—	—	—	—	128.9	63.2	192.1	—	192.1
Balance at April 27, 2008	134.4	67.2	1,130.2	(53.1)	1,838.5	65.4	3,048.2	5.6	3,053.8
Common stock issued	9.2	4.6	177.7	—	—	—	182.3	—	182.3
Exercise of stock options	—	—	0.2	—	—	—	0.2	—	0.2
Stock compensation expense	—	—	3.8	—	—	—	3.8	—	3.8
Sale of warrants	—	—	36.7	—	—	—	36.7	—	36.7
Purchase of call options	—	—	(53.9)	—	—	—	(53.9)	—	(53.9)
Adoption of new accounting guidance on convertible debt	—	—	59.1	—	—	—	59.1	—	59.1
Purchase of stock for trust	—	—	—	(0.6)	—	—	(0.6)	—	(0.6)
Purchase of stock for supplemental employee retirement plan	—	—	—	(11.1)	—	—	(11.1)	—	(11.1)
Change in ownership of noncontrolling interest	—	—	—	—	—	—	—	(0.8)	(0.8)
Comprehensive income (loss):									
Net income (loss)	—	—	—	—	(198.4)	—	(198.4)	(0.7)	(199.1)
Hedge accounting	—	—	—	—	—	(72.0)	(72.0)	—	(72.0)
Pension accounting	—	—	—	—	—	(121.9)	(121.9)	—	(121.9)
Foreign currency translation	—	—	—	—	—	(260.0)	(260.0)	—	(260.0)
Total comprehensive income (loss)	—	—	—	—	(198.4)	(453.9)	(652.3)	(0.7)	(653.0)
Balance at May 3, 2009	143.6	71.8	1,353.8	(64.8)	1,640.1	(388.5)	2,612.4	4.1	2,616.5
Common stock issued	22.2	11.1	283.7	—	—	—	294.8	—	294.8
Exercise of stock options	0.2	0.1	2.0	—	—	—	2.1	—	2.1
Stock compensation expense	—	—	6.6	—	—	—	6.6	—	6.6
Adjustment for redeemable noncontrolling interest	—	—	(19.4)	—	—	—	(19.4)	—	(19.4)
Distributions to noncontrolling interest	—	—	—	—	—	—	—	(1.6)	(1.6)
Purchase of stock for trust	—	—	—	(0.7)	—	—	(0.7)	—	(0.7)
Other	—	—	0.2	—	—	—	0.2	—	0.2
Comprehensive income (loss):									
Net income (loss)	—	—	—	—	(101.4)	—	(101.4)	0.1	(101.3)
Hedge accounting	—	—	—	—	—	52.6	52.6	—	52.6
Pension accounting	—	—	—	—	—	(96.5)	(96.5)	—	(96.5)
Foreign currency translation	—	—	—	—	—	4.9	4.9	—	4.9
Total comprehensive income (loss)	—	—	—	—	(101.4)	(39.0)	(140.4)	0.1	(140.3)
Balance at May 2, 2010	166.0	$83.0	$1,626.9	$(65.5)	$1,538.7	$(427.5)	$2,755.6	$2.6	$2,758.2

See Notes to Consolidated Financial Statements.

NOTES TO CONSOLIDATED FINANCIAL STATEMENTS (in part)

Note 15. Equity (in part)

Increase of Authorized Shares of Common Stock

On August 26, 2009, our shareholders approved an amendment to our Articles of Incorporation to increase the number of authorized shares of our common stock from 200 million to 500 million.

Common Stock Offering

In September 2009 (fiscal 2010), we issued 21,660,649 shares of common stock in a registered public offering at $13.85 per share. In October 2009 (fiscal 2010), we issued an additional 598,141 shares of common stock at $13.85 per share to cover over-allotments from the offering. The net proceeds of $294.8 million from the offering were used to repay our $206.3 million senior unsecured notes, which matured in October 2009 (fiscal 2010), and for working capital and other general corporate purposes.

Common Stock Issued for a Business Combination

5.12

A. SCHULMAN, INC. (AUG)

CONSOLIDATED STATEMENTS OF STOCKHOLDERS' EQUITY

(In thousands, except per share data)	Preferred Stock	Common Stock	Other Capital	Accumulated Other Comprehensive Income (Loss)	Retained Earnings	Treasury Stock	Noncontrolling Interests	Total Equity
Balance at August 31, 2007	$1,057	$41,785	$103,828	$50,092	$507,065	$(279,164)	$5,561	$430,224
Adjustment for adoption of accounting standard on uncertain tax positions					2,078			2,078
Adjusted balance at September 1, 2007	1,057	41,785	103,828	50,092	509,143	(279,164)	5,561	432,302
Comprehensive income:								
Net income					18,049		872	
Foreign currency translation gain				20,715				
Net change in net actuarial losses (net of tax of $1,709)				4,815				
Net change in prior service costs (credit) (net of tax of $138)				4,246				
Net change in unrecognized transition obligations (net of tax of $0)				35				
Total comprehensive income								48,732
Cash dividends paid or accrued:								
Preferred stock, $5 per share					(53)			(53)
Common stock, $0.59 per share					(16,038)			(16,038)
Stock options exercised		206	3,716					3,922
Restricted stock issued, net of forfeitures		245	(245)					—
Redemption of common stock to cover tax withholdings		(5)	(89)					(94)
Purchase of treasury stock						(42,002)		(42,002)
Cash distributions to noncontrolling interests							(900)	(900)
Non-cash stock based compensation			743					743
Amortization of restricted stock			$ 4,152					$ 4,152

(continued)

(In thousands, except per share data)	Preferred Stock	Common Stock	Other Capital	Accumulated Other Comprehensive Income (Loss)	Retained Earnings	Treasury Stock	Noncontrolling Interests	Total Equity
Balance at August 31, 2008	$1,057	$42,231	$112,105	$79,903	$511,101	$(321,166)	$5,533	$430,764
Comprehensive loss:								
Net loss					(2,776)		349	
Foreign currency translation gain (loss)				(30,824)				
Net change in net actuarial losses (net of tax of $1,567)				(7,803)				
Net change in prior service costs (credit) (net of tax of $523)				(2,604)				
Net change in unrecognized transition obligations (net of tax of $0)				42				
Total comprehensive loss								(43,616)
Cash dividends paid or accrued:								
Preferred stock, $5 per share					(53)			(53)
Common stock, $0.60 per share					(15,759)			(15,759)
Stock options exercised		34	552					586
Restricted stock issued, net of forfeitures		45	(45)					—
Redemption of common stock to cover tax withholdings		(15)	(201)					(216)
Purchase of treasury stock						(1,646)		(1,646)
Redemption of preferred stock	(1,055)							(1,055)
Cash distributions to noncontrolling interests							(981)	(981)
Non-cash stock based compensation			16					16
Amortization of restricted stock			2,931					2,931
Balance at August 31, 2009	2	42,295	115,358	38,714	492,513	(322,812)	4,901	370,971
Comprehensive income (loss):								
Net income					43,900		221	
Foreign currency translation gain (loss)				(27,898)				
Net change in net actuarial losses (net of tax of $4,720)				(17,042)				
Net change in prior service costs (credit) (net of tax of $0)				(52)				
Total comprehensive loss								(871)
Cash dividends paid or accrued:								
Common stock, $0.60 per share					(16,754)			(16,754)
Acquisition of ICO		5,100	127,551					132,651
Stock options exercised		214	3,796					4,010
Restricted stock issued, net of forfeitures		123	(123)					—
Redemption of common stock to cover tax withholdings		(42)	(914)					(956)
Issuance of treasury stock						35		35
Redemption of preferred stock	(2)							(2)
Non-cash stock based compensation								—
Amortization of restricted stock			4,066					4,066
Balance at August 31, 2010	$ —	$47,690	$249,734	$(6,278)	$519,659	$(322,777)	$5,122	$493,150

The accompanying notes are an integral part of the consolidated financial statements.

NOTES TO CONSOLIDATED FINANCIAL STATEMENTS (in part)

Note 2—Business Acquisitions (in part)

Mccann Color, Inc.

On March 1, 2010, the Company completed the purchase of McCann Color, Inc. ("McCann Color"), a producer of high-quality color concentrates, based in North Canton, Ohio, for $8.8 million in cash. The business provides specially formulated color concentrates to match precise customer specifications. Its products are used in end markets such as packaging, lawn and garden, furniture, consumer products and appliances. The operations serve customers from its 48,000-square-foot, expandable North Canton facility, which was built in 1998 exclusively to manufacture color concentrates. The facility complements the Company's existing North American masterbatch manufacturing and product development facilities in Akron, Ohio, San Luis Potosi, Mexico, and La Porte, Texas. The results of operations from the McCann Color acquisition are included in the accompanying consolidated financial statements for the period from the acquisition date, March 1, 2010, and are reported in the North America Masterbatch segment.

The acquisition was accounted for in accordance with the FASB revised accounting standard for business combinations. The accounting guidance for business combinations results in a new basis of accounting reflecting the estimated fair values for assets acquired and liabilities assumed. The transaction was financed with available cash. Tangible assets acquired and liabilities assumed were recorded at their estimated fair values of $2.0 million and $0.5 million, respectively. The estimated fair values of finite-lived intangible assets acquired of $4.0 million related to intellectual property and customer relationships are being amortized over their estimated useful lives of 15 years. Goodwill of $3.4 million represents the excess of cost over the estimated fair value of net tangible and intangible assets acquired. The information included herein has been prepared based on the allocation of the purchase price using estimates of the fair value and useful lives of assets acquired and liabilities assumed which were determined with the assistance of independent valuations, quoted market prices and estimates made by management.

Ico, Inc.

On April 30, 2010, the Company acquired ICO, Inc. ("ICO") through a merger by and among the Company, ICO and Wildcat Spider, LLC, a wholly-owned subsidiary of the Company, and which is now known as ICO-Schulman, LLC, pursuant to the terms of the December 2, 2009 Agreement and Plan of Merger ("Merger Agreement"). The results of ICO's operations have been included in the consolidated financial statements since the date of acquisition, April 30, 2010.

The acquisition of ICO presents the Company with an opportunity to expand its presence substantially, especially in the global rotomolding and U.S. masterbatch markets. ICO's business is complementary to the Company's business across markets, product lines and geographies. The acquisition of ICO's operations increases the Company's presence in the U.S. masterbatch market, gains plants in the high-growth market of Brazil and expands the Company's presence in Asia with the addition of several ICO facilities in that region. In Europe, the acquisition allows the Company to add rotomold compounding and size reduction to the Company's capabilities. It also enables growth in countries where the Company currently has a limited presence, such as France, Italy and Holland, as well as leverages its existing facilities serving high-growth markets such as Poland, Hungary and Sweden.

Under the terms of the Merger Agreement, each share of ICO common stock outstanding immediately prior to the merger was converted into the right to receive a pro rata portion of the total consideration of $105.0 million in cash and 5.1 million shares of the Company's common stock. All unvested stock options and shares of restricted stock of ICO became fully vested immediately prior to the merger. Unexercised stock options were exchanged for cash equal to their "in the money" value, which reduced the cash pool available to ICO's stockholders. The following table summarizes the calculation of the estimated fair value of the total consideration transferred (in thousands, except share price):

Estimated fair value of consideration transferred:	
A. Schulman, Inc. common shares issued	5,100
Closing price per share of A. Schulman, Inc. common stock, as of April 30, 2010	$ 26.01
Consideration attributable to common stock	$132,651
Cash paid, including cash paid to settle ICO, Inc.'s outstanding equity awards	$105,000
Total consideration transferred	$237,651

The merger was accounted for in accordance with the FASB revised accounting standard for business combinations. The accounting guidance for business combinations results in a new basis of accounting reflecting the estimated fair values for assets acquired and liabilities assumed. The information included herein has been prepared based on the preliminary allocation of the purchase price using estimates of the fair value and useful lives of assets acquired and liabilities assumed which were determined with the assistance of independent valuations, quoted market prices and estimates made by management. The purchase price allocations are subject to further adjustment until all pertinent information regarding the property, plant and equipment, intangible assets, other long-term assets, goodwill, contingent consideration liabilities, long-term debt, other long-term liabilities and deferred income tax assets and liabilities acquired are fully evaluated by the Company and independent valuations are complete.

Common Stock Issued Upon Conversion of Convertible Debt

5.13

THE TJX COMPANIES, INC. (JAN)

*CONSOLIDATED STATEMENTS OF SHAREHOLDERS'
EQUITY*

(In thousands)	Shares	Common Stock Par Value $1	Additional Paid-In Capital	Accumulated Other Comprehensive Income (Loss)	Retained Earnings	Total
Balance, January 27, 2007	453,650	$453,650	$ —	$(33,989)	$1,870,460	$2,290,121
Comprehensive income:						
Net income	—	—	—	—	771,750	771,750
Gain due to foreign currency translation adjustments	—	—	—	20,998	—	20,998
(Loss) on net investment hedge contracts	—	—	—	(15,823)	—	(15,823)
(Loss) on cash flow hedge contracts	—	—	—	(1,526)	—	(1,526)
Recognition of prior service cost and gains (losses)	—	—	—	1,393	—	1,393
Amount of cash flow hedge reclassified from other comprehensive income to net income	—	—	—	429	—	429
Total comprehensive income						777,221
Implementation of accounting for uncertain tax positions (see note K)	—	—	—	—	(27,178)	(27,178)
Implementation of the measurement provisions relating to retirement obligations (see note L)	—	—	—	(167)	(1,641)	(1,808)
Cash dividends declared on common stock	—	—	—	—	(158,202)	(158,202)
Amortization of share-based compensation expense	—	—	57,370	—	—	57,370
Stock options repurchased by TJX	—	—	(3,266)	—	—	(3,266)
Issuance of common stock under stock incentive plan and related tax effect	7,253	7,253	129,942	—	—	137,195
Common stock repurchased	(32,953)	(32,953)	(184,046)	—	(723,209)	(940,208)
Balance, January 26, 2008	427,950	427,950	—	(28,685)	1,731,980	2,131,245
Comprehensive income:						
Net income	—	—	—	—	880,617	880,617
(Loss) due to foreign currency translation adjustments	—	—	—	(171,225)	—	(171,225)
Gain on net investment hedge contracts	—	—	—	68,816	—	68,816
Recognition of prior service cost and gains (losses)	—	—	—	(1,206)	—	(1,206)
Recognition of unfunded post retirement liabilities	—	—	—	(86,158)	—	(86,158)
Amount of cash flow hedge reclassified from other comprehensive income to net income	—	—	—	677	—	677
Total comprehensive income						691,521
Cash dividends declared on common stock	—	—	—	—	(183,694)	(183,694)
Amortization of share-based compensation expense	—	—	51,229	—	—	51,229
Issuance of common stock upon conversion of convertible debt	1,717	1,717	39,326	—	—	41,043
Stock options repurchased by TJX	—	—	(987)	—	—	(987)
Issuance of common stock under stock incentive plan and related tax effect	7,439	7,439	147,858	—	—	155,297
Common stock repurchased	(24,284)	(24,284)	(237,426)	—	(489,387)	(751,097)
Balance, January 31, 2009	412,822	412,822	—	(217,781)	1,939,516	2,134,557
Comprehensive income:						
Net income	—	—	—	—	1,213,572	1,213,572
Gain due to foreign currency translation adjustments	—	—	—	76,678	—	76,678
Recognition of prior service cost and gains (losses)	—	—	—	8,191	—	8,191
Recognition of unfunded post retirement liabilities	—	—	—	(1,212)	—	(1,212)
Total comprehensive income						1,297,229
Cash dividends declared on common stock	—	—	—	—	(201,490)	(201,490)
Amortization of share-based compensation expense	—	—	55,145	—	—	55,145
Issuance of common stock upon conversion of convertible debt	15,094	15,094	349,994	—	—	365,088
Issuance of common stock under stock incentive plan and related tax effect	8,329	8,329	175,180	—	—	183,509
Common stock repurchased	(26,859)	(26,859)	(580,319)	—	(337,584)	(944,762)
Balance, January 30, 2010	409,386	$409,386	$ —	$(134,124)	$2,614,014	$2,889,276

The accompanying notes are an integral part of the financial
statements.

NOTES TO CONSOLIDATED FINANCIAL STATEMENTS *(in part)*

A. Summary of Accounting Policies *(in part)*

Common Stock and Equity *(in part)*

Equity transactions consist primarily of the repurchase of our common stock under our stock repurchase programs and the amortization of expense and issuance of common stock under our stock incentive plan. In fiscal 2010, we also issued shares upon conversion of convertible notes called for redemption, discussed in Note D. Under our stock repurchase programs we repurchase our common stock on the open market. The par value of the shares repurchased is charged to common stock with the excess of the purchase price over par first charged against any available additional paid-in capital ("APIC") and the balance charged to retained earnings. Due to the high volume of repurchases over the past several years, we have no remaining balance in APIC in any of the years presented. All shares repurchased have been retired.

D. Long-Term Debt and Credit Lines *(in part)*

In February 2001, TJX issued $517.5 million zero coupon convertible subordinated notes due in February 2021 and raised gross proceeds of $347.6 million. The issue price of the notes represented a yield to maturity of 2% per year. During fiscal 2010, TJX called for the redemption of these notes at the original issue price plus accrued original issue discount, and 462,057 of such notes with a carrying value of $365.1 million were converted into 15.1 million shares of TJX common stock at a rate of 32.667 shares per note. TJX paid $2.3 million to redeem the remaining 2,886 notes outstanding that were not converted. Prior to fiscal 2010, a total of 52,557 notes were either converted into common shares of TJX or put back to the Company.

Conversion of Preferred Stock

5.14

THE PROCTER & GAMBLE COMPANY (JUN)

CONSOLIDATED STATEMENTS OF SHAREHOLDERS' EQUITY

(Dollars in millions/Shares in thousands)	Common Shares Outstanding	Common Stock	Preferred Stock	Additional Paid-In Capital	Reserve for ESOP Debt Retirement	Accumulated Other Comprehensive Income (Loss)	Non-controlling Interest	Treasury Stock	Retained Earnings	Total
Balance June 30, 2007	3,131,946	$3,990	$1,406	$59,030	$(1,308)	$617	$252	$(38,772)	$41,797	$67,012
Net earnings									12,075	12,075
Other comprehensive income:										
Financial statement translation						6,543				6,543
Hedges and investment securities, net of $1,664 tax						(2,906)				(2,906)
Defined benefit retirement plans, net of $120 tax						(508)				(508)
Total comprehensive income										$15,204
Cumulative impact for adoption of new accounting guidance[1]									(232)	(232)
Dividends to shareholders:										
Common									(4,479)	(4,479)
Preferred, net of tax benefits									(176)	(176)
Treasury purchases	(148,121)							(10,047)		(10,047)
Employee plan issuances	43,910	12		1,272				1,196		2,480
Preferred stock conversions	4,982		(40)	5				35		—
ESOP debt impacts					(17)				1	(16)
Noncontrolling interest							38			38
Balance June 30, 2008	3,032,717	4,002	1,366	60,307	(1,325)	3,746	290	(47,588)	48,986	69,784
Net earnings									13,436	13,436
Other comprehensive income:										
Financial statement translation						(6,151)				(6,151)
Hedges and investment securities, net of $452 tax						748				748
Defined benefit retirement plans, net of $879 tax						(1,701)				(1,701)
Total comprehensive income										$6,332
Cumulative impact for adoption of new accounting guidance[1]									(84)	(84)
Dividends to shareholders:										
Common									(4,852)	(4,852)
Preferred, net of tax benefits									(192)	(192)
Treasury purchases	(98,862)							(6,370)		(6,370)
Employee plan issuances	16,841	5		804				428		1,237
Preferred stock conversions	4,992		(42)	7				35		—
Shares tendered for Folgers coffee subsidiary	(38,653)							(2,466)		(2,466)
ESOP debt impacts					(15)				15	—
Noncontrolling interest							(7)			(7)
Balance June 30, 2009	2,917,035	4,007	1,324	61,118	(1,340)	(3,358)	283	(55,961)	57,309	63,382
Net earnings									12,736	12,736
Other comprehensive income:										
Financial statement translation						(4,194)				(4,194)
Hedges and investment securities, net of $520 tax						867				867
Defined benefit retirement plans, net of $465 tax						(1,137)				(1,137)
Total comprehensive income										$8,272
Dividends to shareholders:										
Common									(5,239)	(5,239)
Preferred, net of tax benefits									(219)	(219)
Treasury purchases	(96,759)							(6,004)		(6,004)
Employee plan issuances	17,616	1		574				616		1,191
Preferred stock conversions	5,579		(47)	7				40		—
ESOP debt impacts					(10)				27	17
Noncontrolling interest					(2)		41			39
Balance June 30, 2010	2,843,471	$4,008	$1,277	$61,697	$(1,350)	$(7,822)	$324	$(61,309)	$64,614	$61,439

[1] Cumulative impact of adopting new accounting guidance relates to: 2008—uncertainty in income taxes; 2009—split-dollar life insurance arrangements.

See accompanying Notes to Consolidated Financial Statements.

*NOTES TO CONSOLIDATED FINANCIAL
STATEMENTS (in part)*

Note 6—Earnings Per Share

Net earnings less preferred dividends (net of related tax benefits) are divided by the weighted average number of common shares outstanding during the year to calculate basic net earnings per common share. Diluted net earnings per common share are calculated to give effect to stock options and other stock-based awards (see Note 7) and assume conversion of preferred stock (see Note 8).

Net earnings and common shares used to calculate basic and diluted net earnings per share were as follows (in millions):

Years Ended June 30	2010	2009	2008
Net earnings from continuing operations	$10,946	$10,680	$11,291
Preferred dividends, net of tax benefit	(219)	(192)	(176)
Net earnings from continuing operations available to common shareholders	10,727	10,488	11,115
Preferred dividends, net of tax benefit	219	192	176
Diluted net earnings from continuing operations	10,946	10,680	11,291
Net earnings from discontinued operations	1,790	2,756	784
Net earnings	12,736	13,436	12,075

Shares in Millions; Years Ended June 30	2010	2009	2008
Basic weighted average common shares outstanding	2,900.8	2,952.2	3,080.8
Effect of dilutive securities			
Conversion of preferred shares[1]	134.0	139.2	144.2
Exercise of stock options and other unvested equity awards[2]	64.5	62.7	91.8
Diluted weighted average common shares outstanding	3,099.3	3,154.1	3,316.8

[1] Despite being included currently in diluted net earnings per common share, the actual conversion to common stock occurs pursuant to the repayment of the ESOPs' obligations through 2035.

[2] Approximately 101 million in 2010, 92 million in 2009 and 40 million in 2008 of the Company's outstanding stock options were not included in the diluted net earnings per share calculation because the options were out of the money or to do so would have been antidilutive (i.e., the total proceeds upon exercise would have exceeded the market value of the underlying common shares).

*Note 8—Postretirement Benefits and Employee Stock
Ownership Plan (in part)*

Defined Contribution Retirement Plans

We have defined contribution plans which cover the majority of our U.S. employees, as well as employees in certain other countries. These plans are fully funded. We generally make contributions to participants' accounts based on individual base salaries and years of service. Total global defined contribution expense was $344, $364 and $290 in 2010, 2009 and 2008, respectively.

The primary U.S. defined contribution plan (the U.S. DC plan) comprises the majority of the balances and expense for the Company's defined contribution plans. For the U.S. DC plan, the contribution rate is set annually. Total contributions for this plan approximated 15% of total participants' annual wages and salaries in 2010, 2009 and 2008.

We maintain The Procter & Gamble Profit Sharing Trust (Trust) and Employee Stock Ownership Plan (ESOP) to provide a portion of the funding for the U.S. DC plan and other retiree benefits. Operating details of the ESOP are provided at the end of this Note. The fair value of the ESOP Series A shares allocated to participants reduces our cash contribution required to fund the U.S. DC plan.

Employee Stock Ownership Plan

We maintain the ESOP to provide funding for certain employee benefits discussed in the preceding paragraphs.

The ESOP borrowed $1.0 billion in 1989 and the proceeds were used to purchase Series A ESOP Convertible Class A Preferred Stock to fund a portion of the U.S. DC plan. Principal and interest requirements of the borrowing were paid by the Trust from dividends on the preferred shares and from advances provided by the Company. The original borrowing of $1.0 billion has been repaid in full, and advances from the Company of $160 remain outstanding at June 30, 2010. Each share is convertible at the option of the holder into one share of the Company's common stock. The dividend for the current year was equal to the common stock dividend of $1.80 per share. The liquidation value is $6.82 per share.

In 1991, the ESOP borrowed an additional $1.0 billion. The proceeds were used to purchase Series B ESOP Convertible Class A Preferred Stock to fund a portion of retiree health care benefits. These shares, net of the ESOP's debt, are considered plan assets of the other retiree benefits plan discussed above. Debt service requirements are funded by preferred stock dividends, cash contributions and advances provided by the Company, of which $336 is outstanding at June 30, 2010. Each share is convertible at the option of the holder into one share of the Company's common stock. The dividend for the current year was equal to the common stock dividend of $1.80 per share. The liquidation value is $12.96 per share.

Our ESOP accounting practices are consistent with current ESOP accounting guidance, including the permissible continuation of certain provisions from prior accounting guidance. ESOP debt, which is guaranteed by the Company, is recorded as debt (see Note 4) with an offset to the reserve for ESOP debt retirement, which is presented within shareholders' equity. Advances to the ESOP by the Company are recorded as an increase in the reserve for ESOP debt retirement. Interest incurred on the ESOP debt is recorded as interest expense. Dividends on all preferred shares, net of related tax benefits, are charged to retained earnings.

The series A and B preferred shares of the ESOP are allocated to employees based on debt service requirements, net of advances made by the Company to the Trust. The number of preferred shares outstanding at June 30 was as follows:

(Shares in thousands)	2010	2009	2008
Allocated	54,542	56,818	58,557
Unallocated	14,762	16,651	18,665
Total series A	69,304	73,469	77,222
Allocated	20,752	20,991	21,134
Unallocated	41,347	42,522	43,618
Total series B	62,099	63,513	64,752

For purposes of calculating diluted net earnings per common share, the preferred shares held by the ESOP are considered converted from inception.

Tax Benefits of Stock-Based Compensation

5.15

WOLVERINE WORLD WIDE, INC. (DEC)

CONSOLIDATED STATEMENTS OF STOCKHOLDERS' EQUITY AND COMPREHENSIVE INCOME

	Fiscal Year		
(Thousands of dollars, except share and per share data)	2010	2009	2008
Common stock outstanding			
Balance at beginning of the year	$ 62,764	$ 61,656	$ 61,085
Common stock issued under stock incentive plans (2010—1,212,463 shares; 2009—1,108,112 shares; 2008—570,691 shares)	1,212	1,108	571
Balance at end of the year	63,976	62,764	61,656
Additional paid-in capital			
Balance at beginning of the year	81,021	64,696	47,786
Stock-based compensation expense	11,543	8,649	8,164
Amounts associated with common stock issued under stock incentive plans:			
Proceeds over par value	6,289	2,050	5,859
Income tax benefits	4,094	1,427	2,842
Issuance of performance-based shares (2010—215,027 shares; 2009—286,006 shares)	5,197	4,507	—
Issuance of treasury shares (2010—25,829 shares; 2009—32,455 shares; 2008—22,842 shares)	142	(111)	54
Net change in employee notes receivable	—	(197)	(9)
Balance at end of the year	108,286	81,021	64,696
Retained earnings			
Balance at beginning of the year	706,439	666,027	591,706
Net earnings	104,470	61,912	95,821
Cash dividends declared (2010—$0.44 per share; 2009—$0.44 per share; 2008—$0.44 per share)	(21,225)	(21,500)	(21,500)
Balance at end of the year	789,684	706,439	666,027
Accumulated other comprehensive income (loss)			
Balance at beginning of the year	(42,806)	(42,834)	22,268
Foreign currency translation adjustments	(2,929)	15,349	(36,305)
Change in fair value of foreign exchange contracts, net of taxes (2010—$(750); 2009—$3,482; 2008—$(3,447))	1,731	(7,469)	5,978
Pension adjustments, net of taxes (2010—$(1,551); 2009—$4,228; 2008—$18,963)	2,881	(7,852)	(34,775)
Balance at end of the year	(41,123)	(42,806)	(42,834)
Cost of shares in treasury			
Balance at beginning of the year	(325,385)	(319,623)	(244,066)
Common stock acquired for treasury (2010—1,832,193 shares; 2009—454,205 shares; 2008—2,921,264 shares)	(52,190)	(6,566)	(76,129)
Issuance of treasury shares (2010—25,829 shares; 2009—32,455 shares; 2008—22,842 shares)	649	804	572
Balance at end of the year	(376,926)	(325,385)	(319,623)
Total stockholders' equity at end of the year	$543,897	$482,033	$429,922
Comprehensive income			
Net earnings	$104,470	$61,912	$95,821
Foreign currency translation adjustments	(2,929)	15,349	(36,305)
Change in fair value of foreign exchange contracts, net of taxes	1,731	(7,469)	5,978
Pension adjustments, net of taxes	2,881	(7,852)	(34,775)
Total comprehensive income	$106,153	$61,940	$30,719

See accompanying notes to consolidated financial statements.

NOTES TO CONSOLIDATED FINANCIAL STATEMENTS (in part)

All amounts are in thousands of dollars except share and per share data and elsewhere as noted.

1. Summary Of Significant Accounting Policies (in part)

Stock-Based Compensation

The Company accounts for stock-based compensation in accordance with the fair value recognition provisions of FASB ASC Topic 718, *Compensation—Stock Compensation* ("ASC 718"). The Company recognized compensation expense of $11,543, $8,649, and $8,164 and related income tax benefits of $3,552, $2,321, and $1,699 for grants under its stock-based compensation plans in the statements of operations for the years ended January 1, 2011, January 2, 2010, and January 3, 2009, respectively.

Stock-Based/Deferred Compensation

5.16

PAYCHEX, INC. (MAY)

CONSOLIDATED STATEMENTS OF STOCKHOLDERS' EQUITY

(In thousands)	Common Stock		Additional Paid-In Capital	Retained Earnings	Accumulated Other Comprehensive (Loss)/Income	Total
	Shares	Amount				
Balance as of May 31, 2007	382,151	$3,822	$362,982	$1,595,105	$(9,661)	$1,952,248
Net income				576,145		576,145
Unrealized gains on securities, net of tax					25,708	25,708
Total comprehensive income						601,853
Common shares repurchased	(23,658)	(237)	(24,395)	(975,367)		(999,999)
Cash dividends declared				(442,146)		(442,146)
Stock-based compensation			25,535			25,535
Stock-based award transactions	2,007	20	67,517			67,537
Cumulative effect of accounting change for uncertain tax positions				(8,386)		(8,386)
Balance as of May 31, 2008	360,500	3,605	431,639	745,351	16,047	1,196,642
Net income				533,545		533,545
Unrealized gains on securities, net of tax					25,893	25,893
Total comprehensive income						559,438
Cash dividends declared				(447,732)		(447,732)
Stock-based compensation			25,827			25,827
Stock-based award transactions	476	5	8,961	(1,663)		7,303
Balance as of May 31, 2009	360,976	3,610	466,427	829,501	41,940	1,341,478
Net income				476,999		476,999
Unrealized gains on securities, net of tax					469	469
Total comprehensive income						477,468
Cash dividends declared				(448,558)		(448,558)
Stock-based compensation			25,716			25,716
Stock-based award transactions	487	5	7,522	(1,652)		5,875
Balance as of May 31, 2010	361,463	$3,615	$499,665	$ 856,290	$42,409	$1,401,979

See Notes to Consolidated Financial Statements.

NOTES TO CONSOLIDATED FINANCIAL STATEMENTS (in part)

Note A—Description of Business and Significant Accounting Policies (in part)

Stock-based compensation costs: All stock-based awards to employees, including grants of stock options, are recognized as compensation costs in the Consolidated Financial Statements based on their fair values measured as of the date of grant. The Company estimates the fair value of stock option grants using a Black-Scholes option pricing model. This model requires various assumptions as inputs including expected volatility of the Paychex stock price and expected option life. Volatility is estimated based on a combination of historical volatility using weekly stock prices over a period equal to the expected option life and implied market volatility. Expected option life is estimated based on historical exercise behavior.

The Company is required to estimate forfeitures and only record compensation costs for those awards that are expected to vest. The assumptions for forfeitures were determined based on type of award and historical experience. Forfeiture assumptions are adjusted at the point in time a significant change is identified with any adjustment recorded in the period of change, and the final adjustment at the end of the requisite service period to equal actual forfeitures.

The assumptions of volatility, expected option life, and forfeitures all require significant judgment and are subject to change in the future due to factors such as employee exercise behavior, stock price trends, and changes to type or provisions of stock-based awards. Any change in one or more of these assumptions could have a material impact on the estimated fair value of an award and on stock-based compensation costs recognized in the Company's results of operations.

The Company has determined that the Black-Scholes option pricing model, as well as the underlying assumptions used in its application, is appropriate in estimating the fair value of stock option grants. The Company periodically reassesses its assumptions as well as its choice of valuation model, and will reconsider use of this model if additional information becomes available in the future indicating that another model would provide a more accurate estimate of fair value, or if characteristics of future grants would warrant such a change.

Refer to Note B of the Notes to Consolidated Financial Statements for further discussion of the Company's stock-based compensation plans.

Note B—Stock-Based Compensation Plans

The Paychex, Inc. 2002 Stock Incentive Plan, as amended and restated (the "2002 Plan"), effective on October 12, 2005 upon its approval by the Company's stockholders, authorizes grants of up to 29.1 million shares of the Company's common stock. As of May 31, 2010, there were 14.1 million shares available for future grants under the 2002 Plan. No future grants will be made pursuant to the Paychex, Inc. 1998 Stock Incentive Plan, which expired in August 2002; however, options to purchase an aggregate of 1.5 million shares under the plan remain outstanding as of May 31, 2010.

All stock-based awards to employees are recognized as compensation costs in the Consolidated Financial Statements based on their fair values measured as of the date of grant. These costs are recognized as an expense in the Consolidated Statements of Income on a straight-line basis over the requisite service period and increase additional paid-in capital. For grants prior to June 1, 2006, costs were recognized on an accelerated basis over the requisite service period.

Stock-based compensation expense was $25.6 million, $25.7 million, and $25.4 million for fiscal 2010, fiscal 2009, and fiscal 2008, respectively. Related income tax benefits recognized were $7.9 million, $8.0 million, and $7.4 million for the respective fiscal years. Capitalized stock-based compensation costs related to the development of internal use software for these same fiscal years were not significant.

As of May 31, 2010, the total unrecognized compensation cost related to all unvested stock-based awards was $52.0 million and is expected to be recognized over a weighted-average period of 1.7 years.

Stock option grants: Stock option grants entitle the holder to purchase, at the end of the vesting term, a specified number of shares of Paychex common stock at an exercise price per share set equal to the closing market price of the common stock on the date of grant. All stock option grants have a contractual life of ten years from the date of the grant and a vesting schedule as established by the Board of Directors (the "Board"). The Company issues new shares of common stock to satisfy stock option exercises. Non-qualified stock option grants to officers, outside directors, and management are typically approved by the Board in July. Non-qualified stock option grants to officers and management vest 20% per annum while grants to the Board vest one-third per annum.

The Company has granted stock options to virtually all non-management employees with at least 90 days of service, and shares remain outstanding for the following broad-based stock option grants:

Date of Broad-Based Grant	Shares Granted	Exercise Price Per Share	Shares Outstanding as of May 31, 2010	Vesting Schedule
October 2001	1,295,000	$33.17	350,000	25% each October in 2002 through 2005
April 2004	1,655,000	$37.72	755,000	25% each April in 2005 through 2008
October 2006	2,033,000	$37.32	1,294,000	20% each October in 2007 through 2011

Historically, each April and October, the Company has granted options to newly hired employees who met certain criteria. Beginning with grants issued in October 2005, such grants of options vest 20% per annum. Any future grants of stock-based awards are subject to the discretion of the Board.

The following table summarizes stock option activity for the three years ended May 31, 2010:

	Shares Subject to Options (Thousands)	Weighted- Average Exercise Price Per Share	Weighted- Average Remaining Contractual Term (Years)	Aggregate Intrinsic Value[1] (Thousands)
Outstanding as of May 31, 2007	16,268	$34.12		
Granted	971	$40.99		
Exercised	(1,974)	$29.77		
Forfeited	(854)	$36.84		
Expired	(103)	$38.38		
Outstanding as of May 31, 2008	14,308	$35.00		
Granted	1,007	$30.10		
Exercised	(371)	$23.41		
Forfeited	(591)	$36.11		
Expired	(350)	$37.56		
Outstanding as of May 31, 2009	14,003	$34.84		
Granted	1,391	$26.34		
Exercised	(355)	$23.12		
Forfeited	(448)	$33.35		
Expired	(428)	$36.18		
Outstanding as of May 31, 2010	14,163	$34.31	5.4	$4,175
Exercisable as of May 31, 2010	9,770	$34.95	4.5	$ 232

[1] Market price of the underlying stock as of May 28, 2010 less the exercise price.

Other information pertaining to stock option grants is as follows:

In thousands, except per share amounts	Year Ended May 31		
	2010	2009	2008
Weighted-average grant-date fair value of stock options granted (per share)	$ 4.37	$ 6.52	$ 9.84
Total intrinsic value of stock options exercised	$ 1,378	$ 2,576	$25,154
Total fair value of stock options vested	$18,996	$25,842	$32,340

The fair value of stock option grants was estimated at the date of grant using a Black-Scholes option pricing model. The weighted-average assumptions used for valuation under the Black-Scholes model are as follows:

	Year Ended May 31		
	2010	2009	2008
Risk-free interest rate	3.0%	3.2%	4.3%
Dividend yield	4.5%	3.6%	2.9%
Volatility factor	.28	.28	.26
Expected option life in years	6.3	6.3	6.0

Risk-free interest rates are yields for zero coupon U.S. Treasury notes maturing approximately at the end of the expected option life. The estimated volatility factor is based on a combination of historical volatility using weekly stock prices over a period equal to the expected option life and implied market volatility. The expected option life is based on historical exercise behavior.

The Company has determined that the Black-Scholes option pricing model, as well as the underlying assumptions used in its application, are appropriate in estimating the fair value of its stock option grants. The Company periodically assesses its assumptions as well as its choice of valuation model, and will reconsider use of this model if additional information becomes available in the future indicating that another model would provide a more accurate estimate of fair value, or if characteristics of future grants would warrant such a change.

Restricted stock awards: The Board has approved grants of restricted stock awards to the Company's officers and outside directors in accordance with the 2002 Plan. All shares underlying awards of restricted stock are restricted in that they are not transferable until they vest. The recipients of the restricted stock have voting rights and earn dividends, which are paid to the recipient at the time of vesting of the awards. If the recipient leaves Paychex prior to the vesting date for any reason, the shares of restricted stock and the dividends accrued on those shares will be forfeited and returned to Paychex.

For restricted stock awards granted to officers, the shares vest upon the fifth anniversary of the grant date provided the recipient is still an employee of the Company on that date. These awards have a provision for the acceleration of vesting based on achievement of performance targets established by the Board. If the established targets are met for a fiscal year, up to one-third of the award may vest. If all the targets are met for three consecutive years, the award will be fully vested. For outside directors, the shares vest on the third anniversary of the grant date. The fair value of restricted stock awards is equal to the closing market price of the underlying common stock as of the date of grant and is expensed over the requisite service period on a straight-line basis.

The following table summarizes restricted stock activity for the three years ended May 31, 2010:

(In thousands, except per share amounts)	Restricted Shares	Weighted-Average Grant-Date Fair Value Per Share
Nonvested as of May 31, 2007	105	$36.87
Granted	134	$43.91
Vested	(33)	$36.87
Forfeited	(16)	$41.09
Nonvested as of May 31, 2008	190	$41.48
Granted	140	$31.76
Vested	(66)	$39.82
Forfeited	(19)	$36.81
Nonvested as of May 31, 2009	245	$36.74
Granted	153	$24.60
Vested	(9)	$35.79
Forfeited	(19)	$32.66
Nonvested as of May 31, 2010	370	$31.95

Restricted stock units: Beginning in July 2007, the Board approved grants of restricted stock units ("RSUs") to non-officer management as a replacement of non-qualified stock options. RSUs do not have voting rights or earn dividend equivalents during the vesting period. These awards vest 20% per annum over five years with a small population of awards vesting on the fourth anniversary of the grant date. The fair value of RSUs is equal to the closing market price of the underlying common stock as of the date of grant, adjusted for the present value of expected dividends over the vesting period.

The following table summarizes RSU activity for the three years ended May 31, 2010:

(In thousands, except per share amounts)	RSUs	Weighted-Average Grant-Date Fair Value Per Share
Nonvested as of May 31, 2007	—	—
Granted	499	$40.60
Vested	—	—
Forfeited	(29)	$40.60
Nonvested as of May 31, 2008	470	$40.60
Granted	607	$28.30
Vested	(93)	$40.60
Forfeited	(44)	$34.65
Nonvested as of May 31, 2009	940	$32.93
Granted	567	$20.62
Vested	(193)	$34.01
Forfeited	(69)	$28.88
Nonvested as of May 31, 2010	1,245	$27.39

Non-compensatory employee benefit plan: The Company offers an Employee Stock Purchase Plan to all employees under which the Company's common stock can be purchased through a payroll deduction with no discount to the market price and no look-back provision. All transactions occur directly through the Company's transfer agent and no brokerage fees are charged to employees, except for when stock is sold. The plan has been deemed non-compensatory and therefore, no stock-based compensation costs have been recognized for fiscal 2010, fiscal 2009, or fiscal 2008 related to this plan.

Common Stock Extinguishment and Issuance

5.17

SPECTRUM BRANDS HOLDINGS, INC. (SEP)

CONSOLIDATED STATEMENTS OF SHAREHOLDERS' EQUITY (DEFICIT) AND COMPREHENSIVE INCOME (LOSS)

(In thousands)	Common Stock Shares	Common Stock Amount	Additional Paid-In Capital/Other Capital	Accumulated Deficit	Accumulated Other Comprehensive Income (Loss), Net of Tax	Treasury Stock	Total Shareholders' Equity (Deficit)
Balances at September 30, 2007, Predecessor Company	52,765	$690	$669,274	$ (763,370)	$65,664	$(76,086)	$(103,828)
Net loss	—	—	—	(931,545)	—	—	(931,545)
Adjustment of additional minimum pension liability	—	—	—	—	2,459	—	2,459
Valuation allowance adjustment	—	—	—	—	(4,060)	—	(4,060)
Translation adjustment	—	—	—	—	5,236	—	5,236
Other unrealized gains and losses	—	—	—	—	146	—	146
Comprehensive loss							(927,764)
Issuance of restricted stock	408	4	(4)	—	—	—	—
Forfeiture of restricted stock	(268)	(2)	2	—	—	—	—
Treasury shares surrendered	(130)	—	—	—	—	(744)	(744)
Amortization of unearned compensation	—	—	5,098	—	—	—	5,098
Balances at September 30, 2008, Predecessor Company	52,775	$692	$674,370	$(1,694,915)	$69,445	$(76,830)	$(1,027,238)
Net income	—	—	—	1,013,941	—	—	1,013,941
Adjustment of additional minimum pension liability	—	—	—	—	(1,160)	—	(1,160)
Valuation allowance adjustment	—	—	—	—	5,104	—	5,104
Translation adjustment	—	—	—	—	(2,650)	—	(2,650)
Other unrealized gains and losses	—	—	—	—	9,817	—	9,817
Comprehensive income							1,025,052
Issuance of restricted stock	230	(1)	1	—	—	—	—
Forfeiture of restricted stock	(82)	—	—	—	—	—	—
Treasury shares surrendered	(185)	—	—	—	—	(61)	(61)
Amortization of unearned compensation	—	—	2,636	—	—	—	2,636
Cancellation of Predecessor Company common stock	(52,738)	(691)	(677,007)	—	—	76,891	(600,807)
Elimination of Predecessor Company accumulated deficit and accumulated other comprehensive income	—	—	—	680,974	(80,556)	—	600,418
Issuance of new common stock in connection with emergence from Chapter 11 of the Bankruptcy Code	30,000	300	724,796	—	—	—	725,096
Balances at August 30, 2009, Successor Company	30,000	$300	$724,796	$ —	$ —	$ —	$ 725,096

See accompanying notes to consolidated financial statements.

	Common Stock		Additional Paid-In Capital/Other Capital	Accumulated Deficit	Accumulated Other Comprehensive Income (Loss), Net of Tax	Treasury Stock	Total Shareholders' Equity (Deficit)
	Shares	Amount					
Balances at August 30, 2009, Successor Company	30,000	$300	$ 724,796	$ —	$ —	$—	$ 725,096
Net loss	—	—	—	(70,785)	—	—	(70,785)
Adjustment of additional minimum pension liability	—	—	—	—	576	—	576
Valuation allowance adjustment	—	—	—	—	(755)	—	(755)
Translation adjustment	—	—	—	—	5,896	—	5,896
Other unrealized gains and losses	—	—	—	—	851	—	851
Comprehensive loss							(64,217)
Balances at September 30, 2009, Successor Company	30,000	$300	$ 724,796	$ (70,785)	$ 6,568	$—	$ 660,879
Net loss	—	—	—	(189,755)	—	—	(189,755)
Adjustment of additional minimum pension liability	—	—	—	—	(17,773)	—	(17,773)
Valuation allowance adjustment	—	—	—	—	(2,398)	—	(2,398)
Translation adjustment	—	—	—	—	12,596	—	12,596
Other unrealized gains and losses	—	—	—	—	(6,490)	—	(6,490)
Comprehensive income							(203,820)
Extinguishment of Spectrum Brands common stock, pursuant to the Merger	(30,000)	(300)	(724,796)	—	—	—	(725,096)
Issuance of restricted stock	—	—	(9)	—	—	—	(9)
Amortization of unearned compensation	—	—	16,574	—	—	—	16,574
Other capital	—	—	1,298,203	—	—	—	1,298,203
Balances at September 30, 2010, Successor Company	—	$ —	$1,314,768	$(260,540)	$(7,497)	$—	$1,046,731

See accompanying notes to consolidated financial statements.

NOTES TO CONSOLIDATED FINANCIAL STATEMENTS (in part)

(In thousands, except per share amounts)

(2) Voluntary Reorganization Under Chapter 11 (in part)

On February 3, 2009, the Predecessor Company announced that it had reached agreements with certain noteholders, representing, in the aggregate, approximately 70% of the face value of the Company's then outstanding senior subordinated notes, to pursue a refinancing that, if implemented as proposed, would significantly reduce the Predecessor Company's outstanding debt. On the same day, the Debtors filed voluntary petitions under Chapter 11 of the Bankruptcy Code, in the Bankruptcy Court (the "Bankruptcy Filing") and filed with the Bankruptcy Court a proposed plan of reorganization (the "Proposed Plan") that detailed the Debtors' proposed terms for the refinancing. The Chapter 11 cases were jointly administered by the Bankruptcy Court as Case No. 09-50455 (the "Bankruptcy Cases").

The Bankruptcy Court entered a written order (the "Confirmation Order") on July 15, 2009 confirming the Proposed Plan (as so confirmed, the "Plan").

Plan Effective Date

On the Effective Date the Plan became effective, and the Debtors emerged from Chapter 11 of the Bankruptcy Code. Pursuant to and by operation of the Plan, on the Effective Date, all of Predecessor Company's existing equity securities, including the existing common stock and stock options, were extinguished and deemed cancelled. Spectrum Brands filed a certificate of incorporation authorizing new shares of common stock. Pursuant to and in accordance with the Plan, on the Effective Date, Successor Company issued a total of 27,030 shares of common stock and $218,076 of 12% Senior Subordinated Toggle Notes due 2019 (the "12% Notes") to holders of allowed claims with respect to Predecessor Company's 8½% Senior Subordinated Notes due 2013 (the "8½ Notes"), 7⅜% Senior Subordinated Notes due 2015 (the "7⅜ Notes") and Variable Rate Toggle Senior Subordinated Notes due 2013 (the "Variable Rate Notes") (collectively, the "Senior Subordinated Notes"). (See also Note 7, Debt, for a more complete discussion of the 12% Notes.) Also on the Effective Date, Successor Company issued a total of 2,970 shares of common stock to supplemental and sub-supplemental debtor-in-possession facility participants in respect of the equity fee earned under the Debtors' debtor-in-possession credit facility.

Fresh-Start Reporting (in part)

The Company, in accordance with ASC 852, adopted fresh-start reporting as of the close of business on August 30, 2009 since the reorganization value of the assets of the Predecessor Company immediately before the date of confirmation of the Plan was less than the total of all post-petition liabilities and allowed claims, and the holders of the Predecessor Company's voting shares immediately before confirmation of the Plan received less than 50 percent of the voting shares of the emerging entity. The four-column consolidated statement of financial position as of August 30, 2009, included herein, applies effects of the Plan and fresh-start reporting to the carrying values and classifications of assets or liabilities that were necessary.

The Company analyzed the transactions that occurred during the two-day period from August 29, 2009, the day after the Effective Date, and August 30, 2009, the fresh-start reporting date, and concluded that such transactions were not material individually or in the aggregate as such transactions represented less than one-percent of the total net sales for the fiscal year ended September 30, 2009. As a result, the Company determined that August 30, 2009, would be an appropriate fresh-start reporting date to coincide with the Company's normal financial period close for the month of August 2009. Upon adoption of fresh-start reporting, the recorded amounts of assets and liabilities were adjusted to reflect their estimated fair values. Accordingly, the reported historical financial statements of the Predecessor Company prior to the adoption of fresh-start reporting for periods ended on or prior to August 30, 2009 are not comparable to those of the Successor Company.

The four-column consolidated statement of financial position as of August 30, 2009 reflects the implementation of the Plan as if the Plan had been effective on August 30, 2009. Reorganization adjustments have been recorded within the consolidated statement of financial position as of August 30, 2009 to reflect effects of the Plan, including the discharge of Liabilities subject to compromise and the adoption of fresh-start reporting in accordance with ASC 852. The Bankruptcy Court confirmed the Plan based upon a reorganization value of the Company between $2,200,000 and $2,400,000, which was estimated using various valuation methods including: (i) publicly traded company analysis, (ii) discounted cash flow analysis; and (iii) a review and analysis of several recent transactions of companies in similar industries to the Company. These three valuation methods were equally weighted in determining the final range of reorganization value as confirmed by the Bankruptcy Court. Based upon the factors used in determining the range of reorganization value, the Company concluded that $2,275,000 should be used for fresh-start reporting purposes as it most closely approximated fair value.

The following four-column consolidated statement of financial position table identifies the adjustments recorded to the Predecessor Company's August 30, 2009 consolidated statement of financial position as a result of implementing the Plan and applying fresh-start reporting:

	Predecessor Company August 30, 2009	Effects of Plan	Fresh-Start Valuation	Successor Company August 30, 2009
Assets				
Current assets:				
Cash and cash equivalents	$ 86,710	$(25,551)[(a)]	$ —	$ 61,159
Receivables:				
Trade accounts receivable	270,657	—	—	270,657
Other	34,594	—	—	34,594
Inventories	341,738	—	48,762[(m)]	390,500
Deferred income taxes	12,644	1,707[(h)]	9,330[(n)]	23,681
Assets held for sale	10,813	—	1,978[(m)]	12,791
Prepaid expenses and other	40,448	—	(116)[(m)]	40,332
Total current assets	797,604	(23,844)	59,954	833,714
Property, plant and equipment, net	178,786	—	34,699[(m)]	213,485
Deferred charges and other	42,068	—	(6,046)[(m)]	36,022
Goodwill	238,905	—	289,155[(o)]	528,060
Intangible assets, net	677,050	—	782,450[(o)]	1,459,500
Debt issuance costs	18,457	8,949[(b)]	(17,957)[(p)]	9,449
Total assets	$1,952,870	$(14,895)	$1,142,255	$3,080,230
Liabilities and shareholders' equity				
Current liabilities:				
Current maturities of long-term debt	$93,313	$ (3,445)[(c)]	$ (4,329)[(m)]	$ 85,539
Accounts payable	159,370	(204)[(d)]	—	159,166
Accrued liabilities:				
Wages and benefits	80,247	—	—	80,247
Income taxes payable	20,059	—	—	20,059
Restructuring and related charges	26,100	—	—	26,100
Accrued interest	59,724	(59,581)[(e)]	—	143
Other	118,949	9,133[(f)]	(3,503)[(m)]	124,579
Total current liabilities	557,762	(54,097)	(7,832)	495,833

(continued)

	Predecessor Company August 30, 2009	Effects of Plan	Fresh-Start Valuation	Successor Company August 30, 2009
Long-term debt, net of current maturities	$1,329,047	$271,806[g]	$ (75,329)[m]	$1,525,524
Employee benefit obligations, net of current portion	41,385	—	18,712[m]	60,097
Deferred income taxes	106,853	1,707[h]	114,211[n]	222,771
Other	45,982	—	4,927[m]	50,909
Total liabilities	2,081,029	219,416	54,689	2,355,134
Liabilities subject to compromise	1,105,962	(1,105,962)[i]	—	—
Commitments and contingencies				
Shareholders' (deficit) equity:				
Common stock-Old (Predecessor Company)	691	(691)[j]	—	—
Common stock-New (Successor Company)	—	300[j]	—	300
Additional paid-in capital	677,007	47,789[j]	—	724,796
Accumulated (deficit) equity	(1,915,484)	747,362[k]	1,168,122[q]	—
Accumulated other comprehensive income	80,556	—	(80,556)[q]	—
	(1,157,230)	794,760	1,087,566	725,096
Less treasury stock	(76,891)	76,891[l]	—	—
Total shareholders' (deficit) equity	(1,234,121)	871,651	1,087,566	725,096
Total liabilities and shareholders' (deficit) equity	$1,952,870	$(14,895)	$1,142,255	$3,080,230

Effects of Plan Adjustments (in part)

[j] Pursuant to the Plan, the debtor's common stock was canceled and new common stock of the reorganized debtors was issued. The adjustments eliminated Predecessor Company's common stock and additional paid-in capital of $691 and $677,007, respectively, and recorded Successor Company's common stock and additional paid-in capital of $300 and $724,796, respectively, which represents the fair value of the newly issued common stock. The fair value of the newly issued common stock was not separately valued. A fair value of $725,096 was determined by subtracting the fair value of net debt (total debt less cash and cash equivalents), or $1,549,904 from the enterprise value of $2,275,000. The Company issued 30,000 shares at emergence, consisting of 27,030 shares to holders of the Senior Subordinated Notes allowed note holder claims and 2,970 shares in accordance with the terms of the Debtors' debtor-in-possession credit facility.

[k] As a result of the Plan, the adjustment to accumulated (deficit) equity recorded the elimination of the Predecessor Company's common stock, additional paid in capital and treasury stock in the amount of $600,807 and recorded the pre-tax gain on the cancellation of debt in the amount of $146,555. The elimination of the Predecessor Company's common stock, additional paid in capital and treasury stock was calculated as follows:

Elimination of Predecessor Company's common stock (see note (j))	$ 691
Elimination of Predecessor Company's additional paid in capital (see note (j))	677,007
Elimination of Predecessor Company's treasury stock (see note (l))	(76,891)
Elimination of Predecessor Company's common stock	$600,807

The pre-tax gain on the cancellation of debt was calculated as follows:

Extinguishment of Predecessor Company senior subordinated notes	$1,049,885
Extinguishment of Predecessor Company accrued interest on senior subordinated notes	40,497
Issuance of Successor Company 12% Notes (fair value)	(218,731)
Issuance of Successor Company common stock	(725,096)
Pre-tax gain on the cancellation of debt	$ 146,555

[l] Pursuant to the Plan, the adjustment eliminates treasury stock of $76,891 of the Predecessor Company.

Dividends

5.18

REGAL ENTERTAINMENT GROUP (DEC)

CONSOLIDATED STATEMENTS OF DEFICIT AND COMPREHENSIVE INCOME (LOSS)

(In millions, except per share data)	Class A Common Stock Shares	Amount	Class B Common Stock Shares	Amount	Additional Paid-In Capital (Deficit)	Retained Earnings	Accumulated Other Comprehensive Income (Loss)	Total Stockholders' Deficit of Regal Entertainment Group	Non-controlling Interest	Total Deficit
Balances, December 27, 2007	129.5	$0.1	23.8	$—	$(157.6)	$40.9	$(1.6)	$(118.2)	$0.5	$(117.7)
Comprehensive Income:										
Change in fair value of interest rate swap transactions, net of tax	—	—	—	—	—	—	(8.3)	(8.3)	—	(8.3)
Net income attributable to controlling interest	—	—	—	—	—	112.2	—	112.2	—	112.2
Total comprehensive income	—	—	—	—	—	—	—	—	—	103.9
Noncontrolling interest adjustments	—	—	—	—	—	—	—	—	(0.9)	(0.9)
Share-based compensation expense	—	—	—	—	5.5	—	—	5.5	—	5.5
Exercise of stock options	0.1	—	—	—	0.5	—	—	0.5	—	0.5
Tax benefit from exercise of stock options and other	—	—	—	—	0.5	—	—	0.5	—	0.5
Issuance of restricted stock	0.2	—	—	—	—	—	—	—	—	—
ASC Subtopic 470-20 adjustments to additional paid-in capital	—	—	—	—	(35.0)	—	—	(35.0)	—	(35.0)
Impact attributable to 3 ¾% Convertible Senior Notes convertible note hedge and warrant	—	—	—	—	(6.6)	—	—	(6.6)	—	(6.6)
Tax impact attributable to 6 ¼% Convertible Senior Notes convertible note hedge and warrant	—	—	—	—	4.7	—	—	4.7	—	4.7
Net payment on 6 ¼% Convertible Senior Notes convertible note hedge and warrant	—	—	—	—	(6.6)	—	—	(6.6)	—	(6.6)
Cash dividends declared, $1.20 per share	—	—	—	—	(71.2)	(113.0)	—	(184.2)	—	(184.2)
Balances, January 1, 2009	129.8	$0.1	23.8	$—	$(265.8)	$40.1	$(9.9)	$(235.5)	$(0.4)	$(235.9)
Comprehensive Income:										
Change in fair value of interest rate swap transactions, net of tax	—	—	—	—	—	—	(0.4)	(0.4)	—	(0.4)
Net income attributable to controlling interest	—	—	—	—	—	95.5	—	95.5	—	95.5
Total comprehensive income	—	—	—	—	—	—	—	—	—	95.1
Noncontrolling interest adjustments	—	—	—	—	—	—	—	—	(0.4)	(0.4)
Share-based compensation expense	—	—	—	—	5.9	—	—	5.9	—	5.9
Exercise of stock options	0.1	—	—	—	0.1	—	—	0.1	—	0.1
Tax benefits from exercise of stock options, vesting of restricted stock and other	—	—	—	—	(0.9)	—	—	(0.9)	—	(0.9)
Issuance of restricted stock	0.4	—	—	—	—	—	—	—	—	—
Cash dividends declared, $0.72 per share	—	—	—	—	(22.2)	(88.6)	—	(110.8)	—	(110.8)
Balances, December 31, 2009	130.3	$0.1	23.8	$—	$(282.9)	$47.0	$(10.3)	$(246.1)	$(0.8)	$(246.9)
Comprehensive Income:										
Change in fair value of interest rate swap transactions, net of tax	—	—	—	—	—	—	(6.8)	(6.8)	—	(6.8)
Change in fair value of available for sale securities, net of tax	—	—	—	—	—	—	4.9	4.9	—	4.9
Net income attributable to controlling interest	—	—	—	—	—	77.6	—	77.6	—	77.6
Total comprehensive income	—	—	—	—	—	—	—	—	—	75.7
Noncontrolling interest adjustments	—	—	—	—	—	—	—	—	(0.6)	(0.6)
Share-based compensation expense	—	—	—	—	7.2	—	—	7.2	—	7.2
Exercise of stock options	—	—	—	—	0.8	—	—	0.8	—	0.8
Tax benefits from exercise of stock options, vesting of restricted stock and other	—	—	—	—	(0.8)	—	—	(0.8)	—	(0.8)
Issuance of restricted stock	0.3	—	—	—	—	—	—	—	—	—
Extraordinary cash dividend declared, $1.40 per share	—	—	—	—	(195.8)	(20.2)	—	(216.0)	—	(216.0)
Cash dividends declared, $0.72 per share	—	—	—	—	(16.1)	(95.0)	—	(111.1)	—	(111.1)
Balances, December 30, 2010	130.6	$0.1	23.8	$—	$(487.6)	$ 9.4	$(12.2)	$(490.3)	$(1.4)	$(491.7)

See accompanying notes to consolidated financial statements.

NOTES TO CONSOLIDATED FINANCIAL STATEMENTS (in part)

9. Capital Stock and Share-Based Compensation (in part)

Dividends

Regal paid four quarterly cash dividends of $0.18 per share on each outstanding share of the Company's Class A and Class B common stock, or approximately $111.1 million in the aggregate, during the year ended December 30, 2010. In addition, on December 30, 2010, Regal declared an extraordinary cash dividend of $1.40 per share on each outstanding share of its Class A and Class B common stock, or approximately $216.0 million in the aggregate. Stockholders of record at the close of business on December 20, 2010 were paid this dividend on December 30, 2010. Regal paid four quarterly cash dividends of $0.18 per share on each

outstanding share of the Company's Class A and Class B common stock, or approximately $110.8 million in the aggregate, during the year ended December 31, 2009. Finally, Regal paid four quarterly cash dividends of $0.30 per share on each outstanding share of the Company's Class A and Class B common stock, or approximately $184.2 million in the aggregate, during the year ended January 1, 2009.

Tax Charges

5.19

NETAPP, INC. (APR)

CONSOLIDATED STATEMENTS OF STOCKHOLDERS' EQUITY AND COMPREHENSIVE INCOME

(In millions)	Common Stock			Treasury Stock		Retained Earnings	Accumulated Other Comprehensive Income (Loss)	Total
	Shares	Amount	Additional Paid-In Capital	Shares	Treasury Amount			
Balances, April 27, 2007	421.6	$0.4	$2,380.6	(54.6)	$(1,623.7)	$1,226.2	$5.5	$1,989.0
Components of comprehensive income:								
Net income	—	—	—	—	—	309.7	—	309.7
Currency translation adjustment	—	—	—	—	—	—	1.1	1.1
Unrealized gain on investments, net	—	—	—	—	—	—	(7.7)	(7.7)
Unrealized gain on derivatives	—	—	—	—	—	—	1.9	1.9
Total comprehensive income	—	—	—	—	—	—	—	305.0
Issuance of common stock, net of taxes	7.5	—	108.7	—	—	—	—	108.7
Repurchase of common stock	—	—	—	(32.8)	(903.7)	—	—	(903.7)
Stock-based compensation expense	—	—	147.9	—	—	—	—	147.9
Stock-based compensation related to acquisition	—	—	5.2	—	—	—	—	5.2
Income tax benefit from employee stock transactions	—	—	48.2	—	—	—	—	48.2
Balances, April 25, 2008	429.1	0.4	2,690.6	(87.4)	(2,527.4)	1,535.9	0.8	1,700.3
Components of comprehensive income:								
Net income	—	—	—	—	—	64.6	—	64.6
Currency translation adjustment	—	—	—	—	—	—	(4.8)	(4.8)
Unrealized gain on investments, net	—	—	—	—	—	—	(2.0)	(2.0)
Unrealized gain on derivatives	—	—	—	—	—	—	0.8	0.8
Total comprehensive income	—	—	—	—	—	—	—	58.6
Issuance of common stock, net of taxes	7.5	—	85.9	—	—	—	—	85.9
Repurchase of common stock	—	—	—	(16.9)	(400.0)	—	—	(400.0)
Purchase of note hedges	—	—	(254.9)	—	—	—	—	(254.9)
Sale of common stock warrants	—	—	163.1	—	—	—	—	163.1
Convertible debt discount	—	—	248.0	—	—	—	—	248.0
Issuance costs related to equity component of convertible notes	—	—	(5.2)	—	—	—	—	(5.2)
Net tax effect of issuance costs related to convertible notes	—	—	2.2	—	—	—	—	2.2
Stock-based compensation expense	—	—	140.8	—	—	—	—	140.8
Income tax benefit from employee stock transactions	—	—	45.4	—	—	—	—	45.4
Balances, April 24, 2009	436.6	0.4	3,115.9	(104.3)	(2,927.4)	1,600.5	(5.2)	1,784.2
Components of comprehensive income:								
Net income	—	—	—	—	—	400.4	—	400.4
Currency translation adjustment	—	—	—	—	—	—	1.5	1.5
Unrealized gain on investments, net	—	—	—	—	—	—	5.3	5.3
Unrealized gain on derivatives	—	—	—	—	—	—	1.2	1.2
Total comprehensive income	—	—	—	—	—	—	—	408.4
Issuance of common stock, net of taxes	15.0	0.1	197.0	—	—	—	—	197.1
Stock-based compensation expense	—	—	159.6	—	—	—	—	159.6
Income tax charge from employee stock transactions	—	—	(0.9)	—	—	—	—	(0.9)
Settlement of note hedge	—	—	14.2	—	—	—	—	14.2
Taxes on settlement of note hedge	—	—	(32.1)	—	—	—	—	(32.1)
Balances, April 30, 2010	451.6	$0.5	$3,453.7	(104.3)	$(2,927.4)	$2,000.9	$2.8	$2,530.5

See notes to consolidated financial statements.

NOTES TO CONSOLIDATED FINANCIAL STATEMENTS (in part)

14. Income Taxes (in part)

During fiscal 2010, we recorded $32.1 million charge to additional paid in capital related to the establishment of a $26.1 million tax reserve to provide for the uncertainty relating to the tax treatment of the termination of the Lehman Brothers bond hedge, as well as $6.0 million deferred tax liability for related temporary tax return differences in the valuation of the convertible debt as a result of the transaction.

Warrants

5.20

NEWELL RUBBERMAID INC. (DEC)

CONSOLIDATED STATEMENTS OF STOCKHOLDERS' EQUITY AND COMPREHENSIVE INCOME (LOSS)

(Amounts in millions)	Common Stock	Treasury Stock	Add'l Paid-In Capital	Retained Earnings	Accumulated Other Comprehensive Loss	Stockholders' Equity Attributable to Parent	Non-controlling interests	Total Stockholders' Equity
Balance at December 31, 2007	$292.6	$(415.1)	$570.3	$1,894.5	$(123.2)	$2,219.1	$3.0	$2,222.1
Net (loss) income	0	0	0	(52.3)	0	(52.3)	2.0	(50.3)
Foreign currency translation	0	0	0	0	(312.0)	(312.0)	0	(312.0)
Unrecognized pension and other postretirement costs, net of $87.0 of tax benefits	0	0	0	0	(107.4)	(107.4)	0	(107.4)
Gain on derivative instruments, including $22.1 of tax benefits	0	0	0	0	39.5	39.5	0	39.5
Total comprehensive loss						$ (432.2)	$2.0	$ (430.2)
Cash dividends on common stock	0	0	0	(234.5)	0	(234.5)	0	(234.5)
Cash dividends for noncontrolling interests	0	0	0	0	0	0	(3.0)	(3.0)
Exercise of stock options	0.1	0	2.3	0	0	2.4	0	2.4
Pension adjustment, net of $0.2 of tax benefits	0	0	0	(1.1)	0.7	(0.4)	0	(0.4)
Stock-based compensation and other	0.4	(2.9)	34.1	0	0	31.6	0.6	32.2
Balance at December 31, 2008	$293.1	$(418.0)	$606.7	$1,606.6	$(502.4)	$1,586.0	$2.6	$1,588.6
Net income	0	0	0	285.5	0	285.5	0	285.5
Foreign currency translation, including $10.2 of tax benefits	0	0	0	0	75.9	75.9	0	75.9
Unrecognized pension and other postretirement costs, net of $17.4 of tax benefits	0	0	0	0	(109.3)	(109.3)	0	(109.3)
Loss on derivative instruments, including $46.3 of tax expense	0	0	0	0	(49.4)	(49.4)	0	(49.4)
Total comprehensive loss						$ 202.7	0	$ 202.7
Cash dividends on common stock	0	0	0	(71.4)	0	(71.4)	0	(71.4)
Cash dividends for noncontrolling interests	0	0	0	0	0	0	(1.9)	(1.9)
Stock-based compensation and other	0.9	(2.6)	34.7	0	0	33.0	3.5	36.5
Purchase of call options, net of tax	0	0	(43.0)	0	0	(43.0)	0	(43.0)
Issuance and sale of warrants	0	0	32.7	0	0	32.7	0	32.7
Discount on convertible notes, net of issuance costs and tax	0	0	41.0	0	0	41.0	0	41.0
Purchase of noncontrolling interests	0	0	(2.3)	0	0	(2.3)	(0.7)	(3.0)
Balance at December 31, 2009	$294.0	$(420.6)	$669.8	$1,820.7	$(585.2)	$1,778.7	$3.5	$1,782.2
Net income	0	0	0	292.8	0	292.8	0	292.8
Foreign currency translation	0	0	0	0	(13.1)	(13.1)	0	(13.1)
Unrecognized pension and other postretirement costs, net of $30.3 of tax benefits	0	0	0	0	(7.0)	(7.0)	0	(7.0)
Gain on derivative instruments, net of $0 tax	0	0	0	0	0.3	0.3	0	0.3
Total comprehensive income						$ 273.0	0	$ 273.0
Cash dividends on common stock	0	0	0	(55.4)	0	(55.4)	0	(55.4)
Stock-based compensation and other	1.3	(5.1)	35.7	(0.8)	0	31.1	0	31.1
Settlement of call options	0	0	369.5	0	0	369.5	0	369.5
Settlement of warrants	0	0	(298.4)	0	0	(298.4)	0	(298.4)
Common stock issued for convertible notes exchange	37.7	0	600.3	0	0	638.0	0	638.0
Retirement of common stock purchased under the ASB	(25.8)	0	(474.3)	0	0	(500.1)	0	(500.1)
Extinguishment of equity component of convertible notes	0	0	(334.4)	0	0	(334.4)	0	(334.4)
Balance at December 31, 2010	$307.2	$(425.7)	$568.2	$2,057.3	$(605.0)	$1,902.0	$3.5	$1,905.5

See Notes to Consolidated Financial Statements.

NOTES TO CONSOLIDATED FINANCIAL STATEMENTS (in part)

Footnote 10

Convertible Note Hedge and Warrant Transactions

In connection with the issuance of the Convertible Notes in March 2009, the Company entered into separate convertible note hedge transactions and warrant transactions with respect to the Company's common stock to minimize the impact of the potential dilution upon conversion of the Convertible Notes. The Company purchased call options in private transactions to cover 40.1 million shares of the Company's common stock at a strike price of $8.61 per share, subject to adjustment in certain circumstances, for $69.0 million. The call options generally allowed the Company to receive shares of the Company's common stock from counterparties equal to the number of shares of common stock payable to the holders of the Convertible Notes upon conversion. The Company also sold warrants permitting the purchasers to acquire up to 40.1 million shares of the Company's common stock at an exercise price of $11.59 per share, subject to adjustment in certain circumstances, in private transactions for total proceeds of $32.7 million. For each warrant that is exercised, the Company would deliver to the counterparties a number of shares of the Company's common stock equal to the amount by which the Company's stock price exceeds the exercise price, divided by the stock price. As of December 31, 2009, the estimated fair value of the call options and warrants was $306.7 million and $238.9 million, respectively.

The Company analyzed the convertible note hedge transactions and warrant transactions and determined that they met the criteria for classification as equity transactions. As a result, the Company recorded the purchase of the call options as a reduction in additional paid-in capital, net of tax, and the proceeds from the warrants as an increase to additional paid-in capital, and the Company did not recognize subsequent changes in the fair value of the instruments in its financial statements.

In September 2010, in connection with the Plan, the Company negotiated settlement of the convertible note hedge and warrants with the Company receiving $369.5 million from the counterparties for the value of the convertible note hedge and paying the counterparties $298.4 million for the warrants. As of December 31, 2010, the Company had completely settled the convertible note hedge and warrant transactions and recorded a net increase in additional paid-in capital of $71.1 million representing the net value associated with the settlement of the convertible note hedge and warrant transactions.

5.21

LOUISIANA-PACIFIC CORPORATION (DEC)

CONSOLIDATED STATEMENTS OF STOCKHOLDERS' EQUITY

(Dollar and share amounts in millions, except per share amounts)	Common Stock Shares	Common Stock Amount	Treasury Stock Shares	Treasury Stock Amount	Additional Paid-In Capital	Retained Earnings	Accumulated Comprehensive Loss	Total Stockholders' Equity	Redeemable Non Controlling Interest
Balance as of December 31, 2007	116.9	$116.9	13.8	$(302.0)	$439.0	$1,628.6	$(64.5)	$1,818.0	$ —
Correction of beginning balance (see Note 24)						2.8		2.8	
Net loss						(576.6)		(576.6)	(0.2)
Issuance of shares for employee stock plans and for other purposes and other transactions			(0.2)	4.7	0.5			5.2	
Amortization of restricted stock grants					2.1			2.1	
Cash dividends, $0.30 per share						(31.0)		(31.0)	
Tax benefit of employee stock plan transactions					(0.3)			(0.3)	
Acquisition of redeemable non controlling interest								—	18.5
Accretion of redeemable non controlling interest								—	0.4
Other comprehensive loss							(33.6)	(33.6)	
Adjustment to initially apply SFAS 158, net of tax						(0.8)		(0.8)	
Balance as of December 31, 2008	116.9	116.9	13.6	(297.3)	441.3	1,023.0	(98.1)	1,185.8	18.7
Net loss						(120.9)		(120.9)	(0.9)
Issuance of shares for public offering	20.7	20.7			111.6			132.3	
Issuance of shares for employee stock plans and for other purposes			(0.5)	11.2	(2.2)			9.0	
Amortization of restricted stock grants					1.7			1.7	
Issuance and exercise of stock warrants in connection with debt issuance	2.1	2.1			11.4				13.5
Tax benefit of employee stock plan transactions					(1.4)				(1.4)
Other comprehensive income							33.5	33.5	3.3
Balance as of December 31, 2009	139.7	139.7	13.1	(286.1)	562.4	902.1	(64.6)	1,253.5	21.1
Net loss						(39.0)		(39.0)	0.4
Issuance of shares for employee stock plans and for other purposes			(0.2)	6.2	0.8			7.0	
Amortization of restricted stock grants					1.7			1.7	
Issuance and exercise of stock warrants in connection with debt issuance	5.1	5.1			(5.1)			—	
Tax benefit of employee stock plan transactions					(0.4)			(0.4)	
Other comprehensive income (loss)							(5.0)	(5.0)	1.3
Balance as of December 31, 2010	144.8	$144.8	12.9	$(279.9)	$559.4	$863.1	$(69.6)	$1,217.8	$22.8

See Notes to the Financial Statements.

NOTES TO CONSOLIDATED FINANCIAL STATEMENTS (in part)

12. Long-Term Debt (in part)

During 2009, LP issued and sold 375,000 Units consisting of (1) $375 million principal amount at maturity of 13% Senior Secured Notes due 2017 and (2) warrants to purchase 18,395,963 shares of our common stock at an exercise price of $1.39 per share, subject to adjustment in certain circumstances and to mandatory cashless exercise provisions. The units were issued at a discount to the principal amount at maturity of the notes included therein resulting in aggregate gross proceeds of $281.3 million. The effective interest rate of this debt is 19.1% (or 19.7% including the warrants). Simultaneous with the closing of the unit sale, LP used a portion of the proceeds to retire $126.6 million aggregate principal amount of our 8.875% Senior Notes due 2010 for $126.0 million. Subsequently in 2009, LP redeemed 35% of the outstanding Senior Secured Notes ($131.3 million principal amount at maturity) at a price of $858.14 per $1,000 principal amount at maturity or $112.6 million with a portion of the proceeds from the issuance and sale of 20,700,000 shares of common stock through a public offering. In connection with this repurchase, LP recorded a loss on early debt extinguishment of $21.1 million which included $3.7 million associated with the write of the related financing costs.

14. Stockholders' Equity (in part)

Warrants

As part of the unit issuance described in Note 12 above, LP issued warrants to purchase 18,395,963 shares of LP common stock at an exercise price of $1.39 per share subject to mandatory cashless exercise provisions. During the years ended December 31, 2010 and December 31, 2009, warrant exercises resulted in the issuances of 5,108,412 and 2,089,634 shares. At December 31, 2010, the remaining outstanding warrants were exercisable to purchase approximately 9,932,348 shares, at an exercise price of $1.39 per share subject to mandatory cashless exercise provisions. The warrant was valued based upon Black-Scholes option pricing model using expected stock price volatility of 53%; no expected dividends; risk-free interest rate of 2.6%; and an expected life of 8 years which resulted in a fair value per share of $0.72.

COMMON STOCK

DISCLOSURE

5.22 Rule 5-02 of Regulation S-X requires stating on the face of the balance sheet the number of shares issued or outstanding, as appropriate, and the dollar amount. The number of shares authorized should be disclosed on the balance sheet or in the notes. As shown in Table 5-4, consistent with prior years, the majority of the survey entities show common stock at par value.

5.23

TABLE 5-4: COMMON STOCK

Table 5-4 summarizes the reporting bases of common stock.

	2010	2009	2008
Par Value Stock			
Par value	424	467	473
Amount in excess of par	12	11	11
Assigned per share amount	13	—	—
No Par Value Stock			
Assigned per share amount	5	5	7
No assigned per share amount	43	47	40
Other	5	N/C*	N/C*
Issues Outstanding	502	530	531

* N/C = Not compiled. Line item was not included in the table for the year shown.

PREFERRED STOCK

PRESENTATION

5.24 FASB ASC 505-10-50 requires that if preferred stock or other senior stock has a preference in involuntary liquidation, the entity should disclose the liquidation preference of the stock (the relationship between the preference in liquidation and the par or stated value of the shares). That disclosure should be made in the "Equity" section of the balance sheet in the aggregate, either parenthetically or in short.

5.25 FASB ASC 480 requires that an issuer classify certain financial instruments with characteristics of both liabilities and equity as liabilities. Some issuances of stock, such as mandatorily redeemable preferred stock, impose unconditional obligations requiring the issuer to transfer assets or issue its equity shares. FASB ASC 480 requires an issuer to classify such financial instruments as liabilities.

DISCLOSURE

5.26 FASB ASC 505-10-50 requires disclosure of both of the following either on the face of the balance sheet or in the notes thereto:

- The aggregate or per-share amounts at which preferred stock may be called or is subject to redemption through sinking-fund operations or otherwise
- The aggregate and per-share amounts of arrearages in cumulative preferred dividends

Rule 5-02 of SEC Regulation S-X also calls for disclosure of the number of shares authorized and the number of shares issued or outstanding, as appropriate.

5.27

TABLE 5-5: PREFERRED STOCK

Table 5-5 summarizes the reporting bases of preferred stock.

	Number of Entities		
	2010	2009	2008
Par value preferred stock shown at:			
Par value	14	12	9
Liquidation or redemption value	5	7	7
No assigned per share amount	—	3	1
Assigned per share amount	1	—	2
Fair value at issuance date	—	—	—
Other	2	—	—
No par value preferred stock shown at:			
No assigned per share amount	5	7	4
Liquidation or redemption value	3	6	9
Assigned per share amount	4	3	4
Fair value at issuance date	—	—	—
Number of Entities			
Preferred stock outstanding	28	36	34
No preferred stock outstanding	472	464	466
Total Entities	**500**	**500**	**500**

PRESENTATION AND DISCLOSURE EXCERPTS

Preferred Stock

5.28

THE SHERWIN-WILLIAMS COMPANY (DEC)

CONSOLIDATED BALANCE SHEETS (in part)

	December 31		
(Thousands of dollars)	2010	2009	2008
Shareholders' equity:			
Common stock—$1.00 par value: 107,020,728, 109,436,869 and 117,035,117 shares outstanding at December 31, 2010, December 31, 2009 and December 31, 2008, respectively	231,346	228,647	227,147
Preferred stock—convertible, no par value: 216,753 shares outstanding at December 31, 2010, December 31, 2009 and December 31, 2008	216,753	216,753	216,753
Unearned ESOP compensation	(216,753)	(216,753)	(216,753)
Other capital	1,222,909	1,068,963	1,016,362
Retained earnings	4,824,489	4,518,428	4,245,141
Treasury stock, at cost	(4,390,983)	(4,007,633)	(3,472,384)
Cumulative other comprehensive loss	(278,321)	(317,455)	(410,618)
Total shareholders' equity	1,609,440	1,490,950	1,605,648

NOTES TO CONSOLIDATED FINANCIAL STATEMENTS (in part)

Note 11—Capital Stock (in part)

At December 31, 2010, there were 300,000,000 shares of common stock and 30,000,000 shares of serial preferred stock authorized for issuance. Of the authorized serial preferred stock, 3,000,000 shares are designated as cumulative redeemable serial preferred and 1,000,000 shares are designated as convertible serial preferred stock. See Note 12. Effective April 21, 2010, the 2006 Equity and Performance Incentive Plan (2006 Employee Plan) was amended and restated to increase the number of shares that may be issued or transferred by 9,200,000 shares to 19,200,000 shares. See Note 13. An aggregate of 19,835,391, 13,381,449 and 14,884,028 shares of common stock at December 31, 2010, 2009 and 2008, respectively, were reserved for future grants of restricted stock and the exercise and future grants of option rights (see Note 13). Common shares outstanding shown in the following table included 475,628 shares of common stock held in a revocable trust at December 31, 2010, 2009 and 2008, respectively. The revocable trust is used to accumulate assets for the purpose of funding the ultimate obligation of certain non-qualified benefit plans. Transactions between the Company and the trust are accounted for in accordance with the Deferred Compensation—Rabbi Trusts Subtopic of the Compensation Topic of the ASC, which requires the assets held by the trust be consolidated with the Company's accounts.

Note 12—Stock Purchase Plan and Preferred Stock

As of December 31, 2010, 24,624 employees contributed to the Company's ESOP, a voluntary defined contribution plan available to all eligible salaried employees. Participants are allowed to contribute, on a pretax or after-tax basis, up to the lesser of twenty percent of their annual compensation or the maximum dollar amount allowed under the Internal Revenue Code. Prior to July 1, 2009, the Company matched one hundred percent of all contributions up to six percent of eligible employee contributions. Effective July 1, 2009, the ESOP was amended to change the Company match to one-hundred percent on the first three percent of eligible employee contributions and fifty percent on the next two percent of eligible contributions. Such participant contributions may be invested in a variety of mutual funds or a Company common stock fund and may be exchanged between investments as directed by the participant. Participants are permitted to diversify both future and prior Company matching contributions previously allocated to the Company common stock fund into a variety of mutual funds.

The Company made contributions to the ESOP on behalf of participating employees, representing amounts authorized by employees to be withheld from their earnings, of $70,601, $70,025 and $72,812 in 2010, 2009 and 2008, respectively. The Company's matching contributions to the ESOP charged to operations were $37,894, $44,587 and $54,001 for 2010, 2009 and 2008, respectively.

At December 31, 2010, there were 16,845,158 shares of the Company's common stock being held by the ESOP, representing 15.7 percent of the total number of voting shares outstanding. Shares of Company common stock credited to each member's account under the ESOP are voted by the trustee under instructions from each individual plan member. Shares for which no instructions are received are voted by the trustee in the same proportion as those for which instructions are received.

On August 1, 2006, the Company issued 500,000 shares of convertible serial preferred stock, no par value (Series 2 Preferred stock) with cumulative quarterly dividends of $11.25 per share, for $500,000 to the ESOP. The ESOP financed the acquisition of the Series 2 Preferred stock by borrowing $500,000 from the Company at the rate of 5.5 percent per annum. This borrowing is payable over ten years in equal quarterly installments. Each share of Series 2 Preferred stock is entitled to one vote upon all matters presented to the Company's shareholders and generally votes with the common stock together as one class. The Series 2 Preferred stock is held by the ESOP in an unallocated account. As the value of compensation expense related to contributions to the ESOP is earned, the Company has the option of funding the ESOP by redeeming a portion of the preferred stock or with cash. Contributions are credited to the members' accounts at the time of funding. The Series 2 Preferred stock is redeemable for cash or convertible into common stock or any combination thereof at the option of the ESOP based on the relative fair value of the Series 2 Preferred and common stock at the time of conversion. At December 31, 2010, 2009 and 2008, there were no allocated or committed-to-be released shares of Series 2 Preferred stock outstanding. In 2010 and 2009, the Company elected to fund the ESOP with cash. The Company redeemed 107,980 shares of the Series 2 Preferred stock for cash in 2008.

DIVIDENDS

PRESENTATION

5.29   For public entities with respect to any dividends, Rule 3-04 of Regulation S-X requires the amount per share and in the aggregate for each class of shares to be stated. This may be stated on the financial statements or within the note disclosures. Further, Rule 4-08 of Regulation S-X requires disclosure of any restrictions that limit the payment of dividends.

5.30   An entity may distribute certain stock purchase rights that enable the holders of such rights to purchase additional equity in an entity if an outside party acquires or tenders for a substantial minority interest in the subject entity. These are commonly referred to as "poison pill arrangements."

5.31

TABLE 5-6: DIVIDENDS

Table 5-6 shows the nature of distributions made by the survey entities to their shareholders.

	Number of Entities		
	2010	2009	2008
Cash Dividends Paid to Common Stock Shareholders			
Per share amount disclosed in financial statements..	178	176	201
Per share amount disclosed in footnote disclosures	158	152	145
Total..	**336**	**328**	**346**
Cash Dividends Paid to Preferred Stock Shareholders			
Per share amount disclosed in financial statements..	6	7	9
Per share amount disclosed in footnote disclosures	22	15	19
Total..	**28**	**22**	**28**
Stock Dividends...	**5**	**—**	**—**
Dividends in Kind..	**2**	**3**	**7**
Stock Purchase Rights Plan Adopted/Extended......................................	**11**	**12**	**9**

PRESENTATION AND DISCLOSURE EXCERPTS

Cash Dividends

5.32

REPUBLIC SERVICES, INC. (DEC)

*CONSOLIDATED STATEMENT OF STOCKHOLDERS'
EQUITY AND COMPREHENSIVE INCOME*

(In millions)	Total	Comprehensive Income	Common Stock Shares	Common Stock Amount	Additional Paid-In Capital	Retained Earnings	Treasury Stock Shares	Treasury Stock Amount	Other Comprehensive Income (Loss), Net of Tax	Non-controlling Interests
Balance as of December 31, 2007	$1,303.8		195.7	$2.0	$ 38.7	$1,572.3	(10.3)	$(318.3)	$ 9.1	$—
Comprehensive income:										
Net income	73.9	$ 73.9	—	—	—	73.8	—	—	—	0.1
Other comprehensive loss, net of tax:										
Change in the value of derivative instruments, net of tax of $5.4	(8.6)	(8.6)	—	—	—	—	—	—	(8.6)	—
Employee benefit plan liability adjustments, net of tax of $1.9	(3.6)	(3.6)	—	—	—	—	—	—	(3.6)	—
Other comprehensive loss	(12.2)	(12.2)								
Comprehensive income	61.7	$ 61.7								
Cash dividends declared	(168.9)		—	—	—	(168.9)	—	—	—	—
Issuances of common stock other	27.7		1.5	—	27.7	—	—	—	—	—
Issuances of common stock due to the Allied acquisition	6,113.7		195.8	1.9	6,111.8	—	—	—	—	—
Equity issuance costs due to the Allied acquisition	(1.8)		—	—	(1.8)	—	—	—	—	—
Acquisition of noncontrolling interest	1.0		—	—	—	—	—	—	—	1.0
Value of stock options issued to replace Allied stock options	61.2		—	—	61.2	—	—	—	—	—
Issuances of restricted stock and deferred stock units	—		0.4	—	—	—	—	—	—	—
Stock-based compensation	24.0		—	—	24.0	—	—	—	—	—
Adjustment to deferred tax benefits for deferred stock units	(1.5)		—	—	(1.5)	—	—	—	—	—
Purchases of common stock for treasury	(138.4)		—	—	—	—	(4.6)	(138.4)	—	—
Balance as of December 31, 2008	7,282.5		393.4	3.9	6,260.1	1,477.2	(14.9)	(456.7)	(3.1)	1.1
Comprehensive income:										
Net income	496.5	$496.5	—	—	—	495.0	—	—	—	1.5
Other comprehensive income (loss), net of tax:										
Change in the value of derivative instruments, net of tax of $0.2	(0.1)	(0.1)	—	—	—	—	—	—	(0.1)	—
Employee benefit plan liability adjustments, net of tax of $12.8	22.2	22.2	—	—	—	—	—	—	22.2	—
Other comprehensive income	22.1	22.1								
Comprehensive income	518.6	$518.6								
Cash dividends declared	(288.7)		—	—	—	(288.7)	—	—	—	—
Issuances of common stock	40.7		2.3	0.1	40.6	—	—	—	—	—
Stock-based compensation	15.0		—	—	15.4	(0.4)	—	—	—	—
Purchases of common stock for treasury	(1.0)		—	—	—	—	—	(1.0)	—	—
Balance as of December 31, 2009	7,567.1		395.7	4.0	6,316.1	1,683.1	(14.9)	(457.7)	19.0	2.6
Comprehensive income:										
Net income	507.5	$507.5	—	—	—	506.5	—	—	—	1.0
Other comprehensive income (loss), net of tax:										
Change in the value of derivative instruments, net of tax of $4.1	(5.8)	(5.8)	—	—	—	—	—	—	(5.8)	—
Employee benefit plan liability adjustments, net of tax of $6.1	8.7	8.7	—	—	—	—	—	—	8.7	—
Other comprehensive income	2.9	2.9								
Comprehensive income	510.4	$510.4								
Cash dividends declared	(298.8)		—	—	—	(298.8)	—	—	—	—
Issuances of common stock	90.0		4.5	—	90.0	—	—	—	—	—
Stock-based compensation	24.5		—	—	25.0	(0.5)	—	—	—	—
Purchases of common stock for treasury	(43.1)		—	—	—	—	(1.6)	(43.1)	—	—
Distributions paid to noncontrolling interests	(1.2)		—	—	—	—	—	—	—	(1.2)
Balance as of December 31, 2010	$7,848.9		400.2	$4.0	$6,431.1	$1,890.3	(16.5)	$(500.8)	$21.9	$ 2.4

The accompanying notes are an integral part of these financial statements.

NOTES TO CONSOLIDATED FINANCIAL STATEMENTS (in part)

12. Stockholders' Equity (in part)

We initiated a quarterly cash dividend in July 2003. The dividend has been increased from time to time thereafter. In July 2010, the board of directors approved an increase in the quarterly dividend to $0.20 per share. Cash dividends declared were $298.8 million, $288.7 million and $168.9 million for the years ended December 31, 2010, 2009 and 2008, respectively. As of December 31, 2010, we recorded a quarterly dividend payable of $76.7 million to stockholders of record at the close of business on January 3, 2011.

Non-Cash Dividends

5.33

EATON CORPORATION (DEC)

CONSOLIDATED STATEMENTS OF SHAREHOLDERS' EQUITY

(In millions)	Common Shares Shares	Dollars	Capital in Excess of Par Value	Retained Earnings	Accumulated Other Comprehensive Loss	Deferred Compensation Plans	Total Eaton Shareholders' Equity	Noncontrolling Interests	Total Equity
Balance at January 1, 2008	292.0	$146	$2,290	$3,184	$ (423)	$(25)	$ 5,172	$ 59	$ 5,231
Net income	—	—	—	1,058	—	—	1,058	12	1,070
Foreign currency translation and related hedging instruments (net of income tax benefit of $68)	—	—	—	—	(722)	—	(722)	—	(722)
Pensions (net of income tax benefit of $227)	—	—	—	—	(419)	—	(419)	—	(419)
Other postretirement benefits (net of income tax expense of $31)	—	—	—	—	49	—	49	—	49
Cash flow hedges (net of income tax benefit of $12)	—	—	—	—	(23)	—	(23)	—	(23)
Other comprehensive loss							(1,115)	—	(1,115)
Total comprehensive loss							(57)	12	(45)
Effects of changing retirement benefit plans measurement date (net of income tax benefit of $8)	—	—	—	(11)	—	—	(11)	—	(11)
Cash dividends paid	—	—	—	(320)	—	—	(320)	(13)	(333)
Issuance of shares under employee benefit plans-net (net of income tax benefit of $16)	3.4	2	109	(2)	—	2	111	—	111
Sale of shares	37.4	19	1,503	—	—	—	1,522	—	1,522
Purchase of shares	(2.8)	(2)	(33)	(65)	—	—	(100)	—	(100)
Decrease in noncontrolling interests due to sale of business	—	—	—	—	—	—	—	(10)	(10)
Balance at December 31, 2008	330.0	165	3,869	3,844	(1,538)	(23)	6,317	48	6,365

(In millions)	Common Shares Shares	Dollars	Capital in Excess of Par Value	Retained Earnings	Accumulated Other Comprehensive Loss	Deferred Compensation Plans	Total Eaton Shareholders' Equity	Noncontrolling Interests	Total Equity
Balance at December 31, 2008	330.0	165	3,869	3,844	(1,538)	(23)	6,317	48	6,365
Net income	—	—	—	383	—	—	383	2	385
Foreign currency translation and related hedging instruments (net of income tax expense of $45)	—	—	—	—	349	—	349	—	349
Pensions (net of income tax expense of $42)	—	—	—	—	1	—	1	—	—
Other postretirement benefits (net of income tax benefit of $14)	—	—	—	—	(56)	—	(56)	—	(56)
Cash flow hedges (net of income tax expense of $19)	—	—	—	—	36	—	36	—	36
Other comprehensive income							330	—	330
Total comprehensive income							713	2	715
Cash dividends paid	—	—	—	(334)	—	—	(334)	(5)	(339)
Issuance of shares under employee benefit plans-net (net of income tax benefit of $3)	2.3	1	78	—	—	2	81	—	81
Decrease in noncontrolling interests due to sale of business	—	—	—	—	—	—	—	(4)	(4)
Balance at December 31, 2009	332.3	166	3,947	3,893	(1,208)	(21)	6,777	41	6,818

(In millions)	Common Shares Shares	Dollars	Capital in Excess of Par Value	Retained Earnings	Accumulated Other Comprehensive Loss	Deferred Compensation Plans	Total Eaton Shareholders' Equity	Noncontrolling Interests	Total Equity
Balance at December 31, 2009	332.3	166	3,947	3,893	(1,208)	(21)	6,777	41	6,818
Net income	—	—	—	929	—	—	929	8	937
Foreign currency translation and related hedging instruments	—	—	—	—	(78)	—	(78)	—	(78)
Pensions (net of income tax benefit of $30)	—	—	—	—	(61)	—	(61)	—	(61)
Other postretirement benefits (net of income tax benefit of $4)	—	—	—	—	(1)	—	(1)	—	(1)
Other comprehensive loss							(140)	—	(140)
Total comprehensive income							789	8	797
Cash dividends paid	—	—	—	(363)	—	—	(363)	(8)	(371)
Issuance of shares under employee benefit plans-net (net of income tax expense of $3)	7.6	4	146	(4)	—	13	159	—	159
Balance at December 31, 2010	339.9	$170	$4,093	$4,455	$(1,348)	$ (8)	$7,362	$41	$7,403

The number of common shares outstanding, Common shares, Capital in excess of par value and Retained earnings have been restated to give effect to the two-for-one stock split. See Note 1 for additional information.

The notes on pages 24 to 52 are an integral part of the consolidated financial statements.

NOTES TO CONSOLIDATED FINANCIAL STATEMENTS (in part)

Note 1. Summary of Significant Accounting Policies (in part)

General Information (in part)

On January 27, 2011, Eaton's Board of Directors announced a two-for-one stock split of the Company's common shares effective in the form of a 100% stock dividend. The record date for the stock split was February 7, 2011, and the additional shares will be distributed on February 28, 2011. Accordingly, all per share amounts, average shares outstanding, shares outstanding, shares repurchased and equity based compensation presented in the consolidated financial statements and notes have been adjusted retroactively to reflect the stock split. Shareholders' equity has been retroactively adjusted to give effect to the stock split for all periods presented by reclassifying the par value of the additional shares issued in connection with the stock split to Common shares from Retained earnings and Capital in excess of par value.

STOCK SPLITS

RECOGNITION AND MEASUREMENT

5.34   The FASB ASC glossary defines a *stock split* as an issuance by a corporation of its own common shares to its common shareholders without consideration and under conditions indicating that such action is prompted mainly by a desire to increase the number of outstanding shares for the purpose of effecting a reduction in their unit market price and, thereby, of obtaining wider distribution and improved marketability of the shares. It is also sometimes called a stock split-up.

5.35   FASB ASC 505-20 addresses the accounting for stock splits, as well as stock dividends, and provides guidance on determining whether a stock dividend or stock split should be accounted for according to its form or whether it should be accounted for differently.

PRESENTATION AND DISCLOSURE EXCERPTS

Stock Split

5.36

BALL CORPORATION (DEC)

*CONSOLIDATED STATEMENTS OF SHAREHOLDERS'
EQUITY AND COMPREHENSIVE EARNINGS*

	Years Ended December 31		
($ in millions, except share amounts)	2010	2009	2008
Number of Common Shares Issued *(000s)*[a]			
Balance, beginning of year	323,027	321,834	321,358
Shares issued for stock options and other stock plans, net of shares exchanged	2,396	1,193	476
Balance, end of year	325,423	323,027	321,834
Number of Treasury Shares *(000s)*[a]			
Balance, beginning of year	(134,985)	(134,370)	(120,908)
Shares purchased, net of shares reissued[b]	(18,280)	(615)	(13,462)
Balance, end of year	(153,265)	(134,985)	(134,370)
Common Stock			
Balance, beginning of year	$ 830.8	$ 788.0	$ 760.3
Shares issued for stock options and other stock plans, net of shares exchanged (cash and noncash)	49.9	37.3	23.4
Tax benefit from option exercises	12.7	5.5	4.3
Balance, end of year	$ 893.4	$ 830.8	$ 788.0
Retained Earnings			
Balance, beginning of year	$ 2,397.1	$ 2,047.1	$ 1,765.0
Net earnings attributable to Ball Corporation	468.0	387.9	319.5
Common dividends, net of tax benefits	(35.3)	(37.9)	(37.4)
Balance, end of year	$ 2,829.8	$ 2,397.1	$ 2,047.1
Accumulated Other Comprehensive Earnings (Loss) (Note 15)			
Balance, beginning of year	$ (63.8)	$ (182.5)	$ 106.9
Foreign currency translation adjustment	(57.1)	6.6	(48.2)
Pension and other postretirement items, net of tax	(13.4)	(22.6)	(147.8)
Effective financial derivatives, net of tax	49.0	127.7	(93.4)
Mark-to-market gain on available for sale securities, net of tax	3.2	7.0	—
Net other comprehensive earnings (loss) adjustments	(18.3)	118.7	(289.4)
Accumulated other comprehensive earnings (loss)	$ (82.1)	$ (63.8)	$ (182.5)
Treasury Stock			
Balance, beginning of year	$ (1,582.8)	$ (1,566.8)	$ (1,289.7)
Shares purchased, net of shares reissued[b]	(540.3)	(16.0)	(277.1)
Balance, end of year	$ (2,123.1)	$ (1,582.8)	$ (1,566.8)
Noncontrolling Interests			
Balance, beginning of year	$ 1.7	$ 1.5	$ 1.1
Acquisition of equity affiliate	132.9	—	—
Other activity	5.5	0.2	0.4
Balance, end of year	$ 140.1	$ 1.7	$ 1.5
Comprehensive Earnings			
Net earnings attributable to Ball Corporation	$ 468.0	$ 387.9	$ 319.5
Net other comprehensive earnings adjustments (see details above)	(18.3)	118.7	(289.4)
Comprehensive earnings attributable to Ball Corporation	$ 449.7	$ 506.6	$ 30.1

[a] Amounts have been retrospectively adjusted for the two-for-one stock split that was effective on February 15, 2011.
[b] Includes 677,296 shares, 935,948 shares and 901,888 shares reissued in 2010, 2009 and 2008, respectively. The total amounts related to these share reissuances were $19.0 million, $20.9 million and $19.4 million in each of these three years, respectively.

The accompanying notes are an integral part of the consolidated financial statements.

NOTES TO CONSOLIDATED FINANCIAL STATEMENTS (in part)

23. Subsequent Events (in part)

Two-for-One Stock Split

On January 26, 2011, the company's board of directors declared a two-for-one split of Ball's common stock, increased the quarterly dividend to 7 cents per share (on a post-split basis) and authorized the repurchase of 20 million additional common shares (on a post-split basis). The stock split will be effective February 15, 2011, for all shareholders of record on February 4, 2011. As a result of the stock split, all amounts related to shares, share prices and earnings per share have been retroactively restated throughout this Annual report on Form 10-K.

Reverse Stock Split

5.37

MOTOROLA SOLUTIONS, INC. (DEC)

CONSOLIDATED BALANCE SHEETS

	December 31	
(In millions, except per share amounts)	2010	2009
Assets		
Cash and cash equivalents	$ 4,208	$ 2,869
Sigma Fund and short-term investments	4,655	5,094
Accounts receivable, net	3,268	2,845
Inventories, net	1,364	1,097
Deferred income taxes	1,338	1,082
Other current assets	1,342	1,389
Current assets held for sale	979	1,656
Total current assets	17,154	16,032
Property, plant and equipment, net	1,729	1,819
Sigma Fund	70	66
Investments	310	456
Deferred income taxes	1,619	2,283
Goodwill	2,825	2,714
Other assets	1,428	1,680
Non-current assets held for sale	442	553
Total assets	$25,577	$25,603
Liabilities and Stockholders' Equity		
Notes payable and current portion of long-term debt	$605	$536
Accounts payable	2,462	1,998
Accrued liabilities	4,704	4,141
Current liabilities held for sale	939	1,586
Total current liabilities	8,710	8,261
Long-term debt	2,194	3,365
Other liabilities	3,542	3,987
Non-current liabilities held for sale	144	107
Stockholders' Equity		
Preferred stock, $100 par value	—	—
Common stock: 12/31/10—$.01 par value; 12/31/09—$.01 par value	3	3
Authorized shares: 12/31/10—600.0; 12/31/09—600.0		
Issued shares: 12/31/10—337.2; 12/31/09—330.6		
Outstanding shares: 12/31/10—336.3; 12/31/09—330.3		
Additional paid-in capital	8,644	8,231
Retained earnings	4,460	3,827
Accumulated other comprehensive loss	(2,222)	(2,286)
Total Motorola Solutions, Inc. stockholders' equity	10,885	9,775
Noncontrolling interests	102	108
Total stockholders' equity	10,987	9,883
Total liabilities and stockholders' equity	$25,577	$25,603

Presentation gives effect to the Reverse Stock Split, which occurred on January 4, 2011.

See accompanying notes to consolidated financial statements.

NOTES TO CONSOLIDATED FINANCIAL STATEMENTS (in part)

1. Summary of Significant Accounting Policies (in part)

Changes in Presentation (in part)
Reverse Stock Split and Name Change

On November 30, 2010, Motorola Solutions announced the timing and details regarding the Separation and the approval of a reverse stock split at a ratio of 1-for-7. Immediately following the Distribution of Motorola Mobility common stock, the Company completed a 1-for-7 reverse stock split ("the Reverse Stock Split") and changed its name to Motorola Solutions, Inc. All consolidated per share information presented gives effect to the Reverse Stock Split.

CHANGES TO RETAINED EARNINGS

RECOGNITION AND MEASUREMENT

5.38 The retained earnings account is affected by direct charges and credits. The most frequent direct charges to retained earnings are net loss for the year, losses on treasury stock transactions, and cash or stock dividends. The most common direct credit to retained earnings is net income for the year.

PRESENTATION

5.39 In addition to direct charges and credits, the retained earnings account is also affected by opening balance adjustments. Reasons for which the opening balance of retained earnings is properly restated include certain changes in accounting principles, changes in the reporting entity, and corrections of an error in previously issued financial statements.

5.40 FASB ASC 250, *Accounting Changes and Error Corrections*, requires, unless impracticable or otherwise specified by applicable authoritative guidance, retrospective application to prior periods' financial statements of a change in accounting principle. *Retrospective application* is the application of a different accounting principle to prior accounting periods as if that principle had always been used. More specifically, retrospective application involves the following:

- The cumulative effect of the change on periods prior to those presented should be reflected in the carrying amount of assets and liabilities as of the beginning of the first period presented.
- An offsetting adjustment, if any, shall be made to the opening balance of retained earnings or other appropriate component of equity or net assets in the statement of financial position for that period.
- Financial statements for each individual prior period presented should be adjusted to reflect the period-specific effects of applying the new accounting principle.

5.41 FASB ASC 250 also requires any accounting error in the financial statements of a prior period discovered after the financial statements are issued or available to be issued to be reported as an error correction by restating the prior period financial statements. Restatement involves similar requirements as those specified for retrospective application of a change in accounting principle.

5.42 SEC Staff Accounting Bulletin (SAB) No. 108 provides guidance on the consideration of the effects of prior year misstatements in quantifying current year misstatements for the purpose of assessing materiality. SAB No. 108 requires that registrant entities determine the quantitative effect of a financial statement misstatement by using both an income statement ("rollover") and a balance sheet ("iron curtain") approach and evaluate whether, under either approach, the error is material after considering all relevant quantitative and qualitative factors.

5.43

TABLE 5-7: OTHER CHANGES IN RETAINED EARNINGS*

Direct charges and credits—other than net loss, net income, dividends, and stock splits—are summarized in Table 5-7.

	Number of Entities		
	2010	2009	2008
Charges			
Purchase or retirement of capital stock	63	55	91
Treasury stock issued for less than cost	10	36	31
Share-based awards subject to redemption	21	10	5
Preferred stock accretion	1	3	1
Redemption of stock purchase rights	5	N/C^	N/C^
Other—described	47	21	14
Credits			
Tax benefit on stock option exercise	3	6	7
Tax benefit on dividends paid to employee stock ownership plan	3	4	3
Capital stock issued	10	N/C^	N/C^
Other—described	25	21	18

* Appearing in the statement of stockholders' equity or notes to the financial statements, or both.

^ N/C = Not compiled. The line item was not included in the table for the year shown.

PRESENTATION AND DISCLOSURE EXCERPTS

Change in Accounting Principle

5.44

THE DOW CHEMICAL COMPANY (DEC)

CONSOLIDATED STATEMENTS OF EQUITY

	For the Years Ended December 31		
(In millions)	2010	2009	2008
Preferred Stock			
Balance at beginning of year	$4,000	—	—
Preferred stock issued	—	$7,000	—
Preferred stock repurchased	—	(2,500)	—
Preferred stock converted to common stock	—	(500)	—
Balance at end of year	4,000	4,000	—
Common Stock			
Balance at beginning of year	2,906	2,453	$2,453
Common stock issued	25	453	—
Balance at end of year	2,931	2,906	2,453
Additional Paid-in Capital			
Balance at beginning of year	1,913	872	902
Common stock issued	156	2,643	—
Sale of shares to ESOP	—	(1,529)	—
Stock-based compensation and allocation of ESOP shares	217	(73)	(30)
Balance at end of year	2,286	1,913	872
Retained Earnings			
Balance at beginning of year	16,704	17,013	18,004
Net income available for The Dow Chemical Company common stockholders	1,970	336	579
Dividends declared on common stock (Per share: $0.60 in 2010, $0.60 in 2009 and $1.68 in 2008)	(677)	(639)	(1,556)
Other	(13)	(6)	(14)
Impact of adoption of ASU 2009-17, net of tax	(248)	—	—
Balance at end of year	17,736	16,704	17,013
Accumulated Other Comprehensive Loss			
Unrealized Gains (Losses) on Investments at beginning of year	79	(111)	71
Net change in unrealized gains (losses)	32	190	(182)
Balance at end of year	111	79	(111)
Cumulative Translation Adjustments at beginning of year	624	221	723
Translation adjustments	(257)	403	(502)
Balance at end of year	367	624	221
Pension and Other Postretirement Benefit Plans at beginning of year	(4,587)	(4,251)	(989)
Net prior service credit	23	19	16
Net loss	(307)	(355)	(3,278)
Balance at end of year	(4,871)	(4,587)	(4,251)
Accumulated Derivative Gain (Loss) at beginning of year	(8)	(248)	25
Net hedging results	(13)	(65)	(452)
Reclassification to earnings	15	305	179
Balance at end of year	(6)	(8)	(248)
Total accumulated other comprehensive loss	(4,399)	(3,892)	(4,389)
Unearned ESOP Shares			
Balance at beginning of year	(519)	—	—
Shares acquired	(1)	(553)	—
Shares allocated to ESOP participants	44	34	—
Balance at end of year	(476)	(519)	—

(continued)

(In millions)	For the Years Ended December 31		
	2010	**2009**	**2008**
Treasury Stock			
Balance at beginning of year	(557)	(2,438)	(1,800)
Purchases	(14)	(5)	(898)
Sale of shares to ESOP	—	1,529	—
Issuance to employees and employee plans	332	357	260
Balance at end of year	(239)	(557)	(2,438)
The Dow Chemical Company's Stockholders' Equity	21,839	20,555	13,511
Noncontrolling Interests			
Balance at beginning of year	569	69	414
Net income attributable to noncontrolling interests	11	28	75
Purchase of noncontrolling interests' share of subsidiaries	—	—	(376)
Distributions to noncontrolling interests	(8)	(24)	(45)
Acquisition of Rohm and Haas Company noncontrolling interests	—	432	—
Consolidation of variable interest entities	109	46	—
Impact of adoption ASU 2009-17	100	—	—
Other	22	18	1
Balance at end of year	803	569	69
Total Equity	$22,642	$21,124	$13,580

See Notes to the Consolidated Financial Statements.

NOTES TO CONSOLIDATED FINANCIAL STATEMENTS (in part)

Note B—Recent Accounting Guidance (in part)

Recently Adopted Accounting Guidance (in part)

On January 1, 2010, the Company adopted ASU 2009-17, "Consolidations (Topic 810): Improvements to Financial Reporting by Enterprises Involved with Variable Interest Entities," which amended the consolidation guidance applicable to variable interest entities and required additional disclosures concerning an enterprise's continuing involvement with variable interest entities. The Company evaluated the impact of this guidance and determined that the adoption resulted in the consolidation of two additional joint ventures, an owner trust and an entity that was used to monetize accounts receivable. At January 1, 2010, $793 million in assets (net of tax, including the impact on "Investment in nonconsolidated affiliates"), $941 million in liabilities, $100 million in noncontrolling interests and a cumulative effect adjustment to retained earnings of $248 million were recorded as a result of the adoption of this guidance. See Note S for additional information about variable interest entities.

Note S—Variable Interest Entities

On January 1, 2010, the Company adopted ASU 2009-17, "Consolidations (Topic 810): Improvements to Financial Reporting by Enterprises Involved with Variable Interest Entities." ASU 2009-17 amends the consolidation guidance applicable to variable interest entities ("VIEs") and requires additional disclosures concerning an enterprise's continuing involvement with VIEs. The Company evaluated the impact of this guidance and determined that the adoption resulted in the January 1, 2010 consolidation of two additional joint ventures, an owner trust and an entity that is used to monetize accounts receivable. The Company elected prospective application of this guidance at adoption.

The following table summarizes the carrying amount of the assets and liabilities of the two additional joint ventures and the owner trust entity included in the Company's consolidated balance sheet at January 1, 2010.

Assets and Liabilities of Newly Consolidated VIEs Included in the Consolidated Balance Sheet	
(In millions)	**Jan. 1, 2010**
Current assets	$ 37
Property	209
Other noncurrent assets	3
Total assets	$249
Current liabilities	$76
Long-term debt	346
Total liabilities	$422

The carrying amounts of assets and liabilities pertaining to the entity used to monetize accounts receivable, included in the Company's consolidated balance sheet at January 1, 2010, were current assets of $817 million (including $436 million of restricted cash) and current liabilities of $589 million.

Consolidated Variable Interest Entities

The Company holds a variable interest in five joint ventures for which the Company is the primary beneficiary. Three of the joint ventures are development stage enterprises, which will produce propylene oxide and hydrogen peroxide and provide terminal services in Thailand. The Company's variable interest in these joint ventures relates to cost-plus arrangements between the joint venture and the Company, involving the majority of the output on take-or-pay terms and ensuring a guaranteed return to the joint ventures.

Another joint venture will construct, own and operate a membrane chlor-alkali facility to be located at the Company's Freeport, Texas integrated manufacturing complex. The Company's variable interests in this joint venture relate to equity options between the partners and a cost-plus off-take arrangement between the joint venture and the Company, involving proportional purchase commitments on take-or-pay terms and ensuring a guaranteed return to the joint venture. The Company will provide the joint venture with operation and maintenance services, utilities and raw materials; market the joint venture's co-products; and toll convert the other partner's proportional purchase commitments into ethylene dichloride. The joint venture is expected to begin operations in mid-2013.

The fifth joint venture was acquired through the acquisition of Rohm and Haas on April 1, 2009. This joint venture manufactures products in Japan for the semiconductor industry. Each joint venture partner holds several equivalent variable interests, with the exception of a royalty agreement held exclusively between the joint venture and the Company. In addition, the entire output of the joint venture is sold to the Company for resale to third-party customers.

The Company also holds a variable interest in an owner trust, for which the Company is the primary beneficiary. The owner trust leases an ethylene facility in The Netherlands to the Company, whereby substantially all of the rights and obligations of ownership are transferred to the Company. The Company's variable interest in the owner trust relates to a residual value guarantee provided to the owner trust. Upon expiration of the lease, which matures in 2014, the Company may purchase the facility for an amount based on a fair market value determination. At December 31, 2010, the Company had provided to the owner trust a residual value guarantee of $363 million, which represents the Company's maximum exposure to loss under the lease.

As the primary beneficiary of these VIEs, the entities' assets, liabilities and results of operations are included in the Company's consolidated financial statements. The other equity holders' interests are reflected in "Net income attributable to noncontrolling interests" in the consolidated statements of income and "Noncontrolling interests" in the consolidated balance sheets. The following table summarizes the carrying amounts of the entities' assets and liabilities included in the Company's consolidated balance sheets at December 31, 2010 and December 31, 2009:

Assets and Liabilities of Consolidated VIEs

(In millions)	Dec. 31, 2010	Dec. 31, 2009
Current assets (restricted 2010: $228)	$ 228	$102
Property (restricted 2010: $1,388)	1,388	455
Other noncurrent assets (restricted 2010: $122)	122	81
Total assets	$1,738	$638
Current liabilities (nonrecourse 2010: $190)	$ 837	$183
Long-term debt (nonrecourse 2010: $167)	513	125
Other noncurrent liabilities (nonrecourse 2010: $64)	64	43
Total liabilities	$1,414	$351

The Company holds a variable interest in an entity created in June 2010 to monetize accounts receivable of select European entities. The Company is the primary beneficiary of this entity as a result of holding subordinated notes while maintaining servicing responsibilities for the accounts receivable. The carrying amounts of assets and liabilities pertaining to this entity, included in the Company's consolidated balance sheet at December 31, 2010, were current assets of $158 million (zero restricted) and current liabilities of $1 million ($1 million nonrecourse). Prior to the creation of this entity, the Company held a variable interest in another entity that was also used to monetize accounts receivable originated by several European subsidiaries. That arrangement was terminated in June 2010. No gain or loss was recognized as a result of terminating the arrangement.

Amounts presented in the consolidated balance sheets and the table above as restricted assets or nonrecourse obligations relating to consolidated VIEs at December 31, 2010 are adjusted for intercompany eliminations, parental guarantees and residual value guarantees.

In September 2001, Hobbes Capital S.A. ("Hobbes"), a former consolidated foreign subsidiary of the Company, issued $500 million of preferred securities in the form of equity certificates. The certificates provided a floating rate of return (which could be reinvested) based on LIBOR. Under the accounting guidance for consolidation, Hobbes was a VIE and the Company was the primary beneficiary. During the third quarter of 2008, the other partner of Hobbes redeemed its $674 million ownership in Hobbes. The minority ownership was redeemed in a non-cash transaction in exchange for a three-year note payable with a floating rate based on LIBOR, which was repaid in September 2009. Prior to redemption, the preferred return was included in "Net income attributable to noncontrolling interests" in the consolidated statements of income.

Nonconsolidated Variable Interest Entity

The Company holds a variable interest in a joint venture accounted for under the equity method of accounting, acquired through the acquisition of Rohm and Haas on April 1, 2009. The joint venture manufactures crude acrylic acid in the United States and Germany on behalf of the Company and the other joint venture partner. The variable interest relates to a cost-plus arrangement between the joint venture and each joint venture partner. The Company is not the primary beneficiary, as a majority of the joint venture's output is sold to the other joint venture partner, and therefore the entity is not consolidated. At December 31, 2010, the Company's investment in the joint venture was $144 million, classified as "Investment in nonconsolidated affiliates" in the consolidated balance sheets, representing the Company's maximum exposure to loss.

Correction of an Error or Misstatement

5.45

MOLEX INCORPORATED (JUN)

*CONSOLIDATED STATEMENTS OF STOCKHOLDERS'
EQUITY*

	Years Ended June 30		
(In thousands)	2010	2009 (as restated)	2008 (as restated)
Common stock	$ 11,207	$ 11,138	$ 11,107
Paid-in capital:			
Beginning balance	$ 601,459	$ 569,046	$ 520,037
Stock-based compensation	27,034	26,508	24,249
Exercise of stock options	9,012	4,183	22,738
Issuance of stock awards	1,291	1,586	1,743
Other	—	136	279
Ending balance	$ 638,796	$ 601,459	$ 569,046
Retained earnings:			
Beginning balance, as reported	$ 2,355,991	$ 2,785,099	$ 2,650,470
Restatement adjustments (see Note 3)	(94,397)	(93,648)	(93,931)
Beginning balance, as restated	2,261,594	2,691,451	2,556,539
Net income (loss)	76,930	(322,036)	215,720
Dividends	(106,079)	(106,110)	(80,756)
Other	—	(1,711)	(52)
Ending balance	$ 2,232,445	$ 2,261,594	$ 2,691,451
Treasury stock:			
Beginning balance	$(1,089,322)	$(1,009,021)	$ (799,894)
Purchase of treasury stock	—	(76,342)	(199,583)
Exercise of stock options	(8,765)	(3,959)	(9,544)
Other	—	—	—
Ending balance	$(1,098,087)	$(1,089,322)	$(1,009,021)
Accumulated other comprehensive income, net of tax:			
Beginning balance, as reported	$ 183,298	$ 320,615	$ 141,398
Restatement adjustments (see Note 3)	(6,915)	(6,915)	(6,982)
Beginning balance, as restated	176,383	313,700	134,416
Translation adjustments	35,482	(115,029)	165,706
Pension adjustments, net of tax	(12,459)	(22,137)	3,309
Unrealized investment gain (loss), net of tax	1,364	(151)	10,202
Ending balance	$ 200,770	$ 176,383	$ 313,633
Total stockholders' equity	$ 1,985,131	$ 1,961,252	$ 2,576,216
Comprehensive (loss) income, net of tax:			
Net income (loss)	$ 76,930	$ (322,036)	$ 215,720
Translation adjustments	35,482	(115,029)	165,706
Pension adjustments, net of tax	(12,459)	(22,137)	3,309
Unrealized investment gain, net of tax	1,364	(151)	10,202
Total comprehensive income (loss), net of tax	$ 101,317	$ (459,353)	$ 394,937

See accompanying notes to consolidated financial statements.

NOTES TO CONSOLIDATED FINANCIAL STATEMENTS (in part)

3. Restatement of Prior Period Financial Statements

During the fourth quarter of fiscal 2010, we made the following adjustments to the historical consolidated financial statements.

- As discussed in Note 4, we recorded a liability for potential losses related to the unauthorized activities in Japan. We are restating prior period financial statements to record liabilities in the periods in which the unauthorized transactions occurred.

- During the fourth quarter of fiscal 2010, we completed a study to determine if historical tax transactions and balances had been recognized appropriately in accordance with ASC 740. We identified errors in tax-related accounts in prior periods.

Based on our analysis of these adjustments, we concluded that while the adjustments were not material to the operating results of fiscal years 2008 or 2009, there was an overstatement of stockholders' equity in the amount of $101.3 million, which represented 4.9% of total stockholders' equity as of June 30, 2009. Accordingly, we restated the fiscal 2009 and 2008 consolidated financial statements included in this filing. Quarterly results have been restated and are included in Quarterly Financial Information (See Note 21). The restated financial statements did not impact segment reporting.

The effect of the restatement on the consolidated statements of operations for the years ended June 30, 2009 and 2008 follows (in thousands):

		Adjustments		
	As Reported	Japan	Tax	As Restated
Year Ended June 30, 2009:				
Net loss on unauthorized activities in Japan	$ —	$2,685	$ —	$ 2,685
Income (loss) from operations	(346,196)	(2,685)	—	(348,881)
Income (loss) before income taxes	(318,888)	(2,685)	—	(321,573)
Income taxes	2,399	(973)	(963)	463
Net income (loss)	(321,287)	(1,712)	963	(322,036)
Earnings (loss) per share:				
Basic	(1.84)	0.01	(0.01)	(1.84)
Diluted	(1.84)	0.01	(0.01)	(1.84)
Year Ended June 30, 2008:				
Net loss on unauthorized activities in Japan	$ —	$4,717	$ —	$ 4,717
Income (loss) from operations	317,950	(4,717)	—	313,233
Income (loss) before income taxes	338,648	(4,717)	—	333,931
Income taxes	123,211	(1,710)	(3,290)	118,211
Net income (loss)	215,437	(3,007)	3,290	215,720
Earnings (loss) per share:				
Basic	1.19	(0.02)	0.02	1.20
Diluted	1.19	(0.02)	0.02	1.19

The effect of the restatement on the consolidated balance sheet as of June 30, 2009 follows (in thousands):

		Adjustments		
	As Reported	Japan	Tax	As Restated
Deferred income taxes	$ 27,939	$ 63,366	$(3,881)	$ 87,424
Total current assets	1,447,573	63,366	(3,881)	1,507,058
Non-current deferred income taxes	89,332	—	9,944	99,276
Total assets	2,942,157	63,366	6,063	3,011,586
Income taxes payable	4,750	—	(4,063)	687
Accrual for unauthorized activities in Japan	—	174,804	—	174,804
Total current liabilities	714,152	174,804	(4,063)	884,893
Total liabilities	879,593	174,804	(4,063)	1,050,334
Retained earnings	2,355,991	(111,438)	17,041	2,261,594
Accumulated other comprehensive income	183,298	—	(6,915)	176,383
Total stockholders' equity	2,062,564	(111,438)	10,126	1,961,252
Total liabilities and stockholders' equity	2,942,157	63,366	6,063	3,011,586

The effect of the restatement on the consolidated statements of cash flows for the years ended June 30 follows (in thousands):

| | As Reported | Adjustments | | As Restated |
		Japan	Tax	
2009:				
Net income (loss)	$(321,287)	$(1,712)	$ 963	$(322,036)
Deferred income taxes	(26,606)	(973)	(654)	(28,233)
Other current assets and liabilities	(24,967)	2,685	(309)	(22,591)
Cash provided from operating activities	369,898	—	—	369,898
2008:				
Net income (loss)	$ 215,437	$(3,007)	$3,290	$ 215,720
Deferred income taxes	31,096	(1,710)	(600)	28,786
Other current assets and liabilities	(45,798)	4,717	(2,690)	(43,771)
Cash provided from operating activities	479,134	—	—	479,134

4. Net Loss on Unauthorized Activities in Japan

As we previously reported, in April 2010, we launched an investigation into unauthorized activities in Japan. We learned that an individual working in Molex Japan's finance group obtained unauthorized loans from third party lenders, that included in at least one instance the attempted unauthorized pledge of Molex Japan facilities as security, in Molex Japan's name that were used to cover losses resulting from unauthorized trading, including margin trading, in Molex Japan's name. We also learned that the individual misappropriated funds from Molex Japan's accounts to cover losses from unauthorized trading. The individual admitted to forging documentation in arranging and concealing the transactions. We retained outside legal counsel, and they retained forensic accountants, to investigate the matter. The investigation is now substantially complete. Based on our consultation with legal counsel in Japan and the information learned from the substantially completed investigation, we intend to vigorously contest the enforceability of the outstanding unauthorized loans and any attempt by the lender to obtain payment.

At the end of the third quarter of fiscal 2010, we reported the outstanding unauthorized loans as a contingent liability of $162.2 million. Based on the results of the substantially completed investigation, we recorded for accounting purposes an accrued liability for the effect of unauthorized activities pending the resolution of these matters. In particular, we recorded cumulative net losses of $201.9 million, ($128.7 million after-tax) due to these unauthorized activities (see Note 3), which were comprised of (1) the asserted unauthorized loans outstanding as of June 30, 2010 of ¥15.0 billion ($169.7 million), (2) the payment of ¥1.0 billion ($10.8 million) of unauthorized loans on April 5, 2010, (3) misappropriated funds of ¥1.9 billion ($20.5 million), and (4) cumulative investigative costs through June 30, 2010 of $4.8 million, offset by (5) an unauthorized investment account with a balance of ¥0.4 billion ($3.9 million) as of June 30, 2010. We believe these unauthorized activities and related losses occurred from at least as early as 1988 through 2010, with approximately ¥15.4 billion ($167.4 million) occurring prior to June 30, 2007. The accrued liability for these potential net losses was ¥14.7 billion ($165.8 million) as of June 30, 2010.

To the extent we prevail in not having to pay all or any portion of the outstanding unauthorized loans, we would recognize a gain in that amount.

Other Changes in Retained Earnings: Share Repurchase Programs

5.46

RYDER SYSTEM, INC. (DEC)

CONSOLIDATED STATEMENTS OF SHAREHOLDERS' EQUITY

(Dollars in thousands, except per share amounts)	Preferred Stock Amount	Common Stock Shares	Par	Additional Paid-In Capital	Retained Earnings	Accumulated Other Comprehensive Loss	Total
Balance at January 1, 2008	$—	58,041,563	$28,883	729,451	1,160,132	(30,877)	1,887,589
Components of comprehensive income:							
Net earnings	—	—	—	—	199,881	—	199,881
Foreign currency translation adjustments	—	—	—	—	—	(180,819)	(180,819)
Net unrealized loss related to derivatives	—	—	—	—	—	(119)	(119)
Amortization of pension and postretirement items, net of tax of $(1,344)	—	—	—	—	—	2,564	2,564
Pension curtailment, net of tax of $634	—	—	—	—	—	(1,287)	(1,287)
Change in net actuarial loss, net of tax of $188,654	—	—	—	—	—	(333,689)	(333,689)
Total comprehensive loss							(313,469)
Common stock dividends declared and paid—$0.92 per share	—	—	—	—	(52,238)	—	(52,238)
Common stock issued under employee stock option and stock purchase plans[1]	—	1,593,073	934	53,496	—	—	54,430
Benefit plan stock sales[2]	—	1,859	1	282	—	—	283
Common stock repurchases	—	(3,978,436)	(1,989)	(51,737)	(202,406)	—	(256,132)
Share-based compensation	—	—	—	17,076	—	—	17,076
Tax benefits from share-based compensation	—	—	—	7,622	—	—	7,622
Balance at December 31, 2008	—	55,658,059	27,829	756,190	1,105,369	(544,227)	1,345,161
Components of comprehensive income:							
Net earnings	—	—	—	—	61,945	—	61,945
Foreign currency translation adjustments	—	—	—	—	—	96,899	96,899
Net unrealized gain related to derivatives	—	—	—	—	—	149	149
Amortization of pension and postretirement items, net of tax of $(7,930)	—	—	—	—	—	14,287	14,287
Pension curtailment, net of tax of $4,689	—	—	—	—	—	(12,058)	(12,058)
Change in net actuarial loss, net of tax of $(38,906)	—	—	—	—	—	66,031	66,031
Total comprehensive income							227,253
Common stock dividends declared and paid—$0.96 per share	—	—	—	—	(53,334)	—	(53,334)
Common stock issued under employee stock option and stock purchase plans[1]	—	483,270	242	6,906	—	—	7,148
Benefit plan stock sales[2]	—	4,673	2	292	—	—	294
Common stock repurchases	—	(2,726,281)	(1,363)	(37,116)	(77,802)	—	(116,281)
Share-based compensation	—	—	—	16,404	—	—	16,404
Tax benefits from share-based compensation	—	—	—	350	—	—	350
Balance at December 31, 2009	—	53,419,721	26,710	743,026	1,036,178	(378,919)	1,426,995
Components of comprehensive income:							
Net earnings	—	—	—	—	118,170	—	118,170
Foreign currency translation adjustments	—	—	—	—	—	13,009	13,009
Realized gain related to derivatives	—	—	—	—	—	(14)	(14)
Amortization of pension and postretirement items, net of tax of $(6,046)	—	—	—	—	—	10,828	10,828
Pension settlement, net of tax of $(469)	—	—	—	—	—	1,074	1,074
Change in net actuarial loss, net of tax of $13,242	—	—	—	—	—	(22,577)	(22,577)
Total comprehensive income							120,490
Common stock dividends declared and paid—$1.04 per share	—	—	—	—	(54,474)	—	(54,474)
Common stock issued under employee stock option and stock purchase plans[1]	—	740,242	370	16,658	—	—	17,028
Benefit plan stock purchases[2]	—	(3,160)	(2)	(128)	—	—	(130)
Common stock repurchases	—	(2,982,046)	(1,491)	(41,590)	(80,089)	—	(123,170)
Share-based compensation	—	—	—	16,543	—	—	16,543
Tax benefits from share-based compensation	—	—	—	1,031	—	—	1,031
Balance at December 31, 2010	$—	51,174,757	$25,587	735,540	1,019,785	(376,599)	1,404,313

[1] Net of common shares delivered as payment for the exercise price or to satisfy the holders' withholding tax liability upon exercise of options.

[2] Represents open-market transactions of common shares by the trustee of Ryder's deferred compensation plans.

See accompanying notes to consolidated financial statements.

NOTES TO CONSOLIDATED FINANCIAL STATEMENTS (in part)

1. Summary of Significant Accounting Policies (in part)

Share Repurchases

Repurchases of shares of common stock are made periodically in open-market transactions and are subject to market conditions, legal requirements and other factors. The cost of share repurchases is allocated between common stock and retained earnings based on the amount of additional paid-in capital at the time of the share repurchase.

20. Share Repurchase Programs

In February 2010, our Board of Directors authorized a $100 million discretionary share repurchase program over a period not to exceed two years. In 2010, we completed this program and repurchased and retired 2,420,390 shares at an aggregate cost of $100 million.

In December 2009, our Board of Directors authorized a share repurchase program intended to mitigate the dilutive impact of shares issued under our various employee stock, stock option and employee stock purchase plans. Under the December 2009 program, management is authorized to repurchase shares of common stock in an amount not to exceed the number of shares issued to employees under the Company's various employee stock, stock option and employee stock purchase plans from December 1, 2009 through December 15, 2011. The December 2009 program limits aggregate share repurchases to no more than 2 million shares of Ryder common stock. Share repurchases of common stock are made periodically in open-market transactions and are subject to market conditions, legal requirements and other factors. Management may establish a prearranged written plan under Rule 10b5-1 of the Securities Exchange Act of 1934 as part of the December 2009 program, which allow for share repurchases during Ryder's quarterly blackout periods as set forth in the trading plan. During 2010, we repurchased and retired 561,656 shares under this program at an aggregate cost of $23 million. No shares were repurchased under this program during 2009.

In December 2007, our Board of Directors authorized a $300 million discretionary share repurchase program over a period not to exceed two years. Additionally, our Board of Directors authorized a separate two-year anti-dilutive repurchase program. The anti-dilutive program limited aggregate share repurchases to no more than 2 million shares of our common stock. In 2009 and 2008, we repurchased and retired 2,348,909 shares and 2,615,000 shares, respectively, under the $300 million program at an aggregate cost of $100 million and $170 million, respectively. In 2009 and 2008, we repurchased and retired 377,372 shares and 1,363,436 shares, respectively, under the anti-dilutive program at an aggregate cost of $16 million and $86 million, respectively.

Other Changes in Retained Earnings: Accretion to Redemption Value of Preferred Stock

5.47

LAS VEGAS SANDS CORP. (DEC)

CONSOLIDATED STATEMENTS OF EQUITY AND COMPREHENSIVE INCOME (LOSS)

	Preferred Stock	Common Stock	Capital in Excess of Par Value	Accumulated Other Comprehensive Income (Loss)	Retained Earnings	Total Comprehensive Income (Loss)	Noncontrolling Interests	Total
Balance at January 1, 2008	$—	$355	$1,064,878	$(2,493)	$1,197,534		$4,926	$2,265,200
Net loss	—	—	—	—	(163,558)	(163,558)	(4,767)	(168,325)
Currency translation adjustment	—	—	—	20,047	—	20,047	—	20,047
Total comprehensive loss						(143,511)	(4,767)	(148,278)
Exercise of stock options	—	1	6,833	—	—		—	6,834
Tax benefit from stock-based compensation	—	—	1,117	—	—		—	1,117
Stock-based compensation	—	—	59,643	—	—		—	59,643
Issuance of preferred and common stock and warrants, net of transaction costs	298,066	200	1,482,907	—	—		—	1,781,173
Extinguishment of convertible senior notes	—	86	474,914	—	—		—	475,000
Contribution from noncontrolling interests	—	—	—	—	—		2,914	2,914
Accumulated but undeclared dividend requirement on preferred stock issued to Principal Stockholder's family	—	—	—	—	(6,854)		—	(6,854)
Accretion to redemption value of preferred stock issued to Principal Stockholder's family	$—	$ —	$ —	$ —	$ (11,568)		$—	$ (11,568)

(continued)

	Preferred Stock	Common Stock	Capital in Excess of Par Value	Accumulated Other Comprehensive Income (Loss)	Retained Earnings	Total Comprehensive Income (Loss)	Noncontrolling Interests	Total
Balance at December 31, 2008	$298,066	$642	$3,090,292	$17,554	$1,015,554		$ 3,073	$4,425,181
Net loss	—	—	—	—	(354,479)	(354,479)	(14,264)	(368,743)
Currency translation adjustment	—	—	—	10,906	—	10,906	(602)	10,304
Total comprehensive loss						(343,573)	(14,866)	(358,439)
Exercise of stock options	—	—	51	—	—		—	51
Tax shortfall from stock-based compensation	—	—	(4,965)	—	—		—	(4,965)
Stock-based compensation	—	—	49,054	—	—		—	49,054
Exercise of warrants	(63,459)	18	63,441	—	—		—	—
Deemed contribution from Principal Stockholder	—	—	519	—	—		—	519
Sale of and contribution from noncontrolling interest, net of transaction costs	—	—	1,916,459	(1,712)	—		1,101,681	3,016,428
Dividends declared, net of amounts previously accrued	—	—	—	—	(87,843)		—	(87,843)
Accumulated but undeclared dividend requirement on preferred stock issued to Principal Stockholder's family	—	—	—	—	(6,854)		—	(6,854)
Accretion to redemption value of preferred stock issued to Principal Stockholder's family	—	—	—	—	(92,545)		—	(92,545)
Balance at December 31, 2009	234,607	660	5,114,851	26,748	473,833		1,089,888	6,940,587
Net income	—	—	—	—	599,394	599,394	182,209	781,603
Currency translation adjustment	—	—	—	102,771	—	102,771	(4,253)	98,518
Total comprehensive income						702,165	177,956	880,121
Exercise of stock options	—	2	16,453	—	—		—	16,455
Tax shortfall from stock-based compensation	—	—	(195)	—	—		—	(195)
Stock-based compensation	—	—	58,120	—	—		2,698	60,818
Exercise of warrants	(27,251)	46	252,719	—	—		—	225,514
Deemed contribution from Principal Stockholder	—	—	412	—	—		—	412
Acquisition of remaining shares of noncontrolling interest	—	—	2,345	—	—		(2,345)	—
Dividends declared, net of amounts previously accrued	—	—	—	—	(86,546)		—	(86,546)
Accumulated but undeclared dividend requirement on preferred stock issued to Principal Stockholder's family	—	—	—	—	(6,854)		—	(6,854)
Accretion to redemption value of preferred stock issued to Principal Stockholder's family	—	—	—	—	(92,545)		—	(92,545)
Preferred stock inducement premium	—	—	—	—	(6,579)		—	(6,579)
Balance at December 31, 2010	$207,356	$708	$5,444,705	$129,519	$ 880,703		$1,268,197	$7,931,188

The accompanying notes are an integral part of these consolidated financial statements.

NOTES TO CONSOLIDATED FINANCIAL STATEMENTS (in part)

Note 10—Equity (in part)

Preferred Stock Issued to Principal Stockholder's Family

Of the 10,446,300 shares of Preferred Stock issued, the Company issued 5,250,000 shares to the Principal Stockholder's family together with Warrants to purchase up to an aggregate of approximately 87,500,175 shares of its common stock and received gross proceeds of $525.0 million ($523.7 million, net of transaction costs). The allocated carrying values of the Preferred Stock and Warrants on the date of issuance (based on their relative fair values) were $301.1 million and $223.9 million, respectively. The Preferred Stock amount has been recorded as mezzanine equity on the accompanying consolidated balance sheet as the Principal Stockholder and his family have a greater than 50% ownership of the Company (when considering the impact of unexercised warrants and stock options) and therefore have the potential ability to require the Company to redeem their Preferred Stock beginning November 15, 2011.

As the Preferred Stock issued to the Principal Stockholder's family is being accounted for as redeemable at the option of the holder, the balance is being accreted to the redemption value of $577.5 million over three years. As of December 31, 2010 and 2009, $6.9 million of accumulated but undeclared dividends was recorded.

A summary of the Company's Preferred Stock issued its Principal Stockholder's family for the years ended December 31, 2010, 2009 and 2008, is presented below (in thousands, except number of shares):

	Number of Shares	Amount
Balance as of January 1, 2008	—	$ —
Issuance of preferred stock and warrants to purchase common stock, net of transaction costs	5,250,000	299,867
Accretion to redemption value	—	11,568
Accumulated but undeclared dividend requirement	—	6,854
Balance as of December 31, 2008	5,250,000	318,289
Accretion to redemption value	—	92,545
Dividends declared, net of amounts previously accrued	—	45,646
Dividends paid	—	(52,500)
Accumulated but undeclared dividend requirement	—	6,854
Balance as of December 31, 2009	5,250,000	410,834
Accretion to redemption value	—	92,545
Dividends declared, net of amounts previously accrued	—	45,646
Dividends paid	—	(52,500)
Accumulated but undeclared dividend requirement	—	6,854
Balance as of December 31, 2010	5,250,000	$503,379

Other Changes in Retained Earnings: Stock-Based Compensation

5.48

MEDTRONIC, INC. (APR)

CONSOLIDATED STATEMENTS OF SHAREHOLDERS' EQUITY

(In millions)	Common Shares	Common Stock	Retained Earnings	Accumulated Other Comprehensive Loss	Total Shareholders' Equity
Balance April 27, 2007	1,143	$114	$11,448	$ (62)	$11,500
Net earnings	—	—	2,138	—	2,138
Other comprehensive (loss)/income					
Unrealized loss on investments	—	—	—	(47)	(47)
Translation adjustment	—	—	—	14	14
Net change in retirement obligations	—	—	—	37	37
Unrealized loss on foreign currency exchange rate derivatives	—	—	—	(211)	(211)
Total comprehensive income	—	—			1,931
Dividends to shareholders	—	—	(565)	—	(565)
Issuance of common stock under stock purchase and award plans	13	1	402	—	403
Adjustment to deferred tax benefit recorded on adoption of new authoritative guidance for accounting for defined benefit pension and other post-retirement plans	—	—	—	(17)	(17)
Repurchase of common stock	(31)	(3)	(1,541)	—	(1,544)
Excess tax benefit from exercise of stock-based awards	—	—	40	—	40
Stock-based compensation	—	—	217	—	217
Cumulative effect adjustment to retained earnings to initially apply guidance concerning uncertainty in income taxes (Note 14)	—	—	1	—	1
Balance April 25, 2008	1,125	$112	$12,140	$(286)	$11,966
Net earnings	—	—	2,070	—	2,070
Other comprehensive (loss)/income					
Unrealized loss on investments	—	—	—	(54)	(54)
Translation adjustment	—	—	—	(147)	(147)
Net change in retirement obligations	—	—	—	(210)	(210)
Unrealized gain on foreign currency exchange rate derivatives	—	—	—	494	494
Total comprehensive income	—	—			2,153
Dividends to shareholders	—	—	(843)	—	(843)
Issuance of common stock under stock purchase and award plans	11	2	414	—	416
Adjustment for change in plan measurement date pursuant to the new authoritative guidance for accounting for defined benefit pension and other post-retirement plans	—	—	(13)	1	(12)
Repurchase of common stock	(17)	(2)	(757)	—	(759)
Excess tax benefit from exercise of stock-based awards	—	—	24	—	24
Stock-based compensation	—	—	237	—	237
Balance April 24, 2009	1,119	$112	$13,272	$(202)	$13,182
Net earnings	—	—	3,099	—	3,099
Other comprehensive (loss)/income					
Unrealized gain on investments	—	—	—	68	68
Translation adjustment	—	—	—	181	181
Net change in retirement obligations	—	—	—	(214)	(214)
Unrealized loss on foreign currency exchange rate derivatives	—	—	—	(137)	(137)
Reclassification of other-than-temporary losses on marketable securities included in net income	—	—	3	(3)	—
Total comprehensive income					2,997
Dividends to shareholders	—	—	(907)	—	(907)
Issuance of common stock under stock purchase and award plans	5	1	164	—	165
Repurchase of common stock	(27)	(3)	(1,027)	—	(1,030)
Excess tax benefit from exercise of stock-based awards	—	—	(3)	—	(3)
Stock-based compensation	—	—	225	—	225
Balance April 30, 2010	1,097	$110	$14,826	$(307)	$14,629

The accompanying notes are an integral part of these consolidated financial statements.

NOTES TO CONSOLIDATED FINANCIAL STATEMENTS (in part)

13. Stock Purchase and Award Plans (in part)

Stock-Based Compensation Expense Upon the adoption of the fair value recognition provisions of U.S. GAAP for accounting for stock-based compensation, the Company changed its method of recognition and now recognizes stock-based compensation expense based on the substantive vesting period for all new awards. As a result, compensation expense related to stock options granted prior to fiscal year 2007 is being recognized over the stated vesting term of the grant rather than being accelerated upon retirement eligibility.

The amount of stock-based compensation expense recognized during a period is based on the portion of the awards that are ultimately expected to vest. The Company estimates pre-vesting forfeitures at the time of grant by analyzing historical data and revises those estimates in subsequent periods if actual forfeitures differ from those estimates. Ultimately, the total expense recognized over the vesting period will equal the fair value of awards that actually vest.

The following table presents the components and classification of stock-based compensation expense, for options, restricted stock awards and ESPP shares recognized for fiscal years 2010, 2009 and 2008:

	Fiscal Year		
(In millions)	2010	2009	2008
Stock options	$112	$140	$138
Restricted stock awards	98	82	63
Employee stock purchase plan	15	15	16
Total stock-based compensation expense	$225	$237	$217
Cost of products sold	$26	$28	$24
Research and development expense	55	58	52
Selling, general and administrative expense	144	151	141
Total stock-based compensation expense	$225	$237	$217
Income tax benefits	(67)	(69)	(64)
Total stock-based compensation expense, net of tax	$158	$168	$153

In connection with the acquisition of Kyphon in November 2007, the Company assumed Kyphon's unvested stock-based awards. These awards are amortized over 2.5 years, which was their remaining weighted average vesting period at the time of acquisition. For fiscal years 2010, 2009 and 2008 the Company recognized $12 million, $21 million and $24 million respectively, of stock-based compensation expense associated with the assumed Kyphon awards, which is included in the amounts presented above.

SPINOFFS

RECOGNITION AND MEASUREMENT

5.49   The distributions of nonmonetary assets that constitute a business to owners of an entity are commonly referred to as spinoffs. A *business* is defined as an integrated set of activities and assets that is capable of being conducted and managed for the purpose of providing a return in the form of dividends, lower costs, or other economic benefits directly to investors or other owners, members, or participants. Spinoffs are discussed in FASB ASC 505-60.

5.50   The accounting for the distribution of nonmonetary assets to owners of an entity in a spinoff should be based on the recorded amount (after reduction, if appropriate, for an indicated impairment of value). An entity's distribution of the shares of a wholly owned or consolidated subsidiary to its shareholders should be recorded based on the carrying value of the subsidiary. Regardless of whether the spun-off operations will be sold immediately after the spinoff, the transaction should not be accounted for as a sale of the accounting spinnee followed by a distribution of the proceeds. In order to determine the required accounting and reporting in a spinoff transaction, an entity needs to determine which party is the accounting spinnor and which is the accounting spinnee. The accounting spinnee should be reported as a discontinued operation by the accounting spinnor if the spinnee is a component of an entity and meets the conditions for such reporting.

PRESENTATION AND DISCLOSURE EXCERPTS

Spinoffs

5.51

IDT CORPORATION (JUL)

CONSOLIDATED STATEMENTS OF EQUITY

					IDT Corporation Stockholders							
	Common Stock		Class A Common Stock		Class B Common Stock		Additional Paid-In Capital	Treasury Stock	Accumulated Other Comprehensive Income (Loss)	Accumulated Deficit	Non-controlling Interests	Total Equity
(In thousands)	Shares	Amount	Shares	Amount	Shares	Amount						
Balance at July 31, 2008	8,358	$84	3,272	$33	21,301	$213	$717,256	$(285,536)	$6,754	$(96,467)	$5,850	$348,187
Issuance of shares of Class B common stock through employee stock purchase plan	—	—	—	—	36	—	36	—	—	—	—	36
Restricted Class B common stock purchased from employees	—	—	—	—	—	—	—	(45)	—	—	—	(45)
Repurchases of common stock and Class B common stock through repurchase program	—	—	—	—	—	—	—	(8,320)	—	—	—	(8,320)
Stock-based compensation	—	—	—	—	—	—	3,356	—	—	—	—	3,356
Restricted stock issued to employees and directors	883	8	—	—	1,576	16	(24)	—	—	—	—	—
Sales of stock of subsidiaries	—	—	—	—	—	—	180	—	—	—	671	851
Distributions to noncontrolling interests	—	—	—	—	—	—	—	—	—	—	(4,376)	(4,376)
Other	—	—	—	—	—	—	—	—	—	—	(767)	(767)
Change in unrealized gain (loss) on available-for-sale securities	—	—	—	—	—	—	—	—	3,173	—	—	3,173
Foreign currency translation adjustment	—	—	—	—	—	—	—	—	(8,974)	—	—	(8,974)
Net loss for the year ended July 31, 2009	—	—	—	—	—	—	—	—	(155,449)	(155,449)	1,770	(153,679)
Comprehensive (loss) income									$(161,250)			$1,770 $(159,480)
Balance at July 31, 2009	9,241	92	3,272	33	22,913	229	720,804	(293,901)	953	(251,916)	3,148	179,442
Restricted Class B common stock purchased from employee	—	—	—	—	—	—	—	(89)	—	—	—	(89)
Repurchases of common stock and Class B common stock through repurchase program	—	—	—	—	—	—	—	(1,790)	—	—	—	(1,790)
Exercise of stock options, net of 7 shares issued from treasury	—	—	—	—	6	—	(64)	154	—	—	—	90
Stock-based compensation	—	—	—	—	—	—	2,541	—	—	—	—	2,541
Restricted stock issued to employees and directors	—	—	—	—	294	3	(3)	—	—	—	—	—
Sales of stock of subsidiaries	—	—	—	—	—	—	2,415	—	—	—	3,075	5,490
Distributions to noncontrolling interests	—	—	—	—	—	—	—	—	—	—	(2,374)	(2,374)
CTM Spin-Off	—	—	—	—	—	—	(13,992)	—	(177)	—	(1,617)	(15,786)
Change in unrealized gain (loss) on available-for-sale securities	—	—	—	—	—	—	—	—	(311)	—	—	(311)
Foreign currency translation adjustment	—	—	—	—	—	—	—	—	(1,482)	—	(31)	(1,513)
Net income for the year ended July 31, 2010	—	—	—	—	—	—	—	—	20,290	20,290	(17)	20,273
Comprehensive income (loss)									$18,497			$(48) $18,449
Balance at July 31, 2010	9,241	$92	3,272	$33	23,213	$232	$711,701	$(295,626)	$(1,017)	$(231,626)	$2,184	$185,973

See accompanying notes to consolidated financial statements.

NOTES TO CONSOLIDATED FINANCIAL STATEMENTS (in part)

Note 2—Discontinued Operations and Other Dispositions (in part)

CTM Media Holdings, Inc.

On September 14, 2009, the Company completed a pro rata distribution of the common stock of CTM Media Holdings, Inc. ("CTM Holdings") to the Company's stockholders of record as of the close of business on August 3, 2009 (the "CTM Spin-Off"). CTM Holdings' businesses at the time of the CTM Spin-Off included CTM Media Group, IDW Publishing and WMET 1160AM. CTM Holdings and subsidiaries met the criteria to be reported as discontinued operations and accordingly, their assets, liabilities, results of operations and cash flows are classified as discontinued operations for all periods presented. As of September 14, 2009, each of the Company's stockholders of record as of the close of business on the record date received: (i) one share of CTM Holdings Class A common stock for every three shares of the Company's common stock; (ii) one share of CTM Holdings Class B common stock for every three shares of the Company's Class B common stock; (iii) one share of CTM Holdings Class C common stock for every three shares of the Company's Class A common stock; and (iv) cash in lieu of a fractional share of all classes of CTM Holdings' common stock.

In September 2009, prior to the CTM Spin-Off, the Company funded CTM Holdings with an additional $2.0 million in cash.

TREASURY STOCK

PRESENTATION

5.52   Repurchased common stock is often referred to as treasury stock or treasury shares. FASB ASC 505-30 discusses the balance sheet presentation of treasury stock and states that if a corporation's stock is acquired for purposes other than retirement (formal or constructive), or if ultimate disposition has not yet been decided, the cost of acquired stock may be shown separately as a deduction from the total of capital stock, additional paid-in capital, and retained earnings or may be accorded the accounting treatment appropriate for retired stock.

5.53   A repurchase of shares at a price significantly in excess of the current market price creates a presumption that the repurchase price includes amounts attributable to items other than the shares repurchased. A repurchase of shares at a price significantly in excess of the current market price may require an entity to allocate amounts to other elements of the transaction. As shown in Table 5-8, the prevalent balance sheet presentation of treasury stock is to show the cost of treasury stock as a reduction of stockholders' equity.

5.54

TABLE 5-8: TREASURY STOCK—BALANCE SHEET PRESENTATION

	2010	2009	2008
Common Stock			
Cost of treasury stock shown as stockholders' equity deduction	292	316	318
Cost of treasury stock deducted from total capital	18	N/C*	N/C*
Cost of treasury stock deducted from stock of the same class	12	5	10
Par or stated value of treasury stock deducted from issued stock of the same class	—	19	20
Other	1	—	2
Total Presentations	**323**	**340**	**350**
Preferred Stock			
Par value of treasury stock deducted from stock of the same class	1	N/C*	N/C*
Cost of treasury stock shown as stockholders' equity deduction	—	—	—
Other	—	—	—
Total Presentations	**1**	**—**	**—**

	Number of Entities		
Disclosing treasury stock	323	340	350
Not disclosing treasury stock	177	160	150
Total Entities	**500**	**500**	**500**

* N/C = Not compiled. Line item was not included in the table for the year shown.

PRESENTATION AND DISCLOSURE EXCERPTS

Treasury Stock

5.55

THE TJX COMPANIES, INC. (JAN)

CONSOLIDATED BALANCE SHEETS (in part)

	Fiscal Year Ended	
(In thousands)	January 30, 2010	January 31, 2009
Shareholders' equity		
Common stock, authorized 1,200,000,000 shares, par value $1, issued and outstanding 409,386,126 and 412,821,592, respectively	409,386	412,822
Additional paid-in capital	—	—
Accumulated other comprehensive income (loss)	(134,124)	(217,781)
Retained earnings	2,614,014	1,939,516
Total shareholders' equity	2,889,276	2,134,557

CONSOLIDATED STATEMENTS OF SHAREHOLDERS' EQUITY

(In thousands)	Shares	Common Stock Par Value $1	Additional Paid-In Capital	Accumulated Other Comprehensive Income (Loss)	Retained Earnings	Total
Balance, January 27, 2007	453,650	$453,650	$ —	$ (33,989)	$1,870,460	$2,290,121
Comprehensive income:						
Net income	—	—	—	—	771,750	771,750
Gain due to foreign currency translation adjustments	—	—	—	20,998	—	20,998
(Loss) on net investment hedge contracts	—	—	—	(15,823)	—	(15,823)
(Loss) on cash flow hedge contracts	—	—	—	(1,526)	—	(1,526)
Recognition of prior service cost and gains (losses)	—	—	—	1,393	—	1,393
Amount of cash flow hedge reclassified from other comprehensive income to net income	—	—	—	429	—	429
Total comprehensive income						777,221
Implementation of accounting for uncertain tax positions (see note K)	—	—	—	—	(27,178)	(27,178)
Implementation of the measurement provisions relating to retirement obligations (see note L)	—	—	—	(167)	(1,641)	(1,808)
Cash dividends declared on common stock	—	—	—	—	(158,202)	(158,202)
Amortization of share-based compensation expense	—	—	57,370	—	—	57,370
Stock options repurchased by TJX	—	—	(3,266)	—	—	(3,266)
Issuance of common stock under stock incentive plan and related tax effect	7,253	7,253	129,942	—	—	137,195
Common stock repurchased	(32,953)	(32,953)	(184,046)	—	(723,209)	(940,208)
Balance, January 26, 2008	427,950	427,950	—	(28,685)	1,731,980	2,131,245
Comprehensive income:						
Net income	—	—	—	—	880,617	880,617
(Loss) due to foreign currency translation adjustments	—	—	—	(171,225)	—	(171,225)
Gain on net investment hedge contracts	—	—	—	68,816	—	68,816
Recognition of prior service cost and gains (losses)	—	—	—	(1,206)	—	(1,206)
Recognition of unfunded post retirement liabilities	—	—	—	(86,158)	—	(86,158)
Amount of cash flow hedge reclassified from other comprehensive income to net income	—	—	—	677	—	677
Total comprehensive income						691,521
Cash dividends declared on common stock	—	—	—	—	(183,694)	(183,694)
Amortization of share-based compensation expense	—	—	51,229	—	—	51,229
Issuance of common stock upon conversion of convertible debt	1,717	1,717	39,326	—	—	41,043
Stock options repurchased by TJX	—	—	(987)	—	—	(987)
Issuance of common stock under stock incentive plan and related tax effect	7,439	7,439	147,858	—	—	155,297
Common stock repurchased	(24,284)	(24,284)	(237,426)	—	(489,387)	(751,097)
Balance, January 31, 2009	412,822	412,822	—	(217,781)	1,939,516	2,134,557
Comprehensive income:						
Net income	—	—	—	—	1,213,572	1,213,572
Gain due to foreign currency translation adjustments	—	—	—	76,678	—	76,678
Recognition of prior service cost and gains (losses)	—	—	—	8,191	—	8,191
Recognition of unfunded post retirement liabilities	—	—	—	(1,212)	—	(1,212)
Total comprehensive income						1,297,229
Cash dividends declared on common stock	—	—	—	—	(201,490)	(201,490)
Amortization of share-based compensation expense	—	—	55,145	—	—	55,145
Issuance of common stock upon conversion of convertible debt	15,094	15,094	349,994	—	—	365,088
Issuance of common stock under stock incentive plan and related tax effect	8,329	8,329	175,180	—	—	183,509
Common stock repurchased	(26,859)	(26,859)	(580,319)	—	(337,584)	(944,762)
Balance, January 30, 2010	409,386	$409,386	$ —	$(134,124)	$2,614,014	$2,889,276

The accompanying notes are an integral part of the financial statements.

NOTES TO CONSOLIDATED FINANCIAL STATEMENTS (in part)

A. Summary of Accounting Policies (in part)

Common Stock and Equity (in part): Equity transactions consist primarily of the repurchase of our common stock under our stock repurchase programs and the amortization of expense and issuance of common stock under our stock incentive plan. In fiscal 2010, we also issued shares upon conversion of convertible notes called for redemption, discussed in Note D. Under our stock repurchase programs we repurchase our common stock on the open market. The par value of the shares repurchased is charged to common stock with the excess of the purchase price over par first charged against any available additional paid-in capital ("APIC") and the balance charged to retained earnings. Due to the high volume of repurchases over the past several years, we have no remaining balance in APIC in any of the years presented. All shares repurchased have been retired.

I. Capital Stock and Earnings Per Share (in part)

Capital Stock (in part): In December 2009, we completed a $1 billion stock repurchase program which began in fiscal 2009 and initiated another multi-year $1 billion stock repurchase program approved in September 2009. We repurchased and retired 27.0 million shares of our common stock at a cost of $949.9 million during fiscal 2010. TJX reflects stock repurchases in its financial statements on a "settlement" basis. We had cash expenditures under our repurchase programs of $944.8 million in fiscal 2010, $751.1 million in fiscal 2009 and $940.2 million in fiscal 2008, funded primarily by cash generated from operations. We repurchased 26.9 million shares in fiscal 2010, 24.3 million shares in fiscal 2009 and 33.0 million shares in fiscal 2008. As of January 30, 2010, on a "trade date" basis, we had repurchased 5.5 million shares of our common stock at a cost of $205.0 million under the $1 billion stock repurchase program authorized in September 2009. All shares repurchased under our stock repurchase programs have been retired.

In February 2010, TJX's Board of Directors approved a new stock repurchase program that authorizes the repurchase of up to an additional $1 billion of TJX common stock from time to time.

OTHER COMPONENTS OF STOCKHOLDERS' EQUITY

PRESENTATION

5.56 For public entities, Rule 3-04 of Regulation S-X requires that an analysis of the changes in each caption of stockholders' equity and noncontrolling interests presented in the balance sheets should be given in a note or separate statement. This analysis should be presented in the form of a reconciliation of the beginning balance to the ending balance for each period for which an income statement is required to be filed, with all significant reconciling items described by appropriate captions and contributions from, and distributions to, owners shown separately.

5.57 Many of the survey entities present accounts other than capital stock, additional paid-in capital, retained earnings, accumulated other comprehensive income, and treasury stock in the "Stockholders' Equity" section of the balance sheet. Other stockholders' equity accounts appearing on the balance sheets of the survey entities include, but are not limited to, guarantees of employee stock ownership plan debt, unearned or deferred compensation related to employee stock award plans, and amounts owed to an entity by employees for loans to buy company stock, in each instance pursuant to relevant FASB ASC requirements. Other items, such as foreign currency translation adjustments, unrealized gains and losses on certain investments in debt and equity securities, and defined benefit postretirement plan adjustments, are considered components of other comprehensive income. FASB ASC 220, *Comprehensive Income*, permits the presentation of components of other comprehensive income and total comprehensive income in a statement of changes in stockholders' equity.

DISCLOSURE

5.58 In addition, FASB ASC 220 allows disclosure of accumulated balances, by component, included in accumulated other comprehensive income in a statement of changes in stockholders' equity.

5.59 FASB ASC 810, *Consolidation*, establishes accounting and reporting standards for the noncontrolling interest in a subsidiary. It clarifies that a *noncontrolling interest in a subsidiary* is an ownership interest in the consolidated entity that should be reported as equity in the consolidated financial statements but separate from the parent's equity, and clearly identified and labeled. In addition, FASB ASC 810 requires expanded disclosures in the consolidated financial statements that clearly identify and distinguish between the interests of the parent's owners and the interests of the noncontrolling owners of a subsidiary. Those expanded disclosures include a reconciliation of the beginning and ending balances of the equity attributable to the parent and noncontrolling owners and a schedule showing the effects of changes in a parent's ownership interest in a subsidiary on the equity attributable to the parent.

5.60

TABLE 5-9: OTHER STOCKHOLDERS' EQUITY ACCOUNTS

Table 5-9 shows the number of survey company balance sheets presenting other stockholders' equity accounts.

	Number of Entities		
	2010	2009	2008
Noncontrolling interests	240	156	—
Warrants	2	30	21
Unearned compensation	12	17	20
Employee benefit trusts	10	11	13
Guarantees of employee stock ownership plan debt	12	10	13
Receivables from the sale of stock	2	3	5
Other, described	20	N/C*	N/C*

* N/C = Not compiled. Line item was not included in the table for the year shown.

PRESENTATION AND DISCLOSURE EXCERPTS

Unearned Compensation

5.61

COLGATE-PALMOLIVE COMPANY (DEC)

CONSOLIDATED BALANCE SHEETS (in part)

	As of December 31	
(Dollars in millions except per share amounts)	2010	2009
Shareholders' equity		
Preference stock	—	169
Common stock, $1 par value (2,000,000,000 shares authorized, 732,853,180 shares issued)	733	733
Additional paid-in capital	1,132	1,764
Retained earnings	14,329	13,157
Accumulated other comprehensive income (loss)	(2,115)	(2,096)
	14,079	13,727
Unearned compensation	(99)	(133)
Treasury stock, at cost	(11,305)	(10,478)
Total Colgate-Palmolive Company shareholders' equity	2,675	3,116
Noncontrolling interests	142	141
Total shareholders' equity	2,817	3,257
Total liabilities and shareholders' equity	$11,172	$11,134

CONSOLIDATED STATEMENTS OF CHANGES IN SHAREHOLDERS' EQUITY

(Dollars in millions)	Colgate-Palmolive Company Shareholders' Equity							Non-controlling Interests
	Preference Stock	Common Stock	Additional Paid-In Capital	Unearned Compensation	Treasury Stock	Retained Earnings	Accumulated Other Comprehensive Income (Loss)	
Balance, January 1, 2008	$198	$733	$1,518	$(219)	$ (8,904)	$10,628	$(1,667)	$110
Net income						1,957		80
Other comprehensive income, net of tax							(810)	(5)
Dividends declared:								
Series B Convertible Preference stock, net of taxes						(28)		
Common stock						(797)		
Noncontrolling interests in Company's subsidiaries								(64)
Stock-based compensation expense			100					
Shares issued for stock options			61		157			
Treasury stock acquired					(1,073)			
Preference stock conversion	(17)		(66)		83			
Other			(3)	32	40			
Balance, December 31, 2008	$181	$733	$1,610	$(187)	$ (9,697)	$11,760	$(2,477)	$121
Net income						2,291		106
Other comprehensive income, net of tax							381	1
Dividends declared:								
Series B Convertible Preference stock, net of taxes						(30)		
Common stock						(864)		
Noncontrolling interests in Company's subsidiaries								(87)
Stock-based compensation expense			117					
Shares issued for stock options			92		175			
Treasury stock acquired					(1,063)			
Preference stock conversion	(12)		(48)		60			
Other			(7)	54	47			
Balance, December 31, 2009	$169	$733	$1,764	$(133)	$(10,478)	$13,157	$(2,096)	$141
Net income						2,203		110
Other comprehensive income, net of tax							(19)	2
Dividends declared:								
Series B Convertible Preference stock, net of taxes						(34)		
Common stock						(997)		
Noncontrolling interests in Company's subsidiaries								(111)
Stock-based compensation expense			121					
Shares issued for stock options			56		153			
Treasury stock acquired					(2,020)			
Preference stock conversion	(169)		(813)		982			
Other			4	34	58			
Balance, December 31, 2010	$—	$733	$1,132	$(99)	$(11,305)	$14,329	$(2,115)	$142

See Notes to Consolidated Financial Statements.

NOTES TO CONSOLIDATED FINANCIAL STATEMENTS *(in part)*

9. Employee Stock Ownership Plan (in part)

(Dollars in millions except per share amounts)

Annual expense related to the leveraged ESOP, determined as interest incurred on the original notes, plus the higher of either principal payments or the historical cost of Preference stock allocated, less dividends received on the shares held by the ESOP and advances from the Company, was $6 in 2010, $22 in 2009 and $7 in 2008. Unearned compensation, which is shown as a reduction in Shareholders' equity, is the amount of ESOP debt due to the Company.

Deferred Compensation

5.62

NVR, INC. (DEC)

CONSOLIDATED BALANCE SHEETS (in part)

	December 31	
(In thousands, except share and per share data)	**2010**	**2009**
Shareholders' equity:		
Common stock, $0.01 par value; 60,000,000 shares authorized; 20,557,913 and 20,559,671 shares issued as of December 31, 2010 and 2009, respectively	206	206
Additional paid-in-capital	951,234	830,531
Deferred compensation trust—158,894 and 265,278 shares of NVR, Inc. common stock as of December 31, 2010 and 2009, respectively	(27,582)	(40,799)
Deferred compensation liability	27,582	40,799
Retained earnings	4,029,072	3,823,067
Less treasury stock at cost—14,894,357 and 14,609,560 shares as of December 31, 2010 and 2009, respectively	(3,240,138)	(2,896,542)
Total shareholders' equity	1,740,374	1,757,262

CONSOLIDATED STATEMENTS OF SHAREHOLDERS' EQUITY

(In thousands)	Common Stock	Additional Paid-in Capital	Retained Earnings	Treasury Stock	Deferred Compensation Trust	Deferred Compensation Liability	Total
Balance, December 31, 2007	$206	$663,631	$3,529,995	$(3,064,457)	$(75,636)	$75,636	$1,129,375
Net income	—	—	100,892	—	—	—	100,892
Deferred compensation activity	—	—	—	—	786	(786)	—
Purchase of common stock for treasury	—	—	—	—	(128)	128	—
Stock-based compensation	—	41,204	—	—	—	—	41,204
Tax benefit from stock options exercised and deferred compensation distributions	—	50,240	—	—	—	—	50,240
Proceeds from stock options exercised	—	52,078	—	—	—	—	52,078
Treasury stock issued upon option exercise	—	(84,888)	—	84,888	—	—	—
Balance, December 31, 2008	206	722,265	3,630,887	(2,979,569)	(74,978)	74,978	1,373,789
Net income	—	—	192,180	—	—	—	192,180
Deferred compensation activity	—	—	—	—	34,179	(34,179)	—
Stock-based compensation	—	46,302	—	—	—	—	46,302
Tax benefit from stock options exercised and deferred compensation distributions	—	66,448	—	—	—	—	66,448
Proceeds from stock options exercised	—	78,543	—	—	—	—	78,543
Treasury stock issued upon option exercise	—	(83,027)	—	83,027	—	—	—
Balance, December 31, 2009	206	830,531	3,823,067	(2,896,542)	(40,799)	40,799	1,757,262
Net income	—	—	206,005	—	—	—	206,005
Deferred compensation activity	—	—	—	—	13,217	(13,217)	—
Purchase of common stock for treasury	—	—	—	(417,079)	—	—	(417,079)
Stock-based compensation	—	53,136	—	—	—	—	53,136
Tax benefit from stock options exercised and deferred compensation distributions	—	63,558	—	—	—	—	63,558
Proceeds from stock options exercised	—	77,492	—	—	—	—	77,492
Treasury stock issued upon option exercise	—	(73,483)	—	73,483	—	—	—
Balance, December 31, 2010	$206	$951,234	$4,029,072	$(3,240,138)	$(27,582)	$27,582	$1,740,374

See notes to consolidated financial statements

NOTES TO CONSOLIDATED FINANCIAL STATEMENTS (in part)

(Dollars in thousands, except per share data)

9. Equity-Based Compensation, Profit Sharing and Deferred Compensation Plans (in part)

Deferred Compensation Plans

The Company has two deferred compensation plans ("Deferred Comp Plans"). The specific purpose of the Deferred Comp Plans is to i) establish a vehicle whereby named executive officers may defer the receipt of salary and bonus that otherwise would be nondeductible for Company tax purposes into a period where the Company would realize a tax deduction for the amounts paid, and ii) to enable certain of our employees who are subject to the Company's stock hold-ing requirements to acquire shares of our common stock on a pre-tax basis in order to more quickly meet, and maintain compliance with those stock holding requirements. Amounts deferred into the Deferred Comp Plans are invested in NVR common stock, held in a rabbi trust account, and are paid out in a fixed number of shares upon expiration of the deferral period.

The rabbi trust account held 158,894 and 265,278 shares of NVR common stock as of December 31, 2010 and 2009, respectively. During 2010, 106,384 shares of NVR common stock were issued from the rabbi trust related to deferred compensation for which the deferral period ended. There were no shares of NVR common stock contributed to the rabbi trust in 2010, 2009 or 2008. Shares held by the Deferred Comp Plan are treated as outstanding shares in the Company's earnings per share calculation for each of the years ended December 31, 2010, 2009 and 2008.

Deferred Costs—Employee Stock Ownership Plan (ESOP)

5.63

ELI LILLY AND COMPANY (DEC)

CONSOLIDATED BALANCE SHEETS (in part)

	December 31	
(Dollars in millions, shares in thousands)	**2010**	**2009**
Shareholders' Equity (Notes 9 and 11)		
Common stock—no par value		
Authorized shares: 3,200,000		
Issued shares: 1,153,154 (2010) and 1,149,916 (2009)	721.3	718.7
Additional paid-in capital	4,798.5	4,635.6
Retained earnings	12,732.6	9,830.4
Employee benefit trust	(3,013.2)	(3,013.2)
Deferred costs—ESOP	(52.4)	(77.4)
Accumulated other comprehensive loss (Note 16)	(2,670.1)	(2,471.9)
Noncontrolling interests	(7.5)	1.6
	12,509.2	9,623.8
Less cost of common stock in treasury		
2010— 864 shares		
2009— 882 shares	96.4	98.5
	12,412.8	9,525.3

NOTES TO CONSOLIDATED FINANCIAL STATEMENTS (in part)

Note 11. Shareholders' Equity

Changes in certain components of shareholders' equity were as follows:

(In thousands)	Additional Paid-in Capital	Retained Earnings	Deferred Costs- ESOP	Common Stock in Treasury Shares	Common Stock in Treasury Amount
Balance at January 1, 2008	$3,805.2	$11,806.7	$(95.2)	899	$100.5
Net loss		(2,071.9)			
Cash dividends declared per share: $1.90		(2,079.9)			
Retirement of treasury shares	(10.9)			(170)	(11.1)
Issuance of stock under employee stock plans-net	(84.9)			160	9.8
Stock-based compensation	255.3				
ESOP transactions	11.9		8.9		
Balance at December 31, 2008	3,976.6	7,654.9	(86.3)	889	99.2
Net income		4,328.8			
Cash dividends declared per share: $1.96		(2,153.3)			
Retirement of treasury shares	(3.3)			(132)	(3.3)
Issuance of stock under employee stock plans-net	(85.0)			125	2.6
Stock-based compensation	368.5				
ESOP transactions	6.9		8.9		
Employee benefit trust contribution	371.9				
Balance at December 31, 2009	4,635.6	9,830.4	(77.4)	882	98.5
Net income		5,069.5			
Cash dividends declared per share: $1.96		(2,167.3)			
Retirement of treasury shares	(1.0)			(28)	(1.0)
Issuance of stock under employee stock plans-net	(87.6)			10	(1.1)
Stock-based compensation	231.0				
ESOP transactions	20.5		25.0		
Balance at December 31, 2010	$4,798.5	$12,732.6	$(52.4)	864	$ 96.4

As of December 31, 2010, we have purchased $2.58 billion of our announced $3.0 billion share repurchase program. No shares were repurchased in 2010, 2009, or 2008.

We have 5 million authorized shares of preferred stock. As of December 31, 2010 and 2009, no preferred stock has been issued.

We have an employee benefit trust which held 50.0 million and 50.0 million shares of our common stock at December 31, 2010 and 2009, respectively, to provide a source of funds to assist us in meeting our obligations under various employee benefit plans. In February 2009, we contributed an additional 10 million shares to the employee benefit trust, which resulted in a reclassification within equity from additional paid-in capital of $371.9 million and common stock of $6.3 million to the employee benefit trust of $378.2 million. The funding had no net impact on shareholders' equity as we consolidate the employee benefit trust. The cost basis of the shares held in the trust was $3.01 billion and $3.01 billion at December 31, 2010 and 2009, respectively, and is shown as a reduction in shareholders' equity. Any dividend transactions between us and the trust are eliminated. Stock held by the trust is not considered outstanding in the computation of earnings per share. The assets of the trust were not used to fund any of our obligations under these employee benefit plans in 2010, 2009, or 2008.

We have an ESOP as a funding vehicle for the existing employee savings plan. The ESOP used the proceeds of a loan from us to purchase shares of common stock from the treasury. The ESOP issued third-party debt, repayment of which was guaranteed by us (see Note 8). The proceeds were used to purchase shares of our common stock on the open market. Shares of common stock held by the ESOP will be allocated to participating employees annually through 2017 as part of our savings plan contribution. The fair value of shares allocated each period is recognized as compensation expense.

Employee Benefit Trusts

5.64

KB HOME (NOV)

CONSOLIDATED BALANCE SHEETS (in part)

	November 30	
(In thousands, except shares)	2010	2009
Stockholders' equity:		
Preferred stock—$1.00 par value; authorized, 10,000,000 shares; none issued	—	—
Common stock—$1.00 par value; authorized, 290,000,000 shares at November 30, 2010 and 2009; 115,148,586 and 115,120,305 shares issued at November 30, 2010 and 2009, respectively	115,149	115,120
Paid-in capital	873,519	860,772
Retained earnings	717,852	806,443
Accumulated other comprehensive loss	(22,657)	(22,244)
Grantor stock ownership trust, at cost: 11,082,723 and 11,228,951 shares at November 30, 2010 and 2009, respectively	(120,442)	(122,017)
Treasury stock, at cost: 27,095,467 and 27,047,379 shares at November 30, 2010 and 2009, respectively	(931,543)	(930,850)
Total stockholders' equity	631,878	707,224

CONSOLIDATED STATEMENTS OF STOCKHOLDERS' EQUITY

Years Ended November 30, 2010, 2009 and 2008

(In thousands)	Number of Shares — Common Stock	Number of Shares — Grantor Stock Ownership Trust	Number of Shares — Treasury Stock	Common Stock	Paid-in Capital	Retained Earnings	Accumulated Other Comprehensive Income (Loss)	Grantor Stock Ownership Trust	Treasury Stock	Total Stock-holders' Equity
Balance at November 30, 2007	114,976	(12,203)	(25,451)	$114,976	$851,628	$1,968,881	$(22,923)	$(132,608)	$(929,267)	$1,850,687
Comprehensive loss:										
Net loss	—	—	—	—	(976,131)	—	—	—	—	(976,131)
Postretirement benefits adjustment	—	—	—	—	—	—	5,521	—	—	5,521
Total comprehensive loss	—	—	—	—	—	—	—	—	—	(970,610)
Dividends on common stock	—	—	—	—	—	(62,967)	—	—	—	(62,967)
Adoption of new income tax accounting guidance	—	—	—	—	—	(2,459)	—	—	—	(2,459)
Exercise of employee stock options	144	—	—	144	1,443	—	—	—	—	1,587
Restricted stock amortization	—	—	—	—	4,946	—	—	—	—	4,946
Stock-based compensation	—	—	—	—	5,018	—	—	—	—	5,018
Grantor stock ownership trust	—	302	—	—	2,088	—	—	3,282	—	5,370
Treasury stock	—	—	(61)	—	—	—	—	—	(967)	(967)
Balance at November 30, 2008	115,120	(11,901)	(25,512)	115,120	865,123	927,324	(17,402)	(129,326)	(930,234)	830,605
Comprehensive loss:										
Net loss	—	—	—	—	—	(101,784)	—	—	—	(101,784)
Postretirement benefits adjustment	—	—	—	—	—	—	(4,842)	—	—	(4,842)
Total comprehensive loss	—	—	—	—	—	—	—	—	—	(106,626)
Dividends on common stock	—	—	—	—	—	(19,097)	—	—	—	(19,097)
Exercise of employee stock options	—	—	—	—	(4,093)	—	—	—	—	(4,093)
Restricted stock awards	—	—	—	—	(4,846)	—	—	4,846	—	—
Restricted stock amortization	—	—	—	—	1,390	—	—	—	—	1,390
Stock-based compensation	—	—	—	—	2,587	—	—	—	—	2,587
Grantor stock ownership trust	—	672	—	—	611	—	—	2,463	—	3,074
Treasury stock	—	—	(1,535)	—	—	—	—	—	(616)	(616)
Balance at November 30, 2009	115,120	(11,229)	(27,047)	115,120	860,772	806,443	(22,244)	(122,017)	(930,850)	707,224
Comprehensive loss:										
Net loss	—	—	—	—	—	(69,368)	—	—	—	(69,368)
Postretirement benefits adjustment	—	—	—	—	—	—	(413)	—	—	(413)
Total comprehensive loss	—	—	—	—	—	—	—	—	—	(69,781)
Dividends on common stock	—	—	—	—	—	(19,223)	—	—	—	(19,223)
Exercise of employee stock options	29	—	—	29	2,074	—	—	—	—	2,103
Restricted stock awards	—	—	—	—	(307)	—	—	307	—	—
Restricted stock amortization	—	—	—	—	2,297	—	—	—	—	2,297
Stock-based compensation	—	—	—	—	5,777	—	—	—	—	5,777
Cash-settled stock appreciation rights exchange	—	—	—	—	2,348	—	—	—	—	2,348
Grantor stock ownership trust	—	146	—	—	215	—	—	1,268	—	1,483
Treasury stock	—	—	(48)	—	343	—	—	—	(693)	(350)
Balance at November 30, 2010	115,149	(11,083)	(27,095)	$115,149	$873,519	$717,852	$(22,657)	$(120,442)	$(931,543)	$631,878

See accompanying notes.

NOTES TO CONSOLIDATED FINANCIAL STATEMENTS (in part)

Note 18. Employee Benefit and Stock Plans (in part)

Grantor Stock Ownership Trust. On August 27, 1999, the Company established a grantor stock ownership trust (the "Trust") into which certain shares repurchased in 2000 and 1999 were transferred. The Trust, administered by a third-party trustee, holds and distributes the shares of common stock acquired to support certain employee compensation and employee benefit obligations of the Company under its existing stock option, the 401(k) Plan and other employee benefit plans. The existence of the Trust has no impact on the amount of benefits or compensation that is paid under these plans.

For financial reporting purposes, the Trust is consolidated with the Company. Any dividend transactions between the Company and the Trust are eliminated. Acquired shares held by the Trust remain valued at the market price at the date of purchase and are shown as a reduction to stockholders' equity in the consolidated balance sheets. The difference between the Trust share value and the market value on the date shares are released from the Trust is included in paid-in capital. Common stock held in the Trust is not considered outstanding in the computations of earnings (loss) per share. The Trust held 11,082,723 and 11,228,951 shares of common stock at November 30, 2010 and 2009, respectively. The trustee votes shares held by the Trust in accordance with voting directions from eligible employees, as specified in a trust agreement with the trustee.

Warrants

5.65

FEDERAL-MOGUL CORPORATION (DEC)

CONSOLIDATED BALANCE SHEETS (in part)

	December 31	
(Millions of dollars)	**2010**	**2009**
Shareholders' equity:		
Preferred stock ($.01 par value; 90,000,000 authorized shares; none issued)	—	—
Common stock ($.01 par value; 450,100,000 authorized shares; 100,500,000 issued shares; 98,904,500 outstanding shares as of both December 31, 2010 and 2009)	1	1
Additional paid-in capital, including warrants	2,150	2,123
Accumulated deficit	(352)	(513)
Accumulated other comprehensive loss	(505)	(571)
Treasury stock, at cost	(17)	(17)
Total Federal-Mogul shareholders' equity	1,277	1,023
Noncontrolling interests	88	76
Total shareholders' equity	1,365	1,099

NOTES TO CONSOLIDATED FINANCIAL STATEMENTS (in part)

17. Warrants

On December 27, 2007, the Company issued 6,951,871 warrants to purchase common shares of the Company at an exercise price equal to $45.815, exercisable through December 27, 2014. All of these warrants remain outstanding as of December 31, 2010.

Redeemable Preferred Stock

5.66

WHOLE FOODS MARKET, INC. (SEP)

CONSOLIDATED BALANCE SHEETS (in part)

(In thousands)
September 26, 2010 and September 27, 2009

	2010	**2009**
Liabilities and Shareholders' Equity		
Current liabilities:		
Current installments of long-term debt and capital lease obligations	$ 410	$ 389
Accounts payable	213,212	189,597
Accrued payroll, bonus and other benefits due team members	244,427	207,983
Dividends payable	—	8,217
Other current liabilities	289,823	277,838
Total current liabilities	747,872	684,024
Long-term debt and capital lease obligations, less current installments	508,288	738,848
Deferred lease liabilities	294,291	250,326
Other long-term liabilities	62,831	69,262
Total liabilities	1,613,282	1,742,460
Series A redeemable preferred stock, $0.01 par value, 425 shares authorized; zero and 425 shares issued and outstanding at 2010 and 2009, respectively	—	413,052
Shareholders' equity:		
Common stock, no par value, 300,000 shares authorized; 172,033 and 140,542 shares issued and outstanding at 2010 and 2009, respectively	1,773,897	1,283,028
Accumulated other comprehensive income (loss)	791	(13,367)
Retained earnings	598,570	358,215
Total shareholders' equity	2,373,258	1,627,876
Commitments and contingencies		
Total liabilities and shareholders' equity	$3,986,540	$3,783,388

CONSOLIDATED STATEMENTS OF SHAREHOLDERS' EQUITY AND COMPREHENSIVE INCOME

(In thousands)
Fiscal years ended September 26, 2010, September 27, 2009 and September 28, 2008

	Shares Outstanding	Common Stock	Common Stock in Treasury	Accumulated Other Comprehensive Income (Loss)	Retained Earnings	Total Shareholders' Equity
Balances at September 30, 2007	139,240	$1,232,845	$(199,961)	$15,722	$410,198	$1,458,804
Net income	—	—	—	—	114,524	114,524
Foreign currency translation adjustments	—	—	—	(7,714)	—	(7,714)
Reclassification adjustments for amounts included in income, net of income taxes	—	—	—	2,302	—	2,302
Change in unrealized losses, net of income taxes	—	—	—	(9,888)	—	(9,888)
Comprehensive income						99,224
Dividends ($0.60 per common share)	—	—	—	—	(84,012)	(84,012)
Issuance of common stock pursuant to team member stock plans	1,040	17,206	—	—	—	17,206
Retirement of treasury stock	—	—	199,961	—	(199,961)	—
Excess tax benefit related to exercise of team member stock options	—	6,083	—	—	—	6,083
Share-based payment expense	—	10,505	—	—	—	10,505
Cumulative effect of new accounting standard adoption	—	—	—	—	(1,288)	(1,288)
Other	6	(498)	—	—	—	(498)
Balances at September 28, 2008	140,286	1,266,141	—	422	239,461	1,506,024
Net income	—	—	—	—	146,804	146,804
Foreign currency translation adjustments	—	—	—	(8,748)	—	(8,748)
Reclassification adjustments for amounts included in income, net of income taxes	—	—	—	8,440	—	8,440
Change in unrealized losses, net of income taxes	—	—	—	(13,481)	—	(13,481)
Comprehensive income						133,015
Redeemable preferred stock dividends	—	—	—	—	(28,050)	(28,050)
Issuance of common stock pursuant to team member stock plans	256	4,286	—	—	—	4,286
Excess tax benefit related to exercise of team member stock options	—	54	—	—	—	54
Share-based payment expense	—	12,795	—	—	—	12,795
Other	—	(248)	—	—	—	(248)
Balances at September 27, 2009	140,542	1,283,028	—	(13,367)	358,215	1,627,876
Net income	—	—	—	—	245,833	245,833
Foreign currency translation adjustments	—	—	—	1,564	—	1,564
Reclassification adjustments for amounts included in income, net of income taxes	—	—	—	12,943	—	12,943
Change in unrealized losses, net of income taxes	—	—	—	(349)	—	(349)
Comprehensive income						259,991
Redeemable preferred stock dividends	358	5,195	—	—	(5,478)	(283)
Conversion of preferred stock	29,311	413,052	—	—	—	413,052
Issuance of common stock pursuant to team member stock plans	1,822	47,020	—	—	—	47,020
Excess tax benefit related to exercise of team member stock options	—	2,708	—	—	—	2,708
Share-based payment expense	—	22,894	—	—	—	22,894
Balances at September 26, 2010	172,033	$1,773,897	$ —	$ 791	$598,570	$2,373,258

The accompanying notes are an integral part of these consolidated financial statements.

NOTES TO CONSOLIDATED FINANCIAL STATEMENTS (in part)

14. Redeemable Preferred Stock

During the first quarter of fiscal year 2009, the Company issued 425,000 shares of Series A 8% Redeemable, Convertible Exchangeable Participating Preferred Stock, $0.01 par value per share ("Series A Preferred Stock") to affiliates of Leonard Green & Partners, L.P., for approximately $413.1 million, net of approximately $11.9 million in closing and issuance costs. The Series A Preferred Stock was classified as temporary shareholders' equity at September 27, 2009 since the shares were (i) redeemable at the option of the holder and (ii) had conditions for redemption which are not solely within the control of the Company. The holders of the Series A Preferred Stock were entitled to an 8% dividend, payable quarterly on the first day of each calendar quarter in cash. The Company paid cash dividends on the Series A Preferred Stock totaling $8.5 million and approximately $19.8 million during fiscal years 2010 and 2009, respectively.

On October 23, 2009, the Company announced its intention to call all 425,000 outstanding shares of the Series A Preferred Stock for redemption on November 27, 2009 in accordance with the terms governing such Series A Preferred Stock. On November 26, 2009, the holders converted all 425,000 outstanding shares of the Series A Preferred Stock to common stock. The Series A Preferred Stock was converted to common stock based on the quotient of (i) the liquidation preference plus accrued dividends and (ii) 1,000, multiplied by the conversion rate of 68.9655. At the conversion date, the liquidation preference of the Series A Preferred Stock of $425 million and accrued dividends of approximately $5.2 million converted into approximately 29.7 million shares of common stock of the Company.

Noncontrolling Interest

5.67

CF INDUSTRIES HOLDINGS, INC. (DEC)

CONSOLIDATED BALANCE SHEETS (in part)

	December 31	
(In millions, except share and per share amounts)	2010	2009
Equity:		
Stockholders' equity:		
Preferred stock—$0.01 par value, 50,000,000 shares authorized	—	—
Common stock—$0.01 par value, 500,000,000 shares authorized, 2010—71,267,185 and 2009—48,569,985 shares outstanding	0.7	0.5
Paid-in capital	2,732.2	723.5
Retained earnings	1,370.8	1,048.1
Accumulated other comprehensive loss	(53.3)	(43.2)
Total stockholders' equity	4,050.4	1,728.9
Noncontrolling interest	383.0	16.0
Total equity	4,433.4	1,744.9

CONSOLIDATED STATEMENTS OF EQUITY (in part)

	Common Stockholders							
(In millions)	$0.01 Par Value Common Stock	Treasury Stock	Paid-In Capital	Retained Earnings	Accumulated Other Comprehensive Income (Loss)	Total Stockholders' Equity	Non-controlling Interest	Total Equity
Balance at December 31, 2007	$0.6	$—	$ 790.8	$ 416.8	$(21.2)	$1,187.0	$ 17.3	$1,204.3
Net earnings	—	—	—	684.6	—	684.6	116.9	801.5
Other comprehensive income								
Foreign currency translation adjustment	—	—	—	—	(5.4)	(5.4)	(4.7)	(10.1)
Unrealized (loss) on securities—net of taxes	—	—	—	—	(14.5)	(14.5)	—	(14.5)
Defined benefit plans—net of taxes	—	—	—	—	(34.1)	(34.1)	—	(34.1)
Comprehensive income						630.6	112.2	742.8
Issuance of $0.01 par value common stock under employee stock plans	—	—	10.1	—	—	10.1	—	10.1
Stock-based compensation expense	—	—	8.3	—	—	8.3	—	8.3
Excess tax benefit from stock-based compensation	—	—	24.3	—	—	24.3	—	24.3
Purchase of treasury stock	—	(500.2)	—	—	—	(500.2)	—	(500.2)
Cancellation of treasury stock	(0.1)	500.2	(124.1)	(376.0)	—	—	—	—
Cash dividends ($0.40 per share)	—	—	—	(22.0)	—	(22.0)	—	(22.0)
Distributions declared to noncontrolling interest	—	—	—	—	—	—	(106.0)	(106.0)
Effect of exchange rates changes	—	—	—	—	—	—	(10.9)	(10.9)
Balance at December 31, 2008	$0.5	$—	$ 709.4	$ 703.4	$(75.2)	$1,338.1	$ 12.6	$1,350.7
Net earnings	—	—	—	365.6	—	365.6	82.9	448.5
Other comprehensive income								
Foreign currency translation adjustment	—	—	—	—	4.0	4.0	3.3	7.3
Unrealized gain on securities—net of taxes	—	—	—	—	23.7	23.7	—	23.7
Defined benefit plans—net of taxes	—	—	—	—	4.3	4.3	—	4.3
Comprehensive income						397.6	86.2	483.8
Acquisition of treasury stock under employee stock plans	—	(1.8)	—	—	—	(1.8)	—	(1.8)
Issuance of $0.01 par value common stock under employee stock plans	—	1.8	2.9	(1.5)	—	3.2	—	3.2
Stock-based compensation expense	—	—	6.6	—	—	6.6	—	6.6
Excess tax benefit from stock-based compensation	—	—	4.6	—	—	4.6	—	4.6
Cash dividends ($0.40 per share)	—	—	—	(19.4)	—	(19.4)	—	(19.4)
Distributions declared to noncontrolling interest	—	—	—	—	—	—	(92.1)	(92.1)
Effect of exchange rates changes	—	—	—	—	—	—	9.3	9.3
Balance at December 31, 2009	$0.5	$—	$ 723.5	$1,048.1	$(43.2)	$1,728.9	$ 16.0	$1,744.9
Net earnings	—	—	—	349.2	—	349.2	91.5	440.7
Other comprehensive income								
Foreign currency translation adjustment	—	—	—	—	22.8	22.8	1.4	24.2
Unrealized (loss) on securities—net of taxes	—	—	—	—	(14.6)	(14.6)	—	(14.6)
Defined benefit plans—net of taxes	—	—	—	—	(18.3)	(18.3)	—	(18.3)
Comprehensive income						339.1	92.9	432.0
Acquisition of Terra Industries Inc.						—	373.0	373.0
Issuance of $0.01 par value common stock in connection with acquisition of Terra Industries Inc.	0.1	—	881.9	—	—	882.0	—	882.0
Issuance of $0.01 par value common stock in connection with equity offering, net of costs of $41.4 million	0.1	—	1,108.5	—	—	1,108.6	—	1,108.6
Acquisition of treasury stock under employee stock plans	—	(0.7)	—	—	—	(0.7)	—	(0.7)
Issuance of $0.01 par value common stock under employee stock plans	—	0.7	4.6	(0.3)	—	5.0	—	5.0
Stock-based compensation expense	—	—	7.9	—	—	7.9	—	7.9
Excess tax benefit from stock-based compensation	—	—	5.8	—	—	5.8	—	5.8
Cash dividends ($0.40 per share)	—	—	—	(26.2)	—	(26.2)	—	(26.2)
Distributions declared to noncontrolling interest	—	—	—	—	—	—	(101.1)	(101.1)
Effect of exchange rates changes	—	—	—	—	—	—	2.2	2.2
Balance at December 31, 2010	$0.7	$—	$2,732.2	$1,370.8	$(53.3)	$4,050.4	$383.0	$4,433.4

See Accompanying Notes to Consolidated Financial Statements.

NOTES TO CONSOLIDATED FINANCIAL STATEMENTS (in part)

7. Noncontrolling Interest

Canadian Fertilizers Limited (CFL)

CFL is a variable interest entity that owns a nitrogen fertilizer complex in Medicine Hat, Alberta, Canada and supplies fertilizer products to CF Industries, Inc. and Viterra Inc. (Viterra). CF Industries, Inc. owns 49% of CFL's voting common shares and 66% of CFL's nonvoting preferred shares. Viterra owns 34% of the voting common stock and non-voting preferred stock of CFL. The remaining 17% of the voting common stock is owned by GROWMARK, Inc. and La Coop fédérée. CFL is a variable interest entity which we consolidate in our financial statements.

CFL's Medicine Hat complex is the largest nitrogen fertilizer complex in Canada, with two world-scale ammonia plants, a world-scale urea plant and on-site storage facilities for both ammonia and urea. CFL's net sales were $454.0 million, $429.2 million and $710.9 million, for 2010, 2009 and 2008, respectively. CFL's assets and liabilities at December 31, 2010 were $314.0 million and $263.8 million, respectively, and at December 31, 2009 were $356.6 million and $309.0 million, respectively.

CF Industries, Inc. operates the Medicine Hat facility pursuant to a management agreement and purchases approximately 66% of the facility's ammonia and urea production pursuant to a product purchase agreement. Both the management agreement and the product purchase agreement can be terminated by either CF Industries, Inc. or CFL upon a twelve-month notice. Viterra has the right, but not the obligation, to purchase the remaining 34% of the facility's ammonia and urea production under a similar product purchase agreement. To the extent that Viterra does not purchase its 34% of the facility's production, CF Industries, Inc. is obligated to purchase any remaining amounts. However, since 1995, Viterra has purchased at least 34% of the facility's production each year.

Under the product purchase agreements, both CF Industries, Inc. and Viterra pay the greater of operating cost or market price for purchases. The product purchase agreements also provide that CFL will distribute its net earnings to CF Industries, Inc. and Viterra annually based on their respective quantities of product purchased from CFL. The distributions to Viterra are reported as financing activities in the consolidated statements of cash flows, as we consider these payments to be similar to dividends. While general creditors of CFL do not have direct recourse to the general credit of CF Industries, Inc., the product purchase agreement does require CF Industries, Inc. to advance funds to CFL in the event that CFL is unable to meet its debts as they become due. The amount of each advance would be at least 66% of the deficiency and would be more in any year in which CF

Industries, Inc. purchased more than 66% of Medicine Hat's production. A similar obligation also exists for Viterra. CF Industries, Inc. and Viterra currently manage CFL such that each party is responsible for its share of CFL's fixed costs and that CFL's production volume is managed to meet the parties' combined requirements. Based on the contractual arrangements, CF Industries, Inc. is the primary beneficiary of CFL as CF Industries, Inc. receives at least 66% of the economic risks and rewards of CFL.

In accordance with CFL's governing agreements, CFL's earnings are available for distribution to its members based on approval by CFL's shareholders. A portion of the amounts reported as noncontrolling interest in the consolidated statements of operations represent Viterra's 34% interest in the distributed and undistributed earnings of CFL. A portion of the amounts reported as noncontrolling interest on our consolidated balance sheets represent the interests of Viterra and the holders of 17% of CFL's common shares.

Because CFL's functional currency is the Canadian dollar, consolidation of CFL results in a cumulative foreign currency translation adjustment, which is reported in other comprehensive income (loss).

Terra Nitrogen Company L.P. (TNCLP)

TNCLP is a master limited partnership that owns a nitrogen manufacturing facility in Verdigris, Oklahoma. Through our acquisition of Terra in April 2010, we own an aggregate 75.3% of TNCLP through general and limited partnership interests. Outside investors own 24.7% of the limited partnership interests. For financial reporting purposes, the assets, liabilities and earnings of the partnership are consolidated into our financial statements. The outside investors' limited partnership interests in the partnership have been recorded as part of noncontrolling interest in our consolidated financial statements. The noncontrolling interest on the consolidated balance sheets represents the noncontrolling unitholders' interest in the partners' capital of TNCLP.

TNCLP makes cash distributions to the general and limited partners based upon formulas defined within the Agreement of Limited Partnership. Cash available for distribution is defined in the agreement generally as all cash receipts less all cash disbursements, adjusted for changes in certain reserves established as the general partner determines in its reasonable discretion to be necessary. Cash distributions to the limited partners and general partner vary depending on the extent to which the cumulative distributions exceed certain target threshold levels set forth in the Agreement of Limited Partnership.

In each of the applicable quarters of 2010, the minimum quarterly distributions were satisfied, which entitled us to receive increased earnings as provided for in the Agreement of Limited Partnership. The earnings attributed to our general partnership interest in excess of the threshold levels were $49.0 million during 2010.

A reconciliation of the beginning and ending balances of noncontrolling interest and distributions payable to noncontrolling interests on our consolidated balance sheets is provided below.

| | Year Ended December 31 | | | | |
| | 2010 | | | 2009 | 2008 |
(In millions)	CFL	TNCLP	Total	CFL	CFL
Noncontrolling interest:					
Beginning balance	$16.0	$ —	$ 16.0	$ 12.6	$ 17.3
Terra acquistion	—	373.0	373.0	—	—
Earnings attributable to noncontrolling interest	75.8	15.7	91.5	82.9	116.9
Declaration of distributions payable	(78.0)	(23.1)	(101.1)	(92.1)	(106.0)
Effect of exchange rate changes	3.6	—	3.6	12.6	(15.6)
Ending balance	$17.4	$365.6	$383.0	$ 16.0	$ 12.6
Distributions payable to noncontrolling interest:					
Beginning balance	$92.1	$ —	$ 92.1	$106.0	$ 57.6
Declaration of distributions payable	78.0	23.1	101.1	92.1	106.0
Distributions to noncontrolling interest	(93.9)	(23.1)	(117.0)	(112.3)	(52.7)
Effect of exchange rate changes	1.8	—	1.8	6.3	(4.9)
Ending balance	$78.0	$ —	$ 78.0	$ 92.1	$106.0

Section 6: Statement of Cash Flows

GENERAL

PRESENTATION

6.01 Financial Accounting Standards Board (FASB) *Accounting Standards Codification* (ASC) 230, *Statement of Cash Flows*, requires entities to present a statement of cash flows that classifies cash receipts and payments by operating, investing, and financing activities. The information provided in a statement of cash flows, if used with related disclosures and information in the other financial statements, should help investors, creditors, and others do the following:

- Assess the entity's ability to generate positive future net cash flows
- Assess the entity's ability to meet its obligations, its ability to pay dividends, and its needs for external financing
- Assess the reasons for differences between net income and associated cash receipts and payments
- Assess the effects on an entity's financial position of both its cash and noncash investing and financing transactions during the period

6.02 Paragraphs 4–6 of FASB ASC 230-10-45 provide that the statement of cash flows explains the change in cash and cash equivalents during a period. *Cash equivalents* are defined by the FASB ASC glossary to be short-term, highly liquid investments that have both of the following characteristics:

- Readily convertible to known amounts of cash
- So near their maturity that they present an insignificant risk of changes in value because of changes in interest rates

Generally, only investments with original maturities of three months or less qualify under that definition. *Original maturity* means original maturity to the entity holding the investment.

6.03 FASB ASC 230-10-45 states that the amount of cash and cash equivalents at the beginning and end of the period reported on a statement of cash flows should agree with the amount of cash and cash equivalents reported on a statement of financial position. Because not all investments that qualify are required to be treated as cash equivalents, an entity should establish a policy concerning which short-term, highly liquid investments that satisfy the definition of *cash equivalents* are treated as such.

6.04 Paragraphs 7–9 of FASB ASC 230-10-45 explain that generally, cash receipts and payments should be reported separately and not netted. For certain items, the turnover is quick, the amounts are large, and the maturities are short. For certain other items, such as demand deposits of a bank and customer accounts payable of a broker-dealer, the entity is substantively holding or disbursing cash on behalf of its customers. Only the net changes during the period in assets and liabilities with those characteristics need be reported because knowledge of the gross cash receipts and payments related to them may not be necessary to understand the entity's operating, investing, and financing activities. Specifically, provided that the original maturity of the asset or liability is three months or less, cash receipts and payments pertaining to investments (other than cash equivalents),

loans receivable, and debt qualify for net reporting based on this rationale.

6.05 FASB ASC 830-230-45-1 specifies that the effect of exchange rate changes on cash balances held in foreign currencies be reported as a separate part of the reconciliation of the change in cash and cash equivalents during the period in the statement of cash flows. Further, a statement of cash flows of an entity with foreign exchange transactions or foreign operations should report the reporting currency equivalent of foreign currency cash flows using the exchange rates in effect at the time of the cash flows. An appropriately weighted average exchange rate for the period may be used for translation if the result is substantially the same as if the rates at the dates of the cash flows were used.

DISCLOSURE

6.06 FASB ASC 230-10-50-1 explains that an entity should disclose its policy regarding cash equivalent classification, and any change to that policy is a change in accounting principle that should be affected by restating financial statements for earlier years presented for comparative purposes. If the indirect method is used, amounts of interest (net of capitalized amounts) and income tax payments during the period are required to be disclosed.

6.07 Paragraphs 3–6 of FASB ASC 230-10-50 require the disclosure of information about noncash investing and financing activities. Examples of noncash investing and financing transactions include converting debt to equity; acquiring assets by assuming directly-related liabilities, such as purchasing a building by incurring a mortgage to the seller: obtaining an asset by entering into a capital lease; obtaining a building or investment asset by receiving a gift; and exchanging noncash assets or liabilities for other noncash assets or liabilities. If only a few noncash transactions exist, it may be convenient to include them on the same page as the statement of cash flows. Otherwise, the transactions may be reported elsewhere in the financial statements and clearly referenced to the statement of cash flow.

6.08

TABLE 6-1: PRESENTATION OF INTEREST AND INCOME TAX PAYMENTS

Table 6-1 shows where in the financial statements interest and income tax payments are disclosed.

	2010	2009	2008
Interest Payments			
Notes to financial statements..............................	219	244	250
Bottom of statement of cash flows.....................	243	235	237
Within statement of cash flows..........................	9	6	5
Amount not disclosed...	29	15	8
Total Entities...	**500**	**500**	**500**
Income Tax Payments			
Notes to financial statements..............................	223	252	252
Bottom of statement of cash flows.....................	249	241	240
Within statement of cash flows..........................	11	7	6
Amount not disclosed...	17	—	2
Total Entities...	**500**	**500**	**500**

PRESENTATION AND DISCLOSURE EXCERPTS

Cash and Cash Equivalents

6.09

TUTOR PERINI CORPORATION (DEC)

CONSOLIDATED BALANCE SHEETS (in part)

December 31, 2010 and 2009

(In thousands, except share data)	2010	2009
Assets		
Current assets:		
Cash, including cash equivalents of		
$127,879 and $294,807	$ 471,378	$ 348,309
Restricted cash	23,550	—
Accounts receivable, including retainage		
of $271,778 and $544,875	880,614	1,088,386
Costs and estimated earnings in excess		
of billings	139,449	145,678
Deferred tax asset	3,737	1,370
Other current assets	42,314	30,811
Total current assets	1,561,042	1,614,554

CONSOLIDATED STATEMENTS OF CASH FLOWS (in part)

For the Years Ended December 31, 2010, 2009 and 2008

(In thousands)	2010	2009	2008
Net (Decrease) Increase in Cash and Cash Equivalents	123,069	(37,863)	(73,016)
Cash and Cash Equivalents at Beginning of Year	348,309	386,172	459,188
Cash and Cash Equivalents at End of Year	$471,378	$348,309	$386,172

NOTES TO CONSOLIDATED FINANCIAL STATEMENTS (in part)

[1] Summary of Significant Accounting Policies (in part)

(j) Cash, Cash Equivalents and Restricted Cash

Cash equivalents include short-term, highly liquid investments with original maturities of three months or less when acquired.

Cash and cash equivalents as reported in the accompanying Consolidated Balance Sheets consist of amounts held by the Company that are available for general corporate purposes and the Company's proportionate share of amounts held by construction joint ventures that are available only for joint venture-related uses. Joint venture cash and cash equivalents are not restricted to specific uses within those entities; however, the terms of the joint venture agreements limit the ability to distribute those funds and use them for corporate purposes. Cash held by construction joint ventures is distributed from time to time to the Company and to the other joint venture participants in accordance with their percentage interest after the joint venture partners determine that a cash distribution is prudent. Cash distributions received by the Company from its construction joint ventures are then available for general corporate purposes.

At December 31, 2010 and 2009, cash and cash equivalents consisted of the following (in thousands):

	2010	2009
Corporate cash and cash equivalents (available for general corporate purposes)	$455,464	$323,867
Company's share of joint venture cash and cash equivalents (available only for joint venture purposes, including future distributions)	15,914	24,442
	$471,378	$348,309
Restricted Cash	$ 23,550	$ —

Restricted cash is held to secure insurance-related contingent obligations, such as insurance claim deductibles, in lieu of utilizing letters of credit.

Foreign Currency Cash Flows

6.10

H.J. HEINZ COMPANY (APR)

CONSOLIDATED STATEMENTS OF CASH FLOWS

	Fiscal Year Ended		
(Dollars in thousands)	April 28, 2010 (52 Weeks)	April 29, 2009 (52 Weeks)	April 30, 2008 (52 Weeks)
Operating Activities:			
Net income	$ 882,343	$ 937,961	$ 856,478
Adjustments to reconcile net income to cash provided by operating activities:			
Depreciation	254,528	241,294	250,826
Amortization	48,308	40,081	38,071
Deferred tax provision	220,528	108,950	18,543
Net losses/(gains) on disposals	44,860	(6,445)	(15,706)
Pension contributions	(539,939)	(133,714)	(58,061)
Other items, net	90,938	(85,029)	68,851
Changes in current assets and liabilities, excluding effects of acquisitions and divestitures:			
Receivable securitization facility	84,200	—	—
Receivables	37,187	(10,866)	(55,832)
Inventories	48,537	50,731	(133,600)
Prepaid expenses and other current assets	2,113	996	5,748
Accounts payable	(2,805)	(62,934)	89,160
Accrued liabilities	96,533	24,641	28,259
Income taxes	(5,134)	61,216	95,566
Cash provided by operating activities	1,262,197	1,166,882	1,188,303
Investing Activities:			
Capital expenditures	(277,642)	(292,121)	(301,588)
Proceeds from disposals of property, plant and equipment	96,493	5,407	8,531
Acquisitions, net of cash acquired	(11,428)	(293,898)	(151,604)
Proceeds from divestitures	18,637	13,351	63,481
Change in restricted cash	192,736	(192,736)	—
Termination of net investment hedges	—	—	(93,153)
Other items, net	(5,353)	(1,197)	(79,894)
Cash provided by/(used for) investing activities	13,443	(761,194)	(554,227)
Financing Activities:			
Payments on long-term debt	(630,394)	(427,417)	(368,214)
Proceeds from long-term debt	447,056	853,051	—
Net (payments on)/proceeds from commercial paper and short-term debt	(427,232)	(483,666)	483,730
Dividends	(533,552)	(525,293)	(485,246)
Purchases of treasury stock	—	(181,431)	(580,707)
Exercise of stock options	67,369	264,898	78,596
Acquisition of subsidiary shares from noncontrolling interests	(62,064)	—	—
Termination of interest rate swaps	—	—	103,522
Other items, net	(9,099)	(16,478)	10,224
Cash used for financing activities	(1,147,916)	(516,336)	(758,095)
Effect of exchange rate changes on cash and cash equivalents	(17,616)	(133,894)	88,810
Net increase/(decrease) in cash and cash equivalents	110,108	(244,542)	(35,209)
Cash and cash equivalents at beginning of year	373,145	617,687	652,896
Cash and cash equivalents at end of year	$ 483,253	$ 373,145	$ 617,687

See Notes to Consolidated Financial Statements.

Interest and Income Tax Payments

6.11

NORTHROP GRUMMAN CORPORATION (DEC)

CONSOLIDATED STATEMENTS OF CASH FLOWS
(in part)

	Year Ended December 31		
($ in millions)	2010	2009	2008
Operating Activities			
Sources of Cash—Continuing Operations			
Cash received from customers			
Progress payments	$ 6,401	$ 8,561	$ 6,219
Collections on billings	28,079	25,099	26,938
Other cash receipts	61	62	88
Total sources of cash—continuing operations	34,541	33,722	33,245
Uses of Cash—Continuing Operations			
Cash paid to suppliers and employees	(29,775)	(29,250)	(28,817)
Pension contributions	(894)	(858)	(320)
Interest paid, net of interest received	(280)	(269)	(287)
Income taxes paid, net of refunds received	(1,071)	(774)	(712)
Income taxes paid on sale of businesses		(508)	(7)
Excess tax benefits from stock-based compensation	(22)	(2)	(48)
Other cash payments	(46)	(30)	(16)
Total uses of cash—continuing operations	(32,088)	(31,691)	(30,207)
Cash provided by continuing operations	2,453	2,031	3,038
Cash provided by discontinued operations		102	173
Net cash provided by operating activities	2,453	2,133	3,211

Noncash Activities

6.12

IAC/INTERACTIVECORP (DEC)

CONSOLIDATED STATEMENT OF CASH FLOWS
(in part)

	Years Ended December 31		
(In thousands)	2010	2009	2008
Total cash (used in) provided by continuing operations	(494,599)	(479,890)	378,799
Net cash (used in) provided by operating activities attributable to discontinued operations	(4,601)	(20,527)	255,145
Net cash used in investing activities attributable to discontinued operations	(2,944)	(3,965)	(501,701)
Net cash (used in) provided by financing activities attributable to discontinued operations	—	(216)	50,484
Total cash used in discontinued operations	(7,545)	(24,708)	(196,072)
Effect of exchange rate changes on cash and cash equivalents	(1,754)	5,601	(23,035)
Net (decrease) increase in cash and cash equivalents	(503,898)	(498,997)	159,692
Cash and cash equivalents at beginning of period	1,245,997	1,744,994	1,585,302
Cash and cash equivalents at end of period	$ 742,099	$1,245,997	$1,744,994

The accompanying Notes to Consolidated Financial Statements are an integral part of these statements.

NOTES TO CONSOLIDATED FINANCIAL STATEMENTS (in part)

Note 18—Supplemental Cash Flow Information (in part)

During 2010, IAC received a dividend from Meetic, which the Company deemed to be a partial return of its investment. Accordingly, the dividend is reflected as a cash flow from an investing activity in the accompanying consolidated statement of cash flows.

Supplemental Disclosure of Non-Cash Transactions for 2010

On December 1, 2010, in accordance with the Company's stock exchange agreement with Liberty, IAC exchanged $217.9 million in cash and all the outstanding shares of Celebrate Interactive, Inc., a wholly owned subsidiary of IAC that held all the equity interests of Evite, Inc., Giftco, Inc. and IAC Advertising, LLC, for substantially all of Liberty's shares of IAC common stock and all of its shares of Class B common stock, which were valued at $364.2 million based on the closing price of IAC common stock on December 1, 2010.

On March 10, 2010, Match and Meetic completed a transaction in which Match contributed its Latin American business ("Match Latam") and Meetic contributed Parperfeito to a newly formed venture. These contributions, along with a $3.0 million payment from Match to Meetic, resulted in each party owning a 50% equity interest in the newly formed venture, which was valued at $72 million. Match controls the venture through its voting interests. Accordingly, this transaction was accounted for as an acquisition of Parperfeito and a decrease in ownership of Match Latam. No gain or loss was recognized on this transaction as the fair value of the consideration received by Match equaled the fair value of the assets exchanged.

Supplemental Disclosure of Non-Cash Transactions for 2009

The Company recorded a $4.1 million reduction to the Spin-Off distribution. This reflects a reduction in the Company's income tax liability and a corresponding increase in the income tax liability of the Spincos as of the date of the Spin-Off. This reduced tax liability is primarily due to elections made by the Company pursuant to the tax sharing agreement executed in connection with the Spin-Off. The amount is included in the consolidated statement of shareholders' equity as an increase to additional paid-in-capital.

On June 5, 2009, IAC completed the sale of Match Europe to Meetic. In exchange for Match Europe, IAC received a 27% stake in Meetic (approximately 6.1 million shares of Meetic common stock), valued at $154.8 million, plus a promissory note valued at $6.2 million. The promissory note was subsequently paid in the fourth quarter of 2009.

On January 31, 2009, IAC completed the sale of ReserveAmerica to The Active Network, Inc. ("Active"). In exchange for ReserveAmerica, IAC received approximately 3.5 million shares of Active convertible preferred stock, valued at $33.3 million. No gain or loss was recognized on the sale of ReserveAmerica as the fair value of the Active convertible preferred stock received was equivalent to the carrying value of ReserveAmerica.

Supplemental Disclosure of Non-Cash Transactions for 2008

During the year ended December 31, 2008, $12.3 million in aggregate principal amount of Convertible Notes was converted by the holders. Upon conversion, 0.2 million shares of IAC common stock and 0.2 million shares of Expedia common stock were issued to the holders.

After the close of trading on August 20, 2008, IAC completed the Spin-Off. The net assets of the Spincos, net of cash of $728.0 million, of $3.2 billion is included in the accompanying consolidated statement of shareholders' equity as a reduction to additional paid-in capital and retained earnings.

Immediately prior to and in connection with the Spin-Off, the Company exchanged $277.4 million of the Senior Notes for debt of ILG.

CASH FLOWS FROM OPERATING ACTIVITIES

PRESENTATION

6.13 FASB ASC 230-10-45 defines those transactions and events that constitute operating cash receipts and payments. Cash inflows from operating activities include the following:

- Cash receipts from sales of goods or services, including receipts from the collection or sale of accounts and both short- and long-term notes receivable from customers arising from those sales. Goods include certain loans and other debt and equity instruments of other entities that are acquired specifically for resale.
- Cash receipts from returns on loans, other debt instruments of other entities, and equity securities—interest and dividends.
- All other cash receipts that do not stem from transactions defined as investing or financing activities, such as amounts received to settle lawsuits; proceeds of insurance settlements, except for those that are directly related to investing or financing activities, such as destruction of a building; and refunds from suppliers.

Cash outflows from operating activities include the following:

- Cash payments to acquire materials for manufacture or goods for resale, including principal payments on accounts and both short- and long-term notes payable to suppliers for those materials or goods. Goods include certain loans and other debt and equity instruments of other entities that are acquired specifically for resale.
- Cash payments to other suppliers and employees for other goods or services.
- Cash payments to governments for taxes, duties, fines, and other fees or penalties and the cash that would have been paid for income taxes if increases in the value of equity instruments issued under share-based payment arrangements that are not included in the cost of goods or services recognizable for financial reporting purposes also had not been deductible in determining taxable income.
- Cash payments to lenders and other creditors for interest.
- Cash payment made to settle an asset retirement obligation.
- All other cash payments that do not stem from transactions defined as investing or financing activities, such as payments to settle lawsuits, cash contributions to charities, and cash refunds to customers.

6.14 FASB ASC 230-10-45 recommends that the direct method be used to report net cash flow from operating activities, which includes reporting major classes or gross cash receipts and payments and their arithmetic sum. Entities that choose not to provide information about major classes of operating cash receipts and payments by the direct method should determine and report the same amount for net cash flow from operating activities indirectly by adjusting net income of a business entity to reconcile it to net cash flow from operating activities (the indirect or reconciliation method). Regardless of whether the direct or indirect method is used, a reconciliation of net income to net cash flow from operating activities is required to be presented.

6.15 FASB ASC 230-10-45-28 also notes that when reconciling net income to net cash flow from operating activities, a business entity should adjust net income to remove past operating cash receipts and payments and accruals of expected future operating cash receipts and payments, including changes during the period in inventory and receivables and payables pertaining to operating activities. Additionally, all items that are included in net income, such as depreciation and amortization expense, that do not affect net cash provided from, or used for, operating activities should be adjusted for.

6.16

TABLE 6-2: METHOD OF REPORTING CASH FLOWS FROM OPERATING ACTIVITIES

Table 6-2 shows the methods used to report cash flows from operating activities.

	2010	2009	2008
Indirect method	492	495	495
Direct method	8	5	5
Total Entities	**500**	**500**	**500**

6.17

TABLE 6-3: CASH FLOWS FROM OPERATING ACTIVITIES—INCOME STATEMENT RECONCILING ITEMS

Table 6-3 lists the major types of income statement items used by the survey entities to reconcile net income to net cash flow from operating activities.

	2010	2009	2008
Depreciation and/or amortization	497	498	499
Deferred taxes	420	438	438
Employee related costs	366	422	405
Write-down of assets	191	189	155
Gain or loss on sale of property	213	173	162
Tax benefit from share-based compensation plans	159	153	164
Equity in investee's earnings	110	137	142
Gain or loss on sale of assets other than property	94	128	175

6.17

TABLE 6-3: CASH FLOWS FROM OPERATING ACTIVITIES—INCOME STATEMENT RECONCILING ITEMS—CONTINUED

	2010	2009	2008
Provision for doubtful accounts	118	128	116
Intangible asset impairment	89	114	113
Intangible asset amortization	133	111	120
Gain or loss from discontinued operations	102	111	110
Restructuring	93	101	95
Gain or loss on debt extinguishments	88	N/C*	N/C*
Cash surrender value	9	N/C*	N/C*
Cumulative effect of accounting change	1	N/C*	N/C*
Minority interest/noncontrolling interest	19	N/C*	N/C*
Debt discount/premium/issue cost amortization	69	N/C*	N/C*
Accretion of discount/premium on marketable securities/investments	17	N/C*	N/C*
Unrealized gain/loss on marketable securities/derivatives	29	N/C*	N/C*
Foreign currency translation/transaction	50	N/C*	N/C*
Purchased research and/or development cost	10	N/C*	N/C*
Litigation	18	N/C*	N/C*
Other, described	200	N/C*	N/C*

* N/C = Not compiled. The line item was not included in the table for the year shown.

6.18

TABLE 6-4: CASH FLOWS FROM OPERATING ACTIVITIES—BALANCE SHEET RECONCILING ITEMS

Table 6-4 lists the major types of balance sheet items used by the survey entities to reconcile net income to net cash flow from operating activities.

	2010	2009	2008
Accounts receivable	407	460	467
Inventories	369	423	423
Accounts receivable combined with inventories and/or other items	64	27	26
Accounts payable	236	275	266
Accounts payable combined with other items	231	207	213
Income taxes payable	218	205	211
Employee-related liabilities	99	112	107
Current assets and current liabilities are netted	16	N/C*	N/C*
Marketable securities or restricted cash	8	N/C*	N/C*
Deferred income taxes	28	N/C*	N/C*
Other assets, described	135	N/C*	N/C*
Other liabilities, described	192	N/C*	N/C*

* N/C = Not compiled. The line item was not included in the table for the year shown.

PRESENTATION AND DISCLOSURE EXCERPTS

Direct Method

6.19

TECH DATA CORPORATION (JAN)

CONSOLIDATED STATEMENT OF CASH FLOWS

	Year Ended January 31		
(In thousands)	2010	2009	2008
		(As Adjusted- See Note 1)	(As Adjusted- See Note 1)
Cash Flows From Operating Activities:			
Cash received from customers	$ 21,927,372	$ 23,989,567	$ 23,473,295
Cash paid to vendors and employees	(21,320,637)	(23,636,388)	(23,053,048)
Interest paid, net	(14,015)	(20,382)	(14,273)
Income taxes paid	(48,790)	(52,987)	(48,552)
Net cash provided by operating activities	543,930	279,810	357,422
Cash Flows From Investing Activities:			
Acquisition of business, net of cash acquired	(8,153)	(78,266)	(21,503)
Proceeds from sale of business	—	—	7,161
Proceeds from sale of property and equipment	5,491		
Expenditures for property and equipment	(14,486)	(17,272)	(21,474)
Software and software development costs	(14,379)	(15,275)	(16,885)
Net cash used in investing activities	(31,527)	(110,813)	(52,701)
Cash Flows From Financing Activities:			
Proceeds from the issuance of common stock and reissuance of treasury stock	37,959	1,530	12,542
Cash paid for purchase of treasury stock	—	(100,000)	(100,019)
Capital contributions and net borrowings from joint venture partner	23,208	10,810	9,000
Net (repayments) borrowings on revolving credit loans	(19,116)	42,834	(56,297)
Principal payments on long-term debt	(5,654)	(1,786)	(2,371)
Excess tax benefit from stock-based compensation	963	—	212
Net cash provided by (used in) financing activities	37,360	(46,612)	(136,933)
Effect of exchange rate changes on cash and cash equivalents	38,793	(41,702)	14,546
Net increase in cash and cash equivalents	588,556	80,683	182,334
Cash and cash equivalents at beginning of year	528,023	447,340	265,006
Cash and cash equivalents at end of year	$ 1,116,579	$ 528,023	$ 447,340
Reconciliation of Net Income to Net Cash Provided by Operating Activities:			
Net income attributable to shareholders of Tech Data Corporation	$ 180,155	$ 117,278	$ 102,129
Net income (loss) attributable to noncontrolling interest	1,045	(1,822)	(3,559)
Consolidated net income	181,200	115,456	98,570
Adjustments to Reconcile Net Income to Net Cash Provided by (Used in) Operating Activities:			
Loss on disposal of subsidiaries	—	—	14,471
Depreciation and amortization	45,954	51,234	53,881
Provision for losses on accounts receivable	10,953	15,000	11,200
Stock-based compensation expense	11,225	11,990	10,287
Accretion of debt discount on convertible senior debentures	10,278	10,278	10,278
Deferred income taxes	(2,541)	18,221	2,629
Excess tax benefit from stock-based compensation	(963)	—	(212)
Changes in operating assets and liabilities:			
Accounts receivable	(168,152)	(86,423)	57,419
Inventories	116,543	(261,974)	57,904
Prepaid expenses and other assets	21,290	(18,761)	(40,951)
Accounts payable	336,587	374,696	83,845
Accrued expenses and other liabilities	(18,444)	50,093	(1,899)
Total adjustments	362,730	164,354	258,852
Net cash provided by operating activities	$ 543,930	$ 279,810	$ 357,422

The accompanying Notes to Consolidated Financial Statements are an integral part of these financial statements.

Indirect/Reconciliation Method

6.20

EXXON MOBIL CORPORATION (DEC)

CONSOLIDATED STATEMENT OF CASH FLOWS

(Millions of dollars)	Note Reference Number	2010	2009	2008
Cash Flows From Operating Activities				
Net income including noncontrolling interests		$ 31,398	$ 19,658	$ 46,867
Adjustments for noncash transactions				
Depreciation and depletion		14,760	11,917	12,379
Deferred income tax charges/(credits)		(1,135)	—	1,399
Postretirement benefits expense in excess of/(less than) net payments		1,700	(1,722)	57
Other long-term obligation provisions in excess of/(less than) payments		160	731	(63)
Dividends received greater than/(less than) equity in current earnings of equity companies		(596)	(483)	921
Changes in operational working capital, excluding cash and debt				
Reduction/(increase)—Notes and accounts receivable		(5,863)	(3,170)	8,641
—Inventories		(1,148)	459	(1,285)
—Other current assets		913	132	(509)
Increase/(reduction)—Accounts and other payables		9,943	1,420	(5,415)
Net (gain) on asset sales	4	(1,401)	(488)	(3,757)
All other items—net		(318)	(16)	490
Net cash provided by operating activities		$ 48,413	$ 28,438	$ 59,725
Cash Flows From Investing Activities				
Additions to property, plant and equipment		$(26,871)	$(22,491)	$(19,318)
Sales of subsidiaries, investments and property, plant and equipment	4	3,261	1,545	5,985
Decrease/(increase) in restricted cash and cash equivalents	3	(628)	—	—
Additional investments and advances		(1,239)	(2,752)	(2,495)
Collection of advances		1,133	724	574
Additions to marketable securities		(15)	(16)	(2,113)
Sales of marketable securities		155	571	1,868
Net cash used in investing activities		$(24,204)	$(22,419)	$(15,499)
Cash Flows From Financing Activities				
Additions to long-term debt		$ 1,143	$ 225	$ 79
Reductions in long-term debt		(6,224)	(68)	(192)
Additions to short-term debt		598	1,336	1,067
Reductions in short-term debt		(2,436)	(1,575)	(1,624)
Additions/(reductions) in debt with three months or less maturity		709	(71)	143
Cash dividends to ExxonMobil shareholders		(8,498)	(8,023)	(8,058)
Cash dividends to noncontrolling interests		(281)	(280)	(375)
Changes in noncontrolling interests		(7)	(113)	(419)
Tax benefits related to stock-based awards		122	237	333
Common stock acquired		(13,093)	(19,703)	(35,734)
Common stock sold		1,043	752	753
Net cash used in financing activities		$(26,924)	$(27,283)	$(44,027)
Effects of exchange rate changes on cash		$ (153)	$ 520	$ (2,743)
Increase/(decrease) in cash and cash equivalents		$ (2,868)	$(20,744)	$ (2,544)
Cash and cash equivalents at beginning of year		10,693	31,437	33,981
Cash and cash equivalents at end of year		$ 7,825	$ 10,693	$ 31,437

Non-Cash Transactions

The Corporation acquired all the outstanding equity of XTO Energy Inc. in an all-stock transaction valued at $24,659 million in 2010 (see note 19).

The information in the Notes to Consolidated Financial Statements is an integral part of these statements.

Adjustments to Reconcile Net Income: Depreciation and Amortization

6.21

REPUBLIC SERVICES, INC. (DEC)

CONSOLIDATED STATEMENTS OF CASH FLOWS
(in part)

(In millions)	2010	2009	2008
Cash Provided by Operating Activities:			
Net income	$ 507.5	$ 496.5	$ 73.9
Adjustments to reconcile net income to cash provided by operating activities:			
Depreciation and amortization of property and equipment	511.6	520.6	222.6
Landfill depletion and amortization	250.6	278.5	119.7
Amortization of intangible and other assets	71.5	70.6	11.8
Accretion	80.5	88.8	23.9
Non-cash interest expense—debt	52.4	92.1	10.1
Non-cash interest expense—other	48.1	58.1	0.5
Restructuring related charges	(2.0)	34.0	—
Stock-based compensation	24.5	15.0	24.0
Deferred tax provision (benefit)	61.3	(24.6)	(30.4)
Provision for doubtful accounts, net of adjustments	23.6	27.3	36.5
Excess income tax benefit from stock option exercises	(3.5)	(2.5)	2.8
Asset impairments	15.1	7.1	89.8
Loss on extinguishment of debt	160.8	134.1	—
Gain on disposition of assets, net	(11.2)	(147.1)	(1.4)
Other non-cash items	3.8	(0.1)	7.3
Change in assets and liabilities, net of effects from business acquisitions and divestitures:			
Accounts receivable	8.8	53.1	21.1
Prepaid expenses and other assets	(76.6)	(11.9)	15.8
Accounts payable	(34.9)	(6.9)	(164.5)
Restructuring and synergy related expenditures	(20.0)	(66.5)	—
Capping, closure and post-closure expenditures	(111.3)	(100.9)	(27.9)
Remediation expenditures	(50.5)	(56.2)	(43.3)
Other liabilities	(76.4)	(62.6)	119.9
Cash provided by operating activities	1,433.7	1,396.5	512.2

Adjustments to Reconcile Net Income: Gain/Loss on Discontinued Operations/Sale of Business

6.22

DEAN FOODS COMPANY (DEC)

CONSOLIDATED STATEMENTS OF CASH FLOWS
(in part)

	Year Ended December 31		
(In thousands)	2010	2009	2008
Cash Flows From Operating Activities:			
Net income	$ 82,756	$227,847	$183,770
(Income) loss from discontinued operations	2,505	862	(3,158)
(Gain) loss on sale of discontinued operations	(7,521)	(89)	1,275
Adjustments to reconcile net income to net cash provided by operating activities:			
Depreciation and amortization	276,080	253,930	236,820
Share-based compensation expense	36,872	39,371	35,180
Loss on disposition of assets and operations	5,627	12,638	2,968
Write-down of impaired assets	14,186	16,815	20,740
Write-off of financing costs	3,695	—	—
Deferred income taxes	121,043	40,352	67,980
Other	(1,379)	(1,337)	(6,380)
Changes in operating assets and liabilities, net of acquisitions:			
Receivables, net	(25,659)	57,577	58,383
Inventories	4,020	(8,389)	(4,820)
Prepaid expenses and other assets	5,764	5,393	11,055
Accounts payable and accrued expenses	62,931	59,148	64,656
Income taxes receivable/payable	(55,220)	(46,039)	45,037
Net cash provided by operating activities—continuing operations	525,700	658,079	713,506
Net cash provided by operating activities—discontinued operations	8,765	2,475	3,122
Net cash provided by operating activities	534,465	660,554	716,628

Adjustments to Reconcile Net Income: Restructuring Expense

6.23

COHERENT, INC. (SEP)

CONSOLIDATED STATEMENTS OF CASH FLOWS
(in part)

	Year Ended		
(In thousands)	October 2, 2010	October 3, 2009	September 27, 2008
Cash Flows From Operating Activities:			
Net income (loss)	$ 36,916	$(35,319)	$23,403
Adjustments to reconcile net income to net cash provided by operating activities:			
Non-cash restructuring and other charges (recoveries)	4,256	(356)	3,111
Depreciation and amortization	21,657	19,194	23,319
Amortization of intangible assets	8,002	7,466	8,651
Impairment of goodwill	—	19,286	—
Stock-based compensation	8,286	7,415	8,809
Excess tax benefit from stock-based compensation arrangements	(934)	(9)	(749)
Tax benefit from employee stock options	—	—	665
Deferred income taxes	13,287	(12,224)	(1,642)
Loss on disposal of property and equipment	334	594	417
Other non-cash expense	164	128	208
Changes in assets and liabilities, net of effect of acquisitions:			
Accounts receivable	(33,674)	24,854	9,049
Inventories	(14,607)	21,412	(6,491)
Prepaid expenses and other assets	(9,247)	2,302	7,019
Other assets	67	6,245	2,902
Accounts payable	15,122	(4,172)	(1,085)
Income taxes payable/receivable	6,454	1,481	1,717
Other current liabilities	22,838	(13,848)	(8,837)
Other long-term liabilities	(108)	(5,400)	(2,104)
Net cash provided by operating activities	78,813	39,049	68,362

Adjustments to Reconcile Net Income: Gain/Loss on Debt Extinguishments

6.24

SILGAN HOLDINGS INC. (DEC)

CONSOLIDATED STATEMENTS OF CASH FLOWS (in part)

For the years ended December 31, 2010, 2009 and 2008

(Dollars in thousands)	2010	2009	2008
Cash Flows Provided by (Used in) Operating Activities:			
Net income	$144,646	$159,409	$124,992
Adjustments to reconcile net income to net cash provided by operating activities:			
Depreciation and amortization	142,949	145,265	143,964
Amortization of debt issuance costs and discount	2,885	2,044	1,360
Rationalization charges	22,214	1,491	12,180
Loss on early extinguishment of debt	7,548	1,255	—
Deferred income tax provision	21,358	15,316	19,597
Excess tax benefit from stock-based compensation	(2,674)	(2,922)	(3,318)
Other changes that provided (used) cash, net of effects from acquisitions:			
Trade accounts receivable, net	(19,875)	72,059	(49,538)
Inventories	(51,800)	(7,894)	48,898
Trade accounts payable	4,342	(62,547)	66,464
Accrued liabilities	(12,101)	821	(7,798)
Contributions to domestic pension benefit plans	(92,287)	(43,423)	(9,836)
Other, net	20,110	41,900	(1,559)
Net cash provided by operating activities	187,315	322,774	345,406

Adjustments to Reconcile Net Income: Equity in Earnings/Losses of Investee

6.25

DIRECTV (DEC)

CONSOLIDATED STATEMENTS OF CASH FLOWS (in part)

	Years Ended December 31		
(Dollars in millions)	2010	2009	2008
Cash Flows From Operating Activities			
Net income	$2,312	$1,007	$1,613
Income from discontinued operations, net of taxes	—	—	(6)
Income from continuing operations	2,312	1,007	1,607
Adjustments to reconcile income from continuing operations to net cash provided by operating activities:			
Depreciation and amortization	2,482	2,640	2,320
Amortization of deferred revenues and deferred credits	(36)	(48)	(104)
Share-based compensation expense	82	55	51
Equity in earnings from unconsolidated affiliates	(90)	(51)	(55)
Dividends received	78	94	35
Net loss from impairment of investments	—	45	—
Net foreign currency transaction charges	(11)	(62)	—
Liberty transaction and related (gains) charges	(67)	491	—
Deferred income taxes	375	441	107
Other	60	48	31
Change in operating assets and liabilities:			
Accounts receivable	(391)	(141)	95
Inventories	(35)	(12)	18
Prepaid expenses and other	(4)	(5)	(96)
Accounts payable and accrued liabilities	437	(215)	(23)
Unearned subscriber revenues and deferred credits	52	55	8
Other, net	(38)	89	(84)
Net cash provided by operating activities	5,206	4,431	3,910

Adjustments to Reconcile Net Income: Provision for Losses on Accounts Receivable

6.26

ROBERT HALF INTERNATIONAL INC. (DEC)

CONSOLIDATED STATEMENTS OF CASH FLOWS
(in part)

	Years Ended December 31		
(In thousands)	2010	2009	2008
Cash Flows From Operating Activities:			
Net income	$ 66,069	$ 37,263	$250,181
Adjustments to reconcile net income to net cash provided by operating activities:			
Amortization of intangible assets	411	1,460	2,617
Depreciation expense	55,547	63,806	70,593
Stock-based compensation expense—restricted stock and stock units	56,949	60,320	63,571
Stock-based compensation expense—stock options	170	828	5,109
Excess tax benefits from stock-based compensation	(5,814)	(4,751)	(3,688)
Provision for deferred income taxes	7,370	5,752	(6,043)
Provision for doubtful accounts receivable	6,795	(839)	18,137
Changes in assets and liabilities, net of effects of acquisitions:			
(Increase) decrease in accounts receivable	(68,008)	133,541	67,283
Increase (decrease) in accounts payable, accrued expenses, accrued payroll costs and retirement obligations	41,626	(52,210)	(5,238)
Increase (decrease) in income taxes payable	1,490	(3,830)	(12,941)
Change in other assets, net of change in other liabilities	13,278	(1,187)	(2,456)
Net cash flows provided by operating activities	175,883	240,153	447,125

Adjustments to Reconcile Net Income: Impairment/Write-Down of Assets

6.27

ANADARKO PETROLEUM CORPORATION (DEC)

CONSOLIDATED STATEMENTS OF CASH FLOWS
(in part)

	Years Ended December 31		
(Millions)	2010	2009	2008
Cash Flows From Operating Activities			
Net income (loss)	$ 821	$ (103)	$3,283
Less income from discontinued operations, net of taxes	—	—	63
Adjustments to reconcile net income (loss) to net cash provided by operating activities:			
Depreciation, depletion and amortization	3,714	3,532	3,194
Deferred income taxes	(123)	(165)	(22)
Dry hole expense and impairments of unproved properties	682	780	1,005
Impairments	216	115	223
(Gains) losses on divestitures, net	(29)	(44)	(993)
Unrealized (gains) losses on derivatives, net	(114)	717	(922)
Reversal of accrual for DWRRA dispute (Note 15)	—	(657)	—
Other	213	183	125
Changes in assets and liabilities:			
(Increase) decrease in accounts receivable	(172)	(290)	803
Increase (decrease) in accounts payable and accrued expenses	(157)	269	158
Other items—net	196	(411)	(344)
Cash provided by (used in) operating activities—continuing operations	5,247	3,926	6,447
Cash provided by (used in) operating activities—discontinued operations	—	—	(5)
Net cash provided by (used in) operating activities	5,247	3,926	6,442

Adjustments to Reconcile Net Income: Accretion

6.28

NETAPP, INC. (APR)

CONSOLIDATED STATEMENTS OF CASH FLOWS
(in part)

	Year Ended		
(In millions)	April 30, 2010	April 24, 2009	April 25, 2008
Cash Flows From Operating Activities:			
Net income	$400.4	$ 64.6	$309.7
Adjustments to reconcile net income to net cash provided by operating activities:			
Depreciation and amortization	166.0	170.5	148.1
Stock-based compensation	159.8	140.8	148.0
Accretion of discount and issuance costs on notes	50.8	41.0	—
Deferred income taxes	(11.3)	(124.6)	(53.0)
Tax benefit (charges) from stock-based compensation	(0.9)	45.4	48.2
Excess tax benefit from stock-based compensation	(8.6)	(36.7)	(45.4)
Other non-cash items, net	9.7	57.8	(10.0)
Changes in assets and liabilities:			
Accounts receivable	(21.3)	128.7	(27.7)
Inventories	(52.1)	9.1	(15.4)
Other operating assets	(36.8)	(0.8)	(7.6)
Accounts payable	42.7	(27.0)	20.0
Accrued compensation and other current liabilities	53.2	190.5	(24.5)
Deferred revenue	176.7	219.3	401.0
Other operating liabilities	46.7	10.6	117.5
Net cash provided by operating activities	975.0	889.2	1,008.9

Adjustments to Reconcile Net Income: Unrealized Change

6.29

DEVON ENERGY CORPORATION (DEC)

CONSOLIDATED STATEMENTS OF CASH FLOWS
(in part)

	Year Ended December 31		
(In millions)	2010	2009	2008
Cash Flows From Operating Activities:			
Earnings (loss) from continuing operations	$2,333	$(2,753)	$(3,039)
Adjustments to reconcile earnings (loss) from continuing operations to net cash provided by operating activities:			
Depreciation, depletion and amortization	1,930	2,108	3,203
Deferred income tax expense (benefit)	719	(2,014)	(1,562)
Reduction of carrying value of oil and gas properties	—	6,408	9,891
Unrealized change in fair value of financial instruments	107	55	(456)
Other noncash charges	215	288	623
Net decrease (increase) in working capital	(273)	149	(207)
Decrease (increase) in long-term other assets	32	(6)	(53)
Increase (decrease) in long-term other liabilities	(41)	(3)	48
Cash from operating activities—continuing operations	5,022	4,232	8,448
Cash from operating activities—discontinued operations	456	505	960
Net cash from operating activities	5,478	4,737	9,408

CASH FLOWS FROM INVESTING ACTIVITIES

PRESENTATION

6.30 FASB ASC 230 defines those transactions and events that constitute investing cash receipts and payments. Investing activities include making and collecting loans and acquiring and disposing of debt or equity instruments and property, plant, and equipment (PPE) and other productive assets. Investing activities exclude acquiring and disposing of certain loans or other debt or equity instruments that are acquired specifically for resale. Cash flows from purchases, sales, and maturities of available-for-sale securities should be classified as cash flows from investing activities and reported gross in the statement of cash flows. The following are considered cash receipts and payments from investing activities:

- Receipts from collections or sales of loans made by the entity and of other entities' debt instruments, other than cash equivalents and certain debt instruments that are acquired specifically for resale, that were purchased by the entity.
- Receipts from sales of equity instruments of other entities, other than certain equity instruments carried in a trading account, and from returns of investment in those instruments.
- Receipts from sales of PPE and other productive assets.
- Receipts from sales of loans that were not specifically acquired for resale. If loans were acquired as investments, cash receipts from sales of those loans shall be classified as investing cash inflows, regardless of a change in the purpose for holding those loans.
- Disbursements for loans made by the entity and payments to acquire debt instruments of other entities, other than cash equivalents and certain debt instruments that are acquired specifically for resale.
- Payments to acquire equity instruments of other entities, other than certain equity instruments carried in a trading account.
- Payments at the time of purchase or soon before or after purchase to acquire PPE and other productive assets, including interest capitalized as part of the cost of those assets. Generally, only advance payments, the down payment, or other amounts paid at the time of purchase or soon before or after the purchase of PPE and other productive assets are investing cash outflows. However, incurring directly-related debt to the seller is a financing transaction; thus, subsequent payments of principal on that debt are financing cash outflows.

PRESENTATION AND DISCLOSURE EXCERPTS

Property Acquisitions

6.31

TENET HEALTHCARE CORPORATION (DEC)

*CONSOLIDATED STATEMENTS OF CASH FLOWS
(in part)*

(Dollars in millions)	Years Ended December 31		
	2010	2009	2008
Cash flows from investing activities:			
Purchases of property and equipment—continuing operations	(450)	(397)	(452)
Construction of new and replacement hospitals	(13)	(58)	(75)
Purchases of property and equipment—discontinued operations	(13)	(1)	(20)
Purchases of business or joint venture interest	(65)	0	(92)
Proceeds from sales of facilities and other assets—discontinued operations	19	221	160
Proceeds from sales of marketable securities, long-term investments and other assets	84	67	224
Purchases of marketable securities	0	(17)	(26)
Distributions received from (reclassification of) investments in Reserve Yield Plus Fund	1	12	(14)
Proceeds from hospital authority bonds	0	49	8
Proceeds from cash surrender value or basis reduction of insurance policies	0	0	11
Release of escrow funds	15	0	0
Other items, net	2	(1)	2
Net cash used in investing activities	(420)	(125)	(274)

NOTES TO CONSOLIDATED FINANCIAL STATEMENTS (in part)

Note 10. Property and Equipment

The principal components of property and equipment are shown in the table below (dollars in millions):

	December 31	
	2010	2009
Land	$ 352	$ 341
Buildings and improvements	3,984	3,883
Construction in progress	205	264
Equipment	2,863	2,795
	7,404	7,283
Accumulated depreciation and amortization	(3,100)	(2,970)
Net property and equipment	$ 4,304	$ 4,313

Property and equipment is stated at cost, less accumulated depreciation and amortization and impairment write-downs related to assets held and used. At December 31, 2010 and 2009, we had $91 million and $66 million, respectively, of property and equipment purchases accrued for items received but not yet paid. Of these amounts, $87 million and $61 million, respectively, were included in accounts payable.

Investments

6.32

THE SHAW GROUP INC. (AUG)

CONSOLIDATED STATEMENTS OF CASH FLOWS (in part)

(In thousands)	2010	2009	2008
Cash flows from investing activities:			
Purchases of property and equipment	(194,382)	(132,216)	(129,166)
Proceeds from sale of businesses and assets, net of cash surrendered	24,297	25,816	24,022
Sales of restricted short-term investments	90,609	—	—
Purchases of variable interest entity debt	(19,915)	—	—
Investment in, advances to, and return of capital from unconsolidated entities and joint ventures	15,197	(3,670)	(2,927)
Cash withdrawn from restricted and escrowed cash	156,409	247,556	180,874
Cash deposited into restricted and escrowed cash	(105,350)	(320,294)	(169,618)
Purchases of short-term investments	(1,117,553)	(342,219)	—
Proceeds from sale and redemption of short-term investments	899,835	—	—
Purchases of restricted short-term investments	(307,483)	(80,000)	—
Net cash used in investing activities	(558,336)	(605,027)	(96,815)

NOTES TO CONSOLIDATED FINANCIAL STATEMENTS (in part)

Note 1—Description of Business and Summary of Significant Accounting Policies (in part)

Marketable Securities

We categorize our marketable securities as either "trading" or "available-for-sale." These investments are recorded at fair value and are classified as short-term investments in the accompanying consolidated balance sheets. Investments are made based on the Company's investment policy and restrictions contained in our credit facility, which specifies eligible investments and credit quality requirements.

Trading securities are investments held in trust to satisfy obligations under our deferred compensation plans. The changes in fair values on trading securities are recorded as a component of net income in other income (expense), net.

Available-for-sale securities consist of mutual funds, U.S. government and agency obligations, corporate notes and bonds, foreign government and foreign government guaranteed securities, and certificates of deposit at major banks. The changes in fair values, net of applicable taxes, on available-for-sale securities are recorded as unrealized gains (losses) as a component of accumulated other comprehensive income (loss) in stockholders' equity. When fair value of an investment decreases below its cost or amortized cost and in management's opinion that decline is "other-than-temporary," the investment's cost or amortized cost is written down to its fair value and the amount written down is recorded in the statement of operations in other income (expense), net. Management considers a decline "other than temporary" if, among other relevant factors, the fair value is significantly below cost for a period of time. The amount of any write-down is determined by the difference between cost or amortized cost of the investment and its fair value at the time management makes the other-than-temporary determination. During the fiscal year ended August 31, 2010, no other-than-temporary impairment was recognized.

Note 2 – Cash, Cash Equivalents and Short-Term Investments (in part)

At August 31, 2010, the components of our cash, cash equivalents, and short-term investments were as follows (in thousands):

| | | | | | Balance Sheet Classification | |
	Cost Basis	Unrealized Gain	Unrealized (Loss)	Recorded Basis	Cash and Cash Equivalents	Short-Term Investments
Cash	$ 401,277	$ —	$ —	$ 401,277	$401,277	$ —
Money market mutual funds	509,781	—	—	509,781	509,781	—
Certificates of deposit	325,668	—	—	325,668	1,678	323,990
Available-for-sale debt securities:						
Bond mutual funds	75,236	738	—	75,974	—	75,974
Foreign government and foreign government guaranteed securities	42,570	217	—	42,787	—	42,787
Corporate notes and bonds	109,270	320	(381)	109,209	—	109,209
Total	$1,463,802	$1,275	$(381)	$1,464,696	$912,736	$551,960

At August 31, 2009, the components of our cash, cash equivalents, and short-term investments were as follows (in thousands):

| | | | | | Balance Sheet Classification | |
	Cost Basis	Unrealized Gain	Unrealized (Loss)	Recorded Basis	Cash and Cash Equivalents	Short-Term Investments
Cash and cash equivalents	$1,029,138	$—	$—	$1,029,138	$1,029,138	$ —
Time deposits	342,219	—	—	342,219	—	342,219
Total	$1,371,357	$—	$—	$1,371,357	$1,029,138	$342,219

Business Combinations

6.33

CORN PRODUCTS INTERNATIONAL, INC. (DEC)

CONSOLIDATED STATEMENTS OF CASH FLOWS (in part)

| | Years Ended December 31 | | |
(In millions)	2010	2009	2008
Cash provided by (used for) investing activities:			
Capital expenditures	(159)	(146)	(228)
Proceeds from disposal of plants and properties	3	5	9
Payments for acquisitions, net of cash acquired of $82 in 2010	(1,272)	(4)	—
Cash used for investing activities	(1,428)	(145)	(219)

NOTES TO CONSOLIDATED FINANCIAL STATEMENTS (in part)

Note 3—Acquisitions (in part)

On October 1, 2010, the Company completed its acquisition of National Starch, a global provider of specialty starches, from Akzo Nobel N.V., a global coatings and specialty chemicals company, headquartered in The Netherlands. The Company acquired 100 percent of National Starch through asset purchases in certain countries and stock purchases in certain countries. The purchase price was $1.354 billion in cash, subject to certain post-closing adjustments and other finalizations to the valuation. The funding of the purchase price was provided principally from borrowings. See Note 6 for information regarding the Company's borrowing activity. The Company incurred $35 million of acquisition costs and a $20 million charge for bridge loan financing costs related to the acquisition in 2010. The results of National Starch are included in the Company's consolidated results from October 1, 2010 forward.

The acquisition positions the Company with a broader portfolio of products, enhanced geographic reach, and the ability to offer customers a broad range of value-added ingredient solutions for a variety of their evolving needs. National Starch had sales of $1.2 billion in 2009 and provides the Company with, among other things, 11 additional manufacturing facilities in 8 countries, across 5 continents. The acquisition also provides additional sales and technical offices around the world. With the acquisition, the Company now employs approximately 10,700 people in North America, South America, Asia/Africa and Europe. It operates 37 manufacturing facilities in 15 countries; has sales offices in 29 countries, and has research and ingredient development centers in key global markets.

The allocation of the preliminary purchase price to the tangible and identifiable intangible assets acquired and liabilities assumed, based on their fair values as of October 1, 2010, is provided below. Goodwill represents the amount by which the purchase price exceeds the fair value of the net assets acquired. It is estimated that approximately 15 percent of the goodwill associated with this acquisition is deductible for tax purposes.

(In millions)	
Working capital	$ 219
Property, plant and equipment	549
Other assets	119
Intangible assets	359
Goodwill	392
Non-current liabilities assumed	(284)
Total preliminary purchase price	$1,354

All of the Company's acquisitions were accounted for under the purchase method.

Sale of Discontinued Operations

6.34

TEREX CORPORATION (DEC)

CONSOLIDATED STATEMENT OF CASH FLOWS
(in part)

	Year Ended December 31		
(In millions)	2010	2009	2008
Investing Activities of Continuing Operations			
Capital expenditures	(55.0)	(50.4)	(103.6)
Acquisition of businesses, net of cash acquired	(12.8)	(9.8)	(481.5)
Investments in and advances to affiliates	(19.3)	—	—
Proceeds from disposition of discontinued operations	1,002.0	—	—
Investments in derivative securities	(21.1)	—	—
Proceeds from sale of assets	10.0	6.1	20.6
Net cash provided by (used in) investing activities of continuing operations	903.8	(54.1)	(564.5)
Cash Flows from Discontinued Operations			
Net cash (used in) provided by operating activities of discontinued operations	(53.1)	2.9	10.1
Net cash provided by (used in) investing activities of discontinued operations	0.1	(7.0)	(14.8)
Net cash used in financing activities of discontinued operations	—	(0.2)	(0.6)
Net cash used in discontinued operations	(53.0)	(4.3)	(5.3)

NOTES TO CONSOLIDATED FINANCIAL STATEMENTS (in part)

Note D—Discontinued Operations

On February 19, 2010, the Company completed the disposition of its Mining business, which was previously part of the former Materials Processing & Mining segment, to Bucyrus and received approximately $1 billion in cash and approximately 5.8 million shares of Bucyrus common stock. Following this transaction the Company is investing in its current businesses and focusing on products and services where it can maintain and build a strong market presence. The products divested by the Company in the transaction included hydraulic mining excavators, high capacity surface mining trucks, track and rotary blasthole drills, drill tools and highwall mining equipment, as well as the related parts and aftermarket service businesses, including the Company-owned distribution locations. The Company recorded a gain on the sale of its Mining business of approximately $606 million, net of tax for the year ended December 31, 2010. The Company is involved in a dispute with Bucyrus regarding the calculation of the value of the net assets of the Mining business.

Bucyrus has provided the Company with their calculation of the net asset value of the Mining business, which seeks a payment of approximately $149 million from the Company to Bucyrus. The Company believes that the Bucyrus calculation of the net asset value is incorrect and not in accordance with the terms of the definitive agreement. The Company has objected to Bucyrus' calculation and has provided Bucyrus with its calculation of the net asset value, which does not require any payment from the Company to Bucyrus. The Company initiated a court proceeding on October 29, 2010 in the Supreme Court of the State of New York, County of New York, to enforce and protect its rights under the definitive agreement. While the Company believes Bucyrus' position is without merit and it is vigorously opposing it, no assurance can be given as to the final resolution of this dispute or that the Company will not ultimately be required to make a substantial payment to Bucyrus.

The Company accounts for the shares of Bucyrus common stock received as "available for sale" securities as defined in ASC 320, "Investments—Debt and Equity Securities." As such, the carrying value of the Bucyrus common stock will be adjusted on a quarterly basis based on changes in fair value of the stock with the corresponding entry for unrealized gains and losses recorded in Accumulated other comprehensive income. This stock is traded in an active market and measured under the Level 1 fair value category as defined in Note J—"Fair Value Measurements."

On December 31, 2009, the Company completed the sale of substantially all of the assets used in its construction trailer operations, which was formerly part of the AWP segment. The total purchase price received at closing was $3.1 million, comprised of $0.1 million in cash and $3.0 million of promissory notes. The promissory notes are secured by a security agreement and a mortgage on the real estate sold in the transaction.

In March 2010, the Company sold the assets of its Powertrain gears business and pumps business, which were formerly part of the Construction segment. Total proceeds on the sale of these businesses were approximately $2 million.

On March 10, 2010, the Company entered into an agreement to sell its Atlas businesses to Atlas Maschinen. Fil Filipov, a former Terex executive and the father of Steve Filipov, the Company's President, Developing Markets and Strategic Accounts, is the Chairman of Atlas Maschinen. The Atlas product lines divested in the transaction include crawler, wheel and rail excavators, knuckle-boom truck loader cranes and Terex ® Atlas branded material handlers. The transaction also includes the Terex Atlas UK distribution business for truck loader cranes in the United Kingdom and the Terex minority ownership position in an Atlas Chinese joint venture. The Atlas business was previously reported in the Construction segment, with the exception of the knuckle-boom truck loader cranes business, which was reported in the Cranes segment. On April 15, 2010, the Company completed the portion of this transaction related to the Atlas operations in Germany and completed the portion of the transaction related to the operations in the United Kingdom on August 11, 2010. The Company recorded a loss on the sale of Atlas of approximately $17 million, net of tax, for the year ended December 31, 2010.

The following amounts related to the discontinued operations were derived from historical financial information and have been segregated from continuing operations and reported as discontinued operations in the Consolidated Statement of Income (in millions):

	Year Ended December 31		
	2010	2009	2008
Net sales	$ 157.7	$1,346.6	$1,930.7
(Loss) income from discontinued operations before income taxes	$ (9.7)	$ 88.6	$ 233.8
Provision for income taxes	(5.6)	(66.9)	(83.4)
(Loss) income from discontinued operations—net of tax	$ (15.3)	$ 21.7	$ 150.4
Gain (loss) on disposition of discontinued operations	$ 832.7	$ (19.5)	$ —
(Provision for) benefit from income taxes	(243.4)	6.9	—
Gain (loss) on disposition of discontinued operations—net of tax	$ 589.3	$ (12.6)	$ —

The following table provides the amounts of assets and liabilities reported in discontinued operations in the Consolidated Balance Sheet (in millions):

	December 31	
	2010	2009
Cash and cash equivalents	$—	$ 41.7
Trade receivables, net	—	161.3
Inventories	—	479.3
Other current assets	—	41.0
Current assets—discontinued operations	$—	$723.3
Property, plant and equipment - net	$—	$ 67.4
Goodwill	—	70.6
Other assets	—	71.6
Long-term assets—discontinued operations	$—	$209.6
Trade accounts payable	$—	$104.8
Accrued compensation and benefits	—	23.3
Accrued warranties and product liability	—	38.8
Customer advances	—	7.6
Other current liabilities	—	83.0
Current liabilities—discontinued operations	$—	$257.5
Non-current liabilities—discontinued operations	$—	$143.8

The following table provides the amounts of cash and cash equivalents presented in the Consolidated Statement of Cash Flows as of December 31:

	2010	2009	2008
Cash and cash equivalents:			
Cash and cash equivalents— continuing operations	$894.2	$929.5	$450.4
Cash and cash equivalents— discontinued operations	—	41.7	34.0
Total cash and cash equivalents	$894.2	$971.2	$484.4

As a condition of the sale of the Company's Mining business to Bucyrus and the Atlas business to Atlas Maschinen, the parties have entered into transition services agreements. The agreements require Terex to provide the respective counterparties to the transactions with certain general and administrative functions and the use of certain business related assets for a period of time after the close of the sale in exchange for a fee.

Notes Receivable

6.35

BASSETT FURNITURE INDUSTRIES, INCORPORATED (NOV)

CONSOLIDATED STATEMENTS OF CASH FLOWS
(in part)

(In thousands)	2010	2009	2008
Investing activities:			
Purchases of property and equipment	(2,013)	(1,094)	(4,702)
Purchases of retail real estate	—	(2)	(858)
Proceeds from sales and condemnation of property and equipment	4,247	129	2,862
Acquisition of retail licensee stores, net of cash acquired	(378)	(481)	(216)
Proceeds from sales of investments	9,101	26,234	35,817
Purchases of investments	(8,851)	(6,939)	(6,185)
Dividends from affiliates	937	3,847	6,091
Net cash received on licensee notes	494	645	896
Other, net	—	—	(18)
Net cash provided by investing activities	3,537	22,339	33,687

NOTES TO CONSOLIDATED FINANCIAL STATEMENTS (in part)

(In thousands, except share and per share data)

6. Notes Receivable

Notes receivable consists of the following:

	November 27, 2010	November 28, 2009
Notes receivable	$14,914	$19,411
Allowance for doubtful accounts and discounts on notes receivable	(6,748)	(8,950)
Notes receivable, net	8,166	10,461
Less: current portion of notes receivable	(658)	(2,152)
Long term notes receivable	$ 7,508	$ 8,309

Our notes receivable, which bear interest at rates ranging from 2% to 6%, consist primarily of amounts due from our licensees from loans made by the Company to help licensees fund their operations. Approximately 61% and 64% of our notes receivable represent conversions of past due accounts receivable at November 27, 2010 and November 28, 2009, respectively. The net carrying value of notes receivable that are considered to be on non-accrual status for the recognition of interest at November 27, 2010 and November 28, 2009 was $2,277 and $3,083, respectively.

Activity in the allowance for doubtful accounts and discounts was as follows:

	2010	2009
Balance, beginning of the year	$ 8,950	$ 6,596
Additions charged to expense	1,896	6,297
Write-offs	(4,027)	(3,813)
Amortization of discounts	(71)	(130)
Balance, end of the year	$ 6,748	$ 8,950

We amortize the related note discount over the contractual term of the note and cease amortizing the discount to interest income when the present value of expected future cash flows is less than the carrying value of the note. Interest income on the notes, which is included in other loss, net, was $463, $681 and $705 for fiscal 2010, 2009, and 2008, respectively.

During fiscal 2009 we converted past due trade accounts receivable and refinanced an existing note receivable of three licensees. As part of the improvement plans with one of our licensees, we converted $1,100 of past due trade accounts receivable and refinanced an existing note with a remaining balance of $224 into a $1,324 long-term note bearing interest at 4.75%. This note requires interest only payments through 2011 and interest and principal payments due monthly through its maturity on December 31, 2016. Additionally, we converted $550 and $250 of past due trade accounts receivable for two licensees to 4.75% long-term interest bearing notes. The $550 note requires interest only payments through March 16, 2012, and principal and interest payments due monthly through its maturity date of March 16, 2015. The $250 note requires interest only payments through March 16, 2011, with the remaining interest and principal due on April 16, 2011.

The initial carrying value of the notes is determined using present value techniques which consider the fair market rate of interest based on the licensee's risk profile and estimated cash flows to be received. We considered the stated interest rates to be below market due to the overall lack of availability of credit in the financial markets. The following table presents summary fair value information at the inception of these notes:

Face Value of Note Receivable	Discount Rate	Fair Value
$1,324	19.50%	$672
550	5.25%	539
250	19.61%	187

The estimated fair value of our notes receivable portfolio was $8,212 at November 27, 2010 and $10,208 at November 28, 2009. The inputs into these fair value calculations reflect our market assumptions and are not observable. Consequently, the inputs are considered to be Level 3 as specified in the fair value hierarchy in ASC Topic 820, *Fair Value Measurements and Disclosures*. See Note 8.

On a quarterly basis we examine these notes for evidence of impairment, considering factors such as licensee capitalization, projected operating performance, the viability of the market in which the licensee operates and the licensee's operating history, including our cash receipts from the licensee, licensee sales and any underlying collateral. After considering these factors, should we believe that all or a portion of the expected cash flows attributable to the note receivable will not be received, we record an impairment charge on the note by estimating future cash flows and discounting them at the effective interest rate. Any difference between the estimated discounted cash flows and the carrying value of the note is recorded as an increase to the allowance for doubtful accounts.

These notes, as well as our accounts receivable, are generally secured by the filing of security statements in accordance with the Uniform Commercial Code and/or real estate owned by the maker of the note and in some cases, personal guarantees by our licensees.

Capitalized Software

6.36

ARKANSAS BEST CORPORATION (DEC)

CONSOLIDATED STATEMENTS OF CASH FLOWS (in part)

($ thousands)	Year Ended December 31		
	2010	**2009**	**2008**
Investing activities			
Purchases of property, plant and equipment, net of capital leases	(11,422)	(48,044)	(58,729)
Proceeds from asset sales	5,879	4,913	17,073
Purchases of short-term investment securities	(65,171)	(109,806)	(146,655)
Proceeds from sales of short-term investment securities	119,744	133,800	107,404
Business acquisition, net of cash acquired	—	(4,873)	—
Capitalization of internally developed software and other	(4,355)	(5,176)	(5,325)
Net cash provided by (used in) investing activities	44,675	(29,186)	(86,232)

NOTES TO CONSOLIDATED FINANCIAL STATEMENTS (in part)

Note B—Accounting Policies (in part)

Computer Software Developed or Obtained for Internal Use, Including Web Site Development Costs: The Company capitalizes qualifying computer software costs incurred during the "application development stage." For financial reporting purposes, capitalized software costs are amortized by the straight-line method over 2 to 3 years. The amount of costs capitalized within any period is dependent on the nature of software development activities and projects in each period.

Restricted Cash

6.37

XEROX CORPORATION (DEC)

CONSOLIDATED STATEMENTS OF CASH FLOWS (in part)

(In millions)	Year Ended December 31		
	2010	**2009**	**2008**
Cash Flows From Investing Activities:			
Cost of additions to land, buildings and equipment	(355)	(95)	(206)
Proceeds from sales of land, buildings and equipment	52	17	38
Cost of additions to internal use software	(164)	(98)	(129)
Acquisitions, net of cash acquired	(1,734)	(163)	(155)
Net change in escrow and other restricted investments	20	(6)	8
Other investing, net	3	2	3
Net cash used in investing activities	(2,178)	(343)	(441)

NOTES TO CONSOLIDATED FINANCIAL STATEMENTS (in part)

Note 1—Summary of Significant Accounting Policies (in part)

Restricted Cash and Investments

As more fully discussed in Note 17—Contingencies, various litigation matters in Brazil require us to make cash deposits as a condition of continuing the litigation. In addition, several of our secured financing arrangements and other contracts require us to post cash collateral or maintain minimum cash balances in escrow. These cash amounts are classified in our Consolidated Balance Sheets based on when the cash will be contractually or judicially released (refer to Note 10—Supplementary Financial Information for classification of amounts).

Restricted cash amounts at December 31, 2010 and 2009 were as follows:

	2010	2009
Tax and labor litigation deposits in Brazil	$276	$240
Escrow and cash collections related to receivable sales	88	29
Other restricted cash	7	20
Total Restricted Cash and Investments	$371	$289

Insurance Proceeds

6.38

SMITHFIELD FOODS, INC. (APR)

CONSOLIDATED STATEMENTS OF CASH FLOWS
(in part)

	Fiscal Years		
(In millions)	2010	2009	2008
Cash Flows From Investing Activities:			
Capital expenditures	(182.7)	(174.5)	(460.2)
Dispositions	23.3	587.0	—
Insurance proceeds	9.9	—	—
Dividends received	5.3	56.5	—
Investments in partnerships	(1.3)	(31.7)	(6.6)
Proceeds from sale of property, plant and equipment	11.7	21.4	24.7
Business acquisitions, net of cash acquired	—	(17.4)	(41.8)
Net cash flows from investing activities	(133.8)	441.3	(483.9)
Cash Flows From Discontinued Operations:			
Net cash flows from operating activities	—	34.7	4.4
Net cash flows from investing activities	—	(7.0)	(8.2)
Net cash flows from financing activities	—	(0.8)	—
Net cash flows from discontinued operations activities	—	26.9	(3.8)

NOTES TO CONSOLIDATED FINANCIAL STATEMENTS *(in part)*

Note 18. Regulation and Contingencies (in part)

Insurance Recoveries

In July 2009 (fiscal 2010), a fire occurred at the primary manufacturing facility of our subsidiary, Patrick Cudahy, Incorporated (Patrick Cudahy), in Cudahy, WI. The fire damaged a portion of the facility's production space and required the temporary cessation of operations, but did not consume the entire facility. Shortly after the fire, we resumed production activities in undamaged portions of the plant, including the distribution center, and took steps to address the supply needs for Patrick Cudahy products by shifting production to other Company and third party facilities.

The products produced at the facility include precooked and traditional bacon, dry sausage, ham and sliced meats. Patrick Cudahy's operating results are reported in the Pork segment. Annual revenues for Patrick Cudahy's packaged meats business have exceeded $450 million in recent years.

We maintain comprehensive general liability and property insurance, including business interruption insurance, with loss limits that we believe will provide substantial and broad coverage for the currently foreseeable losses arising from this accident. We are working with our insurance carrier to determine the extent of loss. We have received advances totaling $70.0 million toward the ultimate settlement in fiscal 2010. The magnitude and timing of the ultimate settlement is currently unknown. However, we expect the level of insurance proceeds to fully cover the costs and losses incurred from the fire.

We have also been working with a third-party specialist to determine the amount of business interruption losses incurred. Based on an evaluation of business interruption losses incurred, we recognized $31.8 million of the insurance proceeds in cost of sales to offset these previously recorded losses. Additionally, $ 33.0 million of the insurance proceeds was recorded to offset the asset write-offs and other costs incurred. The remaining $5.2 million has been deferred in accrued expenses and other current liabilities to offset future business interruption losses and other reimbursable costs associated with the fire.

Of the $70.0 million in insurance proceeds received during fiscal 2010, $9.9 million has been classified in net cash flows from investing activities in the consolidated condensed statements of cash flows, which represents the portion of proceeds related to destruction of the plant. The remainder of the proceeds was recorded in net cash flows from operating activities in the consolidated condensed statements of cash flows and was attributed to business interruption recoveries and reimbursable costs covered under our insurance policy.

In-Process Research & Development (IPRD)

6.39

JOHNSON & JOHNSON (DEC)

CONSOLIDATED STATEMENTS OF CASH FLOWS
(in part)

(Dollars in millions) (Note 1)	2010	2009	2008
Cash flows from investing activities			
Additions to property, plant and equipment	(2,384)	(2,365)	(3,066)
Proceeds from the disposal of assets	524	154	785
Acquisitions, net of cash acquired (Note 20)	(1,269)	(2,470)	(1,214)
Purchases of investments	(15,788)	(10,040)	(3,668)
Sales of investments	11,101	7,232	3,059
Other (primarily intangibles)	(38)	(109)	(83)
Net cash used by investing activities	(7,854)	(7,598)	(4,187)
Supplemental schedule of noncash investing and financing activities			
Treasury stock issued for employee compensation and stock option plans, net of cash proceeds	$ 673	541	593
Conversion of debt	1	2	—

NOTES TO CONSOLIDATED FINANCIAL STATEMENTS (in part)

20. Business Combinations and Divestitures

Certain businesses were acquired for $1,269 million in cash and $52 million of liabilities assumed during 2010. These acquisitions were accounted for by the purchase method and, accordingly, results of operations have been included in the financial statements from their respective dates of acquisition.

The 2010 acquisitions included: Acclarent, Inc., a privately held medical technology company dedicated to designing, developing and commercializing devices that address conditions affecting the ear, nose and throat (ENT); RespiVert Ltd., a privately held drug discovery company focused on developing small-molecule, inhaled therapies for the treatment of pulmonary diseases and Micrus Endovascular Corporation, a global developer and manufacturer of minimally invasive devices for hemorrhagic and ischemic stroke.

The excess of purchase price over the estimated fair value of tangible assets acquired amounted to $1,185 million and has been assigned to identifiable intangible assets, with any residual recorded to goodwill. Of this amount, approximately $213 million has been identified as the value of IPR&D associated with the acquisitions of Acclarent, Inc., RespiVert Ltd. and Micrus Endovascular Corporation.

The IPR&D related to the acquisition of Acclarent, Inc. was $75 million and is associated with novel, endoscopic, catheter-based devices to meet the needs of ENT patients. The value of the IPR&D was calculated using cash flow projections discounted for the risk inherent in such projects. Probability of success factors ranging from 50–53% were used to reflect inherent clinical and regulatory risk. The discount rate applied was 16%.

The IPR&D related to the acquisition of RespiVert Ltd., was $100 million and is associated with narrow spectrum kinase inhibitors with a unique profile of anti-inflammatory activities as treatments for moderate to severe asthma, Chronic Obstructive Pulmonary Disease (COPD) and Cystic Fibrosis (CF). The value of the IPR&D was calculated using cash flow projections discounted for the risk inherent in such projects. Probability of success factors ranging from 10–12% were used to reflect inherent clinical and regulatory risk. The discount rate applied was 17%.

The IPR&D related to the acquisition of Micrus Endovascular Corporation was $38 million and is associated with ischemic and flow diverter technologies. The value of the IPR&D was calculated using cash flow projections discounted for the risk inherent in such projects. Probability of success factors ranging from 50–75% were used to reflect inherent clinical and regulatory risk. The discount rate applied was 14%.

During 2010, the Company announced an agreement to acquire all outstanding equity of Crucell N.V. that it does not already own for approximately $2.3 billion in a cash tender offer. As of January 2, 2011 the Company held approximately 18% of Crucell's outstanding ordinary shares. Crucell is a global biopharmaceutical company focused on the research & development, production and marketing of vaccines and antibodies against infectious disease worldwide. On February 22, 2011, the Company announced that the tender offer for Crucell has been completed and has declared the offer unconditional.

Certain businesses were acquired for $2,470 million in cash and $875 million of liabilities assumed and non-controlling interests during 2009. These acquisitions were accounted for by the purchase method and, accordingly, results of operations have been included in the financial statements from their respective dates of acquisition.

The 2009 acquisitions included: Mentor Corporation, a leading supplier of medical products for the global aesthetics market; Cougar Biotechnology, Inc., a development stage biopharmaceutical company with a specific focus on oncology; Finsbury Orthopaedics Limited, a privately held UK-based manufacturer and global distributor of orthopaedic implants; Gloster Europe, a privately held developer of innovative disinfection processes and technologies to prevent healthcare-acquired infections and substantially all of the assets and rights of Elan's Alzheimer's Immunotherapy Program through a newly formed company, of which the Company owns 50.1% and Elan owns 49.9%.

The excess of purchase price over the estimated fair value of tangible assets acquired amounted to $2,940 million and has been assigned to identifiable intangible assets, with any residual recorded to goodwill. Of this amount, approximately $1,737 million has been identified as the value of IPR&D primarily associated with the acquisitions of Cougar Biotechnology, Inc. and substantially all of the assets and rights of Elan's Alzheimer's Immunotherapy Program. Additionally, approximately $1,107 million has been identified as the value of other intangible assets, including patents & technology and customer relationships primarily associated with the acquisition of Mentor Corporation.

The IPR&D related to the acquisition of Cougar Biotechnology, Inc. was $971 million and is associated with abiraterone acetate, a late stage, first-in-class compound for the treatment of prostate cancer. The value of the IPR&D was calculated using cash flow projections discounted for the risk inherent in such projects. Probability of success factors ranging from 60–85% were used to reflect inherent clinical and regulatory risk. The discount rate applied was 23.5%.

During 2009, the Company acquired substantially all of the assets and rights of Elan's Alzheimer's Immunotherapy Program through a newly formed company, Janssen Alzheimer Immunotherapy (JAI), of which the Company owns 50.1% and Elan owns 49.9%. In addition, the Company purchased approximately 107 million newly issued American Depositary Receipts (ADRs) of Elan, representing 18.4% of Elan's outstanding ordinary shares. As part of this transaction, the Company paid $885 million to Elan and committed to fund up to $250 million of Elan's share of research and development spending by JAI. Of this total consideration of $1,135 million, $793 million represents the fair value of the 18.4% investment in Elan based on Elan's share price in an actively traded market as of the date of this transaction. The IPR&D related to this transaction was $679 million and is associated with bapineuzumab, a potential first-in-class treatment that is being evaluated for slowing the progression of Alzheimer's Disease. The value of the IPR&D was calculated using cash flow projections discounted for the risk inherent in such projects. Probability of success factors ranging from 40–50% were used to reflect inherent clinical and regulatory risk. The discount rate applied was 26%. The non-controlling interest related to this transaction was $590 million, which the Company has recorded in other non-current liabilities.

Certain businesses were acquired for $1,214 million in cash and $114 million of liabilities assumed during 2008. These acquisitions were accounted for by the purchase method and, accordingly, results of operations have been included in the financial statements from their respective dates of acquisition.

The 2008 acquisitions included: Amic AB, a privately held Swedish developer of in vitro diagnostic technologies for use in point-of-care and near-patient settings; Beijing Dabao Cosmetics Co., Ltd., a company that sells personal care brands in China; SurgRx, Inc., a privately held developer of the advanced bipolar tissue sealing system used in the ENSEAL ® family of devices; HealthMedia, Inc., a privately held company that creates web-based behavior change interventions; LGE Performance Systems, Inc., a privately held company known as Human Performance Institute™, which develops science-based training programs to improve employee engagement and productivity and Omrix Biopharmaceuticals, Inc., a fully integrated biopharmaceutical company that develops and markets biosurgical and immunotherapy products.

The excess of purchase price over the estimated fair value of tangible assets acquired amounted to $891 million and has been assigned to identifiable intangible assets, with any residual recorded to goodwill. Approximately $181 million has been identified as the value of IPR&D associated with the acquisitions of Omrix Biopharmaceuticals, Inc., Amic AB, SurgRx, Inc. and HealthMedia, Inc.

The IPR&D charge related to the acquisition of Omrix Biopharmaceuticals, Inc. was $127 million and is associated with stand-alone and combination biosurgical technologies used to achieve hemostasis. The value of the IPR&D was calculated using cash flow projections discounted for the risk inherent in such projects. Probability of success factors ranging from 60–90% were used to reflect inherent clinical and regulatory risk. The discount rate applied was 14%.

The IPR&D charge related to the acquisition of Amic AB was $40 million and is associated with point-of-care device and 4CAST Chip technologies. The value of the IPR&D was calculated using cash flow projections discounted for the risk inherent in such projects. The discount rate applied was 20%.

The IPR&D charge related to the acquisition of SurgRx, Inc. was $7 million and is associated with vessel cutting and sealing surgical devices. The value of the IPR&D was calculated using cash flow projections discounted for the risk inherent in such projects. Probability of success factors ranging from 90–95% were used to reflect inherent clinical and regulatory risk. The discount rate applied was 18%.

The IPR&D charge related to the acquisition of HealthMedia, Inc. was $7 million and is associated primarily with process enhancements to software technology. The value of the IPR&D was calculated using cash flow projections discounted for the risk inherent in such projects. A probability of success factor of 90% was used to reflect inherent risk. The discount rate applied was 14%.

Supplemental pro forma information for 2010, 2009 and 2008 in accordance with U.S. GAAP standards related to business combinations, and goodwill and other intangible assets, is not provided, as the impact of the aforementioned acquisitions did not have a material effect on the Company's results of operations, cash flows or financial position.

With the exception of the divestiture of the Breast Care Business of Ethicon Endo-Surgery Inc., for which the gain is recorded in other (income) expense in 2010, and the divestiture of the Professional Wound Care business of Ethicon, Inc., which resulted in a gain of $536 million before tax, and is recorded in other (income) expense, net, in 2008, divestitures in 2010, 2009 and 2008 did not have a material effect on the Company's results of operations, cash flows or financial position.

CASH FLOWS FROM FINANCING ACTIVITIES

PRESENTATION

6.40   FASB ASC 230-10-45 defines those transactions and events that constitute financing cash receipts and payments. The following are considered cash receipts and payments from financing activities:

- Proceeds from issuing equity instruments.
- Proceeds from issuing bonds, mortgages, and notes and from other short- or long-term borrowing.
- Receipts from contributions and investment income that, by donor stipulation, are restricted for the purposes of acquiring, constructing, or improving PPE or other long-lived assets or establishing or increasing a permanent or term endowment.
- Proceeds received from derivative instruments that include financing elements at inception, regardless of whether the proceeds were received at inception or over the term of the derivative instrument, other than a financing element inherently included in an at-the-market derivative instrument with no prepayments.
- Cash that is recognizable for financial reporting purposes because it is retained as a result of the tax deductibility of increases in the value of equity instruments issued under share-based payment arrangements that are not included in the cost of goods or services. For this purpose, excess

tax benefits should be determined on an individual award (or portion thereof) basis.

- Payments of dividends or other distributions to owners, including outlays to reacquire the entity's equity instruments.
- Repayments of borrowed amounts.
- Other principal payments to creditors who have extended long-term credit.
- Distributions to counterparties of derivative instruments that include financing elements at inception, other than a financing element inherently included in an at-the-market derivative instrument with no prepayments. The distributions may be either at inception or over the term of the derivative instrument.
- Payments for debt issue costs.

PRESENTATION AND DISCLOSURE EXCERPTS

Debt Proceeds/Repayments

6.41

RYDER SYSTEM, INC. (DEC)

CONSOLIDATED STATEMENTS OF CASH FLOWS
(in part)

(In thousands)	2010	2009	2008
Cash flows from financing activities of continuing operations:			
Net change in commercial paper borrowings	174,939	148,256	(522,312)
Debt proceeds	314,169	2,014	744,004
Debt repaid, including capital lease obligations	(248,668)	(519,710)	(118,641)
Dividends on common stock	(54,474)	(53,334)	(52,238)
Common stock issued	17,028	7,442	54,713
Common stock repurchased	(123,300)	(116,281)	(256,132)
Excess tax benefits from share-based compensation	754	775	6,471
Debt issuance costs	(2,282)	(11,178)	(4,017)
Net cash provided by (used in) financing activities of continuing operations	78,166	(542,016)	(148,152)

ITEM 7. MANAGEMENT'S DISCUSSION AND ANALYSIS OF FINANCIAL CONDITION AND RESULTS OF OPERATIONS (in part)

Financing and Other Funding Transactions (in part)

In September 2010, we issued $300 million of unsecured medium-term notes maturing in March 2016. If the notes are downgraded following, and as a result of, a change of control, the note holder can require us to repurchase all or a portion of the notes at a purchase price equal to 101% of the principal amount plus accrued and unpaid interest. The medium-term notes were issued to take advantage of his-

torically low interest rates and fund capital expenditures and debt maturities.

The following table shows the movements in our debt balance:

(In thousands)	2010	2009
Debt balance at January 1	$2,497,691	2,862,799
Cash-related changes in debt:		
Net change in commercial paper borrowings	174,939	148,256
Proceeds from issuance of medium-term notes	300,000	—
Proceeds from issuance of other debt instruments	14,169	2,014
Retirement of medium-term notes and debentures	(175,000)	(276,000)
Other debt repaid, including capital lease obligations	(73,668)	(243,710)
Net change from discontinued operations	(2,955)	(9,427)
	237,485	(378,867)
Non-cash changes in debt:		
Fair market value adjustment on notes subject to hedging	3,328	(6,290)
Addition of capital lease obligations, including acquisitions	2,164	1,949
Changes in foreign currency exchange rates and other non-cash items	6,334	18,100
Total changes in debt	249,311	(365,108)
Debt balance at December 31	$2,747,002	2,497,691

Capital Stock Proceeds/Payments

6.42

LAM RESEARCH CORPORATION (JUN)

CONSOLIDATED STATEMENTS OF CASH FLOWS
(in part)

(In thousands)	June 27, 2010	June 28, 2009	June 29, 2008
Cash flows from financing activities:			
Principal payments on long-term debt and capital lease obligations	(21,040)	(256,047)	(251,714)
Net proceeds from issuance of long-term debt	336	625	251,915
Excess tax benefit on equity-based compensation plans	10,234	(6,273)	58,904
Treasury stock purchases	(93,032)	(30,946)	(14,552)
Reissuances of treasury stock	17,452	19,797	8,563
Proceeds from issuance of common stock	13,386	12,014	12,694
Net cash provided by (used for) financing activities	(72,664)	(260,830)	65,810

NOTES TO CONSOLIDATED FINANCIAL STATEMENTS (in part)

Note 19. Stock Repurchase Program

On September 8, 2008, the Company announced that its Board of Directors had authorized the repurchase of up to $250 million of Company common stock from the public market or in private purchases, using the Company's available cash. While the repurchase program does not have a defined termination date, it may be suspended or discontinued at any time.

The Company temporarily suspended repurchases under the program during the December 2008 quarter. Subsequently on February 2, 2010, the Board of Directors authorized the resumption of the repurchase program. Repurchases were expected to be made only in the amounts necessary to offset dilution resulting from the Company's equity compensation plans.

Repurchases under the repurchase program were as follows during the periods indicated (in thousands, except per-share data):

Period	Total Number of Shares Repurchased	Total Cost of Repurchase	Average Price Paid Per Share	Amount Available Under Repurchase Program
(In thousands, except per share data)				
Quarter ended September 27, 2009	—	$ —	$ —	$226,942
Quarter ended December 27, 2009	—	$ —	$ —	$226,942
Quarter ended March 28, 2010	2,000	$68,674	$34.34	$158,268
Quarter ended June 27, 2010	697	$27,575	$39.56	$130,693

In addition to shares repurchased under Board authorized repurchase programs shown above, during the twelve months ended June 27, 2010 the Company withheld 285,000 shares through net share settlements to cover tax withholding obligations upon the vesting of restricted stock unit awards under the Company's equity compensation plans.

Exercise of Stock Options

6.43

TEXAS INDUSTRIES, INC. (MAY)

CONSOLIDATED STATEMENTS OF CASH FLOWS (in part)

(In thousands)	Year Ended May 31		
	2010	2009	2008
Financing activities			
Long-term borrowings	—	327,250	366,000
Debt retirements	(245)	(197,772)	(232,366)
Debt issuance costs	(2,552)	(5,470)	(2,160)
Stock option exercises	893	4,641	3,315
Excess tax benefits from stock-based compensation	250	1,596	3,299
Common dividends paid	(8,328)	(8,287)	(8,222)
Net cash provided (used) by financing activities	(9,982)	121,958	129,866

NOTES TO CONSOLIDATED FINANCIAL STATEMENTS (in part)

6. Stock-Based Compensation Plans

The Texas Industries, Inc. 2004 Omnibus Equity Compensation Plan (the "2004 Plan") provides that, in addition to other types of awards, non-qualified and incentive stock options to purchase Common Stock may be granted to employees and non-employee directors at market prices at date of grant. In addition, non-qualified and incentive stock options remain outstanding under our 1993 Stock Option Plan.

Options become exercisable in installments beginning one year after the date of grant and expire ten years after the date of grant. The fair value of each option grant was estimated on the date of grant using the Black-Scholes option pricing model. Options with graded vesting are valued as single awards and the compensation cost recognized using a straight-line attribution method over the shorter of the vesting period or required service period adjusted for estimated forfeitures. The following table sets forth the information about the weighted-average grant date fair value of options granted during the three years ended May 31, 2010 and the weighted-average assumptions used for such grants.

	2010	2009	2008
Weighted average grant date fair value	$16.83	$9.26	$17.59
Weighted average assumptions used:			
Expected volatility	.469	.398	.317
Expected lives	6.5	6.5	6.1
Risk-free interest rates	3.20%	1.60%	3.21%
Expected dividend yields	.83%	1.21%	.59%

Expected volatility is based on an analysis of historical volatility of our common stock. Expected lives of options is determined based on the historical share option exercise experience of our optionees. Risk-free interest rates are determined using the implied yield currently available for zero coupon U.S. treasury issues with a remaining term equal to the expected life of the options. Expected dividend yields are based on the approved annual dividend rate in effect and the market price of our common stock at the time of grant.

A summary of option transactions for the three years ended May 31, 2010, follows:

	Shares Under Option	Weighted-Average Option Price
Outstanding at May 31, 2007	1,483,035	36.31
Granted	212,850	50.63
Exercised	(212,821)	30.01
Canceled	(18,233)	54.49
Outstanding at May 31, 2008	1,464,831	39.08
Granted	397,700	25.15
Exercised	(233,868)	22.09
Canceled	(33,906)	42.25
Outstanding at May 31, 2009	1,594,757	38.03
Granted	320,450	36.15
Exercised	(122,884)	25.50
Canceled	(27,807)	39.20
Outstanding at May 31, 2010	1,764,516	$38.54

Options exercisable at May 31 were 905,066 shares for 2010, 797,662 shares for 2009 and 892,271 shares for 2008 at a weighted-average option price of $39.09, $35.45 and $28.57, respectively. The following table summarizes information about stock options outstanding as of May 31, 2010.

	Range of Exercise Prices		
	$16.04–$27.39	$36.15–$48.60	$50.63–$70.18
Options outstanding			
Shares outstanding	688,768	491,148	584,600
Weighted-average remaining life in years	5.67	7.83	6.29
Weighted-average exercise price	$ 22.12	$ 39.30	$ 57.26
Options exercisable			
Shares exercisable	389,248	169,498	346,320
Weighted-average remaining life in years	3.47	4.47	6.09
Weighted-average exercise price	$ 20.20	$ 44.92	$ 57.47

Outstanding options expire on various dates to January 13, 2020. Shares reserved for future awards under the 2004 Plan totaled 939,815 at May 31, 2010.

As of May 31, 2010, the aggregate intrinsic value (the difference in the closing market price of our common stock of $36.30 and the exercise price to be paid by the optionee) of stock options outstanding was $9.8 million. The aggregate intrinsic value of exercisable stock options at that date was $6.3 million. The total intrinsic value for options exercised (the difference in the market price of our common stock on the exercise date and the price paid by the optionee to exercise the option) was $1.5 million in 2010, $2.4 million in 2009 and $6.9 million in 2008.

We have provided additional stock-based compensation to employees and directors under stock appreciation rights contracts, deferred compensation agreements, restricted stock payments and a former stock awards program. At May 31, 2010, outstanding stock appreciation rights totaled 133,315 shares, deferred compensation agreements to be settled in cash totaled 100,757 shares, deferred compensation agreements to be settled in common stock totaled 2,070 shares, unvested restricted stock payments totaled 14,667 shares and stock awards totaled 3,499 shares. Other credits included $6.0 million at both May 31, 2010 and May 31, 2009 representing accrued compensation which is expected to be settled in cash. Common stock totaling 2.7 million shares at May 31, 2010 and 2.9 million shares at May 31, 2009 have been reserved for the settlement of stock-based compensation.

Total stock-based compensation included in selling, general and administrative expense (credit) was $5.1 million in 2010, $(4.4) million in 2009 and $2.4 million in 2008. The impact of changes in our company's stock price on stock-based awards accounted for as liabilities increased stock-based compensation $0.5 million in 2010 and reduced stock-based compensation $8.4 million in 2009 and $2.6 million in 2008. The total tax expense or benefit recognized in our statements of operations for stock-based compensation was a benefit of $1.0 million in 2010 and an expense of $2.4 million in 2009 and less than $0.1 million in 2008. The total tax benefit realized for stock-based compensation was $0.7 million in 2010, $2.0 million in 2009 and $3.7 million in 2008.

As of May 31, 2010, $10.5 million of total unrecognized compensation cost related to stock options, restricted stock payments and stock awards is expected to be recognized. We currently expect to recognize approximately $3.9 million of this stock-based compensation expense in 2011, $2.9 million in 2012, $1.9 million in 2013, $1.3 million in 2014 and $0.5 million in 2015.

Dividends

6.44

ARMSTRONG WORLD INDUSTRIES, INC. (DEC)

CONSOLIDATED STATEMENTS OF CASH FLOWS (in part)

(Amounts in millions)	Year Ended December 31		
	2010	2009	2008
Cash flows from financing activities:			
Proceeds from revolving credit facility and other debt	50.0	—	25.0
Payments on revolving credit facility and other debt	(25.1)	(1.2)	(27.5)
Issuance of long-term debt	839.3	2.4	5.4
Payments of long-term debt	(462.1)	(25.6)	(20.9)
Financing costs	(18.0)	—	(2.6)
Special dividend paid	(798.6)	(1.3)	(256.4)
Proceeds from exercised stock options	13.3	2.3	—
Purchase of non-controlling interest	(7.8)	(3.3)	—
Net cash (used for) financing activities	(409.0)	(26.7)	(277.0)

NOTES TO CONSOLIDATED FINANCIAL STATEMENTS (in part)

Note 33. Special Cash Dividend

On November 23, 2010 our Board of Directors declared a special cash dividend in the amount of $13.74 per share, or $803.3 million in the aggregate. The special cash dividend, $798.6 million, was paid on December 10, 2010 to shareholders of record as of December 3, 2010. The unpaid portion of the dividend, $4.7 million, is reflected in other long term liabilities and will be paid when the underlying employee shares vest. The dividend was funded in part by the proceeds of the new term loans remaining after repayment of previous debt and in part with existing cash.

Debt Issuance Costs

6.45

HUNTSMAN CORPORATION (DEC)

CONSOLIDATED STATEMENTS OF CASH FLOWS (in part)

(Dollars in millions)	Year Ended December 31		
	2010	2009	2008
Financing Activities:			
Net (repayments) borrowings under revolving loan facilities	$ (6)	$ (14)	$ 11
Revolving loan facility from A/R Programs	254	—	—
Net (repayments) borrowings on overdraft facilities	(2)	(12)	8
Repayments of short-term debt	(175)	(13)	73
Borrowings on short-term debt	212	—	—
Repayments of long-term debt	(1,456)	(542)	(11)
Proceeds from issuance of long-term debt	923	880	263
Repayments of notes payable	(53)	(66)	(55)
Borrowings on notes payable	46	67	48
Debt issuance costs paid	(29)	(5)	(5)
Call premiums related to early extinguishment of debt	(160)	(14)	—
Dividends paid to common stockholders	(96)	(96)	(93)
Dividends paid to preferred stockholders	—	—	(4)
Repurchase and cancellation of stock awards	(6)	(2)	(4)
Proceeds from issuance of common stock	3	—	—
Excess tax benefit related to stock-based compensation	4	—	—
Other, net	(2)	1	(1)
Net cash (used in) provided by financing activities	(543)	184	230

During 2010, 2009 and 2008, the amount of capital expenditures in accounts payable increased (decreased) by $48, $(13) and $9, respectively. The value of share awards that vested during 2010, 2009 and 2008 was $18, $12 and $13, respectively. In connection with our June 23, 2009 acquisition of Baroda, $5 of payables from us to MCIL were forgiven. Beginning July 1, 2010, we began consolidating Arabian Amines Company, our ethyleneamines manufacturing joint venture in Jubail, Saudi Arabia. For more information, see "Note 7. Variable Interest Entities."

During 2010, 2009 and 2008, capital expenditures of $236, $189 and $418, respectively, were reimbursed in part by $34, nil and nil, respectively, from insurance settlement proceeds. During 2010 we received $110 from the settlement of our insurance claims related to the 2006 fire at our Port Arthur Texas plant, $34 of which was considered as a reimbursement of capital expenditures.

NOTES TO CONSOLIDATED FINANCIAL STATEMENTS (in part)

2. Summary of Significant Accounting Policies (in part)

Other Noncurrent Assets

Other noncurrent assets consist primarily of spare parts, deferred debt issuance costs, the overfunded portion related to defined benefit plans for employees and capitalized turnaround costs. Debt issuance costs are amortized using the interest method over the term of the related debt.

9. Other Noncurrent Assets

Other noncurrent assets consisted of the following (dollars in millions):

	December 31	
	2010	2009
Pension assets	$ 75	$ 31
Debt issuance costs	33	16
Capitalized turnaround costs	164	98
Spare parts inventory	81	82
Catalyst assets	21	18
Deposits	55	56
Other noncurrent assets	66	54
Total	$495	$355

Amortization expense of catalyst assets for the years ended December 31, 2010, 2009 and 2008 was $12 million, $14 million and $12 million, respectively.

Lease Obligation Payments

6.46

URS CORPORATION (DEC)

CONSOLIDATED STATEMENTS OF CASH FLOWS (in part)

	Year Ended		
(In thousands)	December 31, 2010	January 1, 2010	January 2, 2009
Cash flows from financing activities:			
Payments on long-term debt	(159,588)	(310,519)	(209,286)
Net payments under lines of credit and short-term notes	(7,607)	(597)	(261)
Net change in overdrafts	14,400	4,376	(15,200)
Payments on capital lease obligations	(7,497)	(6,415)	(7,713)
Excess tax benefits from stock-based compensation	1,306	1,532	4,491
Proceeds from employee stock purchases and exercises of stock options	11,269	15,654	27,186
Distributions to noncontrolling interests	(107,239)	(41,414)	(30,997)
Contributions and advances from noncontrolling interests	8,120	18,575	638
Repurchases of common stock	(128,249)	(41,225)	(42,298)
Net cash from financing activities	(375,085)	(360,033)	(273,440)
Supplemental schedule of noncash investing and financing activities:			
Loan Notes issued and estimated consideration for vested shares exercisable in connection with an acquisition	$ 30,903	$ —	$ —
Equipment acquired with capital lease obligations and equipment note obligations	$ 12,914	$ 8,640	$ 12,429

NOTES TO CONSOLIDATED FINANCIAL STATEMENTS (in part)

Note 9. Indebtedness (in part)

Indebtedness consisted of the following:

(In millions)	December 31, 2010	January 1, 2010
Bank term loans, net of debt issuance costs	$619.6	$763.9
Obligations under capital leases	19.4	16.5
Notes payable, foreign credit lines and loan notes	62.8	24.6
Total Indebtedness	701.8	805.0
Less:		
Current portion of long-term debt	60.5	115.3
Long-term debt	$641.3	$689.7

Other Indebtedness (in part)

Capital Leases. As of December 31, 2010 and January 1, 2010, we had approximately $19.4 million and $16.5 million in obligations under our capital leases, respectively, consisting primarily of leases for office equipment, computer equipment and furniture.

Maturities (in part)

As of December 31, 2010, the amounts of capital leases that mature in the next five years and thereafter were as follows:

(In millions)	Capital Leases
Less than one year	$ 8.0
Second year	8.2
Third year	2.4
Fourth year	1.4
Fifth year	0.4
Total minimum lease payments	20.4
Less: amounts representing interest	1.0
Present value of net minimum lease payments	$19.4

Financial Instrument Settlements

6.47

CHESAPEAKE ENERGY CORPORATION (DEC)

CONSOLIDATED STATEMENTS OF CASH FLOWS (in part)

($ in millions)	Years Ended December 31		
	2010	2009	2008
Cash flows from financing activities:			
Proceeds from credit facilities borrowings	15,117	7,761	13,291
Payments on credit facilities borrowings	(13,303)	(9,758)	(11,307)
Proceeds from issuance of senior notes, net of offering costs	1,967	1,346	2,136
Proceeds from issuance of preferred stock, net of offering costs	2,562	—	—
Proceeds from issuance of common stock, net of offering costs	—	—	2,598
Cash paid to redeem debt	(3,434)	—	(312)
Cash paid for common stock dividends	(189)	(181)	(148)
Cash paid for preferred stock dividends	(92)	(23)	(35)
Proceeds from sale of noncontrolling interest in midstream joint venture	—	588	—
Realized gains on financing derivatives	621	109	(167)
Proceeds from mortgage of building	—	54	—
Proceeds from sale/leaseback of real estate surface assets	—	145	—
Net increase (decrease) in outstanding payments in excess of cash balance	20	(249)	330
Other	(88)	(128)	(30)
Cash provided by (used in) financing activities	3,181	(336)	6,356

NOTES TO CONSOLIDATED FINANCIAL STATEMENTS (in part)

3. Debt (in part)

Our long-term debt consisted of the following at December 31, 2010 and 2009:

($ in millions)	December 31	
	2010	2009
7.5% senior notes due 2013	$ —	$ 364
7.625% senior notes due 2013	500	500
7.0% senior notes due 2014	—	300
7.5% senior notes due 2014	—	300
6.375% senior notes due 2015	—	600
9.5% senior notes due 2015	1,425	1,425
6.625% senior notes due 2016	—	600
6.875% senior notes due 2016	—	670
6.25% euro-denominated senior notes due 2017(a)	796	860
6.5% senior notes due 2017	1,100	1,100
6.25% senior notes due 2018	—	600
6.875% senior notes due 2018	600	—
7.25% senior notes due 2018	800	800
6.625% senior notes due 2020	1,400	—
6.875% senior notes due 2020	500	500
2.75% contingent convertible senior notes due 2035(b)	451	451
2.5% contingent convertible senior notes due 2037(b)	1,378	1,378
2.25% contingent convertible senior notes due 2038(b)	752	763
Corporate revolving bank credit facility	3,612	1,892
Midstream revolving bank credit facility	94	—
Midstream joint venture revolving bank credit facility(c)	—	44
Discount on senior notes(d)	(777)	(921)
Interest rate derivatives(e)	9	69
Total notes payable and long-term debt	$12,640	$12,295

Acquisition of Noncontrolling Interest

6.48

TIFFANY & CO. (JAN)

CONSOLIDATED STATEMENTS OF CASH FLOWS (in part)

(In thousands)	Years Ended January 31		
	2010	2009	2008
Cash flows from financing activities:			
(Repayment of) proceeds from credit facility borrowings, net	(126,811)	103,976	(75,147)
Repayment of long-term debt	(40,000)	(73,483)	(32,301)
Proceeds from issuance of long-term debt	300,000	100,000	—
Repayments of short-term borrowings	(93,000)	(25,473)	—
Proceeds from short-term borrowings	—	116,001	—
Repurchase of Common Stock	(467)	(218,379)	(574,608)
Proceeds from exercise of stock options	71,485	30,357	68,830
Excess tax benefits from share-based payment arrangements	1,349	10,196	18,739
Cash dividends on Common Stock	(84,579)	(82,258)	(69,921)
Purchase of noncontrolling interests	(11,000)	—	—
Financing fees	(6,439)	(645)	—
Net cash provided by (used in) financing activities	10,538	(39,708)	(664,408)

NOTES TO CONSOLIDATED FINANCIAL STATEMENTS (in part)

C. Acquisitions & Dispositions (in part)

In October 2009, the Company acquired all noncontrolling interests in two majority-owned entities that indirectly engage in diamond sourcing and polishing operations through majority-owned subsidiaries in South Africa and Botswana, respectively, for total consideration of $18,000,000, of which $11,000,000 was paid upon closing of the transaction and the remaining $7,000,000 will be paid on or before August 1, 2010. This acquisition is accounted for as an equity transaction since the Company maintained control of the two entities prior to the acquisition. Therefore, the Company recorded a decrease to additional paid-in capital of $20,453,000 in 2009 related to this transaction. In addition, the Company paid $4,000,000 to terminate a third-party management agreement. Management determined that this transaction was separate from the acquisition of the remaining noncontrolling interests; accordingly, the termination fee was recorded within SG&A expenses.

Section 7: Independent Auditors' Report

PRESENTATION IN ANNUAL REPORT

PRESENTATION

7.01 This section reviews the format and content of independent auditors' reports appearing in the annual reports of the 500 survey entities. AU section 508, *Reports on Audited Financial Statements* (AICPA, *Professional Standards*), applies to auditors' reports issued in connection with audits of historical financial statements that are intended to present the financial position, results of operations, and cash flows in conformity with generally accepted accounting principles (GAAP). AICPA Professional Standards apply to audits of non-issuers. PCAOB Auditing Standards apply to audits of issuers.

7.02 Section 103(a) of the Sarbanes-Oxley Act of 2002 authorized the Public Company Accounting Oversight Board (PCAOB) to establish auditing and related professional practice standards to be used by public accounting firms registered with the PCAOB. PCAOB Rule 3100, *Compliance With Auditing and Related Professional Practice Standards* (AICPA, *PCAOB Standards and Related Rules*, Select Rules of the Board), requires auditors to comply with all applicable auditing and related professional practice standards of the PCAOB. On an initial, transitional basis, the PCAOB adopted, as interim standards, the generally accepted auditing standards described in AU section 150, *Generally Accepted Auditing Standards* (AICPA, *Professional Standards*), in existence on April 16, 2003, to the extent not superseded or amended by the PCAOB.

TITLE AND ADDRESSEE

PRESENTATION

Author's Note

Unless otherwise indicated, the auditing standards referred to in the following paragraphs apply to both issuers and non-issuers. Refer to paragraphs 7.01 and 7.02 for further information on AICPA auditing standards and PCAOB auditing standards.

7.03 Paragraph .08(a) of AU section 508 states that the title of an auditor's report should include the word *independent.*

7.04 Paragraph .09 of AU section 508 states the following:

The report may be addressed to the company whose financial statements are being audited or to its board of directors or stockholders. A report on the financial statements of an unincorporated entity should be addressed as circumstances dictate, for example, to the partners, to the general partner, or to the proprietor. Occasionally, an auditor is retained to audit the financial statements of a company that is not a client; in such a case, the report is customarily addressed to the client and not to the directors or stockholders of the company whose financial statements are being audited.

AUDITORS' REPORTS

PRESENTATION

Author's Note

Unless otherwise indicated, the auditing standards referred to in the following paragraphs apply to both issuers and non-issuers. Refer to paragraphs 7.01 and 7.02 for further information on AICPA auditing standards and PCAOB auditing standards.

7.05 Paragraph 8 of AU section 508 presents examples of auditors' standard reports for single-year financial statements and comparative two-year financial statements. The examples presented in paragraph .08 of AU section 508 follows:

INDEPENDENT AUDITORS' REPORT (single year)

We have audited the accompanying balance sheet of X Company as of December 31, 20XX, and the related statements of income, retained earnings, and cash flows for the year then ended. These financial statements are the responsibility of the Company's management. Our responsibility is to express an opinion on these financial statements based on our audit.

We conducted our audit in accordance with auditing standards generally accepted in the United States of America. Those standards require that we plan and perform the audit to obtain reasonable assurance about whether the financial statements are free of material misstatement. An audit includes examining, on a test basis, evidence supporting the amounts and disclosures in the financial statements. An audit also includes assessing the accounting principles used and significant estimates made by management, as well as evaluating the overall financial statement presentation. We believe that our audit provides a reasonable basis for our opinion.

In our opinion, the financial statements referred to above, present fairly, in all material respects, the financial position of X Company as of [at] December 31, 20XX, and the results of its operations and its cash flows for the year then ended in conformity with accounting principles generally accepted in the United States of America.

[*Signature*]
[*Date*]

INDEPENDENT AUDITORS' REPORT (comparative)

We have audited the accompanying balance sheets of X Company as of December 31, 20X2 and 20X1, and the related statements of income, retained earnings, and cash flows for the years then ended. These financial statements are the responsibility of the Company's management. Our responsibility is to express an opinion on these financial statements based on our audits.

We conducted our audits in accordance with auditing standards generally accepted in the United States of America. Those standards require that we plan and perform the audit to obtain reasonable assurance about whether the financial statements are free of material misstatement. An audit includes examining, on a test basis, evidence supporting the amounts and disclosures in the financial statements. An audit also includes assessing the accounting principles used and significant estimates made by management, as well as evaluating the overall financial statement presentation. We believe that our audits provide a reasonable basis for our opinion.

In our opinion, the financial statements referred to above, present fairly, in all material respects, the financial position of X Company as of [at] December 31, 20X2 and 20X1, and the results of its operations and its cash flows for the years then ended in conformity with accounting principles generally accepted in the United States of America.

[*Signature*]
[*Date*]

When performing an integrated audit of financial statements and internal control over financial reporting, if the auditor issues separate reports on the company's financial statements and on internal control over financial reporting, the following paragraph should be added to the auditor's report on the company's financial statements:

> We also have audited, in accordance with the standards of the Public Company Accounting Oversight Board (United States), the effectiveness of X Company's internal control over financial reporting as of December 31, 20x3, based on [identify control criteria] and our report dated [date of report, which should be the same as the date of the report on the financial statements] expressed [include nature of opinions].

7.06   Most of the survey entities present a balance sheet for two years and the other basic financial statements for three years. Footnote 8 to paragraph 8 of AU section 508 explains that if statements of income, retained earnings, and cash flows are presented on a comparative basis for one of more periods, but the balance sheet(s) as of the end of one or more of the prior period(s) is not presented, the phrase "for the years then ended" should be changed to indicate that the auditor's opinion applies to each period for which statements of income, retained earnings, and cash flows are presented, such as "for each of the three years in the period ended [date of latest balance sheet]."

7.07   For audits of public entities (that is, issuers, as defined by the Sarbanes-Oxley Act of 2002, and other entities, when prescribed by the rules of the Securities and Exchange Commission [SEC]), PCAOB Auditing Standard No. 1, *References in Auditors' Reports to the Standards of the Public Company Accounting Oversight Board* (AICPA, *PCAOB Standards and Related Rules,* Auditing Standards), directs auditors to state that the engagement was conducted in accordance with "the standards of the Public Company Accounting Oversight Board (United States)" whenever the auditor has performed the engagement in accordance with the PCAOB's standards. An example of a standard independent registered auditor's report presented in the appendix, "Illustrative Reports," of Auditing Standard No. 1 follows:

REPORT OF INDEPENDENT REGISTERED PUBLIC ACCOUNTING FIRM

We have audited the accompanying balance sheets of X Company as of December 31, 20X3 and 20X2, and the related statements of operations, stockholders' equity, and cash flows for each of the three years in the period ended December 31, 20X3. These financial statements are the responsibility of the Company's management. Our responsibility is to express an opinion on these financial statements based on our audits.

We conducted our audits in accordance with the standards of the Public Company Accounting Oversight Board (United States). Those standards require that we plan and perform the audit to obtain reasonable assurance about whether the financial statements are free of material misstatement. An audit includes examining, on a test basis, evidence supporting the amounts and disclosures in the financial statements. An audit also includes assessing the accounting principles used and significant estimates made by management, as well as evaluating the overall financial statement presentation. We believe that our audits provide a reasonable basis for our opinion.

In our opinion, the financial statements referred to above present fairly, in all material respects, the financial position of the company as of [at] December 31, 20X3 and 20X2, and the results of its operations and its cash flows for each of the three years in the period ended December 31, 20X3, in conformity with U.S. generally accepted accounting principles.

[*Signature*]
[*City and State or Country*]
[*Date*]

7.08   Financial Accounting Standards Board (FASB) *Accounting Standards Codification* (ASC) 220, *Comprehensive Income,* permits entities to report components of comprehensive income in either a separate financial statement or a combined statement of income and comprehensive income. Alternatively, FASB ASC 220 allows components of comprehensive income to be reported in a statement of stockholders' equity. Although an entity may include the term *comprehensive income* in the title of the statement in which it is presented, FASB ASC 220 does not require the use of the term in an entity's financial statements. FASB ASC 220 acknowledges the use of equivalent terms.

7.09 FASB ASC 505-10-50-2 allows for changes in the separate accounts comprising stockholders' equity to be presented either on the face of the basic financial statements or in the form of a separate statement, such as a statement of changes in stockholders' equity.

7.10

TABLE 7-1: INFORMATION RELATED TO AUDITOR'S AND MANAGEMENT'S REPORTS*

	Number of Entities 2010
Auditor's Opinion	
Unqualified opinion, clean	469
Unqualified opinion with emphasis of a matter paragraph	31
Total	500
Management's Report on Internal Control Over Financial Reporting	
Presented in regular audit report	47
Presented as separate report	453
Total	500
Auditor's Report on Internal Control Over Financial Reporting	
Presented in regular audit report	226
Presented as separate report	272
Not presented	2
Total	500
Additional Matters With Regard to Auditors' Reports	
One paragraph presentation of audit report	94
Reference to report of other auditors	2
Opinion expressed on supplemental information	63
Report of management on financial statement	35
Report on internal control over financial reporting indicated ineffective controls	2
Presented in regular audit report	106
Presented as separate report	13

* Note: This material was not tracked in previous editions, so no prior year data are available.

PRESENTATION AND DISCLOSURE EXCERPTS

PricewaterhouseCoopers LLP Auditors' Report

Author's Note

Although most audit reports use the exact format and order of paragraphs, PricewaterhouseCoopers uses a variation of the standard auditor's report that rearranges the standard elements into one paragraph for use in their unqualified opinions only.

7.11

EASTMAN CHEMICAL COMPANY (DEC)

REPORT OF INDEPENDENT REGISTERED PUBLIC ACCOUNTING FIRM

To the Board of Directors and Stockholders of Eastman Chemical Company

In our opinion, the consolidated financial statements listed in the index appearing under Item 15(a)(1) present fairly, in all material respects, the financial position of Eastman Chemical Company and its subsidiaries at December 31, 2010 and 2009, and the results of their operations and their cash flows for each of the three years in the period ended December 31, 2010 in conformity with accounting principles generally accepted in the United States of America. Also in our opinion, the Company maintained, in all material respects, effective internal control over financial reporting as of December 31, 2010, based on criteria established in *Internal Control - Integrated Framework* issued by the Committee of Sponsoring Organizations of the Treadway Commission (COSO). The Company's management is responsible for these financial statements, for maintaining effective internal control over financial reporting and for its assessment of the effectiveness of internal control over financial reporting, included in Management's Report on Internal Control Over Financial Reporting appearing under Item 9A. Our responsibility is to express opinions on these financial statements and on the Company's internal control over financial reporting based on our integrated audits. We conducted our audits in accordance with the standards of the Public Company Accounting Oversight Board (United States). Those standards require that we plan and perform the audits to obtain reasonable assurance about whether the financial statements are free of material misstatement and whether effective internal control over financial reporting was maintained in all material respects. Our audits of the financial statements included examining, on a test basis, evidence supporting the amounts and disclosures in the financial statements, assessing the accounting principles used and significant estimates made by management, and evaluating the overall financial statement presentation. Our audit of internal control over financial reporting included obtaining an understanding of internal control over financial reporting, assessing the risk that a material weakness exists, and testing and evaluating the design and operating effectiveness of internal control based on the assessed risk. Our audits also included performing such other procedures as we considered necessary in the circumstances. We believe that our audits provide a reasonable basis for our opinions.

A company's internal control over financial reporting is a process designed to provide reasonable assurance regarding the reliability of financial reporting and the preparation of financial statements for external purposes in accordance with generally accepted accounting principles. A company's internal control over financial reporting includes those policies and procedures that (i) pertain to the maintenance of records that, in reasonable detail, accurately and fairly reflect the transactions and dispositions of the assets of the company; (ii) provide reasonable assurance that transactions are recorded as necessary to permit preparation of financial statements in accordance with generally accepted accounting principles, and that receipts and expenditures of the company are being made only in accordance with authorizations of management and directors of the company; and (iii) provide reasonable assurance regarding prevention or timely detection of unauthorized acquisition, use, or disposition of the company's assets that could have a material effect on the financial statements.

Because of its inherent limitations, internal control over financial reporting may not prevent or detect misstatements. Also, projections of any evaluation of effectiveness to future periods are subject to the risk that controls may become inadequate because of changes in conditions, or that the degree of compliance with the policies or procedures may deteriorate.

Statement of Operations and Comprehensive Income

7.12

TESORO CORPORATION (DEC)

REPORT OF INDEPENDENT REGISTERED PUBLIC ACCOUNTING FIRM

To the Board of Directors and Stockholders of Tesoro Corporation

We have audited the accompanying consolidated balance sheets of Tesoro Corporation as of December 31, 2010 and 2009, and the related consolidated statements of operations, comprehensive income (loss) and stockholders' equity, and cash flows for each of the three years in the period ended December 31, 2010. These financial statements are the responsibility of the Company's management. Our responsibility is to express an opinion on these financial statements based on our audits.

We conducted our audits in accordance with the standards of the Public Company Accounting Oversight Board (United States). Those standards require that we plan and perform the audit to obtain reasonable assurance about whether the financial statements are free of material misstatement. An audit includes examining, on a test basis, evidence supporting the amounts and disclosures in the financial statements. An audit also includes assessing the accounting principles used and significant estimates made by management, as well as evaluating the overall financial statement presentation. We believe that our audits provide a reasonable basis for our opinion.

In our opinion, the financial statements referred to above present fairly, in all material respects, the consolidated financial position of Tesoro Corporation at December 31, 2010 and 2009, and the consolidated results of its operations and its cash flows for each of the three years in the period ended December 31, 2010, in conformity with U.S. generally accepted accounting principles.

We also have audited, in accordance with the standards of the Public Company Accounting Oversight Board (United States), Tesoro Corporation's internal control over financial reporting as of December 31, 2010, based on criteria established in Internal Control-Integrated Framework issued by the Committee of Sponsoring Organizations of the Treadway Commission and our report dated March 1, 2011 expressed an unqualified opinion thereon.

Statement of Changes in Shareholders' Equity

7.13

DEL MONTE FOODS COMPANY (APR)

REPORT OF INDEPENDENT REGISTERED PUBLIC ACCOUNTING FIRM

The Board of Directors and Stockholders
Del Monte Foods Company

We have audited the accompanying consolidated balance sheets of Del Monte Foods Company and subsidiaries as of May 2, 2010 and May 3, 2009, and the related consolidated statements of income, stockholders' equity and comprehensive income, and cash flows for each of the years in the three-year period ended May 2, 2010. These consolidated financial statements are the responsibility of the Company's management. Our responsibility is to express an opinion on these consolidated financial statements based on our audits.

We conducted our audits in accordance with the standards of the Public Company Accounting Oversight Board (United States). Those standards require that we plan and perform the audit to obtain reasonable assurance about whether the financial statements are free of material misstatement. An audit includes examining, on a test basis, evidence supporting the amounts and disclosures in the financial statements. An audit also includes assessing the accounting principles used and significant estimates made by management, as well as evaluating the overall financial statement presentation. We believe that our audits provide a reasonable basis for our opinion.

In our opinion, the consolidated financial statements referred to above present fairly, in all material respects, the financial position of Del Monte Foods Company and subsidiaries as of May 2, 2010 and May 3, 2009, and the results of their operations and their cash flows for each of the years in the three-year period ended May 2, 2010, in conformity with U.S. generally accepted accounting principles.

We also have audited, in accordance with the standards of the Public Company Accounting Oversight Board (United States), Del Monte Foods Company and subsidiaries' internal control over financial reporting as of May 2, 2010, based on criteria established in Internal Control—Integrated Framework issued by the Committee of Sponsoring Organizations of the Treadway Commission (COSO), and our report dated June 29, 2010 expressed an unqualified opinion on the effectiveness of the Company's internal control over financial reporting.

REFERENCE TO THE REPORT OF OTHER AUDITORS

PRESENTATION

Author's Note

Unless otherwise indicated, the auditing standards referred to in the following paragraphs apply to both issuers and non-issuers. Refer to paragraphs 7.01 and 7.02 for further information on AICPA auditing standards and PCAOB auditing standards.

7.14 When the opinion of a principal auditor is based in part on the report of another auditor, AU section 543, *Part of Audit Performed by Other Independent Auditors* (AICPA, *Professional Standards*), provides guidance to the principal auditor. Paragraph .07 of AU section 543 states the following:

When the principal auditor decides that he will make reference to the audit of the other auditor, his report should indicate clearly, in both the introductory, scope and opinion paragraphs, the division of responsibility as between that portion of the financial statements covered by his own audit and that covered by the audit of the other auditor. The report should disclose the magnitude of the portion of the financial statements audited by the other auditor. This may be done by stating the dollar amounts or percentages of one or more of the following: total assets, total revenues, or other appropriate criteria, whichever most clearly reveals the portion of the financial statements audited by the other auditor. The other auditor may be named but only with his express permission and provided his report is presented together with that of the principal auditor.

7.15 Paragraphs .12–.13 of AU section 508 reaffirm the requirements of AU section 543. Paragraph .13 of AU section 508 and paragraph .09 of AU section 543 present examples of auditors' reports referring to the report of other auditors.

7.16 The auditor's report for 2 survey entities made reference to the report of other auditors. The reference to other auditors in both of these reports is related to investments in unconsolidated affiliates.

PRESENTATION AND DISCLOSURE EXCERPTS

Reference to Other Auditors

7.17

EL PASO CORPORATION (DEC)

REPORT OF INDEPENDENT REGISTERED PUBLIC ACCOUNTING FIRM

The Board of Directors and Stockholders of
El Paso Corporation

We have audited the accompanying consolidated balance sheets of El Paso Corporation (the Company) as of December 31, 2010 and 2009, and the related consolidated statements of income, comprehensive income, equity, and cash flows for each of the three years in the period ended December 31, 2010. Our audits also included the financial statement schedule listed in the Index at Item 15(a). These financial statements and schedule are the responsibility of the Company's management. Our responsibility is to express an opinion on these financial statements and schedule based on our audits. The financial statements of Citrus Corp. and Subsidiaries (a corporation in which the Company has a 50% interest) as of December 31, 2010 and 2009 and for each of the three years in the period ended December 31, 2010 and Four Star Oil & Gas Company (a corporation in which the Company has approximately a 49% interest) for the year ended December 31, 2008 have been audited by other auditors whose reports have been furnished to us, and our opinion on the consolidated financial statements, insofar as it relates to the amounts included from Citrus Corp. and Subsidiaries and Four Star Oil & Gas Company as of the years and for the periods herein referred to, is based solely on the reports of the other auditors. In the consolidated financial statements, the Company's investments in unconsolidated affiliates includes approximately $866 million and $674 million from Citrus Corp. and Subsidiaries as of December 31, 2010 and 2009, respectively, and the Company's earnings from unconsolidated affiliates includes approximately $90 million and $65 million for the years ended December 31, 2010 and 2009, respectively, from Citrus Corp. and Subsidiaries and approximately $147 million for the year ended December 31, 2008, from Citrus Corp. and Subsidiaries and Four Star Oil & Gas Company combined, all of which were audited by other auditors.

We conducted our audits in accordance with the standards of the Public Company Accounting Oversight Board (United States). Those standards require that we plan and perform the audit to obtain reasonable assurance about whether the financial statements are free of material misstatement. An audit includes examining, on a test basis, evidence supporting the amounts and disclosures in the financial statements. An audit also includes assessing the accounting principles used and significant estimates made by management, as well as evaluating the overall financial statement presentation. We believe that our audits and the reports of other auditors provide a reasonable basis for our opinion.

In our opinion, based on our audits and the reports of other auditors, the financial statements referred to above present fairly, in all material respects, the consolidated financial position of El Paso Corporation at December 31, 2010 and 2009, and the consolidated results of its operations and its cash flows for each of the three years in the period ended December 31, 2010 in conformity with U.S. generally accepted accounting principles. Also, in our opinion, the related financial statement schedule, when considered in relation to the basic financial statements taken as a whole, presents fairly in all material respects the information set forth therein.

As discussed in Note 1 to the consolidated financial statements, effective December 31, 2009 the Company changed its reserve estimates and related disclosures as a result of adopting new oil and gas reserve estimation and disclosure requirements.

We also have audited, in accordance with the standards of the Public Company Accounting Oversight Board (United States), El Paso Corporation's internal control over financial reporting as of December 31, 2010, based on criteria established in Internal Control-Integrated Framework issued by the Committee of Sponsoring Organizations of the Treadway Commission and our report dated February 28, 2011 expressed an unqualified opinion thereon.

UNCERTAINTIES

PRESENTATION

Author's Note

Unless otherwise indicated, the auditing standards referred to in the following paragraphs apply to both issuers and non-issuers. Refer to paragraphs 7.01 and 7.02 for further information on AICPA auditing standards and PCAOB auditing standards.

7.18   Paragraph .30 of AU section 508 does not require an explanatory paragraph for *uncertainties*, as defined in paragraph .29 of AU section 508. This does not apply to uncertainties related to going concern situations, for which AU section 341, *The Auditor's Consideration of an Entity's Ability to Continue as a Going Concern* (AICPA, *Professional Standards*), provides guidance.

7.19

TABLE 7-2: REFERENCES TO UNCERTAINTIES IN AUDITORS' REPORTS

Table 7-2 summarizes the nature of uncertainties for which an explanatory paragraph was included in an auditors' report.

	2010	2009	2008
Going concern	—	8	12
Other	19	—	1
Total Uncertainties	**19**	**8**	**13**

PRESENTATION AND DISCLOSURE EXCERPTS

Going Concern

7.20

W. R. GRACE & CO. (DEC)

REPORT OF INDEPENDENT REGISTERED PUBLIC ACCOUNTING FIRM

To the Shareholders and Board of Directors of
W. R. Grace & Co

In our opinion, the accompanying consolidated financial statements present fairly, in all material respects, the financial position of W. R. Grace & Co. and its subsidiaries (the "Company") at December 31, 2010 and December 31, 2009, and the results of their operations and their cash flows for each

of the three years in the period ended December 31, 2010 in conformity with accounting principles generally accepted in the United States of America. In addition, in our opinion, the financial statement schedule listed in the accompanying index presents fairly, in all material respects, the information set forth therein when read in conjunction with the related consolidated financial statements. Also in our opinion, the Company maintained, in all material respects, effective internal control over financial reporting as of December 31, 2010 based on criteria established in Internal Control— Integrated Framework issued by the Committee of Sponsoring Organizations of the Treadway Commission (COSO). The Company's management is responsible for these financial statements and financial statement schedule, for maintaining effective internal control over financial reporting and for its assessment of the effectiveness of internal control over financial reporting, included in the accompanying Management's Report On Internal Control Over Financial Reporting. Our responsibility is to express opinions on these financial statements, on the financial statement schedule, and on the Company's internal control over financial reporting based on our integrated audits. We conducted our audits in accordance with the standards of the Public Company Accounting Oversight Board (United States). Those standards require that we plan and perform the audits to obtain reasonable assurance about whether the financial statements are free of material misstatement and whether effective internal control over financial reporting was maintained in all material respects. Our audits of the financial statements included examining, on a test basis, evidence supporting the amounts and disclosures in the financial statements, assessing the accounting principles used and significant estimates made by management, and evaluating the overall financial statement presentation. Our audit of internal control over financial reporting included obtaining an understanding of internal control over financial reporting, assessing the risk that a material weakness exists, and testing and evaluating the design and operating effectiveness of internal control based on the assessed risk. Our audits also included performing such other procedures as we considered necessary in the circumstances. We believe that our audits provide a reasonable basis for our opinions.

The accompanying consolidated financial statements have been prepared assuming that the Company will continue as a going concern. As discussed in Note 1 to the consolidated financial statements, on April 2, 2001, the Company and substantially all of its domestic subsidiaries voluntarily filed for protection under Chapter 11 of the United States Bankruptcy Code, which raises substantial doubt about the Company's ability to continue as a going concern in its present form. Management's intentions with respect to this matter are described in Note 2. The accompanying consolidated financial statements do not include any adjustments that might result from the outcome of this uncertainty.

A company's internal control over financial reporting is a process designed to provide reasonable assurance regarding the reliability of financial reporting and the preparation of financial statements for external purposes in accordance with generally accepted accounting principles. A company's internal control over financial reporting includes those policies and procedures that (i) pertain to the maintenance of records that, in reasonable detail, accurately and fairly reflect the transactions and dispositions of the assets of the company; (ii) provide reasonable assurance that transactions are recorded as necessary to permit preparation of financial statements in accordance with generally accepted accounting principles, and that receipts and expenditures of the company are being made only in accordance with authorizations of management and directors of the company; and (iii) provide reasonable assurance regarding prevention or timely detection of unauthorized acquisition, use, or disposition of the company's assets that could have a material effect on the financial statements.

Because of its inherent limitations, internal control over financial reporting may not prevent or detect misstatements. Also, projections of any evaluation of effectiveness to future periods are subject to the risk that controls may become inadequate because of changes in conditions, or that the degree of compliance with the policies or procedures may deteriorate.

Fresh-Start Accounting

7.21

SPECTRUM BRANDS HOLDINGS, INC. (SEP)

REPORT OF INDEPENDENT REGISTERED PUBLIC ACCOUNTING FIRM

The Board of Directors and Stockholders
Spectrum Brands, Inc.

We have audited the accompanying consolidated statements of financial position of Spectrum Brands, Inc. and subsidiaries (the Company) as of September 30, 2010 and September 30, 2009 (Successor Company), and the related consolidated statements of operations, shareholders' equity (deficit) and comprehensive income (loss), and cash flows for the year ended September 30, 2010, the period August 31, 2009 to September 30, 2009 (Successor Company), the period October 1, 2008 to August 30, 2009 and the year ended September 30, 2008 (Predecessor Company). In connection with our audit of the consolidated financial statements, we have also audited the financial statement schedule II. These consolidated financial statements and financial statement schedule are the responsibility of the Company's management. Our responsibility is to express an opinion on these consolidated financial statements and financial statement schedule based on our audits.

We conducted our audits in accordance with the standards of the Public Company Accounting Oversight Board (United States). Those standards require that we plan and perform the audit to obtain reasonable assurance about whether the financial statements are free of material misstatement. The Company is not required to have, nor were we engaged to perform, an audit of its internal control over financial reporting. Our audit included consideration of internal control over financial reporting as a basis for designing audit procedures that are appropriate in the circumstances, but not for the purpose of expressing an opinion on the effectiveness of the Company's internal control over financial reporting. Accordingly, we express no such opinion. An audit includes examining, on a test basis, evidence supporting the amounts and disclosures in the financial statements, assessing the accounting principles used and significant estimates made by management, as well as evaluating the overall financial

statement presentation. We believe that our audit provides a reasonable basis for our opinion.

In our opinion, the consolidated financial statements referred to above present fairly, in all material respects, the financial position of Spectrum Brands, Inc. and subsidiaries as of September 30, 2010 and September 30, 2009 (Successor Company), and the results of their operations and their cash flows for the year ended September 30, 2010, the period August 31, 2009 to September 30, 2009 (Successor Company), the period October 1, 2008 to August 30, 2009 and the year ended September 30, 2008 (Predecessor Company) in conformity with U.S. generally accepted accounting principles. Also, in our opinion, the related financial statement schedule, when considered in relation to the basic consolidated financial statements taken as a whole, presents fairly, in all material respects, the information set forth therein.

As discussed in Note 2 to the consolidated financial statements, the Predecessor Company filed a petition for reorganization under Chapter 11 of the United States Bankruptcy Code on February 3, 2009. The Company's plan of reorganization became effective and the Company emerged from bankruptcy protection on August 28, 2009. In connection with their emergence from bankruptcy, the Successor Company Spectrum Brands, Inc. adopted fresh-start reporting in conformity with ASC Topic 852, " *Reorganizations* " formerly American Institute of Certified Public Accountants Statement of Position 90-7, " *Financial Reporting by Entities in Reorganization under the Bankruptcy Code",* effective as of August 30, 2009. Accordingly, the Successor Company's consolidated financial statements prior to August 30, 2009 are not comparable to its consolidated financial statements for periods on or after August 30, 2009.

As discussed in Note 10 to the consolidated financial statements, effective September 30, 2009, the Successor Company adopted the measurement date provision of ASC 715, *"Compensation-Retirement Benefits"* formerly FAS 158, "Employers' *Accounting for Defined Benefit Pension and other Postretirement Plans".*

NOTES TO CONSOLIDATED FINANCIAL STATEMENTS (in part)

Fresh-Start Reporting

The Company, in accordance with ASC 852, adopted fresh-start reporting as of the close of business on August 30, 2009 since the reorganization value of the assets of the Predecessor Company immediately before the date of confirmation of the Plan was less than the total of all post-petition liabilities and allowed claims, and the holders of the Predecessor Company's voting shares immediately before confirmation of the Plan received less than 50 percent of the voting shares of the emerging entity. The four-column consolidated statement of financial position as of August 30, 2009, included herein, applies effects of the Plan and fresh-start reporting to the carrying values and classifications of assets or liabilities that were necessary.

The Company analyzed the transactions that occurred during the two-day period from August 29, 2009, the day after the Effective Date, and August 30, 2009, the fresh-start reporting date, and concluded that such transactions were not material individually or in the aggregate as such transactions represented less than one-percent of the total net sales for the fiscal year ended September 30, 2009. As a result, the Company determined that August 30, 2009, would be an appropriate fresh-start reporting date to coincide with the Company's normal financial period close for the month of August 2009. Upon adoption of fresh-start reporting, the recorded amounts of assets and liabilities were adjusted to reflect their estimated fair values. Accordingly, the reported historical financial statements of the Predecessor Company prior to the adoption of fresh-start reporting for periods ended on or prior to August 30, 2009 are not comparable to those of the Successor Company.

The four-column consolidated statement of financial position as of August 30, 2009 reflects the implementation of the Plan as if the Plan had been effective on August 30, 2009. Reorganization adjustments have been recorded within the consolidated statement of financial position as of August 30, 2009 to reflect effects of the Plan, including the discharge of Liabilities subject to compromise and the adoption of fresh-start reporting in accordance with ASC 852. The Bankruptcy Court confirmed the Plan based upon a reorganization value of the Company between $2,200,000 and $2,400,000, which was estimated using various valuation methods including: (i) publicly traded company analysis, (ii) discounted cash flow analysis; and (iii) a review and analysis of several recent transactions of companies in similar industries to the Company. These three valuation methods were equally weighted in determining the final range of reorganization value as confirmed by the Bankruptcy Court. Based upon the factors used in determining the range of reorganization value, the Company concluded that $2,275,000 should be used for fresh-start reporting purposes as it most closely approximated fair value.

The basis of the discounted cash flow analysis used in developing the reorganization value was based on Company prepared projections which included a variety of estimates and assumptions. While the Company considers such estimates and assumptions reasonable, they are inherently subject to significant business, economic and competitive uncertainties, many of which are beyond the Company's control and, therefore, may not be realized. Changes in these estimates and assumptions may have had a significant effect on the determination of the Company's reorganization value. The assumptions used in the calculations for the discounted cash flow analysis included projected revenue, costs, and cash flows, for the fiscal years ending September 30, 2009, 2010, 2011, 2012 and 2013 and represented the Company's best estimates at the time the analysis was prepared. The Company's estimates implicit in the cash flow analysis included net sales growth of approximately 1.5% for the fiscal year ending September 30, 2010 and 4.0% per year for each of the fiscal years ending September 30, 2011, 2012 and 2013. In addition, selling, general and administrative expenses, excluding depreciation and amortization, were projected to grow at rates relative to net sales, however, certain expense categories for each of the fiscal years ending September 30, 2010, 2011, 2012 and 2013 were reduced for the projected impact of various cost reduction initiatives implemented by the Company during Fiscal 2009 which included lower trade spending, salary freezes, reduced marketing expenses, furloughs, suspension of the Company's match to its 401(k) and reductions in salaries of certain members of management. The analysis also included anticipated levels of reinvestment in the Company's operations through capital expenditures of approximately $25,000 per year. The Company did not include in its estimates the potential effects of litigation, either on the Company or the industry. The foregoing estimates and assumptions are inherently subject to uncertainties and contingencies beyond the control of the Company. Accordingly, there can be no assurance that the estimates, assumptions, and values reflected in the valuations will be realized, and actual results could vary materially.

The publicly traded company analysis identified a group of comparable companies giving consideration to lines of business, business risk, scale and capitalization and leverage. This analysis involved the selection of the appropriate earnings before interest, taxes, depreciation and amortization ("EBITDA") market multiples by segment deemed to be the most relevant when analyzing the peer group. A range of valuation multiples was then identified and applied to the Company's Fiscal 2009 and Fiscal 2010 projections by segment to determine an estimate of reorganization values. The market multiple ranges used by segment were as follows: (i) Global Batteries and Personal Care used a range of 7.0x–8.0x for Fiscal 2009 and 6.5x–7.5x for Fiscal 2010; (ii) Global Pet Supplies used a range of 7.5x–8.5x for Fiscal 2009 and 7.0x–8.0x for Fiscal 2010; and (iii) the Home and Garden Business used a range of 9.0x–10.0x for Fiscal 2009 and 8.0x–9.0x for Fiscal 2010. Theses multiples were based on estimated EBITDA adjusted for certain non-recurring initiatives, as mentioned above.

The recent transactions of companies in similar industries analysis identified transactions of similar companies giving consideration to lines of business, business risk, scale and capitalization and leverage. The analysis considered the business, financial and market environment for which the transactions took place, circumstances surrounding the transaction including the financial position of the buyers and the perceived synergies and benefits that the buyers could obtain from the transaction. This analysis involved the determination of historical acquisition EBITDA multiples by examining public merger and acquisition transactions. A range of valuation multiples was then identified and applied to historical EBITDA by segment to determine an estimate of reorganization values. The multiple ranges used by segment were as follows: (i) Global Batteries and Personal Care used a range of 6.5x–7.5x; (ii) Global Pet Supplies used a range of 9.5x–10.5x; and (iii) the Home and Garden Business used a range of 8.0x–9.0x. These multiples were based on Fiscal 2009 estimated EBITDA adjusted for certain non-recurring initiatives, as mentioned above.

Fresh-start adjustments reflect the allocation of fair value to the Successor Company's long-lived assets and the present value of liabilities to be paid as calculated by the Company.

In applying fresh-start reporting, the Company followed these principles:

- The reorganization value of the entity was allocated to the entity's assets in conformity with the procedures specified by SFAS No. 141, *"Business Combinations"* ("SFAS 141"). The reorganization value exceeded the sum of the amounts assigned to assets and liabilities. This excess was recorded as Successor Company goodwill as of August 30, 2009.
- Each liability existing as of the fresh-start reporting date, other than deferred taxes, has been stated at the present value of the amounts to be paid, determined at appropriate risk adjusted interest rates.
- Deferred taxes were reported in conformity with applicable income tax accounting standards, principally ASC Topic 740: *"Income Taxes,"* formerly SFAS No. 109, *"Accounting for Income Taxes"* ("ASC 740"). Deferred tax assets and liabilities have been recognized for differences between the assigned values and the tax basis of the recognized assets and liabilities.

ATT-SEC 7.21

- Adjustment of all of the property, plant and equipment assets to fair value and eliminating all of the accumulated depreciation.
- Adjustment of the Company's pension plans projected benefit obligation by recognition of all previously unamortized actuarial gains and losses.

The following four-column consolidated statement of financial position table identifies the adjustments recorded to the Predecessor Company's August 30, 2009 consolidated statement of financial position as a result of implementing the Plan and applying fresh-start reporting:

(In thousands, except per share amounts)	Predecessor Company August 30, 2009	Effects of Plan	Fresh-Start Valuation	Successor Company August 30, 2009
Assets				
Current assets:				
Cash and cash equivalents	$ 86,710	$ (25,551)[a]	$ —	$ 61,159
Receivables:				
Trade accounts receivable	270,657	—	—	270,657
Other	34,594	—	—	34,594
Inventories	341,738	—	48,762[m]	390,500
Deferred income taxes	12,644	1,707[h]	9,330[n]	23,681
Assets held for sale	10,813	—	1,978[m]	12,791
Prepaid expenses and other	40,448	—	(116)[m]	40,332
Total current assets	797,604	(23,844)	59,954	833,714
Property, plant and equipment, net	178,786	—	34,699[m]	213,485
Deferred charges and other	42,068	—	(6,046)[m]	36,022
Goodwill	238,905	—	289,155[o]	528,060
Intangible assets, net	677,050	—	782,450[o]	1,459,500
Debt issuance costs	18,457	8,949[b]	(17,957)[p]	9,449
Total assets	$1,952,870	$ (14,895)	$1,142,255	$3,080,230
Liabilities and Shareholders' Equity				
Current liabilities:				
Current maturities of long-term debt	$ 93,313	$ (3,445)[c]	$ (4,329)[m]	$ 85,539
Accounts payable	159,370	(204)[d]	—	159,166
Accrued liabilities:				
Wages and benefits	80,247	—	—	80,247
Income taxes payable	20,059	—	—	20,059
Restructuring and related charges	26,100	—	—	26,100
Accrued interest	59,724	(59,581)[e]	—	143
Other	118,949	9,133[f]	(3,503)[m]	124,579
Total current liabilities	557,762	(54,097)	(7,832)	495,833
Long-term debt, net of current maturities	1,329,047	271,806[g]	(75,329)[m]	1,525,524
Employee benefit obligations, net of current portion	41,385	—	18,712[m]	60,097
Deferred income taxes	106,853	1,707[h]	114,211[n]	222,771
Other	45,982	—	4,927[m]	50,909
Total liabilities	2,081,029	219,416	54,689	2,355,134
Liabilities subject to compromise	1,105,962	(1,105,962)[i]	—	—

(continued)

(In thousands, except per share amounts)	Predecessor Company August 30, 2009	Effects of Plan	Fresh-Start Valuation	Successor Company August 30, 2009
Commitments and contingencies				
Shareholders' (deficit) equity:				
Common stock-Old (Predecessor Company)	691	(691)[j]	—	—
Common stock-New (Successor Company)	—	300[j]	—	300
Additional paid-in capital	677,007	47,789[j]	—	724,796
Accumulated (deficit) equity	(1,915,484)	747,362[k]	1,168,122[q]	—
Accumulated other comprehensive income	80,556	—	(80,556)[q]	—
	(1,157,230)	794,760	1,087,566	725,096
Less treasury stock	(76,891)	76,891[l]	—	—
Total shareholders' (deficit) equity	(1,234,121)	871,651	1,087,566	725,096
Total liabilities and shareholders' (deficit) equity	$ 1,952,870	$(14,895)	$1,142,255	$3,080,230

Effects of Plan Adjustments

[a] The Plan's impact resulted in a net decrease of $25,551 on cash and cash equivalents. The significant sources and uses of cash were as follows:

Sources:	
Amounts borrowed under the exit facility	$ 65,000
Amounts borrowed under new supplemental loan agreement	45,000
Total Sources	$110,000
Uses:	
Repayment of un-reimbursed letters of credit	$ 20,005
Repayment of supplemental loans	45,000
Repayment of certain amounts under the term loan agreement, current portion	3,440
Repayment of certain amounts under the term loan agreement, net of current portion	3,440
Payment of pre-petition foreign exchange contracts recorded in accounts payable	204
Payment of lender cure payments, terminated derivative contracts and other	48,066
Payment of debt issuance costs on exit facility	8,949
Payment of other accrued liabilities	6,447
Total Uses	$135,551
Net Cash Uses	$ (25,551)

[b] The Company incurred $8,949 of debt issuance costs under the exit facility. These debt issuance costs are classified as long-term assets and are amortized over the life of the exit facility.

[c] The adjustment to current maturities of long-term debt reflects the $20,005 payment of the Predecessor Company's un-reimbursed letters of credit, the $45,000 repayment of the Predecessor Company's supplemental loan, and the $3,440 payment of certain amounts under the term loan agreement. The adjustment to current maturities of long-term debt also reflects the $65,000 funding from the exit facility. The adjustment to the current maturities of long-term debt are:

Repayment of unreimbursed letters of credit	$ 20,005
Repayment of supplemental loan	45,000
Repayment of certain amounts under the term loan agreement, current portion	3,440
Amounts borrowed under the exit facility	(65,000)
	$ 3,445

[d] Reflects payment of $204 related to pre-petition foreign exchange derivative contracts.

[e] Total adjustment of $59,581 reflects term lender cure payments of $33,995, terminated interest rate swap derivative contract payments of $12,068 and other accrued interest of $2,003. Additionally, this adjustment includes $11,515 of accrued default interest as provided in the August 2009 amendment of the Senior Term Credit Facility, which was assumed by the Successor Company and included in the principal balance of the loans at emergence (See Note 7, Debt, for additional information).

[f] Reflects the payment of professional fees related to the reorganization in the amount of $6,447 offset by the reclassification of $15,580 related to rejected lease obligations previously recorded as liabilities subject to compromise (see note(i)). These rejected lease obligations were paid by the Successor Company in subsequent periods. As of September 30, 2009, the Company's rejected lease obligation was reduced to $6,181.

(continued)

(g) The adjustment to long-term debt represents the issuance of the 12% Notes at a fair value of $218,731 (face value of $218,076) used, in part, to extinguish the Senior Subordinated Notes of the debtors that were recorded in liabilities subject to compromise (see note (i)), the issuance of the new supplemental loan in the amount of $45,000, offset by the payment of the non-current portion of the term loan in the amount of $3,440 (see note (a)). The excess of fair value over face value of the 12% Notes is recorded in long-term debt and will be accreted as a reduction to interest expense over the life of the note.

Issuance of the 12% Notes (fair value)	$218,731
Amounts borrowed under the new supplemental loan agreement	45,000
Accrued default interest	11,515
Repayment of certain amounts under the term loan agreement, net of current portion	(3,440)
	$271,806

(h) Gain on the cancellation of debt from the extinguishment of the senior subordinated notes as well as the modification of the senior term credit facility, for tax purposes, resulted in a $124,054 reduction in the U.S. net deferred tax asset, exclusive of indefinite-lived intangibles. Due to the Company's full valuation allowance position as of August 30, 2009 on the U.S. net deferred tax asset, exclusive of indefinite-lived intangibles, the tax effect of these items is offset by a corresponding adjustment to the valuation allowance of $124,054. Due to changes in the relative current versus non-current deferred tax asset balances and the corresponding allocation of the domestic valuation allowance, a net $1,707 deferred tax balance reclassification occurred between current and non-current as a result of the effects of the Plan.

(i) The adjustment to liabilities subject to compromise relates to the extinguishment of the Senior Subordinated Notes balance of $1,049,885 and the accrued interest of $40,497 associated with the Senior Subordinated Notes. Additionally, rejected lease obligations of $15,580 were reclassified to other current liabilities (see note (f)).

(j) Pursuant to the Plan, the debtor's common stock was canceled and new common stock of the reorganized debtors was issued. The adjustments eliminated Predecessor Company's common stock and additional paid-in capital of $691 and $677,007, respectively, and recorded Successor Company's common stock and additional paid-in capital of $300 and $724,796, respectively, which represents the fair value of the newly issued common stock. The fair value of the newly issued common stock was not separately valued. A fair value of $725,096 was determined by subtracting the fair value of net debt (total debt less cash and cash equivalents), or $1,549,904 from the enterprise value of $2,275,000. The Company issued 30,000 shares at emergence, consisting of 27,030 shares to holders of the Senior Subordinated Notes allowed note holder claims and 2,970 shares in accordance with the terms of the Debtors' debtor-in-possession credit facility.

(k) As a result of the Plan, the adjustment to accumulated (deficit) equity recorded the elimination of the Predecessor Company's common stock, additional paid in capital and treasury stock in the amount of $600,807 and recorded the pre-tax gain on the cancellation of debt in the amount of $146,555. The elimination of the Predecessor Company's common stock, additional paid in capital and treasury stock was calculated as follows:

Elimination of Predecessor Company's common stock (see note (j))	$ 691
Elimination of Predecessor Company's additional paid in capital (see note (j))	677,007
Elimination of Predecessor Company's treasury stock (see note (l))	(76,891)
Elimination of Predecessor Company's common stock	$600,807

The pre-tax gain on the cancellation of debt was calculated as follows:

Extinguishment of Predecessor Company senior subordinated notes	$1,049,885
Extinguishment of Predecessor Company accrued interest on senior subordinated notes	40,497
Issuance of Successor Company 12% Notes (fair value)	(218,731)
Issuance of Successor Company common stock	(725,096)
Pre-tax gain on the cancellation of debt	$ 146,555

(l) Pursuant to the Plan, the adjustment eliminates treasury stock of $76,891 of the Predecessor Company.

Fresh-Start Valuation Adjustments

(m) Reflects the adjustment of assets and liabilities to estimated fair value, or other measurement specified by SFAS 141, in conjunction with the adoption of fresh-start reporting. Significant adjustments are summarized as followed:

- *Inventories*—An adjustment of $48,762 was recorded to adjust inventory to fair value. Raw materials were valued at current replacement cost, work-in-process was valued at estimated selling prices of finished goods less the sum of costs to complete, cost of disposal and a reasonable profit allowance for completing and selling effort based on profit for similar finished goods. Finished goods were valued at estimated selling prices less the sum of costs of disposal and a reasonable profit allowance for the selling effort.
- *Property, plant and equipment, net*—An adjustment of $34,699 was recorded to adjust the net book value of property, plant and equipment to fair value giving consideration to their highest and best use. Key assumptions used in the valuation of the Company's property, plant and equipment were based on a combination of the cost or market approach, depending on whether market data was available.
- *Current maturities of long-term debt and Long-term debt, net of current maturities*—An adjustment of $79,658 ($4,329 to Current maturities of long-term debt and $75,329 to Long-term debt, net of current maturities) was recorded to adjust the book value of debt to fair value. This adjustment included a decrease of $84,001 which was based on quoted market prices of certain debt instruments as of the Effective Date, offset by an increase of $4,343 related to debt instruments not traded which was calculated giving consideration to the terms of the underlying agreements, using a risk adjusted interest rate of 12%.
- *Employee benefit obligations, net of current portion*—An adjustment of $18,712 was recorded to measure the employee benefit obligations as of the Effective Date. This adjustment primarily reflects the difference between the expected return on plan assets as compared to the fair value of the plan assets as of the Effective Date and the change in the duration weighted discount rate associated with the payment of the benefit obligations from the prior measurement date and the Effective Date. The weighted average discount rate changed from 6.75% at September 30, 2008 to 5.75% at August 30, 2009.

(continued)

(n) Reflects the tax effects of the fresh-start adjustments at statutory tax rates applicable to such adjustments, net of adjustments to the valuation allowance.

(o) Adjustment eliminated the balance of goodwill and other unamortized intangible assets of the Predecessor Company and records Successor Company intangible assets, including reorganization value in excess of amounts allocated to identified tangible and intangible assets, also referred to as Successor Company goodwill. (See Note 6, Goodwill and Intangible Assets, for additional information regarding the Company's goodwill and other intangible assets). The Successor Company's August 30, 2009 statement of financial position reflects the allocation of the business enterprise value to assets and liabilities immediately following emergence as follows:

Business enterprise value	$ 2,275,000
Add: Fair value of non-interest bearing liabilities (non-debt liabilities)	744,071
Less: Fair value of tangible assets, excluding cash	(1,031,511)
Less: Fair value of identified intangible assets	(1,459,500)
Reorganization value of assets in excess of amounts allocated to identified tangible and intangible assets (Successor Company goodwill)	$ 528,060

The following represent the methodologies and significant assumptions used in determining the fair value of intangible assets, other than goodwill.

Certain indefinite-lived intangible assets which include trade names, trademarks and technology, were valued using a relief from royalty methodology. Customer relationships were valued using a multi-period excess earnings method. Certain intangible assets are subject to sensitive business factors of which only a portion are within control of the Company's management. A summary of the key inputs used in the valuation of these assets are as follows:

- The Company valued customer relationships using the income approach, specifically the multi-period excess earnings method. In determining the fair value of the customer relationship, the multi-period excess earnings approach values the intangible asset at the present value of the incremental after-tax cash flows attributable only to the customer relationship after deducting contributory asset charges. The incremental after-tax cash flows attributable to the subject intangible asset are then discounted to their present value. Only expected sales from current customers were used which included an expected growth rate of 3%. The Company assumed a customer retention rate of 95% which was supported by historical retention rates. Income taxes were estimated at a rate of 35% and amounts were discounted using rates between 12%-14%. The customer relationships were valued at $708,000 under this approach.
- The Company valued trade names and trademarks using the income approach, specifically the relief from royalty method. Under this method, the asset values were determined by estimating the hypothetical royalties that would have to be paid if the trade name was not owned. Royalty rates were selected based on consideration of several factors, including consumer product industry practices, the existence of licensing agreements (licensing in and licensing out), and importance of the trademark and trade name and profit levels, among other considerations. Royalty rates used in the determination of the fair values of trade names and trademarks ranged from 1% to 5% of expected net sales related to the respective trade names and trademarks. The Company anticipates using the majority of the trade names and trademarks for an indefinite period. In estimating the fair value of the trademarks and trade names, nets sales were estimated to grow at a rate of (7)%-10% annually with a terminal year growth rate of 2%-6%. Income taxes were estimated at a rate of 35% and amounts were discounted using rates between 12%-14%. Trade name and trademarks were valued at $688,000 under this approach.
- The Company valued technology using the income approach, specifically the relief from royalty method. Under this method, the asset value was determined by estimating the hypothetical royalties that would have to be paid if the technology was not owned. Royalty rates were selected based on consideration of several factors including industry practices, the existence of licensing agreements (licensing in and licensing out), and importance of the technology and profit levels, among other considerations. Royalty rates used in the determination of the fair values of technologies ranged from 7%-8% of expected net sales related to the respective technology. The Company anticipates using these technologies through the legal life of the underlying patent and therefore the expected life of these technologies was equal to the remaining legal life of the underlying patents ranging from 8 to 17 years. In estimating the fair value of the technologies, nets sales were estimated to grow at a rate of 0%-14% annually. Income taxes were estimated at 35% and amounts were discounted using rates between 12%-13%. The technology assets were valued at $63,500 under this approach.

(p) The fresh-start adjustment of $17,957 eliminates the debt issuance costs related to assumed debt, that is, the (senior secured term credit facility).

(q) The Predecessor Company's accumulated deficit and accumulated other comprehensive income is eliminated in conjunction with the adoption of fresh-start reporting. The Predecessor Company recognized a gain of $1,087,566 related to the fresh-start reporting adjustments as follows:

	Gain on Fresh-Start Reporting Adjustments
Establishment of Successor Company's goodwill	$ 528,060
Elimination of Predecessor Company's goodwill	(238,905)
Establishment of Successor Company's other intangible assets	1,459,500
Elimination of Predecessor Company's other intangible assets	(677,050)
Debt fair value adjustments	79,658
Elimination of debt issuance costs	(17,957)
Property, plant and equipment fair value adjustment	34,699
Deferred tax adjustment	(104,881)
Inventory fair value adjustment	48,762
Employee benefit obligations fair value adjustment	(18,712)
Other fair value adjustments	(5,608)
	$1,087,566

LACK OF CONSISTENCY

PRESENTATION

Author's Note

Unless otherwise indicated, the auditing standards referred to in the following paragraphs apply to both issuers and non-issuers. Refer to paragraphs 7.01 and 7.02 for further information on AICPA auditing standards and PCAOB auditing standards.

7.22 As required by paragraphs .16–.18 of AU section 508, if there has been a change in accounting principles or the method of their application that has a material effect on the comparability of the company's financial statements, the auditor should refer to the change in an explanatory paragraph of the report. Such paragraph should follow the opinion paragraph and identify the nature of the change and refer the reader to the note in the financial statements that discusses the change in detail.

7.23

TABLE 7-3: REFERENCES TO LACK OF CONSISTENCY IN AUDITORS' REPORTS

Table 7-3 summarizes the accounting changes for which auditors expressed unqualified opinions, but included explanatory language (following the opinion paragraph) in their reports.

	2010	2009	2008
Income tax uncertainties	8	185	338
Employee benefits	10	107	247
Consolidations/noncontrolling interests	19	66	N/C*
Business combinations	31	38	N/C*
Fair value measurements	2	24	27
Convertible instruments	14	21	N/C*
Stock-based compensation	—	11	85
Earnings per share	5	9	N/C*
Accounting errors/misstatements	3	8	23
Inventories	4	3	7
Impairment of long-lived assets	3	2	1
Variable interest entities	16	2	—
Derivative financial instruments	1	2	—
Revenue recognition	5	2	—
Transfer/servicing of financial assets	6	1	N/C*
Asset retirement obligations	—	—	6
Other—described	33	19	27
Total Entities	**112**	**290**	**402**

* N/C = Not compiled. Line item was not included in the table for the year shown.

PRESENTATION AND DISCLOSURE EXCERPTS

Revenue Recognition

7.24

CSP INC. (SEP)

REPORT OF INDEPENDENT REGISTERED PUBLIC ACCOUNTING FIRM

To the Board of Directors and Shareholders
CSP Inc.

We have audited the accompanying consolidated balance sheets of CSP, Inc. and subsidiaries as of September 30, 2010 and 2009, and the related consolidated statements of operations, shareholders' equity and comprehensive income (loss), and cash flows for the years then ended. These financial statements are the responsibility of the Company's management. Our responsibility is to express an opinion on these financial statements based on our audits.

We conducted our audits in accordance with the standards of the Public Company Accounting Oversight Board (United States). Those standards require that we plan and perform the audit to obtain reasonable assurance about whether the financial statements are free of material misstatement. The Company is not required to have, nor were we engaged to perform an audit of its internal control over financial reporting. Our audit included consideration of internal control over financial reporting as a basis for designing audit procedures that are appropriate in the circumstances, but not for the purpose of expressing an opinion on the effectiveness of the Company's internal control over financial reporting. Accordingly, we express no such opinion. An audit also includes examining, on a test basis, evidence supporting the amounts and disclosures in the financial statements, assessing the accounting principles used and significant estimates made by management, as well as evaluating the overall financial statement presentation. We believe that our audits provide a reasonable basis for our opinion.

In our opinion, the consolidated financial statements referred to above present fairly, in all material respects, the financial position of CSP, Inc. and subsidiaries as of September 30, 2010 and 2009, and the results of their operations and their cash flows for the years then ended in conformity with U.S. generally accepted accounting principles.

As discussed in Note 1 to the financial statements, CSP, Inc. and subsidiaries has changed its method of recognizing certain revenues in 2010 due to the adoption of Accounting Standards Update ("ASU") 2009-13—*Multiple-Deliverable Revenue Arrangements-a Consensus of the FASB Emerging Issues Task Force* and ASU 2009-14—*Certain Revenue Arrangements that Contain Software Elements.*

NOTES TO CONSOLIDATED FINANCIAL STATEMENTS (in part)

1. Summary of Significant Accounting Policies (in part)

Revenue Recognition (in part)

In October 2009, the FASB issued Accounting Standards Update ("ASU") 2009-13 "Multiple-Deliverable Revenue Arrangements—a Consensus of the FASB Emerging

Issues Task Force" ("ASU 2009-13") and ASU 2009-14—
"Certain Revenue Arrangements that Contain Software
Elements." ("ASU 2009-14"). ASU 2009-13 amends existing revenue recognition accounting principles regarding
multiple-deliverable revenue arrangements. The consensus
provides accounting principles and application guidance on
whether multiple deliverables exist, how the arrangement
should be separated, and how the consideration should be
allocated. This guidance eliminates the requirement to establish verifiable, objective evidence of the fair value of undelivered products and services and also eliminates the residual
method of allocating arrangement consideration. The new
guidance provides for separate revenue recognition based
upon management's estimate of the selling price for an undelivered item when there is no other means to determine
the fair value of that undelivered item. Under the previous
guidance, if the fair value of all of the elements in the arrangement was not determinable, then revenue was deferred
until all of the items were delivered or fair value was determined. This pronouncement is effective prospectively for
revenue arrangements entered into or materially modified in
fiscal years beginning on or after June 15, 2010, with early
adoption permitted.

ASU 2009-14 removes the sale of tangible products containing software components and non-software components
that function together to deliver the tangible product's essential functionality from the scope of software revenue recognition guidance.

Adoption of the new revenue recognition guidance has
had an impact on the pattern and timing of revenue recognition. In some cases, revenue that would have been deferred
pursuant to the previously existing multiple-element revenue
recognition guidance, has been recognized pursuant to the
newly issued guidance. This is because in some cases we are
not able to determine VSOE or third-party evidence of the
service element in our arrangements. Under the new guidance, because the requirement to determine fair value of undelivered elements has been eliminated, and we may use
estimated selling price to allocate revenue to elements in an
arrangement, we are now more likely to be able to separate
arrangements into separate units of accounting, and thereby
recognize the delivered elements (typically product revenue)
without having delivered the other elements in the arrangements (typically services). The impact of adopting this new
accounting guidance on revenue for year ended September
30, 2010 was that $3.5 million in additional revenue was rec-
ognized under the newly adopted guidance that wouldn't
have been recognized had we not adopted the new standards. The impact of adopting this new accounting guidance
on net income and EPS was an increase to net income of
$284 thousand for the year ended September 30, 2010, and
an increase of $0.08, to both basic and fully diluted earnings
per share for the year ended September 30, 2010.

The Company has adopted these standards as of October
1, 2009.

Inventory

7.25

GREIF, INC. (OCT)

REPORT OF INDEPENDENT REGISTERED PUBLIC ACCOUNTING FIRM

The Board of Directors and Shareholders of
Greif, Inc.

We have audited the accompanying consolidated balance
sheets of Greif, Inc. and subsidiaries as of October 31, 2010
and 2009, and the related consolidated statements of income, shareholders' equity, and cash flows for each of the
three years in the period ended October 31, 2010. Our audits also included the financial statement schedule listed in
the Index at Item 15(a)(2). These consolidated financial statements and schedule are the responsibility of the Company's
management. Our responsibility is to express an opinion on
these financial statements based on our audits.

We conducted our audits in accordance with the standards
of the Public Company Accounting Oversight Board (United
States). Those standards require that we plan and perform
the audit to obtain reasonable assurance about whether the
financial statements are free of material misstatement. An audit includes examining, on a test basis, evidence supporting
the amounts and disclosures in the financial statements. An
audit also includes assessing the accounting principles used
and significant estimates made by management, as well as
evaluating the overall financial statement presentation. We
believe that our audits provide a reasonable basis for our
opinion.

In our opinion, the financial statements referred to above
present fairly, in all material respects, the consolidated financial position of Greif, Inc. and subsidiaries at October 31,
2010 and 2009, and the consolidated results of their operations and their cash flows for each of the three years in the
period ended October 31, 2010, in conformity with U.S. generally accepted accounting principles. Also, in our opinion,
the related financial statement schedule, when considered in
relation to the basic consolidated financial statements taken
as a whole, presents fairly in all material respects the information set forth therein.

As discussed in Note 4 to the consolidated financial statements, the Company changed its method of accounting for
inventory in 2010 to the FIFO method of inventory valuation
for all locations.

We also have audited, in accordance with the standards
of the Public Company Accounting Oversight Board (United
States), Greif, Inc.'s internal control over financial reporting as
of October 31, 2010, based on criteria established in Internal
Control-Integrated Framework issued by the Committee of
Sponsoring Organizations of the Treadway Commission and
our report dated December 22, 2010 expressed an unqualified opinion thereon.

NOTES TO CONSOLIDATED FINANCIAL STATEMENTS (in part)

Note 4—Inventories

On November 1, 2009, the Company elected to adopt the
FIFO method of inventory valuation for all locations, whereas

in all prior years inventory for certain U.S. locations was valued using the LIFO method. The Company believes that the FIFO method of inventory valuation is preferable because (i) the change conforms to a single method of accounting for all of the Company's inventories on a U.S. and global basis, (ii) the change simplifies financial disclosures, (iii) financial statement comparability and analysis for investors and analysts is improved, and (iv) the majority of the Company's key competitors use FIFO. The comparative consolidated financial statements of prior periods presented have been adjusted to apply the new accounting method retrospectively. The change in accounting principle is reported through retrospective application as described in ASC 250, "Accounting Changes and Error Corrections."

The following consolidated statement of operations line items for the years ending October 31, 2009 and October 31, 2008 were affected by the change in accounting principle (Dollars in thousands):

	For the Year Ended October 31, 2009			For the Year Ended October 31, 2008		
	As Originally Reported	Adjustments	As Adjusted	As Originally Reported	Adjustments	As Adjusted
Cost of products sold	$2,257,141	$ 35,432	$2,292,573	$3,097,760	$(12,025)	$3,085,735
Gross profit	535,076	(35,432)	499,644	692,771	12,025	704,796
Operating profit	235,329	(35,432)	199,897	370,286	12,025	382,311
Income tax expense	37,706	(13,645)	24,061	73,610	4,631	78,241
Net income attributable to Greif, Inc.	$ 132,433	$(21,787)	$ 110,646	$ 234,354	$ 7,394	$ 241,748

The following consolidated balance sheet line items at October 31, 2009 were affected by the change in accounting principle (Dollars in thousands):

	As Originally Reported	Adjustments	As Adjusted
Inventory	$ 227,432	$11,419	$ 238,851
Total assets	$2,812,510	$11,419	$2,823,929
Deferred tax liabilities	$ 156,755	$ 4,397	$ 161,152
Total liabilities	$1,712,940	$ 4,397	$1,717,337
Retained earnings	$1,199,592	$ 7,022	$1,206,614
Total liabilities and shareholders' equity	$2,812,510	$11,419	$2,823,929

The inventories are comprised as follows at October 31 for the year indicated (Dollars in thousands):

	2010	2009
Finished goods	$ 92,469	$ 57,304
Raw materials and work-in process	304,103	181,547
	$396,572	$238,851

Business Combinations

7.26

HEWLETT-PACKARD COMPANY (OCT)

REPORT OF INDEPENDENT REGISTERED PUBLIC ACCOUNTING FIRM

To the Board of Directors and Stockholders of Hewlett-Packard Company

We have audited the accompanying consolidated balance sheets of Hewlett-Packard Company and subsidiaries as of October 31, 2010 and 2009, and the related consolidated statements of earnings, stockholders' equity, and cash flows for each of the three years in the period ended October 31, 2010. Our audits also included the financial statement schedule listed in the Index at Item 15(a)(2). These financial statements and schedule are the responsibility of the Company's management. Our responsibility is to express an opinion on these financial statements and schedule based on our audits.

We conducted our audits in accordance with the standards of the Public Company Accounting Oversight Board (United States). Those standards require that we plan and perform the audit to obtain reasonable assurance about whether the financial statements are free of material misstatement. An audit includes examining, on a test basis, evidence supporting the amounts and disclosures in the financial statements. An audit also includes assessing the accounting principles used and significant estimates made by management, as well as evaluating the overall financial statement presentation. We believe that our audits provide a reasonable basis for our opinion.

In our opinion, the financial statements referred to above present fairly, in all material respects, the consolidated financial position of Hewlett-Packard Company and subsidiaries at October 31, 2010 and 2009, and the consolidated results of their operations and their cash flows for each of the three years in the period ended October 31, 2010, in conformity with U.S. generally accepted accounting principles. Also, in our opinion, the related financial statement schedule, when considered in relation to the basic financial statements taken as a whole, presents fairly in all material respects the information set forth therein.

As discussed in Note 1 to the consolidated financial statements, in fiscal year 2010, Hewlett-Packard Company and subsidiaries changed their method of accounting for business combinations with the adoption of Financial Accounting Standards Board ("FASB") Accounting Standards Codification ("ASC") 805, *Business Combinations*, and their method of accounting for noncontrolling interests with the adoption of the amendments to FASB ASC 810, *Consolidation*, both effective November 1, 2009. In fiscal year 2009, Hewlett-Packard Company and subsidiaries changed their method of accounting for revenue recognition with the adoption of amendments to the FASB ASC resulting from Accounting Standards Update No. 2009-13, *Multiple-Deliverable Revenue Arrangements*, and Accounting Standards Update No. 2009-14, *Certain Revenue Arrangements That Include Software Elements*, both adopted effective November 1, 2008 and their method of accounting for the measurement date provisions for their defined benefit postretirement plans in accordance with the guidance provided in FASB Statement No. 158, *Employers' Accounting for Defined Benefit Pension and Other Postretirement Plans—An Amendment of FASB No. 87, 88, 106 and 132(R)* (codified primarily in FASB ASC Topic 715, *Compensation—Retirement Benefits*).

We also have audited, in accordance with the standards of the Public Company Accounting Oversight Board (United States), Hewlett-Packard Company's internal control over financial reporting as of October 31, 2010, based on criteria established in Internal Control - Integrated Framework issued by the Committee of Sponsoring Organizations of the Treadway Commission and our report dated December 15, 2010, expressed an unqualified opinion thereon.

NOTES TO CONSOLIDATED FINANCIAL STATEMENTS (in part)

Note 1. Summary of Significant Accounting Policies (in part)

Business Combinations

HP has adopted the new accounting standard related to business combinations. HP has included the results of operations of the businesses that it acquired in fiscal 2010 in HP's consolidated results as of the respective dates of acquisition. HP allocates the purchase price of its acquisitions to the tangible assets, liabilities and intangible assets acquired, including in-process research and development ("IPR&D"), based on their estimated fair values. The excess of the purchase price over those fair values is recorded as goodwill. IPR&D is initially capitalized at fair value as an intangible asset with an indefinite life and assessed for impairment thereafter. When the IPR&D project is complete, it is reclassified as an amortizable purchased intangible asset and is amortized over its estimated useful life. If an IPR&D project is abandoned, HP will record a charge for the value of the related intangible asset to HP's Consolidated Statement of Earnings in the period it is abandoned. Acquisition-related expenses and restructuring costs are recognized separately from the business combination and are expensed as incurred.

Consolidation

7.27

JOHNSON CONTROLS, INC. (SEP)

REPORT OF INDEPENDENT REGISTERED PUBLIC ACCOUNTING FIRM

To the Board of Directors and Shareholders of Johnson Controls, Inc.

In our opinion, the consolidated financial statements listed in the accompanying index present fairly, in all material respects, the financial position of Johnson Controls, Inc. and its subsidiaries at September 30, 2010 and 2009, and the results of their operations and their cash flows for each of the three years in the period ended September 30, 2010 in conformity with accounting principles generally accepted in the United States of America. In addition, in our opinion, the financial statement schedule listed in the accompanying index presents fairly, in all material respects, the information set forth therein when read in conjunction with the related consolidated financial statements. Also in our opinion, the Company maintained, in all material respects, effective internal control over financial reporting as of September 30, 2010, based on criteria established in *Internal Control—Integrated Framework* issued by the Committee of Sponsoring Organizations of the Treadway Commission (COSO). The Company's management is responsible for these financial statements and financial statement schedule, for maintaining effective internal control over financial reporting and for its assessment of the effectiveness of internal control over financial reporting, included in Management's Report on Internal Control Over Financial Reporting appearing under Item 9A. Our responsibility is to express opinions on these financial statements, on the financial statement schedule, and on the Company's internal control over financial reporting based on our integrated audits. We conducted our audits in accordance with the standards of the Public Company Accounting Oversight Board (United States). Those standards require that we plan and perform the audits to obtain reasonable assurance about whether the financial statements are free of material misstatement and whether effective internal control over financial reporting was maintained in all material respects. Our audits of the financial statements included examining, on a test basis, evidence supporting the amounts and disclosures in the financial statements, assessing the accounting principles used and significant estimates made by management, and evaluating the overall financial statement presentation. Our audit of internal control over financial reporting included obtaining an understanding of internal control over financial reporting, assessing the risk that a material weakness exists, and testing and evaluating the design and operating effectiveness of internal control based on the assessed risk. Our audits also included performing such other procedures as we considered necessary in the circumstances. We believe that our audits provide a reasonable basis for our opinions.

As discussed in Note 18 to the consolidated financial statements, the Company adopted guidance included in Accounting Standards Codification (ASC) 740, "Income Taxes," prescribing how a company should recognize, measure, present, and disclose uncertain tax positions effective October 1, 2007.

As discussed in Note 14 to the consolidated financial statements, the Company adopted guidance included in Accounting Standards Codification (ASC) 810, "Consolidation," prescribing how a company should account for noncontrolling interests effective October 1, 2009.

A company's internal control over financial reporting is a process designed to provide reasonable assurance regarding the reliability of financial reporting and the preparation of financial statements for external purposes in accordance with generally accepted accounting principles. A company's internal control over financial reporting includes those policies and procedures that (i) pertain to the maintenance of records that, in reasonable detail, accurately and fairly reflect the transactions and dispositions of the assets of the company; (ii) provide reasonable assurance that transactions are recorded as necessary to permit preparation of financial statements in accordance with generally accepted accounting principles, and that receipts and expenditures of the company are being made only in accordance with authorizations of management and directors of the company; and (iii) provide reasonable assurance regarding prevention or timely detection of unauthorized acquisition, use, or disposition of the company's assets that could have a material effect on the financial statements.

Because of its inherent limitations, internal control over financial reporting may not prevent or detect misstatements. Also, projections of any evaluation of effectiveness to future periods are subject to the risk that controls may become inadequate because of changes in conditions, or that the degree of compliance with the policies or procedures may deteriorate.

NOTES TO CONSOLIDATED FINANCIAL STATEMENTS (in part)

1. Summary of Significant Accounting Policies (in part)

Principles of Consolidation

The consolidated financial statements include the accounts of Johnson Controls, Inc. and its domestic and non-U.S. subsidiaries that are consolidated in conformity with accounting principles generally accepted in the United States of America (U.S. GAAP). All significant intercompany transactions have been eliminated. Investments in partially-owned affiliates are accounted for by the equity method when the Company's interest exceeds 20% and the Company does not have a controlling interest. The financial results for the year ended September 30, 2009 include an out of period adjustment of $62 million made in the first and second quarters of fiscal 2009 to correct an error related to the power solutions segment. The correction of the error, which reduces segment income, primarily originated in fiscal 2007 and 2008 and resulted in the overstatement of inventory and understatement of cost of sales in prior periods. The Company determined that the impact of the error on the originating periods was immaterial, and accordingly a restatement of prior period amounts was not considered necessary. The Company also

determined the impact of correcting the error in fiscal 2009 was not material.

Under certain criteria as provided for in Financial Accounting Standards Board (FASB) Accounting Standards Codification (ASC) 810, "Consolidation," the Company may consolidate a partially-owned affiliate when it has less than a 50% ownership. In order to determine whether to consolidate a partially-owned affiliate when the Company has less than a 50% ownership, the Company first determines if the entity is a variable interest entity (VIE). An entity is considered to be a VIE if it has one of the following characteristics: 1) the entity is thinly capitalized; 2) residual equity holders do not control the entity; 3) equity holders are shielded from economic losses or do not participate fully in the entity's residual economics; or 4) the entity was established with non-substantive voting. If the entity meets one of these characteristics, the Company then determines if it is the primary beneficiary of the VIE. The party exposed to the majority of the risks and rewards associated with the VIE is the VIE's primary beneficiary and must consolidate the entity.

Based upon the criteria set forth in ASC 810, the Company has determined that for the reporting periods ended September 30, 2010 and 2009 it was the primary beneficiary in two VIE's in which it holds less than 50% ownership as the Company funds the entities' short-term liquidity needs. Both entities are consolidated within the automotive experience North America segment. The Company did not have a significant variable interest in any unconsolidated VIE's for the presented reporting periods. The carrying amounts and classification of assets and liabilities included in the Company's consolidated statements of financial position for consolidated VIE's are as follows (in millions):

	September 30	
	2010	2009
Current assets	$215	$146
Noncurrent assets	69	101
Total assets	$284	$247
Current liabilities	$174	$103
Noncurrent liabilities	—	—
Total liabilities	$174	$103

Variable Interest Entities

7.28

TIME WARNER INC. (DEC)

REPORT OF INDEPENDENT REGISTERED PUBLIC ACCOUNTING FIRM

The Board of Directors and Shareholders of Time Warner Inc.

We have audited the accompanying consolidated balance sheets of Time Warner Inc. ("Time Warner") as of December 31, 2010 and 2009, and the related consolidated statements of operations, cash flows and equity for each of the three years in the period ended December 31, 2010. Our audits also included the Supplementary Information and Financial Statement Schedule II listed in the index at Item 15(a). These financial statements, supplementary information and schedule are the responsibility of Time Warner's management. Our responsibility is to express an opinion on these financial statements, supplementary information and schedule based on our audits.

We conducted our audits in accordance with the standards of the Public Company Accounting Oversight Board (United States). Those standards require that we plan and perform the audit to obtain reasonable assurance about whether the financial statements are free of material misstatement. An audit includes examining, on a test basis, evidence supporting the amounts and disclosures in the financial statements. An audit also includes assessing the accounting principles used and significant estimates made by management, as well as evaluating the overall financial statement presentation. We believe that our audits provide a reasonable basis for our opinion.

In our opinion, the financial statements referred to above present fairly, in all material respects, the consolidated financial position of Time Warner at December 31, 2010 and 2009, and the consolidated results of its operations and its cash flows for each of the three years in the period ended December 31, 2010, in conformity with U.S. generally accepted accounting principles. Also, in our opinion, the related Supplementary Information and Financial Statement Schedule, when considered in relation to the basic financial statements taken as a whole, present fairly in all material respects the information set forth therein.

As discussed in Note 1 to the accompanying consolidated financial statements, on January 1, 2009 Time Warner retrospectively adopted accounting guidance for non-controlling interests, and accounting guidance which requires that all outstanding unvested share-based payment awards that contain rights to non-forfeitable dividends or dividend equivalents be considered participating securities.

As discussed in Note 1 to the accompanying consolidated financial statements, on January 1, 2010 Time Warner retrospectively adopted the amendments to the accounting guidance pertaining to the accounting for transfers of financial assets and variable interest entities.

We also have audited, in accordance with the standards of the Public Company Accounting Oversight Board (United States), Time Warner's internal control over financial reporting as of December 31, 2010, based on criteria established in Internal Control—Integrated Framework issued by the Committee of Sponsoring Organizations of the Treadway Commission and our report dated February 18, 2011 expressed an unqualified opinion thereon.

NOTES TO CONSOLIDATED FINANCIAL STATEMENTS (in part)

1. Description of Business, Basis of Presentation and Summary of Significant Accounting Policies (in part)

Accounting Guidance Adopted in 2010 (in part)
Amendments to Accounting for Transfers of Financial Assets and VIEs

On January 1, 2010, the Company adopted guidance on a retrospective basis that (i) eliminated the concept of a qualifying special-purpose entity ("SPE"), (ii) eliminated the exception from applying existing accounting guidance related to variable interest entities ("VIEs") that were previously considered qualifying SPEs, (iii) changed the approach for determining the primary beneficiary of a VIE from a quantitative risk and reward model to a qualitative model based on control and (iv) requires the Company to assess each reporting period whether any of the Company's variable interests give it a controlling financial interest in the applicable VIE.

The Company's investments in entities determined to be VIEs principally consist of certain investments at its Networks segment, primarily HBO Asia, HBO South Asia and certain entities that comprise HBO Latin America Group ("HBO LAG"), which operate multi-channel pay and basic cable television services. As of December 31, 2010, the Company held an 80% economic interest in HBO Asia, a 75% economic interest in HBO South Asia and an approximate 80% economic interest in HBO LAG. The Company previously consolidated these entities; however, as a result of adopting this guidance, because voting control is shared with the other partners in each of the three entities, the Company determined that it is no longer the primary beneficiary of these entities and, effective January 1, 2010, accounts for these investments using the equity method. As of December 31, 2010 and December 31, 2009, the Company's aggregate investment in these three entities was $597 million and $362 million, respectively, and was recorded in investments, including available-for-sale securities, in the consolidated balance sheet.

These investments are intended to enable the Company to more broadly leverage its programming and digital strategy in the territories served and to capitalize on the growing multi-channel television market in such territories. The Company provides programming as well as certain services, including distribution, licensing, technological and administrative support, to HBO Asia, HBO South Asia and HBO LAG. These entities are financed through cash flows from their operations, and the Company is not obligated to provide them with any additional financial support. In addition, the assets of these entities are not available to settle the Company's obligations.

The adoption of this guidance with respect to these entities resulted in an increase (decrease) to revenues, operating income and net income attributable to Time Warner Inc. shareholders of $(397) million, $(75) million and $9 million, respectively, for the year ended December 31, 2009 and an increase (decrease) of $(82) million, $(16) million and $4 million, respectively, for the year ended December 31, 2008. The impact on the consolidated balance sheet as of December 31, 2009 and consolidated statement of cash flows for the years ended December 31, 2009 and 2008 was not material.

The Company also held variable interests in two wholly owned SPEs through which the activities of its accounts receivable securitization facilities were conducted. The Company determined it was the primary beneficiary of these entities because of its ability to direct the key activities of the SPEs that most significantly impact their economic performance. Accordingly, as a result of adopting this guidance, the Company consolidated these SPEs, which resulted in an increase to securitized receivables and non-recourse debt of $805 million as of December 31, 2009. In addition, for the year ended December 31, 2008, cash provided by operations increased by $231 million, with an offsetting decrease to cash used by financing activities. There was no change to cash provided by operations for the year ended December 31, 2009. The impact on the consolidated statement of operations for the years ended December 31, 2009 and 2008 was not material. During the first quarter of 2010, the Company repaid the $805 million that was outstanding under these facilities and terminated the two facilities on March 19, 2010 and March 24, 2010, respectively.

Transfer of Financial Assets

7.29

AGCO CORPORATION (DEC)

REPORT OF INDEPENDENT REGISTERED PUBLIC ACCOUNTING FIRM

The Board of Directors and Stockholders
AGCO Corporation

We have audited the accompanying consolidated balance sheets of AGCO Corporation and subsidiaries as of December 31, 2010 and 2009, and the related consolidated statements of operations, stockholders' equity, and cash flows for each of the years in the three-year period ended December 31, 2010. In connection with our audits of the consolidated financial statements, we also have audited the financial statement schedule as listed in Item 15(a)(2). These consolidated financial statements and financial statement schedule are the responsibility of the Company's management. Our responsibility is to express an opinion on these consolidated financial statements and financial statement schedule based on our audits.

We conducted our audits in accordance with the standards of the Public Company Accounting Oversight Board (United States). Those standards require that we plan and perform the audit to obtain reasonable assurance about whether the financial statements are free of material misstatement. An audit includes examining, on a test basis, evidence supporting the amounts and disclosures in the financial statements. An audit also includes assessing the accounting principles used and significant estimates made by management, as well as evaluating the overall financial statement presentation. We believe that our audits provide a reasonable basis for our opinion.

In our opinion, the consolidated financial statements referred to above present fairly, in all material respects, the financial position of AGCO Corporation and subsidiaries as of December 31, 2010 and 2009, and the results of their operations and their cash flows for each of the years in the three-year period ended December 31, 2010, in conformity with U.S. generally accepted accounting principles. Also in our opinion, the related financial statement schedule, when considered in relation to the basic consolidated financial statements taken as a whole, presents fairly, in all material respects, the information set forth therein.

As discussed in Note 1 to the consolidated financial statements, the Company changed its methods of accounting for transfers of financial assets and consolidation of variable interest entities in 2010 due to the adoption of Accounting Standards Updates 2009-16, "Transfers and Servicing (Topic 860): Accounting for Transfers of Financial Assets" and 2009-17, "Consolidations (Topic 810): Improvements to Financial Reporting by Enterprises Involved with Variable Interest Entities".

We also have audited, in accordance with the standards of the Public Company Accounting Oversight Board (United States), AGCO Corporation's internal control over financial reporting as of December 31, 2010, based on criteria established in Internal Control—Integrated Framework issued by the Committee of Sponsoring Organizations of the Treadway Commission (COSO), and our report dated February 25, 2011 expressed an unqualified opinion on the effectiveness of the Company's internal control over financial reporting.

NOTES TO CONSOLIDATED FINANCIAL STATEMENTS (in part)

1. Operations and Summary of Significant Accounting Policies (in part)

Accounts and Notes Receivable (in part)
The Company transfers certain accounts receivable to various financial institutions primarily under its accounts receivable securitization facility in Europe and its accounts receivable sales agreements with its retail finance joint ventures (Note 4). The Company records such transfers as sales of accounts receivable when it is considered to have surrendered control of such receivables under the provisions of ASU 2009-16, "Transfers and Servicing (Topic 860): Accounting for Transfers of Financial Assets" ("ASU 2009-16"). Cash payments are made to the Company's U.S. and Canadian retail finance joint ventures for sales incentive discounts provided to dealers related to outstanding accounts receivables sold. The balance of such sales discount reserves that are classified in "Accrued expenses" as of December 31, 2010 and 2009 were approximately $87.4 million and $94.5 million, respectively.

Recent Accounting Pronouncements (in part)

In December 2009, the FASB issued ASU 2009-16. ASU 2009-16 eliminated the concept of a qualifying special-purpose entity ("QSPE"), changed the requirements for derecognizing financial assets, and added requirements for additional disclosures in order to enhance information reported to users of financial statements by providing greater transparency about transfers of financial assets, including securitization transactions, and an entity's continuing involvement in and exposure to the risks related to transferred financial assets. ASU 2009-16 was effective for fiscal years and interim periods beginning after November 15, 2009. On January 1, 2010, the Company adopted the provisions of ASU 2009-16, and, in accordance with the standard, the Company recognized approximately $113.9 million of accounts receivable sold through its European securitization facilities within the Company's Condensed Consolidated Balance Sheets as of September 30, 2010, with a corresponding liability equivalent to the funded balance of the facility (Note 4).

Convertible Instruments

7.30

SMITHFIELD FOODS, INC. (APR)

REPORT OF INDEPENDENT REGISTERED PUBLIC ACCOUNTING FIRM ON CONSOLIDATED FINANCIAL STATEMENTS

The Board of Directors and Shareholders of
Smithfield Foods, Inc.

We have audited the accompanying consolidated balance sheets of Smithfield Foods, Inc. and subsidiaries as of May 2, 2010 and May 3, 2009, and the related consolidated statements of income, shareholders' equity, and cash flows for each of the three years in the period ended May 2, 2010. Our audits also included the financial statement schedule listed in the Index at Item 15. These financial statements and schedule are the responsibility of the Company's management. Our responsibility is to express an opinion on these financial statements based on our audits.

We conducted our audits in accordance with the standards of the Public Company Accounting Oversight Board (United States). Those standards require that we plan and perform the audit to obtain reasonable assurance about whether the financial statements are free of material misstatement. An audit includes examining, on a test basis, evidence supporting the amounts and disclosures in the financial statements. An audit also includes assessing the accounting principles used and significant estimates made by management, as well as evaluating the overall financial statement presentation. We believe that our audits provide a reasonable basis for our opinion.

In our opinion, the financial statements referred to above present fairly, in all material respects, the consolidated financial position of Smithfield Foods, Inc. and subsidiaries at May 2, 2010 and May 3, 2009, and the consolidated results of their operations and their cash flows for each of the three years in the period ended May 2, 2010, in conformity with U.S. generally accepted accounting principles. Also, in our opinion, the related financial statement schedule, when considered in relation to the basic financial statements taken as a whole, presents fairly in all material respects the information set forth therein.

As discussed in Note 2 to the consolidated financial statements, in fiscal 2010 the Company changed its method for accounting for convertible debt instruments with the adoption of the guidance originally issued in the accounting provisions of Financial Accounting Standards Board (FASB) Staff Position ABP 14-1, *Accounting for Convertible Debt Instruments That May be Settled in Cash upon Conversion* (codified in FASB ASC Topic 470, *Debt*) effective January 1, 2009.

We also have audited, in accordance with the standards of the Public Company Accounting Oversight Board (United States), Smithfield Foods, Inc. and subsidiaries' internal control over financial reporting as of May 2, 2010, based on criteria established in Internal Control-Integrated Framework issued by the Committee of Sponsoring Organizations of the Treadway Commission and our report dated June 18, 2010 expressed an unqualified opinion thereon.

NOTES TO CONSOLIDATED FINANCIAL STATEMENTS (in part)

Note 2. Accounting Changes and New Accounting Guidance (in part)

In May 2008, the FASB issued new accounting guidance for convertible debt instruments that may be settled in cash upon conversion (including partial cash settlement). Under the new guidance, issuers of such instruments should separately account for the liability and equity components in a manner that will reflect the entity's nonconvertible debt borrowing rate when interest cost is recognized in subsequent periods. The amount allocated to the equity component represents a discount to the debt, which is amortized into interest expense using the effective interest method over the life of the debt. We adopted the new accounting guidance in the first quarter of fiscal 2010 and applied it retrospectively to all periods presented. Refer to Note 10—Debt for further discussion of the impact of this new accounting guidance on our consolidated financial statements.

Note 10. Debt (in part)

Convertible Notes

In July 2008 (fiscal 2009), we issued $400.0 million aggregate principal amount of 4% convertible senior notes due June 30, 2013 (the Convertible Notes) in a registered offering. The Convertible Notes are senior unsecured obligations. The Convertible Notes are payable with cash and, at certain times, are convertible into shares of our common stock based on an initial conversion rate, subject to adjustment, of 44.082 shares per $1,000 principal amount of Convertible Notes (which represents an initial conversion price of approximately $22.68 per share). Upon conversion, a holder will receive cash up to the principal amount of the Convertible Notes and shares of our common stock for the remainder, if any, of the conversion obligation.

Prior to April 1, 2013, holders may convert their notes into cash and shares of our common stock, if any, at the applicable conversion rate under the following circumstances:

- During any fiscal quarter if the last reported sale price of our common stock is greater than or equal to 120% of the applicable conversion price for at least 20 trading days during the period of 30 consecutive trading days ending on the last trading day of the preceding fiscal quarter;
- During the five business-day period after any ten consecutive trading-day period in which the trading price per $1,000 principal amount of notes was less than 98% of the last reported sale price of our common stock multiplied by the applicable conversion rate; or
- Upon the occurrence of specified corporate transactions.

On or after April 1, 2013, holders may convert their Convertible Notes at any time prior to the close of business on the third scheduled trading day immediately preceding the maturity date, regardless of the foregoing circumstances.

The Convertible Notes were originally accounted for as a combined debt instrument as the conversion feature did not meet the requirements to be accounted for separately as a derivative financial instrument. In May 2008, the FASB issued new accounting guidance specifying that issuers of convertible debt instruments that may be settled in cash upon conversion (including partial cash settlement) should separately account for the liability and equity components in a manner that will reflect the entity's nonconvertible debt borrowing rate when interest cost is recognized in subsequent periods. The amount allocated to the equity component represents a discount to the debt recorded. This discount represents the amount of additional interest expense to be recognized using the effective interest method over the life of the debt, to accrete the debt to the principal amount due at maturity. We adopted the new accounting guidance beginning in the first quarter of fiscal 2010 (beginning May 4, 2009).

In connection with the issuance of the Convertible Notes, we entered into separate convertible note hedge transactions with respect to our common stock to reduce potential economic dilution upon conversion of the Convertible Notes, and separate warrant transactions (collectively referred to as the Call Spread Transactions). We purchased call options that permit us to acquire up to approximately 17.6 million shares of our common stock, subject to adjustment, which is the number of shares initially issuable upon conversion of the Convertible Notes. In addition, we sold warrants permitting the purchasers to acquire up to approximately 17.6 million shares of our common stock, subject to adjustment. See Note 15—Equity for more information on the Call Spread Transactions.

We incurred fees and expenses associated with the issuance of the Convertible Notes totaling $11.4 million, substantially all of which were capitalized and are being amortized to interest expense over the life of the Convertible Notes.

On the date of issuance of the Convertible Notes, our nonconvertible debt borrowing rate was determined to be 10.2%. Based on that rate of interest, the liability component and equity component of the Convertible Notes were determined to be $304.2 million and $95.8 million, respectively.

The following table presents the effects of the retrospective application of the new accounting guidance on our consolidated condensed balance sheet as of May 3, 2009:

(In millions)	As Originally Presented May 3, 2009	Adjustments	As Adjusted May 3, 2009
Other assets	$ 161.2	$ (2.3)	$ 158.9
Total assets	7,202.5	(2.3)	7,200.2
Long-term debt and capital lease obligations	2,649.9	(82.6)	2,567.3
Other liabilities (original presentation included pension obligations of $340.5 million)	345.7	29.3	375.0
Additional paid-in capital	1,294.7	59.1	1,353.8
Retained earnings	1,648.2	(8.1)	1,640.1
Total shareholders' equity	2,561.4	51.0	2,612.4
Total liabilities and equity	7,202.5	(2.3)	7,200.2

The following table presents the effects of the retrospective application of the new accounting guidance on our consolidated income statement for fiscal 2009:

(In millions, except per share data)	As Originally Presented Fiscal 2009	Adjustments	As Adjusted Fiscal 2009
Interest expense	$209.1	$12.7	$221.8
Loss from continuing operations before income taxes	(369.5)	(12.7)	(382.2)
Income tax benefit	(126.7)	(4.6)	(131.3)
Loss from continuing operations	(242.8)	(8.1)	(250.9)
Net loss	(190.3)	(8.1)	(198.4)
Loss per basic and diluted share:			
Continuing operations	$ (1.72)	$ (.06)	$ (1.78)
Net loss	(1.35)	(.06)	(1.41)

The adoption of the new accounting guidance impacted our results for fiscal 2010 as follows:

(In millions, except per share data)	Fiscal 2010
Interest expense	$16.7
Loss from continuing operations before income taxes	(16.7)
Income tax benefit	(6.1)
Loss from continuing operations	(10.6)
Net loss	(10.6)
Loss per basic and diluted share:	
Continuing operations	$ (.07)
Net loss	(.07)

Note 15. Equity (in part)

New Accounting Guidance for Convertible Notes

As more fully described in Note 10—Debt, the FASB issued new accounting guidance in the first quarter of fiscal 2010, which required us to separately account for the conversion feature of the Convertible Notes as a component of equity, thereby increasing additional paid-in capital by $59.1 million.

Earnings per Share

7.31

CABOT CORPORATION (SEP)

REPORT OF INDEPENDENT REGISTERED PUBLIC ACCOUNTING FIRM

To the Board of Directors and Stockholders of
Cabot Corporation
Boston, Massachusetts

We have audited the accompanying consolidated balance sheets of Cabot Corporation and subsidiaries (the "Company") as of September 30, 2010 and 2009, and the related consolidated statements of operations, changes in stockholders' equity, and cash flows for each of the three years in the period ended September 30, 2010. These consolidated financial statements are the responsibility of the Company's management. Our responsibility is to express an opinion on these financial statements based on our audits.

We conducted our audits in accordance with the standards of the Public Company Accounting Oversight Board (United States). Those standards require that we plan and perform the audit to obtain reasonable assurance about whether the financial statements are free of material misstatement. An audit includes examining, on a test basis, evidence supporting the amounts and disclosures in the financial statements. An audit also includes assessing the accounting principles used and significant estimates made by management, as well as evaluating the overall financial statement presentation. We believe that our audits provide a reasonable basis for our opinion.

In our opinion, such consolidated financial statements present fairly, in all material respects, the financial position of Cabot Corporation and subsidiaries as of September 30, 2010 and 2009, and the results of their operations and their cash flows for each of the three years in the period ended September 30, 2010, in conformity with accounting principles generally accepted in the United States of America.

As discussed in Note B, in 2010 the Company changed (i) its method of accounting for earnings per share; and (ii) its presentation of non-controlling interests. These changes have been applied to all periods presented.

We have also audited, in accordance with the standards of the Public Company Accounting Oversight Board (United States), the Company's internal control over financial reporting as of September 30, 2010, based on the criteria established in *Internal Control—Integrated Framework* issued by the Committee of Sponsoring Organizations of the Treadway Commission and our report dated November 29, 2010 expressed an unqualified opinion on the Company's internal control over financial reporting.

NOTES TO CONSOLIDATED FINANCIAL STATEMENTS (in part)

Note B. Accounting Pronouncements (in part)

New and Adopted (in part)

Cabot adopted new accounting guidance relative to earnings per share on October 1, 2009. This methodology, and the impact on prior periods, is described in Note Q.

Note Q. Earnings Per Share

On October 1, 2009 Cabot began applying the two-class method for calculating earnings per share. Under this method, unvested restricted stock and stock unit awards that receive non-forfeitable rights to dividends or dividend equivalents are treated as a separate class of participating securities. The two-class method calculates earnings per share for common shareholders and participating securities based on the proportionate participation rights of each award type in the Company's undistributed earnings. Diluted earnings per share is calculated using the more dilutive of the treasury stock method or the two-class method. This guidance has been applied to all periods presented herein. The retrospective application of this authoritative guidance increased the Company's basic and diluted net loss per share from $(1.23) to $(1.25) for fiscal 2009 and decreased the Company's basic and diluted net income per share from $1.37 and $1.34, respectively, to $1.32 for both basic and diluted net income per share for fiscal 2008.

The following tables summarize the components of the basic and diluted earnings per common share computations:

(In millions, except per share amounts)	Years Ended September 30		
	2010	2009	2008
Basic EPS:			
Net income (loss) attributable to Cabot Corporation	$ 154	$ (77)	$ 86
Less: Dividends and dividend equivalents to participating securities	1	2	2
Less: Undistributed earnings allocated to participating securities[1]	2	—	1
Earnings (loss) allocated to common shareholders (numerator)	$ 151	$ (79)	$ 83
Weighted average common shares and participating securities outstanding	65	65	65
Less: Participating securities[2]	1	2	2
Adjusted weighted average common shares (denominator)	64	63	63
Income (loss) from continuing operations attributable to Cabot Corporation	$2.37	$(1.24)	$1.32
Loss from discontinued operations	—	(0.01)	—
Net income (loss) attributable to Cabot Corporation	$2.37	$(1.25)	$1.32
Diluted EPS:			
Earnings (loss) allocated to common shareholders	$ 151	$ (79)	$ 83
Plus: Earnings allocated to participating securities	3	2	3
Less: Adjusted earnings allocated to participating securities[3]	(3)	(2)	(3)
Income (loss) available to common shares (numerator)	$ 151	$ (79)	$ 83
Adjusted weighted average common shares outstanding	64	63	63
Effect of dilutive securities:			
Common shares issuable[4]	—	—	—
Adjusted weighted average shares (denominator)	64	63	63
Income (loss) from continuing operations attributable to Cabot Corporation	$2.35	$(1.24)	$1.32
Loss from discontinued operations	—	(0.01)	—
Net income (loss) attributable to Cabot Corporation	$2.35	$(1.25)	$1.32

[1] Undistributed earnings are the earnings which remain after dividends declared during the period are assumed to be distributed to the common and participating shareholders. Undistributed earnings are allocated to common and participating shareholders on the same basis as dividend distributions. In fiscal 2009, undistributed earnings were not allocated to participating securities due to the Company's net loss position. The calculation of undistributed earnings is as follows:

(Dollars in millions)	Years Ended September 30		
	2010	2009	2008
Calculation of undistributed earnings:			
Net income (loss) attributable to Cabot Corporation	$154	$ (77)	$86
Less: Dividends declared on common stock	46	46	45
Less: Dividends declared on participating securities	1	2	2
Undistributed earnings	$107	$(125)	$39
Allocation of undistributed earnings:			
Undistributed earnings allocated to common shareholders	$105	$(125)	$38
Undistributed earnings allocated to participating shareholders	2	—	1
Undistributed earnings	$107	$(125)	$39

[2] Participating securities for fiscal 2010, 2009 and 2008 amounted to approximately 1 million, 2 million and 2 million shares (or other equity awards), respectively, issued under Cabot's equity incentive plans. For fiscal 2010, 2009 and 2008, participating securities consisted of shares of unvested restricted stock and vested restricted stock awards held by employees in which Cabot has a security interest. For fiscal 2010, participating securities also included unvested time-based restricted stock units.

[3] Undistributed earnings are adjusted for the assumed distribution of dividends to the dilutive securities and then reallocated to participating securities.

[4] Represents incremental shares of common stock from the (i) assumed exercise of stock options issued under Cabot's equity incentive plan; (ii) assumed issuance of shares to employees pursuant to the Company's Supplemental Retirement Savings Plan; and (iii) assumed issuance of shares under outstanding performance-based stock unit awards issued under Cabot's equity incentive plans. For fiscal 2010, 193,000 incremental shares of common stock were not included in the calculation of diluted earnings per share because those shares' exercise prices were greater than the average market price of Cabot common stock for that period. For fiscal 2009, 3,833,000 incremental shares of commons stock were excluded from the calculation of diluted earnings per share as those shares would have been antidilutive due to the Company's net loss position. For fiscal 2008, 408,000 incremental shares of common stock were excluded from the calculation of diluted earnings per share because those shares' exercise prices were greater than the average market price of Cabot common stock for that period.

Multiple Element Revenue Transactions

7.32

ADOBE SYSTEMS INCORPORATED (NOV)

REPORT OF INDEPENDENT REGISTERED PUBLIC ACCOUNTING FIRM

The Board of Directors and Stockholders
Adobe Systems Incorporated

We have audited the accompanying consolidated balance sheets of Adobe Systems Incorporated and subsidiaries as of December 3, 2010 and November 27, 2009, and the related consolidated statements of income, stockholders' equity and comprehensive income, and cash flows for each of the years in the three-year period ended December 3, 2010. We also have audited Adobe Systems Incorporated's internal control over financial reporting as of December 3, 2010, based on criteria established in Internal Control—Integrated Framework, issued by the Committee of Sponsoring Organizations of the Treadway Commission (COSO). Adobe System Incorporated's management is responsible for these consolidated financial statements, for maintaining effective internal control over financial reporting, and for its assessment of the effectiveness of internal control over financial reporting, included in the accompanying Management's Annual Report on Internal Control over Financial Reporting appearing under Item 9A. Our responsibility is to express an opinion on these consolidated financial statements and an opinion on the Company's internal control over financial reporting based on our audits.

We conducted our audits in accordance with the standards of the Public Company Accounting Oversight Board (United States). Those standards require that we plan and perform the audits to obtain reasonable assurance about whether the financial statements are free of material misstatement and whether effective internal control over financial reporting was maintained in all material respects. Our audits of the consolidated financial statements included examining, on a test basis, evidence supporting the amounts and disclosures in the financial statements, assessing the accounting principles used and significant estimates made by management, and evaluating the overall financial statement presentation. Our audit of internal control over financial reporting included obtaining an understanding of internal control over financial reporting, assessing the risk that a material weakness exists, and testing and evaluating the design and operating effectiveness of internal control based on the assessed risk. Our audits also included performing such other procedures as we considered necessary in the circumstances. We believe that our audits provide a reasonable basis for our opinions.

A company's internal control over financial reporting is a process designed to provide reasonable assurance regarding the reliability of financial reporting and the preparation of financial statements for external purposes in accordance with generally accepted accounting principles. A company's internal control over financial reporting includes those policies and procedures that (1) pertain to the maintenance of records that, in reasonable detail, accurately and fairly reflect the transactions and dispositions of the assets of the company; (2) provide reasonable assurance that transactions are recorded as necessary to permit preparation of financial statements in accordance with generally accepted accounting principles, and that receipts and expenditures of the company are being made only in accordance with authorizations of management and directors of the company; and (3) provide reasonable assurance regarding prevention or timely detection of unauthorized acquisition, use, or disposition of the company's assets that could have a material effect on the financial statements.

Because of its inherent limitations, internal control over financial reporting may not prevent or detect misstatements. Also, projections of any evaluation of effectiveness to future periods are subject to the risk that controls may become inadequate because of changes in conditions, or that the degree of compliance with the policies or procedures may deteriorate.

In our opinion, the consolidated financial statements referred to above present fairly, in all material respects, the financial position of Adobe Systems Incorporated and subsidiaries as of December 3, 2010 and November 27, 2009, and the results of their operations and their cash flows for each of the years in the three-year period ended December 3, 2010, in conformity with U.S. generally accepted accounting principles. Also in our opinion, Adobe Systems Incorporated maintained, in all material respects, effective internal control over financial reporting as of December 3, 2010, based on criteria established in Internal Control—Integrated Framework, issued by the Committee of Sponsoring Organizations of the Treadway Commission (COSO).

As discussed in notes 1 and 10 to the consolidated financial statements, the Company changed its method of accounting for multiple element revenue transactions in fiscal 2010 and its method for accounting for uncertainty in income taxes in fiscal 2008, resulting from the adoption of new accounting pronouncements.

NOTES TO CONSOLIDATED FINANCIAL STATEMENTS (in part)

Note 1. Basis of Presentation and Significant Accounting Policies (in part)

Significant Accounting Policies (in part)

Multiple Element Arrangements

We enter into multiple element revenue arrangements in which a customer may purchase a combination of software, upgrades, maintenance and support, hosting services, and consulting.

For our software and software related multiple element arrangements, we must: (1) determine whether and when each element has been delivered; (2) determine whether undelivered products or services are essential to the functionality of the delivered products and services; (3) determine the fair value of each element using vendor-specific objective evidence ("VSOE"), and (4) allocate the total price among the various elements. VSOE of fair value is used to allocate a portion of the price to the undelivered elements and the residual method is used to allocate the remaining portion to the delivered elements.

Absent VSOE, revenue is deferred until the earlier of the point at which VSOE of fair value exists for any undelivered element or until all elements of the arrangement have been delivered. However, if the only undelivered element is maintenance and support, the entire arrangement fee is recognized ratably over the performance period. Changes in assumptions or judgments or changes to the elements in a software arrangement could cause a material increase or decrease in the amount of revenue that we report in a particular period.

In October 2009, the Financial Accounting Standards Board ("FASB") amended the accounting standards for certain multiple deliverable revenue arrangements to:

- provide updated guidance on whether multiple deliverables exist, how the deliverables in an arrangement should be separated, and how the consideration should be allocated;
- require an entity to allocate revenue in an arrangement using the best estimated selling price ("BESP") of deliverables if a vendor does not have VSOE of selling price or third-party evidence ("TPE") of selling price; and
- eliminate the use of the residual method and require an entity to allocate revenue using the relative selling price method.

We elected to early adopt this accounting guidance at the beginning of our fiscal quarter of 2010 on a prospective basis for applicable transactions originating or materially modified after November 27, 2009. Our revenue from sales containing non-software related hosting services, custom hosting development and consulting services, and related technical support and training are those impacted.

For multiple element arrangements containing our non-software services, we must: (1) determine whether and when each element has been delivered; (2) determine fair value of each element using the selling price hierarchy of VSOE of fair value, TPE or BESP, as applicable and (3) allocate the total price among the various elements based on the relative selling price method.

This guidance does not generally change the units of accounting for our revenue transactions. For multiple-element arrangements that contain software and non-software elements such as our hosted offerings, we allocate revenue to software or software related elements as a group and any non-software element separately based on the selling price hierarchy. We determine the selling price for each deliverable using VSOE of fair value of selling price, if it exists, or TPE of selling price. If neither VSOE nor TPE of selling price exist for a deliverable, we use its BESP for that deliverable. Revenue allocated to each element is then recognized when the basic revenue recognition criteria are met for each element. Once revenue is allocated to software or software related elements as a group, it follows historic software accounting guidance.

Consistent with our methodology under previous accounting guidance, we determine VSOE for each element based on historical stand-alone sales to third-parties or from the stated renewal rate for the elements contained in the initial arrangement. In determining VSOE, we require that a substantial majority of the selling prices for a product or service fall within a reasonably narrow pricing range.

In certain instances, we are not able to establish VSOE for all deliverables in an arrangement with multiple elements. This may be due to infrequently selling each element separately, not pricing products or services within a narrow range, or only having a limited sales history. When VSOE cannot be established, we attempt to establish the selling price of each element based on TPE. TPE is determined based on competitor prices for similar deliverables when sold separately. Generally, our offerings contain significant differentiation such that the comparable pricing of products with similar functionality cannot be obtained. Furthermore, we are unable to reliably determine what similar competitor products' selling prices are on a stand-alone basis. Therefore, we typically are not able to obtain TPE of selling price.

When we are unable to establish selling prices using VSOE or TPE, we use BESP in our allocation of arrangement consideration. The objective of BESP is to determine the price at which we would transact a sale if the product or service were sold on a stand-alone basis. BESP is generally used for offerings that are not typically sold on a stand-alone basis or for new or highly customized offerings.

We determine BESP for a product or service by considering multiple factors including, but not limited to, major product groupings, geographies, market conditions, competitive landscape, internal costs, gross margin objectives and pricing practices. Significant pricing practices taken into consideration include historic contractually stated prices, volume discounts where applicable and our price lists. The most common fact pattern that emerged through analyzing these factors supports a BESP closely tied to Adobe's list prices. The determination of BESP is made through consultation with and formal approval by our management, taking into consideration our go-to-market strategy.

We regularly review VSOE and have established a review process for TPE and BESP and maintain internal controls over the establishment and updates of these estimates. There was no material impact to revenue during the year ended December 3, 2010 resulting from changes in VSOE, TPE or BESP, nor do we expect a material impact from such changes in the near term.

We have established VSOE for our software maintenance and support services, custom software development services, consulting services and training. We have established BESP for all other offerings, including software products, non-software related hosting services, custom hosting development and consulting services, and technical support and training for hosting services.

Given the nature of our transactions, which are primarily software and software-related, our go-to-market strategies and our pricing practices, total net revenue as reported during the year ended December 3, 2010 is materially consistent with total net revenue that would have been reported if the transactions entered into or materially modified after November 27, 2009 were subject to previous accounting guidance. Additionally, the new accounting standards for revenue recognition, if applied in the same manner to the year ended November 27, 2009, would not have had a material impact on total net revenues for that fiscal year.

Noncontrolling Interest

7.33

HORMEL FOODS CORPORATION (OCT)

REPORT OF INDEPENDENT REGISTERED PUBLIC ACCOUNTING FIRM

To the Board of Directors and Shareholders
Hormel Foods Corporation
Austin, Minnesota

We have audited the accompanying consolidated statements of financial position of Hormel Foods Corporation as of October 31, 2010, and October 25, 2009, and the related consolidated statements of operations, changes in shareholders' investment, and cash flows for each of the three years in the period ended October 31, 2010. These financial statements are the responsibility of the Company's management. Our responsibility is to express an opinion on these financial statements based on our audits.

We conducted our audits in accordance with the standards of the Public Company Accounting Oversight Board (United States). Those standards require that we plan and perform the audit to obtain reasonable assurance about whether the financial statements are free of material misstatement. An audit includes examining, on a test basis, evidence supporting the amounts and disclosures in the financial statements. An audit also includes assessing the accounting principles used and significant estimates made by management, as well as evaluating the overall financial statement presentation. We believe that our audits provide a reasonable basis for our opinion.

In our opinion, the financial statements referred to above present fairly, in all material respects, the consolidated financial position of Hormel Foods Corporation at October 31, 2010, and October 25, 2009, and the consolidated results of its operations and its cash flows for each of the three years in the period ended October 31, 2010, in conformity with U.S. generally accepted accounting principles.

As discussed in Note H of the Notes to Consolidated Financial Statements, effective October 27, 2008, the Company adopted the measurement provisions of Statement of Financial Accounting Standard No. 158, "Employers' Accounting for Defined Benefit Pension and Other Postretirement Plans—an amendment of FASB Statements No. 87, 88, 106 and 132(R)" (codified primarily in FASB ASC 715). As discussed in Note A of the Notes to Consolidated Financial Statements, effective October 26, 2009, the Company adopted new rules regarding the accounting for noncontrolling interests (codified primarily in FASB ASC 810).

We also have audited, in accordance with the standards of the Public Company Accounting Oversight Board (United States), Hormel Foods Corporation's internal control over financial reporting as of October 31, 2010, based on criteria established in *Internal Control-Integrated Framework* issued by the Committee of Sponsoring Organizations of the Treadway Commission and our report dated December 21, 2010, expressed an unqualified opinion thereon.

NOTES TO CONSOLIDATED FINANCIAL STATEMENTS (in part)

Note A—Summary of Significant Accounting Policies (in part)

Accounting Changes and Recent Accounting Pronouncements (in part)

In December 2007, the FASB also updated the guidance within ASC 810, *Consolidation* (ASC 810). The update establishes accounting and reporting standards for the noncontrolling interest in a subsidiary and for the deconsolidation of a subsidiary. It also amends the requirements for certain consolidation procedures for consistency with the requirements of ASC 805. The updated guidance is effective for fiscal years beginning on or after December 15, 2008, and interim periods within those fiscal years. The Company adopted the provisions of ASC 810 at the beginning of fiscal 2010. Adoption did not have a material impact on the consolidated financial statements, but resulted in the following changes in presentation and disclosure: 1) noncontrolling interests were reclas-

sified from other long-term liabilities or accumulated other comprehensive loss (foreign currency translation) to a separate component of shareholders' investment in the Consolidated Statements of Financial Position; 2) consolidated net earnings on the Consolidated Statements of Operations now include the net earnings attributable to both the Company and its noncontrolling interests; 3) the Consolidated Statement of Changes in Shareholders' Investment now identifies the components of shareholders' investment and comprehensive income attributable to the Company's noncontrolling interests; and 4) the Consolidated Statements of Cash Flows now begin with consolidated net earnings attributable to both the Company and its noncontrolling interests, with the net earnings of the noncontrolling interests no longer included within changes in operating assets and liabilities and any distributions to the noncontrolling interests included in financing activities. As required, the prior year consolidated financial statements have also been reclassified to comply with the current year's presentation and disclosure requirements.

EMPHASIS OF A MATTER

PRESENTATION

Author's Note

Unless otherwise indicated, the auditing standards referred to in the following paragraphs apply to both issuers and non-issuers. Refer to paragraphs 7.01 and 7.02 for further information on AICPA auditing standards and PCAOB auditing standards.

7.34 Paragraph .19 of AU section 508 states the following:

In any report on financial statements, the auditor may emphasize a matter regarding the financial statements. Such explanatory information should be presented in a separate paragraph of the auditors' report. Phrases such as "with the foregoing [following] explanation" should not be used in the opinion paragraph if an emphasis paragraph is included in the auditors' report. Emphasis paragraphs are never required; they may be added solely at the auditors' discretion. Examples of matters the auditor may wish to emphasize are—
- That the entity is a component of a larger business enterprise.
- That the entity has had significant transactions with related parties.
- Unusually important subsequent events.
- Accounting matters, other than those involving a change or changes in accounting principles, affecting the comparability of the financial statements with those of the preceding period.

The auditors' reports for 31 survey entities included explanatory information emphasizing a matter regarding the financial statements.

PRESENTATION AND DISCLOSURE EXCERPTS

Emphasis of a Matter

7.35

MOLEX INCORPORATED (JUN)

REPORT OF INDEPENDENT REGISTERED PUBLIC ACCOUNTING FIRM

The Board of Directors and Stockholders of
Molex Incorporated

We have audited the accompanying consolidated balance sheets of Molex Incorporated as of June 30, 2010 and 2009, and the related consolidated statements of operations, stockholders' equity, and cash flows for each of the three years in the period ended June 30, 2010. Our audits also included the financial statement schedule listed in the Index of Part IV, Item 15. These financial statements and schedule are the responsibility of the Company's management. Our responsibility is to express an opinion on these financial statements and schedule based on our audits.

We conducted our audits in accordance with the standards of the Public Company Accounting Oversight Board (United States). Those standards require that we plan and perform the audit to obtain reasonable assurance about whether the financial statements are free of material misstatement. An audit includes examining, on a test basis, evidence supporting the amounts and disclosures in the financial statements. An audit also includes assessing the accounting principles used and significant estimates made by management, as well as evaluating the overall financial statement presentation. We believe that our audits provide a reasonable basis for our opinion.

In our opinion, the consolidated financial statements referred to above present fairly, in all material respects, the consolidated financial position of Molex Incorporated at June 30, 2010 and 2009, and the consolidated results of its operations and its cash flows for each of the three years in the period ended June 30, 2010, in conformity with U.S. generally accepted accounting principles. Also, in our opinion, the related financial statement schedule, when considered in relation to the basic financial statements taken as a whole, presents fairly in all material respects the information set forth therein.

As discussed in Note 3 to the consolidated financial statements, the Company has restated its financial statements as of June 30, 2009 and for each of the two years in the period then ended relating to a fraud matter in Japan and accounting for income taxes.

We also have audited, in accordance with the standards of the Public Company Accounting Oversight Board (United States), the effectiveness of Molex Incorporated's internal control over financial reporting as of June 30, 2010, based on criteria established in Internal Control—Integrated Framework issued by the Committee of Sponsoring Organizations of the Treadway Commission and our report dated August 3, 2010 expressed an unqualified opinion thereon.

DEPARTURES FROM UNQUALIFIED OPINIONS

PRESENTATION

Author's Note

Unless otherwise indicated, the auditing standards referred to in the following paragraphs apply to both issuers and non-issuers. Refer to paragraphs 7.01 and 7.02 for further information on AICPA auditing standards and PCAOB auditing standards.

7.36 AU section 508 does not require auditors to express qualified opinions about the effects of uncertainties or lack of consistency. Under AU section 508, departures from unqualified opinions include opinions qualified because of a scope limitation or departure from GAAP, including inadequate disclosures; adverse opinions; and disclaimers of opinion. Paragraphs .20–.63 of AU section 508 discuss these departures. None of the auditors' reports issued in connection with the financial statements of the survey entities contained a *departure*, as defined by AU section 508.

REPORTS ON COMPARATIVE FINANCIAL STATEMENTS

PRESENTATION

Author's Note

Unless otherwise indicated, the auditing standards referred to in the following paragraphs apply to both issuers and non-issuers. Refer to paragraphs 7.01 and 7.02 for further information on AICPA auditing standards and PCAOB auditing standards.

7.37 Paragraphs .65–.74 of AU section 508 discuss reports on comparative financial statements. None of the auditors' reports for the survey entities expressed an opinion on prior-year financial statements that differed from the opinion originally expressed and none of the auditor reports indicated that a change in auditors had occurred in the current year.

OPINION EXPRESSED ON SUPPLEMENTARY FINANCIAL INFORMATION

PRESENTATION

7.38 Annual reports to security holders may be combined with the required information of SEC Form 10-K and are suitable for filing with the SEC if certain conditions are satisfied. Accordingly, many survey entities prepare an integrated annual report or simply provide to stockholders a copy of Form 10-K in lieu of the annual report. Form 10-K requires inclusion of certain supplementary financial information, including schedules (Article 12 of Regulation S-X), that must be audited. The report on the audit of schedules may be a separate report or combined with the report on the audit of the basic financial statements.

PRESENTATION AND DISCLOSURE EXCERPTS

Supplementary Financial Information

7.39

ALLERGAN, INC. (DEC)

REPORT OF INDEPENDENT REGISTERED PUBLIC ACCOUNTING FIRM

The Board of Directors and Stockholders of Allergan, Inc.

We have audited the accompanying consolidated balance sheets of Allergan, Inc. as of December 31, 2010 and 2009, and the related consolidated statements of earnings, equity, and cash flows for each of the three years in the period ended December 31, 2010. Our audits also included the financial statement schedule listed in the Index at Item 15(a)2. These financial statements and the financial statement schedule are the responsibility of the Company's management. Our responsibility is to express an opinion on these financial statements and schedule based on our audits.

We conducted our audits in accordance with the standards of the Public Company Accounting Oversight Board (United States). Those standards require that we plan and perform the audit to obtain reasonable assurance about whether the financial statements are free of material misstatement. An audit includes examining, on a test basis, evidence supporting the amounts and disclosures in the financial statements. An audit also includes assessing the accounting principles used and significant estimates made by management, as well as evaluating the overall financial statement presentation. We believe that our audits provide a reasonable basis for our opinion.

In our opinion, the consolidated financial statements referred to above present fairly, in all material respects, the consolidated financial position of Allergan, Inc. at December 31, 2010 and 2009, and the consolidated results of its operations and its cash flows for each of the three years in the period ended December 31, 2010, in conformity with U.S. generally accepted accounting principles. Also, in our opinion, the related financial statement schedule, when considered in relation to the basic financial statements taken as a whole, presents fairly in all material respects the information set forth therein.

We also have audited, in accordance with the standards of the Public Company Accounting Oversight Board (United States), Allergan, Inc.'s internal control over financial reporting as of December 31, 2010, based on criteria established in Internal Control—Integrated Framework issued by the Committee of Sponsoring Organizations of the Treadway Commission and our report dated February 28, 2011 expressed an unqualified opinion thereon.

SCHEDULE II

Valuation and Qualifying Accounts
Years Ended December 31, 2010, 2009 and 2008

(In millions)	Balance at Beginning of Year	Additions[a]	Deductions[b]	Balance at End of Year
Allowance for Doubtful Accounts Deducted From Trade Receivables				
2010	$30.3	$ 5.3	$ (6.6)	$29.0
2009	31.4	10.8	(11.9)	30.3
2008	21.4	12.6	(2.6)	31.4

[a] Provision charged to earnings.
[b] Accounts written off, net of recoveries.

DATING OF REPORT

PRESENTATION

Author's Note

Unless otherwise indicated, the auditing standards referred to in the following paragraphs apply to both issuers and non-issuers. Refer to paragraphs 7.01 and 7.02 for further information on AICPA auditing standards and PCAOB auditing standards.

7.40 For non-issuers, AU section 530, *Dating of the Independent Auditor's Report* (AICPA, *Professional Standards*), discusses dating of the independent auditor's report. Paragraphs .01 and .05 of AU section 530 state the following:

> **.01** The auditor's report should not be dated earlier than the date on which the auditor has obtained sufficient appropriate audit evidence to support the opinion. Paragraph .05 describes the procedure to be followed when a subsequent event occurring after the date of the auditor's report is disclosed in the financial statements.
>
> **.05** The independent auditor has two methods available for dating the report when a subsequent event disclosed in the financial statements occurs after the original date of the auditor's report but before the issuance of the related financial statements. The auditor may use "dual dating," for example, "February 16, 20___, except for Note___, as to which the date is March 1, 20___," or may date the report as of the later date. In the former instance, the responsibility for events occurring subsequent to the original report date is limited to the specific event referred to in the note (or otherwise disclosed). In the latter instance, the independent auditor's responsibility for subsequent events extends to the date of the report and, accordingly, the procedures outlined in section 560.12 generally should be extended to that date.
>
> Footnote 1 of paragraph .01 of AU section 530 explains that among other things, sufficient appropriate audit evidence includes evidence that the audit documentation has been reviewed and that the entity's financial statements, including disclosures, have been prepared and that management has asserted that they have taken responsibility for them.

For issuers, amendments were made to the preceding paragraphs in order to conform terminology to the PCAOB's risk assessment standards (Auditing Standard No. 8, *Audit Risk* [AICPA, *PCAOB Standards and Related Rules*, Auditing Standards] through Auditing Standard No. 15, *Audit Evidence* [AICPA, *PCAOB Standards and Related Rules*, Auditing Standards]) and update references to auditing standards that are being superseded or amended. The risk assessment standards are effective for audits of fiscal years beginning on or after December 15, 2010. Paragraphs .01 and 05 of AU section 530 for issuers state the following:

> **.01** The auditor should date the audit report no earlier than the date on which the auditor has obtained sufficient appropriate evidence to support the auditor's opinion. Paragraph .05 describes the procedure to be followed when a subsequent event occurring after the report date is disclosed in the financial statements.
>
> Note: When performing an integrated audit of financial statements and internal control over financial report-

ing, the auditor's reports on the company's financial statements and on internal control over financial reporting should be dated the same date.

> Note: If the auditor concludes that a scope limitation will prevent the auditor from obtaining the reasonable assurance necessary to express an opinion on the financial statements, then the auditor's report date is the date that the auditor has obtained sufficient appropriate evidence to support the representations in the auditor's report.
>
> **.05** The independent auditor has two methods for dating the report when a subsequent event disclosed in the financial statements occurs after the auditor has obtained sufficient appropriate evidence on which to base his or her opinion, but before the issuance of the related financial statements. The auditor may use "dual dating," for example, "February 16, 20___, except for Note___, as to which the date is March 1, 20___," or may date the report as of the later date. In the former instance, the responsibility for events occurring subsequent to the original report date is limited to the specific event referred to in the note (or otherwise disclosed). In the latter instance, the independent auditor's responsibility for subsequent events extends to the later report date and, accordingly, the procedures outlined in section 560.12 generally should be extended to that date.

7.41 None of the survey entities' auditors' reports used dual dating.

AUDITORS' REPORTS ON INTERNAL CONTROL OVER FINANCIAL REPORTING

PRESENTATION

7.42 Section 404(a) of the Sarbanes-Oxley Act of 2002 requires that management of a public entity assess the effectiveness of the entity's internal control over financial reporting as of the end of the entity's most recent fiscal year and include in the entity's annual report management's conclusions about the effectiveness of the entity's internal control structure and procedures. Management is required to state a direct conclusion about whether the entity's internal control over financial reporting is effective. Management's report on internal control over financial reporting is required to include the following:

- A statement of management's responsibility for establishing and maintaining adequate internal control over financial reporting for the entity
- A statement identifying the framework used by management to conduct the required assessment of the effectiveness of the entity's internal control over financial reporting
- An assessment of the effectiveness of the entity's internal control over financial reporting as of the end of the entity's most recent fiscal year, including an explicit statement about whether that internal control over financial reporting is effective
- A statement that the registered public accounting firm that audited the financial statements included in the annual report has issued an attestation report on management's assessment of the entity's internal control over financial reporting

7.43 Under Section 404(b) of the Sarbanes-Oxley Act of 2002, the auditor who audits the public entity's financial statements included in the annual report is required to audit the entity's internal control over financial reporting. In addition, the auditor is required to audit and report on management's assessment of the effectiveness of internal control over financial reporting. Under PCAOB Auditing Standard No. 5, *An Audit of Internal Control Over Financial Reporting That is Integrated with an Audit of Financial Statements* (AICPA, *PCAOB Standards and Related Rules*, Auditing Standards), the auditor's objective in an audit of internal control over financial reporting is to express an opinion on the effectiveness of the entity's internal control over financial reporting. The audit of internal control over financial reporting should be integrated with the audit of the financial statements. Accordingly, independent auditors engaged to audit the financial statements of such entities also are required to audit and report on the entity's internal control over financial reporting as of the end of such fiscal year. Further, if the auditor determines that elements of management's annual report on internal control over financial reporting are incomplete or improperly presented, the auditor should modify the report to include an explanatory paragraph describing the reasons for this determination and identify and fairly describe any material weakness. Paragraph 86 of Auditing Standard No. 5 allows the auditor to issue a combined report (that is, one report containing both an opinion on the financial statements and an opinion on internal control over financial reporting) or separate reports on the entity's financial statements and internal control over financial reporting.

7.44 In September 2010, the SEC approved a final rule related to the Dodd-Frank Wall Street Reform and Consumer Protection Act (Dodd-Frank Act). The Dodd-Frank Act provides that Section 404(b) of the Sarbanes-Oxley Act of 2002 shall not apply with respect to any audit report prepared for an issuer that is neither an accelerated filer nor a large accelerated filer. Prior to the Dodd-Frank Act, a nonaccelerated filer would have been required, under existing SEC rules, to include an attestation report of its registered public accounting firm on internal control over financial reporting in the filer's annual report filed with the SEC for fiscal years ending on or after June 15, 2010. During 2010, all 500 of the entities surveyed presented a management's report on internal control over financial reporting. 498 presented an auditor's report on internal control over financial reporting. 226 of those entities had the auditor's report on internal control over financial reporting combined with the auditor's report on financial statements. The auditor's report on internal control over financial reporting for 2 of the entities surveyed indicated internal control was not effective.

PRESENTATION AND DISCLOSURE EXCERPTS

Separate Report on Internal Control

7.45

IRON MOUNTAIN INCORPORATED (DEC)

MANAGEMENT'S REPORT ON INTERNAL CONTROL OVER FINANCIAL REPORTING

Our management is responsible for establishing and maintaining adequate internal control over financial reporting, as such term is defined in Rule 13a-15(f) of the Exchange Act. Under the supervision and with the participation of our management, including our chief executive officer and chief financial officer, we conducted an evaluation of the effectiveness of our internal control over financial reporting based on the framework in *Internal Control—Integrated Framework* issued by the Committee of Sponsoring Organizations of the Treadway Commission. Based on our evaluation under the framework in *Internal Control—Integrated Framework*, our management concluded that our internal control over financial reporting was effective as of December 31, 2010.

The effectiveness of our internal control over financial reporting has been audited by Deloitte & Touche LLP, an independent registered public accounting firm, as stated in their report which is included herein.

REPORT OF INDEPENDENT REGISTERED PUBLIC ACCOUNTING FIRM

To the Board of Directors and Stockholders of Iron Mountain Incorporated

We have audited the internal control over financial reporting of Iron Mountain Incorporated and subsidiaries (the "Company") as of December 31, 2010, based on criteria established in *Internal Control—Integrated Framework* issued by the Committee of Sponsoring Organizations of the Treadway Commission. The Company's management is responsible for maintaining effective internal control over financial reporting and for its assessment of the effectiveness of internal control over financial reporting, included in the accompanying Management's Report on Internal Control Over Financial Reporting. Our responsibility is to express an opinion on the Company's internal control over financial reporting based on our audit.

We conducted our audit in accordance with the standards of the Public Company Accounting Oversight Board (United States). Those standards require that we plan and perform the audit to obtain reasonable assurance about whether effective internal control over financial reporting was maintained in all material respects. Our audit included obtaining an understanding of internal control over financial reporting, assessing the risk that a material weakness exists, testing and evaluating the design and operating effectiveness of internal control based on the assessed risk, and performing such other procedures as we considered necessary in the circumstances. We believe that our audit provides a reasonable basis for our opinion.

A company's internal control over financial reporting is a process designed by, or under the supervision of, the company's principal executive and principal financial officers, or persons performing similar functions, and effected by the company's board of directors, management, and other personnel to provide reasonable assurance regarding the reliability of financial reporting and the preparation of financial statements for external purposes in accordance with generally accepted accounting principles. A company's internal control over financial reporting includes those policies and procedures that (1) pertain to the maintenance of records that, in reasonable detail, accurately and fairly reflect the transactions and dispositions of the assets of the company; (2) provide reasonable assurance that transactions are recorded as necessary to permit preparation of financial statements in accordance with generally accepted accounting principles, and that receipts and expenditures of the company are being made only in accordance with authorizations of management and directors of the company; and (3) provide reasonable assurance regarding prevention or timely detection of unauthorized acquisition, use, or disposition of the company's assets that could have a material effect on the financial statements.

Because of the inherent limitations of internal control over financial reporting, including the possibility of collusion or improper management override of controls, material misstatements due to error or fraud may not be prevented or detected on a timely basis. Also, projections of any evaluation of the effectiveness of the internal control over financial reporting to future periods are subject to the risk that the controls may become inadequate because of changes in conditions, or that the degree of compliance with the policies or procedures may deteriorate.

In our opinion, the Company maintained, in all material respects, effective internal control over financial reporting as of December 31, 2010, based on the criteria established in *Internal Control—Integrated Framework* issued by the Committee of Sponsoring Organizations of the Treadway Commission.

We have also audited, in accordance with the standards of the Public Company Accounting Oversight Board (United States), the consolidated financial statements as of and for the year ended December 31, 2010 of the Company and our report dated February 28, 2011 expressed an unqualified opinion on those financial statements.

REPORT OF INDEPENDENT REGISTERED PUBLIC ACCOUNTING FIRM

To the Board of Directors and Stockholders of Iron Mountain Incorporated

We have audited the accompanying consolidated balance sheets of Iron Mountain Incorporated and subsidiaries (the "Company") as of December 31, 2010 and 2009, and the related consolidated statements of operations, equity, comprehensive income (loss), and cash flows for each of the three years in the period ended December 31, 2010. These financial statements are the responsibility of the Company's management. Our responsibility is to express an opinion on these financial statements based on our audits.

We conducted our audits in accordance with the standards of the Public Company Accounting Oversight Board (United States). Those standards require that we plan and perform the audit to obtain reasonable assurance about whether the financial statements are free of material misstatement. An audit includes examining, on a test basis, evidence supporting the amounts and disclosures in the financial statements. An

audit also includes assessing the accounting principles used and significant estimates made by management, as well as evaluating the overall financial statement presentation. We believe that our audits provide a reasonable basis for our opinion.

In our opinion, such consolidated financial statements present fairly, in all material respects, the financial position of Iron Mountain Incorporated and subsidiaries as of December 31, 2010 and 2009, and the results of their operations and their cash flows for each of the three years in the period ended December 31, 2010, in conformity with accounting principles generally accepted in the United States of America.

We have also audited, in accordance with the standards of the Public Company Accounting Oversight Board (United States), the Company's internal control over financial reporting as of December 31, 2010, based on the criteria established in *Internal Control—Integrated Framework* issued by the Committee of Sponsoring Organizations of the Treadway Commission and our report dated February 28, 2011 expressed an unqualified opinion on the Company's internal control over financial reporting.

Combined Report on Financial Statements and Internal Control

7.46

TIFFANY & CO. (JAN)

REPORT OF MANAGEMENT

Management's Responsibility for Financial Information. The Company's consolidated financial statements were prepared by management, who are responsible for their integrity and objectivity. The financial statements have been prepared in accordance with accounting principles generally accepted in the United States of America and, as such, include amounts based on management's best estimates and judgments.

Management is further responsible for maintaining a system of internal accounting control designed to provide reasonable assurance that the Company's assets are adequately safeguarded, and that the accounting records reflect transactions executed in accordance with management's authorization. The system of internal control is continually reviewed and is augmented by written policies and procedures, the careful selection and training of qualified personnel and a program of internal audit.

The consolidated financial statements have been audited by PricewaterhouseCoopers LLP, an independent registered public accounting firm. Their report is shown on page K-44. The Audit Committee of the Board of Directors, which is composed solely of independent directors, meets regularly with financial management and the independent registered public accounting firm to discuss specific accounting, financial reporting and internal control matters. Both the independent registered public accounting firm and the internal auditors have full and free access to the Audit Committee. Each year the Audit Committee selects the firm that is to perform audit services for the Company.

Management's Report on Internal Control over Financial Reporting. Management is responsible for establishing and maintaining adequate internal control over financial reporting, as defined in Exchange Act Rule 13a—15(f). Management conducted an evaluation of the effectiveness of internal control over financial reporting based on the framework in Internal Control—Integrated Framework issued by the Committee of Sponsoring Organizations of the Treadway Commission ("COSO"). Based on this evaluation, management concluded that internal control over financial reporting was effective as of January 31, 2010 based on criteria in Internal Control—Integrated Framework issued by the COSO. The effectiveness of the Company's internal control over financial reporting as of January 31, 2010 has been audited by PricewaterhouseCoopers LLP, an independent registered public accounting firm, as stated in their report which is shown on page K-44.

REPORT OF INDEPENDENT REGISTERED PUBLIC ACCOUNTING FIRM

To the Shareholders and Board of Directors of Tiffany & Co.

In our opinion, the accompanying consolidated balance sheets and the related consolidated statements of earnings, of stockholders' equity and comprehensive earnings, and of cash flows present fairly, in all material respects, the financial position of Tiffany & Co. and its subsidiaries (the "Company") at January 31, 2010 and 2009, and the results of their operations and their cash flows for each of the three years in the period ended January 31, 2010 in conformity with accounting principles generally accepted in the United States of America. In addition, in our opinion, the financial statement schedule listed in the index appearing under Item 15(a)(2) presents fairly, in all material respects, the information set forth therein when read in conjunction with the related consolidated financial statements. Also in our opinion, the Company maintained, in all material respects, effective internal control over financial reporting as of January 31, 2010, based on criteria established in *Internal Control—Integrated Framework* issued by the Committee of Sponsoring Organizations of the Treadway Commission (COSO). The Company's management is responsible for these financial statements and financial statement schedule, for maintaining effective internal control over financial reporting and for its assessment of the effectiveness of internal control over financial reporting, included in Management's Report on Internal Control over Financial Reporting under Item 9A. Our responsibility is to express opinions on these financial statements, on the financial statement schedule, and on the Company's internal control over financial reporting based on our integrated audits. We conducted our audits in accordance with the standards of the Public Company Accounting Oversight Board (United States). Those standards require that we plan and perform the audits to obtain reasonable assurance about whether the financial statements are free of material misstatement and whether effective internal control over financial reporting was maintained in all material respects. Our audits of the financial statements included examining, on a test basis, evidence supporting the amounts and disclosures in the financial statements, assessing the accounting principles used and significant estimates made by management, and evaluating the overall financial statement presentation. Our audit of internal control over financial reporting included obtaining an understanding of internal control over financial

reporting, assessing the risk that a material weakness exists, and testing and evaluating the design and operating effectiveness of internal control based on the assessed risk. Our audits also included performing such other procedures as we considered necessary in the circumstances. We believe that our audits provide a reasonable basis for our opinions.

A company's internal control over financial reporting is a process designed to provide reasonable assurance regarding the reliability of financial reporting and the preparation of financial statements for external purposes in accordance with generally accepted accounting principles. A company's internal control over financial reporting includes those policies and procedures that (i) pertain to the maintenance of records that, in reasonable detail, accurately and fairly reflect the transactions and dispositions of the assets of the company; (ii) provide reasonable assurance that transactions are recorded as necessary to permit preparation of financial statements in accordance with generally accepted accounting principles, and that receipts and expenditures of the company are being made only in accordance with authorizations of management and directors of the company; and (iii) provide reasonable assurance regarding prevention or timely detection of unauthorized acquisition, use, or disposition of the company's assets that could have a material effect on the financial statements.

Because of its inherent limitations, internal control over financial reporting may not prevent or detect misstatements. Also, projections of any evaluation of effectiveness to future periods are subject to the risk that controls may become inadequate because of changes in conditions, or that the degree of compliance with the policies or procedures may deteriorate.

GENERAL MANAGEMENT AND SPECIAL-PURPOSE COMMITTEE REPORTS

PRESENTATION

7.47 There were 35 survey entities that presented a report of management on financial statements. These reports may include the following:
- Description of management's responsibility for preparing the financial statements
- Identification of independent auditors
- Statement about management's representations to the independent auditors
- Statement about financial records and related data made available to the independent auditors
- Description of special-purpose committees of the board of directors
- General description of the entity's system of internal control
- Description of the entity's code of conduct

Occasionally, survey entities presented a report of a special-purpose committee, such as the audit committee or compensation committee.

PRESENTATION AND DISCLOSURE EXCERPTS

Report of Management on Financial Statements

7.48

MACY'S, INC. (JAN)

REPORT OF MANAGEMENT

To the Shareholders of
Macy's, Inc.

The integrity and consistency of the Consolidated Financial Statements of Macy's, Inc. and subsidiaries, which were prepared in accordance with accounting principles generally accepted in the United States of America, are the responsibility of management and properly include some amounts that are based upon estimates and judgments.

The Company maintains a system of internal accounting controls, which is supported by a program of internal audits with appropriate management follow-up action, to provide reasonable assurance, at appropriate cost, that the Company's assets are protected and transactions are properly recorded. Additionally, the integrity of the financial accounting system is based on careful selection and training of qualified personnel, organizational arrangements which provide for appropriate division of responsibilities and communication of established written policies and procedures.

The Company's management is responsible for establishing and maintaining adequate internal control over financial reporting, as defined in Exchange Act Rule 13a-15(f) and has issued Management's Report on Internal Control over Financial Reporting.

The Consolidated Financial Statements of the Company have been audited by KPMG LLP. Their report expresses their opinion as to the fair presentation, in all material respects, of the financial statements and is based upon their independent audits.

The Audit Committee, composed solely of outside directors, meets periodically with KPMG LLP, the internal auditors and representatives of management to discuss auditing and financial reporting matters. In addition, KPMG LLP and the Company's internal auditors meet periodically with the Audit Committee without management representatives present and have free access to the Audit Committee at any time. The Audit Committee is responsible for recommending to the Board of Directors the engagement of the independent registered public accounting firm, which is subject to shareholder approval, and the general oversight review of management's discharge of its responsibilities with respect to the matters referred to above.

Report of the Audit Committee

7.49

HARLEY-DAVIDSON, INC. (DEC)

REPORT OF THE AUDIT COMMITTEE

The Audit Committee of the Board of Directors reviews the Company's financial reporting process and the audit process. All of the Audit Committee members are independent in accordance with the Audit Committee requirements of the New York Stock Exchange, Inc.

The Audit Committee of the Board of Directors has reviewed and discussed with management its assessment of the effectiveness of the Company's internal control system over financial reporting as of December 31, 2010. Management has concluded that the internal control system was effective. Additionally, the Company's internal control over financial reporting as of December 31, 2010 was audited by Ernst & Young LLP, the Company's independent registered public accounting firm for the 2010 fiscal year. The audited financial statements of the Company for the 2010 fiscal year were also reviewed and discussed with management as well as with representatives of Ernst & Young LLP. The Audit Committee has also discussed with Ernst & Young LLP, the matters required to be discussed by AU Section 380 of the Public Company Accounting Oversight Board (PCAOB) Auditing Standards, other professional standards and regulatory requirements currently in effect. The Audit Committee has received the written disclosures and the letter from the independent registered public accounting firm required by Rule 3526 of the PCAOB, as currently in effect, and has discussed with representatives of Ernst & Young LLP the independence of Ernst & Young LLP. Based on the review and discussions referred to above, the Audit Committee has recommended to the Board of Directors that the audited financial statements for the 2010 fiscal year be included in the Company's Annual Report on Form 10-K for the 2010 fiscal year.

Appendix of 500 Entities

List of 500 Survey Entities and Where in the Text Excerpts From Their Annual Reports Can Be Found

The following table lists the 500 entities surveyed in this edition of *Accounting Trends & Techniques* (*Trends*) in alphabetical order, as well as where in the text their annual reports are excerpted.

Company Name	Month of Fiscal Year End	Accounting Technique Illustration
3M Company	December	
A. O. Smith Corporation	December	
A. Schulman, Inc.	August	5.12
Abbott Laboratories	December	
ABM Industries Incorporated	October	
Acuity Brands, Inc.	August	
ADC Telecommunications, Inc.	September	
Administaff, Inc.	December	2.114, 2.131, 3.81
Adobe Systems Incorporated	November	2.95, 7.32
Advanced Micro Devices, Inc.	December	3.51
AGCO Corporation	December	7.29
Air Products and Chemicals, Inc.	September	2.178, 3.65
Airgas, Inc.	March	2.30
AK Steel Holding Corporation	December	1.45, 1.114, 2.71
Alberto-Culver Company	September	
Alcoa Inc.	December	4.24
Allegheny Technologies Incorporated	December	3.16
Allergan, Inc.	December	7.39
Alliance One International, Inc.	March	2.162, 3.13, 3.48
Alliant Techsystems Inc.	March	2.202
Altria Group, Inc.	December	3.11
Amazon.com, Inc.	December	
American Greetings Corporation	February	
Ameron International Corporation	November	2.79
AMETEK, Inc.	December	
Amgen Inc.	December	
Amkor Technology, Inc.	December	3.20
Ampco-Pittsburgh Corporation	December	2.193, 3.45
Amphenol Corporation	December	
Anadarko Petroleum Corporation	December	1.117, 3.19, 3.35, 6.27
Analog Devices, Inc.	October	
AnnTaylor Stores Corporation	January	
Apache Corporation	December	3.38, 4.22
Apple Inc.	September	1.30, 3.08
Applied Industrial Technologies, Inc.	June	
Applied Materials, Inc.	October	1.23, 2.12, 2.135
Archer Daniels Midland Company	June	1.70
Arden Group, Inc.	December	1.46
Arkansas Best Corporation	December	2.130, 6.36
Armstrong World Industries, Inc.	December	6.44
Arrow Electronics, Inc.	December	3.61
ArvinMeritor, Inc.	September	
Ashland Inc.	September	
AT&T Inc.	December	1.66
Atmel Corporation	December	
Autodesk, Inc.	January	1.24
Automatic Data Processing, Inc.	June	

Company Name	Month of Fiscal Year End	Accounting Technique Illustration
AutoNation, Inc.	December	
AutoZone, Inc.	August	
Avery Dennison Corporation	December	
Avis Budget Group, Inc.	December	2.148, 3.12
Avnet, Inc.	June	
Avon Products, Inc.	December	
Badger Meter, Inc.	December	2.120
Baker Hughes Incorporated	December	2.99
Ball Corporation	December	1.91, 5.36
Barnes & Noble, Inc.	January	1.98
Bassett Furniture Industries, Incorporated	November	6.35
Baxter International Inc.	December	
BE Aerospace, Inc.	December	
Beckman Coulter, Inc.	December	
Becton, Dickinson and Company	September	
Belden Inc.	December	
Bemis Company, Inc.	December	
Best Buy Co., Inc.	February	2.08
BMC Software, Inc.	March	
Boeing Company, The	December	1.47, 1.107
Bon-Ton Stores, Inc., The	January	2.52
Boston Scientific Corporation	December	1.97, 1.113
Boyd Gaming Corporation	December	1.154
Breeze-Eastern Corporation	March	
Briggs & Stratton Corporation	June	
Brinker International, Inc.	June	2.175
Brink's Company, The	December	2.128, 3.107, 4.25
Bristol-Myers Squibb Company	December	
Brown Shoe Company, Inc.	January	1.72
Brown-Forman Corporation	April	
Brunswick Corporation	December	
Burger King Holdings, Inc.	June	2.149, 2.177
C. R. Bard, Inc.	December	
CA, Inc.	March	
Cablevision Systems Corporation	December	
Cabot Corporation	September	7.31
CACI International Inc	June	2.97, 2.112, 3.97
Cameron International Corporation	December	
Campbell Soup Company	July	
Cardinal Health, Inc.	June	3.40, 4.21
Career Education Corporation	December	
Carlisle Companies Incorporated	December	
Carpenter Technology Corporation	June	
Caterpillar Inc.	December	1.28, 1.95, 3.69
CBS Corporation	December	1.171
CenturyLink, Inc.	December	
Cenveo, Inc.	December	
CF Industries Holdings, Inc.	December	4.10, 5.67
Chesapeake Energy Corporation	December	6.47
Chevron Corporation	December	3.32
Children's Place Retail Stores, Inc., The	January	
Chiquita Brands International, Inc.	December	
Church & Dwight Co., Inc.	December	2.93, 4.18
Cintas Corporation	May	
Cisco Systems, Inc.	July	1.75, 1.121
Cliffs Natural Resources Inc.	December	2.70, 2.201
Clorox Company, The	June	1.65
Coach, Inc.	June	
Coca-Cola Company, The	December	2.77, 3.113, 4.20
Coca-Cola Enterprises Inc.	December	2.98

Company Name	Month of Fiscal Year End	Accounting Technique Illustration
Coherent, Inc.	September	5.09, 6.23
Colgate-Palmolive Company	December	1.37, 5.61
Collective Brands, Inc.	January	1.68
Comcast Corporation	December	1.162, 3.71
Commercial Metals Company	August	
Computer Sciences Corporation	March	
ConAgra Foods, Inc.	May	3.26
ConocoPhillips	December	2.28
Constellation Brands, Inc.	February	
Convergys Corporation	December	
Con-way Inc.	December	
Cooper Tire & Rubber Company	December	
Corn Products International, Inc.	December	1.155, 4.15, 6.33
Corning Incorporated	December	2.78
Costco Wholesale Corporation	August	2.07, 2.32
Covance Inc.	December	
Cracker Barrel Old Country Store, Inc.	July	2.194
Crane Co.	December	2.84
Crown Holdings, Inc.	December	2.38
CSP Inc.	September	7.24
Cummins Inc.	December	
CVS Caremark Corporation	December	
Cytec Industries Inc.	December	
D.R. Horton, Inc.	September	2.31
Dana Holding Corporation	December	
Danaher Corporation	December	
Darden Restaurants, Inc.	May	
Dean Foods Company	December	2.94, 3.59, 3.105, 6.22
Deere & Company	October	2.199
Del Monte Foods Company	April	7.13
Dell Inc.	January	2.85, 2.190, 3.70, 3.92
Devon Energy Corporation	December	2.104, 6.29
Dillard's, Inc.	January	2.125
DIRECTV	December	6.25
Discovery Communications, Inc.	December	
Domino's Pizza, Inc.	December	3.22
Donaldson Company, Inc.	July	
Dover Corporation	December	
Dow Chemical Company, The	December	3.43, 3.74, 5.44
Dun & Bradstreet Corporation, The	December	
E. I. du Pont de Nemours and Company	December	
E. W. Scripps Company, The	December	
Eastman Chemical Company	December	7.11
Eastman Kodak Company	December	1.123, 1.142, 2.105, 2.192
Eaton Corporation	December	2.92, 2.109, 5.33
eBay Inc.	December	2.61
Ecolab Inc.	December	
El Paso Corporation	December	3.05, 7.17
Electronic Arts Inc.	March	
Eli Lilly and Company	December	5.63
EMC Corporation	December	2.121
EMCOR Group, Inc.	December	
Emerson Electric Co.	September	
Energizer Holdings, Inc.	September	4.08
Equifax Inc.	December	
Estee Lauder Companies Inc., The	June	
Exide Technologies	March	
Express Scripts, Inc.	December	
Exxon Mobil Corporation	December	3.85, 4.09, 6.20
Family Dollar Stores, Inc.	August	

Company Name	Month of Fiscal Year End	Accounting Technique Illustration
Federal-Mogul Corporation	December	5.65
FedEx Corporation	May	2.184
Fidelity National Information Services, Inc.	December	3.44
First Solar, Inc.	December	1.166
Fiserv, Inc.	December	
Flowers Foods, Inc.	December	
Fluor Corporation	December	
FMC Corporation	December	2.189
Foot Locker, Inc.	January	
Ford Motor Company	December	
Fortune Brands, Inc.	December	
Fred's, Inc.	January	
Freeport-McMoRan Copper & Gold Inc.	December	
Frontier Communications Corporation	December	1.96, 1.106, 3.33
Furniture Brands International, Inc.	December	1.77, 3.52
GameStop Corp.	January	
Gannett Co., Inc.	December	
Gap, Inc., The	January	
Gardner Denver, Inc.	December	
GenCorp Inc.	November	2.161, 3.114
General Cable Corporation	December	3.72
General Dynamics Corporation	December	2.25, 3.83, 4.23
General Electric Company	December	
General Mills, Inc.	May	
Genuine Parts Company	December	
Georgia Gulf Corporation	December	
Goodrich Corporation	December	
Goodyear Tire & Rubber Company, The	December	2.108, 3.42
Google Inc.	December	3.93, 3.117
Great Atlantic & Pacific Tea Company, Inc., The	February	
Greif, Inc.	October	7.25
Griffon Corporation	September	1.71
Guess?, Inc.	January	
H.J. Heinz Company	April	1.179, 6.10
Halliburton Company	December	1.120
HanesBrands Inc.	December	2.41, 3.50
Harley-Davidson, Inc.	December	1.27, 1.89, 4.19, 7.49
Harman International Industries, Incorporated	June	
Harris Corporation	June	3.34
Harsco Corporation	December	1.144
Hasbro, Inc.	December	
Health Net, Inc.	December	
Herman Miller, Inc.	May	
Hershey Company, The	December	3.84
Hess Corporation	December	
Hewlett-Packard Company	October	7.26
Hill-Rom Holdings, Inc.	September	3.82
HNI Corporation	December	
Home Depot, Inc., The	January	
Honeywell International Inc.	December	2.200
Hormel Foods Corporation	October	7.33
Hovnanian Enterprises, Inc.	October	
Hubbell Incorporated	December	1.81
Huntsman Corporation	December	3.112, 6.45
IAC/InterActiveCorp	December	6.12
IDT Corporation	July	5.51
Illinois Tool Works Inc.	December	
Ingram Micro Inc.	December	1.116
Intel Corporation	December	2.80
International Business Machines Corporation	December	

Company Name	Month of Fiscal Year End	Accounting Technique Illustration
International Flavors & Fragrances Inc.	December	
International Paper Company	December	3.58
Interpublic Group of Companies, Inc., The	December	
Intuit Inc.	July	
Iron Mountain Incorporated	December	1.161, 7.45
ITT Corporation	December	1.157, 3.47
J. C. Penney Company, Inc.	January	2.53, 3.67
J. M. Smucker Company, The	April	
Jabil Circuit, Inc.	August	
Jack in the Box Inc.	September	
Jacobs Engineering Group Inc.	September	2.146
Jarden Corporation	December	
JDS Uniphase Corporation	June	2.54, 2.155
Jo-Ann Stores, Inc.	January	
Johnson & Johnson	December	2.129, 3.28, 6.39
Johnson Controls, Inc.	September	2.145, 3.68, 7.27
Jones Group Inc., The	December	
Joy Global Inc.	October	1.36
Juniper Networks, Inc.	December	
KB Home	November	5.64
Kellogg Company	December	
Kelly Services, Inc.	December	
Kimball International, Inc.	June	1.78, 2.111, 3.18, 3.36
Kimberly-Clark Corporation	December	1.159, 3.63
KLA-Tencor Corporation	June	
Kohl's Corporation	January	2.49, 3.31
Kroger Co., The	January	1.156
L.S. Starrett Company, The	June	2.57
L-3 Communications Holdings, Inc.	December	1.102
Lam Research Corporation	June	1.122, 1.139, 2.107, 2.144, 6.42
Las Vegas Sands Corp.	December	2.195, 5.47
La-Z-Boy Incorporated	April	1.80
Lear Corporation	December	1.101
Lee Enterprises, Incorporated	September	
Leggett & Platt, Incorporated	December	
Lennar Corporation	November	
Lennox International Inc.	December	
Lexmark International, Inc.	December	
Liberty Media Corporation	December	
Liz Claiborne, Inc.	December	
Lockheed Martin Corporation	December	1.74, 1.118, 2.143, 3.14, 3.98
Louisiana-Pacific Corporation	December	5.21
Lowe's Companies, Inc.	January	
LSI Corporation	December	
Lubrizol Corporation, The	December	
Macy's, Inc.	January	7.48
Manitowoc Company, Inc., The	December	
Manpower Inc.	December	
Marriott International, Inc.	December	1.158
Martin Marietta Materials, Inc.	December	
Masco Corporation	December	
Mattel, Inc.	December	
McClatchy Company, The	December	1.119, 1.165, 3.39
McCormick & Company, Incorporated	November	
McDonald's Corporation	December	
McGraw-Hill Companies, Inc., The	December	1.29
McKesson Corporation	March	
MeadWestvaco Corporation	December	2.59
Medtronic, Inc.	April	5.48
Merck & Co., Inc.	December	1.38

Company Name	Month of Fiscal Year End	Accounting Technique Illustration
Meredith Corporation	June	
Meritage Homes Corporation	December	
Mettler-Toledo International Inc.	December	
Micron Technology, Inc.	August	
Microsoft Corporation	June	
Mohawk Industries, Inc.	December	
Molex Incorporated	June	5.45, 7.35
Molson Coors Brewing Company	December	
Monsanto Company	August	
Mosaic Company, The	May	
Motorola Solutions, Inc.	December	5.37
Mueller Industries, Inc.	December	2.191, 3.21
Murphy Oil Corporation	December	
NACCO Industries, Inc.	December	2.198, 3.15
Nash-Finch Company	December	
National Oilwell Varco, Inc.	December	2.139
National Semiconductor Corporation	May	
NCR Corporation	December	
NetApp, Inc.	April	1.105, 1.167, 5.19, 6.28
Netflix, Inc.	December	
New York Times Company, The	December	
Newell Rubbermaid Inc.	December	5.20
NewMarket Corporation	December	
Newmont Mining Corporation	December	
News Corporation	June	
NIKE, Inc.	May	
Noble Energy, Inc.	December	1.140, 3.30
Nordstrom, Inc.	January	
Northrop Grumman Corporation	December	1.143, 6.11
Novell, Inc.	October	
Nucor Corporation	December	
NVR, Inc.	December	5.62
Occidental Petroleum Corporation	December	3.10
Office Depot, Inc.	December	
Olin Corporation	December	
Omnicom Group Inc.	December	
Oracle Corporation	May	1.55, 1.67, 2.11, 3.09
Owens-Illinois, Inc.	December	
PACCAR Inc	December	
Pall Corporation	July	1.52, 2.142, 3.53
Parker-Hannifin Corporation	June	
Paychex, Inc.	May	2.24, 5.16
Peabody Energy Corporation	December	1.124, 3.116
Pentair, Inc.	December	2.154
PepsiCo, Inc.	December	3.49
PerkinElmer, Inc.	December	4.13
Pfizer Inc.	December	1.169, 2.62, 2.186
Phillips-Van Heusen Corporation	January	
Pilgrim's Pride Corporation	December	1.173, 2.160
Pitney Bowes Inc.	December	2.29, 2.187
Plum Creek Timber Company, Inc.	December	
Polaris Industries Inc.	December	3.37
Polo Ralph Lauren Corporation	March	
PolyOne Corporation	December	
Potlatch Corporation	December	
PPG Industries, Inc.	December	2.152, 3.41
Praxair, Inc.	December	1.115
Precision Castparts Corp.	March	
priceline.com Incorporated	December	2.163
Pride International, Inc.	December	

Company Name	Month of Fiscal Year End	Accounting Technique Illustration
Procter & Gamble Company, The	June	1.43, 3.89, 5.14
PulteGroup, Inc.	December	1.32, 2.58
QUALCOMM Incorporated	September	
Quanex Building Products Corporation	October	
Quantum Corporation	March	2.100, 3.73
Quiksilver, Inc.	October	
Qwest Communications International Inc.	December	1.150, 3.04, 5.10
R.R. Donnelley & Sons Company	December	2.168
RadioShack Corporation	December	
Raytheon Company	December	
Regal Beloit Corporation	December	
Regal Entertainment Group	December	5.18
Republic Services, Inc.	December	2.72, 5.32, 6.21
Retail Ventures, Inc.	January	2.153
Reynolds American Inc.	December	1.160, 2.150
Rite Aid Corporation	February	
Robbins & Myers, Inc.	August	1.163
Robert Half International Inc.	December	6.26
Rock-Tenn Company	September	
Rockwell Automation, Inc.	September	
Rockwell Collins, Inc.	September	
RPM International Inc.	May	2.203
Ruddick Corporation	September	
Ryder System, Inc.	December	5.46, 6.41
Ryland Group, Inc., The	December	
Safeway Inc.	December	
SanDisk Corporation	December	1.149
Sanmina-SCI Corporation	September	
Sara Lee Corporation	June	3.76
Schnitzer Steel Industries, Inc.	August	1.22, 2.151
Scholastic Corporation	May	
Scotts Miracle-Gro Company, The	September	
Seaboard Corporation	December	1.103
Sealed Air Corporation	December	
Sealy Corporation	November	2.113
Sears Holdings Corporation	January	
Service Corporation International	December	
SFN Group, Inc.	December	
Shaw Group Inc., The	August	2.60, 4.16, 6.32
Sherwin-Williams Company, The	December	2.51, 2.91, 5.28
Silgan Holdings Inc.	December	6.24
Smithfield Foods, Inc.	April	1.104, 1.141, 5.11, 6.38, 7.30
Smurfit-Stone Container Corporation	December	1.164
Snap-on Incorporated	December	2.50
Snyder's-Lance, Inc.	December	1.73, 2.188
Sonic Automotive, Inc.	December	
Sonoco Products Company	December	
Span-America Medical Systems, Inc.	September	
Sparton Corporation	June	
Spectrum Brands Holdings, Inc.	September	1.172, 3.91, 5.17, 7.21
Spectrum Control, Inc.	November	
Sprint Nextel Corporation	December	2.96
SPX Corporation	December	
St. Jude Medical, Inc.	December	
Standard Pacific Corp.	December	
Standard Register Company, The	December	
Standex International Corporation	June	
Stanley Black & Decker, Inc.	December	2.40
Staples, Inc.	January	
Starbucks Corporation	September	2.23, 4.14

Company Name	Month of Fiscal Year End	Accounting Technique Illustration
Starwood Hotels & Resorts Worldwide, Inc.	December	
Steel Dynamics, Inc.	December	
Steelcase Inc.	February	
Stryker Corporation	December	3.29
Sunoco, Inc.	December	
SuperMedia Inc.	December	
SUPERVALU INC.	February	
Symantec Corporation	March	
SYNNEX Corporation	November	
Sysco Corporation	June	1.53, 3.62
Target Corporation	January	2.42, 3.27
Tech Data Corporation	January	6.19
Teleflex Incorporated	December	
Tellabs, Inc.	December	
Temple-Inland Inc.	December	
Tenet Healthcare Corporation	December	1.168, 6.31
Tenneco Inc.	December	2.39
Terex Corporation,	December	6.34
Tesoro Corporation	December	7.12
Texas Industries, Inc.	May	6.43
Texas Instruments Incorporated	December	
Textron Inc.	December	2.164, 3.99
Thermo Fisher Scientific Inc.	December	
Thomas & Betts Corporation	December	
Thor Industries, Inc.	July	1.25, 3.23
Tiffany & Co.	January	1.109, 1.174, 3.75, 4.11, 6.48, 7.46
Timberland Company, The	December	
Time Warner Inc.	December	1.35, 1.76, 2.81, 7.28
Timken Company, The	December	1.79
TJX Companies, Inc., The	January	5.13, 5.55
Toll Brothers, Inc.	October	
Toro Company, The	October	
Trinity Industries, Inc.	December	1.90
TRW Automotive Holdings Corp.	December	1.34, 2.56
Tupperware Brands Corporation	December	3.94
Tutor Perini Corporation	December	6.09
Twin Disc, Incorporated	June	
Tyson Foods, Inc.	September	
Unifi, Inc.	June	
Unisys Corporation	December	
United Parcel Service, Inc.	December	
United States Steel Corporation	December	
United Stationers Inc.	December	
United Technologies Corporation	December	
Universal Corporation	March	
Universal Forest Products, Inc.	December	
Universal Health Services, Inc.	December	
URS Corporation	December	1.33, 6.46
USG Corporation	December	
V.F. Corporation	December	
Valassis Communications, Inc.	December	2.165, 2.185, 3.17
Valero Energy Corporation	December	
Varian Medical Systems, Inc.	September	
VeriSign, Inc.	December	
Verizon Communications Inc.	December	
Viacom Inc.	September	1.175, 2.147, 3.46
Viad Corp	December	1.40, 4.17
Vishay Intertechnology, Inc.	December	1.44
Visteon Corporation	December	1.31
Vulcan Materials Company	December	3.60, 3.106

Company Name	Month of Fiscal Year End	Accounting Technique Illustration
W. R. Grace & Co.	December	1.42, 2.106, 7.20
W.W. Grainger, Inc.	December	
Walgreen Co.	August	
Wal-Mart Stores, Inc.	January	2.119, 4.12
Walt Disney Company, The	September	
Walter Energy, Inc.	December	
Warnaco Group, Inc., The	December	
Warner Music Group Corp.	September	
Washington Post Company, The	December	
Waste Management, Inc.	December	1.54
Wausau Paper Corp.	December	
Weis Markets, Inc.	December	
WellPoint, Inc.	December	2.138, 4.26
Wendy's/Arby's Group, Inc.	December	1.176, 2.176
Werner Enterprises, Inc.	December	
Western Digital Corporation	June	
Western Refining, Inc.	December	
Western Union Company, The	December	
Weyerhaeuser Company	December	
Whirlpool Corporation	December	
Whole Foods Market, Inc.	September	5.66
Williams-Sonoma, Inc.	January	
Winn-Dixie Stores, Inc.	June	2.173
Winnebago Industries, Inc.	August	3.90
Wolverine World Wide, Inc.	December	1.108, 2.110, 5.15
Worthington Industries, Inc.	May	
Wyndham Worldwide Corporation	December	2.167
Wynn Resorts, Limited	December	
Xerox Corporation	December	1.41, 6.37
Xilinx, Inc.	March	1.69, 2.134
Yahoo! Inc.	December	1.26, 3.88
Yum! Brands, Inc.	December	1.39, 2.174
Zimmer Holdings, Inc.	December	3.54

Pronouncement Index

Note: "*n*" refers to an author's note following the numbered paragraph.

Subject Index

A

Accelerated depreciation methods, 3.83–3.84

Accounting changes and error corrections
    accounting estimates, change in, 1.77–1.78
    accounting principle, changes in, 1.65–1.76
    business combinations, 1.67
    convertible debt, 1.69–1.71
    disclosure, 1.63–1.64
    earnings per share, 1.72
    errors, correction of, 1.79–1.81
    inventory, 1.73
    noncontrolling interests, 1.68
    pensions and other postretirement benefits, 1.66
    presentation, 1.56–1.62
    presentation and disclosure excerpts, 1.65–1.81
    retained earnings, 5.41, 5.45
    revenue recognition, 1.74–1.75
    share-based compensation, 1.65
    stockholders' equity, 5.45
    transfers of financial assets and variable interest
        entities, 1.76

Accounting corrections. *See* Accounting changes and
    error corrections

Accounting estimates
    amortization, 3.78
    changes in, distinguishing from changes in
        accounting principles, 1.61
    depletion, 3.78
    depreciation, 3.78
    disclosure, 1.63
    presentation and disclosure excerpts, 1.77–1.78
    prospective application, 1.60
    significant accounting policies and estimates, 1.43
    use of, 1.40–1.42

Accounting policies
    critical accounting policies, 1.35
    disclosure, 1.18, 1.21, 1.36
    significant accounting policies and
        estimates, 1.43

Accounting principles
    business combinations, 1.67
    changes, distinguishing from changes in
        accounting estimates, 1.61
    changes, when permitted, 1.57
    convertible debt, 1.69–1.71
    disclosure, 1.63
    earnings per share, 1.72
    exceptions, 1.58
    financial assets, transfers, 1.76
    inventory, 1.73
    nonauthoritative accounting guidance sources,
        1.07
    noncontrolling interests, 1.68
    pensions and other postretirement benefits, 1.66
    retained earnings, 5.40, 5.44
    retrospective application, 1.59, 5.40
    revenue recognition, 1.74–1.75
    share-based compensation, 1.65
    variable interest entities, transfers, 1.76

Accounting standards, new 1.33

Accounts receivable. *See also* Current receivables;
    Receivables from related parties; Receivables
    sold or collateralized; Trade receivables and
    payables

Accretion, 6.28

Accumulated depreciation, 2.67

Accumulated other comprehensive income,
    2.196–2.203. *See also* Comprehensive income;
    Other comprehensive income
    component balances, 2.197
    in equity section of balance sheet, 2.198–2.199
    in notes to consolidated financial statements,
        2.202–2.203
    in statement of changes in equity, 2.200–2.201,
        5.58
    pension plans, recognition and measurement,
        3.55
    presentation, 2.196–2.197
    presentation and disclosure excerpts, 2.198–2.203

P

R

income taxes, 3.87, 3.90, 3.91–3.92

Tax effects, disclosure, 4.13–4.15

Tax returns, 1.170

Tax uncertainties, 2.144, 2.187

Taxable investment incentives, 1.166

Taxes other than income taxes, 3.32

Taxes payable, 2.186

Technical Practice Aids (AICPA), 1.07

Technology, intangible assets, 2.97

Title of auditors' report, 7.03

Trade accounts payable
   disclosure, 2.124
   presentation, 2.123
   presentation and disclosure excerpts, 2.125
   recognition and measurement, 2.122

Trade creditors, 2.140

Trade receivables and payables, 2.27, 2.83

Trademarks, 2.94

Tradenames and other intangibles, 2.93

Trading securities, 2.14, 2.15. *See also*
   Available-for-sale securities; Held-to-maturity
   securities; Marketable securities

Transfer of financial assets, 1.76, 7.29

Treasury stock
   balance sheet presentation, 5.54
   presentation, 5.52–5.54
   presentation and disclosure excerpts, 5.55
   stockholders' equity, 5.52–5.55

U

Uncertainties, 7.18–7.21. *See also* Risks and
   uncertainties

Unearned compensation, 5.61

Units-of-production depreciation method, 3.85

Unrealized changes, reconciliation, 6.29

Unsecured long-term debt, 2.160

Unusual items, 3.109, 3.110. *See also* Extraordinary
   items

V

Variable interest entities (VIEs)
   accounting principle, change in, 1.76
   consolidated financial statements, 1.83
   lack of consistency, 7.28
   related party transactions, 1.175

Vendors, 2.32

VIEs. *See* Variable interest entities (VIEs)

Voting interests, 1.83, 1.93

Vulnerability due to certain concentrations,
   1.44–1.47

W

Warranties
   contingencies, 1.121
   expenses and losses, 3.34
   other current liabilities, 2.145
   other noncurrent liabilities, 2.190

Warrants, 5.65

Websites, 2.87

Working capital, 1.99

Write-down of assets
   adjustments to net income (reconciliation), 6.27
   discontinued operations, 3.101, 3.103
   expenses and losses, 3.39

Introducing **eXacct: Financial Reporting Tools & Techniques**.

We appreciate your business and would like to take this opportunity to tell you about **eXacct**, an online tool from the AICPA that builds on our flagship publication *Accounting Trends & Techniques*. For more than 60 years, *Accounting Trends & Techniques* has provided guidance on satisfying U.S. GAAP presentation and disclosure requirements, as well as statistical reporting trends and actual reporting examples from the AICPA's survey of annual reports from 500 of the country's top public companies. **eXacct** adds to this content for a fuller picture of current financial reporting practices and makes it interactive — ready to be searched, filtered, downloaded and used exactly as you need it.

This tool not only provides all available annual report XBRL data files submitted to the SEC by our 500 survey companies, it allows you to search them for specific attributes and disclosures, providing full tag information and highlighting company extensions with the click of a button. **eXacct** allows you to search and view all 500 annual reports in our survey for many of the common disclosures you need. It can sort content by industry, giving you crucial insight into presentation and disclosure methods across a wide variety of industries. With companies from virtually every non-regulated sector represented, you'll get a rich diversity of financial statement disclosure examples that will save you hours of financial reporting time.

Please visit **CPA2Biz.com/tryeXacct** for more information on **eXacct** and what it can do for you.

Thank you for your continued support.